THE ESSENTIAL CASEBOOK
SECOND EDITION

Craig A. Smith

Member of the California Bar

Copyright © 2023 by Craig A. Smith

All rights reserved. This book or any portion thereof may not be reproduced or used in any manner whatsoever without the express written permission of the publisher except for the use of brief quotations in a book review or scholarly journal.

No copyright is claimed in government works that appear in this book.

First Publication: 2015
Second Edition: 2023
ISBN 978-1-7332578-3-1
(Print Edition)

lawschoolhelp.com
PO Box 90103
Santa Barbara, CA 93190
www.lawschoolhelp.com
www.essentialcontractlaw.com

Table Of Contents

CHAPTER 1 1

Nature of Contract And Consideration 1

Definition of "Contract" 1
Elements of a Contract 1
Types of Contracts 1
Express or Implied In Fact Contracts 1
Schaad v. Hazelton 1
ORAL AND WRITTEN CONTRACTS 7
CONSIDERATION 8
The Concept of Detriment 8
Hamer v. Sidway 8
Schumm v. Berg 13
Settlement of Claims or Disputes as Consideration 17
What Is Not Consideration 17
Illusory Promises 17
Strong v. Sheffield 17
Wood v. Lucy, Lady Duff-Gordon 19
The Preexisting Duty Rule 21
Bargained for Exchange 22
Feinberg v. Pfeiffer Co. 22
Mills v. Wyman 26
Relaxation of the Rule That Past Consideration is No Consideration .28
Webb v. McGowin 28
The Requirement of a Bargain 32
Kirksey v. Kirksey 32
Harris v. Time, Inc. 33
Cobaugh v. Klick-Lewis, Inc. 35
Promissory Estoppel; Reliance as an Alternative To Consideration ...37
Ricketts v. Scothorn 37
Feinberg v. Pfeiffer Co. 41
Cotnam v. Wisdom 44
Callano v. Oakwood Park Homes Corp. 47
Assessment Questions Chapter 1 50

CHAPTER 2 51

Mutual Assent 51

Introduction 51
Offer 51
       Lucy v. Zehmer 52
       Owen v. Tunison 55
       Harvey v. Facey 58

Price Quotations Are Not Offers 60
       Lefkowitz v. Great Minneapolis Surplus Store, Inc. 60
       Harris v. Time, Inc. 62
       Donovan v. RRL Corp. 63

Questions 69
Mistaken Offers 69
       Elsinore Union etc. Sch. Dist. v. Kastorff 69
       Donovan v. RRL Corp. 75

Acceptance 79
       International Filter Co. v. Conroe Gin, Ice, & Light Co., ... 80
       Ever-Tite Roofing Corporation v. Green 84
       Davis v. Jacoby 86

Method of Acceptance Required or Merely Suggested? 93
       Allied Steel and Conveyors, Inc., v. Ford Motor Company ... 93

Notification of the Fact of Acceptance for Unilateral Contracts 97
       Carlill v. Carbolic Smoke Ball Company 98

Special Rules for the Sale of Goods, the Uniform Commercial Code .. 99
Scope of Article 2 of the UCC 99
Acceptance by Opening the Package and Retaining the Goods 100
       Dye v. Tamko Bldg. Products, Inc. 100

Shipment of Goods as Acceptance 108
       Corinthian Pharmaceutical Systems, Inc. v. Lederle Laboratories ... 108

Silence is Not Acceptance 112
When Is Acceptance Effective? 113
Acceptance Effective on Dispatch - The "Mailbox Rule" .. 113
       Gibbs v. American Savings & Loan Assn. 113

Revocation of Offers 117
       Dickinson v. Dodds 117
       Yaros v. Trustees of the University of Pennsylvania 121

Acceptance Varying Offer – Counter Offer – Mirror Image Rule 128
    Smith v. Holmwood 128
Abandonment of the Mirror Image Rule Under the UCC 134
    Dorton v. Collins & Aikman Corp. 134
    Steiner v. Mobil Oil Corp. 140
Option Contracts 153
    Marsh v. Lott 153
Merchant's Firm Offer For Sale of Goods 156
Option Contracts and Offers Looking Towards Unilateral Contracts 157
Reliance on an Offer Can Result In Option Contract 157
    Drennan v. Star Paving Co. 157
    Supreme Court of California, 1958 157
The Requirement of Definiteness 162
Contract Must Be Certain as to its Essential Terms 162
    Toys Inc. v. F.M. Burlington Co. 162
Precontractual Liability 166
    Dixon v. Wells Fargo, N.A. 166
Assessment Questions Chapter 2 175

Chapter 3 176

The Statute of Frauds 176

  Introduction 176
  Origins and History 176
  "Party to be Charged" 177
  Contracts That Are Within The Statute of Frauds 177
  Contracts Not To Be Performed Within One Year 177
      White Lighting Company v. Wolfson 178
  "Permanent" Employment Not Within the One-Year Provision 181
  Leases of Longer Than One Year 181
      Bed, Bath & Beyond of La Jolla v. La Jolla Village Square 181
  The Suretyship Clause 185
      Langman v. Alumni Association of University of Virginia 186
  The Main Purpose or Leading Object Rule Exception 188
      Central Ceilings, Inc. v. National Amusements, Inc. 188
  Contracts for the Sale of Goods For a Price of $500 or More 193
      Southwest Engineering Co., Inc. v. Martin Tractor Co. 193
  Satisfying The Writing Requirement 198

Sufficiency of the Note or Memorandum 198
    Crabtree v. Elizabeth Arden Sales Corp. 199
    Brewer v. Horst-Lachmund Co. 204
    Franklin v. Hansen 207

The Signature Requirement 212
    Southwest Engineering Co. Inc. v. Martin Tractor Co. 212

Signatures - You've Got Mail! 214
    JSO Associates, Inc v. Price 214

Excusing The Writing Requirement 216

Partial Performance 216
    Beaver v. Brumlow 216

Estoppel 223
    Monarco v. Lo Greco 223
    Redke v. Silvertrust 226

Reliance Must Be Reasonable 229

UCC Exceptions to the Writing Requirement 230

Non-Objecting Merchant Rule 230
    Harry Rubin & Sons, Inc. v. Con. P. Co. of Am. 230
    St. Ansgar Mills, Inc. v. Streit 232

Subsection 3 Writing Requirement Exceptions 237
    Sedmak v. Charlie's Chevrolet, Inc. 237

Assessment Questions Chapter 3 241

Chapter 4 243

Policing the Bargain 243

Capacity to Contract – Minors and Persons of Unsound Mind 243

Capacity of Minor to Enter Into Contract 243
    Kiefer v. Fred Howe Motors, Inc. 243

Minor's Power to Disaffirm Contracts 246

Necessities of Life 246

Persons of Unsound Mind 246
    Ortelere v. Teachers' Ret. Bd. 247
    Cundick v. Broadbent 249

Overreaching, Pressure in Bargaining, Duress & Undue Influence .. 252

The Pre-Existing Duty Rule (Revisited) 252
    Alaska Packers' Ass'n v. Domenico 252
    Borelli v. Brusseau 256

Relaxation of the Pre-Existing Duty Rule 259
    Watkins & Son, Inc., v. Carrig 259
Duress 263
    Odorizzi v. Bloomfield School District 264
Concealment, and Non-Disclosure 270
    Reed v. King 276
Misrepresentation 280
    Vokes v. Arthur Murray, Inc. 280
Assessment Questions Chapter 4 285

Chapter 5 286

Illegal and Unconscionable Contracts 286

Illegality 286
    Bovard v. American Horse Enterprises 286
    Bradley v. Doherty 290
    Manning v. Bishop of Marquette 294
Licensing Laws 300
Restraints on Trade – Non-Competition Clauses 300
    Hopper v. All Pet Animal Clinic, Inc. 300
    Central Adjustment Bureau, Inc. v. Ingram 306
Prenuptial Agreements and Public Policy 310
    Simeone v. Simeone 310
Surrogacy Contracts 316
    Matter of Baby M. 316
    Johnson v. Calvert 322
Unconscionability 326
    Tuckwiller v. Tuckwiller 327
    American Software, Inc. v. Ali 332
    Donovan v. RRL Corp. 337
Take It or Leave It Contracts 341
    Bolter v. Superior Court (Harris Research, Inc.) 341
Assessment Questions Chapter 5 347

Chapter 6 348

Contract Interpretation 348

    Masterson v. Sine 352
Merger Clauses 355
    A. Kemp Fisheries, Inc. v. Castle & Cooke, Inc., et. al. 356

Exceptions to the Parol Evidence Rule – Mistake and Fraud..........360
    Bollinger v. Central Pennsylvania Quarry Stripping & Const. Co....360
    Riverisland Cold Storage Inc. v. Fresno-Madera Credit Assn. 362

No-Oral-Modification Clauses 371

Extrinsic Evidence to Show the Parties' Intent 371

Plain Meaning Rule Distinguished From Parol Evidence Rule..........372
    Pacific Gas & E. Co. v. G. W. Thomas Drayage & Rigging Co. 372
    Greenfield v. Philles Records..........376
    Trident Center v. Connecticut General Life Ins. Co. 380

General Rules of Contract Interpretation..........384

Contract Construed Most Strictly Against Drafter 384

Words Used Given Their Ordinary Meaning 384

We Interrupt This Casebook for a Fowl Lesson in Poultry 384
    Frigaliment Importing Co., Ltd. v. BNS International Sales Corp..384

Usage of Trade, Course of Performance, Course of Dealing..........390

Usage of Trade 390
    Ermolieff v. R. K. O. Radio Pictures..........390
    Higgins v. California Petroleum & Asphalt Co. et al. 394

Course of Performance 396
    Nanakuli Paving & Rock Co. v. Shell Oil Co...........396
    Whose Meaning Prevails?..........407
    Raffles v. Wichelhaus 407
    Oswald v. Allen..........409
    Colfax Envelope Corp. v. Local No. 458-3M 411

Filling Gaps..........416

Omitted Terms 416

Implied Terms in Contracts for the Sale of Goods..........416

The Implied Warranty of Merchantability 416
    Ambassador Steel Co. v. Ewald Steel Co. 417

The Implied Warranty of Fitness for a Particular Purpose 421
    Tyson v. Ciba-Geigy Corp...........421
    South Carolina Electric & Gas Co. v. Combustion Eng. Inc...........425

Express Warranties..........429
    Smith v. Zimbalist 430
    Keith v. Buchanan 434
    Miller v. Lentine..........439

The Implied Term of "Good Faith" 441

  De La Concha of Hartford, Inc. v. Aetna Life Insurance Co. 442
 Assessment Questions Chapter 6 449
Chapter 7 450
Remedies for Breach of Contract 450
 Introduction 450
 Specific Performance 450
  Klein v. PepsiCo, Inc. 450
  Sedmak v. Charlie's Chevrolet, Inc. 454
  Morris v. Sparrow 458
  Laclede Gas Co. v. Amoco Oil Co. 459
 Questions 464
 Problems in Supervising Specific Performance Orders 464
  Northern Delaware Industrial Dev. Corp. v. E.W. Bliss Co. 464
 Personal Service Contracts and Injunctions 466
  Beverly Glen Music, Inc. v. Warner Communications 467
 Rescission 469
 Damages for Breach 469
  U.S. Naval Institute v. Charter Comm., Inc., ... 470
 Three Protected Interests 473
  Sullivan v. O'Connor 474
  Vitex Manufacturing Corporation, Ltd. v. Caribtex Corporation ... 479
 Buyer's Damages for Seller's Breach of Contract for Sale of Goods ... 483
  Laredo Hides Company, Inc., v. H & H Meat Products Co., Inc. .. 483
 Seller's Damages for Buyer's Breach of Contract for Sale of Goods ... 487
  R.E. Davis Chemical Corp. v. Diasonics, Inc. 487
 Measure of Damages for Incomplete or Defective Construction 491
  Jacob & Youngs v. Kent 491
  Groves v. John Wunder Co. 493
 Limitations On Damages 497
 Avoidability 497
  Rockingham County v. Luten Bridge Co. 497
  Parker v. Twentieth Century-Fox Film Corp. 499
 Foreseeability as a Limitation on Damages 505
  Hadley v. Baxendale 505
  Sun-Maid Raisin Growers v. Victor Packing Co. 509
 Punitive Damages for Breach of Contract 514

  White v. Benkowski 514
Damages for Emotional Distress 517
  Erlich v. Menezes 517
  Ross v. Forest Lawn Memorial Park 524
Certainty as a Limitation on Damages 526
  McDonald v. John P. Scripps Newspaper 526
  Ericson v. Playgirl, Inc. 529
  Fera v. Village Plaza, Inc. 535
Damage Limitation Review 540
Liquidated Damages 540
  Dave Gustafson & Co. v. State 540
  Cellphone Termination Fee Cases 543
Assessment Questions Chapter 7 547

Chapter 8 549

Performance and Breach 549

Introduction 549
Conditions Precedent, Subsequent and Concurrent 549
Express and Constructive (Implied) Conditions 550
  Luttinger v. Rosen 550
  Internatio-Rotterdam, Inc. v. River Brand Rice Mills., Inc. 552
"Pay If Paid" or "Pay When Paid?" Condition or Promise? 556
  Wm. R. Clarke Corp. v. Safeco Ins. Co. 556
Real Estate Brokers and Conditions 562
Conditions of Satisfaction 563
  Gibson v. Cranage 563
Concurrent Conditions 565
  Pittman v. Canham 565
Prevention 569
  Parsons v. Bristol Development Co. 569
Waiver and Estoppel 573
  McKenna v. Vernon 573
  Beverly Way Associates v. Barham 575
Avoidance of Forfeiture as a Basis for Excusing a Condition 580
  Hicks v. Bush 580
  Kingston v. Preston 584
Time for Performance 587

Stewart v. Newbury	587
Substantial Performance	**590**
Time Is of the Essence	**591**
The Perfect Tender Rule	**591**
D.P. Technology Corp. v. Sherwood Tool, Inc.	591
Bartus v. Riccardi	596
Waiver of Breach	**599**
Divisible Contracts	**599**
Gill v. Johnstown Lumber Co.	599
Restitution for a Party in Default	**601**
Britton v. Turner	601
Kirkland v. Archbold	608
Suspending Performance and Terminating the Contract	**611**
Walker & Co. v. Harrison	611
K & G Construction Co. v. Harris	615
Prevention and Cooperation	**619**
United States v. Peck	619
New England Structures, Inc. v. Loranger	620
Repudiation and Anticipatory Breach	**624**
Hochster v. De La Tour	624
Minor v. Minor	629
Cosden Oil & Chemical Co. v. Karl O. Helm Aktiengesellschaft	635
United States v. Seacoast Gas Co.	640
McCloskey & Co. v. Minweld Steel Co.	644
Adequate Assurance of Due Performance	**647**
Pittsburgh-Des Moines Steel v. Brookhaven Manor Water Co.	647
Insolvent Buyers	**651**
Assessment Questions Chapter 8	**652**
Chapter 9	**653**
Mistake, Impracticability and Frustration of Purpose	**653**
Introduction	**653**
Mistake	**653**
Mutual Mistake	**653**
Sherwood v. Walker	654
Wood v. Boynton	658
Renner v. Kehl	661

Unilateral Mistake 665
Donovan v. RRL Corp. 665
Impracticability/Impossibility of Performance 673
Taylor v. Caldwell 674
Cazares v. Saenz 676
Impracticability Under the UCC 680
Transatlantic Financing Corporation v. United States.......................680
Canadian Industrial Alcohol Co. v. Dunbar Molasses Co. 685
Selland Pontiac-GMC, Inc. v. King...687
Drafting Tip – Force Majeure Clauses..690
Crop Failures 690
Squillante v. California Lands, Inc. 690
Frustration of Purpose 691
Krell v. Henry...692
Lloyd v. Murphy 695
20th Century Lites, Inc. v. Goodman..700
Swift Canadian Co. v. Banet 706
Chase Precast v. John J. Paonessa Co. 709
Northern Indiana Public Service Co. v. Carbon County Coal 713
Young v. City of Chicopee...719
Assessment Questions Chapter 9 721

Chapter 10 723

Third Party Rights..723

Introduction..723
Third Party Beneficiary Contracts...723
Lawrence v. Fox..723
Intended Beneficiaries..727
Seaver v. Ransom..727
Johnson v. Holmes Tuttle Lincoln-Mercury 731
Lucas v. Hamm 737
Schauer v. Mandarin Gems of Cal. 740
Incidental Beneficiaries..743
Jones v. Aetna Casualty & Surety Co. 743
Municipal Contracts and Third Parties..746
Luis v. Orcutt Town Water Co..746
Vesting of Third Party's Rights..752

    Karo v. San Diego Symphony Orchestra Ass'n. 752
    Detroit Bank & Trust v. Chicago Flame Hardening 754

Assignment 762
    Herzog v. Irace 762

Assignment Need Not Be in Any Particular Form 765

The Importance of Notice of Assignment 766

Assignment of Future Rights 766

Gratuitous Gift Assignments vs. Assignments for Value 766

Anti-Assignment Clauses 767
    Bel-Ray Company, Inc. v. Chemrite (Pty) Ltd. 767

Assignee Stands In Shoes of Assignor 770
    Delacy Investments, Inc. v. Thurman & Re/Max Real Estate 771
    Chemical Bank v. Rinden Professional Association 776

Holder in Due Course 779

Notice of Assignment Cuts Off Right to Assert Certain Defenses 779

Implied Warranty of Assignment 780

Priority of Assignees of the Same Right 781

Delegation 781

Assignment and Delegation Contrasted 781

Non-Delegable Duties 781
    Taylor v. Palmer 782
    Sally Beauty Company, Inc. v. Nexxus Products Company, Inc. 783

Novation 786

Assessment Questions Chapter 10 787

CHAPTER 1
NATURE OF CONTRACT AND CONSIDERATION

Definition of "Contract"

A contract is an agreement between two or more persons to do or not to do a certain thing or things. (Cal.Civ.Code § 1549; See also, Restatement (Second) of Contracts § 1 (1981) [hereafter cited as Rest.2d].) An indispensable prerequisite to the formation of a contract is mutual agreement, i.e., agreement by all parties to the same terms. Consent is not considered to be mutual unless the parties all agree upon the same thing in the same sense. Mutual assent (which is explored in detail in Chapter 2) is ordinarily established by a process of offer and acceptance.

Elements of a Contract

A valid contract requires:
(1) Parties having legal capacity to contract;
(2) Mutual consent;
(3) A lawful objective; and
(4) A sufficient consideration. (Cal.Civ.Code § 1550)

Types of Contracts

Express or Implied In Fact Contracts

A contract may be express or implied in fact. (Cal.Civ.Code § 1619) In an express contract, the existence and terms of the contract are stated in words or the writings of the parties. (Cal.Civ.Code § 1620) In an implied in fact contract, the existence and terms of the contract are inferred from the conduct of the parties. (Cal.Civ.Code § 1621) The distinction between an express and an implied in fact contract relates only to the manner in which the agreement is shown. Both types are based upon the express or apparent intention of the parties. (See, 1 Witkin, Summary of Cal. Law (10th ed. 2005) Contracts, §§ 102, 103.)

Schaad v. Hazelton
California Court of Appeal Third District, 1946.
72 Cal.App.2d 860, 865, 165 P.2d 517, 519

This action was brought by plaintiff, the daughter of Addie M. Hazelton, deceased, to recover from the estate of said decedent the sum of $21,178.83 claimed to be the reasonable value of services rendered by her to said decedent from July 1, 1926, to March 10, 1943, "in serving as companion, housekeeper, nurse, furnishing transportation, sewing, washing, ironing and otherwise" for said Addie M. Hazelton, "with the understanding and agreement between said Addie M. Hazelton and Plaintiff that said Addie M. Hazelton would compensate Plaintiff for said services by leaving to her ... one-half of all the estate of said Addie M. Hazelton and which estate should include all the property of said Addie M. Hazelton except the home of said Addie M. Hazelton and the home of Earl J. Hazelton." The filing of a claim against the estate of the decedent and its rejection were alleged, a copy of the claim being attached to the complaint. The action was tried before a jury and resulted in a verdict in favor of plaintiff for the sum of $4,300. Thereafter, on motion of defendant, the trial court entered a judgment in favor of defendant notwithstanding the verdict, and this appeal followed.

The only question before this court is whether there was produced before the trial court evidence which, viewed in its most favorable aspect, was sufficient to support the jury's verdict.

J. B. Hazelton and Addie M. Hazelton were husband and wife. They acquired considerable property, including a substantial home and a lumber yard in Orland. They had two children, Marjorie and Earl, both of whom were, in March, 1926, of adult age. The daughter, who was apparently unemployed, was living in the home of her parents, and the son, who was then working for his father in the lumber yard, was married and occupied a home of his own in Orland.

On July 10, 1926, plaintiff married Clarence Schaad. She brought her husband into the home of her parents where they continued to reside until May 1, 1931, when they moved to Willows, and later, to Sacramento. In July, 1934, when Mr. Schaad lost his job they returned to the Hazelton home where they continued to reside. A son was born to the Schaads in 1927, and he, too, lived in the Hazelton home with his parents. On August 5, 1941, J. B. Hazelton and Addie M. Hazelton executed a deed conveying to their daughter the family home in Orland. This deed was deposited with the attorney who had drawn same, with instructions to deliver it to the grantee upon the death of the survivor of the grantors. Prior to his death J. B. Hazelton, who was suffering from cancer, conveyed his property to his wife, and on February 23, 1942, he died.

Mrs. Hazelton died in April, 1943, leaving a will dated April 3, 1942, in which she gave the family home, variously valued at from $8,000 to $15,000, and its contents, appraised at $1,100, to her daughter, reciting that a deed to the home had already been placed in escrow. The will also stated that prior to her husband's death they had agreed between them and their children that all debts owing by their son, and by their daughter and her husband, either to them or the lumber company, were forgiven, and that it was her will that they be canceled. The will devised to plaintiff a life estate in certain other real property with remainder to her children, which property was given value of $5,000 to $8,500, gave the lumber mill and business and other real property to the son, and divided the residue between the two children equally. The whole estate was appraised by the official appraiser at $44,929.86.

Plaintiff produced no evidence whatsoever of any express contract on the part of her mother to compensate her, either by will or otherwise, for any services she might or did perform in the home shared by the two families, nor was there any testimony that either of the parties ever made any reference to any such purported agreement. Appellant does not even contend in her brief that such evidence was produced, but argues that there must have been such an agreement because (a) at the time of a family conference held just before Mr. Hazelton's death he stated to his son that the daughter had been generous in asking that the debts of the son as well as her own be forgiven, and that he wanted them to share the estate equally; (b) that the Schaad boy testified he had heard his grandmother say to his mother, more than once, that the estate was to be settled equally between the son and daughter; (c) that the Schaads paid rent, and (d) that the household expenses were apparently paid from what was called "the bank," into which Mr. Schaad and Mr. Hazelton both put money.

The statement in appellant's brief that the Schaads paid rent is a conclusion based upon the testimony of the Schaad boy that he had seen his mother give his grandmother money for the rent, and had heard his grandmother ask for the rent. . . .

Regarding the services performed by plaintiff in the home of her parents, while there was testimony that she engaged in the general household duties, they appear to have been no different from those which she would have performed for her own family in her own home had she occupied one, except that, owing to operations which Mrs. Hazelton underwent in 1926, and in 1941, she was unable to raise her arms so as to reach the back of her head, and her daughter combed her hair for her, and during her convalescence, assisted in caring for her. It is true that after her operation in 1926 Mrs. Hazelton's health was not good, but it is undenied that except for short periods after her operations, she was able to and did assist with the housework, put up fruit, made the pies, doughnuts, etc., ironed, worked in her garden, washed dishes, did mending, and, during the infancy of the Schaad child, assisted in caring for him. Apparently during the three years that the Schaads lived elsewhere she was able to run her own home. It is undenied, also, that at the time of Mr. Hazelton's last illness a nurse was in attendance for several weeks; and that another woman came in and worked for a few hours a day when Mr. Hazelton's condition was very critical. There was also a nurse in attendance during the month preceding Mrs. Hazelton's death. While there is some testimony that plaintiff, in her own car, at times took her mother to San Francisco and elsewhere and also performed personal services for her, the evidence fails signally to show that the services performed by her in the household were other than those which would naturally be performed by a loving and dutiful daughter in the home of her parents which she and her family shared with them; and their performance is insufficient to give rise to an inference that such services were performed for her mother any more than for her father, or for her husband and her son who alike shared the benefits of same, or that there was any intention on the part of the mother that she should pay for them, or any intention on the part of plaintiff that she should be paid for them.

The statements of the parents that their two children were to share equally in this estate was but natural, and do not imply that the daughter was to be paid for her services in the home; rather the contrary. Furthermore, appellant's claim that in 1926 her mother agreed to compensate her by leaving her one-half of all her estate "except the home of said Addie M. Hazelton and the home of Earl J. Hazelton," is fictitious on its face, since at that time Mrs. Hazelton had no estate, her husband being then living; and it is not reasonable that Mrs. Hazelton could have anticipated that her husband would predecease her, or that should she survive her husband, the home would be excluded from her estate, as it was by the subsequent deed executed by both Mr. and Mrs. Hazelton.

While as a general principle of law where one performs services for another at his instance and request the law implies a promise to pay, and the request may be inferred from circumstances, and that where one accepts or receives the benefit of another's work the law implies a promise to pay what the services are reasonably worth, the rule is founded upon a mere presumption of law which may be rebutted. And where services are rendered between the members of a household or between those closely related by blood, the law will ordinarily presume that they were prompted by motives of love, friendship and kindness, rather than the desire for gain. And, as was said in *Winder v. Winder*, 18 Cal.2d 123, 127-128 [114 P.2d 347, 144 A.L.R. 935], "in order to support a claim for services made by a child or relation who remains with his parent or kin after majority the circumstances must show either an express contract or that compensation was in the contemplation of the parties." Also in that case the court cited and quoted from *Wainwright Trust Co. v. Kinder*, 69 Ind.App. 88 [120 N.E. 419], to the effect that while the intention to pay and the expectation of compensation may be inferred from conduct where equity and justice require compensation, and expectation of compensation may coexist with higher motives prompted by affection or the sense of duty, to warrant the finding of such contract, the elements of intention to pay on the one hand, and expectation of compensation on the other must be found to exist, though they may be inferred from the relation and situation of the parties, the nature and character of the services rendered, and any other facts or circumstances which may reasonably be said to throw any light upon the question at issue.

Appellant relies upon *Winder v. Winder*, asserting that the facts in that case and those in the case before us are parallel. We think them clearly distinguishable, for in the Winder case there was evidence that the mother, who was living alone, induced her son, the plaintiff, to live with her upon her promise to leave her property to him; also that the son paid his mother $25 a month as rent, furnished her with board and personal care, and paid all other expenses except medical, special nursing and hospitalization. There was also evidence that when, after an absence, the son resumed the care of his mother, she reaffirmed her promise to leave the home to him in return for his services. Also there the mother left all of her estate to others, with nothing to plaintiff. None of those facts appear in the present case.

In *Fuller v. Everett*, 100 Cal.App. 593 [280 P. 550], a daughter sought to recover from the estate of her deceased mother for the reasonable value of board and lodging, nursing and personal attendance furnished her mother, alleging that the mother had come to the home of plaintiffs at her own request, and that the services and maintenance were rendered at her special instance and upon a promise to pay therefore. There was testimony that when the mother was ill she said to her daughter that she was going home with her; that the mother thereafter repeatedly remarked that her daughter took fine care of her, and that she would never regret what she had done for the mother; that the mother often said she intended to pay her daughter and pay her well, but never said when or how she would pay her. The court said that this presented appellant's case in its strongest light, but showed no meeting of the minds upon any agreed kind or amount of compensation; that to warrant an inference that one relative became indebted to the other for such service the evidence must be such as reasonably to indicate that it was the expectation of both parties that compensation should be made; that the presumption ordinarily prevailing, that the services were to be paid for, could not be invoked in such cases, but, on the contrary, as was said in Ruble v. Richardson, 188 Cal. 150, 157, [204 P. 572], quoting from 1 Beach on Contracts, "where services are rendered by members of a family, living in one household, to each other, or necessaries are supplied by one near relation to another, the law will presume that they were gratuitous favors merely, prompted by friendship, kindness and the relationship between them. And in such case, before the person rendering the service can recover, the express promise of the party served must be shown or such facts and circumstances as will authorize the jury to find that the services were rendered in the expectation of one of receiving, and by the other of making compensation therefore."

In *Ruble v. Richardson*, plaintiff, who was a niece of a Mrs. Kitchen, brought suit against the executor of Mrs. Kitchen's estate claiming payment for services rendered by her to decedent in whose home she lived as a daughter performing the ordinary services of a daughter. An implied contract to pay for such services was relied upon. The court said that in the absence of evidence of an express contract plaintiff was compelled to rely upon circumstances from which the law might raise an implied promise to compensate her for services rendered; but that evidence that she had performed the ordinary services of a daughter did not raise an inference in law that there was a promise to pay for the services rendered.

In *Murdock v. Murdock*, 7 Cal. 511, plaintiff who was the stepmother of defendants, at the request of defendants resided in their home as mother of the family for several years. Becoming dissatisfied, she left the home, and sued for compensation for her services. The court said that there seemed to have been no mutual expectation of compensation on either side; that plaintiff did not occupy the position of a servant in the family and was not so treated; and that "where a party sustains to others a certain relation, and assumes a certain position, inconsistent with the claim set up, the proof should either show an express contract, or conclusive circumstances from which a contract might be justly implied."

In *Farmer v. Underwood*, 164 Iowa 587 [146 N.W. 18], a daughter and her husband and their family came to live with the daughter's father and mother on their farm. From time to time the son-in-law worked on the farm doing general farm work. Nothing was said by either the father or the son-in-law as to payment of wages, except that some five or six years after the parties began living together, the son-in-law, needing money, stated that he was leaving to seek employment elsewhere, at which time defendant stated that if plaintiff wanted to work he could stay there and defendant would give him $25 per month. The court, in an action by plaintiff to recover for his services, directed a verdict for defendant, and on appeal the judgment was affirmed, the court saying that there was nothing to indicate that defendant at any time understood that plaintiff was working for him in expectation of remuneration, and nothing to indicate that defendant did not understand that plaintiff was there with his family, as a member of defendant's household, receiving support for himself and family, and that the services rendered by him were rendered in that capacity; that no express agreement for compensation was shown and that the facts and circumstances gave rise to no implication that plaintiff intended to charge for his services or that defendant intended to pay him therefore; that before plaintiff could recover, the evidence must disclose a mutual purpose and intent that the services should be paid for before the presumption that they were gratuitously rendered was overcome; and that plaintiff had failed to sustain the burden which rested upon him, to show these matters.

We are satisfied that the evidence relied upon by appellant as giving rise to an inference that the mother intended to pay her daughter for her services in the household, or that appellant contemplated that she should receive payment for same is insufficient, and that plaintiff failed to meet the burden imposed upon her, of proving either an express contract or circumstances from which a contract could be implied. The judgment notwithstanding the verdict is, therefore, affirmed.

Peek, J., and Thompson, J., concurred.

Questions

1. What was the purpose of the plaintiff's action in this case?

2. What was the verdict of the jury in the trial court?

3. What was the basis for the trial court's judgment in favor of the defendant?

4. What evidence did the plaintiff present to support her claim for compensation?

5. According to the court's reasoning, under what circumstances can a claim for compensation be supported in cases involving services rendered within a family or household?

TAKEAWAYS – Implied In Fact Contracts

Where the parties are not members of the same family or close relatives, the burden of proof is on the recipient of the services to show that they were rendered gratuitously or without obligation on his part to pay. (*Sowash v. Emerson* (3d Dist.1916) 32 Cal.App. 13, 161 P. 1018; *Ashley v. Martin* (1st Dist.1916) 100 Cal.App. 217, 279 P. 810.) (This latter allocation of the burden rests upon the presumption that a person rendering services to another at that person's request ordinarily will be compensated.)

ORAL AND WRITTEN CONTRACTS

A contract may be oral, written, or partly oral and partly written. Unless some law provides otherwise, an oral or a partly oral and partly written contract is as valid and enforceable as a written contract. (Cal.Civ.Code § 1622)

Oral Agreement to Be Reduced to Writing

When the parties orally or in writing agree that the terms of a proposed contract are to be reduced to writing and signed by them before it is to be effective, there is no binding agreement until a written contract is signed.

This rule does not mean that a contract already reduced to writing and signed is of no binding force merely because it contemplates a subsequent and more formal instrument. If the parties have orally agreed on all the terms and conditions of a contract with the mutual intention that it shall thereupon become binding, but also agree that a formal written agreement to the same effect shall be prepared and signed, the oral agreement is binding regardless of whether it is subsequently reduced to writing.

The fact that an agreement contemplates subsequent documentation does not invalidate the agreement if the parties have agreed to its existing terms. (See, *Clarke v. Fiedler* (1941) 44 Cal.App.2d 838, 847 [113 P.2d 275] [" 'Any other rule would always permit a party who has entered into a contract like this ... to violate it, whenever the understanding was that it should be reduced to another written form, by simply suggesting other and additional terms and conditions. If this were the rule the contract would never be completed in cases where, by changes in the market, or other events occurring subsequent to the written negotiations, it became the interest of either party to adopt that course in order to escape or evade obligations incurred in the ordinary course of commercial business.' "]; See also, *Smissaert v. Chiodo* (1958) 163 Cal.App.2d 827, 830 [330 P.2d 98].)

Whether it is the intention of the parties that the agreement should be binding at once, or when later reduced to writing or to a more formal writing, is an issue of fact to be determined by reference to the words the parties used, as well as upon all of the surrounding facts and circumstances. (See, 1 Witkin, Summary of Cal. Law (10th ed. 2005) Contracts, § § 134, 135.)

CONSIDERATION

A contract is a promise that the law will enforce. (Rest.2d § 1) However, not every promise is legally enforceable. A promise without sufficient consideration will not be enforced by a court of law. Promises that are not supported by consideration are classified as *gratuitous promises*. A promise to make a gift at sometime in the future would fall into this category. Gratuitous promises are not legally enforceable. What distinguishes enforceable promises from those that are unenforceable is the presence of consideration.

Consideration is any act or forbearance which is of benefit to the promisor or detriment to the promisee. (See, Rest.2d § 71.) It may be either a benefit conferred or agreed to be conferred upon the person making the promise or some other person, or a detriment suffered or agreed to be suffered by the person to whom the promise is made or some other person. (Cal.Civ.Code § 1605)

The Concept of Detriment

Hamer v. Sidway
Court of Appeals of New York, 1891
124 N.Y. 538, 27 N.E. 256

William E. Story agreed to and with William E. Story, 2d, that if he would refrain from drinking liquor, using tobacco, swearing, and playing cards or billiards for money until he should become 21 years of age then he, the said William E. Story, would at that time pay him, the said William E. Story, 2d, the sum of $5,000 for such refraining, to which the said William E. Story, 2d, agreed.

On January 31, 1875, the nephew wrote to his uncle as follows:

'DEAR UNCLE—I am now 21 years old to-day, and I am now my own boss, and I believe, according to agreement, that there is due me $5,000. I have lived up to the contract to the letter in every sense of the word.'

A few days later, and on February sixth, the uncle replied, and, so far as it is material to this controversy, the reply is as follows:

'DEAR NEPHEW—Your letter of the 31st ult. came to hand all right saying that you had lived up to the promise made to me several years ago. I have no doubt but you have, for which you shall have $5,000 as I promised you. I had the money in the bank the day you was 21 years old that I intended for you, and you shall have the money certain. Now, Willie, I don't intend to interfere with this money in any way until I think you are capable of taking care of it, and the sooner that time comes the better it will please me. I would hate very much to have you start out in some adventure that you thought all right and lose this money in one year. * * * This money you have earned much easier than I did, besides acquiring good habits at the same time, and you are quite welcome to the money. Hope you will make good use of it. * * *

W. E. STORY.

'P. S.—You can consider this money on interest.'

PARKER, J.

The question which provoked the most discussion by counsel on this appeal, and which lies at the foundation of plaintiff's asserted right of recovery, is whether by virtue of a contract defendant's testator William E. Story became indebted to his nephew William E. Story, 2d, on his twenty-first birthday in the sum of five thousand dollars. The trial court found as a fact that 'on the 20th day of March, 1869, * * * William E. Story agreed to and with William E. Story, 2d, that if he would refrain from drinking liquor, using tobacco, swearing, and playing cards or billiards for money until he should become 21 years of age then he, the said William E. Story, would at that time pay him, the said William E. Story, 2d, the sum of $5,000 for such refraining, to which the said William E. Story, 2d, agreed,' and that he 'in all things fully performed his part of said agreement.'

The defendant contends that the contract was without consideration to support it, and, therefore, invalid. He asserts that the promisee by refraining from the use of liquor and tobacco was not harmed but benefited; that that which he did was best for him to do independently of his uncle's promise, and insists that it follows that unless the promisor was benefited, the contract was without consideration. A contention, which if well founded, would seem to leave open for controversy in many cases whether that which the promisee did or omitted to do was, in fact, of such benefit to him as to leave no consideration to support the enforcement of the promisor's agreement. Such a rule could not be tolerated, and is without foundation in the law. The Exchequer Chamber, in 1875, defined consideration as follows: 'A valuable consideration in the sense of the law may consist either in some right, interest, profit or benefit accruing to the one party, or some forbearance, detriment, loss or responsibility given, suffered or undertaken by the other.' Courts 'will not ask whether the thing which forms the consideration does in fact benefit the promisee or a third party, or is of any substantial value to anyone. It is enough that something is promised, done, forborne or suffered by the party to whom the promise is made as consideration for the promise made to him.' (Anson's Prin. of Con. 63.)

'In general a waiver of any legal right at the request of another party is a sufficient consideration for a promise.' (Parsons on Contracts, 444.)

'Any damage, or suspension, or forbearance of a right will be sufficient to sustain a promise.' (Kent, vol. 2, 465, 12th ed.)

Pollock, in his work on contracts, page 166, after citing the definition given by the Exchequer Chamber already quoted, says: 'The second branch of this judicial description is really the most important one. Consideration means not so much that one party is profiting as that the other abandons some legal right in the present or limits his legal freedom of action in the future as an inducement for the promise of the first.'

Now, applying this rule to the facts before us, the promisee used tobacco, occasionally drank liquor, and he had a legal right to do so. That right he abandoned for a period of years upon the strength of the promise of the testator that for such forbearance he would give him $5,000. We need not speculate on the effort which may have been required to give up the use of those stimulants. It is sufficient that he restricted his lawful freedom of action within certain prescribed limits upon the faith of his uncle's agreement, and now having fully performed the conditions imposed, it is of no moment whether such performance actually proved a benefit to the promisor, and the court will not inquire into it, but were it a proper subject of inquiry, we see nothing in this record that would permit a determination that the uncle was not benefited in a legal sense. Few cases have been found which may be said to be precisely in point, but such as have been support the position we have taken.

In *Shadwell v. Shadwell* (9 C. B. [N. S.] 159), an uncle wrote to his nephew as follows:

'MY DEAR LANCEY—I am so glad to hear of your intended marriage with Ellen Nicholl, and as I promised to assist you at starting, I am happy to tell you that I will pay to you 150 pounds yearly during my life and until your annual income derived from your profession of a chancery barrister shall amount to 600 guineas, of which your own admission will be the only evidence that I shall require.

'Your affectionate uncle,

'CHARLES SHADWELL.'

It was held that the promise was binding and made upon good consideration.

In *Lakota v. Newton,* an unreported case in the Superior Court of Worcester, Mass., the complaint averred defendant's promise that 'if you (meaning plaintiff) will leave off drinking for a year I will give you $100,' plaintiff's assent thereto, performance of the condition by him, and demanded judgment therefore. Defendant demurred on the ground, among others, that the plaintiff's declaration did not allege a valid and sufficient consideration for the agreement of the defendant. The demurrer was overruled.

In *Talbott v. Stemmons,* the step-grandmother of the plaintiff made with him the following agreement: 'I do promise and bind myself to give my grandson, Albert R. Talbott, $500 at my death, if he will never take another chew of tobacco or smoke another cigar during my life from this date up to my death, and if he breaks this pledge he is to refund double the amount to his mother.' The executor of Mrs. Stemmons demurred to the complaint on the ground that the agreement was not based on a sufficient consideration. The demurrer was sustained and an appeal taken therefrom to the Court of Appeals, where the decision of the court below was reversed. In the opinion of the court it is said that 'the right to use and enjoy the use of tobacco was a right that belonged to the plaintiff and not forbidden by law. The abandonment of its use may have saved him money or contributed to his health, nevertheless, the surrender of that right caused the promise, and having the right to contract with reference to the subject-matter, the abandonment of the use was a sufficient consideration to uphold the promise.' Abstinence from the use of intoxicating liquors was held to furnish a good consideration for a promissory note in *Lindell v. Rokes* (60 Mo. 249). The cases cited by the defendant on this question are not in point. . . .

The trial court found as a fact that 'said letter was received by said William E. Story, 2d, who thereafter consented that said money should remain with the said William E. Story in accordance with the terms and conditions of said letter.' And further, 'That afterwards, on the first day of March, 1877, with the knowledge and consent of his said uncle, he duly sold, transferred and assigned all his right, title and interest in and to said sum of $5,000 to his wife Libbie H. Story, who thereafter duly sold, transferred and assigned the same to the plaintiff in this action.' . . .

The order appealed from should be reversed and the judgment of the Special Term affirmed, with costs payable out of the estate. . . .

Questions

1. What is the defendant's argument regarding the consideration for the contract, and why does the court reject it?

2. According to the court's reasoning, what does the term "consideration" mean in the context of contracts?

3. Provide an example from another case that supports the court's position on consideration.

Consideration Must Have Value

To be sufficient, the consideration must have some value. Something that is completely worthless cannot constitute sufficient consideration. (See 1 Witkin, Summary of California Law (10th ed. 2005) Contracts, §§ 216 - 221.)

Written Contracts Presumed to Be Supported by Consideration

In California, a written instrument is presumptive evidence of consideration. (Cal.Civ.Code § 1614) (However, this is a minority rule as most other jurisdictions do not recognize this presumption.) The burden of showing a want of consideration sufficient to support an instrument lies with the party seeking to invalidate or avoid it. (Cal.Civ.Code § 1615; *Rancho Santa Fe Pharmacy, Inc. v. Seyfert* (4th Dist.1990) 219 Cal.App.3d 875, 884, 268 Cal.Rptr. 505, 510)

Mutual Promises Constitute Consideration (Bilateral Contracts)

Promises by the parties bargained for and given in exchange for each other constitute consideration. (Rest.2d § 75.) In other words, mutual promises constitute consideration. (Cal.Civ.Code, § 1605; *El Rio Oils v. Pacific Coast Asphalt Co.*, 95 Cal.App. 2d 186, 193 [213 P.2d 1].) A single consideration may support several counter-promises. (*H. S. Crocker Co., Inc. v. McFaddin*, 148 Cal.App.2d 639, 645 [307 P.2d 429].)

Introduction to Schumm v. Berg

In the unlikely event you had any doubts about it, the cases and people in this book are real. The next case involves the estate of Wallace Beery, a famous actor of his time who appeared in some 250 movies and even won an Oscar.® Yes, there were scandals in Hollywood long before TMZ.

Schumm v. Berg
Supreme Court of California, 1951.
37 Cal.2d 174, 31 P.2d 39, 21 A.L.R.2d 1051

Wallace Beery

CARTER, J. Plaintiff appeals from a judgment of dismissal entered after defendants' demurrer was sustained without leave to amend in an action against a father's estate on a contract for the support and education of an illegitimate child.

"Whereas, Gloria Schumm is about to marry one, Hans Schumm; and

"Whereas, neither of the parties hereto wish to impose upon said Hans Schumm any responsibility for the maintenance and support of the said child of said Wallace Beery; and

"Whereas, said Wallace Beery deems it to be to his best interests, social and financial, that no suit be instituted against him in any Court for a public adjudication that he is the father of said expected child and for that reason desires to avoid such paternity suit and the unfavorable publicity such suit might entail.

"Now, Therefore, in consideration of the mutual covenants hereof, said Wallace Beery and Gloria Schumm agree as follows:

"(a) The said Gloria Schumm during the remainder of the period of her said pregnancy until the birth of said child shall institute no action or proceeding in any Court to establish judicially the fact that said Wallace Beery is or will be the father of said child.

"(b) Upon the marriage of said Gloria Schumm and Hans Schumm, said expected child if born alive shall be surnamed 'Schumm' and its name if a male shall include said Beery's Christian name 'Wallace,' or if a female, shall include said Beery's nickname 'Wally.'

"(c) Wallace Beery, if said child be born alive, recognizes and acknowledges the claim of Gloria Schumm in behalf of said expected child that he is morally and legally responsible for the support and education of said child in a manner suitable to said Wallace Beery's circumstances, station in life and standard of living from the date of the birth of said child until said child shall become 21 years of age, or until the death of said child, whichever shall occur sooner, and the said Wallace Beery recognizes the claim of Gloria Schumm in behalf of said expected child that he is morally responsible to afford said child a fair start in its adult life, and that considering the wealth and earning capacity of Wallace Beery the sum of $25,000 would be reasonable for such purpose and should be supplied by Wallace Beery to said child for such start.

"(d) Promptly upon the birth of said child, if born alive, said Wallace Beery shall purchase and acquire and deliver to and for said child two fully paid-up policies of a Life Insurance Company, to-wit: (1) one fully paid-up policy to be applied on account of the support and education of said child, whereby the Life Insurance Company shall have agreed to pay to said child beginning as of the date of his birth until he shall have reached the age of 21 years, or until his death, whichever occurs sooner, the sum of $100 per week; (2) a second fully paid-up policy on the Twenty Year Endowment plan, to afford said child a fair start in its adult life, whereby the Life Insurance Company on said child's twenty-first birthday, if he be then living, shall have agreed to pay to said child the sum of $25,000; the said child to have no interest in the life insurance features, if any, of said policies, which shall be exclusively matters of Wallace Beery's own concern; provided however, that said Wallace Beery in lieu of said first mentioned policy to be applied on account of support and education may promptly on the birth of said child designate a Bank in the City of Los Angeles, State of California as Trustee, and forthwith deposit with such Trustee interest or dividend bearing securities sufficient in amount to yield over and above the Trustee's charges and costs, a minimum net income of $100 per week, with provision in the Trust Agreement that the Trustee, beginning from the date of the birth of said child until the said child reaches the age of 21 years, or until said child's death, whichever occurs sooner, shall pay to said child the sum of $100 per week.

"(e) Said child shall be maintained, supported and educated as befitting a child of a prominent public man of wealth. Recognizing that the child's receipts under one of said policies of $100 per week will be wholly inadequate to accomplish the desired result, even without taking into account illness of the child from time to time during its minority, possible accidents, educational and other extraordinary unforeseen expenses, it is stipulated that nothing hereinbefore stated shall be deemed to be an intention on the part of any of the parties hereto to modify, decrease or compromise the legal and moral obligations of Wallace Beery to his said child to provide it during its minority with the necessary funds for its maintenance, support and education according to the station in life and standard of living of Wallace Beery."

Pursuant thereto Gloria married Hans Schumm on August 21, 1947, and on the birth of plaintiff, gave him the name above mentioned including "Wallace" and the surname "Schumm"; no proceeding was instituted until after the birth. Beery refused to comply with any of the provisions of the contract, except he paid nine weekly installments of $25, beginning July 6, 1948. Damages of $104,135 are claimed. Beery died and a claim against his estate was rejected. . . .

Defendants contend that for various reasons there was no consideration for the contract. . . . Beery was not bound because there was no mutuality of obligation. That argument is predicated upon the assumption that the contract was between plaintiff and Beery, which, as pointed out, is not the case. Plaintiff is the third party beneficiary of the contract and there is no performance required of him.

Defendants assert that Gloria's promise not to institute suit and to name plaintiff after Beery is not consideration. We cannot agree with either assertion.

On the first proposition, the argument runs to the effect that it is the illegitimate child's right under section 196a of the Civil Code to enforce the obligation of the father to support it; that the mother has no right except to bring the action in a representative capacity on the child's behalf; that, therefore, in agreeing not to sue she has suffered no detriment, for having no right, she gave up nothing; that a forbearance to sue on a void claim is not good consideration. Before dealing with that contention we note defendants' claim that there was no promise not to institute proceedings, for the promise does not say no action of any kind will be instituted by a guardian or otherwise. The promise (quoted supra) is plain enough. It clearly contemplates that Gloria will not directly or indirectly cause litigation to be instituted involving the question of Beery being the father of the child before the child is born.

The mother does have a definite interest in maintaining the action, for under section 196a the obligation to support is imposed upon both the mother and father. If the mother does not bring an action against the father and he refuses to give support, she will have to bear it. To the extent that she obtains relief against the father in such an action she is relieved of that burden. In agreeing to refrain from suing she is thereby suffering a detriment. It is not a case, therefore, where a person has no right of action and thus could not be benefited by a forbearance to prosecute an action. Gloria had the legal right to bring an action after conception and before birth. (*Davis v. Stroud*, 52 Cal.App.2d 308 [126 P.2d 409]; Kyne v. Kyne, 38 Cal.App.2d 122 [100 P.2d 806].

Gloria's promise to name plaintiff after Beery (given name Wallace) was adequate consideration to support the contract. It was a detriment to Gloria and a benefit to Beery. The privilege of naming a child is valid consideration for a promise. ([Case citations omitted]; Corbin on Contracts, § 127; Williston on Contracts (rev. ed.), § 115.) This is in accord with the principle that the law will not enter into an inquiry as to the adequacy of the consideration. (6 Cal.Jur 189; Williston on Contracts (rev.ed.), § 115; Rest., Contracts, § 81.) Defendants attack the foregoing authorities by asserting that they are dicta or based upon an authority not in point or did not give serious consideration to the question of the sufficiency of the "right to name" as consideration. They have cited no authority to the contrary, however, and two eminent authorities on contracts (Corbin and Williston, supra) have cited them for that proposition. Reason supports the rule, for having a child bear its father's name is commonly considered a privilege and honor, and Beery assumed it was, for he obtained such a promise running to him. Merely because in the cited cases the promise was to use the putative father's surname does not make them distinguishable. That is merely a matter of degree, and as seen, the validity of consideration does not depend on its value. Defendants refer to recitations in the contract that Beery was prominent and did not want the possible adverse publicity resulting from the instigation of a paternal suit. But that was only for the period prior to birth, and as seen, the promise to name the child after him was in his favor and presumably he considered it valuable. . . .

Judgment reversed.

Questions

1. What was the defendants' argument regarding the existence of consideration for the contract, and how did the court respond to it?

2. Why did the court reject the defendants' claim that there was no promise by the plaintiff's mother to refrain from instituting legal proceedings?

3. How did the court establish that the plaintiff's mother suffered a detriment by agreeing not to sue, even though she had the legal right to bring an action?

4. Explain why the court considered the promise to name the child after the defendant as adequate consideration for the contract.

5. What principle did the court rely on to support its view that the law does not inquire into the adequacy of consideration?

Settlement of Claims or Disputes as Consideration

One of the promises made to Beery was that in exchange for his agreement to pay child support, the mother would not bring a paternity action against him in court. This is an example of the settlement or compromise of a disputed claim. The compromise of a claim (even a doubtful one) is supported by consideration so long as the claim is pressed in good faith and is the subject of a bona fide dispute. It is sufficient that the parties entering into the settlement or compromise thought at the time that there was a bona fide question between them, even if it later turns out otherwise. On the other hand, the release from the mere annoyance of unfounded litigation does not furnish valuable consideration. (See, *Fiege v. Boehm* (1956) 210 Md. 352, 123 A2d 316.)

What Is Not Consideration

Having spent some time exploring the meaning of "detriment," it may be helpful to your understanding of that term to examine some things that are not regarded by the courts as the relinquishment of a right or the undertaking to do something that one is not obligated to do. They are illusory promises and the preexisting duty rule.

Illusory Promises

A promise which is conditioned upon the whim of the promisor is not consideration. (See, Rest.2d § 77(1).) In contract law, expressions cloaked in promissory terms, but in reality are noncommittal, are called illusory promises.

Strong v. Sheffield
Court of Appeals of New York, 1895
144 N.Y. 392, 39 N.E. 330

[Action on a promissory note. A judgment for plaintiff, Benjamin B. Strong, against defendant, Louisa A. Sheffield, was reversed by the General Term of the Supreme Court.]

ANDREWS, Ch. J. The contract between a maker or endorser of a promissory note and the payee forms no exception to the general rule that a promise, not supported by a consideration, is *nudum pactum*. The law governing commercial paper which precludes an inquiry into the consideration as against *bona fide* holders for value before maturity, has no application where the suit is between the original parties to the instrument. It is undisputed that the demand note upon which the action was brought was made by the husband of the defendant and indorsed by her at his request and delivered to the plaintiff, the payee, as security for an antecedent debt owing by the husband to the plaintiff. The debt of the husband was past due at the time, and the only consideration for the wife's endorsement, which is or can be claimed, is that as part of the transaction there was an agreement by the plaintiff when the note was given to forbear the collection of the debt, or a request for forbearance, which was followed by forbearance for a period of about two years subsequent to the giving of the note.

There is no doubt that an agreement by the creditor to forbear the collection of a debt presently due is a good consideration for an absolute or conditional promise of a third person to pay the debt, or for any obligation he may assume in respect thereto. Nor is it essential that the creditor should bind himself at the time to forbear collection or to give time. If he is requested by his debtor to extend the time, and a third person undertakes in consideration of forbearance being given to become liable as surety or otherwise, and the creditor does in fact forbear in reliance upon the undertaking, although he enters into no enforceable agreement to do so, his acquiescence in the request, and an actual forbearance in consequence thereof for a reasonable time, furnishes a good consideration for the collateral undertaking. In other words, a request followed by performance is sufficient, and mutual promises at the time are not essential, unless it was the understanding that the promisor was not to be bound, except on condition that the other party entered into an immediate and reciprocal obligation to do the thing requested. The general rule is clearly, and in the main accurately, stated in the note to *Forth* v. *Stanton* (1 Saund. 210, note *b*). The learned reporter says: "And in all cases of forbearance to sue, such forbearance must be either absolute or for a definite time, or for a reasonable time; forbearance for a little, or for some time, is not sufficient." The only qualification to be made is that in the absence of a specified time a reasonable time is held to be intended. The note in question did not in law extend the payment of the debt. It was payable on demand, and although being payable with interest it was in form consistent with an intention that payment should not be immediately demanded, yet there was nothing on its face to prevent an immediate suit on the note against the maker or to recover the original debt.

In the present case the agreement made is not left to inference, nor was it a case of request to forbear, followed by forbearance, in pursuance of the request, without any promise on the part of the creditor at the time. The plaintiff testified that there was an express agreement on his part to the effect that he would not pay the note away, nor put it in any bank for collection, but (using the words of the plaintiff) "I will hold it until such time as I want my money, I will make a demand on you for it." And again: "No, I will keep it until such time as I want it." Upon this alleged agreement the defendant indorsed the note. It would have been no violation of the plaintiff's promise if, immediately on receiving the note, he had commenced suit upon it. Such a suit would have been an assertion that he wanted the money and would have fulfilled the condition of forbearance. The debtor and the defendant, when they became parties to the note, may have had the hope or expectation that forbearance would follow, and there was forbearance in fact. But there was no agreement to forbear for a fixed time or for a reasonable time, but an agreement to forbear for such time as the plaintiff should elect. The consideration is to be tested by the agreement, and not by what was done under it. It was a case of mutual promises, and so intended. We think the evidence failed to disclose any consideration for the defendant's endorsement, and that the trial court erred in refusing so to rule.

The order of the General Term reversing the judgment should be affirmed, and judgment absolute directed for the defendant on the stipulation, with costs in all courts.

Questions

1. What was the alleged agreement between the plaintiff and the defendant regarding the note, and how does it relate to the issue of consideration in the case?

2. What was the consideration claimed for the wife's endorsement in the case?

3. Under what circumstances is an agreement by the creditor to forbear collection of a debt considered a good consideration?

4. What is the general rule regarding promises not supported by consideration?

Wood v. Lucy, Lady Duff-Gordon
Court of Appeals of New York, 1917
222 N.Y. 88, 118 N.E. 214

Appeal from Supreme Court, Appellate Division, First Department.

Action by Otis F. Wood against Lucy, Lady Duff-Gordon. From judgment of the Appellate Division 177 App.Div. 624, 164 N.Y.Supp. 576), which reversed an order denying defendant's motion for judgment on the pleading, and which dismissed the complaint, plaintiff appeals Reversed.

Judge Benjamin Cardozo and Lucy, Lady Duff-Gordon

Cardozo, J. The defendant styles herself "a creator of fashions." Her favor helps a sale. Manufacturers of dresses, millinery, and like articles are glad to pay for a certificate of her approval. The thing which she designs, fabrics, parasols, and what not, have a new value in the public mind when issued in her name. She employed the plaintiff to help her to turn this vogue into money. He was to have the exclusive right, subject always to her approval, to place her indorsements on the designs of others. He was also to have the exclusive right to place her own designs on sale, or to license others to market them. In return she was to have one-half of "all profits and revenues" derived from any contracts he might make. The exclusive right was to last at least on year from April 1, 1915, and thereafter from year to year unless terminated by notice of 90 days. The plaintiff says that he kept the contract on his part, and that the defendant broke it. She placed her indorsement on fabrics, dresses, and millinery without his knowledge and withheld the profits. He sues her for the damages, and the case comes here on demurrer. The agreement of employment is signed by both parties. It has wealth of recitals. The defendant insists, however, that it lacks the elements of a contract. She says that the plaintiff does not bind himself to anything. It is true that he does not promise in so many words that he will use reasonable efforts to place the defendant's indorsements and market her designs. We think, however, that such a promise is fairly to be implied. The law has outgrown its primitive stage of formalism when the precise word was the sovereign talisman, and every slip was fatal. It takes a broader view today. A promise may be lacking, and yet the whole writing may be "instinct with an obligation," imperfectly expressed (Citations omitted). If that is so, there is a contract.

The implication of a promise here finds support in many circumstances. The defendant gave an exclusive privilege. She was to have no right for at least a year to place her own indorsements or market her own designs except through the agency of the plaintiff. The acceptance of the exclusive agency was an assumption of its duties. (Citations omitted) We are not to suppose that one party was to be placed at the mercy of the other. (Citations omitted) Many other terms of the agreement point the same way. We are told at the outset by way of recital that:

"The said Otis F. Wood possesses a business organization adapted to the placing of such indorsements as the said Lucy, Lady Duff-Gordon, has approved."

The implication is that the plaintiff's business organization will be used for the purpose for which it is adapted. But the terms of the defendant's compensation are even more significant. Her sole compensation for the grant of an exclusive agency is to be one-half of all the profits resulting from the plaintiff's efforts. Unless he gave his efforts, she could never get anything. Without an implied promise, the transaction cannot have such business "efficacy, as both parties must have intended that at all events it should have." Bowen, L.J., in The Moorcock, 14 P.D. 64, G8. But the contract does not stop there. The plaintiff goes on to promise that he will account monthly for all moneys received by him, and that he will take out all such patents and copyrights and trademarks as may in his judgment be necessary to protect the rights and articles affected by the agreement. It is true, of course, as the Appellate Division has said, that if he was under no duty to try to market designs or to place certificates of indorsement, his promise to account for profits or take out copyrights would be valueless. But in determining the intention of the parties the promise has a value. It helps to enforce the conclusion that the plaintiff had some duties. His promise to pay the defendant one-half of the profits and revenues resulting from the exclusive agency and to render accounts monthly was a promise to use reasonable efforts to bring profits and revenues into existence. For this conclusion the authorities are ample. . . .

The judgment of the Appellate Division should be reversed, and the order of the Special Term affirmed, with costs in the Appellate Division and in this court.

Questions

1. How does Judge Cardozo interpret the absence of an explicit promise in the contract?

2. What are some circumstances that support the implication of a promise in the case?

3. Why is the defendant's compensation arrangement considered significant in determining the existence of a contract?

4. According to Judge Cardozo, what duties and obligations does the plaintiff have in relation to the contract in question?

Takeaways – Strong v. Sheffield and Wood v. Lucy, Lady Duff Gordon

Why was Strong's promise not to collect "until such time as I want my money," held to be illusory and Wood's promise (which only could be gleaned from reading between the lines) to use reasonable efforts held to be not illusory? The trend of the courts is to avoid construing promises as illusory by, whenever possible, implying conditions of good faith and best efforts in the absence of express language in the contract. Wood v. Lucy, Lady Duff-Gordon is an example of this.

The Preexisting Duty Rule

Merely doing or promising to do that which one is already legally obligated to do is not consideration. To avoid running afoul of the preexisting duty rule, modifications to contracts (unless they are contracts for the sale of goods [see, UCC § 2-209]) must be supported by additional consideration. However, in *Julian v. Gold*, 214 Cal. 74, 76 [3 P.2d 1009], a landlord, without consideration, orally agreed with his tenant to take a lesser sum for monthly rental than that set up in the written lease; he accepted the reduced payments for two years and then sued to recover the difference in rent for the two years past. The court denied recovery on the ground that the oral agreement had already been executed, and stated that "[the] rule is that an executed oral agreement will serve as a modification or release of a written agreement and this [is] without regard to the presence or absence of a consideration."

Bargained for Exchange

Feinberg v. Pfeiffer Co.
Saint Louis Court of Appeals, Missouri, 1959
322 S.W.2d 163

DOERNER, Commissioner. This is a suit brought in the Circuit Court of the City of St. Louis by plaintiff, a former employee of the defendant corporation, on an alleged contract whereby defendant agreed to pay plaintiff the sum of $200 per month for life upon her retirement. A jury being waived, the case was tried by the court alone. Judgment below was for plaintiff for $5,100, the amount of the pension claimed to be due as of the date of the trial, together with interest thereon, and defendant duly appealed.

The parties are in substantial agreement on the essential facts. Plaintiff began working for the defendant, a manufacturer of pharmaceuticals, in 1910, when she was but 17 years of age. By 1947 she had attained the position of bookkeeper, office manager, and assistant treasurer of the defendant, and owned 70 shares of its stock out of a total of 6,503 shares issued and outstanding. Twenty shares had been given to her by the defendant or its then president, she had purchased 20, and the remaining 30 she had acquired by a stock split or stock dividend. Over the years she received substantial dividends on the stock she owned, as did all of the other stockholders. Also, in addition to her salary, plaintiff from 1937 to 1949, inclusive, received each year a bonus varying in amount from $300 in the beginning to $2,000 in the later years.

On December 27, 1947, the annual meeting of the defendant's Board of Directors was held at the Company's offices in St. Louis, presided over by Max Lippman, its then president and largest individual stockholder. The other directors present were George L. Marcus, Sidney Harris, Sol Flammer, and Walter Weinstock, who, with Max Lippman, owned 5,007 of the 6,503 shares then issued and outstanding. At that meeting the Board of Directors adopted the following resolution, which, because it is the crux of the case, we quote in full:

"The Chairman thereupon pointed out that the Assistant Treasurer, Mrs. Anna Sacks Feinberg has given the corporation many years of long and faithful service. Not only has she served the corporation devotedly, but with exceptional ability and skill. The President pointed out that although all of the officers and directors sincerely hoped and desired that Mrs. Feinberg would continue in her present position for as long as she felt able, nevertheless, in view of the length of service which she has contributed provision should be made to afford her retirement privileges and benefits which should become a firm obligation of the corporation to be available to her whenever she should see fit to retire from active duty, however many years in the future such retirement may become effective. It was, accordingly, proposed that Mrs. Feinberg's salary which is presently $350.00 per month, be increased to $400.00 per month, and that Mrs. Feinberg would be given the privilege of retiring from active duty at any time she may elect to see fit so to do upon a retirement pay of $200.00 per month for life, with the distinct understanding that the retirement plan is merely being adopted at the present time in order to afford Mrs. Feinberg security for the future and in the hope that her active services will continue with the corporation for many years to come. After due discussion and consideration, and upon motion duly made and seconded, it was—

"Resolved, that the salary of Anna Sacks Feinberg be increased from $350.00 to $400.00 per month and that she be afforded the privilege of retiring from active duty in the corporation at any time she may elect to see fit so to do upon retirement pay of $200.00 per month, for the remainder of her life."

At the request of Mr. Lippman his sons-in-law, Messrs. Harris and Flammer, called upon the plaintiff at her apartment on the same day to advise her of the passage of the resolution. Plaintiff testified on cross-examination that she had no prior information that such a pension plan was contemplated, that it came as a surprise to her, and that she would have continued in her employment whether or not such a resolution had been adopted. It is clear from the evidence that there was no contract, oral or written, as to plaintiff's length of employment, and that she was free to quit, and the defendant to discharge her, at any time.

Plaintiff did continue to work for the defendant through June 30, 1949, on which date she retired. In accordance with the foregoing resolution, the defendant began paying her the sum of $200 on the first of each month. Mr. Lippman died on November 18, 1949, and was succeeded as president of the company by his widow. Because of an illness, she retired from that office and was succeeded in October, 1953, by her son-in-law, Sidney M. Harris. Mr. Harris testified that while Mrs. Lippman had been president she signed the monthly pension check paid plaintiff, but fussed about doing so, and considered the payments as gifts. After his election, he stated, a new accounting firm employed by the defendant questioned the validity of the payments to plaintiff on several occasions, and in the Spring of 1956, upon its recommendation, he consulted the Company's then attorney, Mr. Ralph Kalish. Harris testified that both Ernst and Ernst, the accounting firm, and Kalish told him there was no need of giving plaintiff the money. He also stated that he had concurred in the view that the payments to plaintiff were mere gratuities rather than amounts due under a contractual obligation, and that following his discussion with the Company's attorney plaintiff was sent a check for $100 on April 1, 1956. Plaintiff declined to accept the reduced amount, and this action followed. Additional facts will be referred to later in this opinion.

(The court's discussion of an evidentiary issue is omitted.)

Appellant's next complaint is that there was insufficient evidence to support the court's findings that plaintiff would not have quit defendant's employ had she not known and relied upon the promise of defendant to pay her $200 a month for life, and the finding that, from her voluntary retirement until April 1, 1956, plaintiff relied upon the continued receipt of the pension installments. The trial court so found, and, in our opinion, justifiably so. Plaintiff testified, and was corroborated by Harris, defendant's witness, that knowledge of the passage of the resolution was communicated to her on December 27, 1947, the very day it was adopted. She was told at that time by Harris and Flammer, she stated, that she could take the pension as of that day, if she wished. She testified further that she continued to work for another year and a half, through June 30, 1949; that at that time her health was good and she could have continued to work, but that after working for almost forty years she thought she would take a rest. Her testimony continued:

"Q. Now, what was the reason—I'm sorry. Did you then quit the employment of the company after you—after this year and a half? A. Yes.

"Q. What was the reason that you left? A. Well, I thought almost forty years, it was a long time and I thought I would take a little rest.

"Q. Yes. A. And with the pension and what earnings my husband had, we figured we could get along.

"Q. Did you rely upon this pension? A. We certainly did."

Q. Being paid? A. Very much so. We relied upon it because I was positive that I was going to get it as long as I lived.

"Q. Would you have left the employment of the company at that time had it not been for this pension? A. No.

"Mr. Allen: Just a minute, I object to that as calling for a conclusion and conjecture on the part of this witness.

"The Court: It will be overruled.

"Q. (Mr. Agatstein continuing): Go ahead, now. The question is whether you would have quit the employment of the company at that time had you not relied upon this pension plan? A. No, I wouldn't.

"Q. You would not have. Did you ever seek employment while this pension was being paid to you—

"A. (interrupting): No.

"Q. Wait a minute, at any time prior—at any other place? A. No, sir.

"Q. Were you able to hold any other employment during that time? A. Yes, I think so.

"Q. Was your health good? A. My health was good."

It is obvious from the foregoing that there was ample evidence to support the findings of fact made by the court below.

We come, then, to the basic issue in the case. While otherwise defined in defendant's third and fourth assignments of error, it is thus succinctly stated in the argument in its brief: "* * * whether plaintiff has proved that she has a right to recover from defendant based upon a legally binding contractual obligation to pay her $200 per month for life."

It is defendant's contention, in essence, that the resolution adopted by its Board of Directors was a mere promise to make a gift, and that no contract resulted either thereby, or when plaintiff retired, because there was no consideration given or paid by the plaintiff. It urges that a promise to make a gift is not binding unless supported by a legal consideration; that the only apparent consideration for the adoption of the foregoing resolution was the "many years of long and faithful service" expressed therein; and that past services are not a valid consideration for a promise. Defendant argues further that there is nothing in the resolution which made its effectiveness conditional upon plaintiff's continued employment, that she was not under contract to work for any length of time but was free to quit whenever she wished, and that she had no contractual right to her position and could have been discharged at any time.

Plaintiff concedes that a promise based upon past services would be without consideration, but contends that there were two other elements which supplied the required element: First, the continuation by plaintiff in the employ of the defendant for the period from December 27, 1947, the date when the resolution was adopted, until the date of her retirement on June 30, 1949. And, second, her change of position, i. e., her retirement, and the abandonment by her of her opportunity to continue in gainful employment, made in reliance on defendant's promise to pay her $200 per month for life.

We must agree with the defendant that the evidence does not support the first of these contentions. There is no language in the resolution predicating plaintiff's right to a pension upon her continued employment. She was not required to work for the defendant for any period of time as a condition to gaining such retirement benefits. She was told that she could quit the day upon which the resolution was adopted, as she herself testified, and it is clear from her own testimony that she made no promise or agreement to continue in the employ of the defendant in return for its promise to pay her a pension. Hence there was lacking that mutuality of obligation which is essential to the validity of a contract. . . .

(The remainder of the opinion in this case is taken up later in this book under the heading of "Reliance as an Alternative to Consideration – Promissory

Estoppel")

Questions

1. According to the defendant, why was there no legally binding contractual obligation to pay the plaintiff the pension?

2. What is the plaintiff's argument regarding the consideration for the promise to pay the pension?

3. Why does the court agree with the defendant that the evidence does not support the plaintiff's claim based on continued employment?

4. What does the court state is lacking in the case, which is essential for the validity of a contract?

Feinberg v. Pfeiffer – The Rest of the Story

Anna Feinberg makes for a very sympathetic plaintiff, and you may be tempted to feel sorry for her. However, the above portion of the opinion was not the end of the story. Although she lost the battle over the issue of whether consideration supported the promise to pay her a lifetime pension, she ultimately prevailed on other grounds. Stay tuned for the rest of the story.

Mills v. Wyman
Supreme Judicial Court of Massachusetts, 1825
3 Pick. 207

[A young man fell ill on his return from a sea voyage and was cared for by the plaintiff for a period of about two weeks. A few days later, after all the young man's expenses had been incurred, the young man's father, wrote to the plaintiff promising to pay those expenses. When the father did not pay, plaintiff sued him. The trial court dismissed the case and the plaintiff appealed.]

PARKER C.J. General rules of law established for the protection and security of honest and fair-minded men, who may inconsiderately make promises without any equivalent, will sometimes screen men of a different character from engagements which they are bound *in foro conscientiae* to perform. This is a defect inherent in all human systems of legislation. The rule that a mere verbal promise, without any consideration, cannot be enforced by action, is universal in its application, and cannot be departed from to suit particular cases in which a refusal to perform such a promise may be disgraceful.

The promise declared on in this case appears to have been made without any legal consideration. The kindness and services towards the sick son of the defendant were not bestowed at his request. The son was in no respect under the care of the defendant. He was twenty-five years old, and had long left his father's family. On his return from a foreign country, he fell sick among strangers, and the plaintiff acted the part of the good Samaritan, giving him shelter and comfort until he died. The defendant, his father, on being informed of this event, influenced by a transient feeling of gratitude, promised in writing to pay the plaintiff for the expenses he had incurred. But he has determined to break this promise, and is willing to have his case appear on record as a strong example of particular injustice sometimes necessarily resulting from the operation of general rules.

A deliberate promise in writing, made freely and without any mistake, one which may lead the party to whom it is made into contracts and expenses, cannot be broken without a violation of moral duty. But if there was nothing paid or promised for it, the law, perhaps wisely, leaves the execution of it to the conscience of him who makes it. It is only when the party making the promise gains something, or he to whom it is made loses something, that the law gives the promise validity....

[Judgment ordered on the nonsuit.]

Questions

1. Why does the court state that the promise made in this case lacks legal consideration?

2. According to the court's reasoning, under what conditions does the law give validity to a promise?

Takeaways – Feinberg v. Pfeiffer and Mills v. Wyman

Receipt of unrequested benefits creates no legal obligation. If a subsequent promise is made to pay for these benefits the promise is unenforceable. Therefore, promises made in recognition of a benefit previously received fail the "bargained-for-exchange" test and are considered to be merely gratuitous promises. In other words, past consideration is no consideration!

Relaxation of the Rule That Past Consideration is No Consideration

Webb v. McGowin
Court of Appeals of Alabama, 1935
27 Ala.App. 82, 168 So. 196

Action by Joe Webb against N. Floyd McGowin and Joseph F McGowin, as executors of the estate of J. Greeley McGowin, deceased From a judgment of nonsuit, plaintiff appeals.

BRICKEN, PRESIDING JUDGE. This action is in assumpsit. The complaint as originally filed was amended. The demurrers to the complaint as amended were sustained, and because of this adverse ruling by the court the plaintiff took a nonsuit, and the assignment of errors on this appeal are predicated upon said action or ruling of the court.

A fair statement of the case presenting the questions for decision is set out in appellant's brief, which we adopt.

"On the 3d day of August, 1925, appellant while in the employ of the W.T. Smith Lumber Company, a corporation, and acting within the scope of his employment, was engaged in clearing the upper floor of Mill No.2 of the company. While so engaged he was in the act of dropping a pine block from the upper floor of the mill to the ground below; this being the usual and ordinary way of clearing the floor, and it being the duty of the plaintiff in the course of his employment to so drop it. The block weighed about 75 pounds.

"As appellant was in the act of dropping the block to the ground below, he was on the edge of the upper floor of the mill. As he started to turn the block loose so that it would drop to the ground, he saw J. Greeley McGowin, testator of the defendants, on the ground below and directly under where the block would have fallen had appellant turned it loose. Had he turned it loose it would have struck McGowin with such force as to have caused him serious bodily harm or death. Appellant could have remained safely on the upper floor of the mill by turning the block loose and allowing it to drop, but had he done this the block would have fallen on McGowin and caused him serious Injuries or death. The only safe and reasonable way to prevent this was for appellant to hold to the block and divert its direction in falling from the place where McGowin was standing and the only safe way to divert it so as to prevent its coming into contact with McGowin was for appellant to fall with it to the ground below. Appellant did this, and by holding to the block and falling with it to the ground below, he diverted the course of its fall in such way that McGowin was not injured. In thus preventing the injuries to McGowin appellant himself received serious bodily injuries, resulting in his right leg being broken, the heel of his right foot torn off and his right arm broken. He was badly crippled for life and rendered unable to do physical or mental labor.

"On September 1, 1925, in consideration of appellant having prevented him from sustaining death or serious bodily harm and in consideration of the injuries appellant had received, McGowin agreed with him to care for and maintain him for the remainder of appellant's life at the rate of $15 every two weeks from the time he sustained his injuries to and during the remainder of appellant's life; it being agreed that McGowin would pay this sum to appellant for his maintenance. Under the agreement McGowin paid or caused to be paid to appellant the sum so agreed on up until McGowin's death on January 1, 1934. After his death the payments were continued to and including January 27, 1934, at which time they were discontinued. Thereupon plaintiff brought suit to recover the unpaid installments accruing up to the time of the bringing of the suit.

'The material averments of the different counts of the original complaint and the amended complaint are predicated upon the foregoing statement of facts."

The action was for the unpaid installments accruing after January 27, 1934, to the time of the suit.

1. The averments of the complaint show that appellant saved McGowin from death or grievous bodily harm. This was a material benefit to him of infinitely more value than any financial aid he could have received. Receiving this benefit, McGowin became morally bound to compensate appellant for the services rendered. Recognizing his moral obligation, he expressly agreed to pay appellant as alleged in the complaint and complied with this agreement up to the time of his death; a period of more than 8 years.

Had McGowin been accidentally poisoned and a physician, without his knowledge or request, had administered an antidote, thus saving his life, a subsequent promise by McGowin to pay the physician would have been valid. Likewise, McGowin's agreement as disclosed by the complaint to compensate appellant for saving him from death or grievous bodily injury is valid and enforceable.

Where the promisee cares for, improves, and preserves the property of the promisor, though done without his request, it is sufficient consideration for the promisor's subsequent agreement to pay for the service, because of the material benefit received. In Boothe v. Fitzpatrick, 36 Vt. 681, the court held that a promise by defendant to pay for the past keeping of a bull which had escaped from defendant's premises and been cared for by plaintiff was valid, although there was no previous request, because the subsequent promise obviated that objection; it being equivalent to a previous request. On the same principle, had the promisee saved the promisor's life or his body from grievous harm, his subsequent promise to pay for the services rendered would have been valid. Such service would have been far more material than caring for his bull. Any holding that saving a man from death or grievous bodily harm is not a material benefit sufficient to uphold a subsequent promise to pay for the service, necessarily rests on the assumption that saving life and preservation of the body from harm have only a sentimental value. The converse of this is true. Life and preservation of the body have material, pecuniary values, measurable in dollars and cents. Because of this, physicians practice their profession charging for services rendered in saving life and curing the body of its ills, and surgeons perform operations. The same is true as to the law of negligence, authorizing the assessment of damages in personal injury cases based upon the extent of the injuries, earnings, and life expectancies of those injured.

In the business of life insurance, the value of a man's life is measured in dollars and cents according to his expectancy, the soundness of his body, and his ability to pay premiums. The same is true as to health and accident insurance.

It follows that if, as alleged in the complaint, appellant saved J. Greeley McGowin from death or grievous bodily harm, and McGowin subsequently agreed to pay him for the service rendered, it became a valid and enforceable contract.

2. It is well settled that a moral obligation is a sufficient consideration to support a subsequent promise to pay where the promisor has received a material benefit, although there was no original duty or liability resting on the promisor. . . . In the case of State ex rel. Bayer v. Funk, supra, the court held that a moral obligation is a sufficient consideration to support all executory promise where the promisor received an actual pecuniary or material benefit for which he subsequently expressly promised to pay.

The case at bar is clearly distinguishable from that class of cases where the consideration is a mere moral obligation or conscientious duty unconnected with receipt by promisor of benefits of a material or pecuniary nature. Park Falls State Bank v. Fordyce, supra. Here the promisor received a material benefit constituting a valid consideration for his promise.

3. Some authorities hold that, for a moral obligation to support a subsequent promise to pay, there must have existed a prior legal or equitable obligation, which for some reason had become unenforceable, but for which the promisor was still morally bound. This rule, however, is subject to qualification in those cases where the promisor having received a material benefit from the promisee, is morally bound to compensate him for the services rendered and in consideration of this obligation promises to pay. In such cases the subsequent promise to pay is an affirmance or ratification of the services rendered carrying with it the presumption that a previous request for the service was made. . . .

Under the decisions above cited, McGowin's express promise to pay appellant for the services rendered was an affirmance or ratification of what appellant had done raising the presumption that the services had been rendered at McGowin's request.

4. The averments of the complaint show that in saving McGowin from death or grievous bodily harm, appellant was crippled for life. This was part of the consideration of the contract declared on. McGowin was benefited. Appellant was injured. Benefit to the promisor or injury to the promisee is a sufficient legal consideration for the promissor's agreement to pay. . . .

5. Under the averments of the complaint the services rendered by appellant were not gratuitous. The agreement of McGowin to pay and the acceptance of payment by appellant conclusively shows the contrary. . . .

(The court's discussion of whether the promise was within the Statute of Frauds, is omitted.)

From what has been said, we are of the opinion that the court below erred in the ruling complained of; that is to say in sustaining the demurrer, and for this error the case is reversed and remanded.

Reversed and remanded.

Questions

1. According to the court, why was the promise by McGowin to compensate the plaintiff valid and enforceable?

2. What is the significance of the promisor receiving a material benefit in cases involving moral obligations?

Takeaways, Mills v. Wyman and Webb v. McGowin

Why the different outcomes in *Mills v. Wyman* and *Webb v. McGowin*? Although the concept that "past consideration is no consideration" was well-entrenched in the common law, it is a notion that is slowly being eroded. California, for example, does not follow the rule that past consideration is no consideration. In California, an existing legal obligation resting upon the promisor, a moral obligation originating in some benefit conferred upon the promisor, or prejudice suffered by the promisee is also a good consideration for a promise, to an extent corresponding with the extent of the obligation, but no further or otherwise. (Cal.Civ.Code § 1606) On this point, California law is consistent with the so-called "minority" rule set forth in the Restatement Second of Contracts that a promise made in recognition of a benefit previously received by the promisor is enforceable to the extent necessary to prevent injustice. (See, Rest.2d § 86.)

The Requirement of a Bargain

Kirksey v. Kirksey
Supreme Court of Alabama, 1845
8 Ala. 131

The plaintiff was the wife of defendant's brother, but had for some time been a widow, and had several children. In 1840, the plaintiff resided on public land, under a contract of lease, she had held over, and was comfortably settled, and would have attempted to secure the land she lived on. The defendant resided in Talladega county, some sixty, or seventy miles off. On the 10th October, 1840, he wrote to her the following letter:

"Dear sister Antillico—Much to my mortification, I heard, that brother Henry was dead, and one of his children. I know that your situation is one of grief, and difficulty. You had a bad chance before, but a great deal worse now. I should like to come and see you, but cannot with convenience at present. . . . I do not know whether you have a preference on the place you live on, or not. If you had, I would advise you to obtain your preference, and sell the land and quit the country, as I understand it is very unhealthy, and I know society is very bad. If you will come down and see me, I will let you have a place to raise your family, and I have more open land than I can tend; and on the account of your situation, and that of your family, I feel like I want you and the children to do well."

Within a month or two after the receipt of this letter, the plaintiff abandoned her possession, without disposing of it, and removed with her family, to the residence of the defendant, who put her in comfortable houses, and gave her land to cultivate for two years, at the end of which time he notified her to remove, and put her in a house, not comfortable, in the woods, which he afterwards required her to leave.

A verdict being found for the plaintiff, for two hundred dollars, the above facts were agreed, and if they will sustain the action, the judgment is to be affirmed, otherwise it is to be reversed.

ORMOND, J. The inclination of my mind, is, that the loss and inconvenience, which the plaintiff sustained in breaking up, and moving to the defendant's, a distance of sixty miles, is a sufficient consideration to support the promise, to furnish her with a house, and land to cultivate, until she could raise her family. My brothers, however think, that the promise on the part of the defendant, was a mere gratuity, and that an action will not lie for its breach. The judgment of the Court below must therefore be, reversed, pursuant to the agreement of the parties.

Questions

1. What was the nature of the defendant's promise to the plaintiff?

2. What was the main point of contention among the judges regarding the validity of the promise?

3. According to the court, what is the significance of the loss and inconvenience suffered by the plaintiff?

4. What was the final decision of the court, and why was the judgment of the lower court reversed?

Takeaways – Kirksey v. Kirksey

Compare the following two statements: 1) "If you come over to my house at noon, I will give you $20." 2) "You can have $20, but you will need to come by my house to pick it up." Do you see a difference between the two statements? One possible distinction is that in one case the speaker is bargaining for the listener's appearance at a certain time and place while in the other case the speaker is simply telling the listener where they need to appear in order to receive a gift. Of these two possibilities, which one do the facts of *Kirksey* fall into?

Harris v. Time, Inc.
Court of Appeals of California, First Appellate District, 1987
191 Cal.App.3d 449, 237 Cal.Rptr. 584

KING, J. Mark Harris, Joshua Gnaizda and Richard Baker appeal from a judgment of dismissal of this class action lawsuit arising from their receipt of a direct mail advertisement from Time, Inc. . . .

It all began one day when Joshua Gnaizda, the three-year-old son of a prominent Bay Area public interest attorney, received what he (or his mother) thought was a tantalizing offer in the mail from Time. The front of the envelope contained two see-through windows partialy revealing the envelope's contents. One window showed Joshua's name and address. The other revealed the following statement: "JOSHUA A. GNAIZDA, I'LL GIVE YOU THIS VERSATILE NEW CALCULATOR WATCH FREE Just for, Opening this Envelope Before Feb. 15, 1985." Beneath the offer was a picture of the calculator watch itself. Joshua's mother opened the envelope and apparently realized she had been deceived by a ploy to get her to open a piece of junk mail. The see-through window had not revealed the full text of Time's offer. Printed below the picture of the calculator watch, and not viewable through the see-through window, were the following additional words: "AND MAILING THIS CERTIFICATE TODAY!" The certificate itself clearly required that Joshua purchase a subscription to Fortune magazine in order to receive the free calculator watch.

As is so often true in life situations these days, the certificate contained both good news and bad news. The good news was that Joshua could save up to 66 percent on the subscription, which might even be tax deductible. Even more important to the bargain hunter, prices might never be this low again. The bad news was that Time obviously had no intention of giving Joshua the versatile new calculator watch just for opening the envelope.

Although most of us, while murmuring an appropriate expletive, would have simply thrown away the mailer, and some might have stood on principle and filed an action in small claims court to obtain the calculator watch, Joshua's father did something a little different: he launched a $15 million lawsuit in San Francisco Superior Court.

The action was prosecuted by Joshua, through his father, and by Mark Harris and Richard Baker, who had also received the same mailer. We are not informed of the ages of Harris and Baker. The complaint alleged one cause of action for breach of contract, three causes of action for statutory unfair advertising, and four causes of action for promissory estoppel and fraud.

The complaint sought the following relief: (1) a declaration that all recipients of the mailer were entitled to receive the promised item or to rescind subscriptions they had purchased, (2) an injunction against future similar mailings, (3) compensatory damages in an amount equal to the value of the item, and (4) $15 million punitive damages to be awarded to a consumer fund "to be used for education and advocacy on behalf of consumer protection and enforcement of laws against unfair business practices." . . .

In sustaining the demurrer as to the cause of action for breach of contract, the court stated no specific grounds for its ruling. Time had argued the complaint did not allege an offer, did not allege adequate consideration, and did not allege notice of performance by the plaintiffs. On appeal, plaintiffs challenge each of these points as a basis for dismissal. . . .

[The court first took up the issue of whether the complaint alleged adequate consideration.] Time also argues that there was no contract because the mere act of opening the envelope was valueless and therefore did not constitute adequate consideration. Technically, this is incorrect. It is basic modern contract law that, with certain exceptions not applicable here (such as illegality or preexisting legal duty), any bargained-for act or forbearance will constitute adequate consideration for a unilateral contract. (Rest.2d, Contracts, § 71; see 1 Witkin, Summary of Cal. Law (8th ed. 1973) Contracts, §§ 162-169, pp. 153-162.) Courts will not require equivalence in the values exchanged or otherwise question the adequacy of the consideration. (*Schumm v. Berg*

(1951) 37 Cal.2d 174, 185 [231 P.2d 39, 21 A.L.R.2d 1051]; Rest.2d, Contracts, § 79.) If a performance is bargained for, there is no further requirement of benefit to the promisor or detriment to the promisee. (Rest.2d, Contracts, § 79, coms. a & b at pp. 200-201.)

Moreover, the act at issue here -- the opening of the envelope, with consequent exposure to Time's sales pitch -- may have been relatively insignificant to the plaintiffs, but it was of great value to Time. At a time when our homes are bombarded daily by direct mail advertisements and solicitations, the name of the game for the advertiser or solicitor is to get the recipient to open the envelope. Some advertisers, like Time in the present case, will resort to ruse or trick to achieve this goal. From Time's perspective, the opening of the envelope was "valuable consideration" in every sense of that phrase.

Thus, assuming (as we must at this juncture) that the allegations of the complaint are true, Time made an offer proposing a unilateral contract, and plaintiffs supplied adequate consideration for that contract when they performed the act of opening the envelope and exposing themselves to the sales pitch within. . . .

Question

Why did the court find that the act of opening the envelope constituted adequate consideration for a unilateral contract?

Cobaugh v. Klick-Lewis, Inc.
Supreme Court of Pennsylvania, 1989
561 A.2d 1248

WIEAND, Judge: On May 17, 1987, Amos Cobaugh was playing in the East End Open Golf Tournament on the Fairview Golf Course in Cornwall, Lebanon County. When he arrived at the ninth tee he found a new Chevrolet Beretta, together with signs which proclaimed: "HOLE-IN-ONE Wins this 1988 Chevrolet Beretta GT Courtesy of KLICK-LEWIS Buick Chevy Pontiac $49.00 OVER FACTORY INVOICE in Palmyra." Cobaugh aced the ninth hole and attempted to claim his prize. Klick-Lewis refused to deliver the car. It had offered the car as a prize for a charity golf tournament sponsored by the Hershey-Palmyra Sertoma Club two days earlier, on May 15, 1987, and had neglected to remove the car and posted signs prior to Cobaugh's hole-in-one. After Cobaugh sued to compel delivery of the car, the parties entered a stipulation regarding the facts and then moved for summary judgment. The trial court granted Cobaugh's motion, and Klick-Lewis appealed. . . .

The facts in the instant case are not in dispute. To the extent that they have not been admitted in the pleadings, they have been stipulated by the parties. Therefore, we must decide whether under the applicable law plaintiff was entitled to judgment as a matter of law. . . .

Appellant argues that it did nothing more than propose a contingent gift and that a proposal to make a gift is without consideration and unenforceable. See: Restatement (Second) of Contracts § 24, Comment b. We cannot accept this argument. Here, the offer specified the performance which was the price or consideration to be given. By its signs, Klick-Lewis offered to award the car as a prize to anyone who made a hole-in-one at the ninth hole. A person reading the signs would reasonably understand that he or she could accept the offer and win the car by performing the feat of shooting a hole-in-one. There was thus an offer which was accepted when appellee shot a hole-in-one. Accord: *Champagne Chrysler-Plymouth, Inc. v. Giles*, 388 So.2d 1343 (Fla.Dist.Ct.App. 1980) (bowling contest); *Schreiner v. Weil Furniture Co.*, 68 So.2d 149 (La.App. 1953) ("Count-the-dots" contest); *Chenard v. Marcel Motors*, 387 A.2d 596 (Me. 1978) (golf tournament); *Grove v. Charbonneau Buick-Pontiac Inc.*, 240 N.W.2d 853 (N.D. Sup.Ct. 1976) (golf tournament); *First Texas Savings Assoc. v. Jergins*, 705 S.W.2d 390 (Tx.Ct.App. 1986) (free drawing).

The contract does not fail for lack of consideration. The requirement of consideration as an essential element of a contract is nothing more than a requirement that there be a bargained for exchange. *Greene v. Oliver Realty, Inc.*, 363 Pa.Super. 534, 541, 526 A.2d 1192, 1195 (1987); *Commonwealth Dept. of Transp. v. First Nat'l Bank*, 77 Pa. Cmwlth. 551, 553, 466 A.2d 753, 754 (1983). Consideration confers a benefit upon the promisor or causes a detriment to the promisee. *Cardamone v. University of Pittsburgh*, 253 Pa.Super. 65, 72 n. 6, 384 A.2d 1228, 1232 n. 6 (1978); *General Mills, Inc. v. Snavely*, 203 Pa.Super. 162, 167, 199 A.2d 540, 543 (1964). By making an offer to award one of its cars as a prize for shooting a hole-in-one at the ninth hole of the Fairview Golf Course, Klick-Lewis benefited from the publicity typically generated by such promotional advertising. In order to win the car, Cobaugh was required to perform an act which he was under no legal duty to perform. The car was to be given in exchange for the feat of making a hole-in-one. This was adequate consideration to support the contract. See, e.g.: *Las Vegas Hacienda, Inc. v. Gibson*, 77 Nev. 25, 359 P.2d 85 (1961) (paying fifty cents and shooting hole-in-one was consideration for prize). See also: *First Texas Savings v. Jergins, supra* (enforcing duty to award prize in free drawing where only performance by plaintiff was completing and depositing entry form). . . .

It is the manifested intent of the offeror and not his subjective intent which determines the persons having the power to accept the offer. Restatement (Second) of Contracts § 29. In this case the offeror's manifested intent, as it appeared from signs posted at the ninth tee, was that a hole-in-one would win the car. The offer was not limited to any prior tournament. . . .

Affirmed.

Questions

1. What did the court feel was more important, the reasonable expectations of the offeree or the actual subjective intentions of the offeror?

2. Would Cobaugh have been entitled to the prize if he didn't notice the "hole-in-one" sign until after he aced the hole?

Promissory Estoppel; Reliance as an Alternative To Consideration

Even in the absence of consideration, a promise may be enforced if there is detrimental reliance. That is, in response to the mere making of a promise, the person to whom the promise was made (the promisee) reasonably and foreseeably changes their position to their detriment. This is known as the doctrine of promissory estoppel.

As set forth in the Restatement Second of Contracts, section 90, three factors are necessary to invoke the doctrine of promissory estoppel.

1) Was there a promise which the promisor reasonably expected to induce action or forbearance? (Foreseeability)

2) Did the promise actually induce such action or forbearance? (Reliance)

3) Can injustice be avoided only by enforcement of the promise? (Injustice)

Section 90 -- the so-called "promissory estoppel" section -- provides that reasonably expected reliance may under some circumstances make binding a promise for which nothing has been given or promised in exchange. (*Earhart v. William Low Co.* (1979) 25 Cal.3d 503, 600 P.2d 1344.) A court may invoke the doctrine of promissory estoppel embodied in section 90 to bind a promisor "when he should reasonably expect a substantial change of position, either by act or forbearance, in reliance on his promise, if injustice can be avoided only by its enforcement." (*Raedeke v. Gibraltar Savings & Loan Assn.* (1974) 10 Cal.3d 665 [111 Cal.Rptr. 693, 517 P.2d 1157].)

Ricketts v. Scothorn
Supreme Court of Nebraska, 1898
57 Neb. 51, 77 N.W. 365, 367, 42 L.R.A. 794

SULLIVAN, J. In the district court of Lancaster County the plaintiff Katie Scothorn recovered judgment against the defendant Andrew D. Ricketts, as executor of the last will and testament of John C. Ricketts, deceased. The action was based upon a promissory note, of which the following is a copy:

"May the first, 1801. I promise to pay to Katie Scothorn on demand, $2,000, to be at 6 per cent per annum. J. C. RICKETTS."

In the petition the plaintiff alleges that the consideration for the execution of the note was that she should surrender her employment as bookkeeper for Mayer Bros, and cease to work for a living. She also alleges that the note was given to induce her to abandon her occupation, and that, relying on it, and on the annual interest, as a means of support, she gave up the employment in which she was then engaged. These allegations of the petition are denied by the executor. The material facts are undisputed. They are as follows: John O. Ricketts, the maker of the note, was the grandfather of the plaintiff. Early in May,—presumably on the day the note bears date,—he called on her at the store where she was working. What transpired between them is thus described by Mr. Flodene, one of the plaintiff's witnesses:

A. Well the old gentleman came in there one morning about 9 o'clock,— probably a little before or a little after, but early in the morning,— and he unbuttoned his vest and took out a piece of paper in the shape of a note; that is the way it looked to me; and he says to Miss Scothorn, "I have fixed out something that you have not got to work any more." He says, "None of my grandchildren work and you don't have to."

Q. Where was she?

A. She took the piece of paper and kissed him; and kissed the old gentleman and commenced to cry.

It seems Miss Scothorn immediately notified her employer of her intention to quit work and that she did soon after abandon her occupation. The mother of the plaintiff was a witness and testified that she had a conversation with her father, Mr. Ricketts, shortly after the note was executed in which he informed her that he had given the note to the plaintiff to enable her to quit work; that none of his grandchildren worked and he did not think she ought to. For something more than a year the plaintiff was without an occupation; but in September, 1892, with the consent of her grandfather, and by his assistance, she secured a position as bookkeeper with Messrs. Funke & Ogden. On June 8, 1894, Mr. Ricketts died. He had paid one year's interest on the note, and a short time before his death expressed regret that he had not been able to pay the balance. In the summer or fall of 1892 he stated to his daughter, Mrs. Scothorn, that if he could sell his farm in Ohio he would pay the note out of the proceeds. He at no time repudiated the obligation.

We quite agree with counsel for the defendant that upon this evidence there was nothing to submit to the jury, and that a verdict should have been directed peremptorily for one of the parties. The testimony of Flodene and Mrs. Scothorn, taken together, conclusively establishes the fact that the note was not given in consideration of the plaintiff pursuing, or agreeing to pursue, any particular line of conduct. There was no promise on the part of the plaintiff to do or refrain from doing anything. Her right to the money promised in the note was not made to depend upon an abandonment of her employment with Mayer Bros, and future abstention from like service. Mr. Ricketts made no condition, requirement, or request. He exacted no quid pro quo. He gave the note as a gratuity and looked for nothing in return. So far as the evidence discloses, it was his purpose to place the plaintiff in a position of independence where she could work or remain idle as she might choose. The abandonment by Miss Scothorn of her position as bookkeeper was altogether voluntary. It was not an act done in fulfillment of any contract obligation assumed when she accepted the note.

The instrument in suit being given without any valuable consideration, was nothing more than a promise to make a gift in the future of the sum of money therein named. Ordinarily, such promises are not enforceable even when put in the form of a promissory note. But it has often been held that an action on a note given to a church, college, or other like institution, upon the faith of which money has been expended or obligations incurred, could not be successfully defended on the ground of a want of consideration. In this class of cases the note in suit is nearly always spoken of as a gift or donation, but the decision is generally put on the ground that the expenditure of money or assumption of liability by the donee, on the faith of the promise, constitutes a valuable and sufficient consideration. It seems to us that the true reason is the preclusion of the defendant, under the doctrine of estoppel, to deny the consideration. Such seems to be the view of the matter taken by the supreme court of Iowa in the case of *Simpson Centenary College v. Tuttle*, 71 Ia. 596, where Rothrock, J., speaking for the court, said:

Where a note, however, is based on a promise to give for the support of the objects referred to, it may still be open to this defense [want of consideration], unless it shall appear that the donee has, prior to any revocation, entered into engagements or made expenditures based on such promise, so that he must suffer loss or injury if the note is not paid. This is based on the equitable principle that, after allowing the donee to incur obligations on the faith that the note would be paid, the donor would be estopped from pleading want of consideration.

And in the case of *Reimensnyder v. Gans*, 110 Pa. St. 17, 2 Atl. Rep. 425, which was an action on a note given as a donation to a charitable object, the court said: "The fact is that, as Ave may see from the case of Ryerss v. Trustees, 33 Pa. St. 114, ft contract of the kind here involved is enforceable rather by way of estoppel than on the ground of consideration in the original undertaking." It has been held that a note given in expectation of the payee performing certain services, but without any contract binding him to serve, will not support an action. *(Hulse v. Hulse,* 84 Eng. Com. Law 709.) But when the payee changes his position to his disadvantage, in reliance on the promise, a right of action does arise. *(McClure v. Wilson*, 43 Ill. 356; *Trustees v. Garvey*, 53 Ill. 401.)

Under the circumstances of this case is there an equitable estoppel which ought to preclude the defendant from alleging that the note in controversy is lacking in one of the essential elements of a valid contract? We think there is. An estoppel *in pais* is defined to be "a right arising from acts, admissions, or conduct which have induced a change of position in accordance with the real or apparent intention of the party against whom they are alleged." Mr. Pomeroy has formulated the following definition:

Equitable estoppel is the effect of the voluntary conduct of a party whereby he is absolutely precluded, both at law and in equity, from asserting rights which might perhaps have otherwise existed, either of property, or contract, or of remedy, as against another person who in good faith relied upon such conduct, and has been led thereby to change his position for the worse, and who on his part acquires some corresponding right either of property, of contract, or of remedy. (2 Pomeroy, Equity Jurisprudence 804.)

According to the undisputed proof, as shown by the record before us, the plaintiff was a working girl, holding a position in which she earned a salary of $10 per week. Her grandfather, desiring to put her in a position of independence, gave her the note, accompanying it with the remark that his other grandchildren did not work, and that she would not be obliged to work any longer. In effect he suggested that she might abandon her employment and rely in the future upon the bounty which he promised, lie, doubtless, desired that she should give up her occupation, but whether he did or not, it is entirely certain that he contemplated such action on her part as a reasonable and probable consequence of his gift. Having intentionally influenced the plaintiff to alter her position for the worse on the faith of the note being paid when due, it would be grossly inequitable to permit the maker, or his executor, to resist payment on the ground that the promise was given without consideration. The petition charges the elements of an equitable estoppel, and the evidence conclusively establishes them. If errors intervened at the trial they could not have been prejudicial. A verdict for the defendant would be unwarranted.

The judgment is right and is [affirmed.]

Questions

1. How did the plaintiff's abandonment of her employment come about after receiving the note?

2. What was the position of the court regarding the enforceability of the note based on consideration?

3. What is the concept of equitable estoppel, and how does it apply to this case?

Feinberg v. Pfeiffer Co.
Saint Louis Court of Appeals, Missouri, 1959
322 S.W.2d 163

(The facts of the case and the first part of the court's opinion were previously set forth at p. 22.)

But as to the second of these contentions we must agree with plaintiff. By the terms of the resolution defendant promised to pay plaintiff the sum of $200 a month upon her retirement. Consideration for a promise has been defined in the Restatement of the Law of Contracts, Section 75, as:

"(1) Consideration for a promise is

(a) an act other than a promise, or

(b) a forbearance, or

(c) the creation, modification or destruction of a legal relation, or

(d) a return promise, bargained for and given in exchange for the promise."

As the parties agree, the consideration sufficient to support a contract may be either a benefit to the promisor or a loss or detriment to the promisee. . . .

Section 90 of the Restatement of the Law of Contracts states that: "A promise which the promisor should reasonably expect to induce action or forbearance of a definite and substantial character on the part of the promisee and which does induce such action or forbearance is binding if injustice can be avoided only by enforcement of the promise." This doctrine has been described as that of "promissory estoppel," as distinguished from that of equitable estoppel or estoppel in pais, the reason for the differentiation being stated as follows:

"It is generally true that one who has led another to act in reasonable reliance on his representations of fact cannot afterwards in litigation between the two deny the truth of the representations, and some courts have sought to apply this principle to the formation of contracts, where, relying on a gratuitous promise, the promisee has suffered detriment. It is to be noticed, however, that such a case does not come within the ordinary definition of estoppel. If there is any representation of an existing fact, it is only that the promisor at the time of making the promise intends to fulfill it. As to such intention there is usually no misrepresentation and if there is, it is not that which has injured the promisee. In other words, he relies on a promise and not on a misstatement of fact; and the term `promissory' estoppel or something equivalent should be used to make the distinction." Williston on Contracts, Rev. Ed., Sec. 139, Vol. 1.

In speaking of this doctrine, Judge Learned Hand said in *Porter v. Commissioner of Internal Revenue*, 2 Cir., 60 F.2d 673, 675, that " . . . `promissory estoppel' is now a recognized species of consideration."

As pointed out by our Supreme Court in *In re Jamison's Estate*, Mo., 202 S.W.2d 879, 887, it is stated in the Missouri Annotations to the Restatement under Section 90 that:

"`There is a variance between the doctrine underlying this section and the theoretical justifications that have been advanced for the Missouri decisions.'"

That variance, as the authors of the Annotations point out, is that:

"This § 90, when applied with § 85, means that the promise described is a contract without any consideration. In Missouri the same practical result is reached without in theory abandoning the doctrine of consideration. In Missouri three theories have been advanced as ground for the decisions (1) *Theory of act for promise.* The induced `action or forbearance' is the consideration for the promise *Underwood Typewriter Co. v. Century Realty Co.* (1909) 220 Mo. 522, 119 S.W. 400, 25 L.R.A., N.S., 1173. See § 76. (2) *Theory of promissory estoppel.* The induced `action or forbearance' works an estoppel against the promisor. (Citing *School District of Kansas City v. Sheidley* (1897) 138 Mo. 672, 40 S. W. 656 [37 L.R.A. 406]) * * * (3) *Theory of bilateral contract.* When the induced `action or forbearance' is begun, a promise to complete is implied, and we have an enforceable bilateral contract, the implied promise to complete being the consideration for the original promise." (Citing cases.)

Was there such an act on the part of plaintiff, in reliance upon the promise contained in the resolution, as will estop the defendant, and therefore create an enforceable contract under the doctrine of promissory estoppel? We think there was. One of the illustrations cited under Section 90 of the Restatement is: "2. A promises B to pay him an annuity during B's life. B thereupon resigns a profitable employment, as A expected that he might. B receives the annuity for some years, in the meantime becoming disqualified from again obtaining good employment. A's promise is binding." This illustration is objected to by defendant as not being applicable to the case at hand. The reason advanced by it is that in the illustration B became "disqualified" from obtaining other employment *before* A discontinued the payments, whereas in this case the plaintiff did not discover that she had cancer and thereby became unemployable until *after* the defendant had discontinued the payments of $200 per month. We think the distinction is immaterial. The only reason for the reference in the illustration to the disqualification of A is in connection with that part of Section 90 regarding the prevention of injustice. The injustice would occur regardless of when the disability occurred. Would defendant contend that the contract would be enforceable if the plaintiff's illness had been discovered on March 31, 1956, the day before it discontinued the payment of the $200 a month, but not if it occurred on April 2nd, the day after? Furthermore, there are more ways to become disqualified for work, or unemployable, than as the result of illness. At the time she retired plaintiff was 57 years of age. At the time the payments were discontinued she was over 63 years of age. It is a matter of common knowledge that it is virtually impossible for a woman of that age to find satisfactory employment, much less a position comparable to that which plaintiff enjoyed at the time of her retirement.

The fact of the matter is that plaintiff's subsequent illness was not the "action or forbearance" which was induced by the promise contained in the resolution. As the trial court correctly decided, such action on plaintiff's part was her retirement from a lucrative position in reliance upon defendant's promise to pay her an annuity or pension. . . .

The Commissioner therefore recommends, for the reasons stated, that the judgment be affirmed.

Questions

1. How does the Restatement's Section 90 define the requirements for a binding promise under the doctrine of promissory estoppel?

2. In the case discussed, why does the defendant argue that the illustration provided under Section 90 of the Restatement is not applicable?

3. Why did the court find the plaintiff's subsequent illness to be immaterial in determining the enforceability of the contract?

Implied In Law Contracts – Quasi Contracts

Unjust Enrichment as a Basis For Restitution

In addition to being express or implied in fact, contracts can be implied in law as well. (Cal.Civ.Code § 1619)

Receipt of a benefit under circumstances where it would be unfair to allow the recipient to keep the benefit without paying the fair value of it can be the basis for a court ordering restitution. (Restitution refers to the interest in the benefits that one party [usually the injured party] has conferred upon the other party [usually the breaching party]. (See, Rest.2d § 373).) This results in what is known as a "quasi-contract," a duty or obligation is created by law for reasons of fairness or justice. For example, where one accepts or receives the benefit of another's work, the law implies a promise to pay what the services are reasonably worth. (*Schaad v. Hazelton, infra.*) Such duty or obligation is not based upon the express or apparent intention of the parties but rather is imposed by law in order to prevent unjust enrichment. Professor Corbin famously described the term *quasi* as "a weasel word that sucks all the meaning of the word that follows it." (Corbin, Contracts (One Volume Ed.) § 19.) Nevertheless, the term "quasi contract" is one that the contracts student needs to be familiar with.

Cotnam v. Wisdom
Supreme Court of Arkansas, 1907
83 Ark. 601, 104 S.W. 164

Action by F. L. Wisdom and another against T. T. Cotnam, administrator of A. M. Harrison, deceased, for services rendered by plaintiffs as surgeons to defendant's intestate. Judgment for plaintiffs. Defendant appeals. Reversed and remanded.

Instructions 1 and 2, given at the instance of plaintiffs, are as follows: (1) If you find from the evidence that plaintiffs rendered professional services as physicians and surgeons to the deceased, A. M. Harrison, in a sudden emergency following the deceased's injury in a street car wreck, in an endeavor to save his life, then you are instructed that plaintiffs are entitled to recover from the estate of the said A. M. Harrison such sum as you may find from the evidence is a reasonable compensation for the services rendered. (2) The character and importance of the operation, the responsibility resting upon the surgeon performing the operation, his experience and professional training, and the ability to pay of the person operated upon, are elements to be considered by you in determining what is a reasonable charge for the services performed by plaintiffs in the particular case.

HILL, C. J. . . . The first question is as to the correctness of this instruction. As indicated therein the facts are that Mr. Harrison, appellant's intestate, was thrown from a street car, receiving serious injuries which rendered him unconscious, and while in that condition the appellees were notified of the accident and summoned to his assistance by some spectator, and performed a difficult operation in an effort to save his life, but they were unsuccessful, and he died without regaining consciousness. The appellant says: "Harrison was never conscious after his head struck the pavement. He did not and could not, expressly or impliedly, assent to the action of the appellees. He was without knowledge or will power. However merciful or benevolent may have been the intention of the appellees, a new rule of law, of contract by implication of law, will have to be established by this court in order to sustain the recovery." Appellant is right in saying that the recovery must be sustained by a contract by implication of law, but is not right in saying that it is a new rule of law, for such contracts are almost as old as the English system of jurisprudence. They are usually called "implied contracts." More properly they should be called "quasi contracts" or "constructive contracts."

The following excerpts from Sceva v. True, 53 N. H. 627, are peculiarly applicable here: We regard it as well settled by the cases referred to in the briefs of counsel, many of which have been commented on at length by Mr. Shirley for the defendant, that an insane person, an idiot, or a person utterly bereft of all sense and reason by the sudden stroke of an accident or disease may be held liable, in assumpsit, for necessaries furnished to him in good faith while in that unfortunate and helpless condition. And the reasons upon which this rest are too broad, as well as too sensible and humane, to be overborne by any deductions which a refined logic may make from the circumstances that in such cases there can be no contract or promise, in fact, no meeting of the minds of the parties. The cases put it on the ground of an implied contract; and by this is not meant, as the defendant's counsel seems to suppose, an actual contract — that is, an actual meeting of the minds of the parties, an actual, mutual understanding, to be inferred from language, acts, and circumstances by the jury — but a contract and promise, said to be implied by the law, where, in point of fact, there was no contract, no mutual understanding, and so no promise. The defendant's counsel says it is usurpation for the court to hold, as a matter of law, that there is a contract and a promise, when all the evidence in the case shows that there was not a contract, nor the semblance of one. It is doubtless a legal fiction, invented and used for the sake of the remedy. If it was originally usurpation, certainly it has now become very inveterate, and firmly fixed in the body of the law. Illustrations might be multiplied, but enough has been said to show that when a contract or promise implied by law is spoken of, a very different thing is meant from a contract in fact, whether express or tacit. The evidence of an actual contract is generally to be found either in some writing made by the parties, or in verbal communications which passed between them, or in their acts and conduct considered in the light of the circumstances of each particular case. A contract implied by law, on the contrary, rests upon no evidence. It has no actual existence. It is simply a mythical creation of the law. The law says it shall be taken that there was a promise, when in point of fact, there was none. Of course this is not good logic, for the obvious and sufficient reason that it is not true. It is a legal fiction, resting wholly for its support on a plain legal obligation, and a plain legal right. If it were true, it would not be a fiction. There is a class of legal rights, with their correlative legal duties, analogous to the obligations quasi ex contractu of the civil law, which seem to he in the region between contracts on the one hand, and torts on the other, and to call for the application of a remedy not strictly furnished either by actions ex contractu or actions ex delicto. The common law supplies no action of duty, as it does of assumpsit and trespass; and hence the somewhat awkward contrivance of this fiction to apply the remedy of assumpsit where there is no true contract and no promise to support it. . . .

In its practical application it sustains recovery for physicians and nurses who render services for infants, insane persons, and drunkards. . . . And services rendered by physicians to persons unconscious or helpless by reason of injury or sickness are in the same situation as those rendered to persons incapable of contracting, such as the classes above described. The court was therefore right in giving the instruction in question.

The defendant sought to require the plaintiff to prove, in addition to the value of the services, the benefit, if any, derived by the deceased from the operation, and alleges error in the court refusing to so instruct the jury. The court was right in refusing to place this burden upon the physicians. . . . So that a surgical operation be conceived and performed with due skill and care, the price to be paid therefore does not depend upon the result. The event so generally lies with the forces of nature that all intelligent men know and understand that the surgeon is not responsible therefore. In absence of express agreement, the surgeon, who brings to such a service due skill and care, earns the reasonable and customary price therefore, whether the outcome be beneficial to the patient or the reverse.

There was evidence in this case proving that it was customary for physicians to graduate their charges by the ability of the patient to pay, and hence, in regard to that element, this case differs from the Alabama case. But the value of the Alabama decision is the reason given which may admit such evidence, viz., because the custom would render the financial condition of the patient a factor to be contemplated by both parties when the services were rendered and accepted. . . . This could not apply to a physician called in an emergency by some bystander to attend a stricken man whom he never saw or heard of before; and certainly the unconscious patient could not, in fact or in law, be held to have contemplated what charges the physician might properly bring against him. In order to admit such testimony, it must be assumed that the surgeon and patient each had in contemplation that the means of the patient would be one factor in determining the amount of the charge for the services rendered. While the law may admit such evidence as throwing light upon the contract and indicating what was really in contemplation when it was made, yet a different question is presented when there is no contract to be ascertained or construed, but a mere fiction of law creating a contract where none existed in order that there might be a remedy for a right. This fiction merely requires a reasonable compensation for the services rendered. The services are the same be the patient prince or pauper, and for them the surgeon is entitled to fair compensation for his time, service, and skill. It was therefore error to admit this evidence, and to instruct the jury in the second instruction that in determining what was a reasonable charge they could consider the "ability to pay of the person operated upon."

It was improper to let it go to the jury that Mr. Harrison was a bachelor and that his estate was left to nieces and nephews. This was relevant to no issue in the case, and its effect might well have been prejudicial. While this verdict is no higher than some of the evidence would justify, yet it is much higher than some of the other evidence would justify, and hence it is impossible to say that this was a harmless error.

Judgment is reversed, and cause remanded.

Questions

1. What are implied contracts, and how do they differ from actual contracts?

2. Explain the concept of a quasi contract or constructive contract.

3. Why was it considered improper to consider the ability to pay of the person operated upon when determining a reasonable charge for the services?

Takeaways – Cotnam v. Wisdom

In the absence of a contractual agreement, a trial court may require an individual to make restitution for unjust enrichment if he has received a benefit which would be unconscionable to retain. A person may be deemed to be unjustly enriched if he (or she) has received a benefit, the retention of which would be unjust. (Restatement, Restitution, § 1, Comment (a).) A person confers a benefit not only where he adds to the property of another, but also where he saves the other from expense or loss. (Restatement, Restitution, § 1(b).)

Callano v. Oakwood Park Homes Corp.
Superior Court of New Jersey, 1966
91 N.J. Super. 105, 219 A.2d 332

COLLESTER, J.A.D. Defendant Oakwood Park Homes Corp. (Oakwood) appeals from a judgment of $475 entered in favor of plaintiffs Julia Callano and Frank Callano in the Monmouth County District Court.

The case was tried below on an agreed stipulation of facts. Oakwood, engaged in the construction of a housing development, in December 1961 contracted to sell a lot with a house to be erected thereon to Bruce Pendergast, who resided in Waltham, Massachusetts. In May 1962, prior to completion of the house, the Callanos, who operated a plant nursery, delivered and planted shrubbery pursuant to a contract with Pendergast. A representative of Oakwood had knowledge of the planting.

Pendergast never paid the Callanos the invoice price of $497.95. A short time after the shrubbery was planted Pendergast died. Thereafter, on July 10, 1962 Oakwood and Pendergast's estate cancelled the contract of sale. Oakwood had no knowledge of Pendergast's failure to pay the Callanos. On July 16, 1962 Oakwood sold the Pendergast property, including the shrubbery located thereon, to Richard and Joan Grantges for an undisclosed amount

The single issue is whether Oakwood is obligated to pay plaintiffs for the reasonable value of the shrubbery on the theory of *quasi*-contractual liability. Plaintiffs contend that defendant was unjustly enriched when the Pendergast contract to purchase the property was cancelled and that an agreement to pay for the shrubbery is implied in law. Defendant argues that the facts of the case do not support a recovery by plaintiffs on the theory of *quasi*-contract.

Contracts implied by law, more properly described as *quasi* or constructive contracts, are a class of obligations which are imposed or created by law without regard to the assent of the party bound, on the ground that they are dictated by reason and justice. They rest solely on a legal fiction and are not contract obligations at all in the true sense, for there is no agreement; but they are clothed with the semblance of contract for the purpose of the remedy, and the obligation arises not from consent, as in the case of true contracts, but from the law or natural equity. Courts employ the fiction of *quasi* or constructive contract with caution. 17 *C.J.S. Contracts* § 6, *pp.* 566-570 (1963).

In cases based on *quasi*-contract liability, the intention of the parties is entirely disregarded, while in cases of express contracts and contracts implied in fact the intention is of the essence of the transaction. In the case of actual contracts the agreement defines the duty, while in the case of *quasi*-contracts the duty defines the contract. Where a case shows that it is the duty of the defendant to pay, the law imparts to him a promise to fulfill that obligation. The duty which thus forms the foundation of a *quasi*-contractual obligation is frequently based on the doctrine of unjust enrichment. It rests on the equitable principle that a person shall not be allowed to enrich himself unjustly at the expense of another, and on the principle of whatsoever it is certain a man ought to do, that the law supposes him to have promised to do. *St. Paul Fire, etc., Co. v. Indemnity Ins. Co. of No. America,* 32 N.J. 17, 22 (1960).

The key words are *enrich* and *unjustly*. To recover on the theory of *quasi*-contract the plaintiffs must prove that defendant was enriched *viz.*, received a benefit, and that retention of the benefit without payment therefore would be unjust.

It is conceded by the parties that the value of the property, following the termination of the Pendergast contract, was enhanced by the reasonable value of the shrubbery at the stipulated sum of $475. However, we are not persuaded that the retention of such benefit by defendant before it sold the property to the Grantges was inequitable or unjust.

Quasi-contractual liability has found application in a myriad of situations. See *Woodruff, Cases on Quasi-Contracts* (3d ed. 1933). However, a common thread runs throughout its application where liability has been successfully asserted, namely, that the plaintiff expected remuneration from the defendant, or if the true facts were known to plaintiff, he would have expected remuneration from defendant, at the time the benefit was conferred. See *Rabinowitz v. Mass. Bonding & Insurance Co.*, 119 N.J.L. 552 (E. & A. 1937); *Power-Matics, Inc. v. Ligotti*, 79 N.J. Super. 294 (App. Div. 1963); *Shapiro v. Solomon*, 42 N.J. Super.377 (App. Div. 1956). It is further noted that *quasi*-contract cases involve either some direct relationship between the parties or a mistake on the part of the person conferring the benefit.

In the instant case the plaintiffs entered into an express contract with Pendergast and looked to him for payment. They had no dealings with defendant, and did not expect remuneration from it when they provided the shrubbery. No issue of mistake on the part of plaintiffs is involved. Under the existing circumstances we believe it would be inequitable to hold defendant liable. Plaintiffs' remedy is against Pendergast's estate, since they contracted with and expected payment to be made by Pendergast when the benefit was conferred. *Cf. Service Fuel Oil Co. v. Hoboken Bank for Savings*, 118 N.J.L. 61 (Sup. Ct. 1937); *La Chance v. Rigoli*, 325 Mass. 25, 91 N.E.2d 204 (Sup. Jud. Ct. 1950); *Gannaway v. Lundstrom*, 204 S.W.2d 999 (Tex. Civ. App. 1947); *Larsen v. New York Dock Co.*, 166 F.2d 687 (Cir. 1948). A plaintiff is not entitled to employ the legal fiction of *quasi*-contract to "substitute one promisor or debtor for another."*Cascaden v. Magryta*, 247 Mich. 267, 225 N.W. 511, 512 (Sup. Ct. 1929).

Plaintiffs place reliance on *De Gasperi v. Valicenti*, 198 Pa. Super. 455, 181 A.2d 862 (Super Ct. 1962), where recovery was allowed on the theory of unjust enrichment. We find the case inapposite. It is clear that recovery on *quasi*-contract was permitted there because of a fraud perpetrated by defendants. There is no contention of fraud on the part of Oakwood in the instant case.

Recovery on the theory of *quasi*-contract was developed under the law to provide a remedy where none existed. Here, a remedy exists. Plaintiffs may bring their action against Pendergast's estate. We hold that under the facts of this case defendant was not unjustly enriched and is not liable for the value of the shrubbery.

Reversed.

Questions

1. According to the court's reasoning, what are the two elements that plaintiffs must prove to recover on the theory of quasi-contract?

2. Why did the court determine that it would be inequitable to hold Oakwood liable for the shrubbery?

3. What alternative remedy did the court suggest for the plaintiffs in this case?

Takeaways – Callano v. Oakwood Park Homes

A party who expends funds and performs services at the request of another, under the reasonable belief that the requesting party will compensate him for such services, may recover in quantum meruit (a Latin term which means, "as much as they deserved") although the expenditures and services do not directly benefit property owned by the requesting party. (*Earhart v. William Low Co.* (1979) 25 Cal.3d 503, 600 P.2d 1344.)

ASSESSMENT QUESTIONS, CHAPTER 1

1. Define consideration in the context of contract law and explain its significance in the formation of a valid contract.

2. Can past consideration be valid consideration for a contract? Justify your answer with relevant legal principles and cases.

3. What is the doctrine of promissory estoppel? How does it differ from the traditional requirement of consideration in contract law?

4. Discuss the concept of adequacy of consideration in contract law. Does the law require consideration to be of equal value between the parties?

5. Can a pre-existing contractual duty serve as valid consideration for a new contract modification? Explain your reasoning, referring to relevant case law.

6. Analyze the scenario where a party promises to do what they are already legally obligated to do. Would this promise be considered valid consideration? Support your answer with legal principles and case examples.

7. Explain the concept of a "conditional gift" and its relevance to the doctrine of consideration in contract law. Provide an example to illustrate your explanation.

8. Can moral or past-due obligations be considered valid consideration in a contract? Discuss the legal principles involved, referencing relevant case law if applicable.

CHAPTER 2
Mutual Assent

Introduction

One of the essential elements to the existence of a contract is the consent of the parties. To form a contract, a manifestation of mutual assent is necessary. Mutual assent may be manifested by written or spoken words, or by conduct. However, conduct alone is not effective as an expression of consent, unless that person intends to engage in the conduct and knows or has reason to know that the other party may infer consent from such conduct. (See, 1 Witkin, Summary of Cal. Law (10th ed. 2005) Contracts, § 116.)

Consent is not mutual unless the parties all agree upon the same thing in the same sense. Ordinarily, it is the outward expression of consent that is controlling. Mutual assent arises out of the reasonable meaning of the words and acts of the parties, and not from any secret or unexpressed intention or understanding. In determining if there was mutual consent, consideration is given to not only the words and conduct of the parties, but also to the circumstances under which the words are used and the conduct occurs. (Cal.Civ.Code § 1580)

Each party's consent must be freely given, mutual, and communicated by each party to the other. (Cal.Civ.Code § 1565) Consent is not freely given if it is obtained by duress, menace, fraud, undue influence, or mistake. (Cal.Civ.Code § 1567)

The typical way to determine whether mutual consent has been given is to analyze whether there has been an offer and acceptance.

Offer

An offer is a manifestation of willingness to enter into a bargain. (Rest.2d § 24.) To be effective it must be so made as to justify another person in understanding that his or her consent to that agreement is invited and will conclude it.

An offer must be sufficiently definite, or must call for such definite terms in the acceptance, that the performance promised is reasonably certain of definition.

Parties may engage in preliminary negotiations, oral or written, before reaching an agreement. These negotiations only result in a binding contract when all of the essential terms are definitely understood and agreed upon even though the parties intend that a formal writing including all of these terms shall be signed later, unless the law requires that the contract be in writing, or unless the apparent agreement is void or voidable. (See, 1 Witkin, Summary of Cal. Law (10th ed. 2005) Contracts, § § 116, 117, 125, 130, 133, 137.)

The individual or entity making the offer is called the offeror. The individual or entity to whom the offer is made is called the offeree. In determining whether an effective offer has been made one could be guided either by the subjective intent of the offeror, or the reasonable expectations of the offeree. Does one of these possibilities carry more weight than the other? This next case should answer that question.

Lucy v. Zehmer

Supreme Court of Appeals of Virginia. 1954
196 Va. 493, 84 S.E.2d 516

BUCHANAN, JUSTICE. This suit was instituted by W.O. Lucy and J.C. Lucy, complainants, against A.H. Zehmer and Ida S. Zehmer, his wife, defendants, to have specific performance of a contract by which it was alleged the Zehmers had sold to W.O. Lucy a tract of land owned by A.H. Zehmer in Dinwiddie county containing 471.6 acres, more or less, known as the Ferguson farm, for $50,000. J.C. Lucy, the other complainant, is a brother of W.O. Lucy, to whom W.O. Lucy transferred a half interest in his alleged purchase.

The instrument sought to be enforced was written by A.H. Zehmer on [Saturday] December 20, 1952, in these words: We hereby agree to sell to W.O. Lucy the Ferguson Farm complete for $50,000.00, title satisfactory to buyer," and signed by the defendants, A.H. Zehmer and Ida S. Zehmer.

The answer of A.H. Zehmer admitted that at the time mentioned W.O. Lucy offered him $50,000 cash for the farm, but that he, Zehmer, considered that the offer was made in jest; that so thinking, and both he and Lucy having had several drinks, he wrote out the memorandum" quoted above and induced his wife to sign it; that he did not deliver the memorandum to Lucy, but that Lucy picked it up, read it, put it in his pocket, attempted to offer Zehmer $5 to bind the bargain, which Zehmer refused to accept, and realizing for the first time that Lucy was serious, Zehmer assured him that he had no intention of selling the farm and that the whole matter was a joke. Lucy left the premises insisting that he had purchased the farm.

Depositions were taken and the decree appealed from was entered holding that the complainants had failed to establish their right to specific performance, and dismissing their bill. The assignment of error is to this action of the court.

The defendants insist that the evidence was ample to support their contention that the writing sought to be enforced was prepared as a bluff or dare to force Lucy to admit that he did not have $50,000; that the whole matter was a joke; that the writing was not delivered to Lucy and no binding contract was ever made between the parties.

It is an unusual, if not bizarre, defense. When made to the writing admittedly prepared by one of the defendants and signed by both, clear evidence is required to sustain it.

In his testimony Zehmer claimed that he "was high as a Georgia pine," and that the transaction was just a bunch of two doggoned drunks bluffing to see who could talk the biggest and say the most." That claim is inconsistent with his attempt to testify in great detail as to what was said and what was done. It is contradicted by other evidence as to the condition of both parties, and rendered of no weight by the testimony of his wife that when Lucy left the restaurant she suggested that Zehmer drive him home. The record is convincing that Zehmer was not intoxicated to the extent of being unable to comprehend the nature and consequences of the instrument he executed, and hence that instrument is not to be invalidated on that ground. C.J.S. Contracts, §, 133, b., p.483; Taliaferro v. Emery, 124 Va. 674, 98 S.E. 627. It was in fact conceded by defendants' counsel in oral argument that under the evi- dence Zehmer was not too drunk to make a valid contract.

The evidence is convincing also that Zehmer wrote two agreements, the first one beginning "I hereby agree to sell. Zehmer first said he could not remember about that, then that "I don't think I wrote but one out." Mrs. Zehmer said that what he wrote was `I hereby agree," but that the "I" was changed to "We" after that night. The agreement that was written and signed is in the record and indicates no such change. Neither are the mistakes in spelling that Zehmer sought to point out readily apparent.

The appearance of the contract, the fact that it was under discussion for forty minutes or more before it was signed; Lucy's objection to the first draft because it was written in the singular, and he wanted Mrs. Zehmer to sign it also; the rewriting to meet that objection and the signing by Mrs. Zehmer; the discussion of what was to be included in the sale, the provision for the examination of the title, the completeness of the instrument that was executed, the taking possession of it by Lucy with no request or suggestion by either of the defendants that he give it back, are facts which furnish persuasive evidence that the execution of the contract was a serious business transaction rather than a casual jesting matter as defendants now contend..

If it be assumed, contrary to what we think the evidence shows, that Zehmer was jesting about selling his farm to Lucy and that the transac- tion was intended by him to be a joke, nevertheless the evidence shows that Lucy did not so understand it but considered it to be a serious business transaction and the contract to be binding on the Zehmers as well as on himself. The very next day he arranged with his brother to put up half the money and take a half interest in the land. The day after that he employed an attorney to examine the title. The next night, Tuesday, he was back at Zehmer's place and there Zehmer told him for the first time, Lucy said, that he wasn't going to sell and he told Zehmer "You know you sold that place fair and square." After receiving the report from his attorney that the title was good he wrote to Zehmer that he was ready to close the deal.

Not only did Lucy actually believe, but the evidence shows he was warranted in believing, that the contract represented a serious business transaction and a good faith sale and purchase of the farm.

In the field of contracts, as generally elsewhere, "We must look to the outward expression of a person as manifesting his intention rather than to his secret and unexpressed intention. 'The law imputes to a person an intention corresponding to the reasonable meaning of his words and acts.'" *First Nat. Exchange Bank of Roanoke v. Roanoke Oil Co.*, 169 Va. 99, 114, 192 S.E. 764, 770.

At no time prior to the execution of the contract had Zehmer indicated to Lucy by word or act that he was not in earnest about selling the farm. They had argued about it and discussed its terms, as Zehmer admitted, for a long time. Lucy testified that if there was any jesting it was about paying $50,000 that night. The contract and the evidence show that he was not expected to pay the money that night. Zehmer said that after the writing was signed he laid it down on the counter in front of Lucy. Lucy said Zehmer handed it to him. In any event there had been what appeared to be a good faith offer and a good faith acceptance, followed by the execution and apparent delivery of a written contract. Both said that Lucy put the writing in his pocket and then offered Zehmer $5 to seal the bargain. Not until then, even under the defendants' evidence, was anything said or done to indicate that the matter was a joke. Both of the Zehmers testified that when Zehmer asked his wife to sign he whispered that it was a joke so Lucy wouldn't hear and that it was not intended that he should hear.

The mental assent of the parties is not requisite for the formation of a contract. If the words or other acts of one of the parties have but one reasonable meaning, his undisclosed intention is immaterial except when an unreasonable meaning which he attaches to his manifestations is known to the other party. Restatement of the Law of Contracts, Vol. I, § 71, p.74....

An agreement or mutual assent is of course essential to a valid contract but the law imputes to a person an intention corresponding to the reasonable meaning of his words and acts. If his words and acts, judged by a reasonable standard, manifest an intention to agree, it is immaterial what may be the real but unexpressed state of his mind. C.J.S. Contracts, §32, p. 361; 12 Am.Jur., Contracts, §19, p. 515.

So a person cannot set up that he was merely jesting when his conduct and words would warrant a reasonable person in believing that he intended a real agreement...

Whether the writing signed by the defendants and now sought to be enforced by the complainant was the result of a serious offer by Lucy and a serious acceptance by the defendants, or was a serious offer by Lucy and an acceptance in secret jest by the defendants, in either event it constituted a binding contract of sale between the parties. . . .

The complainants are entitled to have specific performance of the contract sued on. The decree appealed from is therefore reversed and the cause is remanded for the entry of a proper decree requiring the defendants to perform the contract in accordance with the prayer of the bill.

Reversed and remanded.

Questions

1. What was the defendants' defense regarding the validity of the contract, and why did the court find it unpersuasive?

2. How did the court assess the defendants' claim that the contract was intended as a joke or bluff?

3. According to the court, what factors indicated that the execution of the contract was a serious business transaction?

Takeaways – Lucy v. Zehmer

A proposal that is obviously made in jest, which a reasonable person would not be justified in treating as an offer, does not, upon acceptance, give rise to a valid and enforceable contract. However, if the speaker intends to create in the listener the perception that the speaker is serious and committing him or herself to a particular proposition and a reasonable person standing in the shoes of the offeree would so believe, a valid offer which is capable of acceptance has been made. In other words, contract law enforces the apparent intent of the offeror, which may not be the same as the offeror's actual intent.

Owen v. Tunison
Supreme Judicial Court of Maine, 1932
131 Me. 42, 158 A. 926

BARNES, J. Plaintiff charges that defendant agreed in writing to sell him the Bradley block and lot, situated in Bucksport, for a stated price in cash, that he later refused to perfect the sale, and that plaintiff, always willing and ready to pay the price, has suffered loss on account of defendant's unjust refusal to sell, and claims damages.

From the record it appears that defendant, a resident of Newark, N. J., was, in the fall of 1929, the owner of the Bradley block and lot.

With the purpose of purchasing, on October 23, 1929, plaintiff wrote the following letter:

"Dear Mr. Tunison:

Will you sell me your store property which is located on Main St. in Bucksport, Me. running from Montgomery's Drug Store on one corner to a Grocery Store on the other, for the sum of $6,000.00?"

Nothing more of this letter need be quoted.

On December 5, following, plaintiff received defendant's reply, apparently written in Cannes, France, on November 12, and it reads:

"In reply to your letter of Oct. 23rd which has been forwarded to me in which you inquire about the Bradley Block, Bucksport Me.

Because of improvements which have been added and an expenditure of several thousand dollars it would not be possible for me to sell it unless I was to receive $16,000.00 cash.

The upper floors have been converted into apartments with baths and the b'l'dg put into first class condition.
Very truly yours,

[Signed] R. G. Tunison."

Whereupon, and at once, plaintiff sent to defendant, and the latter received, in France, the following message:

"Accept your offer for Bradley block Bucksport Terms sixteen thousand cash send deed to Eastern Trust and Banking Co Bangor Maine Please acknowledge."

Four days later he was notified that defendant did not wish to sell the property, and on the 14th day of January following brought suit for his damages.

Granted that damages may be due a willing buyer if the owner refuses to tender a deed of real estate, after the latter has made an offer in writing to sell to the former, and such offer has been so accepted, it remains for us to point out that defendant here is not shown to have written to plaintiff an offer to sell.

There can have been no contract for the sale of the property desired, no meeting of the minds of the owner and prospective purchaser, unless there was an offer or proposal of sale. It cannot be successfully argued that defendant made any offer or proposal of sale.

In a recent case the words, "Would not consider less than half" is held "not to be taken as an outright offer to sell for one-half." Sellers v. Warren, 116 Me. 350, 102 A. 40, 41.

Where an owner of millet seed wrote, "I want $2.25 per cwt. for this seed f. o. b. Lowell," in an action for damages for alleged breach of contract to sell at the figure quoted above, the court held: "He [defendant] does not say, 'I offer to sell to you.' The language used is general, and such as may be used in an advertisement, or circular addressed generally to those engaged in the seed business, and is not an offer by which he may be bound, if accepted, by any or all of the persons addressed." Nebraska Seed Co. v. Harsh, 98 Neb. 89, 152 N. W. 310, 311, and cases cited in note L. R. A. 1915F, 824.

Defendant's letter of December 5 in response to an offer of $6,000 for his property may have been written with the intent to open negotiations that might lead to a sale. It was not a proposal to sell.

Judgment for defendant.

Questions

1. What was the content of the plaintiff's initial letter, and how did the defendant respond?

2. How did the court interpret the defendant's letter of December 5, and why did they conclude it was not a proposal to sell?

3. What was the court's decision in this case, and what was their reasoning for reaching that decision?

Takeaways – Owen v. Tunison

Did the defendant make an offer or proposal to sell the property? According to the court's interpretation, what is the significance of the defendant's letter in terms of forming a contract? One of the key factors in determining whether an offer has been made is whether the offeror's communication empowers the offeree to conclude the deal by accepting. Did the defendant's letter in *Owen* empower the plaintiff to "close the contract" or did he indicate he expected the offer to come from the plaintiff?

Harvey v. Facey
A.C. 552 (Privy Council, Jamaica) (1893)

[Harvey and another, solicitors in Kingston, instituted an action to obtain specific performance of an agreement alleged to have been entered into by L. M. Facey for the sale of a property named Bumper Hall Pen. Facey was alleged to have had power and authority to bind his wife Adelaide Facey in selling the property. Harvey also sought an injunction against the Mayor and Council of Kingston to restrain them from taking a conveyance of the property from Facey.]

The case came on for hearing before Mr. Justice Curran who dismissed the action with costs, on the ground that the agreement alleged by the Appellants did not disclose a concluded contract for the sale and purchase of the property. The Court of Appeal reversed the judgment of Mr. Justice Curran, and declared that a binding agreement for the sale and purchase of the property had been proved as between the Appellants and the Respondent L. M. Facey, but that the Appellants had failed to establish that the said L. M. Facey had power to sell the said property without the concurrence of his wife the said Adelaide Facey, or that she had authorised him to enter into the agreement relied on by the Appellants, and that the agreement could not therefore be specifically performed, and the Court ordered that the Appellants should have forty shillings for damages against L. M. Facey in respect of the breach of the agreement, with costs in both Courts against L. M. Facey in respect of the breach of the agreement.

The Appellants obtained leave from the Supreme Court to appeal to Her Majesty in Council, and afterwards obtained special leave from Her :Majesty in Council to appeal in respect of a point not included in the leave granted by the Supreme Court, but the Order in Council provided that the Respondents should he at liberty at the hearing, without special leave, to contest the contract alleged in the pleadings and affirmed by the Court of Appeal.

The Appellants are solicitors carrying on business in partnership at Kingston, and it appears that in the beginning of October 1891 negotiations took place between the Respondent L. M. Facey and the Mayor and Council of Kingston for the sale of the property in question, that Facey had offered to sell it to them for the sum of £900, that the offer was discussed by the Council at their meeting on the 6th of October 1891, and the consideration of its acceptance deferred; that on the 7th of October 1891, L. M. Facey was traveling in the train from Kingston to Porus, and that the Appellants caused a telegram to be sent after him from Kingston addressed to him "on the train for "Porus." in the following words:-

"Will you sell us Bumper Hall Pen? Telegraph lowest cash price-answer paid;" that on the same day L. M. Facey replied by telegram to the Appellants in the following words: "Lowest price for " Bumper Hall Pen £900.";

That on the same day the Appellants replied to the last-mentioned telegram by a telegram addressed to L. M. Facey "on train at Porus" in the words following:

"We agree to buy Bumper Hall Pen for the sum of nine hundred pounds asked by you. Please send us your title deed in order that we may get early possession."

The above telegrams were duly received by the Appellants and by L. M. Facey. [T]heir Lordships concur in the judgment of Justice Curran that there was no concluded contract the Appellants and L. M. Facey to be collected from the aforesaid telegrams. The first telegram asks two questions. The first question is as to the willingness of L. M. Facey to sell to the Appellants; the second question asks the lowest price, and the word "Telegraph" is in its collocation addressed to that second question only. L. M. Facey replied to the second question only, and gives his lowest price. The third telegram from the Appellants treats the answer of L. M. Facey stating his lowest price as an unconditional offer to sell to them at the mice named. Their Lordships cannot treat the telegram from L. M. Facey as binding him in any respect, except to the extent it does by its terms, viz., the lowest price. Everything else is left open, and the reply telegram from the Appellants cannot be treated as an acceptance of an offer to sell to them; it is an offer that required to be accepted by L. M. Facey. The contract could only be completed if L. M. Facey had accepted the Appellants' last telegram. It has been contended for the Appellants that L. M. Facey's telegram should be read as saying "yes" to the first question put in the Appellants' telegram, but there is nothing to support that contention. L. M. Facey's telegram gives a precise answer to a precise question, viz., the price. The contract must appear by the telegrams, whereas the Appellants are obliged to contend that an acceptance of the first question is to be implied. Their Lordships are of opinion that the mere statement of the lowest price at which the vendor would sell contains no implied contract to sell at that price to the persons making the inquiry. . . .

[Reversed and the judgment of Mr. Justice Curran restored.]

Takeaways – Harvey v. Facey

Although reasonable minds could disagree, the court in *Harvey* found the defendant's response to the question of what was their lowest cash price not to be an offer. Given that it was not an offer, how would you best characterize the response? An invitation to make an offer perhaps? Inquiries, invitations to make offers, and preliminary proposals are not offers that are capable of being accepted.

An offer may request that the person to whom it is made (the offeree) manifest their acceptance by either completely performing a requested act or by promising to perform a requested act. When the offer requests that the offeree perform a requested act it is said that the offer looks towards the formation of a *unilateral* contract. When the offer requests that the offeree merely promise to perform the requested act, it is said that the offer looks towards the formation of a *bilateral* contract.

Price Quotations Are Not Offers

It is well settled that quotations of prices are mere invitations to make an offer, Greenberg, *U.C.C. Article 2* § 5.2 at 51; *Corbin on Contracts* §§ 26, 28 (1982); *Interstate Industries, Inc. v. Barclay Industries, Inc.,* 540 F.2d 868, 873 (7th Cir.1976) (price quotation not an offer).

Advertisements as Offers

In *Craft v. Elder Johnston,* 34 Ohio L.A. 605, 38 N.E. 2d 417, the court discussed the legal effect of an advertisement offering for sale, as a one-day special, an electric sewing machine at a named price. The court held that an advertisement was not an offer that was capable of acceptance. This is the general rule.

Lefkowitz v. Great Minneapolis Surplus Store, Inc.
Supreme Court of Minnesota, 1957
251 Minn. 188, 86 N.W.2d 689

Murphy, Justice. This case grows out of the alleged refusal of the defendant to sell to the plaintiff a certain fur piece which it had offered for sale in a newspaper advertisement. It appears from the record that on April 6, 1956, the defendant published the following advertisement in a Minneapolis newspaper:

> SATURDAY 9 A.M.
> 2 BRAND NEW PASTEL
> MINK 3-SKIN SCARFS
> Selling for $89.50
> Out they go
> Saturday. Each $1.00
> 1 BLACK LAPIN STOLE
> Beautiful,
> Worth $139.50 .... $1.00
> FIRST COME
> FIRST SERVED

The record supports the findings of the court that on each of the Saturdays following the publication of the above-described ad the plaintiff was the first to present himself at the appropriate counter in the defendant's store and on each occasion demanded the coat and the stole so advertised and indicated his readiness to pay the sale price of $1. On both occasions, the defendant refused to sell the merchandise to the plaintiff, stating on the first occasion that by a "house rule" the offer was intended for women only and sales would not be made to men, and on the second visit that plaintiff knew defendant's house rules.

On the facts before us we are concerned with whether the advertisement constituted an offer, and, if so, whether the plaintiff's conduct constituted an acceptance.

There are numerous authorities which hold that a particular advertisement in a newspaper or circular letter relating to a sale of articles may be construed by the court as constituting an offer, acceptance of which would complete a contract. . . .

The test of whether a binding obligation may originate in advertisements addressed to the general public is "whether the facts show that some performance was promised in positive terms in return for something requested." 1 Williston, Contracts (Rev. ed.) § 27.

The authorities above cited emphasize that, where the offer is clear, definite, and explicit, and leaves nothing open for negotiation, it constitutes an offer, acceptance of which will complete the contract. . . .

Whether in any individual instance a newspaper advertisement is an offer rather than an invitation to make an offer depends on the legal intention of the parties and the surrounding circumstances. Annotation, 157 A.L.R. 744, 751; 77 C.J.S., Sales, § 25b; 17 C.J.S., Contracts, § 389. We are of the view on the facts before us that the offer by the defendant of the sale of the Lapin fur was clear, definite, and explicit, and left nothing open for negotiation. The plaintiff having successfully managed to be the first one to appear at the seller's place of business to be served, as requested by the advertisement, and having offered the stated purchase price of the article, he was entitled to performance on the part of the defendant. We think the trial court was correct in holding that there was in the conduct of the parties a sufficient mutuality of obligation to constitute a contract of sale.

2. The defendant contends that the offer was modified by a "house rule" to the effect that only women were qualified to receive the bargains advertised. The advertisement contained no such restriction. This objection may be disposed of briefly by stating that, while an advertiser has the right at any time before acceptance to modify his offer, he does not have the right, after acceptance, to impose new or arbitrary conditions not contained in the published offer. . . . Affirmed.

Questions

1. According to the court, what determines whether a newspaper advertisement constitutes an offer?

2. Was the offer in the advertisement considered clear and explicit by the court?

Harris v. Time, Inc.
Court of Appeals of California, First Appellate District, 1987
191 Cal.App.3d 449, 237 Cal.Rptr. 584

[Facts were previously set forth at p. 33.]

A. Offer. On the first point, Time argues there was no contract because the text of the unopened mailer amounted to a mere advertisement rather than an offer.

It is true that advertisements are not typically treated as offers, but merely as invitations to bargain. (1 Corbin on Contracts (1963) § 25, pp. 74-75; Rest.2d, Contracts, § 26, com, b, at p. 76.) There is, however, a fundamental exception to this rule: an advertisement can constitute an offer, and form the basis of a unilateral contract, if it calls for performance of a specific act without further communication and leaves nothing for further negotiation. (Lefkowitz v. Great Minneapolis Surplus Store (1957) 251 Minn. 188 [86 N.W.2d 689, 691]; 1 Corbin on Contracts (1963) §§ 25, 64, pp. 75-76, 264-270; Rest.2d, Contracts, § 26, com. b, at p. 76.) This is a basic rule of contract law, contained in the Restatement Second of Contracts and normally encountered within the first few weeks of law school in cases such as Lefkowitz (furs advertised for sale at specified date and time for "$1.00 First Come First Served") and *Carlill v. Carbolic Smoke Ball Co.* (1893) 1 Q.B. 256 (advertisement of reward to anyone who caught influenza after using seller's medicine). (See, e.g., Murphy & Speidel, Studies in Contract Law (3d ed. 1984) pp. 112, 154.)

The text of Time's unopened mailer was, technically, an offer to enter into a unilateral contract: the promisor made a promise to do something (give the recipient a calculator watch) in exchange for the performance of an act by the promise (opening the envelope). Time was not in the same position as a seller merely advertising price; the proper analogy is to a seller promising to give something to a customer in exchange for the customer's act of coming to the store at a specified time. (Lefkowitz v. Great Minneapolis Surplus Store, supra, 86 N.W.2d 689.)

Questions

1. According to the court, how are advertisements typically treated in contract law, and what is the exception to this rule?

2. What conditions must be met for an advertisement to be considered an offer and form the basis of a unilateral contract?

3. How did the court characterize the text of Time's unopened mailer, and why did they consider it an offer for a unilateral contract?

4. What analogy did the court draw to explain Time's position in relation to the advertisement, and which case supported this analogy?

Takeaways – Lefkowitz and Harris

The general rule is that an advertisement is not an offer. However where the advertisement is clear, definite and explicit and leaves nothing open for negotiation, it constitutes an offer the acceptance of which will result in the formation of a contract.

Donovan v. RRL Corp.
Supreme Court of California, 2001
26 Cal.4th 261, 109 Cal.Rptr.2d 807; 27 P.3d 702

GEORGE, C.J. Defendant RRL Corporation is an automobile dealer doing business under the name Lexus of Westminster. Because of typographical and proofreading errors made by a local newspaper, defendant's advertisement listed a price for a used automobile that was significantly less than the intended sales price. Plaintiff Brian J. Donovan read the advertisement and, after examining the vehicle, attempted to purchase it by tendering the advertised price. Defendant refused to sell the automobile to plaintiff at that price, and plaintiff brought this action against defendant for breach of contract. . . .

While reading the April 26, 1997, edition of the Costa Mesa Daily Pilot, a local newspaper, plaintiff noticed a full-page advertisement placed by defendant. The advertisement promoted a "PRE-OWNED COUP-A-RAMA SALE!/2-DAY PRE-OWNED SALES EVENT" and listed, along with 15 other used automobiles, a 1995 Jaguar XJ6 Vanden Plas. The advertisement described the color of this automobile as sapphire blue, included a vehicle identification number, and stated a price of $25,995. The name Lexus of Westminster was displayed prominently in three separate locations in the advertisement, which included defendant's address along with a small map showing the location of the dealership. The following statements appeared in small print at the bottom of the advertisement: "All cars plus tax, lic., doc., smog & bank fees. On approved credit. Ad expires 4/27/97[.]" . . .

The following day, plaintiff and his spouse drove to Lexus of Westminster and observed a blue Jaguar displayed on an elevated ramp. After verifying that the identification number on the sticker was the same as that listed in defendant's April 26 Daily Pilot advertisement, they asked a salesperson whether they could test drive the Jaguar. Plaintiff mentioned that he had seen the advertisement and that the price "looked really good." The salesperson responded that, as a Lexus dealer, defendant might offer better prices for a Jaguar automobile than would a Jaguar dealer. At that point, however, neither plaintiff nor the salesperson mentioned the specific advertised price.

After the test drive, plaintiff and his spouse discussed several negative characteristics of the automobile, including high mileage, an apparent rust problem, and worn tires. In addition, it was not as clean as the other Jaguars they had inspected. Despite these problems, they believed that the advertised price was a very good price and decided to purchase the vehicle. Plaintiff told the salesperson, "Okay. We will take it at your price, $26,000." When the salesperson did not respond, plaintiff showed him the advertisement. The salesperson immediately stated, "That's a mistake."

After plaintiff asked to speak with an individual in charge, defendant's sales manager also told plaintiff that the price listed in the advertisement was a mistake. The sales manager apologized and offered to pay for plaintiff's fuel, time, and effort expended in traveling to the dealership to examine the automobile. Plaintiff declined this offer and expressed his belief that there had been no mistake. Plaintiff stated that he could write a check for the full purchase price as advertised. The sales manager responded that he would not sell the vehicle at the advertised price. Plaintiff then requested the sales price. After performing some calculations, and based upon defendant's $35,000 investment in the automobile, the sales manager stated that he would sell it to plaintiff for $37,016. Plaintiff responded, "No, I want to buy it at your advertised price, and I will write you a check right now." The sales manager again stated that he would not sell the vehicle at the advertised price, and plaintiff and his spouse left the dealership.

Plaintiff subsequently filed this action against defendant for breach of contract, fraud, and negligence. . . .

An essential element of any contract is the consent of the parties, or mutual assent. (Civ. Code, §§ 1550, subd. (2), 1565, subd. (2).) Mutual assent usually is manifested by an offer communicated to the offeree and an acceptance communicated to the offeror. (1 Witkin, Summary of Cal. Law (9th ed. 1987) Contracts, § 128, p. 153 (hereafter Witkin).) " ' "An offer is the manifestation of willingness to enter into a bargain, so made as to justify another person in understanding that his assent to that bargain is invited and will conclude it." ' [Citations.]" (*City of Moorpark v. Moorpark Unified School Dist.* (1991) 54 Cal.3d 921, 930 (*Moorpark*).) The determination of whether a particular communication constitutes an operative offer, rather than an inoperative step in the preliminary negotiation of a contract, depends upon all the surrounding circumstances. (1 Corbin, Contracts (rev. ed. 1993) § 2.2, p. 105.) The objective manifestation of the party's assent ordinarily controls, and the pertinent inquiry is whether the individual to whom the communication was made had reason to believe that it was intended as an offer. (1 Witkin, *supra*, Contracts, § 119, p. 144; 1 Farnsworth, Contracts (2d ed. 1998) § 3.10, p. 237.)

In the present case, the municipal court ruled that newspaper advertisements for automobiles generally constitute offers that can be accepted by a customer's tender of the purchase price. Its conclusion that defendant's advertisement for the 1995 Jaguar did not constitute an offer was based solely upon the court's factual determination that the erroneous price in the advertisement was the result of a good faith mistake.

Because the existence of an offer depends upon an objective interpretation of defendant's assent as reflected in the advertisement, however, the mistaken price (not reasonably known to plaintiff to be a mistake) is irrelevant in determining the threshold question whether the advertisement constituted an offer. In this situation, mistake instead properly would be considered in deciding whether a contract resulted from the acceptance of an offer containing mistaken terms, or whether any such contract could be voided or rescinded. (See *Chakmak v. H. J. Lucas Masonry, Inc.* (1976) 55 Cal.App.3d 124, 129; Rest.2d Contracts, § 153; 1 Corbin, Contracts, *supra*, § 4.11, pp. 623-627; 2 Williston, Contracts (4th ed. 1991) § 6:57, pp. 682-695.) Thus, the municipal court did not make any factual findings relevant to the issue whether defendant's advertisement constituted an offer, and we shall review the question de novo. (*Richards v. Flower* (1961) 193 Cal.App.2d 233, 235.)

Some courts have stated that an advertisement or other notice disseminated to the public at large generally does not constitute an offer, but rather is presumed to be an invitation to consider, examine, and negotiate. (E.g., *Harris v. Time, Inc.* (1987) 191 Cal.App.3d 449, 455; see Rest.2d Contracts, § 26, com. b, p. 76; 1 Corbin, Contracts, *supra*, § 2.4, p. 116; 1 Farnsworth, Contracts, *supra*, § 3.10, p. 242; 1 Williston, Contracts (4th ed. 1990) § 4:7, pp. 285-287, 294.) Nevertheless, certain advertisements have been held to constitute offers where they invite the performance of a specific act without further communication and leave nothing for negotiation. Advertisements for rewards typically fall within this category, because performing the requested act (e.g., returning a lost article or supplying particular information) generally is all that is necessary to accept the offer and conclude the bargain. (1 Witkin, *supra*, Contracts, § 188, p. 200; Rest.2d Contracts, § 29, com. b, illus. 1, p. 84; 1 Corbin, Contracts, *supra*, § 2.4, p. 119.)

Various advertisements involving transactions in goods also have been held to constitute offers where they invite particular action. For example, a merchant's advertisement that listed particular goods at a specific price and included the phrase "First Come First Served" was deemed to be an offer, because it constituted a promise to sell to a customer at that price in exchange for the customer's act of arriving at the store at a particular time. (*Lefkowitz v. Great Minneapolis Surplus Store* (1957) 251 Minn. 188 [86 N.W. 2d 689, 691]; Rest.2d Contracts, § 26, com. b, illus. 1, p. 76.) Similarly, external wording on the envelope of an item of bulk rate mail promising to give the recipient a watch "just for opening the envelope" before a certain date was held to constitute an operative offer accepted by performance of the act of opening the envelope. (*Harris v. Time, Inc., supra,* 191 Cal.App.3d 449, 455-456.) In addition, an advertisement stating that anyone who purchased a 1954 automobile from a dealer could exchange it for a 1955 model at no additional cost constituted an offer that was accepted when the plaintiff purchased the 1954 vehicle. (*Johnson v. Capital City Ford Co.* (La.Ct.App. 1955) 85 So.2d 75, 79-80; see also *Cobaugh v. Klick-*

Lewis (Pa.Super.Ct. 1989) 561 A.2d 1248, 1249-1250 [sign at golf course stated "hole-in-one wins" an automobile at a specified price].) In such cases, courts have considered whether the advertiser, in clear and positive terms, promised to render performance in exchange for something requested by the advertiser, and whether the recipient of the advertisement reasonably might have concluded that by acting in accordance with the request a contract would be formed. (1 Williston, Contracts, *supra*, § 4:7, pp. 296-297; 1 Corbin, Contracts, *supra*, § 2:4, pp. 116-117; see, e.g., *Chang v. First Colonial Sav. Bank* (1991) 242 Va. 388 [410 S.E.2d 928, 929-930] [bank's newspaper advertisement stating "Deposit $14,000 and receive . . . $20,136.12 upon maturity in 3 1/2 years" constituted an offer that was accepted by the plaintiffs' deposit of that sum for the specified period].)

Relying upon these decisions, defendant contends that its advertisement for the 1995 Jaguar XJ6 Vanden Plas did not constitute an offer, because the advertisement did not request the performance of a specific act that would conclude the bargain. According to defendant, plaintiff's assertion that the advertisement was an offer conflicts with the generally accepted "black-letter" rule that an advertisement that simply identifies goods and specifies a price is an invitation to negotiate.

This court has not previously applied the common law rules upon which defendant relies, including the rule that advertisements generally constitute invitations to negotiate rather than offers. Plaintiff observes that such rules governing the construction of advertisements have been criticized on the ground that they are inconsistent with the reasonable expectations of consumers and lead to haphazard results. (See Eisenberg, *Expression Rules in Contract Law and Problems of Offer and Acceptance* (1994) 82 Cal. L.Rev. 1127, 1166-1172.) Plaintiff urges this court to reject the black-letter advertising rule.

In the present case, however, we need not consider the viability of the black-letter rule regarding the interpretation of advertisements *in general*. Like the Court of Appeal, we conclude that a licensed automobile dealer's advertisement for the sale of a particular vehicle at a specific price--when construed in light of Vehicle Code section 11713.1, subdivision (e)--reasonably justifies a consumer's understanding that the dealer intends the advertisement to constitute an offer and that the consumer's assent to the bargain is invited and will conclude it.

Vehicle Code section 11713.1 sets forth comprehensive requirements governing a licensed automobile dealer's advertisements for motor vehicles. This statute requires, among other things, that an advertisement for a specific automobile identify the vehicle by its identification number or license number (*id.*, subd. (a)), disclose the type of charges that will be added to the advertised price at the time of sale (*id.*, subd. (b)), and refrain from containing various types of misleading information (*id.*, subds. (i), (l), (o), (p), (r)).

In addition, Vehicle Code section 11713.1, subdivision (e) (hereafter section 11713.1(e)), states that it is a violation of the Vehicle Code for the holder of any dealer's license to "[f]ail to sell a vehicle to any person at the advertised total price, exclusive of [specified charges such as taxes and registration fees], while the vehicle remains unsold, unless the advertisement states the advertised total price is good only for a specified time and the time has elapsed."

The administrative regulation implementing section 11713.1(e) states in relevant part: "A specific vehicle advertised by a dealer . . . shall be willingly shown and sold at the advertised price and terms while such vehicle remains unsold . . . , unless the advertisement states that the advertised price and terms are good only for a specific time and such time has elapsed. Advertised vehicles must be sold at or below the advertised price irrespective of whether or not the advertised price has been communicated to the purchaser." (Cal. Code Regs., tit. 13, § 260.04, subd. (b).)

Plaintiff asserts that because a dealer is prohibited by section 11713.1(e) from failing to sell a particular vehicle at the advertised price, an advertisement for such a vehicle cannot be a mere request for offers from consumers or an invitation to negotiate, but instead must be deemed an operative offer that is accepted when a consumer tenders the full advertised price. We agree that, in light of the foregoing regulatory scheme, a licensed automobile dealer's advertisement for a particular vehicle at a specific price constitutes an offer.

As one commentator has observed, legislation can affect consumer expectations and cause reasonable individuals to regard certain retail advertisements for the sale of goods as offers to complete a bargain. (1 Corbin, Contracts, *supra*, § 2.4, p. 118.) By authorizing disciplinary action against a licensed automobile dealer that fails to sell a vehicle at the advertised price, section 11713.1(e) creates a reasonable expectation on the part of consumers that the dealer intends to make an offer to sell at that price, and that the consumer can accept the offer by paying the price specified in the advertisement. Interpreted in light of the regulatory obligations imposed upon dealers, an advertisement for a particular automobile at a specific price constitutes an objective manifestation of the dealer's willingness to enter into a bargain on the stated terms, and justifies the consumer's understanding that his or her assent to the bargain is invited and will conclude it. Such an advertisement therefore constitutes an offer that is accepted when a consumer tenders the advertised price.

Defendant and its supporting amici curiae contend that section 11713.1(e) was not intended to modify the common law of contracts, and that therefore the statute should not be considered in determining whether a contract arose from defendant's advertisement and plaintiff's tender of the advertised price. As we shall explain (pt. IV, *post*), we agree that section 11713.1(e) does not reflect a legislative intent to supplant the common law governing contracts for the sale of motor vehicles by licensed dealers. Nevertheless, the statute does govern the conduct of dealers and thus creates an objective expectation that dealers intend to sell vehicles at the advertised price. Therefore, even though section 11713.1(e) does not alter the applicable common law regarding contractual offers, consumer expectations arising from the statute are relevant in determining whether defendant's advertisement constituted an offer pursuant to governing principles of contract law.

Amicus curiae California Motor Car Dealers Association further asserts that an advertisement for the sale of a vehicle does not constitute an offer because consumers have reason to believe that an automobile dealer does not intend to conclude the bargain until agreement is reached with regard to numerous terms other than price and until the contract is reduced to writing. (See Rest.2d Contracts, §§ 26, 27; 1 Witkin, *supra*, Contracts, § 142, pp. 166-167.) For example, a written contract for the sale of an automobile by a dealer typically includes terms such as the form of payment, warranties, insurance, title, registration, delivery, taxes, documentation fees, and, if applicable, financing. (See *Twaite v. Allstate Ins. Co.* (1989) 216 Cal.App.3d 239, 243; *O'Keefe v. Lee Calan Imports, Inc.* (1970) 128 Ill.App.2d 410 [262 N.E.2d 758, 760]; see also Civ. Code, § 2981 et seq. [requirements for conditional contracts for the sale of motor vehicles].) In addition, specific written disclosures, required by statute, must appear in the contract. (E.g., Veh. Code, § 11713.1, subd. (v) [retail automobile sales contract clearly and conspicuously must disclose whether the vehicle is being sold as used or new], subd. (x) [dealer must disclose on the face of the contract whether the transaction is or is not subject to a fee received by an "autobroker" as defined in the Vehicle Code].)

Plaintiff, on the other hand, contends that the existence of a contract is not defeated by the circumstance that he and defendant might have included additional terms in their ultimate written agreement, or that acceptance of defendant's offer might have been communicated by means other than tender of the purchase price, for example by signing a written contract. Plaintiff relies upon the following principle: "Manifestations of assent that are in themselves sufficient to conclude a contract will not be prevented from so operating by the fact that the parties also manifest an intention to prepare and adopt a written memorial thereof; but the circumstances may show that the agreements are preliminary negotiations." (Rest.2d Contracts, § 27.) Plaintiff also observes that "[a]n offer to make a contract shall be construed as inviting acceptance in any manner and by any medium reasonable in the circumstances," unless otherwise indicated. (Cal. U. Com. Code, § 2206, subd. (1)(a).)

Although dealers are required by statute to prepare a written contract when selling an automobile, and such a contract contains terms other than the price of the vehicle, we agree with plaintiff that a dealer's advertisement specifying a price for a particular vehicle constitutes a sufficient manifestation of the dealer's assent to give rise to a contract. As we have explained, in light of section 11713.1(e) such an advertisement objectively reflects the dealer's intention to sell the vehicle to a member of the public who tenders the full advertised price while the vehicle remains unsold and before the advertisement expires. The price almost always is the most important term of the bargain, and the dealer's intention to include other terms in a written contract does not preclude the existence of mutual assent sufficient to conclude a contract.

In sum, because section 11713.1(e) makes it unlawful for a dealer not to sell a particular vehicle at the advertised price while the vehicle remains unsold and before the advertisement expires, plaintiff reasonably could believe that defendant intended the advertisement to be an offer. Therefore, we conclude that defendant's advertisement constituted an offer that was accepted by plaintiff's tender of the advertised price.

Questions

1. According to the court's ruling, under what circumstances does an advertisement constitute an offer?

2. How does Vehicle Code section 11713.1(e) impact the interpretation of the defendant's advertisement?

Mistaken Offers

Elsinore Union etc. Sch. Dist. v. Kastorff
Supreme Court of California, 1960
54 Cal.2d 380, 6 Cal.Rptr.1, 353 P.2d 713

SCHAUER, J. Defendants, who are a building contractor and his surety, appeal from an adverse judgment in this action by plaintiff school district to recover damages allegedly resulting when defendant Kastorff, the contractor, refused to execute a building contract pursuant to his previously submitted bid to make certain additions to plaintiff's school buildings. We have concluded that because of an honest clerical error in the bid and defendant's subsequent prompt rescission he was not obliged to execute the contract, and that the judgment should therefore be reversed.

Pursuant to plaintiff's call for bids, defendant Kastorff secured a copy of the plans and specifications of the proposed additions to plaintiff's school buildings and proceeded to prepare a bid to be submitted by the deadline hour of 8 p. m., August 12, 1952, at Elsinore, California. Kastorff testified that in preparing his bid he employed work sheets upon which he entered bids of various subcontractors for such portions of the work as they were to do, and that to reach the final total of his own bid for the work he carried into the right hand column of the work sheets the amounts of the respective sub bids which he intended to accept and then added those amounts to the cost of the work which he would do himself rather than through a subcontractor; that there is "a custom among subcontractors, in bidding on jobs such as this, to delay giving ... their bids until the very last moment"; that the first sub bid for plumbing was in the amount of $9,285 and he had received it "the afternoon of the bid-opening," but later that afternoon when "the time was drawing close for me to get my bids together and get over to Elsinore (from his home in San Juan Capistrano) he received a $6,500 bid for the plumbing. Erroneously thinking he had entered the $9,285 plumbing bid in his total column and had included that sum in his total bid and realizing that the second plumbing bid was nearly $3,000 less than the first, Kastorff then deducted $3,000 from the total amount of his bid and entered the resulting total of $89,994 on the bid form as his bid for the school construction. Thus the total included no allowance whatsoever for the plumbing work.

Kastorff then proceeded to Elsinore and deposited his bid with plaintiff. When the bids were opened shortly after 8 p. m. that evening, it was discovered that of the five bids submitted that of Kastorff was some $11,306 less than the next lowest bid. The school superintendent and the four school board members present thereupon asked Kastorff whether he was sure his figures were correct, Kastorff stepped out into the hall to check with the person who had assisted in doing the clerical work on the bid, and a few minutes later returned and stated that the figures were correct. He testified that he did not have his work sheets or other papers with him to check against at the time. The board thereupon, on August 12, 1952, voted to award Kastorff the contract.

The next morning Kastorff checked his work sheets and promptly discovered his error. He immediately drove to the Los Angeles office of the firm of architects which had prepared the plans and specifications for plaintiff, and there saw Mr. Rendon. Mr. Rendon testified that Kastorff "had his maps and estimate work-sheets of the project, and indicated to me that he had failed to carry across the amount of dollars for the plumbing work. It was on the sheet, but not in the total sheet. We examined that evidence, and in our opinion we felt that he had made a clerical error in compiling his bill. ... In other words, he had put down a figure, but didn't carry it out to the 'total' column when he totaled his column to make up his bid. ... He exhibited ... at that time ... his work-sheets from which he had made up his bid." That same morning (August 13) Rendon telephoned the school superintendent and informed him of the error and of its nature and that Kastorff asked to be released from his bid. On August 14 Kastorff wrote a letter to the school board explaining his error and again requesting that he be permitted to withdraw his bid. On August 15, after receiving Kastorff's letter, the board held a special meeting and voted not to grant his request. Thereafter, on August 28, written notification was given to Kastorff of award of the contract to him. Subsequently plaintiff submitted to Kastorff a contract to be signed in accordance with his bid, and on September 8, 1952, Kastorff returned the contract to plaintiff with a letter again explaining his error and asked the board to reconsider his request for withdrawal of his bid.

Plaintiff thereafter received additional bids to do the subject construction; let the contract to the lowest bidder, in the amount of $102,900; and brought this action seeking to recover from Kastorff the $12,906 difference between that amount and the amount Kastorff had bid. Recovery of $4,499.60 is also sought against Kastorff's surety under the terms of the bond posted with his bid.

Defendants in their answer to the complaint pleaded, among other things, that Kastorff had made an honest error in compiling his bid; that "he thought he was bidding, and intended to bid, $9500.00 more, making a total of $99,494.00 as his bid"; that upon discovering his error he had promptly notified plaintiff and rescinded the $89,994 bid. The trial court found that it was true that Kastorff made up a bid sheet, which was introduced in evidence; that the subcontractor's bids thereupon indicated were those received by Kastorff; that he "had 16 subcontracting bids to ascertain from 31 which were submitted"; and that Kastorff had neglected to carry over from the left hand column on the bid sheet to the right hand column on the sheet a portion of the plumbing (and heating) subcontractor's bid. Despite the uncontradicted evidence related hereinabove, including that of plaintiff's architect and of its school superintendent, both of whom testified as plaintiff's witnesses, the court further found, however, that "it is not true that the right hand column of figures was totaled for the purpose of arriving at the total bid to be submitted by E. J. Kastorff ... It cannot be ascertained from the evidence for what purpose the total of the right hand column of figures on the bid sheet was used nor can it be ascertained from the evidence for what purpose the three bid sheets were used in arriving at the total bid." And although finding that "on or about August 15, 1952," plaintiff received Kastorff's letter of August 14 explaining that he "made an error of omitting from my bid the item of Plumbing," the court also found that "It is not true that the plaintiff knew at any time that defendant Kastorff's bid was intended to be other than $89, 994.00 ... It is not true that the plaintiff knew at the time it requested the execution of the contract by defendant Kastorff that he had withdrawn his bid because of an honest error in the compilation thereof. It is not true that plaintiff had notice of an error in the compilation of the bid by defendant Kastorff and tried nevertheless to take advantage of defendant Kastorff by forcing him to enter a contract on the basis of a bid he had withdrawn. ... It is not true that it would be either inequitable or unjust to require defendant Kastorff to perform the contract awarded to him for the sum of $89,994.00, and it is not true that he actually intended to bid for said work the sum of $99,494.00." Judgment was given for plaintiff in the amounts sought, and this appeal by defendants followed.

In reliance upon *M. F. Kemper Const. Co. v. City of Los Angeles* (1951), 37 Cal.2d 696 [235 P.2d 7], and *Lemoge Electric v. County of San Mateo* (1956), 46 Cal.2d 659, 662, 664 [1a, 1b, 2, 3] [297 P.2d 638], defendants urge that where, as defendants claim is the situation here, a contractor makes a clerical error in computing a bid on a public work he is entitled to rescind.

In the *Kemper* case one item on a work sheet in the amount of $301,769 was inadvertently omitted by the contractor from the final tabulation sheet and was overlooked in computing the total amount of a bid to do certain construction work for the defendant city. The error was caused by the fact that the men preparing the bid were exhausted after working long hours under pressure. When the bids were opened it was found that plaintiff's bid was $780,305, and the next lowest bid was $1,049,592. plaintiff discovered its error several hours later and immediately notified a member of defendant's board of public works of its mistake in omitting one item while preparing the final accumulation of figures for its bid. Two days later it explained its mistake to the board and withdrew its bid. A few days later it submitted to the board evidence which showed the unintentional omission of the $301,769 item. The board nevertheless passed a resolution accepting plaintiff's erroneous bid of $780,305, and plaintiff refused to enter into a written contract at that figure. The board then awarded the contract to the next lowest bidder, the city demanded forfeiture of plaintiff's bid bond, and plaintiff brought action to cancel its bid and obtain discharge of the bond. The trial court found that the bid had been submitted as the result of an excusable and honest mistake of a material and fundamental character, that plaintiff company had not been negligent in preparing the proposal, that it had acted promptly to notify the board of the mistake and to rescind the bid, and that the board had accepted the bid with knowledge of the error. The court further found and concluded that it would be unconscionable to require the company to perform for the amount of the bid, that no intervening rights had accrued, and that the city had suffered no damage or prejudice.

On appeal by the city this court affirmed, stating the following applicable rules (pp. 700-703 of 37 Cal.2d): " Once opened and declared, the company's bid was in the nature of an irrevocable option, a contract right of which the city could not be deprived without its consent unless the requirements for rescission were satisfied. [Citations.] ... ... the city had actual notice of the error in the estimates before it attempted to accept the bid, and knowledge by one party that the other is acting under mistake is treated as equivalent to mutual mistake for purposes of rescission. [Citations.] Relief from mistaken bids is consistently allowed where one party knows or has reason to know of the other's error and the requirements for rescission are fulfilled. [Citations.]

"Rescission may be had for mistake of fact if the mistake is material to the contract and was not the result of neglect of a legal duty, if enforcement of the contract as made would be unconscionable, and if the other party can be placed in status quo. [Citations.] In addition, the party seeking relief must give prompt notice of his election to rescind and must restore or offer to restore to the other party everything of value which he has received under the contract. [Citations.]

"Omission of the $301,769 item from the company's bid was, of course, a material mistake. ... [E]ven if we assume that the error was due to some carelessness, it does not follow that the company is without remedy. Civil Code section 1577, which defines mistake of fact for which relief may be allowed, describes it as one not caused by 'the neglect of a legal duty' on the part of the person making the mistake. [6] It has been recognized numerous times that not all carelessness constitutes a 'neglect of legal duty' within the meaning of the section. [Citations.] On facts very similar to those in the present case, courts of other jurisdictions have stated that there was no culpable negligence and have granted relief from erroneous bids. [Citations.] The type of error here involved is one which will sometimes occur in the conduct of reasonable and cautious businessmen, and, under all the circumstances, we cannot say as a matter of law that it constituted a neglect of legal duty such as would bar the right to equitable relief.

"The evidence clearly supports the conclusion that it would be unconscionable to hold the company to its bid at the mistaken figure. The city had knowledge before the bid was accepted that the company had made a clerical error which resulted in the omission of an item amounting to nearly one third of the amount intended to be bid, and, under all the circumstances, it appears that it would be unjust and unfair to permit the city to take advantage of the company's mistake. There is no reason for denying relief on the ground that the city cannot be restored to status quo. It had ample time in which to award the contract without readvertising, the contract was actually awarded to the next lowest bidder, and the city will not be heard to complain that it cannot be placed in status quo because it will not have the benefit of an inequitable bargain. [Citations.] Finally, the company gave notice promptly upon discovering the facts entitling it to rescind, and no offer of restoration was necessary because it had received nothing of value which it could restore. [Citation.] We are satisfied that all the requirements for rescission have been met." . . .

Further, we are persuaded that the trial court's view, . . . "Kastorff had ample time and opportunity after receiving his last subcontractor's bid" to complete and check his final bid, does not convict Kastorff of that "neglect of legal duty" which would preclude his being relieved from the inadvertent clerical error of omitting from his bid the cost of the plumbing. (See Civ. Code, § 1577; *M. F. Kemper Const. Co. v. City of Los Angeles* (1951), supra, 37 Cal.2d 696, 702 .) Neither should he be denied relief from an unfair, inequitable, and unintended bargain simply because, in response to inquiry from the board when his bid was discovered to be much the lowest submitted, he informed the board, after checking with his clerical assistant, that the bid was correct. He did not have his work sheets present to inspect at that time, he did thereafter inspect them at what would appear to have been the earliest practicable moment, and thereupon promptly notified plaintiff and rescinded his bid. Further, as shown in the margin, fn. 5 Kastorff's bid agreement, as provided by plaintiff's own bid form, was to execute a formal written contract only after receiving written notification of acceptance of his bid, and such notice was not given to him until some two weeks following his rescission.

If the situations of the parties were reversed and plaintiff and Kastorff had even executed a formal written contract (by contrast with the preliminary bid offer and acceptance) calling for a fixed sum payment to Kastorff large enough to include a reasonable charge for plumbing but inadvertently through the district's clerical error omitting a mutually intended provision requiring Kastorff to furnish and install plumbing, we have no doubt but that the district would demand and expect reformation or rescission. In the case before us the district expected Kastorff to furnish and install plumbing; surely it must also have understood that he intended to, and that his bid did, include a charge for such plumbing. The omission of any such charge was as unexpected by the board as it was unintended by Kastorff. Under the circumstances the "bargain" for which the board presses (which action we, of course, assume to be impelled by advice of counsel and a strict concept of official duty) appears too sharp for law and equity to sustain.

Plaintiff suggests that in any event the amount of the plumbing bid omitted from the total was immaterial. The bid as submitted was in the sum of $89,994, and whether the sum for the omitted plumbing was $6,500 or $9,285 (the two sub bids), the omission of such a sum is plainly material to the total. In *Lemoge* (*Lemoge Electric v. County of San Mateo* (1956), supra, 46 Cal.2d 659, 661-662) the error which it was declared would have entitled plaintiff to rescind was the listing of the cost of certain materials as $104.52, rather than $10,452, in a total bid of $172,421. Thus the percentage of error here was larger than in Lemoge, and was plainly material.

The judgment is reversed.

Questions

1. What were the findings of the trial court regarding Kastorff's bid and the plaintiff's knowledge of the error?

2. What principles from the *M.F. Kemper Const. Co. v. City of Los Angeles* case were relied upon by the defendants in their argument?

3. What facts or evidence showed that the school board was aware or should have been aware that the bid was mistaken?

Takeaways – Elsinore Union School Dist. v. Kastorff

Relief from mistaken bids is allowed where one party knows or has reason to know of the other's error. Mistake is taken up more completely in Chapter 9.

Donovan v. RRL Corp.
Supreme Court of California, 2001
26 Cal.4th 261, 109 Cal.Rptr.2d 807; 27 P.3d 702

[Facts were previously set forth at p. 63.]

We next consider whether defendant can avoid enforcement of the contract on the ground of mistake.

A party may rescind a contract if his or her consent was given by mistake. (Civ. Code, § 1689, subd. (b)(1).) A factual mistake by one party to a contract, or unilateral mistake, affords a ground for rescission in some circumstances. [4] Civil Code section 1577 states in relevant part: "Mistake of fact is a mistake, not caused by the neglect of a legal duty on the part of the person making the mistake, and consisting in: [¶] 1. An unconscious ignorance or forgetfulness of a fact past or present, material to the contract . . . ."

The Court of Appeal determined that defendant's error did not constitute a mistake of fact within the meaning of Civil Code section 1577. In support of this determination, the court relied upon the following principle: "[A] unilateral misinterpretation of contractual terms, without knowledge by the other party at the time of contract, does not constitute a mistake under either Civil Code section 1577 [mistake of fact] or 1578 [mistake of law]." (*Hedging Concepts, Inc. v. First Alliance Mortgage Co.* (1996) 41 Cal.App.4th 1410, 1422 (*Hedging Concepts*).)

The foregoing principle has no application to the present case. In *Hedging Concepts*, the plaintiff believed that he would fulfill his contractual obligations by introducing potential business prospects to the defendant. The contract, however, required the plaintiff to procure a completed business arrangement. The Court of Appeal held that the plaintiff's subjective misinterpretation of the terms of the contract constituted, at most, a mistake of law. Because the defendant was unaware of the plaintiff's misunderstanding at the time of the contract, the court held that rescission was not a proper remedy. (*Hedging Concepts, supra*, 41 Cal.App.4th at pp. 1418-1422; citing 1 Witkin, *supra*, Contracts, § 379, pp. 345-346 [relief for unilateral mistake of law is authorized only where one party knows of, does not correct, and takes advantage or enjoys the benefit of another party's mistake].) Defendant's mistake in the present case, in contrast, did not consist of a subjective misinterpretation of a contract term, but rather resulted from an unconscious ignorance that the Daily Pilot advertisement set forth an incorrect price for the automobile. Defendant's lack of knowledge regarding the typographical error in the advertised price of the vehicle cannot be considered a mistake of law. Defendant's error constituted a mistake of fact, and the Court of Appeal erred in concluding otherwise. As we shall explain, the Court of Appeal also erred to the extent it suggested that a unilateral mistake of fact affords a ground for rescission only where the other party is aware of the mistake.

Under the first Restatement of Contracts, unilateral mistake did not render a contract voidable unless the other party knew of or caused the mistake. (1 Witkin, *supra*, Contracts, § 370, p. 337; see Rest., Contracts, § 503.) In *Germain etc. Co. v. Western Union etc. Co.* (1902) 137 Cal. 598, 602, this court endorsed a rule similar to that of the first Restatement. Our opinion indicated that a seller's price quotation erroneously transcribed and delivered by a telegraph company contractually could bind the seller to the incorrect price, unless the buyer knew or had reason to suspect that a mistake had been made. Some decisions of the Court of Appeal have adhered to the approach of the original Restatement. (See, e.g., *Conservatorship of O'Connor* (1996) 48 Cal.App.4th 1076, 1097-1098, and cases cited therein.) Plaintiff also advocates this approach and contends that rescission is unavailable to defendant, because plaintiff was unaware of the mistaken price in defendant's advertisement when he accepted the offer.

The Court of Appeal decisions reciting the traditional rule do not recognize that in *M. F. Kemper Const. Co. v. City of L. A.* (1951) 37 Cal.2d 696, 701 (*Kemper*), we acknowledged but rejected a strict application of the foregoing Restatement rule regarding unilateral mistake of fact. The plaintiff in *Kemper* inadvertently omitted a $301,769 item from its bid for the defendant city's public works project--approximately one-third of the total contract price. After discovering the mistake several hours later, the plaintiff immediately notified the city and subsequently withdrew its bid. Nevertheless, the city accepted the erroneous bid, contending that rescission of the offer was unavailable for the plaintiff's unilateral mistake.

Our decision in *Kemper* recognized that the bid, when opened and announced, resulted in an irrevocable option contract conferring upon the city a right to accept the bid, and that the plaintiff could not withdraw its bid unless the requirements for rescission of this option contract were satisfied. (*Kemper*, *supra*, "37 Cal.2d at pp. 700, 704.) We stated: "Rescission may be had for mistake of fact if the mistake is material to the contract and was not the result of neglect of a legal duty, if enforcement of the contract as made would be unconscionable, and if the other party can be placed in status quo. [Citations.]" (*Id.* at p. 701.) Although the city knew of the plaintiff's mistake before it accepted the bid, and this circumstance was relevant to our determination that requiring the plaintiff to perform at the mistaken bid price would be unconscionable (*id.* at pp. 702-703), we authorized rescission of the city's option contract even though the city had not known of or contributed to the mistake before it opened the bid.

Similarly, in *Elsinore Union etc. Sch. Dist. v. Kastorff* (1960) 54 Cal.2d 380 (*Elsinore*), we authorized the rescission of an erroneous bid even where the contractor had assured the public agency, after the agency inquired, that his figures were accurate, and where the agency already had accepted the bid before it was aware of the mistake. In this situation, the other party clearly had no reason to know of the contractor's mistake before it accepted the bid.

The decisions in *Kemper* and *Elsinore* establish that California law does not adhere to the original Restatement's requirements for rescission based upon unilateral mistake of fact--i.e., only in circumstances where the other party knew of the mistake or caused the mistake. Consistent with the decisions in *Kemper* and *Elsinore*, the Restatement Second of Contracts authorizes rescission for a unilateral mistake of fact where "the effect of the mistake is such that enforcement of the contract would be unconscionable." (Rest.2d Contracts, § 153, subd. (a).) The comment following this section recognizes "a growing willingness to allow avoidance where the consequences of the mistake are so grave that enforcement of the contract would be unconscionable." (*Id.*, com. a, p. 394.) Indeed, two of the illustrations recognizing this additional ground for rescission in the Restatement Second of Contracts are based in part upon this court's decisions in *Kemper* and *Elsinore*. (Rest.2d Contracts, § 153, com. c, illus. 1, 3, pp. 395, 396, and Reporter's Note, pp. 400-401; see also *Schultz v. County of Contra Costa* (1984) 157 Cal.App.3d 242, 249-250 [applying section 153, subdivision (a), of the Restatement Second of Contracts], disagreed with on another ground in *Van Petten v. County of San Diego* (1995) 38 Cal.App.4th 43, 50-51; 1 Witkin, *supra*, Contracts, § 370, p. 337 [reciting the rule of the same Restatement provision].) Although the most common types of mistakes falling within this category occur in bids on construction contracts, section 153 of the Restatement Second of Contracts is not limited to such cases. (Rest.2d Contracts, § 153, com. b, p. 395.)

Because the rule in section 153, subdivision (a), of the Restatement Second of Contracts, authorizing rescission for unilateral mistake of fact where enforcement would be unconscionable, is consistent with our previous decisions, we adopt the rule as California law. As the author of one treatise recognized more than 40 years ago, the decisions that are inconsistent with the traditional rule "are too numerous and too appealing to the sense of justice to be disregarded." (3 Corbin, Contracts (1960) § 608, p. 675, fn. omitted.) We reject plaintiff's contention and the Court of Appeal's conclusion that, because plaintiff was unaware of defendant's unilateral mistake, the mistake does not provide a ground to avoid enforcement of the contract.

Having concluded that a contract properly may be rescinded on the ground of unilateral mistake of fact as set forth in section 153, subdivision (a), of the Restatement Second of Contracts, we next consider whether the requirements of that provision, construed in light of our previous decisions, are satisfied in the present case. Where the plaintiff has no reason to know of and does not cause the defendant's unilateral mistake of fact, the defendant must establish the following facts to obtain rescission of the contract: (1) the defendant made a mistake regarding a basic assumption upon which the defendant made the contract; (2) the mistake has a material effect upon the agreed exchange of performances that is adverse to the defendant; (3) the defendant does not bear the risk of the mistake; and (4) the effect of the mistake is such that enforcement of the contract would be unconscionable. We shall consider each of these requirements below.

A significant error in the price term of a contract constitutes a mistake regarding a basic assumption upon which the contract is made, and such a mistake ordinarily has a material effect adverse to the mistaken party. (See, e.g., *Elsinore, supra,* 54 Cal.2d at p. 389 [7 percent error in contract price]; *Lemoge Electric v. County of San Mateo* (1956) 46 Cal.2d 659, 661-662 [6 percent error]; *Kemper, supra,* 37 Cal.2d at p. 702 [28 percent error]; *Brunzell Const. Co. v. G. J. Weisbrod, Inc.* (1955) 134 Cal.App.2d 278, 286 [20 percent error]; Rest.2d Contracts, § 152, com. b, illus. 3, p. 387 [27 percent error].) In establishing a material mistake regarding a basic assumption of the contract, the defendant must show that the resulting imbalance in the agreed exchange is so severe that it would be unfair to require the defendant to perform. (Rest.2d Contracts, § 152, com. c, p. 388.) Ordinarily, a defendant can satisfy this requirement by showing that the exchange not only is less desirable for the defendant, but also is more advantageous to the other party. (*Ibid.*)

Measured against this standard, defendant's mistake in the contract for the sale of the Jaguar automobile constitutes a material mistake regarding a basic assumption upon which it made the contract. Enforcing the contract with the mistaken price of $25,995 would require defendant to sell the vehicle to plaintiff for $12,000 less than the intended advertised price of $37,995--an error amounting to 32 percent of the price defendant intended. The exchange of performances would be substantially less desirable for defendant and more desirable for plaintiff. . . .

Questions

1. What are the requirements for rescission of a contract based on a unilateral mistake of fact, according to California law?

2. What is the significance of a significant error in the price term of a contract in establishing a material mistake?

3. Why did the court determine that enforcing the contract with the mistaken price in the sale of the Jaguar automobile would be unfair to the defendant?

Takeaways - Donovan v. RRL Corp.

Was the plaintiff in *Donovan* aware that the advertised price was an error? If so, that may have offered an easier basis for deciding the case, as the long-established rule is that one cannot snap up or pounce on an offer they know contains a mistake. (See, *Tyra v. Cheney*, 152. N.W. 835 (Minn.1915).)

California Civil Code section 1577 does not include language regarding allocation of the risk of mistake to one party, but rather excludes from the definition of "mistake of fact" any mistake resulting from the neglect of a legal duty. Pursuant to section 1577 and the Restatement Second of Contracts section 157, the neglect of a legal duty amounting to a breach of the duty of good faith and fair dealing bars relief from mistake, whether or not the other party has reason to know of the mistake.

Acceptance

Acceptance is a manifestation of willingness to be bound by the terms of the offer made in the manner invited or required by the offer. (Rest.2d § 50(1).) An acceptance of an offer must be absolute and unconditional. All of the terms of the offer must be accepted without change or condition. (Cal.Civ.Code § 1585) Acceptance results in the formation of a contract, both parties are bound and neither party can withdraw from the bargain without incurring liability to the other.

An offer may invite or require acceptance to be made by an affirmative answer in words, or by performing or refraining from performing a specified act. (Rest.2d § 30.) When an offer seeks an affirmative answer in words (i.e., a promise to perform) as the means of acceptance, we say that the offer looks towards the formation of a bilateral contract. If an offer seeks a completed performance of a specified act as the means of acceptance, we say the offer looks towards the formation of a *unilateral* contract.

To be effective, an acceptance of an offer that looks to formation of a *bilateral* contract (a promise in exchange for a return promise) must be communicated to the person who made the offer. If the offer prescribes any conditions concerning the communication of its acceptance, the conditions must be conformed to, but in the absence of such conditions, any reasonable and usual mode of communication may be adopted.

Performance of the conditions of an offer, or the acceptance of the consideration offered with a proposal, is an acceptance even though a notice of acceptance is not transmitted. (See, Cal.Civ.Code § 1584; See also, 1 Witkin, Summary of Cal. Law (10th ed. 2005) Contracts, § § 183, 185, 187-189, 191, 192, 195.)

International Filter Co. v. Conroe Gin, Ice, & Light Co.,
Commission of Appeals of Texas, 1925
277 S.W. 631

NICKELS, J. Plaintiff in error, an Illinois corporation, is a manufacturer of machinery, apparatus, etc., for the purification of water in connection with the manufacture of ice, etc., having its principal office in the city of Chicago. Defendant in error is a Texas corporation engaged in the manufacture of ice, etc., having its plant, office, etc., at Conroe, Montgomery county, Tex.

On February 10, 1920, through its traveling solicitor, Waterman, plaintiff in error, at Conroe, submitted to defendant in error, acting through Henry Thompson, its manager, a written instrument, addressed to defendant in error, which (with immaterial portions omitted) reads as follows:

"Gentlemen: We propose to furnish, f. o. b. Chicago, one No. two Junior (steel tank) International water softener and filter to purify water of the character shown by sample to be submitted. * * * Price: Twelve hundred thirty ($1,230.00) dollars. * * * This proposal is made in duplicate and becomes a contract when accepted by the purchaser and approved by an executive officer of the International Filter Company, at its office in Chicago. Any modification can only be made by duly approved supplementary agreement signed by both parties.

"This proposal is submitted for prompt acceptance, and unless so accepted is subject to change without notice.

"Respectfully submitted,
"International Filter Co.
"W. W. Waterman."

On the same day the "proposal" was accepted by defendant in error through notation made on the paper by Thompson reading as follows:
"Accepted Feb. 10, 1920.
"Conroe Gin, Ice & Light Co.,
"By Henry Thompson, Mgr."

The paper as thus submitted and "accepted" contained the notation, "Make shipment by Mar. 10." The paper, in that form, reached the Chicago office of plaintiff in error, and on February 13, 1920, P. N. Engel, its president and vice president, indorsed thereon: "O. K. Feb. 13, 1920, P. N. Engel." February 14, 1920, plaintiff in error wrote and mailed, and in due course defendant in error received, the following letter:

"Feb. 14, 1920.

"Attention of Mr. Henry Thompson, Manager.

"Conroe Gin, Ice & Light Co., Conroe, Texas--Gentlemen: This will acknowledge and thank you for your order given Mr. Waterman for a No. 2 Jr. steel tank International softener and filter, for 110 volt, 60 cycle, single phase current--for shipment March 10th.

"Please make shipment of the sample of water promptly so that we may make the analysis and know the character of the water before shipment of the apparatus. Shipping tag is enclosed, and please note the instructions to pack to guard against freezing.

"Yours very truly,
"International Filter Co.,
"M. B. Johnson."

By letter of February 28, 1920, defendant in error undertook to countermand the "order," which countermand was repeated and emphasized by letter of March 4, 1920. By letter of March 2, 1920 (replying to the letter of February 28th), plaintiff in error denied the right of countermand, etc., and insisted upon performance of the "contract." The parties adhered to the respective positions thus indicated, and this suit resulted.

Plaintiff in error sued for breach of the contract alleged to have been made in the manner stated above. The defense is that no contract was made because: (1) Neither Engel's indorsement of "O. K.," nor the letter of February 14, 1920, amounted to approval "by an executive officer of the International Filter Company, at its office in Chicago." (2) Notification of such approval, or acceptance, by plaintiff in error was required to be communicated to defendant in error; it being insisted that this requirement inhered in the terms of the proposal and in the nature of the transaction and, also, that Thompson, when he indorsed "acceptance" on the paper stated to Waterman, as agent of plaintiff in error, that such notification must be promptly given; it being insisted further that the letter of February 14, 1920, did not constitute such acceptance or notification of approval, and therefore defendant in error, on February 28, 1920, etc., had the right to withdraw, or countermand, the unaccepted offer. Thompson testified in a manner to support the allegation of his statement to Waterman. There are other matters involved in the suit which must be ultimately determined, but the foregoing presents the issues now here for consideration.

The case was tried without a jury, and the judge found the facts in favor of defendant in error on all the issues indicated above, and upon other material issues. The judgment was affirmed by the Court of Civil Appeals,

We agree with the honorable Court of Civil Appeals upon the proposition that Mr. Engel's indorsement of "O. K." amounted to an approval "by an executive officer of the International Filter Company, at its office in Chicago," within the meaning of the so-called "proposal" of February 10th. The paper then became a "contract," according to its definitely expressed terms, and it became then, and thereafter it remained, an enforceable contract, in legal contemplation, unless the fact of approval by the filter company was required to be communicated to the other party and unless, in that event, the communication was not made.

We are not prepared to assent to the ruling that such communication was essential. There is no disposition to question the justice of the general rules stated in support of that holding, yet the existence of contractual capacity imports the right of the offeror to dispense with notification; and he does dispense with it "if the form of the offer," etc., "shows that this was not to be required." 9 Cyc. 270, 271; Carlill v. Carbolic Smoke Ball Co., 1 Q. B. 256 (and other references in note 6, 9 Cyc. 271). The case just cited, it seems to us, correctly states the rule:

"As notification of acceptance is required for the benefit of the person who makes the offer, the person who makes the offer may dispense with notice to himself if he thinks it desirable to do so, and I suppose there can be no doubt that where a person in an offer made by him to another person, expressly or impliedly intimates a particular mode of acceptance as sufficient to make the bargain binding, it is only necessary for the other person to whom such offer is made to follow the indicated method of acceptance; and if the person making the offer, expressly or impliedly intimates in his offer that it will be sufficient to act on the proposal without communicating acceptance of it to himself, performance of the condition is a sufficient acceptance without notification."

The Conroe Gin, Ice & Light Company executed the paper for the purpose of having it transmitted, as its offer, to the filter company at Chicago. It was so transmitted and acted upon. Its terms embrace the offer, and nothing else, and by its terms the question of notification must be judged, since those terms are not ambiguous.

The paper contains two provisions which relate to acceptance by the filter company. One is the declaration that the offer shall "become a contract * * * when approved by an executive officer of the International Filter Company, at its Chicago office." The other is thus stated: "This proposal is submitted for prompt acceptance, and unless so accepted is subject to change without notice." The first provision states "a particular mode of acceptance as sufficient to make the bargain binding," and the filter company (as stated above) followed "the indicated method of acceptance." When this was done, so the paper declares, the proposal "became a contract." The other provision does not in any way relate to a different method of acceptance by the filter company. Its sole reference is to the time within which the act of approval must be done; that is to say, there was to be a "prompt acceptance," else the offer might be changed "without notice." The second declaration merely required the approval thereinbefore stipulated for to be done promptly; if the act was so done, there is nothing in the second provision to militate against, or to conflict with, the prior declaration that, thereupon, the paper should become "a contract."

A holding that notification of that approval is to be deduced from the terms of the last-quoted clause is not essential in order to give it meaning or to dissolve ambiguity. On the contrary, such a construction of the two provisions would introduce a conflict, or ambiguity, where none exists in the language itself, and defeat the plainly expressed term wherein it is said that the proposal "becomes a contract * * * when approved by an executive officer." There is not anything in the language used to justify a ruling that this declaration must be wrenched from its obvious meaning and given one which would change both the locus and time prescribed for the meeting of the minds. The offeror said that the contract should be complete if approval be promptly given by the executive officer at Chicago; the court cannot properly restate the offer so as to make the offeror declare that a contract shall be made only when the approval shall have been promptly given at Chicago and that fact shall have been communicated to the offeror at Conroe. In our opinion, therefore, notice of the approval was not required.

The letter of February 14th, however, sufficiently communicated notice, if it was required. Here the fact of acceptance in the particular method prescribed by the offeror is established aliunde the letter--Engel's "O. K." indorsed on the paper at Chicago did that. The form of notice, where notice is required, may be quite a different thing from the acceptance itself; the latter constitutes the meeting of the minds, the former merely relates to that pre-existent fact. The rules requiring such notice, it will be marked, do not make necessary any particular form or manner, unless the parties themselves have so prescribed. Whatever would convey, by word or fair implication, notice of the fact would be sufficient. And this letter, we think, would clearly indicate to a reasonably prudent person, situated as was the defendant in error, the fact of previous approval by the filter company. If the Gin, Ice & Light Company had acted to change its position upon it as a notification of that fact, it must be plain that the filter company would have been estopped to deny its sufficiency.

We recommend that the judgment of the Court of Civil Appeals be reversed, and that the cause be remanded to that court for its disposition of all questions not passed upon by it heretofore and properly before it for determination.

Questions

1. What was the written instrument submitted by the plaintiff to the defendant?

2. How did the defendant indicate their acceptance of the proposal?

3. What were the two provisions in the proposal regarding acceptance by the filter company?

4. According to the court's ruling, was notification of approval by the filter company required?

Takeaways – International Filter

Were the offeror and the preparer of the offer one and the same? If you have ever purchased an automobile from a dealer you should think about who was the offeror in that transaction and who provided the offer form that was to be filled out? This is common in business transactions.

Where an offer is made by one party to another when they are not together, the acceptance of it by the offeree must be manifested by some appropriate act. A mental determination to accept which is not manifested by some appropriate act is not an acceptance which will bind the offeror. (*White v. Corlies & Tift* 46 N.Y. 467 (1871).)

Ever-Tite Roofing Corporation v. Green
83 So.2d 449 (La.App., 1955)

Defendants executed and signed an instrument June 10, 1953, for the purpose of obtaining the services of plaintiff in re-roofing their residence situated in Webster Parish, Louisiana. The document set out in detail the work to be done and the price therefor to be paid in monthly installments. This instrument was likewise signed by plaintiff's sale representative, who, however, was without authority to accept the contract for and on behalf of the plaintiff. This alleged contract contained these provisions:

"This agreement shall become binding only upon written acceptance hereof, by the principal or authorized officer of the Contractor, *or upon commencing performance of the work.*"

Inasmuch as this work was to be performed entirely on credit, it was necessary for plaintiff to obtain credit reports and approval from the lending institution which was to finance said contract. With this procedure defendants were more or less familiar and knew their credit rating would have to be checked and a report made. On receipt of the proposed contract in plaintiff's office on the day following its execution, plaintiff requested a credit report, which was made after investigation and which was received in due course and submitted by plaintiff to the lending agency. Additional information was requested by this institution, which was likewise in due course transmitted to the institution, which then gave its approval.

The day immediately following this approval, which was either June 18 or 19, 1953, plaintiff engaged its workmen and two trucks, loaded the trucks with the necessary roofing materials and proceeded from Shreveport to defendants' residence for the purpose of doing the work and performing the services allegedly contracted for the defendants. Upon their arrival at defendants' residence, the workmen found others in the performance of the work which plaintiff had contracted to do. Defendants notified plaintiff's workmen that the work had been contracted to other parties two days before and forbade them to do the work.

The basis of the judgment appealed was that defendants had timely notified plaintiff before "commencing performance of work". The trial court held that notice to plaintiff's workmen upon their arrival with the materials that defendants did not desire them to commence the actual work was sufficient and timely to signify their intention to withdraw from the contract. With this conclusion we find ourselves unable to agree.* * *

Defendants evidently knew this work was to be processed through plaintiff's Shreveport office. The record discloses no unreasonable delay on plaintiff's part in receiving, processing or accepting the contract or in commencing the work contracted to be done. No time limit was specified in the contract within which it was to be accepted or within which the work was to be begun. It was nevertheless understood between the parties that some delay would ensue before the acceptance of the contract and the commencement of the work, due to the necessity of compliance with the requirements relative to financing the job

The general rule of law is that an offer proposed may be withdrawn before its acceptance and that no obligation is incurred thereby. This is, however, not without exceptions. For instance, Restatement of the Law of Contracts stated:

"(1) The power to create a contract by acceptance of an offer terminates at the time specified in the offer, or, if no time is specified, at the end of a reasonable time.

"What is a reasonable time is a question of fact depending on the nature of the contract proposed, the usages of business and other circumstances of the case which the offeree at the time of his acceptance either knows or has reason to know."

These principles are recognized in the Civil Code.

The obligation of a contract not being complete, until the acceptance, or in cases where it is implied by law, until the circumstances, which raise such implication, are known to the party proposing; *he may therefore revoke his offer or proposition before such acceptance, but not without allowing such reasonable time as from the terms of his offer he has given, or from the circumstances of the case he may be supposed to have intended to give to the party, to communicate his determination."* (Emphasis supplied.)

Therefore, since the contract did not specify the time within which it was to be accepted or within which the work was to have been commenced, a reasonable time must be allowed therefor in accordance with the facts and circumstances and the evident intention of the parties. A reasonable time is contemplated where no time is expressed. What is a reasonable time depends more or less upon the circumstances surrounding each particular case. The delays to process defendants' application were not unusual. The contract was accepted by plaintiff by the commencement of the performance of the work contracted to be done. This commencement began with the loading of the trucks with the necessary materials in Shreveport and transporting such materials and the workmen to defendants' residence. Actual commencement or performance of the work therefore began before any notice of dissent by defendants was given plaintiff. The proposition and its acceptance thus became a completed contract.

By their aforesaid acts defendants breached the contract. They employed others to do the work contracted to be done by plaintiff and forbade plaintiff's workmen to engage upon that undertaking. By this breach defendants are legally bound to respond to plaintiff in damages.

Questions

1. When did the plaintiff engage its workmen and trucks to commence the work?

2. According to the court's ruling, what constituted the commencement of the performance of the work in this case?

Davis v. Jacoby
Supreme Court of California, 1934
1 Cal.2d 370, 4 P.2d 1026

THE COURT. Plaintiffs appeal from a judgment refusing to grant specific performance of an alleged contract to make a will. The facts are not in dispute and are as follows:

The plaintiff Caro M. Davis was the niece of Blanche Whitehead who was married to Rupert Whitehead. Prior to her marriage in 1913 to her coplaintiff Frank M. Davis, Caro lived for a considerable time at the home of the Whiteheads, in Piedmont, California. The Whiteheads were childless and extremely fond of Caro.

The record is replete with uncontradicted testimony of the close and loving relationship that existed between Caro and her aunt and uncle. During the period that Caro lived with the Whiteheads she was treated as and often referred to by the Whiteheads as their daughter. In 1913, when Caro was married to Frank Davis the marriage was arranged at the Whitehead home and a reception held there. After the marriage Mr. and Mrs. Davis went to Mr. Davis' home in Canada, where they have resided ever since. During the period 1913 to 1931 Caro made many visits to the Whiteheads, several of them being of long duration. The Whiteheads visited Mr. and Mrs. Davis in Canada on several occasions. After the marriage and continuing down to 1931 the closest and most friendly relationship at all times existed between these two families. They corresponded frequently, the record being replete with letters showing the loving relationship.

By the year 1930 Mrs. Whitehead had become seriously ill. She had suffered several strokes and her mind was failing. Early in 1931 Mr. Whitehead had her removed to a private hospital. The doctors in attendance had informed him that she might die at any time or she might linger for many months. Mr. Whitehead had suffered severe financial reverses. He had had several sieges of sickness and was in poor health. The record shows that during the early part of 1931 he was desperately in need of assistance with his wife, and in his business affairs, and that he did not trust his friends in Piedmont. On March 18, 1931, he wrote to Mrs. Davis telling her of Mrs. Whitehead's condition and added that Mrs. Whitehead was very wistful. * * * on April 12, 1931, Mr. Whitehead again wrote, addressing his letter to "Dear Frank and Caro", and in this letter made the definite offer, which offer it is claimed was accepted and is the basis of this action. In this letter he first pointed out that Blanche, his wife, was in a private hospital and that "she cannot last much longer ... my affairs are not as bad as I supposed at first. Cutting everything down I figure 150,000 can be saved from the wreck." He then enumerated the values placed upon his various properties and then continued "my trouble was caused by my friends taking advantage of my illness and my position to skin me. * * * So if you can come, Caro will inherit everything and you will make our lives happier and see Blanche is provided for to the end.

"Will you let me hear from you as soon as possible, I know it will be a sacrifice but times are still bad and likely to be, so by settling down you can help me and Blanche and gain in the end. If I had you here my mind would get better and my courage return, and we could work things out."

This letter was received by Mr. Davis at his office in Windsor, Canada, about 9:30 A. M. April 14, 1931. After reading the letter to Mrs. Davis over the telephone, and after getting her belief that they must go to California, Mr. Davis immediately wrote Mr. Whitehead a letter, which, after reading it to his wife, he sent by air mail. This letter was lost, but there is no doubt that it was sent by Davis and received by Whitehead, in fact the trial court expressly so found. Mr. Davis testified in substance as to the contents of this letter. After acknowledging receipt of the letter of April 12, 1931, Mr. Davis unequivocally stated that he and Mrs. Davis accepted the proposition of Mr. Whitehead and both would leave Windsor to go to him on April 25th. This letter of acceptance also contained the information that the reason they could not leave prior to April 25th was that Mr. Davis had to appear in court on April 22d as one of the executors of his mother's estate. The testimony is uncontradicted and ample to support the trial court's finding that this letter was sent by Davis and received by Whitehead. In fact under date of April 15, 1931, Mr. Whitehead again wrote to Mr. Davis and stated "Your letter by air mail received this a. m. Now, I am wondering if I have put you to unnecessary trouble and expense, if you are making any money don't leave it, as things are bad here. ... You know your business and I don't and I am half crazy in the bargain, but I don't want to hurt you or Caro.

"Then on the other hand if I could get some one to trust and keep me straight I can save a good deal, about what I told you in my former letter."

This letter was received by Mr. Davis on April 17, 1931, and the same day Mr. Davis telegraphed to Mr. Whitehead "Cheer up--we will soon be there, we will wire you from the train."

Between April 14, 1931, the date the letter of acceptance was sent by Mr. Davis, and April 22d, Mr. Davis was engaged in closing out his business affairs, and Mrs. Davis in closing up their home and in making other arrangements to leave. On April 22, 1931, Mr. Whitehead committed suicide. Mr. and Mrs. Davis were immediately notified and they at once came to California. From almost the moment of her arrival Mrs. Davis devoted herself to the care and comfort of her aunt, and gave her aunt constant attention and care until Mrs. Whitehead's death on May 30, 1931. On this point the trial court found: "from the time of their arrival in Piedmont, Caro M. Davis administered in every way to the comforts of Blanche Whitehead and saw that she was cared for and provided for down to the time of the death of Blanche Whitehead on May 30, 1931; during said time Caro M. Davis nursed Blanche Whitehead, cared for her and administered to her wants as a natural daughter would have done toward and for her mother".

This finding is supported by uncontradicted evidence and in fact is conceded by respondents to be correct. In fact the record shows that after their arrival in California Mr. and Mrs. Davis fully performed their side of the agreement.

After the death of Mrs. Whitehead, for the first time it was discovered that the information contained in Mr. Whitehead's letter of March 30, 1931, in reference to the contents of his and Mrs. Whitehead's wills was incorrect. By a duly witnessed will dated February 28, 1931, Mr. Whitehead, after making several specific bequests, had bequeathed all of the balance of his estate to his wife for life, and upon her death to respondents Geoff Doubble and Rupert Ross Whitehead, his nephews. Neither appellant was mentioned in his will. It was also discovered that Mrs. Whitehead by a will dated December 17, 1927, had devised all of her estate to her husband. The evidence is clear and uncontradicted that the relationship existing between Whitehead and his two nephews, respondents herein, was not nearly as close and confidential as that existing between Whitehead and appellants.

After the discovery of the manner in which the property had been devised was made, this action was commenced upon the theory that Rupert Whitehead had assumed a contractual obligation to make a will whereby "Caro Davis would inherit everything"; that he had failed to do so; that plaintiffs had fully performed their part of the contract; that damages being insufficient, quasi specific performance should be granted in order to remedy the alleged wrong, upon the equitable principle that equity regards that done which ought to have been done. The requested relief is that the beneficiaries under the will of Rupert Whitehead, respondents herein, be declared to be involuntary trustees for plaintiffs of Whitehead's estate.

It should also be added that the evidence shows that as a result of Frank Davis leaving his business in Canada he forfeited not only all insurance business he might have written if he had remained, but also forfeited all renewal commissions earned on past business. According to his testimony this loss was over $8,000.

The trial court found that the relationship between Mr. and Mrs. Davis and the Whiteheads was substantially as above recounted and that the other facts above stated were true; that prior to April 12, 1931, Rupert Whitehead had suffered business reverses and was depressed in mind and ill in body; that his wife was very ill; that because of his mental condition he "was unable to properly care for or look after his property or affairs"; that on April 12, 1931, Rupert Whitehead in writing made an offer to plaintiffs that, if within a reasonable time thereafter plaintiffs would leave and abandon their said home in Windsor, and if Frank M. Davis would abandon or dispose of his said business, and if both the plaintiffs would come to Piedmont in the said county of Alameda where Rupert Whitehead then resided and thereafter reside at said place and be with or near him, and, if Frank M. Davis would thereupon and thereafter look after the business and affairs of said Rupert Whitehead until his condition improved to such an extent as to permit him so to do, and if the plaintiffs would look after and administer to the comforts of Blanche Whitehead and see that she was properly cared for until the time of her death, that, in consideration thereof, Caro M. Davis would inherit everything that Rupert Whitehead possessed at the time of his death and that by last will and testament Rupert Whitehead would devise and bequeath to Caro M. Davis all property and estate owned by him at the time of his death, other than the property constituting the community interest of Blanche Whitehead; that shortly prior to April 12, 1931, Rupert Whitehead informed plaintiffs of the supposed terms of his will and the will of Mrs. Whitehead. The court then finds that the offer of April 12th was not accepted. As already stated, the court found that plaintiffs sent a letter to Rupert Whitehead on April 14th purporting to accept the offer of April 12th, and also found that this letter was received by the Whiteheads, but finds that in fact such letter was not a legal acceptance. The court also found that the offer of April 12th was "fair and just and reasonable, and the consideration therefor, namely, the performance by plaintiffs of the terms and conditions thereof, if the same had been performed, would have been an adequate consideration for said offer and for the agreement that would have resulted from such performance; said offer was not, and said agreement would not have been, either harsh or oppressive or unjust to the heirs at law, or devisees, or legatees, of Rupert Whitehead, or to each or any of them, or otherwise".

The court also found that plaintiffs did not know that the statements made by Whitehead in reference to the wills were not correct until after Mrs. Whitehead's death, that after plaintiffs arrived in Piedmont they cared for Mrs. Whitehead until her death and "Blanche Whitehead was greatly comforted by the presence, companionship and association of Caro M. Davis, and by her administering to her wants".

The theory of the trial court and of respondents on this appeal is that the letter of April 12th was an offer to contract, but that such offer could only be accepted by performance and could not be accepted by a promise to perform, and that said offer was revoked by the death of Mr. Whitehead before performance. In other words, it is contended that the offer was an offer to enter into a unilateral contract, and that the purported acceptance of April 14th was of no legal effect.

The distinction between unilateral and bilateral contracts is well settled in the law. It is well stated in section 12 of the American Institute's Restatement of the Law of Contracts as follows:

"A unilateral contract is one in which no promisor receives a promise as consideration for his promise. A bilateral contract is one in which there are mutual promises between two parties to the contract; each party being both a promisor and a promisee."

This definition is in accord with the law of California. (Christman v. Southern Cal. Edison Co., 83 Cal.App. 249 [256 P. 618].)

In the case of unilateral contracts no notice of acceptance by performance is required. Section 1584 of the Civil Code provides, "Performance of the conditions of a proposal, ... is an acceptance of the proposal." (See Cuthill v. Peabody, 19 Cal.App. 304 [125 P. 926]; Los Angeles Traction Co. v. Wilshire, 135 Cal. 654 [67 P. 1086].)

Although the legal distinction between unilateral and bilateral contracts is thus well settled, the difficulty in any particular case is to determine whether the particular offer is one to enter into a bilateral or unilateral contract. Some cases are quite clear cut. Thus an offer to sell which is accepted is clearly a bilateral contract, while an offer of a reward is a clear-cut offer of a unilateral contract which cannot be accepted by a promise to perform, but only by performance. (Berthiaume v. Doe, 22 Cal.App. 78 [133 P. 515].) Between these two extremes is a vague field where the particular contract may be unilateral or bilateral depending upon the intent of the offerer and the facts and circumstances of each case. The offer to contract involved in this case falls within this category. By the provisions of the Restatement of the Law of Contracts it is expressly provided that there is a presumption that the offer is to enter into a bilateral contract. Section 31 provides:

"In case of doubt it is presumed that an offer invites the formation of a bilateral contract by an acceptance amounting in effect to a promise by the offeree to perform what the offer requests, rather than the formation of one or more unilateral contracts by actual performance on the part of the offeree."

Professor Williston in his Treatise on Contracts, volume 1, section 60, also takes the position that a presumption in favor of bilateral contracts exists.

In the comment following section 31 of the Restatement the reason for such presumption is stated as follows:

"It is not always easy to determine whether an offerer requests an act or a promise to do the act. As a bilateral contract immediately and fully protects both parties, the interpretation is favored that a bilateral contract is proposed."

While the California cases have never expressly held that a presumption in favor of bilateral contracts exists, the cases clearly indicate a tendency to treat offers as offers of bilateral rather than of unilateral contracts. (Roth v. Moeller, 185 Cal. 415 [197 P. 62]; Boehm v. Spreckels, 183 Cal. 239 [191 P. 5]; see, also, Wood v. Lucy, Lady Duff- Gordon, 222 N.Y. 88 [118 N.E. 214].)

Keeping these principles in mind we are of the opinion that the offer of April 12th was an offer to enter into a bilateral as distinguished from a unilateral contract. Respondents argue that Mr. Whitehead had the right as offerer to designate his offer as either unilateral or bilateral. That is undoubtedly the law. It is then argued that from all the facts and circumstances it must be implied that what Whitehead wanted was performance and not a mere promise to perform. We think this is a non sequitur, in fact the surrounding circumstances lead to just the opposite conclusion. These parties were not dealing at arm's length. Not only were they related, but a very close and intimate friendship existed between them. The record indisputably demonstrates that Mr. Whitehead had confidence in Mr. and Mrs. Davis, in fact that he had lost all confidence in everyone else. The record amply shows that by an accumulation of occurrences Mr. Whitehead had become desperate, and that what he wanted was the promise of appellants that he could look to them for assistance. He knew from his past relationship with appellants that if they gave their promise to perform he could rely upon them. The correspondence between them indicates how desperately he desired this assurance. Under these circumstances he wrote his offer of April 12th, above quoted, in which he stated, after disclosing his desperate mental and physical condition, and after setting forth the terms of his offer: "Will you let me hear from you as soon as possible--I know it will be a sacrifice but times are still bad and likely to be, so by settling down you can help me and Blanche and gain in the end." By thus specifically requesting an immediate reply Whitehead expressly indicated the nature of the acceptance desired by him--namely, appellants' promise that they would come to California and do the things requested by him. This promise was immediately sent by appellants upon receipt of the offer, and was received by Whitehead. It is elementary that when an offer has indicated the mode and means of acceptance, an acceptance in accordance with that mode or means is binding on the offerer.

Another factor which indicates that Whitehead must have contemplated a bilateral rather than a unilateral contract, is that the contract required Mr. and Mrs. Davis to perform services until the death of both Mr. and Mrs. Whitehead. It is obvious that if Mr. Whitehead died first some of these services were to be performed after his death, so that he would have to rely on the promise of appellants to perform these services. It is also of some evidentiary force that Whitehead received the letter of acceptance and acquiesced in that means of acceptance.

Shaw v. King, 63 Cal.App. 18 [218 P. 50], relied on by respondents is clearly not in point. In that case there was no written acceptance, nor was there an acceptance by partial or total performance.

For the foregoing reasons we are of the opinion that the offer of April 12, 1931, was an offer to enter into a bilateral contract which was accepted by the letter of April 14, 1931. Subsequently appellants fully performed their part of the contract. Under such circumstances it is well settled that damages are insufficient and specific performance will be granted. (Wolf v. Donahue, 206 Cal. 213 [273 P. 547].) Since the consideration has been fully rendered by appellants the question as to mutuality of remedy becomes of no importance. (6 Cal.Jur., sec. 140.)

Respondents also contend the complaint definitely binds appellants to the theory of a unilateral contract. This contention is without merit. The complaint expressly alleges the parties entered into a contract. It is true that the complaint also alleged that the contract became effective by performance. However, this is an action in equity. Respondents were not misled. No objection was made to the testimony offered to show the acceptance of April 14th. A fair reading of the record clearly indicates the case was tried by the parties on the theory that the sole question was whether there was a contract--unilateral or bilateral.

For the foregoing reasons the judgment appealed from is reversed.

Questions

1. How did Frank and Caro Davis accept the offer?

2. What was the legal distinction between unilateral and bilateral contracts in this case?

3. According to the trial court's finding, did the offer of April 12th constitute a unilateral or bilateral contract?

Takeaways – Ever-Tite and Davis

Unless otherwise indicated by the language or the circumstances, an offer invites acceptance in any manner and by any medium that is reasonable. (Rest.2d § 30(2).) Traditionally, any ambiguity as to whether the offer invited a promise as a means of acceptance or a performance as a means of acceptance was resolved in favor of the presumption that an offeror seeks a promise rather than a performance. (See First Restatement § 31.) However, this presumption was changed by Restatement Second section 32 which provides that in case of doubt, the choice is up to the offeree to accept by either promising to perform or by rendering performance.

Method of Acceptance Required or Merely Suggested?

Allied Steel and Conveyors, Inc., v. Ford Motor Company
U.S. Court of Appeals for the Sixth Circuit, 1960
277 F2d 907

On August 19, 1955, Ford ordered from Allied numerous items of machinery and equipment. The consideration to be paid was $71,325.00. Under the terms of the order, Allied was to install the machinery and equipment on Ford's premises for an additional consideration of $6,900.00, with a provision that should Ford elect to install the machinery with its own labor, Allied would furnish a supervisor to direct the installation on a per diem basis. The order further provided that "the signing and returning to Buyer by Seller of the Acknowledgment Copy shall constitute acceptance by Seller of this Purchase Order and of all of its terms and conditions." The order was submitted on printed forms regularly used by Ford, and was designated "Purchase Order No. 15145." Item 15 of the printed form provided that if Allied was required to perform work on Ford's premises, Allied would be responsible for all damages or injuries occurring as a result of the fault or negligence of its own employees, including any damages or injuries to Ford's employees and property. Attached to the Purchase Order and made a part thereof was a printed form designated Form 3618, which included an indemnity provision broader in scope than Item 15 of the purchase order, requiring the Seller to assume full responsibility not only for the fault or negligence of its own employees but also for the fault or negligence of Ford's employees, arising out of or in connection with Allied's work. This provision in Form 3618, however, was marked "VOID." On December 16, 1955, Ford submitted to Allied its Amendment No. 1 to the purchase order, deleting the item of $6,900.00 for the cost of installation by Allied and providing that the installation would be done by Ford. The original Purchase Order and Amendment No. 1 were both duly accepted by Allied and the agreements were performed.

Subsequently, on July 26, 1956, Ford submitted to Allied Amendment No. 2 to Purchase Order 15145, and it is this Amendment which is the focal point of the present controversy. By the amendment Ford proposed to purchase additional machinery to be installed on Ford's premises by Allied, at a total cost of $173,700.00. Amendment No. 2, as did Amendment No. 1, provided:

"This purchase order agreement is not binding until accepted. Acceptance should be executed on acknowledgment copy which should be returned to buyer." The copy of Ford's Form 3618 attached to Amendment No. 2 was identical to the printed Form 3618 which was attached to the original Purchase Order, but the broad indemnity provision in Form 3618, making Allied liable for the negligent acts of both its own and Ford's employees, was not marked "VOID." The record makes it clear that the reason for not voiding the broad indemnity provision of Form 3618 attached to Amendment No. 2 was that the installation work on Ford's premises was to be performed by Allied's employees, whereas under the original purchase order as amended by Amendment No. 1 the installation work was to be done by Ford's own employees. Another pertinent provision of Form 3618 was:

"Such of the terms and conditions of Seller's Purchase Order as are inconsistent with the provisions hereinabove set forth are hereby superseded."

The acknowledgment copy of Amendment No. 2 was duly executed by Allied on or about November 10, 1956, and was received by Ford on November 12, 1956. At that time Allied had already begun installation of the machinery on the Ford premises, although the exact date upon which the installation was commenced is not shown in the record. On September 5, 1956, in the course of the installation, one Hankins, an employee of Allied, sustained personal injuries as a result of the negligence of Ford's employees. Hankins later filed an action against Ford in the District Court for the Eastern District of Michigan, Southern Division. After the complaint was filed, Ford added Allied, Hankins' employer, as a third-party defendant, relying upon the indemnity provisions of Form 3618, and demanding judgment against Allied "* * * for all sums that may be adjudged against the defendant, Ford Motor Company, in favor of plaintiff, John T. Hankins." The trial before a jury resulted in verdicts for $12,500.00 in favor of Hankins and against Ford, and in favor of Ford and against Allied for the same amount. This appeal by Allied followed denial by the District Court of its motion for judgment notwithstanding the verdict of the jury and entry of judgment against it in favor of Ford upon the third-party complaint.

It was Allied's insistence at the trial, as it is here, that the agreement evidenced by Amendment No. 2 which was signed and returned to Ford on November 10, 1956, was not in effect on September 5, 1956, when Hankins was injured; and further, that, in any event, it was the intention of the parties to void the broad indemnity provision in Form 3618 attached to Amendment No. 2, thus leaving in effect Item 15 contained in the original Purchase Order which made Allied liable only for its own negligence. Although the agreements contained in Amendment No. 2 were fully performed by the parties and Allied received full payment for its goods and services, the point made by Allied is that it did not become bound by the provisions of such amendment until November 1956, when it actually signed and returned to Ford the acknowledgment copy of Amendment No. 2. It argues that it was under no contractual obligation on September 5, 1956, the date of Hankins' injury, to indemnify Ford against Ford's negligent acts.

Allied first says that the contractual provisions evidenced by Amendment No. 2 were not in effect at the time of the Hankins injury because it had not been accepted at that time by Allied in the formal manner expressly required by the amendment itself. It argues that a binding acceptance of the amendment could be effected only by Allied's execution of the acknowledgment copy of the amendment and its return to Ford.

With this argument we cannot agree. It is true that an offeror may prescribe the manner in which acceptance of his offer shall be indicated by the offeree, and an acceptance of the offer in the manner prescribed will bind the offeror. And it has been held that if the offeror prescribes an exclusive manner of acceptance, an attempt on the part of the offeree to accept the offer in a different manner does not bind the offeror *in the absence of a meeting of the minds on the altered type of acceptance.* Venters v. Stewart, Ky.App., 261 S.W.2d 444, 446; Shortridge v. Ghio, Mo.App., 253 S.W.2d 838, 845. On the other hand, if an offeror merely suggests a permitted method of acceptance, other methods of acceptance are not precluded. Restatement, Contracts, Sec. 61; Williston on Contracts, Third Ed. Secs. 70, 76. Moreover, it is equally well settled that if the offer requests a return promise and the offeree without making the promise actually does or tenders what he was requested to promise to do, there is a contract if such performance is completed or tendered within the time allowable for accepting by making a promise. In such a case a tender operates as a promise to render complete performance. Restatement, Contracts, Sec. 63; Williston on Contracts, Third Ed. Sec. 75.

Applying these principles to the case at bar, we reach the conclusion, first, that execution and return of the acknowledgment copy of Amendment No. 2 was merely a suggested method of acceptance and did not preclude acceptance by some other method; and, second, that the offer was accepted and a binding contract effected when Allied, with Ford's knowledge, consent and acquiescence, undertook performance of the work called for by the amendment. The only significant provision, as we view the amendment, was that it would not be binding until it was accepted by Allied. This provision was obviously for the protection of Ford, Albright v. Stegeman Motorcar Co., 168 Wis. 557, 170 N.W. 951, 952, 19 A.L.R. 463, and its import was that Ford would not be bound by the amendment unless Allied agreed to all of the conditions specified therein. The provision for execution and return of the acknowledgment copy, as we construe the language used, was not to set forth an exclusive method of acceptance but was merely to provide a simple and convenient method by which the assent of Allied to the contractual provisions of the amendment could be indicated. The primary object of Ford was to have the work performed by Allied upon the terms prescribed in the amendment, and the mere signing and return of an acknowledgment copy of the amendment before actually undertaking the work itself cannot be regarded as an essential condition to completion of a binding contract.

It is well settled that acceptance of an offer by part performance in accordance with the terms of the offer is sufficient to complete the contract. . . .

But what will constitute an acceptance depends frequently upon circumstances. A direct, unequivocal, written acceptance of an offer to purchase is satisfactory evidence of the fact, but, if the parties have not stipulated otherwise, the acceptance need not be in any particular form nor evidenced by express words; the delivery by the vendor of a part of the property referred to in the offer to buy, may take the place of words as proof of acceptance."

Other authorities are to the effect that the acceptance of a contract may be implied from acts of the parties. Malooly v. York Heating & Vent. Corp., 270 Mich. 240, 253, 258 N.W. 622; and may be shown by proving acts done on the faith of the order, including shipment of the goods ordered, Petroleum Products Distributing Co. v. Alton Tank Line, 165 Iowa 398, 403, 146 N.W. 52. Cf. Texas Co. v. Hudson, 155 La. 966, 971, 99 So. 714, 716. It would seem necessarily to follow that an offeree who has unjustifiably led the offerer to believe that he had acquired a contractual right, should not be allowed to assert an actual intent at variance with the meaning of his acts.

It has been argued on behalf of Allied, by way of analogy, that Ford could have revoked the order when Allied began installing the machinery without first having executed its written acceptance. If this point should be conceded, cf. Venters v. Stewart, supra, it would avail Allied nothing. For, after Allied began performance by installing the machinery called for, and Ford acquiesced in the acts of Allied and accepted the benefits of the performance, Ford was estopped to object and could not thereafter be heard to complain that there was no contract. Sparks v. Mauk, 170 Cal. 122, 148 P. 926. The judgment of the District Court is [a]ffirmed.

Questions

1. How did the court interpret the requirement for acceptance in the amendment?

2. What was the significance of the provision for execution and return of the acknowledgment copy of Amendment No. 2?

3. Can an acceptance of a contract be implied from acts of the parties? Provide examples from the case.

4. What is the effect when an offeree begins performance without executing a written acceptance and the offeror acquiesces to their actions?

Takeaways – Allied Steel

Was there a way for Ford to have avoided this problem? Could they have specified that the only method of effectively accepting would have been to have executed and returned the acknowledgment copy? Consider what Professor Corbin had to say on this subject.

"[T]here is no question that the offeror can require notice of acceptance in any form he pleases. He can require that it shall be in any language and transmitted in any manner. He may require notice to be given by a nod of the head, by flags, by wig wag, by a smoke signal on a high hill. He may require that it be by letter, telegraph or radio, and that there shall be no contract unless and until he is himself made conscious of it." (Corbin on Contracts § 67 p. 109 [One Vol. Ed.].)

This is why it is said that the offeror is the "master of the offer." They may dictate the manner and means by which the offer is to be accepted. Any deviation from a manner of acceptance which is required or exclusive results in any purported acceptance being ineffective.

The offer may specify the manner in which acceptance is to be communicated. If it does, that method becomes the exclusive method and means of acceptance. But if the offer prescribes no means, any reasonable and usual mode of acceptance may be used. (See Rest.2d §30.)

Notification of the Fact of Acceptance for Unilateral Contracts

When an offer seeks from the promisee a return promise as the manifestation of willingness to be bound, notice of acceptance is seldom an issue as the making of the promise usually (but not always) communicates the fact of acceptance. However,

98 CHAPTER 2 MUTUAL ASSENT

when an offer asks for a completed performance on the part of the offeree, the offeror may not be aware that the offer has been accepted. What steps, if any, must the offeree in such a situation take to ensure that the offeror is made aware of the fact of acceptance?

Carlill v. Carbolic Smoke Ball Company
1 Q.B. 256 (C.A. 1893)

(The plaintiff, in response to an advertisement that promised a £100 reward to any person who contracted influenza after purchasing and using the defendant's patent medicine known as a "smoke ball" according to certain instruction. The plaintiff purchased and used the product as directed and contracted the flu, but the defendant refused to pay the £100 reward. After considering a number of issues, the court then turned to the question of whether the plaintiff was required to notify the defendant that she had accepted their offer by using the product as directed.)

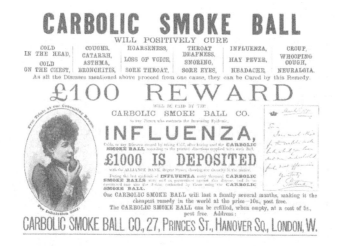

LINDLEY, L.J. But then it is said, "Supposing that the performance of the conditions is an acceptance of the offer, that acceptance ought to have been notified." Unquestionably, as a general proposition, when an offer is made, it is necessary in order to make a binding contract, not only that it should be accepted, but that the acceptance should be notified. But is that so in cases of this kind? I apprehend that they are an exception to that rule, or, if not an exception, they are open to the observation that the notification of the acceptance need not precede the performance. This offer is a continuing offer. It was never revoked, and if notice of acceptance is required — which I doubt very much, for I rather think the true view is that which was expressed and explained by Lord Blackburn in the case of Brogden v. Metropolitan Ry. Co. 2 App Cas 666, 691 — if notice of acceptance is required, the person who makes the offer gets the notice of acceptance contemporaneously with his notice of the performance of the condition. If he gets notice of the acceptance before his offer is revoked, that in principle is all you want. I, however, think that the true view, in a case of this kind, is that the person who makes the over shews by his language and from the nature of the transaction that he does not expect and does not require notice of the acceptance apart from notice of the performance.

Questions

1. Is notification of acceptance always necessary to form a binding contract?

2. Why does the court consider the case of a continuing offer to be an exception to the general rule of acceptance notification?

3. What is the significance of the offer in this case being a continuing offer?
How does the court., reason that the requirement of notice of acceptance is fulfilled in this case?

Takeaways – Carlill v. Carbolic Smoke Ball

Is Justice Lindley saying that Mrs. Carlill was not required to notify the seller that she had accepted its offer or is he saying that the seller dispensed with any requirement that it be notified? Ordinarily, notice of acceptance of an offer looking towards formation of a unilateral contract is unnecessary, but the offeror may elect to request notification. (Rest.2d §54(1).)

Special Rules for the Sale of Goods, the Uniform Commercial Code

Scope of Article 2 of the UCC

The thrust of the Uniform Commercial Code (UCC) is to facilitate commerce by making it easier to do business. To that end, the UCC relaxes the rules of contract formation. However, the UCC and its liberalized rules of contract formation do not apply to every type of contract. Article 2 of the UCC applies only to contracts for the sale of goods. (UCC §§ 2-102, 2-105 (1); *English v. Ralph Williams Ford* (1971) 17 Cal.App.3d 1038, 1046.) UCC section 2-105 defines "goods" as "all things (including specially manufactured goods) which are movable at the time of identification to the contract for sale."

Throughout this book you will encounter many cases where the more liberalized rules of the UCC apply rather than the long-established rules of the common law which will apply to contracts for the furnishing of services, employment contracts, or contracts for the purchase and sale of real property. The UCC's treatment of shipment of goods as an act of acceptance is merely the first of these instances.

Acceptance by Opening the Package and Retaining the Goods

Dye v. Tamko Bldg. Products, Inc.
United States Court of Appeals, Eleventh Circuit
908 F.3d 675 (2018)

NEWSOM, Circuit Judge: You've undoubtedly heard of—and for that matter probably accepted the terms of—a "shrinkwrap" agreement, which binds a software (or small-electronics) purchaser to an inside-the-box contract if she opens the product and retains it for some specified time. In this cyber age, you've also almost certainly assented to the terms of a "clickwrap" or "scrollwrap" agreement — for instance, by hitting "I accept" when installing the latest operating system for your smartphone. This case—not quite as hip but governed by the same basic principles—requires us to determine the enforceability of what, for lack of a better label, we'll call a "shinglewrap" agreement.

Boiled to its essence, the question we must decide is this: Where a roofing-shingle manufacturer displays on the exterior wrapping of every package of shingles the entirety of its product-purchase agreement —including, as particularly relevant here, a mandatory-arbitration provision — are homeowners whose roofers ordered, opened, and installed the shingles bound by the agreement's terms? Applying Florida law, we conclude that the homeowners are bound—and must therefore arbitrate any product-related claims that they allege against the manufacturer. In particular, we hold (1) that the manufacturer's packaging here sufficed to convey a valid offer of contract terms, (2) that unwrapping and retaining the shingles was an objectively reasonable means of accepting that offer, and (3) that the homeowners' grant of express authority to their roofers to buy and install shingles necessarily included the act of accepting purchase terms on the homeowners' behalf.

Tamko Building Products is a Missouri-based roofing company. Its "Heritage 30" shingles come with (appropriately) a 30-year limited warranty, which is printed—in full—on the outside wrapper of every shingle package. Although most of the warranty is set in ordinary Roman type, several key portions—including those most significant to this appeal—are rendered in a more conspicuous font. Each package wrapper, for instance, displays the all-capped word "IMPORTANT" and warns the purchaser—again in all caps—to "READ CAREFULLY BEFORE OPENING [THE] BUNDLE." The wrapper further explains (1) that the consumer must notify Tamko of any warranty-related claims "within thirty (30) days following discovery of the problem with the Shingles" and (2) that the warranty and other purchase terms are available not only on the face of the wrapper itself but also on Tamko's website and via a toll-free telephone number.

As particularly relevant to this appeal, Tamko's limited warranty contains a mandatory-arbitration clause—which, significantly, is also printed in its entirety, and in all caps, on the outside of every shingle wrapper. In pertinent part, that clause states as follows:

> MANDATORY BINDING ARBITRATION: EVERY CLAIM, CONTROVERSY, OR DISPUTE OF ANY KIND WHATSOEVER (EACH AN "ACTION") BETWEEN YOU AND TAMKO (INCLUDING ANY OF TAMKO'S EMPLOYEES AND AGENTS) RELATING TO OR ARISING OUT OF THE PRODUCT SHALL BE RESOLVED BY FINAL AND BINDING ARBITRATION, REGARDLESS OF WHETHER THE ACTION SOUNDS IN WARRANTY, CONTRACT, STATUTE, OR ANY OTHER LEGAL OR EQUITABLE THEORY. . . .

Enter Douglas Bohn and Stephen Dye. Both are Florida residents whose homes are fitted with Tamko's Heritage 30 shingles. Bohn hired Duffield Home Improvements to install a new roof on his Middleburg, Florida home. After a few years, he noticed that his shingles were crumbling and that asphalt granules were shedding and collecting in his gutters. Similarly, Dye hired Tampa Roofing Company to replace the roof on his house in Tampa, Florida. Shortly after installation, Dye too noticed his shingles cracking and granules littering his patio.

Bohn and Dye filed a putative class action seeking damages and declaratory relief on behalf of a class of building owners who had used Tamko shingles. Their complaint alleged that Tamko manufactured its Heritage 30 shingles with less asphalt than necessary to comply with industry standards and building codes, which caused the shingles to crack and split. The complaint included claims for breach of express and implied warranties, strict products liability, negligence, and violations of the Florida Deceptive and Unfair Trade Practices Act. In response, Tamko filed a motion to compel arbitration and an accompanying motion to dismiss or stay court proceedings. Tamko contended that by unwrapping and retaining its shingles the homeowners had accepted the terms of its purchase agreement and were thus bound, pursuant to the agreement's plain terms, to arbitrate their claims.

The district court granted Tamko's motion and dismissed the homeowners' complaint. The court reasoned that the homeowners were bound to arbitrate because through their roofers, whom they had hired to buy and install the shingles, they had accepted the terms of Tamko's purchase agreement, including its mandatory-arbitration provision. This appeal followed.

On appeal, we must determine whether Tamko's warranty-emblazoned shingle wrappers set forth a valid offer that gave purchasers an adequate opportunity to assent to its terms—most notably, the mandatory-arbitration clause—and, if so, whether the roofers, as the homeowners' agents for the purposes of purchasing and installing shingles, bound the homeowners to arbitrate by unwrapping the shingle packages. We consider each issue in turn.

First up, we consider whether the shingle wrappers conveyed a valid offer of Tamko's contract terms — in particular, that any product-related dispute must be arbitrated rather than litigated. Of course they did, Tamko says, asserting that the law is well-settled that opening and retaining a product constitutes acceptance of terms printed on the product's packaging. The homeowners, by contrast, contend that consumers aren't on notice that shingles come wrapped in purchase terms and can't assent to terms of which they are unaware. The nub of the dispute is whether Tamko's shingle wrappers provide a reasonable opportunity for consumers to review and accept the company's terms of purchase.

Florida law provides the rules of decision here. Applying Florida law, we recently held that "[a] valid contract— premised on the parties' requisite willingness to contract—may be `manifested through written or spoken words, or inferred in whole or in part from the parties' conduct.'" [Citations omitted] see also Fla. Stat. § 672.204(1) ("A contract for sale of goods may be made in any manner sufficient to show agreement, including conduct by both parties which recognizes the existence of such a contract."). Somewhat more specifically, courts applying Florida law have clarified (1) that "[a] vendor, as master of the offer," is free to "invite acceptance by conduct" and in so doing to "propose limitations on the kind of conduct that constitutes acceptance," and (2) that a consumer may, in turn, "accept by performing the acts the vendor proposes to treat as acceptance." [Citations omitted] (quoting ProCD, Inc. v. Zeidenberg, 86 F.3d 1447, 1449 (7th Cir. 1996)).

These settled principles give rise to two fundamental inquiries: (1) Would "a reasonable, objective person" have understood an offer as an "invitation to contract," and (2) did that person's "words and acts, judged by a reasonable standard, manifest an intention to agree?" Kolodziej, 774 F.3d at 741-42 (quotation omitted). In considering these questions, a court must examine the content of the offer, the circumstances in which the offer was made, and the conduct of the parties—all the while keeping firmly in mind that "[t]he law imputes to a person an intention corresponding to the reasonable meaning of his words and acts." Id. at 742 (quoting Lucy v. Zehmer, 196 Va. 493, 84 S.E.2d 516, 522 (1954), "the classic case describing and applying what we now know as the objective standard of assent").

As particularly relevant here, courts applying Florida law have recognized that a vendor's prerogative to specify conduct that constitutes acceptance includes inviting acceptance by unwrapping a product. Take, for instance, TracFone Wireless, Inc. v. Pak China Group Co. Ltd., a shrinkwrap case cited extensively by both parties. There, a cellphone manufacturer's retail packaging displayed "conspicuous language" specifically "restricting the use of the Phones for TracFone Prepaid Wireless service and prohibit[ing] the consumer from tampering or altering the software or hardware in the Phone." TracFone, 843 F.Supp.2d at 1298. The language further stated that "[b]y purchasing or opening this package" the consumer agreed to the manufacturer's terms as printed on the wrapper and in the enclosed user guide. Id. Applying Florida law, the court held that a consumer's act of opening the package constituted an acceptance of the manufacturer's terms, thereby creating a valid contract. Id. at 1298-99. Management Computer Controls, Inc. v. Charles Perry Construction, Inc., 743 So.2d 627 (Fla. 1st Dist. Ct. App. 1999), is similar. There, a computer-software vendor sent a product to a customer with its licensing agreement affixed to the outside of the box, which was itself sealed with an orange sticker warning that "[b]y opening this packet, you indicate your acceptance of the [company's] license agreement." Id. at 629. The court deemed this a valid offer and held that the consumer "agreed to the terms of the license agreement by breaking the seal on the software." Id. at 631.

This case is cut from the same cloth. Tamko's purchase terms were printed in full on the exterior of every package of shingles, accompanied by text alerting purchasers of an "IMPORTANT" message that they should "READ CAREFULLY BEFORE OPENING [THE] BUNDLE." The agreement required consumers to notify Tamko "within thirty (30) days following discovery of the potential problem with the Shingles," and further—most importantly here—featured an all-caps, mandatory-arbitration clause.[5] As in the shrinkwrap cases, Tamko's packaging provided conspicuous notice of its offer—something a reasonable, objective person would understand as an invitation to contract. See Kolodziej, 774 F.3d at 741. For the homeowners' part, opening and retaining the shingles was the (quite ordinary, reasonable) conduct from which their assent can be "inferred." See id.

The homeowners acknowledge that Florida law recognizes "shrinkwrap" contracting but contend that the nature of the product here calls for a different analysis. It's a fair point. Software packaging of the sort typically involved in a shrinkwrap case is fairly small, usually delivered directly to (and sometimes retained by) the end user, and often includes at least some notice of terms printed both on the outside and inside of the package. By contrast, shingle packages are large and unwieldy, are often delivered to contractors rather than end users, are quite unlikely to be kept following installation, and in this case sported terms printed only once on the outer wrapping. These differences matter, the argument presumably goes, because Florida law tasks courts with determining whether "a reasonable, objective person" would have understood Tamko's packaging as "an invitation to contract." Kolodziej, 774 F.3d at 741. And it's just not clear that consumers have the same realistic opportunity to review shingle (or floorboard, siding, or tile) packaging as they would software packaging.

To be sure, there are distinctions between small-box and big-box items, but those distinctions neither alter the underlying principles nor require a different result. Indeed, they arguably cut in different ways. On the one hand, for instance, it's surely true that a consumer (or his agent—more on that below) is less likely to keep shingle packaging than software packaging after unwrapping the product. On the other hand, one of the things that has historically made shrinkwrap cases tricky is that the full purchase terms "are typically provided inside the packaging of consumer goods," while the outer packaging bears only a notice or excerpt of those terms—leading courts to hold that valid acceptance occurs not upon purchase or opening, but rather only upon the purchaser's "failure to return the product after reading, or at least having a realistic opportunity to read, the terms and conditions of the contract included with the product." Schnabel v. Trilegiant Corp., 697 F.3d 110, 121-22 (2d Cir. 2012) (emphasis added). Here, by contrast—in the quintessential belt-and-suspenders move—Tamko has emblazoned its entire purchase-agreement (complete with terms, warnings, and the all-important arbitration clause) in haec verba on the outside of every package of shingles. No hidden terms—no buried treasure.

Moreover, and in any event, that big-box items come with purchase terms and conditions should hardly come as a surprise to modern consumers. Post-purchase, acceptance-by-retention warranties are ubiquitous today—think furniture, home appliances, sporting goods, etc. It's not only objectively reasonable to assume that such items come with terms and conditions, it's also eminently reasonable to assume that by opening and retaining those items a consumer necessarily accepts the accompanying terms and conditions. See Kolodziej, 774 F.3d at 742 ("[T]he law imputes to a person an intention corresponding to the reasonable meaning of his words and acts." (quotations omitted)).

Indeed, this expectation—and with it, fair notice—has been building for some time. More than 20 years ago, in Hill v. Gateway 2000, 105 F.3d 1147 (7th Cir. 1997), the Seventh Circuit rejected a suggestion that its earlier decision in ProCD, Inc. v. Zeidenberg, 86 F.3d 1447 (7th Cir. 1996)—the seminal case on shrinkwrap contracts—applied only to software, for precisely this reason. See Hill, 105 F.3d at 1149 ("ProCD is about the law of contract, not the law of software."). The Hill court explained that "[p]ractical considerations support allowing vendors to enclose the full legal terms with their products," employing a "simple approve-or-return" model in place of a "costly and ineffectual" requirement that sellers narrate their terms of purchase "telephonic[ally]." Id. When it comes to warranties and other purchase terms, the Hill court explained, "[c]ompetent adults are bound by such documents, read or unread." Id.; see also id. at 1148 ("A contract need not be read to be effective; people who accept [the contract] take the risk that the unread terms may in retrospect prove unwelcome.").

All of that applies a fortiori two decades hence, in the age of Amazon Prime. As fewer and fewer purchases are consummated face to face, and more and more are made online, consumers should (and must) know that vendors will often employ a "simple approve-or-return" model, enclosing their full legal terms with a product at shipment. Indeed, the sort of "costly and ineffectual" telephonic recitation of terms that the Hill court posited is a vanishingly small exception to the norm.[7] Really, how often does the modern consumer, following a large purchase, call a vendor to sit through a verbal oration of warranty terms? Or insist on signing and returning a form to convey acceptance of her latest online purchase, instead of just, oh, say, keeping it?

That's not to imply that consumers can't choose to seek out purchase terms by other means should they so choose. Indeed, one key reason that the Hill court rejected the "I-didn't-read-it" excuse was that consumers could discover the terms of their desired purchases in one of several ways, such as by "ask[ing] the vendor to send a copy before deciding whether to buy," by "consult[ing] public sources (computer magazines, the Web sites of vendors)," or by "inspect[ing] the documents after the product's delivery." 105 F.3d at 1150. And of course, as we have emphasized, the same is true here—Tamko's purchase terms were available not only on its packaging but also on its website and over the phone, such that a diligent consumer could easily have discovered and reviewed them before or after purchase.

At the end of the day, the point is simply this: modern consumers are on notice that products come with warranties and other terms and conditions of purchase. And they are free to research (or not), request (or not), and read (or not) those terms before unwrapping their purchases. As to the case before us, Florida law makes clear that providing conspicuously printed product packaging is an OK way to convey purchase terms. Florida consumers who purchase, open, and retain a product are thus bound in accordance with warranty terms conspicuously printed on that product's packaging, whether they actually take the time to read them or not.

We can summarize using what this Court has referred to as the "million-dollar question" in evaluating assent: "What did the part[ies] say and do?" Kolodziej, 774 F.3d at 743. By conspicuously printing its purchase terms on its shingle wrappers, Tamko made a valid offer in accordance with Florida law. As master of that offer, Tamko was free to invite acceptance by specified conduct, and it did—inviting consumers to accept by opening the shingles and retaining them for more than 30 days. By doing exactly this, the homeowners here "accept[ed] by performing" the acts that Tamko "propose[d] to treat as acceptance," thus "manifest[ing] an intention to agree." TracFone, 843 F.Supp.2d at 1298; Kolodziej, 774 F.3d at 742. We therefore hold that Tamko made a valid offer— again, including an offer to arbitrate, rather than litigate, all product-related claims—and that its offer was accepted.

Hang on just a minute, the homeowners contend: Even if this was a valid means of making an offer, they didn't accept it— their roofers did. After all, the homeowners say, they never saw the shingle packaging and thus never had a reasonable opportunity to consider Tamko's purchase terms—arbitration clause included—so they can't possibly be bound by them. Attributing the roofers' acceptance to them would be, the homeowners assert, an "ill-advised" and "unsupported" expansion of agency law. We disagree. Imputing the roofers' notice and acceptance of Tamko's purchase terms to the homeowners requires no expansion, but rather fits squarely within established agency-law principles and precedent.

Let's start with the basics. "[A]n agency relationship requires `(1) the principal to acknowledge that the agent will act for it; (2) the agent to manifest an acceptance of the undertaking; and (3) control by the principal over the actions of the agent.'" Franza v. Royal Caribbean Cruises, Ltd., 772 F.3d 1225, 1236 (11th Cir. 2014) (quotation omitted). Importantly here, we have further held—applying Florida law—that a grant of agency authority also necessarily implies "the authority to do acts that are `incidental to it, usually accompany it, or are reasonably necessary to accomplish it.'" . . . .

Neither party seriously disputes that the roofers were the homeowners' agents for purposes of purchasing and installing shingles. Both homeowners expressly delegated those tasks to their roofers, their roofers accepted those tasks by signing contracts, and the homeowners maintained control over their roofers' completion of those tasks pursuant to those contracts. See Franza, 772 F.3d at 1236. The question, then, is whether accepting Tamko's purchase terms—including an arbitration provision —was "incidental to," "usually accompany[ing]," or "reasonably necessary to accomplish" the purchase and installation of the shingles. See Delray Beach, 622 F.3d at 1342-43.

The homeowners admit that they contracted with their roofers to buy shingles, and even that the roofers might have known that by opening the shingles, they—i.e., the roofers—were entering into an agreement with Tamko. But the homeowners dispute that this necessarily means that the roofers accepted Tamko's purchase terms—including, as we keep saying, the arbitration clause—on the homeowners' behalf. Had they made clear that their roofers could enter into binding contracts on their behalf, the homeowners contend, that grant might have encompassed agreeing to the arbitration provision. But, they say, a "circumscribed contract... to buy and install shingles does not bring with it the authority to enter into any other contract whatsoever regarding those shingles."

We think the homeowners are missing the point. Accepting the purchase terms is not "any other contract ... regarding those shingles"—it is the contract regarding those shingles. Purchasing a product necessarily and by definition encompasses accepting the terms of that purchase. The homeowners here expressly delegated to their roofers the task of purchasing shingles, and yet they now contest terms—in particular, those requiring mandatory arbitration—that are part and parcel of that purchase. In the language of our precedent, accepting purchase terms is "incidental to," "usually accompany[ing]," and "reasonably necessary to" the act of purchasing. And Florida law is clear that, in this respect at least, arbitration terms are no different from any others: "[A]n agent can bind a principal to an arbitration agreement just like any other contract." Fi-Evergreen Woods, LLC v. Estate of Robinson, 172 So.3d 493, 497 (Fla. 5th Dist. Ct. App.2015).

Even aside from our "incidental-to" precedent, it is axiomatic under Florida law—and more generally—that knowledge or notice that an agent acquires while acting within the course and scope of his authority is generally imputed to his principal. See, e.g., Chang v. JPMorgan Chase Bank, N.A., 845 F.3d 1087, 1095 (11th Cir. 2017); Restatement (Third) Of Agency § 5.03 ("For purposes of determining a principal's legal relations with a third party, notice of a fact that an agent knows or has reason to know is imputed to the principal if knowledge of the fact is material to the agent's duties to the principal[.]"). Here, Tamko's purchase terms were printed on the shingle packaging, which the homeowners agree their roofers opened. Because the notice that their roofers acquired while acting within the scope of their authority to purchase and install the shingles is properly imputed to them, the homeowners cannot now plead ignorance of the offer's existence.

To summarize, then, acceptance of Tamko's purchase terms—arbitration clause and all—was incidental to, and reasonably necessary to accomplish, the homeowners' express grant of agency authority to their roofers to purchase and install shingles, and in any event, the roofers' notice of the terms printed on the shingle wrappers is properly imputed to the homeowners.

As "master of the offer," Tamko invited purchasers to accept its contract terms by opening and retaining the shingles—a reasonable means of acceptance-by-conduct under Florida law. The homeowners, through their roofer agents, validly accepted those terms—Tamko's binding arbitration provision included. We therefore affirm the district court's decision to grant Tamko's motion to compel arbitration and to dismiss the homeowners' complaint.

AFFIRMED.

Questions

1. According to the court, what are the two fundamental inquiries in determining whether an offer has been made and accepted under Florida law?

2. What were the key features of Tamko's shingle packaging that the court considered in determining whether it conveyed a valid offer of contract terms?

3. In the context of post-purchase acceptance-by-retention warranties, why did the court find it reasonable for consumers to assume that by opening and retaining a product, they accept the accompanying terms and conditions?

Shipment of Goods as Acceptance

Corinthian Pharmaceutical Systems, Inc. v. Lederle Laboratories

United States District Court, S.D. Indiana, Indianapolis Division, 1989
724 F.Supp. 605

. . . This is a straightforward sale of goods problem resembling those found in a contracts or sales casebook. The fundamental question is whether Lederle Labs agreed to sell Corinthian Pharmaceuticals 1,000 vials of DTP vaccine at $64.32 per vial. As shown below, the undisputed material facts mandate the conclusion as a matter of law that no such agreement was ever formed.

[Defendant Lederle Laboratories is a pharmaceutical manufacturer and distributor that makes a number of drugs, including the DTP vaccine. Plaintiff Corinthian Pharmaceutical is a distributor of drugs that purchases supplies from manufacturers such as Lederle Labs and then resells the product to physicians and other providers. One of the products that Corinthian buys and distributes with some regularity is the DTP vaccine.]

From 1985 through early 1986, Corinthian made a number of purchases of the vaccine from Lederle Labs. During this period of time, the largest single order ever placed by Corinthian with Lederle was for 100 vials. When Lederle Labs filled an order it sent an invoice to Corinthian.

During this period of time, product liability lawsuits concerning DTP increased, and insurance became more difficult to procure. As a result, Lederle decided in early 1986 to self-insure against such risks. In order to cover the costs of self-insurance, Lederle concluded that a substantial increase in the price of the vaccine would be necessary.

In order to communicate the price change to its own sales people, Lederle's Price Manager prepared "PRICE LETTER NO. E-48." This document was dated May 19, 1986, and indicated that effective May 20, 1986, the price of the DTP vaccine would be raised from $51.00 to $171.00 per vial. Price letters such as these were routinely sent to Lederle's sales force, but did not go to customers. Corinthian Pharmaceutical did not know of the existence of this internal price letter until a Lederle representative presented it to Corinthian several weeks after May 20, 1986.

Additionally, Lederle Labs also wrote a letter dated May 20, 1986, to its customers announcing the price increase and explaining the liability and insurance problems that brought about the change. Corinthian somehow gained knowledge of this letter on May 19, 1986, the date before the price increase was to take effect. In response to the knowledge of the impending price increase, Corinthian immediately ordered 1000 vials of DTP vaccine from Lederle. Corinthian placed its order on May

19, 1986, by calling Lederle's "Telgo" system. The Telgo system is a telephone computer ordering system that allows customers to place orders over the phone by communicating with a computer. After Corinthian placed its order with the Telgo system, the computer gave Corinthian a tracking number for its order. On the same date, Corinthian sent Lederle two written confirmations of its order. On each form Corinthian stated that this "order is to receive the $64.32 per vial price."

On June 3, 1986, Lederle sent invoice 1771 to Corinthian for 50 vials of DTP vaccine priced at $64.32 per vial. The invoice contained the standard Lederle conditions noted above. The 50 vials were sent to Corinthian and were accepted. At the same time, Lederle sent its customers, including Corinthian, a letter regarding DTP

This letter stated that the "enclosed represents a partial shipment of the order for DTP vaccine, which you placed with Lederle on May 19, 1986." The letter stated that under Lederle's standard terms and conditions of sale the normal policy would be to invoice the order at the price when shipment was made. However, in light of the magnitude of the price increase, Lederle had decided to make an exception to its terms and conditions and ship a portion of the order at the lower price. The letter further stated that the balance would be priced at $171.00, and that shipment would be made during the week of June 16. The letter closed, "If for any reason you wish to cancel the balance of your order, please contact [us] ... on or before June 13."

Based on these facts, plaintiff Corinthian Pharmaceutical brings this action seeking specific performance for the 950 vials of DTP vaccine that Lederle Labs chose not to deliver. In support of its summary judgment motion, Lederle urges a number of alternative grounds for disposing of this claim, including that no contract for the sale of 1000 vials was formed, that if one was formed, it was governed by Lederle's terms and conditions, and that the 50 vials sent to Corinthian were merely an accommodation. . . .

A. *LEDERLE LABS NEVER AGREED TO SELL 1,000 VIALS AT THE LOWER PRICE:*

Initially, it should be noted that this is a sale of goods covered by the Uniform Commercial Code, and that both parties are merchants under the Code. The parties do not discuss which state's laws are to apply to action, but because the Code is substantially the same in all states having any connection to this dispute, the Court will, for ease of reference, refer in general to the U.C.C. with relevant interpretations from Indiana and other states.

The starting point in this analysis is where did the first offer originate. An offer is "the manifestation of willingness to enter into a bargain, so made as to justify another person in understanding that his assent to that bargain is invited and will conclude it." H. Greenberg, *Rights and Remedies Under U.C.C. Article 2* § 5.2 at 50 (1987) [*hereinafter* "Greenberg, *U.C.C. Article 2*"], (*quoting* 1 *Restatement (Second), Contracts* § 4 (1981)). The only possible conclusion in this case is that Corinthian's "order" of May 19, 1986, for 1,000 vials at $64.32 was the first offer. Nothing that the seller had done prior to this point can be interpreted as an offer.

First, the price lists distributed by Lederle to its customers did not constitute offers. It is well settled that quotations are mere invitations to make an offer, Greenberg, *U.C.C. Article 2* § 5.2 at 51; *Corbin on Contracts* §§ 26, 28 (1982), particularly where, as here, the price lists specifically stated that prices were subject to change without notice and that all orders were subject to acceptance by Lederle. Greenberg, *U.C.C. Article 2* § 5.2 at 51; *Quaker State Mushroom v. Dominick's Finer Foods,* 635 F.Supp. 1281, 1284 (N.D. Ill.1986) (No offer where price quotation is subject to change and orders are subject to seller's confirmation); *Interstate Industries, Inc. v. Barclay Industries, Inc.,* 540 F.2d 868, 873 (7th Cir.1976) (price quotation not an offer).

Second, neither Lederle's internal price memorandum nor its letter to customers dated May 20, 1986, can be construed as an offer to sell 1,000 vials at the lower price. There is no evidence that Lederle intended Corinthian to receive the internal price memorandum, nor is there anything in the record to support the conclusion that

Thus, as a matter of law, the first offer was made by Corinthian when it phoned in and subsequently confirmed its order for 1,000 vials at the lower price. The next question, then, is whether Lederle ever accepted that offer.

Under the Code, an acceptance need not be the mirror-image of the offer. U.C.C. § 2-207. However, the offeree must still do some act that manifests the intention to accept the offer and make a contract. Under § 2-206, an offer to make a contract shall be construed as inviting acceptance in any manner and by any medium reasonable in the circumstances. The first question regarding acceptance, therefore, is whether Lederle accepted the offer prior to sending the 50 vials of vaccine.

The record is clear that Lederle did not communicate or do any act prior to shipping the 50 vials that could support the finding of an acceptance. When Corinthian placed its order, it merely received a tracking number from the Telgo computer. Such an automated, ministerial act cannot constitute an acceptance. *See, e.g., Foremost Pro Color, Inc. v. Eastman Kodak Co.,* 703 F.2d 534, 539 (9th Cir.1983) (logging purchase orders as received did not manifest acceptance); *Southern Spindle & Flyer Co. v. Milliken & Co.,* 53 N.C. App. 785, 281 S.E.2d 734, 736 (1981) (seller's acknowledgement of receipt of purchase order did not constitute assent to its terms). Thus, there was no acceptance of Corinthian's offer prior to the deliver of 50 vials.

The next question, then, is what is to be made of the shipment of 50 vials and the accompanying letter. Section 2-206(b) of the Code speaks to this issue:

[A]n order or other offer to buy goods for prompt or current shipment shall be construed as inviting acceptance either by a prompt promise to ship or by the prompt or current shipment of conforming or non-conforming goods, *but such a shipment of non-conforming goods does not constitute an acceptance if the seller seasonably notifies the buyer that the shipment is offered only as an accommodation to the buyer.*

§ 2-206 (emphasis added). Thus, under the Code a seller accepts the offer by shipping goods, whether they are conforming or not, but if the seller ships non-conforming goods *and* seasonably notifies the buyer that the shipment is a mere accommodation, then the seller has not, in fact, accepted the buyer's offer. See, Greenberg, *U.C.C. Article 2* § 5.5 at 53.

In this case, the offer made by Corinthian was for 1,000 vials at $64.32. In response, Lederle Labs shipped only 50 vials at $64.32 per vial, and wrote Corinthian indicating that the balance of the order would be priced at $171.00 per vial and would be shipped during the week of June 16. The letter further indicated that the buyer could cancel its order by calling Lederle Labs. Clearly, Lederle's shipment was non-conforming, for it was for only 1/20th of the quantity desired by the buyer. *See* § 2-106(2) (goods or conduct are conforming when they are in accordance with the obligations under the contract); *Michiana Mack, Inc. v. Allendale Rural Fire Protection,* 428 N.E.2d 1367, 1370 (Ind.App.1981) (non-conformity describes goods and conduct). The narrow issue, then, is whether Lederle's response to the offer was a shipment of non-conforming goods not constituting an acceptance because it was offered only as an accommodation under § 2-206.

An accommodation is an arrangement or engagement made as a favor to another. *Black's Law Dictionary* (5th ed. 1979). The term implies no consideration. *Id.* In this case, then, even taking all inferences favorably for the buyer, the only possible conclusion is that Lederle Labs' shipment of 50 vials was offered merely as an accommodation; that is to say, Lederle had no obligation to make the partial shipment, and did so only as a favor to the buyer. The accommodation letter, which Corinthian is sure it received, clearly stated that the 50 vials were being sent at the lower price as an exception to Lederle's general policy, and that the balance of the offer would be invoiced at the higher price. The letter further indicated that Lederle's proposal to ship the balance of the order at the higher price could be rejected by the buyer. Moreover, the standard terms of Lederle's invoice stated that acceptance of the order was expressly conditioned upon buyer's assent to the seller's terms.

Under these undisputed facts, § 2-206(1)(b) was satisfied. Where, as here, the notification is properly made, the shipment of nonconforming goods is treated as a counteroffer just as at common law, and the buyer may accept or reject the counteroffer under normal contract rules. 2 W. Hawkland, *Uniform Commercial Code Series* § 2-206:04 (1987).

Thus, the end result of this analysis is that Lederle Lab's price quotations were mere invitations to make an offer, that by placing its order Corinthian made an offer to buy 1,000 vials at the low price, that by shipping 50 vials at the low price Lederle's response was non-conforming, but the nonconforming response was a mere accommodation and thus constituted a counteroffer. Accordingly, there being no genuine issues of material fact on these issues and the law being in favor of the seller, summary judgment must be granted for Lederle Labs.

Questions

1. According to the court's analysis, who made the first offer in this case?

2. Why did the court conclude that Lederle Labs' price lists did not constitute offers?

3. Did Lederle Labs accept Corinthian Pharmaceutical's offer before shipping the 50 vials?

4. Under the Uniform Commercial Code, what conditions must be met for a shipment of non-conforming goods to be considered an acceptance?

5. How did Lederle Labs characterize the shipment of 50 vials in their letter to Corinthian Pharmaceutical? What options did Corinthian have in response to this shipment?

Takeaways – Corinthian Pharmaceutical

UCC § 2-206(1)(b) provides that an offer can be accepted by any reasonable "medium" including the commencement of performance. Unless otherwise unambiguously indicated, an offer to buy goods for "prompt shipment" is to be construed as inviting acceptance either by promise or by the act of shipment itself. This is not radically different from the common law rule which provides in cases of doubt as to whether the offeror is seeking a promise to perform or a completed performance as an act of acceptance, the choice as to how to accept is left up to the offeree. (See, Rest.2d §§ 32 and 62.)

Silence is Not Acceptance

Since acceptance must be communicated, ordinarily silence cannot constitute an offer to enter into a bilateral contract.

Unsolicited Merchandise Suppose you receive merchandise in the mail that you never requested. If the accompanying note says, "if you do not return this to me, you will owe me X number of dollars," are you bound to either return it or pay for it? For the answer see, Cal.Civ.Code § 1584.5 which reads in part: "The receipt of any goods etc. shall for all purposes be deemed an unconditional gift to the recipient who may use or dispose of the goods in any manner he sees fit without obligation on his part to the sender." Note that this is a statutory exception to the rule that use of consideration constitutes acceptance. See also, 39 U.S.C. § 3009(b).

When Is Acceptance Effective?

Acceptance Effective on Dispatch - The "Mailbox Rule"

A written notice of acceptance is effective when placed into the course of transmission and beyond the control of the offeree. This is regardless of whether it ever reaches the offeror. (Rest.2d § 63.) If the accepting party uses an unauthorized or unreasonable means of transmittal, the acceptance is not effective until actually received by the person who made the offer within any time limit set forth or implied in the offer. (Cal.Civ.Code § 1583)

Gibbs v. American Savings & Loan Assn.
Court of Appeals of California, Second Appellate District, 1990
217 Cal.App.3d 1372, 266 Cal.Rptr. 517

LUCAS, P. J. James and Barbara Gibbs appeal from judgment against them and in favor of American Savings & Loan Association (American Savings) in their action to enforce a purported contract for the sale of real property. We affirm.

In August 1984, James and Barbara Gibbs (the Gibbses) submitted an offer for $180,000 to American Savings to purchase a house in Woodland Hills which American Savings had taken back through foreclosure. American Savings, through its employee, Dorothy Folkman, agreed that the Gibbs could move into the subject property and rent it until the close of escrow. No action was taken on this offer.

On March 27, 1985, pursuant to a request by Ms. Folkman, the Gibbs submitted a new offer because American Savings could not find their original offer. The purchase price was again $180,000. On the morning of June 6, 1985, the Gibbses received a counteroffer from American Savings containing several additional terms and conditions, but with no mention of purchase price. According to Barbara Gibbs, she immediately drove to her husband's jobsite where she and her husband signed this counteroffer. She drove to her office, typed an envelope with a certified mail tag, placed the counter-offer in the envelope, and before 10 o'clock that morning, she handed it to the mail clerk at her office, instructing him to mail it for her.

At approximately 11 a.m. that same morning, Barbara Gibbs had a telephone conversation with Dorothy Folkman in which Folkman said the counteroffer was in error, since American Savings had intended to increase the sales price to $198,000. Folkman also advised the Gibbses that because of this error, the counteroffer was revoked.

American Savings took the position that no contract had been formed. The Gibbses insisted that they had accepted the counteroffer before it was revoked and that a contract thus existed. The Gibbses brought the within action for damages, specific performance, breach of contract and declaratory relief. After trial, the court found that Barbara Gibbs did not place the acceptance of the counteroffer in the course of transmission when she gave it to the mail clerk in her office on June 6, 1985; thus there was no acceptance on that date. The postmark on the envelope was June 7, 1985. Dorothy Folkman's oral revocation of the counteroffer on June 6, 1985, preceded the Gibbses' acceptance of that counteroffer on June 7 and therefore no contract for sale of the property was ever formed. The Gibbses appeal from the judgment thereafter entered. . . .

[W]e find substantial evidence supports the trial court's judgment. Barbara Gibbs testified that she received the counteroffer from American Savings at about 8:45 or 9 a.m. on June 6, 1985. She and her husband signed the counteroffer at 9:39 a.m. that day. She then drove about one mile to her office, prepared an envelope and certified mail receipt, and gave the ready-to-mail, signed counteroffer to the mail clerk in her office for mailing. This purportedly occurred before 10 a.m. on June 6.

Barbara Gibbs further testified that the clerk brought the mail to the Woodland Hills Post Office and returned with her receipt by 10:15 a.m. on June 6. However, the certified mail receipt was not produced at trial, and the envelope in which the signed counteroffer was mailed to American Savings was postmarked June 7, 1985, not June 6. According to the Domestic Mail Manual of the United States Postal Service, section 144.471, the date shown in the meter postmark of any type of mail must be the actual date of deposit. Section 144.534 of the manual provides that metered mail bearing the wrong date of mailing shall be run through a canceling machine or otherwise postmarked to show the proper date. The postmarked envelope constitutes substantial evidence that the acceptance was mailed on June 7, not June 6.

Civil Code section 1583 provides: "Consent is deemed to be fully communicated between the parties as soon as the party accepting a proposal has put his acceptance in the course of transmission to the proposer, ..." This rule has long been interpreted to require that the acceptance be placed out of the control of the accepting party in order to be considered "in the course of transmission." (*Ivey v. Kern County Land Co.* (1896) 115 Cal. 196, 201 [46 P. 926].) Typically, this is found when the acceptance is delivered to the post office. (*Morello v. Growers Grape Prod. Assn.*

(1947) 82 Cal.App.2d 365, 370-371 [186 P.2d 463].) California's "'effective upon posting'" rule, as codified in section 1583, thus holds that an acceptance of an offer is effective and deemed communicated upon its deposit in the mail. (*Palo Alto Town & Country Village, Inc. v. BBTC Company* (1974) 11 Cal.3d 494, 500-501 [113 Cal.Rptr. 705, 521 P.2d 1097].)

The postmark on the counteroffer in the case before us shows such deposit occurred on June 7, 1985, not on June 6. The counteroffer was not placed in the course of transmission beyond the control of the offeree when Barbara Gibbs gave it to the mail clerk in her office with instructions to deliver it to the post office. It was placed in the course of transmission within the meaning of Civil Code section 1583 when it was deposited with the United States Postal Service on June 7, 1985.

It is basic contract law that an offer may be revoked any time prior to acceptance. (Civ. Code, § 1586.) Both Barbara Gibbs and Dorothy Folkman from American Savings testified that they spoke together on the telephone on the morning of June 6, 1985. During that call, Folkman became aware of American Savings' error in failing to include the $198,000 purchase price in the counteroffer, advised Barbara Gibbs of the error and stated that American Savings was revoking the counteroffer. Inasmuch as the counteroffer was revoked on June 6, prior to the Gibbses' acceptance, no contract was formed.

A similar result was reached in the Florida case of *Kendel v. Pontius* (Fla. 1971) 244 So.2d 543, 544. In *Kendel*, the buyers delivered their signed acceptance to their attorney who was to mail it to the seller. Before the attorney mailed the signed acceptance to the seller, the seller revoked the offer. The court held delivery to the buyers' attorney did not constitute posting. No contract was formed because the seller's revocation preceded the mailing of the acceptance.

We find no reason to depart from this well-reasoned law. . . .

The judgment is affirmed.

Questions

1. What is the requirement for an acceptance to be considered "in the course of transmission?"

2. Why did the court conclude that no contract was formed in this case?

Takeaways – Gibbs v. American Savings

Although revocation and rejection of an offer are effective when received, the general rule is that a contract is made when the acceptance is dispatched, even though the letter of acceptance is lost and never reaches the offeror. This is the rule of old English case of *Adams v. Lindsell* (1818) 106 Eng. Rep. 250 (K.B.).

The Restatement Second of Contracts, section 63(a) provides, among other things, that if an acceptor entrusts a notice of acceptance or acceptance to his or her agent for transmittal, the acceptance is not effective until the agent puts this notice or acceptance out of his or her possession. The possession of the agent is the possession of the principal.

Termination of the Power of Acceptance

Like most other things in life, offers don't last forever. An offer may be revoked any time prior to acceptance. (Cal.Civ.Code § 1586) This is so even though the offer is stated to be good or irrevocable for a specified period. An offer is revoked when notice of the revocation is communicated to the offeree before the offeree's acceptance is communicated to the offeror. (Cal.Civ.Code, § 1587, subd. 1.) Both revocation and acceptance can be communicated by any usual and reasonable mode and notice of revocation or acceptance is complete when placed in the course of transmission to the recipient. (*Bellasi v. Shackelford* (1962) 201 Cal.App.2d 265, 267-268 [19 Cal.Rptr. 925]; Civ.Code, §§ 1582, 1583.) Note that with respect to revocation and rejection of offers, the "majority" rule is that revocation and rejection of an offer are effective when received. However, in California, rejection is effective upon dispatch. (Cal.Civ.Code §§ 1587 and 1583.)

According to Restatement Second section 36, an offer is revoked by,

1. *Express revocation* By the person who made the offer, giving notice of revocation to the person to whom the offer has been made, in the same manner required to communicate the acceptance; or

2. *Implied revocation* By the person who made the offer, taking some action inconsistent with keeping the offer open, and the person to whom the offer is made receiving reliable information of that fact; or

3. *Lapse* By the lapse of the time set forth in the offer for the acceptance, or if no time is set forth, the lapse of a reasonable time without communication of the acceptance; or by the failure of the person accepting the offer to fulfill a condition precedent to acceptance; or

4. *Rejection* Manifestation on the part of the person to whom the offer is made that they are not accepting the offer; or

5. *Counteroffer* A counter-proposal made by the person to whom the offer is made; or

6. *Death or Incapacity of the Offeror* By the death or insanity of the person making the offer. (See also, Cal.Civ.Code § 1587.)

Revocation of Offers

Dickinson v. Dodds
In the Court of Appeal, Chancery Division, 1876
LR 2 Ch.D. 463

On Wednesday, the 10th of June, 1874, the Defendant John Dodds signed and delivered to the Plaintiff, George Dickinson, a memorandum, of which the material part was as follows:--

"I hereby agree to sell to Mr. George Dickinson the whole of the dwelling-houses, garden ground, stabling, and outbuildings thereto belonging, situate at Croft, belonging to me, for the sum of £800. As witness my hand this tenth day of June, 1874." £800.

(Signed) John Dodds."; "

P.S.--This offer to be left over until Friday, 9 o'clock, A.M. J. D. (the twelfth), 12th June, 1874.

The bill alleged that Dodds understood and intended that the Plaintiff should have until Friday 9 A.M. within which to determine whether he would or would not purchase, and that he should absolutely have until that time the refusal of the property at the price of £800, and that the Plaintiff in fact determined to accept the offer on the morning of Thursday, the 11th of June, but did not at once signify his acceptance to Dodds, believing that he had the power to accept it until 9 A.M. on the Friday.

In the afternoon of the Thursday the Plaintiff was informed by a Mr. Berry that Dodds had been offering or agreeing to sell the property to Thomas Allan, the other Defendant. Thereupon the Plaintiff, at about half-past seven in the evening, went to the house of Mrs. Burgess, the mother-in-law of Dodds, where he was then staying, and left with her a formal acceptance in writing of the offer to sell the property. According to the evidence of Mrs. Burgess this document never in fact reached Dodds, she having forgotten to give it to him.

On the following (Friday) morning, at about seven o'clock, Berry, who was acting as agent for Dickinson, found Dodds at the Darlington railway station, and handed to him a duplicate of the acceptance by Dickinson, and explained to Dodds its purport. He replied that it was too late, as he had sold the property. A few minutes later Dickinson himself found Dodds entering a railway carriage, and handed him another duplicate of the notice of acceptance, but Dodds declined to receive it, saying, "You are too late. I have sold the property."

It appeared that on the day before, Thursday, the 11th of June, Dodds had signed a formal contract for the sale of the property to the Defendant Allan for £800, and had received from him a deposit of £40.

The bill in this suit prayed that the Defendant Dodds might be decreed specifically to perform the contract of the 10th of June, 1874; that he might be restrained from conveying the property to Allan; that Allan might be restrained from taking any such conveyance;

JAMES, L.J. after referring to the document of the 10th of June, 1874, continued:-- The document, though beginning "I hereby agree to sell," was nothing but an offer, and was only intended to be an offer, for the Plaintiff himself tells us that he required time to consider whether he would enter into an agreement or not. Unless both parties had then agreed there was no concluded agreement then made; it was in effect and substance only an offer to sell. The Plaintiff, being minded not to complete the bargain at that time, added this memorandum--"This offer to be left over until Friday, 9 o'clock A.M., 12th June, 1874." That shews it was only an offer. There was no consideration given for the undertaking or promise, to whatever extent it may be considered binding, to keep the property unsold until 9 o'clock on Friday morning; but apparently Dickinson was of opinion, and probably Dodds was of the same opinion, that he (Dodds) was bound by that promise, and could not in any way withdraw from it, or retract it, until 9 o'clock on Friday morning, and this probably explains a good deal of what afterwards took place. But it is clear settled law, on one of the clearest principles of law, that this promise, being a mere nudum pactum, was not binding, and that at any moment before a complete acceptance by Dickinson of the offer, Dodds was as free as Dickinson himself. Well, that being the state of things, it is said that the only mode in which Dodds could assert that freedom was by actually and distinctly saying to Dickinson, "Now I withdraw my offer." It appears to me that there is neither principle nor authority for the proposition that there must be an express and actual withdrawal of the offer, or what is called a retraction. It must, to constitute a contract, appear that the two minds were at one, at the same moment of time, that is, that there was an offer continuing up to the time of the acceptance. If there was not such a continuing offer, then the acceptance comes to nothing. Of course it may well be that the one man is bound in some way or other to let the other man know that his mind with regard to the offer has been changed; but in this case, beyond all question, the Plaintiff knew that Dodds was no longer minded to sell the property to him as plainly and clearly as if Dodds had told him in so many words, "I withdraw the offer." This is evident from the Plaintiff's own statements in the bill.

The Plaintiff says in effect that, having heard and knowing that Dodds was no longer minded to sell to him, and that he was selling or had sold to some one else, thinking that he could not in point of law withdraw his offer, meaning to fix him to it, and endeavoring to bind him," I went to the house where he was lodging, and saw his mother-in-law, and left with her an acceptance of the offer, knowing all the while that he had entirely changed his mind. I got an agent to watch for him at 7 o'clock the next morning, and I went to the train just before 9 o'clock, in order that I might catch him and give him my notice of acceptance just before 9 o'clock, and when that occurred he told my agent, and he told me, you are too late, and he then threw back the paper." It is to my mind quite clear that before there was any attempt at acceptance by the Plaintiff, he was perfectly well aware that Dodds had changed his mind, and that he had in fact agreed to sell the property to Allan. It is impossible, therefore, to say there was ever that existence of the same mind between the two parties which is essential in point of law to the making of an agreement. I am of opinion, therefore, that the Plaintiff has failed to prove that there was any binding contract between Dodds and himself.

MELLISH, L.J.:-- I am of the same opinion. The first question is, whether this document of the 10th of June, 1874, which was signed by Dodds, was an agreement to sell, or only an offer to sell, the property therein mentioned to Dickinson; and I am clearly of opinion that it was only an offer, although it is in the first part of it, independently of the postscript, worded as an agreement. I apprehend that, until acceptance, so that both parties are bound, even though an instrument is so worded as to express that both parties agree, it is in point of law only an offer, and, until both parties are bound, neither party is bound. It is not necessary that both parties should be bound within the Statute of Frauds, for, if one party makes an offer in writing, and the other accepts it verbally, that will be sufficient to bind the person who has signed the written document. But, if there be no agreement, either verbally or in writing, then, until acceptance, it is in point of law an offer only, although worded as if it were an agreement. But it is hardly necessary to resort to that doctrine in the present case, because the postscript calls it an offer, and says, "This offer to be left over until Friday, 9 o'clock A.M." Well, then, this being only an offer, the law says--and it is a perfectly clear rule of law--that, although it is said that the offer is to be left open until Friday morning at 9 o'clock, that did not bind Dodds. He was not in point of law bound to hold the offer over until 9 o'clock on Friday morning. He was not so bound either in law or in equity. Well, that being so, when on the next day he made an agreement with Allan to sell the property to him, I am not aware of any ground on which it can be said that that contract with Allan was not as good and binding a contract as ever was made. Assuming Allan to have known (there is some dispute about it, and Allan does not admit that he knew of it, but I will assume that he did) that Dodds had made the offer to Dickinson, and had given him till Friday morning at 9 o'clock to accept it, still in point of law that could not prevent Allan from making a more favorable offer than Dickinson, and entering at once into a binding agreement with Dodds.

Then Dickinson is informed by Berry that the property has been sold by Dodds to Allan. Berry does not tell us from whom he heard it, but he says that he did hear it, that he knew it, and that he informed Dickinson of it. Now, stopping there, the question which arises is this--If an offer has been made for the sale of property, and before that offer is accepted, the person who has made the offer enters into a binding agreement to sell the property to somebody else, and the person to whom the offer was first made receives notice in some way that the property has been sold to another person, can he after that make a binding contract by the acceptance of the offer? I am of opinion that he cannot. The law may be right or wrong in saying that a person who has given to another a certain time within which to accept an offer is not bound by his promise to give that time; but, if he is not bound by that promise, and may still sell the property to some one else, and if it be the law that, in order to make a contract, the two minds must be in agreement at some one time, that is, at the time of the acceptance, how is it possible that when the person to whom the offer has been made knows that the person who has made the offer has sold the property to someone else, and that, in fact, he has not remained in the same mind to sell it to him, he can be at liberty to accept the offer and thereby make a binding contract? It seems to me that would be simply absurd. If a man makes an offer to sell a particular horse in his stable, and says, "I will give you until the day after to-morrow to accept the offer," and the next day goes and sells the horse to somebody else, and receives the purchase-money from him, can the person to whom the offer was originally made then come and say, "I accept," so as to make a binding contract, and so as to be entitled to recover damages for the non-delivery of the horse? If the rule of law is that a mere offer to sell property, which can be withdrawn at any time, and which is made dependent on the acceptance of the person to whom it is made, is a mere nudum pactum, how is it possible that the person to whom the offer has been made can by acceptance make a binding contract after he knows that the person who has made the offer has sold the property to some one else? It is admitted law that, if a man who makes an offer dies, the offer cannot be accepted after he is dead, and parting with the property has very much the same effect as the death of the owner, for it makes the performance of the offer impossible. I am clearly of opinion that, just as when a man who has made an offer dies before it is accepted it is impossible that it can then be accepted, so when once the person to whom the offer was made knows that the property has been sold to some one else, it is too late for him to accept the offer, and on that ground I am clearly of opinion that there was no binding contract for the sale of this property by Dodds to Dickinson, and even if there had been, it seems to me that the sale of the property to Allan was first in point of time. However, it is not necessary to consider, if there had been two binding contracts, which of them would be entitled to priority in equity, because there is no binding contract between Dodds and Dickinson.

Questions

1. What did Dickinson add to the document to indicate that it was only an offer and not a binding agreement?

2. Why did the court state that the promise to keep the property unsold until 9 o'clock on Friday morning was not binding?

3. Is it necessary for an offer to be expressly and actually withdrawn for there to be no contract?

Takeaways – Dickinson v. Dodds

Revocation of an offer can be express, as when the offeror tells the offeree in words that the offer is no longer effective, (Rest.2d. § 42) or it can be indirect which occurs when the offeror takes definite action that is inconsistent with keeping the offer open and the offeree acquires reliable information to that effect. (Rest.2d § 43.) However, this latter rule does not apply where the offeror takes no action or takes equivocal action; e.g., where he or she merely negotiates with a third person, or makes a binding contract with a third person expressly subject to the rights of the offeree. (Comment d to Restatement Second section 43.) What kind of revocation do the facts in *Dickinson v. Dodds* show? An express revocation or an indirect one?

Lapse of Offer

Yaros v. Trustees of the University of Pennsylvania
742 A. 2d 1118 (1999)

ORIE MELVIN, J.: This is an appeal from an Order ... granting appellee Dr. Nancy Yaros's Motion to Enforce Settlement against appellant, the Trustees of the University of Pennsylvania ("University"). For the reasons that follow, we affirm.

The record reveals Dr. Yaros brought a negligence action against the University after she fell at one of its ice skating rinks. ... Testimony began on January 26, 1998. On that date, the University offered Dr. Yaros a settlement offer of $750,000.00. Attorney Haaz informed Attorney Orlando that Dr. Yaros would accept $1.5 million in settlement up until the time she testified, after which she would not settle for any amount. The trial continued, two defense witnesses took the stand, and then Dr. Yaros testified. No settlement was reached at that time.

On January 29, 1998, after the conclusion of testimony, the University offered Dr. Yaros $750,000.00 in settlement. Attorney Orlando made the offer to Attorney Haaz during a ten minute recess prior to closing arguments. At the close of the conversation Attorney Orlando told Attorney Haaz "you've got to get back to me."

When he made this statement, Attorney Orlando looked at the clock and placed his palms sideward. No time limitations regarding the offer were communicated, nor was it indicated that the offer was only open until closing arguments began. Attorney Haaz stated he would talk to his client now. After the offer was made Attorney Haaz left the courtroom to speak to his client. Attorney Orlando also left the courtroom to go to the men's restroom. Attorney Haaz returned to the courtroom without Dr. Yaros, who was in the restroom. Attorney Haaz asked the trial court for two minutes to speak to his client before closings, to which the court agreed. At that time Attorney Orlando assumed Attorney Haaz had not discussed the offer with Dr. Yaros. Upon Dr. Yaros's return, Attorney Haaz did not confer with her and closing arguments commenced immediately. Earlier that day, Judge Ribner informed both counsel he expected closing arguments to be finished by 5:00 p.m. so he could charge the jury the next day. During the University's closing, Dr. Yaros authorized Attorney Haaz to accept the offer. After the University ended its closing, Attorney Haaz gave his rebuttal. At a sidebar conference following closings Attorney Haaz stated Dr. Yaros accepted the University's settlement offer. Attorney Orlando replied by stating, "I don't know if it's still there, judge." The next day, prior to jury deliberations Dr. Yaros orally moved to enforce the settlement. Judge Ribner denied the motion pending evidentiary hearings on the matter and the jury's verdict. The jury came back with a defense verdict. Following trial, Dr. Yaros filed . . . a Motion to Enforce Settlement. One evidentiary hearing was held before Judge Ribner. However, upon his retirement the case was reassigned to the Honorable Sandra Mazer Moss, who conducted hearings on January 12 and 15, 1999. On February 22, 1999, Judge Mazer Moss granted Dr. Yaros's Motion to Enforce Settlement. This timely appeal followed.

On appeal, the University raises several allegations of error in connection with the trial court's enforcement of the settlement. It presents the following issues for our review: . . .

2. Whether the Trial Court erred in granting [Dr. Yaros's] Motion to Enforce Settlement, even though, as a matter of law, [Dr. Yaros's] conduct constituted a rejection of the settlement offer?

3. Whether the Trial Court erred in granting [Dr. Yaros's] Motion to Enforce Settlement, even though, as a matter of law, [Dr. Yaros] did not accept the settlement offer within a reasonable time under the circumstances, and therefore allowed the offer to lapse?

4. Whether the Trial Court's factual finding that [Dr. Yaros] accepted the University's offer within a reasonable period of time was against the weight of the evidence, capricious and erroneous as a matter of law? . . .

The trial court found the University's offer was not withdrawn and Dr. Yaros accepted it within a reasonable amount of time under the circumstances. In analyzing whether this was a valid and enforceable settlement agreement the trial court relied upon the standards set forth in Vaskie v. West American Ins. Co., 383 Pa.Super. 76, 556 A.2d 436 (1989), wherein this Court stated:

> Under such circumstances, i.e. where an offer does not specify an expiration date or otherwise limit the allowable time for acceptance, it is both hornbook law and well-established in Pennsylvania that the offer is deemed to be outstanding for a reasonable period of time. . . .; Restatement (Second) Contracts Section 41 (1981).

The University asserts the above legal standard is only a general rule. It maintains the "conversation rule" as stated in Restatement (Second) Contracts § 41, comment d governs. That comment provides as follows:

> d. Direct negotiations. Where the parties bargain face to face or over the telephone, the time for acceptance does not ordinarily extend beyond the end of the conversation unless a contrary intention is indicated. A contrary intention may be indicated by express words or by the circumstances. For example, the delivery of a written offer to the offeree, or an expectation that some action will be taken before acceptance, may indicate that a delayed acceptance is invited.

Our Court has adopted the legal standard enunciated in comment d. Textron, Inc. v. Froelich, 223 Pa.Super. 506, 302 A.2d 426, 427 (1973) (stating "an oral offer ordinarily terminates at the end of the conversation"); Boyd v. Merchants' and Farmers' Peanut Co., 25 Pa. Superior Ct. 199, 204 (1904) (stating "[w]hen an offer is made to another orally and he goes away without accepting it, it would seem that ordinarily the offer would be considered as having lapsed"). In Textron, the Court acknowledged that this standard does not preclude the possibility that an oral offer continues past the conversation and noted the general rule that if no time is specified, the offer terminates at the end of a reasonable amount of time. Id. at 427. Furthermore, the Court stated while there may be times when a judge could find as a matter of law that an oral offer terminates with the end of the conversation, if there is any doubt as to what is a reasonable interpretation, the decision should be left to the fact-finder. Id. The University insists that because of the face to face nature of the negotiations, the offer terminated at the end of the conversation between counsel or at the very latest at the beginning of closing arguments.

Because the parties' counsel conducted face to face negotiations it appears comment d initially provides the more on point legal standard; however, this does not affect the trial court's ultimate decision. The offer by the University clearly extended beyond the end of counsels' conversation, during the court recess when Attorney Haaz walked out of the courtroom to speak with his client about the settlement offer. A contrary intention was clearly indicated by Attorney Orlando when he ended the conversation with Attorney Haaz by stating "get back to me." Thus, the time for acceptance by Dr. Yaros extended beyond the end of the conversation between the parties' attorneys. The question that then arises is how long was the offer open. The University maintains it intended the offer was only open until the beginning of closing arguments, and such intention was clear. It submits that although Attorney Orlando did not articulate explicitly a definite time limit for Dr. Yaros's acceptance, its intention was manifested by the fact closing arguments were imminent, the established pattern of including an event condition with a settlement offer, and the verbal and non-verbal expressions used.

The enforceability of settlement agreements is determined according to principles of contract law. [Citation omitted] "[I]n the case of a disputed oral contract, what was said and done by the parties as well as what was intended by what was said and done by them are questions of fact." [Citation omitted]. We find preposterous the University's assertion that its intention regarding the time limitation of the offer was clear. The trial court made a factual determination that no time or event conditions were ever placed on the settlement offer. Here, the duration of the offer was not even clear to its trial counsel Attorney Orlando or its risk manager, Erika Gross. After Dr. Yaros accepted the offer Attorney Orlando stated, "I don't know if it's still there, judge." Certainly, if Attorney Orlando, the offeror, was unclear of whether the offer was still open after closing arguments were complete, it's incredulous to argue the offeree, Dr. Yaros, was clearly aware that the offer would lapse once closing arguments began. Moreover, we reject the University's claim that verbal and non-verbal conduct made the time limitation of the offer apparent. The University argues Attorney Orlando's statement "you've got to get back to me" can only be interpreted as "you've got to get back to me with an answer as soon as possible— which is, when we both come back into the courtroom: you from your discussion with your client and I from the Men's Room, so we can conclude this negotiation in the next few minutes before closings.". We will not reject the trial court's findings in favor of such a strained interpretation of the statement, "you've got to get back to me," or conduct like Attorney Haaz's statement that he needed two minutes to speak with his client and Attorney Orlando's non-verbal act of looking at the clock and "put[ting] [his] palms sidewards."

Additionally, the University makes much of the fact that Dr. Yaros had earlier during the trial imposed an event condition on a settlement offer. During trial Attorney Haaz informed Attorney Orlando that Dr. Yaros would accept a settlement in a certain dollar amount only up until the time she testified. The University now maintains this established a pattern of including an event condition with a settlement offer. While the prior course of dealings between the parties is instructive, in this case it cuts against the University's argument. In the parties' prior course of dealings, Dr. Yaros and her counsel explicitly informed the University of the event condition. There was no such explanation when the University made its offer just prior to closing arguments. Moreover, the offer remained open during the course of several witnesses' testimony. Under such circumstances, the prior course of dealing between the parties did not establish closing argument was an event which would terminate the offer.

The University next argues Dr. Yaros's conduct constituted a rejection of the offer. Specifically, it maintains that because Attorney Haaz did not confer with Dr. Yaros when she returned to the courtroom just prior to closings and because Dr. Yaros participated in closing and rebuttal arguments without accepting the offer, it was justified in inferring she had in fact rejected the offer. The trial court found Dr. Yaros never rejected the offer. The court further rebuffed the University's contention that it could infer its offer had been rejected when closing arguments commenced.

An offer is rejected when the offeror is justified in inferring from the words or conduct of the offeree that the offeree intends not to accept the offer or to take it under further advisement. Restatement (Contracts) § 36; Smaligo v. Fireman's Fund Ins. Co., 432 Pa. 133, 139, 247 A.2d 577, 580 (1968). In Smaligo, an insurance company made a settlement offer informing the offeree plaintiffs that proceeding forward with the case would be viewed as a rejection. The plaintiffs proceeded to arbitration. This Court agreed with the trial court that plaintiffs' action clearly showed that they did not intend to accept the offer. Unlike Smaligo, this is not a situation where the offeree was placed on notice that certain conduct would constitute a rejection of the offer. While an offeree need not be put on specific notice that certain conduct will be viewed by the offeror as a rejection of the offer, not all conduct can justify an offeror in inferring that the offer has been rejected. In this case we can find no error in the trial court's finding that the University was not justified in inferring that proceeding to closing arguments would constitute a rejection of the settlement offer. There is no per se rule that commencing with closing arguments constitutes a rejection of a settlement offer. Nor do we wish to create one here. It would produce a situation where an offeror would have the unfair advantage of unilaterally asserting after the offer has been accepted that an unspecified, undefined and uncommunicated event at trial constituted a rejection. Moreover, we agree with Dr. Yaros's observation that since the University believed she had not had an opportunity to consult with her counsel and was unaware of the settlement offer, it would not be justified in inferring that proceeding to closing arguments constituted a rejection of the offer. How the University could interpret the actions of Dr. Yaros and Attorney Haaz as a rejection of its offer when the University was under the impression Dr. Yaros was unaware of the offer at that time is beyond our understanding.

The University finally argues the settlement offer lapsed because, as a matter of law, Dr. Yaros did not accept it within a reasonable amount of time. It submits the trial court's factual finding that Dr. Yaros accepted the offer within a reasonable amount of time was against the weight of the evidence. Where an offer does not specify an expiration date or otherwise limit the allowable time for acceptance, the offer is deemed to be outstanding for a reasonable period of time. First Home Savings Bank, FSB v. Nernberg, 436 Pa.Super. 377, 648 A.2d 9, 15 (1994); Vaskie,

556 A.2d at 438. In Vaskie, this Court examined the issue of whether reasonableness is a question of law or of fact:

What is a reasonable time is ordinarily a question of fact to be decided by the jury and is dependent upon the numerous circumstances surrounding the transaction... Such circumstances as the nature of the contract, the relationship or situation of the parties and their course of dealing, and usages of the particular business are all relevant.

However, there are situations where the question of what is a reasonable time for acceptance may be decided by the court as a matter of law. As stated in Boyd, supra:

What is a reasonable time for acceptance is a question of law for the court in such commercial transactions as happen in the same way, day after day, and present the question upon the same data in continually recurring instances; and where the time taken is so clearly reasonable or unreasonable that there can be no question of doubt as to the proper answer to the question. Where the answer to the question is one dependent on many different circumstances, which do not continually recur in other cases of like character, and with respect to which no certain rule of law could be laid down, the question is one of fact for the jury.

Id. at 438-439. After holding numerous evidentiary hearings, the trial court treated this issue as a question of fact, finding the time period was reasonable under the circumstances. The University believes this is a question of law because trials happen in the same manner every day in the sense that the significant events of trial such as opening arguments, the presentation of evidence, and closing arguments proceed in the same manner in every trial. While trials do commence in the same manner, "the course and nature of settlement negotiations varies greatly from case to case." Id. at 440. There are individual circumstances distinct to this case, such as when and how the offer was made, which will not necessarily continually recur in other cases. Thus, we believe the trial court was correct in treating this as a question of fact.

As a reviewing court we will not disturb the findings of a trial judge sitting as the finder of fact unless there is a determination that those findings are not based upon competent evidence. [Citation omitted] In reviewing the trial court's findings, the victorious party is entitled to have the evidence viewed in the light most favorable to him and all the evidence must be taken as true and all unfavorable inferences rejected. [Citation omitted] Moreover, the trial court's decision should not be overturned unless the trial court's factual findings were capricious or against the weight of the evidence. [Citation omitted]

In support of its contention that a reasonable amount of time to accept the offer had lapsed, the University rehashes the same arguments we have already addressed. The University maintains, although it did not articulate explicitly a definite time limit for acceptance, it limited the duration of the offer through its words and body language. As we have already found such conduct would not put Dr. Yaros on notice of any event condition on the offer, we will not discuss it further.

The University also submits the seventy minutes Dr. Yaros took to accept the offer was unreasonable in light of the fact the offer occurred during trial. It maintains there is an urgency that accompanies a response when an offer is made during the course of trial, and in such a context the actual amount of minutes from offer to acceptance is irrelevant. In effect, the University maintains where an offer is made immediately before closing arguments it is unreasonable for the offer to stay open beyond the commencement of closings, which in this case occurred approximately ten minutes after the offer was made.

In this regard the University makes much of the trial court's finding that closing arguments are not significant trial court events, instead arguing that "academic research, the wisdom of modern trial practitioners and more than two thousand years of jurisprudential history" require us to vacate the trial court's order. The University's argument is misplaced because the trial court made its observation regarding the significance of closings to address the University's argument that a rejection could be inferred when Dr. Yaros participated in closings. Whether or not closing arguments are significant trial events does not support the University's contention that the occurrence of closing arguments automatically causes a settlement offer to lapse. There are many significant events during the course of a trial. Settlement offers are accepted at all stages of trial. Even assuming a closing argument is a significant trial event, such an occurrence does not necessarily determine whether an offeree accepted an offer within a reasonable period of time. It is but one consideration. Here, the trial court found the offer was accepted within a reasonable amount of time under the circumstances. We will not disturb that finding. Under the facts of this case, we cannot say the trial court erred in finding Dr. Yaros accepted the offer within a reasonable amount of time or such a finding was against the weight of the evidence. In conclusion, we find no abuse of discretion or error of law in the trial court's enforcement of the settlement.

Order affirmed.

Questions

1. Refer to Restatement Second section 36. Which manners of termination of the offer was the University arguing should apply?

2. How did the trial court determine that Dr. Yaros had not rejected the settlement offer?

Acceptance Varying Offer – Counter Offer – Mirror Image Rule

Smith v. Holmwood
California Court of Appeals, Third District, 1965
231 Cal.App.2d 549, 41 Cal.Rptr. 907

VAN DYKE, J. This is an appeal by defendant from a judgment in favor of plaintiffs. . . .

Holmwood, the defendant and appellant, owned 800 acres of land in the region of Lake Tahoe. He dealt with a real estate broker, one White, who in turn dealt with plaintiffs and respondents concerning the sale and purchase of the property. The dealings between the parties took the following form: Respondents gave to White for transmission to appellant a document dated November 16, 1958, entitled, "This Is An Offer" and signed by two of respondents as offerors. In material part the document read as follows: "The undersigned Ralph L. Smith, Glenn H. Millage and Nello Malerbi, Hereby Offer to Purchase from Loren Holmwood, on the following terms and conditions, the property [description].

"1. The purchase price shall be the sum of $250,000.00."

"2. The purchase price shall be paid as follows:"

"a. $1,000.00 cash to be paid upon the acceptance of the within offer. Said acceptance to be in writing by Loren Holmwood the owner."

"b. $4,000.00 cash to be paid to the owner within 30 days after the date of the acceptance of the within offer in writing by the owner.

"c. $25,000.00 cash to be paid to the owner on or before May 31, 1959."

"d. The balance of the purchase price shall be paid according to the terms of the promissory note to be executed by the offerors, a copy of which is attached to this offer and made a part hereof; said note to be secured by a deed of trust to be executed by the offerors, a copy of which is attached hereto and made a part hereof for all purposes."

The document contained many other provisions unnecessary here to relate.

White presented this offer to appellant on November 17. It was not accepted by him, although in almost all respects it was satisfactory. However, the written offer contained a provision that out of the 800 acres appellant reserved the right to select and have conveyed to him without consideration a parcel of two acres located in a certain area described in the offer. This was unsatisfactory to appellant because of the limited location. Appellant signed and delivered to White for communication to respondents a document reading as follows:

"Regarding offer from Ralph L. Smith, Glenn H. Millage and Nello Malerbi to Loren Holmwood, dated Nov. 16, 1958 and relative to 800 acres of land in Placer County, Calif., which is attached hereto and made a part hereof:"

"The Undersigned Loren Holmwood accepts the said offer subject to the following change:"

"Relative to item 6 of said offer. The seller reserves the right to select the two acres described in said item 6 at any place in the said section 23 except within 200 feet of the big spring."

"Other items of the original offer are acceptable."

/s/ Loren Holmwood"

This document contained in the left lower part the word "Accepted," below which appeared three signature lines--the names of the respondents being typed below the signature lines.

White transmitted the document signed by appellant to the respondents who signed it and gave it to White for transmission to appellant with a letter reading as follows:

"November 19, 1958."

"Ed. White,"

2616 J St.,

Sacramento, Calif.

Dear Sir:

This is to advise you that the offer dated Nov. 16, 1958, and your (representing Mr. Loren Holmwood) counter offer of Nov. 17, 1958, covering 800 acres more or less in Placer County, Calif., owned by Mr. Loren Holmwood, from Ralph Smith, Glenn Millage and Nello Malerbi has been accepted. Copies of properly signed documents will be forwarded to you under separate cover.""

White then wrote to appellant telling him that "Regarding offer of Ralph Smith, Glenn Millage and Nello Malerbi dated November 16, 1958 and your counter of November 17, 1958, ..."

"I am pleased to inform you that I have been advised, in writing, ... that your conditional acceptance of the original offer has been accepted by the offerors."

In the meantime appellant had consulted an attorney who on November 22, 1958, mailed to respondents a letter telling them that appellant had "rescinded" any contract that existed by reason of fraud in the procurement of the same. On December 12, 1958, the sum of $5,000 was tendered by respondents to appellant who refused the tender. Prior to that no money had been paid or tendered by respondents to appellant.

The parties are in agreement, and we think necessarily so, that the question of contract or none depends upon what was done prior to the letter from appellant's attorney to respondents. The trial court decided that the contract had arisen, notwithstanding no money had been paid, and decreed specific performance. We think this was error.

Respondents' offer to purchase was rejected by appellant when he offered to sell on different terms, the difference being his refusal to sell without modifying the provisions concerning the reserved two acres contained in the respondents' offer. It is familiar law that an offer to sell must be accepted precisely as made and that any qualifications insisted upon by the offeree amounts to a rejection of the offer and in a proper case the making of a counteroffer. The parties are agreed that appellant did refuse respondents' offer and did make a counteroffer of his own. Appellant claims this counteroffer was never accepted. Respondents claim that it was and the court so found. Appellant contends that in order to accept his counteroffer respondents had to pay the $1,000 as a material part of that acceptance. Respondents contend that the payment of the $1,000 was not necessary to acceptance but was merely a first payment of a purchase price agreed upon in the contract which was completed and went into effect when they, through White, notified appellant that they were accepting, or had accepted, his counteroffer. If the prescribed mode of acceptance of an offer to sell property requires the payment of a sum of money, the offer is not accepted unless the money be paid or tendered, and a simple notice of acceptance, however executed, unaccompanied by the payment of the prescribed sum amounts to no more than a counteroffer and does not give rise to a contract unless this counteroffer is in turn accepted by the first offeror. . . .

On the rule that acceptance must in every respect correspond with the offer before a contract results see generally . . . [Rest.2d § 58] 1 Williston on Contracts (3d ed.) section 73, page 238. From Williston we quote the following: "In order to make a bargain it is necessary that the acceptor shall give in return for the offeror's promise exactly the consideration which the offeror requests. If an act is requested, that very act and no other must be given."

The documents interchanged between the parties when read in connection with the acts hereinbefore described accomplished the following: Respondents offered to buy the property upon terms which required them to pay $1,000 cash to appellant "upon the acceptance" in writing of their offer. This offer appellant rejected and it no longer stood as an offer. Appellant then offered to sell, adopting, save for the modification he made, all the terms of respondents' previous offer. Thus he required on his part a written acceptance of his offer concurrently with the payment of $1,000 cash. The payment of this sum was an act "requested" and "that very act and no other" had to be given; otherwise no contract arose. There is no dispute concerning the facts insofar as material to the discussion here. The money was never paid nor even tendered until after the appellant's offer was revoked.

The judgment appealed from is reversed with directions to enter judgment for defendant.

PIERCE, P. J. I dissent. I would reverse the judgment with directions for a new trial. I agree, and it is elementary, that a binding bilateral contract exists only where there has been an offer and a communicated acceptance: and where the offer requires that a notification of an acceptance be accompanied by an act (e.g., payment of a sum of money) no contract comes into being unless and until both the notification and the act have been accomplished. On the other hand, if the parties so decide, no policy of the law prevents their agreement that a binding contract shall occur upon the communication of the acceptance of the offer and without payment of the first installment of the purchase price even though it be agreed that such payment is to follow promptly--as a contractual obligation of the buyer immediately after the communicated acceptance. Whether the case falls into the one category or the other depends upon the intent of the parties.

That was the question presented to the trial court and which is presented to us--what did the parties intend here?

In the answer of that question the rules by which courts are bound are these: If the agreement is in writing and the terms of the written instrument are clear, the parole evidence rule requires that the search for intent shall begin and end by giving effect to this language. If it is unclear, then resort may be had to parole evidence not to vary the terms of the instrument but to ascertain what the parties meant by what they said under the various guide rules prescribed for the interpretation of ambiguous writings. This is also Hornbook law.

Inquiry in this case centers upon the interpretation of the sentence: "The purchase price shall be paid as follows: a. *$1,000.00 cash to be paid upon the acceptance of the within offer.* Said acceptance to be in writing by Loren Holmwood the owner." (Italics supplied.) And in these sentences I would emphasize the word "upon."

Depending upon context the word "upon" when denoting time can mean either "before," "after," or "simultaneously with" the fact to which it relates. (67 C.J.S.

495, and cases cited.)

The majority opinion finds that as used here the meaning of the language used was too clear to admit interpretation. Had this statement been made in a seller's offer to a buyer, I would agree; and the cases cited in the majority opinion so hold either expressly or by inference. But here the statement quoted was not made originally in a seller's offer to a buyer. It was a proposal being made by buyers to a seller who was located at a place some distance away and since the offer was not accompanied by a payment of a thousand dollars as earnest money it was made with the knowledge that some period of time must elapse after the communicated acceptance of the offer before the thousand dollars payment could be made.

From this fact I draw the conclusion that, whatever the ultimate intent of the parties may have been, it was not the buyers' original intent that a binding contract would occur only when they, after the seller's notification of acceptance, delivered the thousand dollars to the seller. So to construe their intent would be to give them complete control over the inception of the contract. Under such a construction the buyers would have merely been taking a revocable option until the contract was brought into being by their sending a thousand dollars to the seller. That, to me, was clearly not their intent.

Reasonably construed, the buyers' offer obviously intended a binding contract as soon as the seller communicated his acceptance of the proposed terms with payment of a thousand dollars by the buyers to follow promptly thereafter as their obligation under the contract.

Did the asserted "conditional acceptance" of the buyers' offer (legally a counteroffer) incorporating by reference the buyers' expression of terms change this intent? Possibly, but, as I see it, not so clearly and unambiguously that resort may not be had to parole evidence to determine what the parties really intended.

There are factors present here which permit reasonable inference that when the seller replied to the offer he did not regard payment of the thousand dollars as the sine qua non of the contract's birth. In his letter of "conditional acceptance" the seller seems preoccupied with a new condition being imposed--the location of the 2 acres to be reserved. In fact, importance of the thousand dollars was not apparent in the seller's mind even after the buyers' acceptance of the counteroffer. Having received such acceptance, he consulted his attorney and it seems clear that both the seller and his attorney then considered that a contract existed because the latter, at the seller's instance, then wrote the buyers "rescinding" the contract--upon the ground of "fraud."

In summary, I consider the meaning of the word "upon" by a buyer in the context of this written instrument and its incorporation by reference in the seller's counteroffer sufficiently unclear to permit a trial court to receive parole evidence to determine the true intent of the parties. And I think that the case should be reversed for a new trial to permit determination of the parties' intent. . . .

Questions

1. What were the terms and conditions stated in the document dated November 16, 1958, offered by the respondents to the appellant?

2. How did the appellant respond to the offer made by the respondents?

3. What was the appellant's counteroffer, and how did the respondents indicate their acceptance?

4. According to the appellant, what was necessary for acceptance of his counteroffer to occur?

5. Was the payment of $1,000 cash a requirement for acceptance of the appellant's counteroffer? Why or why not?

Takeaways – Smith v. Holmwood

An acceptance must be absolute and unqualified. A qualified acceptance is a new proposal. (Rest.2d §§ 58 and 59; Cal.Civ.Code § 1585.) In other words, an acceptance, which adds qualifications or conditions or which in any way varies from the terms of the original offer, is treated as a rejection and counter offer. This is true no matter how trivial or insignificant the qualification or condition. This is known as the "Mirror Image Rule." A change in the terms set forth in the offer, or a conditional acceptance, is a rejection of the offer. Once an offer has been rejected, it cannot be accepted unless the person who made the offer remakes the offer following the rejection. A change in terms, or a conditional or qualified acceptance communicated to the person who made the original offer, is a counter offer. (Cal.Civ.Code § 1585) A counter offer may be accepted, rejected totally, or rejected by a further counter offer. A contract results only when an offer or a counter offer is absolutely and unconditionally accepted. As the following case demonstrates, this rigid rule of the common law has been relaxed with respect contracts for the sale of goods.

Abandonment of the Mirror Image Rule Under the UCC

Dorton v. Collins & Aikman Corp.
United States Court of Appeals
453 F.2d 1161 (1972)

CELEBREZZE, Circuit Judge.. . . . .The suit arose after a series of over 55 transactions during 1968, 1969, and 1970 in which Plaintiffs-Appellees [hereinafter The Carpet Mart], carpet retailers in Kingsport, Tennessee, purchased carpets from Defendant-Appellant [hereinafter Collins & Aikman]. . . . Collins & Aikman moved for a stay pending arbitration, asserting that The Carpet Mart was bound to an arbitration agreement which appeared on the reverse side of Collins & Aikman's printed sales acknowledgment forms. Holding that there existed no binding arbitration agreement between the parties, the District Court denied the stay. For the reasons set forth below, we remand the case to the District Court for further findings. . . .The primary question before us on appeal is whether the District Court, in denying Collins & Aikman's motion for a stay pending arbitration, erred in holding that The Carpet Mart was not bound by the arbitration agreement appearing on the back of Collins &

Aikman's acknowledgment forms. . . .

In each of the more than 55 transactions, one of the partners in The Carpet Mart, or, on some occasions, Collins & Aikman's visiting salesman, telephoned Collins & Aikman's order department in Dalton, Georgia, and ordered certain quantities of carpets listed in Collins & Aikman's catalogue. . . . After each oral order was placed, the price, if any, quoted by the buyer was checked against Collins & Aikman's price list, and the credit department was consulted to determine if The Carpet Mart had paid for all previous shipments. After it was found that everything was in order, Collins & Aikman's order department typed the information concerning the particular order on one of its printed acknowledgment forms. Each acknowledgment form bore one of three legends: "Acknowledgment," "Customer Acknowledgment," or "Sales Contract." The following provision was printed on the face of the forms bearing the "Acknowledgment" legend:

> "The acceptance of your order is subject to all of the terms and conditions on the face and reverse side hereof, including arbitration, all of which are accepted by buyer; it supersedes buyer's order form, if any. It shall become a contract either (a) when signed and delivered by buyer to seller and accepted in writing by seller, or (b) at Seller's option, when buyer shall have given to seller specification of assortments, delivery dates, shipping instructions, or instructions to bill and hold as to all or any part of the merchandise herein described, or when buyer has received delivery of the whole or any part thereof, or when buyer has otherwise assented to the terms and conditions hereof."

Similarly, on the face of the forms bearing the "Customer Acknowledgment" or "Sales Contract" legends the following provision appeared:

> "This order is given subject to all of the terms and conditions on the face and reverse side hereof, including the provisions for arbitration and the exclusion of warranties, all of which are accepted by Buyer, supersede Buyer's order form, if any, and constitute the entire contract between Buyer and Seller. This order shall become a contract as to the entire quantity specified either (a) when signed and delivered by Buyer to Seller and accepted in writing by Seller or (b) when Buyer has received and retained this order for ten days without objection, or (c) when Buyer has accepted delivery of any part of the merchandise specified herein or has furnished to Seller specifications or assortments, delivery dates, shipping instructions, or instructions to bill and hold, or when Buyer has otherwise indicated acceptance of the terms hereof."

The small print on the reverse side of the forms provided, among other things, that all claims arising out of the contract would be submitted to arbitration in New York City. Each acknowledgment form was signed by an employee of Collins & Aikman's order department and mailed to The Carpet Mart on the day the telephone order was received or, at the latest, on the following day. The carpets were thereafter shipped to The Carpet Mart, with the interval between the mailing of the acknowledgment form and shipment of the carpets varying from a brief interval to a period of several weeks or months. Absent a delay in the mails, however, The Carpet Mart always received the acknowledgment forms prior to receiving the carpets. In all cases The Carpet Mart took delivery of and paid for the carpets without objecting to any terms contained in the acknowledgment form.

In holding that no binding arbitration agreement was created between the parties through the transactions above, the District Court relied on [UCC § 2-207], ...

The District Court found that Subsection 2-207(3) controlled the instant case, quoting the following passage from 1 W. Hawkland, A Transactional Guide to the Uniform Commercial Code § 1.090303, at 19-20 (1964):

> "If the seller . . . ships the goods and the buyer accepts them, a contract is formed under subsection (3). The terms of this contract are those on which the purchase order and acknowledgment agree, and the additional terms needed for a contract are to be found throughout the U.C.C.
>
> . . . [T]he U.C.C. does not impose an arbitration term on the parties where their contract is silent on the matter. Hence, a conflict between an arbitration and an no-arbitration clause would result in the no-arbitration clause becoming effective."

Under this authority alone the District Court concluded that the arbitration clause on the back of Collins & Aikman's sales acknowledgment had not become a binding term in the 50-odd transactions with The Carpet Mart.

In reviewing this determination by the District Court, we are aware of the problems which courts have had in interpreting Section 2-207. This section of the UCC has been described as a "murky bit of prose," Southwest Engineering Co. v. Martin Tractor Co., 205 Kan. 684, 694, 473 P.2d 18, 25 (1970), as "not too happily drafted," Roto-Lith Ltd. v. F. P. Bartlett & Co., 297 F.2d 497, 500 (1st Cir. 1962), and as "one of the most important, subtle, and difficult in the entire Code, and well it may be said that the product as it finally reads is

not altogether satisfactory." Duesenberg & King, Sales and Bulk Transfers under the Uniform Commercial Code, (Vol. 3, Bender's Uniform Commercial Code Service) § 3.03, at 3-12 (1969). Despite the lack of clarity in its language, Section 2-207 manifests definite objectives which are significant in the present case.

As Official Comment No. 1 indicates, UCC § 2-207 was intended to apply to two situations:

"The one is where an agreement has been reached either orally or by informal correspondence between the parties and is followed by one or both of the parties sending formal acknowledgments or memoranda embodying the terms so far as agreed upon and adding terms not discussed. The other situation is one in which a wire or letter expressed and intended as the closing or confirmation of an agreement adds further minor suggestions or proposals such as `ship by Tuesday,' `rush,' `ship draft against bill of lading inspection allowed,' or the like." [UCC § 2-207], Official Comment 1.

Although Comment No. 1 is itself somewhat ambiguous, it is clear that Section 2-207, and specifically Subsection 2-207(1), was intended to alter the "ribbon matching" or "mirror" rule of common law, under which the terms of an acceptance or confirmation were required to be identical to the terms of the offer or oral agreement, respectively. 1 W. Hawkland, supra, at 16; R. Nordstrom, Handbook of the Law of Sales, Sec. 37, at 99-100 (1970). Under the common law, an acceptance or a confirmation which contained terms additional to or different from those of the offer or oral agreement constituted a rejection of the offer or agreement and thus became a counter-offer. The terms of the counter-offer were said to have been accepted by the original offeror when he proceeded to perform under the contract without objecting to the counter-offer. Thus, a buyer was deemed to have accepted the seller's counter-offer if he took receipt of the goods and paid for them without objection.

Under Section 2-207 the result is different. This section of the Code recognizes that in current commercial transactions, the terms of the offer and those of the acceptance will seldom be identical. Rather, under the current "battle of the forms," each party typically has a printed form drafted by his attorney and containing as many terms as could be envisioned to favor that party in his sales transactions. Whereas under common law the disparity between the fine-print terms in the parties' forms would have prevented the consummation of acontract when these forms are exchanged, Section 2-207 recognizes that in many, but not all, cases the parties do not impart such significance to the terms on the printed forms. See 1 W. Hawkland, supra; § 1.0903, at 14, § 1.090301, at 16. Subsection 2-207(1) therefore provides that "[a] definite and seasonable expression of acceptance or a written confirmation . . . operates as an acceptance even though it states terms additional to or different from those offered or agreed upon, unless acceptance is expressly made conditional on assent to the additional or different terms." Thus, under Subsection (1), a contract is recognized notwithstanding the fact that an acceptance or confirmation contains terms additional to or different from those of the offer or prior agreement, provided that the offeree's intent to accept the offer is definitely expressed, see Sections 2-204 and 2-206, and provided that the offeree's acceptance is not expressly conditioned on the offeror's assent to the additional or different terms. When a contract is recognized under Subsection (1), the additional terms are treated as "proposals for addition to the contract" under Subsection (2), which contains special provisions under which such additional terms are deemed to have been accepted when the transaction is between merchants. Conversely, when no contract is recognized under Subsection 2-207(1)—either because no definite expression of acceptance exists or, more specifically, because the offeree's acceptance is expressly conditioned on the offeror's assent to the additional or different terms—the entire transaction aborts at this point. If, however, the subsequent conduct of the parties—particularly, performance by both parties under what they apparently believe to be a contract—recognizes the existence of a contract, under Subsection 2-207(3) such conduct by both parties is sufficient to establish a contract, notwithstanding the fact that no contract would have been recognized on the basis of their writings alone. Subsection 2-207(3) further provides how the terms of contracts recognized thereunder shall be determined.

With the above analysis and purposes of Section 2-207 in mind, we turn to their application in the present case. We initially observe that the affidavits and the acknowledgment forms themselves raise the question of whether Collins & Aikman's forms constituted acceptances or confirmations under Section 2-207. The language of some of the acknowledgment forms ("The acceptance of your order is subject to . . .") and the affidavit of Mr. William T. Hester, Collins & Aikman's marketing operations manager, suggest that the forms were the only acceptances issued in response to The Carpet Mart's oral offers. However, in his affidavit Mr. J. A. Castle, a partner in The Carpet Mart, asserted that when he personally called Collins & Aikman to order carpets, someone from the latter's order department would agree to sell the requested carpets, or, alternatively, when Collins & Aikman's visiting salesman took the order, he would agree to the sale, on some occasions after he had used The Carpet Mart's telephone to call Collins & Aikman's order department. Absent the District Court's determination of whether Collins & Aikman's acknowledgment forms were acceptances or, alternatively, confirmations of prior oral agreements, we will consider the application of section 2-207 to both situations for the guidance of the District Court on remand.

Viewing Collins & Aikman's acknowledgment forms as acceptances under Subsection 2-207(1), we are initially faced with the question of whether the arbitration provision in Collins & Aikman's acknowledgment forms were in fact "additional to or different from" the terms of The Carpet Mart's oral offers. In the typical case under Section 2-207, there exist both a written purchase order and a written acknowledgment, and this determination can be readily made by comparing the two forms. In the present case, where the only written forms were Collins & Aikman's sales acknowledgments, we believe that such a comparison must be made between the oral offers and the written acceptances. Although the District Court apparently assumed that The Carpet Mart's oral orders did not include in their terms the arbitration provision which appeared in Collins & Aikman's acknowledgment forms, we believe that a specific finding on this point will be required on remand.

Assuming, for purposes of analysis, that the arbitration provision was an addition to the terms of The Carpet Mart's oral offers, we must next determine whether or not Collins & Aikman's acceptances were "expressly made conditional on assent to the additional . . . terms" therein, within the proviso of Subsection 2-207(1). As set forth in full above, the provision appearing on the face of Collins & Aikman's acknowledgment forms stated that the acceptances (or orders) were "subject to all of the terms and conditions on the face and reverse side hereof, including arbitration, all of which are accepted by buyer." The provision on the "Acknowledgment" forms further stated that Collins & Aikman's terms would become the basis of the contract between the parties "either (a) when signed and delivered by buyer to seller and accepted in writing by seller, or (b) at Seller's option, when buyer shall have given to seller specification of assortments, delivery dates, shipping instructions, or instructions to bill and hold as to all or any part of the merchandise herein described, or when buyer has received delivery of the whole or any part thereof, or when buyer has otherwise assented to the terms and conditions hereof."

Similarly, the provision on the "Customer Acknowledgment" and "Sales Contract" forms stated that the terms therein would become the basis of the contract "either (a) when signed and delivered by Buyer to Seller and accepted in writing by Seller or (b) when Buyer has received and retained this order for ten days without objection, or (c) when Buyer has accepted delivery of any part of the merchandise specified herein or has furnished to Seller specifications or assortments, delivery dates, shipping instructions to bill and hold, or when Buyer has otherwise indicated acceptance of the terms hereof."

Although Collins & Aikman's use of the words "subject to" suggests that the acceptances were conditional to some extent, . . . we believe that [the proviso] was intended to apply only to an acceptance which clearly reveals that the offeree is unwilling to proceed with the transaction unless he is assured of the offeror's assent to the additional or different terms therein. See 1 W. Hawkland, supra, § 1.090303, at 21. That the acceptance is predicated on the offeror's assent must be "directly and distinctly stated or expressed rather than implied or left to inference." Webster's Third International Dictionary (defining "express").

Although the UCC does not provide a definition of "assent," it is significant that Collins & Aikman's printed acknowledgment forms specified at least seven types of action or inaction on the part of the buyer which—sometimes at Collins & Aikman's option—would be deemed to bind the buyer to the terms therein. These ranged from the buyer's signing and delivering the acknowledgment to the seller—which indeed could have been recognized as the buyer's assent to Collins & Aikman's terms—to the buyer's retention of the acknowledgment for ten days without objection— which could never have been recognized as the buyer's assent to the additional or different terms where acceptance is expressly conditional on that assent.

To recognize Collins & Aikman's acceptances as "expressly conditional on [the buyer's] assent to the additional . . . terms" therein, within the proviso of Subsection 2-207(1), would thus require us to ignore the specific language of that provision. Such an interpretation is not justified in view of the fact that Subsection 2-207(1) is clearly designed to give legal recognition to many contracts where the variance between the offer and acceptance would have precluded such recognition at common law.

Because Collins & Aikman's acceptances were not expressly conditional on the buyer's assent to the additional terms within the proviso of Subsection 2-207(1), a contract is recognized under Subsection (1), and the additional terms are treated as "proposals" for addition to the contract under Subsection 2-207(2). Since both Collins & Aikman and The Carpet Mart are clearly "merchants" as that term is defined in Subsection 2-104(1), the arbitration provision will be deemed to have been accepted by The Carpet Mart under Subsection 2-207(2) unless it materially altered the terms of The Carpet Mart's oral offers. [UCC § 2-207(2) (b)]. We believe that the question of whether the arbitration provision materially altered the oral offer under Subsection 2-207(2) (b) is one which can be resolved only by the District Court on further findings of fact in the present case.[8] If the arbitration provision did in fact materially alter The Carpet Mart's offer, it could not become a part of the contract "unless expressly agreed to" by The Carpet Mart. [UCC § 2-207], Official Comment No. 3.

We therefore conclude that if on remand the District Court finds that Collins & Aikman's acknowledgments were in fact acceptances and that the arbitration provision was additional to the terms of The Carpet Mart's oral orders, contracts will be recognized under Subsection 2-207(1). The arbitration clause will then be viewed as a "proposal" under Subsection 2-207(2) which will be deemed to have been accepted by The Carpet Mart unless it materially altered the oral offers.

If the District Court finds that Collins & Aikman's acknowledgment forms were not acceptances but rather were confirmations of prior oral agreements between the parties, an application of Section 2-207 similar to that above will be required. Subsection 2-207(1) will require an initial determination of whether the arbitration provision in the confirmations was "additional to or different from" the terms orally agreed upon. Assuming that the District Court finds that the arbitration provision was not a term of the oral agreements between the parties, the arbitration clause will be treated as a "proposal" for addition to the contract under Subsection 2-207(2). . . . Regardless of whether the District Court finds Collins & Aikman's acknowledgment forms to have been acceptances or confirmations, if the arbitration provision was additional to, and a material alteration of, the offers or prior oral agreements, The Carpet Mart will not be bound to that provision absent a finding that it expressly agreed to be bound thereby. . . .

For the reasons set forth above, the case is remanded to the District Court for further findings consistent with this opinion.

Questions

1. What was the primary question before the appellate court in this case regarding the arbitration agreement?

2. How did the District Court interpret UCC § 2-207 in relation to the arbitration agreement?

3. What are the objectives of Section 2-207 of the UCC?

4. How does Subsection 2-207(1) of the UCC alter the common law "mirror" rule regarding acceptance and confirmation of terms?

5. How does Subsection 2-207(3) of the UCC determine the terms of contracts in cases where no contract is recognized under Subsection 2-207(1)?

Steiner v. Mobil Oil Corp.
Supreme Court of California, 1977
20 Cal.3d 90, 569 P.2d 751, 141 Cal.Rptr. 157

TOBRINER, J. In this case, over one year after apparently accepting plaintiff's offer, the Mobil Oil Corporation sought to impose upon plaintiff the very contractual terms which plaintiff expressly rejected in his offer. As justification for its conduct, Mobil asserted that the crucial provision of plaintiff's offer was lost in the labyrinth of the Mobil bureaucracy, and thus that Mobil decision-makers had no opportunity to pass on plaintiff's offer as such. [1a] As we shall see, however, the trial court correctly concluded that section 2207 of the California Uniform Commercial Code bars Mobil from in this way converting its own error into plaintiff's misfortune.

Section 2207, subdivision (1), provides that parties may form an agreement, even if the terms of offer and acceptance do not entirely converge, if the offeree gives a definite expression of acceptance, and if the terms of acceptance do not explicitly condition agreement upon the offeror's consent to the offeree's new proposed terms. In this case, as the trial court found, defendant Mobil did not condition its acceptance of plaintiff's offer upon plaintiff's agreement to Mobil's alteration of plaintiff's offer and thus a contract was formed. Section 2207, subdivision (2), provides in turn that, if the terms of the offer and acceptance differ, the terms of the offer become part of a contract between merchants if the offer expressly limits acceptance to its own terms, or if the varying terms of the acceptance materially alter the terms of the offer. As the trial court found, under either of these clauses, the terms of Steiner's offer must prevail, because Steiner's offer was expressly conditional upon Mobil's agreement to provide a guaranteed discount, and Mobil's substitution of a discount terminable at its discretion materially affected Steiner's interests.

Accordingly, the trial court did not err in granting judgment for plaintiff, and we shall thus affirm its judgment.

1. The facts in this case

Defendant Mobil Oil Corporation, in appealing from a judgment for plaintiff Steiner, does not challenge the facts as found by the trial court, but rather confines itself to an attack on the trial court's conclusions of law. The facts in this case, thus, are not in dispute.

Joseph R. Steiner is an independent service station operator. He purchases the gasoline which he sells from Mobil, but, except for any incidental rights which the gasoline contract confers, Mobil owns no interest in Steiner's property.

In 1971, the third party who leased the service station property to Steiner informed him that the property was for sale. Steiner contacted Mobil sales representative Tony Montemarano. Montemarano informed Steiner that Mobil would not purchase the property, but that Mobil was interested in assisting Steiner in making the purchase.

Thereafter, Steiner entered into extended negotiations with J. S. Chenen, Mobil's area manager and Montemarano's superior. Steiner and Chenen agreed that Mobil would supply the down payment on the property, amounting to $30,000. In return, Steiner would enter into a 10-year contract with Mobil. The contract would treat the cash advance as a prepaid competitive allowance, to be amortized over the 10-year period through Steiner's purchase of 5.8 million gallons of gasoline.

The negotiations did not terminate with the agreement concerning the down payment. Steiner had concluded that he would not be able to do business successfully if he were compelled to purchase gasoline from Mobil at the standard tank wagon price. As the trial court found, Steiner told Chenen that he, Steiner, "needed a firm competitive allowance for the length of his distributor's agreement to make his cash flow adequate to meet the payments on the property." Steiner and Chenen agreed that a satisfactory arrangement with Mobil would include not only the $30,000 prepaid competitive allowance, but also a further competitive allowance reducing Mobil's tank wagon price by 1.4 cents per gallon. Mobil would also supply Steiner with $3,000 worth of improvements.

As Chenen made clear to Steiner, neither Chenen nor his immediate supervisor, district manager D. L. Dalbec, possessed the authority to accept the negotiated terms on Mobil's behalf. The negotiations therefore did not culminate in an agreement as such but rather in a proposal to be submitted to R. D. Pfaff, the division general manager, who did possess authority to agree to the proposal on Mobil's behalf.

Moreover, the proposal did not take the form of a documented single contract. Chenen and Steiner utilized a series of standard Mobil forms in putting together the proposal, modifying the forms where necessary. Steiner signed those of the forms, such as the basic retail dealer contract, which required his signature. The package of documents which comprised the proposal, therefore, needed only Pfaff's approval to become effective.

Near the close of the process of negotiating and assembling the proposal, Steiner obtained a copy of the standard Mobil form which would embody the 1.4 cents per gallon competitive allowance. This form, which did not require Steiner's signature, stated: "This allowance may be changed or discontinued by us at any time upon notice to you in writing ...." Upon receipt of the form Steiner immediately contacted Chenen by telephone, told Chenen that he would not go ahead with the deal if Mobil could revoke the competitive allowance at any time, and demanded assurances that no such revocation would occur.

In order to placate Steiner, Chenen, after consultation and authorization from Dalbec, sent Steiner a letter, dated December 2, 1971, which declared "[¶] The ten year Retail Dealer Contract dated December 15, 1971, effective January 1, 1972, is signed by you on the basis that Mobil grant a $30,000 Prepaid Competitive Allowance, and a $.014 Competitive Allowance at time of delivery. [¶] If Mobil management does not accept in full the above conditions outlined in your competitive offer, the above mentioned contract will be void."

The trial court found that "Chenen was authorized by Mobil to write the letter" to Steiner. Moreover, as the trial court also found, because of the letter, "through ... Chenen and Dalbec Mobil had both knowledge and notice" of Steiner's demand for a guaranteed competitive allowance. "Mobil had reason to know that the transaction and agreement would be materially affected and that plaintiff would not enter therein if [the guaranteed discount] term was not part of the 'package.'" The trial court further concluded that, for Chenen and Dalbec, the transmission of Steiner's offer to division general manager Pfaff "was part of their regular duties" and thus that Chenen and Dalbec "were obligated, in the exercise of good faith and ordinary care and diligence, to communicate the substance of plaintiff's [offer] to Pfaff."

In fact, however, Chenen and Dalbec did not transmit to Pfaff the letter which Chenen had sent to Steiner; Mobil's copy of that letter remained in the district office files. In preparing the proposal for submission to Pfaff, Chenen and Dalbec assembled a package which included the various documents that Steiner had executed, the standard form providing the revocable 1.4 cents per gallon competitive allowance, and various memoranda explaining the advantages of the deal for Mobil. Early in 1972, several months after Chenen and Dalbec had transmitted the proposal to him, Pfaff approved it as submitted.

Chenen informed Steiner of Pfaff's approval by telephone. Steiner had called Chenen to find out what was happening with the proposal which they had negotiated. Chenen told Steiner that Mobil had a check for him, and that the next thing for Steiner to do was to open an escrow account and proceed with the purchase of the property.

Subsequently, Montemarano delivered to Steiner at his service station a manila folder containing the documents approved by Pfaff. These documents, the trial court found, were "numerous and complex in nature." Nonetheless, there was no cover letter describing the contents of the folder. Although the folder included Mobil's standard competitive allowance form, with its clause providing for revocation at will, Montemarano did not call this fact to Steiner's attention.

Thus, as the trial court found, at no time after Chenen sent Steiner the December 2 letter "did Mobil advise [Steiner] that a non-cancelable allowance would not be part of the agreement." Moreover, Steiner "did not at any time reread all of the documents delivered to him by Mobil, particularly the form letter ... setting forth the provision regarding the 1.4 cents per gallon competitive allowance being cancelable." Mobil did not "specifically bring" to Steiner's attention "the statements made in the form letter ... concerning the cancelable condition of the competitive allowance."

By April 1972, Steiner had completed the process of acquiring the service station property. Beginning in March, Mobil afforded Steiner the benefit of the 1.4

cents per gallon competitive allowance in billing him for gasoline and continued to do so until the summer of 1973. On July 16, 1973, Chenen informed Steiner by letter that, in accordance with the provisions of Mobil's notice of competitive allowance, Mobil would reduce Steiner's discount to 0.5 cents per gallon as of August 1, 1973.

Steiner brought this suit in the Los Angeles County Superior Court, seeking declaratory and monetary relief. The trial court, sitting without a jury, found that Mobil "had reason to know" that Steiner would not enter into an agreement unless Mobil agreed that he "was to have a non-cancelable ... competitive allowance ... to run as long as the distributor agreement was in force." Moreover, the trial court found, in returning the package of documents to Steiner, "Mobil intended to make a contract, not to make a counter offer." The trial court concluded that "in the exercise of good faith and reasonable care and diligence Mobil was required to specifically bring to the attention of plaintiff the statements made in the form letter sent by Dalbec concerning the cancelable condition of the competitive allowance."

The trial court ruled that, under California Uniform Commercial Code section 2207, Mobil had entered into a contract with Steiner which guaranteed Steiner a 1.4 cents per gallon discount for 10 years. "Mobil made a definite and seasonable expression of acceptance of plaintiff's offer, although its reply contained a material term different from that offer." Moreover, "[i]n accepting plaintiff's offer Mobil did not either orally or in writing expressly condition its acceptance upon plaintiff's assent to the different terms as to the competitive allowance in Mobil's acceptance." The trial court granted Steiner a declaratory judgment to that effect, and awarded Steiner damages of $4,953.63. Mobil appeals the trial court's judgment.

2. Under California Uniform Commercial Code section 2207, Steiner's contract with Mobil grants Steiner a 1.4 cents per gallon discount for the duration of the contract.

Neither Mobil nor Steiner disputes the trial court's conclusion that the sales provisions of the California Uniform Commercial Code apply in this case. Moreover, Mobil and Steiner do not challenge the trial court's conclusion that the outcome of this case turns on the applicability of section 2207. As we shall see, the relevant provisions of that statute confirm the trial court's conclusion that Mobil breached its agreement with Steiner when it unilaterally reduced Steiner's competitive discount. Initially, we shall identify the considerations which underlie section 2207 and thus structure our interpretation of the statute. Thereafter, we shall proceed to the application of section 2207 itself.

Under traditional common law, no contract was reached if the terms of the offer and the acceptance varied. "In order to make a bargain it is necessary that the acceptor shall give in return for the offeror's promise exactly the consideration which the offeror requests." (1 Williston, The Law of Contracts (1st ed. 1920) § 73, p. 128.)

This "mirror image" rule of offer and acceptance was plainly both unfair and unrealistic in the commercial context. "The fact that the parties did intend a contract to be formed and both had a reasonable commercial understanding that the deal was closed, is ignored." (Murray, Intention Over Terms: An Exploration of UCC 2-207 and New Section 60, Restatement of Contracts (1969) 37 Fordham L.Rev. 317, 319.)

Section 2207 rejects the "mirror image" rule. (See e.g., Roto-Lith, Ltd. v. F. P. Bartlett & Co. (1st Cir. 1962) 297 F.2d 497, 500.) "This section of the Code recognizes that in current commercial transactions, the terms of the offer and those of the acceptance will seldom be identical." (*Dorton v. Collins & Aikman Corp.* (6th Cir. 1972) 453 F.2d 1161, 1166.)

Under section 2207, for example, the parties may conclude a contract despite the fact that, after reaching accord, they exchanged forms which purport to memorialize the agreement, but which differ because each party has drafted his form "to give him advantage." (White & Summers, Uniform Commercial Code (1972) p. 23; see, e.g., Rite Fabrics, Inc. v. Stafford-Higgins Co., Inc. (S.D.N.Y. 1973) 366 F.Supp. 1.) Similarly, the parties may form a contract even if the terms of offer and acceptance differ because one or the other party, in stating its initial position, relies upon "forms drafted to cover the majority of [its] transactions in a uniform, standard manner" (Duesenberg & King, Sales and Bulk Transfers under the Uniform Commercial Code (1976) § 3.02, p. 3-9), and subsequently fails to amend its form to reflect the deal which the other party claims was actually negotiated. (See, e.g., Ebasco Services Inc. v. Pennsylvania Power & L. Co. (E.D.Pa. 1975) 402 F. Supp. 421, 434-435.)

In place of the "mirror image" rule, section 2207 inquires as to whether the parties intended to complete an agreement: "Under this Article a proposed deal which in commercial understanding has in fact been closed is recognized as a contract." (§ 2207, Cal. U. Com. Code, com. 2.) If the parties intend to contract, but the terms of their offer and acceptance differ, section 2207 authorizes a court to determine which terms are part of the contract, either by reference to the parties' own dealings (see § 2207, subds. (1), (2)), or by reference to other provisions of the code. (See § 2207, subd. (3).)

Section 2207 is thus of a piece with other recent developments in contract law. Instead of fastening upon abstract doctrinal concepts like offer and acceptance, section 2207 looks to the actual dealings of the parties and gives legal effect to that conduct. Much as adhesion contract analysis teaches us not to enforce contracts until we look behind the facade of the formalistic standardized agreement in order to determine whether any inequality of bargaining power between the parties renders contractual terms unconscionable, or causes the contract to be interpreted against the more powerful party, section 2207 instructs us not to refuse to enforce contracts until we look below the surface of the parties' disagreement as to contract terms and determine whether the parties undertook to close their deal. Section 2207 requires courts to put aside the formal and academic stereotypes of traditional doctrine of offer and acceptance and to analyze instead what really happens. In this spirit, we turn to the application of section 2207 in this case.

Section 2207, subdivision (1), provides: "A definite and seasonable expression of acceptance or a written confirmation which is sent within a reasonable time operates as an acceptance even though it states terms additional or different from those offered or agreed upon, unless acceptance is expressly made conditional on assent to the additional or different terms."

In this case, as the trial court found, Mobil provided "[a] definite and seasonable expression of acceptance." Steiner offered to enter into a 10-year dealer contract with Mobil only if Mobil, among other things, agreed to advance Steiner $30,000, and to give Steiner a 1.4 cents per gallon competitive discount on the price of Mobil gasoline for the duration of the contract. When Steiner telephoned Chenen, Mobil's employee, to inquire as to the fate of Steiner's offer, Chenen told Steiner that Mobil had a check for him, that he should open an escrow account, and that he should go ahead with the purchase of the service station property -- in context a clear statement that Mobil had approved the deal.

Moreover, through Montemarano, another Mobil employee, Mobil returned to Steiner various executed documents in an envelope unaccompanied by any cover. The documents provided written confirmation of the deal. The fact that Mobil returned the documents without in any way calling Steiner's attention to them is further evidence that Mobil regarded the process of negotiation as over and the deal as complete.

As the trial court also found, Mobil did not in any way make its acceptance "expressly ... conditional" on Steiner's "assent to the additional or different terms." Chenen, in telling Steiner to go ahead with the purchase, did not suggest that Mobil had conditioned its acceptance. In returning the executed documents, Mobil enclosed no cover letter; again, it did not use the occasion in any way to condition expressly its acceptance.

Thus, neither of the restrictions which limit section 2207, subdivision (1)'s application are relevant in this case. Despite the fact that the terms of Mobil's acceptance departed partially from the terms of Steiner's offer, Mobil and Steiner did form a contract. To determine the terms of this contract, we turn to section 2207, subdivision (2).

Section 2207, subdivision (2), provides: "... additional terms are to be construed as proposals for addition to the contract. Between merchants such terms become part of the contract unless: [¶] (a) The offer expressly limits acceptance to the terms of the offer; [¶] (b) They materially alter it; or [¶] (c) Notification of objection to them has already been given or is given within a reasonable time after notice of them is received."

Under section 2207, subdivision (2), Mobil's revocable discount provision does not become part of the agreement between Steiner and Mobil. In order to become part of the agreement, Mobil's provision must not fall within any of the categories defined by section 2207, subdivision (2), subsections (a), (b), and (c). Mobil's term, however, clearly comes within subsections (a) and (b).

Subsection (a) provides that no additional term can become part of the agreement if Steiner's offer "expressly limit[ed] acceptance to the terms of the offer." (§ 2207, subd. (2)(a).) Mobil concedes that Steiner's offer provided that the competitive allowance of 1.4 cents per gallon would run for the full length of the 10-year dealer contract. Chenen's December 2 letter to Steiner explicitly acknowledges Mobil's awareness that "[i]f Mobil management does not accept in full the above conditions outlined in your competitive offer, the above mentioned contract is void."

Moreover, Mobil's acceptance falls within subsection (b) since without question the acceptance "materially alter[ed]" the terms of Steiner's offer. (See § 2207, subd. (2)(b).) The Uniform Commercial Code comment notes that a variation is material if it would "result in surprise or hardship if incorporated without express awareness by the other party. ..." (§ 2-207, U. Com. Code, com. 4.) Here, Steiner clearly indicated to Mobil in the course of the negotiations that, without the 1.4 cents per gallon discount, he could not economically operate the service station. Mobil's alteration, therefore, amended the terms of the offer to Steiner's significant detriment; accordingly, the alteration was necessarily "material."

To reiterate, subsections (a), (b), and (c) of section 2207, subdivision (2), operate in the alternative. If any one of the three subsections applies, the variant terms of an acceptance do not become part of an agreement. Here, as we have seen, the provisions of both subsections (a) and (b) are met. Mobil's declaration that the 1.4 cents per gallon discount was terminable at Mobil's discretion did not become part of the contract. Instead, Steiner and Mobil formed a contract incorporating the terms of Steiner's offer: Under this contract, Steiner was guaranteed a 1.4 cents per gallon discount throughout the 10-year period of the dealer contract.

Thus, on their face, subdivisions (1) and (2) of section 2207 confirm the trial court's conclusion that Mobil breached its agreement with Steiner. We now turn to Mobil's opposing argument that we should adopt an interpretation of section 2207 which conflicts with the trial court's conclusion.

3. Contrary to Mobil's argument, California Uniform Commercial Code sections 2204 and 2207 do not incorporate the traditional rule that parties to a

contract must mutually assent to all essential terms.

We set forth Mobil's contentions, which, although elaborately developed, can be simply stated. Section 2207 does not apply if the general contract formation rules of section 2204 are not met. Section 2204 does not change the traditional rule that, in order to create an enforceable contract, the parties must mutually assent to all essential terms of the supposed agreement. In order to square section 2207 with section 2204, Mobil argues, we must construe section 2207, subdivision (1), to provide that there is no "definite" acceptance unless the parties agree to all essential terms. Moreover, Mobil contends, we must also hold that, under the same section, an acceptance which alters an essential term of an offer is an acceptance "expressly made conditional on assent" to the variant term. Finally, Mobil concludes that, since its acceptance, in changing the duration of the discount, modified an essential term of Steiner's offer, i.e., price, we must find that Steiner cannot claim a continued discount.

As we shall explain, Mobil's arguments do not survive scrutiny. The official comments accompanying section 2204, other provisions of the code, and the case law interpreting section 2204, all support the conclusion that section 2204 does not require mutual assent to all essential terms. Mobil's interpretations of the definite agreement and conditional acceptance provisions of section 2207, subdivision (1), likewise conflict with other subdivisions of section 2207.

a. California Uniform Commercial Code section 2204 does not incorporate the traditional requirement of mutual assent to all essential terms.

Section 2204 incorporates three subdivisions. The third of these subdivisions directly refutes Mobil's claims. "Even though one or more terms are left open a contract for sale does not fail for indefiniteness if the parties have intended to make a contract and there is a reasonably certain basis for giving an appropriate remedy." (§ 2204, subd. (3).)

Section 2204, subdivision (3), does not, by its terms, require parties to a contract to assent to all essential terms. Instead, this provision states that a court, if it is to enforce a contract, must first make two findings. Initially, the court must find some basis for concluding that the parties engaged in a process of offer and acceptance, rather than inconclusive negotiations. Second, the court must find that it possesses sufficient information about the parties' incomplete transaction to apply the provisions of the California Uniform Commercial Code which fill in the gaps in parties' contracts. As we have already seen, both of these minimal requirements are met in this case: the parties did not engage in inconclusive negotiations, and section 2207 readily fills in the terms of their contract.

To overcome the literal language of section 2204, subdivision (2), Mobil argues that the traditional requirement of "a meeting of the minds upon the essential features of the agreement" (Ellis v. Klaff (1950) 96 Cal.App.2d 471, 478 [216 P.2d 15]; see Roffinella v. Roffinella (1923) 191 Cal. 753, 758 [218 P. 397]) is so fundamental that the code could not conceivably have rejected it. The California code comment, however, explicitly states: "'[A] meeting of the minds on the essential features of the agreement' is not required. ...." (§ 2204, com. 2.)

Other code provisions sustain the comment's view. As we have already pointed out, section 2207, subdivision (2)(b), expressly acknowledges the possibility that parties may reach a contract without agreeing to all "material" terms. Mobil does not attempt to distinguish "material" from "essential" terms; in any event, we do not think that it could successfully do so. Section 2305, subdivision (1), provides an even more dramatic refutation of Mobil's argument. As we have noted, Mobil treats price as an "essential" term. Nonetheless, this section states: "The parties if they so intend can conclude a contract for sale even though the price is not settled." (§ 2305, subd. (1).)

The case law interpreting section 2204 reinforces the interpretation offered by the code comment and the implication of other code provisions: the rules of contract formation under the California Uniform Commercial Code do not include the principle that the parties must agree to all essential terms in order to form a contract. Courts have held that, under section 2204, subdivision (3), parties may form a contract even though they do not agree as to the terms of payment (Southwest Engineering Co. v. Martin Tractor Co. (1970) 205 Kan. 684 [473 P.2d 18, 23-24]), the time or place for performance (Taunton v. Allenberg Cotton Company, Inc. (M.D.Ga. 1973) 378 F.Supp. 34, 39), or the quantity of the goods sold (City of Louisville v. Rockwell Manufacturing Co. (6th Cir. 1973) 482 F.2d 159, 164) -- all terms which might appear to be "essential" to an agreement.

More significantly, in view of Mobil's emphasis on the essential character of price terms, a number of courts have held that, under section 2204, subdivision (3), the parties may frame a contract without fully agreeing as to price. (See, e.g., Alter & Sons, Inc. v. United Engineers & Constructors, Inc. (S.D.Ill. 1973) 366 F.Supp. 959, 965; J. W. Knapp Co. v. Sinas (1969) 19 Mich.App. 427 [172 N.W.2d 867, 869]; see also Oskey Gasoline and Oil Company, Inc. v. OKC Refining Inc., supra, 364 F.Supp. 1137, 1144.) Concededly, one court has suggested in dictum that section 2204, subdivision (3), incorporates the requirement of assent to essential terms. (See Blackhawk Heat. & P. Co., Inc. v. Data Lease Fin. Corp. (Fla. 1974) 302 So.2d 404, 408.) We think, however, that the Delaware Supreme Court stated the prevailing view: "[T]he omission of even an important term does not prevent the finding under [section 2204, subdivision (3)] that the parties intended to make a contract." (Pennsylvania Co. v. Wilmington Trust Co. (1960) 39 Del.Ch. 453, 463 [166 A.2d 726].)

b. California Uniform Commercial Code section 2207, subdivision (1), should not be narrowly read to conform to the principle of mutual assent to all essential terms.

As we have seen, section 2204 quite clearly does not incorporate the rule that parties must mutually assent to all essential terms. Mobil has thus failed to establish the premise that it would postulate as justifying a narrow reading of section 2207, subdivision (1). We shall, however, briefly consider Mobil's other and further arguments concerning the construction of section 2207, and show that these arguments, taken in isolation, are consistent neither with the language of section 2207, subdivision (1), nor with the logic of section 2207 as a whole.

Initially, Mobil focuses on section 2207, subdivision (1)'s requirement of a "definite ... expression of acceptance." Mobil would define "definite" by reference to the extent of the difference between offer and acceptance: the more significant the divergence, the less definitely a response is an acceptance. This construction suffers from two flaws. First, in section 2207, subdivision (1), "definite" modifies "expression" and not "acceptance," and thus refers to the process of offer and acceptance and not to the terms of the acceptance itself. Second, in any event, section 2207 as a whole bars any interpretation of "definite" which, as Mobil urges, would exclude from the ranks of acceptances all but collateral variations on the terms of offers. Section 2207, subdivision (2)(b)'s concern with material variations necessarily implies that acceptances incorporating such variations can satisfy the requirements of subdivision (1).

Mobil would also construe the final clause of section 2207, subdivision (1), which provides that, if acceptance "is expressly made conditional on assent to ... additional or different terms," the "acceptance" does not operate as an acceptance but as a counteroffer. Specifically Mobil argues that we should read this provision broadly, by adopting the interpretation advanced in Roto-Lith, Ltd. v. F. P. Bartlett & Co., supra, 297 F.2d at page 500: "a response which states a condition materially altering the obligation solely to the disadvantage of the offeror is an 'acceptance ... expressly ... conditional on assent to the additional ... terms.'"

Again, however, Mobil's construction does not accord with the language of the section. Such an interpretation of the conditional acceptance clause would transform acceptances into counteroffers without regard to whether the acceptance is in fact, as section 2207, subdivision (1), requires, "expressly made conditional on assent to ... additional or different terms." Moreover, under Mobil's reading, the conditional acceptance clause of section 2207, subdivision (1), would largely duplicate the function of the material variation clause of section 2207, subdivision (2)(b).

As Mobil concedes, courts and commentators alike have repeatedly criticized the *Roto-Lith* interpretation of section 2207, subdivision (1). (See, e.g., *Dorton v. Collins*

& *Aikman Corp.*, supra, 453 F.2d at p. 1168 & fn. 5; Duesenberg & King, supra, § 3.04 [1], pp. 3-40 to 3-49; 76 Harv.L.Rev. (1963) 1481.) Most courts have rejected *Roto-Lith*, and have instead interpreted the conditional acceptance clause literally, as we did earlier. (See *Ebasco Services Inc. v. Pennsylvania Power & L. Co.*, supra, 402 F.Supp. at pp. 437-438.) Recognizing the superiority of the majority view, we reject Mobil's attempt to advance the Roto-Lith interpretation of section 2207, subdivision (1).

4. Conclusion.

In this case, as we have seen, the trial court correctly concluded that under section 2207 the guaranteed discount included in the terms of Steiner's offer, and not Mobil's standard revocable discount provision, became part of the agreement between Mobil and Steiner. Mobil cannot assert as a defense the failure of its own bureaucracy to respond to, or even fully recognize, Steiner's efforts to modify the standard Mobil dealer contract. The judgment is affirmed.

Questions

1. According to UCC § 2-207, what is the purpose of the statute in relation to contract formation?

2. Under UCC § 2-207, how does the statute handle situations where the terms of the offer and acceptance differ?

3. In this case, how did the trial court interpret UCC § 2-207 in relation to the contract between Steiner and Mobil?

4. According to the court's ruling, what obligation did Mobil have in regards to communicating the terms of the agreement to Steiner?

Takeaways – Dorton & Steiner

An exception to the common law mirror image rule exists in the context of contracts for the sale of goods.

Pursuant to section 2-207, a definite and seasonable expression of acceptance operates as an acceptance, in spite of the fact that it contains additional or different terms. Additional terms are treated as *proposals* for addition to the contract. The additional terms do not become part of the contract without further assent of the parties. However, if both parties to the contract are "merchants," as defined by UCC § 2-104, then the additional terms become part of the contract, unless, (1) the terms of the offer limited acceptance to the original terms; (2) the additional terms materially alter the contract or; (3) timely notice of objection is given to the additional terms.

So why, you may ask, relax the mirror image rule? As the *Steiner* court points out, section 2-207 recognizes that in current commercial transactions, the terms of the offer and those of the acceptance will seldom be identical. If the mirror image rule were retained for transactions involving the sale of goods, contracts would still be formed but always on the terms of the last counter-offer. 2-207 changes that by permitting a contract to be formed on the terms of the original offer along with any additional terms contained in the confirmatory memo or the expression of acceptance so long as those terms are more or less harmless.

Even if the writings of the parties are not sufficient to form a contract, conduct of the parties that recognizes the existence of a contract will be sufficient to bind the parties to a contract. In such a case, the terms of the contract are those terms on which the writings of the parties agree, together with the relevant "gap-filler" provisions of the UCC. "Gap filler" provisions are default rules that the UCC implicates when parties fail to settle on a particular contract term. (See, e.g. UCC § 2-305 [open price term].)

UCC § 2-207 rejects the common law mirror image rule and converts many common law counteroffers into acceptances. A document may be an acceptance under 2-207(1) and yet differ substantially from the offer. 2-207(2)(b) provides that a contract can be formed under 2-207(1) even though the acceptance includes a term that "materially alters" the offer. (See, *Dorton v. Collins & Aikman Corp.* 453 F2d 1161 (1972).)

The question of the relevance of the distinction between "additional" and "different" terms has become a matter of some controversy among courts and commentators. Section 2-207, subdivision (1) refers to acceptances in which terms are either "additional to or different from" the terms of an offer. Section 2-207, subdivision (2), however, expressly concerns itself with only "additional terms." Noting this difference, several courts and commentators have concluded that section 2-207, subdivision (2) applies if an acceptance adds terms to an offer, but does not apply if an acceptance alters the terms of an offer. (See, e.g., *American Parts Co., Inc. v. American Arbitration Ass'n* (1967) 8 Mich.App. 156 [154 N.W.2d 5, 11].) Other courts and commentators, however, suggest that section 2-207, subdivision (2) applies without regard to whether the varying terms of an acceptance differ from or add to an offer. (See, e.g., *Ebasco Services Inc. v. Pennsylvania Power & L. Co.*, 402 F.Supp. 421, 440 & fn. 27; Comment, Section 2-207 of the Uniform Commercial Code -- New Rules for the "Battle of the Forms" (1971) 32 U.Pitt.L.Rev. 209, 211.)

In *Steiner, supra,* The Supreme Court concluded that the applicability of section 2-207, subdivision (2) should not turn upon a characterization of the varying terms of an acceptance as "additional" or "different." First, Uniform Commercial Code comment 3 specifically states that "[w]hether or not additional or different terms will become part of the agreement depends upon the provisions of subsection (2)." (See also UCC com. 2.) Second, the distinction between "additional" and "different" terms is ambiguous. Since an offer's silence with respect to a particular issue may indicate an intention to adopt the code's gap-filling provisions, even an acceptance of a term which at first glance appears to be plainly "additional" is at least arguably "different." (See *Air Products & Chem., Inc. v. Fairbanks Morse, Inc.* (1973) 58 Wis.2d 193 [206 N.W.2d 414, 424].) Third, the distinction between additional and different terms serves no clear purpose. If additional and different terms are treated alike for purposes of section 2-207, subdivision (2), an offeror does not, as some contend, lose "the ability to retain control over the terms of his offer." (*Duesenberg & King*, supra, at p. 3-37.) Under section 2-207, subdivision (2), if the offeror wishes to retain such control, he may do so by framing his offer so that it "expressly limits acceptance to the terms of the offer. ..." (§ 2-207, subd. (2)(a).) (Footnote 5 of *Steiner* opinion.)

Option Contracts

As you have seen, the offeror has the power to revoke or withdraw an offer anytime prior to acceptance. But suppose the offeror promises not to withdraw or revoke? E.g., "I'll give you until next Friday to make up your mind." An option contract is a promise not to withdraw or revoke an offer for a stated period of time. However, unless separate consideration is given in exchange for the promise not to revoke or withdraw the offer, the promise is merely a gratuitous promise and unenforceable. (Rest.2d § 87.) Under the California rule, the holder of a formal option loses the right to exercise it once it has communicated a formal rejection, and this is so even though the purported exercise occurs within the time specified in the option agreement. (*Landberg v. Landberg* (1972) 24 Cal.App.3d 742, 757 [101 Cal.Rptr. 335].)

Marsh v. Lott
Court of Appeals of California, Second District, 1908
8 Cal.App. 384, 97 P. 163

SHAW, J. Action for specific performance of a contract, whereby plaintiff asserts that in consideration of 25 cents he was given an option to purchase, for the sum of $100,000, certain real estate owned by defendant. Judgment was rendered for defendant. Plaintiff appeals from the judgment, and from an order denying his motion for a new trial.

The contract, specific performance of which is sought, is as follows: "For and in consideration of the sum of twenty-five cents to me in hand paid, I hereby give Robt. Marsh & Co. an option to purchase, at any time up to and including June 1st,

1905, with privilege of 30 days extension, from date hereof, the following described property, to wit: South 1/2 of lot 9 & all of lot 8, block 101, Bellevue Terrace tract, and all of the property owned by myself in above block, for the sum of one hundred thousand dollars, payable thirty thousand cash, balance on or before 4 years, 4 1/2 % net. I agree to furnish an unlimited certificate of title showing said property to be free from all encumbrance, and to convey the same in such condition by deed of grant, bargain and sale, & pay regular commission. M.A. Lott. [Seal.] Date: Feb. 25th, 1905. Property: 90x165. Building: 6 flats--2 cottages. Rents: $260.00." On June 1, 1905, plaintiff notified defendant in writing that he exercised the right accorded by said contract regarding the extension of time therein specified, and elected to extend the same for a period of 30 days. On June 2, 1905, defendant, by a written instrument served upon plaintiff, revoked said option, and notified him that she withdrew said property from sale.

On June 29, 1905, within the extended time, plaintiff left at the residence of defendant an instrument, of which the following is a copy: "June 29, 1905. Mrs. M.A. Lott, 507 South Olive Street, City. Dear Madame: Referring to your agreement with me dated February 25, 1905, by which you gave me the privilege of purchasing the south half of lot nine and the whole of lot eight, in block one hundred and one, Bellevue Terrace tract, in this city, I again tender you in gold coin of the United States the sum of $30,000 as provided in said agreement, and demand of you performance on your part as in said agreement provided. This tender will also be made to your attorney, J. Wiseman MacDonald, Esq., as per request this morning when I tendered you $30,000 in gold coin at your residence on said property. Yours truly, Robert Marsh & Company."

The contention of appellant is that certain findings are not supported by the evidence. The findings material to a consideration of the case are as follows: The court found that the sum of 25 cents paid for the option was an inadequate and insufficient consideration for the same, and that the said option contract was not just and reasonable to defendant and no adequate consideration was paid to her for it. By finding 9 it appears that "after such revocation and withdrawal of said option, plaintiff, under the name of Robert Marsh & Co., on the 29th day of June, 1905, in an instrument left at the defendant's house, offered to pay to the defendant the sum of $30,000, and under the said name demanded from defendant a conveyance of the said property, but plaintiff did not at any time actually tender $30,000, or any sum at all in cash, to the defendant, nor did he, in his, or any other name, at any time, tender or offer to defendant any note or mortgage, or other evidence of indebtedness in the amount of $70,000, or any sum at all, either carrying interest at 4 1/2 per cent. net, or at any rate at all, nor did he, in his own name, or any other name, at any time, offer to pay defendant the balance of $70,000, on or before four years from the date of said option, or at any time, with interest at 4 1/2 per cent. net, or with or without interest." And by finding 10 it appears that "plaintiff has not duly or at all performed all and every provision and thing on his part in said option agreement contained. He has made no tender or offer to defendant, save as is set forth in finding No. 9 hereof. Plaintiff is willing to perform the matters on the part of Robert Marsh & Co. to be performed according to the terms of the said option, and is able to pay the sum of thirty thousand dollars."

If there was no sufficient consideration for the option, then it was a mere nudum pactum, and defendant's revocation thereof, notwithstanding her promise to the contrary, was effectual in terminating any right of plaintiff to consummate the purchase. Page on Contracts, § 35; Wristen v. Bowles, 82 Cal. 84, 22 Pac. 1136; Brown v. San Francisco Savings Union, 134 Cal. 448, 66 Pac. 592. If, on the other hand, the offer was to remain open a fixed time and was made upon a valuable consideration, equity will ignore the attempted revocation, and treat a subsequent acceptance, made within the time defined in the option, exactly as if no attempted revocation had been made. [Citations omitted]

Subdivision 1 of section 3391, of the Civil Code makes an adequate consideration for the contract one of the conditions for the specific enforcement thereof. The provision, however, has reference to the consideration to be paid for the property, the right to purchase which at a stipulated price within a given time is the subject of the option. It has no application to the sufficiency of the consideration paid for the executed contract, whereby defendant transferred to plaintiff the right to elect to purchase at the stipulated price. It is not the option which it is sought to enforce, but that which, by plaintiff's acceptance of defendant's offer, has ripened into an executory contract, whereby, for an adequate consideration, the one agrees to buy and the other agrees to sell. "The sale of an option is an executed contract; that is to say, the lands are not sold, the contract is not executed as to them, but the option is as completely sold and transferred in praesenti as a piece of personal property instantly delivered on payment of the price." Ide v. Leiser, 10 Mont. 5, 24 Pac. 695, 24 Am.St.Rep. 17. From the very nature of the case no standard exists whereby to determine the adequate value of an option to purchase specific real estate. The land has a market value susceptible of ascertainment, but the value of an option upon a piece of real estate might, and oftentimes does, depend upon proposed or possible improvements in the particular vicinity. To illustrate: If A., having information that the erection of a gigantic department store is contemplated in a certain locality, wishes an option for a specified time to purchase property owned by B. in the vicinity of such proposed improvement, and takes the option on B.'s property at the full market price at the time, must he pay a greater sum therefor because of his knowledge and the fact of B.'s ignorance of the proposed improvement? It is not possible that B., upon learning of the proposed improvement, can, in the absence of facts constituting fraud, etc., revoke or rescind the option upon the claim that he sold and transferred the right specified therein for an inadequate consideration. In our judgment any money consideration, however small, paid and received for an option to purchase property at its adequate value is binding upon the seller thereof for the time specified therein, and is irrevocable for want of its adequacy.

The provisions of section 3391, Civ.Code, are but a codification of equitable principles that have existed from time immemorial, and the sufficiency of the price paid for an option has never been measured by its adequacy. In Warvelle on Vendors (2d Ed.) § 125, it is said: "If the option is given for a valuable consideration, whether adequate or not, it cannot be withdrawn or revoked within the time fixed, and it will be binding and obligatory upon the owner, or his assigns with notice, until it expires by its own limitation." In Mathews Slate Co. v. New Empire Slate Co. (C.C.) 122 Fed. 972, it is said: "This court is of the opinion that if two persons enter into a contract in writing under seal, by which the one party, in consideration of $1, the payment of which is acknowledged, agrees to sell and convey to the other party within a specified time certain lands and premises, on payment by the other party of a specified consideration, such contract is valid and binding, and ought to be and may be specifically enforced. The seller has the right to fix his price, and covenant and agree that, on receiving that price within a certain time, he will convey the premises, and, if within that time the purchaser of the option tenders the money and demands a conveyance, he is entitled to it. To hold otherwise is to destroy the efficacy of such contracts and agreements." Mr. Freeman in his note to the case of Mueller v. Nortmann, 96 Am.St.Rep. 997, says: "An option given by the owner of land for a valuable consideration, whether adequate or not, agreeing to sell it to another at a fixed price if accepted within a specified time, is binding upon the owner and all his successors in interest with knowledge thereof." [Citations omitted] It therefore follows that the purported revocation made by defendant on June 2, 1905, was ineffectual for the purpose of terminating plaintiff's right to exercise the privilege of electing to accept the offer prior to the time designated therein for its expiration.

* * *

Questions

1. What was the consideration paid for the option contract in this case?

2. According to the court's opinion, is the adequacy of consideration a determining factor for the validity of an option contract?

Merchant's Firm Offer For Sale of Goods

An exception to the rule that an irrevocable option must be supported by consideration is found in UCC § 2-205. (Remember, the UCC only applies to sales of goods and 2-205 applies only to "merchants" [these are buyers or sellers who deal regularly in goods of the kind or hold themselves out as having special expertise with regard to the goods. [UCC § 2-104(1)].) This section converts a common law offer into a firm offer. However, it only applies if (1) an offer has been made (2) by a merchant (3) in a signed writing (4) which gives assurance that it will be held open.

Option Contracts and Offers Looking Towards Unilateral Contracts

Performance of the act requested by the offeror ordinarily constitutes acceptance in the case of an offer looking towards the formation a unilateral contract. Since there can be no acceptance until performance is fully completed the traditional view was that such an offer could be revoked at any time up until performance was completed. However, section 45 of the Second Restatement states a different rule holding that an offer looking towards formation of a unilateral contract is in effect an option contract in that once the offeree has started to perform, the offeror is not free to withdraw the offer until the offeree has had a reasonable time to complete performance. The rationale behind the rule is to protect the offeree who has begun to perform in reliance on the offer.

Reliance on an Offer Can Result In Option Contract

Drennan v. Star Paving Co.
Supreme Court of California, 1958
51 Cal.2d 409, 333 P.2d 757

TRAYNOR, J. Defendant appeals from a judgment for plaintiff in an action to recover damages caused by defendant's refusal to perform certain paving work according to a bid it submitted to plaintiff.

On July 28, 1955, plaintiff, a licensed general contractor, was preparing a bid on the "Monte Vista School Job" in the Lancaster school district. Bids had to be submitted before 8 p. m. Plaintiff testified that it was customary in that area for general contractors to receive the bids of subcontractors by telephone on the day set for bidding and to rely on them in computing their own bids. Thus on that day plaintiff's secretary, Mrs. Johnson, received by telephone between 50 and 75 subcontractors' bids for various parts of the school job. As each bid came in, she wrote it on a special form, which she brought into plaintiff's office. He then posted it on a master cost sheet setting forth the names and bids of all subcontractors. His own bid had to include the names of subcontractors who were to perform one-half of one per cent or more of the construction work, and he had also to provide a bidder's bond of 10 per cent of his total bid of $317,385 as a guarantee that he would enter the contract if awarded the work.

Late in the afternoon, Mrs. Johnson had a telephone conversation with Kenneth R. Hoon, an estimator for defendant. He gave his name and telephone number and stated that he was bidding for defendant for the paving work at the Monte Vista School according to plans and specifications and that his bid was $7,131.60. At Mrs. Johnson's request he repeated his bid. Plaintiff listened to the bid over an extension telephone in his office and posted it on the master sheet after receiving the bid form from Mrs. Johnson. Defendant's was the lowest bid for the paving. Plaintiff computed his own bid accordingly and submitted it with the name of defendant as the subcontractor for the paving. When the bids were opened on July 28th, plaintiff's proved to be the lowest, and he was awarded the contract.

On his way to Los Angeles the next morning plaintiff stopped at defendant's office. The first person he met was defendant's construction engineer, Mr. Oppenheimer. Plaintiff testified: "I introduced myself and he immediately told me that they had made a mistake in their bid to me the night before, they couldn't do it for the price they had bid, and I told him I would expect him to carry through with their original bid because I had used it in compiling my bid and the job was being awarded them. And I would have to go and do the job according to my bid and I would expect them to do the same."

Defendant refused to do the paving work for less than $15,000. Plaintiff testified that he "got figures from other people" and after trying for several months to get as low a bid as possible engaged L & H Paving Company, a firm in Lancaster, to do the work for $10,948.60.

The trial court found on substantial evidence that defendant made a definite offer to do the paving on the Monte Vista job according to the plans and specifications for $7,131.60, and that plaintiff relied on defendant's bid in computing his own bid for the school job and naming defendant therein as the subcontractor for the paving work. Accordingly, it entered judgment for plaintiff in the amount of $3,817 (the difference between defendant's bid and the cost of the paving to plaintiff) plus costs.

Defendant contends that there was no enforceable contract between the parties on the ground that it made a revocable offer and revoked it before plaintiff communicated his acceptance to defendant.

There is no evidence that defendant offered to make its bid irrevocable in exchange for plaintiff's use of its figures in computing his bid. Nor is there evidence that would warrant interpreting plaintiff's use of defendant's bid as the acceptance thereof, binding plaintiff, on condition he received the main contract, to award the subcontract to defendant. In sum, there was neither an option supported by consideration nor a bilateral contract binding on both parties.

Plaintiff contends, however, that he relied to his detriment on defendant's offer and that defendant must therefore answer in damages for its refusal to perform. Thus the question is squarely presented: Did plaintiff's reliance make defendant's offer irrevocable

Section 90 of the Restatement of Contracts states: "A promise which the promisor should reasonably expect to induce action or forbearance of a definite and substantial character on the part of the promisee and which does induce such action or forbearance is binding if injustice can be avoided only by enforcement of the promise." This rule applies in this state. . . .

Defendant's offer constituted a promise to perform on such conditions as were stated expressly or by implication therein or annexed thereto by operation of law. (See 1 Williston, Contracts [3d ed.], § 24A, p. 56, § 61, p. 196.) Defendant had reason to expect that if its bid proved the lowest it would be used by plaintiff. It induced "action ... of a definite and substantial character on the part of the promisee."

Had defendant's bid expressly stated or clearly implied that it was revocable at any time before acceptance we would treat it accordingly. It was silent on revocation, however, and we must therefore determine whether there are conditions to the right of revocation imposed by law or reasonably inferable in fact. In the analogous problem of an offer for a unilateral contract, the theory is now obsolete that the offer is revocable at any time before complete performance. Thus section 45 of the Restatement of Contracts provides: "If an offer for a unilateral contract is made, and part of the consideration requested in the offer is given or tendered by the offeree in response thereto, the offeror is bound by a contract, the duty of immediate performance of which is conditional on the full consideration being given or tendered within the time stated in the offer, or, if no time is stated therein, within a reasonable time." In explanation, comment b states that the "main offer includes as a subsidiary promise, necessarily implied, that if part of the requested performance is given, the offeror will not revoke his offer, and that if tender is made it will be accepted. Part performance or tender may thus furnish consideration for the subsidiary promise. Moreover, merely acting in justifiable reliance on an offer may in some cases serve as sufficient reason for making a promise binding (see § 90)."

Whether implied in fact or law, the subsidiary promise serves to preclude the injustice that would result if the offer could be revoked after the offeree had acted in detrimental reliance thereon. Reasonable reliance resulting in a foreseeable prejudicial change in position affords a compelling basis also for implying a subsidiary promise not to revoke an offer for a bilateral contract.

The absence of consideration is not fatal to the enforcement of such a promise. It is true that in the case of unilateral contracts the Restatement finds consideration for the implied subsidiary promise in the part performance of the bargained-for exchange, but its reference to section 90 makes clear that consideration for such a promise is not always necessary. The very purpose of section 90 is to make a promise binding even though there was no consideration "in the sense of something that is bargained for and given in exchange." (See 1 Corbin, Contracts 634 et seq.) Reasonable reliance serves to hold the offeror in lieu of the consideration ordinarily required to make the offer binding. In a case involving similar facts the Supreme Court of South Dakota stated that "we believe that reason and justice demand that the doctrine [of section 90] be applied to the present facts. We cannot believe that by accepting this doctrine as controlling in the state of facts before us we will abolish the requirement of a consideration in contract cases, in any different sense than an ordinary estoppel abolishes some legal requirement in its application. We are of the opinion, therefore, that the defendants in executing the agreement [which was not supported by consideration] made a promise which they should have reasonably expected would induce the plaintiff to submit a bid based thereon to the Government, that such promise did induce this action, and that injustice can be avoided only by enforcement of the promise." (Northwestern Engineering Co. v. Ellerman, 69 S.D. 397, 408 [10 N.W.2d 879]; see also Robert Gordon, Inc. v. Ingersoll-Rand Co., 117 F.2d 654, 661; cf. James Baird Co. v. Gimbel Bros., 64 F.2d 344.)

When plaintiff used defendant's offer in computing his own bid, he bound himself to perform in reliance on defendant's terms. Though defendant did not bargain for this use of its bid neither did defendant make it idly, indifferent to whether it would be used or not. On the contrary it is reasonable to suppose that defendant submitted its bid to obtain the subcontract. It was bound to realize the substantial possibility that its bid would be the lowest, and that it would be included by plaintiff in his bid. It was to its own interest that the contractor be awarded the general contract; the lower the subcontract bid, the lower the general contractor's bid was likely to be and the greater its chance of acceptance and hence the greater defendant's chance of getting the paving subcontract. Defendant had reason not only to expect plaintiff to rely on its bid but to want him to. Clearly defendant had a stake in plaintiff's reliance on its bid. Given this interest and the fact that plaintiff is bound by his own bid, it is only fair that plaintiff should have at least an opportunity to accept defendant's bid after the general contract has been awarded to him.

It bears noting that a general contractor is not free to delay acceptance after he has been awarded the general contract in the hope of getting a better price. Nor can he reopen bargaining with the subcontractor and at the same time claim a continuing right to accept the original offer. (See R. J. Daum Const. Co. v. Child, 122 Utah 194 [247 P.2d 817, 823].) In the present case plaintiff promptly informed defendant that plaintiff was being awarded the job and that the subcontract was being awarded to defendant.

Defendant contends, however, that its bid was the result of mistake and that it was therefore entitled to revoke it. It relies on the rescission cases of M. F. Kemper Const. Co. v. City of Los Angeles, 37 Cal.2d 696 [235 P.2d 7], and Brunzell Const. Co. v. G. J. Weisbrod, Inc., 134 Cal.App.2d 278 [285 P.2d 989]. (See also Lemoge Electric v. San Mateo County, 46 Cal.2d 659, 662 [297 P.2d 638].) In those cases, however, the bidder's mistake was known or should have been to the offeree, and the offeree could be placed in status quo. Of course, if plaintiff had reason to believe that defendant's bid was in error, he could not justifiably rely on it, and section 90 would afford no basis for enforcing it. (Robert Gordon, Inc. v. Ingersoll-Rand Co., 117 F.2d 654, 660.) Plaintiff, however, had no reason to know that defendant had made a mistake in submitting its bid, since there was usually a variance of 160 per cent between the highest and lowest bids for paving in the desert around Lancaster. He committed himself to performing the main contract in reliance on defendant's figures. Under these circumstances defendant's mistake, far from relieving it of its obligation, constitutes an additional reason for enforcing it, for it misled plaintiff as to the cost of doing the paving. Even had it been clearly understood that defendant's offer was revocable until accepted, it would not necessarily follow that defendant had no duty to exercise reasonable care in preparing its bid. It presented its bid with knowledge of the substantial possibility that it would be used by plaintiff; it could foresee the harm that would ensue from an erroneous underestimate of the cost. Moreover, it was motivated by its own business interest. Whether or not these considerations alone would justify recovery for negligence had the case been tried on that theory (see Biakanja v. Irving, 49 Cal.2d 647, 650 [320 P.2d 16]), they are persuasive that defendant's mistake should not defeat recovery under the rule of section 90 of the Restatement of Contracts. As between the subcontractor who made the bid and the general contractor who reasonably relied on it, the loss resulting from the mistake should fall on the party who caused it.

Leo F. Piazza Paving Co. v. Bebek & Brkich, 141 Cal.App.2d 226 [296 P.2d 368], and Bard v. Kent, 19 Cal.2d 449 [122 P.2d 8, 139], are not to the contrary. In the Piazza case the court sustained a finding that defendants intended, not to make a firm bid, but only to give the plaintiff "some kind of an idea to use" in making its bid; there was evidence that the defendants had told plaintiff they were unsure of the significance of the specifications. There was thus no offer, promise, or representation on which the defendants should reasonably have expected the plaintiff to rely. The Bard case held that an option not supported by consideration was revoked by the death of the optionor. The issue of recovery under the rule of section 90 was not pleaded at the trial, and it does not appear that the offeree's reliance was "of a definite and substantial character" so that injustice could be avoided "only by the enforcement of the promise." . . .

The judgment is affirmed.

Questions

1. What was the plaintiff's reliance on defendant's bid when preparing his own bid for the Monte Vista School Job?

2. According to Section 90 of the Restatement of Contracts, what conditions must be met for a promise to be binding?

Takeaways – Drennan v. Star Paving

Restatement Second of Contracts section 87 states that "an offer which the offeror should reasonably expect to induce action or forbearance of a substantial character on the part of the offeree before acceptance and does induce such action or forbearance is binding as an option contract to the extent necessary to avoid injustice." Compare this language to that of Restatement Second section 90. What is the difference? (Note that the Drennan case was decided before the Restatement Second of Contracts was promulgated and section 87 made its debut.)

The Requirement of Definiteness

Contract Must Be Certain as to its Essential Terms

Toys Inc. v. F.M. Burlington Co.
Supreme Court of Vermont, 1990
582 A.2d 123

On November 1, 1979, the parties entered into a lease for space in a shopping mall owned by defendant. The lease was for an initial five-year term, April 1, 1980 through February 28, 1985, and plaintiff was given an option to renew for five additional years. The option provision in the lease is as follows: Tenant shall be provided one option to extend the lease for five years, provided that tenant was not in default of the lease at any time during the initial term upon the same terms and conditions except: (a) there shall be no further right to renew; (b) the fixed minimum rental shall be renegotiated to the then prevailing rate within the mall. Should the tenant wish to renew, tenant shall give one year's written notice of intention to exercise the option.

On February 7, 1984, Toys Inc. wrote to F.M. Burlington, pursuant to the lease, and said, "[P]lease be advised that Toys, Inc. hereby notifies F.M. Burlington Company of its intent to exercise its option to renew." F.M. Burlington responded on February 24, 1984. In that letter defendant confirmed that plaintiff was exercising its option to renew and then stated the prevailing rate per square foot in the mall.

On March 1, 1984, plaintiff responded. This letter stated that "Toys, Inc.'s notice of intent to renew was premised on a substantially different understanding of the prevailing rate." It described a conversation with defendant's leasing agent that involved the quotation of a prevailing rental rate well below that stated in defendant's letter of February 24th and included the understanding that "we would be completely free to renegotiate the issue of a fixed minimum rent without being bound to a prevailing rate." The letter concluded, "I trust . . . that in the coming months we will be able to renegotiate a mutually agreeable rent structure."

On March 2, 1984, defendant responded by letter stating: You are of course completely free to renegotiate the rate without reference to the prevailing rate. However, as far as the rights of the Tenant under the option are concerned, the prevailing rate . . . is $10.00 [per square foot]. The prevailing rate is subject to change until such time as an agreement for renewal is reached.

On July 17, 1984, the parties met and seemed to come to an understanding as to a rent structure for the renewal term. The new rent structure was not significantly different from that specified by defendant in February, except that the first-year rent was lower than the prevailing rate and the last-year rent was higher than the prevailing rate. Over the five-year period, the new rent averaged to the prevailing rate. Defendant wrote to plaintiff the next day describing the terms and stated "[i]f this offer is accepted, please have a copy of this letter executed and returned to me. This offer is valid through August 1, 1984." (Emphasis added.) Plaintiff responded with a request for more time to consider the offer and was given until August 15, 1984.

On August 15, 1984, plaintiff wrote to defendant: It is necessary for my clients at this time to ask for an additional two (2) week extension from [August 15, 1984], in which to accept your offer as set forth in your July 18, 1984 correspondence. Please let me know if there is a problem with the above request. Defendant did not respond, and plaintiff did not accept or reject the "offer" of July 17, 1984. During this time, plaintiff was seeking an alternative location for its toy store in case negotiations with defendant did not work out. Sometime in the late summer or early fall, plaintiff began pursuing the purchase of a building in which to locate its store. In October, a loan application was submitted to a financing source for funds to purchase the building. The next communication between the parties to this action was a letter from defendant dated November 1, 1984 and informing plaintiff that "Burlington Square is listing store no. 20 for lease effective March 1, 1985."

On November 9, 1984, plaintiff wrote to defendant: On February 7, 1984, my clients informed you in writing of their intention to exercise the option to renew in the above matter. At this time we would like to be advised of the prevailing rate so that a lease can be signed as soon as possible. In reference to your November 1, 1984[,] letter, we would consider any attempt on your part to lease store No. 20 to any party other than Toys, Inc., a breach of our lease.

Although the paper jousting continued, negotiations between the parties ceased. Defendant took the position that plaintiff had failed to accept the prevailing rate in February and that they had let the July offer lapse. Plaintiff stated that it had exercised the option to renew with the February 7th letter and defendant was bound at its prevailing rate. Plaintiff left the mall and purchased the building for which it earlier sought financing. Plaintiff then sued for breach of contract. After discovery and based generally on the facts set forth above, defendant moved for summary judgment, arguing that: (1) the option provision in the lease is actually an unenforceable agreement to agree; (2) even if a valid option existed, it was never effectively exercised by plaintiff; (3) if plaintiff had a right of renewal, it waived it through its conduct. The trial court found that the lease provision created a binding option, that plaintiff exercised the option by letter on February 7, 1984, and that plaintiff never waived its acceptance of the renewal. Accordingly, it awarded summary judgment to the plaintiff. Defendant renews its same arguments here, urging that we grant it summary judgment or, alternatively, remand for trial. . . .

We agree with the trial court that summary judgment for plaintiff was appropriate on the first issue raised by defendant. The lease provision created a valid option for plaintiff to renew for an additional five years. Defendant characterizes the lease renewal provision as merely an agreement to agree and therefore not enforceable. If defendant's construction were correct, the lease provision would not create an enforceable option. See Reynolds v. Sullivan, 136 Vt. 1, 3, 383 A.2d 609, 611 (1978). In Reynolds we held that a preliminary option agreement that was vague and uncertain in its terms "would be an impossibility to enforce." Id. The test is whether the option agreement contains "all material and essential terms to be incorporated in the subsequent document." Id. The agreement in Reynolds was labeled as preliminary and specifically provided that the parties "agree to enter an agreement for an option" and that "more specific terms will be stated in the option to purchase." Id. at 2, 383 A.2d at 610.

It is not necessary under Reynolds that the option agreement contain all the terms of the contract as long as it contains a practicable, objective method of determining the essential terms. See Krupinsky v. Birsky, 129 Vt. 400, 405, 278 A.2d 757, 760 (1971) (option contract valid even though it "did not fix a price certain" where "it did appoint a mode of determining the price"); Restatement (Second) of Contracts { 33 comment (a), { 34(1) (1981) ("The terms of a contract may be reasonably certain even though it empowers one or both parties to make a selection of terms in the course of performance."). We must construe the option agreement in a way to give it binding effect if possible. See Agway, Inc. v. Marotti, 149 Vt. 191, 194, 540 A.2d 1044, 1046 (1988) (before voiding a contract for vagueness, indefiniteness or uncertainty of expression, Court must attempt to construe the contract to avoid the defect). We are also mindful that defendant drafted the language of the option clause and that a doubtful provision in a written instrument is construed against the party responsible for drafting it. See Trustees of Net Realty v. AVCO Financial Services, 147 Vt. 472, 475-76, 520 A.2d 981, 983 (1986).

The option agreement states that "the fixed minimum rental shall be renegotiated to the then prevailing rate within the mall." We believe that this language sets forth a definite, ascertainable method of determining the price term for the lease extension. Within days after plaintiff stated its original intent to exercise its option, defendant replied by quoting the "prevailing rate within the mall" at that time. Neither defendant nor plaintiff have disputed the accuracy of this calculation.

Defendant puts much emphasis on the use of the term "renegotiate" in the renewal clause, as showing an intent to reach a future agreement. While the choice of wording could have been more precise, we agree with the plaintiff that the term means that the then-existing "prevailing rate" would be determined by agreement, and does not mean that the parties would start from a clean slate in renegotiating a rent term. Even if we give defendant the benefit of all inferences and reasonable doubt, we find no genuine issue of fact bearing on whether there was an enforceable option to renew and hold as a matter of law that a valid option existed.

Questions

1. How did the defendant argue that the lease provision was an unenforceable agreement to agree?

2. How did the court determine whether the lease provision created a valid option for the plaintiff to renew?

3. What factors did the court consider when determining whether the option agreement contained all material and essential terms?

Takeaways – Toys Inc.

When a consideration is executory, (yet to be performed) it is not indispensable that the contract should specify its amount or the means of ascertaining it. It may be left to the decision of a third person, or regulated by any specified standard. (Cal.Civ.Code § 1610.) Though an essential term is uncertain or not agreed upon, if the contract provides a means or formula by which that essential term can be determined, the contract is enforceable. Performance by the parties may also render clear what was uncertain, and the contract becomes enforceable. (See, 1 Witkin, Summary of Cal. Law (10th ed. 2005) Contracts, §§ 139, 146, 147.)

A contract will be enforced if it is sufficiently definite for the court to ascertain the parties' obligations and to determine whether those obligations have been performed or breached. (*Boyd v. Bevilacqua* (1966) 247 Cal.App.2d 272, 287 [55 Cal.Rptr. 610]; *Hennefer v. Butcher* (1986) 182 Cal.App.3d 492, 500- 501 [227 Cal.Rptr. 318]; *Robinson & Wilson, Inc. v. Stone* (1973) 35 Cal.App.3d 396, 407 [110 Cal.Rptr. 675].) Stated otherwise, the contract will be enforced if it is possible to reach a fair and just result even if, in the process, the court is required to fill in some gaps. (*Okun v. Morton* (1988) 203 Cal.App.3d 805, 817 [250 Cal.Rptr. 220].) When an agreement does not specify a time for performance, it is implied that it is to be performed within a reasonable time, and what is a reasonable time is a question of fact. (See *Smith v. Galio*, 95 N.M. 4, 7, 617 P.2d 1325, 1328 (Ct. App. 1980).)

Where any of the essential terms of an apparent agreement are left for future determination, and it is understood by the parties that the agreement is not complete until they are settled, or where it is understood that the agreement is incomplete until reduced to writing and signed by the parties, no contract results until this is done.

An agreement definite in its essential terms is not rendered unenforceable by reason of uncertainty in some minor, nonessential detail. Such details may be left to the further agreement of the parties.

"Where the matters left for future agreement are unessential, each party will be forced to accept a reasonable determination of the unsettled point, or if possible the unsettled point may be left unperformed and the remainder of the contract be enforced." (*City of Los Angeles v. Superior Court* (1959) 51 Cal.2d 423, 433, 333 P.2d 745, 750.)

Precontractual Liability

We know that a contract is formed when an offer is accepted. May a promise ever be enforced in the absence of an acceptance? Courts have long permitted the parties the freedom to negotiate without risk of contractual liability if the negotiations fall short of ending in an enforceable agreement. This is based upon the assumption that a party assumes the risk of loss if the other party breaks off contract negotiations prior to reaching an agreement. However, if during the course of negotiations one party has conferred a benefit on the other party, the recipient may be required to make restitution, that is, return the benefit. To what extent can reliance and restitution provide remedies for failed negotiations?

Dixon v. Wells Fargo, N.A.
798 F.Supp.2d 336, 2011

YOUNG, District Judge. Frank and Deana Dixon (collectively "the Dixons") bring this cause of action against Wells Fargo Bank, N.A. ("Wells Fargo"), seeking (1) an injunction prohibiting Wells Fargo from foreclosing on their home; (2) specific performance of an oral agreement to enter into a loan modification; and (3) damages. . . .

The Dixons reside at their home in Scituate, Plymouth County, Massachusetts. Compl. Wells Fargo is a corporation doing business in the Commonwealth of Massachusetts. Wells Fargo alleges that it is the holder of a mortgage on the Dixons' home.

On or about June 8, 2009, the Dixons orally agreed with Wells Fargo to take the steps necessary to enter into a mortgage loan modification.. As part of this agreement, Wells Fargo instructed the Dixons to stop making payments on their loan. It was contemplated that the unpaid payments would be added to the note as modified. In addition, Wells Fargo requested certain financial information, which the Dixons promptly supplied.

Notwithstanding the Dixons' diligent efforts and reliance on Wells Fargo's promise, Wells Fargo has failed, and effectively refused, to abide by the oral agreement to modify the existing mortgage loan.

On or about December 8, 2010, the Dixons received notice from the Massachusetts Land Court that Wells Fargo was proceeding with a foreclosure on their home. *Id.* The return date on the order of notice in the Land Court was January 10, 2011, and so the Dixons sought a temporary restraining order in the Superior Court to prevent the loss of their home.

The Dixons state that, on information and belief, the fair market value of their home is in excess of the mortgage loan balance and any arrearage. . . .

B. Promissory Estoppel

The gravamen of the Dixons' complaint is that Wells Fargo promised to engage in negotiations to modify their loan, provided that they took certain "steps necessary to enter into a mortgage modification." Compl. ¶ 7. On the basis of Wells Fargo's representation, the Dixons stopped making payments on their loan and submitted the requested financial information—only to learn subsequently that the bank had initiated foreclosure proceedings against them. They contend that Wells Fargo ought have anticipated their compliance with the terms of its promise to consider them for a loan modification. Not only was it reasonable that they would rely on the promise, but also their reliance left them considerably worse off, for by entering into default they became vulnerable to foreclosure.

The question whether these allegations are sufficient to state a claim for promissory estoppel requires a close look at the doctrine's evolution in the law of Massachusetts. In *Loranger Const. Corp. v. E.F. Hauserman Co.,* 376 Mass. 757, 384 N.E.2d 176 (1978), the Supreme Judicial Court recognized the enforceability of a promise on the basis of detrimental reliance, but declined to "use the expression `promissory estoppel,' since it tends to confusion rather than clarity." *Id.* at 760-61, 384 N.E.2d 176. The court reasoned that "[w]hen a promise is enforceable in whole or in part by virtue of reliance, it is a `contract,' and it is enforceable pursuant to a `traditional contract theory' antedating the modern doctrine of consideration." *Id.* at 761, 384 N.E.2d 176. Since *Loranger,* the court has adhered to its view that "an action based on reliance is equivalent to a contract action, and the party bringing such an action must prove all the necessary elements of a contract other than consideration." *Rhode Island Hosp. Trust Nat'l Bank v. Varadian,* 419 Mass. 841, 850, 647 N.E.2d 1174 (1995).

"An essential element in the pleading and proof of a contract claim is, of course, the `promise' sought to be enforced." *Kiely v. Raytheon Co.,* 914 F.Supp. 708, 712 (D.Mass.1996) (O'Toole, J.). Thus, even where detrimental reliance acts as a substitute for consideration, the promise on which a claim for promissory estoppel is based must be interchangeable with an offer "in the sense of `commitment.'" *Cataldo Ambulance Serv., Inc. v. City of Chelsea,* 426 Mass. 383, 386 n. 6, 688 N.E.2d 959 (1998). The promise must demonstrate "an intention to act or refrain from acting in a specified way, so as to justify a promisee in understanding that a *commitment* has been made." *Varadian,* 419 Mass. at 849-50, 647 N.E.2d 1174 (quoting Restatement (Second) of Contracts § 2 (1981)). That the representation is of future, rather than present, intention will not preclude recovery, so long as the promisor's expectation to be legally bound is clear. *See Sullivan v. Chief Justice for Admin. & Mgt. of Trial Court,* 448 Mass. 15, 28 & n. 9, 858 N.E.2d 699 (2006) (quoting *Boylston Dev. Group, Inc. v. 22 Boylston St. Corp.,* 412 Mass. 531, 542 n. 17, 591 N.E.2d 157 (1992)).

In addition to demonstrating a firm commitment, the putative promise, like any offer, must be sufficiently "definite and certain in its terms" to be enforceable. *Moore v. La-Z-Boy, Inc.,* 639 F.Supp.2d 136, 142 (D.Mass.2009) (Stearns, J.) (quoting *Kiely,* 914 F.Supp. at 712). "[I]f an essential element is reserved for the future agreement of both parties, as a general rule, the promise can give rise to no legal obligation until such future agreement." 1 Richard A. Lord, Williston on Contracts § 4:29 (4th ed. 1990); *see Lucey v. Hero Int'l Corp.,* 361 Mass. 569, 574-75, 281 N.E.2d 266 (1972). Under well-settled Massachusetts law, "an agreement to enter into a contract which leaves the terms of that contract for future negotiation is too indefinite to be enforced." *Caggiano v. Marchegiano,* 327 Mass. 574, 580, 99 N.E.2d 861 (1951); . . . Restatement (Second) of Contracts § 33, comment (c) ("The more terms the parties leave open, the less likely it is that they have intended to conclude a binding agreement.").

The longstanding reluctance of courts to enforce open-ended "agreements to agree" reflects a belief that, unless a "fall-back standard" exists to supply the missing terms, there is no way to know what ultimate agreement, if any, would have resulted. E. Allan Farnsworth, *Precontractual Liability and Preliminary Agreements: Fair Dealing and Failed Negotiations,* 87 Colum. L.Rev. 217, 255-56 (1987). It is the vague and indefinite nature of that potential final agreement—not the preliminary agreement to agree—that troubles courts. *See Armstrong v. Rohm & Haas Co., Inc.,* 349 F.Supp.2d 71, 78 (D.Mass. 2004) (Saylor, J.) (holding that an agreement must be sufficiently definite to enable courts to give it an exact meaning). Judges are justifiably unwilling to endorse one party's aspirational view of the terms of an unrealized agreement. *See* Farnsworth, *supra* at 259. Just as "[i]t is no appropriate part of judicial business to rewrite contracts freely entered into," *RCI Northeast Servs. Div. v. Boston Edison Co.,* 822 F.2d 199, 205 (1st Cir.1987), courts must not force parties into contracts into which they have not entered freely, *Armstrong,* 349 F.Supp.2d at 80 (holding a promise unenforceable where the court could not "supply the missing terms without `writing a contract for the parties which they themselves did not make'" (quoting *Held v. Zamparelli*, 13 Mass.App. Ct. 957, 958, 431 N.E.2d 961 (1982))).

Moreover, parties ought be allowed to step away unscathed if they are unable to reach a deal. *Cf. R.W. Int'l Corp. v. Welch Food, Inc.,* 13 F.3d 478, 484-85 (1st Cir. 1994). To impose rights and duties at "the stage of `imperfect negotiation,'" *Lafayette Place Assocs.,* 427 Mass. at 517, 694 N.E.2d 820, would be to interfere with the liberty to contract—or not to contract. Thus, the concern is that if a court were to order specific performance of an agreement to agree, where the material terms of the final agreement were left open by the parties, not only would there be "little, if anything, to enforce," *Lambert v. Fleet Nat'l Bank,* 449 Mass. 119, 123, 865 N.E.2d 1091 (2007), but also future negotiations would be chilled. *Cf. American Broad. Cos., Inc. v. Wolf,* 52 N.Y.2d 394, 438 N.Y.S.2d 482, 420 N.E.2d 363, 368-69 (1981) (denying request for specific performance of general contract negotiation clause as inhibitive of free competition).

Wells Fargo would have this Court end its inquiry here. The complaint plainly alleges that the parties had an "agreement to enter into a loan modification agreement," but as matter of law "[a]n agreement to reach an agreement is a contradiction in terms and imposes no obligations on the parties thereto." *Rosenfield,* 290 Mass. at 217, 195 N.E. 323. As such, the complaint would appear to fail to state a claim.

During the course of opposing Wells Fargo's motion to dismiss, however, the Dixons have made clear that they do not seek specific performance of a promised loan modification. *See* Pls.' Supplemental Mem. Opp'n 1-2. They admit that there was no guarantee of a modification by Wells Fargo, only a verbal commitment to determine their eligibility for a modification if they followed the bank's prescribed steps. Thus, the Dixons' request that Wells Fargo be held to its promise to consider them for a loan modification is not a covert attempt to bind the bank to a final agreement it had not contemplated. There is no risk that this Court, were it to uphold the promissory estoppel claim, would be "trapping" Wells Fargo into a vague, indefinite, and unintended loan modification masquerading as an agreement to agree. *Teachers Ins. & Annuity Ass'n of Am. v. Tribune Co.,* 670 F.Supp. 491, 497 (S.D.N.Y.1987).

Furthermore, because the parties had not yet begun to negotiate the terms of a modification, the Court questions whether Wells Fargo's promise ought even be characterized as a preliminary agreement to agree. Instead, it more closely resembles an "agreement to negotiate." *See* Farnsworth, *supra* at 263-69; *cf. Aceves v. U.S. Bank, N.A.,* 192 Cal.App.4th 218, 120 Cal. Rptr.3d 507, 514 (2011) ("[T]he question here is simply whether U.S. Bank made and kept a promise to *negotiate* with Aceves, not whether . . . the bank promised to make a loan or, more precisely, to modify a loan.").

To be sure, Massachusetts courts have tended to treat agreements to negotiate as variants of open-ended agreements to agree. The view that "[a]n agreement to negotiate does not create a binding contract," *Sax*, 639 F.Supp.2d at 171, again reflects a concern that a promise of further negotiations is too indefinite, too undefined in scope, to be enforceable. *See Bell*, 359 Mass. at 763, 270 N.E.2d 926 (finding an agreement to negotiate "for as long as the parties agreed" to be "void for vagueness"). This is particularly true where the parties have not specified the terms on which they will continue negotiating. *See* Farnsworth, *supra* at 264. Conventional wisdom holds that courts ought not "strain[] to find an agreement to negotiate in the absence of a clear indication of assent" by the parties to a governing standard of conduct, e.g., "good faith" or "best efforts," *Id.* at 266-67, because "there is no meaningful content in a general duty to negotiate, standing alone," Steven J. Burton & Eric G. Anderson, Contractual Good Faith § 8.4.2, at 361 (1995). *See Pinnacle Books, Inc. v. Harlequin Enters. Ltd.*, 519 F.Supp. 118, 122 (S.D.N.Y.1981). As with open-ended agreements to agree, judicial enforcement of vague agreements to negotiate would risk imposing on parties contractual obligations they had not taken on themselves.

In this case, Wells Fargo and the Dixons had not yet contemplated the terms of a loan modification, but they had contemplated negotiations. Their failure to elaborate on the boundaries of that duty to negotiate, however, would seem to militate against enforcement of it. Yet, Wells Fargo made a specific promise to consider the Dixons' eligibility for a loan modification if they defaulted on their payments and submitted certain financial information. *See* Burton & Andersen, *supra* § 8.2.2, at 332-33 (recognizing that, while there is no general duty to negotiate in good faith, public policy favors imposing noncontractual liability "when one person wrongfully harms another" by making a promise intended to induce reliance); Lucian Arye Bebchuk & Omri Ben-Shahar, *Precontractual Reliance*, 30 J. Legal Stud. 423, 424 (2001) ("A party may be liable for the other party's reliance costs on three possible grounds: if it induced this reliance through misrepresentation, if it benefited from the reliance, or if it made a specific promise during negotiations."); Farnsworth, *supra* at 236 (referring to the "specific promises that one party makes to another in order to interest the other party in the negotiations" as a "common basis for precontractual liability"). Importantly, it was not a promise made in exchange for a bargained-for legal detriment, as there was no bargain between the parties; rather, the legal detriment that the Dixons claim to have suffered was a direct consequence of their reliance on Wells Fargo's promise. Joseph Perillo, Calamari & Perillo on Contracts § 6.1, at 218 (6th ed. 2009). Under the theory of promissory estoppel, "[a] negotiating party may not with impunity break a promise made during negotiations if the other party has relied on it." Farnsworth, *supra* at 236.

Promissory estoppel has developed into "an attempt by the courts to keep remedies abreast of increased moral consciousness of honesty and fair representations in all business dealings." *Peoples Nat'l Bank of Little Rock v. Linebarger*

Constr. Co., 219 Ark. 11, 240 S.W.2d 12, 16 (1951). While it began as "a substitute for (or the equivalent of) consideration" in the context of an otherwise binding contract, Perillo, *supra* § 6.1, at 218, "promissory estoppel has come to be a doctrine employed to rescue failing contracts where the cause of the failure is not related to consideration," *Id.* § 6.3, at 229. It now "provides a remedy for many promises or agreements that fail the test of enforceability under many traditional contract doctrines," *Id.* § 6.1, at 218, but whose enforcement is "necessary to avoid injustice," Restatement (Second) of Contracts § 90, comment (b).

Admittedly, the courts of Massachusetts have yet to formally embrace promissory estoppel as more than a consideration substitute. *See, e.g., Varadian,* 419 Mass. at 850, 647 N.E.2d 1174. Nonetheless, without equivocation, they have adopted section 90 of the Restatement (Second) of Contracts, which reads, "A promise which the promisor should reasonably expect to induce action or forbearance on the part of the promisee or a third person and which does induce such action or forbearance is binding if injustice can be avoided only by enforcement of the promise." *See Chedd-Angier Prod. Co. v. Omni Publ'ns Int'l, Ltd.,* 756 F.2d 930, 937 (1st Cir.1985); *Loranger Constr. Corp.,* 376 Mass. at 760-61, 384 N.E.2d 176; *McAndrew v. School Comm.,* 20 Mass.App. Ct. 356, 363, 480 N.E.2d 327 (1985); *see also Anzalone v. Administrative Office of Trial Court,* 457 Mass. 647, 661, 932 N.E.2d 774 (2010) (using the term "promissory estoppel" and defining estoppel similarly to the Restatement); *Sullivan,* 448 Mass. at 27-28, 858 N.E.2d 699 (same). Nowhere in the comments to section 90 nor in section 2 of the Restatement, which defines the word "promise," is there an explicit "requirement that the promise giving rise to the cause of action must be so comprehensive in scope as to meet the requirements of an offer that would ripen into a contract if accepted by the promisee." *Hoffman v. Red Owl Stores, Inc.,* 26 Wis.2d 683, 133 N.W.2d 267, 275 (1965). In fact, the Restatement "has expressly approved" promissory estoppel's use to protect reliance on indefinite promises. . . .

Massachusetts's continued insistence that a promise be definite— at least to a degree likely not met in the present case— is arguably in tension with its adoption of the Restatement's more relaxed standard. This tension is not irreconcilable, however. Tracing the development of promissory estoppel through the case law reveals a willingness on courts' part to enforce even an indefinite promise made during preliminary negotiations where the facts suggest that the promisor's words or conduct were designed to take advantage of the promisee. The promisor need not have acted fraudulently, deceitfully, or in bad faith. *McLearn v. Hill,* 276 Mass. 519, 524-25, 177 N.E. 617 (1931). Rather, "[f]acts falling short of these elements may constitute conduct contrary to general principles of fair dealing and to the good conscience which ought to actuate individuals and which it is the design of courts to enforce." *Id.* at 524, 177 N.E. 617. As the Supreme Judicial Court remarked in an early promissory estoppel case:

[I]t is not essential that the representations or conduct giving rise to [the doctrine's] application should be fraudulent in the strictly legal significance of that term, or with intent to mislead or deceive; the test appears to be whether in all the circumstances of the case conscience and duty of honest dealing should deny one the right to repudiate the consequence of his representations or conduct; whether the author of a proximate cause may justly repudiate its natural and reasonably anticipated effect; fraud, in the sense of a court of equity, properly including all acts, omissions, and concealments which involve a breach of legal or equitable duty, trust, or confidence, justly reposed, and are injurious to another or by which an undue and unconscientious advantage is taken of another. *Id.* at 525, 177 N.E. 617 (quoting *Howard v. West Jersey & Seashore R.R.,* 102 N.J. Eq. 517, 141 A. 755, 757 (N.J.Ch.1928), *aff'd,* 104 N.J. Eq. 201, 144 A. 919 (N.J. 1929)).

Typically, where the Massachusetts courts have applied the doctrine of promissory estoppel to enforce an otherwise unenforceable promise, "there has been a pattern of conduct by one side which has dangled the other side on a string.". . . In (*Greenstein v. Flatley,* 19 Mass.App.Ct. 351, 352-54, 474 N.E.2d 1130 (1985)), where a landlord submitted a lease to a prospective tenant and then strung him along for more than four months before repudiating the lease he had submitted, the Massachusetts Appeals Court concluded that the conduct of the landlord "was calculated to misrepresent the true situation to the [tenant], keep him on a string, and make the [tenant] conclude—reasonably—that the deal had been made and that only a bureaucratic formality remained." 19 Mass. App.Ct. at 356, 474 N.E.2d 1130. Because this conduct "was misleading, it fit[] comfortably `within at least the penumbra of some common-law, statutory, or other established concept of unfairness.'" *Id.* (quoting *PMP Assocs., Inc. v. Globe Newspaper Co.,* 366 Mass. 593, 596, 321 N.E.2d 915 (1975)); *see* Avery Katz, *When Should an Offer Stick? The Economics of Promissory Estoppel in Preliminary Negotiations,* 105 Yale L.J. 1249, 1254 (1996) ("The doctrine of promissory estoppel is commonly explained as promoting the same purposes as the tort of misrepresentation: punishing or deterring those who mislead others to their detriment and compensating those who are misled."). . . .

In *Cohoon v. Citizens Bank,* No. 002774, 2000 WL 33170737 (Mass.Super. Nov. 11, 2000) (Agnes, J.), the parties orally agreed to a discounted payoff in full satisfaction of the plaintiff's original mortgage obligation. The defendant encouraged the plaintiff to default on a mortgage payment to ensure approval of the discounted payoff. Until that time, the plaintiff had made timely payments. *Id.* Once in default, however, the defendant sold the note to a buyer who promptly commenced foreclosure. *Id.* The court upheld the plaintiff's claim for promissory estoppel because, "[t]aking the facts in the light most favorable to the plaintiff, it could be found that [the defendant] encouraged [the plaintiff] to delay mortgage payment and, as a result of that reliance, the eventual buyer. . . took advantage of [the plaintiff's] vulnerable state by initiating foreclosure on [the plaintiff's] property interest." *Id.* While the court indicated that, to prevail at trial, the plaintiff would need to establish that he "was misled or induced to believe that by defaulting he would achieve the discounted purchase of the note that he was seeking," *Id.* at, he was at least entitled to "th[is] opportunity to prove facts in support of his claim of detrimental reliance."

In the present case, Wells Fargo convinced the Dixons that to be eligible for a loan modification they had to default on their payments, and it was only because they relied on this representation and stopped making their payments that Wells Fargo was able to initiate foreclosure proceedings. While there is no allegation that its promise was dishonest, Wells Fargo distinctly gained the upper hand by inducing the Dixons to open themselves up to a foreclosure action. In specifically telling the Dixons that stopping their payments and submitting financial information were the "steps necessary to enter into a mortgage modification," Wells Fargo not only should have known that the Dixons would take these steps believing their fulfillment would lead to a loan modification, but also must have intended that the Dixons do so. The bank's promise to consider them for a loan modification if they took those steps necessarily "involved as matter of fair dealing an undertaking on [its] part not to [foreclose] based upon facts coming into existence solely from" the making of its promise. *McLearn,* 276 Mass. at 523-24, 177 N.E. 617; *see Aceves,* 120 Cal.Rptr.3d at 514 ("U.S. Bank agreed to 'work with [Aceves] on a mortgage reinstatement and loan modification' if she no longer pursued relief in the bankruptcy court. . . . [This promise] indicates that U.S. Bank would not foreclose on Aceves's home without first engaging in negotiations with her to reinstate and modify the loan on mutually agreeable terms."); *cf. Vigoda v. Denver Urban Renewal Auth.,* 646 P.2d 900, 905 (Colo.1982) (ruling that the plaintiff's allegation that she incurred losses in reasonable reliance on the defendant's promise to negotiate in good faith was sufficient to state a claim for relief). Wells Fargo's decision to foreclose without warning was unseemly conduct at best. In the opinion of this Court, such conduct presents "an identifiable occasion for applying the principle of promissory estoppel." *Greenstein,* 19 Mass.App.Ct. at 356-57, 474 N.E.2d 1130.

As the cases reveal, where, like here, the promisor opportunistically has strung along the promisee, the imposition of liability despite the preliminary stage of the negotiations produces the most equitable result. This balancing of the harms "is explicitly made an element of recovery under the doctrine of promissory estoppel by the last words of [section 90 of the Restatement], which make the promise binding only if injustice can be avoided by its enforcement." Metzger & Phillips, *supra* at 849. Binding the promisor to a promise made to take advantage of the promisee is also the most efficient result. *Cf.* Richard Craswell, *Offer, Acceptance, and Efficient Reliance,* 48 Stan. L.Rev. 481, 538 (1996). In cases of opportunism, "[the] willingness to impose a liability rule can be justified as efficient since such intervention may be the most cost-effective means of controlling opportunistic behavior, which both parties would seek to control ex ante as a means of maximizing joint gains. Because private control arrangements may be costly, the law-supplied rule may be the most effective means of controlling opportunism and maximizing joint gain." Juliet P. Kostritsky, *The Rise and Fall of Promissory Estoppel or Is Promissory Estoppel Really as Unsuccessful as Scholars Say It Is:*

A New Look at the Data, 37 Wake Forest L.Rev. 531, 574 (2002); *see* Katz, *supra* at 1309 (contending that promissory estoppel can help "regulat[e] the opportunistic exercise of bargaining power" during preliminary negotiations); Schwartz & Scott, *supra* at 667 (remarking that protecting the party who has relied "will deter some strategic behavior").

There remains the concern that, by imposing precontractual liability for specific promises made to induce reliance during preliminary negotiations, courts will restrict parties' freedom to negotiate by reading in a duty to bargain in good faith not recognized at common law. While this concern does not fall on deaf ears, it can be effectively minimized by limiting the promisee's recovery to his or her reliance expenditures. . . .

This Court, therefore, holds that the complaint states a claim for promissory estoppel: Wells Fargo promised to engage in negotiating a loan modification if the Dixons defaulted on their payments and provided certain financial information, and they did so in reasonable reliance on that promise, only to learn that the bank had taken advantage of their default status by initiating foreclosure proceedings. Assuming they can prove these allegations by a preponderance of the evidence, their damages appropriately will be confined to the value of their expenditures in reliance on Wells Fargo's promise.

Questions

1. How does the court distinguish between an agreement to agree and an agreement to negotiate?

2. Why do courts hesitate to enforce open-ended agreements to agree or negotiate?

3. In this case, what specific promise did Wells Fargo make to the Dixons, and how does it relate to the theory of promissory estoppel?

Takeaways – Dixon v. Wells Fargo

In addition to being a basis for the enforcement of promises that are unsupported by consideration (e.g. *Feinberg v. Pfeiffer,* p. 39) or making offers irrevocable because of reliance (e.g. *Drennan v. Star Paving.* p. 130) promissory estoppel can also impose fair-dealing requirements on parties involved in pre-contractual negotiations despite the absence of an intent to be bound by a contract.

ASSESSMENT QUESTIONS, CHAPTER 2

1. Expain mutual assent and its significance in contract formation.

2. What is the difference between an offer and an invitation to make an offer?

3. What are the requirements for a valid acceptance?

4. Can silence be considered as acceptance in contract law? Why or why not?

5. What is the mailbox rule? How does it affect the timing of acceptance in contract formation?

6. Describe the mirror image rule. How does it relate to the concept of mutual assent?

7. What are the exceptions to the mirror image rule?

CHAPTER 3
THE STATUTE OF FRAUDS

Introduction
Origins and History

The Statute of Frauds originated in 17th century England to combat the use of fraud and perjury by litigants in court proceedings to establish oral contracts. *See* 2 E. Allan Farnsworth, *Contracts* § 6.1, at 82-83 (2d ed. 1990). At the time, court rules prohibited parties to a lawsuit from testifying as witnesses in their case, and, consequently, an oral contract could only be established with testimony of third parties. *See Azevedo v. Minister,* 86 Nev. 576, 471 P.2d 661, 663 (1970). This prohibition allowed witnesses to be persuaded to give false testimony on behalf of a party in an effort to establish an oral contract, leaving the other party at a distinct disadvantage. *See* James J. O'Connell, Jr., *Boats Against a Current: The Courts and the Statute of Frauds,* 47 Emory L.J. 253, 257 (1998).

In 1677, in response to this unsavory practice of using perjury to establish oral contracts, Parliament enacted the Statute of Frauds to require certain contracts to be supported by written evidence to be enforceable. 29 Car. 2, ch. 3 (1677) (Eng.); *see* Hugh E. Willis, *Statute of Frauds—A Legal Anachronism,* 3 Ind. L.J. 427, 427 (1928). The statute included contracts which were not only particularly susceptible to fraud, but those which posed serious consequences of fraud, including contracts for the sale of goods or property. *See* O'Connell, 47 Emory L.J. at 258.

In addition to being aimed at preventing fraud and perjury it is also recognized that the Statute of Frauds serves a "cautionary" purpose. Requiring that certain types of contracts be evidenced by a written note or memorandum, signed by the party to be charged, should be a reminder to the parties of the significance and consequences of entering into agreements that are within the scope of the statute.

Despite a difference in the court rules which gave rise to this statute of frauds, our American legal culture quickly adopted the principle. James J. White & Robert S. Summers, *Uniform Commercial Code* § 2—1, at 50 (2d ed.1980). Currently, every state has a Statute of Frauds, although there are variations in scope among the different states.

California's basic Statute of Frauds, which is based on the original English Statute of Frauds enacted in 1677 (and is typical of many other states), is set forth, in part, below.

California Civil Code section 1624

(a) The following contracts are invalid, unless they, or some note or memorandum thereof, are in writing and subscribed by the party to be charged or by the party's agent:

(1) An agreement that by its terms is not to be performed within a year from the making thereof.

(2) A special promise to answer for the debt, default, or miscarriage of another, except in the cases provided for in Section 2794.

(3) An agreement for the leasing for a longer period than one year, or for the sale of real property, or of an interest therein; such an agreement, if made by an agent of the party sought to be charged, is invalid, unless the authority of the agent is in writing, subscribed by the party sought to be charged.

(4) An agreement authorizing or employing an agent, broker, or any other person to purchase or sell real estate, or to lease real estate for a longer period than one year, or to procure, introduce, or find a purchaser or seller of real estate or a lessee or lessor of real estate where the lease is for a longer period than one year, for compensation or a commission.

(5) An agreement that by its terms is not to be performed during the lifetime of the promisor.

(6) An agreement by a purchaser of real property to pay an indebtedness secured by a mortgage or deed of trust upon the property purchased, unless assumption of the indebtedness by the purchaser is specifically provided for in the conveyance of the property.

"Party to be Charged"

The reference in the rule to the "party to be charged" means the individual or entity against whom the agreement is being enforced. I.e., the person or entity that is trying to avoid liability under the contract.

Contracts That Are Within The Statute of Frauds

"A contract is said to be 'within the statute' if its provisions are such that its operation and enforceability depend upon compliance with the requirements of the statute; it is said to be 'not within the statute' if its operation and enforceability do not depend on such compliance. According to this usage, a contract may be 'within the statute' even though it is completely in writing and duly signed and delivered, so that the requirements of the statute are fully satisfied." (Corbin, Contracts (One Vol.Ed) § 276.)

Contracts Not To Be Performed Within One Year

A contract that by its terms is not to be completely performed within a year from the making thereof is within the Statute of Frauds. (See Rest.2d § 130) The year is calculated from the time of formation to the completion of performance, so even a performance that will take a day is within the one-year provision if it is to begin at some time in the future and will not be complete until more than a year after the contract was originally formed.

White Lighting Company v. Wolfson
California Supreme Court
68 Cal.2d 336, 438 P.2d 345, 66 Cal.Rptr. 697 (1968)

TOBRINER, J. . . . Plaintiff White Lighting Company, hereinafter "White," sued defendant Wolfson to recover $850 for money due and owing. Wolfson denied the indebtedness and filed his first cross-complaint against White, Shaft (the president, controlling owner, and a director of White), Beber (an officer and director of White), and Basin (a corporation) on November 9, 1964. The cross-complaint alleged in substance that Wolfson and cross-defendants entered into an oral employment contract which obligated White to employ Wolfson on a "permanent" basis; . . . and that White and cross-defendants Shaft and Beber had breached an oral termination of employment agreement. The trial court sustained general and special demurrers to the cross-complaint with leave to amend. . . .

The second amended cross-complaint contained five counts. The trial court sustained general demurrers to the first count (oral employment contract), the second count (oral termination of employment contract), . . . without leave to amend. . . .

The causes of action alleged in the first two counts are not barred by the statute of frauds . . .

Wolfson alleged as the first count of the second amended cross-complaint that during October 1963 cross-defendants promised him that if he would continue with White as vice president and sales manager he would receive a salary of $300 per week, automobile and other business expenses, and one percent of the annual gross sales of White exceeding one million dollars per year, payable quarterly commencing November 1, 1963. Although Wolfson relied to his detriment on these oral representations and performed all the conditions, cross-defendants refused not only to comply with the promise as to the percentage of gross receipts but also to give Wolfson any information by which he could determine if any amount was owing to him. Although Wolfson's employment was to be on a "permanent" basis, it was not to continue for any specified period. To this count the trial court sustained a general demurrer without leave to amend on the ground that the alleged oral employment contract violated the statute of frauds. (Civ. Code, 1624, subd. 1.)

Even though part of an employee's compensation is to be measured by annual receipts of the employer, the statute of frauds does not apply to an employment contract unless its terms provide that the employee cannot completely perform it within one year from the making of the contract. Civil Code section 1624, subdivision 1, invalidates "an agreement that by its terms is not to be performed within a year from the making thereof" unless the contract "or some note or memorandum thereof, is in writing and subscribed by the party to be charged or by his agent." The cases hold that section 1624, subdivision 1, applies only to those contracts which, by their terms, cannot possibly be performed within one year (E.g., Hollywood Motion Picture Equipment Co. v. Furer (1940) 16 Cal.2d 184, 187 [105 P.2d 299]; Keller v. Pacific Turf Club (1961) 192 Cal.App.2d 189, 195-196 [13 Cal.Rptr. 346].) [fn. 2]

The contractual provision that Wolfson would receive one percent of the annual gross sales of White exceeding one million dollars per year does not in itself convert the oral employment contract into one which by its terms cannot be performed within a year. Decisions involving other oral employment contracts with similar terms as to compensation support this conclusion. Thus the statute of frauds does not apply to employment contracts for an indefinite period merely because the contract provides that payment will be forthcoming on termination of the employment relationship. (Lloyd v. Kleefisch (1941) 48 Cal.App.2d 408, 414 [120 P.2d 97].) Nor does the statute of frauds apply to employment contracts because the compensation for the services is to be measured by their value to the employer over a period of more than one year. (Reed Oil Co. v. Cain (1925) 169 Ark. 309 [275 S.W. 333].) Moreover, in Pecarovich v. Becker (1952) 113 Cal.App.2d 309, 315-316 [248 P.2d 123], the court held that the statute of frauds does not apply to an oral contract relating to the services and annual salary of a football coach for a three-year period; the court explained that the contract authorized the employer to terminate the employment relationship at the end of each year by payment of a named sum.

Our conclusion coincides with the position unanimously taken by the few courts that have dealt with oral employment contracts involving bonus or profit-sharing provisions. Thus in Dennis v. Thermoid Co. (1942) 128 N.J.L. 303, 305 [25 A.2d 886], the court held that a provision for a bonus payable at the end of the year did not render an oral employment contract not performable within that year.

Since in the instant case the alleged oral contract may be terminated at will be either party, it can, under its terms, be performed within one year. When Wolfson's employment relationship with White was terminated, Wolfson had completely performed; White's performance consisted of nothing more than compensating Wolfson. (See Roberts v. Wachter (1951) 104 Cal.App.2d 271, 280-281 [231 P.2d 534].) Moreover, as we have explained, the inclusion of the provision for a bonus ascertainable only after one year does not invalidate the oral agreement under the statute of frauds. . . .

[T]he judgment of dismissal is reversed and the cause is remanded to the trial court. . . .

Questions

1. Why did the trial court sustain a general demurrer without leave to amend to the first count of Wolfson's second amended cross-complaint?

2. According to Civil Code section 1624, subdivision 1, when does the statute of frauds apply to an employment contract?

3. Why did the court conclude that the alleged oral employment contract between Wolfson and White did not violate the statute of frauds?

Takeaways – White Lighting v. Wilson

As you have gathered from the Court's opinion, with respect to the one-year provision, the important words are "by its terms"; i.e., only those contracts which expressly preclude performance within a year are unenforceable. If it is merely unlikely that it will be so performed, or the period of performance is indefinite, the statute does not apply. An oral agreement which, according to the intention of the parties, as shown by the terms of the contract, might be fully performed within a year from the time it was made, is not within the statute, although the time of its performance is uncertain, and might probably extend, and be expected by the parties to extend, and does in fact extend, beyond the year. "The question is not what that probable, or expected, or actual performance of the contract was, but whether the contract, according to the reasonable interpretation of its terms, required that it should not be performed within the year." *Warner v Texas & P.R, Co.* 164 U.S. 418 (1896) The facts of *Warner* are the basis of Illustration 3, to Rest.2d § 130.

An oral contract that may be terminated at the will of either party can, under its terms, be performed within one year and therefore is not within the one-year provision of the Statute of Frauds. (*White Lighting Co. v. Wolfson*, 68 Cal.2d 336, 438 P.2d 345, 66 Cal.Rptr. 697 (1968).)

"In its actual application, however, the courts have been perhaps even less friendly to this provision [the "one year" section] than to the other provisions of the statute [of frauds]. They have observed the exact words of this provision and have interpreted them literally and very narrowly. ... To fall within the words of the provision, therefore, the agreement must be one of which it can truly be said at the very moment it is made, 'This agreement is not to be performed within one year'; in general, the cases indicate that there must not be the slightest possibility that it can be fully performed within one year." (Corbin on Contracts, [One Volume Edition] § 444, at p. 446.)

"Permanent" Employment Not Within the One-Year Provision

In 1897, the Supreme Judicial Court of Massachusetts rejected an employer's contention that the statute of frauds invalidated an oral agreement for "permanent employment" so long as the plaintiff, an enameler, performed his work satisfactorily. The Court rejected the employer's defense. "It has been repeatedly held that, if an agreement whose performance would otherwise extend beyond a year may be completely performed within a year on the happening of some contingency, it is not within the statute of frauds. [Citations.] In this case, we say nothing of other contingencies. The contract would have been completely performed if the defendant had ceased to carry on business within a year." (*Carnig v. Carr* (1897) 167 Mass. 544 [46 N.E. 117, 118].)

Leases of Longer Than One Year

Bed, Bath & Beyond of La Jolla v. La Jolla Village Square
California Court of Appeal, 1997
60 Cal.Rptr. 2d. 830

JONES, J. Plaintiff Bed, Bath & Beyond of La Jolla, Inc., negotiated for a lease of retail space in a shopping center owned by La Jolla Village Square Venture Partners. The negotiated terms of the lease were reduced to a written agreement which was signed by plaintiff but never by La Jolla. Instead, La Jolla leased the subject premises for higher rent than that negotiated by plaintiff to defendant Linens 'N Things, Inc., a retail business in direct competition with plaintiff. fn. 2 Plaintiff filed an action against La Jolla and Linens 'N Things, asserting causes of action for specific performance, breach of contract and fraud against La Jolla and causes of action for interference with contractual relations and prospective economic advantage against Linens 'N Things. The court granted summary adjudication against plaintiff on each of its causes of action except the one for fraud, concluding the alleged lease agreement was within the statute of frauds and Linens 'N Things' "fair competition" privilege was a complete defense to plaintiff's claim for interference with prospective economic advantage. Plaintiff later voluntarily dismissed its fraud cause of action.

On appeal plaintiff contends: (1) the alleged lease agreement between plaintiff and La Jolla is not rendered unenforceable by the statute of frauds; . . . We affirm.

Factual and Procedural Background

From May 1992 through January 1993 plaintiff negotiated with representatives of La Jolla for a lease of retail space in La Jolla Village Square, a shopping center La Jolla was then in the process of building. In February 1993 La Jolla's legal representative in the negotiations presented plaintiff with four copies of a proposed written lease agreement and guaranty agreement to be executed by plaintiff and its guarantor, plaintiff's parent corporation. The cover letter accompanying these documents requested they be executed by plaintiff and its guarantor and returned to

La Jolla's legal representative for "execution by the Landlord." Plaintiff signed the lease and its parent corporation signed the guaranty. The documents were then returned to La Jolla for execution.

La Jolla never executed the lease. In late March 1993 the representative of La Jolla who negotiated the proposed lease with plaintiff informed plaintiff that La Jolla intended to lease the subject premises to Linens 'N Things, plaintiff's competitor. Prior to that communication plaintiff was unaware that La Jolla had been negotiating with Linens 'N Things.

In April 1993 plaintiff filed its complaint in the instant action and later filed a first amended complaint. The first amended complaint included causes of action for specific performance, breach of contract, and fraud against La Jolla and causes of action for intentional interference with "economic relationship" and intentional interference with "prospective business agreement" against Linens 'N Things. The first amended complaint also included a cause of action for injunctive relief against all defendants, seeking to enjoin La Jolla from leasing the subject premises to Linens 'N Things.

Plaintiff's claims were challenged by two separate motions for summary adjudication. First, La Jolla and Linens 'N Things jointly moved for summary adjudication as to plaintiff's first, second, third and fifth causes of action for specific performance, breach of contract, injunctive relief, and intentional interference with contractual relations, respectively. The court granted defendants' motion, concluding: "The Statute of Frauds, as set forth in Civil Code sections 1091 and 1624[, subdivision (d)] and Code of Civil Procedure section 1971, requires that the lease alleged by plaintiff be in writing, duly subscribed by the party to be charged. The factual predicate to each of the causes of action [challenged by defendants' motion] is a valid, enforceable lease." . . .

Plaintiff's principal contention on appeal is that the trial court erred by ruling the lease between plaintiff and La Jolla is subject to the statute of frauds. We conclude the trial court correctly ruled the statute of frauds renders the alleged lease agreement unenforceable.

Three different "statutes of fraud" apply to bar enforcement of the alleged lease agreement in this case. Civil Code section 1624, subdivision (d) specifies, as a type of contract which is invalid unless it is in writing and subscribed by the party to be charged, "[a]n agreement ... to lease real estate for a longer period than one year ...."

Civil Code section 1091 provides: "An estate in real property, other than an estate at will or for a term not exceeding one year, can be transferred only by operation of law, or by an instrument in writing, subscribed by the party disposing of the same, or by his agent thereunto authorized by writing."

Similarly, Code of Civil Procedure section 1971 provides, in pertinent part: "No estate or interest in real property, other than for leases for a term not exceeding one year, ... can be created, granted, assigned, surrendered, or declared, otherwise than by operation of law, or a conveyance or other instrument in writing, subscribed by the party creating, granting, assigning, surrendering, or declaring the same, or by the party's lawful agent thereunto authorized by writing." (Italics added.)

Thus, Civil Code section 1624, subdivision (d) requires that an agreement to lease property for a term longer than one year be in writing and signed by the "party to be charged" while Civil Code section 1091 and Code of Civil Procedure section 1971 more specifically require that a lease of property for a term longer than one year be in writing and signed by the lessor. (See Kevich v. R.L.C., Inc. (1959) 173 Cal.App.2d 315, 321 [343 P.2d 402].) Whether viewed as an oral agreement or written agreement, plaintiff's alleged lease agreement is unenforceable because it is undisputed that La Jolla, the lessor and "party to be charged," never signed the draft instrument that plaintiff signed. (Tabata v. Murane (1944) 24 Cal.2d 221, 228 [148 P.2d 605] [agreements which are invalid under Civil Code section 1624 are unenforceable].)

Plaintiff contends the lease agreement is not subject to the statute of frauds because it possibly could have been performed within one year from the date of its making. Plaintiff's argument rests on two provisions in the unexecuted written lease. Article 3, subdivision (b) of the lease provided the tenant could terminate the lease before the rental term commenced if the landlord failed to begin certain preparatory work on the leased premises by June 1, 1993, or substantially complete that work by December 31, 1993. Article 3, subdivision (c) gave the landlord the right to terminate the lease before commencement of the rental term if the landlord was unable to obtain the various governmental permits and approvals required for construction of the premises despite exercising diligence and good faith in attempting to do so.

As authority for its position that these provisions take the lease out of the statute of frauds, plaintiff relies primarily on Fisher v. Parsons (1963) 213 Cal.App.2d 829 [29 Cal.Rptr. 210]. In Fisher, the plaintiff lessor sued the defendant lessee for breach of an oral lease agreement under which the defendant promised to rent office space in the plaintiff's building as long as the defendant remained in business and required office space. (Id. at pp. 832-833.) The Fisher court held the lease was not subject to the statute of frauds because its term possibly could have been less than one year. The court rejected the defendant's attempt to distinguish Civil Code section 1624, subdivision (a) concerning agreements that cannot be performed within one year generally, and the provision in subdivision (d) concerning agreements to lease real property for a period of more than one year. The court stated: "Respondent's effort to differentiate between subdivisions 1 and 4 of the statute of frauds must prove sterile. Those subdivisions are applied indiscriminately to leases in this state and as if they were exact equivalents. Subdivision 1 refers to an agreement 'that by its terms is not to be performed within a year from the making thereof.' Subdivision 4: 'An agreement for the leasing for a longer period than one year.' The language of the two subdivisions expresses the same thought, that the agreement or lease must be so worded that it cannot be performed within a year." (Fisher v. Parsons, supra, 213 Cal.App.2d at p. 837.)

We disagree with Fisher that subdivisions (a) and (d) of Civil Code section 1624 express the same thought. Subdivision (a) applies to agreements in general which cannot be performed within one year, whereas subdivision (d) applies to lease agreements where the term or duration of the lease is longer than one year. Subdivision (d) is a more specific provision than subdivision (a) because the focus of subdivision (d) is not the overall agreement to lease, which may be terminable within one year of its making and prior to commencement of the actual lease term, but rather on the duration or term of the lease.

It is a settled rule of statutory construction that statutes relating to the same subject matter must be read together and harmonized if possible. (Brown v. West Covina Toyota (1994) 26 Cal.App.4th 555, 565-566 [32 Cal.Rptr.2d 85].) When Civil Code section 1624, subdivision (d) is read in conjunction with Civil Code section 1091 and Code of Civil Procedure section 1971, it is clear the Legislature intended that an agreement to lease real property for a term exceeding one year cannot be enforced by a lessee unless it is in writing and signed by the lessor.

The distinction between subdivisions (a) and (d) of Civil Code section 1624 was immaterial in Fisher because the oral lease in that case was of an indefinite term which could have expired in less than one year from the date it commenced. Fisher applied the principle of subdivision (a)-i.e., that an oral contract is invalid only when by its own terms it cannot be performed within one year from the date it is made-to subdivision (d), concluding "[s]ubdivision [(d)] does not apply to a lease for an indefinite term which can be performed within a year." (Fisher v. Parsons, supra, 213 Cal.App.2d at p. 837.) Fisher could apply either subdivision (a) or (d) of Civil Code section 1624 indiscriminately because the result under either provision was the same.

In contrast, the distinction between subdivisions (a) and (d) of Civil Code section 1624 is critical in the instant case. If we were to strictly apply subdivision (a) without regard to subdivision (d), plaintiff's alleged agreement to lease arguably would not fall within the statute of frauds because it could be performed within one year (assuming termination prior to commencement of the lease term due to failure of a condition precedent constitutes "performance"). On the other hand, application of Civil Code section 1624, subdivision (d), along with Civil Code section 1091 and Code of Civil Procedure section 1971, renders the alleged lease unenforceable despite its pre-commencement termination provisions because the actual term of the lease exceeds one year.

It is a fundamental principle that " ' "[a] specific provision relating to a particular subject will govern a general provision, even though the general provision standing alone would be broad enough to include the subject to which the specific provision relates." ' [Citations.]" (Prudential Reinsurance Co. v. Superior Court (1992) 3 Cal.4th 1118, 1148 [14 Cal.Rptr.2d 749, 842 P.2d 48] (dis. opn. of Kline, J.).) Since Civil Code section 1624, subdivision (d) concerning agreements to lease real property for a term longer than one year is a more specific provision than Civil Code section 1624, subdivision (a) concerning agreements in general that cannot be performed within one year from the date of making, subdivision (d) controls over subdivision (a) where the two provisions conflict.

Therefore, we hold that an agreement to lease real property for a term exceeding one year is within the statute of frauds of Civil Code section 1624, subdivision (d) regardless whether such agreement provides that it may be canceled or terminated within one year of the date of its making and prior to commencement of the lease term. Accordingly, the trial court correctly concluded the alleged lease agreement in the instant case was unenforceable under the statute of frauds, as it was an agreement to lease real property for a term exceeding one year and was not signed by the lessor, La Jolla.

Questions

1. Which statutes of frauds were found to be applicable in this case, and what requirements did they impose on the lease agreement?

2. How did the plaintiff argue that the lease agreement was not subject to the statute of frauds?

3. What was the court's reasoning in distinguishing between subdivisions (a) and (d) of Civil Code section 1624 and applying subdivision (d) to render the lease agreement unenforceable?

The Suretyship Clause

A promise to answer for the debt or duty of another is within the Statute of Frauds. If you have ever been asked to co-sign someone else's loan, you can thank the suretyship clause of the Statute of Frauds. Oral promises to pay someone else's debt if they flake out on it are unenforceable.

Langman v. Alumni Association of University of Virginia
Virginia Supreme Court, 1994
442 S.E.2d 669

The deed that is the subject of this litigation is dated December 30, 1986. It states that Langman and Stowe, as grantors, convey to the Alumni Association, as grantee, the Ferdinand's Arcade property in fee simple. The consideration recited is "the love and respect which the Grantors have for the University of Virginia."

The deed states that the property is subject to the lien of the deed of trust securing the $600,000 debt to Dominion Federal. The next sentence reads, "The Grantee does hereby assume payment of such obligation and agrees to hold the Grantors harmless from further liability on such obligation." The deed was not signed by a representative of the Alumni Association, nor was there a space provided for the grantee's signature. . . .

The evidence also established an oral agreement between Stowe and the Alumni Association whereby Stowe undertook, after the conveyance of Ferdinand's Arcade to the Alumni Association, to "follow through, manage [the] property, collect the rents, and get it sold." Beginning in 1987, Stowe assumed the management of the property and its tenants, and saw that both the operating expenses and the mortgage debt were paid out of the property's income. When the income was insufficient to meet these expenses, Stowe paid the shortfall from his own funds. . . .

In the summer of 1989, Stowe apparently became unable to continue making up the shortfalls in expenses on the Ferdinand's Arcade property, including the debt service. At that time, his building and development corporation entered Chapter 11 bankruptcy proceedings.

In August 1989, Trustbank, the successor in interest to Dominion Federal, notified Langman that the note secured by the Ferdinand's Arcade property was in default, and it called upon her to cure the default. Langman in turn demanded that the Alumni Association make the required payments, but the Alumni Association disclaimed any responsibility for payment of the mortgage debt. Langman paid the amounts demanded under a reservation of rights and commenced this litigation. . . .

We . . . disagree with the Alumni Association's contention that the trial court erred in holding that the statute of frauds does not bar enforcement of a mortgage assumption clause that is not signed by the grantee.

Code § 11-2 provides, in material part:

Unless a promise, contract, agreement, representation, assurance, or ratification, or some memorandum or note thereof, is in writing and signed by the party to be charged or his agent, no action shall be brought in any of the following cases:

4. To charge any person upon a promise to answer for the debt, default, or misdoings of another[.]

The Alumni Association argues that the "suretyship" provision of the statute of frauds, Code § 11-2(4), required the Alumni Association to sign a written agreement to assume the mortgage. Citing Lawson v. States Construction Co., 193 Va. 513, 517, 69 S.E.2d 450, 453 (1952), the Alumni Association contends that this Court has held that any "collateral" promise to answer for the debts of another must comply with Code § 11-2(4). The Alumni Association asserts that, because Langman would remain secondarily liable to Dominion Federal on the mortgage debt even after an effective assumption of the debt, the Alumni Association's agreement to assume the mortgage was a "collateral" promise falling within the scope of Code § 11-2(4). We disagree.

A grantee who assumes an existing mortgage is not a surety. The grantee makes no promise to the mortgagee to pay the debt of another, but promises the grantor to pay to the mortgagee the debt the grantee owes to the grantor. This is an original undertaking. Blanton v. Keneipp, 155 Va. 668, 678, 156 S.E. 413, 416 (1931); 2 Devlin, supra, §§ 1056, 1073-74; 2 Leonard A. Jones, A Treatise on the Law of Mortgages of Real Property § 750 (7th ed. 1915); 5 Herbert T. Tiffany, The Law of Real Property § 1437 (3d ed. 1939); see also Goode v. Bryant, 118 Va. 314, 322-23, 87 S.E. 588, 591-92 (1915).

A collateral undertaking to which Code § 11-2(4) applies is one in which the promisor is merely a surety or guarantor, receives no direct benefit, and is liable only if the debtor defaults. Colonial Ford Truck Sales, Inc. v. Schneider, 228 Va. 671, 676, 325 S.E.2d 91, 93-94 (1985). Here, the Alumni Association received a direct benefit and did not merely act as surety for the grantors. Therefore, we conclude that the trial court did not err in ruling that the statute of frauds does not bar enforcement of the mortgage assumption clause.

Questions

1. According to the court's interpretation, why did the statute of frauds not bar enforcement of the mortgage assumption clause?

2. How did the court define a collateral undertaking to which the statute of frauds applies?

3. Why did the court conclude that the Alumni Association's agreement to assume the mortgage was not a collateral promise falling within the scope of the statute of frauds?

4. What were the key factors that led the court to determine that the Alumni Association received a direct benefit and did not merely act as a surety in this case?

The Main Purpose or Leading Object Rule Exception

Central Ceilings, Inc. v. National Amusements, Inc.
Appeals Court of Massachusetts, 2007
70 Mass. App. Ct. 172

PERRETTA, J. Central Ceilings, Inc. (Central), brought the present action against National Amusements, Inc. (National), seeking damages sustained as a result of a breach of an oral agreement it had with National. . . . a jury found that National was in breach of an oral promise to pay Central for its work. On appeal, National argues that the judge erred in denying its motions for a directed verdict, for judgment notwithstanding the verdict, and for a new trial. The principal issue before us on National's appeal is whether enforcement of the oral agreement is barred by the Statute of Frauds, G. L. c. 259, § 1, Second (the Statute). We agree with the judge's conclusion that the "main purpose" exception to the Statute was applicable and affirm the judgment.

1. The facts. There was evidence to show the following facts. National is the owner of a cinema theater complex in Lawrence. This dispute arose out of the construction of that complex (the Project). On or about March 10, 2000, National entered into a contract with Old Colony Construction Corporation (Old Colony), the general contractor, with an anticipated completion date of June 28, 2000. Central submitted a bid to Old Colony that Old Colony accepted on March 17, 2000, making Central a "core" subcontractor; specifically, Central was to do the drywall, acoustical, carpentry, and hardware installation work at the Project.

Meeting the anticipated completion date of June 28, 2000, proved difficult if not improbable due, in part, to delays caused by problems related to groundwater at the construction site. . . .

As matters stood as of the end of June, the completion date of September 3, 2000, was highly aggressive, if not unrealistic.

National, however, wanted to have the theater complex open for the Labor Day weekend because summer holiday weekends, with their large audiences and blockbuster releases, represented substantial revenue opportunities. In other words, National tried to schedule the opening of its new theater complex to coincide with a holiday or the release of blockbuster movies so as to open with a "splash." Put otherwise, there was evidence to show that National had an interest in having the Project completed and its theater complex opened before a competitor's theater in the same area opened.

There was another problem with the Project. In the spring of 2000, Old Colony was experiencing severe cash flow problems. These difficulties were due in large measure to its failure timely to bill National for work performed on the Project as well as on earlier projects. Old Colony owed substantial sums to its subcontractors, including Central, for work done on past projects. In June, 2000, Old Colony owed Central over one million dollars for its work on prior projects. Old Colony was not paying invoices in a timely fashion, and some of its checks were returned as uncollected. As a consequence, when the groundwater problem was starting to be resolved and work could have been continued, many subcontractors were refusing to return to the Project.

While the revised architectural redesign plans were complete, they called for a change in the scope of the work to be performed by Central. As things stood at the end of June, Central estimated that it would need to increase its manpower substantially on the Project in order to meet a September completion date.

It is against the backdrop of these problems that Joseph McPherson, a Central manager, informed Old Colony's project manager, Patrick Hogan, that Central would not go forward with its work unless he obtained "assurances" of payment from National. He demanded that Hogan arrange for him to meet with National's then vice-president of construction, Peter Brady.

Just prior to the July 4, 2000, holiday, Brady, Hogan, McPherson and others met. There was discussion of the fact that Old Colony owed Central substantial sums of money and that the revised scope of the work would require additional funding if Central were to accomplish its work by Labor Day. McPherson indicated that Central would not continue its work on the Project without a payment commitment from National. He told Brady, "[Y]ou've got to guarantee me the payments. You've got to guarantee me that I will get funded for this project." Brady said that "he would guarantee [McPherson]." However, his promise to McPherson was not made conditional upon Old Colony's prior default in paying for the work. It was ultimately agreed by Brady and McPherson that Central would continue to work under the direction of Old Colony and that National would pay half the amount due Central on the Monday after Labor Day and the balance ten days thereafter. Central set to work the day after this meeting and achieved substantial completion of its work by August 25, 2000.

In November of 2000, National issued a joint check to Old Colony and Central in the amount $679,949.75, ... The amount of the check was a partial payment of what Central claimed it was owed, but National refused to pay Central its claimed unpaid balance of $593,237.25. In the course of reconciling its account for the Project, National discovered that Brady had collaborated with the president of Old Colony in a scheme to defraud National on a number of construction projects, including the project in issue, by inflating Old Colony's contract price above what was necessary to accomplish the work and then splitting the overage.

In March, 2001, Central brought this action alleging breach of contract against Old Colony and seeking to establish a lien on National's property pursuant to G. L. c. 254. After a default judgment was entered against Old Colony in the amount of $593,237.25, plus interest and costs, Central amended its complaint to add claims against National for breach of its agreement to pay Central for its work at the Project, quantum meruit, and violations of G. L. c. 93A. The quantum meruit and G. L. c. 93A claims, as well as Central's request for a lien on National's property, were dismissed at various stages of the litigation, leaving for trial its claim against National for breach of contract.

2. The special questions and post trial motions. In response to special questions, the jury found that (1) Brady did promise to pay Central the debt of Old Colony for Central's work on the Project; (2) Brady had the actual or apparent authority to make such a promise on behalf of National; (3) National's promise was supported by valid consideration; (4) the main purpose of the agreement between National and Central was to bestow a benefit upon National to which it was not already entitled; (5) National was in breach of its promise; and (6) Central was entitled to receive $593,237.25 from National as a result of that breach. . . .

3. The issues. National argues on appeal that Brady's alleged oral promise to McPherson at the meeting prior to July 4, 2000, was, at best, a promise "to answer for the debt . . . of another," G. L. c. 259, § 1, Second, and was unenforceable as it was not in writing. Ibid. . . .

4. Discussion. In taking up National's various allegations of error, we begin with its argument that, if successful, would be decisive of the appeal, that is, whether the evidence was sufficient to show that Central's claim was barred by G. L. c. 259, § 1, Second.

a. The Statute of Frauds. General Laws, c. 159, § 1, Second, provides:

"No action shall be brought: . . . [t]o charge a person upon a special promise to answer for the debt, default or misdoings of another . . . [u]nless the promise, contract or agreement upon which such action is brought, or some memorandum or note thereof, is in writing and signed by the party to be charged therewith or by some person thereunto by him lawfully authorized."

In ruling on National's post trial motions, the judge applied the long-recognized exception to the Statute, the so-called "leading object" or "main purpose" exception. In Ames v. Foster, 106 Mass. 400 , 403 (1871), the court stated:

"[A] case is not within the statute, where, upon the whole transaction, the fair inference is, that the leading object or purpose and the effect of the transaction was the purchase or acquisition by the promisor from the promisee of some property, lien or benefit which he did not before possess, but which enured to him by reason of his promise, so that the debt for which he is liable may fairly be deemed to be a debt of his own, contracted in such purchase or acquisition." . . .

c. *National's defenses to Central's claims.* National contends that the oral promise made between it and Central is within the Statute, and because Central never released Old Colony from liability, Central's claims are barred by the Statute. Its argument suggests that in order to be excluded from the operation of the Statute, the agreement in issue must effect a novation, that is, the creditor, Central, must accept the new promisor, National, as its debtor in place of the original obligor, Old Colony. National also argues that there was no evidence of a benefit flowing to it "sufficient" to bring the oral promise within the "leading object" exception to the Statute.

In support of both its contentions, National cites to a line of decisions in general accord with the proposition that "[a] promise by an owner . . . or a mortgagee . . . of land, to pay a contractor what another owes him if he will finish the building according to his contract, [is] within the statute, although the owner or mortgagee obtains a benefit." . . . The court's conclusion in these cases, that the owner or mortgagee had merely promised to pay the debt of another, rested in whole or part on the fact that the subcontractor had not released the general contractor from liability. See Gill, 111 Mass. at 503-504; Ribock, 218 Mass. at 7; Slotnick, 252 Mass. at 305; Collins, 276 Mass. at 107. See also Greenberg v. Weisman, 345 Mass. 700, 702 (1963) (acknowledging but distinguishing general proposition on basis that where original contract no longer in existence due to general contractor's repudiation of contract with subcontractor, novation not required to establish new contract with owner).

Our analysis of National's claims begins with the premise that "[i]f liability on the part of another . . . is extinguished by a novation . . . the promise is 'original' and not within the statute." Colpitts v. L.C. Fisher Co., 289 Mass. at 234. The Statute is implicated only where a "promisor purports to add his liability to a continuing liability on the part of a principal debtor." Ibid. See American Fireworks Co. of Mass. v. Morrison, 300 Mass. 531 , 536 (1938); 4 Corbin, Contracts § 15.20, at 309-310 (rev.ed. 1997); 9 Williston, Contracts § 22:5, at 244-245 (4th ed. 1999).

Novation, however, is but one ground on which a promise is removed from the operation of the Statute. The "leading object" exception to the Statute addresses a separate and distinct set of circumstances. They are that (1) a third party is indebted; (2) there is no novation; and (3) the third party's duty to the creditor will be terminated by the performance promised by the defendant. See 4 Corbin, Contracts, supra § 16.12 at 362. Under the "leading object" exception to the Statute, an oral agreement that does not effect a novation may nonetheless be enforceable if the facts and circumstances of the transaction show that the promise was given primarily or solely to serve the promisor's own interests. In the decisions relied upon by National, it does not appear that the "leading object" exception to the Statute was expressly rejected as a basis for enforcing an oral contract.

In another line of decisions, it is recognized that a property owner's promise to pay subcontractors or suppliers may, in appropriate circumstances, come within the "leading object" exception to the Statute. See Hayes v. Guy, 348 Mass. at 756-757; Barboza v. Liberty Contractors Co., 18 Mass. App. Ct. at 971. See also Gegan, Some Exceptions to the Suretyship Statute of Frauds: A Tale of Two Courts, 79 St. John's L. Rev. 319, 353 (2005). Based upon these authorities the question now before us is whether the circumstances presented in the instant case are such as to bring it within the "leading object" exception to the Statute.

There was evidence here to show that (1) National wanted to open the theater at the Project by the end of August so as to capture large audiences over the Labor Day weekend and thereby tap the revenue and business opportunities associated with a movie premier and the Labor Day weekend; (2) as of the beginning of July, the work to be completed for the anticipated opening would have to be completed in a "tight time frame"; (3) Central was one of the "core" subcontractors on the Project and was responsible for significant portions of the work to be completed; (4) Central had completed its preliminary work and was poised to start building; and (5) given the circumstances, Central was one of the few subcontractors in Massachusetts, if not the only one, capable of delivering the necessary work in the time frame desired by National.

Under these circumstances, we conclude that the evidence was sufficient to warrant a finding that National's promise -- made through Brady, who was found by the jury to have the apparent authority to make such a promise -- was given to secure Central's continued and expedited performance at the Project and that the satisfaction of any obligation on the part of Old Colony was merely incidental to that promise. See Hayes v. Guy, 348 Mass. at 757; Barboza v. Liberty Contractors Co., 18 Mass. App. Ct. at 971-972.

Judgment affirmed.

Question

1. What exception to the Statute of Frauds did the court apply in this case, and what are the requirements for invoking this exception?

2. What were the specific circumstances that the court considered to determine whether the "leading object" exception to the Statute of Frauds applied?

3. How did the court differentiate between the requirement of novation and the "leading object" exception?

4. Based on the evidence presented, why did the court conclude that National's promise to pay Central's debt was primarily intended to secure Central's continued and expedited performance rather than simply assuming Old Colony's liability?

Takeaways – Central Ceilings

A promise to answer for the debt, duty or obligation of another is within the Statute of Frauds. This is known as the suretyship clause. There is a major exception to this suretyship provision which is known as the "main purpose" or "leading object" rule. That rule says that where the consideration for the promise is beneficial to the promisor, and the circumstances indicate that she gave the promise mainly for her own monetary gain or business advantage, the writing requirement of the Statute of Frauds does not apply, in spite of the fact that the promise may be in form one to pay the debt of another.

Contracts for the Sale of Goods For a Price of $500 or More

UCC § 2-201(1) provides "Except as otherwise provided in this section a contract for the sale of goods for the price of $500 or more is not enforceable by way of action or defense unless there is some writing sufficient to indicate that a contract for sale has been made between the parties and signed by the party against whom enforcement is sought or by his authorized agent or broker. A writing is not insufficient because it omits or incorrectly states a term agreed upon but the contract is not enforceable under this paragraph beyond the quantity of goods shown in such writing."

Southwest Engineering Co., Inc. v. Martin Tractor Co.
Supreme Court of Kansas, 1970
205 Kan. 684, 473 P.2d 18

FONTRON, J. This is an action to recover damages for breach of contract. Trial was had to the court which entered judgment in favor of the plaintiff. The defendant has appealed.

Southwest Engineering Company, Inc., the plaintiff, is a Missouri corporation engaged in general contracting work, while the defendant, Martin Tractor Company, Inc., is a Kansas corporation. The two parties will be referred to hereafter either as plaintiff, or Southwest, on the one hand and defendant, or Martin, on the other.

We glean from the record that in April, 1966, the plaintiff was interested in submitting a bid to the United States Corps of Engineers for the construction of certain runway lighting facilities at McConnell Air Force Base at Wichita. However, before submitting a bid, and on April 11, 1966, the plaintiff's construction superintendent, Mr. R.E. Cloepfil, called the manager of Martin's engine department,

Mr. Ken Hurt, who at the time was at Colby, asking for a price on a standby generator and accessory equipment. Mr. Hurt replied that he would phone him back from Topeka, which he did the next day, quoting a price of $18,500. This quotation was re-confirmed by Hurt over the phone on April 13.

Southwest submitted its bid on April 14, 1966, using Hurt's figure of $18,500 for the generating equipment, and its bid was accepted. On April 20, Southwest notified Martin that its bid had been accepted. Hurt and Cloepfil thereafter agreed over the phone to meet in Springfield on April 28. On that date Hurt flew to Springfield, where the two men conferred at the airfield restaurant for about an hour. Hurt took to the meeting a copy of the job specifications which the government had supplied Martin prior to the letting.

At the Springfield meeting it developed that Martin had upped its price for the generator and accessory equipment from $18,500 to $21,500. Despite this change of position by Martin, concerning which Cloepfil was understandably amazed, the two men continued their conversation and, according to Cloepfil, they arrived at an agreement for the sale of a D353 generator and accessories for the sum of $21,500. In addition it was agreed that if the Corps of Engineers would accept a less expensive generator, a D343, the aggregate price to Southwest would be $15,000. The possibility of providing alternate equipment, the D343, was suggested by Mr. Hurt, apparently in an attempt to mollify Mr. Cloepfil when the latter learned that Martin had reneged on its price quotation of April 12. It later developed that the Corps of Engineers would not approve the cheaper generator and that Southwest eventually had to supply the more expensive D353 generator.

At the conference, Mr. Hurt separately listed the component parts of each of the two generators on the top half of a sheet of paper and set out the price after each item. The prices were then totaled. On the bottom half of the sheet Hurt set down the accessories common to both generators and their cost. This handwritten memorandum, as it was referred to during the trial, noted a 10 per cent discount on the aggregate cost of each generator, while the accessories were listed at Martin's cost. The price of the D353 was rounded off at $21,500 and the D343 at $15,000. The memorandum was handed to Cloepfil while the two men were still at the airport. We will refer to this memorandum further during the course of this opinion.

On May 2, 1966, Cloepfil addressed a letter to the Martin Tractor Company, directing Martin to proceed with shop drawings and submittal documents for the McConnell lighting job and calling attention to the fact that applicable government regulations were required to be followed. Further reference to this communication will be made when necessary.

Some three weeks thereafter, on May 24, 1966, Hurt wrote Cloepfil the following letter:

"MARTIN TRACTOR COMPANY, INC. Topeka Chanute Concordia Colby CATERPILLAR "P.O. Box 1698 Topeka, Kansas May 24, 1966 Mr. R.E. Cloepfil Southwest Engineering Co., Inc. P.O. Box 3314, Glenstone Station Springfield, Missouri 65804

Dear Sir:

Due to restrictions placed on Caterpillar products, accessory suppliers, and other stipulations by the district governing agency, we cannot accept your letter to proceed dated May 2, 1966, and hereby withdraw all verbal quotations. Regretfully, /s/ Ken Hurt Ken Hurt, Manager Engine Division"

On receipt of this unwelcome missive, Cloepfil telephoned Mr. Hurt who stated they had some work underway for the Corps of Engineers in both the Kansas City and Tulsa districts and did not want to take on any other work for the Corps at that time. Hurt assured Cloepfil he could buy the equipment from anybody at the price Martin could sell it for. Later investigation showed, however, that such was not the case.

In August of 1966, Mr. Cloepfil and Mr. Anderson, the president of Southwest, traveled to Topeka in an effort to persuade Martin to fulfill its contract. Hurt met them at the company office where harsh words were bandied about. Tempers eventually cooled off and at the conclusion of the verbal melee, hands were shaken all around and Hurt went so far as to say that if Southwest still wanted to buy the equipment from them to submit another order and he would get it handled. On this promising note the protagonists parted.

After returning to Springfield, Mr. Cloepfil, on September 6, wrote Mr. Hurt placing an order for a D353 generator (the expensive one) and asking that the order be given prompt attention, as their completion date was in early December. This communication was returned unopened.

A final effort to communicate with Martin was attempted by Mr. Anderson when the unopened letter was returned. A phone call was placed for Mr. Martin, himself, and Mr. Anderson was informed by the girl on the switchboard that Martin was in Colorado Springs on a vacation. Anderson then placed a call to the motel where he was told Mr. Martin could be reached. Martin refused to talk on the call, on learning the caller's name, and Anderson was told he would have to contact his office.

Mr. Anderson then replaced his call to Topeka and reached either the company comptroller or the company treasurer who responded by cussing him and saying "Who in the hell do you think you are? We don't have to sell you a damn thing."

Southwest eventually secured the generator equipment from Foley Tractor Co. of Wichita, a company which Mr. Hurt had one time suggested, at a price of $27,541. The present action was then filed, seeking damages of $6,041 for breach of the contract and $9,000 for loss resulting from the delay caused by the breach. The trial court awarded damages of $6,041 for the breach but rejected damages allegedly due to delay. The defendant, only, has appealed; there is no cross-appeal by plaintiff.

The basic disagreement centers on whether the meeting between Hurt and Cloepfil at Springfield resulted in an agreement which was enforceable under the provisions of the Uniform Commercial Code (sometimes referred to as the Code), which was enacted by the Kansas Legislature at its 1965 session. K.S.A. 84-2-201 (1), being part of the Code, provides:

"Except as otherwise provided in this section a contract for the sale of goods for the price of $500 or more is not enforceable by way of action or defense unless there is some writing sufficient to indicate that a contract for sale has been made between the parties and signed by the party against whom enforcement is sought or by his authorized agent or broker. A writing is not insufficient because it omits or incorrectly states a term agreed upon but the contract is not enforceable under this paragraph beyond the quantity of goods shown in such writing."

Southwest takes the position that the memorandum prepared by Hurt at Springfield supplies the essential elements of a contract required by the foregoing statute, i.e., that it is (1) a writing signed by the party sought to be charged, (2) that it is for the sale of goods and (3) that quantity is shown. In addition, the reader will have noted that the memorandum sets forth the prices of the several items listed.

It cannot be gainsaid that the Uniform Commercial Code has effected a somewhat radical change in the law relating to the formation of enforceable contracts as such has been expounded by this and other courts. In the Kansas Comment to 84-2-201, which closely parallels the Official UCC Comment, the following explanation is given:

"Subsection (1) relaxes the interpretations of many courts in providing that the required writing need not contain all the material terms and that they need not be stated precisely. All that is required is that the writing afford a basis for believing that the offered oral evidence rests on a real transaction. Only three definite and invariable requirements as to the writing are made by this subsection. First, it must evidence a contract for the sale of goods; second, it must be `signed,' a word which includes any authentication which identifies the party to be charged; and third, it must specify quantity. Terms relating to price, time, and place of payment or delivery, the general quality of goods, or any particular warranties may all be omitted."

From legal treatises, as well, we learn that the three invariable requirements of an enforceable written memorandum under 84-2-201 are that it evidence a sale of goods, that it be signed or authenticated and that it specify quantity. In Vernon's Kansas Statutes Annotated, Uniform Commercial Code, Howe and Navin, the writers make this clear:

"Under the Code the writing does not need to incorporate all the terms of the transaction, nor do the terms need to be stated precisely. The Code does require that the writing be broad enough to indicate a contract of sale between the parties; that the party against whom enforcement is sought, or his agent, must have signed the writing; and that the quantity dealt with must be stated. Any error concerning the quantity stated in the memorandum prevents enforcement of the agreement beyond the precise quantity stated."

The defendant does not seriously question the interpretation accorded the statute by eminent scriveners and scholars, but maintains, nonetheless, that the writing in question does not measure up to the stature of a signed memorandum within the purview of the Code; that the instrument simply sets forth verbal quotations for future consideration in continuing negotiations.

But on this point the trial court found there was an agreement reached between Hurt and Cloepfil at Springfield; that the formal requirements of K.S.A. 84-2-201 were satisfied; and that the memorandum prepared by Hurt contains the three essentials of the statute in that it evidences a sale of goods, was authenticated by Hurt and specifies quantity. Beyond that, the court specifically found that Hurt had apparent authority to make the agreement; that both Southwest and Martin were "merchants" as defined in K.S.A. 84-2-104; that the agreement reached at Springfield included additional terms not noted in the writing: (1) Southwest was to install the equipment; (2) Martin was to deliver the equipment to Wichita and (3) Martin was to assemble and supply submittal documents within three weeks; and that Martin's letter of May 24, 1966, constituted an anticipatory breach of the contract.

We believe the record supports all the above findings. With particular reference to the preparation and sufficiency of the written memorandum, the following evidence is pertinent:

Mr. Cloepfil testified that he and Hurt sat down at a restaurant table and spread out the plans which Hurt had brought with him; that they went through the specifications item by item and Hurt wrote each item down, together with the price thereof; that while the specifications called for a D353 generator, Hurt thought the D343 model might be an acceptable substitute, so he gave prices on both of them and Southwest could take either one of the two which the Corps of Engineers would approve; that Hurt gave him (Cloepfil) the memorandum "as a record of what we had done, the agreement we had arrived at our meeting in the restaurant at the airport." . . .

Neither confirmation nor acceptance by Southwest was needed on May 2 to breathe life into the agreement previously concluded at Springfield, for it was memorialized in writing at the time of making. In an article entitled "The Law of Sales Under the Uniform Commercial Code, 17 Rutgers Law Review 14, Professor Calvin W. Corman writes:

"The Code Provision merely requires that the writing be sufficient to indicate that a contract for sale has been made between the parties."

In our opinion the instant memorandum amply satisfies that requirement, affording a substantial basis for the belief that it rests on a real transaction. (See Harry Rubin & Sons, Inc. v. Con. P. Co. of Am., 396 Pa. 506, 512, 153 A.2d 472.)

We find no error in this case and the judgment of the trial court is affirmed.

Questions

1. According to the court, what are the three requirements for a written memorandum to be considered an enforceable contract under the Uniform Commercial Code (UCC)?

2. What was the court's finding regarding the sufficiency of the written memorandum prepared by Mr. Hurt during the meeting in Springfield?

Takeaways -Southwest Engineering

The writing requirement under the UCC's version of the Statute of Frauds is more relaxed than the common law writing requirement. To satisfy the writing requirement for a sale of goods, all that is required is that the note or memorandum evidence a sale of goods, that it be signed or authenticated, and that it specify quantity term.

Satisfying The Writing Requirement

Sufficiency of the Note or Memorandum

The Statute of Frauds does not require that the contract itself be in writing, it only requires that the contract be evidenced in writing by "some note or memorandum thereof." That is an important distinction to keep in mind. The next case examines the writing requirement for non-sales contracts that are not within the scope of Article 2 of the UCC.

Crabtree v. Elizabeth Arden Sales Corp.
Court of Appeals of New York, 1953
305 N.Y. 48, 110 N.E.2d 551

FULD, Judge. In September of 1947, Nate Crabtree entered into preliminary negotiations with Elizabeth Arden Sales Corporation, manufacturers and sellers of cosmetics, looking toward his employment as sales manager. Interviewed on September 26th, by Robert P. Johns, executive vice-president and general manager of the corporation, who had apprised him of the possible opening, Crabtree requested a three-year contract at $25,000 a year. Explaining that he would be giving up a secure well-paying job to take a position in an entirely new field of endeavor which he believed would take him some years to master he insisted upon an agreement for a definite term. And he repeated his desire for a contract for three years to Miss Elizabeth Arden, the corporation's president. When Miss Arden finally indicated that she was prepared to offer a two-year contract, based on an annual salary of $20,000 for the first six months, $25,000 for the second six months and $30,000 for the second year, plus expenses of $5,000 a year for each of those years, Crabtree replied that that offer was 'interesting'. Miss Arden thereupon had her personal secretary make this memorandum on a telephone order blank that happened to be at hand:

"EMPLOYMENT AGREEMENT WITH NATE CRABTREE

Date Sept. 26-1947
6:PM
At 681-5th Ave
* * *
Begin 20000.
6 months 25000.
6 months 30000.
5000. per year
Expense money
(2 years to make good)
Arrangement with
Mr. Crabtree
By Miss Arden
Present Miss Arden
Mr. John
Mr. Crabtree
Miss OLeary"

A few days later, Crabtree 'phoned Mr. Johns and telegraphed Miss Arden; he accepted the 'invitation to join the Arden organization', and Miss Arden wired back her 'welcome'. When he reported for work, a 'pay-roll change' card was made up and initialed by Mr. Johns, and then forwarded to the payroll department. Reciting that it was prepared on September 30, 1947, and was to be effective as of October 22d, it specified the names of the parties, Crabtree's 'Job Classification' and, in addition, contained the notation that 'This employee is to be paid as follows:

"First six months of employment $20,000. per annum
Next six months of employment $25,000. per annum
After one year of employment $30,000. per annum

Approved by RPJ (initialed)"

After six months of employment, Crabtree received the scheduled increase from $20,000 to $25,000, but the further specified increase at the end of the year was not paid. Both Mr. Johns and the comptroller of the corporation, Mr. Carstens, told Crabtree that they would attempt to straighten out the matter with Miss Arden, and, with that in mind, the comptroller prepared another 'pay-roll change' card, to which his signature is appended, noting that there was to be a 'Salary increase' from $25,000 to $30,000 a year, 'per contractual arrangements with Miss Arden'. The latter, however, refused to approve the increase and, after further fruitless discussion, plaintiff left defendant's employ and commenced this action for breach of contract.

At the ensuing trial, defendant denied the existence of any agreement to employ plaintiff for two years, and further contended that, even if one had been made, the statute of frauds barred its enforcement. The trial court found against defendant on both issues and awarded plaintiff damages of about $14,000, and the Appellate Division, two justices dissenting, affirmed. Since the contract relied upon was not to be performed within a year, the primary question for decision is whether there was a memorandum of its terms, subscribed by defendant, to satisfy the statute of frauds, Personal Property Law, § 31.

Each of the two payroll cards the one initialed by defendant's general manager, the other signed by its comptroller unquestionably constitutes a memorandum under the statute. That they were not prepared or signed with the intention of evidencing the contract, or that they came into existence subsequent to its execution, is of no consequence, see Marks v. Cowdin, 226 N.Y. 138, 145, 123 N.E. 139, 141; Spiegel v. Lowenstein, 162 App.Div. 443, 448-449, 147 N.Y.S. 655, 658; see, also, Restatement, Contracts, §§ 209, 210, 214; it is enough, to meet the statute's demands, that they were signed with intent to authenticate the information contained therein and that such information does evidence the terms of the contract. See Marks v. Cowdin, supra, 226 N.Y. 138, 123 N.E. 139; Bayles v. Strong, 185 N.Y. 582, 78 N.E. 1099, affirming 104 App.Div. 153, 93 N.Y.S. 346; Spiegel v. Lowenstein, supra, 162 App.Div. 443, 448, 147 N.Y.S. 655, 658; see, also, 2 Corbin on Contracts (1951), pp. 732-733, 763-764; 2 Williston on Contracts (Rev. ed., 1936), pp. 1682-1683. Those two writings contain all of the essential terms of the contract the parties to it, the position that plaintiff was to assume, the salary that he was to receive except that relating to the duration of plaintiff's employment. Accordingly, we must consider whether that item, the length of the contract, may be supplied by reference to the earlier unsigned office memorandum, and, if so, whether its notation, '2 years to make good', sufficiently designates a period of employment.

The statute of frauds does not require the 'memorandum * * * to be in one document. It may be pieced together out of separate writings, connected with one another either expressly or by the internal evidence of subject-matter and occasion.' (Citations omitted) Where each of the separate writings has been subscribed by the party to be charged, little if any difficulty is encountered. (Citations omitted) Where, however, some writings have been signed, and others have not as in the case before us there is basic disagreement as to what constitutes a sufficient connection permitting the unsigned papers to be considered as part of the statutory memorandum. The courts of some jurisdictions insist that there be a reference, of varying degrees of specificity, in the signed writing to that unsigned, and, if there is no such reference, they refuse to permit consideration of the latter in determining whether the memorandum satisfies the statute. (Citations omitted) That conclusion is based upon a construction of the statute which requires that the connection between the writings and defendant's acknowledgment of the one not subscribed, appear from examination of the papers alone, without the aid of parol evidence. The other position which has gained increasing support over the years is that a sufficient connection between the papers is established simply by a reference in them to the same subject matter or transaction. See, e. g., Frost v. Alward, 176 Cal. 691, 169 P. 379; Lerned v. Wannemacher, 9 Allen, 412, 91 Mass. 412. The statute is not pressed 'to the extreme of a literal and rigid logic', Marks v. Cowdin, supra, 226 N.Y. 138, 144, 123 N.E. 139, 141, and oral testimony is admitted to show the connection between the documents and to establish the acquiescence, of the party to be charged, to the contents of the one unsigned. See Beckwith v. Talbot, 95 U.S. 289, 24 L.Ed. 496; Oliver v. Hunting, 44 Ch.D. 205, 208-209; see, also, 2 Corbin, op. cit., §§ 512-518; cf. Restatement, Contracts, § 208, subd. (b), par. (iii).

The view last expressed impresses us as the more sound, and, indeed although several of our cases appear to have gone the other way, (Citations omitted) this court has on a number of occasions approved the rule, and we now definitively adopt it, permitting the signed and unsigned writings to be read together, provided that they clearly refer to the same subject matter or transaction. (Citations omitted)

The language of the statute 'Every agreement * * * is void, unless * * * some note or memorandum thereof be in writing, and subscribed by the party to be charged', Personal Property Law, § 31-does not impose the requirement that the signed acknowledgment of the contract must appear from the writings alone, unaided by oral testimony. The danger of fraud and perjury, generally attendant upon the admission of parol evidence, is at a minimum in a case such as this. None of the terms of the contract are supplied by parol. All of them must be set out in the various writings presented to the court, and at least one writing, the one establishing a contractual relationship between the parties, must bear the signature of the party to be charged, while the unsigned document must on its face refer to the same transaction as that set forth in the one that was signed. Parol evidence to portray the circumstances surrounding the making of the memorandum serves only to connect the separate documents and to show that there was assent, by the party to be charged, to the contents of the one unsigned. If that testimony does not convincingly connect the papers, or does not show assent to the unsigned paper, it is within the province of the judge to conclude, as a matter of law, that the statute has not been satisfied. True, the possibility still remains that, by fraud or perjury, an agreement never in fact made may occasionally be enforced under the subject matter or transaction test. It is better to run that risk, though, than to deny enforcement to all agreements, merely because the signed document made no specific mention of the unsigned writing. As the United States Supreme Court declared, in sanctioning the admission of parol evidence to establish the connection between the signed and unsigned writings. 'There may be cases in which it would be a violation of reason and common sense to ignore a reference which derives its significance from such (parol) proof. If there is ground for any doubt in the matter, the general rule should be enforced. But where there is no ground for doubt, its enforcement would aid, instead of discouraging, fraud.' Beckwith v. Talbot, supra, 95 U.S. 289, 292, 24 L.Ed. 496.

Turning to the writings in the case before us the unsigned office memo, the payroll change form initialed by the general manager Johns, and the paper signed by the comptroller Carstens it is apparent, and most patently, that all three refer on their face to the same transaction. The parties, the position to be filled by plaintiff, the salary to be paid him, are all identically set forth; it is hardly possible that such detailed information could refer to another or a different agreement. Even more, the card signed by Carstens notes that it was prepared for the purpose of a 'Salary increase per contractual arrangements with Miss Arden'. That certainly constitutes a reference of sorts to a more comprehensive 'arrangement,' and parol is permissible to furnish the explanation. The corroborative evidence of defendant's assent to the contends of the unsigned office memorandum is also convincing. Prepared by defendant's agent, Miss Arden's personal secretary, there is little likelihood that that paper was fraudulently manufactured or that defendant had not assented to its contents. Furthermore, the evidence as to the conduct of the parties at the time it was prepared persuasively demonstrates defendant's assent to its terms. Under such circumstances, the courts below were fully justified in finding that the three papers constituted the 'memorandum' of their agreement within the meaning of the statute.

Nor can there be any doubt that the memorandum contains all of the essential terms of the contract. (Citations omitted) Only one term, the length of the employment, is in dispute. The September 26th office memorandum contains the notation, '2 years to make good'. What purpose, other than to denote the length of the contract term, such a notation could have, is hard to imagine. Without it, the employment would be at will, see Martin v. New York Life Ins. Co., 148 N.Y. 117, 121, 42 N.E. 416, 417, and its inclusion may not be treated as meaningless or purposeless. Quite obviously, as the courts below decided, the phrase signifies that the parties agreed to a term, a certain and definite term, of two years, after which, if plaintiff did not 'make good', he would be subject to discharge. And examination of other parts of the memorandum supports that construction. Throughout the writings, a scale of wages, increasing plaintiff's salary periodically, is set out; that type of arrangement is hardly consistent with the hypothesis that the employment was meant to be at will. The most that may be argued from defendant's standpoint is that '2 years to make good', is a cryptic and ambiguous statement. But, in such a case, parol evidence is admissible to explain its meaning. See Martocci v. Greater New York Brewery, 301 N.Y. 57, 63, 92 N.E.2d 887, 889; Marks v. Cowdin, supra, 226 N.Y. 138, 143-144, 123 N.E. 139, 140, 141; 2 Williston, op. cit., § 576; 2 Corbin, op. cit., § 527. Having in mind the relations of the parties, the course of the negotiations and plaintiff's insistence upon security of employment, the purpose of the phrase or so the trier of the facts was warranted in finding was to grant plaintiff the tenure he desired. The judgment should be affirmed, with costs.

Judgment affirmed.

Questions

1. Explain the court's reasoning regarding the connection between separate writings to satisfy the statute of frauds in this case.

2. What was the court's rationale for considering the unsigned office memorandum, the payroll change form initialed by the general manager, and the paper signed by the comptroller as part of the memorandum of agreement?

3. How did the court justify the admission of parol evidence to establish the connection between the signed and unsigned writings and to show the party's assent to the contents of the unsigned paper?

Takeaways- Crabtree v. Elizabeth Arden

What kind of "writing" will be sufficient to satisfy the Statute? The Statute does not require the memo to be in one document. It may be pieced together out of separate writings connected with one another. Signed and unsigned writings may be read together, provided that they clearly refer to the same subject matter or transaction. Also note that the memorandum need not presently exist. If it has been lost or destroyed, the Statute is satisfied so long as it once existed.

Brewer v. Horst-Lachmund Co.
Supreme Court of California, 1900
127 Cal. 643, 60 P. 418

GRAY, C. This is an action for a breach of contract of sale and purchase brought by the vendor against the vendee. The complaint sets out an agreement whereby plaintiff agreed to sell, and defendant agreed to buy, of plaintiff fifty-seven thousand one hundred and ten pounds of hops at eleven and five-eighths cents per pound; that plaintiff tendered the hops and defendant refused to take or pay for them, and that thereupon plaintiff sold said hops to a third person for the best obtainable price, which was eight hundred and thirty dollars and ninety-three cents less than defendant had agreed to pay therefor. Plaintiff obtained judgment for said eight hundred and thirty dollars and ninety-three cents, and defendant appeals. The case comes here on the judgment-roll.

The answer sets up the statute of frauds, alleging that the agreement sued on "was an agreement for the sale of goods and chattels at a price exceeding two hundred dollars; and defendant did not accept or receive any part of said goods and chattels, and did not pay any part of the purchase money therefor; and said sale was not made at auction; and said agreement was not, nor was any sufficient, proper, or adequate memorandum or note thereof, in writing, subscribed by defendant, or by any agent of defendant."

The court found as to the contract that Fred E. Alter was the general agent in the state of California and was empowered to make contracts therein for defendant. That C. A. Wagner was defendant's agent in the county of Sacramento, empowered to solicit samples in that and adjoining counties from hop growers and transmit the same to defendant's said general agent at Santa Rosa, California, "and to contract with such growers for the purchase from them in behalf of defendant corporation of such of said hops as might by the latter be desired, subject to the approval of the defendant corporation, through its general agent said Alter." That plaintiff was a hop grower, having a farm near Ben Ali, Sacramento county, and in September, 1897, said Wagner, as agent for defendant, obtained samples of a certain lot of hops, consisting of two hundred and ninety-six bales, weighing fifty-seven thousand one hundred and ten pounds, belonging to said plaintiff, and transmitted said samples to Alter at Santa Rosa, at the same time informing said Alter of the fact that said samples were from the lot aforesaid comprising two hundred and ninety-six bales of the last pickings of hops grown by plaintiff during the year 1897 upon his said farm; that at the same time said Wagner designated said samples by the trade number or symbol "13"; that it was and is the custom which prevails generally among dealers in hops to mark and designate by number the different samples furnished them by growers, and such custom was followed by defendant in the transaction herein set forth. That hops are sold, according to the custom of trade and usage in California, by the pound. That on October 11, 1897, plaintiff and defendant's agent, Wagner, entered into an oral contract, subject to the approval of Alter, whereby plaintiff sold and defendant bought the aforesaid lot of hops, provided the same were in quality equal to the samples marked "13," and it was agreed that defendant should inspect the hops on or before October 16th. On the same day, October 11th, Wagner telegraphed to Santa Rosa as follows:

> October 11, 1897.
> Horst & Lachmund Co., Santa Rosa, Cal.
>
> Bought thirteen at eleven five-eighths net you; confirm purchase by wire to Brewer, nineteen sixteen M street, inspection on or before Saturday. Do you want fifteen at eleven quarter?
>
> "C. A. WAGNER."

Alter received this message the same day, and thereupon sent to plaintiff, and plaintiff received, the following telegram:

> Santa Rosa, Cala., Oct. 11-97.
> Geo. Brewer, 1916 M street, Sacramento, Cala.
>
> We confirm purchase Wagner eleven five-eight cents. like sample.
>
> "(Signed) HORST AND LACHMUND CO."

That these telegrams are the only written evidence of the contract between the parties. That the said Alter knew that the number or symbol designated "13," used in the telegram first set out above, referred to and meant the hops belonging to plaintiff, as aforesaid, comprising said two hundred and ninety-six bales or thereabouts, and were the last pickings of plaintiff's hops grown upon his said farm in 1897, and also knew the situation of the hops and the other facts hereinbefore mentioned. And that defendant subsequently inspected the hops, and, without any lawful or just cause, rejected them and refused to receive them when tendered by plaintiff.

The only question presented for decision is, did these telegrams constitute a sufficient note or memorandum of the contract to satisfy the requirements of the statute of frauds? The trial court, by its judgment, answered this question in the affirmative. And, in view of all the facts found, we think the court reached the proper conclusion. If there were nothing to look to but the telegrams, the court might find it difficult, if not impossible, to determine the nature of the contract, or that any contract was entered into between the parties. But the court is permitted to interpret the memorandum (consisting of the two telegrams) by the light of all the circumstances under which it was made; and if, when the court is put into possession of all the knowledge which the parties to the transaction had at the time, it can be plainly seen from the memorandum who the parties to the contract were, what the subject of the contract was, and what were its terms, then the court should not hesitate to hold the memorandum sufficient. Oral evidence may be received to show in what sense figures or abbreviations were used; and their meaning may be explained as it was understood between the parties. (*Mann v. Higgins*, 83 Cal. 66; *Berry v. Kowalsky*, 95 Cal. 134; 29 Am. St. Rep. 101; *Callahan v. Stanley*, 57 Cal. 476.) Also: "Parol evidence is always admissible to explain the surrounding circumstances, and situation and relations of the parties, at and immediately before the execution of the contract, in order to connect the description with the only thing intended, and thereby to identify the subject matter, and to explain all terms and phrases used in a local or special sense." (*Preble v. Abrahams*, 88 Cal. 245; *Towle v. Carmelo etc. Co.*, 99 Cal. 397.) Interpreting the telegrams by the foregoing rules, it is not difficult to see that the parties to the contract are George Brewer, of 1916 M street, Sacramento, California, vendor, and Horst and Lachmund Company, of Santa Rosa, California, vendee; that the contract was one of purchase and sale, and the subject of it was the property represented in the first telegram by "thirteen" and well known by the parties to consist of two hundred and ninety-six bales of hops, and to be the last pickings of hops grown by plaintiff upon his farm in Sacramento county during the year 1897, and that the price to be paid for said hops was eleven and five-eighths cents per pound.

The two telegrams bear the same date; on their face the last one was sent to plaintiff in response to the first; and it is clear that they should be read together to determine whether they constitute the note or memorandum required by the statute of frauds. (*Elbert v. Los Angeles Gas Co.*, 97 Cal. 244; *Breckinridge v. Crocker*, 78 Cal. 529.) We are satisfied that the telegrams, thus read by the light of the circumstances surrounding the parties, are sufficient to take the contract out of the statute of frauds. Any other conclusion than the one here reached would certainly impair the usefulness of modern appliances to modern business, tend to hamper trade, and increase the expense thereof. . . .

Questions

1. How did the court interpret the telegrams in light of the surrounding circumstances to determine the parties, subject matter, and terms of the contract?

2. Why did the court state that it would be difficult, if not impossible, to determine the nature of the contract solely based on the telegrams?

3. What role does oral evidence play in interpreting the figures or abbreviations used in the telegrams and understanding their meaning as intended by the parties?

4. According to the court's reasoning, why is it permissible to consider the surrounding circumstances, situation, and relations of the parties when interpreting

the contract?

5. What would be the potential implications if the court had concluded that the telegrams did not constitute a sufficient note or memorandum to satisfy the requirements of the statute of frauds?

Takeaways – Brewer v. Horst-Lachmund, Co.

It is not necessary that the memo be prepared with the intent that it evidence a contract, nor is it fatal that it was prepared after the contract was executed.

Franklin v. Hansen
California Supreme Court, 1963
59 Cal.2d 570, 381 P.2d 386, 30 Cal.Rptr. 530

PEEK, J. In this appeal the defendant Charles P. Hansen seeks a reversal of a judgment in the amount of $5,000 in favor of plaintiff Donald V. Franklin, a licensed real estate broker, for claimed commissions in procuring a buyer for defendant's real property.

Defendant owned residential property in Newport Beach. Plaintiff had acted as an agent for defendant in the rental of the property and had informed defendant that he would like to represent defendant in selling the property. A sale price of $115,000 was agreed upon and although plaintiff obtained several offers for the property over a period of several months, all were for less than the agreed price. Defendant eventually agreed that he would accept an offer for $100,000. None of the transactions between the parties up to this point were in writing, defendant having assured plaintiff that a signed listing would be unnecessary as his word was good.

On January 15, 1960, plaintiff obtained an offer for $100,000 and telephoned defendant, requesting an authorization by telegram to sell the property. In response, defendant sent the following telegram: "Los Angeles, California ... D. V. Franklin, 208 Marine Balboa Island California. This is confirm that I will sell 608 South Bay Front Balboa Island for 100,000 cash this offer good until noon 1-19-60. Chas. P. Hansen."

On January 19, 1960, plaintiff again telephoned defendant and advised that he had sold the property and had accepted a check for $5,000 as a down payment. Defendant stated that he was pleasantly surprised, that delivery could take place when the present lease terminated in a few months, and consented to the suggested escrow agent. But when a standard form deposit receipt providing for payment of a 5 per cent commission to plaintiff was presented to defendant, he refused to sign, and indicated that he wished "to get out of the deal." On January 22 defendant and the prospective buyers appeared at plaintiff's office. When the buyers refused to waive their rights under the agreement defendant admitted that he was "stuck" with the sale and that plaintiff would receive his commission. Subsequently, however, he refused to sign any of the documents necessary to complete the sale of the property, and also refused to pay the agreed commission.

Plaintiff's complaint alleges breach of a commission contract, reciting defendant's promise to abide by the verbal listing of the property, the telegram in "confirmation thereof," the arrangements for the sale of the property, the defendant's refusal to proceed with the sale and his promise to pay the 5 per cent commission notwithstanding.

Relying on the statute of frauds defendant demurred to the complaint for commissions, which demurrer was overruled. The trial court heard, over defendant's objections, parol evidence as to all transactions between the parties and awarded judgment as prayed by plaintiff. Defendant contends on this appeal that neither the telegram nor any other writing constituted a sufficient memorandum or ratification of a contract of employment to satisfy the statute of frauds.

Section 1624 of the Civil Code provides in part: "The following contracts are invalid, unless the same, or some note or memorandum thereof, is in writing and subscribed by the party to be charged or by his agent: ... 5. An agreement authorizing or employing an agent or broker to purchase or sell real estate for compensation or a commission." (See also Code Civ. Proc., § 1973, subd. 5; Civ. Code, § 2310.)

We have before considered the nature of a memorandum sufficient to satisfy subdivision 5 of section 1624. (See Pacific Southwest Dev. Corp. v. Western Pac. R. R. Co., 47 Cal.2d 62 [301 P.2d 815].) There a broker sued to recover compensation for services rendered to a buyer in procuring an option to purchase real property. The broker's offer of proof demonstrated substantial services rendered to the buyer, but the only writing subscribed by the buyer was a letter to the broker as follows: " 'I am in a position to take an option on the Lenfest property at $3,000.00 per acre. We would not wish to pay more than $1,500.00 for the option and would want it for 90 days, with a contingent extension of time long enough to have the property rezoned. ... If you think this proposal is worth your trip, let me know perhaps by telephone tomorrow and I will arrange to meet you at San Jose--maybe we can get the deal signed up. ...' " (47 Cal.2d 62, 68.)

At page 69 in the foregoing case the court stated: "The only writing with which defendant can be charged here is the letter of August 29, 1950 ..., and as above quoted, it made no reference to the fact of employment by defendant of plaintiff or to any compensation. True, the latter reference is not essential if there is a contract of employment, for a reasonable amount as a commission will be inferred. [Citations.] But where there is a failure to mention the fact of employment, the further fact that there is no mention of a commission is significant. The authorities require that a writing 'subscribed by the party to be charged, or his agent' must unequivocally show the fact of employment of the broker seeking to recover a real estate commission [citations]. It must therefore be concluded that the writings here are insufficient under the statute of frauds to sustain plaintiff's claim."

Here, too, as to the content thereof, the writing in the instant case is similar to that in the cited case since it also fails to expressly recite or make reference to the existence of any employment contract or to any compensation. In both cases parol evidence demonstrated that the real nature of the agreement between the parties was one of employment; that the broker in each instance rendered substantial, bargained-for-services which culminated in the achievement of the objective for which employed; and that neither broker was guilty of overreaching or improper and unethical practices. It does not appear that we can give full effect to the Pacific Southwest Dev. Corp. case and at the same time sustain the instant award.

The sufficiency of a writing to satisfy the statute of frauds cannot be established by evidence which is extrinsic to the writing itself. (Code Civ. Proc., § 1973.) While a telegram, sufficient in content, may satisfy the statute (Niles v. Hancock, 140 Cal. 157 [73 P. 840]; Gibson v. De La Salle Institute, 66 Cal.App.2d 609 [152 P.2d 774]), still it must contain the essential elements of a specific, consummated agreement. (Zellner v. Wassman, 184 Cal. 80 [193 P. 84]; Fritz v. Mills, 170 Cal. 449 [150 P. 375].) Where it discloses no promise or agreement and cannot be made clear as to its significance without resort to parol evidence, it is inadequate. (Ellis v. Klaff, 96 Cal.App.2d 471 [216 P.2d 15]; Sherwood v. Lowell, 34 Cal.App. 365 [167 P. 554].) But where it imports the essentials of a contractual obligation although it fails to do so in an explicit, definite or complete manner, it is always permissible to show the circumstances which attended its making. Thus in Gibson v. De La Salle Institute, supra, 66 Cal.App.2d 609, parol evidence was resorted to in explanation of certain trade terms contained in a telegram offer. Likewise in Brewer v. Horst & Lachmund Co., 127 Cal. 643 [60 P. 418, 50 L.R.A. 240], an agent, using certain code words, wired his principal that he had purchased goods, and the principal sent a confirming telegram to the seller, also utilizing code words. Extrinsic evidence was held admissible in explanation of the two telegrams and they together were deemed to satisfy the statute of frauds. Such evidence is also admissible to resolve ambiguities on the face of the memorandum (Balfour v. Fresno Canal & Irr. Co., 109 Cal. 221, 225-226 [41 P. 876]), or to ascertain a term of the agreement by resort to another document referred to in the memorandum. (Searles v. Gonzales, 191 Cal. 426 [216 P. 1003, 28 A.L.R. 78].) But in each of the foregoing instances the memorandum itself demonstrated the existence of a contractual intent on the part of the one to be charged, and extrinsic evidence was necessary only to define the limits thereof.

The telegram in the instant case fails to use any words in recognition of a contractual obligation for a commission. While it may be a sufficient memorandum of an agreement to sell the property, it is the alleged commission agreement which is sought to be enforced. There are no ambiguities to be resolved or references to extrinsic materials which would aid in ascertaining a meaning not made definite on the face of the document. True, the writer purports to "confirm," but he also states in definite and certain language that which he confirms. The meaning of the telegram is clear and definite--it requires no aid in its interpretation, and it does not imply, infer or suggest a commission agreement. It is only by resort to extrinsic matters not suggested by the writing that it is possible to determine with any justification that defendant had agreed to compensate plaintiff for his services. This is not sufficient under the established law.

It is suggested in a number of cases, and urged in the instant case, that a more liberal construction of the statute of frauds should be employed to protect a broker from being defrauded by a landowner. (See Note 80 A.L.R. 1457.) The statute, of course, does not purport to afford a greater degree of protection to an agent or broker, as distinguished from a principal. Real estate brokers are licensed as such only after they have demonstrated a knowledge of the laws relating to real estate transactions (Bus. & Prof. Code, §§ 10150, 10153), and it would seem that they would thus require less protection against pitfalls encountered in transactions regulated by those laws. In Pacific Southwest Dev. Corp. v. Western Pac. R. R. Co., supra, 47 Cal.2d 62, the court stated at page 70: "Plaintiff is a licensed real estate broker and, as such, is presumed to know that contracted for real estate commissions are invalid and unenforceable unless put in writing and subscribed by the person to be charged. [Citations.] Nevertheless, plaintiff failed to secure proper written authorization to protect itself in the transaction. Rather it assumed the risk of relying upon claimed oral promises of defendant, and it has no cause for complaint if its efforts go unrewarded."

Moreover, the cases on which plaintiff relies as giving more favorable treatment to an agent or broker are distinguishable. Thus in Kennedy v. Merickel, 8 Cal.App. 378 [97 P. 81], a writing which expressly provided for the payment of commissions, although the amount was left uncertain, was held at page 381 to be "a sufficient compliance with the statute." As authority for the foregoing statement the court relied on Imperato v. Wasboe, 47 Misc. 150 [93 N.Y.S. 489], wherein the following memorandum was held sufficient under the New York statute: "Mr. P. Imperato, Real Estate Broker--Dear Sir: ... There will be no need of my meeting you if you haven't a party who desires to purchase my house No. 416 East 124th Street at $15,000, as I am not very anxious to dispose of my property, and I do not intend to sell for any less. Very truly yours, O. Wasboe." Significantly the memorandum addresses the agent as a "Real Estate Broker" and recognizes that the agent is acting in such capacity (i.e., "... if you haven't a party who desires to purchase my house ..."). Authorization to sell at $15,000 was held by the New York court to have been sufficiently established by the writing.

Again, in Toomy v. Dunphy, 86 Cal. 639, 640 [25 P. 130], a note which recited: " 'Henry Toomy can arrange for the sale of my ranch in Nevada, as per within memorandum,' " was held to sufficiently establish the employment of Toomy as an agent, and the fact of consideration for such services was implied therefrom.

Of the cases to which we are referred, the foregoing lends plaintiff most support. But in each case the writing evidenced at least the employment relationship, whereas the memorandum in the case before us is silent as to the existence of such a relationship.

Written evidence of the employment relationship has always been deemed an essential requirement of the statute of frauds. In addition to the Pacific Southwest Dev. Corp. case, supra, other decisions have held that the failure to expressly provide for employment is fatal to the sufficiency of any memorandum. Thus, in Morrill v. Barneson, 30 Cal.App.2d 598 [86 P.2d 924], a letter which fully described the property, the sale price and terms thereof, and provided for the payment of the "regular 5% commission," was held insufficient because it failed to expressly create an employment relationship with anyone. In Herzog v. Blatt, 80 Cal.App.2d 340 [180 P.2d 30], a memorandum in the form of an offer to accept "8400 net" for designated property was also held insufficient because it too failed to authorize anyone to act for the owner. And in Kleinsorge & Heilbron v. Liness, 17 Cal.App. 534 [120 P. 444], a writing setting forth the price, terms and description of property offered for sale by the signer thereof, which writing was delivered to the plaintiff real estate brokers although not expressly addressed to them, was held insufficient as not bearing written evidence of a contract of employment or authorization. For the proposition that a sufficient writing "must unequivocally show on its face the fact of employment of the broker" see also Blanchard v. Pauley, 92 Cal.App.2d 244, 247 [206 P.2d 864]; Sanstrum v. Gonser, 140 Cal.App.2d 732 [295 P.2d 532]; Edens v. Stoddard, 126 Cal.App.2d 56, 60 [271 P.2d 610]; Hooper v. Mayfield, 114 Cal.App.2d 801, 807 [251 P.2d 330].

Plaintiff herein has neither alleged nor urged the application of an equitable estoppel, pursuant to which doctrine a party to an oral agreement might be estopped to rely on the statute of frauds in instances where the elements of the doctrine can be established. (See Monarco v. Lo Greco, 35 Cal.2d 621, 626 [220 P.2d 737].)

In view of the foregoing we are compelled to the conclusion that the memorandum in the case now before us is obviously insufficient to satisfy the requirements of the statute of frauds under the prevailing standards. Accordingly, the judgment is reversed.

Questions

1. Why did the court find the telegram sent by the defendant insufficient to establish a commission agreement?

2. Discuss the court's reasoning behind its refusal to apply a more liberal construction of the statute of frauds to protect the broker.

The Signature Requirement

See Rest.2d § 134 and UCC 1-201 (37).

Southwest Engineering Co. Inc. v. Martin Tractor Co.
205 Kan. 684, 1970, 473 P.2d 18

(Facts of the case were set forth previously at p. 192.)

We digress at this point to note Martin's contention that the memorandum is not signed within the meaning of (UCC) 2-201. The sole authentication appears in hand-printed form at the top left-hand corner in these words: "Ken Hurt, Martin Tractor, Topeka, Caterpillar." The court found this sufficient, and we believe correctly so.

[UCC 1-201 (37)] provides as follows:

"`Signed' includes any symbol executed or adopted by a party with present intention to authenticate a writing."

The official U.C.C. Comment states in part:

"The inclusion of authentication in the definition of `signed' is to make clear that as the term is used in this Act a complete signature is not necessary. Authentication may be printed, stamped or written; ... It may be on any part of the document and in appropriate cases may be found in a billhead or letterhead.... The question always is whether the symbol was executed or adopted by the party with present intention to authenticate the writing."

Hurt admittedly prepared the memorandum and has not denied affixing his name thereto. We believe the authentication sufficiently complies with the statute.

Donovan v. RRL Corp.
California Supreme Court, 2001
26 Cal.4th 261, 109 Cal.Rptr.2d 807, 27 P.3d 702

[Facts were previously set forth at p. 63.]

GEORGE, C.J.- Defendant contends that even if its advertisement constituted an offer that was accepted by plaintiff's tender of the purchase price, plaintiff is not authorized by law to enforce the resulting contract, because there was no signed writing that satisfied the requirements of the statute of frauds for the sale of goods. Plaintiff, on the other hand, maintains that defendant's name, as it appeared in the newspaper advertisement for the sale of the vehicle, constituted a signature within the meaning of the statute.

The applicable statute of frauds states in relevant part: "Except as otherwise provided in this section a contract for the sale of goods for the price of five hundred dollars ($500) or more is not enforceable by way of action or defense unless there is some writing sufficient to indicate that a contract for sale has been made between the parties and *signed by the party against whom enforcement is sought or by his or her authorized agent or broker.* A writing is not insufficient because it omits or incorrectly states a term agreed upon[,] but the contract is not enforceable under this paragraph beyond the quantity of goods shown in the writing." (Cal. U. Com. Code, § 2201, subd. (1),.)

The California Uniform Commercial Code defines the term "signed" as including "any symbol executed or adopted by a party with present intention to authenticate a writing." [Cal. U. Com. Code, § 1201, subd. (37).] The comment regarding the corresponding provision of the Uniform Commercial Code states: "The inclusion of authentication in the definition of 'signed' is to make clear that as the term is used in [the code] a complete signature is not necessary. Authentication may be printed, stamped, or written; it may be by initials or by thumbprint. It may be on any part of the document and in appropriate cases may be found in a billhead or letterhead. No catalog of possible authentications can be complete and the court must use common sense and commercial experience in passing upon these matters. The question always is whether the symbol was executed or adopted by the party with present intention to authenticate the writing." (U. Com. Code com., reprinted at 23A West's Ann. Cal. U. Com. Code (1964 ed.) foll. § 1201, p. 65; see 1 Witkin, *supra*, Contracts, § 281, p. 273 [citing California decisions generally consistent with this comment]; Rest.2d Contracts, § 134.)

Some decisions have relaxed the signature requirement considerably to accommodate various forms of electronic communication. For example, a party's printed or typewritten name in a telegram has been held to satisfy the statute of frauds. (E.g., *Hessenthaler v. Farzin* (Pa.Super.Ct. 1989) 564 A.2d 990, 993-994; *Hillstrom v. Gosnay* (1980) 188 Mont. 388 [614 P.2d 466, 470].) Even a tape recording identifying the parties has been determined to meet the signature requirement of the Uniform Commercial Code. (*Ellis Canning Company v. Bernstein* (D.Colo. 1972) 348 F.Supp. 1212, 1228.)

When an advertisement constitutes an offer, the printed name of the merchant is intended to authenticate the advertisement as that of the merchant. (See Rest.2d Contracts, § 131, com. d, illus. 2, p. 335 [newspaper advertisement constituting an offer to purchase certain goods, with offeror's name printed therein, satisfies the requirements of the statute of frauds].) In other words, where the advertisement reasonably justifies the recipient's understanding that the communication was intended as an offer, the offeror's intent to authenticate his or her name as a signature can be established from the face of the advertisement.

In the present case, the parties presented no evidence with regard to whether defendant intended that its name in the advertisement constitute a signature. Therefore, the issue whether the appearance of defendant's name supports a determination that the writing was "signed" is closely related to the question whether the advertisement constituted an offer. Those characteristics of the advertisement justifying plaintiff's belief that defendant intended it to be an offer also support a finding that defendant intended that its name serve as an authentication.

As established above, defendant's advertisement reflected an objective manifestation of its intention to make an offer for the sale of the vehicle at the stated price. Defendant's printed name in the advertisement similarly evidenced an intention to authenticate the advertisement as an offer and therefore constituted a signature satisfying the statute of frauds.

Questions

1. What does the comment regarding 1-201 (37) of the Uniform Commercial Code state about the definition of "signed" and the requirement for authentication?

2. How does the court's reasoning support the finding that the defendant's printed name in the advertisement constitutes a signature satisfying the statute of frauds?

Signatures - You've Got Mail!

JSO Associates, Inc v. Price
Supreme Court, New York, 2008
2008 WL 904703

[In an action to recover a finder's fee, the parties exchanged numerous emails. After concluding that the emails sent by the defendant otherwise satisfied the Statute of Frauds writing requirement, the court turned to the issue of whether they were "signed."]

The court will now consider whether the memorandum was signed. Edward Price's name appears in the email address at the top of the "SunOpta" email. However, the email closes, "I'll talk to you later." and, except for Edward's name in the email address, is otherwise unsigned. It has been stated that, "The subscription which the statute [of frauds] demands is a writing at the end of the memorandum". Thus, a "scrawl at the top of the memorandum" is insufficient to satisfy the writing requirement(Id). However, *Steinberg* was decided in a different technological era, when email and home computers had not even entered the public imagination. Moreover, the requirement of a signature at the bottom was to minimize the opportunity for fraudulent additions to the memorandum, a practice which is not feasible with electronic communication.

"Electronic signatures" on such formal documents as tax returns or SEC filings are now becoming commonplace. On the other hand, the law is still developing as to the kind and location of signature which will satisfy the statute of frauds for less formal types of electronic communication, such as email and instant messaging. Nonetheless, the court must look for assurance as to the source of the email and the authority of the person who sent it. While technology has advanced since the Court of Appeals decided *Morris Cohon & Co.,* the decision's rationale still provides helpful guidance, "The Statute of Frauds was designed to guard against the peril of perjury; to prevent the enforcement of unfounded fraudulent claims. But,...the Statute of Frauds was not enacted to afford persons a means of evading just obligations; nor was it intended to supply a cloak of immunity to hedging litigants lacking integrity; nor was it adopted to enable defendants to interpose the Statute as a bar to a contract fairly, and admittedly made"

The court holds that where there is no question as to the source and authenticity of an email, the email is "signed" for purposes of the statute of frauds if defendant's name clearly appears in the email as the sender As noted, Edward Price's name appears as the sender of the "SunOpta" email. Additionally, half an hour later, Edward sent Jerry another email concerning the SunOpta deal which was signed, "Edward," in the traditional letter writing fashion. Thus, the court concludes that the "SunOpta" email was sufficiently signed by Edward Price to satisfy the statute of frauds signature requirement.

Questions

1. According to the court, why was the requirement of a signature at the bottom of the memorandum established in the past?

2. How does the court justify considering electronic communication, such as email, for satisfying the statute of frauds signature requirement?

3. In what circumstances does the court consider an email to be "signed" for purposes of the statute of frauds?

4. What rationale does the court provide for interpreting the statute of frauds in a way that prevents evading just obligations?

5. What evidence does the court rely on to conclude that the "SunOpta" email was sufficiently signed to satisfy the statute of frauds signature requirement?

Excusing The Writing Requirement

There are several basis on which a court can enforce an oral contract that is within the Statute of Frauds even though the writing requirement has not been complied with. They are partial performance of the oral contract and estoppel to assert the Statute of Frauds as a defense.

Partial Performance

Beaver v. Brumlow
Court of Appeals of New Mexico, 2010
148 N.M. 172, 231 P.3d 628

VIGIL, Judge. This case is about a verbal agreement made by Warren and Betty Beaver (Sellers) to sell land for a home site to Michael and Karen Brumlow (Buyers). Sellers reneged on the agreement after Mr. Brumlow left Sellers' employment and started working for a competitor. The trial court ordered specific performance of the oral agreement, and Sellers appeal. Sellers acknowledge that the evidence was sufficient for the trial court to find that they made the agreement with Buyers. Nevertheless, Sellers contend that specific enforcement of the verbal agreement is barred pursuant to the statute of frauds. We disagree and affirm. . . .

Buyer Michael Brumlow worked for Sellers in their race horse transportation business for approximately ten years, beginning in 1994, and ending in 2004. In October 2000, Sellers purchased twenty-four acres of property in the Village of Ruidoso Downs, and in approximately June or July of 2001, Mr. Brumlow asked Seller Warren Beaver if he would sell some of the land to put a home on. Mr. Beaver agreed, and the parties walked the specific boundaries of the property that Sellers would sell to Buyers.

Sellers allowed Buyers to rely on their representations to Buyers that Sellers would sell Buyers the subject property. Buyers went into possession of the land with Sellers' consent. In reliance on Sellers' agreement to sell, Buyer Karen Brumlow cashed in her IRA and 401-K retirement plans, at a substantial penalty, to pay for the home and improvements. Buyers purchased a double-wide home and moved it onto the property. Mr. Beaver signed an application with the Village of Ruidoso Downs for placement of the home on the property he agreed to sell to Buyers. In reliance on the agreement, Buyers also skirted the mobile home, poured concrete footers and a concrete foundation for the home, built a deck and two sets of stairs to access the home, had electricity and a water supply run to the property, had a septic system installed, had a propane system installed, brought a Tuff Shed for storage onto the property, and landscaped the property. Mr. Beaver signed the application/approval required by the Village of Ruidoso Downs for the construction of the septic system. In reliance on the agreement, Buyers spent approximately $85,000.

Sellers sought legal advice as to the manner in which to sell the property to Buyers, and the parties discussed with Sellers' attorney the requirement of a survey, and either a real estate contract or a note and mortgage. A fair inference from the record is that formal documents were not prepared and executed because Sellers discovered that their property was encumbered with a mortgage containing a due on sale clause. Throughout their time on the land, Buyers repeatedly requested that their contract be formalized, and Sellers responded, "We will work it out."

A date certain was never determined for the sale of the property or transfer of title to the property, nor was a price actually determined. However, Mr. Brumlow assumed he would pay whatever the market would bear in that particular neighborhood. He testified he thought the price would be "whatever it was worth.

Sellers drove by Buyers' home location daily during the time Buyers were making improvements to the land and setting up the home without ever expressing an intent not to sell the subject property to Buyers. Sellers never attempted to interrupt Buyers' quiet possession of the property during the years of possession. Sellers allowed Buyers to rely on their representations to Buyers that Sellers would sell Buyers the subject property for years without notifying Buyers they intended to renege on their promise

In March 2004, Mr. Brumlow gave Mr. Beaver a two-week notice of termination of his employment with Sellers, intending to go to work for a competitor of Sellers in the race horse transportation business. The relationship between the parties rapidly deteriorated, and Sellers changed their mind and decided not to sell the agreed upon tract of land to Buyers because of hurt or anger. Sellers then attempted to restructure the agreement as a "lease" as opposed to a sale, and then attempted to terminate the "lease" and evict Buyers. Sellers prepared and required Buyers to sign an "Agreement." The "Agreement" required Buyers to pay Sellers $400 per month, and Buyers complied, believing it was payment for the land. When Buyers began writing "Land Payment" on the checks, Sellers stopped cashing the checks and alleged that the "Agreement" was for rental, although the "Agreement" did not contain the words "Rent," "Rental," "Lease," or "Leasehold." Buyers attempted to amicably resolve the dispute by offering to pay cash in the amount of the fair market value for the property and to have the property surveyed at their expense. Sellers refused.

Sellers then filed a suit for ejectment against Buyers, seeking to remove them from the property by alleging that Buyers were in violation of a rental agreement. Buyers denied the existence of a rental agreement and affirmatively alleged that their occupancy was pursuant to an agreement to purchase the property. Buyers also filed counterclaims which included claims for breach of contract, fraud, and prima facie tort. Sellers pleaded the statute of frauds as a defense.

The trial court concluded that Sellers entered into a contract with Buyers to sell them a specific portion of their land and that Sellers reneged on their agreement to sell the property to Buyers. The trial court further determined that Sellers changed their mind three years after making the contract, chose not to honor it, and attempted to unilaterally restructure the contract into a lease, which was never intended. In committing these acts, the trial court concluded, Sellers committed a prima facie tort, which they knew would harm Buyers. Addressing the statute of frauds defense, the trial court concluded that while the parties had no written agreement, the verbal agreement was proven by clear, cogent, and convincing evidence and that part performance of the contract by both Buyers and Sellers was sufficient to remove the contract from the statute of frauds. Furthermore, the trial court concluded, requiring a cash payment of the fair market value, as determined by a professional appraiser, was a proper equitable remedy.

The trial court allowed Buyers a choice of remedy: money damages for the prima facie tort or specific performance of the contract. Buyers chose specific performance. The property was appraised at a value of $10,000 by a professional appraiser, and a survey of the property to be sold was prepared. The final judgment directs that Buyers tender to Sellers the amount of $10,000 by depositing that amount into the trust account of Buyers' attorney within thirty days from the entry of the judgment, and that Sellers prepare and execute a good and sufficient warranty deed to Buyers for the property as described in the testimony of Mr. Brumlow and as depicted on the survey of the property. Upon receipt of the warranty deed executed by Sellers, payment of the $10,000 is to be made to Sellers. All other claims and counterclaims were dismissed with prejudice. Sellers appeal.

Sellers contend that specific enforcement of the oral contract is barred pursuant to the statute of frauds because: (1) Buyers' part performance was not "unequivocally referable" to the verbal agreement; and (2) the verbal agreement was not certain as to the purchase price and time of performance. Sellers also argue that specific performance was improper because Buyers had an adequate remedy at law in damages. For the following reasons, we disagree and affirm....

While the underlying reasons justifying adoption of the statute of frauds no longer exist, retention of the statute has been justified for three primary reasons: the statute still serves an evidentiary function, and thereby lessens the danger of perjured testimony (the original reason for the statute); the requirement of a writing causes the parties to reflect on the importance of the agreement; and the writing requirement makes it easier to distinguish agreements which are enforceable from those which are not....

Notwithstanding its language, judicial construction of the statute of frauds has resulted in limiting its application in order to overcome the harshness and injustice of a literal and mechanical application of its terms. McIntosh, 469 P.2d at 180. One well settled exception, recognized in New Mexico, is the doctrine of part performance. Alvarez v. Alvarez, 72 N.M. 336, 341, 383 P.2d 581, 584 (1963).

"Where an oral contract not enforceable under the statute of frauds has been performed to such extent as to make it inequitable to deny effect thereto, equity may consider the contract as removed from operation of the statute of frauds and decree specific performance." Id. In this case, the trial court concluded:

[T]he evidence is clear, cogent and convincing so as to remove the case from the application of the [s]tatute of [f]rauds and that there is significant partial performance by both parties, [Buyers] in expending so much time, energy and money developing the parcel of property and [Sellers] in applying for permission to have the personal property placed on the land, seeking advice of counsel as to the manner in which to sell the property and allowing [Buyers] to rely on their representations and to reside on the property for years. The [c]ourt finds that applying the [s]tatute of [f]rauds would be unfair and inequitable.

Sellers do not contend that proof of the oral contract is lacking; in fact, they concede that the evidence is sufficient. Moreover, Sellers do not argue that the partial performance of Buyers was insufficient to overcome the statute of frauds or that their own partial performance was insufficient. Sellers' sole argument is that the character of Buyers' performance was not sufficiently indicative of an oral agreement to sell land to qualify as partial performance. See Burns v. McCormick, 135 N.E. 273, 273 (N.Y. 1922) ("Not every act of part performance will move a court of equity, though legal remedies are inadequate, to enforce an oral agreement affecting rights in land. There must be performance ?unequivocally referable' to the agreement, performance which alone and without the aid of words of promise is unintelligible or at least extraordinary unless as an incident of ownership, assured, if not existing."); Woolley v. Stewart, 118 N.E. 847, 848 (N.Y. 1918) ("An act which admits of explanation without reference to the alleged oral contract or a contract of the same general nature and purpose is not, in general, admitted to constitute a part performance."), quoted with approval in Alvarez, 72 N.M. at 342, 383 P.2d at 585.

A court of equity [therefore] requires that a part performance relied on to take the case out of the statute [of frauds] should be of a character, not only consistent with the reasonable presumption that what was done was done on the faith of such a contract, but also that it would be unreasonable to presume that it was done on any other theory.

Alvarez, 72 N.M. at 342, 383 P.2d at 585 (internal quotation marks and citation omitted).

Sellers argue that Buyers' acts are not "unequivocally referable" to their agreement because Buyers' actions could also be consistent with those taken by a person who needs a place to live and who is given an opportunity to reside on another person's property. Sellers argue that if there is an alternative explanation for the actions taken in reliance of the oral contract, those actions are not "unequivocally referable" to the contract, and application of the part performance doctrine is improper. We disagree.

In Nashan v. Nashan, 119 N.M. 625, 630-31, 894 P.2d 402, 407-08 (Ct. App. 1995), we discussed the interrelationship of the factors that may be considered in determining whether a contract to convey land has been proven and whether it would be inequitable to enforce the contract. We said:

Whatever the purpose of each test, however, the main questions are the same for a court faced with a case such as this one was there actually an oral agreement such as that alleged by the plaintiff, and if so would it be inequitable to deny enforcement to the agreement? The factors should not be applied mechanically to determine whether the plaintiff's performance has met a particular test. Instead, the case must be viewed as a whole to determine whether specific performance of the agreement is required
.Id. at 631, 894 P.2d at 408. Thus, we reject the suggestion that the "unequivocally referable" concept means that outside of the contract, there can be no other plausible explanation for the part performance. In fact, we described the "unequivocally referable" concept in plain language as "meaning that an outsider, knowing all of the circumstances of a case except for the claimed oral agreement, would naturally and reasonably conclude that a contract existed regarding the land, of the same general nature as that alleged by the claimant." Id. at 630, 894 P.2d at 407 (citing Smith v. Smith, 466 So. 2d 922, 925 (Ala. 1985)). We did not say that the performance must relate exclusively to the oral contract; rather, the performance must lead an outsider to "naturally and reasonably" conclude that the contract alleged actually exists. Two key specific factors, approved by this Court and many other courts, in coming to such a conclusion, are taking possession of the property, and making valuable, permanent, and substantial improvements to the property. Id. at 630-31, 894 P.2d at 407-08. Where these two factors coincide, specific performance usually results. Id.

In this case, Buyers went into possession of the specific land Sellers agreed to convey with Sellers' consent. In reliance on the agreement, Buyers cashed IRA and 401-K retirement plans at a substantial penalty, purchased a double-wide mobile home, and with Sellers' consent, moved it onto the property. Buyers also erected valuable temporary and permanent improvements on the land, and landscaped the property with Sellers' consent. In reliance on the agreement, Buyers spent approximately $85,000 in purchasing the home and making improvements. We hold Buyers' actions were sufficient part performance in reliance on the oral agreement to take the agreement outside of the statute of frauds. . .

The trial court concluded:

[T]he terms of the contract were that [Sellers] would sell to [Buyers] the piece of property included in the demarcation of the landmarks as testified to by [Mr. Brumlow]. While the purchase price was never agreed upon, the [c]ourt finds that [Buyers] should pay to [Sellers] the fair market value of the property as determined by an objective appraiser, in one lump sum, within sixty days of the [c]ourt's decision. Imposing fair market value and requiring a cash payment is the equitable remedy.

Sellers assert that by ruling that the purchase price would be established by an appraisal and that the terms of the payment would be in cash payable within thirty days, the trial court "formulated an agreement between the parties that never existed" and it "enforced terms and conditions on the parties that they had not had a meeting of the minds upon" . . .

This case is . . . analogous to Colcott v. Sutherland, 36 N.M. 370, 16 P.2d 399 (1932), in which our Supreme Court suggested that a claim for specific performance of a contract involving land will not fail for failure to specify a price where the contract is otherwise complete, and there has been part performance of the contract by a transfer of possession. Id. at 374-75, 16 P.2d at 401-02. In Colcott, the buyer alleged that the owner agreed to sell the buyer two acres from a parcel he owned for the sum of $150 per acre, provided that the buyer gave the seller an option to buy the land back if the buyer decided to move a gin he was planning on constructing on the land in the future. Id. at 371-72, 16 P.2d at 400. In reliance on the agreement, the buyer alleged he went into possession of the land and constructed the gin at a cost of $25,000. Id. at 372, 16 P.2d at 400. However, the parties never agreed on a price at which the seller could repurchase the property, nor did they agree on a means for determining the repurchase price. Id. at 374, 16 P.2d at 401. On this basis, the seller asserted that the allegations failed to state a claim for specific performance because there was no contract. Id. at 373-74, 16 P.2d at 400-01. Our Supreme Court said:

The parties having thus agreed, what is the effect of the omission to stipulate the price for a repurchase? [The seller] contends that it results in incompleteness and uncertainty fatal to the remedy of specific performance. [The buyer] says there is no incompleteness or uncertainty, since the law's implication binds the parties to a reasonable price, and equity has means to determine it. This may be entirely sound.

Id. at 374-75, 16 P.2d at 401 (emphasis added) (citing John Norton Pomeroy & John C. Mann, Specific Performance of Contracts § 148, at 380-82 (3d ed. 1926)). However, the suit was not for specific performance of the seller's option to repurchase; it was to enforce the contract to sell to the buyer. Accordingly, the Court did not decide whether an action would lie for specific performance of the option itself. Id. While our Supreme Court did not decide the issue, its statement that the buyer's position "may be entirely sound" and citation to Pomeroy & Mann is highly suggestive of its answer. In its entirety, the Pomeroy reference states:

> In all contracts of sale, assignment, and the like, the price is, of course, a material term. It must either be fixed by the agreement itself, or means must be therein provided for ascertaining it with certainty. In the absence of such provision, either stating it or furnishing a mode for fixing it, the agreement would be plainly incomplete, and could not be enforced; and if the contract is written, this term must appear in the memorandum or written instrument. This rule, of course, does not apply to gifts, which, under certain circumstances of parol performance by the donee, will, as has already been shown, be enforced by courts of equity. There is an apparent but not real exception to this general proposition. A valid contract of sale may be made without any stipulation as to the price, the law in such case implying that the price is the reasonable value of the thing which is the subject-matter of the agreement. This is, however, no exception to, but rather a special instance of, the foregoing rule; because such a contract does, in fact, by operation of the law, furnish a means of exactly ascertaining and fixing the price. . . .

Buyers proved to the satisfaction of the trial court by clear, cogent, and convincing evidence that Sellers entered into a contract to sell specific land to Buyers, as reflected in its conclusions of law quoted above. In addition, there was significant specific part performance by both Buyers and Sellers in reliance on the contract they made. In particular, Buyers cashed their retirement plans, went into possession of the property, moved their home onto the property, and made significant improvements to the land at a total cost of approximately $85,000, all with the knowledge and consent of Sellers for several years. Buyers assumed they would have to pay whatever the property was worth, and Sellers consulted an attorney to draft the sale documents. When Buyers repeatedly asked that the contract be formalized, Sellers' response was, "We will work it out." Thus, it is through no fault of Buyers that formal contract documents were not written with a set price and terms. Under these circumstances, it was within the equitable jurisdiction of the trial court to set the price at the fair market value as determined by an objective appraiser. We take particular note that Sellers do not dispute on appeal the fairness of the price established by the trial court.

Sellers would have us invalidate what was unquestionably a valid contract based on a mechanical application of contract law. We decline to do so. See Herrera v. Herrera, 1999-NMCA-034, ¶ 13, 126 N.M. 705, 974 P.2d 675 (noting that the purpose of the statute of frauds is to prevent fraud and perjury, not to prevent the performance or enforcement of oral contracts that have been made or to create a loophole of escape for a person who seeks to repudiate a contract he admits was made). Sellers do not seem to acknowledge that this is a case under the equitable jurisdiction of the trial court. "In the general juristic sense, equity means the power to meet the moral standards of justice in a particular case by a tribunal having discretion to mitigate the rigidity of the application of strict rules of law so as to adapt the relief to the circumstances of the particular case." Henry L. McClintock, Principles of Equity § 1, at 1 (2d ed. 1948). We hold that there was no error committed by the trial court by decreeing specific performance of the contract for Sellers to sell, and Buyers to buy, the subject property for its fair market value. . . .

The Judgment of the trial court is affirmed.

Questions

1. How does the court justify the retention of the statute of frauds despite the fact that its original justifications no longer exist?

2. What is the doctrine of part performance and how does it apply in this case?

3. According to the court, what factors must be considered in determining whether a contract to convey land has been proven and whether it would be inequitable to enforce the contract?

4. What actions taken by the buyers are considered sufficient part performance to take the oral agreement outside of the statute of frauds?

5. How does the court determine the sufficiency of the verbal agreement in terms of the purchase price and time of performance?

Takeaways – Beaver v. Brumlow

A court generally will enforce an alleged oral contract pursuant to the doctrine of part performance only if a party can adequately demonstrate, in reliance on said agreement, possession of the property, improvements thereon, or payment of a substantial part of the purchase price. Or, to put it more succinctly, moved onto the land and built something grand. (Rest.2d § 129)

Estoppel

Monarco v. Lo Greco
Supreme Court of California, 1950
35 Cal.2d 621, 220 P.2d 737

TRAYNOR, J. Natale and Carmela Castiglia were married in 1919 in Colorado. Carmela had three children, John, Rosie and Christie, by a previous marriage. Rosie was married to Nick Norcia. Natale had one grandchild, plaintiff Carmen Monarco, the son of a deceased daughter by a previous marriage. Natale and Carmela moved to California where they invested their assets, amounting to approximately $4,000, in a half interest in agricultural property. Rosie and Nick

Norcia acquired the other half interest. Christie, then in his early teens, moved with the family to California. Plaintiff remained in Colorado. In 1926, Christie, then 18 years old, decided to leave the home of his mother and stepfather and seek an independent living. Natale and Carmela, however, wanted him to stay with them and participate in the family venture. They made an oral proposal to Christie that if he stayed home and worked they would keep their property in joint tenancy so that it would pass to the survivor who would leave it to Christie by will except for small devises to John and Rosie. In performance of this agreement Christie remained home and worked diligently in the family venture. He gave up any opportunity for further education or any chance to accumulate property of his own. He received only his room and board and spending money. When he married and suggested the possibility of securing some present interest to support his wife, Natale told him that his wife should move in with the family and that Christie need not worry, for he would receive all the property when Natale and Carmela died. Natale and Carmela placed all of their property in joint tenancy and in 1941 both executed wills leaving all their property to Christie with the exception of small devises to Rosie and John and $500 to plaintiff. Although these wills did not refer to the agreement, their terms were agreed upon by Christie, Natale and Carmela. The venture was successful, so that at the time of Natale's death his and Carmela's interest was worth approximately $100,000. Shortly before his death Natale became dissatisfied with the agreement and determined to leave his half of the joint property to his grandson, the plaintiff. Without informing Christie or Carmela he arranged the necessary conveyances to terminate the joint tenancies and executed a will leaving all of his property to plaintiff. This will was probated and the court entered its decree distributing the property to plaintiff. After the decree of distribution became final, plaintiff brought these actions for partition of the properties and an accounting. By cross-complaint Carmela asked that plaintiff be declared a constructive trustee of the property he received as a result of Natale's breach of his agreement to keep the property in joint tenancy. On the basis of the foregoing facts the trial court gave judgment for defendants and cross-complainant, and plaintiff has appealed.

The controlling question is whether plaintiff is estopped from relying upon the statute of frauds (Civ. Code § 1624; Code Civ. Proc. § 1973) to defeat the enforcement of the oral contract. The doctrine of estoppel to assert the statute of frauds has been consistently applied by the courts of this state to prevent fraud that would result from refusal to enforce oral contracts in certain circumstances. Such fraud may inhere in the unconscionable injury that would result from denying enforcement of the contract after one party has been induced by the other seriously to change his position in reliance on the contract . . . . Thus not only may one party have so seriously changed his position in reliance upon, or in performance of, the contract that he would suffer an unconscionable injury if it were not enforced, but the other may have reaped the benefits of the contract so that he would be unjustly enriched if he could escape its obligations. . . .

In this case both elements are present. In reliance on Natale's repeated assurances that he would receive the property when Natale and Carmela died, Christie gave up any opportunity to accumulate property of his own and devoted his life to making the family venture a success. That he would be seriously prejudiced by a refusal to enforce the contract is made clear by a comparison of his position with that of Rosie and Nick Norcia. Because the Norcias were able to make a small investment when the family venture was started, their interest, now worth approximately $100,000, has been protected. Christie, on the other hand, forbore from demanding any present interest in the venture in exchange for his labors on the assurance that Natale's and Carmela's interest would pass to him on their death. Had he invested money instead of labor in the venture on the same oral understanding, a resulting trust would have arisen in his favor. (Byers v. Doheny, 105 Cal.App. 484, 493-495 [287 P. 988]; see, Restatement, Trusts, § 454, comment J., illus. 12.) His 20 years of labor should have equal effect. On the other hand, Natale reaped the benefits of the contract. He and his devisees would be unjustly enriched if the statute of frauds could be invoked to relieve him from performance of his own obligations thereunder.

It is contended, however, that an estoppel to plead the statute of frauds can only arise when there have been representations with respect to the requirements of the statute indicating that a writing is not necessary or will be executed or that the statute will not be relied upon as a defense. This element was present in the leading case of Seymour v. Oelrichs, 156 Cal. 782 [106 P. 88, 134 Am.St.Rep. 154], and it is not surprising therefore that it has been listed as a requirement of an estoppel in later cases that have held on their facts that there was or was not an estoppel. . . . Likewise in the case of partly performed oral contracts for the sale of land specific enforcement will be decreed whether or not there have been representations going to the requirements of the statute, because its denial would result in a fraud on the plaintiff who has gone into possession or made improvements in reliance on the contract. . . . In reality it is not the representation that the contract will be put in writing or that the statute will not be invoked, but the promise that the contract will be performed that a party relies upon when he changes his position because of it. Moreover, a party who has accepted the benefits of an oral contract will be unjustly enriched if the contract is not enforced whether his representations related to the requirements of the statute or were limited to affirmations that the contract would be performed.

It is settled that neither the remedy of an action at law for damages for breach of contract nor the quasi-contractual remedy for the value of services rendered is adequate for the breach of a contract to leave property by will in exchange for services of a peculiar nature involving the assumption or continuation of a close family relationship. . . . The facts of this case clearly bring it within the foregoing rule.

The judgments are affirmed.

Questions

1. Explain the doctrine of estoppel to assert the statute of frauds and its application in this case.

2. How did Christie change his position in reliance on the oral contract, and why would he suffer unconscionable injury if the contract were not enforced?

3. Compare the positions of Christie and Rosie/Nick Norcia in terms of their interests in the family venture, and explain why Christie should be protected.

4. Is it necessary for there to be explicit representations regarding the requirements of the statute of frauds in order to establish an estoppel? Explain the court's reasoning.

Takeaways – Monarco v. LoGreco

A defendant is precluded from asserting the Statute of Frauds as a defense where the plaintiff would be unconscionably injured or the defendant unjustly enriched, and plaintiff in reliance on the oral promise has changed his position. In other words, detrimental reliance can excuse compliance with the writing requirement.

The idea of estoppel to assert the Statute of Frauds is recognized in Restatement Second of Contracts, section 139. Note once again, that the language of that section closely tracks the language of section 90 on promissory estoppel. Comment b to Restatement Second section 139 states: "Like § 90 this Section states a flexible principle, but the requirement of consideration is more easily displaced than the requirement of a writing. The reliance must be foreseeable by the promisor, and enforcement must be necessary to avoid injustice. Subsection (2) lists some of the relevant factors in applying the latter requirement."

Redke v. Silvertrust
Supreme Court of California, 1971
6 Cal.3d 94, 90 P.2d 805, 98 Cal.Rptr. 293

BURKE, J. Plaintiff Mitzi Lee Redke brought an action in Los Angeles Superior Court to enforce the terms of an oral agreement allegedly made for her benefit between her mother Ann Hayden, and her stepfather, Samuel Hayden, both of whom are now deceased, whereupon Sam agreed to bequeath certain of Ann's separate property to Mitzi. Defendants, who are the executors of Sam's estate, co-trustees of a trust created by him, and testamentary trustees under Ann's will, appeal from a judgment in Mitzi's favor. We have concluded that, except for one minor modification, the judgment should be affirmed.

The pertinent facts underlying the dispute are as follows: In 1955, Sam, a widower with three adult children, married Ann, mother of Mitzi and Warren. By 1963, Ann's separate property had grown from approximately $20,000-$40,000 to over a million dollars, largely a result of Sam's assistance in managing her investments. Ann executed a will and an inter vivos trust which provided that half of her separate property would be placed in a marital deduction trust for Sam, giving him a general power of appointment over that property; the remaining half was to be placed in trust for her children, Mitzi and Warren. Sam executed a similar will and trust leaving half of his property to Ann, and half in trust for Mitzi and Warren.

On February 22, 1963, Warren died unexpectedly from a heart attack. Ann, who was suffering from terminal cancer, was informed of her son's death the following day. That news was a shock to Ann, and she immediately became concerned about providing for Mitzi, whose husband was also ill. Consequently, she informed Sam, in the presence of her nurse, Mitzi and another person, that she wanted to call her lawyers to change her will and trust to leave all of her separate property to Mitzi. Sam assured her that no such changes were necessary, and promised that if Ann died, Sam would leave his share of Ann's property to Mitzi upon his own death and would see that Mitzi received all of Ann's property. Ann agreed. Thereafter, the only substantial changes made in Ann or Sam's estate plans prior to Ann's death were amendments to their trusts to give Warren's share of their trust estates to Mitzi; Ann also executed a document transferring to her trust most of her remaining property.

Ann died on April 5, 1963. On the following day, Sam offered to give to Mitzi Ann's jewelry and furs, a matter discussed separately below. Sam also reaffirmed to various persons, including Mitzi, his promise to leave Mitzi his share of Ann's property. Nevertheless, within a few months following Ann's death, Sam met and married Ruth Allender and shortly thereafter amended his trust and will eliminating all provision for Mitzi and naming as beneficiaries his new wife and his natural children. Sam died in 1965, and Mitzi filed creditor's claims against his estate based upon the oral agreement and the separate gift of furs and jewelry.

At trial, defendants denied the existence of the alleged oral agreement and contended, among other things, that such an agreement would be unenforceable under the statute of frauds and void as contrary to public policy, being an illegal evasion of federal and state death taxes. The trial court made extensive findings which, in effect, recognized the existence of the oral agreement and upheld its validity and enforceability. The court held that upon Ann's death Sam became constructive trustee for the benefit of Mitzi of all of Ann's separate property, furs and jewelry received by Sam from and after Ann's death, together with all income, interest and profits derived therefrom. The court's judgment ordered defendants to deliver to Mitzi certain designated stock valued at $392,186.48, with dividends and increments thereto, plus 7 percent interest from the date of judgment. In addition to this stock,

Mitzi was awarded $457,916.06, plus 7 percent interest from the date of judgment. Mitzi also obtained judgment for all damages which she or Ann's estate may incur by reason of Sam's negligence or misconduct.

1. The Oral Agreement

In general, a contract to make a particular testamentary disposition of property is valid and enforceable. As in every contract, "there is an implied covenant of good faith and fair dealing that neither party will do anything which injures the right of the other to receive the benefits of the agreement. [Citations.] Where the parties contract to make a particular disposition of property by will, the agreement necessarily includes a promise not to breach the contract by revoking the will and failing to dispose of the property as agreed." (Brown v. Superior Court, 34 Cal.2d 559, 564-565 [212 P.2d 878]; Brewer v. Simpson, 53 Cal.2d 567, 588-589 [2 Cal.Rptr. 609, 349 P.2d 289].) If the contract is executed between spouses, a failure to perform it constitutes a violation of their confidential relationship and is constructive fraud which justifies the imposition of a constructive trust. (Day v. Greene, 59 Cal.2d 404, 411 [29 Cal.Rptr. 785, 380 P.2d 385, 94 A.L.R.2d 802].)

The trial court correctly determined that the statute of frauds did not render the agreement unenforceable. "Although the statute requires that an agreement to make a provision by will be in writing (Civ. Code, § 1624, subd. 6; Code Civ. Proc., § 1973, subd. 6), a party will be estopped from relying on the statute where fraud would result from refusal to enforce an oral contract [citation]. The doctrine of estoppel has been applied where an unconscionable injury would result from denying enforcement after one party has been induced to make a serious change of position in reliance on the contract or where unjust enrichment would result if a party who has received the benefits of the other's performance were allowed to invoke the statute. [Citation.]" (Day v. Greene, supra, 59 Cal.2d 404, 409-410; see Monarco v. Lo Greco, 35 Cal.2d 621, 623 [220 P.2d 737]; Notten v. Mensing, 3 Cal.2d 469, 474 [45 P.2d 198]; Mintz v. Rowitz, 13 Cal.App.3d 216, 223-225 [91 Cal.Rptr. 435].)

The trial court found that Ann, by reason of her trust and confidence in Sam, and in reliance upon his oral promise, changed her position to her detriment, and to Mitzi's detriment, by not changing her will and trust to make Mitzi her sole beneficiary; she changed her position by maintaining the status quo despite her concern over her daughter's welfare. Defendants do not question the evidentiary support for this finding, nor do they dispute the applicable law set forth above. They do, however, contend that Sam and Ann subsequently abandoned the agreement, a factual question which the trial court resolved in plaintiff's favor. There was ample evidence to support the court's finding that the agreement was not abandoned, including the fact that after Ann's death, Sam affirmed to five witnesses, including Mitzi, his agreement to leave his share of Ann's property to Mitzi. We conclude that the trial court correctly held that defendants are estopped to rely upon the statute of frauds. . . .

The judgment is modified by striking therefrom the award of post-judgment interest upon any stocks found to have been delivered by defendants to plaintiff in compliance with the terms of the judgment. As so modified, the judgment is affirmed and the cause is remanded to the Los Angeles County Superior Court for further proceedings not inconsistent with this opinion. Plaintiff shall receive her costs on appeal.

Questions

1. How does the doctrine of estoppel apply to the enforcement of an oral contract to make a provision by will?

2. According to the court's reasoning, why did the statute of frauds not render the oral agreement unenforceable in this case?

Takeaways – Redke v. Silvertrust

A defendant is precluded from asserting the statute of frauds where the plaintiff would be unconscionably injured or the defendant unjustly enriched, and plaintiff in reliance on the oral promise has changed his position. (*Monarco v. Lo Greco* (1950) 35 Cal.2d 621 [220 P.2d 737].) In other words, reliance by one party on an oral contract may "estop" the other from setting up a defense based upon the statute of frauds. Where a contract, which is required by law to be in writing, is prevented from being put into writing by the fraud of a party thereto, any other party who is by such fraud led to believe that it is in writing, and acts upon such belief to his prejudice, may enforce it against the fraudulent party. (Cal.Civ.Code § 1623)

Reliance Must Be Reasonable

The reliance required to estop or preclude the assertion of lack of compliance with the Statute of Frauds writing requirement must be reasonable. For example, a real estate broker's reliance on an oral contract to pay a commission is not reasonable in light of the broker's presumed knowledge (by virtue of being trained and licensed) of the requirements of the Statute of Frauds. (*Phillippe v. Shapell Industries* (1987) 43 Cal.3d 1247, 743 P.2d 1279, 241 Cal.Rptr. 22)

UCC Exceptions to the Writing Requirement

Non-Objecting Merchant Rule

Harry Rubin & Sons, Inc. v. Con. P. Co. of Am.
Supreme Court of Pennsylvania, 1959
396 Pa. 506, 512, 153 A.2d 472

JUSTICE BENJAMIN R. JONES, This is an appeal from the action of the Court of Common Pleas No. 1 of Philadelphia County, which sustained, in part, the appellees' preliminary objections to the appellants' complaint in assumpsit.

Rubin-Arandell, in their complaint, alleged that on three different dates — August 22nd, 25th and 28th, 1958 — they entered into three separate oral agreements, all for the sale of goods in excess of $500, with one Carl Pearl, an officer and agent of Consolidated-Lustro, for the purchase of plastic hoops and materials for use in assembling plastic hoops, and that Consolidated-Lustro failed to deliver a substantial portion of the hoops and material as required by the terms of the oral agreements. The court below, passing upon Consolidated-Lustro's preliminary objections, held that two of the alleged oral agreements violated the statute of frauds provision of the Uniform Commercial Code and were unenforceable. Rubin-Arandell contend that certain memoranda (attached as exhibits to the complaint) were sufficient to take both oral agreements out of the statute of frauds. Rubin-Arandell also contend that the court below erred in rejecting their claim for damages for loss of good will because of their inability to supply their customers with plastic hoops by reason of Consolidated-Lustro's breach of the agreements.

The statute of frauds provision of the Uniform Commercial Code, supra, states: "§ 2-201. Formal Requirements: Statute of Frauds (1) Except as otherwise provided in this section a contract for the sale of goods for the price of $500 or more is not enforceable by way of action or defense unless there is some writing sufficient to indicate that a contract for sale has been made between the parties and signed by the party against whom enforcement is sought or by his authorized agent or broker. A writing is not insufficient because it omits or incorrectly states a term agreed upon but the contract is not enforceable under this paragraph beyond the quantity of goods shown in such writing. (2) Between merchants if within a reasonable time a writing in confirmation of the contract and sufficient against the sender is received and the party receiving it has reason to know its contents, it satisfies the requirements of subsection (1) against such party unless written notice of objection to its contents is given within ten days after it is received."

As between merchants, the present statute of frauds provision (i.e. under § 2-201 (2), supra) significantly changes the former law by obviating the necessity of having a memorandum signed by the party sought to be charged. The present statutory requirements are: (1) that, within a reasonable time, there be a writing in confirmation of the oral contract; (2) that the writing be sufficient to bind the sender; (3) that such writing be received; (4) that no reply thereto has been made although the recipient had reason to know of its contents. Section 2-201 (2) penalizes a party who fails to "answer a written confirmation of a contract within ten days" of the receipt of the writing by depriving such party of the defense of the statute of frauds.

The memoranda upon which Rubin-Arandell rely consist of the purchase order on the Lustro form signed by Rubin stating the quantity ordered as 30,000 hoops with a description, the size and the price of the hoops listed and the letter of August 25th from Rubin to Consolidated requesting the entry of a similar order for an additional 60,000 hoops at a fixed price: "As per our phone conversation of today." This letter closes with the significant sentence that: "It is our understanding that these [the second order for 60,000 hoops] will be produced upon completion of the present order for 30,000 hoops."

Consolidated-Lustro's objection to the memoranda in question is that by employment of the word "order" rather than "contract" or "agreement, the validity of such memoranda depended upon acceptance thereof by Consolidated-Lustro and could not be "in confirmation of the contract[s]" as required by § 2-201 (2). We believe, however, that the letter of August 25th sufficiently complies with § 2-201 (2) to remove both oral contracts from the statute of frauds. The word "order" as employed in this letter obviously contemplated a binding agreement, at least, on the part of the sender, and in all reason, should have been interpreted in that manner by the recipient. The sender in stating that "It is our understanding that these will be produced upon completion of the present order for 30,000 hoops," was referring to the initial order as an accomplished fact, not as an offer depending upon acceptance for its validity. Any doubt that may exist as to the sender's use of the word "order" is clearly dispelled by its use in the communication confirming a third contract. This letter of August 28th, 1958, states: "Pursuant to our phone conversation of yesterday, you may enter our order for the following [number, description and price] . . . . This order is to be entered based upon our phone conversation, in which you *agreed* to ship us your entire production of this Hoop material at the above price. . . ." (Emphasis supplied) The letter of August 25th was a sufficient confirmation in writing of the two alleged oral contracts, and, in the absence of a denial or rejection on the part of the recipient within ten days, satisfied the requirements of § 2-201 (2) of the Uniform Commercial Code.

Under the statute of frauds as revised in the Code "All that is required is that the writing afford a basis for believing that the offered oral evidence rests on a real transaction." Its object is the elimination of certain formalistic requirements adherence to which often resulted in injustice, rather than the prevention of fraud. The present memoranda fulfill the requirement of affording a belief that the oral contracts rested on a real transaction and the court below erred in holding otherwise. Nor are Consolidated-Lustro harmed by such a determination since Rubin-Arandell must still sustain the burden of persuading the trier of fact that the contracts were in fact made orally prior to the written confirmation.

Question

According to the court's reasoning, why does the letter of August 25th satisfy the requirements of subdivision (2) of Section 2-201 of the Uniform Commercial Code?

St. Ansgar Mills, Inc. v. Streit
Supreme Court of Iowa, 2000
613 NW 2d 289

CADY, Justice. A grain dealer appeals from an order by the district court granting summary judgment in an action to enforce an oral contract for the sale of corn based on a written confirmation. The district court held the oral contract was unenforceable because the written confirmation was not delivered within a reasonable time after the oral contract as a matter of law. We reverse the decision of the district court and remand for further proceedings.

I. Background Facts and Proceedings.

St. Ansgar Mills, Inc. is a family-owned agricultural business located in Mitchell County. As a part of its business, St. Ansgar Mills buys corn from local grain farmers and sells corn to livestock farmers for feed. The price of the corn sold to farmers is established by trades made on the Chicago Board of Trade for delivery with reference to five contract months. The sale of corn for future delivery is hedged by St. Ansgar Mills through an offsetting futures position on the Chicago Board of Trade.

A sale is typically made when a farmer calls St. Ansgar Mills and requests a quote for a cash price of grain for future delivery based on the Chicago Board of Trade price for the delivery. The farmer then accepts or rejects the price. If the price is accepted, St. Ansgar Mills protects the price through a licensed brokerage house by acquiring a hedge position on the Chicago Board of Trade. This hedge position, however, obligates St. Ansgar Mills to purchase the corn at the stated price at the time of delivery. Thus, St. Ansgar Mills relies on the farmer who purchased the grain to accept delivery at the agreed price.

Duane Streit . . . raises hogs. He owns. . . a hog finishing operation. . . purchased . . . from his father in 1993.

Duane and his father have been long-time customers of St. Ansgar Mills. Since 1989, Duane entered into numerous contracts with St. Ansgar Mills for the purchase of large quantities of corn and other grain products. Duane would generally initiate the purchase agreement by calling St. Ansgar Mills on the telephone to obtain a price quote. If an oral contract was made, an employee of St. Ansgar Mills would prepare a written confirmation of the sale and either mail it to Duane to sign and return, or wait for Duane or John to sign the confirmation when they would stop into the business.

John would regularly stop by St. Ansgar Mills sometime during the first ten days of each month and pay the amount of the open account Duane maintained at St. Ansgar Mills for the purchase of supplies and other materials. On those occasions when St. Ansgar Mills sent the written confirmation to Duane, it was not unusual for Duane to fail to sign the confirmation for a long period of time. He also failed to return contracts sent to him. Nevertheless, Duane had never refused delivery of grain he purchased by telephone prior to the incident which gave rise to this case.

On July 1, 1996, John telephoned St. Ansgar Mills to place two orders for the purchase of 60,000 bushels of corn for delivery in December 1996 and May 1997. This order followed an earlier conversation between Duane and St. Ansgar Mills. After the order was placed, St. Ansgar Mills completed the written confirmation but set it aside for John to sign when he was expected to stop by the business to pay the open account. The agreed price of the December corn was $3.53 per bushel. The price of the May corn was $3.73 per bushel.

John failed to follow his monthly routine of stopping by the business during the month of July. St. Ansgar Mills then asked a local banker who was expected to see John to have John stop into the business.

John did not stop by St. Ansgar Mills until August 10, 1996. On that date, St. Ansgar Mills delivered the written confirmation to him.

Duane later refused delivery of the corn orally purchased on July 1, 1996. The price of corn had started to decline shortly after July 1, and eventually plummeted well below the quoted price on July 1. After Duane refused delivery of the corn, he purchased corn for his hog operations on the open market at prices well below the contract prices of July 1. St. Ansgar Mills later told Duane it should have followed up earlier with the written confirmation and had no excuse for not doing so.

St. Ansgar Mills then brought this action for breach of contract. It sought damages of $152,100, which was the difference between the contract price of the corn and the market price at the time Duane refused delivery.

Duane filed a motion for summary judgment. He claimed the oral contract alleged by St. Ansgar Mills was governed by the provisions of the Uniform Commercial Code, and was unenforceable as a matter of law under the statute of frauds. He claimed the written confirmation delivered to John on August 10, 1996 did not satisfy the statute of frauds for two reasons. First, he was not a merchant. Second, the confirmation was not received within a reasonable time after the alleged oral agreement.

The district court determined a jury question was presented on whether Duane was a merchant under the Uniform Commercial Code. However, the district court found the written confirmation did not satisfy the writing requirements of the statute of frauds because the delivery of the confirmation to John, as Duane's agent, did not occur within a reasonable time after the oral contract as a matter of law. The district court found the size of the order, the volatility of the grain market, and the lack of an explanation by St. Ansgar Mills for failing to send the confirmation to Duane after John failed to stop by the business as expected made the delay between July 1 and August 10 unreasonable as a matter of law.

St. Ansgar Mills appeals. It claims a jury question was presented on the issue of whether a written confirmation was received within a reasonable time. . . .

Although the statute of frauds has been deeply engrained into our law, many of the forces which originally gave rise to the rule are no longer prevalent. White & Summers § 2—1, at 51. This, in turn, has caused some of the rigid requirements of the rule to be modified.

One statutory exception or modification to the statute of frauds which has surfaced applies to merchants. *Id.* § 554.2201(2). Under section 554.2201(2), the writing requirements of section 554.2201(1) are considered to be satisfied if, within a reasonable time, a writing in confirmation of the contract which is sufficient against the sender is received and the merchant receiving it has reason to know of its contents, unless written notice of objection of its contents is given within ten days after receipt. *Id.* Thus, a writing is still required, but it does not need to be signed by the party against whom the contract is sought to be enforced. The purpose of this exception was to put professional buyers and sellers on equal footing by changing the former law under which a party who received a written confirmation of an oral agreement of sale, but who had not signed anything, could hold the other party to a contract without being bound. *See* White & Summers § 2—3, at 55; *Kimball County Grain Coop. v. Yung,* 200 Neb. 233, 263 N.W.2d 818, 820 (1978). It also encourages the common, prudent business practice of sending memoranda to confirm oral agreements. White & Summers § 2—3, at 55.

While the written confirmation exception imposes a specific ten-day requirement for a merchant to object to a written confirmation, it employs a flexible standard of reasonableness to establish the time in which the confirmation must be received. Iowa Code § 554.2201(2). The Uniform Commercial Code specifically defines a reasonable time for taking action in relationship to "the nature, purpose and circumstances" of the action. *Id.* § 554.1204(2). Additionally, the declared purpose of the Uniform Commercial Code is to permit the expansion of commercial practices through the custom and practice of the parties. *See* Iowa Code Ann. § 554.1102 cmt. 2 (course of dealings, usage of trade or course of performance are material in determining a reasonable time). Furthermore, the Uniform Commercial Code relies upon course of dealings between the parties to help interpret their conduct. Iowa Code § 554.1205(1). Thus, all relevant circumstances, including custom and practice of the parties, must be considered in determining what constitutes a reasonable time under section 554.2201(2).

Generally, the determination of the reasonableness of particular conduct is a jury question. . . . Thus, the reasonableness of time between an oral contract and a subsequent written confirmation is ordinarily a question of fact for the jury. . . .It is only in rare cases that a determination of the reasonableness of conduct should be decided by summary adjudication. *Harvey,* 388 F.2d at 125. Summary judgment is appropriate only when the evidence is so one-sided that a party must prevail at trial as a matter of law. . . .

There are a host of cases from other jurisdictions which have considered the question of what constitutes a reasonable time under the written confirmation exception of the Uniform Commercial Code. *See Gestetner Corp. v. Case Equip. Co.,* 815 F.2d 806, 810 (1st Cir.1987) (roughly five month delay reasonable in light of merchants' relationship and parties' immediate action under contract following oral agreement); *Serna, Inc. v. Harman,* 742 F.2d 186, 189 (5th Cir.1984) (three and one-half month delay reasonable in light of the parties' interaction in the interim, and non-fluctuating prices, thus no prejudice); *Cargill, Inc. v. Stafford,* 553 F.2d 1222, 1224 (10th Cir.1977) (less than one month delay unreasonable despite misdirection of confirmation due to mistaken addressing); *Starry Constr. Co. v. Murphy Oil USA, Inc.,* 785 F.Supp. 1356, 1362-63 (D.Minn. 1992) (six month delay for confirmation of modification order for additional oil unreasonable as a matter of law in light of Persian Gulf War, thus increased prices and demand); *Rockland Indus., Inc. v. Frank Kasmir Assoc.,* 470 F.Supp. 1176, 1179 (N.D.Tex.1979) (letter sent eight months after alleged oral agreement for two-year continuity agreement unreasonable in light of lack of evidence supporting reasonableness of delay); *Yung,* 263 N.W.2d at 820 (six month delay in confirming oral agreement delivered one day prior to last possible day of delivery unreasonable); *Azevedo,* 471 P.2d at 666 (ten week delay reasonable in light of immediate performance by both parties following oral agreement); *Lish v. Compton,* 547 P.2d 223, 226-27 (Utah 1976) (twelve day delay "outside the ambit which fair-minded persons could conclude to be reasonable" in light of volatile price market and lack of excuse for delay other than casual delay). Most of these cases, however, were decided after a trial on the merits and cannot be used to establish a standard or time period as a matter of law. Only a few courts have decided the question as a matter of law under the facts of the case. *Compare Starry,* 785 F.Supp. at 1362-63 (granting summary judgment), *and Lish,* 547 P.2d at 226-27 (removing claim from jury's consideration), *with Barron v. Edwards,* 45 Mich.App. 210, 206 N.W.2d 508, 511 (1973) (remanding for further development of facts, summary judgment improper). However, these cases do not establish a strict principle to apply in this case. The resolution of each case depends upon the particular facts and circumstances.

In this case, the district court relied upon the large amount of the sale, volatile market conditions, and lack of an explanation by St. Ansgar Mills for failing to send the written confirmation to Duane in determining St. Ansgar Mills acted unreasonably as a matter of law in delaying delivery of the written confirmation until August 10, 1996. Volatile market conditions, combined with a large sale price, would normally narrow the window of reasonable time under section 554.2201(2). However, they are not the only factors to consider. Other relevant factors which must also be considered in this case reveal the parties had developed a custom or practice to delay delivery of the confirmation. The parties also maintained a long-time amicable business relationship and had engaged in many other similar business transactions without incident. There is also evidence to infer St. Ansgar Mills did not suspect John's failure to follow his customary practice in July of stopping by the business was a concern at the time. These factors reveal a genuine dispute over the reasonableness of the delay in delivering the written confirmation, and make the resolution of the issue appropriate for the jury. Moreover, conduct is not rendered unreasonable solely because the acting party had no particular explanation for not pursuing different conduct, or regretted not pursuing different conduct in retrospect. The reasonableness of conduct is determined by the facts and circumstances existing at the time.

Considering our principles governing summary adjudication and the need to resolve the legal issue by considering the particular facts and circumstances of each case, we conclude the trial court erred by granting summary judgment. We reverse and remand the case for further proceedings.

Reversed and remanded.

Questions

1. How does the UCC define a reasonable time in relation to taking action?

2. Why did the district court find that the delay in delivering the written confirmation was unreasonable as a matter of law?

3. What factors, besides market conditions and sale price, should be considered in determining the reasonableness of the delay in delivering the written confirmation?

Takeaways – Rubin and St. Ansgar Mills

These cases illustrate the "non-objecting" merchant rule. I.e., a contract that is within the UCC version of the Statute of Frauds is enforceable against a non-signing party when he receives a written confirmation signed by the opposing party (i.e. would be enforceable against the opposing party) and he fails to object within 10 days. However, for this section to be operable, both parties to the contract must be "merchants."

Subsection 2 obviates the necessity of having a memorandum signed by the party to be charged. Instead, a written confirmation may take the place of a memorandum, between merchants, if within a reasonable time a writing in confirmation of the contract and sufficient against the sender is received and the party receiving it has reason to know its contents, it is sufficient against such party unless written notice of objection to its contents is given within 10 days after it is received. (UCC 2-201(2).)

Subsection 3 Writing Requirement Exceptions

Sedmak v. Charlie's Chevrolet, Inc.
Missouri Court of Appeals, 1981
622 SW 2d 694

[The Sedmaks, alleged they entered into a contract with defendant, Charlie's Chevrolet, Inc. (Charlie's), to purchase a Corvette automobile for approximately $15,000.00. Dr. Sedmak telephoned defendant's sales manager to ask him if a specific Corvette could be ordered. Kells indicated that he would require a deposit on the car, so Mrs. Sedmak went to Charlie's and gave the sale's manager a check for $500.00. She was given a receipt for that amount bearing the names of Kells and Charlie's Chevrolet, Inc. When the sales manager later told the Sedmaks they could not purchase the car for the manufacturer's retail price because demand for the car had inflated its value beyond the suggested price the Sedmaks filed this suit for specific performance.]

SATZ, Judge. Charlie's next complains that if there were an oral contract, it is unenforceable under the Statute of Frauds. The trial court concluded the contract was removed from the Statute of Frauds either by the written memoranda concerning the transaction or by partial payment made by the Sedmaks. We find the latter ground a sufficient answer to defendant's complaint. We discuss it and do not consider or address the former ground.

Prior to our adoption of the Uniform Commercial Code, part payment for goods was sufficient to remove the entire contract from the Statute of Frauds. § 432.020 RSMo 1949; *Woodburn v. Cogdal*, 39 Mo. 222, 228 (1866); *See Coffman v.*

Fleming, 301 Mo. 313, 256 S.W. 731, 732-733 (1923). This result followed from the logical assumption that money normally moves from one party to another not as a gift but for a bargain. The basis of this rule is the probative value of the act—part payment shows the existence of an agreement. *3 Sales & Bulk Transfers Under U.C.C.*, (Bender), § 2.04[5] at 2-96. However, "[t]his view overlooks the fact that, although ... part payment of the price does indicate the existence of an agreement, [it does] not reveal [the agreement's] quantity term, a key provision without which the court cannot reconstruct the contract fairly and provide against fraudulent claims." *1 Hawkland, A Transactional Guide To The Uniform Commercial Code* (1964), § 1.1202 at 28. Thus, under this rule a buyer who orally purchased one commercial unit for $10.00 could falsely assert he purchased 100 units and, then, by also asserting a $10.00 payment was part payment on the 100 units, he could, in theory and in practice, convince the trier of fact that the contract entered into was for 100 units. The Code attempts to correct this defect by providing that part payment of an oral contract satisfies the Statute of Frauds *only* "with respect to goods for which payment has been made and accepted ...." § 400.2-201(3)(c) RSMo 1978. Under this provision, part payment satisfies the Statute of Frauds, not for the entire contract, but only for that quantity of goods to which part payment can be apportioned. This change simply reflects the rationale that part payment alone does not establish the oral contract's quantity term.

In correcting one problem, however, the change creates another problem when, as in the instant case, payment for a single unit sale has been less than full. Obviously, this part payment cannot be apportioned and, thus, the question arises how shall this subsection of the Code be applied. The few courts that have considered this question have used opposing logic and, thus, reached opposing answers. At least one court reads and applies the changed provision literally and denies the enforcement of the oral contract because payment has not been received in full. *Williamson v. Martz*, 11 Pa. Dist. & Co.R.2d 33, 35 (1956). The *Williamson* Court reasoned:

"Under the code, part payment takes the case out of the statute only to the extent for which payment has been made. The code therefore makes an important change by denying the enforcement of the contract where in the case of a single object the payment made is less than the full amount." *Id.* At 35.

Charlie's argues for this view. Other courts infer that part payment for one unit is still sufficient evidence that a contract existed between the parties and enforce the oral contract. *Lockwood v. Smigel*, 18 Cal. App.3d 800, 96 Cal.Rptr. 289 (1971); *Starr v. Freeport Dodge, Inc.*, 54 Misc.2d 271, 282 N.Y.S.2d 58 (N.Y.Dist.1967); *see also*, *Paloukos v. Intermountain Chevrolet Company*, 99 Idaho 740, 588 P.2d 939, 944 (1978); *Bertram Yacht Sales, Inc. v. West*, 209 So.2d 677, 679 (Fla.App.1968); *Thomaier v. Hoffman Chevrolet, Inc.*, 64 A.D.2d 492, 410 N.Y.S.2d 645, 648-649 (1978). We are persuaded by the cogency of the logic supporting this view.

Admittedly, § 400.2-201(3)(c) does validate a divisible contract only for as much of the goods as has been paid for. However, this subsection was drafted to provide a method for enforcing oral contracts where there is a quantity dispute. *See Lockwood v. Smigel, supra,* 18 Cal. App.3d 800, 96 Cal.Rptr. at 291; *see also, 1 Hawkland, supra* at 28. The subsection does not necessarily resolve the Statute of Frauds problem where there is no quantity dispute. Neither the language of the subsection nor its logical dictates necessarily invalidate an oral contract for an indivisible commercial unit where part payment has been made and accepted. If there is no dispute as to quantity, the part payment still retains its probative value to prove the existence of the contract.

Moreover, where, as here, there is no quantity dispute, part payment evidences the existence of a contract as satisfactorily as would a written memorandum of agreement under the liberalized criteria of the Code. The Code establishes only three basic requirements for a written memorandum to take an oral contract out of the Statute of Frauds. "First, it must evidence a contract for the sale of goods; second it must be `signed,' a word which includes any authentication which identifies the party to be charged; and third, it must specify a quantity." § 400.2-201 RSMo 1978, U.C.C., Comment 1. Here, part payment evidences the contract for the sale of goods—the car. The party to be charged— Charlie's—is identified as the one who received payment. The quantity is not in dispute because the Sedmaks are claiming to have purchased one unit—the car. Thus, part payment here evidences the existence of a contract as satisfactorily as would a written memorandum of agreement under the Code. *Lockwood v. Smigel,* 18 Cal. App.3d 800, 96 Cal.Rptr. 289, 291 (1971); *see also Paloukos v. Intermountain Chevrolet Co.,* 99 Idaho 740, 588 P.2d 939, 944 (1978).

Finally, the Code has not changed the basic policy of the Statute of Frauds.

"The purpose of the Statute of Frauds is to prevent the enforcement of alleged promises that were never made; it is not, and never has been, to justify the contractors in repudiating promises that were in fact made." *Corbin, The Uniform Commercial Code; Should It Be Enacted?* 59 Yale L.J. 821, 829 (1950).

Enforcement of the oral contract here carries out the purpose of the Statute of Frauds. Denial of the contract's existence frustrates that purpose. The present contract could not have contemplated less than one car. If the part payment is believed, it must have been intended to buy the entire car not a portion of the car. Thus, denying the contract because part payment cannot be apportioned encourages fraud rather than discouraging it. "The Statute of Frauds would be used to cut down the trusting buyer rather than to protect the one who, having made his bargain, parted with a portion of the purchase price as an earnest of his good faith." *Starr v. Freeport Dodge, Inc., supra,* 54 Misc.2d 271, 282 N.Y.S.2d at 61.

We hold, therefore, that where, as here, there is no dispute as to quantity, part payment for a single indivisible commercial unit validates an oral contract under § 400.2-201(3)(c) RSMo 1978.

Questions

1. According to the court's reasoning, what was the basis for the rule that part payment for goods removed the contract from the Statute of Frauds?

2. What change did the Uniform Commercial Code (UCC) make regarding part payment to satisfy the Statute of Frauds?

3. How do opposing courts differ in their interpretation and application of the UCC provision regarding part payment for a single unit sale?

4. Why does the court argue that part payment should still retain its probative value in proving the existence of a contract when there is no quantity dispute?

5. Based on the court's reasoning, why does the enforcement of the oral contract in this case fulfill the purpose of the Statute of Frauds?

Problem

John, a car enthusiast, contacts a custom car builder named Alex to inquire about the possibility of having a unique and specially designed sports car built. After several discussions, they agree on the specifications and design details of the car. However, they never formalize their agreement in writing.

Alex, understanding that the car is specifically tailored to John's preferences and not suitable for sale to others, starts working on the project. He purchases the necessary materials, allocates his team's time, and begins the manufacturing process. He invests a significant amount of time and resources into the project, indicating his commitment to fulfill the agreement.

Before Alex completes the car or delivers it to John, John sends him a message stating that he no longer wishes to proceed with the project and intends to repudiate the agreement.

In this scenario, even though the contract between John and Alex does not satisfy the requirements of UCC 2-201 (1) (i.e., it is not in writing), it is still enforceable under subsection (3)(a) of the rule. The goods, which is the specially manufactured sports car, is likely not suitable for sale to others in the ordinary course of Alex's business. Furthermore, Alex has made a substantial beginning of manufacturing the car and has committed resources to its procurement.

Therefore, based on these circumstances, Alex can enforce the contract against John and seek appropriate remedies for the breach.

Takeaways – UCC 2-201 (3)

UCC 2-201(3) provides: A contract which does not satisfy the requirements of subsection (1) but which is valid in other respects is enforceable

(a) if the goods are to be specially manufactured for the buyer and are not suitable for sale to others in the ordinary course of the seller's business and the seller, before notice of repudiation is received and under circumstances which reasonably indicate that the goods are for the buyer, has made either a substantial beginning of their manufacture or commitments for their procurement; or

(b) if the party against whom enforcement is sought admits in his pleading, testimony or otherwise in court that a contract for sale was made, but the contract is not enforceable under this provision beyond the quantity goods admitted; or

(c) with respect to goods for which payment has been made and accepted or which have been received and accepted.

ASSESSMENT QUESTIONS, CHAPTER 3

1. What is the Statute of Frauds and what is its purpose in contract law?

2. List the types of contracts that typically fall within the scope of the Statute of Frauds.

3. Explain the writing requirement under the Statute of Frauds. What information must be included in the written memorandum?

4. Can an electronic communication, such as an email, satisfy the writing requirement under the Statute of Frauds?

5. Describe the concept of part performance and its significance in relation to the Statute of Frauds.

6. Provide three exceptions to the Statute of Frauds where a contract can be enforceable even without a written memorandum.

7. What is the effect of noncompliance with the Statute of Frauds? Does it render a contract completely unenforceable?

8. Discuss the role of promissory estoppel in overcoming the Statute of Frauds. When can promissory estoppel be invoked?

9. What is the "one-year rule" under the Statute of Frauds? How does it impact the enforceability of certain contracts?

10. How does the UCC modify the writing requirement for certain types of contracts?

11. What is the role of the signature requirement under the Statute of Frauds? Can a signature be electronic or digital?

Chapter 4
Policing the Bargain

Capacity to Contract – Minors and Persons of Unsound Mind

Capacity

Certain classes of persons are deemed by the law to have a limited ability to contract. Typically these classes of persons include minors (also referred to in many of the cases by the more archaic term, "infants") and the mentally infirm.

Capacity of Minor to Enter Into Contract

With respect to minors, the general rule is that the contract of a minor, other than for the necessities of life, is voidable at the minor's option. In other words, minors only incur voidable contractual obligations. (See Rest.2d § 14) The rationale behind this rule is that minors are immature and should be protected from their own bad judgment as well as those who would take advantage of them.

Kiefer v. Fred Howe Motors, Inc.
Supreme Court of Wisconsin, 1968
39 Wis. 2d 20, 158 N.W.2d 288

Wilkie, J. . . . The law governing agreements made during infancy reaches back over many centuries. The general rule is that "... the contract of a minor, other than for necessaries, is either void or voidable at his option." The only other exceptions to the rule permitting disaffirmance are statutory or involve contracts which deal with duties imposed by law such as a contract of marriage or an agreement to support an illegitimate child. The general rule is not affected by the minor's status as emancipated or unemancipated.

Appellant does not advance any argument that would put this case within one of the exceptions to the general rule, but rather urges that this court, as a matter of public policy, adopt a rule that an emancipated minor over eighteen years of age be made legally responsible for his contracts.

The underpinnings of the general rule allowing the minor to disaffirm his contracts were undoubtedly the protection of the minor. It was thought that the minor was immature in both mind and experience and that, therefore, he should be protected from his own bad judgments as well as from adults who would take advantage of him. The doctrine of the voidability of minors' contracts often seems commendable and just. If the beans that the young naive Jack purchased from the crafty old man in the fairy tale "Jack and the Bean Stalk" had been worthless rather than magical, it would have been only fair to allow Jack to disaffirm the bargain and reclaim his cow. However, in today's modern and sophisticated society the "infancy doctrine" seems to lose some of its gloss.

Paradoxically, we declare the infant mature enough to shoulder arms in the military, but not mature enough to vote; mature enough to marry and be responsible for his torts and crimes, but not mature enough to assume the burden of his own contractual indiscretions. In Wisconsin, the infant is deemed mature enough to use a dangerous instrumentality a motor vehicle at sixteen, but not mature enough to purchase it without protection until he is twenty-one.

No one really questions that a line as to age must be drawn somewhere below which a legally defined minor must be able to disaffirm his contracts for nonnecessities. The law over the centuries has considered this age to be twenty-one. Legislatures in other states have lowered the age. We suggest that the appellant might better seek the change it proposes in the legislative halls rather than this court. A recent law review article in the Indiana Law

Journal explores the problem of contractual disabilities of minors and points to three different legislative solutions leading to greater freedom to contract. The first approach is one gleaned from the statutes of California and New York, which would allow parties to submit a proposed contract to a court which would remove the infant's right of disaffirmance upon a finding that the particular contract is fair. This suggested approach appears to be extremely impractical in light of the expense and delay that would necessarily accompany the procedure. A second approach would be to establish a rebuttable presumption of incapacity to replace the strict rule. This alternative would be an open invitation to litigation. The third suggestion is a statutory procedure that would allow a minor to petition a court for the removal of disabilities. Under this procedure a minor would only have to go to court once, rather than once for each contract as in the first suggestion.

Undoubtedly, the infancy doctrine is an obstacle when a major purchase is involved. However, we believe that the reasons for allowing that obstacle to remain viable at this point outweigh those for casting it aside. Minors require some protection from the pitfalls of the marketplace. Reasonable minds will always differ on the extent of the protection that should be afforded. For this court to adopt a rule that the appellant suggests and remove the contractual disabilities from a minor simply because he becomes emancipated, which in most cases would be the result of marriage, would be to suggest that the married minor is somehow vested with more wisdom and maturity than his single counterpart. However, logic would not seem to dictate this result especially when today a youthful marriage is oftentimes indicative of a lack of wisdom and maturity.

Disaffirmance. The appellant questions whether there has been an effective disaffirmance of the contract in this case.

Williston, while discussing how a minor may disaffirm a contract, states: "Any act which clearly shows an intent to disaffirm a contract or sale is sufficient for the purpose. Thus a notice by the infant of his purpose to disaffirm ... a tender or even an offer to return the consideration or its proceeds to the vendor, ... is sufficient."

The testimony of Steven Kiefer and the letter from his attorney to the dealer clearly establish that there was an effective disaffirmance of the contract.

Misrepresentation. Appellant's last argument is that the respondent should be held liable in tort for damages because he misrepresented his age. Appellant would use these damages as a set-off against the contract price sought to be reclaimed by respondent.

The 19th-century view was that a minor's lying about his age was inconsequential because a fraudulent representation of capacity was not the equivalent of actual capacity. This rule has been altered by time. There appear to be two possible methods that now can be employed to bind the defrauding minor: He may be estopped from denying his alleged majority, in which case the contract will be enforced or contract damages will be allowed; or he may be allowed to disaffirm his contract but be liable in tort for damages. Wisconsin follows the latter approach. . . .

Questions

1. What is the general rule regarding contracts made by minors, and what are the exceptions to this rule?

2. According to the court, what were the underpinnings of the general rule allowing minors to disaffirm their contracts?

3. How does the court address the argument that an emancipated minor over eighteen should be legally responsible for their contracts?

4. What are the two possible methods that can be employed to bind a defrauding minor who misrepresented their age, according to the court?

Takeaways – Kiefer v. Fred Howe Motors

Could the trial court have found that the car was a "necessity?" In *Kiefer*, a dissenting justice thought so. "Automobiles for parents under 21 years of age to go to and from work in our current society may well be a necessity. . . "

Minor's Power to Disaffirm Contracts

A minor may avoid a contract by disaffirming it. A contract of a minor may be disaffirmed by the minor before majority (reaching the age of 18 in most states) or within a reasonable time afterwards. (Cal.Fam.Code § 6710) If a minor disaffirms the contract she is bound to return any consideration which she still has in her possession. However, if she no longer has the consideration she need not return it. Failure to timely disaffirm results in ratification of the contract. Ratification may be express, by conduct, or by failure to timely disaffirm. Retaining and using the property for more than a reasonable time after attaining the age of majority is ratification by inaction. Ratification cannot take place at any time prior to reaching the age of majority.

The power of disaffirm and avoid the contract lies solely with the minor. The adult party to the transaction cannot avoid the contract on the ground that the other party was a minor without the capacity to contract.

In California, a minor cannot make a contract relating to real property or any interest therein, or make a contract relating to any personal property not in the immediate possession or control of the minor. (Cal.Fam.Code § 6701(b)(c).)

Necessities of Life

A minor cannot disaffirm a contract to pay the reasonable value of things necessary for the support of the minor or the minor's family. So what are "necessities" or "necessaries" for purposes of determining whether a minor person can enter into a binding contract? Obviously food, shelter and clothing are necessaries as are medical services. Necessaries are relative to the minor's status in life. Education is a necessary but the kind of education which is necessary depends on the circumstances of the minor. At least one court has sought to expand the scope of necessaries. "In our view, the concept of `necessaries' should be enlarged to include such articles of property and such services as are reasonably necessary to enable the infant to earn the money required to provide the necessities of life for himself and those who are legally dependent upon him." If an infant borrows money for the purpose of purchasing necessaries and so uses it, the infant is liable to the lender as if the lender had supplied the necessaries. (*Gastonia Personnel Corp. v. Rogers* 172 S.E. 2d 19 (N.C. 1970).)

Persons of Unsound Mind

Under Restatement 2d §15, a contract is voidable if a party "by reason of mental illness or defect is unable to understand in a reasonable manner the nature and consequences of the transaction or is unable to act in a reasonable manner in relation to the transaction and the other party has reason to know of this condition." A similar rule applies to the contracts of an intoxicated person. (Rest.2d § 16)

Ortelere v. Teachers' Ret. Bd.
Court of Appeals of the State of New York, 1969
25 N.Y.2d 196, 250 N.E.2d 460

BREITEL, J. . . . The particular issue arises on the evidently unwise and foolhardy selection of benefits by a 60-year-old teacher, on leave for mental illness and suffering from cerebral arteriosclerosis, after service as a public schoolteacher and participation in a public retirement system for over 40 years. The teacher died a little less than two months after making her election of maximum benefits, payable to her during her life, thus causing the entire reserve to fall in. She left surviving her husband of 38 years of marriage and two grown children. . . . [In 1965, without telling her husband, she obtained a loan from the retirement system in the largest amount possible, $8,760, and made an irrevocable election to take the maximum retirement benefits of $450 a month during her lifetime. This revoked an earlier election under which she would have received only $375 a month but her husband would have taken the unexhausted reserve on her death. The new election left him with no benefits in the event of her death. Two months later she died. Her husband sued to set aside her election on the ground of mental incompetence. Her psychiatrist testified that she was incapable of making a decision of any kind and that victims of involutional melancholia "can't think rationally." From a judgment for Mr. Ortelere, the Board appealed to the Appellate Division which reversed and dismissed the complaint. The plaintiff appealed.]

Traditionally, in this State and elsewhere, contractual mental capacity has been measured by what is largely a cognitive test . . . Under this standard the "inquiry" is whether the mind was "so affected as to render him wholly and absolutely incompetent to comprehend and understand the nature of the transaction" . . . A requirement that the party also be able to make a rational judgment concerning the particular transaction qualified the cognitive test (*Paine v. Aldrich*, 133 N.Y. 544, 546; Note, "Civil Insanity": The New York Treatment of the Issue of Mental Incompetency in Non-Criminal Cases, 44 Cornell L. Q. 76). Conversely, it is also well recognized that contractual ability would be affected by insane delusions intimately related to the particular transaction (*Moritz v. Moritz*, 153 App. Div. 147, affd. 211 N.Y. 580; see Green, Judicial Tests of Mental Incompetency, 6 Mo. L. Rev. 141, 151).

These traditional standards governing competency to contract were formulated when psychiatric knowledge was quite primitive. They fail to account for one who by reason of mental illness is unable to control his conduct even though his cognitive ability seems unimpaired. When these standards were evolving it was thought that all the mental faculties were simultaneously affected by mental illness. (Green, Mental Incompetency, 38 Mich. L. Rev. 1189, 1197-1202.) This is no longer the prevailing view (Note, Mental Illness and the Law of Contracts, 57 Mich. L. Rev. 1020, 1033-1036). . . .

It is quite significant that Restatement, 2d, Contracts, states the modern rule on competency to contract. This is in evident recognition, and the Reporter's Notes support this inference, that, regardless of how the cases formulated their reasoning, the old cognitive test no longer explains the results. Thus, the new Restatement section reads: "(1) A person incurs only voidable contractual duties by entering into a transaction if by reason of mental illness or defect * * * (b) he is unable to act in a reasonable manner in relation to the transaction and the other party has reason to know of his condition." (Restatement, 2d, Contracts [T.D. No. 1, April 13, 1964], § 18C.) [renumbered 15]. . . .

The system was, or should have been, fully aware of Mrs. Ortelere's condition. They, or the Board of Education, knew of her leave of absence for medical reasons and the resort to staff psychiatrists by the Board of Education. Hence, the other of the conditions for avoidance is satisfied.

Lastly, there are no significant changes of position by the system other than those that flow from the barest actuarial consequences of benefit selection.

Nor should one ignore that in the relationship between retirement system and member, and especially in a public system, there is not involved a commercial, let alone an ordinary commercial, transaction. Instead the nature of the system and its announced goal is the protection of its members and those in whom its members have an interest. It is not a sound scheme which would permit 40 years of contribution and participation in the system to be nullified by a one-instant act committed by one known to be mentally ill. This is especially true if there would be no substantial harm to the system if the act were avoided. On the record none may gainsay that her selection of a "no option" retirement while under psychiatric care, ill with cerebral arteriosclerosis, aged 60, and with a family in which she had always manifested concern, was so unwise and foolhardy that a fact finder might conclude that it was explainable only as a product of psychosis.

On this analysis it is not difficult to see that plaintiff's evidence was sufficient to sustain a finding that, when she acted as she did on February 11, 1965, she did so solely as a result of serious mental illness, namely, psychosis. Of course, nothing less serious than medically classified psychosis should suffice or else few contracts would be invulnerable to some kind of psychological attack. Mrs. Ortelere's psychiatrist testified quite flatly that as an involutional melancholia in depression she was incapable of making a voluntary "rational" decision. Of course, as noted earlier, the trial court's finding and perhaps some of the testimony attempted to fit into the rubrics of the traditional rules. For that reason rather than reinstatement of the judgment at Trial Term there should be a new trial under the proper standards frankly considered and applied.

[Reversed]

Questions

1. What were the traditional standards for determining mental capacity to contract, and how do they differ from the modern understanding?

2. According to the Restatement (2d) of Contracts, what conditions must be met for a person with mental illness or defect to incur only voidable contractual duties?

3. How does the court argue that the retirement system should have been aware of Mrs. Ortelere's mental condition and that one of the conditions for avoidance is satisfied?

4. Why does the court consider the relationship between the retirement system and its members to be different from an ordinary commercial transaction?

Takeaways – Ortelere v. Teacher's Retirement Bd.

A person is rebuttably presumed to be of unsound mind if the person is substantially unable to manage his or her own financial resources or resist fraud or undue influence. (Cal.Civ.Code § 39(b).) A person entirely without understanding has no power to make a contract of any kind, but the person is liable for the reasonable value of things furnished to the person necessary for the support of the person or the person's family. (Cal.Civ.Code § 38)

Cundick v. Broadbent
United States Court of Appeals for the Tenth Circuit, 1967
383 F.2d 157

Irma Cundick, guardian ad litem for her husband, Darwin Cundick, brought this diversity suit in Wyoming to set aside an agreement for the sale of (1) livestock and equipment; (2) shares of stock in a development company; and (3) base range land in Wyoming. The alleged grounds for nullification were that at the time of the transaction Cundick was mentally incompetent to execute the agreement; that Broadbent, knowing of such incompetency, fraudulently represented to Cundick that the purchase price for the property described in the agreement was fair and just and that Cundick relied upon the false representations when he executed the agreement and transferred the property. The complaint further states that the guardian ad litem had offered to restore and does now offer to do so, but Broadbent has refused.

Upon a trial of the case without a jury, Judge Kerr made findings of fact in which he narrated the details of the months-long transaction. Specifically, he found that the various papers and documents embodying the agreement between the parties were prepared by Cundick's counsel and signed by Cundick in the presence of his counsel and his wife with her consent and approval; that the purchase price was paid and the transaction carried out between the date on which the agreement was executed, September 2, 1963, and the middle of February, 1964; that during this time neither Cundick nor his wife ever complained that he was incompetent or mentally incapable of transacting his own affairs, or that he was unable to understand and appreciate the effect of the transaction in which he had participated. He further found that Cundick's conduct during the critical time was the conduct and behavior of a competent person and there was no indication or evidence of any kind that Cundick was defrauded, imposed upon, deceived or overreached; that Cundick's election to rescind the agreement was not made until March, 1964, at which time the contract had been practically carried out; and that the election to rescind was not, therefore, sufficiently prompt.

The court concluded that Cundick failed to sustain the burden of proving that at the time of the transaction he was mentally incapable of managing his affairs; or that Broadbent knew of any mental deficiency when they entered into the agreement; or that Broadbent knowingly overreached him. The appeal is from a judgment dismissing the action. For reasons we shall state, the judgment is affirmed.

The contentions on appeal are twofold and stated alternatively: (1) that at the time of the transaction Cundick was totally incompetent to contract; that the agreement between the parties was therefore void ab initio, hence incapable of ratification; and (2) that in any event Cundick was mentally infirm and Broadbent knowingly overreached him; that the contract was therefore voidable, was not ratified — hence rescindable.

At one time, in this country and in England, it was the law that since a lunatic or non compos mentis had no mind with which to make an agreement, his contract was wholly void and incapable of ratification. But, if his mind was merely confused or weak so that he knew what he was doing yet was incapable of fully understanding the terms and effect of his agreement, he could indeed contract, but such contract would be voidable at his option. See Dexter v. Hall, 15 Wall. 9, 82 U.S. 9, 21 L. Ed. 73; see also Principles of Contract by Sir Fredrick Pollock, 4th ed. 1888, p. 158. But in recent times courts have tended away from the concept of absolutely void contracts toward the notion that even though a contract be said to be void for lack of capacity to make it, it is nevertheless ratifiable at the instance of the incompetent party. The modern rule, and the weight of authority, seems to be as stated in 2 Jaeger's Williston on Contracts, 3d ed., § 251, in which an Eighth Circuit case is cited and quoted to the effect that " * * * the contractual act by one claiming to be mentally deficient, but not under guardianship, absent fraud, or knowledge of such asserted incapacity by the other contracting party, is not a void act but at most only voidable at the instance of the deficient party; and then only in accordance with certain equitable principles." Rubenstein v. Dr. Pepper Co., 8 Cir., 228 F.2d 528. See also Williston, Secs. 253 and 254.

In recognition of different degrees of mental competency the weight of authority seems to hold that mental capacity to contract depends upon whether the allegedly disabled person possessed sufficient reason to enable him to understand the nature and effect of the act in issue. Even average intelligence is not essential to a valid bargain. Williston on Contracts, 2d ed., § 256. In amplification of this principle, it has been said that if a maker of a contract " * * has sufficient mental capacity to retain in his memory without prompting the extent and condition of his property and to comprehend how he is disposing of it and to whom and upon what consideration, then he possesses sufficient mental capacity to execute such instrument." (Citations omitted) The Wyoming court adheres to the general principle that "Mere weakness of body or mind, or of both, do not constitute what the law regards as mental incompetency sufficient to render a contract voidable. * * * A condition which may be described by a physician as senile dementia may not be insanity in a legal sense." (Citations omitted.) Weakmindedness is, however, highly relevant in determining whether the deficient party was overreached and defrauded. . . .

There was, to be sure, evidence of a change in his personality and attitude toward his business affairs during this period. But the record is conspicuously silent concerning any discussion of his mental condition among his family and friends in the community where he lived and operated his ranch. Certainly, the record is barren of any discussion or comment in Broadbent's presence. It seems incredible that Cundick could have been utterly incapable of transacting his business affairs, yet such condition be unknown on this record to his family and friends, especially his wife who lived and worked with him and participated in the months-long transaction which she now contends was fraudulently conceived and perpetrated. . . .

The narrated facts of this case amply support the trial court's finding to the effect that Broadbent did not deceive or overreach Cundick. In the absence of any evidence that Broadbent knew of Cundick's mental deficiency, the only evidence from which it can be said that Broadbent took advantage or overreached him is the proof concerning the value of the property sold under the contract. As to that, there is positive evidence that the property was worth very much more than what Broadbent paid for it. But as we have noted, there was evidence to the effect that after the original contract was signed and some complaint made about the purchase price, the parties agreed to raise the price and the contract was so modified. . . .

The Court finally concluded that the contract as amended was not unconscionable, unfair or inequitable. From the whole record we cannot say its conclusions in that respect are unsupported by the evidence. In this view of the case we have no occasion to consider whether the contract, if voidable, was in fact ratified.

[Affirmed]

Questions

1. How does the court differentiate between mental incompetency and weakness of mind in relation to contract validity?

2. What evidence supports the court's finding that the defendant did not deceive or overreach the mentally incompetent party?

3. Why does the court conclude that the contract, as amended, was not unconscionable, unfair, or inequitable, and how does this affect the issue of ratification?

Takeaways – Cundick v. Broadbent

Transactions by a person of weak understanding are subject to close scrutiny. This principle recognizes the fact that such persons can easily be taken advantage of. Therefore, evidence of weakness of mind and circumstances showing unfair dealing and inadequacy of consideration may present a situation where agreements that have been entered into should be rescinded. Williston, Contracts, § 256; 23 Am.Jur., Fraud and Deceit, § 15; 17 C.J.S. Contracts § 133(1).

Overreaching, Pressure in Bargaining, Duress & Undue Influence

The Pre-Existing Duty Rule (Revisited)

Alaska Packers' Ass'n v. Domenico
United States Court of Appeals, Ninth Circuit, 1902
117 F. 99

[This case was based upon a contract alleged to have been entered into between the libelants and the appellant corporation on the 22d day of May, 1900, at Pyramid Harbor, Alaska, by which it is claimed the appellant promised to pay each of the libelants, [In admiralty or maritime law, a "libelant" refers to the party who initiates a legal action by filing a libel or a complaint in a maritime court. The libelant is typically the party bringing a claim or seeking redress in a maritime dispute, such as a claim for damages, breach of contract, salvage, or personal injury. The libelant presents their case and seeks a judgment or remedy from the court against the respondent, who is the opposing party in the litigation.] among other things, the sum of $100 for services rendered and to be rendered. In its answer the respondent denied the execution, on its part, of the contract sued upon, averred that it was without consideration, and for a third defense alleged that the work performed by the libelants for it was performed under other and different contracts than that sued on, and that, prior to the filing of the libel, each of the libelants was paid by the respondent the full amount due him thereunder, in consideration of which each of them executed a full release of all his claims and demands against the respondent.

The evidence shows without conflict that on March 26, 1900, at the city and county of San Francisco, the libelants entered into a written contract with the appellants, whereby they agreed to go from San Francisco to Pyramid Harbor, Alaska, and return, on board such vessel as might be designated by the appellant, and to work for the appellant during the fishing season of 1900, at Pyramid Harbor, as sailors and fishermen, agreeing to do "regular ship's duty, both up and down, discharging and loading; and to do any other work whatsoever when requested to do so by the captain or agent of the Alaska Packers' Association." By the terms of this agreement, the appellant was to pay each of the libelants $50 for the season. Under these contracts, the libelants sailed on board the Two Brothers for Pyramid Harbor, where the appellants had about $150,000 invested in a salmon cannery. The libelants arrived there early in April of the year mentioned, and began to unload the vessel and fit up the cannery. A few days thereafter, to wit, May 19th, they stopped work in a body, and demanded of the company's superintendent there in charge $100 for services in operating the vessel to and from Pyramid Harbor, instead of the sums stipulated for in and by the contracts; stating that unless they were paid this additional wage they would stop work entirely, and return to San Francisco. The evidence showed, and the court below found, that it was impossible for the appellant to get other men to take the places of the libelants, the place being remote, the season short and just opening; so that, after endeavoring for several days without success to induce the libelants to proceed with their work in accordance with their contracts, the company's superintendent, on the 22d day of May, so far yielded to their demands as to instruct his clerk to copy the contracts executed in San Francisco, including the words "Alaska Packers' Association" at the end, substituting, for the $50 and $60 payments, respectively, of those contracts, the sum of $100. Upon the return of the libelants to San Francisco at the close of the fishing season, they demanded pay in accordance with the terms of the alleged contract of May 22d, when the company denied its validity, and refused to pay other than as provided for by the contracts of March 26th and April 5th, respectively. The libelants sued on the promise to pay the sum of $100.]

Ross, Circuit Judge. On the trial in the court below, the libelants undertook to show that the fishing nets provided by the respondent were defective, and that it was on that account that they demanded increased wages. On that point, the evidence was substantially conflicting, and the finding of the court was against the libelants the court saying:

"The contention of libelants that the nets provided them were rotten and unserviceable is not sustained by the evidence. The defendants' interest required that libelants should be provided with every facility necessary to their success as fishermen, for on such success depended the profits defendant would be able to realize that season from its packing plant, and the large capital invested therein. In view of this self-evident fact, it is highly improbable that the defendant gave libelants rotten and unserviceable nets with which to fish. It follows from this finding that libelants were not justified in refusing performance of their original contract." . . .

The real questions in the case as brought here are questions of law, and, in the view that we take of the case, it will be necessary to consider but one of those. Assuming that the appellant's superintendent at Pyramid Harbor was authorized to make the alleged contract of May 22d, and that he executed it on behalf of the appellant, was it supported by a sufficient consideration? From the foregoing statement of the case, it will have been seen that the libelants agreed in writing, for certain stated compensation, to render their services to the appellant in remote waters where the season for conducting fishing operations is extremely short, and in which enterprise the appellant had a large amount of money invested; and, after having entered upon the discharge of their contract, and at a time when it was impossible for the appellant to secure other men in their places, the libelants, without any valid cause, absolutely refused to continue the services they were under contract to perform unless the appellant would consent to pay them more money. Consent to such a demand, under such circumstances, if given, was, in our opinion, without consideration, for the reason that it was based solely upon the libelants' agreement to render the exact services, and none other, that they were already under contract to render. The case shows that they willfully and arbitrarily broke that obligation. . . .

Certainly, it cannot be justly held, upon the record in this case, that there was any voluntary waiver on the part of the appellant of the breach of the original contract. The company itself knew nothing of such breach until the expedition returned to San Francisco, and the testimony is uncontradicted that its superintendent at Pyramid Harbor, who, it is claimed, made on its behalf the contract sued on, distinctly informed the libelants that he had no power to alter the original or to make a new contract, and it would, of course, follow that, if he had no power to change the original, he would have no authority to waive any rights thereunder. The circumstances of the present case bring it, we think, directly within the sound and just observations of the supreme court of Minnesota in the case of King v. Railway Co., 61 Minn. 482, 63 N.W. 1105:

"No astute reasoning can change the plain fact that the party who refuses to perform, and thereby coerces a promise from the other party to the contract to pay him an increased compensation for doing that which he is legally bound to do, takes an unjustifiable advantage of the necessities of the other party. Surely it would be a travesty on justice to hold that the party so making the promise for extra pay was estopped from asserting that the promise was without consideration. A party cannot lay the foundation of an estoppel by his own wrong, where the promise is simply a repetition of a subsisting legal promise. There can be no consideration for the promise of the other party, and there is no warrant for inferring that the parties have voluntarily rescinded or modified their contract. The promise cannot be legally enforced, although the other party has completed his contract in reliance upon it."

In *Lingenfelder v. Brewing Co.*, 103 Mo. 578, 15 S.W. 844, the court, in holding void a contract by which the owner of a building agreed to pay its architect an additional sum because of his refusal to otherwise proceed with the contract, said:

"It is urged upon us by respondents that this was a new contract. New in what? Jungenfeld was bound by his contract to design and supervise this building. Under the new promise, he was not to do anything more or anything different. What benefit was to accrue to Wainwright? He was to receive the same service from Jungenfeld under the new, that Jungenfeld was bound to tender under the original, contract. What loss, trouble, or inconvenience could result to Jungenfeld that he had not already assumed? No amount of metaphysical reasoning can change the plain fact that Jungenfeld took advantage of Wainwright's necessities, and extorted the promise of five per cent. on the refrigerator plant as the condition of his complying with his contract already entered into. . . .

"To permit plaintiff to recover under such circumstances would be to offer a premium upon bad faith, and invite men to violate their most sacred contracts that they may profit by their own wrong. That a promise to pay a man for doing that which he is already under contract to do is without consideration is conceded by respondents. * * * What we hold is that, when a party merely does what he has already obligated himself to do, he cannot demand an additional compensation therefor; and although, by taking advantage of the necessities of his adversary, he obtains a promise for more, the law will regard it as nudum pactum, and will not lend its process to aid in the wrong." . . . .

It results from the views above expressed that the judgment must be reversed. . . .

Question

Why did the court conclude that the alleged contract of May 22nd lacked sufficient consideration?

Takeaways – Alaska Packers' Ass'n.

The pre-existing duty rule (Rest.2d § 73) states that doing or promising to do what one is already legally obligated to do cannot be consideration for a promise because one has not incurred detriment. *Alaska Packers* stands for the proposition that a party cannot pressure the opposing party into modifying a contract by threatening not to perform their contractual duties.

Borelli v. Brusseau
California Court of Appeal, 1993
12 Cal.App.4th 647; 16 Cal.Rptr. 2d 16

[Plaintiff sought specific performance of a promise by her deceased husband, Michael J. Borelli (decedent), to transfer certain property to her in return for her promise to care for him at home after he had suffered a stroke.]

PERLEY, J. In March 1983, February 1984, and January 1987, decedent was admitted to a hospital due to heart problems. As a result, "decedent became concerned and frightened about his health and longevity." He discussed these fears and concerns with appellant and told her that he intended to "leave" the following property to her.

1. "An interest" in a lot in Sacramento, California.
2. A life estate for the use of a condominium in Hawaii.
3. A 25 percent interest in Borelli Meat Co.
4. All cash remaining in all existing bank accounts at the time of his death.
5. The costs of educating decedent's stepdaughter, Monique Lee.
6. Decedent's entire interest in a residence in Kensington, California.
7. All furniture located in the residence.
8. Decedent's interest in a partnership.
9. Health insurance for appellant and Monique Lee.

In August 1988, decedent suffered a stroke while in the hospital. "Throughout the decedent's August, 1988 hospital stay and subsequent treatment at a rehabilitation center, he repeatedly told [appellant] that he was uncomfortable in the hospital and that he disliked being away from home. The decedent repeatedly told [appellant] that he did not want to be admitted to a nursing home, even though it meant he would need round-the-clock care, and rehabilitative modifications to the house, in order for him to live at home."

"In or about October, 1988, [appellant] and the decedent entered an oral agreement whereby the decedent promised to leave to [appellant] the property listed [above], including a one hundred percent interest in the Sacramento property. ... In exchange for the decedent's promise to leave her the property ... [appellant] agreed to care for the decedent in his home, for the duration of his illness, thereby avoiding the need for him to move to a rest home or convalescent hospital as his doctors recommended. The agreement was based on the confidential relationship that existed between [appellant] and the decedent."

Appellant performed her promise but the decedent did not perform his. Instead his will bequeathed her the sum of $100,000 and his interest in the residence they owned as joint tenants. The bulk of decedent's estate passed to respondent, who is decedent's daughter.

"It is fundamental that a marriage contract differs from other contractual relations in that there exists a definite and vital public interest in reference to the marriage relation. The 'paramount interests of the community at large,' quoting from the Phillips case [Phillips v. Phillips (1953) 41 Cal.2d 869] is a matter of primary concern." (Hendricks v. Hendricks (1954) 125 Cal.App.2d 239, 242 270 P.2d 80].)

"The laws relating to marriage and divorce (Civ. Code, [former] §§ 55-181) have been enacted because of the profound concern of our organized society for the dignity and stability of the marriage relationship. This concern relates primarily to the status of the parties as husband and wife. The concern of society as to the property rights of the parties is secondary and incidental to its concern as to their status." (Sapp v. Superior Court (1953) 119 Cal.App.2d 645, 650 [260 P.2d 119].)

"Marriage is a matter of public concern. The public, through the state, has interest in both its formation and dissolution. ... The regulation of marriage and divorce is solely within the province of the Legislature except as the same might be restricted by the Constitution." (Haas v. Haas (1964) 227 Cal.App.2d 615, 617 [38 Cal.Rptr. 811].)

In accordance with these concerns the following pertinent legislation has been enacted: Civil Code section 242- "Every individual shall support his or her spouse ...." Civil Code section 4802-"[A] husband and wife cannot, by any contract with each other, alter their legal relations, except as to property. ..." Civil Code section 5100- "Husband and wife contract toward each other obligations of mutual respect, fidelity, and support." Civil Code section 5103-"[E]ither husband or wife may enter into any transaction with the other ... respecting property, which either might if unmarried." Civil Code section 5132-"[A] married person shall support the person's spouse while they are living together. ...."

The courts have stringently enforced and explained the statutory language. [3] "Although most of the cases, both in California and elsewhere, deal with a wife's right to support from the husband, in this state a wife also has certain obligations to support the husband." (In re Marriage of Higgason (1973) 10 Cal.3d 476, 487 [110 Cal.Rptr. 897, 516 P.2d 289], disapproved on other grounds in In re Marriage of Dawley (1976) 17 Cal.3d 342, 352 [131 Cal.Rptr. 3, 551 P.2d 323].)

"Indeed, husband and wife assume mutual obligations of support upon marriage. These obligations are not conditioned on the existence of community property or income." (See v. See (1966) 64 Cal.2d 778, 784 [51 Cal.Rptr. 888, 415 P.2d 776].) "In entering the marital state, by which a contract is created, it must be assumed that the parties voluntarily entered therein with knowledge that they have the moral and legal obligation to support the other." (Department of Mental Hygiene v. Kolts (1966) 247 Cal.App.2d 154, 165 [55 Cal.Rptr. 437].)

Moreover, interspousal mutual obligations have been broadly defined. "[Husband's] duties and obligations to [wife] included more than mere cohabitation with her. It was his duty to offer [wife] his sympathy, confidence [citation], and fidelity." (In re Marriage of Rabie (1974) 40 Cal.App.3d 917, 922 [115 Cal.Rptr. 594].) When necessary, spouses must "provide uncompensated protective supervision services for" each other. (Miller v. Woods (1983) 148 Cal.App.3d 862, 877 [196 Cal.Rptr. 69].)

Estate of Sonnicksen (1937) 23 Cal.App.2d 475, 479 [73 P.2d 643] and Brooks v. Brooks (1941) 48 Cal.App.2d 347, 349-350 [119 P.2d 970], each hold that under the above statutes and in accordance with the above policy a wife is obligated by the marriage contract to provide nursing-type care to an ill husband. Therefore, contracts whereby the wife is to receive compensation for providing such services are void as against public policy; and there is no consideration for the husband's promise. . . .

These cases indicate that the marital duty of support under Civil Code sections 242, 5100, and 5132 includes caring for a spouse who is ill. They also establish that support in a marriage means more than the physical care someone could be hired to provide. Such support also encompasses sympathy (In re Marriage of Rabie, supra, 40 Cal.App.3d at p. 922) comfort (Krouse v. Graham, supra, 19 Cal.3d at pp. 66-67) love, companionship and affection (Rodriguez v. Bethlehem Steel Corp., supra, 12 Cal.3d at pp. 404-405). Thus, the duty of support can no more be "delegated" to a third party than the statutory duties of fidelity and mutual respect (Civ. Code, § 5100). Marital duties are owed by the spouses personally. This is implicit in the definition of marriage as "a personal relation arising out of a civil contract between a man and a woman." (Civ. Code, § 4100.)

We therefore adhere to the long-standing rule that a spouse is not entitled to compensation for support, apart from rights to community property and the like that arise from the marital relation itself. Personal performance of a personal duty created by the contract of marriage does not constitute a new consideration supporting the indebtedness, alleged in this case.

We agree with the dissent that no rule of law becomes sacrosanct by virtue of its duration, but we are not persuaded that the well-established rule that governs this case deserves to be discarded. If the rule denying compensation for support originated from considerations peculiar to women, this has no bearing on the rule's gender-neutral application today. There is as much potential for fraud today as ever, and allegations like appellant's could be made every time any personal care is rendered. This concern may not entirely justify the rule, but it cannot be said that all rationales for the rule are outdated.

Speculating that appellant might have left her husband but for the agreement she alleges, the dissent suggests that marriages will break up if such agreements are not enforced. While we do not believe that marriages would be fostered by a rule that encouraged sickbed bargaining, the question is not whether such negotiations may be more useful than unseemly. The issue is whether such negotiations are antithetical to the institution of marriage as the Legislature has defined it. We believe that they are.

The dissent maintains that mores have changed to the point that spouses can be treated just like any other parties haggling at arm's length. Whether or not the modern marriage has become like a business, and regardless of whatever else it may have become, it continues to be defined by statute as a personal relationship of mutual support. Thus, even if few things are left that cannot command a price, marital support remains one of them.

Questions

1. What is the pre-existing duty rule, and how does it relate to the case at hand?

2. According to the court, why does the pre-existing duty rule apply in this case?

3. How did the court interpret the concept of support within the context of the pre-existing duty rule?

Relaxation of the Pre-Existing Duty Rule

Watkins & Son, Inc., v. Carrig
Supreme Court of New Hampshire, 1941
91 N.H. 459, 21 A.2d, 591, 138 A.L.R. 131

Assumpsit, for work done. By a written contract between the parties the plaintiff agreed to excavate a cellar for the defendant for a stated price. Soon after the work was commenced solid rock was encountered. The plaintiff's manager notified the defendant, a meeting between them was held, and it was orally agreed that the plaintiff should remove the rock at a stipulated unit price about nine times greater than the unit price for excavating upon which the gross amount to be paid according to the written contract was calculated. The rock proved to constitute about two–thirds of the space to be excavated.

ALLEN, Chief Justice. When the written contract was entered into, no understanding existed between the parties that no rock would be found in the excavating. The plaintiff's manager made no inquiry or investigation to find out the character of the ground below the surface, no claim is made that the defendant misled him, and the contract contains no reservations for unexpected conditions. It provides that "all material" shall be removed from the site, and its term that the plaintiff is "to excavate" is unqualified. In this situation a defense of mutual mistake is not available. A space of ground to be excavated, whatever its character, was the subject matter of the contract, and the offer of price on that basis was accepted. Leavitt v. Dover, 67 N.H. 94, 32 A. 156, 68 Am.St.Rep. 640. If the plaintiff was unwise in taking chances, it is not relieved, on the ground of mistake, from the burden incurred in being faced with them. The case differs from that of King Co. v. Aldrich, 81 N.H. 42, 121 A. 434, in which the parties did not contract for the property delivered in purported performance of the contract actually made.

The referee's finding that the written contract was "superseded" by an oral contract when the rock was discovered is construed to mean that the parties agreed to rescind the written contract as though it had not been made and entered into an oral one as though it were the sole and original one. The defendant either thought that the contract did not require the excavation of rock on the basis of the contract price or was willing to forgo his rights under the contract in respect to rock. It was important to him that the work should not be delayed, and other reasons may have contributed to induce him to the concession he made. In any event, he consented to a special price for excavating rock, whatever his rights under the contract. The plaintiff on the strength of the promise proceeded with the work.

But the defendant contends that the facts do not support a claim of two independent and separate transactions, one in rescission of the written contract as though it were nugatory, and one in full substitution of it. All that is shown, as he urges, is one transaction by which he was to pay more for the excavating than the written contract provided, with that contract otherwise to remain in force. And upon the basis of this position he relies upon the principle of contract law that his promise to pay more was without consideration, as being a promise to pay the plaintiff for performance of its obligation already in force and outstanding. Whether the contract was rescinded with a new one to take its place or whether it remained in force with a modification of its terms, is not important. In the view of a modification, the claim of a promise unsupported by consideration is as tenable as under the view of a rescission. A modification involves a partial rescission.

In the situation presented the plaintiff entered into a contractual obligation. Facts subsequently learned showed the obligation to be burdensome and the contract improvident. On insistent request by the plaintiff, the defendant granted relief from the burden by a promise to pay a special price which overcame the burden. The promise was not an assumption of the burden; the special price was fair and the defendant received reasonable value for it.

The issue whether the grant of relief constituted a valid contract is one of difficulty. The basic rule that a promise without consideration for it is invalid leads to its logical application that a promise to pay for what the promisor already has a right to receive from the promisee is invalid. The promisee's performance of an existing duty is no detriment to him, and hence nothing is given by him beyond what is already due the promisor. But the claim is here made that the original contract was rescinded, either in full or in respect to some of its terms, by mutual consent, and since any rescission mutually agreed upon is in itself a contract, the claim of a promise to pay for performance of a subsisting duty is unfounded. The terms of the contract of rescission are of course valid if the rescission is valid. The defendant's answer to this claim is well stated in this quotation from Williston, Contr., 2d Ed., § 130a: "But calling an agreement an agreement for rescission does not do away with the necessity of consideration, and when the agreement for rescission is coupled with a further agreement that the work provided for in the earlier agreement shall be completed and that the other party shall give more than he originally promised, the total effect of the second agreement is that one party promises to do exactly what he had previously bound himself to do, and the other party promises to give an additional compensation therefor."

With due respect for this eminent authority, the argument appears to clothe consideration with insistence of control beyond its proper demands. With full recognition of the legal worthlessness of a bare promise and of performance of a subsisting duty as a void consideration, a result accomplished by proper means is not necessarily bad because it would be bad if the means were improper or were not employed. . . .

In common understanding there is, importantly, a wide divergence between a bare promise and a promise in adjustment of a contractual promise already outstanding. A promise with no supporting consideration would upset well and long-established human interrelations if the law did not treat it as a vain thing. But parties to a valid contract generally understand that it is subject to any mutual action they may take in its performance. Changes to meet changes in circumstances and conditions should be valid if the law is to carry out its function and service by rules conformable with reasonable practices and understandings in matters of business and commerce. . . . Merger of the rescission and promise into one transaction does not destroy them as elements composing the transaction. . . .

The case is one of a simple relinquishment of a right pertaining to intangible personalty. The defendant intentionally and voluntarily yielded to a demand for a special price for excavating rock. In doing this he yielded his contract right to the price it provided. Whether or not he thought he had the right, he intended, and executed his intent, to make no claim of the right. The promise of a special price for excavating rock necessarily imported a release or waiver of any right by the contract to hold the plaintiff to the lower price the contract stipulated. In mutual understanding the parties agreed that the contract price was not to control. The contract right being freely surrendered, the issue of contract law whether the new promise is valid is not doubtful. If the totality of the transaction was a promise to pay more for less, there was in its inherent makeup a valid discharge of an obligation.

Although the transaction was single, the element of discharge was distinct in precedence of the new promise.

The foregoing views are considered to meet the reasonable needs of standard and ethical practices of men in their business dealings with each other. Conceding that the plaintiff threatened to break its contract because it found the contract to be improvident, yet the defendant yielded to the threat without protest, excusing the plaintiff, and making a new arrangement. Not insisting on his rights but relinquishing them, fairly he should be held to the new arrangement. The law is a means to the end. It is not the law because it is the law, but because it is adapted and adaptable to establish and maintain reasonable order. If the phrase justice according to law were transposed into law according to justice, it would perhaps be more accurately expressive. In a case like this, of conflicting rules and authority, a result which is considered better to establish "fundamental justice and reasonableness" (Cavanaugh v. Boston & M. Railroad, 76 N.H. 68, 72, 79 A. 694, 696), should be attained. It is not practical that the law should adopt all precepts of moral conduct, but it is desirable that its rules and principles should not run counter to them in the important conduct and transactions of life.

Exceptions overruled.

Questions

1. What was the defendant's argument regarding the modification of the contract, and how did the court address it?

2. What factors did the court consider in determining the validity of the new promise made by the defendant?

Takeaways – Watkins & Son v. Carrig

Threatening not to perform one's contractual obligations has never been countenanced by contract law. (See, *Alaska Packers* above) But suppose there has been a change in circumstances between the time of contract formation and before a party has performed their obligations? Restatement 2d §89(a) provides that a promise modifying an executory contract (one that has not been fully performed) is binding if the modification is fair and equitable in view of circumstances not anticipated by the parties when the contract was made.

UCC § 2-209 provides that a contract for the sale of goods can be modified without the necessity of new consideration provided that the modification is made in good faith.

Getting Around the Pre-Existing Duty Rule – Introducing "New" Consideration

Accord and Satisfaction

Traditionally, the common law has sanctioned a subtle form of duress or coercion known as "accord and satisfaction." An accord and satisfaction is the offering of some performance different from that originally called for and the acceptance of the different performance as a full and complete performance. Take the following example: You've agreed with a cabinetmaker to perform some work at your home. The agreed price is $1,000.00 but you feel that she has botched the job and that the cost of remedying the defect would be $150.00. You send her a check for $850.00 explaining why you feel that is a fair amount and state that the check is being offered in "full payment" of the amount owed under the agreement. A "payment in full "check operates as an accord and satisfaction where the creditor negotiates the check with full awareness of the terms on which it was offered. Traditionally, a creditor could write all manner of disclaimer on the check to no avail. If she accepted the check with awareness of the basis on which it was offered she entered into a valid accord and satisfaction. This was true irrespective of whether the creditor's "acceptance" took the form of simply cashing the check, holding the check uncashed for an unreasonable period of time, protesting the condition orally or on the check before cashing it or striking the "payment in full" language before negotiating the check, and without regard to whether it represents only the amount that the debtor admits owing.

The process of accord and satisfaction is validated by UCC § 3-311 and in California by Civil Code §§ 1521-1526. However, the California procedure is different from that set out above in a non-trivial way. Civil Code section 1526 provides that a payment in full check does not operate as an accord and satisfaction if the creditor strikes out the restrictive words or can prove that she cashed the check without knowledge of the restriction. In order to show that the creditor should have known of the restriction the debtor must give notice in writing to the creditor "not less than 15 days nor more than 90 days prior to receipt of the check or draft . . . that a check or draft will be tendered with a restrictive endorsement and that acceptance and cashing of the check or draft will constitute an accord and satisfaction." Then and only then will an accord and satisfaction have been entered into upon the creditor's cashing of the check. (Cal.Civ.Code § 1526(b)(2).)

Duress

The Restatement addresses the problem of duress in sections 175 and 176. "If a party's manifestation of assent is induced by an improper threat by the other party that leaves the victim no reasonable alternative, the contract is voidable by the victim." (Rest.2d §175(1).)

Duress is not limited to threats against the person. It may also consist of threats to business or property interests. However, since an essential element of duress is the making of an *improper* threat (see Rest.2d § 176 for definition of what constitutes an improper threat) the filing of a civil lawsuit or the threat to file such a lawsuit cannot constitute duress.

A contract is voidable on the ground of duress when it is established that the party making the claim was forced to agree to it by means of a wrongful threat precluding the exercise of his free will. However, a mere threat to break a contract does not constitute duress. A threat to breach a contract constitutes duress if the threatened breach would, if carried out, result in irreparable injury because of the absence of an adequate legal or equitable remedy, or other reasonable alternative. (*Austin Instrument, Inc. v. Loral Corp.* 29 N.Y.2d 124, 324 N.Y.S.2d 22, 272 N.E.2d 533 (1971).)

Undue Influence

Closely related to the concept of duress, but different, is the concept of undue influence. As you read the next case ask yourself how the two concepts differ.

Odorizzi v. Bloomfield School District
Court of Appeal of California, 1966
246 Cal. App. 2d 123; 54 Cal. Rptr. 533

Plaintiff Donald Odorizzi was employed during 1964 as an elementary school teacher by defendant Bloomfield School District and was under contract with the district to continue to teach school the following year as a permanent employee. On June 10 he was arrested on criminal charges of homosexual activity, and on June 11 he signed and delivered to his superiors his written resignation as a teacher, a resignation which the district accepted on June 13. In July the criminal charges against Odorizzi were dismissed and in September he sought to resume his employment with the district. On the district's refusal to reinstate him he filed suit for declaratory and other relief.

Odorizzi's amended complaint asserts his resignation was invalid because obtained through duress, fraud, mistake, and undue influence and given at a time when he lacked capacity to make a valid contract. Specifically, Odorizzi declares he was under such severe mental and emotional strain at the time he signed his resignation, having just completed the process of arrest, questioning by the police, booking, and release on bail, and having gone for 40 hours without sleep, that he was incapable of rational thought or action. While he was in this condition and unable to think clearly, the superintendent of the district and the principal of his school came to his apartment. They said they were trying to help him and had his best interests at heart, that he should take their advice and immediately resign his position with the district, that there was no time to consult an attorney, that if he did not resign immediately the district would suspend and dismiss him from his position and publicize the proceedings, his "aforedescribed arrest" and cause him "to suffer extreme embarrassment and humiliation"; but that if he resigned at once the incident would not be publicized and would not jeopardize his chances of securing employment as a teacher elsewhere. Odorizzi pleads that because of his faith and confidence in their representations they were able to substitute their will and judgment in place of his own and thus obtain his signature to his purported resignation. A demurrer to his amended complaint was sustained without leave to amend. . . .

In our view the facts in the amended complaint are insufficient to state a cause of action for duress, menace, fraud, or mistake, but they do set out sufficient elements to justify rescission of a consent because of undue influence. We summarize our conclusions on each of these points.

1. No duress or menace has been pleaded. Duress consists in unlawful confinement of another's person, or relatives, or property, which causes him to consent to a transaction through fear. (Civ. Code, § 1569.) Duress is often used interchangeably with menace (*Leeper* v. *Beltrami*, 53 Cal.2d 195, 203 [1 Cal.Rptr. 12, 347 P.2d 12, 77 A.L.R.2d 803]), but in California menace is technically a threat of duress or a threat of injury to the person, property, or character of another. (Civ. Code, § 1570; Rest., Contracts, §§ 492, 493.) We agree with respondent's contention that neither duress nor menace was involved in this case, because the action or threat in duress or menace must be unlawful, and a threat to take legal action is not unlawful unless the party making the threat knows the falsity of his claim. (*Leeper* v. *Beltrami*, 53 Cal.2d 195, 204 [1 Cal.Rptr. 12, 347 P.2d 12, 77 A.L.R.2d 803].) The amended complaint shows in substance that the school representatives announced their intention to initiate suspension and dismissal proceedings under Education Code, sections 13403, 13408 et seq. at a time when the filing of such proceedings was not only their legal right but their positive duty as school officials. (Ed. Code, § 13409; *Board of Education* v. *Weiland*, 179 Cal.App.2d 808 [4 Cal.Rptr. 286].) Although the filing of such proceedings might be extremely damaging to plaintiff's reputation, the injury would remain incidental so long as the school officials acted in good faith in the performance of their duties. (*Schumm* v. *Berg*, 37 Cal.2d 174, 185-186 [231 P.2d 39, 21 A.L.R.2d 1051].) Neither duress nor menace was present as a ground for rescission.

(The court's discussion of fraud and mistake, which it found to be lacking, is omitted.)

4. However, the pleading does set out a claim that plaintiff's consent to the transaction had been obtained through the use of undue influence.

Undue influence, in the sense we are concerned with here, is a shorthand legal phrase used to describe persuasion which tends to be coercive in nature, persuasion which overcomes the will without convincing the judgment. (*Estate of Ricks*, 160 Cal. 467, 480-482 [117 P. 539].) The hallmark of such persuasion is high pressure, a pressure which works on mental, moral, or emotional weakness to such an extent that it approaches the boundaries of coercion. In this sense, undue influence has been called overpersuasion. (*Kelly* v. *McCarthy*, 6 Cal.2d 347, 364 [57 P.2d 118].) Misrepresentations of law or fact are not essential to the charge, for a person's will may be overborne without misrepresentation. By statutory definition undue influence includes "taking an unfair advantage of another's weakness of mind, or . . . taking a grossly oppressive and unfair advantage of another's necessities or distress." (Civ. Code, § 1575.) While most reported cases of undue influence involve persons who bear a confidential relationship to one another, a confidential or authoritative relationship between the parties need not be present when the undue influence involves unfair advantage taken of another's weakness or distress. (*Wells Fargo Bank* v. *Brady*, 116 Cal.App.2d 381, 398 [254 P.2d 71]; *Buchmayer* v. *Buchmayer*, 68 Cal.App.2d 462, 467 [157 P.2d 9].)

We paraphrase the summary of undue influence given the jury by Sir James P. Wilde in *Hall* v. *Hall*, L.R. 1, P. & D. 481, 482 (1868): To make a good contract a man must be a free agent. Pressure of whatever sort which overpowers the will without convincing the judgment is a species of restraint under which no valid contract can be made. Importunity or threats, if carried to the degree in which the free play of a man's will is overborne, constitute undue influence, although no force is used or threatened. A party may be led but not driven, and his acts must be the offspring of his own volition and not the record of someone else's.

In essence undue influence involves the use of excessive pressure to persuade one vulnerable to such pressure, pressure applied by a dominant subject to a servient object. In combination, the elements of undue susceptibility in the servient person and excessive pressure by the dominating person make the latter's influence undue, for it results in the apparent will of the servient person being in fact the will of the dominant person.

Undue susceptibility may consist of total weakness of mind which leaves a person entirely without understanding (Civ. Code, § 38); or, a lesser weakness which destroys the capacity of a person to make a contract even though he is not totally incapacitated (Civ. Code, § 39; *Peterson* v. *Ellebrecht*, 205 Cal.App.2d 718, 721-722 [23 Cal.Rptr. 349]); or, the first element in our equation, a still lesser weakness which provides sufficient grounds to rescind a contract for undue influence (Civ. Code, § 1575; *Faulkner* v. *Beatty*, 161 Cal.App.2d 547, 551 [327 P.2d 41]; *Stewart* v. *Marvin*, 139 Cal.App.2d 769, 775 [294 P.2d 114]). Such lesser weakness need not be long-lasting nor wholly incapacitating, but may be merely a lack of full vigor due to age (*Wells Fargo Bank* v. *Brady*, 116 Cal.App.2d 381, 397-398 [254 P.2d 71]), physical condition

(*Weger* v. *Rocha*, 138 Cal.App. 109, 114-115 [32 P.2d 417]), emotional anguish (*Moore* v. *Moore*, 56 Cal. 89, 93; 81 Cal. 195, 197-198 [22 P. 589, 874]), or a combination of such factors. The reported cases have usually involved elderly, sick, senile persons alleged to have executed wills or deeds under pressure. (*Malone* v. *Malone*, 155 Cal.App.2d 161 [317 P.2d 65] [constant importuning of a senile husband]; *Stewart* v. *Marvin*, 139 Cal.App.2d 769 [294 P.2d 114] [persistent nagging of elderly spouse].) In some of its aspects this lesser weakness could perhaps be called weakness of spirit. But whatever name we give it, this first element of undue influence resolves itself into a lessened capacity of the object to make a free contract.

In the present case plaintiff has pleaded that such weakness at the time he signed his resignation prevented him from freely and competently applying his judgment to the problem before him. Plaintiff declares he was under severe mental and emotional strain at the time because he had just completed the process of arrest, questioning, booking, and release on bail and had been without sleep for forty hours. It is possible that exhaustion and emotional turmoil may wholly incapacitate a person from exercising his judgment. As an abstract question of pleading, plaintiff has pleaded that possibility and sufficient allegations to state a case for rescission.

Undue influence in its second aspect involves an application of excessive strength by a dominant subject against a servient object. Judicial consideration of this second element in undue influence has been relatively rare, for there are few cases denying persons who persuade but do not misrepresent the benefit of their bargain. Yet logically, the same legal consequences should apply to the results of excessive strength as to the results of undue weakness. Whether from weakness on one side, or strength on the other, or a combination of the two, undue influence occurs whenever there results "that kind of influence or supremacy of one mind over another by which that other is prevented from acting according to his own wish or judgment, and whereby the will of the person is overborne and he is induced to do or forbear to do an act which he would not do, or would do, if left to act freely." (*Webb* v. *Saunders*, 79 Cal.App.2d 863, 871 [181 P.2d 43].) Undue influence involves a type of mismatch which our statute calls unfair advantage. (Civ. Code, § 1575.) Whether a person of subnormal capacities has been subjected to ordinary force or a person of normal capacities subjected to extraordinary force, the match is equally out of balance. If will has been overcome against judgment, consent may be rescinded.

The difficulty, of course, lies in determining when the forces of persuasion have overflowed their normal banks and become oppressive flood waters. There are second thoughts to every bargain, and hindsight is still better than foresight. Undue influence cannot be used as a pretext to avoid bad bargains or escape from bargains which refuse to come up to expectations. A woman who buys a dress on impulse, which on critical inspection by her best friend turns out to be less fashionable than she had thought, is not legally entitled to set aside the sale on the ground that the saleswoman used all her wiles to close the sale. A man who buys a tract of desert land in the expectation that it is in the immediate path of the city's growth and will become another Palm Springs, an expectation cultivated in glowing terms by the seller, cannot rescind his bargain when things turn out differently. If we are temporarily persuaded against our better judgment to do something about which we later have second thoughts, we must abide the consequences of the risks inherent in managing our own affairs. (*Estate of Anderson*, 185 Cal. 700, 706-707 [198 P. 407].)

However, overpersuasion is generally accompanied by certain characteristics which tend to create a pattern. The pattern usually involves several of the following elements: (1) discussion of the transaction at an unusual or inappropriate time, (2) consummation of the transaction in an unusual place, (3) insistent demand that the business be finished at once, (4) extreme emphasis on untoward consequences of delay, (5) the use of multiple persuaders by the dominant side against a single servient party, (6) absence of third-party advisers to the servient party, (7) statements that there is no time to consult financial advisers or attorneys. If a number of these elements are simultaneously present, the persuasion may be characterized as excessive. The cases are illustrative:

Moore v. *Moore*, 56 Cal. 89, 93, and 81 Cal. 195 [22 P. 589, 874]. The pregnant wife of a man who had been shot to death on October 30 and buried on November 1 was approached by four members of her husband's family on November 2 or 3 and persuaded to deed her entire interest in her husband's estate to his children by a prior marriage. In finding the use of undue influence on Mrs. Moore, the court commented: "It was the second day after her late husband's funeral. It was at a time when she would naturally feel averse to transacting any business, and she might reasonably presume that her late husband's brothers would not apply to her at such a time to transact any important business, unless it was of a nature that would admit of no delay. And as it would admit of delay, the only reason which we can discover for their unseemly haste is, that they thought that she would be more likely to comply with their wishes then than at some future time, after she had recovered from the shock which she had then so recently experienced. If for that reason they selected that time for the accomplishment of their purpose, it seems to us that they not only took, but that they designed to take, an unfair advantage of her weakness of mind. If they did not, they probably can explain why they selected that inappropriate time for the transaction of business which might have been delayed for weeks without injury to anyone. In the absence of any explanation, it appears to us that the time was selected with reference to just that condition of mind which she alleges that she was then in.

"Taking an unfair advantage of another's weakness of mind is undue influence, and the law will not permit the retention of an advantage thus obtained. (Civ. Code, § 1575.)"

Weger v. *Rocha*, 138 Cal.App. 109 [32 P.2d 417]. Plaintiff, while confined in a cast in a hospital, gave a release of claims for personal injuries for a relatively small sum to an agent who spent two hours persuading her to sign. At the time of signing plaintiff was in a highly nervous and hysterical condition and suffering much pain, and she signed the release in order to terminate the interview. The court held that the release had been secured by the use of undue influence....

The difference between legitimate persuasion and excessive pressure, like the difference between seduction and rape, rests to a considerable extent in the manner in which the parties go about their business. For example, if a day or two after Odorizzi's release on bail the superintendent of the school district had called him into his office during business hours and directed his attention to those provisions of the Education Code compelling his leave of absence and authorizing his suspension on the filing of written charges, had told him that the district contemplated filing written charges against him, had pointed out the alternative of resignation available to him, had informed him he was free to consult counsel or any adviser he wished and to consider the matter overnight and return with his decision the next day, it is extremely unlikely that any complaint about the use of excessive pressure could ever have been made against the school district.

But, according to the allegations of the complaint, this is not the way it happened, and if it had happened that way, plaintiff would never have resigned. Rather, the representatives of the school board undertook to achieve their objective by overpersuasion and imposition to secure plaintiff's signature but not his consent to his resignation through a high-pressure carrot-and-stick technique -- under which they assured plaintiff they were trying to assist him, he should rely on their advice, there wasn't time to consult an attorney, if he didn't resign at once the school district would suspend and dismiss him from his position and publicize the proceedings, but if he did resign the incident wouldn't jeopardize his chances of securing a teaching post elsewhere.

Plaintiff has thus pleaded both subjective and objective elements entering the undue influence equation and stated sufficient facts to put in issue the question whether his free will had been overborne by defendant's agents at a time when he was unable to function in a normal manner. It was sufficient to pose "... the ultimate question ... whether a free and competent judgment was merely influenced, or whether a mind was so dominated as to prevent the exercise of an independent judgment." (Williston on Contracts, § 1625 [rev. ed.]; Rest., Contracts, § 497, com. c.) The question cannot be resolved by an analysis of pleading but requires a finding of fact.

We express no opinion on the merits of plaintiff's case, or the propriety of his continuing to teach school (Ed. Code, § 13403), or the timeliness of his rescission (Civ. Code, § 1691). We do hold that his pleading, liberally construed, states a cause of action for rescission of a transaction to which his apparent consent had been obtained through the use of undue influence.

The judgment is reversed.

Questions

1. According to the court, what is the distinction between duress and menace?

2. How does the court define undue influence in this case?

3. What elements constitute undue susceptibility in the context of undue influence?

4. Explain the two aspects of undue influence as described by the court.

5. According to the court, what characteristics create a pattern of excessive persuasion in cases of undue influence?

Concealment and Non-Disclosure

Concealment and Liability for Non-Disclosure

The traditional rule was that in a bargaining transaction there is generally no duty to disclose information to the other party. I.e. no liability for "bare non-disclosure." (See, *Swinton v. Whitinsville Savings Bank,* 311 Mass. 677, 42 N.E.2d 808 (1942).) Generally where material facts are known to one party and not to the other, failure to disclose them is not actionable fraud unless there is some relationship between the parties which gives rise to a duty to disclose such known facts. A duty to disclose known facts arises where the party having knowledge of the facts is in a fiduciary or a confidential relationship. A fiduciary or a confidential relationship exists whenever under the circumstances trust and confidence reasonably may be and are reposed by one person in the integrity and fidelity of another. (See, 5 Witkin, Summary of Cal.Law (10th ed. 2005) Torts §§ 793-798.) Examples of a fiduciary or confidential relationship include, but are not limited to; broker and customer, attorney and client, principal and agent, physician and patient and husband and wife. Historically, the relationship of buyer and seller has been regarded as an "arms-length" relationship and not a special or confidential relationship. However, the traditional common law rule of no duty to disclose in the absence of a special relationship, is being eroded.

Kannavos v. Annino
Supreme Judicial Court of Massachusetts, 1969
356 Mass. 42, 247 N.E.2d 708

CUTTER, J. These bills in equity are brought by the vendees of real estate, fixtures, and personal property in Ingersoll Grove, Springfield, against the vendors, to rescind the purchases made in 1965. The amended bills alleged that the vendees bought in reliance on the vendors' fraudulent misrepresentations and concealment of material facts. Demurrers to the amended bills were overruled. The facts are stated on the basis of a confirmed master's report. By final decree rescission of the purchases was ordered. The vendors appealed.

Kannavos and his wife acquired 11 Ingersoll Grove from the vendors (who are the trustees of Annino Realty Trust) on June 28, 1965. Kannavos and Bellas bought 71-73 and 79 Ingersoll Grove from the vendors on July 12, 1965. The situation as to each purchase is substantially the same.

Mrs. Annino (who at all pertinent times "was authorized to act and did act on behalf of ... Annino Realty Trust") had bought the Ingersoll Grove properties in 1961 and 1962. At that time there was a single family house on each property. Each house was, under the Springfield zoning ordinance, in a Residence A district, where multi-family uses are prohibited. This zoning has remained in effect at all times since 1961. Despite the zoning provisions, Mrs. Annino converted each single family house into a multi-family apartment building. Each was furnished and rented as a multi-family dwelling. All the work of conversion was done "without obtaining any building permit," as each trustee of the realty trust knew. Each trustee also knew that the use of the buildings for multi-family purposes was in violation of the zoning ordinance.

In 1965 Kenneth F. Foote was retained as real estate broker "to try to sell the properties." He caused advertisements, of which the following is an example, to appear in Springfield newspapers: "Income gross $9,600 yr. in lg. single house, converted to 8 lovely, completely furn. (includ. TV and china) apts. 8 baths, ideal for couple to live free with excellent income. By apt. only. Foote Realty." Each advertisement clearly advertised, in some form of words, the particular property as being income property of multi-family use.

Kannavos, a self-employed hairdresser, about thirty-eight years old, read one advertisement. He "wanted to acquire some income real estate." He got in touch with Foote, who showed him the 11 Ingersoll Grove property and gave him income and expense figures obtained from Mrs. Annino. Kannavos executed a purchase agreement to buy 11 Ingersoll Grove. The vendees had no lawyer representing them with respect to the negotiations, the agreement, or the final closing. An attorney representing a mortgagee, under a mortgage obtained by the vendees, drew and recorded the papers used at the closing, at which the vendors were also represented by an attorney "to check the adjustments."

"No statements were made by the ... [vendors], by ... Foote... [or by either attorney] at any time during the negotiations or closing, to the ... [vendees] with respect to zoning or building permits. The ... [vendees] made no inquiry of the" vendors, Foote, or the vendors' "attorney at any time before or during the closing with respect to zoning or building permits. All statements made by the" vendors, Foote, or the vendors' attorney to the vendees "were substantially true and the ... [vendees] do not complain of any spoken misrepresentation."

Mrs. Annino and Foote both represented to the vendees "that the property ... consisted of eight ... furnished apartments which were being rented to the public for multi-family purposes. They knew that Kannavos' reason for buying the property was to rent the apartments to the public.... Kannavos had no prior experience with real estate. He was unaware of any zoning or building permit violation and would not have purchased the property if he had known of any such violation."

The sale of the other properties (71-73 and 79 Ingersoll Grove) occurred in substantially similar circumstances. Discussion of other property owned by the vendors started shortly before Kannavos acquired 11 Ingersoll Grove. The vendees saw an advertisement of the houses at 71-73 and 79 Ingersoll Grove in July, 1965, and then went to see them. Mrs. Annino and Foote "represented to ... Kannavos and Bellas, that the property [71-73 and 79 Ingersoll Grove] was rented as multi-dwelling property and that Bellas and Kannavos could continue to operate it as multi-dwelling property. The ... [vendees] continued to operate the buildings as multi-dwelling property up to and including the date of the hearing. The operation showed a profit...." The vendors represented to Bellas that "71-73 [and] 79 Ingersoll Grove would be a good investment for him as rental multi-family real estate."

"By ... registered letters dated July 26, 1965 ... the city... notified Bellas and Kannavos with respect to ... 79 Ingersoll Grove that the property was being used for multi-family purposes in violation of the building code and zoning ordinance ... that the wiring was illegal and should be corrected by a licensed electrician with a valid building permit ... and that the plumbing was in violation of the building code and should be corrected by a licensed plumber with a valid building permit.... By three registered letters of July 26, 1965 with respect to ... 71-73 Ingersoll Grove, Bellas and Kannavos were notified by the Building Commissioner ... of the same violations of zoning, wiring, and plumbing."

The two groups of vendees "had no actual knowledge of the zoning or building code violations until ... notified" by the city authorities. The vendees promptly through their attorney "notified the ... [vendors] of the rescission of" each sale. "Each property is worth substantially less if operated only as a single family dwelling instead of [as] a multifamily dwelling." The city has started civil proceedings "to abate the use of each property as [a] multi-family" dwelling.

From his subsidiary findings summarized above the master concluded, among other things, that the vendors made no actual spoken misrepresentations; that they "intentionally withheld" from the vendees that the operation of the buildings "was in violation of the zoning ordinance"; that the vendors "represented... that the buildings ... were being used as multi-family dwellings and ... in each case that the ... [vendees] could continue" so to operate them; and that the vendees "would not have bought the real estate if ... [they] had known of the violations of the zoning ordinance, or the building code." He also concluded that the vendees "relied upon representations of the ... [vendors] and the appearances of the real estate in that it was being used for multi-family purposes" and that they "made no independent inquiry concerning any violation of the zoning ordinance or building code." . . .

1. We assume that, if the vendors had been wholly silent and had made no references whatsoever to the use of the Ingersoll Grove houses, they could not have been found to have made any misrepresentation. See Swinton v. Whitinsville Sav. Bank, 311 Mass. 677, 678-679,[6] where this court affirmed an order sustaining a demurrer to a declaration in an action of tort brought by a purchaser of a house. The seller knew that the house was infested with termites and remained silent. This court (per Qua, J. at p. 678) said, "There is no allegation of any false statement or representation, or of the uttering of a half truth which may be tantamount to a falsehood. There is no intimation that the defendant by any means prevented the plaintiff from acquiring information as to the condition of the house. There is nothing to show any fiduciary relation between the parties, or that the plaintiff stood in a position of confidence toward or dependence upon the defendant. So far as appears the parties made a business deal at arm's length. The charge is concealment and nothing more; and it is concealment in the simple sense of mere failure to reveal, with nothing to show any peculiar duty to speak." The court (p. 679) indicated that it was applying a long standing "rule of nonliability for bare nondisclosure" (emphasis supplied).

As in the Swinton case, the parties here were dealing at arm's length, the vendees were in no way prevented from acquiring information, and the vendors stood in no fiduciary relationship to the vendees. In two aspects, however, the present cases differ from the Swinton case: viz. (a) The vendees themselves could have found out about the zoning violations by inquiry through public records, whereas in the Swinton case the purchaser would have probably discovered the presence of termites only by retaining expert investigators; and (b) there was something more here than the "bare nondisclosure" of the seller in the Swinton case.

(a) We deal first with the affirmative actions by the vendors, their conduct, advertising, and statements. Was enough said and done by the vendors so that they were bound to disclose more to avoid deception of the vendees and reliance by them upon a half truth? In other words, did the statements made by the vendors in their advertising and otherwise take the cases out of the "rule of nonliability for bare nondisclosure" applied in the Swinton case?

Although there may be "no duty imposed upon one party to a transaction to speak for the information of the other ... if he does speak with reference to a given point of information, voluntarily or at the other's request, he is bound to speak honestly and to divulge all the material facts bearing upon the point that lie within his knowledge. Fragmentary information may be as misleading ... as active misrepresentation, and half-truths may be as actionable as whole lies...." See Harper & James, Torts, § 7.14. See also Restatement: Torts, § 529; Williston, Contracts (2d ed.) §§ 1497-1499. The existence of substantially this principle was assumed in the Swinton case, 311 Mass. 677, 678, in the first sentence of the passage from that case quoted above. Massachusetts decisions have applied this principle. See Kidney v. Stoddard, 7 Met. 252, 254-255 (a father represented that his son was entitled to credit but failed to disclose that the son was a minor; statement treated as a fraudulent representation); Burns v. Dockray, 156 Mass. 135, 137 (assertion that title was good [see Lyman v. Romboli, 293 Mass. 373, 374] but omitting to refer to the possible insanity of one whose incompetence might cloud title); Van Houten v. Morse, 162 Mass. 414, 417-419 (partial disclosure by a woman to her fiancé about a prior divorce). See also International Trust Co. v. Myers, 241 Mass. 509, 512-513; White Tower Management Corp. v. Taglino, 302 Mass. 453, 454-455; Boston Five Cents Sav. Bank v. Brooks, 309 Mass. 52, 55-56 ("Deception need not be direct.... Declarations and conduct calculated to mislead ... which ... do mislead one ... acting reasonably are enough to constitute fraud"). Cf. Wade v. Ford Motor Co. 341 Mass. 596, 597-598.

The master's report provides ample basis for treating the present cases as within the decisions just cited. The original advertisements in effect offered the houses as investment properties and referred to them as single houses converted to apartments. The investment aspect of the houses was emphasized by Foote's action in furnishing income and expense figures. There was an express assertion that 11 Ingersoll Grove was "being rented to the public for multi-family purposes" and that Kannavos and Bellas "could continue to operate ... [the other properties] as multi-dwelling property." The master's conclusions indicate that this statement applied to all the properties. The buildings were divided into apartments. The sales included refrigerators, stoves, and other furnishings appropriate for apartment use, as well as real estate. The vendors knew that the vendees were planning to continue to use the buildings for apartments, and yet the vendors still failed to disclose the zoning and building violations. We conclude that enough was done affirmatively to make the disclosure inadequate and partial, and, in the circumstances, intentionally deceptive and fraudulent.

(b) The second difference between these cases and the Swinton case is the character of the defect not disclosed. In the Swinton case, the presence of predatory insects threatened the structure sold. In the absence of any seller's representations whatsoever, there was no duty to disclose this circumstance, even though doubtless it would have been difficult to discover. In the present cases, the defect in the premises related to a matter of public regulation, the zoning and building ordinances. Its applicability to these premises could have been discovered by these vendees or by the vendees' counsel if, acting with prudence, they had retained counsel, which they did not. The bank mortgagee's counsel presumably was looking only to the protection of the bank's security position. Nevertheless, where there is reliance on fraudulent representations or upon statements and action treated as fraudulent, our cases have not barred plaintiffs from recovery merely because they "did not use due diligence ... [when they] could readily have ascertained from ... records" what the true facts were. See Yorke v. Taylor, 332 Mass. 368, 373. There this court allowed rescission because of the negligent misrepresentation, innocent but false, of the current assessed value of the property being sold. Here the representations made by the advertising and the vendors' conduct and statements in effect were that the property was multi-family housing suitable for investment and that the housing could continue to be used for that purpose. Because the vendors did as much as they did do, they were bound to do more. Failing to do so, they were responsible for misrepresentation. We think the situation is comparable to that in Yorke v. Taylor, 332 Mass. 368, 374, even though there the misrepresentation was "not consciously false" and here it was by half truth.

We hold that the vendors' conduct entitled the vendees to rescind. . . .

Questions

1. What principle is applied in Massachusetts to determine when a party is bound to speak honestly and divulge all material facts in a transaction?

2. Explain why the court concluded that the vendors' conduct and statements in this case were intentionally deceptive and fraudulent.

3. How does the court address the argument that the vendees could have discovered the zoning and building violations by conducting their own due diligence or consulting public records?

Reed v. King

Court of Appeals of California, 1983
145 Cal.App.3d 261, 193 Cal.Rptr. 130

BLEASE, J. In the sale of a house, must the seller disclose it was the site of a multiple murder?

Dorris Reed purchased a house from Robert King. Neither King nor his real estate agents (the other named defendants) told Reed that a woman and her four children were murdered there 10 years earlier. However, it seems "truth will come to light; murder cannot be hid long." (Shakespeare, Merchant of Venice, act II, scene II.) Reed learned of the gruesome episode from a neighbor after the sale. She sues seeking rescission and damages. King and the real estate agent defendants successfully demurred to her first amended complaint for failure to state a cause of action. Reed appeals the ensuing judgment of dismissal. We will reverse the judgment.

We take all issuable facts pled in Reed's complaint as true. King and his real estate agent knew about the murders and knew the event materially affected the market value of the house when they listed it for sale. They represented to Reed the premises were in good condition and fit for an "elderly lady" living alone. They did not disclose the fact of the murders. At some point King asked a neighbor not to inform Reed of that event. Nonetheless, after Reed moved in neighbors informed her no one was interested in purchasing the house because of the stigma. Reed paid $76,000, but the house is only worth $65,000 because of its past.

The trial court sustained the demurrers to the complaint on the ground it did not state a cause of action. The court concluded a cause of action could only be stated "if the subject property, by reason of the prior circumstances, were presently the object of community notoriety ...." Reed declined the offer of leave to amend.

Does Reed's pleading state a cause of action? Concealed within this question is the nettlesome problem of the duty of disclosure of blemishes on real property which are not physical defects or legal impairments to use.

Reed seeks to state a cause of action sounding in contract, i.e. rescission, or in tort, i.e., deceit. In either event her allegations must reveal a fraud. (See Civ. Code, §§ 1571-1573, 1689, 1709-1710.) "The elements of actual fraud, whether as the basis of the remedy in contract or tort, may be stated as follows: There must be (1) a false representation or concealment of a material fact (or, in some cases, an opinion) susceptible of knowledge, (2) made with knowledge of its falsity or without sufficient knowledge on the subject to warrant a representation, (3) with the intent to induce the person to whom it is made to act upon it; and such person must (4) act in reliance upon the representation (5) to his damage." (1 Witkin, Summary of Cal. Law (8th ed. 1973) Contracts, § 315.)

The trial court perceived the defect in Reed's complaint to be a failure to allege concealment of a material fact. "Concealment" and "material" are legal conclusions concerning the effect of the issuable facts pled. As appears, the analytic pathways to these conclusions are intertwined.

Concealment is a term of art which includes mere nondisclosure when a party has a duty to disclose. (See, e.g., Lingsch v. Savage (1963) 213 Cal.App.2d 729, 738 [29 Cal.Rptr. 201, 8 A.L.R.3d 537]; Rest.2d Contracts, § 161; Rest.2d Torts, § 551; Rest., Restitution, § 8, esp. com. b.) Reed's complaint reveals only nondisclosure despite the allegation King asked a neighbor to hold his peace. There is no allegation the attempt at suppression was a cause in fact of Reed's ignorance. (See Rest.2d Contracts, §§ 160, 162-164; Rest.2d Torts, § 550; Rest., Restitution, § 9.) Accordingly, the critical question is: does the seller have a duty to disclose here? Resolution of this question depends on the materiality of the fact of the murders.

In general, a seller of real property has a duty to disclose: "where the seller knows of facts materially affecting the value or desirability of the property which are known or accessible only to him and also knows that such facts are not known to, or within the reach of the diligent attention and observation of the buyer, the seller is under a duty to disclose them to the buyer. [Citations omitted.]" (Lingsch v. Savage, supra, 213 Cal.App.2d at p. 735.) This broad statement of duty has led one commentator to conclude: "The ancient maxim caveat emptor ('let the buyer beware.') has little or no application to California real estate transactions." (1 Miller & Starr, Current Law of Cal. Real Estate (rev.ed. 1975) § 1:80.)

Whether information "is of sufficient materiality to affect the value or desirability of the property ... depends on the facts of the particular case." (Lingsch, supra, 213 Cal.App.2d at p. 737.) Materiality "is a question of law, and is part of the concept of right to rely or justifiable reliance." (3 Witkin, Cal. Procedure (2d ed. 1971) Pleading, § 578, p. 2217.) Accordingly, the term is essentially a label affixed to a normative conclusion. Three considerations bear on this legal conclusion: the gravity of the harm inflicted by nondisclosure; the fairness of imposing a duty of discovery on the buyer as an alternative to compelling disclosure, and the impact on the stability of contracts if rescission is permitted.

Numerous cases have found nondisclosure of physical defects and legal impediments to use of real property are material. (See 1 Miller & Starr, supra, § 181.) However, to our knowledge, no prior real estate sale case has faced an issue of nondisclosure of the kind presented here. (Compare Earl v. Saks & Co., supra, 36 Cal.2d 602; Kuhn v. Gottfried (1951) 103 Cal.App.2d 80, 85-86 [229 P.2d 137].) Should this variety of ill-repute be required to be disclosed? Is this a circumstance where "non-disclosure of the fact amounts to a failure to act in good faith and in accordance with reasonable standards of fair dealing[?]" (Rest.2d Contracts, § 161, subd. (b).)

The paramount argument against an affirmative conclusion is it permits the camel's nose of unrestrained irrationality admission to the tent. If such an "irrational" consideration is permitted as a basis of rescission the stability of all conveyances will be seriously undermined. Any fact that might disquiet the enjoyment of some segment of the buying public may be seized upon by a disgruntled purchaser to void a bargain. In our view, keeping this genie in the bottle is not as difficult a task as these arguments assume. We do not view a decision allowing Reed to survive a demurrer in these unusual circumstances as indorsing the materiality of facts predicating peripheral, insubstantial, or fancied harms.

The murder of innocents is highly unusual in its potential for so disturbing buyers they may be unable to reside in a home where it has occurred. This fact may foreseeably deprive a buyer of the intended use of the purchase. Murder is not such a common occurrence that buyers should be charged with anticipating and discovering this disquieting possibility. Accordingly, the fact is not one for which a duty of inquiry and discovery can sensibly be imposed upon the buyer.

Reed alleges the fact of the murders has a quantifiable effect on the market value of the premises. We cannot say this allegation is inherently wrong and, in the pleading posture of the case, we assume it to be true. If information known or accessible only to the seller has a significant and measurable effect on market value and, as is alleged here, the seller is aware of this effect, we see no principled basis for making the duty to disclose turn upon the character of the information. Physical usefulness is not and never has been the sole criterion of valuation. Stamp collections and gold speculation would be insane activities if utilitarian considerations were the sole measure of value. (See also Civ. Code, § 3355 [deprivation of property of peculiar value to owner]; Annot. (1950) 12 A.L.R.2d 902 [Measure of Damages for Conversion or Loss of, or Damage to, Personal Property Having No Market Value].)

Reputation and history can have a significant effect on the value of realty. "George Washington slept here" is worth something, however physically inconsequential that consideration may be. Ill-repute or "bad will" conversely may depress the value of property. Failure to disclose such a negative fact where it will have a foreseeably depressing effect on income expected to be generated by a business is tortious. (See Rest.2d Torts, § 551, illus. 11.) Some cases have held that unreasonable fears of the potential buying public that a gas or oil pipeline may rupture may depress the market value of land and entitle the owner to incremental compensation in eminent domain. (See Annot., Eminent Domain: Elements and Measure of Compensation for Oil or Gas Pipeline Through Private Property (1954) 38 A.L.R.2d 788, 801-804.)

Whether Reed will be able to prove her allegation the decade-old multiple murder has a significant effect on market value we cannot determine. If she is able to do so by competent evidence she is entitled to a favorable ruling on the issues of materiality and duty to disclose. Her demonstration of objective tangible harm would still the concern that permitting her to go forward will open the floodgates to rescission on subjective and idiosyncratic grounds.

A more troublesome question would arise if a buyer in similar circumstances were unable to plead or establish a significant and quantifiable effect on market value. However, this question is not presented in the posture of this case. Reed has not alleged the fact of the murders has rendered the premises useless to her as a residence. As currently pled, the gravamen of her case is pecuniary harm. We decline to speculate on the abstract alternative.

The judgment is reversed.

Questions

1. What are the essential elements of a cause of action based on fraud in contract?

2. What did the trial court perceive to be the defect in Reed's complaint regarding the duty to disclose?

3. According to the court, what are the three considerations that bear on the legal conclusion of materiality?

4. Why did the court consider the fact of the murders to be a material fact in this case?

Takeaways – Kannavos and Reed

Generally, where one party to a transaction has sole knowledge or access to material facts and knows that such facts are not known or reasonably discoverable by the other party, then a duty to disclose exists. (*Goodman v. Kennedy* (1976) 18 Cal.3d 335, 347 [134 Cal.Rptr. 375, 556 P.2d 737].) A duty to disclose known facts arises in the absence of a fiduciary or a confidential relationship where one party knows of material facts and also knows that such facts are neither known nor readily accessible to the other party. Whether a fact has to be voluntarily disclosed in the absence of an inquiry by the other party often depends on whether or not the fact in question is "material." A fact is material when it would influence the other party's decision as to whether or not to proceed with the transaction.

The following have been held to be of sufficient materiality to require disclosure: the home sold was constructed on filled land (*Burkett v. J.A. Thompson & Son* (1957) 150 Cal.App.2d 523, 526 [310 P.2d 56]); improvements were added without a building permit and in violation of zoning regulations (*Barder v. McClung* (1949) 93 Cal.App.2d 692, 697 [209 P.2d 808]) or in violation of building codes

(*Curran v. Heslop* (1953) 115 Cal.App.2d 476, 480-481 [252 P.2d 378]); the structure was condemned (*Katz v. Department of Real Estate* (1979) 96 Cal.App.3d 895, 900 [158 Cal.Rptr. 766]); the structure was termite-infested (*Godfrey v. Steinpress* (1982) 128 Cal.App.3d 154 [180 Cal.Rptr. 95]); there was water infiltration in the soil (*Barnhouse v. City of Pinole* (1982) 133 Cal.App.3d 171, 187-188 [183 Cal.Rptr. 881]); the amount of net income a piece of property would yield was overstated. (*Ford v. Cournale* (1973) 36 Cal.App.3d 172, 179-180 [111 Cal.Rptr. 334, 81 A.L.R.3d 704].) (Footnote 5, *Reed v. King, supra.*)

Is there a duty to disclose the presence of noisy neighbors? (See, *Shapiro v. Sutherland* (1998) 64 Cal.App.4th 1534, 76 Cal.Rptr.2d 101.)

Misrepresentation

A misrepresentation is "an assertion that is not in accord with the facts." (Rest.2d §159) Misrepresentation whether it is intentional or negligent is grounds for rescinding a contract.

Vokes v. Arthur Murray, Inc.
District Court of Appeal of Florida, 1968
212 So.2d 906

PIERCE, Judge. . . . Plaintiff Mrs. Audrey E. Vokes, a widow of 51 years and without family, had a yen to be 'an accomplished dancer' with the hopes of finding 'new interest in life'. So, on February 10, 1961, a dubious fate, with the assist of a motivated acquaintance, procured her to attend a 'dance party' at Davenport's 'School of Dancing' where she whiled away the pleasant hours, sometimes in a private room, absorbing his accomplished sales technique, during which her grace and poise were elaborated upon and her rosy future as 'an excellent dancer' was painted for her in vivid and glowing colors. As an incident to this interlude, he sold her eight 1/2-hour dance lessons to be utilized within one calendar month therefrom, for the sum of $14.50 cash in hand paid, obviously a baited 'come on'.

Thus she embarked upon an almost endless pursuit of the terpsichorean art during which, over a period of less than sixteen months, she was sold fourteen 'dance courses' totaling in the aggregate 2302 hours of dancing lessons for a total cash outlay of $31,090.45, all at Davenport's dance emporium. All of these fourteen courses were evidenced by execution of a written 'Enrollment Agreement—Arthur Murray's School of Dancing' with the addendum in heavy black print, 'No one will be informed that you are taking dancing lessons. Your relations with us are held in strict confidence', setting forth the number of 'dancing lessons' and the 'lessons in rhythm sessions' currently sold to her from time to time, and always of course accompanied by payment of cash of the realm.

These dance lesson contracts and the monetary consideration therefor of over $31,000 were procured from her by means and methods of Davenport and his associates which went beyond the unsavory, yet legally permissible, perimeter of 'sales puffing' and intruded well into the forbidden area of undue influence, the suggestion of falsehood, the suppression of truth, and the free exercise of rational judgment, if what plaintiff alleged in her complaint was true. From the time of her first contact with the dancing school in February, 1961, she was influenced unwittingly by a constant and continuous barrage of flattery, false praise, excessive compliments, and panegyric encomiums, to such extent that it would be not only inequitable, but unconscionable, for a Court exercising inherent chancery power to allow such contracts to stand.

She was incessantly subjected to overreaching blandishment and cajolery. She was assured she had 'grace and poise'; that she was 'rapidly improving and developing in her dancing skill'; that the additional lessons would 'make her a beautiful dancer, capable of dancing with the most accomplished dancers'; that she was 'rapidly progressing in the development of her dancing skill and gracefulness', etc., etc. She was given 'dance aptitude tests' for the ostensible purpose of 'determining' the number of remaining hours instructions needed by her from time to time.

At one point she was sold 545 additional hours of dancing lessons to be entitled to award of the 'Bronze Medal' signifying that she had reached 'the Bronze Standard', a supposed designation of dance achievement by students of Arthur Murray, Inc.

Later she was sold an additional 926 hours in order to gain the 'Silver Medal', indicating she had reached 'the Silver Standard', at a cost of $12,501.35.

At one point, while she still had to her credit about 900 unused hours of instructions, she was induced to purchase an additional 24 hours of lessons to participate in a trip to Miami at her own expense, where she would be 'given the opportunity to dance with members of the Miami Studio'.

She was induced at another point to purchase an additional 123 hours of lessons in order to be not only eligible for the Miami trip but also to become 'a life member of the Arthur Murray Studio', carrying with it certain dubious emoluments, at a further cost of $1,752.30.

At another point, while she still had over 1,000 unused hours of instruction she was induced to buy 151 additional hours at a cost of $2,049.00 to be eligible for a 'Student Trip to Trinidad', at her own expense as she later learned.

Also, when she still had 1100 unused hours to her credit, she was prevailed upon to purchase an additional 347 hours at a cost of $4,235.74, to qualify her to receive a 'Gold Medal' for achievement, indicating she had advanced to 'the Gold Standard'.

On another occasion, while she still had over 1200 unused hours, she was induced to buy an additional 175 hours of instruction at a cost of $2,472.75 to be eligible 'to take a trip to Mexico'.

Finally, sandwiched in between other lesser sales promotions, she was influenced to buy an additional 481 hours of instruction at a cost of $6,523.81 in order to 'be classifies as a Gold Bar Member, the ultimate achievement of the dancing studio'.

All the foregoing sales promotions, illustrative of the entire fourteen separate contracts, were procured by defendant Davenport and Arthur Murray, Inc., by false representations to her that she was improving in her dancing ability, that she had excellent potential, that she was responding to instructions in dancing grace, and that they were developing her into a beautiful dancer, whereas in truth and in fact she did not develop in her dancing ability, she had no 'dance aptitude', and in fact had difficulty in 'hearing that musical beat'. The complaint alleged that such representations to her 'were in fact false and known by the defendant to be false and contrary to the plaintiff's true ability, the truth of plaintiff's ability being fully known to the defendants, but withheld from the plaintiff for the sole and specific intent to deceive and defraud the plaintiff and to induce her in the purchasing of additional hours of dance lessons'. It was averred that the lessons were sold to her 'in total disregard to the true physical, rhythm, and mental ability of the plaintiff'. In other words, while she first exulted that she was entering the 'spring of her life', she finally was awakened to the fact there was 'spring' neither in her life nor in her feet.

The complaint prayed that the Court decree the dance contracts to be null and void and to be cancelled, that an accounting be had, and judgment entered against, the defendants 'for that portion of the $31,090.45 not charged against specific hours of instruction given to the plaintiff'. The Court held the complaint not to state a cause of action and dismissed it with prejudice. We disagree and reverse.

. . . Defendants contend that contracts can only be rescinded for fraud or misrepresentation when the alleged misrepresentation is as to a material fact, rather than an opinion, prediction or expectation, and that the statements and representations set forth at length in the complaint were in the category of 'trade puffing', within its legal orbit.

It is true that 'generally a misrepresentation, to be actionable, must be one of fact rather than of opinion'. Tonkovich v. South Florida Citrus Industries, Inc., Fla.App.1966, 185 So.2d 710; Kutner v. Kalish, Fla.App.1965, 173 So.2d 763. But this rule has significant qualifications, applicable here. It does not apply where there is a fiduciary relationship between the parties, or where there has been some artifice or trick employed by the representor, or where the parties do not in general deal at 'arm's length' as we understand the phrase, or where the representee does not have equal opportunity to become apprised of the truth or falsity of the fact represented. 14 Fla.Jur. Fraud and Deceit, s 28; Kitchen v. Long, 1914, 67 Fla. 72, 64 So. 429. As stated by Judge Allen of this Court in Ramel v. Chasebrook Construction Company, Fla.App.1961, 135 So.2d 876: '* * * A statement of a party having * * * superior knowledge may be regarded as a statement of fact although it would be considered as opinion if the parties were dealing on equal terms.'

It could be reasonably supposed here that defendants had 'superior knowledge' as to whether plaintiff had 'dance potential' and as to whether she was noticeably improving in the art of terpsichore. And it would be a reasonable inference from the undenied averments of the complaint that the flowery eulogiums heaped upon her by defendants as a prelude to her contracting for 1944 additional hours of instruction in order to attain the rank of the Bronze Standard, thence to the bracket of the Silver Standard, thence to the class of the Gold Bar Standard, and finally to the crowning plateau of a Life Member of the Studio, proceeded as much or more from the urge to 'ring the cash register' as from any honest or realistic appraisal of her dancing prowess or a factual representation of her progress.

Even in contractual situations where a party to a transaction owes no duty to disclose facts within his knowledge or to answer inquiries respecting such facts, the law is if he undertakes to do so he must disclose the Whole truth. Ramel v. Chasebrook Construction Company, supra; Beagle v. Bagwell, Fla.App.1964, 169 So.2d 43. From the face of the complaint, it should have been reasonably apparent to defendants that her vast outlay of cash for the many hundreds of additional hours of instruction was not justified by her slow and awkward progress, which she would have been made well aware of if they had spoken the 'whole truth'.

In Hirschman v. Hodges, etc., 1910, 59 Fla. 517, 51 So. 550, it was said that— '* * * what is plainly injurious to good faith ought to be considered as a fraud sufficient to impeach a contract', and that an improvident agreement may be avoided—'* * * because of surprise, or mistake, Want of freedom, undue influence, the suggestion of falsehood, or the suppression of truth'.

We repeat that where parties are dealing on a contractual basis at arm's length with no inequities or inherently unfair practices employed, the Courts will in general 'leave the parties where they find themselves'. But in the case sub judice, from the allegations of the unanswered complaint, we cannot say that enough of the accompanying ingredients, as mentioned in the foregoing authorities, were not present which otherwise would have barred the equitable arm of the Court to her. In our view, from the showing made in her complaint, plaintiff is entitled to her day in Court.

It accordingly follows that the order dismissing plaintiff's last amended complaint with prejudice should be and is reversed.

Questions

1. What legal principle did the defendants argue to support their contention that the contracts cannot be rescinded?

2. Under what circumstances does the rule that misrepresentations must be of material fact, rather than opinion, not apply?

3. How did the court determine whether the statements made by the defendants were factual or mere opinion?

4. What duty does a party owe when voluntarily disclosing facts or answering inquiries about those facts?

5. What factors did the court consider in determining whether the plaintiff's complaint stated a cause of action?

Takeaways - Vokes v. Arthur Murray

As a general rule, the misrepresentation must be one of fact and not of opinion. Ordinarily, expressions of opinion are not treated as representations of fact upon which to base actionable fraud. However, when one party possesses or holds himself or herself out as possessing superior knowledge or special information regarding the subject of a representation, and the other party is so situated that he or she may reasonably rely upon such supposed superior knowledge or special information, a representation made by the party possessing or holding himself herself out as possessing such knowledge or information will be treated as a representation of fact. This is so, even though the representation, if made by any other person, might be regarded as an expression of opinion. When a party states an opinion as a fact, in such a manner that it is reasonable to rely and act upon it as a fact, it may be treated as a representation of fact. (See, 5 Witkin, Summary of Cal.Law (10th ed. 2005) Torts § 774.)

In California, any contract for dance studio lessons entered into in reliance upon any willful and false, fraudulent, or misleading information, representation, notice, or advertisement of the seller is void and unenforceable. (Cal.Civ.Code § 1812.60)

Promise Without Intention To Perform

A promise made without intention of performing it, constitutes misrepresentation. (See, Cal.Civ.Code § 1572)

ASSESSMENT QUESTIONS, CHAPTER 4

1. Discuss the concept of contractual capacity for minors. What are the rights and liabilities of minors when entering into contracts?

2. Can a minor disaffirm a contract at any time? Explain the limitations and exceptions to a minor's right to disaffirm.

3. What is the concept of ratification in relation to contracts made by minors? Explain when and how ratification occurs.

4. Describe the capacity requirements for individuals with mental incapacity to contract. What legal standards are used to determine mental incapacity?

5. What is the duty to disclose in contract law? Under what circumstances does a party have an obligation to disclose certain information?

6. Can silence or non-disclosure constitute misrepresentation? Explain the principle of caveat emptor and its relation to the duty to disclose.

7. Describe the doctrine of concealment and its role in the duty to disclose. When does a party have a duty to disclose hidden defects or information?

8. Define misrepresentation in the context of contract law. What are the key elements that must be established to prove misrepresentation?

9. Distinguish between innocent, negligent, and fraudulent misrepresentation. Provide an example for each.

10. Explain the concept of materiality in misrepresentation. Why is materiality important in determining the effect of a misrepresentation on a contract?

CHAPTER 5
ILLEGAL AND UNCONSCIONABLE CONTRACTS

Illegality

Illegal contracts are also said to be contracts that are against public policy. (See, Rest.2d § 178) Courts will not enforce illegal bargains. Nor will they allow restitution for illegal contracts. There are three categories of illegal contracts: 1) Those contrary to express statutes; 2) those contrary to the policy of express statutes; 3) those otherwise contrary to good morals. (Cal.Civ.Code § 1667.)

Bovard v. American Horse Enterprises
California Court of Appeal, 1988
201 Cal.App. 3d 832

Robert Bovard appeals from the judgment dismissing his supplemental complaint against defendants, American Horse Enterprises, Inc., and James T. Ralph. Bovard contends the trial court erroneously concluded the contract upon which his action was founded was illegal and void as contrary to public policy. . .

On the third day of trial, Bovard testified as to the nature of the business conducted by American Horse Enterprises, Inc., at the time the corporation was sold to Ralph. Bovard explained the corporation made jewelry and drug paraphernalia, which consisted of "roach clips" and "bongs" used to smoke marijuana and tobacco. At that point the trial court excused the jury and asked counsel to prepare arguments on the question whether the contract for sale of the corporation was illegal and void.

The following day, after considering the arguments of counsel, the trial court dismissed the supplemental complaint. The court found that the corporation predominantly produced paraphernalia used to smoke marijuana and was not engaged significantly in jewelry production, and that Bovard had recovered the corporate machinery through self-help. The parties do not challenge these findings. The court acknowledged that the manufacture of drug paraphernalia was not itself illegal in 1978 when Bovard and Ralph contracted for the sale of American Horse Enterprises, Inc. However, the court concluded a public policy against the manufacture of drug paraphernalia was implicit in the statute making the possession, use and transfer of marijuana unlawful. (See Health & Saf. Code, §§ 11357, 11358, 11359, 11360.) The trial court held the consideration for the contract was contrary to the policy of express law, and the contract was therefore illegal and void. Finally, the court found the parties were in pari delicto and thus with respect to their contractual dispute should be left as the court found them.

"The consideration of a contract must be lawful within the meaning of section sixteen hundred and sixty-seven." (Civ. Code, § 1607.) "That is not lawful which is: [¶] 1. Contrary to an express provision of law; [¶] 2. Contrary to the policy of express law, though not expressly prohibited; or, [¶] 3. Otherwise contrary to good morals." (Civ. Code, § 1667.) "If any part of a single consideration for one or more objects, or of several considerations for a single object, is unlawful, the entire contract is void." (Civ. Code, § 1608.)

The trial court concluded the consideration for the contract was contrary to the policy of the law as expressed in the statute prohibiting the possession, use and transfer of marijuana. [1a] Whether a contract is contrary to public policy is a question of law to be determined from the circumstances of the particular case. (Kallen v. Delug (1984) 157 Cal.App.3d 940, 951 [203 Cal.Rptr. 879]; Russell v. Soldinger (1976) 59 Cal.App.3d 633, 642 [131 Cal.Rptr. 145].) Here, the critical facts are not in dispute. Whenever a court becomes aware that a contract is illegal, it has a duty to refrain from entertaining an action to enforce the contract. (Russell v. Soldinger, supra; Santoro v. Carbone (1972) 22 Cal.App.3d 721, 732 [99 Cal.Rptr. 488], disapproved on another ground in Liodas v. Sahadi (1977) 19 Cal.3d 278, 287 [137 Cal.Rptr. 635, 562 P.2d 316].) Furthermore the court will not permit the parties to maintain an action to settle or compromise a claim based on an illegal contract. (Union Collection Co. v. Buckman (1907) 150 Cal. 159, 165 [88 P. 708]; see also First Nat. Bk. v. Thompson (1931) 212 Cal. 388, 405 [298 P. 808].)

The question whether a contract violates public policy necessarily involves a degree of subjectivity. Therefore, "... courts have been cautious in blithely applying public policy reasons to nullify otherwise enforceable contracts. This concern has been graphically articulated by the California Supreme Court as follows: 'It has been well said that public policy is an unruly horse, astride of which you are carried into unknown and uncertain paths, ... While contracts opposed to morality or law should not be allowed to show themselves in courts of justice, yet public policy requires and encourages the making of contracts by competent parties upon all valid and lawful considerations, and courts so recognizing have allowed parties the widest latitude in this regard; and, unless it is entirely plain that a contract is violative of sound public policy, a court will never so declare. "The power of the courts to declare a contract void for being in contravention of sound public policy is a very delicate and undefined power, and, like the power to declare a statute unconstitutional, should be exercised only in cases free from doubt." [Citation.] ... "No court ought to refuse its aid to enforce a contract on doubtful and uncertain grounds. The burden is on the defendant to show that its enforcement would be in violation of the settled public policy of this state, or injurious to the morals of its people." [Citation.]'" (Moran v. Harris (1982) 131 Cal.App.3d 913, 919-920 [182 Cal.Rptr. 519, 28 A.L.R.4th 655], quoting Stephens v. Southern Pacific Co. (1895) 109 Cal. 86, 89-90 [41 P. 783].)

Bovard places great reliance on Moran v. Harris, supra, 131 Cal.App. 3d 913, to support his argument the trial court erred in finding the contract violative of public policy. In Moran, two lawyers entered into a fee splitting agreement relative to a case referred by one to the other. The agreement was made in 1972, 10 months before the adoption of a rule of professional conduct prohibiting such agreements. In 1975, the attorney to whom the case had been referred settled the case, but then refused to split the attorney's fees with the referring attorney. (Id., at pp. 916-917.) The trial court held the fee splitting contract violated public policy. The appellate court reversed, noting the rule of professional conduct had been amended effective January 1, 1979, to permit fee splitting agreements; thus there was no statute or rule prohibiting fee splitting agreements either at the time the attorneys' contract was formed or after January 1, 1979, during the pendency of the action to enforce the fee splitting contract. Therefore, the court held there was no basis for a finding that the contract violated public policy. (Id., at pp. 920-921.)

Here, in contrast to Moran, there is positive law on which to premise a finding of public policy, although the trial court did not find the manufacture of marijuana paraphernalia against public policy on the basis of the later enacted ordinance or statute prohibiting such manufacture. Rather, the court's finding was based on a statute prohibiting the possession, use and transfer of marijuana which long antedated the parties' contract.

Moran suggests factors to consider in analyzing whether a contract violates public policy: "Before labeling a contract as being contrary to public policy, courts must carefully inquire into the nature of the conduct, the extent of public harm which may be involved, and the moral quality of the conduct of the parties in light of the prevailing standards of the community. [Citations.]" (Id., at p. 920.)

These factors are more comprehensively set out in the Restatement Second of Contracts section 178: "(1) A promise or other term of an agreement is unenforceable on grounds of public policy if legislation provides that it is unenforceable or the interest in its enforcement is clearly outweighed in the circumstances by a public policy against the enforcement of such terms.

"(a) the parties' justified expectations,
"(b) any forfeiture that would result if enforcement were denied, and
"(c) any special public interest in the enforcement of the particular term.
"(a) the strength of that policy as manifested by legislation or judicial decisions,
"(b) the likelihood that a refusal to enforce the term will further that policy,
"(c) the seriousness of any misconduct involved and the extent to which it was deliberate, and
"(d) the directness of the connection between that misconduct and the term."

Applying the Restatement test to the present circumstances, we conclude the interest in enforcing this contract is very tenuous. Neither party was reasonably justified in expecting the government would not eventually act to geld American Horse Enterprises, a business harnessed to the production of paraphernalia used to facilitate the use of an illegal drug. Moreover, although voidance of the contract imposed a forfeiture on Bovard, he did recover the corporate machinery, the only assets of the business which could be used for lawful purposes, i.e., to manufacture jewelry. Thus, the forfeiture was significantly mitigated if not negligible. Finally, there is no special public interest in the enforcement of this contract, only the general interest in preventing a party to a contract from avoiding a debt.

On the other hand, the Restatement factors favoring a public policy against enforcement of this contract are very strong. As we have explained, the public policy against manufacturing paraphernalia to facilitate the use of marijuana is strongly implied in the statutory prohibition against the possession, use, etc., of marijuana, a prohibition which dates back at least to 1929. (See Stats. 1929, ch. 216, § 1, p. 380.) Obviously, refusal to enforce the instant contract will further that public policy not only in the present circumstances but by serving notice on manufacturers of drug paraphernalia that they may not resort to the judicial system to protect or advance their business interests. Moreover, it is immaterial that the business conducted by American Horse Enterprises was not expressly prohibited by law when Bovard and Ralph made their agreement since both parties knew that the corporation's products would be used primarily for purposes which were expressly illegal. We conclude the trial court correctly declared the contract contrary to the policy of express law and therefore illegal and void. . . .

The judgment dismissing the supplemental complaint, the order striking the memorandum of costs and taxing costs, and the judgment dismissing the cross-complaint are affirmed. The parties are to bear their own costs on appeal.

Questions

1. What were the critical facts considered by the trial court in determining whether the contract was contrary to public policy?

2. According to the court's reasoning, what factors should be considered when analyzing whether a contract violates public policy?

3. In the *Moran v. Harris* case, why did the appellate court find that the fee splitting contract did not violate public policy?

4. How did the court apply the Restatement test to determine whether the contract should be enforced in this case?

5. Based on the court's reasoning, why did the trial court conclude that the contract for the sale of American Horse Enterprises was illegal and void?

Takeaways – Bovard

In *Bovard* the court referred to the fact that the parties to the agreement "were in pari delicto." The maxim "*in pari delicto*" (which roughly translates to "equally blameworthy) declares that the defendant will prevail when the parties are of equal guilt. In other words, the plaintiff cannot enforce an illegal contract. See generally Wade, Restitution of Benefits Acquired Through Illegal Transactions, 95 U. Pa. L. Rev. 261 (1947); Nathanson v. Weis, Voisin, Cannon, Inc., supra. Where the parties are not equally culpable, the defense of *in pari delicto* is not appropriate. In other words, where the conduct of the party who seeks to enlist support of the doctrine outrages public sensibilities more than the conduct of the party against whom the doctrine is sought to be applied, courts will not support application of the doctrine of *in pari delicto."* (*Goldberg v. Sanglier* 639 P2d 1347 (Wash.1982); Courts will not only not enforce illegal contracts or contracts that are against public policy, they will not order restitution for such contracts. (Rest.2d § 197) If a party to a contract is found to be not *"in pari delicto"* they can at least get restitution.

"In determining whether the subject of a given contract violates public policy, courts must rely on the state of the law as it existed at the time the contract was made." (*Moran v. Harris,* (1982) 131 Cal.App.3d 913 at p. 918.)

All contracts which have for their object, directly or indirectly, to exempt any one from responsibility for his own fraud, or willful injury to the person or property of another, or violation of law, whether willful or negligent, are against the policy of the law. (Cal.Civ.Code § 1668)

As a general rule, if a contract can be performed legally, a court will presume that the parties intended a lawful mode of performance. (*West Covina Enterprises, Inc. v. Chalmers* (1958) 49 Cal.2d 754, 759 [322 P.2d 13].)

Bradley v. Doherty
30 Cal.App.3d 991 (1973)
106 Cal. Rptr. 725

BRAY, J. Plaintiff appeals from two separate but related orders of the San Mateo County Superior Court: (1) judgment sustaining demurrer without leave to amend the fifth cause of action, and (2) order dissolving temporary injunction and denying plaintiff's motion for preliminary injunction. . . .

Appellant's complaint contains nine causes of action. . . . The fifth cause of action alleges that respondents fraudulently obtained $70,000 from appellant by "betting on sides or hands of various plays or games." . . .

Respondents filed general and special demurrers to the complaint. The special demurrers were sustained. . . .

The sustaining of the demurrer to the fifth cause of action without leave to amend was proper.

The court sustained the demurrer on the ground that the allegations of the fifth count showed that appellant was attempting to collect $70,000 which he had lost in betting on the outcome of pinball games, that appellant was in pari delicto and that, under California law, as betting is illegal, one engaged in betting cannot recover his losses even though the gambling game is fixed and crooked. Appellant concedes that such is the law in this state but contends that the doctrine of in pari delicto should be held unconstitutional if applied to a gambling game which is fixed, or to a compulsive gambler.

"The general rule is that the courts will not recognize such an illegal contract [betting] and will not aid the parties thereto, but will leave them where it finds them. This rule has been rigidly enforced in this state to deny any relief in the courts to parties seeking to recover either their stakes or their winnings under a wagering contract which is in violation of law,... [Citations omitted] "The rule applies even though the winner wins the gambling by fraud or deceit. [Citations omitted]

In Wallace v. Opinham (1946) 73 Cal. App.2d 25 [165 P.2d 709], a demurrer was properly sustained to a complaint alleging that the plaintiff was cheated out of a sum of money when his opponents in a card game of "Twenty-One" used marked cards, the court refusing to aid or assist plaintiff to enforce rights growing out of the illegal card game in the absence of a statute authorizing a recovery of gambling losses. The court pointed out that it had frequently been decided that courts would not become the arbiters of incidental acts of participants in gambling games which were prohibited by law, and that public policy precluded courts from declaring and distinguishing between degrees of turpitude of parties who engaged in outlawed transactions, since otherwise, courts might be compelled to decide which party had cheated the most. (Id. at p. 27.)

"Clearly, if the gaming, whatever be its character, is conducted according to rule, the one losing money in a wager upon the result would be denied any remedy at law. It is difficult to perceive how he could be entitled to greater consideration because of cheating if the game was conducted fairly, or the result prearranged. If such facts shall enter into the consideration of one's right to recover money lost in betting, then it inevitably follows that the courts must sit as arbiters of every game upon which money is wagered, act as judge of the race-course, and umpire the prize-ring." (Schmitt v. Gibson (1910) 12 Cal. App. 407, 415-416 [107 P. 517].) Penal Code section 337a provides: "Every person ... 6. Who lays, makes, offers or accepts any bet or bets, or wager or wagers, upon the result, or purported result, of any ... mechanical apparatus, is punishable by imprisonment in the county jail for a period of not more than one year or in the state prison for a period not exceeding two years."

Appellant argues incorrectly that the California courts have reevaluated the doctrine of in pari delicto since the Wallace decision. He cites Tri-Q, Inc. v. Sta-Hi Corp. (1965) 63 Cal.2d 199 [45 Cal. Rptr. 878, 404 P.2d 486], an action to enjoin violation of the Unfair Practices Act. There the court found that the corporate officer who joined in an agreement that recited consideration which was not the true consideration, did not enter into the agreement with any wrongful purpose and that his only moral fault arose out of his knowledge of the corporation's illegal purposes and actions. In effect, the court found that the officer was not in pari delicto.

Norwood v. Judd (1949) 93 Cal. App.2d 276 [209 P.2d 24], dealt with a situation where one partner had secured a contractor's license in his own name rather than in that of the partnership. It was held that this lack of a valid license for the partnership did not prevent the other partner from obtaining an accounting. The court pointed out "that this is not a case where the parties engaged in a business prohibited by statute or public policy, or where a license would not have been issued had application been made." (Id. at p. 283.) The court distinguished a business "which has been illegally conducted for lack of license ... from an unlawful and forbidden enterprise, ..." (Id., p. 285, quoting Denning v. Taber, 70 Cal. App.2d 253, 257 [160 P.2d 900].) The court stated that X statutes are passed primarily for the protection and safety of the public, and not for "the benefit of a greedy partner who seeks to keep for himself all of the fruits of the partnership enterprise to the exclusion of another partner entitled to share therein." (Id. at p. 286.)

The case at bench falls within the distinction made in Norwood between businesses that are conducted illegally because of failure to obtain a license and those that are unlawful and forbidden enterprises. Norwood cited with approval the case of Hooper v. Barranti (1947) 81 Cal. App.2d 570 [184 P.2d 688], wherein two persons agreed to operate a tavern in partnership under a license held by one of them. In Hooper, the partnership agreement itself provided for the conducting of the bar business for 15 months without a proper license. Furthermore, in Hooper it was impossible for the parties to enter into a lawful agreement because one of the proposed partners was a noncitizen, and aliens could not secure a liquor license as a partner or otherwise. In Hooper, the action for an accounting was dismissed on the grounds that the claim could proceed only from the partnership agreement, and that the agreement was illegal. In the case at bar we are talking about a forbidden enterprise under Penal Code section 337a, subdivision 6. As stated in Hooper, an action may not be maintained on an illegal agreement.

In Smith v. Turner (1965) 238 Cal. App.2d 141 [47 Cal. Rptr. 582], plaintiffs, inexperienced in corporate matters, paid a seller for shares of stock before a permit to issue the shares was recieved. The commissioner of corporations therefore refused to issue the permit. Plaintiffs began to fear they would not receive the shares and they therefore signed false receipts for the return of the money, so that the permit would be granted. In an action for recovery of their money, plaintiffs were held not to be in pari delicto with the defendant. The court pointed out that the plaintiffs were not experienced in corporate matters while the defendant was and, moreover, plaintiffs belong to the class of persons the securities laws were intended to protect. (Id. at p. 149.)

Appellant attempts to avoid the application of the cases applying the in pari delicto rule to gambling by stating that the cases cited did not contain allegations such as are in his complaint, of the gambling being conducted by negligence, negligent supervision, fraud and theft. The answer to that is that no matter what the happenings were called, nor how they were brought about, the simple fact is that they constituted gambling prohibited by law and voluntarily entered into by the parties.

Appellant does not belong to the class of persons to be protected under section 337a of the Penal Code, nor was the activity illegal for mere failure to obtain a permit or license, nor was the wrongful purpose of the activity shared solely by appellant — both appellant and respondents knew they were engaging in gambling. (1) The gambling activity engaged in in the instant case can only be classified as an unlawful and forbidden enterprise to which the doctrine of in pari delicto applies.

It is true that there are some jurisdictions which do not follow the California rule (see Annot., Recovery of money or property lost through cheating or fraud in forbidden gambling or game, 39 A.L.R.2d 1213). However, appellant has not shown that the California rule is other than herein set forth. . . .

As it clearly appears that because of the necessary application of the doctrine of in pari delicto appellant cannot state a cause of action, the court correctly sustained the demurrer without leave to amend. . . .

The judgment and order are affirmed.

Questions

1. Why did the court sustain the demurrer to the fifth cause of action without leave to amend?

2. What is the general rule applied by the California courts regarding illegal contracts and wagering contracts?

3. In *Wallace v. Opinham*, why did the court refuse to aid or assist the plaintiff in enforcing rights arising from the illegal card game?

4. How did the court in *Tri-Q, Inc. v. Sta-Hi Corp.* distinguish the doctrine of in pari delicto?

5. According to the court's reasoning, why does the doctrine of in pari delicto apply in the case at bench?

Manning v. Bishop of Marquette
Supreme Court of Michigan,
345 Mich 130; 76 NW2d 75 (1956)

SMITH, J. This is not an easy case. The difficulty arises from the fact that the plaintiff, though grievously injured, is said to be a law violator, whose turpitude bars her from recovery. She had, in truth, been playing bingo at Cathedral Hall, St. Peter's Cathedral, in Marquette. She was injured while leaving the church property, and was awarded damages. Her case is analogized to that of a woman aborted who sought to recover damages from the doctor, Nash v. Meyer, 54 Idaho 283 (31 P2d 273); to that of a participant in a fist fight suing his adversary, Galbraith v. Fleming, 60 Mich 403; and to that involving the consort of a strumpet, who, having lost his wallet, sued the hotel, alleging that he came within the statutory definition of a "guest," Curtis v. Murphy, 63 Wis 4 (22 NW 825, 53 Am Rep 242). We have meditated long on the case. A rogue does not appeal to our conscience. Yet even a rogue may have a cause of action and so, a fortiori, may Mrs. Manning, who is no rogue.

In more detail, this was the situation: On Tuesday, May 23, 1950, Mrs. Manning, a resident of the city of Marquette, at about 7:15 p.m., went to St. Peter's Cathedral to attend a bingo game regularly sponsored by the church. It is estimated that approximately 400 persons were in attendance at the game on this particular evening. The game was open to the public and the cards necessary for playing were available for the price of $1 each. About 10:15 p.m. the game was concluded and plaintiff, along with the rest of the crowd, left the hall. (The exit consisted of double doors, illuminated on the outside by an ornamental light fixture above and to the right of the doors as one leaves the building.) Plaintiff came out of the left side of the right-hand door and walked toward the left on the private walk in preparation to turning left where it joins the public sidewalk. The night was dark and plaintiff was in the middle of a crowd. As she walked along in this company and in the darkness, she "stepped into this hole" and fell to the ground, sustaining serious injuries.

Action was brought against Bishop Thomas L. Noa, of Marquette, individually and as trustee of St. Peter's Cathedral. Upon motion granted below, the Bishop in his individual capacity was dismissed as a party defendant and he appears here as Bishop of the Diocese, holding title to the premises as trustee for St. Peter's Cathedral Parish and, as conceded, the person who "individually or through his agents, employees and assigns, operated St. Peter's Cathedral." The action so brought was in tort, and was based upon the negligence of defendant in failing to maintain "the walkways and means of egress from the premises in a reasonably safe condition." In the one case plaintiff Lucille A. Manning claims damages for personal injuries sustained as a result of her fall....

Defendant has taken a general appeal from a judgment for plaintiff, entered upon the jury's verdict and from the trial court's denial of his motion for a directed verdict made at the conclusion of plaintiff's case....

Our doors are open to both the virtuous and the villainous. We do not, however, lend our aid to the furtherance of an unlawful project, nor do we decide, as between 2 scoundrels, who cheated whom the more. Rarely, indeed, are such cases brought before us, possibly from the result of the highwayman's case, reported in 2 Evans', Pothier on Obligations (3d Am ed), pp 2, 3:

"There is a tradition that a suit was instituted by a highwayman against his companion to account for his share of the plunder, and a copy of the proceedings has been published as found amongst the papers of a deceased attorney. It was a bill in the Exchequer, which avoided stating in direct terms the criminality of the engagement, and is founded upon a supposed dealing as copartners in rings, watches, et cetera, but the mode of dealing may be manifestly inferred. The tradition receives some degree of authenticity, by the order of the court being such as would in all probability ensue from such an attempt. The order was, that the bill should be dismissed with costs for impertinence, and the solicitor fined 50 £. The printed account is accompanied by a memorandum which states the particular times and places where the plaintiff and defendant were afterwards executed. Europ Mag, 1787, vol 2, p 360 (a)."

Whether or not the case is suppositious, it well illustrates a general principle. For more modern discussion see Piechowiak v. Bissell, 305 Mich 486, involving a charge of malicious prosecution by one of the parties to a criminal conspiracy against the other.

Inasmuch as the bearing of asserted illegality of plaintiff's actions upon a recovery for tort is involved, a problem involving complex considerations of individual and public morality, we deem it prudent to point out that our opinion is narrowly circumscribed. We have not a case of "splitting up the loot," i.e., an action for the conversion of property obtained under an illegal contract. Nor do we have the case where the defendant was acting in concert with plaintiff, for here defendant is charged only with negligence. We are not, moreover, faced with the case in which plaintiff was injured during her participation in an unlawful act, such as rioters injuring one another in the general turmoil. In all such cases the plaintiff must prove the illegal transaction in order to make out his case. But in the case at bar the game is over. The evening has come to a close and the day's pursuits, wicked or pure, are over. The plaintiff is proceeding by normal means of egress, and, it is asserted, in the exercise of due care, towards her domicile, when she is hurt while still on the church premises. Will the action lie? Or is it to be barred by the evil range of the evening's activities? That is to say, is this properly a case where recovery cannot be had because of the unlawful act of the plaintiff, which was a contributing cause of the damage suffered?

Assuming, but not deciding, that, as Mrs. Manning abandoned her evening's diversions and started for home, she still wore a halo of illegality, or, as defendant puts it, still "was tarred with the illegal transaction," is she outside the law, precluded from recovery? We find no warrant for the position. It goes too far. In order to have such effect an unlawful act must be one which the law recognizes as having a causal connection with the injury complained of. If the unlawful act was merely collateral to the cause of action sued upon, and did not proximately contribute to the injury, recovery is not barred. 52 Am Jur, Torts, § 92. A moment's reflection will confirm the justice of the rule. A passenger on a railroad train should be able to recover for the negligence of his carrier, resulting in the train's derailment and his injury therefrom, even though he was swearing like a trooper at the time he was hurt, in direct violation of CL 1948, § 466.10 (Stat Ann § 22.269), which forbids the utterance of profane language in the hearing of other passengers on a railroad train. Would his case be weaker if he were on his way home from hunting deer out of season? Was Mrs. Manning's prior bingo game a substantial causal factor? We must, and do, distinguish between legal or proximate cause and cause in a philosophical sense. As Dean Prosser puts it (Prosser on Torts [1st ed], p 312):

"In a philosophical sense, the consequences of an act go forward to eternity, and the causes of an event go back to the discovery of America and beyond. `The fatal trespass done by Eve was cause of all our woe.' But any attempt to impose responsibility upon such a basis would result in infinite liability for all wrongful acts, and would `set society on edge and fill the courts with endless litigation.'"

Consistent with the foregoing was the decision of the Connecticut court in Bagre v. Daggett Chocolate Co., 126 Conn 659 (13 A2d 757), that plaintiff was not barred from her action for injuries arising from her biting into a hard metallic substance in a piece of candy, even though the box of candy had been won at a bingo game. There was "absence of any causal relation between this illegal act and the injury." Similar in principle is our decision in Van Auken v. Chicago & West Michigan R. Co., 96 Mich 307 (22 LRA 33), wherein a traveler on the Sabbath recovered for injuries received because of the railroad's negligence.

The principles described above are well stated by the Mississippi court in Meador v. Hotel Grover, 193 Miss 392, 405, 406 (9 So2d 782), in the following words:

"For a plaintiff to be barred of an action for negligent injury under the principle of public policy implicit in the maxim ex dolo malo non oritur actio, his injury must have been suffered while and as a proximate result of committing an illegal act. The unlawful act must be at once the source of both his criminal responsibility and his civil right. The injury must be traceable to his own breach of the law and such breach must be an integral and essential part of his case. Where the violation of law is merely a condition and not a contributing cause of the injury, a recovery may be permitted. (Citing cases.)

"The mere status of a plaintiff as a lawbreaker at the time of his injury is not sufficient of itself to bar him from resort to the courts. With respect to the particular act out of which the injury arose, his right to invoke the power of the law to protect can be neutralized only by the power of the law to punish. Before he can be held in pari delicto with defendant he must first be in delicto. Regardless of the propriety for a private or public condemnation of one for a moral delinquency, matters which affect his personal character or reputation are no concern of the courts in their examination of his rights as a litigant. Plaintiff by his conduct did not place himself outside the law. He is not caput lupinum. 4 Black Comm 320. Even illegality as such is but an abstraction and of itself neither causes injury nor creates disability. The status of the deceased as a violator of the law is thus made an irrelevant inquiry."

It is not enough, then, to bar a plaintiff's recovery, that some illegal act be a remote link in the chain of causation.

But, defendant also urges upon us, the illegality complained of infects as well the matter of plaintiff's status on the property itself. We should not, as defendant puts it, "permit plaintiff to use her own illegal conduct as a foundation of her claim that she was on defendant's premises as an invitee, without which status her case falls." In support of the argument we are cited to the Canadian case of Danluk v. Birkner [Ontario], (1946) 3 DLR 172. In this case plaintiff was in a gambling establishment operated by the defendant. An alarm buzzer sounded, indicating a police raid. Plaintiff ran to a door, unhooked the latch, threw it open, and hurriedly escaped from the building. Unfortunately, there were no stairs leading to the ground from this particular door. It opened onto nothing. Plaintiff was seriously injured. In reversing an award of damages, the Ontario court of appeal held, in part, that plaintiff "has not the status in law of an invitee" because, it said, the business (in connection with which the invitation onto the premises is extended) must be a lawful business. Denied, also, was his status as a licensee. "The court will not take cognizance of that which the parties may say was the `consent' given by the occupier," since it involved "`consent' to the frequenter committing the crime."

The reasoning thus set forth we cannot accept. It confuses the fact of consent or invitation with the purpose for which it was given. The editorial note prefacing the report of the case in (1946) 3 DLR, supra, presents a well-reasoned criticism of the opinion, commenting, in part, as follows:

"The main grounds on which the court supports its judgment raise an issue of first impression in this country so far as negligence actions are concerned. Heretofore our courts have not denied recovery to a plaintiff whose conduct might involve criminal or penal consequences; e.g., where he has been injured in a collision while engaged in dangerous driving; or where he has been driving without a license. Why should the criminal liability of the plaintiff in the present case be any more a ground for denying recovery? Presumably, the court would have allowed recovery if the plaintiff had been a plumber called in to do repairs. But suppose he had placed a bet or had entered with that purpose? There is another forum for punishing criminal or penal acts, and to afford the present defendant immunity is to offer him the same subsidy that is granted charitable organizations in some jurisdictions."

Research, however, discloses that the case was not allowed to remain so ruled. The supreme court of Canada, Danluck v. Birkner and Cassey, (1947) SCR 484 ([1947] 3 DLR 337), examined the matter, and, although approving the result below (on the theory that even if plaintiff were an invitee to whom a duty was owed by the occupiers, their duty did not, in the circumstances, extend to the manner of making his exit) was careful to point out that "we must not be taken as approving the grounds upon which the court below proceeded." No more do we.

With the elimination of the defenses revolving around the illegalities charged, there is little left to the appeal. There was an abundance of testimony to take the case to the jury, involving the allegedly dangerous condition of the premises (a view of which had been moved and granted, as a part of plaintiff's case), the conditions of illumination, plaintiff's freedom from contributory negligence, and other necessary elements of her recovery. There was no error in submitting the case to the jury.

Affirmed.

Questions

1. What legal principle is discussed in the case regarding the recovery of damages by a plaintiff who has engaged in illegal activities?

2. How does the court distinguish between an unlawful act that bars recovery and one that is collateral to the cause of action?

3. According to the court's reasoning, why should the fact that the plaintiff participated in an illegal bingo game not preclude her from seeking recovery for her injuries?

4. In what circumstances does the court state that an unlawful act must have a causal connection with the injury in order to bar recovery?

5. How does the court address the argument that the plaintiff's illegal actions should bar her from recovery in the case?

6. According to the court's reasoning, what is required for an unlawful act to bar a plaintiff from recovery?

Takeaways – Bradly and Bishop

Can you explain the differing outcomes in *Bradley* and *Manning*? As the *Manning* court so colorfully observed, "even a rogue may have a cause of action." Is a pinball player more of a rogue than a bingo player? Mrs. Manning had ceased her illegal activity and was on her way home when she was injured. The court found that there was not a substantial causal relationship between Mrs. Manning's prior bingo game and her fall in the parking lot. The bingo game was a "remote link in the chain of causation." But suppose she had been sitting at the bingo table and accidentally struck in the face by the patron sitting next to her when that patron suddenly jumped up flayling her arms and shouting bingo! Would she have a claim agaiint the Bishop? The exuberent patron?

Want to Bet?

The New York Court of Appeals in *Intercontinental Hotels Corp v Golden*, 15 NY2d 9, 14-15; 203 NE2d 210, 212-213; 254 NYS2d 527, 530-531 (1964), declined to determine public policy "by mere reference to the laws" of New York: "Strong public policy is found in prevailing social and moral attitudes of the community."

In holding enforceable in New York a gambling debt incurred in Puerto Rico where gambling was legal and judicially enforceable, the Court was motivated in part by "the changing attitudes of the People of the State of New York."

"The legalization of pari-mutuel betting and the operation of bingo games, as well as a strong movement for legalized off-track betting, indicate that the New York public does not consider authorized gambling a violation of `some prevalent conception of good morals, [or] some deep-rooted tradition of the common weal. "The trend in New York State demonstrates an acceptance of licensed gambling transactions as a morally acceptable activity, not objectionable under the prevailing standards of lawful and approved social conduct in a community. Our newspapers quote the odds on horse races, football games, basketball games and print the names of the winners of the Irish Sweepstakes and the New Hampshire lottery. Informed public sentiment in New York is only against unlicensed gambling, which is unsupervised, unregulated by law and which affords no protection to customers and no assurance of fairness or honesty in the operation of the gambling devices."

The Court further noted that public policy would not be furthered by allowing the defendant to manipulate "public policy" to his advantage: "[I]njustice would result if citizens of this State were allowed to retain the benefits of the winnings in a State where such gambling is legal, but to renege if they were losers."

Licensing Laws

Should a contract to perform a service that requires a license be voided on the grounds that the party rendering the service did not possess the required license? The general rule is that if the reason for requiring a license is to protect the public by ensuring that the licensee has a minimum level of skill or competence, then the lack of a license makes the contract unenforceable. On the other hand, if the purpose behind requiring a license is merely to raise revenue, then the lack of a license does not prohibit enforcement of the contract. (Rest.2d § 181.)

Restraints on Trade – Non-Competition Clauses

Hopper v. All Pet Animal Clinic, Inc.
Supreme Court of Wyoming, 1993
1993 WY 125, 861 P.2d 531

TAYLOR, Justice. Following her graduation from Colorado State University, Dr. Glenna Hopper (Dr. Hopper) began working part-time as a veterinarian at the All Pet Animal Clinic, Inc. (All Pet) in July of 1988. All Pet specialized in the care of small animals; mostly domesticated dogs and cats, and those exotic animals maintained as household pets. Dr. Hopper practiced under the guidance and direction of the President of All Pet, Dr. Robert Bruce Johnson (Dr. Johnson).

Dr. Johnson, on behalf of All Pet, offered Dr. Hopper full-time employment in February of 1989. The oral offer included a specified salary and potential for bonus earnings as well as other terms of employment. According to Dr. Johnson, he conditioned the offer on Dr. Hopper's acceptance of a covenant not to compete, the specific details of which were not discussed at the time. Dr. Hopper commenced full-time employment with All Pet under the oral agreement in March of 1989 and relocated to Laramie, discontinuing her commute from her former residence in Colorado.

A written Employment Agreement incorporating the terms of the oral agreement was finally executed by the parties on December 11, 1989. Ancillary to the provisions for employment, the agreement detailed the terms of a covenant not to compete:

This agreement may be terminated by either party upon 30 days' notice to the other party. Upon termination, Dr. Hopper agrees that she will not practice small animal medicine for a period of three years from the date of termination within 5 miles of the corporate limits of the City of Laramie, Wyoming. Dr. Hopper agrees that the duration and geographic scope of that limitation is reasonable.

The agreement was antedated to be effective to March 3, 1989. . . .

One year later, reacting to a rumor that Dr. Hopper was investigating the purchase of a veterinary practice in Laramie, Dr. Johnson asked his attorney to prepare a letter which was presented to Dr. Hopper. The letter, dated June 17, 1991, stated:

I have learned that you are considering leaving us to take over the small animal part of Dr. Meeboer's practice in Laramie.

When we negotiated the terms of your employment, we agreed that you could leave upon 30 days' notice, but that you would not practice small animal medicine within five miles of Laramie for a three-year period. We do not have any non-competition agreement for large-animal medicine, which therefore does not enter into the picture.

I am willing to release you from the non-competition agreement in return for a cash buy-out. I have worked back from the proportion of the income of All-Pet and Alpine which you contribute and have decided that a reasonable figure would be $40,000.00, to compensate the practice for the loss of business which will happen if you practice small-animal medicine elsewhere in Laramie.

If you are willing to approach the problem in the way I suggest, please let me know and I will have the appropriate paperwork taken care of.
Sincerely,
[Signed]
R. Bruce Johnson,
D.V.M.

Dr. Hopper responded to the letter by denying that she was going to purchase Dr. Meeboer's practice. Dr. Hopper told Dr. Johnson that the Employment Agreement was not worth the paper it was written on and that she could do anything she wanted to do. Dr. Johnson [then] terminated Dr. Hopper's employment . . .

Subsequently, Dr. Hopper purchased Gem City Veterinary Clinic (Gem City), the practice of Dr. Melanie Manning. Beginning on July 15, 1991, Dr. Hopper operated Gem City, in violation of the covenant not to compete, within the City of Laramie and with a practice including large and small animals. Under Dr. Hopper's guidance, Gem City's client list grew from 368 at the time she purchased the practice to approximately 950 at the time of trial. A comparison of client lists disclosed that 187 clients served by Dr. Hopper at Gem City were also clients of All Pet or Alpine. Some of these shared clients received permissible large animal services from Dr.

Hopper. Overall, the small animal work contributed from fifty-one to fifty-two percent of Dr. Hopper's gross income at Gem City.

All Pet and Alpine filed a complaint against Dr. Hopper on November 15, 1991 seeking injunctive relief and damages for breach of the covenant not to compete contained in the Employment Agreement. . . .

The district court, in its Findings of Fact, Conclusions of Law and Judgment, determined that the covenant not to compete was enforceable as a matter of law and contained reasonable durational and geographic limits necessary to protect All Pet's and Alpine's special interests. . . . Dr. Hopper was enjoined from practicing small animal medicine within five miles of the corporate limits of the City of Laramie for a period of three years. . . .

A. The Enforceability of a Covenant Not to Compete

The common law policy against contracts in restraint of trade is one of the oldest and most firmly established. Restatement (Second) of Contracts §§ 185-188 (1981) (Introductory Note at 35). See Dutch Maid Bakeries v. Schleicher, 58 Wyo. 374, 131 P.2d 630, 634 (1942). The traditional disfavor of such restraints means covenants not to compete are construed against the party seeking to enforce them. Commercial Bankers Life Ins. Co. of America v. Smith, 516 N.E.2d 110, 112 (Ind. App. 1987). The initial burden is on the employer to prove the covenant is reasonable and has a fair relation to, and is necessary for, the business interests for which protection is sought. Tench v. Weaver, 374 P.2d 27, 29 (Wyo. 1962).

Two principles, the freedom to contract and the freedom to work, conflict when courts test the enforceability of covenants not to compete. Ridley v. Krout, 63 Wyo. 252, 180 P.2d 124, 128 (1947). There is general recognition that while an employer may seek protection from improper and unfair competition of a former employee, the employer is not entitled to protection against ordinary competition. See, e.g., Duffner v. Alberty, 19 Ark. App. 137, 718 S.W.2d 111, 112 (1986) and American Sec. Services, Inc. v. Vodra, 222 Neb. 480, 385 N.W.2d 73, 78 (1986). The enforceability of a covenant not to compete depends upon a finding that the proper balance exists between the competing interests of the employer and the employee. See Restatement (Second) of Agency § 393 cmt. e (1958) (noting that without a covenant not to compete, an agent, employee, can compete with a principal despite past employment and can begin preparations for future competition, such as purchasing a competitive business, before leaving present employment).

Wyoming adopted a rule of reason inquiry from the Restatement of Contracts testing the validity of a covenant not to compete. Dutch Maid Bakeries, 131 P.2d at 634 (citing Restatement of Contracts §§ 513-515 (1932)); Ridley, 180 P.2d at 127. The present formulation of the rule of reason is contained in Restatement (Second) of Contracts, supra, § 188:

(1) A promise to refrain from competition that imposes a restraint that is ancillary to an otherwise valid transaction or relationship is unreasonably in restraint of trade if
  (a) the restraint is greater than is needed to protect the promisee's legitimate interest, or
  (b) the promisee's need is outweighed by the hardship to the promisor and the likely injury to the public.
(2) Promises imposing restraints that are ancillary to a valid transaction or relationship include the following:
  (a) a promise by the seller of a business not to compete with the buyer in such a way as to injure the value of the business sold;
  (b) a promise by an employee or other agent not to compete with his employer or other principal;
  (c) a promise by a partner not to compete with the partnership.

See also Restatement (Second) of Contracts, supra, §§ 186-187. An often quoted reformulation of the rule of reason inquiry states that "[a] restraint is reasonable only if it (1) is no greater than is required for the protection of the employer, (2) does not impose undue hardship on the employee, and (3) is not injurious to the public." Harlan M. Blake, Employee Agreements Not to Compete, 73 Harv. L.Rev. 625, 648-49 (1960)....

[W]e turn to the rule of reason inquiry....

The special interests of All Pet and Alpine identified by the district court as findings of fact are not clearly erroneous. Dr. Hopper moved to Laramie upon completion of her degree prior to any significant professional contact with the community. Her introduction to All Pet's and Alpine's clients, client files, pricing policies, and practice development techniques provided information which exceeded the skills she brought to her employment. While she was a licensed and trained veterinarian when she accepted employment, the additional exposure to clients and knowledge of clinic operations her employers shared with her had a monetary value for which the employers are entitled to reasonable protection from irreparable harm. See Reddy, 298 S.E.2d at 912-14 (discussing the economic analysis applied to restrictive covenants). The proven loss of 187 of All Pet's and Alpine's clients to Dr. Hopper's new practice sufficiently demonstrated actual harm from unfair competition.

The reasonableness, in a given fact situation, of the limitations placed on a former employee by a covenant not to compete are determinations made by the court as a matter of law. See, e.g., Jarrett v. Hamilton, 179 Ga. App. 422, 346 S.E.2d 875,

304 CHAPTER 5 ILLEGAL AND UNCONSCIONABLE CONTRACTS

876 (1986). Therefore, the district court's conclusions of law about the reasonableness of the type of activity, geographic, and durational limits contained in the covenant are subject to de novo review.

. . [I]n Cukjati, 772 S.W.2d at 216, 218, the Court of Appeals of Texas held a covenant not to compete was unreasonable because it limited a veterinarian from practicing within twelve miles of his former employer's clinic in North Irving, a community within the Dallas-Fort Worth metropolitan area. Because evidence from that proceeding disclosed that Dallas area residents are unlikely to travel more than a few miles for pet care, the court found the restriction unreasonable. Id. at 218. The number of veterinarians and the demands upon their services obviously varies between Laramie, Wyoming and metropolitan Dallas, Texas, creating a different usage pattern. We believe the reasonableness of individual limitations contained in a specific covenant not to compete must be assessed based upon the facts of that proceeding. Ridley, 180 P.2d at 131. . . .

Enforcement of the practice restrictions Dr. Hopper accepted as part of her covenant not to compete does not create an unreasonable restraint of trade. While the specific terms of the covenant failed to define the practice of small animal medicine, the parties' trade usage provided a conforming standard of domesticated dogs and cats along with exotic animals maintained as household pets. As a veterinarian licensed to practice in Wyoming, Dr. Hopper was therefore permitted to earn a living in her chosen profession without relocating by practicing large animal medicine, a significant area of practice in this state. The restriction on the type of activity contained in the covenant was sufficiently limited to avoid undue hardship to Dr. Hopper while protecting the special interests of All Pet and Alpine. . . .

The public will not suffer injury from enforcement of the covenant. . . .

The geographical limit contained in the covenant not to compete restricts Dr. Hopper from practicing within a five mile radius of the corporate limits of Laramie. As a matter of law, this limit is reasonable in this circumstance. The evidence presented at trial indicated that the clients of All Pet and Alpine were located throughout the county. Despite Wyoming's rural character, the five mile restriction effectively limited unfair competition without presenting an undue hardship. Dr. Hopper could, for example, have opened a practice at other locations within the county.

A durational limitation should be reasonably related to the legitimate interest which the employer is seeking to protect. Restatement (Second) of Contracts, supra, § 188 cmt. b. . . .

A one year durational limit sufficiently secures All Pet's and Alpine's interests in pricing policies and practice development information. Pricing policies at All Pet and Alpine were changed yearly, according to Dr. Johnson, to reflect changes in material and service costs provided by the clinics as well as new procedures. Practice development information, especially in a learned profession, loses its value quickly as technological change occurs and new reference material become available. We hold, as a matter of law, that enforcement of a one year durational limit is reasonable and sufficiently protects the interests of All Pet and Alpine without violating public policy. . . . Because we hold that the covenant's three year durational term imposed a partially unreasonable restraint of trade, we remand for a modification of the judgment to enjoin Dr. Hopper from unfair competition for a duration of one year from the date of termination. . . .

A well-drafted covenant not to compete preserves a careful and necessary economic balance in our society. While there are many layers to the employer-employee relationship, preventing unfair competition from employees who misuse trade secrets or special influence over customers serves public policy. Tempering the balance is the need to protect employees from unfair restraints on competition which defeat broad policy goals in favor of small business and individual advancement. Courts, in reviewing covenants not to compete, must consider these policy implications in assessing the reasonableness of the restraint as it applies to both employer and employee.

Affirmed as modified and remanded for issuance of a judgment in conformity herewith.

Questions

1. What is the initial burden on the employer regarding the enforceability of a covenant not to compete?

2. What are the three factors that determine the reasonableness of a covenant not to compete?

3. How did the court determine the reasonableness of the geographic limit in this case?

4. Why did the court find that the restriction on the type of activity in the covenant not to compete was reasonable?

5. What was the court's ruling regarding the durational limit in the covenant not to compete, and what factors influenced their decision?

Central Adjustment Bureau, Inc. v. Ingram
Supreme Court of Tennessee, 1984
678 S.W.2d 28

DROWOTA, Justice. . . . [T]he Court addresses the issue of whether a covenant not to compete, the geographic and time limitations of which are unnecessarily broad, can be judicially modified so as to make the covenant reasonable and enforceable.

The plaintiff-employer, Central Adjustment Bureau, a Texas corporation whose home office is in Dallas, Texas, is qualified to do business in Tennessee as a collector of past-due debts. It has 25 branch offices throughout the United States, including a branch in Nashville, Tennessee. The defendants are former employees who left Central Adjustment Bureau (hereinafter CAB) in 1979 to form Ingram & Associates, a company which competed directly with CAB. All of the defendants had signed covenants not to compete with CAB. After the defendants left, CAB brought suit in Chancery Court seeking both compensatory and injunctive relief. According to CAB's allegations, the defendants were liable in tort and for breach of the non-competition covenants.

The Chancellor found that the non-competition covenants were unreasonably broad with regard to geographical and time limitations. The Chancellor, however, modified these restrictions enforcing them as modified by injunctive relief. . . .

The Court of Appeals reversed the Chancellor on the issue of the covenant not to compete, holding . . . that the covenants were unenforceable because they were unreasonably broad in their geographic and time limitations. . . .

As a general rule, restrictive covenants in employment contracts will be enforced if they are reasonable under the particular circumstances. Allright Auto Parks, Inc. v. Berry, 219 Tenn. 280, 409 S.W.2d 361 (1966). The rule of reasonableness applies to consideration as well as to other matters such as territorial and time limitations. Di Deeland v. Colvin, 208 Tenn. 551, 554, 347 S.W.2d 483, 484 (1961). Whether there is adequate consideration to support a non-competition covenant signed during an on-going employment relationship depends upon the facts of each case. Davies & Davies Agency, Inc. v. Davies, 298 N.W.2d 127 (Minn. 1980).

We agree with both the Chancellor and the Court of Appeals that the restrictions were unreasonably broad. As enforced by the Chancellor, however, the covenants were reasonable. The question before this Court is whether the Chancellor had the authority to modify a covenant not to compete which is otherwise unreasonably broad. Tennessee courts have not previously addressed this question. As a case of first impression, therefore, it is appropriate to look for guidance to decisions by courts having considered this question. See generally, Annot. 61 A.L.R.3d 397 (1975) (collecting cases).

At one time the majority of courts employed the "all or nothing at all" rule. Under this rule, a court either enforces the contract as written or rejects it altogether. A covenant containing a term greater than necessary to protect the employer's interest is void in its entirety. Courts employing this rule reason that partial enforcement delegates to courts, when the covenants prove excessive, power to make private agreements.

The recent trend, however, has been away from the all or nothing at all rule in favor of some form of judicial modification. Several courts have explicitly overruled their own prior case law and adopted judicial modification. Our research indicates some form of judicial modification has now been adopted by the majority of jurisdictions. See, Annot. 61 A.L.R.3d 397 (1975). We think that under appropriate circumstances, some form of judicial modification should be permitted, especially when, as in the case before us, the covenant specifically provides for modification.

Courts have taken one of two approaches in modifying restrictive covenants. The "blue pencil" rule provides that an unreasonable restriction against competition may be modified and enforced to the extent that a grammatically meaningful reasonable restriction remains after the words making the restriction unreasonable are stricken. Solari Industries, Inc. v. Malady, supra, 264 A.2d at 57. For example, in a restriction on soliciting business clients in "Toledo, Ohio, and the United States" the court would "blue pencil" or mark out "Ohio, and the United States" leaving the covenant enforceable in Toledo. See, Briggs v. Butler, 140 Ohio St. 499, 45 N.E.2d 757 (1942).

The blue pencil rule has the advantage of simplicity and prevents a court from actually rewriting private agreements. On the other hand, the contract still fails if the offending provision cannot be stricken. Often a divisible term contains an integral part of the agreement so that "blue penciling" the provision emasculates the contract. Raimonde v. Van Vlerah, 42 Ohio St.2d 21, 325 N.E.2d 544 (1975). The rule has been criticized as emphasizing form over substance. Bess v. Bothman, 257 N.W.2d 791 (Minn. 1977). It has been rejected as against the weight of authority and criticized by writers such as Williston and Corbin. See, RESTATEMENT (SECOND) OF CONTRACTS § 184 reporter's note; 6A Corbin on Contracts, §§ 1390 and 1394 (1968); 14 Williston on Contracts, § 1647B, 1647C (3d ed. 1972).

The most recent trend, therefore, has been to abandon the "blue pencil" rule in favor of a rule of reasonableness. See, e.g., Ehlers v. Iowa Warehouse Co., supra; Bess v. Bothman, supra; Karpinski v. Ingrasci, 28 N.Y.2d 45, 320 N.Y.S.2d 1, 268 N.E.2d 751 (1971); Solari Industries, Inc. v. Malady, supra; and Raimonde v. Van Vlerah, supra. This rule provides that unless the circumstances indicate bad faith on the part of the employer, a court will enforce covenants not to compete to the extent that they are reasonably necessary to protect the employer's interest "without imposing undue hardship on the employee when the public interest is not adversely affected." Ehlers v. Iowa Warehouse Co., supra, at 370.

We are persuaded that the rule of reasonableness is the better rule. It is consistent with and an extension of the rule of reasonableness set forth in Allright Auto Parks v. Berry, supra. In adopting it, we do not intend a retreat from the general rule precluding courts from creating new contracts for parties. See, Bob Pearsall Motors, Inc. v. Regal Chrysler-Plymouth, Inc., 521 S.W.2d 578 (Tenn. 1975). We are guided instead by the special nature of covenants not to compete already discussed. Further, as noted by two leading commentators on contracts:

"This is not making a new contract for the parties; it is a choice among the possible effects of the one that they made, establishing the one that is the most desirable for the contractors and the public at large. Partial enforcement involves much less of a variation from the effects intended by the parties than total nonenforcement would. If the arguments in favor of partial enforcement are convincing, no court need hesitate to give them effect." Williston & Corbin, On the Doctrine of Beit v. Beit, 23 Conn.B.J. 40, 49-50 (1949).

We recognize the force of the objection that judicial modification could permit an employer to insert oppressive and unnecessary restrictions into a contract knowing that the courts can modify and enforce the covenant on reasonable terms. Especially when the contract allows the employer attorney's fees, the employer may have nothing to lose by going to court, thereby provoking needless litigation. See, Rector-Phillips-Morse, Inc. v. Vroman, supra, 489 S.W.2d at 5. If there is credible evidence to sustain a finding that a contract is deliberately unreasonable and oppressive, then the covenant is invalid. Ehlers v. Iowa Warehouse Co., supra, at 374. Even in the absence of evidence sufficient to support a finding of invalidity, a court may well find in the course of determining reasonableness that a contractual provision for attorney's fees is unreasonable either in whole or in part.

In the instant case, we hold that the Chancellor acted properly in enforcing the contract on reasonable terms against the defendants. We further find no credible evidence to sustain a finding of bad faith on the part of CAB or to warrant invalidation of the contractual provision on attorney's fees.

The judgment of the Court of Appeals as to all defendants is reversed and the judgment of the Chancellor is affirmed.

Questions

1. What was the Court of Appeals' decision regarding the enforceability of the covenant not to compete in the case?

2. According to the court, what is the general rule regarding the enforcement of restrictive covenants in employment contracts?

3. What are the two approaches that courts have taken in modifying restrictive covenants?

4. Why did the court decide to adopt the rule of reasonableness in this case?

5. What factors did the court consider in determining whether the covenant not to compete should be enforced on reasonable terms?

Takeaways – Central Adjustment Bureau v. Ingram

If a non-competition clause is determined to be against public policy because it is too broad with respect to duration of time or geographical area, does the court have the option of rewriting it? *Central Adjustment Bureau* suggests three possibilities: an "all or nothing rule," a "blue pencil rule" and a "rule of reasonableness." Which rule did the court opt for and which one do you think is the better rule?

Drafting Tip – Illegality

Even if part of a contract is determined to be unenforceable because it is illegal, against public policy or unconscionable, that does not necessarily mean that the remainder of the contractual terms cannot be enforced. The careful drafter who wants to ensure that the valid portions of a contract remain enforceable might use language such as:

"If any provision of this Contract is held unenforceable, then such provision will be modified to reflect the parties' intention. All remaining provisions of this Contract shall remain in full force and effect."

Prenuptial Agreements and Public Policy

Simeone v. Simeone
Supreme Court of Pennsylvania, 1990
525 Pa. 392, 581 A.2d 162

FLAHERTY, Justice. At issue in this appeal is the validity of a prenuptial agreement executed between the appellant, Catherine E. Walsh Simeone, and the appellee, Frederick A. Simeone. At the time of their marriage, in 1975, appellant was a twenty-three year old nurse and appellee was a thirty-nine year old neurosurgeon. Appellee had an income of approximately $90,000 per year, and appellant was unemployed. Appellee also had assets worth approximately $300,000. On the eve of the parties' wedding, appellee's attorney presented appellant with a prenuptial agreement to be signed. Appellant, without the benefit of counsel, signed the agreement. Appellee's attorney had not advised appellant regarding any legal rights that the agreement surrendered. The parties are in disagreement as to whether appellant knew in advance of that date that such an agreement would be presented for signature. Appellant denies having had such knowledge and claims to have signed under adverse circumstances, which, she contends, provide a basis for declaring it void.

The agreement limited appellant to support payments of $200 per week in the event of separation or divorce, subject to a maximum total payment of $25,000. The parties separated in 1982, and, in 1984, divorce proceedings were commenced. Between 1982 and 1984 appellee made payments which satisfied the $25,000 limit. In 1985, appellant filed a claim for alimony pendente lite. A master's report upheld the validity of the prenuptial agreement and denied this claim. Exceptions to the master's report were dismissed by the Court of Common Pleas of Philadelphia County. The Superior Court affirmed. Simeone v. Simeone, 380 Pa.Super. 37, 551 A.2d 219 (1988).

We granted allowance of appeal because uncertainty was expressed by the Superior Court regarding the meaning of our plurality decision in Estate of Geyer, 516 Pa. 492, 533 A.2d 423 (1987) (Opinion Announcing Judgment of the Court). The Superior Court viewed Geyer as permitting a prenuptial agreement to be upheld if it either made a reasonable provision for the spouse or was entered after a full and fair disclosure of the general financial positions of the parties and the statutory rights being relinquished. Appellant contends that this interpretation of Geyer is in error insofar as it requires disclosure of statutory rights only in cases where there has not been made a reasonable provision for the spouse. Inasmuch as the courts below held that the provision made for appellant was a reasonable one, appellant's efforts to overturn the agreement have focused upon an assertion that there was an inadequate disclosure of statutory rights. Appellant continues to assert, however, that the payments provided in the agreement were less than reasonable. . . .

There is no longer validity in the implicit presumption that supplied the basis for Geyer and similar earlier decisions. Such decisions rested upon a belief that spouses are of unequal status and that women are not knowledgeable enough to understand the nature of contracts that they enter. Society has advanced, however, to the point where women are no longer regarded as the "weaker" party in marriage, or in society generally. Indeed, the stereotype that women serve as homemakers while men work as breadwinners is no longer viable. Quite often today both spouses are income earners. Nor is there viability in the presumption that women are uninformed, uneducated, and readily subjected to unfair advantage in marital agreements. Indeed, women nowadays quite often have substantial education, financial awareness, income, and assets.

Accordingly, the law has advanced to recognize the equal status of men and women in our society. See, e.g., Pa. Const. art. 1, § 28 (constitutional prohibition of sex discrimination in laws of the Commonwealth). Paternalistic presumptions and protections that arose to shelter women from the inferiorities and incapacities which they were perceived as having in earlier times have, appropriately, been discarded. See Geyer, 516 Pa. at 509-14, 533 A.2d at 431-33 (dissenting opinion of Mr. Chief Justice Nix setting forth detailed history of case law evidencing a shift away from the former paternalistic approach of protecting women towards a newer approach of equal treatment). It would be inconsistent, therefore, to perpetuate the standards governing prenuptial agreements that were described in Geyer and similar decisions, as these reflected a paternalistic approach that is now insupportable.

Further, Geyer and its predecessors embodied substantial departures from traditional rules of contract law, to the extent that they allowed consideration of the knowledge of the contracting parties and reasonableness of their bargain as factors governing whether to uphold an agreement. Traditional principles of contract law provide perfectly adequate remedies where contracts are procured through fraud, misrepresentation, or duress. Consideration of other factors, such as the knowledge of the parties and the reasonableness of their bargain, is inappropriate. See Geyer, 516 Pa. at 516-17, 533 A.2d at 434-35 (Flaherty, J. dissenting). Prenuptial agreements are contracts, and, as such, should be evaluated under the same criteria as are applicable to other types of contracts. See Geyer, 516 Pa. at 508, 533 A.2d at 431 ("These agreements are nothing more than contracts and should be treated as such." (Nix, C.J. dissenting)). Absent fraud, misrepresentation, or duress, spouses should be bound by the terms of their agreements.

Contracting parties are normally bound by their agreements, without regard to whether the terms thereof were read and fully understood and irrespective of whether the agreements embodied reasonable or good bargains. See Standard Venetian Blind Co. v. American Empire Insurance Co., 503 Pa. 300, 305, 469 A.2d 563, 566 (1983) (failure to read a contract does not warrant avoidance or nullification of its provisions); Estate of Brant, 463 Pa. 230, 235, 344 A.2d 806, 809 (1975); Bollinger v.

Central Pennsylvania Quarry Stripping & Construction Co., 425 Pa. 430, 432, 229 A.2d 741, 742 (1967) ("Once a person enters into a written agreement he builds around himself a stone wall, from which he cannot escape by merely asserting he had not understood what he was signing."); Montgomery v. Levy, 406 Pa. 547, 550, 177 A.2d 448, 450 (1962) (one is legally bound to know the terms of the contract entered). Based upon these principles, the terms of the present prenuptial agreement must be regarded as binding, without regard to whether the terms were fully understood by appellant. Ignorantia non excusat.

Accordingly, we find no merit in a contention raised by appellant that the agreement should be declared void on the ground that she did not consult with independent legal counsel. To impose a per se requirement that parties entering a prenuptial agreement must obtain independent legal counsel would be contrary to traditional principles of contract law, and would constitute a paternalistic and unwarranted interference with the parties' freedom to enter contracts.

Further, the reasonableness of a prenuptial bargain is not a proper subject for judicial review. Geyer and earlier decisions required that, at least where there had been an inadequate disclosure made by the parties, the bargain must have been reasonable at its inception. See Geyer, 516 Pa. at 503, 533 A.2d at 428. Some have even suggested that prenuptial agreements should be examined with regard to whether their terms remain reasonable at the time of dissolution of the parties' marriage.

By invoking inquiries into reasonableness, however, the functioning and reliability of prenuptial agreements is severely undermined. Parties would not have entered such agreements, and, indeed, might not have entered their marriages, if they did not expect their agreements to be strictly enforced. If parties viewed an agreement as reasonable at the time of its inception, as evidenced by their having signed the agreement, they should be foreclosed from later trying to evade its terms by asserting that it was not in fact reasonable. Pertinently, the present agreement contained a clause reciting that "each of the parties considers this agreement fair, just and reasonable. . . ."

Further, everyone who enters a long-term agreement knows that circumstances can change during its term, so that what initially appeared desirable might prove to be an unfavorable bargain. Such are the risks that contracting parties routinely assume. Certainly, the possibilities of illness, birth of children, reliance upon a spouse, career change, financial gain or loss, and numerous other events that can occur in the course of a marriage cannot be regarded as unforeseeable. If parties choose not to address such matters in their prenuptial agreements, they must be regarded as having contracted to bear the risk of events that alter the value of their bargains.

We are reluctant to interfere with the power of persons contemplating marriage to agree upon, and to act in reliance upon, what they regard as an acceptable distribution scheme for their property. A court should not ignore the parties' expressed intent by proceeding to determine whether a prenuptial agreement was, in the court's view, reasonable at the time of its inception or the time of divorce. These are exactly the sorts of judicial determinations that such agreements are designed to avoid. Rare indeed is the agreement that is beyond possible challenge when reasonableness is placed at issue. Parties can routinely assert some lack of fairness relating to the inception of the agreement, thereby placing the validity of the agreement at risk. And if reasonableness at the time of divorce were to be taken into account an additional problem would arise. Virtually nonexistent is the marriage in which there has been absolutely no change in the circumstances of either spouse during the course of the marriage. Every change in circumstance, foreseeable or not, and substantial or not, might be asserted as a basis for finding that an agreement is no longer reasonable.

In discarding the approach of Geyer that permitted examination of the reasonableness of prenuptial agreements and allowed inquiries into whether parties had attained informed understandings of the rights they were surrendering, we do not depart from the longstanding principle that a full and fair disclosure of the financial positions of the parties is required. Absent this disclosure, a material misrepresentation in the inducement for entering a prenuptial agreement may be asserted. Hillegass, 431 Pa. at 152-53, 244 A.2d at 676-77. Parties to these agreements do not quite deal at arm's length, but rather at the time the contract is entered into stand in a relation of mutual confidence and trust that calls for disclosure of their financial resources. Id., 431 Pa. at 149, 244 A.2d at 675; Gelb Estate, 425 Pa. 117, 120, 228 A.2d 367, 369 (1967). It is well settled that this disclosure need not be exact, so long as it is "full and fair." Kaufmann Estate, 404 Pa. 131, 136 n. 8, 171 A.2d 48, 51 n. 8 (1961). In essence therefore, the duty of disclosure under these circumstances is consistent with traditional principles of contract law. . . .

Appellant's final contention is that the agreement was executed under conditions of duress in that it was presented to her at 5 p.m. on the eve of her wedding, a time when she could not seek counsel without the trauma, expense, and embarrassment of postponing the wedding. The master found this claim not credible. The courts below affirmed that finding, upon an ample evidentiary basis.

Although appellant testified that she did not discover until the eve of her wedding that there was going to be a prenuptial agreement, testimony from a number of other witnesses was to the contrary. Appellee testified that, although the final version of the agreement was indeed presented to appellant on the eve of the wedding, he had engaged in several discussions with appellant regarding the contents of the agreement during the six month period preceding that date. Another witness testified that appellant mentioned, approximately two or three weeks before the wedding, that she was going to enter a prenuptial agreement. Yet another witness confirmed that, during the months preceding the wedding, appellant participated in several discussions of prenuptial agreements. And the legal counsel who prepared the agreement for appellee testified that, prior to the eve of the wedding, changes were made in the agreement to increase the sums payable to appellant in the event of separation or divorce. He also stated that he was present when the agreement was signed and that appellant expressed absolutely no reluctance about signing. It should be noted, too, that during the months when the agreement was being discussed appellant had more than sufficient time to consult with independent legal counsel if she had so desired. See generally Carrier v. William Penn Broadcasting Corp., 426 Pa. 427, 431, 233 A.2d 519, 521 (1967) (concept of duress as applied to contracting parties). Under these circumstances, there was plainly no error in finding that appellant failed to prove duress.

Hence, the courts below properly held that the present agreement is valid and enforceable. . . .

Order affirmed.

PAPADAKOS, Justice, concurring. . . .I cannot join the opinion authored by Mr. Justice Flaherty, because, it must be clear to all readers, it contains a number of unnecessary and unwarranted declarations regarding the "equality" of women. Mr. Justice Flaherty believes that, with the hard-fought victory of the Equal Rights Amendment in Pennsylvania, all vestiges of inequality between the sexes have been erased and women are now treated equally under the law. I fear my colleague does not live in the real world. If I did not know him better I would think that his statements smack of male chauvinism, an attitude that "you women asked for it, now live with it." If you want to know about equality of women, just ask them about comparable wages for comparable work. Just ask them about sexual harassment in the workplace. Just ask them about the sexual discrimination in the Executive Suites of big business. And the list of discrimination based on sex goes on and on.

I view prenuptial agreements as being in the nature of contracts of adhesion with one party generally having greater authority than the other who deals in a subservient role. I believe the law protects the subservient party, regardless of that party's sex, to insure equal protection and treatment under the law.

The present case does not involve the broader issues to which the gratuitous declarations in question are addressed, and it is injudicious to offer declarations in a case which does not involve those issues. Especially when those declarations are inconsistent with reality.

McDERMOTT, Justice, dissenting. . . Were a contract of marriage, the most intimate relationship between two people, not the surrender of freedom, an offering of self in love, sacrifice, hope for better or for worse, the begetting of children and the offer of effort, labor, precious time and care for the safety and prosperity of their union, then the majority would find me among them. . . .

> At the time of dissolution of the marriage, a spouse should be able to avoid the operation of a pre-nuptial agreement upon clear and convincing proof that, despite the existence of full and fair disclosure at the time of the execution of the agreement, the agreement is nevertheless so inequitable and unfair that it should not be enforced in a court of this state. Although the spouse attempting to avoid the operation of the agreement will admittedly have a difficult burden given the standard of proof, and the fact of full and fair disclosure, we must not close our courts to relief where to enforce an agreement will result in unfairness and inequity. The majority holds to the view, without waiver, that parties, having contracted with full and fair disclosure, should be made to suffer the consequences of their bargains. In so holding, the majority has given no weight to the other side of the scales: the state's paramount interest in the preservation of marriage and the family relationship, and the protection of parties to a marriage who may be rendered wards of the state, unable to provide for their own reasonable needs. Our sister states have found such treatment too short a shrift for so fundamental a unit of society. . . .

Questions

1. How does the court in this case challenge the notion of unequal status between spouses and the stereotype of women as homemakers?

2. According to the court, why should prenuptial agreements be evaluated under the same criteria as other types of contracts?

3. Why does the court argue against examining the reasonableness of prenuptial agreements at the time of divorce?

4. What is the court's stance on the requirement for independent legal counsel in prenuptial agreements?

5. What is the court's view on the duty of disclosure in prenuptial agreements and how does it relate to traditional principles of contract law?

Takeaways – Simeone v. Simeone

> It is fair to say that up until the latter half of the 20th century, women enjoyed the status of "favoreds" under the law. Contract law presumed in many instances that they lacked bargaining power and, in some situations, business sophistication. *Simeone*, and cases like it, demonstrate that the favored status of women no longer exists.

Should public policy take into account the socio-economic position of parties to a contract?

Surrogacy Contracts

Matter of Baby M.
Supreme Court of New Jersey, 1988
109 N.J. 396, 537 A.2d 1227

WILENTZ, C.J. In this matter the Court is asked to determine the validity of a contract that purports to provide a new way of bringing children into a family. For a fee of $10,000, a woman agrees to be artificially inseminated with the semen of another woman's husband; she is to conceive a child, carry it to term, and after its birth surrender it to the natural father and his wife. The intent of the contract is that the child's natural mother will thereafter be forever separated from her child. The wife is to adopt the child, and she and the natural father are to be regarded as its parents for all purposes. The contract providing for this is called a "surrogacy contract," the natural mother inappropriately called the "surrogate mother."

We invalidate the surrogacy contract because it conflicts with the law and public policy of this State. While we recognize the depth of the yearning of infertile couples to have their own children, we find the payment of money to a "surrogate" mother illegal, perhaps criminal, and potentially degrading to women. Although in this case we grant custody to the natural father, the evidence having clearly proved such custody to be in the best interests of the infant, we void both the termination of the surrogate mother's parental rights and the adoption of the child by the wife/stepparent. We thus restore the "surrogate" as the mother of the child. We remand the issue of the natural mother's visitation rights to the trial court, since that issue was not reached below and the record before us is not sufficient to permit us to decide it de novo.

We find no offense to our present laws where a woman voluntarily and without payment agrees to act as a "surrogate" mother, provided that she is not subject to a binding agreement to surrender her child. Moreover, our holding today does not preclude the Legislature from altering the current statutory scheme, within constitutional limits, so as to permit surrogacy contracts. Under current law, however, the surrogacy agreement before us is illegal and invalid.

INVALIDITY AND UNENFORCEABILITY OF SURROGACY CONTRACT

We have concluded that this surrogacy contract is invalid. Our conclusion has two bases: direct conflict with existing statutes and conflict with the public policies of this State, as expressed in its statutory and decisional law.

One of the surrogacy contract's basic purposes, to achieve the adoption of a child through private placement, though permitted in New Jersey "is very much disfavored." Sees v. Baber, 74 N.J. 201, 217 (1977). Its use of money for this purpose and we have no doubt whatsoever that the money is being paid to obtain an adoption and not, as the Sterns argue, for the personal services of Mary Beth Whitehead is illegal and perhaps criminal. N.J.S.A. 9:3-54. In addition to the inducement of money, there is the coercion of contract: the natural mother's irrevocable agreement, prior to birth, even prior to conception, to surrender the child to the adoptive couple. Such an agreement is totally unenforceable in private placement adoption. Sees, 74 N.J. at 212-14. Even where the adoption is through an approved agency, the formal agreement to surrender occurs only after birth (as we read N.J.S.A. 9:2-16 and -17, and similar statutes), and then, by regulation, only after the birth mother has been offered counseling. N.J.A.C. 10:121A-5.4(c). Integral to these invalid provisions of the surrogacy contract is the related agreement, equally invalid, on the part of the natural mother to cooperate with, and not to contest, proceedings to terminate her parental rights, as well as her contractual concession, in aid of the adoption, that the child's best interests would be served by awarding custody to the natural father and his wife all of this before she has even conceived, and, in some cases, before she has the slightest idea of what the natural father and adoptive mother are like.

The foregoing provisions not only directly conflict with New Jersey statutes, but also offend long-established State policies. These critical terms, which are at the heart of the contract, are invalid and unenforceable; the conclusion therefore follows, without more, that the entire contract is unenforceable.

A. Conflict with Statutory Provisions

The surrogacy contract conflicts with: (1) laws prohibiting the use of money in connection with adoptions; (2) laws requiring proof of parental unfitness or abandonment before termination of parental rights is ordered or an adoption is granted; and (3) laws that make surrender of custody and consent to adoption revocable in private placement adoptions.

(1) Our law prohibits paying or accepting money in connection with any placement of a child for adoption. N.J.S.A. 9:3-54a. Violation is a high misdemeanor. N.J.S.A. 9:3-54c. Excepted are fees of an approved agency (which must be a non-profit entity, N.J.S.A. 9:3-38a) and certain expenses in connection with childbirth. N.J.S.A. 9:3-54b.[4]

Considerable care was taken in this case to structure the surrogacy arrangement so as not to violate this prohibition. . . . Nevertheless, it seems clear that the money was paid and accepted in connection with an adoption.. . .

The prohibition of our statute is strong. Violation constitutes a high misdemeanor, N.J.S.A. 9:3-54c, a third-degree crime, N.J.S.A. 2C:43-1b, carrying a penalty of three to five years imprisonment. N.J.S.A. 2C:43-6a(3). The evils inherent in baby-bartering are loathsome for a myriad of reasons. The child is sold without regard for whether the purchasers will be suitable parents. N. Baker, Baby Selling: The Scandal of Black Market Adoption 7 (1978). The natural mother does not receive the benefit of counseling and guidance to assist her in making a decision that may affect her for a lifetime. In fact, the monetary incentive to sell her child may, depending on her financial circumstances, make her decision less voluntary. . . .

The provision in the surrogacy contract whereby the mother irrevocably agrees to surrender custody of her child and to terminate her parental rights conflicts with the settled interpretation of New Jersey statutory law. There is only one irrevocable consent, and that is the one explicitly provided for by statute: a consent to surrender of custody and a placement with an approved agency or with DYFS. The provision in the surrogacy contract, agreed to before conception, requiring the natural mother to surrender custody of the child without any right of revocation is one more indication of the essential nature of this transaction: the creation of a contractual system of termination and adoption designed to circumvent our statutes.

B. Public Policy Considerations

The surrogacy contract's invalidity, resulting from its direct conflict with the above statutory provisions, is further underlined when its goals and means are measured against New Jersey's public policy. The contract's basic premise, that the natural parents can decide in advance of birth which one is to have custody of the child, bears no relationship to the settled law that the child's best interests shall determine custody. . . .

Under the contract, the natural mother is irrevocably committed before she knows the strength of her bond with her child. She never makes a totally voluntary, informed decision, for quite clearly any decision prior to the baby's birth is, in the most important sense, uninformed, and any decision after that, compelled by a preexisting contractual commitment, the threat of a lawsuit, and the inducement of a $10,000 payment, is less than totally voluntary. Her interests are of little concern to those who controlled this transaction. . . .

Worst of all, however, is the contract's total disregard of the best interests of the child. There is not the slightest suggestion that any inquiry will be made at any time to determine the fitness of the Sterns as custodial parents, of Mrs. Stern as an adoptive parent, their superiority to Mrs. Whitehead, or the effect on the child of not living with her natural mother.

This is the sale of a child, or, at the very least, the sale of a mother's right to her child, the only mitigating factor being that one of the purchasers is the father. Almost every evil that prompted the prohibition on the payment of money in connection with adoptions exists here.

The differences between an adoption and a surrogacy contract should be noted, since it is asserted that the use of money in connection with surrogacy does not pose the risks found where money buys an adoption. Katz, "Surrogate Motherhood and the Baby-Selling Laws," 20 Colum.J.L. & Soc.Probs. 1 (1986).

First, and perhaps most important, all parties concede that it is unlikely that surrogacy will survive without money. Despite the alleged selfless motivation of surrogate mothers, if there is no payment, there will be no surrogates, or very few. That conclusion contrasts with adoption; for obvious reasons, there remains a steady supply, albeit insufficient, despite the prohibitions against payment. The adoption itself, relieving the natural mother of the financial burden of supporting an infant, is in some sense the equivalent of payment.

Second, the use of money in adoptions does not produce the problem conception occurs, and usually the birth itself, before illicit funds are offered. With surrogacy, the "problem," if one views it as such, consisting of the purchase of a woman's procreative capacity, at the risk of her life, is caused by and originates with the offer of money.

Third, with the law prohibiting the use of money in connection with adoptions, the built-in financial pressure of the unwanted pregnancy and the consequent support obligation do not lead the mother to the highest paying, ill-suited, adoptive parents. She is just as well-off surrendering the child to an approved agency. In surrogacy, the highest bidders will presumably become the adoptive parents regardless of suitability, so long as payment of money is permitted.

Fourth, the mother's consent to surrender her child in adoptions is revocable, even after surrender of the child, unless it be to an approved agency, where by regulation there are protections against an ill-advised surrender. In surrogacy, consent occurs so early that no amount of advice would satisfy the potential mother's need, yet the consent is irrevocable.

In the scheme contemplated by the surrogacy contract in this case, a middle man, propelled by profit, promotes the sale. Whatever idealism may have motivated any of the participants, the profit motive predominates, permeates, and ultimately governs the transaction. The demand for children is great and the supply small. The availability of contraception, abortion, and the greater willingness of single mothers to bring up their children has led to a shortage of babies offered for adoption. See N. Baker, Baby Selling: The Scandal of Black Market Adoption, supra; Adoption and

Foster Care, 1975: Hearings on Baby Selling Before the Subcomm. On Children and Youth of the Senate Comm. on Labor and Public Welfare, 94th Cong.1st Sess. 6 (1975) (Statement of Joseph H. Reid, Executive Director, Child Welfare League of America, Inc.). The situation is ripe for the entry of the middleman who will bring some equilibrium into the market by increasing the supply through the use of money. . . .

The point is made that Mrs. Whitehead agreed to the surrogacy arrangement, supposedly fully understanding the consequences. Putting aside the issue of how compelling her need for money may have been, and how significant her understanding of the consequences, we suggest that her consent is irrelevant. There are, in a civilized society, some things that money cannot buy. In America, we decided long ago that merely because conduct purchased by money was "voluntary" did not mean that it was good or beyond regulation and prohibition. West Coast Hotel Co. v. Parrish, 300 U.S. 379, 57 S.Ct. 578, 81 L.Ed. 703 (1937). Employers can no longer buy labor at the lowest price they can bargain for, even though that labor is "voluntary," 29 U.S.C. § 206 (1982), or buy women's labor for less money than paid to men for the same job, 29 U.S.C. § 206(d), or purchase the agreement of children to perform oppressive labor, 29 U.S.C. § 212, or purchase the agreement of workers to subject themselves to unsafe or unhealthful working conditions, 29 U.S.C. §§ 651 to 678. (Occupational Safety and Health Act of 1970). There are, in short, values that society deems more important than granting to wealth whatever it can buy, be it labor, love, or life. Whether this principle recommends prohibition of surrogacy, which presumably sometimes results in great satisfaction to all of the parties, is not for us to say. We note here only that, under existing law, the fact that Mrs. Whitehead "agreed" to the arrangement is not dispositive. . . .

The surrogacy contract is based on, principles that are directly contrary to the objectives of our laws. It guarantees the separation of a child from its mother; it looks to adoption regardless of suitability; it totally ignores the child; it takes the child from the mother regardless of her wishes and her maternal fitness; and it does all of this, it accomplishes all of its goals, through the use of money.

Beyond that is the potential degradation of some women that may result from this arrangement. In many cases, of course, surrogacy may bring satisfaction, not only to the infertile couple, but to the surrogate mother herself. The fact, however, that many women may not perceive surrogacy negatively but rather see it as an opportunity does not diminish its potential for devastation to other women.

In sum, the harmful consequences of this surrogacy arrangement appear to us all too palpable. In New Jersey the surrogate mother's agreement to sell her child is void. Its irrevocability infects the entire contract, as does the money that purports to buy it.

CONCLUSION

This case affords some insight into a new reproductive arrangement: the artificial insemination of a surrogate mother. The unfortunate events that have unfolded illustrate that its unregulated use can bring suffering to all involved. Potential victims include the surrogate mother and her family, the natural father and his wife, and most importantly, the child. Although surrogacy has apparently provided positive results for some infertile couples, it can also, as this case demonstrates, cause suffering to participants, here essentially innocent and well-intended.

We have found that our present laws do not permit the surrogacy contract used in this case. Nowhere, however, do we find any legal prohibition against surrogacy when the surrogate mother volunteers, without any payment, to act as a surrogate and is given the right to change her mind and to assert her parental rights. Moreover, the Legislature remains free to deal with this most sensitive issue as it sees fit, subject only to constitutional constraints.

If the Legislature decides to address surrogacy, consideration of this case will highlight many of its potential harms. We do not underestimate the difficulties of legislating on this subject. In addition to the inevitable confrontation with the ethical and moral issues involved, there is the question of the wisdom and effectiveness of regulating a matter so private, yet of such public interest. Legislative consideration of surrogacy may also provide the opportunity to begin to focus on the overall implications of the new reproductive biotechnology in vitro fertilization, preservation of sperm and eggs, embryo implantation and the like. The problem is how to enjoy the benefits of the technology especially for infertile couples while minimizing the risk of abuse. The problem can be addressed only when society decides what its values and objectives are in this troubling, yet promising, area.

The judgment is affirmed in part, reversed in part, and remanded for further proceedings consistent with this opinion.

Questions

1. What are the two basis on which the court concluded that the surrogacy contract is invalid?

2. According to the court, how does the surrogacy contract conflict with existing statutes?

3. Explain why the court considered the surrogacy contract to be in violation of public policy.

4. What are the major differences between adoption and a surrogacy contract in terms of the use of money?

5. Why did the court consider the consent of the surrogate mother to be irrelevant in determining the validity of the surrogacy contract?

Johnson v. Calvert
California Supreme Court, 1993
5 Cal4th 87, 851 P. 2d 776

PANELLI, J. In this case we address several of the legal questions raised by recent advances in reproductive technology. When, pursuant to a surrogacy agreement, a zygote formed of the gametes of a husband and wife is implanted in the uterus of another woman, who carries the resulting fetus to term and gives birth to a child not genetically related to her, who is the child's "natural mother" under California law? . . . [I]s such an agreement barred by any public policy of this state?

We conclude that the husband and wife are the child's natural parents, and that this result does not offend . . . public policy.

Mark and Crispina Calvert are a married couple who desired to have a child. Crispina was forced to undergo a hysterectomy in 1984. Her ovaries remained capable of producing eggs, however, and the couple eventually considered surrogacy. In 1989 Anna Johnson heard about Crispina's plight from a coworker and offered to serve as a surrogate for the Calverts.

On January 15, 1990, Mark, Crispina, and Anna signed a contract providing that an embryo created by the sperm of Mark and the egg of Crispina would be implanted in Anna and the child born would be taken into Mark and Crispina's home "as their child." Anna agreed she would relinquish "all parental rights" to the child in favor of Mark and Crispina. In return, Mark and Crispina would pay Anna $10,000 in a series of installments, the last to be paid six weeks after the child's birth. Mark and Crispina were also to pay for a $200,000 life insurance policy on Anna's life.

The zygote was implanted on January 19, 1990. Less than a month later, an ultrasound test confirmed Anna was pregnant.

Unfortunately, relations deteriorated between the two sides. Mark learned that Anna had not disclosed she had suffered several stillbirths and miscarriages. Anna felt Mark and Crispina did not do enough to obtain the required insurance policy. She also felt abandoned during an onset of premature labor in June.

In July 1990, Anna sent Mark and Crispina a letter demanding the balance of the payments due her or else she would refuse to give up the child. The following month, Mark and Crispina responded with a lawsuit, seeking a declaration they were the legal parents of the unborn child. Anna filed her own action to be declared the mother of the child, and the two cases were eventually consolidated. The parties agreed to an independent guardian ad litem for the purposes of the suit.

The child was born on September 19, 1990, and blood samples were obtained from both Anna and the child for analysis. The blood test results excluded Anna as the genetic mother. The parties agreed to a court order providing that the child would remain with Mark and Crispina on a temporary basis with visits by Anna.

At trial in October 1990, the parties stipulated that Mark and Crispina were the child's genetic parents. After hearing evidence and arguments, the trial court ruled that Mark and Crispina were the child's "genetic, biological and natural" father and mother, that Anna had no "parental" rights to the child, and that the surrogacy contract was legal and enforceable against Anna's claims. The court also terminated the order allowing visitation. Anna appealed from the trial court's judgment. The Court of Appeal . . . affirmed. We granted review. . . .

In deciding the issue of maternity under the Act we have felt free to take into account the parties' intentions, as expressed in the surrogacy contract, because in our view the agreement is not, on its face, inconsistent with public policy.

Preliminarily, Mark and Crispina urge us to interpret the Legislature's 1992 passage of a bill that would have regulated surrogacy as an expression of this state's public policy despite the fact that Governor Wilson's veto prevented the bill from becoming law. Senate Bill No. 937 contained a finding that surrogate contracts are not against sound public and social policy. (Sen. Bill No. 937 (1991-1992 Reg. Sess.).) Had Senate Bill No. 937 become law, there would be no room for argument to the contrary. The veto, however, raises a question whether the legislative declaration truly expresses California's public policy.

In the Governor's veto message we find, not unequivocal agreement with the Legislature's public policy assessment, but rather reservations about the practice of surrogate parenting. "Surrogacy is a relatively recent phenomenon. The full moral and psychological dimensions of this practice are not yet clear. In fact, they are just beginning to emerge. Only two published court opinions in California have treated this nettlesome subject.... Comprehensive regulation of this difficult moral issue is premature.... [¶] To the extent surrogacy continues to be practical, it can be governed by the legal framework already established in the family law area." (Governor's veto message to Sen. on Sen. Bill No. 937 (Sept. 26, 1992) Sen. Daily File (1991-1992 Reg. Sess.) p. 68.) Given this less than ringing endorsement of surrogate parenting, we conclude that the passage of Senate Bill No. 937, in and of itself, does not establish that surrogacy contracts are consistent with public policy. (Of course, neither do we draw the opposite conclusion from the fact of the Governor's veto.)

Anna urges that surrogacy contracts violate several social policies. Relying on her contention that she is the child's legal, natural mother, she cites the public policy embodied in Penal Code section 273, prohibiting the payment for consent to adoption of a child. She argues further that the policies underlying the adoption laws of this state are violated by the surrogacy contract because it in effect constitutes a prebirth waiver of her parental rights.

We disagree. Gestational surrogacy differs in crucial respects from adoption and so is not subject to the adoption statutes. The parties voluntarily agreed to participate in in vitro fertilization and related medical procedures before the child was conceived; at the time when Anna entered into the contract, therefore, she was not vulnerable to financial inducements to part with her own expected offspring. As discussed above, Anna was not the genetic mother of the child. The payments to Anna under the contract were meant to compensate her for her services in gestating the fetus and undergoing labor, rather than for giving up "parental" rights to the child. Payments were due both during the pregnancy and after the child's birth. We are, accordingly, unpersuaded that the contract used in this case violates the public policies embodied in Penal Code section 273 and the adoption statutes. For the same reasons, we conclude these contracts do not implicate the policies underlying the statutes governing termination of parental rights. (See Welf. & Inst. Code, § 202.)

It has been suggested that gestational surrogacy may run afoul of prohibitions on involuntary servitude. (See U.S. Const., Amend. XIII; Cal. Const., art. I, § 6; Pen. Code, § 181.) Involuntary servitude has been recognized in cases of criminal punishment for refusal to work. (Pollock v. Williams (1944) 322 U.S. 4, 18 [88 L.Ed. 1095, 1104, 64 S.Ct. 792, 799]; see, generally, 7 Witkin, Summary of Cal. Law (9th ed. 1988) Constitutional Law, §§ 411-414, pp. 591-596.) We see no potential for that evil in the contract at issue here, and extrinsic evidence of coercion or duress is utterly lacking. We note that although at one point the contract purports to give Mark and Crispina the sole right to determine whether to abort the pregnancy, at another point it acknowledges: "All parties understand that a pregnant woman has the absolute right to abort or not abort any fetus she is carrying. Any promise to the contrary is unenforceable." We therefore need not determine the validity of a surrogacy contract purporting to deprive the gestator of her freedom to terminate the pregnancy.

Finally, Anna and some commentators have expressed concern that surrogacy contracts tend to exploit or dehumanize women, especially women of lower economic status. Anna's objections center around the psychological harm she asserts may result from the gestator's relinquishing the child to whom she has given birth. Some have also cautioned that the practice of surrogacy may encourage society to view children as commodities, subject to trade at their parents' will.

We are all too aware that the proper forum for resolution of this issue is the Legislature, where empirical data, largely lacking from this record, can be studied and rules of general applicability developed. However, in light of our responsibility to decide this case, we have considered as best we can its possible consequences.

We are unpersuaded that gestational surrogacy arrangements are so likely to cause the untoward results Anna cites as to demand their invalidation on public policy grounds. Although common sense suggests that women of lesser means serve as surrogate mothers more often than do wealthy women, there has been no proof that surrogacy contracts exploit poor women to any greater degree than economic necessity in general exploits them by inducing them to accept lower-paid or otherwise undesirable employment. We are likewise unpersuaded by the claim that surrogacy will foster the attitude that children are mere commodities; no evidence is offered to support it. The limited data available seem to reflect an absence of significant adverse effects of surrogacy on all participants.

The argument that a woman cannot knowingly and intelligently agree to gestate and deliver a baby for intending parents carries overtones of the reasoning that for centuries prevented women from attaining equal economic rights and professional status under the law. To resurrect this view is both to foreclose a personal and economic choice on the part of the surrogate mother, and to deny intending parents what may be their only means of procreating a child of their own genes. Certainly in the present case it cannot seriously be argued that Anna, a licensed vocational nurse who had done well in school and who had previously borne a child, lacked the intellectual wherewithal or life experience necessary to make an informed decision to enter into the surrogacy contract. . . .

The judgment of the Court of Appeal is affirmed.

ARABIAN, J., Concurring.

I concur in the decision to find under the Uniform Parentage Act that Crispina Calvert is the natural mother of the child she at all times intended to parent and raise as her own with her husband Mark, the child's natural father. That determination answers the question on which this court granted review, and in my view sufficiently resolves the controversy between the parties to warrant no further analysis. I therefore decline to subscribe to the dictum in which the majority find surrogacy contracts "not... inconsistent with public policy."

Surrogacy contracts touch upon one of the most, if not the most, sensitive subjects of human endeavor. Not only does the birth of a new generation perpetuate our species, it allows every parent to contribute, both genetically and socially, to our collective understanding of what it means to be human. Every child also offers the opportunity of a unique lifetime relationship, potentially more satisfying and fulfilling than any other pursuit. (See Adoption of Kelsey S. (1992) 1 Cal.4th 816, 837 [4 Cal. Rptr.2d 615, 823 P.2d 1216].)

The multiplicity of considerations at issue in a surrogacy situation plainly transcend traditional principles of contract law and require careful, nonadversarial analysis. For this reason, I do not think it wise for this court to venture unnecessarily into terrain more appropriately cleared by the Legislature in the first instance. . . .

Questions

1. How did the court address the argument that surrogacy contracts violated the policies underlying adoption laws?

2. What were the main objections raised against surrogacy contracts, and how did the court evaluate these objections?

Takeaways – Baby M. and Johnson v. Calvert

As you can tell from the court's decisions in the above two cases, surrogacy contracts are controversial. Whether surrogacy contracts are viewed as personal service agreements or agreements for the sale of the child born as the result of the agreement, commentators critical of contractual surrogacy view these contracts as contrary to public policy and thus not enforceable. (Radin, Market-Inalienability, supra, 100 Harv.L.Rev. at p. 1924, fn. 261; Capron & Radin, Choosing Family Law Over Contract Law as a Paradigm for Surrogate Motherhood, supra, in Surrogate Motherhood, at pp. 62-63; see also Krimmel, Can Surrogate Parenting Be Stopped? An Inspection of the Constitutional and Pragmatic Aspects of Outlawing Surrogate Mother Arrangements (1992) 27 Val.U.L.Rev. 1, 4-5.) However, as we know from *Johnson*, there are states that will enforce surrogacy contracts.

Unconscionability

The doctrine of unconscionability permits a court to refuse to enforce a contract if it feels it is unfair. In the context of contract law, unconscionability means absence of meaningful choice on the part of one of the parties together with contract terms which are unreasonably favorable to the other party. If a court determines a contract or part of a contract to be unconscionable it may grant any of three forms of relief: (1) the court may refuse to enforce the entire contract, (2) or any part of it, or (3) the court may limit the application of a particular clause to prevent an unconscionable result. (Rest.2d § 208, UCC 2-302)

Tuckwiller v. Tuckwiller
Supreme Court of Missouri, 1967
413 S.W.2d 274

WELBORN, Commissioner. This is an appeal from a decree ordering specific performance of a contract to devise real estate. The residuary legatee to which the proceeds of the property would have passed under the owner's will and the executor have appealed.

At her death at the age of 73 years, on June 14, 1963, Flora Metta Morrison was the owner of a 160-acre farm in Saline County. The inventory value of the farm was $34,400.00. By her will, dated September 7, 1961, the farm and the remainder of the residuary estate of the decedent were to be converted into cash and the proceeds given to the trustees of Davidson College to establish a student loan fund in memory of the decedent's mother. By the will, John Tuckwiller, a nephew of the decedent and the husband of the plaintiff, was given an option to purchase the farm at its appraised value. Ruby Tuckwiller, plaintiff below, based her action for specific performance upon a written contract with the decedent, entered into May 3, 1963, whereby plaintiff was to care for Mrs. Morrison during her lifetime, for which the farm was to be devised to plaintiff

The Hudson family farm consisted of three separate tracts in the same general neighborhood. Since 1958, Flora Metta Morrison had owned the 160-acre tract here in question and her sister, Dr. Virginia O. Hudson, had owned a 140-acre tract and an 80-acre tract, called the home place on which the Hudson family home was located.

In November, 1958, John Tuckwiller and his family moved into the "home place" and operated the three farms on a rental basis. By the arrangement between John and Dr. Virginia Hudson, three rooms in the home place were reserved for the use of Doctor Hudson and Metta whenever they saw fit to make use of them.

Flora Metta Hudson was born at the home place. She attended Missouri Valley College, Central Missouri State College at Warrensburg and Columbia University, receiving master's degrees from the latter two. Around 1920, she married a Morrison whose name does not otherwise appear and she was not married at the time of her death. After her marriage, she taught in the Philippine Islands for some twenty years. In the 1940's, she went to New York and worked for the Red Cross and at Saks Fifth Avenue. After the Tuckwillers moved into the home place, she visited them two or three times per year. In 1961, the apartment building in which she lived in New York was demolished and she had no particular place of residence. She went to Paris in the fall and winter of 1961 and subsequently visited relatives in various parts of this country. She came to the home place in October, 1962, and stayed until just before Thanksgiving. She left and visited in Oklahoma, Arkansas, Texas and New Mexico before returning to the home place in January, 1963.

Mrs. Morrison had Parkinson's disease, "a progressive relentless disease which progresses as time goes on, and it goes to the various stages from minimum involvement to complete involvement of the musculature." Mrs. Morrison had had the disease for two or three years and her condition was worse upon her return to the home place in January, 1963, than it had been on her previous visit. She went to New York for a few days in January, 1963, but did no further traveling after her return to the farm.

John Tuckwiller's wife, Ruby, had been employed at the State School in Marshall since February 1, 1960. In 1963, she was employed in the food service department at a salary of $206 per month. Ruby and Metta were quite congenial and Metta expressed frequent appreciation of the care and attention which she received from Ruby. Aware of the course of the disease from which she suffered, Mrs. Morrison was concerned about the prospect of her eventual disability and confinement in a nursing home for care. She began to urge Ruby to quit her job at the State School and to care for Mrs. Morrison in the home place the rest of her life. In April, 1963, Ruby did begin to use her accrued vacation time and remained at home, but she was unwilling at that time to forego her employment and undertake Mrs. Morrison's care.

On April 11, 1963, Mrs. Morrison had been quite dizzy, had staggered and fallen. When she fell again the following day, an ambulance was called and she was taken to the hospital at Marshall. There she was diagnosed as having suffered a cardiovascular accident (stroke) with a secondary diagnosis of Parkinsonism. There was evidence of some mental confusion during her hospitalization. According to her physician, she knew where she was, but did not know why she was there. She was discharged from the hospital on April 20. Upon an examination at a house call on May 2, her physician found Mrs. Morrison mentally clear. A lifelong friend whom Mrs. Morrison visited on the morning of May 3 stated that mentally "she was just as clear as a bell." As she left the friend's house, Mrs. Morrison remarked, "I'm not done for."

However, according to her physician Mrs. Morrison was aware that Parkinsonism was a "time consuming disease," which, "if [it] progresses far enough, [its victims] will become invalids... depending one hundred percent on outside care." Upon her return from the hospital, Mrs. Morrison had talked further to Mrs. Tuckwiller about providing care for her. Mrs. Tuckwiller was reluctant to give up her job at which she worked regular hours for what she felt might involve several years of exacting care. However, on May 3, in the late afternoon and in the presence of plaintiff's husband, an agreement was reached which plaintiff put in writing as follows:

"My offer to Aunt Metta is as follows

"I will take care of her for her lifetime; by that I mean provide her 3 meals per day a good bed do any possible act of nursing and provide her every pleasure possible.
"In exchange she will will me her (Corum) farm at her death keeping all money made from it during her life. She will maintain expense of her medicine."

The writing was signed by Mrs. Morrison at that time. . . .

On Monday morning, May 6, Mrs. Tuckwiller went to the State School and resigned her job. On the same morning, Mrs. Morrison called the attorney who had drawn her earlier will for an appointment to change her will. An appointment was made for 10:00 A.M., May 7. However, shortly after noon on May 6, Mrs. Morrison again fainted and fell at the "home place." An ambulance was called to take her to the hospital. Some thirty to forty-five minutes elapsed before the ambulance arrived and Mrs. Morrison remained on the floor. In the meantime, Mrs. Morrison "came out" and was able to talk. When the ambulance arrived she was placed on a stretcher. At that point, Mrs. Morrison said: "Wait a minute; I have got some business I want to tend to." She asked Mrs. Tuckwiller to "get that piece of paper. . . that we have our agreement on." She wanted it witnessed. She handed the paper to one of the ambulance attendants, told him what it was and asked him to sign it. A second ambulance attendant also signed the paper. Mrs. Morrison, according to John Tuckwiller, then asked Mrs. Tuckwiller to put the date on it "so it will come after my will" and the date May 6, 1963 was written on it. One of the ambulance attendants, called as a witness for plaintiff, testified that Mrs. Morrison said that "she had some business she wanted to get taken care of first." He recalled further conversation, although he did not recall what was said. The other attendant who testified for defendants did not recall hearing Mrs. Morrison say anything. He said that he signed the paper at Mrs. Tuckwiller's request.

Mrs. Morrison was again taken to the hospital at Marshall. Her attending physician found some mental confusion at that time. However, she improved and was discharged on May 11, again with a diagnosis of cardiovascular accident. The hospitalization prevented Mrs. Morrison from keeping her appointment for May 7 with her attorney. She returned to the home place and had been there only two hours when she again fainted and fell. She was put to bed and when her condition continued to worsen, she was readmitted to the hospital on May 15, where she remained until her death on June 14, from a cerebral vascular accident. During her final illness, Mrs. Morrison was attended by two special nurses. Mrs. Tuckwiller also spent much time at the hospital, assisting as she could. Mrs. Tuckwiller's daughters also assisted in Mrs. Morrison's care and one made a claim against the estate for her services. None of the hospital expenses were paid by Mrs. Tuckwiller.

At the trial, plaintiff offered evidence that the life expectancy of a 73-year old person ranged from 8.69 to 9.35 years. The defendants' evidence was limited to the hospital records of Mrs. Morrison's three hospitalizations, the testimony above referred to of one of the ambulance attendants, and testimony of a nursing home operator that the cost for care and service there was $200 per month.

The trial court, while recognizing that some money value might be placed upon the services rendered during the six weeks' period, concluded that at the time the "Contract was made the type, kind and duration of the services required, were so uncertain that they could not be measured by a money standard." The court concluded that the contract was not inequitable when it was made, that plaintiff had performed her obligations under the contract and that it would not be inequitable to decree specific performance.

On this appeal, the defendants' sole contention is that specific performance should not be decreed because "the meager services rendered decedent by plaintiff are easily ascertainable and plaintiff can be compensated by the payment of money, and specific performance of the alleged contract . . . results in unjust enrichment to plaintiff, is inequitable and unconscionable, and is based on inadequate consideration, and is grossly unjust to defendant Davidson College." . . . .

[I]n determining whether or not a contract is so unfair or inequitable or is unconscionable so as to deny its specific performance, the transaction must be viewed prospectively, not retrospectively. The same rule applies with respect to sufficiency of consideration.

Viewed in this light, we find that plaintiff gave up her employment with which she was well satisfied and undertook what was at the time of the contract an obligation of unknown and uncertain duration, involving duties which, in the usual course of the disease from which Mrs. Morrison suffered, would have become increasingly onerous. . . .

Viewed from the standpoint of Mrs. Morrison, the contract cannot be considered unfair. She was appreciative of the care and attention which plaintiff had given her prior to the agreement. Although, as defendants suggest, such prior services cannot provide the consideration essential to a binding contract, such prior services and the past relation of the parties may properly be considered in connection with the fairness of the contract and adequacy of the consideration. 5A Corbin on Contracts, 1165, p. 227. Aware of her future outlook and having no immediate family to care for her, Mrs. Morrison was understandably appreciative of the personal care and attention of plaintiff and concerned with the possibility of routine impersonal care over a long period of time in a nursing home or similar institution. Having no immediate family which might be the object of her bounty, she undoubtedly felt more free to agree to dispose of the farm without insisting upon an exact quid pro quo. Her insistence that the contract be witnessed prior to her hospitalization is clear evidence of her satisfaction with the bargain as was her unsuccessful effort to change her will to carry out her agreement. . . .

Properly viewed from the standpoint of the parties at the time of the agreement, we find that the contract was fair, not unconscionable, and supported by an adequate consideration. Although not conceding that such conclusion is correct, defendants argue, in effect, that in view of the obviously brief duration of plaintiff's services and their value in comparison with the value of the farm, plaintiff should be obliged to accept the offered payment of the reasonable value of her services and denied the relief of specific performance. Defendants point out that the trial court found that valuing the services which plaintiff rendered might be "possible." That conclusion is undoubtedly correct and unquestionably the monetary value of plaintiff's services would have been a quite small proportion (perhaps one percent) of the value of the farm. Once, however, the essential fairness of the contract and the adequacy of the consideration are found, the fact that the subject of the contract is real estate answers any question of adequacy of the legal remedy of monetary damages. "Whenever a contract concerning real property is in its nature and incidents entirely unobjectionable that is, when it possesses none of those features which . . . appeal to the discretion of the court it is as much a matter of course for a court of equity to decree a specific performance of it, as it is for a court of law to give damages for the breach of it." Pomeroy's Specific Performance of Contracts (3d ed.), 10, p. 23.

Questions

1. What was the main issue raised by the defendants in their appeal against the decree ordering specific performance?

2. How did the trial court evaluate the fairness and equity of the contract between the parties?

3. Why did the court consider the contract to be fair from the perspective of Mrs. Morrison?

4. How did the court address the argument regarding the value of plaintiff's services compared to the value of the farm?

Takeaways - Tuckwiller v. Tuckwiller

After reading this case a football fan might conclude that courts don't engage in "Monday morning quarterbacking." As applied to the facts of this case, how is that so and why is that so?

American Software, Inc. v. Ali
California Court of Appeal, 1996
46 Cal.App.4th 1386, 54 Cal.Rptr.2d 477

KING, J. The appellant, American Software, Inc., appeals from a decision of the trial court granting a former employee, respondent Melane Ali, unpaid commissions based upon software sales she generated while in American Software's employ but which were remitted by customers after she voluntarily severed her employment. The key issue in this appeal is whether a provision of Ali's employment contract which, generally speaking, terminates her right to receive commissions on payments received on her accounts 30 days after severance of her employment is unconscionable, and therefore, unenforceable. The trial court found that Ali was entitled to recover the disputed commissions because this contractual provision was unconscionable. We disagree and reverse.

Ali was an account executive for American Software from September 5, 1991, to March 2, 1994. The employment relationship commenced after Ali was approached by a professional recruiter on behalf of American Software and was terminated when Ali voluntarily resigned because she had a job offer from one of American Software's competitors. Ali was hired to sell and market licensing agreements for software products to large companies. These products are designed to the customer's specifications for the purpose of integrating the customer's accounting, manufacturing, sales and distribution processes.

In exchange for her services, American Software agreed to pay Ali a base monthly salary plus a draw. If products were sold during the month, any commissions paid were reduced by the amount of the draw. However, the draw portion of the salary was paid regardless of whether or not the salesperson earned commissions to cover the draw. Any negative amount would be carried over from month-to-month until such time as the commissions were large enough to cover the previous draws, or until such time as the employment relationship was severed. If the amount of draws exceeded commissions at the time of termination, American Software would suffer the loss. At the time of her resignation, Ali's annual guaranteed salary, exclusive of commissions, was $75,000. Her base monthly salary was $3,333 per month and her nonrefundable draw was $2,917.

The terms and conditions of Ali's employment were set out in a written contract which was prepared by American Software. Ali reviewed the contract, and had an attorney, who she described as a "buddy," review it prior to employment. Of pertinence to the instant controversy, the contract included the specific circumstances under which Ali was to receive commissions after termination of employment with American Software. The employment agreement first states that "[c]ommissions are considered earned when the payment is received by the Company." It goes on to provide: "In the event of termination, the right of all commissions which would normally be due and payable are forfeited 30 days following the date of termination in the case of voluntary termination and 90 days in the case of involuntary termination."

Based on her testimony at trial, there is no question that Ali was aware of this provision prior to her execution of the agreement and commencement of work at American Software. She testified she reviewed the two-and-one-half-page contract for one-half hour and caused certain handwritten deletions and revisions to be made to it, most notably deleting a provision requiring her to reimburse American Software $5,000 for the recruiter's fee in the event that she terminated her employment within a year. Ali testified that she signed the employment contract even though she believed certain provisions were unenforceable in California.

After Ali left American Software's employment, she sought additional commissions in connection with transactions with IBM and Kaiser Foundation Health Plan. American Software received payment from both companies more than 30 days after Ali's resignation.

After Ali's claim for unpaid commissions was denied by the Labor Commissioner, she sought de novo review in the superior court. (Lab. Code, § 98.2.) The trial court awarded Ali approximately $30,000 in unpaid commissions after finding that the contract provision regarding post employment commissions was unconscionable and thus, unenforceable. The trial court found the evidence "overwhelming that the forfeiture provision inures to the benefit of the party with superior bargaining power without any indication of a reason for tying such benefit to the timing of a payment, rather than to the service actually provided in completing the sale." American Software timely appealed.

In 1979, our Legislature enacted Civil Code section 1670.5, which codified the established doctrine that a court can refuse to enforce an unconscionable provision in a contract. . . . While the term "unconscionability" is not defined by statute, the official comment explains the term as follows: "The basic test is whether, in the light of the general background and the needs of the particular case, the clauses involved are so one-sided as to be unconscionable under the circumstances existing at the time of the making of the contract.... The principle is one of the
of oppression and unfair surprise [citation] and not of disturbance of allocation of risks because of superior bargaining power." (Legis. committee com., Deering's Ann. Civ. Code (1994 ed.) § 1670.5, pp. 328-329.)

Most California cases analyze unconscionability as having two separate elements-procedural and substantive. [Citations omitted] Substantive unconscionability focuses on the actual terms of the agreement, while procedural unconscionability focuses on the manner in which the contract was negotiated and the circumstances of the parties. California courts generally require a showing of both procedural and substantive unconscionability at the time the contract was made. (See

A & M Produce Co. v. FMC Corp. (1982) 135 Cal.App.3d 473, 487 [186 Cal.Rptr. 114, 38 A.L.R.4th 1].) Some courts have indicated that a sliding scale applies-for example, a contract with extraordinarily oppressive substantive terms will require less in the way of procedural unconscionability. [Citations omitted]

Indicia of procedural unconscionability include "oppression, arising from inequality of bargaining power and the absence of real negotiation or a meaningful choice" and "surprise, resulting from hiding the disputed term in a prolix document." (Vance v. Villa Park Mobilehome Estates, supra, 36 Cal.App.4th at p. 709.) Substantive unconscionability is indicated by contract terms so one-sided as to "shock the conscience." (California Grocers Assn. v. Bank of America (1994) 22 Cal.App.4th 205, 214 [27 Cal.Rptr.2d 396], italics in original.) A less stringent standard of "reasonableness" was applied in A & M Produce Co. v. FMC Corp., supra, 135 Cal.App.3d at pages 486-487. This standard was expressly rejected by Division Two of this court in California Grocers Assn. as being inherently subjective. (California Grocers Assn., supra, at p. 214.) We agree. With a concept as nebulous as "unconscionability" it is important that courts not be thrust in the paternalistic role of intervening to change contractual terms that the parties have agreed to merely because the court believes the terms are unreasonable. The terms must shock the conscience.

The critical juncture for determining whether a contract is unconscionable is the moment when it is entered into by both parties-not whether it is unconscionable in light of subsequent events. (Civ. Code, § 1670.5.) Unconscionability is ultimately a question of law for the court. (Ilkhchooyi v. Best, supra, 37 Cal.App.4th at p. 411; Vance v. Villa Park Mobilehome Estates, supra, 36 Cal.App.4th at p. 709; Patterson v. ITT Consumer Financial Corp. (1993) 14 Cal.App.4th 1659, 1663 [18 Cal.Rptr.2d 563].)

In assessing procedural unconscionability, the evidence indicates that Ali was aware of her obligations under the contract and that she voluntarily agreed to assume them. In her business as a salesperson it is reasonable to assume she had become familiar with contracts and their importance. In fact, in Ali's testimony, she indicated that as part of her responsibilities for American Software, she helped negotiate the terms of a contract with IBM representing over a million dollars in sales. The salient provisions of the employment contract are straightforward, and the terms used are easily comprehensible to the layman. She had the benefit of counsel. fn. 3 Nor is this a situation in which one party to the contract is confronted by an absence of meaningful choice. The very fact that Ali had enough bargaining "clout" to successfully negotiate for more favorable terms on other provisions evidences the contrary. She admits that she was aware of the post employment commissions clause, but did not attempt to negotiate for less onerous terms. fn. 4 In short, this case is a far cry from those cases where fine print, complex terminology, and presentation of a contract on a take-it-or-leave-it basis constitutes the groundwork for a finding of unconscionability.

Nor do we find substantive unconscionability. Ali's arguments of substantive unconscionability rest largely on events that occurred several years after the contract was entered into-her loss of sizable commissions on sales she had solicited during her employment but where payment was delayed for various reasons so that it was not received within 30 days after her departure. However, as indicated by the very wording of California's unconscionability statute, we must analyze the circumstances as they existed "at the time [the contract] was made" to determine if gross unfairness was apparent at that time. (Civ. Code, § 1670.5, subd. (a).)

When viewed in light of the circumstances as they existed on August 23, 1991, when the instant contract was executed, we cannot say the contract provision with respect to compensation after termination was so unfair or oppressive in its mutual obligations as to "shock the conscience." (California Grocers Assn. v. Bank of America, supra, 22 Cal.App.4th at p. 214.) If the official notes accompanying Uniform Commercial Code section 2-302, upon which Civil Code section 1670.5 is based, is to be relied upon as a guide, fn. 5 the contract terms are to be evaluated "in the light of the general commercial background and the commercial needs of the particular trade or case, ..." (U. Com. Code, § 2-302, com. 1). Corbin suggests that the test is whether the terms are "so extreme as to appear unconscionable according to the mores and business practices of the time and place." (1 Corbin, Contracts (1963) § 128, p. 551.)

Our survey of case law indicates that the contract provision challenged here is commonplace in employment contracts with sales representatives, such as Ali, who have ongoing responsibilities to "service" the account once the sale is made. (See, e.g., Chretian v. Donald L. Bren Co. (1984) 151 Cal.App.3d 385, 389 [198 Cal.Rptr. 523]; J.S. DeWeese Co. v. Hughes-Treitler Mfg. (Mo.App. 1994) 881 S.W.2d 638, 644-646; see also Entis v. Atlantic Wire & Cable Corporation (2d Cir. 1964) 335 F.2d 759, 762.) In briefing below, the rationale for deferring commissions until payment is actually received by the customer was explained by American Software: "[I]f the entire commission were to be deemed earned by merely obtaining buyers, the burden of servicing those buyers pending receipt of revenues would fall on American Software's other salespersons unfamiliar with the earlier transaction who would receive nothing for their efforts." In Watson v. Wood Dimension, Inc. (1989) 209 Cal.App.3d 1359, 1363-1365 [257 Cal.Rptr. 816], the court upheld an award of post-termination commissions for a reasonable period of time based on quantum meruit in the total absence of contractual provisions governing the situation. If a court can impose these terms on parties in the absence of an agreement, then it is difficult to see how such terms can be considered "unconscionable" when the parties agree to them.

Nor do we find that the terms of this contract represent "an overly harsh allocation of risks ... which is not justified by the circumstances under which the contract was made." (Carboni v. Arrospide, supra, 2 Cal.App.4th at p. 83.) The contract terms with regard to Ali's compensation involved certain risks to both parties to the bargain. The contract in the instant case placed a risk on Ali that she would lose commissions from her customers if payment was not received by American Software within 30 days after her resignation. American Software took the risk that at the time of Ali's termination, she would not have earned sufficient commissions to cover the substantial draws "credited" to her. This is part of the bargaining process-it does not necessarily make a contract unconscionable. The contract simply does not appear to be "overly harsh or one-sided, with no justification for it at the time of the agreement." (Vance v. Villa Park Mobilehome Estates, supra, 36 Cal.App.4th at p. 709.)

Much of the parties' arguments in this case revolve around Ellis v. McKinnon Broadcasting Co. (1993) 18 Cal.App.4th 1796 [23 Cal.Rptr.2d 80]. In Ellis the court examined a provision in an employment contract denying the plaintiff, an advertising salesperson, commissions on advertising if the employer had not yet received payment for the advertising prior to termination of the salesperson's employment. The employer collected nearly $100,000 in advertising fees from the plaintiff's sales after he voluntarily left his employment two years later, which meant that the plaintiff would have been entitled to approximately $20,000 in commissions had he continued his employment. The court described the pivotal inquiry as assessing "the substantive reasonableness of the challenged provision" and proceeded to find elements of procedural unconscionability, unfair surprise, and oppression, as well as substantive unconscionability. (Id. at pp. 1805-1806, italics added.)

Despite the many analogous facts and issues, we reach a different conclusion than Ellis. In this instance, the conflicting result can most easily be explained by the fact that the Ellis court closely followed the A&M Produce analytical structure in considering whether the commissions provision was "reasonable"-an approach we have specifically rejected in favor of the more rigorous "shock the conscience" standard enunciated in California Grocers Assn. v. Bank of America supra, 22 Cal.App.4th at page 214. We also find the result in Ellis hard to reconcile with other California appellate decisions which have shown considerable restraint in second-guessing provisions in employment contracts governing payment of sales commissions upon termination of employment. (See, e.g., Chretian v. Donald L. Bren, Co., supra, 151 Cal.App.3d at pp. 389-390; Neal v. State Farm Ins. Cos. (1961) 188 Cal.App.2d 690 [10 Cal.Rptr. 781].) A critical review of Ellis in the legal literature observes, "[T]he test on unconscionability is not whether the parties could have written a better or more reasonable contract. The proper test in these cases is whether the bargain is so one-sided as to shock the conscience and whether there was some bargaining impropriety resulting from surprise or oppression. The Neal and Chretian courts, unlike the court in Ellis, displayed the proper restraint and deference to agreements that were not egregiously one-sided in the allocation of risks." (Prince, Unconscionability in California: A Need for Restraint and Consistency (1995) 46 Hastings L.J. 459, 545.)

In the present case, there are no unclear or hidden terms in the employment agreement and no unusual terms that would shock the conscience, all leading to the conclusion that the contract accurately reflects the reasonable expectations of the parties. Overall, the evidence establishes that this employment contract was the result of an arm's-length negotiation between two sophisticated and experienced parties of comparable bargaining power and is fairly reflective of prevailing practices in employing commissioned sales representatives. Therefore, the contract fails to qualify as unconscionable.

The judgment is reversed.

Questions

1. Explain the difference between procedural unconscionability and substantive unconscionability.

2. What are the indicia of procedural unconscionability mentioned in the case?

3. According to the court, when should the critical juncture for determining unconscionability be?

Takeaways – American Software

Whether a contract is unconscionable is a matter of law which "must be determined on a case by case basis . . . giving particular attention to whether, at the time of execution of the agreement, the contract provision could result in unfair surprise and was oppressive to the allegedly disadvantaged party." (*Zapatha v. Dairy Mart, Inc.,* 381 Mass. 284, 291, 293, 408 N.E.2d 1370, 1375, 1376 (1980).

Donovan v. RRL Corp.
California Supreme Court, 2001
26 Cal.4th 261, 109 Cal.Rptr.2d 807; 27 P.3d 702

[Facts were set forth previously at p. 63.]

The final factor defendant must establish before obtaining rescission based upon mistake is that enforcement of the contract for the sale of the 1995 Jaguar XJ6 Vanden Plas at $25,995 would be unconscionable. Although the standards of unconscionability warranting rescission for mistake are similar to those for unconscionability justifying a court's refusal to enforce a contract or term, the general rule governing the latter situation (Civ. Code, § 1670.5) is inapplicable here, because unconscionability resulting from mistake does not appear at the time the contract is made. (Rest.2d Contracts, § 153, com. c, p. 395; 1 Witkin, *supra*, Contracts, § 370, pp. 337-338.)

An unconscionable contract ordinarily involves both a procedural and a substantive element: (1) oppression or surprise due to unequal bargaining power, and (2) overly harsh or one-sided results. (*Armendariz v. Foundation Health Psychcare Services, Inc.* (2000) 24 Cal.4th 83, 114.) Nevertheless, " 'a sliding scale is invoked which disregards the regularity of the procedural process of the contract formation, that creates the terms, in proportion to the greater harshness or unreasonableness of the substantive terms themselves.' [Citations.]" (*Ibid.*) For example, the Restatement Second of Contracts states that "[i]nadequacy of consideration does not of itself invalidate a bargain, but gross disparity in the values exchanged may be an important factor in a determination that a contract is unconscionable and may be sufficient ground, without more, for denying specific performance." (Rest.2d Contracts, § 208, com. c, p. 108.) In ascertaining whether rescission is warranted for a unilateral mistake of fact, substantive unconscionability often will constitute the determinative factor, because the oppression and surprise ordinarily results from the mistake--not from inequality in bargaining power. Accordingly, even though defendant is not the weaker party to the contract and its mistake did not result from unequal bargaining power, defendant was surprised by the mistake, and in these circumstances overly harsh or one-sided results are sufficient to establish unconscionability entitling defendant to rescission.

Our previous cases support this approach. In *Kemper, supra*, , we held that enforcement of the city's option to accept a construction company's bid, which was 28 percent less than the intended bid, would be unconscionable. Our decision reasoned that (1) the plaintiff gave prompt notice upon discovering the facts entitling it to rescind, (2) the city therefore was aware of the clerical error before it exercised the option, (3) the city already had awarded the contract to the next lowest bidder, (4) the company had received nothing of value it was required to restore to the city, and (5) "the city will not be heard to complain that it cannot be placed in statu quo because it will not have the benefit of an inequitable bargain." (*Id.* at p. 703.) Therefore, "under all the circumstances, it appears that it would be unjust and unfair to permit the city to take advantage of the company's mistake." (*Id.* at pp. 702-703.) Nothing in our decision in *Kemper* suggested that the mistake resulted from surprise related to inequality in the bargaining process. (Accord, *Farmers Sav. Bank, Joice v. Gerhart* (Iowa 1985) 372 N.W.2d 238, 243-245 [holding unconscionable the enforcement of sheriff's sale against bank that overbid because of a mistake caused by negligence of its own attorney].) Similarly, in *Elsinore, supra*, 54 Cal.2d 380, we authorized rescission of a bid based upon a clerical error, without suggesting any procedural unconscionability, even where the other party afforded the contractor an opportunity to verify the accuracy of the bid before it was accepted.

In the present case, enforcing the contract with the mistaken price of $25,995 would require defendant to sell the vehicle to plaintiff for $12,000 less than the intended advertised price of $37,995--an error amounting to 32 percent of the price defendant intended. Defendant subsequently sold the automobile for slightly more than the intended advertised price, suggesting that that price reflected its actual market value. Defendant had paid $35,000 for the 1995 Jaguar and incurred costs in advertising, preparing, displaying, and attempting to sell the vehicle. Therefore, defendant would lose more than $9,000 of its original investment in the automobile. Plaintiff, on the other hand, would obtain a $12,000 windfall if the contract were enforced, simply because he traveled to the dealership and stated that he was prepared to pay the advertised price.

These circumstances are comparable to those in our prior decisions authorizing rescission on the ground that enforcing a contract with a mistaken price term would be unconscionable. Defendant's 32 percent error in the price exceeds the amount of the errors in cases such as *Kemper* and *Elsinore*. For example, in *Elsinore*, *supra*, "54 Cal.2d at page 389, we authorized rescission for a $6,500 error in a bid that was intended to be $96,494--a mistake of approximately 7 percent in the intended contract price. As in the foregoing cases, plaintiff was informed of the mistake as soon as defendant discovered it. Defendant's sales manager, when he first learned of the mistake in the advertisement, explained the error to plaintiff, apologized, and offered to pay for plaintiff's fuel, time, and effort expended in traveling to the dealership to examine the automobile. Plaintiff refused this offer to be restored to the status quo and did not seek in this action to recover damages for the incidental costs he incurred because of the erroneous advertisement. Like the public agencies in *Kemper* and *Elsinore*, plaintiff should not be permitted to take advantage of defendant's honest mistake that resulted in an unfair, one-sided contract. (Cf. *Drennan v. Star Paving Co.* (1958) 51 Cal.2d 409, 415-416 [no rescission of mistaken bid where other party detrimentally altered his position in reasonable reliance upon the bid and could not be restored to the status quo].)

The circumstance that section 11713.1(e) makes it unlawful for a dealer not to sell a vehicle at the advertised price does not preclude a finding that enforcing an automobile sales contract containing a mistaken price would be unconscionable. Just as the statute does not eliminate the defense of mistake, as established above, the statute also does not dictate that enforcing a contract with an erroneous advertised price necessarily must be considered equitable and fair for purposes of deciding whether the dealer is entitled to rescission on the ground of mistake. In *Kemper, supra*, 37 Cal.2d 696, we concluded that it would be unconscionable to bar rescission of a bid pursuant to a city charter provision prohibiting the withdrawal of bids, where "it appear[ed] that it would be unjust and unfair to permit the city to take advantage of the company's mistake." (*Id.* at p. 703.) Thus, notwithstanding the public interest underlying the charter provision, our decision in *Kemper* precluded the city from relying upon that provision to impose absolute contractual liability upon the contractor. (*Id.* at p. 704.)

Accordingly, section 11713.1(e) does not undermine our determination that, under the circumstances, enforcement of the contract for the sale of the 1995 Jaguar XJ6 Vanden Plas at the $25,995 mistaken price would be unconscionable. The other requirements for rescission on the ground of unilateral mistake have been established. Defendant entered into the contract because of its mistake regarding a basic assumption, the price. The $12,000 loss that would result from enforcement of the contract has a material effect upon the agreed exchange of performances that is adverse to defendant. Furthermore, defendant did not neglect any legal duty within the meaning of Civil Code section 1577 or breach any duty of good faith and fair dealing in the steps leading to the formation of the contract. Plaintiff refused defendant's offer to compensate him for his actual losses in responding to the advertisement. "The law does not penalize for negligence beyond requiring compensation for the loss it has caused." (3 Corbin, Contracts, *supra*, § 609, p. 684.) In this situation, it would not be reasonable for this court to allocate the risk of the mistake to defendant.

Questions

1. What are the two elements typically involved in determining whether a contract is unconscionable?

2. What are the requirements that need to be established for rescission based on unilateral mistake, according to the court's decision?

3. How does the concept of substantive unconscionability apply to the determination of rescission in cases of unilateral mistake?

Takeaways – American Software and Donovan

As the court points out in each case, an unconscionable contract ordinarily involves both a procedural and a substantive element: (1) oppression or surprise due to unequal bargaining power, and (2) overly harsh or one-sided results. Another way to think of procedural unconscionability is in terms of how did questionable clause find its way into the contract? Was it slipped into the contract via fine print on the backside? Was a party dissuaded from reading the contract by being told, "Oh don't worry about that, it's just our standard terms."? These are common examples of procedural unconscionability. In *Donovan* what did the procedural unconscionability consist of? And in *American Software,* was there any procedural unconscionability at all?

Take It or Leave It Contracts

Bolter v. Superior Court (Harris Research, Inc.)
California Court of Appeal, Fourth Dist., 2001
87 Cal.App.4th 900, 104 Cal.Rptr.2d 888

O'LEARY, J. Franchise owners, Florence Bolter (doing business as Bolter's Chem-Dry), Sandra Valdez (doing business as Canyon Chem-Dry), and Stephen R. Knight (doing business as Knight's Chem-Dry) filed the underlying writ petition challenging the court's ruling their breach of contract action against Harris Research, Inc., must be arbitrated in Utah. The franchisees acknowledge their franchise agreements mandate that all disputes be arbitrated in Utah, but claim the provision is unconscionable and violates Business and Professions Code section 20040.5. Finding their first contention has merit, we grant the writ relief requested.

Harris is the franchisor of a carpet cleaning operation known as "Chem-Dry" businesses. In the early 1980's, petitioners first purchased their Chem-Dry franchises, operating their small businesses in Orange County. Over the years, when their franchise agreements lapsed, petitioners executed renewals and sometimes new franchise agreements.

In April 1998, petitioners filed a complaint seeking damages and declaratory relief, alleging Harris breached the franchise contracts and the covenants of good faith and fair dealing. Petitioners claimed Harris continually modified the franchise agreements at every opportunity to "liberalize the obligations of [Harris]" and "constrict the rights of the franchisees." They said Harris threatened to terminate their franchises if they refused to execute the newer agreements.

Petitioners have many complaints about franchise agreements signed within the past four years. For example, the new agreements provide that if petitioners terminate their franchises, they will be forced to surrender their customer lists and clients' telephone numbers. Petitioners say they must make their income tax returns available upon request and claim Harris enforces strict advertising restrictions contained in the agreement against petitioners but not other franchisees. Additionally, petitioners assert Harris has saturated their franchise territories, diminishing the value of their franchises. Finally, petitioners are outraged by Harris's new requirement they purchase from Harris an overpriced water extraction system called the Velda, and its expensive fixtures and attachments. When petitioners originally bought their franchises, they utilized a "carbonated method of carpet cleaning," which did not involve the bulky, heavy equipment used by carpet steam or water extraction systems.

In their complaint, petitioners claimed that "at the time [Harris] commenced the wrongful conduct upon which this action is based, all [petitioners] had extant written agreements with [Harris] providing that jurisdiction would be in, and the governing law would be of, the State of California" but "some of the more recent agreements provide that the franchisee shall submit to the jurisdiction of the State of Utah in any litigation involving the contract ...."

On April 18, 2000, the court issued an order granting Harris's motion to compel arbitration in Utah and dismissing the case. On May 1, 2000, the court signed a document prepared by Harris containing the "findings of fact and conclusions of law" in support of the order. It included the statement, inter alia, "The arbitration provisions in the franchise agreements, even if adhesive, are not unconscionable and do not impose an unreasonable burden on [petitioners]." Petitioners filed the underlying writ petition, and we issued an order to show cause and temporarily stayed the arbitration proceedings.

[W]e find the answer to this case lies in general contract law principles. Keeping in mind the values of judicial economy, we confine our analysis accordingly.

"A written provision in a contract to submit to arbitration a dispute arising out of the contract is valid, irrevocable and enforceable except on 'such grounds as exist at law or in equity for the revocation of any contract.' (9 U.S.C. § 2 [contracts subject to the FAA]; Code Civ. Proc., § 1281 [contracts governed by state arbitration law].) Accordingly, the existence of a valid agreement to arbitrate is determined by reference to state law principles regarding the formation, revocation and enforceability of contracts generally. [Citations.]" (*Kinney v. United HealthCare Services, Inc.* (1999) 70 Cal.App.4th 1322, 1327-1328 [83 Cal.Rptr.2d 348].)

Contrary to Harris's belief, arbitration agreements are not subject to a different standard than other contracts. As recently noted by the Supreme Court, "[U]nder both federal and California law, arbitration agreements are valid, irrevocable, and enforceable, save upon such grounds as exist at law or in equity for the revocation of *any* contact." (*Armendariz v. Foundation Health Psychcare Services, Inc.* (2000) 24 Cal.4th 83, 98 [99 Cal.Rptr.2d 745, 6 P.3d 669], fn. omitted,.) It further explained, "[A]lthough we have spoken of a 'strong public policy of this state in favor of resolving disputes by arbitration' [citation], Code of Civil Procedure section 1281 makes clear that an arbitration agreement is to be rescinded on the same ground as other contracts or contract terms. In this respect, arbitration agreements are neither favored nor disfavored, but simply placed on an equal footing with other contracts." (*Id.* at pp. 126-127.)

Turning to the case at hand, we first address petitioners' argument the mandatory arbitration provisions contained in their franchise agreements were unconscionable and therefore unenforceable. The doctrine of unconscionability is a judicially created doctrine which was codified in 1979 when the Legislature enacted Civil Code section 1670.5. (*Armendariz v.* Foundation Health Psychcare Services, Inc, supra, 24 Cal.4th at pp. 113-114.) That section provides in relevant part, "If the court as a matter of law finds the contract or any clause of the contract to have been unconscionable at the time it was made the court may refuse to enforce the contract ...." (Civ. Code, § 1670.5, subd. (a).) While the statute does not attempt to precisely define "unconscionable," there is a large body of case law recognizing the term has "both a procedural and a substantive element, both of which must be present to render a contract unenforceable. [Citation.] The procedural element focuses on the unequal bargaining positions and hidden terms common in the context of adhesion contracts. [Citation.] While courts have defined the substantive element in various ways, it traditionally involves contract terms that are so one-sided as to 'shock the conscience,' or that impose harsh or oppressive terms. [Citation.]" (*24 Hour Fitness, Inc. v. Superior Court* (1998) 66 Cal.App.4th 1199, 1212-1213 [78 Cal.Rptr.2d 533].)

Both elements need not be present to the same degree. "[T]he more substantively oppressive the contract term, the less evidence of procedural unconscionability is required to come to the conclusion that the term is unenforceable, and vice versa." (*Armendariz v. Foundation Health Psychcare Services, Inc., supra,* 24 Cal.4th at p. 114.) Additionally, a "claim of unconscionability often cannot be determined merely by examining the face of a contract, but will require inquiry into its [commercial] setting, purpose, and effect." (*Perdue v. Crocker National Bank* (1985) 38 Cal.3d 913, 926 [216 Cal.Rptr. 345, 702 P.2d 503].)

Thus, "[u]nconscionability analysis begins with an inquiry into whether the contract is one of adhesion. [Citation.] 'The term [contract of adhesion] signifies a standardized contract, which, imposed and drafted by the party of superior bargaining strength, relegates to the subscribing party only the opportunity to adhere to the contract or reject it.' [Citation.]" (*Armendariz v. Foundation Health Psychcare Services, Inc., supra,* 24 Cal.4th at p. 113.) [2b] Such was the case here: Harris made no attempt to refute petitioners' characterization of it as a "large wealthy international franchiser." And it is undisputed petitioners have limited financial means, owning small "one-man operated" Dry-Chem franchises. Petitioners were told they must agree to the new franchise terms in order to *continue* running their franchises. Only a person contemplating whether to purchase a franchise for the first time would have been in the position to reject Harris's "take it or leave it" attitude. Harris was certainly aware established franchise owners simply could not afford to dispute, much less attempt to negotiate, the place and manner arbitration was to occur. Perhaps this is why Harris did not focus on this issue below or on appeal.

When a contract is adhesive, "the court must then determine whether 'other factors are present which, ... operate to render it [unenforceable].' [Citation.]" (*Armendariz v. Foundation Health Psychcare Services, Inc., supra,* 24 Cal.4th at p. 113.) Harris maintains the court correctly determined the arbitration provisions in the franchise agreements, even if adhesive, do not impose an unreasonable burden on petitioners. Citing to *Lagatree v. Luce, Forward, Hamilton & Scripps* (1999) 74 Cal.App.4th 1105, 1124 [88 Cal.Rptr.2d 664], Harris argues adhesive arbitration agreements are valid and enforceable because " ' "[t]here is nothing inherently unfair or oppressive about arbitration clauses." ... In fact, ... the FAA shows a strong federal policy in favor of arbitration....' [Citations.]"

We acknowledge there is much authority, including the cases Harris relies upon, holding adhesive arbitration provisions are not per se unconscionable. (*Izzi v. Mesquite Country Club* (1986) 186 Cal.App.3d 1309, 1318 [231 Cal.Rptr. 315].) However, it is also generally recognized that "there may be arbitration provisions which do give an advantage to one party.... In those cases, ... it is not the requirement of arbitration alone which makes the provision unfair but rather the place or manner in which the arbitration is to occur." (*Strotz v. Dean Witter Reynolds, Inc.* (1990) 223 Cal.App.3d 208, 216, fn. 7 [272 Cal.Rptr. 680], overruled on other grounds in *Rosenthal v. Great Western Fin. Securities Corp.* (1996) 14 Cal.4th 394, 407 [58 Cal.Rptr.2d 875, 926 P.2d 1061].) It is those provisions, regarding "place and manner," which we take issue with here.

The agreement provides, in relevant part, as follows: All disputes regarding the franchise agreement "[s]hall be submitted for arbitration to the Salt Lake City, Utah office of the [AAA] on demand of either party. Notwithstanding the foregoing, any controversies, disputes or claims related to or based on the marks may, at [Harris's] sole election, be brought and maintained in any court of competent jurisdiction. Such arbitration proceedings shall be conducted in Salt Lake City, Utah and, except as otherwise provided in this Agreement, shall be heard by one arbitrator in accordance with the then current commercial arbitration rules of the [AAA]. ... [¶] The arbitrator shall have the right to award or include in his or her award any relief which he or she deems proper in the circumstances, ... [except] exemplary or punitive damages.... [¶] [Harris] and [franchisee] agree that all arbitration shall be conducted on an individual, not class-wide, basis and that an arbitration proceeding between [Harris] and [franchisee] shall not be consolidated with any other arbitration proceeding involving [Harris] and any other natural person, association, corporation, partnership or other entity." In addition, the agreement provided, "All matters relating to arbitration shall be governed by the [FAA] ... [and] this Agreement and the franchise shall be governed by the laws of the State of Utah."

In order to assess the reasonableness of Harris's "place and manner" restrictions, the respective circumstances of the parties become relevant. As explained above, Harris is a large international corporation and petitioners are small "Mom and Pop" franchisees located in California. When petitioners first purchased their Chem-Dry franchises in the early 1980's, Harris was headquartered in California, and the franchise agreement did not contain an arbitration provision. Thus, they never anticipated Harris would relocate its headquarters to Utah and mandate that all disputes be litigated there.

Under the circumstances, the "place and manner" terms are unduly oppressive: The agreement requires franchisees wishing to resolve any dispute to close down their shops, pay for airfare and accommodations in Utah, and absorb the increased costs associated in having counsel familiar with Utah law. To rub salt in the wound, the agreement provides franchisees are precluded from consolidating arbitrations to share these increased costs among themselves. And the potential to recoup expenses with a favorable verdict is limited by the restriction against exemplary or punitive damages.

Because Dry-Chem franchises are by nature small businesses, it is simply not a reasonable or affordable option for franchisees to abandon their offices for any length of time to litigate a dispute several thousand miles away. As Sandra Valdez explained, "I labor hard and daily to make a living from my franchise, and I have complete responsibility, myself, for running the franchise out of my home. I attend to all the advertising, administrative and selling efforts. It is necessary for me to be home daily in order to receive calls from potential customers, schedule cleanings, and do all that must ordinarily be done in connection with such a family-run business."

Likewise, Stephen Knight, who owns three Chem-Dry franchises, stated he is "basically a one-man operation." He has several employees who do the cleaning, but he personally attends to all the administrative duties such as taking phone calls from customers and scheduling cleaning jobs. He claimed he would lose much of his business if forced to litigate the matter outside California. Florence Bolter declared she is 66 years old and solely responsible for running her franchises. She also cares for her husband who is "severely ill" and "could not get by in [her] absence."

Moreover, petitioners declared they are all suffering from severe financial hardships and could not afford to maintain their claims if forced to litigate the matter out of state. Knight attested he is "barely able to afford [the] costs [of the suit] as it is" in California. Valdez echoed these sentiments, explaining it has "become more and more difficult to make a living" due to Harris's misconduct, which is the basis of the lawsuit. She said the franchise was purchased for $32,500, but she would "be fortunate now if we could sell it for $10,000 to $15,000." Similarly, Florence Bolter said she recently had to declare bankruptcy.

Harris's prohibition against consolidation, limitation on damages and forum selection provisions have no justification other than as a means of maximizing an advantage over the petitioners. Arguably, Harris understood those terms would effectively preclude its franchisees from ever raising any claims against it, knowing the increased costs and burden on their small businesses would be prohibitive. As aptly stated in *Armendariz*, "Arbitration was not intended for this purpose." (*Armendariz v. Foundation Health Psychcare Services, Inc., supra,* 24 Cal.4th at p. 118.)

Petitioners assert the presence of unconscionable "place and manner" provisions leads to the conclusion the arbitration agreement as a whole is unenforceable. They submit Harris's "position has always been that the parties entered into an agreement to arbitrate in the State of Utah, as opposed to an agreement to arbitrate, and a separate agreement as to venue." We disagree. It is not necessary to throw the baby out with the bath water, i.e., the unconscionable provisions can be severed and the rest of the agreement enforced.

This is a remedy contemplated by the Legislature. Civil Code section 1670.5, subdivision (a) provides that, "If the court ... finds the contract or any clause of the contract to have been unconscionable ... the court may refuse to enforce the contract, or it may enforce the remainder of the contract without the unconscionable clause, or it may so limit the application of any unconscionable clause as to avoid any unconscionable result." The Legislative Committee comment explains, "Under this section the court, in its discretion, may refuse to enforce the contract as a whole if it is permeated by the unconscionability, or it may strike any single clause or group of clauses which are so tainted or which are contrary to the essential purpose of the agreement, or it may simply limit unconscionable clauses so as to avoid unconscionable results." (Legis. Com. com., 9 West's Ann. Civ. Code, foll. § 1670.5 (1985 ed.) p. 494.)

We find no legal ground to grant petitioners' request to strike the entire arbitration agreement. "[P]ermeation is indicated by the fact that there is no single provision a court can strike or restrict in order to remove the unconscionable taint from the agreement." (*Armendariz v. Foundation Health* Psychcare Services, Inc., supra, 24 Cal.4th at pp. 124-125.) As explained, we did not find the requirement of arbitration alone to be unduly unfair but rather the "place and manner" in which the arbitration was to occur. The unconscionable provisions contained in the agreement relating to the arbitration of all controversies, disputes or claims in Salt Lake City, Utah, are clearly severable from the remainder of the arbitration agreement. (Cf. *id.* at pp. 123-127 [court found arbitration agreement permeated by an unlawful purpose due to number of defects].) Unconscionability can be cured by striking those provisions, leaving an otherwise valid and complete agreement to submit disputes to arbitration.

Let a writ of mandate issue directing the superior court to vacate its judgment and enter a new and different order striking the provisions of the agreement mandating that all arbitrations take place in the State of Utah. This court's previously issued stay order is dissolved. Petitioners shall recover their costs on appeal.

Questions

1. According to the court, how should the validity of an arbitration agreement be determined?

2. What is the significance of a contract being characterized as adhesive?

3. Why did the court find the "place and manner" restrictions in the arbitration provision unduly oppressive?

4. How did the financial circumstances of the franchisees affect the court's analysis of the arbitration provision?

Takeaways – Bolter v. Superior Court

The term contract of adhesion signifies a standardized contract, imposed and drafted by the party of superior bargaining strength, which relegates to the subscribing party only the opportunity to adhere to the contract or reject it. The adhesive or "take-it-or-leave-it" aspect goes to the element of procedural unconscionability. However, the presence of procedural unconscionability is not grounds for declaring the entire contract to be unconscionable. There must also be substantive unconscionability. What did the substantive unconscionability consists of in *Bolter*?

ASSESSMENT QUESTIONS, CHAPTER 5

1. Explain the types of contracts that are typically considered contrary to public policy.

2. What are the consequences of entering into a contract that is contrary to public policy?

3. Explain the doctrine of restraint of trade and its relation to public policy. Under what circumstances may a contract be deemed unenforceable due to restraint of trade?

4. What is required for a covenant not to compete to be enforceable in a court of law?

5. Describe contracts that are considered to be unconscionable. What factors are evaluated in determining unconscionability?

6. What is procedural unconscionability? Substantive unconscionability?

Chapter 6
Contract Interpretation

Introduction

Words are imperfect. They are oftentimes ambiguous and vague. In addition, what words are to be resorted to in interpreting the meaning of a contract? Are we limited to the contract itself or can we resort to outside (what courts and lawyers like to call "extrinsic") evidence to interpret the meaning of the contract? Can we look to evidence of what was said in the negotiations that led up to the contract? Can we look to prior drafts of the contract? Can a court implicate or supply terms that are omitted in order to fill gaps in the contract? These are just some of the questions that will be raised in this chapter. We start with an examination of the parol evidence rule which addresses what evidence can be resorted to in order to explain or interpret the meaning of a written contract.

The Parol Evidence Rule

An agreement reduced to final written form and intended by the parties to be the complete statement of their agreement is called an "integrated" agreement. (See, Rest.2d § 209(3).) In such a case, extrinsic (i.e,. not contained in the final written agreement) evidence of prior or contemporaneous negotiations or agreements is inadmissible to vary or contradict the terms of the written integrated agreement. (See, Rest.2d § 213, UCC 2-202) The parol evidence rule prohibits the introduction of any extrinsic evidence, whether oral or written, to vary, alter or add to the terms of an integrated agreement. (*Tahoe National Bank v. Phillips* (1971) 4 Cal.3d 11, 23 [92 Cal.Rptr. 704, 480 P.2d 320].)

Put another way, conversations, discussions and negotiations culminating in a written instrument are not admissible in evidence. The execution of a contract in writing, whether the law requires it to be written or not, supersedes all the negotiations or stipulations concerning its matter which preceded or accompanied the execution of the instrument. (Cal.Civ.Code § 1625) The rule only comes into operation when there is a single and final written agreement setting forth the understanding of the parties. When that takes place, prior and contemporaneous negotiations, oral or written, are excluded; or, as it is sometimes said, the written agreement supersedes these prior or contemporaneous negotiations.

Whether or not a writing was intended by the parties to be the final and complete expression of their agreement, i.e., an integrated agreement, is a question of fact. However, in a jury trial, it is the judge and not the jury who determines whether the parties intended the writing to be a final expression of their agreement with respect to such terms as are included therein and whether the writing is intended also as a complete and exclusive statement of the terms of the agreement. (Cal.Code.Civ.Proc. §1856 (d).)

As an aside, it should be pointed out that the label "parol evidence rule" is a misnomer on several counts. First of all, it is not limited to "oral" evidence (as the Latin term *parol* might suggest) but it excludes all extrinsic evidence, both oral and written, of prior or contemporaneous negotiations. Secondly, it's not a rule of "evidence" (you won't find it in the Federal Rules of Evidence or any state evidence codes) but rather it is a substantive rule of contract law.

Gianni v. R. Russell Co., Inc.
Supreme Court of Pennsylvania, 1924
281 Pa. 320

JUSTICE SCHAFFER. Plaintiff had been a tenant of a room in an office building in Pittsburgh wherein he conducted a store, selling tobacco, fruit, candy and soft drinks. Defendant acquired the entire property in which the storeroom was located and its agent negotiated with plaintiff for a further leasing of the room. A lease for three years was signed. It contained a provision that the lessee should "use the premises only for the sale of fruit, candy, soda water," etc., with the further stipulation that "it is expressly understood that the tenant is not allowed to sell tobacco in any form, under penalty of instant forfeiture of this lease." The document was prepared following a discussion about renting the room between the parties and after an agreement to lease had been reached. It was signed after it had been left in plaintiff's hands and admittedly had been read over to him by two persons, one of whom was his daughter.

Plaintiff sets up that in the course of his dealings with defendant's agent it was agreed that, in consideration of his promises not to sell tobacco and to pay an increased rent, and for entering into the agreement as a whole, he should have the exclusive right to sell soft drinks in the building. No such stipulation is contained in the written lease. Shortly after it was signed, defendant demised the adjoining room in the building to a drug company without restricting the latter's right to sell soda water and soft drinks. Alleging that this was in violation of the contract which defendant had made with him and that the sale of these beverages by the drug company had greatly reduced his receipts and profits, plaintiff brought this action for damages for breach of the alleged oral contract and was permitted to recover. Defendant has appealed.

Plaintiff's evidence was to the effect that the oral agreement had been made at least two days, possibly longer, before the signing of the instrument and that it was repeated at the time he signed; that relying upon it he executed the lease. Plaintiff called one witness who said he heard defendant's agent say to plaintiff, at a time admittedly several days before the execution of the lease, that he would have the exclusive right to sell soda water and soft drinks, to which the latter replied if that was the case he accepted the tenancy. Plaintiff produced no witness who was present when the contract was executed to corroborate his statement as to what then occurred. Defendant's agent denied that any such agreement was made, either preliminary to or at the time of the execution of the lease.

Appellee's counsel argues this is not a case in which an endeavor is being made to reform a written instrument because of something omitted as a result of fraud, accident or mistake, but is one involving the breach of an independent oral agreement which does not belong in the writing at all and is not germane to its provisions. We are unable to reach this conclusion.

"Where parties, without any fraud or mistake, have deliberately put their engagements in writing, the law declares the writing to be not only the best, but the only, evidence of their agreement": Martin v. Berens, 67 Pa. 459, 463; Irvin v. Irvin, 142 Pa. 271, 287.

"All preliminary negotiations, conversations and verbal agreements are merged in and superseded by the subsequent written contract . . . and unless fraud, accident or mistake be averred, the writing constitutes the agreement between the parties, and its terms cannot be added to nor subtracted from by parol evidence": Union Storage Co. v. Speck, 194 Pa. 126, 133; Vito v. Birkel, 209 Pa. 206, 208.

The writing must be the entire contract between the parties if parol evidence is to be excluded and to determine whether it is or not the writing will be looked at and if it appears to be a contract complete within itself "couched in such terms as import a complete legal obligation without any uncertainty as to the object or extent of the engagement, it is conclusively presumed that the whole engagement of the parties, and the extent and manner of their undertaking, were reduced to writing": Seitz v. Brewers' Refrigerating Machine Co., 141 U.S. 510, 517.

When does the oral agreement come within the field embraced by the written one? This can be answered by comparing the two, and determining whether parties, situated as were the ones to the contract, would naturally and normally include the one in the other if it were made. If they relate to the same subject-matter and are so interrelated that both would be executed at the same time, and in the same contract, the scope of the subsidiary agreement must be taken to be covered by the writing. This question must be determined by the court.

In the case at bar the written contract stipulated for the very sort of thing which plaintiff claims has no place in it. It covers the use to which the storeroom was to be put by plaintiff and what he was and what he was not to sell therein; he was "to use the premises only for the sale of fruit, candy, soda water, etc.," and was not "allowed to sell tobacco in any form." Plaintiff claims his agreement not to sell tobacco was part of the consideration for the exclusive right to sell soft drinks. Since his promise to refrain was included in the writing it would be the natural thing to have included the promise of exclusive rights. Nothing can be imagined more pertinent to these provisions which were included than the one appellee avers.

In cases of this kind, where the cause of action rests entirely on an alleged oral understanding concerning a subject which is dealt with in a written contract, it is presumed that the writing was intended to set forth the entire agreement as to that particular subject.

"In deciding upon this intent [as to whether a certain subject was intended to be embodied by the writing], the chief and most satisfactory index . . . is found in the circumstances whether or not the *particular element of the alleged extrinsic negotiation is dealt with at all* in the writing. If it is mentioned, covered, or dealt with in the writing, then presumably the writing was meant to represent all of the transaction on that element; if it is not, then probably the writing was not intended to embody that element of the negotiation": Wigmore on Evidence (2d ed.) vol. 5, page 309.

As the written lease is the complete contract of the parties and since it embraces the field of the alleged oral contract, evidence of the latter is inadmissible under the parol evidence rule.

"The [parol evidence] rule also denies validity to a subsidiary agreement within [the] scope [of the written contract] if sued on as a separate contract, although except for [that rule], the agreement fulfills all the requisites of valid contract": 2 Williston, Contracts 1222; . . ..

There are, of course, certain exceptions to the parol evidence rule but this case does not fall within any of them. Plaintiff expressly rejects any idea of fraud, accident or mistake and they are the foundation upon which any basis for admitting parol evidence to set up an entirely separate agreement within the scope of a written contract must be built. The evidence must be such as would cause a chancellor to reform the instrument and that would be done only for these reasons (Pioso v. Bitzer, 209 Pa. 503) and this holds true where this essentially equitable relief is being given, in our Pennsylvania fashion, through common law forms.

We have stated on several occasions recently that we propose to stand for the integrity of written contracts: (Citations omitted) We reiterate our position in this regard.

The judgment of the court below is reversed and is here entered for defendant.

Questions

1. According to the court, under what circumstances can parol evidence be excluded from a written contract?

2. What argument did the plaintiff's counsel make regarding the nature of the oral agreement and its relationship to the written lease?

3. How did the court evaluate whether the oral agreement should be considered part of the written contract?

4. What exceptions to the parol evidence rule did the court mention, and why did they not apply in this case?

Masterson v. Sine
Supreme Court of California, 1968
68 Cal.2d 222, 436 P.2d 561

TRAYNOR, C. J. Dallas Masterson and his wife Rebecca owned a ranch as tenants in common. On February 25, 1958, they conveyed it to Medora and Lu Sine by a grant deed "Reserving unto the Grantors herein an option to purchase the above described property on or before February 25, 1968" for the "same consideration as being paid heretofore plus their depreciation value of any improvements Grantees may add to the property from and after two and a half years from this date." Medora is Dallas' sister and Lu's wife. Since the conveyance Dallas has been adjudged bankrupt. His trustee in bankruptcy and Rebecca brought this declaratory relief action to establish their right to enforce the option.

The case was tried without a jury. Over defendants' objection the trial court . . . determined that the parol evidence rule precluded admission of extrinsic evidence offered by defendants to show that the parties wanted the property kept in the Masterson family and that the option was therefore personal to the grantors and could not be exercised by the trustee in bankruptcy.

The court entered judgment for plaintiffs, declaring their right to exercise the option, specifying in some detail how it could be exercised, and reserving jurisdiction to supervise the manner of its exercise and to determine the amount that plaintiffs will be required to pay defendants for their capital expenditures if plaintiffs decide to exercise the option.

Defendants appeal. They contend that extrinsic evidence (as to the option provision's) meaning should not have been admitted. The trial court properly refused to frustrate the obviously declared intention of the grantors to reserve an option to repurchase by an overly meticulous insistence on completeness and clarity of written expression. . . . It properly admitted extrinsic evidence to explain the language of the deed ... to the end that the consideration for the option would appear with sufficient certainty to permit specific enforcement. . . . The trial court erred, however, in excluding the extrinsic evidence that the option was personal to the grantors and therefore non-assignable.

When the parties to a written contract have agreed to it as an "integration"--a complete and final embodiment of the terms of an agreement--parol evidence cannot be used to add to or vary its terms. When only part of the agreement is integrated, the same rule applies to that part, but parol evidence may be used to prove elements of the agreement not reduced to writing.

The crucial issue in determining whether there has been an integration is whether the parties intended their writing to serve as the exclusive embodiment of their agreement. The instrument itself may help to resolve that issue. It may state, for example, that "there are no previous understandings or agreements not contained in the writing," and thus express the parties' "intention to nullify antecedent understandings or agreements." (See 3 Corbin, Contracts (1960) § 578, p. 411.) Any such collateral agreement itself must be examined, however, to determine whether the parties intended the subjects of negotiation it deals with to be included in, excluded from, or otherwise affected by the writing. Circumstances at the time of the writing may also aid in the determination of such integration. . . .

California cases have stated that whether there was an integration is to be determined solely from the face of the instrument and that the question for the court is whether it "appears to be a complete ... agreement. ..." . . Neither of these strict formulations of the rule, however, has been consistently applied. The requirement that the writing must appear incomplete on its face has been repudiated in many cases where parol evidence was admitted "to prove the existence of a separate oral agreement as to any matter on which the document is silent and which is not inconsistent with its terms"--even though the instrument appeared to state a complete agreement. . . . Even under the rule that the writing alone is to be consulted, it was found necessary to examine the alleged collateral agreement before concluding that proof of it was precluded by the writing alone. (See 3 Corbin, Contracts (1960) § 582, pp. 444-446.) It is therefore evident that "The conception of a writing as wholly and intrinsically self-determinative of the parties' intent to make it a sole memorial of one or seven or twenty-seven subjects of negotiation is an impossible one." (9 Wigmore, Evidence (3d ed. 1940) § 2431, p. 103.) For example, a promissory note given by a debtor to his creditor may integrate all their present contractual rights and obligations, or it may be only a minor part of an underlying executory contract that would never be discovered by examining the face of the note.

In formulating the rule governing parol evidence, several policies must be accommodated. One policy is based on the assumption that written evidence is more accurate than human memory. (Germain Fruit Co. v. J. K. Armsby Co. (1908) 153

Cal. 585, 595 [96 P. 319].) This policy, however, can be adequately served by excluding parol evidence of agreements that directly contradict the writing. Another policy is based on the fear that fraud or unintentional invention by witnesses interested in the outcome of the litigation will mislead the finder of facts. (Citations omitted) McCormick has suggested that the party urging the spoken as against the written word is most often the economic underdog, threatened by severe hardship if the writing is enforced. In his view the parol evidence rule arose to allow the court to control the tendency of the jury to find through sympathy and without a dispassionate assessment of the probability of fraud or faulty memory that the parties made an oral agreement collateral to the written contract, or that preliminary tentative agreements were not abandoned when omitted from the writing. (See McCormick, Evidence (1954) § 210.) He recognizes, however, that if this theory were adopted in disregard of all other considerations, it would lead to the exclusion of testimony concerning oral agreements whenever there is a writing and thereby often defeat the true intent of the parties. (See McCormick, op. cit. supra, § 216, p. 441.)

Evidence of oral collateral agreements should be excluded only when the fact finder is likely to be misled. The rule must therefore be based on the credibility of the evidence. One such standard, adopted by section 240(1)(b) of the Restatement of Contracts, permits proof of a collateral agreement if it "is such an agreement as might naturally be made as a separate agreement by parties situated as were the parties to the written contract." (Italics added; see McCormick, Evidence (1954) § 216, p. 441; see also 3 Corbin, Contracts (1960) § 583, p. 475, § 594, pp. 568-569; 4 Williston, Contracts (3d ed. 1961) § 638, pp. 1039-1045.) The draftsmen of the Uniform Commercial Code would exclude the evidence in still fewer instances: "If the additional terms are such that, if agreed upon, they would certainly have been included in the document in the view of the court, then evidence of their alleged making must be kept from the trier of fact." (Com. 3, § 2-202, italics added.)

The option clause in the deed in the present case does not explicitly provide that it contains the complete agreement, and the deed is silent on the question of assignability. Moreover, the difficulty of accommodating the formalized structure of a deed to the insertion of collateral agreements makes it less likely that all the terms of such an agreement were included. . . . The statement of the reservation of the option might well have been placed in the recorded deed solely to preserve the grantors' rights against any possible future purchasers, and this function could well be served without any mention of the parties' agreement that the option was personal. There is nothing in the record to indicate that the parties to this family transaction, through experience in land transactions or otherwise, had any warning of the disadvantages of failing to put the whole agreement in the deed. This case is one, therefore, in which it can be said that a collateral agreement such as that alleged "might naturally be made as a separate agreement." A fortiori, the case is not one in which the parties "would certainly" have included the collateral agreement in the deed.

It is contended, however, that an option agreement is ordinarily presumed to be assignable if it contains no provisions forbidding its transfer or indicating that its performance involves elements personal to the parties. . . . The fact that there is a written memorandum, however, does not necessarily preclude parol evidence rebutting a term that the law would otherwise presume. In American Industrial Sales Corp. v. Airscope, Inc., supra, 44 Cal.2d 393, 397-398, we held it proper to admit parol evidence of a contemporaneous collateral agreement as to the place of payment of a note, even though it contradicted the presumption that a note, silent as to the place of payment, is payable where the creditor resides. . . . In the absence of a controlling statute the parties may provide that a contract right or duty is nontransferable. . . . Moreover, even when there is no explicit agreement--written or oral--that contractual duties shall be personal, courts will effectuate a presumed intent to that effect if the circumstances indicate that performance by a substituted person would be different from that contracted for. . . .

In the present case defendants offered evidence that the parties agreed that the option was not assignable in order to keep the property in the Masterson family. The trial court erred in excluding that evidence.

The judgment is reversed.

Questions

1. How did the court determine whether the grant deed was an integrated agreement?

2. What policies and considerations did the court take into account when formulating the parol evidence rule?

3. Why did the court conclude that the option agreement in the deed could be considered a collateral agreement?

Merger Clauses

The determinative factor as to whether or not the parol evidence rule will apply and exclude extrinsic evidence is whether the parties intended their written agreement to be "integrated," i.e., was it the complete and final agreement of the parties. While it is not completely conclusive on the question of whether the parties intended the writing to be the final, full and complete expression of their agreement, the presence of a "merger" or "integration" clause declaring that intention is strong evidence of that fact. A typical "merger clause" might be written as follows:

This Agreement and the exhibits attached hereto contain the entire agreement of the parties with respect to the subject matter of this Agreement, and supersede all prior negotiations, agreements and understandings with respect thereto. This Agreement may only be amended by a written document duly executed by all parties."

A. Kemp Fisheries, Inc. v. Castle & Cooke, Inc., et. al.
U.S. Court of Appeal Ninth Circuit (Wash.) 1989
852 F.2d 493

EUGENE A. WRIGHT, Circuit Judge: In this case we consider whether the court properly admitted parol evidence to determine the terms of the Charter Agreement between A. Kemp Fisheries, Inc. and Bumble Bee Samoa, Inc., a subsidiary of Castle & Cooke, Inc. We conclude that the court applied the parol evidence rule incorrectly and reverse its judgment.

A. Kemp Fisheries Inc. and Bumble Bee Samoa, Inc., a fully owned subsidiary of Castle & Cooke, Inc., agreed that Kemp would charter, with an option to purchase, the M/V CITY OF SAN DIEGO. Kemp needed the vessel to fish for herring and salmon in Alaska from April to August 1983. In February of that year they signed a letter of intent that incorporated certain telexes exchanged in their negotiations. This letter served as their agreement "[p]ending preparation and execution of final documentation required for the bareboat charter and option to purchase." To compensate Bumble Bee for removing the vessel from the market Kemp paid a nonrefundable deposit of $50,000.

After reviewing drafts of the agreement with Kemp's attorney, Bumble Bee sent the final bare boat Charter Agreement late in March. Louis Kemp, the charterer's president, found that the agreement differed from his understanding of the arrangement. Specifically, he understood that Bumble Bee had agreed that the engines would be in good working order and had represented orally that the freezing system would meet Kemp's specific needs. The agreement contained no such provisions and in fact, disclaimed all warranties, express or implied. Despite his reservations, Kemp signed it without voicing his concerns to Bumble Bee. He took the vessel in early April and sailed to Alaska for the May herring season.

In the midst of herring season, two of the three auxiliary engines that powered the SAN DIEGO's freezing system broke down. After repairing one engine, Kemp switched from freezing to curing the herring because it lacked confidence that the engine would last. Kemp sold the cured herring for a price below that for frozen herring.

In preparation for salmon season at the end of June, Kemp repaired the auxiliary engines and rented an additional engine. Although the engines were operating at full power and suffered no breakdowns, the salmon froze in a block and the flesh was "honey combed." Kemp's buyer rejected most of it. Kemp took it to a shore-based freezing plant in Bellingham where it was thawed and refrozen. It sold the salmon for 75 cents a pound, 50 cents less than the price it would have received for properly frozen salmon.

Kemp sued Bumble Bee and Castle & Cooke in admiralty for breach of the Charter Agreement, intentional and negligent misrepresentation, estoppel, and rescission. It claimed that Bumble Bee agreed to provide engines in good working order and represented that the freezing system would meet its specific needs.

The trial judge found that the Charter Agreement signed in March was ambiguous and admitted parol evidence to clarify the parties' intent. She concluded that the letter of intent and referenced telexes reflected the parties' final intent and indicated that no other negotiations would occur. From evidence of their negotiations, she found that Bumble Bee warranted the vessel to be seaworthy and the engines to be in good working condition, and represented orally that the vessel's freezing system could meet Kemp's specific requirements. She held Bumble Bee liable for all of Kemp's damages because the "inability of the M/V CITY OF SAN DIEGO to freeze herring and salmon within the parameters specified by Bumble Bee is solely the result of Bumble Bee's breach of warranties." Bumble Bee appeals.

In the Charter Agreement, the parties agreed that "the Charter Party shall be governed by and enforced under the laws of the State of California." We apply California law in our analysis.

The parol evidence rule provides:

When the parties to a written contract have agreed to it as an "integration"--a complete and final embodiment of the terms of an agreement-- parol evidence cannot be used to add to or vary its terms. When only part of the agreement is integrated, the same rule applies to that part, but parol evidence may be used to prove elements of the agreement not reduced to writing. *Masterson v. Sine,* 68 Cal.2d 222, 65 Cal. Rptr. 545, 547, 436 P.2d 561 (1968) (citations omitted). *See also* Cal.Civ.Code § 1625, Cal.Code Civ.P. § 1856(a), and *Battery Steamship Corp. v. Refineria Panama, S.A.,* 513 F.2d 735, 738 (2d Cir.1975) (the federal common law parol evidence rule).

If a contract is integrated, the parol evidence rule operates to exclude evidence that is not "relevant to prove a meaning to which the language of the instrument is reasonably susceptible." *Pacific Gas and Elec. Co. v. G.W. Thomas Drayage & R. Co.,* 69 Cal.2d 33, 69 Cal.Rptr. 561, 564, 442 P.2d 641, 644 (1968). "[E]xtrinsic evidence is not admissible to add to, detract from, or vary the terms of a written contract." *Id.* 69 Cal.Rptr. at 565, 442 P.2d at 645. If a contract is not integrated, the parol evidence rule does not apply. The court can admit all evidence relevant to the parties' intent, including negotiations and prior agreements.

"The crucial issue in determining whether there has been an integration is whether the parties intended their writings to serve as the exclusive embodiment of their agreement." *Marani v. Jackson,* 183 Cal.App.3d 695, 228 Cal.Rptr. 518, 521 (1 Dist. 1986) (quoting *Salyer Grain & Milling Co. v. Henson,* 13 Cal.App.3d 493, 91

Cal.Rptr. 847 (5 Dist.1970)). To make this determination, the court considers: the language and completeness of the written agreement and whether it contains an integration clause, the terms of the alleged agreement and whether they contradict those in the writing, whether the agreement might naturally be made as a separate agreement, and whether the jury might be misled by the introduction of the parol testimony. A court also considers the circumstances surrounding the transaction and its subject matter, nature and object. *Marani,* 228 Cal.Rptr. at 522 (citations omitted).

The Charter Agreement is an integrated contract. The agreement itself is complete and comprehensive. It covers in great detail the various rights and responsibilities of the parties. Although the Charter does not contain an integration clause, the letter of intent shows clearly that the parties intended that the Charter would be the "final documentation" of their agreement.

The alleged agreements regarding the warranties of the vessel's seaworthiness, engines, and freezing system are not collateral agreements that would normally be made in a separate contract. These alleged understandings directly contradict the Charter's waiver of all warranties. In addition, the agreement specifies Bumble Bee's responsibility for testing and repairing the freezing system and preparing the vessel for Kemp. If Bumble Bee warranted the freezing system and the engines, the Charter Agreement would typically provide that.

The circumstances surrounding this transaction also support our conclusion that the contract is integrated. Kemp and Bumble Bee are corporations familiar with business transactions. Kemp's attorney reviewed the Charter with Bumble Bee in the month before it signed. Bumble Bee incorporated some of Kemp's changes into the final Charter presented in March. Kemp had ample opportunity to express its understanding of the deal. Nothing suggests that this agreement was not recognized by both parties as final and complete.

The judge admitted parol evidence to resolve ambiguities and contradictions within sub-paragraphs 3B, E and F. Sub-paragraph 3B provides:

B. Prior to delivery of the Vessel, Owner shall maintain the Vessel in good condition and shall cause the Vessel to be surveyed, on its own account, by a competent surveyor chosen by Owner, which survey shall show that the Vessel meets TA 2003 insurance requirements and is in all respects tight, staunch, strong and seaworthy.

Sub-paragraphs 3E and F provide:

E. Delivery to Charterer shall constitute full performance by Owner of all of Owner's obligations hereunder, and thereafter Charterer shall not be entitled to make or assert any claim against Owner on account of any representations or warranties, express or implied, with respect to the Vessel. F. Charterer's acceptance of delivery of the Vessel, its equipment, gear and non-consumable stores shall constitute conclusive evidence that the same have been inspected by Charterer and are accepted by Charterer as suitable for the intended use hereunder and, as between the parties, the seaworthiness and suitability of the Vessel, its equipment, gear and non-consumable stores are deemed admitted.

The judge construed sub-paragraph 3B as an express warranty of seaworthiness and sub-paragraphs 3E and F as a waiver of that warranty. To resolve this conflict, she turned to parol evidence.

The court erred. The parol evidence rule requires that courts consider extrinsic evidence to determine whether the contract is ambiguous. *Drayage,* 69 Cal.Rptr. at 565-66, 442 P.2d at 645-46 ("[R]ational interpretation requires at least a preliminary consideration of all credible evidence offered to prove the intention of the parties."); *Trident Center v. Connecticut General Life Ins. Co.,* 847 F.2d 564, 569 (9th Cir.1988). But if the extrinsic evidence advances an interpretation to which the language of the contract is not reasonably susceptible, the evidence is not admissible. *Drayage,* 69 Cal.Rptr. at 564, 442 P.2d at 644: "The test of admissibility of extrinsic evidence to explain the meaning of a written instrument is ... whether the offered evidence is relevant to prove a meaning to which the language of the instrument is reasonably susceptible." *Cf. Trident,* at 570 n. 6. The Charter Agreement is not "reasonably susceptible" to the court's interpretation that it warrants the seaworthiness of the vessel, the condition of the engines, and the capacity of the freezing system.

Sub-paragraph 3B concerns the condition of the vessel prior to delivery. It imposes on Bumble Bee an obligation to maintain the vessel in "good," not seaworthy condition, and to see that a "competent surveyor" surveys it to show that it is "tight, staunch, strong and seaworthy" for insurance purposes. It guarantees neither the accuracy of the survey nor the seaworthiness of the vessel.

Sub-paragraphs 3E and F address Bumble Bee's obligations after delivery. They provide that once Kemp accepts delivery, Bumble Bee's responsibility for the condition of the vessel ceases. They make clear that Kemp's acceptance of delivery releases Bumble Bee from responsibility for the vessel's condition and cannot be interpreted reasonably to warrant seaworthiness.

Nor should the court similarly have admitted evidence that Bumble Bee warranted the condition of the engines and the capacity of the freezing system. Paragraphs 3B, E and F do not even mention the engines or the freezing system and are not "reasonably susceptible" to that interpretation.

The court erred in admitting parol evidence and in enforcing warranties of seaworthiness, the engines, and freezing capacity. The Charter Agreement contains none of these warranties. . . .

The judgment is REVERSED and is rendered for the defendant. The Charter Agreement is an integrated contract and contained all the parties' agreements. It is not ambiguous and the court erred in admitting parol evidence on the warranty of seaworthiness, the capacity of the freezing system, and the engines. . . . Bumble Bee is not liable for Kemp's losses.

Questions

1. What is the purpose of the parol evidence rule?

2. How does the court determine whether a contract is integrated or not?

3. Why did the court conclude that the Charter Agreement in this case was an integrated contract?

4. Why did the court find that the Charter Agreement was not ambiguous?

5. What was the error made by the trial judge in admitting parol evidence in this case?

Takeaways – A. Kemp Fisheries

Was there an integration clause in the contract in *A. Kemp Fisheries*? If not, what factors caused the court to conclude that the parties' agreement was an integrated one and that extrinsic evidence of what was said or agreed to during negotiations was barred?

Exceptions to the Parol Evidence Rule – Mistake and Fraud

Bollinger v. Central Pennsylvania Quarry Stripping & Const. Co.

Supreme Court of Pennsylvania, 1967
425 Pa. 430

JUSTICE MUSMANNO. Mahlon Bollinger and his wife, Vinetta C. Bollinger, filed an action in equity against the Central Pennsylvania Quarry Stripping and Construction Company asking that a contract entered into between them be reformed so as to include therein a paragraph alleged to have been omitted by mutual mistake and that the agreement, as reformed, be enforced.

The agreement, as executed, provided that the defendant was to be permitted to deposit on the property of the plaintiffs, construction waste as it engaged in work on the Pennsylvania Turnpike in the immediate vicinity of the plaintiff's property.

The Bollingers claimed that there had been a mutual understanding between them and the defendant that, prior to depositing such waste on the plaintiffs' property, the defendant would remove the topsoil of the plaintiffs' property, pile on it the waste material and then restore the topsoil in a way to cover the deposited waste. The Bollingers averred that they had signed the written agreement without reading it because they assumed that the condition just stated had been incorporated into the writing.

When the defendant first began working in the vicinity of the plaintiffs' property, it did first remove the topsoil, deposited the waste on the bare land, and then replaced the topsoil. After a certain period of time, the defendant ceased doing this and the plaintiffs remonstrated. The defendant answered there was nothing in the written contract which required it to make a sandwich of its refuse between the bare earth and the topsoil. It was at this point that the plaintiffs discovered that that feature of the oral understanding had been omitted from the written contract. The plaintiff husband renewed his protest and the defendant's superintendent replied he could not remove the topsoil because his equipment for that operation had been taken away. When he was reminded of the original understanding, the superintendent said, in effect, he couldn't help that.

The plaintiffs then filed their action for reformation of the contract, the court granted the requested relief, and the defendant firm appealed. We said in *Bugen v. New York Life Insurance Co.*, 408 Pa. 472: "A court of equity has the power to reform the written evidence of a contract and make it correspond to the understanding of the parties . . . However, the mistake must be mutual to the parties to the contract." The fact, however, that one of the parties denies that a mistake was made does not prevent a finding of mutual mistake. *Kutsenkow v. Kutsenkow*, 414 Pa. 610, 612.

Once a person enters into a written agreement he builds around himself a stone wall, from which he cannot escape by merely asserting he had not understood what he was signing. However, equity would completely fail in its objectives if it refused to break a hole through the wall when it finds, after proper evidence, that there was a mistake between the parties, that it was real and not feigned, actual and not hypothetical.

The Chancellor, after taking testimony, properly concluded: "We are satisfied that plaintiffs have sustained the heavy burden placed upon them. Their understanding of the agreement is corroborated by the undisputed evidence. The defendant did remove and set aside the top soil on part of the area before depositing its waste and did replace the top soil over such waste after such depositing. It follows it would not have done so had it not so agreed. Further corroboration is found in the testimony that it acted similarly in the case of plaintiffs' neighbor Beltzner."

After the court handed down its Decree Nisi, the defendant petitioned for a rehearing on the ground of after-discovered evidence. Even assuming, without so deciding, that the so-called after-discovered evidence qualified as such, it is not clear that it was sufficiently material or relevant to bring about a change in the result reached by the chancellor, and he so stated in his opinion. We are satisfied that the proffered evidence would not be inconsistent with the chancellor's findings.

Decree affirmed, costs on the appellant.

Questions

1. According to the court's reasoning, what is the basis for granting the plaintiffs' request for reformation of the contract?

2. How does the court address the defendant's argument that there was no mutual mistake in the contract?

3. Explain why the court emphasizes the importance of proper evidence in determining the existence of a mistake between the parties.

4. What evidence did the plaintiffs present to support their claim of mutual understanding regarding the depositing of waste material?

Takeaways – Bollinger

Where a mistake or imperfection of the writing is put in issue by the pleadings, the parol evidence rule does not exclude evidence relevant to that issue. In other words, the parol evidence rule does not bar evidence of mistake with respect to the written agreement. (Rest.2d § 214(d); Cal.Code.Civ.Proc. §1856 (e).)

Riverisland Cold Storage Inc. v. Fresno-Madera Credit Assn.
California Supreme Court, 2013
55 Cal.4th 1169, 291 P.3d 316

CORRIGAN, J. The parol evidence rule protects the integrity of written contracts by making their terms the exclusive evidence of the parties' agreement. However, an established exception to the rule allows a party to present extrinsic evidence to show that the agreement was tainted by fraud. Here, we consider the scope of the fraud exception to the parol evidence rule.

As we discuss below, the fraud exception is a longstanding one, and is usually stated in broad terms. However, in 1935 this court adopted a limitation on the fraud exception: evidence offered to prove fraud "must tend to establish some independent fact or representation, some fraud in the procurement of the instrument or some breach of confidence concerning its use, and not a promise directly at variance with the promise of the writing." (*Bank of America etc. Assn. v. Pendergrass* (1935) 4 Cal.2d 258, 263, 48 P.2d 659 (*Pendergrass*).) The *Pendergrass* rule has been criticized but followed by California courts, for the most part, though some have narrowly construed it. The Court of Appeal in this case adopted such a narrow construction, deciding that evidence of an alleged oral misrepresentation of the written terms themselves is not barred by the *Pendergrass* rule.

Plaintiffs, who prevailed below, not only defend the Court of Appeal's holding but, alternatively, invite us to reconsider *Pendergrass*. There are good reasons for doing so. The *Pendergrass* limitation finds no support in the language of the statute codifying the parol evidence rule and the exception for evidence of fraud. It is difficult to apply. It conflicts with the doctrine of the Restatements, most treatises, and the majority of our sister-state jurisdictions. Furthermore, while intended to prevent fraud, the rule established in *Pendergrass* may actually provide a shield for fraudulent conduct. Finally, *Pendergrass* departed from established California law at the time it was decided, and neither acknowledged nor justified the abrogation. We now conclude that *Pendergrass* was ill-considered, and should be overruled. . . .

Plaintiffs Lance and Pamela Workman fell behind on their loan payments to defendant Fresno–Madera Production Credit Association (Credit Association or Association). They restructured their debt in an agreement, dated March 26, 2007, which confirmed outstanding loans with a total delinquency of $776, 380.24. In the new agreement, the Credit Association promised it would take no enforcement action until July 1, 2007, if the Workmans made specified payments. As additional collateral, the Workmans pledged eight separate parcels of real property. They initialed pages bearing the legal descriptions of these parcels.

The Workmans did not make the required payments. On March 21, 2008, the Credit Association recorded a notice of default. Eventually, the Workmans repaid the loan and the Association dismissed its foreclosure proceedings. The Workmans then filed this action, seeking damages for fraud and negligent misrepresentation, and including causes of action for rescission and reformation of the restructuring agreement. They alleged that the Association's vice president, David Ylarregui, met with them two weeks before the agreement was signed, and told them the Association would extend the loan for two years in exchange for additional collateral consisting of two ranches. The Workmans further claimed that when they signed the agreement Ylarregui assured them its term was two years and the ranches were the only additional security. As noted, the contract actually contemplated only three months of forbearance by the Association, and identified eight parcels as additional collateral. The Workmans did not read the agreement, but simply signed it at the locations tabbed for signature.

The Credit Association moved for summary judgment. It contended the Workmans could not prove their claims because the parol evidence rule barred evidence of any representations contradicting the terms of the written agreement. In opposition, the Workmans argued that Ylarregui's misrepresentations were admissible under the fraud exception to the parol evidence rule. Relying on *Pendergrass, supra,* 4 Cal.2d 258, 48 P.2d 659, the trial court granted summary judgment, ruling that the fraud exception does not allow parol evidence of promises at odds with the terms of the written agreement.

The Court of Appeal reversed. It reasoned that *Pendergrass* is limited to cases of promissory fraud. The court considered false statements about the contents of the agreement itself to be factual misrepresentations beyond the scope of the *Pendergrass* rule. We granted the Credit Association's petition for review. . . .

The parol evidence rule is codified in Code of Civil Procedure section 1856 and Civil Code section 1625. It provides that when parties enter an integrated written agreement, extrinsic evidence may not be relied upon to alter or add to the terms of the writing. (*Casa Herrera, Inc. v. Beydoun* (2004) 32 Cal.4th 336, 343, 9 Cal.Rptr.3d 97, 83 P.3d 497 (*Casa Herrera*).) "An integrated agreement is a writing or writings constituting a final expression of one or more terms of an agreement." (Rest.2d Contracts, § 209, subd. (1); see *Alling v. Universal Manufacturing Corp.* (1992) 5 Cal.App.4th 1412, 1433, 7 Cal.Rptr.2d 718.) There is no dispute in this case that the parties' agreement was integrated.

Although the parol evidence rule results in the exclusion of evidence, it is not a rule of evidence but one of substantive law. (*Casa Herrera, supra,* 32 Cal.4th at p. 343, 9 Cal.Rptr.3d 97, 83 P.3d 497.) It is founded on the principle that when the parties put all the terms of their agreement in writing, the writing itself becomes the agreement. The written terms supersede statements made during the negotiations. Extrinsic evidence of the agreement's terms is thus *irrelevant,* and cannot be relied upon. (*Casa Herrera,* at p. 344, 9 Cal.Rptr.3d 97, 83 P.3d 497.) "[T]he parol evidence rule, unlike the statute of frauds, does not merely serve an evidentiary purpose; it determines the enforceable and incontrovertible terms of an integrated written agreement." (*Id.* at p. 345, 9 Cal.Rptr.3d 97, 83 P.3d 497; cf. *Sterling v. Taylor* (2007) 40 Cal.4th 757, 766, 55 Cal.Rptr.3d 116, 152 P.3d 420 [explaining evidentiary function of statute of frauds].) The purpose of the rule is to ensure that the parties' final understanding, deliberately expressed in writing, is not subject to change. (*Casa Herrera,* at p. 345, 9 Cal.Rptr.3d 97, 83 P.3d 497.)

Section 1856, subdivision (f) establishes a broad exception to the operation of the parol evidence rule: "Where the validity of the agreement is the fact in dispute, this section does not exclude evidence relevant to that issue." This provision rests on the principle that the parol evidence rule, intended to protect the *terms* of a valid written contract, should not bar evidence challenging the *validity* of the agreement itself. "Evidence to prove that the instrument is void or voidable for mistake, fraud, duress, undue influence, illegality, alteration, lack of consideration, or another invalidating cause is admissible. This evidence does not contradict the terms of an effective integration, because it shows that the purported instrument has no legal effect." (2 Witkin, Cal. Evidence (5th ed. 2012) Documentary Evidence, § 97, p. 242; see also *id.,* §§ 66 & 72, pp. 206 & 211.) The fraud exception is expressly stated in section 1856, subdivision (g): "This section does not exclude other evidence ... to establish ... fraud."

Despite the unqualified language of section 1856, which broadly permits evidence relevant to the validity of an agreement and specifically allows evidence of fraud, the *Pendergrass* court decided to impose a limitation on the fraud exception. The facts of *Pendergrass* are similar in certain respects to those here. Borrowers fell behind on their payments. They and the bank executed a new promissory note, which was secured by additional collateral and payable on demand. Soon after it was signed, the bank seized the encumbered property and sued to enforce the note. In defense, the borrowers claimed the bank had promised not to interfere with their farming operations for the remainder of the year, and to take the proceeds of those operations in payment. They alleged that the bank had no intention of performing these promises, but made them for the fraudulent purpose of obtaining the new note and additional collateral. (*Pendergrass, supra,* 4 Cal.2d at pp. 259–262, 48 P.2d 659.)

The *Pendergrass* court concluded that further proceedings were required to determine whether the lender had pursued the proper form of action. (*Pendergrass, supra,* 4 Cal.2d at pp. 262–263, 48 P.2d 659.) However, the court also considered whether oral testimony would be admissible to establish the lender's alleged promise not to require payment until the borrowers sold their crops. "This promise is in direct contravention of the unconditional promise contained in the note to pay the money on demand. The question then is: Is such a promise the subject of parol proof for the purpose of establishing fraud as a defense to the action or by way of canceling the note, assuming, of course, that it can be properly coupled with proof that it was made without any intention of performing it?" (*Id.* at p. 263, 48 P.2d 659.)

"Our conception of the rule which permits parol evidence of fraud to establish the invalidity of the instrument is that it must tend to establish some independent fact or representation, some fraud in the procurement of the instrument or some breach of confidence concerning its use, and not a promise directly at variance with the promise of the writing. We find apt language in *Towner v. Lucas' Exr.* [(1857)] 54 Va. (13 Gratt.) 705, 716, in which to express our conviction: 'It is reasoning in a circle, to argue that fraud is made out, when it is shown by oral testimony that the obligee contemporaneously with the execution of a bond, promised not to enforce it. Such a principle would nullify the rule: for conceding that such an agreement is proved, or any other contradicting the written instrument, the party seeking to enforce the written agreement according to its terms, would always be guilty of fraud. The true question is, Was there any such agreement? And this can only be established by legitimate testimony. For reasons founded in wisdom and to prevent frauds and perjuries, the rule of the common law excludes such oral testimony of the alleged agreement; and as it cannot be proved by legal evidence, the agreement itself in legal contemplation, cannot be regarded as existing in fact.'" (*Pendergrass, supra,* 4 Cal.2d at pp. 263–264, 48 P.2d 659.)

Despite some criticism, *Pendergrass* has survived for over 75 years and the Courts of Appeal have followed it, albeit with varying degrees of fidelity. [Citations omitted] Until now, this court has not revisited the *Pendergrass* rule.

The primary ground of attack on *Pendergrass* has been that it is inconsistent with the principle, reflected in the terms of section 1856, that a contract may be invalidated by a showing of fraud. (*Coast Bank v. Holmes* (1971) 19 Cal.App.3d 581, 591, 97 Cal.Rptr. 30; Sweet, *supra,* 49 Cal. L.Rev. at p. 887; Note, *Parol Evidence: Admissibility to Show That a Promise Was Made Without Intention to Perform It* (1950) 38 Cal. L.Rev. 535, 538 (Note); see also *Pacific State Bank v. Greene* (2003) 110 Cal.App.4th 375, 390, 392, 1 Cal.Rptr.3d 739.) Evidence is deemed admissible for the purpose of proving fraud, without restriction, in the Restatements. (Rest.2d Contracts, § 214, subd. (d), and coms. c & d, pp. 134–135; see also *id.,* § 166, com. c, p. 452; Rest.2d Torts, § 530, com. c, p. 65.) Most of the treatises agree that evidence of fraud is not affected by the parol evidence rule.[Citations omitted]

Underlying the objection that *Pendergrass* overlooks the impact of fraud on the validity of an agreement is a more practical concern: its limitation on evidence of fraud may itself further fraudulent practices. As an Oregon court noted: "Oral promises made without the promisor's intention that they will be performed could be an effective means of deception if evidence of those fraudulent promises were never admissible merely because they were at variance with a subsequent written agreement." (*Howell v. Oregonian Publishing Co.* (1987) 85 Or.App. 84, 735 P.2d 659, 661; see Sweet, *supra,* 49 Cal. L.Rev. at p. 896 ["Promises made without the intention on the part of the promisor that they will be performed are unfortunately a facile and effective means of deception"].) Corbin observes: "The best reason for allowing fraud and similar undermining factors to be proven extrinsically is the obvious one: if there was fraud, or a mistake or some form of illegality, it is unlikely that it was bargained over or will be recited in the document. To bar extrinsic evidence would be to make the parol evidence rule a shield to protect misconduct or mistake." (6 Corbin on Contracts, *supra,* § 25.20[A], p. 280.)

Pendergrass has been criticized on other grounds as well. The distinction between promises deemed consistent with the writing and those considered inconsistent has been described as "tenuous." (*Coast Bank v. Holmes, supra,* 19 Cal.App.3d at p. 591, 97 Cal.Rptr. 30; see *Simmons v. Cal. Institute of Technology* (1949) 34 Cal.2d 264, 274, 209 P.2d 581; Note, *supra,* 38 Cal. L.Rev. at p. 537 [discussing *Simmons*]; Sweet, *supra,* 49 Cal. L.Rev. at p. 896 ["any attempt to forecast results in this area is a hazardous undertaking"].) The distinction between false promises and misrepresentations of fact has been called "very troublesome." (Sweet, *supra,* 49 Cal.

L.Rev. at p. 895.) It has also been noted that some courts have resisted applying the *Pendergrass* limitation by various means, leading to uncertainty in the case law. (See *Duncan v. The McCaffrey Group, Inc., supra,* 200 Cal.App.4th at pp. 369, 376–377, 133 Cal.Rptr.3d 280; Sweet, *supra,* 49 Cal. L.Rev. at pp. 885–886; *id.* at p. 907 ["The California experience demonstrates that even where a restrictive rule is adopted, many devices will develop to avoid its impact"]; Note, *The Fraud Exception to the Parol Evidence Rule: Necessary Protection for Fraud Victims or Loophole for Clever Parties?* (2009) 82 So.Cal. L.Rev. 809, 829 (*Fraud Exception*) [reviewing cases, and concluding that "inconsistent application of the fraud exception ... undermines the belief that the *Pendergrass* rule is clear, defensible, and viable"].)

In 1977, the California Law Revision Commission ignored *Pendergrass* when it proposed modifications to the statutory formulation of the parol evidence rule. The Commission advised the Legislature to conform the terms of section 1856 with rulings handed down by this court, observing: "As the parol evidence rule exists in California today, it bears little resemblance to the statutory statement of the rule." (Recommendation Relating to Parol Evidence Rule, 14 Cal. Law Revision Com. Rep., *supra,* pp. 147–148.) The Commission identified three opinions for consideration in designing revisions to the statute. (*Id.* at p. 148, fns. 6, 7, & 10, citing *Delta Dynamics, Inc. v. Arioto* (1968) 69 Cal.2d 525, 72 Cal.Rptr. 785, 446 P.2d 785, *Pacific Gas & E. Co. v. G.W. Thomas Drayage etc. Co.* (1968) 69 Cal.2d 33, 69 Cal.Rptr. 561, 442 P.2d 641, and *Masterson v. Sine* (1968) 68 Cal.2d 222, 65 Cal.Rptr. 545, 436 P.2d 561.)

Conspicuously omitted was any mention of *Pendergrass* and its nonstatutory limitation on the fraud exception. The Commission's discussion of the parol evidence rule set out the fraud exception without restriction, citing *Coast Bank v. Holmes, supra,* 19 Cal.App.3d 581, 97 Cal.Rptr. 30, which was strongly critical of *Pendergrass.* (Recommendation Relating to Parol Evidence Rule, 14 Cal. Law Revision Com. Rep., *supra,* p. 148.) The Commission's proposed revisions were adopted by the Legislature. They included no substantive changes to the statutory language allowing evidence that goes to the validity of an agreement, and evidence of fraud in particular. (Recommendation, at p. 152; see Stats.1978, ch. 150, § 1, pp. 374–375.)

On the other hand, *Pendergrass* has had its defenders. Its limitation on evidence of fraud has been described as "an entirely defensible decision favoring the policy considerations underlying the parol evidence rule over those supporting a fraud cause of action." (*Price v. Wells Fargo Bank, supra,* 213 Cal.App.3d at p. 485, 261 Cal.Rptr. 735; accord, *Duncan v. The McCaffrey Group, Inc., supra,* 200 Cal.App.4th at p. 369, 133 Cal.Rptr.3d 280; *Banco Do Brasil, S.A. v. Latian, Inc.* (1991) 234 Cal.App.3d 973, 1010, 285 Cal.Rptr. 870.) The *Price* court observed that "[a] broad doctrine of promissory fraud may allow parties to litigate disputes over the meaning of contract terms armed with an arsenal of tort remedies inappropriate to the resolution of commercial disputes." (*Price, supra,* at p. 485, 261 Cal.Rptr. 735; see also *Banco Do Brasil,* at pp. 1010–1011, 285 Cal.Rptr. 870.)

We note as well that the *Pendergrass* approach is not entirely without support in the treatises and law reviews. Wigmore, in a comment relied upon by the bank in *Pendergrass* and referred to indirectly by the *Pendergrass* court, has opined that an intent not to perform a promise should not be considered fraudulent for purposes of the parol evidence rule. (IX Wigmore, Evidence (Chadbourn rev. 1981) § 2439, p. 130; see Sweet, *supra*, 49 Cal. L.Rev. at p. 883; *Pendergrass, supra*, 4 Cal.2d at p. 264, 48 P.2d 659.) A recent law review comment, while critical of *Pendergrass*, favors limiting the scope of the fraud exception and advocates an even stricter rule for sophisticated parties. (*Fraud Exception, supra*, 82 So.Cal. L.Rev. at pp. 812–813.)

There are multiple reasons to question whether *Pendergrass* has stood the test of time. It has been criticized as bad policy. Its limitation on the fraud exception is inconsistent with the governing statute, and the Legislature did not adopt that limitation when it revised section 1856 based on a survey of California case law construing the parol evidence rule. *Pendergrass*'s divergence from the path followed by the Restatements, the majority of other states, and most commentators is cause for concern, and leads us to doubt whether restricting fraud claims is necessary to serve the purposes of the parol evidence rule. Furthermore, the functionality of the *Pendergrass* limitation has been called into question by the vagaries of its interpretations in the Courts of Appeal.

We respect the principle of stare decisis, but reconsideration of a poorly reasoned opinion is nevertheless appropriate. It is settled that if a decision departed from an established general rule without discussing the contrary authority, its weight as precedent is diminished. . . . Accordingly, we review the state of the law on the scope of the fraud exception when *Pendergrass* was decided, to determine if it was consistent with California law at that time.

Earlier cases from this court routinely stated without qualification that parol evidence was admissible to prove fraud. (E.g., *Martin v. Sugarman* (1933) 218 Cal. 17, 19, 21 P.2d 428; *Ferguson v. Koch* (1928) 204 Cal. 342, 347, 268 P. 342; *Mooney v. Cyriacks* (1921) 185 Cal. 70, 80, 195 P. 922; *Maxson v. Llewelyn* (1898) 122 Cal. 195, 199, 54 P. 732; *Hays v. Gloster* (1891) 88 Cal. 560, 565, 26 P. 367; *Brison v. Brison* (1888) 75 Cal. 525, 528, 17 P. 689; see also 10 Cal.Jur. (1923) Evidence § 203, pp. 937–938; Sweet, *supra*, 49 Cal. L.Rev. at pp. 880–882.) As the *Ferguson* court declared, "Parol evidence is always admissible to prove fraud, and it was never intended that the parol evidence rule should be used as a shield to prevent the proof of fraud." (*Ferguson, supra*, 204 Cal. at p. 347, 268 P. 342.)

Historically, this unconditional rule was applied in cases of promissory fraud. For instance, in *Langley v. Rodriguez* (1898) 122 Cal. 580, 55 P. 406, the trial court excluded evidence of an oral promise by a packing company agent to make an advance payment to a grower. This court reversed, stating: "The oral promise to pay part of the agreed price in advance of the curing of the crop was in conflict with the provision of the written contract that payment would be made on delivery of the raisins at the packing-house, and if the promise was honestly made it was undoubtedly within the rule forbidding proof of a contemporaneous or prior oral agreement to detract from the terms of a contract in writing. The rule cannot be avoided by showing that the promise outside the writing has been broken; such breach in itself does not constitute fraud. [Citations.] But a promise made without any intention of performing it is one of the forms of actual fraud (Civ.Code, sec.1572); and cases are not infrequent where relief against a contract reduced to writing has been granted on the ground that its execution was procured by means of oral promises fraudulent in the particular mentioned, however variant from the terms of the written engagement into which they were the means of inveigling the party. [Citations.]" (*Langley, supra,* 122 Cal. at pp. 581–582, 55 P. 406; see also, e.g., *Hays v. Gloster, supra,* 88 Cal. at p. 565, 26 P. 367; *Brison v. Brison, supra,* 75 Cal. at p. 528, 17 P. 689.)

Interestingly, two years after *Pendergrass* this court fell back on the old rule in *Fleury v. Ramacciotti* (1937) 8 Cal.2d 660, 67 P.2d 339, a promissory fraud case. Ramacciotti, a mortgage debtor, claimed he had signed a renewal note without reading it, relying on a false promise that the note included a provision barring a deficiency judgment. (*Id.* at p. 661, 67 P.2d 339.) The trial court ruled in Ramacciotti's favor. The *Fleury* court affirmed, stating summarily: "Plaintiff's contention that the evidence was admitted in violation of the parol evidence rule is of course untenable, for although a written instrument may supersede prior negotiations and understandings leading up to it, fraud may always be shown to defeat the effect of an agreement." (*Id.* at p. 662, 67 P.2d 339; see also *Stock v. Meek* (1950) 35 Cal.2d 809, 815–816, 221 P.2d 15 [mistake of law case, quoting old rule and language from Rest. of Contracts permitting extrinsic evidence of mistake or fraud].)

Thus, *Pendergrass* was plainly out of step with established California law. Moreover, the authorities to which it referred, upon examination, provide little support for the rule it declared. The *Pendergrass* court relied primarily on *Towner v. Lucas' Exr., supra,* 54 Va. 705, quoting that opinion at length. (*Pendergrass, supra,* 4 Cal.2d at pp. 263–264, 48 P.2d 659.) In *Towner*, a debtor relied on an oral promise of indemnity against payment on surety bonds. However, no fraud was alleged, nor was it claimed that the promise had been made without the intent to perform, an essential element of promissory fraud. (*Towner, supra,* 54 Va. at pp. 706, 722; see *Langley v. Rodriguez, supra,* 122 Cal. at p. 581, 55 P. 406; 5 Witkin, Summary of Cal. Law, *supra,* Torts, § 781, p. 1131.) While dicta in *Towner* provides some support for the *Pendergrass* rule, the *Towner* court appeared to be principally concerned with the consequences of a rule that mere proof of nonperformance of an oral promise at odds with the writing would establish fraud. (*Towner, supra,* 54 Va. at p. 716; see Sweet, *supra,* 49 Cal. L.Rev. at pp. 884–885.)

Pendergrass also cited a number of California cases. Yet not one of them considered the fraud exception to the parol evidence rule. . . .

Accordingly, we conclude that *Pendergrass* was an aberration. It purported to follow section 1856 (*Pendergrass, supra,* 4 Cal.2d at p. 264, 48 P.2d 659), but its restriction on the fraud exception was inconsistent with the terms of the statute, and with settled case law as well. *Pendergrass* failed to account for the fundamental principle that fraud undermines the essential validity of the parties' agreement. When fraud is proven, it cannot be maintained that the parties freely entered into an agreement reflecting a meeting of the minds. Moreover, *Pendergrass* has led to instability in the law, as courts have strained to avoid abuses of the parol evidence rule. The *Pendergrass* court sought to " 'prevent frauds and perjuries' " (*id.* at p. 263, 48 P.2d 659), but ignored California law protecting against promissory fraud. The fraud exception has been part of the parol evidence rule since the earliest days of our jurisprudence, and the *Pendergrass* opinion did not justify the abridgment it imposed. For these reasons, we overrule *Pendergrass,* and its progeny, and reaffirm the venerable maxim stated in *Ferguson v. Koch, supra,* 204 Cal. at page 347, 268 P. 342: "[I]t was never intended that the parol evidence rule should be used as a shield to prevent the proof of fraud." . . .

We affirm the Court of Appeal's judgment.

Questions

1. What is the fraud exception to the parol evidence rule, and what limitation was imposed on it by the *Pendergrass* case?

2. How did the Court of Appeal in this case interpret and apply the fraud exception?

3. What are the reasons provided in the case for reconsidering and overruling the *Pendergrass* rule?

Takeaways – Riverisland Cold Storage

Riverisland highlights a distinction between two types of fraud: fraud in the inducement and fraud in the execution. Fraud in the inducement refers to false statements made to persuade someone to enter into an agreement. Fraud in the execution, on the other hand, refers to false statements made regarding the content of the written agreement. Historically, most courts have ruled that only evidence of fraud in the inducement is an exception to the parol evidence rule and is not barred by the rule. The premise of not creating an exception for fraud in the execution is that since the falsity of any statements or representations as to the content of the document could be revealed simply by reading the document, no one could reasonably rely on any false statements regarding the content of the document. How does *Riverisland* change that rule?

No-Oral-Modification Clauses

The parol evidence rule has no application to oral agreements made *subsequent* to the execution of a written contract. The parties are always free to modify their agreement (subject to the limitations of the pre-existing duty rule) if they so choose. May the parties agree in advance to forego this right? One way of accomplishing this might be the inclusion of a "no oral modification clause." Such a clause typically says, "This written contract can only be modified by a writing. Oral modifications will not be effective." By including a no oral modification clause, the parties have in effect created their own private statute of frauds with respect to their agreement.

UCC 2-209(2) provides that a signed agreement which excludes modification or rescission except by a signed writing cannot be otherwise modified or rescinded. (Between merchants there must be a signed agreement containing the no oral modification clause.) However, 2-209(4) provides that an attempt at modification which does not satisfy a contractual requirement that modifications be in writing may nevertheless operate as a waiver. Attempted modification is effective as a waiver only if there is reliance. I.e., there is no waiver unless the party seeking to enforce the oral modification has relied to its detriment on the modification. If there has been detrimental reliance, the right to insist that all modifications be in writing has been waived.

Extrinsic Evidence to Show the Parties' Intent

So far, we have only examined whether extrinsic evidence can be resorted to for purposes of introducing a term that was not included in the writing. In other words, in addition to the written agreement itself, are there any other terms, such a previous negotiations or representations, that should be included in what the parties agreed to and therefore is considered to be part of their "contract?" We now turn to a different question. What happens when a contract has been reduced to writing and a dispute arises as to the meaning of what has been written down? Can anything other than the words of the contract themselves be looked to in order to determine what the word or term in question means and/or what the parties intended? May the parties resort to extrinsic evidence to explain or interpret a word or term that is included in the writing?

Up until the first half of the twentieth century, courts honored what was known as the "plain meaning rule." The plain meaning rule states that if a writing, or if a word or term in the writing, appears to be plain and unambiguous on its face, its meaning must be determined from the face of the instrument (sometimes more graphically referred to as the "four corners" of the instrument) without resort to extrinsic evidence. However the plain meaning (or 4 corners) rule no longer enjoys universal acceptance. The Restatement Second of Contracts has rejected the plain meaning rule. (See Rest.2d § 214(c).) This is true even if there the writing is integrated and there is no ambiguity. However, the trial judge must initially decide whether the asserted meaning is one to which the language taken in context, is reasonably susceptible in the light of all the evidence. If it is not then that asserted meaning may not be attached to the language in question. (See Rest.2d §§ 210, 215.)

Plain Meaning Rule Distinguished From Parol Evidence Rule

Although both the plain meaning rule and parol evidence rule revolve around the issue of whether extrinsic evidence can be admitted into evidence and taken into consideration, the rules are separate and distinct. The parol evidence rule is a limitation on the ability to use extrinsic evidence to vary or contradict the terms of the agreement. The plain meaning rule is concerned with whether extrinsic evidence can ever be resorted to as an aid in interpreting or explaining a word, term or clause contained in the agreement.

Pacific Gas & E. Co. v. G. W. Thomas Drayage & Rigging Co.
Supreme Court of California, 1968
69 Cal.2d 33, 442 P2d 641

Defendant appeals from a judgment for plaintiff in an action for damages for injury to property under an indemnity clause of a contract.

In 1960 defendant entered into a contract with plaintiff to furnish the labor and equipment necessary to remove and replace the upper metal cover of plaintiff's steam turbine. Defendant agreed to perform the work "at [its] own risk and expense" and to "indemnify" plaintiff "against all loss, damage, expense and liability resulting from ... injury to property, arising out of or in any way connected with the performance of this contract." Defendant also agreed to procure not less than $50,000 insurance to cover liability for injury to property. Plaintiff was to be an additional named insured, but the policy was to contain a cross-liability clause extending the coverage to plaintiff's property.

During the work the cover fell and injured the exposed rotor of the turbine. Plaintiff brought this action to recover $25,144.51, the amount it subsequently spent on repairs. During the trial it dismissed a count based on negligence and thereafter secured judgment on the theory that the indemnity provision covered injury to all property regardless of ownership.

Defendant offered to prove by admissions of plaintiff's agents, by defendant's conduct under similar contracts entered into with plaintiff, and by other proof that in the indemnity clause the parties meant to cover injury to property of third parties only and not to plaintiff's property. Although the trial court observed that the language used was "the classic language for a third party indemnity provision" and that "one could very easily conclude that ... its whole intendment is to indemnify third parties," it nevertheless held that the "plain language" of the agreement also required defendant to indemnify plaintiff for injuries to plaintiff's property. Having determined that the contract had a plain meaning, the court refused to admit any extrinsic evidence that would contradict its interpretation.

When the court interprets a contract on this basis, it determines the meaning of the instrument in accordance with the "... extrinsic evidence of the judge's own linguistic education and experience." (3 Corbin on Contracts (1960 ed.) [1964 Supp. § 579, p. 225, fn. 56].) The exclusion of testimony that might contradict the linguistic background of the judge reflects a judicial belief in the possibility of perfect verbal expression. (9 Wigmore on Evidence (3d ed. 1940) § 2461, p. 187.) This belief is a remnant of a primitive faith in the inherent potency fn. 2 and inherent meaning of words.

The test of admissibility of extrinsic evidence to explain the meaning of a written instrument is not whether it appears to the court to be plain and unambiguous on its face, but whether the offered evidence is relevant to prove a meaning to which the language of the instrument is reasonably susceptible. . . .

A rule that would limit the determination of the meaning of a written instrument to its four-corners merely because it seems to the court to be clear and unambiguous, would either deny the relevance of the intention of the parties or presuppose a degree of verbal precision and stability our language has not attained.

Some courts have expressed the opinion that contractual obligations are created by the mere use of certain words, whether or not there was any intention to incur such obligations. Under this view, contractual obligations flow, not from the intention of the parties but from the fact that they used certain magic words. Evidence of the parties' intention therefore becomes irrelevant.

In this state, however, the intention of the parties as expressed in the contract is the source of contractual rights and duties. A court must ascertain and give effect to this intention by determining what the parties meant by the words they used. Accordingly, the exclusion of relevant, extrinsic, evidence to explain the meaning of a written instrument could be justified only if it were feasible to determine the meaning the parties gave to the words from the instrument alone.

If words had absolute and constant referents, it might be possible to discover contractual intention in the words themselves and in the manner in which they were arranged. Words, however, do not have absolute and constant referents. "A word is a symbol of thought but has no arbitrary and fixed meaning like a symbol of algebra or chemistry, ..." (Pearson v. State Social Welfare Board (1960) 54 Cal.2d 184, 195 [5 Cal.Rptr. 553, 353 P.2d 33].) The meaning of particular words or groups of words varies with the "... verbal context and surrounding circumstances and purposes in view of the linguistic education and experience of their users and their hearers or readers (not excluding judges). ... A word has no meaning apart from these factors; much less does it have an objective meaning, one true meaning." (Corbin, The Interpretation of Words and the Parol Evidence Rule (1965) 50 Cornell L.Q. 161, 187.) Accordingly, the meaning of a writing "... can only be found by interpretation in the light of all the circumstances that reveal the sense in which the writer used the words. The exclusion of parol evidence regarding such circumstances merely because the words do not appear ambiguous to the reader can easily lead to the attribution to a written instrument of a meaning that was never intended. [Citations omitted.]"

Although extrinsic evidence is not admissible to add to, detract from, or vary the terms of a written contract, these terms must first be determined before it can be decided whether or not extrinsic evidence is being offered for a prohibited purpose. The fact that the terms of an instrument appear clear to a judge does not preclude the possibility that the parties chose the language of the instrument to express different terms. That possibility is not limited to contracts whose terms have acquired a particular meaning by trade usage, but exists whenever the parties' understanding of the words used may have differed from the judge's understanding.

Accordingly, rational interpretation requires at least a preliminary consideration of all credible evidence offered to prove the intention of the parties. (Civ. Code, § 1647; Code Civ. Proc., § 1860; see also 9 Wigmore on Evidence, op. cit. supra, § 2470, p. 227.) Such evidence includes testimony as to the "circumstances surrounding the making of the agreement ... including the object, nature and subject matter of the writing ..." so that the court can "place itself in the same situation in which the parties found themselves at the time of contracting." (Universal Sales Corp. v. California Press Mfg. Co., supra, 20 Cal.2d 751, 761; Lemm v. Stillwater Land & Cattle Co., supra, 217 Cal. 474, 480-481.) If the court decides, after considering this evidence, that the language of a contract, in the light of all the circumstances, "is fairly susceptible of either one of the two interpretations contended for ..." .. , extrinsic evidence relevant to prove either of such meanings is admissible.

In the present case the court erroneously refused to consider extrinsic evidence offered to show that the indemnity clause in the contract was not intended to cover injuries to plaintiff's property. Although that evidence was not necessary to show that the indemnity clause was reasonably susceptible of the meaning contended for by defendant, it was nevertheless relevant and admissible on that issue. Moreover, since that clause was reasonably susceptible of that meaning, the offered evidence was also admissible to prove that the clause had that meaning and did not cover injuries to plaintiff's property. Accordingly, the judgment must be reversed. . . .

The judgment is reversed.

Questions

1. What was the main issue in the case regarding the interpretation of the contract's indemnity clause?

2. How did the trial court interpret the language of the indemnity clause and why did it refuse to consider extrinsic evidence?

3. According to the court, what is the test of admissibility of extrinsic evidence in interpreting a written contract?

4. Why did the court state that a rule limiting the determination of the contract's meaning to its four corners would deny the relevance of the parties' intention?

5. What was the court's conclusion regarding the admissibility of extrinsic evidence in this case and why did it reverse the judgment?

Takeaways – Pacific Gas & Electric

Is extrinsic evidence being offered here to vary or contradict the terms of the written agreement or is it being offered to interpret or explain a term in the contract that is ambiguous? The court noted that "extrinsic evidence is not admissible to add to, detract from, or vary the terms of a written contract." But it also observed that "[a] court must ascertain and give effect to [the parties'] intention by determining what the parties meant by the words they used." Do you see the distinction?

If you don't, don't feel bad. One person's interpretation may very well be the other person's contradiction. As an example, extrinsic evidence that "north" meant "south" would be barred as a variance or contradiction but extrinsic evidence that "north" meant "magnetic north" (as opposed to "true north") would probably be admissible as explaining or interpreting the term "north." (*Jenny Lind Co. v. Bower* (1858) 11 Cal. 194, 197-199)

Should extrinsic evidence be admitted to show that the word "ton" in a contract meant a long ton or 2,240 pounds and not the statutory ton of 2,000 pounds? (*Higgins v. California Petroleum etc. Co.* (1898) 120 Cal. 629, 630-632 [52 P. 1080]) Should extrinsic evidence of trade usage or custom be admitted to show that the term "United Kingdom" in a motion picture distribution contract includes Ireland? (See, *Ermolieff v. R.K.O. Radio Pictures, Inc.* (1942) 19 Cal.2d 543, 549-552 [122 P.2d 3]) Both of these cases are considered later in this chapter as examples of extrinsic evidence of "trade usage" as permissible sources for explaining or interpreting terms that otherwise appear to be unambiguous on their face.

According to the court in *Pacific Gas & Electric*, the test of admissibility of extrinsic evidence to explain the meaning of a written instrument is not whether it appears to the court to be plain and unambiguous on its face, but whether the offered evidence is relevant to prove a meaning to which the language of the instrument is reasonably susceptible.

Greenfield v. Philles Records
Court of Appeals of the State of New York, 2002
98 N.Y.2d 562 . 780 N.E.2d 166, 750 N.Y.S.2d 565

GRAFFEO, J. In this contract dispute between a singing group and their record producer, we must determine whether the artists' transfer of full ownership rights to the master recordings of musical performances carried with it the unconditional right of the producer to redistribute those performances in any technological format. In the absence of an explicit contractual reservation of rights by the artists, we conclude that it did.

The Ronettes

In the early 1960s, Veronica Bennett (now known as Ronnie Greenfield), her sister Estelle Bennett and their cousin Nedra Talley, formed a singing group known as "The Ronettes." They met defendant Phil Spector, a music producer and composer, in 1963 and signed a five-year "personal services" music recording contract (the Ronettes agreement) with Spector's production company, defendant Philles Records, Inc. The plaintiffs agreed to perform exclusively for Philles Records and in exchange, Philles Records acquired an ownership right to the recordings of the Ronettes' musical performances. The agreement also set forth a royalty schedule to compensate plaintiffs for their services. After signing with Philles Records, plaintiffs received a single collective cash advance of approximately $15,000.

The Ronettes recorded several dozen songs for Philles Records, including "Be My Baby," which sold over a million copies and topped the music charts. Despite their popularity, the group disbanded in 1967 and Philles Records eventually went out of business. Other than their initial advance, plaintiffs received no royalty payments from Philles Records.

Beyond their professional relationship, however, was the story of the personal relationship between Spector and plaintiff Ronnie Greenfield. They married in 1968 but separated after a few years. Greenfield initiated a divorce proceeding against Spector in California and a settlement was reached in 1974. As part of that agreement, Spector and Greenfield executed mutual general releases that purported to resolve all past and future claims and obligations that existed between them, as well as between Greenfield and Spector's companies.

Defendants subsequently began to capitalize on a resurgence of public interest in 1960s music by making use of new recording technologies and licensing master recordings of the Ronettes' vocal performances for use in movie and television productions, a process known in entertainment industry parlance as "synchronization." The most notable example was defendants' licensing of "Be My Baby" in 1987 for use in the motion picture "Dirty Dancing." Defendants also licensed master recordings to third parties for production and distribution in the United States (referred to as domestic redistribution), and sold compilation albums containing performances by the Ronettes. While defendants earned considerable compensation from such licensing and sales, no royalties were paid to any of the plaintiffs.

As a result, plaintiffs commenced this breach of contract action in 1987, alleging that the 1963 agreement did not provide Philles Records with the right to license the master recordings for synchronization and domestic redistribution, and demanded royalties from the sales of compilation albums. Although defendants initially denied the existence of a contract, in 1992 they stipulated that an unexecuted copy of the contract would determine the parties' rights. Defendants thereafter argued that the agreement granted them absolute ownership rights to the master recordings and permitted the use of the recordings in any format, subject only to royalty rights. Following extensive pretrial proceedings (160 AD2d 458; 243 AD2d 353; 248 AD2d 212), Supreme Court ruled in plaintiffs' favor and awarded approximately $3 million in damages and interest.

The Appellate Division affirmed, concluding that defendants' actions were not authorized by the agreement with plaintiffs because the contract did not specifically transfer the right to issue synchronization and third-party domestic distribution licenses. Permitting plaintiffs to assert a claim for unjust enrichment, the Court found that plaintiffs were entitled to the music recording industry's standard

50% royalty rate for income derived from synchronization and third-party licensing. We granted leave to appeal.

We are asked on this appeal to determine whether defendants, as the owners of the master recordings of plaintiffs' vocal performances, acquired the contractual right to issue licenses to third parties to use the recordings in connection with television, movies and domestic audio distribution. The agreement between the parties consists of a two-page document, which apparently was widely used in the 1960s by music producers signing new artists. Plaintiffs executed the contract without the benefit of counsel. The parties' immediate objective was to record and market the Ronettes' vocal performances and "mak[e] therefrom phonograph records and/or tape recordings and other similar devices (excluding transcriptions)." The ownership rights provision of the contract provides:

"All recordings made hereunder and all records and reproductions made therefrom together with the performances embodied therein, shall be entirely [Philles'] property, free of any claims whatsoever by you or any person deriving any rights of interest from you. Without limitation of the foregoing, [Philles] shall have the right to make phonograph records, tape recordings or other reproductions of the performances embodied in such recordings by any method now or hereafter known, and to sell and deal in the same under any trade mark or trade names or labels designated by us, or we may at our election refrain therefrom."

Plaintiffs concede that the contract unambiguously gives defendants unconditional ownership rights to the master recordings, but contend that the agreement does not bestow the right to exploit those recordings in new markets or mediums since the document is silent on those topics. Defendants counter that the absence of specific references to synchronization and domestic licensing is irrelevant. They argue that where a contract grants full ownership rights to a musical performance or composition, the only restrictions upon the owner's right to use that property are those explicitly enumerated by the grantor/artist.

Despite the technological innovations that continue to revolutionize the recording industry, long-settled common-law contract rules still govern the interpretation of agreements between artists and their record producers. The fundamental, neutral precept of contract interpretation is that agreements are construed in accord with the parties' intent "The best evidence of what parties to a written agreement intend is what they say in their writing" (Slamow v Del Col, 79 NY2d 1016, 1018 [1992]). Thus, a written agreement that is complete, clear and unambiguous on its face must be enforced according to the plain meaning of its terms .

Extrinsic evidence of the parties' intent may be considered only if the agreement is ambiguous, which is an issue of law for the courts to decide (see W.W.W. Assoc. v Giancontieri, supra at 162). A contract is unambiguous if the language it uses has "a definite and precise meaning, unattended by danger of misconception in the purport of the [agreement] itself, and concerning which there is no reasonable basis for a difference of opinion" Thus, if the agreement on its face is reasonably susceptible of only one meaning, a court is not free to alter the contract to reflect its personal notions of fairness and equity.

The pivotal issue in this case is whether defendants are prohibited from using the master recordings for synchronization, and whatever future formats evolve from new technologies, in the absence of explicit contract language authorizing such uses. Stated another way, does the contract's silence on synchronization and domestic licensing create an ambiguity which opens the door to the admissibility of extrinsic evidence to determine the intent of the parties? We conclude that it does not and, because there is no ambiguity in the terms of the Ronettes agreement, defendants are entitled to exercise complete ownership rights, subject to payment of applicable royalties due plaintiffs. . . .

Defendants further claim that Greenfield is barred from sharing in those royalties because she executed a general release in connection with her divorce from Spector. We look to California law to analyze the scope of Greenfield's release because that is the state where the release was executed and the divorce was finalized. In contrast to the "four corners" rule that New York has long applied, California courts preliminarily consider all credible evidence of the parties' intent in addition to the language of the contract "[t]he test of admissibility of extrinsic evidence to explain the meaning of a written instrument is not whether it appears to the court to be plain and unambiguous on its face, but whether the offered evidence is relevant to prove a meaning to which the language of the instrument is reasonably susceptible" (Pacific Gas & Elec. Co. v G.W. Thomas Drayage & Rigging Co., 69 Cal 2d 33, 37, 442 P2d 641, 644 [1968]).

During proceedings in New York, Supreme Court determined that the extrinsic evidence supported Greenfield's allegation that her right to compensation under the 1963 recording contract was not an intended subject of the release. That finding of fact, affirmed by the Appellate Division, is supported by the record. We find no reason to reverse the Appellate Division's interpretation of California law (see e.g. Rudman v Cowles Communications, 30 NY2d 1, 10 [1972]). Plaintiff Greenfield is therefore entitled to her share of any damages assessed against defendants.

We have reviewed the parties' remaining contentions; they are either academic or meritless.

Accordingly, the order of the Appellate Division should be modified, without costs, and the case remitted to Supreme Court for further proceedings in accordance with this opinion and, as so modified, affirmed.

Questions

1. What did the plaintiffs argue regarding the exploitation of the recordings in new markets or mediums? How did the defendants counter that argument?

2. According to the court, when can extrinsic evidence of the parties' intent be considered in contract interpretation? How did the court apply this principle to the case?

3. Why did the court look to California law to analyze the scope of Greenfield's release? How did the court determine the effect of the release on Greenfield's right to compensation under the recording contract?

4. Having read the leading cases from the highest courts of California and New York, what is the distinction between the New York approach and the California approach to using extrinsic evidence to interpret or explain words or terms that otherwise appear to be plain and unambiguous?

Trident Center v. Connecticut General Life Ins. Co.
U.S. Court of Appeal Ninth Circuit (Cal.), 1988
847 F.2d 564

KOZINSKI, Circuit Judge: The parties to this transaction are, by any standard, highly sophisticated business people: Plaintiff is a partnership consisting of an insurance company and two of Los Angeles' largest and most prestigious law firms; defendant is another insurance company. Dealing at arm's length and from positions of roughly equal bargaining strength, they negotiated a commercial loan amounting to more than $56 million. The contract documents are lengthy and detailed; they squarely address the precise issue that is the subject of this dispute; to all who read English, they appear to resolve the issue fully and conclusively.

Plaintiff nevertheless argues here, as it did below, that it is entitled to introduce extrinsic evidence that the contract means something other than what it says. This case therefore presents the question whether parties in California can ever draft a contract that is proof to parol evidence. Somewhat surprisingly, the answer is no. . . .

The facts are rather simple. Sometime in 1983 Security First Life Insurance Company and the law firms of Mitchell, Silberberg & Knupp and Manatt, Phelps, Rothenberg & Tunney formed a limited partnership for the purpose of constructing an office building complex on Olympic Boulevard in West Los Angeles. The partnership, Trident Center, the plaintiff herein, sought and obtained financing for the project from defendant, Connecticut General Life Insurance Company. The loan documents provide for a loan of $56,500,000 at 12 1/4 percent interest for a term of 15 years, secured by a deed of trust on the project. The promissory note provides that "[m]aker shall not have the right to prepay the principal amount hereof in whole or in part" for the first 12 years. Note at 6. In years 13-15, the loan may be prepaid, subject to a sliding prepayment fee. The note also provides that in case of a default during years 1-12, Connecticut General has the option of accelerating the note and adding a 10 percent prepayment fee.

Everything was copacetic for a few years until interest rates began to drop. The 12 1/4 percent rate that had seemed reasonable in 1983 compared unfavorably with 1987 market rates and Trident started looking for ways of refinancing the loan to take advantage of the lower rates. Connecticut General was unwilling to oblige, insisting that the loan could not be prepaid for the first 12 years of its life, that is, until January 1996.

Trident then brought suit in state court seeking a declaration that it was entitled to prepay the loan now, subject only to a 10 percent prepayment fee. Connecticut General promptly removed to federal court and brought a motion to dismiss, claiming that the loan documents clearly and unambiguously precluded prepayment during the first 12 years. The district court agreed and dismissed Trident's complaint. The court also "*sua sponte,* sanction[ed] the plaintiff for the filing of a frivolous lawsuit." Order of Dismissal, No. CV 87-2712 JMI (Kx), at 3 (C.D. Cal. June 8, 1987). Trident appeals both aspects of the district court's ruling.

Trident makes two arguments as to why the district court's ruling is wrong. First, it contends that the language of the contract is ambiguous and proffers a construction that it believes supports its position. Second, Trident argues that, under California law, even seemingly unambiguous contracts are subject to modification by parol or extrinsic evidence. Trident faults the district court for denying it the opportunity to present evidence that the contract language did not accurately reflect the parties' intentions.

As noted earlier, the promissory note provides that Trident "shall not have the right to prepay the principal amount hereof in whole or in part before January 1996." Note at 6. It is difficult to imagine language that more clearly or unambiguously expresses the idea that Trident may not unilaterally prepay the loan during its first 12 years. Trident, however, argues that there is an ambiguity because another clause of the note provides that "[i]n the event of a prepayment resulting from a default hereunder or the Deed of Trust prior to January 10, 1996 the prepayment fee will be ten percent (10%)." Note at 6-7. Trident interprets this clause as giving it the option of prepaying the loan if only it is willing to incur the prepayment fee.

We reject Trident's argument out of hand. . . .

Trident argues in the alternative that, even if the language of the contract appears to be unambiguous, the deal the parties actually struck is in fact quite different. It wishes to offer extrinsic evidence that the parties had agreed Trident could prepay at any time within the first 12 years by tendering the full amount plus a 10 percent prepayment fee. As discussed above, this is an interpretation to which the contract, as written, is not reasonably susceptible. Under traditional contract principles, extrinsic evidence is inadmissible to interpret, vary or add to the terms of an unambiguous integrated written instrument. *See* 4 S. Williston, *supra* p. 5, § 631, at 948-49; 2 B. Witkin, *California Evidence* § 981, at 926 (3d ed. 1986).

Trident points out, however, that California does not follow the traditional rule. Two decades ago the California Supreme Court in *Pacific Gas & Electric Co. v. G.W. Thomas Drayage & Rigging Co.,* 69 Cal.2d 33, 442 P.2d 641, 69 Cal.Rptr. 561 (1968), turned its back on the notion that a contract can ever have a plain meaning discernible by a court without resort to extrinsic evidence. The court reasoned that contractual obligations flow not from the words of the contract, but from the intention of the parties. "Accordingly," the court stated, "the exclusion of relevant, extrinsic, evidence to explain the meaning of a written instrument could be justified only if it were feasible to determine the meaning the parties gave to the words from the instrument alone." 69 Cal.2d at 38, 442 P.2d 641, 69 Cal.Rptr. 561. This, the California Supreme Court concluded, is impossible: "If words had absolute and constant referents, it might be possible to discover contractual intention in the words themselves and in the manner in which they were arranged. Words, however, do not have absolute and constant referents." *Id.* In the same vein, the court noted that "[t]he exclusion of testimony that might contradict the linguistic background of the judge reflects a judicial belief in the possibility of perfect verbal expression. This belief is a remnant of a primitive faith in the inherent potency and inherent meaning of words." *Id.* at 37, 442 P.2d 641, 69 Cal.Rptr. 561 (citation and footnotes omitted).

Under *Pacific Gas,* it matters not how clearly a contract is written, nor how completely it is integrated, nor how carefully it is negotiated, nor how squarely it addresses the issue before the court: the contract cannot be rendered impervious to attack by parol evidence. If one side is willing to claim that the parties intended one thing but the agreement provides for another, the court must consider extrinsic evidence of possible ambiguity. If that evidence raises the specter of ambiguity where there was none before, the contract language is displaced and the intention of the parties must be divined from self-serving testimony offered by partisan witnesses whose recollection is hazy from passage of time and colored by their conflicting interests. *See Delta Dynamics, Inc. v. Arioto,* 69 Cal.2d 525, 532, 446 P.2d 785, 72 Cal.Rptr. 785 (1968) (Mosk, J., dissenting). We question whether this approach is more likely to divulge the original intention of the parties than reliance on the seemingly clear words they agreed upon at the time. *See generally Morta v. Korea Ins. Co.,* 840 F.2d 1452, 1460 (9th Cir.1988).

Pacific Gas casts a long shadow of uncertainty over all transactions negotiated and executed under the law of California. As this case illustrates, even when the transaction is very sizeable, even if it involves only sophisticated parties, even if it was negotiated with the aid of counsel, even if it results in contract language that is devoid of ambiguity, costly and protracted litigation cannot be avoided if one party has a strong enough motive for challenging the contract. While this rule creates much business for lawyers and an occasional windfall to some clients, it leads only to frustration and delay for most litigants and clogs already overburdened courts.

It also chips away at the foundation of our legal system. By giving credence to the idea that words are inadequate to express concepts, *Pacific Gas* undermines the basic principle that language provides a meaningful constraint on public and private conduct. If we are unwilling to say that parties, dealing face to face, can come up with language that binds them, how can we send anyone to jail for violating statutes consisting of mere words lacking "absolute and constant referents"? How can courts ever enforce decrees, not written in language understandable to all, but encoded in a dialect reflecting only the "linguistic background of the judge"? Can lower courts ever be faulted for failing to carry out the mandate of higher courts when "perfect verbal expression" is impossible? Are all attempts to develop the law in a reasoned and principled fashion doomed to failure as "remnant[s] of a primitive faith in the inherent potency and inherent meaning of words"?

Be that as it may. While we have our doubts about the wisdom of Pacific *Gas,* we have no difficulty understanding its meaning, even without extrinsic evidence to guide us. As we read the rule in California, we must reverse and remand to the district court in order to give plaintiff an opportunity to present extrinsic evidence as to the intention of the parties in drafting the contract. It may not be a wise rule we are applying, but it is a rule that binds us.

The judgment of the district court is REVERSED.

Questions

1. How did Trident attempt to use extrinsic evidence to support its position, and what was the court's response to this argument?

2. What is the significance of the California Supreme Court's decision in *Pacific Gas & Electric Co. v. G.W. Thomas Drayage & Rigging Co.?*

3. Despite expressing doubts about the wisdom of *Pacific Gas*, what ruling did the court make in this case based on the rule established in that decision?

General Rules of Contract Interpretation

Contract Construed Most Strictly Against Drafter

Any ambiguities caused by the drafter of the contract must be resolved against the drafter or the party employing them. In cases of uncertainty the language of a contract should be interpreted most strongly against the party who caused the uncertainty to exist. (Rest.2d § 206; Cal.Civ.Code § 1654).

Words Used Given Their Ordinary Meaning

The words of a contract are to be understood in their ordinary and popular sense, rather than according to their strict legal meaning, unless used by the parties in a technical sense, or unless a special meaning is given to them by usage, in which case the latter must be followed. (Rest.2d § 202 93); Cal.Civ.Code § 1644.)

We Interrupt This Casebook for a Fowl Lesson in Poultry

Frigaliment Importing Co., Ltd. v. BNS International Sales Corp.
U.S. District Court for the Southern District of New York, 1960
190 F. Supp. 116

FRIENDLY, Circuit Judge. The issue is, what is chicken? Plaintiff says "chicken" means a young chicken, suitable for broiling and frying. Defendant says "chicken" means any bird of that genus that meets contract specifications on weight and quality, including what it calls "stewing chicken" and plaintiff pejoratively terms "fowl". Dictionaries give both meanings, as well as some others not relevant here. To support its, plaintiff sends a number of volleys over the net; defendant essays to return them and adds a few serves of its own. Assuming that both parties were acting in good faith, the case nicely illustrates Holmes' remark "that the making of a contract depends not on the agreement of two minds in one intention, but on the agreement of two sets of external signs not on the parties' having *meant* the same thing but on their having *said* the same thing." The Path of the Law, in Collected Legal Papers, p. 178. I have concluded that plaintiff has not sustained its burden of persuasion that the contract used "chicken" in the narrower sense.

The action is for breach of the warranty that goods sold shall correspond to the description, . . . Two contracts are in suit. In the first, dated May 2, 1957, defendant, a New York sales corporation, confirmed the sale to plaintiff, a Swiss corporation, of

> "US Fresh Frozen Chicken, Grade A, Government Inspected, Eviscerated 2½-3 lbs. and 1½-2 lbs. Each
> all chicken individually wrapped in cryovac, packed in secured fiber cartons or wooden boxes, suitable for export

> 75,000 lbs. 2½-3 lbs........@$33.00
> 25,000 lbs. 1½-2 lbs........@$36.50
> per 100 lbs. FAS New York
> scheduled May 10, 1957 pursuant to instructions from Penson & Co., New York."

The second contract, also dated May 2, 1957, was identical save that only 50,000 lbs. of the heavier "chicken" were called for, the price of the smaller birds was $37 per 100 lbs., and shipment was scheduled for May 30. The initial shipment under the first contract was short but the balance was shipped on May 17. When the initial shipment arrived in Switzerland, plaintiff found, on May 28, that the 2½-3 lbs. birds were not young chicken suitable for broiling and frying but stewing chicken or "fowl"; indeed, many of the cartons and bags plainly so indicated. Protests ensued. Nevertheless, shipment under the second contract was made on May 29, the 2½-3 lbs. birds again being stewing chicken. Defendant stopped the transportation of these at Rotterdam.

This action followed. Plaintiff says that, notwithstanding that its acceptance was in Switzerland, New York law controls under the principle of Rubin v. Irving Trust Co., 1953, 305 N.Y. 288, 305, 113 N.E.2d 424, 431; defendant does not dispute this, and relies on New York decisions. I shall follow the apparent agreement of the parties as to the applicable law.

Since the word "chicken" standing alone is ambiguous, I turn first to see whether the contract itself offers any aid to its interpretation. Plaintiff says the 1½-2 lbs. birds necessarily had to be young chicken since the older birds do not come in that size, hence the 2½-3 lbs. birds must likewise be young. This is unpersuasive a contract for "apples" of two different sizes could be filled with different kinds of apples even though only one species came in both sizes. Defendant notes that the contract called not simply for chicken but for "US Fresh Frozen Chicken, Grade A, Government Inspected." It says the contract thereby incorporated by reference the Department of Agriculture's regulations, which favor its interpretation; I shall return to this after reviewing plaintiff's other contentions.

The first hinges on an exchange of cablegrams which preceded execution of the formal contracts. The negotiations leading up to the contracts were conducted in New York between defendant's secretary, Ernest R. Bauer, and a Mr. Stovicek, who was in New York for the Czechoslovak government at the World Trade Fair. A few days after meeting Bauer at the fair, Stovicek telephoned and inquired whether defendant would be interested in exporting poultry to Switzerland. Bauer then met with Stovicek, who showed him a cable from plaintiff dated April 26, 1957, announcing that they "are buyer" of 25,000 lbs. of chicken 2½-3 lbs. weight, Cryovac packed, grade A Government inspected, at a price up to 33¢ per pound, for shipment on May 10, to be confirmed by the following morning, and were interested in further offerings. After testing the market for price, Bauer accepted, and Stovicek sent a confirmation that evening. Plaintiff stresses that, although these and subsequent cables between plaintiff and defendant, which laid the basis for the additional quantities under the first and for all of the second contract, were predominantly in German, they used the English word "chicken"; it claims this was done because it understood "chicken" meant young chicken whereas the German word, "Huhn," included both "Brathuhn" (broilers) and "Suppenhuhn" (stewing chicken), and that defendant, whose officers were thoroughly conversant with German, should have realized this. Whatever force this argument might otherwise have is largely drained away by Bauer's testimony that he asked Stovicek what kind of chickens were wanted, received the answer "any kind of chickens," and then, in German, asked whether the cable meant "Huhn" and received an affirmative response....

Plaintiff's next contention is that there was a definite trade usage that "chicken" meant "young chicken." Defendant showed that it was only beginning in the poultry trade in 1957, thereby bringing itself within the principle that "when one of the parties is not a member of the trade or other circle, his acceptance of the standard must be made to appear" by proving either that he had actual knowledge of the usage or that the usage is "so generally known in the community that his actual individual knowledge of it may be inferred." 9 Wigmore, Evidence (3d ed. 1940) § 2464. Here there was no proof of actual knowledge of the alleged usage; indeed, it is quite plain that defendant's belief was to the contrary. In order to meet the alternative requirement, the law of New York demands a showing that "the usage is of so long continuance, so well established, so notorious, so universal and so reasonable in itself, as that the presumption is violent that the parties contracted with reference to it, and made it a part of their agreement."

Plaintiff endeavored to establish such a usage by the testimony of three witnesses and certain other evidence. Strasser, resident buyer in New York for a large chain of Swiss cooperatives, testified that "on chicken I would definitely understand a broiler." However, the force of this testimony was considerably weakened by the fact that in his own transactions the witness, a careful businessman, protected himself by using "broiler" when that was what he wanted and "fowl" when he wished older birds. Indeed, there are some indications, dating back to a remark of Lord Mansfield, Edie v. East India Co., 2 Burr. 1216, 1222 (1761), that no credit should be given "witnesses to usage, who could not adduce instances in verification." 7 Wigmore, Evidence (3d ed. 1940), § 1954; ... While Wigmore thinks this goes too far, a witness' consistent failure to rely on the alleged usage deprives his opinion testimony of much of its effect. Niesielowski, an officer of one of the companies that had furnished the stewing chicken to defendant, testified that "chicken" meant "the male species of the poultry industry. That could be a broiler, a fryer or a roaster", but not a stewing chicken; however, he also testified that upon receiving defendant's inquiry for "chickens", he asked whether the desire was for "fowl or frying chickens" and, in fact, supplied fowl, although taking the precaution of asking defendant, a day or two after plaintiff's acceptance of the contracts in suit, to change its confirmation of its order from "chickens," as defendant had originally prepared it, to "stewing chickens." Dates, an employee of Urner-Barry Company, which publishes a daily market report on the poultry trade, gave it as his view that the trade meaning of "chicken" was "broilers and fryers." In addition to this opinion testimony, plaintiff relied on the fact that the Urner-Barry service, the Journal of Commerce, and Weinberg Bros. & Co. of Chicago, a large supplier of poultry, published quotations in a manner which, in one way or another, distinguish between "chicken," comprising broilers, fryers and certain other categories, and "fowl," which, Bauer acknowledged, included stewing chickens. This material would be impressive if there were nothing to the contrary. However, there was, as will now be seen.

Defendant's witness Weininger, who operates a chicken eviscerating plant in New Jersey, testified "Chicken is everything except a goose, a duck, and a turkey. Everything is a chicken, but then you have to say, you have to specify which category you want or that you are talking about." Its witness Fox said that in the trade "chicken" would encompass all the various classifications. Sadina, who conducts a food inspection service, testified that he would consider any bird coming within the classes of "chicken" in the Department of Agriculture's regulations to be a chicken. The specifications approved by the General Services Administration include fowl as well as broilers and fryers under the classification "chickens." Statistics of the Institute of American Poultry Industries use the phrases "Young chickens" and "Mature chickens," under the general heading "Total chickens." and the Department of Agriculture's daily and weekly price reports avoid use of the word "chicken" without specification.

Defendant advances several other points which it claims affirmatively support its construction. Primary among these is the regulation of the Department of Agriculture, 7 C.F.R. § 70.300-70.370, entitled, "Grading and Inspection of Poultry and Edible Products Thereof." and in particular § 70.301 which recited:

"*Chickens.* The following are the various classes of chickens:
(a) Broiler or fryer . . .
(b) Roaster . . .
(c) Capon . . .
(d) Stag . . .
(e) Hen or stewing chicken or fowl . . .
(f) Cock or old rooster . . .

Defendant argues, as previously noted, that the contract incorporated these regulations by reference. Plaintiff answers that the contract provision related simply to grade and Government inspection and did not incorporate the Government definition of "chicken," and also that the definition in the Regulations is ignored in the trade. However, the latter contention was contradicted by Weininger and Sadina;

and there is force in defendant's argument that the contract made the regulations a dictionary, particularly since the reference to Government grading was already in plaintiff's initial cable to Stovicek.

Defendant makes a further argument based on the impossibility of its obtaining broilers and fryers at the 33¢ price offered by plaintiff for the 2½-3 lbs. birds. There is no substantial dispute that, in late April, 1957, the price for 2½-3 lbs. broilers was between 35 and 37¢ per pound, and that when defendant entered into the contracts, it was well aware of this and intended to fill them by supplying fowl in these weights. It claims that plaintiff must likewise have known the market since plaintiff had reserved shipping space on April 23, three days before plaintiff's cable to Stovicek, or, at least, that Stovicek was chargeable with such knowledge. It is scarcely an answer to say, as plaintiff does in its brief, that the 33¢ price offered by the 2½-3 lbs. "chickens" was closer to the prevailing 35¢ price for broilers than to the 30¢ at which defendant procured fowl. Plaintiff must have expected defendant to make some profit certainly it could not have expected defendant deliberately to incur a loss.

Finally, defendant relies on conduct by the plaintiff after the first shipment had been received. On May 28 plaintiff sent two cables complaining that the larger birds in the first shipment constituted "fowl." Defendant answered with a cable refusing to recognize plaintiff's objection and announcing "We have today ready for shipment 50,000 lbs. chicken 2½-3 lbs. 25,000 lbs. broilers 1½-2 lbs.," these being the goods procured for shipment under the second contract, and asked immediate answer "whether we are to ship this merchandise to you and whether you will accept the merchandise." After several other cable exchanges, plaintiff replied on May 29 "Confirm again that merchandise is to be shipped since resold by us if not enough pursuant to contract chickens are shipped the missing quantity is to be shipped within ten days stop we resold to our customers pursuant to your contract chickens grade A you have to deliver us said merchandise we again state that we shall make you fully responsible for all resulting costs."[2] Defendant argues, that if plaintiff was sincere in thinking it was entitled to young chickens, plaintiff would not have allowed the shipment under the second contract to go forward, since the distinction between broilers and chickens drawn in defendant's cablegram must have made it clear that the larger birds would not be broilers. However, plaintiff answers that the cables show plaintiff was insisting on delivery of young chickens and that defendant shipped old ones at its peril. Defendant's point would be highly relevant on another disputed issue whether if liability were established, the measure of damages should be the difference in market value of broilers and stewing chicken in New York or the larger difference in Europe, but I cannot give it weight on the issue of interpretation. Defendant points out also that plaintiff proceeded to deliver some of the larger birds in Europe, describing them as "poulets"; defendant argues that it was only when plaintiff's customers complained about this that plaintiff developed the idea that "chicken" meant "young chicken." There is little force in this in view of plaintiff's immediate and consistent protests.

When all the evidence is reviewed, it is clear that defendant believed it could comply with the contracts by delivering stewing chicken in the 2½-3 lbs. size. Defendant's subjective intent would not be significant if this did not coincide with an objective meaning of "chicken." Here it did coincide with one of the dictionary meanings, with the definition in the Department of Agriculture Regulations to which the contract made at least oblique reference, with at least some usage in the trade, with the realities of the market, and with what plaintiff's spokesman had said. Plaintiff asserts it to be equally plain that plaintiff's own subjective intent was to obtain broilers and fryers; the only evidence against this is the material as to market prices and this may not have been sufficiently brought home. In any event it is unnecessary to determine that issue. For plaintiff has the burden of showing that "chicken" was used in the narrower rather than in the broader sense, and this it has not sustained.

This opinion constitutes the Court's findings of fact and conclusions of law. Judgment shall be entered dismissing the complaint with costs.

Questions

1. What evidence did the plaintiff present to support its contention that "chicken" meant young chicken?

2. What arguments did the defendant present to support its interpretation of "chicken?"

3. What factors did the court consider in reaching its conclusion regarding the interpretation of "chicken" in the contracts?

Takeaways – Frigaliment

Sections 201 through 203 of the Restatement 2nd provide some general rules and standards of preference to be followed in the process of interpretation. Restatement 2d section 201(1) provides that where the parties attach the same meaning to the terms used in their agreement, the interpretation of the agreement should be in accord with that meaning even if a third party might interpret the language differently. The converse is also true: whatever an objective observer might think, if the contracting parties attach different meanings to the same term, then neither is bound by the understanding of the other unless one of them knew or had reason to know what the other understood the disputed term to mean. Which one of those rules applies to *Frigaliment*?

Usage of Trade, Course of Performance, Course of Dealing

The terms set forth in a writing intended by the parties as a final expression of their agreement may be explained or supplemented by course of dealing or usage of trade or by course of performance. (UCC § 1-303(d), Cal.Code.Civ.Proc. §1856 (c).)

Usage of Trade

"Usage of trade" is defined as any practice or method of dealing in a place, vocation, or trade as to justify an expectation that it will be observed with respect to the transaction in question. (UCC § 1-303(c))

Technical words in a contract must "be interpreted as usually understood by persons in the profession or business to which they relate, unless clearly used in a different sense." (Cal.Civ.Code § 1645,) A contract is to be interpreted according to the law and usage of the place where it is to be performed or, if it does not indicate a place of performance, according to the law and usage of the place where it is made. (Cal.Civ.Code § 1646)

Ermolieff v. R. K. O. Radio Pictures
Supreme Court of California, 1942
19 Cal.2d 543, 122 P.2d 3

CARTER, J. Plaintiff and defendant are producers and distributors in the motion picture industry. Plaintiff was the owner and producer of a foreign language motion picture entitled "Michael Strogoff," based on a novel by Jules Verne, which prior to July 6, 1936, he had produced in the German and French languages. On that date the parties entered into a contract in which plaintiff granted to defendant the exclusive right to produce and distribute an English version of that picture in only those "countries or territories of the world" listed on an exhibit annexed to the contract. On the exhibit is listed among other places "The United Kingdom." Plaintiff reserved the rights in the picture in both foreign and English language in all countries or territories not listed in the exhibit. The contract was modified in December, 1936, and September, 1937, to add other countries or territories to the list. Plaintiff commenced the instant action on May 8, 1940, pleading the contract and its modifications and alleging that defendant had produced an English version of the picture under the title "Soldier and a Lady" in the United States and elsewhere; and that a controversy has arisen between the parties as to the countries and territories granted to defendant and those reserved by plaintiff under the contract and its modifications. Those allegations were admitted by defendant and it alleges that the only controversy between the parties is with respect to the area referred to as "The United Kingdom"; that the only dispute is whether "The United Kingdom," in which the contract grants rights to defendant, includes Eire or the Irish Free State; and that there is a custom and usage in the motion picture industry that that term does include Eire and that such usage is a part of the contract. Both the complaint and the answer pray for declaratory relief, namely, a declaration of their rights with respect to those areas embraced in the contract which are in dispute.

It was stipulated that the sole issue with respect to the territory embraced in the contract was whether defendant or plaintiff held the rights in the picture in Eire, which in turn depended upon whether The United Kingdom included Eire; that defendant did distribute the picture in Eire, and that The United Kingdom, from a political and legal viewpoint, did not include Eire, the latter being independent from it. . . .

In the instant case plaintiff in his complaint claimed a controversy with respect to the respective rights of the parties under the contract. Defendant in its answer set forth with particularity the controversy as being whether The United Kingdom included Eire. It was stipulated that that was the sole controversy and the case was tried on that issue. The court denied defendant's claim that the case was not within the purview of section 1060 and granted declaratory relief. While it is true that defendant has already distributed pictures in Eire, it is also true that if plaintiff is correct in his assertion that Eire is not included in The United Kingdom, he has reserved the right in the contract to distribute pictures there. If defendant is correct it has the right to make a further distribution of pictures in Eire. Defendant's contention must therefore fail.

Defendant asserts, however, that the judgment must be reversed because of the granting of plaintiff's motion to strike defendant's evidence that according to the custom and usage of the moving picture industry Eire is included in The United Kingdom. With that contention we agree. Both plaintiff and defendant are engaged in the business of producing and distributing moving pictures and rights in connection therewith. Defendant's evidence consisted of the testimony of several witnesses familiar with the distribution of motion pictures to the effect that in contracts covering the rights to produce pictures the general custom and usage was that the term "The United Kingdom" included Eire, the Irish Free State. Plaintiff's motion to strike out all of that evidence on the ground that it was incompetent, irrelevant and immaterial was granted. Plaintiff, reserving his objection to defendant's evidence, offered contrary evidence concerning such custom and usage.

The correct rule with reference to the admissibility of evidence as to trade usage under the circumstances here presented is that while words in a contract are ordinarily to be construed according to their plain, ordinary, popular or legal meaning, as the case may be, yet if in reference to the subject matter of the contract, particular expressions have by trade usage acquired a different meaning, and both parties are engaged in that trade, the parties to the contract are deemed to have used them according to their different and peculiar sense as shown by such trade usage. Parol evidence is admissible to establish the trade usage, and that is true even though the words are in their ordinary or legal meaning entirely unambiguous, inasmuch as by reason of the usage the words are used by the parties in a different sense. (See Code of Civil Procedure, sec. 1861; Civil Code, secs. 1644, 1646, 1655; Jenny Lind Co. v. Bower & Co., 11 Cal. 194; Callahan v. Stanley, 57 Cal. 476; Higgins v. California Petroleum etc. Co., 120 Cal. 629 [52 P. 1080]; Caro v. Mattei, 39 Cal.App. 253 [178 P. 537]; Wigmore on Evidence, vol. IX, sec. 2463, p. 204; Restatement, Contracts, secs. 246, 248; 89 A.L.R. 1228.) The basis of this rule is that to accomplish a purpose of paramount importance in interpretation of documents, namely, to ascertain the true intent of the parties, it may well be said that the usage evidence does not alter the contract of the parties, but on the contrary gives the effect to the words there used as intended by the parties. The usage becomes a part of the contract in aid of its correct interpretation.

Plaintiff relies upon such cases as Brant v. California Dairies, Inc., 4 Cal.2d 128 [48 PaCal.2d 13], and Wells v. Union Oil Co., 25 Cal.App.2d 165 [76 PaCal.2d 696], as announcing a rule contrary to the one above stated. However, in those cases evidence of custom or usage was not offered, and no contention was made therein that the words employed in the contracts there involved had any other than their ordinary, popular or legal meaning in reference to the subject matter of said contracts. That is not the case here. Plaintiff also cites other authorities. In New York Cent. R. R. Co. v. Frank H. Buck Co., 2 Cal.2d 384 [41 PaCal.2d 547], and the cases therein cited, the rule stated is merely that where the terms of the contract are expressly and directly contrary to the precise subject matter embraced in the custom or usage, parol evidence of that custom or usage is not admissible. The provision in the contract was tantamount to a clause that custom or usage shall not be a part of the contract. They did not involve a situation where the evidence was introduced to define a term in the contract. In the case at bar it cannot be said that there was a provision of that character. The contract stated that the defendant's rights existed only in the countries or territories listed in the annexed exhibit and plaintiff reserved the rights in all other countries or territories. "Territories" is a more comprehensive term than countries, and may well include more than one political entity or nation. The term "The United Kingdom" as a territory or area, does not necessarily limit that area to a political entity known as The United Kingdom. The fact that it is expressly stipulated in the contract that defendant has no rights in any countries not named in the exhibit, does not alter the situation. It falls short of being tantamount to an express and direct agreement that Eire shall not be considered as included in The United Kingdom. The door is still open to evidence of custom and usage with reference to the scope of The United Kingdom. The foregoing comments are equally applicable to the other cases cited by plaintiff, namely, Withers v. Moore, 140 Cal. 591 [74 P. 159]; May v. American Trust Co., 135 Cal.App. 385 [27 PaCal.2d 101]; Brandenstein v. Jackling, 99 Cal.App. 438 [278 P. 880]; Fish v. Correll, 4 Cal.App. 521 [88 P. 489], and California Jewelry Co. v. Provident Loan Assn., 6 Cal.App.2d 506 [45 PaCal.2d 271].

Plaintiff urges that since judicial notice may be taken and it was stipulated that Eire is independent of The United Kingdom and not a part thereof, the custom and usage evidence is not admissible to contradict that stipulation or notice. That notice and stipulation add nothing material to the situation. In any case where a word in a contract had an unquestioned common meaning there could be no dispute as to that common meaning, but the custom and usage is evidence of the peculiar sense in which it was used. The stipulation would add nothing that was not already plain on the face of the contract.

It is contended that the parties placed a practical construction on the contract which negatived presence of custom and usage as a part thereof. The contract was modified on December 1, 1936, and September 8, 1937, to include countries not mentioned in the original contract. Eire was not among the added areas and nothing was said therein with reference to the territory embraced by The United Kingdom. Malta and Gibraltar which are political subdivisions of The United Kingdom were added. It does not necessarily follow that these modifications constituted a construction of the contract by the parties to the effect that Eire was not included in the term "The United Kingdom," nor that evidence of custom or usage was removed from the picture. Indeed, it may reasonably follow from those modifications that the criterion to be used in construing the area embraced within The United Kingdom was not the political or legal boundaries thereof. It may well be said to indicate an uncertainty as to the extent of the area embraced by that term because upon plaintiff's present reasoning The United Kingdom is circumscribed by the political and legal boundaries thereof. That being the case, there would be no occasion for the modification because Malta and Gibraltar being political subdivisions of The United Kingdom would be embraced in the contract as originally written. For those reasons, it is also a fair inference to conclude, that the parties because of the modifications, had some meaning in their mind for the term "The United Kingdom," other than that territory which is a political and legal part thereof.

Finally, plaintiff asserts that the custom and usage evidence was inadmissible because a custom and usage to be available must be known by the parties or so generally known that knowledge must be presumed, citing Security Commercial & Savings Bank of San Diego v. Southern Trust & Commerce Bank, 74 Cal.App. 734 [241 P. 945]. But in this case defendant's excluded evidence showed that the custom was general in the moving picture industry and both parties were engaged in the production of motion pictures. As plaintiff expresses it in his brief, "Respondent (plaintiff) is a world famous producer." It is stated in Restatement, Contracts, section 248, page 352:

"Where both parties to a transaction are engaged in the same occupation, or belong to the same group of persons, the usages of that occupation or group are operative, unless one of the parties knows or has reason to know that the other party has an inconsistent intention."

Plaintiff further urges in support of the exclusion of the evidence of usage; that the witnesses were biased, that it was a "low quality of proof," that it was insufficient and the like. These are matters that go to the weight of the evidence, rather than to its admissibility. With that we are not concerned. There is no necessity for a detailed analysis of the evidence. It is clear that the trial court did not purport to weigh or evaluate that evidence. It disregarded it in toto as is evinced by its order striking it out. On retrial of the action, if the parties so desire, the trial court may consider and give such weight to such evidence as may be introduced.

The judgment is reversed.

Questions

1. According to the court, what is the correct rule regarding the admissibility of evidence as to trade usage?

2. Why did the court disagree with the plaintiff's contention that evidence of custom and usage should be excluded?

Higgins v. California Petroleum & Asphalt Co. et al.
Supreme Court of California, 1898
120 Cal. 629, 52 P. 1080

TEMPLE, J. Plaintiff brought this action to recover certain royalties on certain bituminous rock and liquid asphaltum mined by defendants, for which they agreed to pay 'the sum of fifty cents per ton for each and every gross ton.' The trial court found 'that the term 'gross ton,' as used in the lease, * * * means two thousand two hundred and forty,' and gave judgment for plaintiff accordingly. From this judgment, plaintiff appeals on the judgment roll alone. His contention is that the ton contemplated by the contract is a ton of two thousand pounds. A contract of precisely the same terms in respect of the question now presented, was before this court in Higgins v. Asphalt Co., 109 Cal. 304, 41 Pac. 1087. It was held in that case that the ton referred to, upon the facts as they there appeared, was 'equal to two thousand pounds avoirdupois, and no more.' The only question involved here is whether the finding above quoted supports the judgment. Appellant claims that this 'is simply a conclusion of law based upon the contract,' and, * * * 'if a finding of fact, it is error, as it is found from the contract itself.' By section 3215 of the Political Code it is provided that 'twenty hundred weight constitute a ton.' The contention of appellant is that the statute defines the meaning and use of the word 'ton' (section 3215, Pol. Code); and that the lease is unambiguous, and cannot be explained or contradicted by parol evidence. Therefore, there could have been no evidence at the trial justifying the finding of the court that the phrase 'gross ton,' used in the lease, meant a long ton of 2,240 pounds.

Some decisions are cited apparently holding that a contract of this nature must be conclusively presumed to refer to the statutory weights and measures, at least in the absence of a direct and express reference in the contract to a different standard; and in this connection it is argued that the adjective 'gross' does not refer to measure,--that is, to the number of pounds in the ton,--but to the condition of the commodity when weighed, to wit, that the crude and unrefined asphalt is to be weighed, and not the refined product. I think the question is entirely settled by section 1861 of the Code of Civil Procedure, which reads as follows: 'The terms of a writing are presumed to have been used in their primary and general acceptation, but evidence is nevertheless admissible that they have a local, technical or otherwise peculiar signification, and were so used and understood in the particular instance, in which case the agreement must be construed accordingly.' I know no reason why this rule would not apply as well to a statutory weight or measure as to any other term used in a writing. Suppose there had been a bill of exceptions in this case, showing that upon the trial it was proven (1) that there was a usage throughout the state among all dealing in asphaltum that the crude material was dealt in according to a gross ton of 2,240 pounds; (2) that there was a custom to the same effect in Santa Barbara county; that in fact, by the usage and custom, the phrase 'gross ton' is always used to indicate the long ton, just as, by commercial usage, the last phrase is used to indicate that 2,240 pounds is meant; (3) that the parties, acting under this very contract, had in numerous settlements recognized the fact that 'gross ton' meant the long ton, and not the statutory ton. And we might add to this that there had been previous contracts between these same parties, of the same general character, but in which the phrase had been so defined. Would not such evidence have been admissible, and would it not have supported the finding? I think it would.

Of course, appellant would contend that, even under section 1861, such evidence cannot be received, unless the contract expressly indicates a local, technical, or peculiar signification. But the section plainly provides that it may be shown by evidence that the language is used in a technical, local, or peculiar sense, and not merely that evidence may be introduced to show what such meaning is when language is so used. This view is somewhat strengthened by the fact, as shown in respondents' brief, that the phrase 'gross ton' is often used in lieu of the phrase 'long ton,' with which we are all familiar in commercial reports, and which always indicates a ton containing 2,240 pounds. It is said that in the case of Higgins v. Asphalt Co., supra, this identical lease was construed, and that it was between the same parties. Possibly, had the evidence been brought up on this appeal, we would now construe it in the same way. But that case does not constitute the law of this case, and here we are asked to decide whether there could possibly have been evidence which would have sustained the finding objected to. I think the finding was not necessarily a mere conclusion of law,--that is, a construction of the language of the lease,--but may have been based upon evidence. Judgment affirmed.

Questions

1. What is the primary issue in this case regarding the interpretation of the term "gross ton"?

2. How does the appellant argue that the term "ton" should be defined in this case?

3. According to section 3215 of the Political Code, what does the statute define as a ton?

4. How does the respondent argue that the term "gross ton" should be interpreted in this case?

5. What legal principle does the court rely on to support its interpretation of the term "gross ton"?

Takeaways – Ermolieff and Higgins

A law student goes to a lumber yard and asks for a "2 x 4." Has there been a breach of contract when the student gets the piece of lumber home, measures it and discovers that it is only 1-1/2" x 3-1/2"? If 1-1/2" x 3-1/2" passes for 2 x 4 in the lumber industry, then there has been no breach because of the concept of trade usage. Trade usage is "relevant to show that the expectation of the parties that a given usage would be observed was justified." (*Nanakuli Paving & Rock Co.,* 664 F.2d at 785.) Both parties need not be consciously aware of the particular trade usage at issue. "It is enough if the trade usage is such as to 'justify an expectation' of its observance." (*Id.* at 792.)

Course of Performance

Nanakuli Paving & Rock Co. v. Shell Oil Co.
United States Court of Appeals, Ninth Circuit, 1981
664 F.2d 772

Nanakuli, the second largest asphaltic paving contractor in Hawaii, had bought all its asphalt requirements from 1963 to 1974 from Shell under two long-term supply contracts; its suit charged Shell with breach of the later 1969 contract. The jury returned a verdict of $220,800 for Nanakuli on its first claim, which is that Shell breached the 1969 contract in January, 1974, by failing to price protect Nanakuli on 7200 tons of asphalt at the time Shell raised the price for asphalt from $44 to $76. Nanakuli's theory is that price-protection, as a usage of the asphaltic paving trade in Hawaii, was incorporated into the 1969 agreement between the parties, as demonstrated by the routine use of price protection by suppliers to that trade, and reinforced by the way in which Shell actually performed the 1969 contract up until 1974. Price protection, appellant claims, required that Shell hold the price on the tonnage Nanakuli had already committed because Nanakuli had incorporated that price into bids put out to or contracts awarded by general contractors and government agencies. The District Judge set aside the verdict and granted Shell's motion for judgment n. o. v., which decision we vacate. We reinstate the jury verdict because we find that, viewing the evidence as a whole, there was substantial evidence to support a finding by reasonable jurors that Shell breached its contract by failing to provide protection for Nanakuli in 1974. We do not believe the evidence in this case was such that, giving Nanakuli the benefit of all inferences fairly supported by the evidence and without weighing the credibility of the witnesses, only one reasonable conclusion could have been reached by the jury. . . .

Nanakuli offers two theories for why Shell's failure to offer price protection in 1974 was a breach of the 1969 contract. First, it argues, all material suppliers to the asphaltic paving trade in Hawaii followed the trade usage of price protection and thus it should be assumed, under the U.C.C., that the parties intended to incorporate price protection into their 1969 agreement. This is so, Nanakuli continues, even though the written contract provided for price to be "Shell's Posted Price at time of delivery," F.O.B. Honolulu. Its proof of a usage that was incorporated into the contract is reinforced by evidence of the commercial context, which under the U.C.C. should form the background for viewing a particular contract. The full agreement must be examined in light of the close, almost symbiotic relations between Shell and Nanakuli on the island of Oahu, whereby the expansion of Shell on the island was intimately connected to the business growth of Nanakuli. The U.C.C. looks to the actual performance of a contract as the best indication of what the parties intended those terms to mean. Nanakuli points out that Shell had price protected it on the two occasions of price increases under the 1969 contract other than the 1974 increase. In 1970 and 1971 Shell extended the old price for four and three months, respectively, after an announced increase.

Nanakuli's second theory for price protection is that Shell was obliged to price protect Nanakuli, even if price protection was not incorporated into their contract, because price protection was the commercially reasonable standard for fair dealing in the asphaltic paving trade in Hawaii in 1974. . . .

Shell presents three arguments for upholding the judgment n. o. v. or, on cross appeal, urging that the District Judge erred in admitting certain evidence. First, it says, the District Court should not have denied Shell's motion *in limine* to define trade, for purposes of trade usage evidence, as the sale and purchase of asphalt in Hawaii, rather than expanding the definition of trade to include other suppliers of materials to the asphaltic paving trade. Asphalt, its argument runs, was the subject matter of the disputed contract and the only product Shell supplied to the asphaltic paving trade. Shell protests that the judge, by expanding the definition of trade to include the other major suppliers to the asphaltic paving trade, allowed the admission of highly prejudicial evidence of routine price protection by all suppliers of aggregate.

Asphaltic concrete paving is formed by mixing paving asphalt with crushed rock, or aggregate, in a "hot-mix" plant and then pouring the mixture onto the surface to be paved. Shell's second complaint is that the two prior occasions on which it price protected Nanakuli, although representing the only other instances of price increases under the 1969 contract, constituted mere waivers of the contract's price term, not a course of performance of the contract, A course of performance of the contract, in contrast to a waiver, demonstrates how the parties understand the terms of their agreement. . . . Shell's final argument is that, even assuming its prior price protection constituted a course of performance and that the broad trade definition was correct and evidence of trade usages by aggregate suppliers was admissible, price protection could not be construed as reasonably consistent with the express price term in the contract, in which case the Code provides that the express term controls.

We hold that the judge did not abuse his discretion in defining the applicable trade, for purposes of trade usages, as the asphaltic paving trade in Hawaii, rather than the purchase and sale of asphalt alone . . . Additionally, we hold that, under the facts of this case, a jury could reasonably have found that Shell's acts on two occasions to price protect Nanakuli were not ambiguous and therefore indicated Shell's understanding of the terms of the agreement with Nanakuli rather than being a waiver by Shell of those terms.

Lastly we hold that, although the express price terms of Shell's posted price of delivery may seem, at first glance, inconsistent with a trade usage of price protection at time of increases in price, a closer reading shows that the jury could have reasonably construed price protection as consistent with the express term. . . .

Trade Usage Before And After 1969

The key to price protection being so prevalent in 1969 that both parties would intend to incorporate it into their contract is found in one reality of the Oahu asphaltic paving market: the largest paving contracts were let by government agencies and none of the three levels of government — local, state, or federal — allowed escalation clauses for paving materials. If a paver bid at one price and another went into effect before the award was made, the paving company would lose a great deal of money, since it could not pass on increases to any government agency or to most general contractors. Extensive evidence was presented that, as a consequence, aggregate suppliers routinely price protected paving contractors in the 1960's and 1970's, as did the largest asphaltic supplier in Oahu, Chevron. Nanakuli presented documentary evidence of routine price protection by aggregate suppliers as well as two witnesses: Grosjean, Vice-President for Marketing of Ameron H.C. D., and Nihei, Division Manager of Lone Star Industries for Pacific Cement and Aggregate (P.C. A.). Both testified that price protection to their knowledge had always been practiced: at H.C. D. for many years prior to Grosjean's arrival in 1962 and at P.C. A. routinely since Nihei's arrival in 1960. Such protection consisted of advance notices of increases, coupled with charging the old price for work committed at that price or for enough time to order the tonnage committed. The smallness of the Oahu market led to complete trust among suppliers and pavers. H.C. D. did not demand that Nanakuli or other pavers issue purchase orders or sign contracts for aggregate before incorporating its aggregate prices into bids. Nanakuli would merely give H.C. D. raised its prices, without documentation. "Their word and letter is good enough for us," Grosjean testified. Nihei said P.C. A. at the time of price increases would get a list of either particular projects bid by a paver or simply total tonnage bid at the old price. "We take either one. We take their word for it." None of the aggregate companies had a contract with Nanakuli expressly stating price protection would be given;. . .

Shell's Course Of Performance Of The 1969 Contract

The Code considers actual performance of a contract as the most relevant evidence of how the parties interpreted the terms of that contract. In 1970 and 1971, the only points at which Shell raised prices between 1969 and 1974, it price protected Nanakuli by holding its old price for four and three months, respectively, after announcing a price increase. . . .

Scope Of Trade Usage

The validity of the jury verdict in this case depends on four legal questions. First, how broad was the trade to whose usages Shell was bound under its 1969 agreement with Nanakuli: did it extend to the Hawaiian asphaltic paving trade or was it limited merely to the purchase and sale of asphalt, which would only include evidence of practices by Shell and Chevron? Second, were the two instances of price protection of Nanakuli by Shell in 1970 and 1971 waivers of the 1969 contract as a matter of law or was the jury entitled to find that they constituted a course of performance of the contract? Third, could the jury have construed an express contract term of Shell's posted price at delivery as reasonably consistent with a trade usage and Shell's course of performance of the 1969 contract of price protection, which consisted of charging the old price at times of price increases, either for a period of time or for specific tonnage committed at a fixed price in non-escalating contracts? Fourth, could the jury have found that good faith obliged Shell to at least give advance notice of a $32 increase in 1974, that is, could they have found that the commercially reasonable standards of fair dealing in the trade in Hawaii in 1974 were to give some form of price protection?

The Code defines usage of trade as "any practice or method of dealing having such regularity of observance in a *place, vocation or trade* s to justify an expectation that it will be observed with respect to the transaction in question." *Id.*§ 490:1-205(2) (emphasis supplied). . . . a usage need not necessarily be one practiced by members of the party's own trade or vocation to be binding *if* it is so commonly practiced in a locality that a party should be aware of it. . . . A party is always held to conduct generally observed by members of his chosen trade because the other party is justified in so assuming unless he indicates otherwise. He is held to more general business practices to the extent of his actual knowledge of those practices or to the degree his ignorance of those practices is not excusable: they were so generally practiced he should have been aware of them.

No U.C.C. cases have been found on this point, but the court's reading of the Code language is similar to that of two of the best-known commentators on the U.C.C.:

Under pre-Code law, a trade usage was not operative against a party who *was not a member of the trade unless* he actually knew of it or *the other party could reasonably believe he knew of it.*

J. White R. Summers, *Uniform Commercial Code,*§ 12-6 at 371 (1972) (emphasis supplied) (citing 3 A. Corbin, *Corbin on Contracts* § 557 at 248 (1960)). *See also* Restatement of Contracts § 247, Comment b (1932); 5 S. Williston, *Williston on Contracts* § 661 at 113-18 (3d. ed. 1961). White and Summers add (emphasis supplied):

This view has been carried forward by 1-205(3), ... [U]sage of the trade is only binding on *members of the trade involved or persons* who know or *should know about it.* Persons who should be aware of the trade usage doubtless *include those who regularly deal with members of the relevant trade,* and also members of a second trade that commonly deals with members of a relevant trade (for example, farmers should know something of seed selling).

White Summers, *supra,* § 12-6 at 371. Using that analogy, even if Shell did not "regularly deal" with aggregate supplies, it did deal constantly and almost exclusively on Oahu with one asphalt paver. It therefore should have been aware of the usage of Nanakuli and other asphaltic pavers to bid at fixed prices and therefore receive price protection from their materials suppliers due to the refusal by government agencies to accept escalation clauses. Therefore, we do not find the lower court abused its discretion or misread the Code as applied to the peculiar facts of this case in ruling that the applicable trade was the asphaltic paving trade in Hawaii. An asphalt seller should be held to the usages of trade in general as well as those of asphalt sellers and common usages of those to whom they sell. Certainly, under the unusual facts of this case it was not unreasonable for the judge to extend trade usages to include practices of other material suppliers toward Shell's primary and perhaps only customer on Oahu. He did exclude, on Shell's motion *in limine,* evidence of cement suppliers. He only held Shell to routine practices in Hawaii by the suppliers of the two major ingredients of asphaltic paving, that is, asphalt and aggregate. Those usages were only practiced towards two major pavers. It was not unreasonable to expect Shell to be knowledgeable about so small a market. In so ruling, the judge undoubtedly took into account Shell's half-million dollar investment in Oahu strictly because of a long-term commitment by Nanakuli, its actions as partner in promoting Nanakuli's expansion on Oahu, and the fact that its sales on Oahu were almost exclusively to Nanakuli for use in asphaltic paving. The wisdom of the pre-trial ruling was demonstrated by evidence at trial that Shell's agent in Hawaii stayed in close contact with Nanakuli and was knowledgeable about both the asphaltic paving market in general and Nanakuli's bidding procedures and economics in particular.

Shell argued not only that the definition of trade was too broad, but also that the practice itself was not sufficiently regular to reach the level of a usage and that Nanakuli failed to show with enough precision how the usage was carried out in order for a jury to calculate damages. The extent of a usage is ultimately a jury question. The Code provides, "The existence and scope of such a usage are to be proved as facts." Haw.Rev.Stat. § 490:1-205(2). The practice must have "such regularity of observance . . . as to justify an expectation that it will be observed. . . ." *Id.* The Comment explains:

> The ancient English tests for "custom" are abandoned in this connection. Therefore, it is not required that a usage of trade be "ancient or immemorial," "universal" or the like . . . . [F]ull recognition is thus available for new usages and for usages currently observed by the great majority of decent dealers, even though dissidents ready to cut corners do not agree.

Id., Comment 5. The Comment's demand that "not universality but only the described 'regularity of observance'" is required reinforces the provision only giving "effect to usages of which the parties 'are or should be aware' . . . ."*Id.,* Comment 7. A "regularly observed" practice of protection, of which Shell "should have been aware," was enough to constitute a usage that Nanakuli had reason to believe was incorporated into the agreement.

Nanakuli went beyond proof of a regular observance. It proved and offered to prove that price protection was probably a universal practice by suppliers to the asphaltic paving trade in 1969. It had been practiced by H.C. D. since at least 1962, by P.C. A. since well before 1960, and by Chevron routinely for years, with the last specific instance before the contract being March, 1969, as shown by documentary evidence. The only usage evidence missing was the behavior by Shell, the only other asphalt supplier in Hawaii, prior to 1969. That was because its only major customer was Nanakuli and the judge ruled prior course of dealings between Shell and Nanakuli inadmissible. Shell did not point in rebuttal to one instance of failure to price protect by any supplier to an asphalt paver in Hawaii before its own 1974 refusal to price protect Nanakuli. Thus, there clearly was enough proof for a jury to find that the practice of price protection in the asphaltic paving trade existed in Hawaii in 1969 and was regular enough in its observance to rise to the level of a usage that would be binding on Nanakuli and Shell. . .

Waiver or Course of Performance

Course of performance under the Code is the action of the parties in carrying out the contract at issue, whereas course of dealing consists of relations between the parties *prior* to signing that contract. Evidence of the latter was excluded by the District Judge; evidence of the former consisted of Shell's price protection of Nanakuli in 1970 and 1971. Shell protested that the jury could not have found that those two instances of price protection amounted to a course of performance of its 1969 contract, relying on two Code comments. First, one instance does not constitute a course of performance. "A single occasion of conduct does not fall within the language of this section. . . ." Haw.Rev. Stat. § 490:2-208, Comment 4. Although the Comment rules out one instance, it does not further delineate how many acts are needed to form a course of performance. The prior occasions here were only two, but they constituted the only occasions before 1974 that would call for such conduct. In addition, the language used by a top asphalt official of Shell in connection with the first price protection of Nanakuli indicated that Shell felt that Nanakuli was entitled to some form of price protection. On that occasion in 1970 Blee, who had negotiated the contract with Nanakuli and was familiar with exactly what terms Shell was bound to by that agreement, wrote of the need to "bargain" with Nanakuli over the extent of price protection to be given, indicating that some price protection was a legal right of Nanakuli's under the 1969 agreement.

Shell's second defense is that the Comment expresses a preference for an interpretation of waiver.

3. Where it is difficult to determine whether a particular act merely sheds light on the meaning of the agreement or represents a waiver of a term of the agreement, the preference is in favor of "waiver" whenever such construction, plus the application of the provisions on the reinstatement of rights waived . . ., is needed to preserve the flexible character of commercial contracts and to prevent surprise or other hardship.

Id., Comment 3. The preference for waiver only applies, however, where acts are ambiguous. It was within the province of the jury to determine whether those acts were ambiguous, and if not, whether they constituted waivers or a course of performance of the contract. The jury's interpretation of those acts as a course of performance was bolstered by evidence offered by Shell that it again price protected Nanakuli on the only two occasions of post-1974 price increases, in 1977 and 1978.

Express Terms As Reasonably Consistent With Usage In Course of Performance

Perhaps one of the most fundamental departures of the Code from prior contract law is found in the parol evidence rule and the definition of an agreement between two parties. Under the U.C.C., an agreement goes beyond the written words on a piece of paper. " `Agreement' means the bargain of the parties in fact as found in their language or by implication from other circumstances including course of dealing or usage of trade or course of performance as provided in this chapter (sections 490:1-205 and 490:2-208)."*Id.*§ 490:1-201(3). Express terms, then, do not constitute the entire agreement, which must be sought also in evidence of usages, dealings, and performance of the contract itself. . . . Course of dealings is more important than usages of the trade, being specific usages between the two parties to the contract. "[C]ourse of dealing controls usage of trade." *Id.* § 490:1-205(4).

A commercial agreement, then, is broader than the written paper and its meaning is to be determined not just by the language used by them in the written contract but "by their action, read and interpreted in the light of commercial practices and other surrounding circumstances. The measure and background for interpretation are set by the commercial context, which may explain and supplement even the language of a formal or final writing."*Id.,*Comment 1. Performance, usages, and prior dealings are important enough to be admitted always, even for a final and complete agreement; only if they cannot be reasonably reconciled with the express terms of the contract are they not binding on the parties. "The express terms of an agreement and an applicable course of dealing or usage of trade shall be construed wherever reasonable as consistent with each other; but when such construction is unreasonable express terms control both course of dealing and usage of trade and course of dealing controls usage of trade."*Id.* § 490:1-205(4). . . .

Our study of the Code provisions and Comments, then, form the first basis of our holding that a trade usage to price protect pavers at times of price increases for work committed on nonescalating contracts could reasonably be construed as consistent with an express term of seller's posted price at delivery. Since the agreement of the parties is broader than the express terms and includes usages, which may even add terms to the agreement, and since the commercial background provided by those usages is vital to an understanding of the agreement, we follow the Code's mandate to proceed on the assumption that the parties have included those usages unless they cannot reasonably be construed as consistent with the express terms. . . .

Some guidelines can be offered as to how usage evidence can be allowed to modify a contract. First, the court must allow a check on usage evidence by demanding that it be sufficiently definite and widespread to prevent unilateral post-hoc revision of contract terms by one party. The Code's intent is to put usage evidence on an objective basis.

Although the Code abandoned the traditional common law test of nonconsensual custom and views usage as a way of determining the parties' probable intent . . . thus abolishing the requirement that common law custom be universally practiced, trade usages still must be well settled. . . . Here the evidence was overwhelming that all suppliers to the asphaltic paving trade price protected customers under the same types of circumstances. Chevron's contract with H.B. was a similar long-term supply contract between a buyer and seller with very close relations, on a form supplied by the seller, covering sales of asphalt, and setting the price at seller's posted price, with no mention of price protection. . . .

[In addition, here] the express price terms was "Shell's Posted Price at time of delivery." A total negation of that term would be that the buyer was to set the price. It is a less than complete negation of the term that an unstated exception exists at times of price increases, at which times the old price is to be charged, for a certain period or for a specified tonnage, on work already committed at the lower price on nonescalating contracts. Such a usage forms a broad and important exception to the express term, but does not swallow it entirely. Therefore, we hold that, under these particular facts, a reasonable jury could have found that price protection was incorporated into the 1969 agreement between Nanakuli and Shell and that price protection was reasonably consistent with the express term of seller's posted price at delivery.

Good Faith In Setting Price

Nanakuli offers an alternative theory why Shell should have offered price protection at the time of the price increases of 1974. Even if the price protection was not a term of the agreement, Shell could not have exercised good faith in carrying out its 1969 contract with Nanakuli when it raised its price by $32 effective January 1 in a letter written December 31st and only received on January 4, given the universal practice of advance notice of such an increase in the asphaltic paving trade. The Code provides, "A price to be fixed by the seller or by the buyer means a price for him to fix in good faith," Haw.Rev.Stat. § 490:2-305(2). For a merchant good faith means "the observance of reasonable commercial standards of fair dealing in the trade."*Id.*490:2-103(1)(b). The comment to Section 2-305 explains, "[I]n the normal case a 'posted price' . . . satisfies the good faith requirement." *Id.,* Comment 3. However, the words "in the normal case" mean that, although a posted price will usually be satisfactory, it will not be so under all circumstances. In addition, the dispute here was not over the amount of the increase — that is, the price that the seller fixed — but over the manner in which that increase was put into effect. It is true that Shell, in order to observe the good faith standards of the trade in 1974, was not bound by the practices of aggregate companies, which did not labor under the same disabilities as did asphalt suppliers in 1974. However, Nanakuli presented evidence that Chevron, in raising its price to $76, gave at least six weeks' advance notice, in accord with the long-time usage of the asphaltic paving trade. Shell, on the other hand, gave absolutely no notice, from which the jury could have concluded that Shell's manner of carrying out the price increase of 1974 did not conform to commercially reasonable standards. In both the timing of the announcement and its refusal to protect work already bid at the old price, Shell could be found to have breached the obligation of good faith imposed by the Code on all merchants. "Every contract or duty within this chapter imposes an obligation of good faith in its performance or enforcement," *Id.*§ 490:1-203, which for merchants entails the observance of commercially reasonable standards of fair dealing in the trade. The Comment to 1-203 reads:

> This section sets forth a basic principle running thought this Act. The principle involved is that in commercial transactions good faith is required in the performance and enforcement of all agreements or duties. Particular applications of this general principle appear in specific provisions of the Act . . . It is further implemented by Section 1-205 on course of dealing and usage of trade.

Id.§ 490:1-203, Comment. Chevron's conduct in 1974 offered enough relevant evidence of commercially reasonable standards of fair dealing in the asphalt trade in Hawaii in 1974 for the jury to find that Shell's failure to give sufficient advance notice and price protect Nanakuli after the imposition of the new price did not conform to good faith dealings in Hawaii at that time.

Because the jury could have found for Nanakuli on its price protection claim under either theory, we reverse the judgment of the District Court and reinstate the jury verdict for Nanakuli in the amount of $220,800, plus interest according to law.

KENNEDY, Circuit Judge, concurring specially: The case involves specific pricing practices, not an allegation of unfair dealing generally. Our opinion should not be interpreted to permit juries to import price protection or a similarly specific contract term from a concept of good faith that is not based on well-established custom and usage or other objective standards of which the parties had clear notice. Here, evidence of custom and usage regarding price protection in the asphaltic paving trade was not contradicted in major respects, and the jury could find that the parties knew or should have known of the practice at the time of making the contract. In my view, these are necessary predicates for either theory of the case, namely, interpretation of the contract based on the course of its performance or a finding that good faith required the seller to hold the price. With these observations, I concur.

Questions

1. What are Nanakuli's two theories for why Shell's failure to offer price protection in 1974 was a breach of the 1969 contract?

2. How does Nanakuli argue that the trade usage of price protection should be incorporated into the 1969 agreement?

3. What evidence did Nanakuli present to support the claim that price protection was a common practice in the asphaltic paving trade in Hawaii?

4. How does Shell argue against the admission of evidence regarding trade usages by other suppliers in the asphaltic paving trade?

5. According to the court's ruling, why was Shell bound by the usages of the asphaltic paving trade in Hawaii, even if it did not regularly deal with other suppliers in the trade?

Takeaways – Nanakuli Paving

UCC § 2-202 permits resort to course of dealing and trade usage to explain or supplement a contract. Admissibility of this kind of evidence is not dependent upon ambiguity within the contract. The test of the admissibility of course of dealing and trade usage is not whether the contract appears on its face to be complete in every detail, but whether the evidence of course of dealing and trade usage can be construed as consistent with the express terms of the contract. Course of dealing and trade usage are not synonymous with verbal understandings, terms and conditions. 2-202 draws a distinction between supplementing a written contract by consistent additional terms and supplementing it by course of dealing and trade usage. There is no limitation on the introduction of evidence of course of dealing and trade usage as once again, the admissibility of such evidence is not dependent on ambiguity in the contract.

In a part of the opinion omitted from the excerpt of the case, the *Nanakuli* court observed:

"Federal courts usually have been lenient in not ruling out consistent additional terms or trade usage for apparent inconsistency with express terms. The leading case on the subject is *Columbia Nitrogen Corp. v. Roister Co.*, 451 F.2d 3 (4th Cir. 1971). Columbia, the buyer, had in the past primarily produced and sold nitrogen to Royster. When Royster opened a new plant that produced and sold nitrogen to Royster the parties reversed roles and signed a sales contract for Royster to sell excess phosphate to Columbia. The contract terms set out the price that would be charged by Royster and the amount to be sold. It provided for the price to go up if certain events occurred but did not provide for price declines. When the price of nitrogen fell precipitously, Columbia refused to accept the full amount of nitrogen specified in the contract after Royster refused to renegotiate the contract price. The District Judge's exclusion of usage of the trade and course of dealing to explain the express quantity term in the contract was reversed. Columbia had offered to prove that the Quantity set out in the contract was a mere projection to be adjusted according to market forces.

Ambiguity was not necessary for the admission of evidence of usage and prior dealings. Even though the lengthy contract was the result of long and careful negotiations and apparently covered every contingency, the appellate court ruled that "the test of admissibility is not whether the contract appears on its face to be complete in every detail, but whether the proffered evidence of course of dealing and trade usage reasonably can be construed as consistent with the express terms of the agreement." *Id.* at 9. The express quantity term could be reasonably construed as consistent with a usage that such terms would be mere projections for several reasons: (1) the contract did not expressly state that usage and dealings evidence would be excluded; (2) the contract was silent on the adjustment of price or quantities in a declining market; (3) the minimum tonnage was expressed in the contract as Products Supplied, not Products Purchased; (4) the default clause of the contract did not state a penalty for failure to take delivery; and (5) apparently most important in the court's view, the parties had deviated from similar express terms in earlier contracts in times of declining market. *Id.* at 9-10. As here, the contract's merger clause said that there were no oral agreements. The court explained that its ruling "reflects the reality of the market place and avoids the overly legalistic interpretations which the Code seeks to abolish." *Id.* at 10. The Code assigns dealing and usage evidence "unique and important roles" and therefore "overly simplistic and overly legalistic interpretation of a contract should be shunned." (*Nanakuli, supra,* 664 F.2d 772, 797.)

Whose Meaning Prevails?

Raffles v. Wichelhaus
Court of the Exchequer, 1864
2 Hurl. & C. 906

A ship named Peerless

Declaration. For that it was agreed between the plaintiff and the defendants, to wit, at Liverpool, that the plaintiff should sell to the defendants, and the defendants buy of the plaintiff, certain goods, to wit, 125 bales of Surat cotton, guaranteed middling fair merchant's Dhollorah, to arrive ex Peerless from Bombay; and that the cotton should be taken from the quay, and that the defendants would pay the plaintiff for the same at a certain rate, to wit, at the rate of 17.25 d. per pound, within a certain time then agreed upon after the arrival of said goods in England. Averments: that the said goods did arrive by said ship from Bombay to England, to wit, at Liverpool, and the plaintiff was then and there ready and willing and offered to deliver that said goods to the defendants, etc. Breach: that the defendants refused to accept the said goods or pay the plaintiff for them.

Plea. That the said ship mentioned in the said agreement was meant and intended by the defendant to be the ship called the Peerless, which sailed from Bombay, to wit, in October; and that the plaintiff was not ready and willing, and did not offer to deliver to the defendants any bales of cotton which arrived by the last-mentioned ship, but instead thereof was only ready and willing, and offered to deliver to the defendants 125 bales of Surat cotton which arrived by another and different ship, which was also called the Peerless, and which sailed from Bombay, to wit, in December.

Demurrer, and joinder therein.

Milward, in support of the demurrer. The contract was for the sale of a number of bales of cotton of a particular description, which the plaintiff was ready to deliver. It is immaterial by what ship the cotton was to arrive, so that it was a ship called the Peerless. The words, "to arrive ex Peerless," only mean that if the vessel is lost on the voyage, the contract is to be at an end. [Pollock, C.B. It would be a question for the jury whether both parties meant the same ship to be called the Peerless.] That would be so if the contract was for the sale of a ship called the Peerless; but it is for the sale of cotton on board a ship of that name. [Pollock, C.B. The defendant only bought that cotton which was to arrive by a particular ship. It may as well be said, that if there is a contract for the purchase of certain goods in a warehouse A., that is satisfied by the delivery of goods of the same description in warehouse B.] In that case there would be goods in both warehouses; here, it does not appear that the plaintiff had any goods on board the other Peerless. [Martin, B. It is imposing on the defendant a different contract from that which he entered into. Pollock, C.B. It is like a contract for the purchase of wine coming from a particular estate in Spain or France, where there are two estates of the same name.] The defendant has no right to contradict, by parol evidence, a written contract good upon the face of it. He does not impute misrepresentation or fraud, but only says he fancied the ship a different one. Intention is of no avail, unless stated at the time of contract. [Pollock, C.B. One vessel sailed in October, the other in December.] The time of sailing is no part of the contract.

Mellish (Cohen with him), in support of the plea. There is nothing on the face of the contract to show that any particular ship called the Peerless was meant; but the moment it appears that two ships called the Peerless were about to sail from Bombay there is a latent ambiguity, and parol evidence may be given for the purpose of showing that the defendant meant one Peerless and the plaintiff another. That being so, there was no consensus ad item, and therefore no binding contract. He was then stopped by the Court.

Per Curiam. Judgment for the defendants.

Questions

1. What was the argument of the defendants regarding the interpretation of the contract and the identity of the ship called the Peerless?

2. What was the contention of the defendants in relation to the use of parol evidence to determine the intent of the parties involved? How did they argue that the presence of two ships called the Peerless created ambiguity in the contract?

Oswald v. Allen
United States Court of Appeals, Second Circuit, 1969
417 F.2d 43

MOORE, Circuit Judge. Dr. Oswald, a coin collector from Switzerland, was interested in Mrs. Allen's collection of Swiss coins. In April of 1964 Dr. Oswald was in the United States and arranged to see Mrs. Allen's coins. The parties drove to the Newburgh Savings Bank of Newburgh, New York, where two of her collections referred to as the Swiss Coin Collection and the Rarity Coin Collection were located in separate vault boxes. After examining and taking notes on the coins in the Swiss Coin Collection, Dr. Oswald was shown several valuable Swiss coins from the Rarity Coin Collection. He also took notes on these coins and later testified that he did not know that they were in a separate "collection." The evidence showed that each collection had a different key number and was housed in labeled cigar boxes.

On the return to New York City, Dr. Oswald sat in the front seat of the car while Mrs. Allen sat in the back with Dr. Oswald's brother, Mr. Victor Oswald, and Mr. Cantarella of the Chase Manhattan Bank's Money Museum, who had helped arrange the meeting and served as Dr. Oswald's agent. Dr. Oswald could speak practically no English and so depended on his brother to conduct the transaction. After some negotiation a price of $50,000 was agreed upon. Apparently the parties never realized that the references to "Swiss coins" and the "Swiss Coin Collection" were ambiguous. The trial judge found that Dr. Oswald thought the offer he had authorized his brother to make was for all of the Swiss coins, while Mrs. Allen thought she was selling only the Swiss Coin Collection and not the Swiss coins in the Rarity Coin Collection.

On April 8, 1964, Dr. Oswald wrote to Mrs. Allen to "confirm my purchase of all your Swiss coins (gold, silver and copper) at the price of $50,000.00." The letter mentioned delivery arrangements through Mr. Cantarella. In response Mrs. Allen wrote on April 15, 1964, that "Mr. Cantarella and I have arranged to go to Newburgh Friday April 24." This letter does not otherwise mention the alleged contract of sale or the quantity of coins sold. On April 20, realizing that her original estimation of the number of coins in the Swiss Coin Collection was erroneous, Mrs. Allen offered to permit a re-examination and to undertake not to sell to anyone else. Dr. Oswald cabled from Switzerland to Mr. Alfred Barth of the Chase Manhattan Bank, giving instruction to proceed with the transaction. Upon receiving the cable, Barth wrote a letter to Mrs. Allen stating Dr. Oswald's understanding of the agreement and requesting her signature on a copy of the letter as a "mere formality." Mrs. Allen did not sign and return this letter. On April 24, Mrs. Allen's husband told Barth that his wife did not wish to proceed with the sale because her children did not wish her to do so.

Appellant attacks the conclusion of the Court below that a contract did not exist since the minds of the parties had not met. The opinion below states:

"* * * plaintiff believed that he had offered to buy all Swiss coins owned by the defendant while defendant reasonably understood the offer which she accepted to relate to those of her Swiss coins as had been segregated in the particular collection denominated by her as the `Swiss Coin Collection' * * *."

There was ample evidence upon which the trial judge could rely in reaching this decision.

In such a factual situation the law is settled that no contract exists. The Restatement of Contracts [2d § 201] adopts the rule of *Raffles v. Wichelhaus*, 2 Hurl. C. 906, 159 Eng. Rep. 375 (Ex. 1864). Professor Young states that rule as follows:

"when any of the terms used to express an agreement is ambivalent, and the parties understand it in different ways, there cannot be a contract unless one of them should have been aware of the other's understanding."

Young, Equivocation in Agreements, 64 Colum.L.Rev. 619, 621 (1964). Even though the mental assent of the parties is not requisite for the formation of a contract the facts found by the trial judge clearly place this case within the small group of exceptional cases in which there is "no sensible basis for choosing between conflicting understandings." Young, at 647. The rule of *Raffles v. Wichelhaus* is applicable here.

Questions

1. According to the trial judge's decision, why did the court conclude that no contract existed between Dr. Oswald and Mrs. Allen? Explain the conflicting understandings of the parties regarding the sale of the Swiss coins.

2. What legal principle does the Restatement of Contracts 2d § 201 adopt regarding contracts formed when the parties have different understandings of ambiguous terms? How does this principle apply to the case at hand?

3. What is the significance of the *Raffles v. Wichelhaus* case in determining the existence of a contract? How does it relate to the present case?

4. Can a contract be formed even if the parties do not have the same mental assent or understanding of the terms? Explain the general rule and how it applies to this specific case.

5. Under what circumstances would the court consider a case to be an exception to the general rule regarding conflicting understandings in contract formation? How does the trial judge's findings in this case support the application of this exception?

Takeaways – Raffles and Oswald

In *Raffles* did the parties attach the same meaning to "Peerless?" In *Oswald*, did the parties attach the same meaning to the term "Swiss coins?" If they did not, did either party have reason to know of the other party's understanding of those terms?" And if neither did, then what is the consequence of that? (See, Rest.2d § 201)

Colfax Envelope Corp. v. Local No. 458-3M
United States Court of Appeals for the Seventh Circuit, 1994
20 F.3d 750

POSNER, Chief Judge. This appeal in a suit over a collective bargaining agreement presents a fundamental issue of contract law, that of drawing the line between an ambiguous contract, requiring interpretation, and a contract that, because it cannot be said to represent the agreement of the parties at all, cannot be interpreted, can only be rescinded and the parties left to go their own ways. Colfax, the plaintiff, is a manufacturer of envelopes. It does some printing of its envelopes, and the seventeen employees who do the printing are represented by the defendant union. Colfax has two printing presses. One prints 78-inch-wide sheets in four colors. The other prints 78-inch-wide sheets in five colors, but most of the time Colfax prints only four-color sheets on it.

Colfax has so few printing employees that it does not bother to participate in the collective bargaining negotiations between the union and the Chicago Lithographers Association, an association for collective bargaining of the other Chicago printing companies whose employees are represented by this union. Instead, whenever the union and the CLA sign a new collective bargaining agreement, the union sends Colfax a summary of the changes that the new agreement has made in the old one. If Colfax is content with the changes, the union sends it a copy of the complete new agreement, which Colfax signs and returns. If Colfax doesn't like the terms negotiated by the CLA, it is free to do its own bargaining with the union.

The collective bargaining agreements specify minimum manning requirements for each type of press used by the printers. The agreement in force between 1987 and 1991 fixed those minima as three men for four-color presses printing sheets 45 to 50 inches wide and four men for four-color presses printing sheets wider than 50 inches. Five-color presses printing sheets more than 55 inches wide required five men unless only four colors were printed, in which event only four men were required. The upshot was that under these agreements, all of which Colfax had signed, Colfax had to man each of its presses (which were 78-inch presses) with four men except on the rare occasions when it printed five-color sheets on its second press, and then it had to add a man.

In 1991 the union negotiated a new agreement with the CLA and sent a summary of the changes to Colfax. The letter enclosing the summary asked Colfax to indicate whether it agreed to the terms in the summary. (This may have been a departure from past practice, in which Colfax signed the complete agreement rather than the summary, but if so neither party makes anything of it.) In a section on manning requirements, the summary lists "4C 60" Press--3 Men" and "5C 78" Press--4 Men." Believing (in part because union members who claimed to be familiar with the new agreement had told Colfax that Colfax would really like the changes in it) that this meant that all presses operated as four-color presses would now require only three men to man them, Colfax's president and majority shareholder, Charles Patten, signed the union's letter, indicating acceptance of the terms in the summary. Later a copy of the actual agreement arrived, but it contained a crucial typo, which supported Patten's understanding of the summary. When a corrected copy of the agreement finally arrived, the manning requirements stated in it were different from what Patten had understood from the summary. Four-color presses between 45 and 60 inches required three men, but all four-color presses over 60 inches required four men. The changes had not benefited Colfax at all, and because it was under competitive pressure, it would have liked to negotiate better terms. Patten refused to sign the agreement but the union took the position that Colfax was bound to it by its acceptance of the summary.

Colfax brought this suit under section 301 of the Taft-Hartley Act, 29 U.S.C. § 185, for a declaration that it has no collective bargaining contract with the union because the parties never agreed on an essential term--the manning requirements for Colfax's printing presses. The union counterclaimed for an order to arbitrate. The union's position was that Colfax had accepted the new agreement, which requires arbitration of all disputes "arising out of the application or interpretation of this contract." The district judge granted summary judgment for the union, concluding that the reference to the new manning requirement for a four-color 60-inch press in the summary of changes that Colfax had accepted referred unambiguously to 60-inch presses and had no application to any other presses, such as Colfax's 78-inch presses. Colfax has appealed.

One way to describe the issue that divides the parties is that they disagree about the meaning of the term "4C 60" Press--3 Men." Colfax believes that it means four-color presses printing sheets 60 inches and over, while the union believes that it means four-color presses 60 inches and under (down to 45 inches). Remember that the previous agreement had allowed the use of three-man crews on four-color presses between 45 and 50 inches. The union interprets the change as extending the upper bound of the three-man range to 60 inches. Ordinarily a dispute over the meaning of a contractual term is, if the contract contains an arbitration clause, for the arbitrator to decide. But sometimes the difference between the parties goes so deep that it is impossible to say that they ever agreed--that they even have a contract that a court or arbitrator might interpret. In the famous though enigmatic and possibly misunderstood case of Raffles v. Wichelhaus, 2 H. & C. 906, 159 Eng.Rep. 375 (Ex. 1864), the parties made a contract for the delivery of a shipment of cotton from Bombay to England on the ship Peerless. Unbeknownst to either party, there were two ships of that name sailing from Bombay on different dates. One party thought the contract referred to one of the ships, and the other to the other. The court held that there was no contract; there had been no "meeting of the minds." See generally A.W. Brian Simpson, "Contracts for Cotton to Arrive: The Case of the Two Ships Peerless," 11 Cardozo L.Rev. 287 (1989).

The premise--that a "meeting of the minds" is required for a binding contract--obviously is strained. 2 E. Allan Farnsworth, Contracts Sec. 7.9, at p. 251 (1990). Most contract disputes arise because the parties did not foresee and provide for some contingency that has now materialized--so there was no meeting of minds on the matter at issue--yet such disputes are treated as disputes over contractual meaning, not as grounds for rescinding the contract and thus putting the parties back where they were before they signed it. So a literal meeting of the minds is not required for an enforceable contract, which is fortunate, since courts are not renowned as mind readers. Let us set the concept to one side, therefore, and ask how (else) to explain Raffles v. Wichelhaus and cases like it. It seems to us as it has to other courts that a contract ought to be terminable without liability and the parties thus allowed to go their own ways when there is "no sensible basis for choosing between conflicting understandings" of the contractual language, as the court said in an American Raffles-like case, Oswald v. Allen, 417 F.2d 43, 45 (2d Cir. 1969), quoting William F. Young, Jr., "Equivocation in the Making of Agreements," 64 Colum. L. Rev. 619, 647 (1964). In Oswald the misunderstanding arose because the parties did not speak the same language (literally). In Balistreri v. Nevada Livestock Production Credit Association, 214 Cal.App.3d 635, 262 Cal.Rptr. 862 (1989), the parents of an aspiring farmer thought they had pledged property they owned in Sebastopol to secure a loan to their son, and indeed the lender's cover letter described the property as "your Sebastopol residence." But the actual deed of trust listed the parents' home in Petaluma as the collateral. The court held that there had been no meeting of the minds.

Raffles and Oswald were cases in which neither party was blameable for the mistake; Balistreri a case in which both were equally blameable, the parents for having failed to read the deed of trust, the lender for having drafted a misleading cover letter. It is all the same. Restatement (Second) of Contracts Secs. 20(1) (a), (b) (1981). If neither party can be assigned the greater blame for the misunderstanding, there is no nonarbitrary basis for deciding which party's understanding to enforce, so the parties are allowed to abandon the contract without liability. Neel v. Lang, 236 Mass. 61, 127 N.E. 512 (1920); Konic International Corp. v. Spokane Computer Services, Inc., 109 Idaho 527, 529, 708 P.2d 932, 934 (App.1985). These are not cases in which one party's understanding is more reasonable than the other's. Compare Restatement, supra, Sec. 20(2) (b). If rescission were permitted in that kind of case, the enforcement of every contract would be at the mercy of a jury, which might be persuaded that one of the parties had genuinely held an idiosyncratic idea of its meaning, so that there had been, in fact, no meeting of the minds. Cf. Young, supra, at 646. Intersubjectivity is not the test of an enforceable contract.

The clearest cases for rescission on the ground that there was "no meeting of the minds" (or, better, that there was a "latent ambiguity" in the sense that neither party knew that the contract was ambiguous) are ones in which an offer is garbled in transmission. The cases we have cited are all of that character, if "transmission" is broadly construed. Vickery v. Ritchie, 202 Mass. 247, 88 N.E. 835 (1909), provides a further illustration. A landowner and a contractor signed what they believed to be duplicate copies of a contract for the construction of a Turkish bath house. Because of a fraud by the architect for which neither the contractor nor the landowner could be blamed, the copy signed by the landowner stated the price as $23,000 and the copy signed by the contractor stated it as $34,000. Through no fault of their own, the parties had signed different contracts. Or consider Konic International Corp. v. Spokane Computer Services, Inc., supra. The seller quoted a price of "fifty-six twenty," which the buyer thought meant $56.20. In fact the seller had meant $5,620. In both cases rescission was permitted, the first being a case in which neither party was at fault, the second one in which both were equally at fault, being careless in their utterance and interpretation, respectively, of an ambiguous oral formula.

Our case is superficially similar. The actual terms of the 1991 agreement were muddied in the summary that the union gave Colfax and that Colfax signed, making it possible that the parties had different understandings. The difference between this case and the others is that Colfax, unlike the hapless promisors in the cases we have cited, should have realized that the contract was unclear. The buyer in Konic thought--really thought--that he was being quoted a price of $56.20, and no doubt fell off his stool when he discovered that the price was a hundred times greater than he thought. But the expression "4C 60" Press" does not on its face speak to the minimum manning requirement for a 4C 78" Press. The union's interpretation, that the phrase merely extended the upper bound of the old range for three-man four-color presses from 50 to 60 inches, may or may not be correct. The fact that the union restated and clarified the interpretation in the corrected agreement that it sent Colfax is not decisive on the question, because it is the summary rather than the corrected full agreement that is the contract between these parties. But Colfax, if reasonable, could not have doubted from reading the summary that interpretations of the kind that the union and the district judge later placed upon it would be entirely plausible. Colfax had a right to hope that its interpretation would prevail but it had no right to accept the offer constituted by the summary on the premise that either its interpretation was correct or it could walk away from the contract. "Heads I win, tails you lose," is not the spirit that animates the principle that latent ambiguity is a ground for rescission of a contract.

It is common for contracting parties to agree--that is, to signify agreement--to a term to which each party attaches a different meaning. It is just a gamble on a favorable interpretation by the authorized tribunal should a dispute arise. Parties often prefer to gamble in this way rather than to take the time to try to iron out all their possible disagreements, most of which may never have any consequence. Colfax gambled on persuading an arbitrator that the reference in the summary to the four-color 60-inch press meant what Colfax believes it means. The union gambled on the arbitrator's adopting the meaning that the union later made clear in the full agreement--but, to repeat, if there is a contract it is (the parties agree) the summary, read in light of the collective bargaining agreement that was being modified, that is the contract between these parties.

When parties agree to a patently ambiguous term, they submit to have any dispute over it resolved by interpretation. That is what courts and arbitrators are for in contract cases--to resolve interpretive questions founded on ambiguity. It is when parties agree to terms that reasonably appear to each of them to be unequivocal but are not, cases like that of the ship Peerless where the ambiguity is buried, that the possibility of rescission on grounds of mutual misunderstanding, or, the term we prefer, latent ambiguity, arises. A reasonable person in Colfax's position would have realized that its interpretation of the term "4C 60" Press--3 Men" might not coincide with that of the other party or of the tribunal to which a dispute over the meaning of the term would be submitted. It threw the dice, and lost, and that is the end of the case. It cannot gamble on a favorable interpretation and, if that fails, repudiate the contract with no liability. Cf. Prudential Ins. Co. v. Miller Brewing Co., 789 F.2d 1269, 1278 (7th Cir. 1986). . . .

Questions

1. How does the court distinguish between an ambiguous contract requiring interpretation and a contract that cannot be interpreted and can only be rescinded?

2. According to the court, when is a contract considered terminable without liability, and the parties are allowed to go their separate ways?

3. In cases of mutual misunderstanding or latent ambiguity, what is the basis for permitting rescission of a contract?

4. Why did the court conclude that Colfax's acceptance of the summary of changes in the collective bargaining agreement constituted a binding contract between the parties?

Takeaways – Colfax Envelope

Contract law has long-drawn a distinction between latent ambiguity and patent ambiguity, allowing rescission for the former but not for the latter. What kind of ambiguity was involved in *Colfax*? In *Oswald v. Allen*? In *Raffles v. Wichelhaus*?

Filling Gaps
Omitted Terms

What happens when the parties, whether intentionally or inadvertently, leave out or omit a term from their contract? Restatement Second section 204 provides that when the parties omit a term from their contract which is essential to the determination of their rights the court will supply a term which is reasonable. If the contract is for the sale of goods Article 2 of the UCC provides for a number of statutory terms to be used to fill gaps in the contract when missing terms cannot be supplied through resort to course of performance, course of dealing or usage of trade. (See, e.g. UCC §§ 2-305, 2-308) If not for these "gap filler" terms, a contract for the sale of goods might otherwise be unenforceable because the terms of the contract are too indefinite. The implication of these gap filling terms is usually preceded by the phrase, "Unless otherwise agreed . . . ."

Implied Terms in Contracts for the Sale of Goods

The Implied Warranty of Merchantability

In sales of goods by merchants certain warranties or guarantees with regard to quality or performance of the goods will be implied by law. This is regardless of whether anything is said by the seller about quality or performance and, unless effectively disclaimed, the warranty becomes part of the contract. The first of these warranties is the Implied Warranty of Merchantability. Under the Code the warranty accompanies any sale of goods by a merchant who deals regularly in goods of that kind. (UCC § 2-314)

Ambassador Steel Co. v. Ewald Steel Co.
Michigan Court of Appeals, 1971
33 Mich. App. 495, 190 N.W.2d 275

FITZGERALD, J. Plaintiff and defendant are both merchants in the business of the sale of steel. On or about October 4 and 5, 1966, plaintiff sold a certain amount of steel to defendant. The purchase price of the steel was $9,856.44, of which defendant paid $4,107.60, leaving an unpaid balance of $5,748.84. Plaintiff brought an action in the common pleas court to recover the balance due, ...

Defendant admitted the purchase price of the steel, but claimed a setoff, alleging that plaintiff breached its implied warranty of merchantability in that plaintiff failed to supply defendant with "commercial quality" steel, that is, steel with a carbon content of 1010 to 1020. The defect came to light when the company to whom the defendant in turn sold the steel informed defendant that the steel cracked after being welded onto railroad cars. As a result of this, defendant's customer charged back its losses to defendant. Defendant thus claimed the setoff against plaintiff.

The trial court allowed defendant to set off the entire amount of the chargeback, with the exception of a claim for overhead, and entered a judgment for plaintiff in the amount of $1,055.78. Plaintiff appealed to the circuit court, contending the judgment was inadequate. The circuit court affirmed, plaintiff applied for leave to appeal to this court and we granted it. . . .

The first issue can be stated in the following form:

As between dealers in steel, is there an implied warranty that the steel is merchantable for the purpose for which it is used, where plaintiff was not advised by defendant of the use to which the steel was to be put?

Plaintiff contends on appeal that because defendant did not inform plaintiff of the purposes for which the steel was to be used, defendant cannot claim that it was not fit for the purpose for which it was used. Defendant, however, appears to be relying on a different implied warranty, that of merchantability, and not that of particular fitness.

Section 2-314 of the Uniform Commercial Code provides, in part:

"(1) Unless excluded or modified * * *, a warranty that the goods shall be merchantable is implied in a contract for their sale if the seller is a merchant with respect to goods of that kind. * * *

"(2) Goods to be merchantable must be at least such as:

(a) pass without objection in the trade under the contract description; and

(b) * * *

(c) are fit for the ordinary purposes for which such goods are used; and

(d) run, within the variations permitted by the agreement, of even kind, quality and quantity within each unit and among all units involved; and

(e) * * *

(f) * * *

"(3) Unless excluded or modified * * *, other implied warranties may arise from course of dealing or usage of trade." (MCLA § 440.2314 [Stat Ann 1964 Rev § 19.2314]).

This section is further explained in the Comments of National Conference of Commissioners following the section, which states:

"2. The question when the warranty is imposed turns basically on the meaning of the terms of the agreement as recognized in the trade. Goods delivered under an agreement made by a merchant in a given line of trade must be of a quality comparable to that generally acceptable in that line of trade under the description or other designation of the goods used in the agreement."

Thus, unless there is an exclusion or modification, when, as here, a merchant sells such goods, an implied warranty arises that the goods would pass without objection in the trade under the contract description; also, that they are fit for the ordinary purposes for which the goods are used.

The implied warranty of merchantability is decidedly different from the implied warranty for a particular purpose that arises under MCLA § 440.2315 (Stat Ann 1964 Rev § 19.2315). The particular purpose warranty is defined by the official UCC comment as:

"2. A `particular purpose' differs from the ordinary purpose for which the goods are used in that it envisages a specific use by the buyer which is peculiar to the nature of his business whereas the ordinary purposes for which goods are used are those envisaged in the concept of merchantability and go to uses which are customarily made of the goods in question. For example, shoes are generally used for the purpose of walking upon ordinary ground, but a seller may know that a particular pair was selected to be used for climbing mountains."

It appears, then, that the warranty of merchantability warrants that the goods sold are of average quality within the industry, whereas a warranty of fitness for a particular purpose warrants that the goods sold are fit for the purposes for which they are intended. The latter is also further qualified by the requirement that the seller must know, at the time of sale, the particular purpose for which the goods are required and also that the buyer is relying on the seller to select or furnish suitable goods.

In the instant case, it is undisputed that the plaintiff was not made aware of the purpose for which the steel was to be used. Therefore, the implied warranty of fitness for a particular purpose did not arise under MCLA § 440.2315 (Stat Ann 1964 Rev § 19.2315).

The question then becomes whether or not the steel sold by plaintiff to defendant was subject to the implied warranty of merchantability under MCLA § 440.2314 (Stat Ann 1964 Rev § 19.2314). Although defendant sold the goods to a third party, MCLA § 440.2314 (Stat Ann 1964 Rev § 19.2314) Comment 1 states that the warranty of merchantability applies to goods sold for resale as well as those for sale. And, as we previously stated, Comment 2 of the same section states that the question of when the warranty is imposed turns basically on the meaning of the terms as recognized in the trade.

MCLA § 440.1205(2) (Stat Ann 1964 Rev § 19.1205[2]) defines a usage of trade as "any practice or method of dealing having such regularity of observance in a place, vocation or trade as to justify an expectation that it will be observed with respect to the transaction in question".

MCLA § 440.1205(3) (Stat Ann 1964 Rev § 19.1205[3]) provides, "A course of dealing between parties and any usage of trade in the vocation in which they are engaged or of which they are or should be aware give particular meaning to and supplement or qualify terms of an agreement".

Testimony in the transcript indicates that defendant made no specific request concerning the particular quality of steel they ordered. However, there was also ample testimony below to the effect that when an order is placed without specification as to the particular quality desired, custom and usage of the steel business is that a "commercial quality" steel, that is, steel with a carbon content between 1010 and 1020, is to be used. Further testimony was to the effect that if one desired steel other than "commercial quality" it must be specified in the order, according to local custom and usage. The testimony indicated that the steel sold by plaintiff to defendant was not within the commercial range, thus the steel cracked after being welded. Therefore, plaintiff breached the implied warranty of merchantability in selling to defendant steel of a different quality than ordinarily sold in the custom and usage of the steel business, and not fit for the ordinary purposes for which such goods are used. MCLA § 440.2314 (Stat Ann 1964 Rev § 19.2314).

Plaintiff raises the point that they were not notified of the purpose to which the steel was to be put.

Apparently plaintiff implies that the use made of the steel was a particular purpose and thus not an ordinary purpose. We have already held that plaintiff is not liable for any implied warranty for fitness for a particular purpose. Furthermore, we need not decide whether this was a particular purpose, because the quality of steel that should have been delivered under the general warranty of merchantability, but was not, was sufficient to satisfy the use in the instant case. . . .

Plaintiff next raises the issue that defendant did not sustain the burden of proving that plaintiff had breached the contract. We agree; defendant did not sustain the burden of proving plaintiff had breached the contract. However, defendant did not need to do so. What defendant needed to do, and what the record shows he did do, was prove that plaintiff had breached its implied warranty of merchantability. Defendant proved below that plaintiff impliedly warranted the steel sold as being of "commercial quality", that the plaintiff did not, in fact, sell to defendant steel that was of "commercial quality", and that if the steel had been of "commercial quality" it would not have cracked after being welded onto the railroad cars. This is sufficient to sustain an action for breach of warranty. See UCC, § 2-314, Official Comment 13. . . .

Therefore, the lower court should be, and hereby is, affirmed.

Questions

1. Under what conditions does the implied warranty of merchantability arise in a contract for the sale of goods?

2. How does the court define a "particular purpose" under the Uniform Commercial Code?

3. Was the plaintiff notified of the purpose for which the steel was to be used? How does this affect the defendant's claim of breach of warranty?

4. How did the defendant prove that the plaintiff breached the implied warranty of merchantability in this case?

Takeaways – Ambassador Steel

It has been said that the implied warranty of merchantability is really a "no-worse-than-anything-else-on-the-market" test. (See, UCC § 2-314(2).) Can you explain why this is so?

The Implied Warranty of Fitness for a Particular Purpose

Tyson v. Ciba-Geigy Corp.
Court of Appeals of North Carolina, 1986
82 N.C.App. 626, 347 S.E.2d 473

[Plaintiff, who wanted to plant "no-till" soybeans approached defendant to purchase certain weed killers. After plaintiff described to defendant's sales representative the characteristics of his land and the fact that he wanted to plant no-till soybeans, the representative told him that Dual SE, mixed with Paraquat would be as good as and cheaper than other weed killers. The weed killers recommended by defendant did not kill the crabgrass resulting in a very low yield of soybeans. Plaintiff sued.]

HEDRICK, Chief Judge. Finally, plaintiff contends that the trial court erred in granting defendant Farm Chemical's motion for directed verdict on the issue of breach of implied warranty. We agree with this contention. [UCC 2-315] defines implied warranty of fitness for particular purpose as follows:

Where the seller at the time of contracting has reason to know any particular purpose for which the goods are required and that the buyer is relying on the seller's skill or judgment to select or furnish suitable goods, there is unless excluded or modified under the next section [Sec. 25-2-316] an implied warranty that the goods shall be fit for such purpose.

The evidence in the present case, when considered in the light most favorable to plaintiff, tends to show that plaintiff contacted defendant Farm Chemical to order the herbicides Lasso and Lorox, for the no-till cultivation of soybeans. He spoke with Mr. Gregory, an employee of Farm Chemical, on the telephone and told him that he was planning the no-till cultivation of soybeans on 145 acres of his land and described the type of soil on the land. Mr. Gregory gave Dual 8E a good recommendation and told plaintiff that it would "do a good job," would be less expensive to use than the chemicals he had used the previous year and would also be less risky to use on plaintiff's type of land. He further told plaintiff that Dual 8E could be mixed with Paraquat and a surfactant to replace Lasso and Lorox. He also told plaintiff the amount of Dual 8E per acre that he should use. Plaintiff testified that based upon Mr. Gregory's recommendation and his past business dealings with Farm Chemical, he decided to use Dual 8E and ordered thirty-five gallons from Farm Chemical. Vance Tyson testified that he mixed the chemicals in accordance with Mr. Gregory's instructions, but that the Dual 8E was ineffective in killing crabgrass. Plaintiff also introduced evidence tending to show that Dual 8E must be mixed with Sencor, Lexone or Lorox and either Ortho Paraquat CL or Roundup. This evidence is sufficient to support a finding that the seller, Farm Chemical, had reason to know of the particular purpose, the no-till cultivation of soybeans, for which the product was required and that plaintiff was relying on its recommendation when he ordered the Dual 8E. There is no evidence in the record indicating that defendant Farm Chemical disclaimed any warranties relating to the Dual 8E. Thus, the evidence in the record is sufficient for a jury to find that Farm Chemical made an implied warranty relating to the fitness of the Dual 8E for plaintiff's purpose and that this warranty was breached. We hold, therefore, that the trial court erred in directing a verdict for defendant Farm Chemical on the issue of breach of an implied warranty of fitness for particular purpose.

Questions

1. What is the definition of the implied warranty of fitness for a particular purpose under UCC-2-315?

2. How does the court determine whether an implied warranty of fitness for a particular purpose exists in a contract for the sale of goods?

3. What evidence did the plaintiff present to support their claim that the seller had reason to know of the particular purpose for which the goods were required?

4. Why did the court conclude that the seller, Farm Chemical, made an implied warranty relating to the fitness of the Dual 8E for the plaintiff's purpose?

5. What was the error committed by the trial court in regard to the issue of breach of an implied warranty of fitness for a particular purpose in this case?

Keith v. Buchanan
California Court of Appeal, Second District, Division Six (1985)
173 Cal.App.3d 13, 220 Cal. Rptr. 392

OCHOA, J. . . . Plaintiff, Brian Keith, purchased a sailboat from defendants in November 1978 for a total purchase price of $75,610. Even though plaintiff belonged to the Waikiki Yacht Club, had attended a sailing school, had joined the Coast Guard Auxiliary, and had sailed on many yachts in order to ascertain his preferences, he had not previously owned a yacht. He attended a boat show in Long Beach during October 1978 and looked at a number of boats, speaking to sales representatives and obtaining advertising literature. In the literature, the sailboat which is the subject of this action, called an "Island Trader 41," was described as a seaworthy vessel. In one sales brochure, this vessel is described as "a picture of sure-footed seaworthiness." In another, it is called "a carefully well-equipped, and very seaworthy liveaboard vessel." Plaintiff testified he relied on representations in the sales brochures in regard to the purchase. Plaintiff and a sales representative also discussed plaintiff's desire for a boat which was ocean-going and would cruise long distances.

Plaintiff asked his friend, Buddy Ebsen, who was involved in a boat building enterprise, to inspect the boat. Mr. Ebsen and one of his associates, both of whom had extensive experience with sailboats, observed the boat and advised plaintiff that the vessel would suit his stated needs. A deposit was paid on the boat, a purchase contract was entered into, and optional accessories for the boat were ordered. After delivery of the vessel, a dispute arose in regard to its seaworthiness.

Plaintiff filed the instant lawsuit alleging causes of action in breach of express warranty and breach of implied warranty. The trial court granted defendants' Code of Civil Procedure section 631.8 motion for judgment at the close of plaintiff's case. The court found that no express warranty was established by the evidence because none of the defendants had undertaken in writing to preserve or maintain the utility or performance of the vessel, nor to provide compensation for any failure in utility or performance. It found that the written statements produced at trial were opinions or commendations 19*19 of the vessel. The court further found that no implied warranty of fitness was created because the plaintiff did not rely on the skill and judgment of defendants to select and furnish a suitable vessel, but had rather relied on his own experts in selecting the vessel. . . .

II. IMPLIED WARRANTY

Appellant . . . claimed breach of the implied warranty of fitness for a particular purpose in regard to the sale of the subject vessel. An implied warranty of fitness for a particular purpose arises when a "seller at the time of contracting has reason to know any particular purpose for which the goods are required and that the buyer is relying on the seller's skill or judgment to select or furnish suitable goods," which are fit for such purpose. (Cal. U. Com. Code, § 2315.) The Consumer Warranty Act makes such an implied warranty applicable to retailers, distributors, and manufacturers. (Civ. Code, §§ 1791.1, 1792.1, 1792.2, subd. (a).) An implied warranty of fitness for a particular purpose arises only where (1) the purchaser at the time of contracting intends to use the goods for a particular purpose, (2) the seller at the time of contracting has reason to know of this particular purpose, (3) the buyer relies on the seller's skill or judgment to select or furnish goods suitable for the particular purpose, and (4) the seller at the time of contracting has reason to know that the buyer is relying on such skill and judgment. (Metowski v. Traid Corp. (1972) 28 Cal. App.3d 332, 341 [104 Cal. Rptr. 599].)

The reliance elements are important to the consideration of whether an implied warranty of fitness for a particular purpose exists. "If the seller had no reason to know that he was being relied upon, his conduct in providing goods cannot fairly be deemed a tacit representation of their suitability for a particular purpose. And if the buyer did not in fact rely, then the principal justification for imposing a fitness warranty disappears." (See Warranties in Commercial Transactions, supra, at p. 89.) The major question in determining the existence of an implied warranty of fitness for a particular purpose is the reliance by the buyer upon the skill and judgment of the seller to select an article suitable for his needs. (Bagley v. International Harvester Co. (1949) 91 Cal. App.2d 922, 925 [206 P.2d 43]; Drumar M. Co. v. Morris Ravine M. Co. (1939) 33 Cal. App.2d 492, 495-496 [92 P.2d 424].)

The trial court found that the plaintiff did not rely on the skill and judgment of the defendants to select a suitable vessel, but that he rather relied on his own experts. "Our sole task is to determine `whether the evidence, viewed in the light most favorable to [respondent], sustains [these] findings.' [Citations.] Moreover, `in examining the sufficiency of the evidence to support a questioned finding an appellate court must accept as true all evidence tending to establish the correctness of the finding as made, taking into account, as well, all inferences which might reasonably have been thought by the trial court to lead to the same conclusion.' [Citations.] If appellate scrutiny reveals that substantial evidence supports the trial court's findings and conclusions, the judgment must be affirmed." (Board of Education v. Jack M. (1977) 19 Cal.3d 691, 697 [139 Cal. Rptr. 700, 566 P.2d 602].)

A review of the record reveals ample evidence to support the trial court's finding. Appellant had extensive experience with sailboats at the time of the subject purchase, even though he had not previously owned such a vessel. He had developed precise specifications in regard to the type of boat he wanted to purchase. He looked at a number of different vessels, reviewed their advertising literature, and focused on the Island Trader 41 as the object of his intended purchase. He also had friends look at the boat before making the final decision to purchase. The trial court's finding that the buyer did not rely on the skill or judgment of the seller in the selection of the vessel in question is supported by substantial evidence.

Questions

1. What are the elements required to establish an implied warranty of fitness for a particular purpose under the UCC?

2. How does the court determine whether the buyer relied on the skill and judgment of the seller in selecting goods for a particular purpose?

3. What factors did the court consider in this case to determine whether the buyer relied on the seller's skill and judgment in selecting the sailboat?

4. What did the trial court conclude regarding the buyer's reliance on the seller's skill and judgment in this case?

Takeaways – Tyson & Keith

Where a seller has reason to know at the time of contract formation that the buyer desires goods to be used for a particular purpose and that the buyer is relying on the seller's skill and judgment in selecting or furnishing suitable goods, a warranty is implied by law that the goods will be fit for that purpose. (UCC § 2-315) This is in contrast to the warranty of merchantability which sets a standard of fitness for ordinary purposes.

Thus, to establish a valid warranty of fitness for a particular purpose, "the seller must know, at the time of sale, the particular purpose for which the goods are required and also that the buyer is relying on the seller to select or furnish suitable goods." *Ambassador Steel Co. v. Ewald Steel Co.*, 33 Mich.App. 495, 501, 190 N.W.2d 275 (1971).

Note that a warranty of fitness for particular purpose can arise even though the seller is not a "merchant" with respect to the goods of the kind. (Compare UCC § 2-314 with § 2-315) Also, a disclaimer of the warranty of merchantability might not disclaim the implied warranty of fitness.

Excluding and Disclaiming Implied Warranties

Can the parties keep implied warranties out of the contract?

South Carolina Electric & Gas Co. v. Combustion Eng. Inc.
Court of Appeals of South Carolina, 1984
283 S.C. 182, 322 S.E.2d 453

GOOLSBY, Judge: The appellant South Carolina Electric and Gas Company (SCE&G) seeks to recover damages in excess of $350,000 that SCE&G alleges it sustained as a result of a fire that occurred when a flexible metal hose ruptured and sprayed heated fuel oil across the surface of a steam generating boiler at the Arthur Williams Station, a power generating plant owned by SCE&G. The circuit court granted summary judgment in favor of the respondent Combustion Engineering, Inc. (Combustion), which manufactured and sold the boiler and its ancillary equipment to SCE&G, and the respondent Daniel International Corporation (Daniel), which constructed the power plant and installed the boiler as well as the pipes and hoses that connected to it.

SCE&G appeals the grant of summary judgment in favor of Combustion on causes of action for (1) breach of an implied warranty that the boiler unit was fit for a particular purpose, (2) breach of an implied warranty that the boiler unit was merchantable, and (3) negligence in the design of the fuel piping. . . .

I. Case Against Combustion
A. Implied Warranties

SCE&G entered into the contract with Combustion for the sale of the boiler unit in early 1970. The sales contract contains an item labeled "WARRANTY," that expressly warrants the equipment to be free "from defects in material and workmanship for a period of one year." Because the boiler became operational on March 18, 1973, and the fire that brought on this litigation occurred over two years later on May 19, 1975, the one-year warranty provision had expired at the time of the fire.

The warranty item also contains a disclaimer of warranties provision. It states that "[t]here are no other warranties, whether expressed or implied, other than title."

The circuit court, in granting Combustion summary judgment on each cause of action alleging a breach of an implied warranty, ruled that the disclaimer excludes an implied warranty of merchantability as well as an implied warranty for fitness for a particular purpose.

SCE&G, however, maintains that Combustion was not entitled to summary judgment. It argues that the disclaimer, as a matter of law, does not exclude the implied warranties alleged in its complaint because the disclaimer does not meet the requirements of Subsection (2) of [UCC 2-316] and that a question of fact exists as to whether the disclaimer can come within the exceptions to Subsection (2) permitted by Subsection (3) of that statute.

We agree with SCE&G that the disclaimer does not satisfy the requirements of Subsection (2). First of all, the disclaimer nowhere mentions the word "merchantability," as it must do under Subsection (2) to exclude an implied warranty of merchantability.

Further, the written language of the disclaimer, as a matter of law, is not "conspicuous," as Subsection (2) requires it to be to exclude an implied warranty of fitness for a particular purpose as well as an implied warranty of merchantability. Indeed, the written agreement is twenty-two typewritten pages in length and is mostly single-spaced. The disclaimer itself appears on page 17 of the agreement in the last sentence of a two-paragraph item. It is indistinctive both as to color and as to type. See [UCC 1-201(10)] ("A... clause is conspicuous when it is so written that a reasonable person against whom it is to operate ought to have noticed it.... Language in the body of a form is `conspicuous' if it is in larger or other contrasting type or color"); [Citations Omitted]

Moreover, the item containing the disclaimer is misleading in that it is suggestive of "a grant of warranty rather than a disclaimer" because the heading of the item, printed in underlined capital letters, simply reads "WARRANTY." [Citations Omitted]

But the question remains concerning whether a genuine issue of material fact exists as to whether the disclaimer, as the circuit court found, falls within the exception prescribed by Subsection (3)(a). Subsection (3)(a) permits, as do Subsections (3)(b) and (c), the exclusion of implied warranties when "the circumstances surrounding the transaction are in themselves sufficient to call the buyer's attention to the fact that no implied warranties are made or that a certain implied warranty is excluded." [UCC 2-316 official comment 6]

In support of its motion for summary judgment, Combustion submitted the affidavit of Kurt W. Johnson that identified several documents exchanged between Combustion and SCE&G relative to the purchase by SCE&G of the boiler from Combustion. The first document, dated August 15, 1968 and entitled "Proposal No. 16268-E," originated with Combustion. It included the disclaimer at issue here. Five months later on January 31, 1969, SCE&G wrote Combustion stating that its August 1968 proposal was unacceptable in certain respects. SCE&G advised Combustion that it required that any purchase order filled by Combustion be subject to certain prescribed conditions. One condition was that Combustion agree "to be bound in relation to [its] equipment by the ... warranties implied by the laws of the State of South Carolina."

Combustion responded to SCE&G's letter on February 19, 1969, and informed SCE&G that it could not accept the conditions relating to implied warranties. Combustion insisted that it "have a limitation on the warranty period and a limitation on the remedy for breach of any warranty, expressed or implied." On February 21, 1969, SCE&G replied to Combustion's letter of two days before and advised Combustion that it agreed that the "warranties implied by [the] laws of the State of South Carolina shall be limited" to the warranty item included in the original proposal.

The parties differ concerning whether the correspondence mentioned above forms part of the contract and whether it constitutes evidence extrinsic to the contract. SCE&G maintains that the correspondence is not part of the contract and that consideration of it by the circuit court to determine whether the disclaimer is effective demonstrates conclusively that the disclaimer is ambiguous. SCE&G relies on the settled rule that the intention of the parties to an ambiguous contract is a question of fact for the jury to determine and is not a question that a court should decide on summary judgment. See Wheeler v. Globe & Rutgers Fire Insurance Co., 125 S.C. 320, 325, 118 S.E. 609 (1923) ("where a contract is not clear, or is ambiguous and capable of one or more constructions, what the parties really intended, as a matter of fact, should be submitted to a jury").

We need not decide whether the correspondence forms part of the contract because we think that the language of the disclaimer itself is unambiguous. In plain language, the disclaimer excludes all warranties other than the express one-year warranty and the warranty of title.

Although we do not use the correspondence to resolve an ambiguity in the language employed by the disclaimer, we do consider the correspondence to determine whether the language of the disclaimer was unbargained for and unexpected by SCE&G, the buyer. If the evidentiary material presented in connection with Combustion's motion for summary judgment shows that no genuine issue of fact exists as to whether the language of disclaimer was unbargained for and unexpected and that, as a matter of fact, the language was bargained for and expected, SCE&G could not rightly claim, irrespective of the requirements of Subsection (2), that the language does not exclude the two implied warranties asserted by Combustion. See [UCC 2-316 official comment 1 (Subsections (2) and (3) designed to protect the buyer from "unexpected and unbargained language of disclaimer"). In such a case, summary judgment for Combustion would be entirely proper.

As we view the record, Combustion was entitled to summary judgment as a matter of law on the causes of action alleging breaches of implied warranties of merchantability and fitness for a particular purpose. . . .

The correspondence exchanged between Combustion and SCE&G relating to the warranty item and submitted in support of Combustion's motion for summary judgment discloses that the language of disclaimer included in the warranty item came as no surprise to SCE&G and that SCE&G in fact bargained with Combustion over a period of seven months concerning it. SCE&G makes no factual showing to the contrary. As the correspondence indicates, the disclaimer, which is written in simple language, was subjected to detailed review by SCE&G and was agreed upon by SCE&G only after Combustion refused to accept SCE&G's condition that Combustion be bound by the "warranties implied by the laws of the State of South Carolina."

In addition, both corporations are commercially sophisticated and possess relatively equal bargaining strength. The sheer size of the transaction itself ($12,139,786.00) and the length of the negotiations (approximately nineteen months) suggest as much. As in AMF Incorporated v. Computer Automation, Inc., 573 F. Supp. 924, 930 (S.D. Ohio 1983), which also involved "commercially sophisticated businesses," it would strain "credulity to hold that a business like [SCE&G] was not, or should not have been, aware of the language disclaiming implied warranties."

We therefore hold that an effective disclaimer of implied warranties under Subsection (3)(a) was shown; thus, the language of the disclaimer at issue here was effective notwithstanding its failure to satisfy the requirements of Subsection (2). See

Tennessee Carolina Transportation Inc. v. Strick Corp., 283 N.C. 423, 196 S.E. (2d) 711 (1973) (dictum that actual awareness by a nonconsumer buyer of a disclaimer prior to entering into a sales contract and possession of substantially equivalent bargaining power satisfies purpose of "conspicuous" requirement); cf. Country Clubs, Inc. v. Allis-Chalmers Manufacturing Co., 430 F. (2d) 1394, 1397 (6th Cir.1970) (exclusion of implied warranties of merchantability upheld under Subsection 3(c) where course of dealing indicated buyer "had acquiesced in the limited warranty provision" and sale involved experienced businessmen dealing at arm's length).

Questions

1. According to SCE&G, why does the disclaimer in the sales contract not exclude the implied warranties alleged in its complaint?

2. What are the requirements of Subsection (2) of UCC 2-316 and how does the disclaimer fail to meet these requirements?

What does Subsection (3)(a) of UCC 2-316 permit in relation to the exclusion of implied warranties, and how does Combustion argue that it satisfies this provision?

How does the court determine whether the language of the disclaimer was unbargained for and unexpected by SCE&G, and what conclusion does the court reach based on the evidence presented in this case?

Takeaways – South Carolina Electric and Gas Co.

UCC § 2-316 provides that all implied warranties may be excluded by a disclaimer in language that "in common understanding calls the buyer's attention to the exclusion of warranties and makes plain that there is no implied warranty." Examples of sufficient language are "as is," "as they stand," and "with all faults."

Under 2-316(3)(b) implied warranties may be excluded by the buyer's examination of goods or his or her refusal to examine them. In other words, inspection (or reasonable opportunity for inspection) excludes implied warranties.

Express Warranties

Not all warranties under the UCC are implied by law. A seller's statement of fact, a promise or a description of the goods may constitute an express warranty. (UCC § 2-313)

Smith v. Zimbalist
California Court of Appeal, 1934
2 Cal.App.2d 324, 38 P.2d 170

Houser, J. From the "findings of fact" made pursuant to the trial of the action, it appears that plaintiff, who was of the age of eighty-six years, although not a dealer in violins, had been a collector of rare violins for many years; "that defendant was a violinist of great prominence, internationally known, and himself the owner and collector of rare and old violins made by the old masters"; that at the suggestion of a third person, and without the knowledge by plaintiff of defendant's intention in the matter, defendant visited plaintiff at the home of the latter and there asked plaintiff if he might see plaintiff's collection of old violins; that in the course of such visit and inspection, "plaintiff showed a part of his collection to defendant; that defendant picked up one violin and asked plaintiff what he would take for the violin, calling it a 'Stradivarius'; that plaintiff did not offer his violins, or any of them, for sale, but on account of his age, after he had been asked what he would take for them, said he would not charge as much as a regular dealer, but that he would sell it for $5,000; that thereafter defendant picked up another violin, calling it a 'Guarnerius', and asked plaintiff what he would take for that violin, and plaintiff said if defendant took both violins, he could have them for $8,000; that the defendant said 'all right', thereupon stating his financial condition and asking if he could pay $2,000 cash and the balance in monthly payments of $1,000." Thereupon a memorandum was signed by defendant as follows:

"I hereby acknowledge receipt of one violin by Joseph Guarnerius and one violin by Stradivarius dated 1717 purchased by me from George Smith for the total sum of Eight Thousand Dollars toward which purchase price I have paid Two Thousand Dollars the balance I agree to pay at the rate of one thousand dollars on the fifteenth day of each month until paid in full."

In addition thereto, a "bill of sale" in the following language was signed by plaintiff:

"This certifies that I have on this date sold to Mr. Efrem Zimbalist one Joseph Guarnerius violin and one Stradivarius violin dated 1717, for the full price of $8,000.00 on which has been paid $2,000.00.

"The balance of $6,000.00 to be paid $1,000.00 fifteenth of each month until paid in full. I agree that Mr. Zimbalist shall have the right to exchange these for any others in my collection should he so desire."

That at the time said transaction was consummated each of the parties thereto "fully believed that said violins were made one by Antonius Stradivarius and one by Josef Guarnerius"; that preceding the closing of said transaction "plaintiff made no representations and warranties as to said violins, or either of them, as to who their makers were, but believed them to have been made one by Antonius Stradivarius and one by Josef Guarnerius in the early part of the eighteenth century; that plaintiff did not fraudulently make any representations or warranties to defendant at the time of said purchase"; that there was "a preponderance of evidence to the effect that said violins are not Stradivarius or Guarnerius violins, nor made by either Antonius Stradivarius or Josef Guarnerius, but were in fact made as imitations thereof, and were not worth more than $300.00".

The action which is the foundation of the instant appeal was brought by plaintiff against defendant to recover judgment for the unpaid balance of the purchase price of the two violins.

As is shown by the conclusions of law reached by the trial court from such facts, the theory upon which the case was decided was that the transaction in question was the result of "a mutual mistake on the part of plaintiff and defendant", and consequently that plaintiff was not entitled to recover judgment. From a judgment rendered in favor of defendant, plaintiff has appealed to this court.

In urging a reversal of the judgment, it is the contention of appellant that the doctrine of caveat emptor should have been applied to the facts in the case; that is to say, that in the circumstances shown by the evidence and reflected in the findings of fact, the trial court should have held that defendant bought the violins at his own risk and peril.

The substance of the argument presented by appellant is a recast of the decision at nisi prius in the case of Jendwine v. Slade, (1797) 2 Espinasse, 572. The syllabus in that case is as follows:

"The putting down the name of an artist in a catalogue as the painter of any picture, is not such a warranty as will subject the party selling to an action, if it turns out that he might be mistaken, and that it was not the work of the artist to whom it was attributed." . . .

In Hawkins v. Pemberton, (1872) 51 N.Y. 198 [10 Am. Rep. 595], where a sale by auction had been made of what was assumed to be "blue vitriol", but which in fact was "mixed vitriol", after an extensive review of the authorities it was held that the contract was unenforceable. And in the same case, in referring to the case of Chandelor v. Lopus, (1603) 2 Cr. Jac. 4, 79 English Rep. 3 (Full Reprint), upon the decision of which many of the former cases relied as an authority, in part the court said: "The doctrine (there) laid down is that a mere affirmation or representation as to the character or quality of goods sold will not constitute a warranty; and that doctrine has long since been exploded and the case itself is no longer regarded as good law in this country or England." (Citing authorities.) . . .

A case which in its facts closely resembles those in the instant case is that of Power v. Barham, (1836) 4 Ad. & E., 473, 111 English Repts., Full Reprint, (K. B.) 865. Therein the early case of Jendwine v. Slade, 2 Espinasse, 572 (1797), to which reference hereinbefore has been had, is cited and "distinguished". The syllabus in Power v. Barham, supra, is as follows: "In assumpsit for breach of a warranty of pictures, it was proved, among other things, that the defendant, at the time of the sale, gave the following bill of parcels: "Four pictures, Views in Venice, Canaletto, 1601'. The Judge left it to the jury upon this and the rest of the evidence, whether the defendant had contracted that the pictures were those of the artist named, or whether his name had been used merely as matter of description, or intimation of opinion, the jury found for the plaintiff, saying that the bill of parcels amounted to a warranty: Held, that the question had been rightly left to jury, and that the verdict was not to be disturbed." . . .

In the case of Henshaw v. Robins, 9 Met. (50 Mass.) 83 [43 Am. Dec. 367], where the authorities are reviewed, the facts and the law are indicated in the syllabus as follows: "When a bill of parcels is given, upon a sale of goods, describing the goods, or designating them by a name well understood, such bill is to be considered as a warranty that the goods sold are what they are thus described or designated to be. And this rule applies, though the goods are examined by the purchaser, at or before the sale, if they are so prepared, and present such an appearance, as to deceive skillful dealers." . . .

The governing principle of law to the effect that an article described in a "bill of parcels", or, as in the instant case, in a "bill of sale", amounts to a warranty that such article in fact conforms to such description and that the seller is bound by such description, has been applied in this state in the case of Flint v. Lyon, 4 Cal. 17, wherein it was held that where the defendant purchased an entire cargo of flour which was described as "Haxall" flour, he was not required by the contract to accept the same flour which in reality was "Gallego" flour, but which was of as excellent quality as "Haxall" flour. Therein, in part, the court said:

"What the inducement was to the defendant to purchase Haxall, we know not; but having purchased that particular brand, he was entitled to it, and could not be compelled to accept any other as a substitute. The use of the word 'Haxall' in the sale note amounted to a warranty that the flour was Haxall. (Citing authorities.) How, then, stands the case? The contract was founded in mistake, both parties supposing they were contracting concerning a certain article which had no existence, consequently the contract was void for want of the substance of the thing contracted for. Could then the acceptance of a different article than the one sold by Gorham, the sub-vendee, conclude the defendant? Certainly not! ..."

Although it may be that by some authorities a different rule may be indicated, it is the opinion of this court that, in accord with the weight of the later authorities to which attention hereinbefore has been directed, the strict brule of caveat emptor may not be applied to the facts of the instant case, but that such rule is subject to the exception thereto to the effect that on the purported sale of personal property the parties to the proposed contract are not bound where it appears that in its essence each of them is honestly mistaken or in error with reference to the identity of the subject-matter of such contract. In other words, in such circumstances, no enforceable sale has taken place. But if it may be said that a sale, with a voidable condition attached, was the outcome of the transaction in the instant case, notwithstanding the "finding of fact" by the trial court that "plaintiff made no representations and warranties as to said violins", from a consideration of the language employed by the parties in each of the documents that was exchanged between them (to which reference hereinbefore has been had), together with the general conduct of the parties, and particularly the acquiescence by plaintiff in the declaration made by defendant regarding each of the violins and by whom it was made,--it becomes apparent that, in law, a warranty was given by plaintiff that one of the violins was a Guarnerius and that the other was a Stradivarius.

The findings of fact unquestionably show that each of the parties believed and assumed that one of said violins was a genuine Guarnerius and that the other was a genuine Stradivarius; the receipt given by defendant to plaintiff for said violins so described them, and the "bill of sale" given by plaintiff to defendant certifies that plaintiff "sold to Mr. Efrem Zimbalist (defendant) one Joseph Guarnerius violin and one Stradivarius violin dated 1717 for the full price of $8,000.00 on which has been paid $2,000.00. ..."

Without burdening this opinion with the citation of additional authorities, it may suffice to state that, although the very early decisions may hold to a different rule, all the more modern authorities, including many of those in California to which attention has been directed (besides the provision now contained in section 1734, Civ. Code), are agreed that the description in a bill of parcels or sale note of the thing sold amounts to a warranty on the part of the seller that the subject-matter of the sale conforms to such description. (See, generally, 22 Cal.Jur. 994; 55 Cor. Jur. 738 et seq.; 24 R. C. L. 171; and authorities respectively there cited.)

It is ordered that the judgment be and it is affirmed.

Questions

1. How did the court interpret the language and conduct of the parties to determine the existence of a warranty?

2. What exception to the strict rule of caveat emptor did the court recognize in this case?

3. Based on the court's analysis, what was the effect of the plaintiff's description of the violins in the "bill of sale" on the transaction?

Takeaways – Smith v. Zimbalist

If goods are sold by any description which has been made part of the basis of the bargain, the goods are subject to the seller's warranty that they will conform to that description. (UCC § 2-313(1)(b))

Keith v. Buchanan
California Court of Appeal Second District, Division Six (1985)
173 Cal.App.3d 13, 220 Cal. Rptr. 392

(The facts of the case are set forth at page 422)

I. EXPRESS WARRANTY

California Uniform Commercial Code section 2313[1] provides, inter alia, that express warranties are created by (1) any affirmation of fact or promise made by the seller to the buyer which relates to the goods and becomes part of the basis of the bargain, and (2) any description of the goods which is made part of the basis of the bargain. Formal words such as "warranty" or "guarantee" are not required to make a warranty, but the seller's affirmation of the value of the goods or an expression of opinion or commendation of the goods does not create an express warranty. . . .

California Uniform Commercial Code section 2313, regarding express warranties, was enacted in 1963 and consists of the official text of Uniform Commercial Code section 2-313 without change. (3) In deciding whether a statement made by a seller constitutes an express warranty under this provision, the court must deal with three fundamental issues. First, the court must determine whether the seller's statement constitutes an "affirmation of fact or promise" or "description of the goods" under California Uniform Commercial Code section 2313, subdivision (1)(a) or (b), or whether it is rather "merely the seller's opinion or commendation of the goods" under section 2313, subdivision (2). Second, assuming the court finds the language used susceptible to creation of a warranty, it must then be determined whether the statement was "part of the basis of the bargain." Third, the court must determine whether the warranty was breached. (See Sessa v. Riegle (E.D.Pa. 1977) 427 F. Supp. 760, 765.)

A warranty relates to the title, character, quality, identity, or condition of the goods. The purpose of the law of warranty is to determine what it is that the seller has in essence agreed to sell. (A.A. Baxter Corp. v. Colt Industries, Inc. (1970) 10 Cal. App.3d 144, 153 [88 Cal. Rptr. 842].) "Express warranties are chisels in the hands of buyers and sellers. With these tools, the parties to a sale sculpt a monument representing the goods. Having selected a stone, the buyer and seller may leave it almost bare, allowing considerable play in the qualities that fit its contours. Or the parties may chisel away inexactitudes until a well-defined shape emerges. The seller is bound to deliver, and the buyer to accept, goods that match the sculpted form. [Fn.

omitted.]" (Special Project: Article Two Warranties in Commercial Transactions, Express Warranties — Section 2-313 (1978-79) 64 Cornell L.Rev. 30 (hereafter cited as Warranties in Commercial Transactions) at pp. 43-44.)

A. Affirmation of fact, promise or description versus statement of opinion, commendation or value.

"The determination as to whether a particular statement is an expression of opinion or an affirmation of a fact is often difficult, and frequently is dependent upon the facts and circumstances existing at the time the statement is made." (Willson v. Municipal Bond Co. (1936) 7 Cal.2d 144, 150 [59 P.2d 974].) Recent decisions have evidenced a trend toward narrowing the scope of representations which are considered opinion, sometimes referred to as "puffing" or "sales talk," resulting in an expansion of the liability that flows from broad statements of manufacturers or retailers as to the quality of their products. Courts have liberally construed affirmations of quality made by sellers in favor of injured consumers. (Hauter v. Zogarts (1975) 14 Cal.3d 104, 112 [120 Cal. Rptr. 681, 534 P.2d 377, 7 A.L.R.3d 1282]; see also 55 Cal.Jur.3d, Sales, § 74, p. 580.) It has even been suggested "that in an age of consumerism all seller's statements, except the most blatant sales pitch, may give rise to an express warranty." (1 Alderman and Dole, A Transactional Guide to the Uniform Commercial Code (2d ed. 1983) p. 89.)

Courts in other states have struggled in efforts to create a formula for distinguishing between affirmations of fact, promises, or descriptions of goods on the one hand, and value, opinion, or commendation statements on the other. The code comment indicates that the basic question is: "What statements of the seller have in the circumstances and in objective judgment become part of the basis of the bargain?" The commentators indicated that the language of subsection (2) of the code section was included because "common experience discloses that some statements or predictions cannot fairly be viewed as entering into the bargain." (See U. Com. Code com. 8 to Cal. U. Com. Code, § 2313, West's Ann. Com. Code (1964) p. 250, Deering's Cal. Codes Ann. p. 143.)

Statements made by a seller during the course of negotiation over a contract are presumptively affirmations of fact unless it can be demonstrated that the buyer could only have reasonably considered the statement as a statement of the seller's opinion. Commentators have noted several factors which tend to indicate an opinion statement. These are (1) a lack of specificity in the statement made, (2) a statement that is made in an equivocal manner, or (3) a statement which reveals that the goods are experimental in nature. (See Warranties in Commercial Transactions, supra, at pp. 61-65.)

It is clear that statements made by a manufacturer or retailer in an advertising brochure which is disseminated to the consuming public in order to induce sales can create express warranties. (Fundin v. Chicago Pneumatic Tool Co. (1984) 152 Cal. App.3d 951, 957 [199 Cal. Rptr. 789]; see also Community Television Services v. Dresser Industries (8th Cir.1978) 586 F.2d 637, 640, cert. den. 1979; Fargo Mach. & Tool Co. v. Kearney & Trecker Corp. (E.D.Mich. 1977) 428 F. Supp. 364, 370-371; Colorado-Ute Elec. Ass'n, Inc. v. Envirotech Corp. (D.Colo. 1981) 524 F. Supp. 1152, 1156; Neville Const. Co. v. Cook Paint and Varnish Co. (8th Cir.1982) 671 F.2d 1107, 1110.) In the instant case, the vessel purchased was described in sales brochures as "a picture of sure-footed seaworthiness" and "a carefully well-equipped and very seaworthy vessel." The seller's representative was aware that appellant was looking for a vessel sufficient for long distance ocean-going cruises. The statements in the brochure are specific and unequivocal in asserting that the vessel is seaworthy. Nothing in the negotiation indicates that the vessel is experimental in nature. In fact, one sales brochure assures prospective buyers that production of the vessel was commenced "after years of careful testing." The representations regarding seaworthiness made in sales brochures regarding the Island Trader 41 were affirmations of fact relating to the quality or condition of the vessel.

B. "Part of the basis of the bargain" test.

Under former provisions of law, a purchaser was required to prove that he or she acted in reliance upon representations made by the seller. (Grinnell v. Charles Pfizer & Co. (1969) 274 Cal. App.2d 424, 440 [79 Cal. Rptr. 369].) California Uniform Commercial Code section 2313 indicates only that the seller's statements must become "part of the basis of the bargain." According to official comment 3 to this Uniform Commercial Code provision, "no particular reliance ... need be shown in order to weave [the seller's affirmations of fact] into the fabric of the agreement. Rather, any fact which is to take such affirmations, once made, out of the agreement requires clear affirmative proof." (See U. Com. Code com. 3 to Cal. U. Com. Code, § 2313, 23A West's Ann. Com. Code (1964 ed.) p. 249, Deering's Ann. Cal. U. Com. Code (1970 ed.) p. 142.)

The California Supreme Court, in discussing the continued viability of the reliance factor, noted that commentators have disagreed in regard to the impact of this development. Some have indicated that it shifts the burden of proving nonreliance to the seller, and others have indicated that the code eliminates the concept of reliance altogether. (Hauter v. Zogarts, supra, 14 Cal.3d at pp. 115-116.) The court did not resolve this issue, but noted that decisions of other states prior to that time had "ignored the significance of the new standard and have held that consumer reliance still is a vital ingredient for recovery based on express warranty." (Id., at p. 116, fn. 13; see also Fogo v. Cutter Laboratories, Inc. (1977) 68 Cal. App.3d 744, 760 [137 Cal. Rptr. 417].)

The shift in language clearly changes the degree to which it must be shown that the seller's representation affected the buyer's decision to enter into the agreement. A buyer need not show that he would not have entered into the agreement absent the warranty or even that it was a dominant factor inducing the agreement. A warranty statement is deemed to be part of the basis of the bargain and to have been relied upon as one of the inducements for the purchase of the product. In other words, the buyer's demonstration of reliance on an express warranty is "not a prerequisite for breach of warranty, as long as the express warranty involved became part of the bargain. See White & Summers, Uniform Commercial Code (2d ed. 1980) § 94. If, however, the resulting bargain does not rest at all on the representations of the seller, those representations cannot be considered as becoming any part of the `basis of the bargain.' ..." (Allied Fidelity Ins. Co. v. Pico (1983) 99 Nev. 15 [656 P.2d 849, 850].)

The official Uniform Commercial Code comment in regard to section 2-313 "indicates that in actual practice affirmations of fact made by the seller about the goods during a bargain are regarded as part of the description of those goods; hence no particular reliance on such statements need be shown in order to weave them into the fabric of the agreement." (Young & Cooper, Inc. v. Vestring (1974) 214 Kan. 311 [521 P.2d 281, 291]; Brunner v. Jensen (1974) 215 Kan. 416 [524 P.2d 1175, 1185].) It is clear from the new language of this code section that the concept of reliance has been purposefully abandoned. (Interco Inc. v. Randustrial Corp. (Mo. App. 1976) 533 S.W.2d 257, 261; see also Winston Industries, Inc. v. Stuyvesant Insurance Co., Inc. (1975) 55 Ala.App. 525 [317 So.2d 493, 497].)

The change of the language in section 2313 of the California Uniform Commercial Code modifies both the degree of reliance and the burden of proof in express warranties under the code. The representation need only be part of the basis of the bargain, or merely a factor or consideration inducing the buyer to enter into the bargain. A warranty statement made by a seller is presumptively part of the basis of the bargain, and the burden is on the seller to prove that the resulting bargain does not rest at all on the representation.

The buyer's actual knowledge of the true condition of the goods prior to the making of the contract may make it plain that the seller's statement was not relied upon as one of the inducements for the purchase, but the burden is on the seller to demonstrate such knowledge on the part of the buyer. Where the buyer inspects the goods before purchase, he may be deemed to have waived the seller's express warranties. But, an examination or inspection by the buyer of the goods does not necessarily discharge the seller from an express warranty if the defect was not actually discovered and waived. (Doak Gas Engine Co. v. Fraser (1914) 168 Cal. 624, 627 [143 P. 1024]; Munn v. Earle C. Anthony, Inc. (1918) 36 Cal. App. 312, 315 [171 P. 1082]; Capital Equipment Enter., Inc. v. North Pier Terminal Co. (1969) 117 Ill. App.2d 264 [254 N.E.2d 542, 545].)

Appellant's inspection of the boat by his own experts does not constitute a waiver of the express warranty of seaworthiness. Prior to the making of the contract, appellant had experienced boat builders observe the boat, but there was no testing of the vessel in the water. Such a warranty (seaworthiness) necessarily relates to the time when the vessel has been put to sea (Werner v. Montana (1977) 117 N.H. 721 [378 A.2d 1130, 1134-1135]) and has been shown to be reasonably fit and adequate in materials, construction, and equipment for its intended purposes (Daly v. General Motors Corp. (1978) 20 Cal.3d 725, 739 [144 Cal. Rptr. 380, 575 P.2d 1162]; Vittone v. American President Lines (1964) 228 Cal. App.2d 689, 693-694 [39 Cal. Rptr. 758]).

In this case, appellant was aware of the representations regarding seaworthiness by the seller prior to contracting. He also had expressed to the seller's representative his desire for a long distance ocean-going vessel. Although he had other experts inspect the vessel, the inspection was limited and would not have indicated whether or not the vessel was seaworthy. It is clear that the seller has not overcome the presumption that the representations regarding seaworthiness were part of the basis of this bargain.

Questions

1. According to the court's reasoning, when does an express warranty arise in a sale of goods?

2. What are the three fundamental issues that the court must consider when determining whether a statement made by a seller constitutes an express warranty under Uniform Commercial Code section 2-313?

4. Why did the court find that a warranty was given by the plaintiff regarding the identity of the violins being sold?

5. According to the court's interpretation of the law, what is the significance of the description of the goods in a bill of parcels or a bill of sale? How does it affect the seller's liability for the conformity of the goods to the description?

Miller v. Lentine
Supreme Judicial Court of Maine, 1985
495 A.2d 1229

NICHOLS, Justice. In this case involving allegations of breach of an express warranty, [UCC § 2-313], and mutual mistake in the contract of sale between the Plaintiff, Hale W. Miller, and the Defendant, Sal Lentine, of an outboard motor, the Plaintiff appeals the Superior Court's (Knox County) denial of his appeal. The Plaintiff argues that the District Court erred in the following respects: (1) in concluding that the Defendant's representations were merely "puffing;" (2) in concluding that the contract entered into was not based on mutual mistake; and (3) in finding certain facts concerning the discovery and cause of defects in the motor.

We disagree and affirm the judgment.

In the Spring of 1983, the Plaintiff, who was in the market for an outboard motor, noticed a used 1980 235 horsepower outboard motor on display in the shop of Coastal Diversified Marine in Owls Head. He inquired of Albert Hallowell in the shop as to the owner and price of the motor and learned that it was owned by the Defendant, who was then in New Jersey, was offered for $3,500.00, and was in good condition with only 30-35 running hours on it, but had been involved in an accident when the boat to which the motor was attached fell off a trailer. The Plaintiff spoke by telephone with the Defendant and was told in addition to the information he had already received that the motor had a broken skega lower part designed to protect the propeller if an object is struck, was in "perfect running condition," and should not cause him any trouble.

The Plaintiff paid a deposit of $350.00 to the Defendant and subsequently sent the balance of $3,150.00 on or about March 21, 1983. There was no written agreement between the parties. Upon the Plaintiff's request, Hallowell installed a new propeller on the motor. Hallowell tested the motor and noted no problems. The Plaintiff took delivery of the motor on May 8, 1983 and launched his boat with the motor on it that same day. The Defendant testified that at that time he noted a problem with its idling. It was not, however, until sometime thereafter that the Plaintiff asked Hallowell to make adjustments. The Plaintiff had not sought an opportunity to operate it prior to purchase. About one month after purchase, the Plaintiff had difficulty with the motor and brought it to Hallowell for repairs in the first week of June. Hallowell fixed the motor after "digging deeper and deeper" and splitting the power head open to find the crankshaft defective from rust. He found the rest of the motor in excellent condition. The Plaintiff paid $1,457.90 for the repairs. Later other problems, including a misalignment of the drive shaft, a burned out voltage regulator, and a wrong size gas tank, were discovered.

Turning to the Plaintiff's contention that the District Court erred in concluding that there was no express warranty breached, we first note that the question whether particular language gives rise to an express warranty is generally one for the trier of fact. Cuthbertson v. Clark Equipment Co., 448 A.2d 315, 320 (Me. 1982) (citation omitted). Thus, we review the District Court's finding for clear error. See Auto Sales & Finance Co. v. Seavey, 401 A.2d 648, 650 (Me.1979).

The term "puffing" is frequently used to denote "dealer's talk," "sales talk," and "praise of goods by the seller." See 77 C.J.S. Sales § 310 (1952 & Supp.1984); Annot., 94 A.L.R.3d 729 (1979); 8 Williston on Contracts § 971A at 493 (3d Ed.1964). Very often it is difficult to distinguish puffing statements from affirmations of fact relating to goods. See id.; Downie v. Abex Corp., 741 F.2d 1235, 1240 (10th Cir.1984); J. White & R. Summers, Uniform Commercial Code 329 (1980). In the instant case, the District Court found that the Defendant told the Plaintiff, prior to the latter's purchase, that the motor in question was in "perfect running condition" and that the Plaintiff should have no problem with it. The question then became whether those statements created an express warranty or merely disclosed the seller's opinion. See 11 M.R.S.A. § 2-313(2).

Courts in other jurisdictions are divided on the issue of whether language similar to "perfect running condition" and "should not give you any trouble" creates an express warranty. The circumstances surrounding the agreement, including the knowledge of both parties, should be considered in determining whether an express warranty was formed. See Peterson v. North American Plant Breeders, 218 Neb. 258, 354 N.W.2d 625, 630 (1984). Given the District Court's finding that during a telephone conversation with the Plaintiff the Defendant described certain damage to the motor, we cannot now say that that court committed clear error in concluding that the Defendant's other statements as to the condition of the motor constituted nothing more than "sales talk." . . .

Judgment affirmed.

Questions

1. According to the court's decision, what factors should be considered in determining whether a statement creates an express warranty or is merely "sales talk"?

2. How does the court determine whether a statement in this case constituted an express warranty or the seller's opinion?

3. Explain the court's rationale for considering the circumstances surrounding the agreement and the knowledge of both parties in determining the existence of an express warranty.

4. Why did the court find that the Defendant's statements about the motor being in "perfect running condition" and causing no trouble were not sufficient to create an express warranty in this case?

Takeaways – Keith and Miller

In deciding whether a statement made by a seller constitutes an express warranty, two questions must be addressed. 1. Does the seller's statement constitute an affirmation of fact or promise or description of the goods? 2. If so, was the statement part of the basis of the bargain?

As you have gathered, in determining whether an express warranty has been made courts distinguish between statements of fact, which are actionable, and statements of opinion (sometimes referred to as "puffing" or "sales talk") which are not actionable. One court has distinguished between statement of fact and mere expression of opinion as follows: "Did seller assume to assert a fact of which buyer was ignorant, or did he merely express a judgment on something as to which each of them might be expected to have an opinion?" (*Gen. Supply v. Phillips* (1972) 490 SW2d 913.)

For cases holding an express warranty was made: *Taylor v. Alfama*, 145 Vt. 4, 481 A.2d 1059, 1060 (1984) (car in "mint condition"); *Pake v. Byrd*, 55 N.C.App. 551, 286 S.E.2d 588 (1982) ("good tractor" and "it operated as good as when it was new"); *Jones v. Kellner*, 5 Ohio App.3d 242, 451 N.E.2d 548 (App.1982) (car "mechanically A-1); *Ekizian v. Capurro*, 111 Misc.2d 372, 444 N.Y.S.2d 361 (1981) (engine "runs good"); *Valley Datsun v. Martinez*, 578 S.W.2d 485 (Tex.Civ.App.1979) (camper in "excellent condition").

For cases holding that the seller's statement did not create an express warranty: (watering system "would provide years of trouble-free service"); (racehorse "sound"); (trailer in "perfect condition").

The Implied Term of "Good Faith"

As we have seen, when during performance of a contract a situation arises that wasn't covered by an express term of the contract a court will have to resort to a gap filler to supply a term. One of the most important gap fillers is the obligation to act in "good faith." It is an implied term of every contract. (Rest.2d § 205, UCC § 1-304) This duty of good faith, also known as the implied covenant of good faith and fair dealing, means that neither party shall do anything to deprive the other of the fruits of the contract.

De La Concha of Hartford, Inc. v. Aetna Life Insurance Co.
Supreme Court of Connecticut, 2004
269 Conn. 424, 849 A.2d 382

[In 1975, the plaintiff, De La Concha of Hartford, Inc., leased space from the defendant in the new Hartford Civic Center to sell tobacco and tobacco-related products. The Civic Center is an enclosed mall with retail stores facing inward toward a central court and not generally visible from the street. It also contained a coliseum used for events and exhibitions, and an arena for sporting contests. Interdependency of the retailers was particularly important. Consumers who came to the Civic Center to make an intended purchase at one store frequently made an impulse purchase at another store. On the one hand, full occupancy of the Civic Center helped all the retailers to prosper. On the other hand, low occupancy gave the Civic Center a deserted feeling that depressed the sales of the remaining retailers. While the Civic Center was essentially fully occupied when it opened, the defendant was never able to find an anchor tenant. The Civic Center's occupancy rate fluctuated with the Hartford economy. Yet, even when fully occupied, the defendant lost money as the owner of the Civic Center.

In 1995, the defendant's new manager for the Civic Center analyzed the financial outlook and found that the Civic Center had lost more than $50 million in twenty years, had few substantial tenants and was hemorrhaging thousands of dollars for lack of rental income and high operating expenses. The manager explored the possibilities of closing the Civic Center, selling it or finding a partner able to run it profitably. Because the manager deemed the sale of the Civic Center as the most likely alternative, but could not foresee what use the potential purchaser might make of the Civic Center, he undertook a policy of entering into short-term leases or leases giving the defendant the right to recapture the premises in order to make the Civic Center more saleable. In 1995, the defendant essentially terminated its efforts to promote the Civic Center and substantially cut its promotion budget. It stopped television, radio, and newspaper advertising and promotional events at the Civic Center. For the next three years, the defendant limited its capital expenditures to safety measures and maintaining the physical integrity of the premises.

The plaintiff's sales peaked at $550,027 (partly as a result of a boom in cigar sales), over 70 percent higher than they had been just five years ear-lier. That year. the defendant finally decided to sell the Civic Center and, in 1999, the defendant agreed to sell the Civic Center to Northland, Inc., for development into a high rise residential complex with some retail stores.

The plaintiff continued in operation, but with declining business. The plaintiff also started to default in its rent. In 2000, however, the plaintiff sought to exercise its option to renew its lease for another five years. The plaintiff was then behind in paying rent and had failed to maintain its annual sales of at least $262,500, a condition for renewal of the lease. The defendant rejected the plaintiffs option to renew. The plaintiff closed its business in 2001]

PALMER, J. This appeal arises out of a dispute between the plaintiff, De La Concha of Hartford, Inc., the lessee of certain retail space in the Hartford Civic Center (Civic Center), and the defendant, Aetna Life Insurance Company, the former owner of the Civic Center and lessor of the space leased by the plaintiff. The plaintiff commenced this action alleging, inter alia, that the defendant had breached the implied covenant of good faith and fair dealing and had violated the Connecticut Unfair Trade Practices Act (CUTPA), General Statutes § 42-110a et seq., by changing its leasing and promotional practices at the Civic Center during the plaintiff's tenancy and by refusing to renew the plaintiff's lease. . . .

We turn now to the legal principles governing each of the plaintiff's two claims. With respect to the plaintiff's allegation that the defendant breached the implied covenant of good faith and fair dealing, "[i]t is axiomatic that the . . . duty of good faith and fair dealing is a covenant implied into a contract or a contractual relationship. See *Magnan* v. *Anaconda Industries, Inc.,* 193 Conn. 558, 566, 479 A.2d 781 (1984); see also 2 Restatement (Second), Contracts § 205 (1979) ([e]very contract imposes upon each party a duty of good faith and fair dealing in its performance and its enforcement)." (Internal quotation marks omitted.) *Hoskins* v. *Titan Value Equities Group, Inc.,* 252 Conn. 789, 793, 749 A.2d 1144 (2000). In other words, every contract carries an implied duty "requiring that neither party do anything that will injure the right of the other to receive the benefits of the agreement." (Internal quotation marks omitted.) *Gaudio* v. *Griffin Health Services Corp.,* 249 Conn. 523, 564, 733 A.2d 197 (1999) (*Callahan, C. J.,* dissenting). "The covenant of good faith and fair dealing presupposes that the terms and purpose of the contract are agreed upon by the parties and that what is in dispute is a party's discretionary application or interpretation of a contract term." (Internal quotation marks omitted.) *Celentano* v. *Oaks Condominium Assn.,* 265 Conn. 579, 617, 830 A.2d 164 (2003).

"To constitute a breach of [the implied covenant of good faith and fair dealing], the acts by which a defendant allegedly impedes the plaintiff's right to receive benefits that he or she reasonably expected to receive under the contract must have been taken in bad faith." *Alexandru* v. *Strong,* 81 Conn. App. 68, 80-81, 837 A.2d 875, cert. denied, 268 Conn. 906, 845 A.2d 406 (2004), citing *Gupta* v. *New Britain General Hospital,* 239 Conn. 574, 598, 687 A.2d 111 (1996). "Bad faith in general implies both actual or constructive fraud, or a design to mislead or deceive another, or a neglect or refusal to fulfill some duty or some contractual obligation, not prompted by an honest mistake as to one's rights or duties, but by some interested or sinister motive. . . . Bad faith means more than mere negligence; it involves a dishonest purpose." (Citation omitted; internal quotation marks omitted.) *Habetz* v. *Condon,* 224 Conn. 231, 237, 618 A.2d 501 (1992).

With respect to the plaintiff's CUTPA claim, "Connecticut courts, when determining whether a practice violates CUTPA, will consider (1) whether the practice, without necessarily having been previously considered unlawful, offends public policy as it has been established by statutes, the common law, or otherwise—whether, in other words, it is within at least the penumbra of some common-law, statutory, or other established concept of unfairness; (2) whether it is immoral, unethical, oppressive, or unscrupulous; (3) whether it causes substantial injury to consumers (or competitors or other businessmen). . . . Thus, a violation of CUTPA may be established by showing either an actual deceptive practice . . . or a practice amounting to a violation of public policy. . . . Whether a practice is unfair and thus violates CUTPA is an issue of fact. . . . The facts found must be viewed within the context of the totality of circumstances which are uniquely available to the trial court." (Citations omitted; internal quotation marks omitted.) *Ancona v. Manafort Bros., Inc.,* 56 Conn. App. 701, 714-15, 746 A.2d 184, cert. denied, 252 Conn. 953, 749 A.2d 1202 (2000).

With these legal principles in mind, we consider first the plaintiff's contention that the trial court improperly rejected its claim that the defendant breached the implied covenant of good faith and fair dealing. At trial, the plaintiff maintained that, because the economic viability of any one retail tenant of an enclosed mall, such as the Civic Center, depends upon the occupancy rate of the entire mall, the defendant had an obligation, implied under its lease, to make good faith efforts to promote and to maintain the mall. In support of this contention, the plaintiff relies on two provisions in the lease: the gross sales provision, which afforded the plaintiff the right to renew its lease provided its gross sales exceeded $262,500, and the promotional fund provision, which required the defendant to contribute not less than 25 percent of the total amount that the Civic Center tenants had paid into the promotional fund. According to the plaintiff, the gross sales provision of the lease impliedly obligated the defendant to refrain from conduct that created any unfair or unnecessary risk of adversely affecting the plaintiff's sales. The plaintiff further claimed that the promotional fund provision gave rise to a duty on the part of the defendant to make reasonable efforts to promote and to maintain the Civic Center for the purpose of achieving an occupancy rate that was consistent with the economic well-being of the tenants, including the plaintiff.

The plaintiff asserted that the defendant failed to meet its obligation to promote the Civic Center and to make reasonable efforts to maintain the occupancy rate at an acceptable level. In particular, the plaintiff claimed that the evidence established, as a matter of law, that the defendant, once it had decided to sell the Civic Center, engaged in a "scheme" or course of conduct to "starve out" the plaintiff and other tenants so as to make the Civic Center more appealing to potential purchasers who, in the absence of tenants, would have greater flexibility in deciding how to maximize profitability. The plaintiff asserted that, in furtherance of this strategy, the defendant, beginning in or around 1995, elected not to promote or to market the Civic Center and, in addition, declined to enter into new leases or lease renewals on terms that would be attractive to existing or prospective tenants. In support of the latter claim, the plaintiff pointed to the defendant's decision to enter into short-term leases and lease renewals only, and to require a provision in each such lease permitting the defendant to "recapture," or terminate, the lease on relatively short notice. In the plaintiff's view, these recapture provisions were likely to increase vacancies at the Civic Center.

Finally, the plaintiff challenged the propriety of the defendant's refusal to renew the plaintiff's lease in 2000 on the ground that the plaintiff had failed to attain gross annual sales of $262,500. Specifically, the plaintiff claimed that the defendant's rejection of the plaintiff's option to renew was unreasonable and in violation of the lease's implied covenant of good faith and fair dealing because the plaintiff's failure to reach gross sales of $262,500 was due in large part to the defendant's failure to promote the Civic Center as required under the lease.

In rejecting the plaintiff's claims, the trial court found that the defendant had not breached any express term of the lease nor had it engaged in any conduct prohibited by the lease's implied covenant of good faith and fair dealing. In particular, the court found that, although the defendant had an obligation to conduct itself in conformity with the express lease provisions and with the plaintiff's justified expectations in light of those provisions, the defendant's conduct had satisfied that standard. In this regard, the trial court noted: "The Civic Center was an economic venture in which [the defendant] was engaged . . . not only as a good citizen of Hartford but also to make a profit. Clearly, [the defendant's] reasonable expectations did not include continuing to promote the Civic Center when it was losing hundreds of thousands of dollars every year. Nor did it assume an obligation as a guarantor of the plaintiff's prosperity. . . .

"Here, [the defendant] acted reasonably to cut its losses arising from the operation of the Civic Center in light of the departure of the [Hartford] Whalers, the expansion of shopping malls in the suburbs and the deteriorating economic situation in downtown Hartford.

With regard to the promotional fund provision of the lease, the court found that the defendant had contributed substantially more to promoting and marketing the Civic Center than that required under the lease. The court further found that even if the defendant had failed, at some point during the plaintiff's tenancy, to meet its responsibility under the lease to promote the Civic Center, any such failure would have had "no effect" on the plaintiff's financial condition because, by that time, "no matter how much the [defendant] had expended on promoting the [Civic] [C]enter, [any such expenditure] would not have made the slightest . . . difference in [the maintenance and acquisition of] new tenants or in . . . the economic viability of the [Civic] [C]enter."

The trial court also found that the plaintiff had failed to establish that the defendant acted in bad faith at any time. In particular, the trial court concluded that, although the defendant had "pursued its own self-interest in limiting its losses in the operation of the Civic Center . . . it did not do so because of a dishonest purpose, a furtive design or ill will toward the plaintiff."

Finally, the trial court rejected the plaintiff's claim that the defendant had violated the lease's implied covenant of good faith and fair dealing by refusing to renew the plaintiff's lease. The court concluded that the defendant had acted reasonably and within its rights under the lease in rejecting the plaintiff's option to renew because the plaintiff, having failed to pay rent for the several months preceding its renewal request, was in default and, therefore, not entitled to the renewal that it had sought.

To the extent that the plaintiff contends that the defendant was obligated to conduct itself in good faith and in a manner consistent with the reasonable expectations of the parties in view of the provisions of the lease, we agree with that contention. Although the actual lease terms provide the most significant guidepost in determining the parties' reasonable expectations, it is also true, as the plaintiff asserts, that the defendant was prohibited, under the lease's implied covenant of good faith and fair dealing, from engaging in purposeful conduct that is inimical to the material terms of the lease. We conclude, however, that the trial court's determination that the evidence did not support the plaintiff's allegations of such conduct is amply supported by the record.

As we have indicated, the thrust of the plaintiff's claim was that, once the defendant had decided to sell the Civic Center, it took steps to "starve out" the tenants to make the Civic Center more marketable. Contrary to the plaintiff's claim, the evidence supported the trial court's finding that the defendant's decision to sell the Civic Center and the steps it took to implement that decision were undertaken reasonably and in good faith, and for the purpose of extricating itself from a well-intended but unsuccessful business venture that resulted in the defendant's loss of more than $50 million over the course of approximately twenty years. In particular, the evidence established that the defendant went to considerable lengths to *retain* existing tenants and to attract new ones; indeed, the defendant offered certain tenants substantial rent reductions to induce them to renew their leases. With respect to the defendant's decision to enter into short-term leases with recapture provisions, a number of tenants or potential tenants *themselves* insisted on such terms in light of the precarious state of the Hartford economy.[9] For example, one tenant, Successories of Connecticut, Inc., sought the right to terminate its lease upon sixty days' notice; T.J. Maxx, a principal tenant of the Civic Center mall, threatened to exercise its lease termination option and to leave the Civic Center unless the defendant agreed to a year-to-year tenancy; and Pizzeria Uno, a potential tenant concerned about the possible departure of the Hartford Whalers, indicated that it would not lease space in the Civic Center unless it was afforded a right of early termination. Thus, as Romano, the Civic Center's asset manager, explained: "There was no desire on my part to empty out the [Civic Center] mall because we didn't know if a full mall or an empty mall would be desirable to a buyer because, again . . . we didn't know what the end game was, so it didn't make sense to empty out the mall, nor did it make sense to fill it up with a lot of long-term lease obligations. What made sense was to have it be flexible so that it [could] take on a life it needed to take on."

Moreover, some existing tenants simply refused to renew their leases, not because of the terms offered by the defendant but, rather, because of the bleak retail climate in downtown Hartford. In light of the weak economy, it also was difficult, if not impossible, for the defendant to attract new tenants to the Civic Center. As Romano testified: "It was very hard to attract retail tenants to downtown Hartford because of the general economic nature of downtown Hartford. Again, it had suffered through serious job loss from [the late 1980s to the mid 1990s]. Retail had left downtown. You had expanded retail options in the suburbs, which were the new shopping areas of choice, and so it was difficult to get retailers even interested to even look at leasing space in the Civic Center mall, and if [you have] them entertaining a discussion with you, the discussion of the economics of what it would take to have them open up in the mall and whether or not you could make any money off of that . . . it was just hard to make the numbers work for both sides."

The trial court reasonably concluded, moreover, that the defendant's conduct subsequent to its decision to sell the Civic Center, including its efforts to minimize operating losses by eliminating direct expenditures for promotional activities, had no material bearing on the plaintiff's gross sales. As the evidence indicated and the trial court found, the weak Hartford economy and the end of the cigar boom combined to cause the reduction in the plaintiff's gross sales from 1998 through 2000, not the management policies implemented by the defendant in the face of substantial annual operating deficits.

The plaintiff also cannot prevail on its claim that those policies, which were predicated in large part on the defendant's decision to keep the Civic Center open until a buyer could be secured rather than to close the Civic Center and to buy out existing leases, necessarily demonstrated that the defendant's conduct was motivated by bad faith. On the contrary, the defendant was free to take appropriate action to reduce the losses it had incurred for many years, and the evidence fully supported the trial court's conclusion that the ameliorative measures that the defendant had taken were reasonably designed to achieve that end. The defendant, moreover, had no obligation to buy out the plaintiff's lease or even to relieve the plaintiff of its responsibilities under the lease. Nor was the defendant otherwise obliged to ensure the plaintiff's fiscal well-being. In sum, the record does not support the plaintiff's contention that the trial court was clearly erroneous in finding that the defendant's actions were motivated not by some improper purpose or scheme but, rather, by a legitimate interest in curtailing its losses.

For all of the foregoing reasons, we conclude that the trial court properly found that the management policies that the defendant had implemented after it had decided to sell the Civic Center did not violate the lease's implied covenant of good faith and fair dealing. In light of the court's findings regarding the propriety of those policies, the plaintiff's claim that the defendant violated the lease's implied covenant of good faith and fair dealing by rejecting the plaintiff's option to renew its lease also is without merit; because the defendant was not responsible either for the plaintiff's failure to pay rent or for its failure to attain gross annual revenue of at least $262,500, the defendant was entitled, under the express provisions of the lease, to decline the renewal of the lease for those reasons. . . . The judgment is affirmed.

Questions

1. What is the implied covenant of good faith and fair dealing in a contract, and how does it apply to the lease agreement between the plaintiff and the defendant in this case?

2. According to the court's ruling, what standard must be met for a breach of the implied covenant of good faith and fair dealing to occur? How does "bad faith" play a role in determining such a breach?

3. How did the plaintiff argue that the defendant breached the implied covenant of good faith and fair dealing in this case?

4. Did the court find that the defendant violated the lease's implied covenant of good faith and fair dealing in this regard? Why or why not?

5. Why did the court reject the plaintiff's claim that the defendant violated the lease's implied covenant of good faith and fair dealing by refusing to renew the plaintiff's lease? What was the court's reasoning behind this decision?

Takeaways – De La Concha

A law student, in order to earn some extra money, agrees with the Dean of the school to clean the inside of the building every Saturday. If the student shows up on a Saturday and is locked out of the building, has the Dean violated the duty of good faith? Every contract carries an implied duty "requiring that neither party do anything that will injure the right of the other to receive the benefits of the agreement." If one party's ability to successfully perform their contractual obligations depends on the other party's cooperation, can cooperation be withheld without violating the implied duty of good faith?

ASSESSMENT QUESTIONS, CHAPTER 6

1. Define contract interpretation in the context of contract law. Why is it important in determining the rights and obligations of the parties involved?

2. Discuss the role of the parol evidence rule in contract interpretation. When can extrinsic evidence be admitted to interpret a contract?

3. Describe the process of interpreting ambiguous terms in a contract. What factors do courts consider in resolving ambiguity?

4. Discuss the impact of trade usage and course of dealing on contract interpretation. How do these factors influence the interpretation of contractual terms?

5. Can prior negotiations or preliminary agreements be considered in contract interpretation? Explain the principle of merger or integration clauses.

6. Describe the concept of implied terms in contract interpretation. When and how can a court imply terms into a contract?

CHAPTER 7
REMEDIES FOR BREACH OF CONTRACT

Introduction

If one of the parties to the contract breaches it by not performing their contractual obligations and causes harm to the other party, the law entitles the injured party to pursue a remedy. Remedies for breach of contract are either specific or substitutionary.

It would be natural to assume that if a party breaches a contract by failing to do what they promised to do, either by not performing at all or by incompletely or defectively performing, a court would order them to specifically perform their contractual obligations as promised. However, the remedy of specific performance is the exception rather than the rule. The law has a preference for the substitutionary remedy of monetary damages. The amount of harm caused by the breach is quantified in dollars and cents and awarded to the injured non-breaching party as a substitute for the breaching party's performance. The reasons for preferring a substitutionary remedy over a specific remedy are both historical and practical. In England, where our common law system originated, only the courts of equity could order specific performance which is why it is referred to today as an "equitable remedy." Monetary damages, which could be ordered by the English courts of law, is referred to as a "legal remedy." It is only where the injured party can show that the legal remedy of monetary damages is inadequate to put them in as good a position as they would have been in had the contract been completely performed can they be awarded the equitable remedy of specific performance. (Rest.2d § 359(1))

Specific Performance

Klein v. PepsiCo, Inc.
Court of Appeals, 4th Circuit, 1988
845 F. 2d 76

ERVIN, Circuit Judge: This case turns on whether a contract was formed between Universal Jet Sales, Inc. ("UJS") and PepsiCo, Inc., ("PepsiCo") for the sale of a Gulfstream G-II corporate jet to UJS for resale to one Eugene V. Klein. If a contract was formed, the question remains whether the district court acted within his discretion by ordering specific performance of the contract. We believe the district court properly found that a contract was formed; however, we conclude that the remedy of specific performance is inappropriate. Accordingly, we affirm in part, reverse and remand in part.

In March 1986, Klein began looking for a used corporate jet; specifically, he wanted a G-II. He contacted Patrick Janas, President of UJS, who provided information to Klein about several aircraft including the PepsiCo aircraft. Klein's pilot and mechanic, Mr. Sherman and Mr. Quaid, inspected the PepsiCo jet in New York. Mr. James Welsch served as the jet broker for PepsiCo.

Klein asked that the jet be flown to Arkansas for his personal inspection. On March 29, 1986, he inspected the jet. Mr. Rashid, PepsiCo Vice President for Asset Management and Corporate Service, accompanied the jet to Arkansas and met Mr. Klein. Janas also went to Arkansas. Klein gave Janas $200,000 as a deposit on the jet, and told Janas to offer $4.4 million for the aircraft.

On March 31, 1986, Janas telexed the $4.4 million offer to Welsch. The telex said the offer was subject to a factory inspection satisfactory to the purchaser, and a definitive contract. On April 1, PepsiCo counteroffered with a $4.7 million asking price. After some dickering, Welsch offered the jet for $4.6 million. Janas accepted the offer by telex on April 3. Janas then planned to sell the aircraft to Klein for $4.75 million. In Finding of Fact number 18, JA 85, Judge Williams declared that a contract had been formed at this point.

Judge Williams ruled that a contract was evidenced by Janas' confirming telex which "accepted" PepsiCo's offer to sell the jet, and noted that a $100,000 down payment would be wired. The telex also asked for the proper name of the company selling the aircraft. See JA 86 Finding of Fact number 22.

On April 3, Janas sent out copies of the Klein/UJS agreement and the UJS-PepsiCo agreement to the respective parties. Janas also sent a bill of sale to PepsiCo (to Rashid). PepsiCo sent the bill of sale to the escrow agent handling the deal on April 8. Mr. Rochoff, PepsiCo's corporate counsel, spoke with Janas about the standard contract sent by Janas to PepsiCo. He noted only that the delivery date should be changed.

On Monday, April 7, the aircraft was flown to Savannah, Georgia for the pre-purchase inspection. Quaid was present at the inspection for Klein. Archie Walker, PepsiCo's chief of maintenance, was present for the seller. Walker and Quaid discussed a list of repairs to be made to the jet. Most of the problems were cured during the inspection. However, one cosmetic problem was to be corrected in New York, and there were cracks in the engine blades of the right engine.

On April 8, a boroscopic examination conducted by Aviall revealed eight to eleven cracks on the turbine blades. Walker told Rashid that the cost of repairing the blades would be between $25,000 to $28,000. Judge Williams found in Finding of Fact numbers 34 through 37 that PepsiCo, through Walker and Rashid, agreed to pay for the repair to the engine.

On April 9, the plane was returned to New York. Rashid wanted the plane grounded; however, it was sent to retrieve the stranded PepsiCo Chairman of the Board from Dulles airport that same evening. Donald Kendall, the Chairman, on April 10, called Rashid and asked that the jet be withdrawn from the market. Rashid called Welsch who effected the withdrawal. On the 11th Janas told Klein that PepsiCo refused to tender the aircraft. The deal was supposed to close on Friday, April 11.

On April 14, Klein telexed UJS demanding delivery of the aircraft. That same day, UJS telexed PepsiCo demanding delivery and expressing satisfaction with the pre-purchase inspection. On April 15, PepsiCo responded with a telex to UJS saying that it refused to negotiate further because discussions had not reached the point of agreement; in particular, Klein was not prepared to go forward with the deal.

Judge Williams, in a lengthy opinion, made numerous findings of fact. Such findings are reviewed only for clear error. *Davis v. Food Lion,* 792 F.2d 1274, 1277 (4th Cir.1986). If the findings are based on determinations of witness credibility, are consistent, and are corroborated by extrinsic evidence, they are virtually never clearly erroneous. *Brown v. Baltimore and Ohio R. Co.,* 805 F.2d 1133, 1140 (4th Cir.1986).

Judge Williams' decision to grant specific performance is reviewed only for an abuse of discretion. *Haythe v. May,* 223 Va. 359, 288 S.E.2d 487 (1982); *Horner v. Bourland,* 724 F.2d 1142, 1144-45 (5th Cir.1984). Keeping these standards in mind, we now turn to the first issue, whether the district court clearly erred in finding that a contract arose between PepsiCo and UJS.

[The appellate court ruled that the trial court correctly found that a contract was formed between the parties.]

Ultimately, then, a contract exists between PepsiCo and UJS for the sale of one G-II Gulfstream aircraft. Because PepsiCo failed to deliver the aircraft, the district court ordered relief in the form of specific performance. We now consider the appropriateness of the relief ordered.

The Virginia Code § 8.2-716 permits a jilted buyer of goods to seek specific performance of the contract if the goods sought are unique, or in other proper circumstances. Judge Williams ruled that: 1) the G-II aircraft involved in this case is unique and 2) Klein's inability to cover with a comparable aircraft is strong evidence of "other proper circumstances." JA 111-112, Conclusions of Law No. 31 and No. 32. These conclusions are not supported in the record.

We note first that Virginia's adoption of the Uniform Commercial Code does not abrogate the maxim that specific performance is inappropriate where damages are recoverable and adequate. *Griscom v. Childress,* 183 Va. 42, 31 S.E.2d 309, 311 (1944). In this case Judge Williams repeatedly stated that money damages would make Klein whole. JA 668-9, 582. Klein argued that he wanted the plane to resell it for a profit. JA 669. Finally, an increase in the cost of a replacement does not merit the remedy of specific performance. *Hilmor Sales Co. v. Helen Neuschalfer Division of Supronics Corp.,* 6 U.C.C.Rep.Serv. 325 (N.Y.Sup.Ct.1969). There is no room in this case for the equitable remedy of specific performance.

Turning now to the specific rulings of the court below, Judge Williams explained that the aircraft was unique because only three comparable aircraft existed on the market. Therefore, Klein would have to go through considerable expense to find a replacement. JA 110. Klein's expert testified that there were twenty-one other G-II's on the market, three of which were roughly comparable. JA 838-9, 1284-88. Klein's chief pilot said that other G-II's could be purchased. JA 259. Finally, we should note that UJS bought two G-II's which they offered to Klein after this deal fell through, JA 796-7, and Klein made bids on two other G-II's after PepsiCo withdrew its aircraft from the market. JA 277, 666, 694. Given these facts, we find it very difficult to support a ruling that the aircraft was so unique as to merit an order of specific performance.

Judge Williams ruled further that Klein's inability to cover his loss is an "other proper circumstance" favoring specific performance. Klein testified himself that he didn't purchase another G-II because prices had started to rise. JA 693. Because of the price increase, he decided to purchase a G-III aircraft. As noted earlier, price increases alone are no reason to order specific performance. Because money damages would clearly be adequate in this case, and because the aircraft is not unique within the meaning of the Virginia Commercial Code, we reverse the grant of specific performance and remand the case to the district court for a trial on damages.

Affirmed in Part, Reversed and Remanded in Part.

Questions

1. Why did the district court (the trial court) conclude that specific performance was an appropriate remedy in this case?

2. Why did the appellate court conclude that specific performance was not an appropriate remedy in this case? What were the factors the court considered in reaching this conclusion?

Takeaways – Klein v. Pepsico

The UCC authorizes specific performance when the seller breaches a contract for the sale of goods. UCC § 2-716 permits a disappointed buyer of goods to seek specific performance of the contract if the goods sought are unique. Was the corporate jet which was the subject of the contract "unique?" Could Klein have purchased a substitute jet? If the answer is "yes" then why was he not awarded specific performance?

Rest.2d § 360 lists three factors for the court to consider in determining whether damages are an adequate legal remedy. They are:

(a) the difficulty of proving damage with reasonable certainty,

(b) the difficulty of procuring a suitable substitute performance by means of money awarded as damages, and

(c) the likelihood that an award of damages could not be collected.

Which, if any, do you suppose were factors in the court's decision in *Klein v. Pepsico*?

Sedmak v. Charlie's Chevrolet, Inc.
Missouri Court of Appeals, 1981
622 SW 2d 694

SATZ, Judge. This is an appeal from a decree of specific performance. We affirm.

In their petition, plaintiffs, Dr. and Mrs. Sedmak (Sedmaks), alleged they entered into a contract with defendant, Charlie's Chevrolet, Inc. (Charlie's), to purchase a Corvette automobile for approximately $15,000.00. The Corvette was one of a limited number manufactured to commemorate the selection of the Corvette as the Pace Car for the Indianapolis 500. Charlie's breached the contract, the Sedmaks alleged, when, after the automobile was delivered, an agent for Charlie's told the Sedmaks they could not purchase the automobile for $15,000.00 but would have to bid on it.

The trial court found the parties entered into an oral contract and also found the contract was excepted from the Statute of Frauds. The court then ordered Charlie's to make the automobile "available for delivery" to the Sedmaks. Charlie's raises three points on appeal: . . . (3) specific performance is an improper remedy because the Sedmaks did not show their legal remedies were inadequate. . . .

[T]he record reflects the Sedmaks to be automobile enthusiasts, who, at the time of trial, owned six Corvettes. In July, 1977, "Vette Vues," a Corvette fancier's magazine to which Dr. Sedmak subscribed, published an article announcing Chevrolet's tentative plans to manufacture a limited edition of the Corvette. The limited edition of approximately 6,000 automobiles was to commemorate the selection of the Corvette as the Indianapolis 500 Pace Car. The Sedmaks were interested in acquiring one of these Pace Cars to add to their Corvette collection. In November, 1977, the Sedmaks asked Tom Kells, sales manager at Charlie's Chevrolet, about the availability of the Pace Car. Mr. Kells said he did not have any information on the car but would find out about it. Kells also said if Charlie's were to receive a Pace Car, the Sedmaks could purchase it.

On January 9, 1978, Dr. Sedmak telephoned Kells to ask him if a Pace Car could be ordered. Kells indicated that he would require a deposit on the car, so Mrs. Sedmak went to Charlie's and gave Kells a check for $500.00. She was given a receipt for that amount bearing the names of Kells and Charlie's Chevrolet, Inc. At that time, Kells had a pre-order form listing both standard equipment and options available on the Pace Car. Prior to tendering the deposit, Mrs. Sedmak asked Kells if she and Dr. Sedmak were "definitely going to be the owners." Kells replied, "yes." After the deposit had been paid, Mrs. Sedmak stated if the car was going to be theirs, her husband wanted some changes made to the stock model. She asked Kells to order the car equipped with an L82 engine, four speed standard transmission and AM/FM radio with tape deck. Kells said that he would try to arrange with the manufacturer for these changes. Kells was able to make the changes, and, when the car arrived, it was equipped as the Sedmaks had requested.

Kells informed Mrs. Sedmak that the price of the Pace Car would be the manufacturer's retail price, approximately $15,000.00. The dollar figure could not be quoted more precisely because Kells was not sure what the ordered changes would cost, nor was he sure what the "appearance package"—decals, a special paint job—would cost. Kells also told Mrs. Sedmak that, after the changes had been made, a "contract"—a retail dealer's order form— would be mailed to them. However, no form or written contract was mailed to the Sedmaks by Charlie's.

On January 25, 1978, the Sedmaks visited Charlie's to take delivery on another Corvette. At that time, the Sedmaks asked Kells whether he knew anything further about the arrival date of the Pace Car. Kells replied he had no further information but he would let the Sedmaks know when the car arrived. Kells also requested that Charlie's be allowed to keep the car in their showroom for promotional purposes until after the Indianapolis 500 Race. The Sedmaks agreed to this arrangement.

On April 3, 1978, the Sedmaks were notified by Kells that the Pace Car had arrived. Kells told the Sedmaks they could not purchase the car for the manufacturer's retail price because demand for the car had inflated its value beyond the suggested price. Kells also told the Sedmaks they could bid on the car. The Sedmaks did not submit a bid. They filed this suit for specific performance.

Mr. Kells' testimony about his conversations with the Sedmaks regarding the Pace Car differed markedly from the Sedmaks' testimony. Kells stated that he had no definite price information on the Pace Car until a day or two prior to its arrival at Charlie's. He denied ever discussing the purchase price of the car with the Sedmaks. He admitted, however, that after talking with the Sedmaks on January 9, 1978, he telephoned the zone manager and requested changes be made to the Pace Car. He denied the changes were made pursuant to Dr. Sedmak's order. He claimed the changes were made because they were "more favorable to the automobile" and were changes Dr. Sedmak "preferred." In ordering the changes, Kells said he was merely taking Dr. Sedmak's advice because he was a "very knowledgeable man on the

Corvette." There is no dispute, however, that when the Pace Car arrived, it was equipped with the options requested by Dr. Sedmak.

Mr. Kells also denied the receipt for $500.00 given him by Mrs. Sedmak on January 9, 1978, was a receipt for a deposit on the Pace Car. On direct examination, he said he "accepted a five hundred dollar ($500) deposit from the Sedmaks to assure them the first opportunity of purchasing the car." On cross-examination, he said: "We were accepting bids and with the five hundred dollar ($500) deposit it was to give them the first opportunity to bid on the car." Then after acknowledging that other bidders had not paid for the opportunity to bid, he explained the deposit gave the Sedmaks the "last opportunity" to make the final bid. Based on this evidence, the trial court found the parties entered into an oral contract for the purchase and sale of the Pace Car at the manufacturer's suggested retail price. . . .

Charlie's contends the Sedmaks failed to show they were entitled to specific performance of the contract. We disagree. Although it has been stated that the determination whether to order specific performance lies within the discretion of the trial court, *Landau v. St. Louis Public Service Co.*, 273 S.W.2d 255, 259 (Mo. 1954), this discretion is, in fact, quite narrow. When the relevant equitable principles have been met and the contract is fair and plain, "'specific performance goes as a matter of right.'" *Miller v. Coffeen*, 280 S.W.2d 100, 102 (Mo.1955). Here, the trial court ordered specific performance because it concluded the Sedmaks "have no adequate remedy at law for the reason that they cannot go upon the open market and purchase an automobile of this kind with the same mileage, condition, ownership and appearance as the automobile involved in this case, except, if at all, with considerable expense, trouble, loss, great delay and inconvenience." Contrary to defendant's complaint, this is a correct expression of the relevant law and it is supported by the evidence.

Under the Code, the court may decree specific performance as a buyer's remedy for breach of contract to sell goods "where the goods are unique or in other proper circumstances." § 400.2-716(1) RSMo 1978. The general term "in other proper circumstances" expresses the drafters' intent to "further a more liberal attitude than some courts have shown in connection with the specific performance of contracts of sale." § 400.2-716, U.C.C., Comment 1. This Comment was not directed to the courts of this state, for long before the Code, we, in Missouri, took a practical approach in determining whether specific performance would lie for the breach of contract for the sale of goods and did not limit this relief only to the sale of "unique" goods. *Boeving v. Vandover*, 240 Mo.App. 117, 218 S.W.2d 175 (1945). In *Boeving*, plaintiff contracted to buy a car from defendant. When the car arrived, defendant refused to sell. The car was not unique in the traditional legal sense but, at that time, all cars were difficult to obtain because of war-time shortages. The court held specific performance was the proper remedy for plaintiff because a new car "could not be obtained elsewhere except at considerable expense, trouble or loss, which cannot be estimated in advance and under such circumstances [plaintiff] did not have an adequate remedy at law." *Id.* at 177-178. Thus, *Boeving*, presaged the broad and liberalized language of § 400.2-716(1) and exemplifies one of the "other proper circumstances" contemplated by this subsection for ordering specific performance. § 400.2-716, Missouri Code Comment 1. The present facts track those in *Boeving*.

The Pace Car, like the car in *Boeving*, was not unique in the traditional legal sense. It was not an heirloom or, arguably, not one of a kind. However, its "mileage, condition, ownership and appearance" did make it difficult, if not impossible, to obtain its replication without considerable expense, delay and inconvenience. Admittedly, 6,000 Pace Cars were produced by Chevrolet. However, as the record reflects, this is limited production. In addition, only one of these cars was available to each dealer, and only a limited number of these were equipped with the specific options ordered by plaintiffs. Charlie's had not received a car like the Pace Car in the previous two years. The sticker price for the car was $14,284.21. Yet Charlie's received offers from individuals in Hawaii and Florida to buy the Pace Car for $24,000.00 and $28,000.00 respectively. As sensibly inferred by the trial court, the location and size of these offers demonstrated this limited edition was in short supply and great demand. We agree, with the trial court. This case was a "proper circumstance" for ordering specific performance.

Judgment affirmed.

Questions

1. Why did the trial court find that the Sedmaks were entitled to specific performance of the contract?

2. What is the basis for the trial court's conclusion that the Sedmaks have no adequate remedy at law?

3. According to the court's reasoning, what circumstances make this case a "proper circumstance" for ordering specific performance?

4. How does the court's interpretation of the Code differ from a strict interpretation of the term "unique goods"?

5. How did the limited production and demand for the Pace Car contribute to the court's decision to order specific performance?

Takeaways – Sedmak v. Charlie's Chevrolet

Why were the Sedmak's entitled to get specific performance and Klein wasn't? Neither the car nor the corporate jet were truly one-of-a-kind items. What language in UCC § 2-716 would support the Sedmak's entitlement to specific performance?

Morris v. Sparrow
Supreme Court of Arkansas, 1956
225 Ark. 1019, 287 S.W.2d 583

ROBINSON, Justice. Appellee Archie Sparrow filed this suit for specific performance, seeking to compel appellant Morris to deliver possession of a certain horse, which Sparrow claims Morris agreed to give him as part consideration for work done by Sparrow. The appeal is from a decree requiring the delivery of the horse.

Morris owns a cattle ranch near Mountain View, Arkansas, and he also participates in rodeos. Sparrow is a cowboy, and is experienced in training horses; occasionally he takes part in rodeos. He lives in Florida; while at a rodeo in that state, he and Morris made an agreement that they would go to Morris' ranch in Arkansas and, later, the two would go to Canada. After arriving at the Morris ranch, they changed their plans and decided that, while Morris went to Canada, Sparrow would stay at the ranch and do the necessary work. The parties are in accord that Sparrow was to work 16 weeks for a money consideration of $400. But, Sparrow says that as an additional consideration he was to receive a brown horse called Keno, owned by Morris. However, Morris states that Sparrow was to get the horse only on condition that his work at the ranch was satisfactory, and that Sparrow failed to do a good job. Morris paid Sparrow the amount of money they agreed was due, but did not deliver the horse.

At the time Sparrow went to Morris' ranch, the horse in question was practically unbroken; but during his spare time, Sparrow trained the horse and, with a little additional training, he will be a first class roping horse.

First there is the issue of whether Sparrow can maintain, in equity, a suit to enforce, by specific performance, a contract for the delivery of personal property. Although it has been held that equity will not ordinarily enforce, by specific performance, a contract for the sale of chattels, it will do so where special and peculiar reasons exist which render it impossible for the injured party to obtain relief by way of damages in an action at law. McCallister v. Patton, 214 Ark. 293, 215 S.W.2d 701. Moreover, specific performance is authorized by Ark.Stats. § 68-1468, which provides : "Where the seller has broken a contract to deliver specific or ascertained goods, a court having the powers of a court of equity may, if it thinks fit, on the application of the buyer, by its judgment or decree direct that the contract shall be performed specifically, without giving the seller the option of retaining the goods on payment of damages. * * *" Certainly when one has made a roping horse out of a green, unbroken pony, such a horse would have a peculiar and unique value; if Sparrow is entitled to prevail, he has a right to the horse instead of its market value in dollars and cents.

Morris claims that the part of the agreement whereby Sparrow was to receive the horse was conditional, depending on Sparrow doing a good job, and that he did not do such a job. Both parties were in Chancery Court and the Chancellor had a better opportunity than this court to evaluate the testimony of the witnesses; we cannot say the Chancellor's finding in favor of Sparrow is against the preponderance of the evidence. . . . Affirmed.

Questions

1. Under what circumstances will equity enforce a contract for the delivery of personal property by specific performance?

2. What is the basis for the court's authority to order specific performance in cases involving the breach of a contract for the delivery of specific or ascertained goods?

3. Why does the court consider the horse in question to have a peculiar and unique value?

4. What is Morris's argument regarding the conditional nature of Sparrow's entitlement to the horse? How did the court evaluate this argument?

Takeaways – Morris v. Sparrow

UCC § 2-716 provides that specific performance may be available "where the goods are unique or in other proper circumstances." Was Keno, the unbroken horse, "unique" or was it Sparrow's time spent in breaking the horse, his investment in the horse, that was unique? Is this an example of some "other proper circumstance?"

Laclede Gas Co. v. Amoco Oil Co.
United States Court of Appeals for the Eighth Circuit, 1975
522 F.2d 33

The Laclede Gas Company (Laclede), a Missouri corporation, brought this diversity action alleging breach of contract against the Amoco Oil Company (Amoco), a Delaware corporation. It sought relief in the form of a mandatory injunction prohibiting the continuing breach or, in the alternative, damages. The district court held a bench trial on the issues of whether there was a valid, binding contract between the parties and whether, if there was such a contract, Amoco should be enjoined from breaching it. It then ruled that the "contract is invalid due to lack of mutuality" and denied the prayer for injunctive relief. The court made no decision regarding the requested damages. Laclede Gas Co. v. Amoco Oil Co., 385 F. Supp. 1332, 1336 (E.D. Mo. 1974). This appeal followed, and we reverse the district court's judgment.

On September 21, 1970, Midwest Missouri Gas Company (now Laclede), and American Oil Company (now Amoco), the predecessors of the parties to this litigation, entered into a written agreement which was designed to provide central propane gas distribution systems to various residential developments in Jefferson County, Missouri, until such time as natural gas mains were extended into these areas. The agreement contemplated that as individual developments were planned the owners or developers would apply to Laclede for central propane gas systems. If Laclede determined that such a system was appropriate in any given development, it could request Amoco to supply the propane to that specific development. This request was made in the form of a supplemental form letter, as provided in the September 21 agreement; and if Amoco decided to supply the propane, it bound itself to do so by signing this supplemental form.

Once this supplemental form was signed the agreement placed certain duties on both Laclede and Amoco. Basically, Amoco was to "(i)nstall, own, maintain and operate . . . storage and vaporization facilities and any other facilities necessary to provide (it) with the capability of delivering to (Laclede) commercial propane gas suitable . . . for delivery by (Laclede) to its customers' facilities." Amoco's facilities were to be "adequate to provide a continuous supply of commercial propane gas at such times and in such volumes commensurate with (Laclede's) requirements for meeting the demands reasonably to be anticipated in each Development while this Agreement is in force." Amoco was deemed to be "the supplier," while Laclede was "the distributing utility."

For its part Laclede agreed to "(i)nstall, own, maintain and operate all distribution facilities" from a "point of delivery" which was defined to be "the outlet of (Amoco) header piping." Laclede also promised to pay Amoco "the Wood River Area Posted Price for propane plus four cents per gallon for all amounts of commercial propane gas delivered" to it under the agreement.

Since it was contemplated that the individual propane systems would eventually be converted to natural gas, one paragraph of the agreement provided that Laclede should give Amoco 30 days written notice of this event, after which the agreement would no longer be binding for the converted development.

Another paragraph gave Laclede the right to cancel the agreement. However, this right was expressed in the following language:

This Agreement shall remain in effect for one (1) year following the first delivery of gas by (Amoco) to (Laclede) hereunder. Subject to termination as provided in Paragraph 11 hereof (dealing with conversions to natural gas), this Agreement shall automatically continue in effect for additional periods of one (1) year each unless (Laclede) shall, not less than 30 days prior to the expiration of the initial one (1) year period or any subsequent one (1) year period, give (Amoco) written notice of termination.

There was no provision under which Amoco could cancel the agreement.

For a time the parties operated satisfactorily under this agreement, and some 17 residential subdivisions were brought within it by supplemental letters. However, for various reasons, including conversion to natural gas, the number of developments under the agreement had shrunk to eight by the time of trial. These were all mobile home parks.

During the winter of 1972-73 Amoco experienced a shortage of propane and voluntarily placed all of its customers, including Laclede, on an 80% Allocation basis, meaning that Laclede would receive only up to 80% Of its previous requirements. Laclede objected to this and pushed Amoco to give it 100% Of what the developments needed. Some conflict arose over this before the temporary shortage was alleviated.

Then, on April 3, 1973, Amoco notified Laclede that its Wood River Area Posted Price of propane had been increased by three cents per gallon. Laclede objected to this increase also and demanded a full explanation. None was forthcoming. Instead Amoco merely sent a letter dated May 14, 1973, informing Laclede that it was "terminating" the September 21, 1970, agreement effective May 31, 1973. It claimed it had the right to do this because "the Agreement lacks 'mutuality.'"

The district court felt that the entire controversy turned on whether or not Laclede's right to "arbitrarily cancel the Agreement" without Amoco having a similar right rendered the contract void "for lack of mutuality" and it resolved this question in the affirmative. We disagree with this conclusion and hold that settled principles of contract law require a reversal....

Since he found that there was no binding contract, the district judge did not have to deal with the question of whether or not to grant the injunction prayed for by Laclede. He simply denied this relief because there was no contract. Laclede Gas Co. v. Amoco Oil Co., supra, 385 F. Supp. At 1336.

Generally the determination of whether or not to order specific performance of a contract lies within the sound discretion of the trial court. [Citation omitted]

However, this discretion is, in fact, quite limited; and it is said that when certain equitable rules have been met and the contract is fair and plain "specific performance goes as a matter of right." [Citation omitted]

With this in mind we have carefully reviewed the very complete record on appeal and conclude that the trial court should grant the injunctive relief prayed. We are satisfied that this case falls within that category in which specific performance should be ordered as a matter of right. [Citation omitted]

Amoco contends that four of the requirements for specific performance have not been met. Its claims are: (1) there is no mutuality of remedy in the contract; (2) the remedy of specific performance would be difficult for the court to administer without constant and long-continued supervision; (3) the contract is indefinite and uncertain; and (4) the remedy at law available to Laclede is adequate. The first three contentions have little or no merit and do not detain us for long.

There is simply no requirement in the law that both parties be mutually entitled to the remedy of specific performance in order that one of them be given that remedy by the court. [Citation omitted]

While a court may refuse to grant specific performance where such a decree would require constant and long-continued court supervision, this is merely a discretionary rule of decision which is frequently ignored when the public interest is involved. [Citation omitted].

Here the public interest in providing propane to the retail customers is manifest, while any supervision required will be far from onerous.

Section 370 of the Restatement of Contracts (1932) provides:

Specific enforcement will not be decreed unless the terms of the contract are so expressed that the court can determine with reasonable certainty what is the duty of each party and the conditions under which performance is due.

We believe these criteria have been satisfied here. As discussed in part I of this opinion, as to all developments for which a supplemental agreement has been signed, Amoco is to supply all the propane which is reasonably foreseeably required, while Laclede is to purchase the required propane from Amoco and pay the contract price therefor. The parties have disagreed over what is meant by "Wood River Area Posted Price" in the agreement, but the district court can and should determine with reasonable certainty what the parties intended by this term and should mold its decree, if necessary accordingly. Likewise, the fact that the agreement does not have a definite time of duration is not fatal since the evidence established that the last subdivision should be converted to natural gas in 10 to 15 years. This sets a reasonable time limit on performance and the district court can and should mold the final decree to reflect this testimony.

It is axiomatic that specific performance will not be ordered when the party claiming breach of contract has an adequate remedy at law. [Citation omitted] This is especially true when the contract involves personal property as distinguished from real estate.

However, in Missouri, as elsewhere, specific performance may be ordered even though personalty is involved in the "proper circumstances." Mo.Rev.Stat. § 400.2-716(1); Restatement of Contracts, supra, § 361. And a remedy at law adequate to defeat the grant of specific performance "must be as certain, prompt, complete, and efficient to attain the ends of justice as a decree of specific performance." [Citation omitted]

One of the leading Missouri cases allowing specific performance of a contract relating to personalty because the remedy at law was inadequate is Boeving v. Vandover, 240 Mo.App. 117, 218 S.W.2d 175, 178 (1949). In that case the plaintiff sought specific performance of a contract in which the defendant had promised to sell him an automobile. At that time (near the end of and shortly after World War II) new cars were hard to come by, and the court held that specific performance was a proper remedy since a new car "could not be obtained elsewhere except at considerable expense, trouble or loss, which cannot be estimated in advance."

We are satisfied that Laclede has brought itself within this practical approach taken by the Missouri courts. As Amoco points out, Laclede has propane immediately available to it under other contracts with other suppliers. And the evidence indicates that at the present time propane is readily available on the open market. However, this analysis ignores the fact that the contract involved in this lawsuit is for a long-term supply of propane to these subdivisions. The other two contracts under which Laclede obtains the gas will remain in force only until March 31, 1977, and April 1, 1981, respectively; and there is no assurance that Laclede will be able to receive any propane under them after that time. Also it is unclear as to whether or not Laclede can use the propane obtained under these contracts to supply the Jefferson County subdivisions, since they were originally entered into to provide Laclede with propane with which to "shave" its natural gas supply during peak demand periods. Additionally, there was uncontradicted expert testimony that Laclede probably could not find another supplier of propane willing to enter into a long-term contract such as the Amoco agreement, given the uncertain future of worldwide energy supplies. And, even if Laclede could obtain supplies of propane for the affected developments through its present contracts or newly negotiated ones, it would still face considerable expense and trouble which cannot be estimated in advance in making arrangements for its distribution to the subdivisions.

Specific performance is the proper remedy in this situation, and it should be granted by the district court. [Reversed and remanded.]

Questions

1. What were the four contentions raised by Amoco in its argument against specific performance, and how did the appellate court address each contention?

2. Explain the significance of the "mutuality of remedy" requirement in contract law and how it applied to this case.

3. What criteria did the appellate court consider in determining whether specific performance should be granted in this case?

4. Why did the appellate court conclude that Laclede's remedy at law was inadequate and that specific performance was the appropriate remedy?

Problems in Supervising Specific Performance Orders

Northern Delaware Industrial Dev. Corp. v. E.W. Bliss Co.
Court of Chancery of Delaware, 1968
245 A.2d 431

MARVEL, Vice Chancellor: Plaintiffs and defendant are parties to a contract dated May 26th, 1966, under the terms of which defendant agreed to furnish all labor, services, materials and equipment necessary to expand and modernize a steel fabricating plant owned by the plaintiff Phoenix Steel Corporation at Claymont, Delaware. A massive undertaking is called for in the contract, the total price for the work to be performed by the defendant being set in the contract at $27,500,000 and the area of contract performance extending over a plant site of approximately sixty acres.

Work on the project has not progressed as rapidly as contemplated in the contract and what plaintiffs now seek is an order compelling defendant to requisition 300 more workmen for a night shift, thus requiring defendant to put on the job, as it allegedly contracted to do, the number of men required to make up a full second shift at the Phoenix plant site during the period when one of the Phoenix mills must be shut down in order that its modernization may be carried out under the contract. And while the present record is sparse, there seems to be no doubt but that defendant has fallen behind the work completion schedules set forth in such contract. What plaintiffs apparently seek is a speeding up of work at the site by means of a court-ordered requisitioning by defendant of more laborers. . . .

The sole matter now for decision is a question raised by the Court at argument on defendant's motion, namely whether or not this Court should exercise its jurisdiction to grant plaintiffs' application for an order for specific performance of an alleged contractual right to have more workers placed on the massive construction project here involved, and order the requisitioning of 300 workers for a night shift, this being the number of laborers deemed by plaintiffs to be appropriate properly to bring about prompt completion of the job at hand.

On the basis of the record before me, viewed in the light of the applicable law, I am satisfied that this Court should not, as a result of granting plaintiffs' prayer for specific performance of an alleged term of a building contract, become committed to supervising the carrying out of a massive, complex, and unfinished construction contract, a result which would necessarily follow as a consequence of ordering defendant to requisition laborers as prayed for,. . .

It is not that a court of equity is without jurisdiction in a proper case to order the completion of an expressly designed and largely completed construction project, particularly where the undertaking to construct is tied in with a contract for the sale of land and the construction in question is largely finished, Valley Builders, Inc. v. Stein, 41 Del.Ch. 259, 193 A.2d 793, and Lee Builders v. Wells, 33 Del.Ch. 315, 92 A.2d 710, rev'd on other grounds, 34 Del.Ch. 107, 99 A.2d 620. Furthermore, this is not a case which calls for a building plan so precisely definite as to make compliance therewith subject to effective judicial supervision, Wilmont Homes, Inc. v. Weiler, 42 Del.Ch. 8, 202 A.2d 576, but rather an attempt to have the Court as the result of ordering a builder to speed up general work by hiring a night shift of employees (a proposal which was merely "contemplated" by the subcontractor, Dick) to become deeply involved in supervision of a complex construction project located on plaintiffs' property.

The point is that a court of equity should not order specific performance of any building contract in a situation in which it would be impractical to carry out such an order, Jones v. Parker, 163 Mass. 564, 40 N. E. 1044, and Restatement, Contracts § 371, unless there are special circumstances or the public interest is directly involved

I conclude that to grant specific performance, as prayed for by plaintiffs, would be inappropriate in view of the imprecision of the contract provision relied upon and the impracticability if not impossibility of effective enforcement by the Court of a mandatory order designed to keep a specific number of men on the job at the site of a steel mill which is undergoing extensive modernization and expansion. If plaintiffs have sustained loss as a result of actionable building delays on defendant's part at the Phoenix plant at Claymont, they may, at an appropriate time, resort to law for a fixing of their claimed damages.

ON REARGUMENT

In their motion for reargument plaintiffs argue that what they actually seek is not an order which would make the Court the supervisor of a vast building project but rather one directing the performance of a ministerial act, namely the hiring by defendant of more workers. Plaintiffs also contend that they should have an opportunity to supplement the record for the purpose of demonstrating that construction labor is available in the area as well as establishing that perhaps fewer than 300 additional workers could adequately insure defendant's performance of the contract here in issue. These contentions, if factually sustainable, do not, of course, affect the Court's power to decline to exercise its jurisdiction to order specific performance of a construction contract.

Plaintiffs, in seeking specific performance of what they now term defendant's ministerial duty to hire a substantial number of additional laborers, run afoul of the well-established principle that performance of a contract for personal services, even of a unique nature, will not be affirmatively and directly enforced. . . . Defendant's motion for reargument is denied.

Questions

1. According to the court, under what circumstances would a court of equity order specific performance of a building contract?

2. Why does the court conclude that granting specific performance in this case would be inappropriate?

3. What argument did plaintiffs raise in their motion for reargument?

4. How does the court respond to plaintiffs' argument regarding defendant's alleged ministerial duty to hire more workers?

Takeaways – Northern Delaware Industrial

Did the plaintiff have an adequate legal remedy? If not, why did the court refuse to order specific performance? What other things besides adequacy of remedy does a court take into consideration in deciding whether or not to grant specific performance?

Personal Service Contracts and Injunctions

An injunction is an order of the court commanding a party to do, or not to do, a certain thing. An order for specific performance is a type of injunction. Injunctions can be framed in the negative ordering a party not to do something. Can an individual be ordered to perform as promised for another party? Can they be ordered or enjoined not to perform as a means of pressuring them to honor their contractual obligations?

Beverly Glen Music, Inc. v. Warner Communications
178 Cal.App.3d 1142, 224 Cal. Rptr. 260 (1986)

KINGSLEY, Acting P.J. The plaintiff appeals from an order denying a preliminary injunction against the defendant, Warner Communications, Inc. We affirm.

In 1982, plaintiff Beverly Glen Music, Inc., signed to a contract a then-unknown singer, Anita Baker. Ms. Baker recorded an album for Beverly Glen which was moderately successful, grossing over $1 million. In 1984, however, Ms. Baker was offered a considerably better deal by defendant Warner Communications. As she was having some difficulties with Beverly Glen, she accepted Warner's offer and notified plaintiff that she was no longer willing to perform under the contract. Beverly Glen then sued Ms. Baker and sought to have her enjoined from performing for any other recording studio. The injunction was denied, however, as, under Civil Code section 3423, subdivision Fifth, California courts will not enjoin the breach of a personal service contract unless the service is unique in nature and the performer is guaranteed annual compensation of at least $6,000, which Ms. Baker was not.

Following this ruling, the plaintiff voluntarily dismissed the action against Ms. Baker. Plaintiff, however, then sued Warner Communications for inducing Ms. Baker to breach her contract and moved the court for an injunction against Warner to prevent it from employing her. This injunction, too, was denied, the trial court reasoning that what one was forbidden by statute to do directly, one could not accomplish through the back door. It is from this ruling that the plaintiff appeals.

From what we can tell, this is a case of first impression in California. While there are numerous cases on the general inability of an employer to enjoin his former employee from performing services somewhere else, apparently no one has previously thought of enjoining the new employer from accepting the services of the breaching employee. While we commend the plaintiff for its resourcefulness in this regard, we concur in the trial court's interpretation of the maneuver.

"It is a familiar rule that a contract to render personal services cannot be specifically enforced." (Foxx v. Williams (1966) 244 Cal. App.2d 223, 235 [52 Cal. Rptr. 896].) An unwilling employee cannot be compelled to continue to provide services to his employer either by ordering specific performance of his contract, or by injunction. To do so runs afoul of the Thirteenth Amendment's prohibition against involuntary servitude. (Poultry Producers etc. v. Barlow (1922) 189 Cal. 278, 288 [208 P. 93].) However, beginning with the English case of Lumley v. Wagner (1852) 42 Eng. Rep. 687, courts have recognized that, while they cannot directly enforce an affirmative promise (in the Lumley case, Miss Wagner's promise to perform at the plaintiff's opera house), they can enforce the negative promise implied therein (that the defendant would not perform for someone else that evening). Thus, while it is not possible to compel a defendant to perform his duties under a personal service contract, it is possible to prevent him from employing his talents anywhere else. The net effect is to pressure the defendant to return voluntarily to his employer by denying him the means of earning a living. Indeed, this is its only purpose, for, unless the defendant relents and honors the contract, the plaintiff gains nothing from having brought the injunction.

The California Legislature, however, did not adopt this principle when in 1872 it enacted Civil Code section 3423, subdivision Fifth, and Code of Civil Procedure section 526, subdivision 5. These sections both provided that an injunction could not be granted: "To prevent the breach of a contract the performance of which would not be specifically enforced." In 1919, however, these sections were amended, creating an exception for: "a contract in writing for the rendition or furnishing of personal services from one to another where the minimum compensation for such service is at the rate of not less than six thousand dollars per annum and where the promised service is of a special, unique, unusual, extraordinary or intellectual character...."

The plaintiff has already unsuccessfully argued before the trial court that Ms. Baker falls within this exception. It has chosen not to appeal that judgment, and is therefore barred from questioning that determination now. The sole issue before us then is whether plaintiff — although prohibited from enjoining Ms. Baker from performing herself — can seek to enjoin all those who might employ her and prevent them from doing so, thus achieving the same effect.

We rule that plaintiff cannot. Whether plaintiff proceeds against Ms. Baker directly or against those who might employ her, the intent is the same: to deprive Ms. Baker of her livelihood and thereby pressure her to return to plaintiff's employ. Plaintiff contends that this is not an action against Ms. Baker but merely an equitable claim against Warner to deprive it of the wrongful benefits it gained when it "stole" Ms. Baker away. Thus, plaintiff contends, the equities lie not between the plaintiff and Ms. Baker, but between plaintiff and the predatory Warner Communications company. Yet if Warner's behavior has actually been predatory, plaintiff has an adequate remedy by way of damages. An injunction adds nothing to plaintiff's recovery from Warner except to coerce Ms. Baker to honor her contract. Denying someone his livelihood is a harsh remedy. The Legislature has forbidden it but for one exception. To expand this remedy so that it could be used in virtually all breaches of a personal service contract is to ignore over 100 years of common law on this issue. We therefore decline to reverse the order.

Questions

1. What is the main issue being appealed in this case?

2. According to Civil Code section 3423, subdivision Fifth, under what conditions will California courts enjoin the breach of a personal service contract?

3. How does the court distinguish between directly enforcing an affirmative promise and enforcing a negative promise implied in a personal service contract?

4. What is the purpose of seeking an injunction in a personal service contract dispute?

5. Why does the court rule that the plaintiff cannot seek to enjoin those who might employ the breaching employee, even though they cannot directly enjoin the employee from performing?

Rescission

Rescission is the cancellation of a contract by mutual agreement of the parties. Mistake or fraud are the most typical grounds for rescission. But parties can also mutually agree to rescind even if there are no grounds for rescission and even if neither party has committed a breach. How free should the parties be to rescind or abandon their agreement? There is justified concern for the effects of an overly indulgent rescission policy on the stability of bargains. "The power to cancel a contract is a most extraordinary power. It is one which should be exercised with great caution,--nay, I may say, with great reluctance,--unless in a clear case. A too free use of this power would render all business uncertain, and, as has been said, make the length of a chancellor's foot the measure of individual rights. The greatest liberty of making contracts is essential to the business interests of the country. In general, the parties must look out for themselves." (*Colton v. Stanford* (1880) 82 Cal. 351, 398 [23 P. 16].)

Damages for Breach

The measure of damages for the breach of a contract is that amount of money which will compensate the injured party for all the detriment or loss caused by the breach, or which in the ordinary course of things, would be likely to result therefrom. The injured party should receive those damages naturally arising from the breach, or those damages which might have been reasonably contemplated or foreseen by both parties, at the time they made the contract, as the probable result of the breach. (Rest.2d § 351.) As nearly as possible, the injured party should receive the equivalent of the benefits of performance, (Cal.Civ.Code § 3300) provided the damages are "clearly ascertainable in both their nature and origin" (Cal.Civ.Code, § 3301 and see Rest.2d § 352) As a corollary to this rule, no person can recover a greater amount in damages for the breach of an obligation than he or she could have gained had all parties fully performed. (Cal.Civ.Code § 3358) In other words, a plaintiff in a breach of contract action is entitled to the benefits he or she would have obtained if both parties had fully performed, but no more. (Rest.2d § 344(a).)

U.S. Naval Institute v. Charter Comm., Inc.,
United States Court of Appeals, Second Circuit, 1991
936 F.2d 692

KEARSE, Circuit Judge. . . . Naval, as the assignee of the author's copyright in [The Hunt for] Red October, entered into a licensing agreement with Berkley in September 1984 (the "Agreement"), granting Berkley the exclusive license to publish a paperback edition of the Book "not sooner than October 1985." Berkley shipped its paperback edition to retail outlets early, placing those outlets in position to sell the paperback prior to October 1985. As a result, retail sales of the paperback began on September 15, 1985, and early sales were sufficiently substantial that the Book was near the top of paperback bestseller lists before the end of September 1985.

Naval commenced the present action when it learned of Berkley's plans for early shipment, and it unsuccessfully sought a preliminary injunction. After trial, the district judge dismissed the complaint. He ruled that Berkley had not breached the Agreement because it was entitled, in accordance with industry custom, to ship prior to the agreed publication date. On appeal, we reversed. Though we upheld the district court's finding that the Agreement did not prohibit the early shipments themselves, we concluded that if the "not sooner than October 1985" term of the Agreement had any meaning whatever, it meant at least that Berkley was not allowed to cause such voluminous paperback retail sales prior to that date, and that Berkley had therefore breached the Agreement. Naval I, 875 F.2d at 1049-51. Accordingly, we remanded for entry of a judgment awarding Naval appropriate relief.

On the remand, Naval . . . sought judgment awarding it all of Berkley's profits from pre-October 1985 sales of the Book; it estimated those profits at $724,300. . . .

The district judge held that Berkley's profits "attributable to the infringement" were only those profits that resulted from "sales to customers who would not have bought the paperback but for the fact it became available in September." He found that most of the September paperback sales were made to buyers who would not have bought a hardcover edition in September, and therefore only those September sales that displaced hardcover sales were attributable to the infringement. Berkley's profit on the displacing copies totaled $7,760.12, and the court awarded that amount to Naval. . . .

The damages awarded by the district court on remand had two components: (1) Naval's lost profits resulting from Berkley's early publication of the paperback edition of the Book, and (2) Berkley's profits attributable to its assumed infringement. For the reasons discussed above, the latter component of the award cannot stand.

The former component, however, may properly measure damages under a breach-of-contract theory.

Since the purpose of damages for breach of contract is to compensate the injured party for the loss caused by the breach, 5 Corbin On Contracts Sec. 1002, at 31 (1964), those damages are generally measured by the plaintiff's actual loss, see, e.g., Restatement (Second) of Contracts Sec. 347 (1981). While on occasion the defendant's profits are used as the measure of damages, see, e.g., Cincinnati Siemens-Lungren Gas Illuminating Co. v. Western Siemens-Lungren Co., 152 U.S. 200, 204-07, 14 S. Ct. 523, 525-26, 38 L. Ed. 411 (1894); Murphy v. Lifschitz, 183 Misc. 575, 577, 49 N.Y.S.2d 439, 441 (Sup.Ct.N.Y. County 1944), aff'd mem., 268 A.D. 1027, 52 N.Y.S.2d 943 (1st Dep't), aff'd mem., 294 N.Y. 892, 63 N.E.2d 26 (1945), this generally occurs when those profits tend to define the plaintiff's loss, for an award of the defendant's profits where they greatly exceed the plaintiff's loss and there has been no tortious conduct on the part of the defendant would tend to be punitive, and punitive awards are not part of the law of contract damages. See generally Restatement (Second) of Contracts Sec. 356 comment a ("The central objective behind the system of contract remedies is compensatory, not punitive."); id. comment b (agreement attempting to fix damages in amount vastly greater than what approximates actual loss would be unenforceable as imposing a penalty); id. Sec. 355 (punitive damages not recoverable for breach of contract unless conduct constituting the breach is also a tort for which such damages are recoverable).

Here, the district court found that Berkley's alleged $724,300 profits did not define Naval's loss because many persons who bought the paperback in September 1985 would not have bought the book in hardcover but would merely have waited until the paperback edition became available. This finding is not clearly erroneous, and we turn to the question of whether the district court's finding that Naval suffered $35,380.50 in actual damages was proper.

In reaching the $35,380.50 figure, the court operated on the premise that, but for the breach by Berkley, Naval would have sold in September the same number of hardcover copies it sold in August. Berkley challenges that premise as speculative and argues that since Naval presented no evidence as to what its September 1985 sales would have been, Naval is entitled to recover no damages. It argues alternatively that the court should have computed damages on the premise that sales in the second half of September, in the absence of Berkley's premature release of the paperback edition, would have been made at the same rate as in the first half of September. Evaluating the district court's calculation of damages under the clearly erroneous standard of review, see Thyssen, Inc. v. S.S. Fortune Star, 777 F.2d 57, 60 (2d Cir. 1985), we reject Berkley's contentions.

The record showed that, though there was a declining trend of hardcover sales of the Book from March through August 1985, Naval continued to sell its hardcover copies through the end of 1985, averaging some 3,000 copies a month in the latter period. It plainly was not error for the district court to find that the preponderance of the evidence indicated that Berkley's early shipment of 1,400,000 copies of its paperback edition, some 40% of which went to retail outlets and led to the Book's rising close to the top of the paperback bestseller lists before the end of September 1985, caused Naval the loss of some hardcover sales prior to October 1985.

As to the quantification of that loss, we think it was within the prerogative of the court as finder of fact to look to Naval's August 1985 sales. Though there was no proof as to precisely what the unimpeded volume of hardcover sales would have been for the entire month of September, any such evidence would necessarily have been hypothetical. But it is not error to lay the normal uncertainty in such hypotheses at the door of the wrongdoer who altered the proper course of events, instead of at the door of the injured party. See, e.g., Lamborn v. Dittmer, 873 F.2d 522, 532-33 (2d Cir. 1989); Lee v. Joseph E. Seagram & Sons, Inc., 552 F.2d 447, 455-56 (2d Cir. 1977); W.L. Hailey & Co. v. County of Niagara, 388 F.2d 746, 753 (2d Cir. 1967). See generally Bigelow v. RKO Radio Pictures, Inc., 327 U.S. 251, 264-65, 66 S. Ct. 574, 579-80, 90 L. Ed. 652 (1946); Restatement (Second) of Contracts Sec. 352 comment a ("Doubts are generally resolved against the party in breach."). The court was not required to use as the starting point for its calculations Naval's actual sales in the first half of September, i.e., those made prior to the first retail sale of the paperback edition. Berkley has not called to our attention any evidence in the record to indicate that the sales in a given month are normally spread evenly through that month. Indeed, it concedes that " [t]o a large degree, book sales depend on public whim and are notoriously unpredictable...." Thus, nothing in the record foreclosed the possibility that, absent Berkley's breach, sales of hardcover copies in the latter part of September would have outpaced sales of those copies in the early part of the month. Though the court accurately described its selection of August 1985 sales as its benchmark as "generous," it was not improper, given the inherent uncertainty, to exercise generosity in favor of the injured party rather than in favor of the breaching party.

In all the circumstances, we cannot say that the district court's calculation of Naval's damages was clearly erroneous. . . .

For the foregoing reasons, we reverse so much of the judgment as granted Naval $7,760.12 as an award of Berkley's profits.

Questions

1. What was the court's finding regarding Naval's actual damages resulting from Berkley's early publication of the paperback edition?

2. How did the court determine the amount of Naval's actual damages?

3. Why did the court reject Berkley's argument regarding the calculation of damages based on sales in the second half of September?

4. What was the court's reasoning for reversing the award of Berkley's profits to Naval?

Takeaways – U.S. Naval Institute

What was wrong with taking Berkley's profits and awarding them to Naval Institute? What rule or principle of contract damages did this violate?

Three Protected Interests

Monetary damages for breach of contract can be grouped into three protected interests:

The **expectation interest** which represents the injured party's interest in their prospect of gain from the contract. The expectation interest seeks to place the injured party in the position they would have been in had the contract been fully performed. (Rest.2d § 344(a))

The **reliance interest** which represents the injured party's interest in being reimbursed for their change of position in anticipation of the contract being performed. The reliance interest seeks to put the injured party in the position she would have been in had she never entered into the contract. (Rest.2d § 344(b))

The **restitution interest** which represents the injured party's interest in having returned to him any benefits or consideration he conferred on or furnished to the breaching party. (Rest.2d § 344(c))

The overarching goal of the substitutionary remedy of monetary damages is to put the injured party in the position that she would have been in had the contract been fully performed as promised. The injured party in a breach of contract action is entitled to the benefits he or she would have obtained if both parties had fully performed, but no more. Court's first look to see if monetary damages can satisfy the expectation interest. However, as you will see, there are a number of limitations of monetary damages for breach of contract and there are situations where the expectation interest cannot be fulfilled due to those limitations. In those situations the court will seek to compensate the injured party by fulfilling the reliance or restitution interest.

Sullivan v. O'Connor
Supreme Judicial Court of Massachusetts, 1973
363 Mass. 579, 296 N.E.2d 183

KAPLAN, J. The plaintiff patient secured by a jury verdict of $13,500 against the defendant surgeon for breach of contract in respect to an operation upon the plaintiff's nose.... [T]he plaintiff alleged that she, as patient, entered into a contract with the defendant, a surgeon, wherein the defendant promised to perform plastic surgery on her nose and thereby to enhance her beauty and improve her appearance; that he performed the surgery but failed to achieve the promised result; rather the result of the surgery was to disfigure and deform her nose, to cause her pain in body and mind, and to subject her to other damage and expense....

On the plaintiff's demand, the case was tried by jury. At the close of the evidence, the judge put to the jury, as special questions, the issues of liability ... and instructed them accordingly. The jury returned a verdict for the plaintiff on the contract count... The judge then instructed the jury on the issue of damages.

As background to the instructions and the parties' exceptions, we mention certain facts as the jury could find them. The plaintiff was a professional entertainer, and this was known to the defendant. The agreement was as alleged in the declaration. More particularly, judging from exhibits, the plaintiff's nose had been straight, but long and prominent; the defendant undertook by two operations to reduce its prominence and somewhat to shorten it, thus making it more pleasing in relation to the plaintiff's other features. Actually the plaintiff was obliged to undergo three operations, and her appearance was worsened. Her nose now had a concave line to about the midpoint, at which it became bulbous; viewed frontally, the nose from bridge to midpoint was flattened and broadened, and the two sides of the tip had lost symmetry. This configuration evidently could not be improved by further surgery. The plaintiff did not demonstrate, however, that her change of appearance had resulted in loss of employment. Payments by the plaintiff covering the defendant's fee and hospital expenses were stipulated at $622.65.

The judge instructed the jury, first, that the plaintiff was entitled to recover her out-of-pocket expenses incident to the operations. Second, she could recover the damages flowing directly, naturally, proximately, and foreseeably from the defendant's breach of promise. These would comprehend damages for any disfigurement of the plaintiff's nose that is, any change of appearance for the worse including the effects of the consciousness of such disfigurement on the plaintiff's mind, and in this connection the jury should consider the nature of the plaintiff's profession. Also consequent upon the defendant's breach, and compensable, were the pain and suffering involved in the third operation, but not in the first two. As there was no proof that any loss of earnings by the plaintiff resulted from the breach, that element should not enter into the calculation of damages.

By his exceptions the defendant contends that the judge erred in allowing the jury to take into account anything but the plaintiff's out-of-pocket expenses (presumably at the stipulated amount). The defendant excepted to the judge's refusal of his request for a general charge to that effect, and, more specifically, to the judge's refusal of a charge that the plaintiff could not recover for pain and suffering connected with the third operation or for impairment of the plaintiff's appearance and associated mental distress

The plaintiff on her part excepted to the judge's refusal of a request to charge that the plaintiff could recover the difference in value between the nose as promised and the nose as it appeared after the operations. However, the plaintiff in her brief expressly waives this exception and others made by her in case this court overrules the defendant's exceptions; thus she would be content to hold the jury's verdict in her favor.

We conclude that the defendant's exceptions should be overruled. . . .

If an action on the basis of contract is allowed, we have next the question of the measure of damages to be applied where liability is found. Some cases have taken the simple view that the promise by the physician is to be treated like an ordinary commercial promise, and accordingly that the successful plaintiff is entitled to a standard measure of recovery for breach of contract "compensatory" ("expectancy") damages, an amount intended to put the plaintiff in the position he would be in if the contract had been performed, or, presumably, at the plaintiff's election, "restitution" damages, an amount corresponding to any benefit conferred by the plaintiff upon the defendant in the performance of the contract disrupted by the defendant's breach. See Restatement: Contracts § 329 and comment a, §§ 347, 384. Thus in Hawkins v. McGee, 84 N.H. 114, the defendant doctor was taken to have promised the plaintiff to convert his damaged hand by means of an operation into a good or perfect hand, but the doctor so operated as to damage the hand still further. The court, following the usual expectancy formula, would have asked the jury to estimate and award to the plaintiff the difference between the value of a good or perfect hand, as promised, and the value of the hand after the operation. (The same formula would apply, although the dollar result would be less, if the operation had neither worsened nor improved the condition of the hand.) If the plaintiff had not yet paid the doctor his fee, that amount would be deducted from the recovery. There could be no recovery for the pain and suffering of the operation, since that detriment would have been incurred even if the operation had been successful; one can say that this detriment was not "caused" by the breach. But where the plaintiff by reason of the operation was put to more pain than he would have had to endure, had the doctor performed as promised, he should be compensated for that difference as a proper part of his expectancy recovery. It may be noted that on an alternative court for malpractice the plaintiff in the Hawkins case had been nonsuited; but on ordinary principles this could not affect the contract claim, for it is hardly a defense to a breach of contract that the promiser acted innocently and without negligence. The New Hampshire court further refined the Hawkins analysis in McQuaid v. Michou, 85 N.H. 299, all in the direction of treating the patient-physician cases on the ordinary footing of expectancy....

Other cases, including a number in New York, without distinctly repudiating the Hawkins type of analysis, have indicated that a different and generally more lenient measure of damages is to be applied in patient-physician actions based on breach of alleged special agreements to effect a cure, attain a stated result, or employ a given medical method. This measure is expressed in somewhat variant ways, but the substance is that the plaintiff is to recover any expenditures made by him and for other detriment (usually not specifically described in the opinions) following proximately and foreseeably upon the defendant's failure to carry out his promise. Robins v. Finestone, 308 N.Y. 543, 546.... This, be it noted, is not a "restitution" measure, for it is not limited to restoration of the benefit conferred on the defendant (the fee paid) but includes other expenditures, for example, amounts paid for medicine and nurses; so also it would seem according to its logic to take in damages for any worsening of the plaintiff's condition due to the breach. Nor is it an "expectancy" measure, for it does not appear to contemplate recovery of the whole difference in value between the condition as promised and the condition actually resulting from the treatment. Rather the tendency of the formulation is to put the plaintiff back in the position he occupied just before the parties entered upon the agreement, to compensate him for the detriments he suffered in reliance upon the agreement. This kind of intermediate pattern of recovery for breach of contract is discussed in the suggestive article by Fuller and Perdue, The Reliance Interest in Contract Damages, 46 Yale L.J. 52, 373, where the authors show that, although not attaining the currency of the standard measures, a "reliance" measure has for special reasons been applied by the courts in a variety of settlings, including noncommercial settings. See 46 Yale L.J. at 396-401.

For breach of the patient-physician agreements under consideration, a recovery limited to restitution seems plainly to meager, if the agreements are to be enforced at all. On the other hand, an expectancy recovery may well be excessive. The factors, already mentioned, which have made the cause of action somewhat suspect, also suggest moderation as to the breadth of the recovery that should be permitted. Where, as in the case at bar and in a number of the reported cases, the doctor has been absolved of negligence by the trier, an expectancy measure may be thought harsh. We should recall here that the fee paid by the patient to the doctor for the alleged promise would usually be quite disproportionate to the putative expectancy recovery. To attempt, moreover, to put a value on the condition that would or might have resulted, had the treatment succeeded as promised, may sometimes put an exceptional strain on the imagination of the fact finder. As a general consideration, Fuller and Perdue argue that the reasons for granting damages for broken promises to the extent of the expectancy are at their strongest when the promises are made in a business context, when they have to do with the production or distribution of goods or the allocation of functions in the market place; they become weaker as the context shifts from a commercial to a noncommercial field. 46 Yale L.J. at 60-63.

There is much to be said, then, for applying a reliance measure to the present facts, and we have only to add that our cases are not unreceptive to the use of that formula in special situations. We have, however, had no previous occasion to apply it to patient-physician cases.

The question of recovery on a reliance basis for pain and suffering or mental distress requires further attention. We find expressions in the decisions that pain and suffering (or the like) are simply not compensable in actions for breach of contract. The defendant seemingly espouses this proposition in the present case. True, if the buyer under a contract for the purchase of a lot of merchandise, in suing for the seller's breach, should claim damages for mental anguish caused by his disappointment in the transaction, he would not succeed; he would be told, perhaps, that the asserted psychological injury was not fairly foreseeable by the defendant as a probable consequence of the breach of such a business contract. See Restatement: Contracts, § 341 and comment a. But there is no general rule barring such items of damage in actions for breach of contract. It is all a question of the subject matter and background of the contract, and when the contract calls for an operation on the person of the plaintiff, psychological as well as physical injury may be expected to figure somewhere in the recovery, depending on the particular circumstances. The point is explained in Stewart v. Rudner, 349 Mich. 459, 469. Cf. Frewen v. Page, 238 Mass. 499; McClean v. University Club, 327 Mass. 68. Again, it is said in a few of the New York cases, concerned with the classification of actions for statute of limitations purposes, that the absence of allegations demanding recovery for pain and suffering is characteristic of a contract claim by a patient against a physician, that such allegations rather belong in a claim for malpractice. See Robins v. Finestone, 308 N.Y. 543, 547; Budoff v. Kessler, 2 App. Div.2d (N.Y.) 760. These remarks seem unduly sweeping. Suffering or distress resulting from the breach going beyond that which was envisaged by the treatment as agreed, should be compensable on the same ground as the worsening of the patient's conditions because of the breach. Indeed it can be argued that the very suffering or distress "contracted for" that which would have been incurred if the treatment achieved the promised result should also be compensable on the theory underlying the New York cases. For that suffering is "wasted" if the treatment fails. Otherwise stated, compensation for this waste is arguably required in order to complete the restoration of the status quo ante.

In the light of the foregoing discussion, all the defendant's exceptions fail: the plaintiff was not confined to the recovery of her out-of-pocket expenditures; she was entitled to recover also for the worsening of her condition, and for the pain and suffering and mental distress involved in the third operation. These items were compensable on either an expectancy or a reliance view. We might have been required to elect between the two views if the pain and suffering connected with the first two operations contemplated by the agreement, or the whole difference in value between the present and the promised conditions, were being claimed as elements of damage. But the plaintiff waives her possible claim to the former element, and to so much of the latter as represents the difference in value between the promised condition and the condition before the operations.

Plaintiff's exceptions waived. Defendant's exceptions overruled.

Questions

1. According to the judge's instructions, what damages could the plaintiff recover for?

2. What are the two different measures of damages discussed in the case?

3. Why does the court suggest applying a reliance measure of damages in patient-physician cases?

Takeaways – Sullivan v. O'Connor

Did the award of damages put the plaintiff in the position she would have been in had the surgeon's promise been performed? Of the three protected interests mentioned in the introduction preceding this case, which one(s) did the court allow plaintiff to recover for?

Recovery on a reliance basis for breach of the physician's promise looks to restoration of the patent's condition before the injury. What would recovery on an expectation basis look to?

Restatement Second section 347. Measure of Damages in General

Subject to the limitations stated in §§ 350-53, the injured party has a right to damages based on his expectation interest as measured by

(a) the loss in value to him of the other party's performance caused by its failure or deficiency, plus

(b) any other loss, including incidental or consequential loss, less

(c) any cost or other loss that he has avoided by not having to perform.

A breakdown of this rule looks like this:

Damages = (a) loss in value + (b) other loss – (c) cost and loss avoided.

Vitex Manufacturing Corporation, Ltd. v. Caribtex Corporation

United States Court of Appeals, Third Circuit, 1967
377 F.2d 795

Staley, Chief Judge. This is an appeal by Caribtex Corporation from a judgment of the District Court of the Virgin Islands finding Caribtex in breach of a contract entered into with Vitex Manufacturing Company, Ltd., and awarding $21,114 plus interest to Vitex for loss of profits. The only substantial question raised by Caribtex is whether it was error for the district court, sitting without a jury, not to consider overhead as part of Vitex's costs in determining the amount of profits lost. We conclude that under the facts presented, the district court was not compelled to consider Vitex's overhead costs, and we will affirm the judgment.

Before discussing the details of the controversy between the parties, it will be helpful to briefly describe the peculiar legal setting in which this suit arose. At the time of the events in question, there were high tariff barriers to the importation of foreign wool products. However, under § 301 of the Tariff Act of 1930, 19 U.S.C.A. § 1301a, repealed but the provision continued under Revised Tariff Schedules, 19 U.S.C.A. § 1202, note 3(a) (i) (ii) (1965), if such goods were imported into the Virgin Islands and were processed in some manner so that their finished value exceeded their importation value by at least 50%, then the high tariffs to importation into the continental United States would be avoided. Even after the processing, the foreign wool enjoyed a price advantage over domestic products so that the business flourished. However, to keep the volume of this business at such levels that Congress would not be stirred to change the law, the Virgin Islands Legislature imposed "quotas" on persons engaging in processing, limiting their output. 33 V.I.C. § 504 (Supp.1966).

Vitex was engaged in the business of chemically shower-proofing imported cloth so that it could be imported duty-free into the United States. For this purpose, Vitex maintained a plant in the Virgin Islands and was entitled to process a specific quantity of material under the Virgin Islands quota system. Caribtex was in the business of importing cloth into the islands, securing its processing, and exporting it to the United States.

In the fall of 1963, Vitex found itself with an unused portion of its quota but no customers, and Vitex closed its plant. Caribtex acquired some Italian wool and subsequently negotiations for a processing contract were conducted between the principals of the respective companies in New York City. Though the record below is clouded with differing versions of the negotiations and the alleged final terms, the trial court found upon substantial evidence in the record that the parties did enter into a contract in which Vitex agreed to process 125,000 yards of Caribtex's woolen material at a price of 26 cents per yard.

Vitex proceeded to re-open its Virgin Islands plant, ordered the necessary chemicals, recalled its work force and made all the necessary preparations to perform its end of the bargain. However, no goods were forthcoming from Caribtex, despite repeated demands by Vitex, apparently because Caribtex was unsure that the processed wool would be entitled to duty-free treatment by the customs officials. Vitex subsequently brought this suit to recover the profits lost through Caribtex's breach.

Vitex alleged, and the trial court found, that its gross profits for processing said material under the contract would have been $31,250 and that its costs would have been $10,136, leaving Vitex's damages for loss of profits at $21,114. On appeal, Caribtex asserted numerous objections to the detailed computation of lost profits. While the record below is sometimes confusing, we conclude that the trial court had substantial evidence to support its findings on damages. It must be remembered that the difficulty in exactly ascertaining Vitex's costs is due to Caribtex's wrongful conduct in repudiating the contract before performance by Vitex. Caribtex will not be permitted to benefit by the uncertainty it has caused. Thus, since there was a sufficient basis in the record to support the trial court's determination of substantial damages, we will not set aside its judgment. Stentor Elec. Mfg. Co. v. Klaxon Co., 115 F.2d 268 (C.A.3, 1940), rev'd other grounds 313 U.S. 487, 61 S. Ct. 1020, 85 L. Ed. 1477 (1941); 5 Williston, Contracts § 1345 (rev. ed. 1937).

Caribtex first raised the issue at the oral argument of this appeal that the trial court erred by disregarding Vitex's overhead expenses in determining lost profits. In general, overhead " . . . may be said to include broadly the continuous expenses of the business, irrespective of the outlay on a particular contract." Grand Trunk W. R. R. Co. v. H. W. Nelson Co., 116 F.2d 823, 839 (C.A. 6, 1941). Such expenses would include executive and clerical salaries, property taxes, general administration expenses, etc. Although Vitex did not expressly seek recovery for overhead, if a portion of these fixed expenses should be allocated as costs to the Caribtex contract, then under the judgment of the district court Vitex tacitly recovered these expenses as part of its damages for lost profits, and the damages should be reduced accordingly. Presumably, the portion to be allocated to costs would be a pro rata share of Vitex's annual overhead according to the volume of business Vitex would have done over the year if Caribtex had not breached the contract.

Although there is authority to the contrary, we feel that the better view is that normally, in a claim for lost profits, overhead should be treated as a part of gross profits and recoverable as damages, and should not be considered as part of the seller's costs. A number of cases hold that since overhead expenses are not affected by the performance of the particular contract, there should be no need to deduct them in computing lost profits. E. g., Oakland California Towel Co. v. Sivils, 52

Cal.App.2d 517, 520, 126 P.2d 651, 652 (1942); Jessup & Moore Paper Co. v. Bryant Paper Co., 297 Pa. 483, 147 A. 519, 524 (1929); Annot., 3 A.L.R.3d 689 (1965) (collecting cases on both sides of the controversy). The theory of these cases is that the seller is entitled to recover losses incurred and gains prevented in excess of savings made possible, Restatement, Contracts § 329 (made part of the law of the Virgin Islands, 1 V.I.C. § 4); since overhead is fixed and non-performance of the contract produced no overhead cost savings, no deduction from profits should result.

The soundness of the rule is exemplified by this case. Before negotiations began between Vitex and Caribtex, Vitex had reached a lull in business activity and had closed its plant. If Vitex had entered into no other contracts for the rest of the year, the profitability of its operations would have been determined by deducting its production costs and overhead from gross receipts yielded in previous transactions. When this opportunity arose to process Caribtex's wool, the only additional expenses Vitex would incur would be those of re-opening its plant and the direct costs of processing, such as labor, chemicals and fuel oil. Overhead would have remained the same whether or not Vitex and Caribtex entered their contract and whether or not Vitex actually processed Caribtex's goods. Since this overhead remained constant, in no way attributable-to or affected-by the Caribtex contract, it would be improper to consider it as a cost of Vitex's performance to be deducted from the gross proceeds of the Caribtex contract.

However, Caribtex may argue that this view ignores modern accounting principles, and that overhead is as much a cost of production as other expenses. It is true that successful businessmen must set their prices at sufficient levels to recoup all their expenses, including overhead, and to gain profits. Thus, the price the businessman should charge on each transaction could be thought of as that price necessary to yield a pro rata portion of the company's fixed overhead, the direct costs associated with production, and a "clear" profit. Doubtless this type of calculation is used by businessmen and their accountants. Pacific Portland Cement Co. v. Food Mach. & Chem. Corp., 178 F.2d 541 (C.A.9, 1949). However, because it is useful for planning purposes to allocate a portion of overhead to each transaction, it does not follow that this allocate share of fixed overhead should be considered a cost factor in the computation of lost profits on individual transactions.

First, it must be recognized that the pro rata allocation of overhead costs is only an analytical construct. In a similar manner one could allocate a pro rata share of the company's advertising cost, taxes and/or charitable gifts. The point is that while these items all are paid from the proceeds of the business, they do not normally bear such a direct relationship to any individual transaction to be considered a cost in ascertaining lost profits.

Secondly, even were we to recognize the allocation of overhead as proper in this case, we should uphold the tacit award of overhead expense to Vitex as a "loss incurred." Conditioned Air Corp. v. Rock Island Motor Transit Co., 253 Iowa 961, 114 N.W.2d 304, 3 A.L.R.3d 679, cert. denied, 371 U.S. 825, 83 S. Ct. 46, 9 L. Ed. 2d 64 (1962). By the very nature of this allocation process, as the number of transaction over which overhead can be spread becomes smaller, each transaction must bear a greater portion or allocate share of the fixed overhead cost. Suppose a company has fixed overhead of $10,000 and engages in five similar transactions; then the receipts of each transaction would bear $2000 of overhead expense. If the company is now forced to spread this $10,000 over only four transactions, then the overhead expense per transaction will rise to $2500, significantly reducing the profitability of the four remaining transactions. Thus, where the contract is between businessmen familiar with commercial practices, as here, the breaching party should reasonably foresee that his breach will not only cause a loss of "clear" profit, but also a loss in that the profitability of other transactions will be reduced. Resolute Ins. Co. v. Percy Jones, Inc., 198 F.2d 309 (C.A.10, 1952); Cf. In re Kellett Aircraft Corp., 191 F.2d 231 (C.A.3, 1951). Therefore, this loss is within the contemplation of "losses caused and gains prevented," and overhead should be considered to be a compensable item of damage.

Significantly, the Uniform Commercial Code, adopted in the Virgin Islands, 11A V.I.C. §§ 1-101 et seq., and in virtually every state today, provides for the recovery of overhead in circumstances similar to those presented here. Under 11A V.I.C. § 2-708, the seller's measure of damage for non-acceptance or repudiation is the difference between the contract price and the market price, but if this relief is inadequate to put the seller in as good position as if the contract had been fully performed, " ... then the measure of damages is the profit (including reasonable overhead) which the seller would have made from full performance by the buyer ... ." 11A V.I.C. § 2-708(2). (Emphasis added.) While this contract is not controlled by the Code, the Code is persuasive here because it embodies the foremost modern legal thought concerning commercial transactions. Indeed, it may overrule some of the cases denying recovery for overhead. E. g., Wilhelm Lubrication Co. v. Brattrud, 197 Minn. 626, 632, 268 N.W. 634, 636, 106 A.L.R. 1279 (1936). . . .

The judgment of the district court will be affirmed.

Questions

1. According to the court, why was the district court not compelled to consider Vitex's overhead costs in determining the amount of profits lost?

2. What is the court's view regarding the treatment of overhead expenses in claims for lost profits? Provide an explanation.

3. How does the court address the argument that overhead is a cost of production and should be considered in the computation of lost profits?

Takeaways – Vitex v. Caribtex

What were Vitex's damages based upon? Virtually every party that has contractual obligations will incur costs in performing those obligations. If they are excused from performing by virtue of the other party's breach how does that cost of performing (that they no longer have) figure into the damage calculation? This is what is known as *cost avoided*. And suppose as a result of the breach, Vitex had been able to take on another textile processing job. One that pays less, but one they would not have been able to take on had there been no breach. Any money they made from that job would be *loss avoided* and would be deducted from their damages.

Buyer's Damages for Seller's Breach of Contract for Sale of Goods

Laredo Hides Company, Inc., v. H & H Meat Products Co., Inc.
Court of Civil Appeals of Texas, 1974
513 S.W.2d 210

BISSETT, Justice. This is a breach of contract case. Laredo Hides Company, Inc., the buyer, sued H & H Meat Products Company, Inc., the seller, to recover damages for breach of a written contract for the sale of cattle hides. Trial was to the court without a jury. A take nothing judgment in favor of defendant was rendered. Plaintiff has appealed.

The controlling facts of the case are undisputed. H & H Meat Products Company, Inc. (H & H) is a meat processing and packing corporation, located in Mercedes, Texas. It sells cattle hides as a by-product of its business. Laredo Hides Company, Inc. (Laredo Hides) is a corporation, located in Laredo, Texas. It purchases cattle hides from various meat packers in the United States and ships them to tanneries in Mexico.

A written contract dated February 29, 1972, was executed whereby Laredo Hides agreed to by H & H's entire cattle hide production during the period March through December, 1972. Among other provisions, the contract provided:

"Terms: Cash upon delivery, deliveries to be made at least twice a month."

The agreement was signed on behalf of Laredo Hides by Camilio Prada (Prada), its president, and on behalf of H & H by Liborio Hinojosa (Hinojosa), its vice president and general manager. [After two deliveries of hides a $9,000 check sent by Laredo to H & H was delayed in the mail and failed to arrive before a deadline set by H & H.] . . .

Hinojosa treated the failure to make payment before 4:30 p. m. on March 21, 1972, as a breach of the agreement which gave H & H a right to cancel the contract.

On March 30, 1972, Prada called Hinojosa and asked if a shipment of hides would be ready on the following Saturday, April 1, 1972. Hinojosa unequivocally told him that he was not going to sell him anymore hides, and further advised that it was useless for him to send a truck for the hides, since at 4:30 p. m., Tuesday, March 21st, he had made up his mind to terminate the contract. [In an omitted part of the opinion the court ruled this action was precipitous and was a breach on the seller's part.]

Laredo Hides, on March 3, 1972, had contracted with a Mexican tannery for the sale of all the hides which it expected to purchase from H & H under the February 29, 1972, contract. Following the cancellation by H & H of the contract, Laredo Hides, in order to meet the requirements of its contract with the tannery, was forced to purchase hides on the open market in substitution for the hides which were to have been delivered to it under the contract with H & H.

H & H's total production during the months April through December, 1972, was 17,218 hides. Under the contract with H & H, the price was $9.75 per hide for bull, steer and heifer hides, and $9.75 per hide for cow hides if the shipment was under 5% cow hides. In the event the shipment was more than 5% cow hides, the price on the excess of cow hides over 5% was reduced to $7.50 per cow hide. The market price for hides steadily increased following the execution of the contract in question. By December 31, 1972, the average cost of bull hides was about $33.00 each and the average cost of cow, heifer and steer hides was about $22.00 each. The total additional cost to Laredo Hides of purchasing substitute hides from other suppliers was $142,254.48. The additional costs (transportation and handling charges) to Laredo Hides which resulted because of the purchases from third parties amounted to $3,448.95. . . .

Since this case must be reversed, we now confront the issue of damages. The guidelines for determining a buyer's remedies in a case where there is a breach of a contract for the sale of goods by a seller are found in Chapter 2 of the Texas Business and Commerce Code. Among other remedies afforded by the Code, when there is a repudiation of the contract by the seller or a failure to make delivery of the goods under contract, the buyer may cover under § 2.711. He may have damages under § 2.712 "by making in good faith and without unreasonable delay any reasonable purchase of or contract to purchase goods in substitution for those due from the seller", and "may recover from the seller as damages the difference between the cost of cover and the contract price together with any incidental or consequential damages" provided by the chapter; or, he may, under § 2.713, have damages measured by "the difference between the market price at the time when the buyer learned of the breach and the contract price together with any incidental and consequential damages" provided by the chapter.

Laredo Hides instituted suit in May, 1972, and filed its amended petition (its trial pleading) on October 24, 1972, when performance was still due by H & H under the contract. It prayed for specific performance, or in the alternative "... damages at least in the amount of one hundred thousand dollars ($100,000), the same being the damages proximately caused by defendant's breach of the contract..." There was never a trial amendment of this petition. There were no exceptions by H & H to Laredo Hides' pleadings. Trial commenced on February 28, 1973 was recessed on March 2, 1973, resumed on May 15, 1973, and ended May 16, 1973. Judgment was signed and rendered on August 6, 1973.

Laredo Hides offered uncontroverted evidence of the hide production of H & H from April to December, 1972. It also established the price for the same number of hides which it was forced to buy elsewhere. There was testimony that purchases had to be made periodically throughout 1972 since Laredo Hides had no storage facilities, and the hides would decompose if allowed to age. Furthermore, White, a C.P.A., testified as to statistical summaries which he made showing the cost of buying substitute hides. These summaries were made from invoices which are also in evidence. All of this evidence was admitted without objection. Clearly, Laredo Hides elected to pursue the remedy provided by § 2.712 of the Code, and by its pleadings and evidence brought itself within the purview of the "cover" provisions contained therein.

It is not necessary under § 2.712 that the buyer establish market price. Duesenberg and King, Sales and Bulk Transfers under the U.C.C.§ 14.04 Matthew Bender (1974). Where the buyer complies with the requirements of § 2.712, his purchase is presumed proper and the burden of proof is on the seller to show that "cover" was not properly obtained. Spies, Sales, Performance and Remedies, 44 Tex.L.Rev. 629, 638 (1966). There was no evidence offered by H & H to negate this presumption or to "establish expenses saved in consequence of the seller's breach", as permitted by § 2.712.

The difference between the cover price and the contract price is shown to be $134,252.82 for steer hides and $8,001.66 for bull hides, or a total of $142,254.48. In addition, Laredo Hides offered evidence of increased transportation costs of $1,435.77, and increased handling charges of $2,013.18. These are clearly recoverable as incidental damages where the buyer elects to "cover". §§ 2.715(a); 2.712(b). . . .

There is no evidence that Laredo Hides, in any manner, endeavored to increase its damages sustained when H & H refused to deliver any more hides to it. Laredo Hides, in purchasing the hides in substitution of the hides which should have been delivered under the contract, acted promptly and in a reasonable manner. The facts of this case regarding the issue of liability of H & H and the issues pertaining to damages suffered by Laredo Hides, have been fully and completely developed in the court below. The facts upon which judgment should have been rendered for Laredo Hides by the trial court are conclusively established. It, therefore, becomes the duty of this Court to render judgment which the trial court should have rendered. . . .

Applying the rules announced by the above cited cases and authorities to the instant case, we hold that the record does not support the findings of fact made by the trial judge and there is no legal justification for the conclusion of law reached by the court. Accordingly, the judgment of the trial court is reversed, and judgment is here rendered for Laredo Hides in the amount of $152,960.04, together with interest thereon at the rate of 6% per annum from August 6, 1973, the date judgment was rendered by the trial court, until paid.

Reversed and rendered.

Questions

1. What remedies are available to a buyer under the UCC when there is a breach of a contract for the sale of goods?

2. How did Laredo Hides establish its damages under UCC § 2-712?

Takeaways – Laredo Hides v. H & H Meat

The basic measure of damages available to a buyer for a seller's nondelivery or repudiation is the difference between the market price and the contract price. (UCC § 2-713) The market price to be used as the basis of the calculation is the market to which a buyer would normally go to effect cover. (§ 2-713, subd. (2); Market price is measured as of the time the buyer learned of the breach at which time he could be expected to seek cover. (§ 2-713, subd. (1))

However, when the seller breaches a contract for the sale of goods, the buyer may elect to "cover," i.e. go out on the open market and buy similar goods in substitution for those due under the contract. When the buyer covers, the measure of damages the buyer is entitled to is the difference between the contract price and the price of the goods purchased in substitution together with any incidental or consequential damages. (UCC § 2-712)

When a party to a contract breaks his promise, the victim of the breach may replace the promised performance with a substitute performance. The substitute-price formula awards the victim of breach the cost of replacing a performance with a substitute performance. (73 Cal.LR 1439)

UCC § 2-712 provides: "(1) After a breach within [UCC § 2-711, which specifies, inter alia, remedies available upon nondelivery or repudiation] the buyer may 'cover' by making in good faith and without unreasonable delay any reasonable purchase of or contract to purchase goods in substitution for those due from the seller. [¶] (2) The buyer may recover from the seller as damages the difference between the cost of cover and the contract price together with any incidental or consequential damages as hereinafter defined (UCC § 2- 715), but less expenses saved in consequence of the seller's breach. [¶] (3) Failure of the buyer to effect cover within this section does not bar him from any other remedy."

Sections 2-712 and 2-713 of the Uniform Commercial Code are sometimes referred to as "cover" and "hypothetical cover," since the former involves an actual entry into the market by the buyer while the latter does not. (See Childres, Buyer's Remedies: The Danger of Section 2-713 (1978) 72 Nw.U.L.Rev. 837, 841.)

So why allow the jilted buyer the option of choosing between two possible remedies? Here is one explanation offered by Professors White & Summers: "Since cover was not a recognized remedy under pre-[UCC] law, it made sense under that law to say that the contract-market formula put [the] buyer in the same position as performance would have on the assumption that the buyer would purchase substitute goods. If things worked right, the market price would approximate the cost of the substitute goods and buyer would be put 'in the same position ....' But under the {UCC}, 2-712 does this job with greater precision, and 2-713 reigns over only those cases in which the buyer does not purchase a substitute." (White & Summers, Uniform Commercial Code § 6-4.)

The Code remedy of "cover" gives the buyer the right to recover the cost of a good faith purchase of substitute goods made without unreasonable delay. (2-712(1)(2)) The Code permits recovery of lost profits as consequential damages. (2-715) 2-715(2)(a) bars consequential damages where the loss could have been avoided by "cover."

Seller's Damages for Buyer's Breach of Contract for Sale of Goods

R.E. Davis Chemical Corp. v. Diasonics, Inc.
United States Court of Appeals, Seventh Circuit, 1991
924 F.2d 709

CUDAHY, Circuit Judge. Though uncomplicated on its face, this contract dispute has spawned a protracted cycle of litigation. . . .

Diasonics is a Delaware corporation engaged in the business of manufacturing and marketing medical diagnostic equipment. R.E. Davis Chemical Corporation (Davis), an Illinois business, contracted to purchase one such device, a .35 tesla nuclear magnetic resonance instrument (MRI), from Diasonics at the price of $1,500,000 pursuant to a written agreement dated February 23, 1984. By the terms of the agreement, upon payment of the full purchase price Davis was to be furnished a $225,000 research grant "based on [an] approved program of development activities." Appellee's Br. at 3. The agreement also afforded Davis the option to upgrade the MRI to a high-field/spectroscopy system by June 1, 1985--approximately

15 months after delivery of the MRI was scheduled--at an additional cost of $700,000. Davis advanced a $300,000 deposit for the MRI but failed to take delivery, thereby breaching the contract. After Davis repudiated the contract, Diasonics resold the MRI to a third party at the contract price.

When Diasonics refused to refund the $300,000 deposit, Davis filed suit demanding return of the down payment pursuant to section 2-718(2) of the Uniform Commercial Code (the UCC). Ill.Rev.Stat. ch. 26, para. 2-718(2) (1985). Diasonics counterclaimed, alleging that it was entitled to recover the profit it lost on the sale under UCC 2-708(2) because it was a lost volume seller. Ill.Rev.Stat. ch. 26, para. 2-708(2) (1985). The district court entered summary judgment for Davis, holding that lost volume sellers are not eligible for recovery of lost profits but rather are limited to damages measured by the difference between the resale price and the contract price together with incidental damages under UCC 2-706(1). Ill.Rev.Stat. ch. 26, para. 2-706(1) (1985). Concluding that the Illinois Supreme Court would follow the majority of jurisdictions, which allow lost volume sellers to recoup their lost profits under UCC 2-708(2), we reversed and remanded the case with instructions that the district court calculate Diasonics' damages under 2-708(2) if Diasonics can establish, not only that it had the capacity to make the sale to Davis as well as the sale to the resale buyer, but also that it would have been profitable for it to make both sales ... [and that Diasonics] probably would have made the second sale absent the breach.

On remand, Diasonics filed a motion in limine to preclude Davis from introducing evidence of the additional expenses Diasonics would have been forced to incur had Davis performed its part of the bargain and elected to exercise the upgrade option. The district court granted this motion at the start of the three-day bench trial. Concluding that Diasonics had adequately established damages for its lost profit amounting to $453,050, the district court ultimately entered judgment for Diasonics in the sum of $153,050 ($453,050 less the $300,000 deposit which Diasonics retained).

On appeal, Davis challenges the district court's verdict on the following grounds. First, Davis would prohibit Diasonics from recovering the profit it lost on the sale because Diasonics failed to precisely identify the buyer to whom it resold the MRI. Davis also quibbles with Diasonics' damage computations, asserting that they are inconsistent, incomplete and unreliable. In their stead, Davis proffers its own more favorable accounting figures. Finally, Davis contends that the district court erred by refusing to allow it a $225,000 credit for the research grant and by excluding evidence of the loss Diasonics would have sustained had Davis exercised its upgrade option.

Ordinarily, a seller's damages for a buyer's breach of contract are measured by the difference between the contract price and the market price. In some situations, however, this sum is inadequate to place the seller in as good a position as performance would have done. For example, a broken contract costs a lost volume seller--one with a finite quantity of customers and the capacity to make an additional sale--its profit on one sale. To be made whole, a lost volume seller must thus recover damages equal to the profit it lost on the sale.

In accordance with this reasoning, in Diasonics I, 826 F.2d at 681, we adopted for the first time in Illinois the rule that a lost volume seller is entitled to recoup its lost profit. We held that in order to qualify as a lost volume seller, a plaintiff must establish the following three factors:

(1) that it possessed the capacity to make an additional sale,

(2) that it would have been profitable for it to make an additional sale, and

(3) that it probably would have made an additional sale absent the buyer's breach.

Diasonics has adduced ample evidence to establish its status as a lost volume seller. The evidence is undisputed that Diasonics possessed the capacity to manufacture one more MRI. Diasonics also demonstrated that it was, in the words of Judge Kocoras, "beating the bushes for all possible sales." Tr. at 3. Douglas McCutcheon, controller of Diasonics' MRI Division, testified at trial that Diasonics' sales force pursued "every possible lead" and attempted to "identify every possible qualified customer" in 1984. The fact that Diasonics was still a young company struggling to acquire business in an extremely competitive market at the time of Davis' breach lends independent corroboration to McCutcheon's statements. Based upon this evidence, the district court's finding that Diasonics probably would have made an additional sale but for Davis' breach is not clearly erroneous.

Davis offers no evidence to controvert the proof adduced by Diasonics that it both possessed the capacity to manufacture additional MRIs and was actively soliciting every possible customer for MRI sales in 1984. Instead, Davis clutches at one footnote in our previous opinion to justify its contention that Diasonics must precisely identify the resale buyer. In this case, it appears that the generic MRI units manufactured by Diasonics were interchangeable and thus were not identified to any particular customer until just prior to delivery. The mere fact that Diasonics was unable to specify the particular unit Davis contracted to buy and trace the exact resale buyer for that unit thus should not foreclose it from recovering lost profits. Without more evidence, we decline to impose upon Diasonics the burden of proving the exact buyer who purchased this particular system in order to qualify as a lost volume seller. . . .

Diasonics is entitled to the benefit of its bargain, no more, no less.

AFFIRMED IN PART, REVERSED IN PART, AND REMANDED for further proceedings not inconsistent with this opinion.

Questions

1. What factors must a plaintiff establish to qualify as a lost volume seller, according to the court's reasoning in *Diasonics*?

2. How did the court determine that Diasonics possessed the capacity to make an additional sale and was actively pursuing all possible leads?

3. Why did the court reject Davis' argument that Diasonics should have precisely identified the resale buyer in order to recover lost profits?

4. What is the usual measure of damages for a seller's breach of contract, and in what circumstances is this measure considered inadequate?

5. Explain the court's reasoning behind awarding damages to Diasonics based on the lost profit it suffered as a lost volume seller.

Takeaways – Diasonics

The measure of damages when the buyer breaches a contract for the sale of goods is the difference between the market price at the time and place for delivery and the unpaid contract price together with any incidental damages but less expenses saved in consequence of the buyer's breach. (UCC § 2-708(1))

In many transactions, the market price will be equal to the contract price and the seller can sell elsewhere at the contract price. In this situation, the resale or market price theories of damages do not fully compensate the seller, because he makes only one profitable sale where he could have made two. The UCC permits a calculation of damages to be based on "the profit (including reasonable overhead) which the seller would have made from full performance by the buyer," whenever damages measured by market price or resale proceeds are "inadequate to put the seller in as good a position as performance would have done." (UCC § 2-708(2)) Damages include incidental expenses and "due allowance for costs reasonably incurred" less "due credit for payments or proceeds of resale."

The "lost volume seller" is the seller who had the capacity not only make the sale that was the subject of the buyer's breach but one additional sale. (One that has a predictable and finite number of customers and that has the capacity either to sell to all new buyers or to make the one additional sale represented by the resale after the breach.) Unless, the seller is allowed to recover the profit from the sale that is the subject of the breach, the seller is not fully compensated. If the seller would have made the profit represented by the resale whether or not the breach occurred, damages measured by the difference between the contract price and the market price cannot put the lost volume seller in as good a position as he or she would have been in had the original buyer performed.

Measure of Damages for Incomplete or Defective Construction

Jacob & Youngs v. Kent
Court of Appeals of New York, 1921
230 N.Y. 239,, 129 N.E. 889, 23 A.L.R. 1429

CARDOZO, J. The plaintiff built a country residence for the defendant at a cost of upwards of $77,000, and now sues to recover a balance of $3,483.46, remaining unpaid. The work of construction ceased in June, 1914, and the defendant then began to occupy the dwelling. There was no complaint of defective performance until March, 1915. One of the specifications for the plumbing work provides that "all wrought iron pipe must be well galvanized, lap welded pipe of the grade known as 'standard pipe' of Reading manufacture." The defendant learned in March, 1915, that some of the pipe, instead of being made in Reading, was the product of other factories. The plaintiff was accordingly directed by the architect to do the work anew. The plumbing was then encased within the walls except in a few places where it had to be exposed. Obedience to the order meant more than the substitution of other pipe. It meant the demolition at great expense of substantial parts of the completed structure. The plaintiff left the work untouched, and asked for a certificate that the final payment was due. Refusal of the certificate was followed by this suit.

The evidence sustains a finding that the omission of the prescribed brand of pipe was neither fraudulent nor willful. It was the result of the oversight and inattention of the plaintiff's subcontractor. Reading pipe is distinguished from Cohoes pipe and other brands only by the name of the manufacturer stamped upon it at intervals of between six and seven feet. Even the defendant's architect, though he inspected the pipe upon arrival, failed to notice the discrepancy. The plaintiff tried to show that the brands installed, though made by other manufacturers, were the same in quality, in appearance, in market value and in cost as the brand stated in the contract, that they were, indeed, the same thing, though manufactured in another place. The evidence was excluded, and a verdict directed for the defendant. The Appellate Division reversed, and granted a new trial. . . .

In the circumstances of this case, we think the measure of the allowance is not the cost of replacement, which would be great, but the difference in value, which would be either nominal or nothing. Some of the exposed sections might perhaps have been replaced at moderate expense. The defendant did not limit his demand to them, but treated the plumbing as a unit to be corrected from cellar to roof. In point of fact, the plaintiff never reached the stage at which evidence of the extent of the allowance became necessary. The trial court had excluded evidence that the defect was unsubstantial, and in view of that ruling there was no occasion for the plaintiff to go farther with an offer of proof. We think, however, that the offer, if it had been made, would not of necessity have been defective because directed to difference in value. It is true that in most cases the cost of replacement is the measure (Spence v. Ham, supra). The owner is entitled to the money which will permit him to complete, unless the cost of completion is grossly and unfairly out of proportion to the good to be attained. When that is true, the measure is the difference in value. Specifications call, let us say, for a foundation built of granite quarried in Vermont. On the completion of the building, the owner learns that through the blunder of a subcontractor part of the foundation has been built of granite of the same quality quarried in New Hampshire. The measure of allowance is not the cost of reconstruction. "There may be omissions of that which could not afterwards be supplied exactly as called for by the contract without taking down the building to its foundations, and at the same time the omission may not affect the value of the building for use or otherwise, except so slightly as to be hardly appreciable" (Handy v. Bliss, 204 Mass. 513, 519. Cf. Foeller v. Heintz, 137 Wis. 169, 178; Oberlies v. Bullinger, 132 N. Y. 598, 601; 2 Williston on Contracts, sec. 805, p. 1541). The rule that gives a remedy in cases of substantial performance with compensation for defects of trivial or inappreciable importance, has been developed by the courts as an instrument of justice. The measure of the allowance must be shaped to the same end.

The order should be affirmed, and judgment absolute directed in favor of the plaintiff upon the stipulation, with costs in all courts.

Question

What measure did the court propose for determining the allowance or damages in this case, and why did they reject the cost of replacement as the measure?

Takeaways – Jacob & Youngs v. Kent

When a building contract is incompletely or defectively performed the owner is entitled to damages measured by the cost of repairing the defect or of finishing the construction job. However, if that cost is wholly out of proportion to the loss in value (the difference in value between if built as promised and as it stands) then the measure of damages is merely the difference between the value of the structure if built to specifications and the value it has as constructed. This in some cases will mean that the owner is entitled only to nominal damages. (Rest.2d § 348(2).)

Groves v. John Wunder Co.
Supreme Court of Minnesota, 1939
205 Minn. 163, 286 N.W. 235

STONE, Justice. Action for breach of contract. Plaintiff got judgment for a little over $15,000. Sorely disappointed by that sum, he appeals.

In August, 1927, S. J. Groves & Sons Company, a corporation (hereinafter mentioned simply as Groves), owned a tract of 24 acres of Minneapolis suburban real estate. It was served or easily could be reached by railroad trackage. It is zoned as heavy industrial property. But for lack of development of the neighborhood its principal value thus far may have been in the deposit of sand and gravel which it carried. The Groves company had a plant on the premises for excavating and screening the gravel. Nearby defendant owned and was operating a similar plant.

In August, 1927, Groves and defendant made the involved contract. For the most part it was a lease from Groves, as lessor, to defendant, as lessee; its term seven years. Defendant agreed to remove the sand and gravel and to leave the property "at a uniform grade, substantially the same as the grade now existing at the roadway * * * on said premises, and that in stripping the overburden * * * it will use said overburden for the purpose of maintaining and establishing said grade."

Under the contract defendant got the Groves screening plant. The transfer thereof and the right to remove the sand and gravel made the consideration moving from Groves to defendant, except that defendant incidentally got rid of Groves as a competitor. On defendant's part it paid Groves $105,000. So that from the outset, on Groves' part the contract was executed except for defendant's [165] right to continue using the property for the stated term. (Defendant had a right to renewal which it did not exercise.)

Defendant breached the contract deliberately. It removed from the premises only "the richest and best of the gravel" and wholly failed, according to the findings, "to perform and comply with the terms, conditions, and provisions of said lease * * * with respect to the condition in which the surface of the demised premises was required to be left." Defendant surrendered the premises, not substantially at the grade required by the contract "nor at any uniform grade." Instead, the ground was "broken, rugged, and uneven." Plaintiff sues as assignee and successor in right of Groves.

As the contract was construed below, the finding is that to complete its performance 288,495 cubic yards of overburden would need to be excavated, taken from the premises, and deposited elsewhere. The reasonable cost of doing that was found to be upwards of $60,000. But, if defendant had left the premises at the uniform grade required by the lease, the reasonable value of the property on the determinative date would have been only $12,160. The judgment was for that sum, including interest, thereby nullifying plaintiff's claim that cost of completing the contract rather than difference in value of the land was the measure of damages. The gauge of damage adopted by the decision was the difference between the market value of plaintiff's land in the condition it was when the contract was made and what it would have been if defendant had performed. The one question for us arises upon plaintiff's assertion that he was entitled, not to that difference in value, but to the reasonable cost to him of doing the work called for by the contract which defendant left undone.

Defendant's breach of contract was wilful. There was nothing of good faith about it. Hence, that the decision below handsomely rewards bad faith and deliberate breach of contract is obvious. That is not allowable. Here the rule is well settled, and has been since Elliott v. Caldwell, 43 Minn. 357, 45 N.W. 845, 9 L.R.A. 52, that, where the contractor wilfully and fraudulently varies from the terms of a construction contract, he cannot sue thereon and have the benefit of the equitable doctrine of substantial performance. That is the rule generally. See Annotation, "Wilful or intentional variation by contractor from terms of contract in regard to material or work as affecting measure of damages," 6 A.L.R. 137.

Jacob & Youngs, Inc. v. Kent, 230 N.Y. 239, 243, 244, 129 N.E. 889, 891, 23 A.L.R. 1429, is typical. It was a case of substantial performance of a building contract. (This case is distinctly the opposite.) Mr. Justice Cardozo, in the course of his opinion, stressed the distinguishing features. "Nowhere," he said, "will change be tolerated, however, if it is so dominant or pervasive as in any real or substantial measure to frustrate the purpose of the contract." Again, "the willful transgressor must accept the penalty of his transgression."

In reckoning damages for breach of a building or construction contract, the law aims to give the disappointed promisee, so far as money will do it, what he was promised. 9 Am.Jur. Building and Construction Contracts, § 152. It is so ruled by a long line of decisions in this state, beginning with Carli v. Seymour, Sabin & Co., 26 Minn. 276, 3 N.W. 348, where the contract was for building a road. There was a breach. Plaintiff was held entitled to recover what it would cost to complete the grading as contemplated by the contract. For our other similar cases, see 2 Dunnell, Minn. Dig. (2 ed. & Supp.) §§ 2561, 2565.

Never before, so far as our decisions show, has it even been suggested that lack of value in the land furnished to the contractor who had bound himself to improve it any escape from the ordinary consequences of a breach of the contract. . . .

Even in case of substantial performance in good faith, the resulting defects being remediable, it is error to instruct that the measure of damage is "the difference in value between the house as it was and as it would have been if constructed according to contract." The "correct doctrine" is that the cost of remedying the defect is the "proper" measure of damages. Snider v. Peters Home Building Co., 139 Minn. 413, 414, 416, 167 N.W. 108.

Value of the land (as distinguished from the value of the intended product of the contract, which ordinarily will be equivalent to its reasonable cost) is no proper part of any measure of damages for wilful breach of a building contract. The reason is plain.

The summit from which to reckon damages from trespass to real estate is its actual value at the moment. The owner's only right is to be compensated for the deterioration in value caused by the tort. That is all he has lost. 1 But not so if a contract to improve the same land has been breached by the contractor who refuses to do the work, especially where, as here, he has been paid in advance. The summit from which to reckon damages for that wrong is the hypothetical peak of accomplishment (not value) which would [168] have been reached had the work been done as demanded by the contract.

The owner's right to improve his property is not trammeled by its small value. It is his right to erect thereon structures which will reduce its value. If that be the result, it can be of no aid to any contractor who declines performance. As said long ago in Chamberlain v. Parker, 45 N.Y. 569, 572: "A man may do what he will with his own, * * * and if he chooses to erect a monument to his caprice or folly on his premises, and employs and pays another to do it, it does not lie with a defendant who has been so employed and paid for building it, to say that his own performance would not be beneficial to the plaintiff." To the same effect is Restatement, Contracts, § 346, p. 576, Illustrations of Subsection (1), par. 4.

Suppose a contractor were suing the owner for breach of a grading contract such as this. Would any element of value, or lack of it, in the land have any relevance in reckoning damages? Of course not. The contractor would be compensated for what he had lost, i. e., his profit. Conversely, in such a case as this, the owner is entitled to compensation for what he has lost, that is, the work or structure which he has been promised, for which he has paid, and of which he has been deprived by the contractor's breach.

To diminish damages recoverable against him in proportion as there is presently small value in the land would favor the faithless contractor. It would also ignore and so defeat plaintiff's right to contract and build for the future. To justify such a course would require more of the prophetic vision than judges possess. This factor is important when the subject matter is trackage property in the margin of such an area of population and industry as that of the Twin Cities.

The genealogy of the error pervading the argument contra is easy to trace. It begins with Seely v. Alden, 61 Pa. 302, 100 Am.Dec. 642, a tort case for pollution of a stream. Resulting depreciation in value of plaintiff's premises, of course, was the measure of damages. About 40 years later, in Bigham v. Wabash-Pittsburg T. Ry., 223 Pa. 106, 72 A. 318, the measure of damages of the earlier tort case was used in one for breach of contract, without comment or explanation to show why. . . .

The objective of this contract of present importance was the improvement of real estate. That makes irrelevant the rules peculiar to damages to chattels, arising from tort or breach of contract. . . . In tort, the thing lost is money value, nothing more. But under a construction contract, the thing lost by a breach such as we have here is a physical structure or accomplishment, a promised and paid for alteration in land. That is the "injury" for which the law gives him compensation. Its only appropriate measure is the cost of performance.

It is suggested that because of little or no value in his land the owner may be unconscionably enriched by such a reckoning. The answer is that there can be no unconscionable enrichment, no advantage upon which the law will frown, when the result is but to give one party to a contract only what the other has promised; particularly where, as here, the delinquent has had full payment for the promised performance.

It is said by the Restatement, Contracts, § 346, comment b: "Sometimes defects in a completed structure cannot be physically remedied without tearing down and rebuilding, at a cost that would be imprudent and unreasonable. The law does not require damages to be measured by a method requiring such economic waste. If no such waste is involved, the cost of remedying the defect is the amount awarded as compensation for failure to render the promised performance."

The "economic waste" declaimed against by the decisions applying that rule has nothing to do with the value in money of the real estate, or even with the product of the contract. The waste avoided is only that which would come from wrecking a physical structure, completed, or nearly so, under the contract. The cases applying that rule go no further. Illustrative are Buchholz v. Rosenberg, 163 Wis. 312, 156 N.W. 946; Burmeister v. Wolfgram, 175 Wis. 506, 185 N.W. 517. Absent such waste, as it is in this case, the rule of the Restatement, Contracts, § 346, is that "the cost of remedying the defect is the amount awarded as compensation for failure to render the promised performance." That means that defendants here are liable to plaintiff for the reasonable cost of doing what defendants promised to do and have willfully declined to do.

It follows that there must be a new trial. The initial question will be as to the proper construction of the contract. Thus far the case has been considered from the standpoint of the construction adopted by plaintiff and acquiesced in, very likely for strategic reasons, by defendants. The question has not been argued here, so we intimate no opinion concerning it, but we put the question whether the contract required removal from the premises of any overburden. The requirement in that respect was that the overburden should be used for the purpose of "establishing and maintaining" the grade. A uniform slope and grade were doubtless required. But whether, if it could not be accomplished without removal and deposit elsewhere of large amounts of overburden, the contract required as a condition that the grade everywhere should be as low as the one recited as "now existing at the roadway" is a question for initial consideration below.

The judgment must be reversed with a new trial to follow.

Questions

1. What was the measure of damages sought by the plaintiff in this case?

2. According to the court's ruling, what is the appropriate measure of damages for a breach of a building contract?

3. Why did the court reject the argument that lack of value in the land should diminish the damages recoverable for the breach of a building contract?

Takeaways – Groves v. John Wunder

So how do you reconcile the different outcomes in this case and *Jacob & Youngs*? Neither builder built the house to specifications as promised yet one gets off with only paying nominal damages while the other is likely on the hook for the full cost of remedying the defect. Perhaps the answer lies in this sentence? "[T]he willful transgressor must accept the penalty of his transgression."

Limitations On Damages

Avoidability

Rockingham County v. Luten Bridge Co.
U.S. Circuit Court of Appeals, Fourth Circuit, 1929
35 F.2d 301

PARKER, Circuit Judge. This was an action at law instituted in the court below by the Luten Bridge Company, as plaintiff, to recover of Rockingham county, North Carolina, an amount alleged to be due under a contract for the construction of a bridge. The county admits the execution and breach of the contract, but contends that notice of cancellation was given the bridge company before the erection of the bridge was commenced, and that it is liable only for the damages which the company would have sustained, if it had abandoned construction at that time....

As the county now admits the execution and validity of the contract, and the breach on its part, the ultimate question in the case is one as to the measure of plaintiff's recovery, and the exceptions must be considered with this in mind. Upon these exceptions, three principal questions arise for our consideration, viz.: . . . (3) whether plaintiff, if the notices are to be deemed action by the county, can recover under the contract for work done after they were received, or is limited to the recovery of damages for breach of contract as of that date. . . .

Coming, then, to the third question i. e., as to the measure of plaintiff's recovery we do not think that, after the county had given notice, while the contract was still executory, that it did not desire the bridge built and would not pay for it, plaintiff could proceed to build it and recover the contract price. It is true that the county had no right to rescind the contract, and the notice given plaintiff amounted to a breach on its part; but, after plaintiff had received notice of the breach, it was its duty to do nothing to increase the damages flowing therefrom. If A enters into a binding contract to build a house for B, B, of course, has no right to rescind the contract without A's consent. But if, before the house is built, he decides that he does not want it, and notifies A to that effect, A has no right to proceed with the building and thus pile up damages. His remedy is to treat the contract as broken when he receives the notice, and sue for the recovery of such damages as he may have sustained from the breach, including any profit which he would have realized upon performance, as well as any other losses which may have resulted to him. In the case at bar, the county decided not to build the road of which the bridge was to be a part, and did not build it. The bridge, built in the midst of the forest, is of no value to the county because of this change of circumstances. When, therefore, the county gave notice to the plaintiff that it would not proceed with the project, plaintiff should have desisted from further work. It had no right thus to pile up damages by proceeding with the erection of a useless bridge.

The contrary view was expressed by Lord Cockburn in Frost v. Knight, L. R. 7 Ex. 111, but, as pointed out by Prof. Williston (Williston on Contracts, vol. 3, p. 2347), it is not in harmony with the decisions in this country. The American rule and the reasons supporting it are well stated by Prof. Williston as follows:

"There is a line of cases running back to 1845 which holds that, after an absolute repudiation or refusal to perform by one party to a contract, the other party cannot continue to perform and recover damages based on full performance. This rule is only a particular application of the general rule of damages that a plaintiff cannot hold a defendant liable for damages which need not have been incurred; or, as it is often stated, the plaintiff must, so far as he can without loss to himself, mitigate the damages caused by the defendant's wrongful act. The application of this rule to the matter in question is obvious. If a man engages to have work done, and afterwards repudiates his contract before the work has been begun or when it has been only partially done, it is inflicting damage on the defendant without benefit to the plaintiff to allow the latter to insist on proceeding with the contract. The work may be useless to the defendant, and yet he would be forced to pay the full contract price. On the other hand, the plaintiff is interested only in the profit he will make out of the contract. If he receives this it is equally advantageous for him to use his time otherwise."...

Judgment reversed.

Questions

1. According to the court's reasoning, why couldn't the plaintiff proceed to build the bridge and recover the contract price after receiving notice of the county's breach?

2. What analogy does the court use to explain the plaintiff's duty upon receiving notice of the breach?

3. How does the court explain the effect of the county's decision not to build the road on the value of the bridge?

4. What is the American rule regarding damages in cases of absolute repudiation or refusal to perform a contract, as described by Professor Williston?

Takeaways – Rockingham County v. Luten Bridge

A party cannot recover for loss which they could have avoided or mitigated through their reasonable efforts. (Rest.2d § 350.) This is often referred to as the "duty to mitigate." But calling it a "duty" is a misnomer. The non-breaching party is not under an affirmative obligation to mitigate. They just can't recover any damages they could have reasonably avoided.

Parker v. Twentieth Century-Fox Film Corp.
Supreme Court of California, 1970
3 Cal.3d 176, 474 P.2d 689

BURKE, J. Defendant Twentieth Century-Fox Film Corporation appeals from a summary judgment granting to plaintiff the recovery of agreed compensation under a written contract for her services as an actress in a motion picture. As will appear, we have concluded that the trial court correctly ruled in plaintiff's favor and that the judgment should be affirmed.

Shirley MacLaine Parker

Plaintiff is well known as an actress, and in the contract between plaintiff and defendant is sometimes referred to as the "Artist." Under the contract, dated August 6, 1965, plaintiff was to play the female lead in defendant's contemplated production of a motion picture entitled "Bloomer Girl." The contract provided that defendant would pay plaintiff a minimum "guaranteed compensation" of $53,571.42 per week for 14 weeks commencing May 23, 1966, for a total of $750,000. Prior to May 1966 defendant decided not to produce the picture and by a letter dated April 4, 1966, it notified plaintiff of that decision and that it would not "comply with our obligations to you under" the written contract.

By the same letter and with the professed purpose "to avoid any damage to you," defendant instead offered to employ plaintiff as the leading actress in another film tentatively entitled "Big Country, Big Man" (hereinafter, "Big Country"). The compensation offered was identical, as were 31 of the 34 numbered provisions or articles of the original contract. Unlike "Bloomer Girl," however, which was to have been a musical production, "Big Country" was a dramatic "western type" movie. "Bloomer Girl" was to have been filmed in California; "Big Country" was to be produced in Australia. Also, certain terms in the proffered contract varied from those of the original. fn. 2 Plaintiff was given one week within which to accept; she did not and the offer lapsed. Plaintiff then commenced this action seeking recovery of the agreed guaranteed compensation.

The complaint sets forth two causes of action. The first is for money due under the contract; the second, based upon the same allegations as the first, is for damages resulting from defendant's breach of contract. Defendant in its answer admits the existence and validity of the contract, that plaintiff complied with all the conditions, covenants and promises and stood ready to complete the performance, and that defendant breached and "anticipatorily repudiated" the contract. It denies, however, that any money is due to plaintiff either under the contract or as a result of its breach, and pleads as an affirmative defense to both causes of action plaintiff's allegedly deliberate failure to mitigate damages, asserting that she unreasonably refused to accept its offer of the leading role in "Big Country."

Plaintiff moved for summary judgment under Code of Civil Procedure section 437c, the motion was granted, and summary judgment for $750,000 plus interest was entered in plaintiff's favor. This appeal by defendant followed. . . .

As stated, defendant's sole defense to this action which resulted from its deliberate breach of contract is that in rejecting defendant's substitute offer of employment plaintiff unreasonably refused to mitigate damages.

The general rule is that the measure of recovery by a wrongfully discharged employee is the amount of salary agreed upon for the period of service, less the amount which the employer affirmatively proves the employee has earned or with reasonable effort might have earned from other employment. [Citations omitted] However, before projected earnings from other employment opportunities not sought or accepted by the discharged employee can be applied in mitigation, the employer must show that the other employment was comparable, or substantially similar, to that of which the employee has been deprived; the employee's rejection of or failure to seek other available employment of a different or inferior kind may not be resorted to in order to mitigate damages. . . .

In the present case defendant has raised no issue of reasonableness of efforts by plaintiffs to obtain other employment; the sole issue is whether plaintiff's refusal of defendant's substitute offer of "Big Country" may be used in mitigation. Nor, if the "Big Country" offer was of employment different or inferior when compared with the original "Bloomer Girl" employment, is there an issue as to whether or not plaintiff acted reasonably in refusing the substitute offer. Despite defendant's arguments to the contrary, no case cited or which our research has discovered holds or suggests that reasonableness is an element of a wrongfully discharged employee's option to reject, or fail to seek, different or inferior employment lest the possible earnings therefrom be charged against him in mitigation of damages.

Applying the foregoing rules to the record in the present case, with all intendments in favor of the party opposing the summary judgment motion--here, defendant--it is clear that the trial court correctly ruled that plaintiff's failure to accept defendant's tendered substitute employment could not be applied in mitigation of damages because the offer of the "Big Country" lead was of employment both different and inferior, and that no factual dispute was presented on that issue. The mere circumstance that "Bloomer Girl" was to be a musical review calling upon plaintiff's talents as a dancer as well as an actress, and was to be produced in the City of Los Angeles, whereas "Big Country" was a straight dramatic role in a "Western Type" story taking place in an opal mine in Australia, demonstrates the difference in kind between the two employments; the female lead as a dramatic actress in a western style motion picture can by no stretch of imagination be considered the equivalent of or substantially similar to the lead in a song-and-dance production. Additionally, the substitute "Big Country" offer proposed to eliminate or impair the director and screenplay approvals accorded to plaintiff under the original "Bloomer Girl" contract and thus constituted an offer of inferior employment. No expertise or judicial notice is required in order to hold that the deprivation or infringement of an employee's rights held under an original employment contract converts the available "other employment" relied upon by the employer to mitigate damages, into inferior employment which the employee need not seek or accept. (See Gonzales v. Internal. Assn. of Machinists, supra, 213 Cal.App.2d 817, 823-824; and fn. 5, post.) . . .

In view of the determination that defendant failed to present any facts showing the existence of a factual issue with respect to its sole defense-- plaintiff's rejection of its substitute employment offer in mitigation of damages--we need not consider plaintiff's further contention that for various reasons, including the provisions of the original contract set forth in footnote 1, ante, plaintiff was excused from attempting to mitigate damages.

The judgment is affirmed.

SULLIVAN, Acting C. J. (dissenting) The basic question in this case is whether or not plaintiff acted reasonably in rejecting defendant's offer of alternate employment. The answer depends upon whether that offer (starring in "Big Country, Big Man") was an offer of work that was substantially similar to her former employment (starring in "Bloomer Girl") or of work that was of a different or inferior kind. To my mind this is a factual issue, which the trial court should not have determined on a motion for summary judgment. The majority have not only repeated this error but have compounded it by applying the rules governing mitigation of damages in the employer-employee context in a misleading fashion. Accordingly, I respectfully dissent.

The familiar rule requiring a plaintiff in a tort or contract action to mitigate damages embodies notions of fairness and socially responsible behavior which are fundamental to our jurisprudence. Most broadly stated, it precludes the recovery of damages which, through the exercise of due diligence, could have been avoided. Thus, in essence, it is a rule requiring reasonable conduct in commercial affairs. This general principle governs the obligations of an employee after his employer has wrongfully repudiated or terminated the employment contract. Rather than permitting the employee simply to remain idle during the balance of the contract period, the law requires him to make a reasonable effort to secure other employment. He is not obliged, however, to seek or accept any and all types of work which may be available. Only work which is in the same field and which is of the same quality need be accepted.

Over the years the courts have employed various phrases to define the type of employment which the employee, upon his wrongful discharge, is under an obligation to accept. Thus in California alone it has been held that he must accept employment which is "substantially similar" (Lewis v. Protective Security Life Ins. Co. (1962) 208 Cal.App.2d 582, 584 [25 Cal.Rptr. 213]; de la Falaise v. Gaumont-British Picture Corp. (1940) 39 Cal.App.2d 461, 469 [103 P.2d 447]); "comparable employment" (Erler v. Five Points Motors, Inc. (1967) 249 Cal.App.2d 560, 562 [57 Cal.Rptr. 516]; Harris v. Nat. Union etc. Cooks, Stewards (1953) 116 Cal.App.2d 759, 761 [254 P.2d 673]); employment "in the same general line of the first employment" (Rotter v. Stationers Corp. (1960) 186 Cal.App.2d 170, 172 [8 Cal. Rptr. 690]); "equivalent to his prior position" (De Angeles v. Roos Bros., Inc. (1966) 244 Cal.App.2d 434, 443 [52 Cal.Rptr. 783]); "employment in a similar capacity" (Silva v. McCoy (1968) 259 Cal.App.2d 256, 260 [66 Cal.Rptr. 364]); employment which is "not ... of a different or inferior kind...." (Gonzales v. Internat. Assn. of Machinists (1963) 213 Cal.App.2d 817, 822 [29 Cal.Rptr. 190].)

For reasons which are unexplained, the majority cite several of these cases yet select from among the various judicial formulations which they contain one particular phrase, "Not of a different or inferior kind," with which to analyze this case. I have discovered no historical or theoretical reason to adopt this phrase, which is simply a negative restatement of the affirmative standards set out in the above cases, as the exclusive standard. Indeed, its emergence is an example of the dubious phenomenon of the law responding not to rational judicial choice or changing social conditions, but to unrecognized changes in the language of opinions or legal treatises. However, the phrase is a serviceable one and my concern is not with its use as the standard but rather with what I consider its distortion.

The relevant language excuses acceptance only of employment which is of a different kind. (Gonzales v. Internat. Assn. of Machinists, supra, 213 Cal.App.2d 817, 822; Harris v. Nat. Union etc. Cooks, Stewards, supra, 116 Cal.App.2d 759, 761; de la Falaise v. Gaumont-British Picture Corp., supra, 39 Cal.App.2d 461, 469.) It has never been the law that the mere existence of differences between two jobs in the same field is sufficient, as a matter of law, to excuse an employee wrongfully discharged from one from accepting the other in order to mitigate damages. Such an approach would effectively eliminate any obligation of an employee to attempt to minimize damage arising from a wrongful discharge. The only alternative job offer an employee would be required to accept would be an offer of his former job by his former employer.

Although the majority appear to hold that there was a difference "in kind" between the employment offered plaintiff in "Bloomer Girl" and that offered in "Big Country" an examination of the opinion makes crystal clear that the majority merely point out differences between the two films (an obvious circumstance) and then apodictically assert that these constitute a difference in the kind of employment. The entire rationale of the majority boils down to this; that the "mere circumstances" that "Bloomer Girl" was to be a musical review while "Big Country" was a straight drama "demonstrates the difference in kind" since a female lead in a western is not "the equivalent of or substantially similar to" a lead in a musical. This is merely attempting to prove the proposition by repeating it. It shows that the vehicles for the display of the star's talents are different but it does not prove that her employment as a star in such vehicles is of necessity different in kind and either inferior or superior.

I believe that the approach taken by the majority (a superficial listing of differences with no attempt to assess their significance) may subvert a valuable legal doctrine. The inquiry in cases such as this should not be whether differences between the two jobs exist (there will always be differences) but whether the differences which are present are substantial enough to constitute differences in the kind of employment or, alternatively, whether they render the substitute work employment of an inferior kind. . . .

I remain convinced that the relevant question in such cases is whether or not a particular contract provision is so significant that its omission creates employment of an inferior kind. This question is, of course, intimately bound up in what I consider the ultimate issue: whether or not the employee acted reasonably. This will generally involve a factual inquiry to ascertain the importance of the particular contract term and a process of weighing the absence of that term against the countervailing advantages of the alternate employment. . . . .

Questions

1. What is the general rule regarding the measure of recovery for a wrongfully discharged employee?

2. Under what circumstances can projected earnings from other employment opportunities be applied in mitigation of damages?

3. How did the court determine that the substitute offer of employment in "Big Country" was different and inferior compared to the original employment in "Bloomer Girl"?

Takeaways – Parker v. Twentieth Century-Fox

A wrongfully discharged or terminated employee is entitled to recover monetary damages caused by the breach. Damages for breach of the employment contract are the amount of compensation agreed upon for the period determined to be a reasonable period that plaintiff's employment would have continued but for the breach of the employment contract less any compensation actually earned by the employee during that period.

An employee who is damaged as a result of a breach of an employment contract by the employer has a duty to take steps to minimize the loss by making a reasonable effort to find comparable employment. If the employee through reasonable efforts could have found comparable employment, any amount that the employee could reasonably have earned by obtaining comparable employment through reasonable efforts shall be deducted from the amount of damages awarded to employee.

So why is the wrongfully discharged employee required to mitigate her damages by seeking similar alternative work? One of the footnotes in the *Parker* case had this to say. "The values of the doctrine of mitigation of damages in this context are that it minimizes the unnecessary personal and social (e.g.. nonproductive use of labor, litigation) costs of contractual failure. If a wrongfully discharged employee can, through his own action and without suffering financial or psychological loss in the process, reduce the damages accruing from the breach of contract, the most sensible policy is to require him to do so. I fear the majority opinion will encourage precisely opposite conduct." (*Parker v. Twentieth Century-Fox, supra,* fn. 5)

Foreseeability as a Limitation on Damages

Hadley v. Baxendale
Court of Exchequer, 1854
9 Exch. 341, 156 Eng.Rep. 145

At the trial before Crompton, J., at the last Gloucester Assizes, it appeared that the plaintiffs carried on an extensive business as millers at Gloucester; and that on the 11th on May, their mill was stopped by a breakage of the crank shaft by which the mill was worked. The steam-engine was manufactured by Messrs. Joyce & Co., the engineers, at Greenwich, and it became necessary to send the shaft as a pattern for a new one to Greenwich. The fracture was discovered on the 12th, and on the 13th the plaintiffs sent one of their servants to the office of the defendants, who are the well-known carriers trading under the name of Pickford & Co., for the purpose of having the shaft carried to Greenwich. The plaintiffs' servant told the clerk that the mill was stopped, and that the shaft must be sent immediately; and in answer to the inquiry when the shaft would be taken, the answer was, that if it was sent up by twelve o'clock any day, it would be delivered at Greenwich on the following day. On the following day the shaft was taken by the defendants, before noon, for the purpose of being conveyed to Greenwich, and the sum of 2l. 4s. was paid for its carriage for the whole distance; at the same time the defendants' clerk was told that a special entry, if required, should be made to hasten its delivery. The delivery of the shaft at Greenwich was delayed by some neglect; and the consequence was, that the plaintiffs did not receive the new shaft for several days after they would otherwise have done, and the working of their mill was thereby delayed, and they thereby lost the profits they would otherwise have received.

On the part of the defendants, it was objected that these damages were too remote, and that the defendants were not liable with respect to them. The learned Judge left the case generally to the jury, who found a verdict with £25 damages beyond the amount paid into Court.

Whateley, in last Michaelmas Term, obtained a rule nisi for a new trial, on the ground of misdirection.

Alderson, B. We think that there ought to be a new trial in this case; but, in so doing, we deem it to be expedient and necessary to state explicitly the rule which the Judge, at the next trial, ought, in our opinion, to direct the jury to be governed by when they estimate the damages.

It is, indeed, of the last importance that we should do this; for, if the jury are left without any definite rule to guide them, it will, in such cases as these, manifestly lead to the greatest injustice. The Courts have done this on several occasions; and, in Blake v. Midland Railway Company, 18 Q.B. 93, the Court granted a new trial on this very ground, that the rule had not been definitely laid down to the jury by the learned Judge at Nisi Prius.

"There are certain established rules," this Court says, in Alder v. Keighley, 15 M. & W. 117,"according to which the jury ought to find." And the Court, in that case, adds: "and here there is a clear rule, that the amount which would have been received if the contract had been kept, is the measure of damages if the contract is broken."

Now we think the proper rule in such a case as the present is this:-- Where two parties have made a contract which one of them has broken, the damages which the other party ought to receive in respect of such breach of contract should be such as may fairly and reasonably be considered either arising naturally, i.e., according to the usual course of things, from such breach of contract itself, or such as may reasonably be supposed to have been in the contemplation of both parties, at the time they made the contract, as the probable result of the breach of it. Now, if the special circumstances under which the contract was actually made were communicated by the plaintiffs to the defendants, and thus known to both parties, the damages resulting from the breach of such a contract, which they would reasonably contemplate, would be the amount of injury which would ordinarily follow from a breach of contract under these special circumstances so known and communicated. But, on the other hand, if these special circumstances were wholly unknown to the party breaking the contract, he, at the most, could only be supposed to have had in his contemplation the amount of injury which would arise generally, and in the great multitude of cases not affected by any special circumstances, from such a breach of contract. For, had the special circumstances been known, the parties might have specially provided for the breach of contract by special terms as to the damages in that case; and of this advantage it would be very unjust to deprive them.

Now the above principles are those by which we think the jury ought to be guided in estimating the damages arising out of any breach of contract. It is said, that other cases such as breaches of contract in the nonpayment of money, or in the not making a good title of land, are to be treated as exceptions from this, and as governed by a conventional rule. But as, in such cases, both parties must be supposed to be cognizant of that well-known rule, these cases may, we think, be more properly classed under the rule above enunciated as to cases under known special circumstances, because there both parties may reasonably be presumed to contemplate the estimation of the amount of damages according to the conventional rule.

Now, in the present case, if we are to apply the principles above laid down, we find that the only circumstances here communicated by the plaintiffs to the defendants at the time of the contract was made, were, that the article to be carried was the broken shaft of a mill, and that the plaintiffs were the millers of the mill. But how do these circumstances shew reasonably that the profits of the mill must be stopped by an unreasonable delay in the delivery of the broken shaft by the carrier to the third person? Suppose the plaintiffs had another shaft in their possession put up or putting up at the time, and that they only wished to send back the broken shaft to the engineer who made it; it is clear that this would be quite consistent with the above circumstances, and yet the unreasonable delay in the delivery would have no effect upon the intermediate profits of the mill. Or, again, suppose that, at the time of the delivery to the carrier, the machinery of the mill had been in other respects defective, then, also, the same results would follow. Here it is true that the shaft was actually sent back to serve as a model for the new one, and that the want of a new one was the only cause of the stoppage of the mill, and that the loss of profits really arose from not sending down the new shaft in proper time, and that this arose from the delay in delivering the broken one to serve as a model. But it is obvious that, in the great multitude of cases of millers sending off broken shafts to third persons by a carrier under ordinary circumstances, such consequences would not, in all probability, have occurred; and these special circumstances were here never communicated by the plaintiffs to the defendants.

It follows therefore, that the loss of profits here cannot reasonably be considered such a consequence of the breach of contract as could have been fairly and reasonably contemplated by both the parties when they made this contract. For such loss would neither have flowed naturally from the breach of this contract in the great multitude of such cases occurring under ordinary circumstances, nor were the special circumstances, which, perhaps, would have made it a reasonable and natural consequence of such breach of contract, communicated to or known by the defendants. The Judge ought, therefore, to have told the jury that upon the facts then before them they ought not to take the loss of profits into consideration at all in estimating the damages. There must therefore be a new trial in this case.

Questions

1. According to the court, what factors should be considered when estimating damages resulting from a breach of contract?

2. Why did the court determine that the loss of profits claimed by the plaintiffs was not a reasonable and natural consequence of the breach of contract in this case?

Takeaways – Hadley v. Baxendale

Contract damages are limited to losses that might reasonably be contemplated or foreseen by the parties. (Rest.2d § 351, Cal.Civ.Code, § 3300) Special damages beyond the expectation of the parties are not recoverable. The measure of general damages for the breach of a contract is that amount which will compensate the injured party for all the detriment or loss caused by the breach, or which in the ordinary course of things, would be likely to result therefrom. The injured party should receive those damages naturally arising from the breach, or those damages which might have been reasonably contemplated or foreseen by both parties, at the time they made the contract, as the probable result of the breach.

The decision in *Hadley* draws an important distinction between "general damages" on the one hand and "special damages" on the other. Now is a good time to familiarize yourself with that distinction.

General Damages

"General damages" are those that flow naturally and typically as a consequence of the breach. General damages are always recoverable because it is presumed that the natural and probable consequences of breach are always within the contemplation of the parties and therefore "foreseeable."

Special Damages

"Special damages" are those that result as a direct consequence of the breach but are peculiar or unique to the injured party's particular situation or circumstances. Special damages are recoverable when special circumstances exist which cause some unusual injury to the non-breaching party. The plaintiff can only recover special damages if defendant knew or should have known of the existence of special circumstances at the time defendant entered into the contract. Any award for special damages must be reasonable. (See, 1 Witkin, Summary of Cal.Law (10th ed. 2005) Contracts § 871-874.)

One category of special damages would be lost profits. These are special damages because not every victim of a breach is looking to resell the property which was the subject of the contract or using the property in their occupation or profession. When the non-breaching party plans to turn around and resell the subject matter of the contract, (or needs it to earn a living) not only do they have the loss of the difference in value between the contract price and the market price (their general damages) They also have special damages in the form of lost profits. Loss of profits, present or future, as an element of special damages, may be recovered for a breach of contract if:

(1) The loss is the direct and natural consequence of the breach,

(2) It is reasonably probable that the profits would have been earned except for the breach, and

(3) The amount of loss can be shown with reasonable certainty.

If future loss of profits is reasonably certain, any reasonable basis for determining the amount of the probable profits lost is acceptable. (See, Cal.Civ.Code § 3301; 1 Witkin, Summary of Cal.Law (10th ed. 2005) Contracts § 879 - 882.)

In order to earn some extra money, a law student uses her car on weekends to drive for Uber, a ride sharing service. If she takes the car to the mechanic on Thursday and he promises to get it back to her by 5pm Friday but fails to do so, she is entitled to the rental value of the car for each day its delivery is delayed for those represent her general damages. The natural and typical consequence of the breach is loss of her car and the substitutionary remedy is the amount of money it would cost to secure a replacement vehicle on a per day basis. Her loss of profits from not being able to drive for Uber would be her special damages (assuming she didn't rent a replacement car). However, to be recoverable, the car mechanic would have to have been on notice that she was using her car to earn money driving for Uber.

Sun-Maid Raisin Growers v. Victor Packing Co.
California Court of Appeals, 1983
146 Cal.App.3d 787, 194 Cal.Rptr. 612

FRANSON, Acting P. J. Plaintiff and respondent Sun-Maid Raisin Growers of California (hereinafter Sun-Maid) filed a complaint against defendants and appellants Victor Packing Company and Pyramid Packing Company (hereinafter appellants or Victor). The complaint for injunctive relief, specific performance and damages alleged appellants had breached agreements to sell Sun-Maid 1,800 tons of raisins from the 1975 raisin crop by repudiating the contracts and refusing to deliver 610 tons of raisins which remained to be delivered under the contracts. The repudiation allegedly occurred on August 10, 1976.

After a court trial, judgment was issued in favor of Sun-Maid, holding appellants jointly liable for damages of $247,383, and Victor additionally liable for damages of $59,956, for a total of $307,339. In addition, Sun-Maid recovered its costs of suit. Findings of fact and conclusions of law were filed. After denial of appellants' motion for new trial, a timely appeal was filed. . . . .

V. Damages Were Foreseeable

Appellants' precise argument on appeal is that the damages award of $295,339.40 for lost profits is excessive because "the amount of lost profits was unforeseeable by either party when the contracts were formed," citing Hadley v. Baxendale (1854) 9 Ex. 341, 156 Eng.Rep. 145. According to appellants, the foreseeability requirement applies not only to the fact that some profits might be lost as a result of the breach but also to the amount of profits thereby lost. Thus, "the foreseeability of extraordinary profits must itself be proved, even if the fact of ordinary ... profits is either presumed or otherwise proved to be within the parties' contemplation." Appellants hinge their argument on the fact that the new crop in September was reduced in quantity and quality by "disastrous" rains which resulted in an extraordinary increase in the market price of raisins in November and December 1976.

Preliminarily, we observe that appellants made no foreseeability objection to Sun-Maid's evidence of damages at trial. It was only in appellants' post-trial brief that they argued the point. Furthermore, appellants filed no objections to Sun-Maid's proposed findings on damages and made no request for a specific finding on the foreseeability question.

We also observe that unless it can be ruled on as a matter of law, the question whether the buyer's consequential damages were foreseeable by the seller is one of fact to be determined by the trier of fact. (See Annot. (1979) 96 A.L.R.3d 299, 329, § 4b.) If supported by the evidence, the decision cannot be overturned on appeal.

The basic measure of damages for a seller's nondelivery or repudiation is the difference between the market price and the contract price. (Cal. U. Com. Code, § 2713.) The market price to be used as the basis of the calculation is the market to which a buyer would normally go to effect cover. (§ 2713, subd. (2); 1 Cal. Commercial Law (Cont.Ed.Bar 1966) § 12.15, pp. 562-563.) Market price is measured as of the time the buyer learned of the breach--in this case August 10--at which time he could be expected to seek cover. (§ 2713, subd. (1).)

If evidence of a price prevailing at the appropriate time or place "is not readily available," the price prevailing within a reasonable time before or after may be used. (§ 2723, subd. (2).)
In addition to the difference between the market price and the contract price, the buyer can recover incidental damages such as expenses of cover (§ 2715, subd. (1)) and consequential damages such as lost profits (§ 2715, subd. (2)(a)) to the extent they could not have been avoided by cover. The inability to cover after a prompt and

reasonable effort to do so is a prerequisite to recovery of consequential damages. (Ibid) If the buyer is only able to cover in part, he is entitled to the net cost of cover (the difference between the cover price and the contract price plus expenses) together with any consequential damages as hereinafter defined (§ 2715) but less expenses saved in consequence of the seller's breach (§ 2712).

Under section 2715, subdivision (2)(a), consequential damages include "[a]ny loss resulting from general or particular requirements and needs of which the seller at the time of contracting had reason to know and which could not reasonably be prevented by cover or otherwise; ..." The "reason to know" language concerning the buyer's particular requirements and needs arises from Hadley v. Baxendale, supra, 9 Ex. 347, 156 Eng.Rep. 145 (see Dunn, Recovery of Damages for Lost Profits in California (1974-75) 9 U.S.F.L.Rev. 415). The code, however, has imposed an objective rather than a subjective standard in determining whether the seller should have anticipated the buyer's needs. Thus, actual knowledge by the seller of the buyer's requirements is not required. The only requirement under section 2715, subdivision (2)(a), is that the seller reasonably should have been expected to know of the buyer's exposure to loss. (Id, at pp. 420-421.)

Furthermore, comment 6 to section 2715 provides that if the seller knows that the buyer is in the business of reselling the goods, the seller is charged with knowledge that the buyer will be selling the goods in anticipation of a profit. "Absent a contractual provision against consequential damages a seller in breach [will] therefore always be liable for the buyer's resulting loss of profit." (1 Cal. Commercial Law, supra, § 12.20, p. 568, citing Stott v. Johnston (1951) 36 Cal.2d 864 [229 P.2d 348, 28 A.L.R.2d 580].)

Finally, a buyer's failure to take any other steps by which the loss could reasonably have been prevented bars him from recovering consequential damages. (§ 2715, subd. (2)(a).) This is merely a codification of the rule that the buyer must attempt to minimize damages. (1 Witkin, Summary of Cal. Law (8th ed. 1973) Contracts, §§ 639-640, 670-674.)

In the present case, the evidence fully supports the finding that after appellants' breach of the contract on August 10, 1976, Sun-Maid acted in good faith in a commercially reasonable manner and was able to cover by purchase of only some 200 tons of substitute raisins at a cost of 43 cents per pound. ($860 per packed weight ton.) There were no other natural Thompson seedless free tonnage raisins available for purchase in the market at or within a reasonable time after appellants' breach. Although the evidence indicates that Sun-Maid actually was able to purchase an additional 410 tons of raisins after the September rainfall in their efforts to effect cover, these were badly damaged raisins which had to be reconditioned at a substantial cost to bring them up to market condition. According to Sun-Maid, if the trial court had used the total cost of cover of the full 610 tons as the measure of damages rather than lost profits on resale, their damages would have totaled $377,720.

Although the trial court did not specify why it determined damages by calculating lost profits instead of the cost of cover (no findings were requested), the court probably found that damages should be limited to the amount that would have put Sun-Maid in "as good a position as if the other party had fully performed." (§ 1106.) Thus, Sun-Maid was awarded the lesser of the actual cost of cover (treating the reconditioning of the 410 tons as a cost) and the loss of prospective profits.

In contending the foreseeability requirement applies to the amount of the lost profits and not just to the fact of lost profits, appellants apparently acknowledge that they knew at the time of contracting that Sun-Maid would be reselling the raisins to its customers in the domestic market. Appellants have no alternative to this concession since they were experienced packers and knew that Sun-Maid marketed raisins year round in the domestic market. They also knew that Sun-Maid substituted reserve raisins into their free tonnage in place of appellants' raisins which were shipped to Japan. Furthermore, appellants must be presumed to have known that if they did not deliver the full quota of raisins provided under the contracts (1,800 tons) by the end of the crop year or before such reasonable time as thereafter might be agreed to, Sun-Maid would be forced to go into the market to attempt to cover its then existing orders for sale of raisins. This is exactly what occurred. When Peterson called Sahatdjian on August 10 and requested some 38 tons of raisins and Sahatdjian refused the order, Peterson stated, "Well, we have orders here to fill; and I'll have to tell Frank Light about it." Within five minutes, Light called Sahatdjian and demanded to know what was going on. Sahatdjian again refused to deliver as requested but said he "would be glad" to deliver when the new crop came in.

A reasonable inference arises that apart from appellants' breach of contract, they intended to fulfill their obligations to Sun-Maid by acquiring raisins from the new crop which would be available in October. The fact that Sun-Maid requested only 38 tons on August 10 suggests that Sun-Maid also understood that appellants intended to deliver the balance of the raisins from the new crop.

The contemplation of the parties in August was consistent with Sun-Maid's industry-wide announcement in November 1975 that it needed raisins for sale in the domestic market "through 1976."

When the contract for sale involves repeated occasions for performance by either party with the knowledge of the nature of the performance and opportunity for objection to it by the other, any performance accepted or acquiesced in without objection shall be relevant to determining the meaning of the agreement. (§ 2208, subd. (1).) Since appellants had delivered only 1,190 tons by August and the amount of each delivery had been within their discretion, Sun-Maid's reliance on appellants' future performance of the contract by accepting orders from the domestic market must have been within the parties' contemplation. Thus, appellants had "reason to know" that their failure to deliver the 610 tons before the new crop came in would result in lost profits on resales by Sun-Maid. . . .

The possibility of "disastrous" rain damage to the 1976 raisin crop was clearly foreseeable to appellants. Such rains have occurred at sporadic intervals since raisins have been grown in the San Joaquin Valley. Raisin packers fully understand the great risk in contracting to sell raisins at a fixed price over a period of time extending into the next crop year. The market price may go up or down depending on consumer demand and the supply and quality of raisins. If the seller does not have sufficient inventory to fulfill his delivery obligations within the time initially required or as subsequently modified by the parties, he will have to go into the market to purchase raisins. The fact that he may be surprised by an extraordinary rise in the market price does not mean that the buyer's prospective profits on resale are unforeseeable as a matter of law.

Once the trial court found that the contracts did not end either by March 1 or June 30, appellants were required to deliver the balance of the raisins by September 1 or by such further time as the parties would have agreed to if the contracts had not been breached on August 10. Sun-Maid's damages for the cost of cover and lost profits on prospective resale were the natural, foreseeable and inevitable result of appellants' failure to deliver according to the contracts.

The judgment is affirmed.

Questions

1. According to the court's ruling, what is the standard for determining whether the buyer's consequential damages were foreseeable by the seller?

2. Explain the court's reasoning behind the measure of damages for a seller's nondelivery or repudiation.

3. Why did the court determine that the damages should be limited to the amount that would have put Sun-Maid in "as good a position as if the other party had fully performed"?

4. What factors did the court consider in determining whether the seller should have anticipated the buyer's needs and potential loss?

5. Why did the court conclude that Sun-Maid's damages for the cost of cover and lost profits on prospective resale were the natural, foreseeable, and inevitable result of appellants' failure to deliver according to the contracts?

Punitive Damages for Breach of Contract

White v. Benkowski
Supreme Court of Wisconsin, 1967
37 Wis. 2D 285, 155 N.W.2d 74

[In 1962, the Whites bought a house that lacked its own water supply but was connected by pipes to a well on the adjacent property owned by the Benkowskis. The Whites entered into a written contract with the Benkowskis whereby the latter promised to supply water to the Whites' home for ten years. Although the relationship between the neighbors began as a friendly one, within two years it had become hostile. During March and June of 1964 the Benkowskis shut off the water supply on nine occasions. The Whites sued the Benkowskis for breach of contract, seeking compensatory and punitive damages. The jury found that the Benkowskis had shut off the water maliciously in order to harass the Whites. The jury awarded the Whites $10 in compensatory damages and $2,000 in punitive damages. The trial judge reduced the compensatory award to $1 and allowed no recovery at all for punitive damages. The Whites appealed.]

WILKIE, J. Two issues are raised on this appeal.

1. Was the trial court correct in reducing the award of compensatory damages from $10 to $1?

2. Are punitive damages available in actions for breach of contract?

Reduction of Jury Award.

The evidence of damage adduced during the trial here was that the water supply had been shut off during several short periods. Three incidents of inconvenience resulting from these shut-offs were detailed by the plaintiffs. Mrs. White testified that the lack of water in the bathroom on one occasion caused an odor and that on two other occasions she was forced to take her children to a neighbor's home to bathe them. Based on this evidence, the court instructed the jury that:

". . .in an action for a breach of contract the plaintiff is entitled to such damages as shall have been sustained by him which resulted naturally and directly from the breach if you find that the defendants did in fact breach the contract. Such damages include pecuniary loss and inconvenience suffered as a natural result of the breach and are called compensatory damages. In this case the plaintiffs have proved no pecuniary damages which you or the Court could compute. In a situation where there has been a breach of contract which you find to have damaged the plaintiff but form which the plaintiffs have proven no actual damages, the plaintiffs may recover nominal damages

"By nominal damages is meant trivial trivial sum of money."

Plaintiffs did not object to this instruction. In the trial court's decision on motions after verdict it states that the court so instructed the jury because, based on the fact that the plaintiffs paid for services they did not receive, their loss in proportion to the contract rate was approximately 25 cents. This rationale indicates that the court disregarded or overlooked Mrs. White's testimony of inconvenience. In viewing the evidence most favorable to the plaintiffs, there was some injury. The plaintiffs are not required to ascertain their damages with mathematical precision, but rather the trier of fact must set damages a reasonable amount. Notwithstanding this instruction, the jury set the plaintiffs' damages at $10. The court was in error in reducing that amount to $1.

The jury finding of $10 in actual damages, though small, takes it out of the mere nominal status. The award is predicated on an actual injury. This was not the situation present in Sunderman v. Warnken. [247 Wis. 472, 29 N.W.2d 496 (1947)] Sunderman was a wrongful-entry action by a tenant against his landlord. No actual injury could be shown by the mere fact that the landlord entered the tenant's apartment, therefore damages were nominal and no punitive award could be made. Here there was credible evidence which showed inconvenience and thus actual injury, and the jury's finding as to compensatory damages should be reinstated.

Punitive Damages.

"If a man shall steal an ox, or a sheep, and kill it, or sell it; he shall restore five oxen for an ox, and four sheep for a sheep."

Over one hundred years ago this court held that, under proper circumstances, a plaintiff was entitled to recover exemplary or punitive damages. . . .

In Wisconsin compensatory damages are given to make whole the damage or injury suffered by the injured party. On the other hand, punitive damages are given". . . . on the basis of punishment to the injured party not because he has been injured, which injury has been compensated with compensatory damages, but to punish the wrongdoer for his malice and to deter others from like conduct."

Thus we reach the question of whether the plaintiffs are entitled to punitive damages for a breach of the water agreement. The overwhelming weight of authority supports the proposition that punitive damages are not recoverable in actions for breach of contract. In Chitty on Contracts, the author states that the right to receive punitive damages for breach on contract is now confined to the single case of damages for breach of a promise to marry.

Simpson states: "Although damages in excess of compensation for loss are in some instances permitted in tort actions by way of punishment ... in contract actions the damages recoverable are limited to compensation for pecuniary loss sustained by the breach." Corbin states that as a general rule punitive damages are not recoverable for breach of contract.

In Wisconsin, the early case of Gordon v. Brewster [7 Wis. 309 (1858)] involved the breach of an employment contract. The trial court instructed the jury that if the nonperformance of the contract was attributable to the defendant's wrongful act of discharging the plaintiff, then that would go to increase the damages sustained. On appeal, this court said that the instruction was unfortunate and might have led the jurors to suppose that they could give something more than actual compensation in a breach of contract case. We find no Wisconsin case in which breach of contract (other than breach of promise to marry)[14] has led to the award of punitive damages.

Persuasive authority from other jurisdictions supports the proposition (without exception) that punitive damages are not available in breach of contract actions. This is true even if the breach, as in the instant case, is wilful.

Although it is well recognized that breach of a contractual duty may be a tort, in such situations the contract creates the relation out of which grows the duty to use care in the performance of a responsibility prescribed by the contract. Not so here. No tort was pleaded or proved.

Reversed in part by reinstating the jury verdict relating to compensatory damages and otherwise affirmed. Costs to appellants.

Questions

1. What is the distinction between compensatory damages and punitive damages?

2. According to the court's analysis, are punitive damages available in actions for breach of contract?

Takeaways – White v. Benkowski

Damages for breach of contract may not be punitive or exemplary and may not be imposed as a form of chastisement. (Rest.2d § 355, Cal.Civ.Code, § 3294; *Foley v. Interactive Data Corp.* (1988) 47 Cal.3d 654, 254 Cal.Rptr. 211, 765 P.2d 373.) Punitive damages are awarded in a tort action to punish malicious or willful and wanton conduct. The purpose of such an award is to deter or make an example of the defendant.

Damages for Emotional Distress

As a general rule, damages will not be awarded to compensate for the mental distress or emotional trauma that may be caused by a breach of contract. (Rest.2d § 353) The next two cases demonstrate the general rule and an exception.

Erlich v. Menezes
Supreme Court of California, 1999
21 Cal.4th 543, 87 Cal.Rptr.2d 886, 981 P.2d 978

BROWN, J. We granted review in this case to determine whether emotional distress damages are recoverable for the negligent breach of a contract to construct a house. A jury awarded the homeowners the full cost necessary to repair their home as well as damages for emotional distress caused by the contractor's negligent performance. Since the contractor's negligence directly caused only economic injury and property damage, and breached no duty independent of the contract, we conclude the homeowners may not recover damages for emotional distress based upon breach of a contract to build a house.

Both parties agree with the facts as ascertained by the Court of Appeal. Barry and Sandra Erlich contracted with John Menezes, a licensed general contractor, to build a "dream house" on their ocean-view lot. The Erlichs moved into their house in December 1990. In February 1991, the rains came. "[T]he house leaked from every conceivable location. Walls were saturated in [an upstairs bedroom], two bedrooms downstairs, and the pool room. Nearly every window in the house leaked. The living room filled with three inches of standing water. In several locations water 'poured in streams' from the ceilings and walls. The ceiling in the garage became so saturated ... the plaster liquefied and fell in chunks to the floor."

Menezes's attempts to stop the leaks proved ineffectual. Caulking placed around the windows melted, " 'ran down [the] windows and stained them and ran across the driveway and ran down the house [until it] ... looked like someone threw balloons with paint in them at the house.' " Despite several repair efforts, which included using sledgehammers and jackhammers to cut holes in the exterior walls and ceilings, application of new waterproofing materials on portions of the roof and exterior walls, and more caulk, the house continued to leak-from the windows, from the roofs, and water seeped between the floors. Fluorescent light fixtures in the garage filled with water and had to be removed.

"The Erlichs eventually had their home inspected by another general contractor and a structural engineer. In addition to confirming defects in the roof, exterior stucco, windows and waterproofing, the inspection revealed serious errors in the construction of the home's structural components. None of the 20 shear, or load-bearing walls specified in the plans were properly installed. The three turrets on the roof were inadequately connected to the roof beams and, as a result, had begun to collapse. Other connections in the roof framing were also improperly constructed. Three decks were in danger of 'catastrophic collapse' because they had been finished with mortar and ceramic tile, rather than with the light-weight roofing material originally specified. Finally, the foundation of the main beam for the two-story living room was poured by digging a shallow hole, dumping in 'two sacks of dry concrete mix, putting some water in the hole and mixing it up with a shovel.' " This foundation, required to carry a load of 12,000 pounds, could only support about 2,000. The beam is settling and the surrounding concrete is cracking.

According to the Erlichs' expert, problems were major and pervasive, concerning everything "related to a window or waterproofing, everywhere that there was something related to framing," stucco, or the walking deck.

Both of the Erlichs testified that they suffered emotional distress as a result of the defective condition of the house and Menezes's invasive and unsuccessful repair attempts. Barry Erlich testified he felt "absolutely sick" and had to be "carted away in an ambulance" when he learned the full extent of the structural problems. He has a permanent heart condition, known as superventricular tachyarrhythmia, attributable, in part, to excessive stress. Although the condition can be controlled with medication, it has forced him to resign his positions as athletic director, department head and track coach.

Sandra Erlich feared the house would collapse in an earthquake and feared for her daughter's safety. Stickers were placed on her bedroom windows, and alarms and emergency lights installed so rescue crews would find her room first in an emergency.

Plaintiffs sought recovery on several theories, including breach of contract, fraud, negligent misrepresentation, and negligent construction. Both the breach of contract claim and the negligence claim alleged numerous construction defects.

Menezes prevailed on the fraud and negligent misrepresentation claims. The jury found he breached his contract with the Erlichs by negligently constructing their home and awarded $406,700 as the cost of repairs. Each spouse was awarded $50,000 for emotional distress, and Barry Erlich received an additional $50,000 for physical pain and suffering and $15,000 for lost earnings.

By a two-to-one majority, the Court of Appeal affirmed the judgment, including the emotional distress award. The majority noted the breach of a contractual duty may support an action in tort. The jury found Menezes was negligent. Since his negligence exposed the Erlichs to "intolerable living conditions and a constant, justifiable fear about the safety of their home," the majority decided the Erlichs were properly compensated for their emotional distress.

The dissent pointed out that no reported California case has upheld an award of emotional distress damages based upon simple breach of a contract to build a house. Since Menezes's negligence directly caused only economic injury and property damage, the Erlichs were not entitled to recover damages for their emotional distress.

We granted review to resolve the question.

In an action for breach of contract, the measure of damages is "the amount which will compensate the party aggrieved for all the detriment proximately caused thereby, or which, in the ordinary course of things, would be likely to result therefrom" (Civ. Code, § 3300), provided the damages are "clearly ascertainable in both their nature and origin" (Civ. Code, § 3301). In an action not arising from contract, the measure of damages is "the amount which will compensate for all the detriment proximately caused thereby, whether it could have been anticipated or not" (Civ. Code, § 3333).

"Contract damages are generally limited to those within the contemplation of the parties when the contract was entered into or at least reasonably foreseeable by them at that time; consequential damages beyond the expectation of the parties are not recoverable. [Citations.] This limitation on available damages serves to encourage contractual relations and commercial activity by enabling parties to estimate in advance the financial risks of their enterprise." (*Applied Equipment Corp. v. Litton Saudi Arabia Ltd.* (1994) 7 Cal.4th 503, 515 [28 Cal.Rptr.2d 475, 869 P.2d 454] (*Applied Equipment*).) "In contrast, tort damages are awarded to [fully] compensate the victim for [all] injury suffered. [Citation.]" (*Id.* at p. 516.)

" '[T]he distinction between tort and contract is well grounded in common law, and divergent objectives underlie the remedies created in the two areas. Whereas contract actions are created to enforce the intentions of the parties to the agreement, tort law is primarily designed to vindicate "social policy." [Citation.]' " (*Hunter v. Upright, Inc.* (1993) 6 Cal.4th 1174, 1180 [26 Cal.Rptr.2d 8, 864 P.2d 88], quoting *Foley v. Interactive Data Corp.* (1988) 47 Cal.3d 654, 683 [254 Cal.Rptr. 211, 765 P.2d 373] (*Foley*).) While the purposes behind contract and tort law are distinct, the boundary line between them is not (*Freeman & Mills, Inc. v. Belcher Oil Co.* (1995) 11 Cal.4th 85, 106 [44 Cal.Rptr.2d 420, 900 P.2d 669] (conc. and dis. opn. of Mosk, J.) (*Freeman & Mills*)) and the distinction between the remedies for each is not " 'found ready made.' " (*Ibid.*, quoting Holmes, The Common Law (1881) p. 13.) These uncertain boundaries and the apparent breadth of the recovery available for tort actions create pressure to obliterate the distinction between contracts and torts-an expansion of tort law at the expense of contract principles which Grant Gilmore aptly dubbed "con*torts*." In this case we consider whether a negligent breach of a contract will support an award of damages for emotional distress-either as tort damages for negligence or as consequential or special contract damages.

In concluding emotional distress damages were properly awarded, the Court of Appeal correctly observed that "the same wrongful act may constitute both a breach of contract and an invasion of an interest protected by the law of torts." (*North American Chemical Co. v. Superior Court* (1997) 59 Cal.App.4th 764, 774 [69 Cal.Rptr.2d 466], citing 3 Witkin, Cal. Procedure (4th ed. 1996) Actions, § 139, pp. 203-204.) Here, the court permitted plaintiffs to recover both full repair costs as normal contract damages and emotional distress damages as a tort remedy. . . .

Having concluded tort damages are not available, we finally consider whether damages for emotional distress should be included as consequential or special damages in a contract claim. "Contract damages are generally limited to those within the contemplation of the parties when the contract was entered into or at least reasonably foreseeable by them at the time; consequential damages beyond the expectations of the parties are not recoverable. [Citations.] This limitation on available damages serves to encourage contractual relations and commercial activity by enabling parties to estimate in advance the financial risks of their enterprise." (*Applied Equipment, supra*, 7 Cal.4th at p. 515.)

" '[W]hen two parties make a contract, they agree upon the rules and regulations which will govern their relationship; the risks inherent in the agreement and the likelihood of its breach. The parties to the contract in essence create a mini-universe for themselves, in which each voluntarily chooses his contracting partner, each trusts the other's willingness to keep his word and honor his commitments, and in which they define their respective obligations, rewards and risks. Under such a scenario, it is appropriate to enforce only such obligations as each party voluntarily assumed, and to give him only such benefits as he expected to receive; this is the function of contract law.' " (*Applied Equipment, supra*, 7 Cal.4th at p. 517.)

Accordingly, damages for mental suffering and emotional distress are generally not recoverable in an action for breach of an ordinary commercial contract in California. (*Kwan v. Mercedes-Benz of North America, Inc.* (1994) 23 Cal.App.4th 174, 188 [28 Cal.Rptr.2d 371] (*Kwan*); *Sawyer v. Bank of America* (1978) 83 Cal.App.3d 135, 139 [145 Cal.Rptr. 623].) "Recovery for emotional disturbance will be excluded unless the breach also caused bodily harm or the contract or the breach is of such a kind that serious emotional disturbance was a particularly likely result." (Rest.2d Contracts, § 353.) The Restatement specifically notes the breach of a contract to build a home is not "particularly likely" to result in "serious emotional disturbance." (*Ibid.*)

Cases permitting recovery for emotional distress typically involve mental anguish stemming from more personal undertakings the traumatic results of which were unavoidable. (See, e.g., *Burgess v. Superior Court, supra*, 2 Cal.4th 1064 [infant injured during childbirth]; *Molien v. Kaiser Foundation Hospitals* (1980) 27 Cal.3d 916 [167 Cal.Rptr. 831, 616 P.2d 813, 16 A.L.R.4th 518] [misdiagnosed venereal disease and subsequent failure of marriage]; *Kately v. Wilkinson* (1983) 148 Cal.App.3d 576 [195 Cal.Rptr. 902] [fatal waterskiing accident]; *Chelini v. Nieri* (1948) 32 Cal.2d 480

[196 P.2d 915] [failure to adequately preserve a corpse].) Thus, when the express object of the contract is the mental and emotional well-being of one of the contracting parties, the breach of the contract may give rise to damages for mental suffering or emotional distress. (See *Wynn v. Monterey Club* (1980) 111 Cal.App.3d 789, 799-801 [168 Cal.Rptr. 878] [agreement of two gambling clubs to exclude husband's gambling-addicted wife from clubs and not to cash her checks]; *Ross v. Forest Lawn Memorial Park* (1984) 153 Cal.App.3d 988, 992-996 [203 Cal.Rptr. 468, 42 A.L.R.4th 1049] [cemetery's agreement to keep burial service private and to protect grave from vandalism]; *Windeler v. Scheers Jewelers* (1970) 8 Cal.App.3d 844, 851-852 [88 Cal.Rptr. 39] [bailment for heirloom jewelry where jewelry's great sentimental value was made known to bailee].)

Cases from other jurisdictions have formulated a similar rule, barring recovery of emotional distress damages for breach of contract except in cases involving contracts in which emotional concerns are the essence of the contract. (See, e.g., *Hancock v. Northcutt* (Alaska 1991) 808 P.2d 251, 258 ["contracts pertaining to one's dwelling are not among those contracts which, if breached, are particularly likely to result in serious emotional disturbance"; typical damages for breach of house construction contracts can appropriately be calculated in terms of monetary loss]; *McMeakin v. Roofing & Sheet Metal Supply* (1990) 1990 Okla.Civ.App. 101 [807 P.2d 288] [affirming order granting summary judgment in favor of defendant roofing company after it negligently stacked too many brick tiles on roof, causing roof to collapse and completely destroy home, leading to plaintiff's heart attack one month later]; *Day v. Montana Power Co.* (1990) 242 Mont. 195 [789 P.2d 1224] [owner of restaurant that was destroyed in gas explosion allegedly caused by negligence of utility company employee not entitled to recover damages for emotional distress]; *Creger v. Robertson* (La.Ct.App. 1989) 542 So.2d 1090 [reversing award for emotional distress damages caused by foul odor emanating from a faulty foundation, preventing plaintiff from entertaining guests in her residence]; *Groh v. Broadland Builders, Inc.* (1982) 120 Mich.App. 214 [327 N.W.2d 443] [reversing order denying motion to strike allegations of mental anguish in case involving malfunctioning septic tank system, and noting adequacy of monetary damages to compensate for pecuniary loss of "having to do the job over," as distinguished from cases allowing recovery because situation could never be adequately corrected].)

Plaintiffs argue strenuously that a broader notion of damages is appropriate when the contract is for the construction of a home. Amici curiae urge us to permit emotional distress damages in cases of negligent construction of a personal residence when the negligent construction causes gross interference with the normal use and habitability of the residence.

Such a rule would make the financial risks of construction agreements difficult to predict. Contract damages must be clearly ascertainable in both nature and origin. (Civ. Code, § 3301.) A contracting party cannot be required to assume limitless responsibility for all consequences of a breach and must be advised of any special harm that might result in order to determine whether or not to accept the risk of contracting. (1 Witkin, Summary of Cal. Law (9th ed. 1987) Contracts, § 815, p. 733.)

Moreover, adding an emotional distress component to recovery for construction defects could increase the already prohibitively high cost of housing in California, affect the availability of insurance for builders, and greatly diminish the supply of affordable housing. The potential for such broad-ranging economic consequences-costs likely to be paid by the public generally-means the task of fashioning appropriate limits on the availability of emotional distress claims should be left to the Legislature. (See Tex. Prop. Code Ann. § 27.001 et seq. (1999); Haw. Rev. Stat. § 663-8.9 (1998).)

Permitting damages for emotional distress on the theory that certain contracts carry a lot of emotional freight provides no useful guidance. Courts have carved out a narrow range of exceptions to the general rule of exclusion where emotional tranquility is the contract's essence. Refusal to broaden the bases for recovery reflects a fundamental policy choice. A rule which focuses not on the risks contracting parties voluntarily assume but on one party's reaction to inadequate performance, cannot provide any principled limit on liability.

The discussion in *Kwan*, a case dealing with the breach of a sales contract for the purchase of a car, is instructive. "[A] contract for [the] sale of an automobile is not essentially tied to the buyer's mental or emotional well-being. Personal as the choice of a car may be, the central reason for buying one is usually transportation.... [¶] In spite of America's much-discussed 'love affair with the automobile,' disruption of an owner's relationship with his or her car is not, in the normal case, comparable to the loss or mistreatment of a family member's remains [citation], an invasion of one's privacy [citation], or the loss of one's spouse to a gambling addiction [citation]. In the latter situations, the contract exists primarily to further or protect emotional interests; the direct and foreseeable injuries resulting from a breach are also primarily emotional. In contrast, the undeniable aggravation, irritation and anxiety that may result from [the] breach of an automobile warranty are secondary effects deriving from the decreased usefulness of the car and the frequently frustrating process of having an automobile repaired. While [the] purchase of an automobile may sometimes lead to severe emotional distress, such a result is not ordinarily foreseeable from the nature of the contract." (*Kwan, supra*, 23 Cal.App.4th at p. 190.)

Most other jurisdictions have reached the same conclusion. (See *Sanders v. Zeagler* (La. 1997) 686 So.2d 819, 822-823 [principal object of a contract for the construction of a house was to obtain a place to live and emotional distress damages were not recoverable]; *Hancock v. Northcutt, supra*, 808 P.2d at pp. 258-259 [no recovery for emotional distress as a result of defective construction; typical damages for breach of house construction contracts can appropriately be calculated in terms of monetary loss]; *City of Tyler v. Likes* (Tex. 1997) 962 S.W.2d 489, 497 [mental anguish based solely on property damage is not compensable as a matter of law].)

We agree. The available damages for defective construction are limited to the cost of repairing the home, including lost use or relocation expenses, or the diminution in value. (*Orndorff v. Christiana Community Builders* (1990) 217 Cal.App.3d 683 [266 Cal.Rptr. 193].) The Erlichs received more than $400,000 in traditional contract damages to correct the defects in their home. While their distress was undoubtedly real and serious, we conclude the balance of policy considerations-the potential for significant increases in liability in amounts disproportionate to culpability, the court's inability to formulate appropriate limits on the availability of claims, and the magnitude of the impact on stability and predictability in commercial affairs-counsel against expanding contract damages to include mental distress claims in negligent construction cases. . . .

The judgment of the Court of Appeal is reversed and the matter is remanded for further proceedings consistent with this opinion.

Questions

1. What was the court's reasoning behind concluding that the homeowners may not recover damages for emotional distress based on breach of a contract to build a house?

2. According to the court's decision, what is the distinction between tort damages and contract damages?

3. Under what circumstances does the court allow recovery for emotional distress damages in a breach of contract case, according to the court's decision?

Takeaways – Erlich v. Menezes

Damages for mental suffering may not be recovered in an action for breach of an ordinary commercial contract. "Recovery for emotional disturbance will be excluded unless the breach also caused bodily harm or the contract or the breach is of such a kind that serious emotional disturbance was a particularly likely result." (Rest.2d § 353) The rule against emotional distress damages for breach of contract has been applied in California to bar such damages, for example, for breach of a choral singer's employment contract (*Westwater v. Grace Church* (1903) 140 Cal. 339, 341-343 [73 P. 1055])

Ross v. Forest Lawn Memorial Park
California Court of Appeal
153 Cal.App.3d 988, 203 Cal. Rptr. 468 (1984)

ASHBY, J. Appellant Francine Ross appeals from the dismissal of her fourth amended complaint against respondent Forest Lawn following the granting of a demurrer without leave to amend. Appellant is attempting to establish respondent's liability for events surrounding the funeral and burial services of her 17-year-old daughter, Kristie.

We accept as true the following facts, as alleged in the complaint. Appellant and respondent entered into a contract whereby Kristie's funeral and burial would be handled by respondent, a corporation engaged in business as a cemetery. At the time the arrangements were being made appellant advised respondent that she wanted the funeral and burial services to be private. Only family members and invited guests were to be permitted to attend. In particular, appellant requested that no "punk rockers" be allowed at the services. Kristie had been a punk rocker. Appellant was fearful that her daughter's former associates would disrupt the private services, and so advised respondent. Respondent agreed to use all reasonable efforts and means to comply with appellant's request.

Many punk rockers attended both the funeral services in the chapel and the gravesite burial services. Neither their appearance nor comportment was in accord with traditional, solemn funeral ceremonies. Some were in white face makeup and black lipstick. Hair colors ranged from blues and greens to pinks and oranges. Some were dressed in leather and chains and twirled baton-like weapons, while yet another wore a dress decorated with live rats. The uninvited guests were drinking and using cocaine, and were physically and verbally abusive to family members and their guests. A disturbance ensued and grew to the point that police had to be called to restore order.

Later that day, in light of what took place at the burial, appellant became concerned that the punk rockers might return to the grave and vandalize or desecrate it. She requested respondent's agents to especially guard Kristie's grave, and they agreed to do so. Upon returning to the gravesite the next day, however, appellant discovered that the flowers and surface of the grave had been disturbed. Appellant then arranged to have Kristie's body moved to another, secret gravesite.

Appellant requested permission to hire someone to guard the original grave overnight until the body could be moved to the new grave. Respondent's agent first gave her the permission and then informed her that she could not have a private guard for the night....

We find that the complaint does express a duty to provide appellant with a private funeral. The duty is based on the oral contract between the parties by which respondent agreed to accommodate appellant by excluding uninvited guests. The fact that by its title the first cause of action purports to be in tort is of no consequence. "`[T]he nature of an action and the issues involved are to be determined, not from the appellation given the pleading, but from the facts alleged and the relief that they support. [Citation omitted.]'" (De Lancie v. Superior Court (1982) 31 Cal.3d 865, 869 [183 Cal. Rptr. 866, 647 P.2d 142].) . . .

Respondent maintains that because appellant has not alleged physical injury no recovery is permissible. Respondent's duty to provide a private funeral and burial arose from respondent's agreement to do so. Appellant seeks damages for emotional rather than physical injury that resulted from respondent's failure to exclude the unwanted guests. The contract was a lawful contract which by its nature put respondent on notice that a breach would result in emotional and mental suffering by appellant. [Citations omitted] Appellant's claim to damages for emotional distress is compensable as a result of a breach of contract. [Citations omitted]

Sustaining the demurrer without leave to amend was an abuse of discretion. [Citations omitted]

The order dismissing the complaint is reversed.

Question

How did the court justify its decision to sustain the appellant's claim for emotional distress damages despite the absence of physical injury?

Takeaways Erlich and Ross

How do you account for the different outcomes in *Erlich* and *Ross*? While the general rule is that no emotional distress damages are permitted for breach of contract California courts, as well as the courts of other states, have recognized the existence of extraordinary contracts, ones "which so affect the vital concerns of the individual that severe mental distress is a foreseeable result of breach. For many years, our courts have recognized that damages for mental distress may be recovered for breach of a contract of this nature. [Citations.]" (*Allen v. Jones* (1980) 104 Cal.App.3d 207, 211 [163 Cal.Rptr. 445].) Stated another way, the exceptional contracts are those whose terms "relate to matters which concern directly the comfort, happiness, or personal welfare of one of the parties, or the subject matter of which is such as directly to affect or move the affection, self-esteem, or tender feelings of that party ...." (*Westervelt v. McCullough* (1924) 68 Cal.App. 198, 208-209 [228 P. 734].)

In the typical contract case, it is not foreseeable that breach will cause emotional distress. Thus, a rule has evolved that damages for emotional distress are generally not recoverable in an action for breach of contract. However, some contracts-including mortuary and crematorium contracts-so affect the vital concerns of the contracting parties that severe emotional distress is a foreseeable result of a breach. (*Allen v. Jones* (1980) 104 Cal.App.3d 207, 211 [163 Cal.Rptr. 445].) The right to recover damages for emotional distress for breach of mortuary and crematorium contracts has been well established in California. (See, e.g., *Chelini v. Nieri* (1948) 32 Cal.2d 480, 481-482 [196 P.2d 915].) "Even in the context of an action for breach of contract, where recovery of damages solely for emotional distress resulting from a breach is not normally allowed, the provision of services related to the disposition of human remains has been distinguished because of the unique nature of the services." (*Christensen v. Superior Court*, supra, 54 Cal.3d 868 at pp. 894-895.)

Certainty as a Limitation on Damages

In order to be recoverable, damages must be established with reasonable certainty. (Rest.2d §352) Damages must be clearly ascertainable and reasonably certain, both in their nature and origin. Damages which are speculative, remote, imaginary, contingent, or merely possible cannot serve as a legal basis for recovery. (Cal.Civ.Code § 3301; *Earp v. Nobmann* (1981) 122 Cal.App.3d 270, 294 [175 Cal.Rptr. 767].)

McDonald v. John P. Scripps Newspaper
California Court of Appeal, 1989
210 Cal.App.3d 100, 257 Cal.Rptr. 473

GILBERT, J. Gavin [L. McDonald] was a contestant in the 1987 Scripps Howard National Spelling Bee, sponsored in Ventura County by the newspaper, the Ventura County Star-Free Press. The contest is open to all students through the eighth grade who are under the age of 16. Gavin won competitions at the classroom and school-wide levels. This earned him the chance to compete against other skilled spellers in the county-wide spelling bee. The best speller in the county wins a trip to Washington D.C. and a place in the national finals. The winner of the national finals is declared the national champion speller.

Gavin came in second in the county spelling bee. Being adjudged the second best orthographer in Ventura County is an impressive accomplishment, but pique overcame self-esteem. The spelling contest became a legal contest.

We search in vain through the complaint to find a legal theory to support this metamorphosis. Gavin alleges that two other boys, Stephen Chen and Victor Wang, both of whom attended a different school, also competed in the spelling contest. Stephen had originally lost his school-wide competition to Victor. Stephen was asked to spell the word "horsy." He spelled it "h-o-r-s-e-y." The spelling was ruled incorrect. Victor spelled the same word "h-o-r-s-y." He then spelled another word correctly, and was declared the winner.

Contest officials, who we trust were not copy editors for the newspaper sponsoring the contest, later discovered that there are two proper spellings of the word "horsy," and that Stephen's spelling was correct after all.

Contest officials asked Stephen and Victor to again compete between themselves in order to declare one winner. Victor, having everything to lose by agreeing to this plan, refused. Contest officials decided to allow both Victor and Stephen to advance to the county-wide spelling bee, where Gavin lost to Stephen.

Taking Vince Lombardi's aphorism to heart, "Winning isn't everything, it's the only thing," Gavin filed suit against the Ventura County Star-Free Press and the Scripps Howard National Spelling Bee alleging breach of contract, breach of implied covenant of good faith and fair dealing, and intentional and negligent infliction of emotional distress.

In his complaint, Gavin asserts that contest officials violated spelling bee rules by allowing Stephen Chen to compete at the county level. He suggests that had Stephen not progressed to the county-wide competition, he, Gavin, would have won. For this leap of faith he seeks compensatory and punitive damages.

The trial court sustained Scripps's demurrer without leave to amend because the complaint fails to state a cause of action. The action was dismissed, and Gavin appeals.

Gavin asserts that he has set forth the necessary elements of a cause of action for breach of contract, and that these elements are: "(1) The contract; (2) Plaintiff's performance; (3) Defendant's breach; (4) Damage to plaintiff. 4 Witkin, California Procedure, Pleading, § 464 (3rd Ed. 1985)."

Gavin's recitation of the law is correct, but his complaint wins no prize. He omitted a single word in the fourth element of an action for breach of contract, which should read "damage to plaintiff therefrom." (4 Witkin, Cal. Procedure (3d ed. 1985) Pleading, § 464, p. 504.) Not surprisingly, the outcome of this case depends on that word. A fundamental rule of law is that "whether the action be in tort or contract compensatory damages cannot be recovered unless there is a causal connection between the act or omission complained of and the injury sustained." (Capell Associates, Inc. v. Central Valley Security Co. (1968) 260 Cal.App.2d 773, 779 [67 Cal.Rptr. 463]; State Farm Mut. Auto. Ins. Co. v. Allstate Ins. Co. (1970) 9 Cal.App.3d 508, 528 [88 Cal.Rptr. 246]; Civ. Code, §§ 3300, 3333.)

The erudite trial judge stated Gavin's shortcoming incisively. "I see a gigantic causation problem ...." Relying on the most important resource a judge has, he said, "common sense tells me that this lawsuit is nonsense."

Even if Gavin and Scripps had formed a contract which Scripps breached by allowing Stephen Chen to compete at the county level in violation of contest rules, nothing would change. Gavin cannot show that he was injured by the breach. Gavin lost the spelling bee because he misspelled a word, and it is irrelevant that he was defeated by a contestant who "had no right to advance in the contest."

Gavin argues that had the officials "not violated the rules of the contest, Chen would not have advanced, and would not have had the opportunity to defeat" Gavin. Of course, it is impossible for Gavin to show that he would have spelled the word correctly if Stephen were not his competitor. Gavin concedes as much when he argues that he would not have been damaged if defeated by someone who had properly advanced in the contest. That is precisely the point.

Gavin cannot show that anything would have been different had Stephen not competed against him. Nor can he show that another competitor would have also misspelled that or another word, thus allowing Gavin another opportunity to win. "It is fundamental that damages which are speculative, remote, imaginary, contingent, or merely possible cannot serve as a legal basis for recovery." (Earp v. Nobmann (1981) 122 Cal.App.3d 270, 294 [175 Cal.Rptr. 767].)

Gavin offers to amend the complaint by incorporating certain rules of the spelling bee which purportedly show that the decision to allow Stephen to advance in the competition was procedurally irregular. This offer to amend reflects a misunderstanding of the trial court's ruling. The fatal defect in the complaint is that Gavin cannot show that but for Stephen Chen's presence in the spelling bee, Gavin would have won. . . .

In Shapiro v. Queens County Jockey Club (1945) 184 Misc. 295 [53 N.Y.S.2d 135], plaintiff's horse was the only horse to run the full six furlongs in the sixth race at Aqueduct Race Track after racing officials declared a false start. A half hour later the sixth race was run again, and plaintiff's horse came in fifth out of a total of six.

The Shapiro court held that plaintiff had no cause of action against the race track. Plaintiff could not support the theory that his horse would have won the second time around if all the other horses had also run the six furlongs after the false start. Plaintiff was not content to merely chalk up his loss to a bad break caused by the vicissitudes of life. The lesson to be learned is that all of us, like high-strung horses at the starting gate, are subject to life's false starts. The courts cannot erase the world's imperfections.

The Georgia Supreme Court in Georgia High School Ass'n v. Waddell (1981) 248 Ga. 542 [285 S.E.2d 7], decided it was without authority to review the decision of a football referee regarding the outcome of the game. The court stated that the referee's decision did not present a justiciable controversy. Nor does the decision of the spelling bee officials present a justiciable controversy here.

Our decision at least keeps plaintiff's bucket of water from being added to the tidal wave of litigation that has engulfed our courts. . . .

As for the judgment of the trial court, we'll spell it out. A-F-I-R-M-E-D.

Questions

1. According to the court's reasoning, why is it important for the plaintiff to establish a causal connection between the defendant's act or omission and the injury sustained?

2. How did the court respond to the plaintiff's argument that the officials' violation of the contest rules caused his loss in the spelling bee?

Ericson v. Playgirl, Inc.
Court of Appeals of California, 1977
73 Cal.App.3d 850

FLEMING, Acting P. J. Were damages awarded here for breach of contract speculative and conjectural, or were they clearly ascertainable and reasonably certain, both in nature and in origin?

The breach of contract arose from the following circumstances: plaintiff John Ericson, in order to boost his career as an actor, agreed that defendant Playgirl, Inc. could publish without compensation as the centerfold of its January 1974 issue of Playgirl photographs of Ericson posing naked at Lion Country Safari. No immediate career boost to Ericson resulted from the publication. In April 1974 defendant wished to use the pictures again for its annual edition entitled Best of Playgirl, a publication with half the circulation of Playgirl and without advertising. Ericson agreed to a rerun of his pictures in Best of Playgirl on two conditions: that certain of them be cropped to more modest exposure, and that Ericson's photograph occupy a quarter of the front cover, which would contain photographs of five other persons on its remaining three-quarters. Defendant honored the first of these conditions but not the second, in that as the result of an editorial mixup Ericson's photograph did not appear on the cover of Best of Playgirl. Ericson thereupon sued for damages, not for invasion of privacy from unauthorized publication of his pictures, but for loss of the publicity he would have received if defendant had put Ericson's picture on the cover as it had agreed to do.

All witnesses testified that the front cover of a magazine is not for sale, that a publisher reserves exclusive control over the front cover because its format is crucial to circulation, that consequently it is impossible to quote a direct price for front cover space. Witnesses also agreed that a picture on the front cover of a national magazine can provide valuable publicity for an actor or entertainer, but that it is difficult to put a price on this publicity. Analogies were sought in the cost of advertising space inside and on the back cover of national magazines. In July 1974 a full-page advertisement in Playgirl cost $7,500 to $8,000, a quarter page $2,500, and the back cover $11,000. However, Best of Playgirl carried no advertising and enjoyed only half the circulation of its parent magazine.

The trial court awarded plaintiff damages of $12,500, expressly basing its award on the testimony of Richard Cook, western advertising manager for TV Guide. According to Cook, the value to an entertainer of an appearance on the cover of a national magazine is "probably close to $50,000, and I base that on this: That magazine lays on the newsstand, a lot of people that never buy it see it, and everybody that does buy it certainly sees it." Cook said that the circulation of a magazine affects the value of a cover appearance, as does the magazine's demographics, i.e., the specific audience it reaches. He based his opinion on his knowledge of Playgirl, for he had no knowledge of the circulation, demographics, or even existence of Best of Playgirl. He also quantified his opinion by stating that if the picture only occupied a quarter of the cover instead of the full cover, the value of the appearance would be only a fourth of $50,000, which was the figure used by the trial court in fixing plaintiff's damages for loss of publicity at $12,500.

On appeal the sole substantial issue is that of damages, for it is clear the parties entered a contract which defendant breached.

In reviewing the issue of damages we first note that the cause of action is for breach of contract and not for a tort such as invasion of privacy. Defendant is not charged with committing a civil wrong but merely with failing to keep its promise. From this classification of the action as breach of contract, three important consequences affecting the measure of damages follow:

1. Damages may not be punitive or exemplary and may not be imposed as a form of chastisement (Civ. Code, § 3294).

2. Damages are limited to losses that might reasonably be contemplated or foreseen by the parties. (Civ. Code, §§ 3300, 3358; Hadley v. Baxendale (1854) 156 Eng. Rep. 145.)

3. Damages must be clearly ascertainable and reasonably certain, both in their nature and origin. (Civ. Code, § 3301.)

In each of these respects damages for breach of contract differ from damages in tort (see Civ. Code, §§ 3294, 3333); accordingly, tort precedents on the measure of damages have no direct relevancy here. Of limited application, too, is the tort rule that when calculation of the fact and amount of damages has been made difficult by defendant's wrong, courts will adopt whatever means are at hand to right the wrong. (Bigelow v. R.K.O. Radio Pictures (1946) 327 U.S. 251, 265-266 [90 L.Ed. 652, 660-661, 66 S.Ct. 574]; Zinn v. Ex-Cell-O-Corp. (1944) 24 Cal.2d 290, 297-298 [149 P.2d

177]; cf. Cal. Lettuce Growers, Inc. v. Union Sugar Co. (1955) 45 Cal.2d 474, 486-487 [289 P.2d 785, 49 A.L.R.2d 496].)

Plaintiff's claim of damages for breach of contract was based entirely on the loss of general publicity he would have received by having his photograph appear, alongside those of five others, on the cover of Best of Playgirl. Plaintiff proved that advertising is expensive to buy, that publicity has value for an actor. But what he did not prove was that loss of publicity as the result of his nonappearance on the cover of Best of Playgirl did in fact damage him in any substantial way or in any specific amount. Plaintiff's claim sharply contrasts with those few breach of contract cases that have found damages for loss of publicity reasonably certain and reasonably calculable, as in refusals to continue an advertising contract. In such cases the court has assessed damages at the market value of the advertising, less the agreed contract price. (See Metropolitan Broadcasting Corporation v. Lebowitz (D.C.Cir. 1961) 293 F.2d 524 [110 App.D.C. 336, 90 A.L.R.2d 1193]; Annot., 90 A.L.R.2d 1199.) Plaintiff's claim for damages more closely resembles those which have been held speculative and conjectural, as in the analogous cases of Jones v. San Bernardino Real Estate Board (1959) 168 Cal.App.2d 661, 665 [336 P.2d 606], where the court declined to award purely conjectural damages for loss of commissions, contacts, business associations, and clientele allegedly occasioned by plaintiff's expulsion from a local realty board; and of Fisher v. Hampton (1975) 44 Cal.App.3d 741 [118 Cal.Rptr. 811], where the court rejected an award of damages for defendant's failure to drill a $35,000 oil well when geological reports opined that oil would not be found and no evidence whatever established that plaintiff had been damaged. Under normal legal rules plaintiff's claim for damages failed to satisfy the requirements of reasonable foreseeability (Civ. Code, § 3300) and reasonable certainty (Civ. Code, § 3301), and therefore took on a punitive hue (Civ. Code, § 3294).

Plaintiff, however, contends that special rules of foreseeability and certainty of damages apply to loss of publicity by actors, entertainers, and other performing artists dependent upon public patronage for the success of their careers. In substance, plaintiff argues that for artists the loss of any kind of publicity is harmful and detrimental to their careers; hence for them any loss of publicity in breach of contract is compensable in damages. In order to evaluate this contention we must consider the nature and kind of publicity that plaintiff has lost.

All persons who offer personal services to the general public rely on goodwill to establish and maintain custom (cf. Bus. & Prof. Code, § 14100), and at first blush it seems reasonable to assume that the better known they are, the more likely they are to attract custom. But to be accurate we must make this assumption more precise. We must ask the question -- better known for what? A lawyer who is a famous yachtsman may not necessarily attract legal business; a dentist world-renowned as a mountain climber may not necessarily improve his practice of dentistry as a consequence of his renown; a hairdresser who swims the Catalina Channel in record time may not necessarily increase the patronage of her beauty salon. For publicity to be of value and result in custom it must relate to the specific aspect of the human activity that is involved. General publicity bears little relation to the repute that leads to custom and trade, for it is specific reputation that brings about gain or loss of business. (Cf. Civ. Code, §§ 46, subd. 3, 48a, subd. 4(b).) It follows that damages for loss of publicity in breach of contract must be tied to loss of publicity for some particular event, such as a musical concert or a prize fight, or loss of publicity for some continuing activity, such as the conduct of a specific business at a specific location or the practice of a particular skill or art. Consequently, damages from loss of general publicity alone will almost always be wholly speculative and conjectural.

Plaintiff, however, insists that actors and performing artists fall in a special category apart from other purveyors of personal services. He argues that an actor needs an audience to perform; that an actor must be visible to patrons of his art to become successful; that only by becoming publicly visible can an actor become favorably known to patrons of his art and to producers of dramatic productions who provide him with employment; therefore all publicity is valuable to an actor, and the loss by an actor of any publicity is injurious and damaging. To a considerable extent the argument is sound -- except for the breadth of its final conclusion. In our view it is not any kind of publicity, celebrity, or notoriety that is valuable to an artist's career, but instead the publicity which is valuable to the artist is publicity related to the performance of his art. Publicity of this sort, gained by the performance or production of his art, is the type of publicity that creates good will, reputation, and custom, and which taken at the flood leads to fame and fortune. Hence the importance to actors of appearances on the stage and screen, to musicians of appearances in concerts, and to writers and composers of credits for the works they have written or composed. Loss of publicity of this type as a result of breach of contract is compensable to an actor, musician, or writer, because the lost publicity is directly connected with the performance of his art, grows out of his profession, and directly affects his earning power.

The compensability in damages for an artist's loss of publicity in connection with his art as a result of breach of contract was established by a series of English cases that culminated in Herbert Clayton and Jack Waller Ld. v. Oliver [1930] A.C. 209. In that case the House of Lords squarely held that an actor whose contract of employment has been breached has a cause of action not only for loss of salary but for loss of publicity resulting from the denial of the opportunity to appear in public in his professional capacity. California has adopted the English rule in Colvig v. R.K.O. General, Inc. (1965) 232 Cal.App.2d 56 [42 Cal.Rptr. 473]. But an examination of the cases allowing recovery of damages for loss of publicity as a result of breach of contract discloses that in each instance the lost publicity grew out of the loss of the artist's exercise of his profession, i.e., loss of the opportunity to act, to broadcast, to sing, to conduct an orchestra, to entertain; or resulted from the loss of credit to the artist for professional services connected with a particular work, i.e., a script, play, musical composition, design, production, and the like. Publicity in both these categories performs a similar function in that it permits patrons and producers to evaluate the artist's merits in connection with the performance of his art. Damages for the loss of such publicity does not present insuperable difficulties in calculation, for the artist's future earnings can be directly correlated to his box office appeal or to his known record of successes. But even here proof of damages from loss of publicity must be reasonably certain and specific, and those claims that appear speculative and conjectural are rejected. For example, in Zorich v. Petroff (1957) 152 Cal.App.2d 806, 811 [313 P.2d 118], the court declined to award damages to an associate producer of a motion picture for defendant's failure to give him screen credit. In that case the motion picture was a failure, no evidence of actual damage was introduced, and the court opined that screen credit, if given, might have turned out to be a liability rather than an asset.

A yawning gulf exists between the cases that involve loss of professional publicity and the instant case in which plaintiff complains of loss of mere general publicity that bears no relation to the practice of his art. His situation is comparable to that of an actor who hopes to obtain wide publicity by cutting the ribbon for the opening of a new resort-hotel complex, by sponsoring a golf or tennis tournament, by presenting the winning trophy at the national horse show, or by acting as master of ceremonies at a televised political dinner. Each of these activities may generate wide publicity that conceivably could bring the artist to the attention of patrons and producers of his art and thus lead to professional employment. Yet none of it bears any relation to the practice of his art. Plaintiff's argument, in essence, is that for an actor all publicity is valuable, and the loss of any publicity as a result of breach of contract is compensable. Carried to this point, we think his claim for damages becomes wholly speculative. It is possible, as plaintiff suggests, that a television programmer might have seen his photograph on the cover of Best of Playgirl, might have scheduled plaintiff for a talk show, and that a motion picture producer viewing the talk show might recall plaintiff's past performances, and decide to offer him a role in his next production. But it is equally plausible to speculate that plaintiff might have been hurt professionally rather than helped by having his picture appear on the cover of Best of Playgirl, that a motion picture producer whose attention had been drawn by the cover of the magazine to its contents depicting plaintiff posing naked in Lion Country Safari might dismiss plaintiff from serious consideration for a role in his next production. The speculative and conjectural nature of such possibilities speaks for itself.

Assessment of the value of general publicity unrelated to professional performance takes us on a random walk whose destination is as unpredictable as the lottery and the roulette wheel. When, as at bench, damages to earning capacity and loss of professional publicity in the practice of one's art are not involved, we think recovery of compensable damages for loss of publicity is barred by the Civil Code requirement that damages for breach of contract be clearly foreseeable and clearly ascertainable. (§§ 3300, 3301.)

Plaintiff relies heavily on the somewhat analogous case of Leavy v. Cooney (1963) 214 Cal.App.2d 496 [29 Cal.Rptr. 580]. In that case Leavy, the prosecutor in the notorious Chessman case, appeared as narrator and participant in a motion picture depicting the prosecution and imprisonment of Chessman, under an agreement that the picture would be shown only on television as a news broadcast and not in motion picture theaters. Defendant breached that agreement. In affirming an award of compensatory damages of $7,500 to plaintiff, the court pointed out that plaintiff's professional reputation could well have been damaged by the publicity occasioned by the breach of contract, that it was within the jury's discretion to assess the detriment caused. (214 Cal.App.2d at pp. 501-502.) Two critical factors distinguish Leavy from the cause before us: First, the publicity in Leavy intimately and directly related to the prosecutor's practice of his profession. Second, the publicity was unwanted, and defendant's conduct constituted the tort of invasion of privacy as well as breach of contract. At bench, the gist of plaintiff's claim is the precise opposite, for he seeks damages for loss of wanted publicity. No injury to personal rights and no relation to professional activities are involved. We conclude that the damages awarded by the trial court are speculative and conjectural, and that plaintiff failed to establish any ascertainable loss for which he is entitled to compensatory damages.

Plaintiff, however, is entitled to recover nominal damages for breach of contract. We evaluate plaintiff's right to nominal damages by analogy to Civil Code section 3344, which provides minimum statutory damages of $300 for knowing commercial use of a person's name or likeness without his consent. The statute's obvious purpose is to specify an amount for nominal damages in situations where actual damages are impossible to assess. Accordingly, although we find no support for any assessment of compensatory damages in plaintiff's favor because of the wholly speculative nature of the detriment suffered by plaintiff as a result of his nonappearance on a fourth of the cover of Best of Playgirl, plaintiff is entitled to nominal damages for breach of contract, which we fix in the sum of $300.

The judgment is modified to reduce the amount of damages to $300, and, as so modified, the judgment is affirmed.

Question

Why did the court find the plaintiff's claim for damages to be speculative and conjectural?

Takeaways – McDonald and Ericson

Damages must be established with reasonable certainty both with respect to the fact of damage and the amount of damage. What was the plaintiff's problem in *Ericson*? Was he unable to establish that he was damaged at all? The dollar amount by which he was damaged? Both?

For other examples of where damage claims were rejected for lack of certainty see *Jones v. San Bernardino Real Estate Board* (1959) 168 Cal.App.2d 661, 665 [336 P.2d 606], where the court declined to award purely conjectural damages for loss of commissions, contacts, business associations, and clientele allegedly occasioned by plaintiff's expulsion from a local realty board, and *Fisher v. Hampton* (1975) 44 Cal.App.3d 741 [118 Cal.Rptr. 811], where the court rejected an award of damages for defendant's failure to drill a $35,000 oil well when geological reports opined that oil would not be found and no evidence whatever established that plaintiff had been damaged.

Fera v. Village Plaza, Inc.
Supreme Court of Michigan, 1976
396 Mich. 639, 242 N.W.2d 372

KAVANAGH, C.J. Plaintiffs received a jury award of $200,000 for loss of anticipated profits in their proposed new business as a result of defendants' breach of a lease. The Court of Appeals reversed. 52 Mich App 532; 218 NW2d 155 (1974). We reverse and reinstate the jury's award.

On August 20, 1965 plaintiffs and agents of Fairborn-Village Plaza executed a ten-year lease for a "book and bottle" shop in defendants' proposed shopping center. This lease provided for occupancy of a specific location at a rental of $1,000 minimum monthly rent plus 5% of annual receipts in excess of $240,000. A $1,000 deposit was paid by plaintiffs.

After this lease was executed, plaintiffs gave up approximately 600 square feet of their leased space so that it could be leased to another tenant. In exchange, it was agreed that liquor sales would be excluded from the percentage rent override provision of the lease.

Complications arose, including numerous work stoppages. Bank of the Commonwealth received a deed in lieu of foreclosure after default by Fairborn and Village Plaza. Schostak Brothers managed the property for the bank.

When the space was finally ready for occupancy, plaintiffs were refused the space for which they had contracted because the lease had been misplaced, and the space rented to other tenants. Alternative space was offered but refused by plaintiffs as unsuitable for their planned business venture.

Plaintiffs initiated suit in Wayne Circuit Court, alleging inter alia a claim for anticipated lost profits. The jury returned a verdict for plaintiffs against all defendants for $200,000.

The Court of Appeals reversed and remanded for new trial on the issue of damages only, holding that the trial court "erroneously permitted lost profits as the measure of damages for breach of the lease". 52 Mich App 532, 542; 218 NW2d 155, 160.

In Jarrait v Peters, 145 Mich 29, 31-32; 108 NW 432 (1906), plaintiff was prevented from taking possession of the leased premises. The jury gave plaintiff a judgment which included damages for lost profits. This Court reversed:

"It is well settled upon authority that the measure of damages when a lessor fails to give possession of the leased premises is the difference between the actual rental value and the rent reserved. 1 Sedgwick on Damages (8th ed), § 185. Mr. Sedgwick says:

"'If the business were a new one, since there could be no basis on which to estimate profits, the plaintiff must be content to recover according to the general rule.'

"The rule is different where the business of the lessee has been interrupted. . . .

"The evidence admitted tending to show the prospective profits plaintiff might have made for the ensuing two years should therefore have been excluded under the objections made by defendant, and the jury should have been instructed that the plaintiff's damages, if any, would be the difference between the actual rental value of the premises and the rent reserved in the lease."

Six years later, in Isbell v Anderson Carriage Co, 170 Mich 304, 318; 136 NW 457 (1912), the Court wrote:

"It has sometimes been stated as a rule of law that prospective profits are so speculative and uncertain that they cannot be recognized in the measure of damages. This is not because they are profits, but because they are so often not susceptible of proof to a reasonable degree of certainty. Where the proof is available, prospective profits may be recovered, when proven, as other damages. But the jury cannot be asked to guess. They are to try the case upon evidence, not upon conjecture."

These cases and others since should not be read as stating a rule of law which prevents every new business from recovering anticipated lost profits for breach of contract. The rule is merely an application of the doctrine that "[i]n order to be entitled to a verdict, or a judgment, for damages for breach of contract, the plaintiff must lay a basis for a reasonable estimate of the extent of his harm, measured in money". 5 Corbin on Contracts, § 1020, p 124. The issue becomes one of sufficiency of proof. "The jury should not [be] allowed to speculate or guess upon this question of the amount of loss of profits". Kezeli v River Rouge Lodge IOOF, 195 Mich 181, 188; 161 NW 838 (1917). . . .

The rule was succinctly stated in Shropshire v Adams, 40 Tex Civ App 339, 344; 89 SW 448, 450 (1905):

"Future profits as an element of damage are in no case excluded merely because they are profits but because they are uncertain. In any case when by reason of the nature of the situation they may be established with reasonable certainty they are allowed."

It is from these principles that the "new business"/"interrupted business" distinction has arisen.

"If a business is one that has already been established a reasonable prediction can often be made as to its future on the basis of its past history. * * * If the business * * * has not had such a history as to make it possible to prove with reasonable accuracy what its profits have been in fact, the profits prevented are often but not necessarily too uncertain for recovery." 5 Corbin on Contracts, § 1023, pp 147, 150-151. Cf Jarrait v Peters, supra.

The Court of Appeals based its opinion reversing the jury's award on two grounds: First, that a new business cannot recover damages for lost profits for breach of a lease. We have expressed our disapproval of that rule. Secondly, the Court of Appeals held plaintiffs barred from recovery because the proof of lost profits was entirely speculative. We disagree.

The trial judge in a thorough opinion made the following observations upon completion of the trial.

"On the issue of lost profits, there were days and days of testimony. The defendants called experts from the Michigan Liquor Control Commission and from Cunningham Drug Stores, who have a store in the area, and a man who ran many other stores. The plaintiffs called experts and they, themselves, had experience in the liquor sales business, in the book sales business and had been representatives of liquor distribution firms in the area.

"The issue of the speculative, conjectural nature of future profits was probably the most completely tried issue in the whole case. Both sides covered this point for days on direct and cross-examination. The proofs ranged from no lost profits to two hundred and seventy thousand dollars over a ten-year period as the highest in the testimony. A witness for the defendants, an expert from Cunningham Drug Company, testified the plaintiffs probably would lose money. Mr. Fera, an expert in his own right, testified the profits would probably be two hundred and seventy thousand dollars. The jury found two hundred thousand dollars. This is well within the limits of the high and the low testimony presented by both sides, and a judgment was granted by the jury. . . .

"The court cannot invade the finding of fact by the jury, unless there is no testimony to support the jury's finding. There is testimony to support the jury's finding. We must realize that witness Stein is an interested party in this case, personally. He is an officer or owner in Schostak Brothers. He may personally lose money as a result of this case. The jury had to weigh this in determining his credibility. How much credibility they gave his testimony was up to them. How much weight they gave to counter-evidence was up to them. . . .

"The court must decide whether or not the jury had enough testimony to take this fact from the speculative-conjecture category and find enough facts to be able to make a legal finding of fact. This issue [damages for lost profits] was the most completely tried issue in the whole case. Both sides put in testimony that took up days and encompassed experts on both sides. This fact was adequately taken from the category of speculation and conjecture by the testimony and placed in the position of those cases that hold that even though loss of profits is hard to prove, if proven they should be awarded by the jury. In this case, the jury had ample testimony to make this decision from both sides. . . .

As Judge Wickens observed, the jury was instructed on the law concerning speculative damages. The case was thoroughly tried by all the parties. Apparently, the jury believed the plaintiffs. That is its prerogative.

The testimony presented during the trial was conflicting. The weaknesses of plaintiffs' specially prepared budget were thoroughly explored on cross-examination. Defendants' witnesses testified concerning the likelihood that plaintiffs would not have made profits if the contract had been performed. There was conflicting testimony concerning the availability of a liquor license. All this was spread before the jury. The jury weighed the conflicting testimony and determined that plaintiffs were entitled to damages of $200,000.

As we stated in Anderson v Conterio, 303 Mich 75, 79; 5 NW2d 572 (1942):

"The testimony * * * is in direct conflict, and that of plaintiff * * * was impeached to some extent. However, it cannot be said as a matter of law that the testimony thus impeached was deprived of all probative value or that the jury could not believe it. The credibility of witnesses is for the jury, and it is not for us to determine who is to be believed."

The trial judge, who also listened to all of the conflicting testimony, denied defendants' motion for a new trial, finding that the verdict was justified by the evidence. We find no abuse of discretion in that decision. . . .

While we might have found plaintiffs' proofs lacking had we been members of the jury, that is not the standard of review we employ. "As a reviewing court we will not invade the fact-finding of the jury or remand for entry of judgment unless the factual record is so clear that reasonable minds may not disagree." Hall v Detroit, 383 Mich 571, 574; 177 NW2d 161 (1970). This is not the situation here.

The Court of Appeals is reversed and the trial court's judgment on the verdict is reinstated.

COLEMAN, J. (concurring in part, dissenting in part).

Although anticipated profits from a new business may be determined with a reasonable degree of certainty such was not the situation regarding loss of profits from liquor sales as proposed by plaintiffs.

First, plaintiffs had no license and a Liquor Control Commission regional supervisor and a former commissioner testified that the described book and bottle store could not obtain a license. Further, the proofs of possible profits from possible liquor sales if a license could have been obtained were too speculative. The speculation of possible licensing plus the speculation of profits in this case combine to cause my opinion that profits from liquor sales should not have been submitted to the jury.

I . . . would have allowed proof of loss from the bookstore operation to go to the jury, but not proof of loss from liquor sales. His remedy is also approved. I would affirm the trial court judgment conditioned upon plaintiffs' consenting within 30 days following the release of this opinion, to "remitting that portion of the judgment in excess of $60,000. Otherwise, the judgment should be reversed and a new trial had". Plaintiffs are also entitled to the $1,000 deposit.

Questions

1. What was the trial judge's opinion regarding the issue of lost profits and the sufficiency of proof presented during the trial?

2. What happened in the Court of Appeals?

3. What was the reasoning behind the Supreme Court's disapproval of the rule that a new business cannot recover damages for lost profits for breach of a lease?

Takeaways – Fera v. Village Plaza

The difficulty of estimating anticipated profits from a new start-up business has in many cases led the courts to classify those damages as uncertain and conjectural and to therefore deny recovery for loss of future profits. However, this uncertainty can be overcome with a satisfactory evidentiary showing of certainty.

Damage Limitation Review

There are several limitations on awarding damages to make the nonbreaching party whole. A party cannot recover for loss which she could have avoided through her reasonable efforts. (Rest.2d §350) Damages are limited to those losses which were foreseeable, i.e., in the contemplation of the parties at the time the contract was entered into. (Rest.2d §351.) In order to be recoverable damages must be established with reasonable certainty. (Rest.2d §352) In other words, damages which are speculative, remote, imaginary, contingent, or merely possible cannot be recovered. Damages for the mental distress that may result from the breach of a contract are not recoverable. (Rest.2d § 353)

Liquidated Damages

The parties may agree in advance to the amount of damages that will be imposed in the event of a breach. Such an agreement is known as a liquidated damage clause. The validity of a clause for liquidated damages requires that the parties to the contract "agree therein upon an amount which shall be presumed to be the amount of damages sustained by a breach thereof ...." This amount must represent the result of a reasonable endeavor by the parties to estimate a fair average compensation for any loss that may be sustained. (Rest.2d § 356, UCC 2-718(1). *Rice v. Schmid* (1941) 18 Cal.2d 382, 386 [115 P.2d 498, 138 A.L.R. 589];)" (*Better Food Mkts. v. Amer. Dist. Teleg. Co.,* (1953) 40 Cal.2d 179, 186-187.) As we have seen, damages for breach cannot be punitive. Therefore a penalty clause masquerading as a liquidated damages clause will be unenforceable.

Dave Gustafson & Co. v. State
Supreme Court of South Dakota, 1968
156 N.W.2d 185

HANSON, Presiding Judge. In this action by a contractor against the State of South Dakota and its Highway Commission the single question is whether a provision in a state highway construction contract is one for liquidated damages, as the trial court found, or is a penalty.

On October 5, 1963 plaintiff, Dave Gustafson & Company, entered into a contract with the State Highway Commission for the construction of the sub base, base and bituminous surfacing of a new public highway between Wessington Springs and Woonsocket. Plaintiff performed a total dollar amount of work in the amount of $530,724.14. Upon completion the new highway replaced the pre-existing portion of State Trunk Highway No. 34 between the two towns. During construction the old portion of Highway 34 remained open for travel by the public in substantially the same manner as it had been for the past five years. After the new highway was completed the old portion of the road was also left open for use as a public highway.

Plaintiff failed to complete the new highway on the date fixed. There was a delay of 67 working days for which there was no extension of time requested or granted. Therefore the state withheld $14,070.00 as liquidated damages from the amount due plaintiff computed according to the contract scale of daily damage for delay in construction. As this project totaled $530,742.14, the per diem daily damage was $210. This daily damage multiplied by the 67 day delay equals the sum withheld. [The trial court upheld the state's claim and Gustafson appealed.]

... The court said [in a previous case] "A provision for payment of a stipulated sum as a liquidation of damages will ordinarily be sustained if it appears that at the time the contract was made the damages in the event of a breach will be incapable or very difficult of accurate estimation, that there was a reasonable endeavor by the parties as stated to fix fair compensation, and that the amount stipulated bears a reasonable relation to probable damages and not disproportionate to any damages reasonably to be anticipated."

This case reflects the modern tendency not to "look with disfavor upon 'liquidated damages' provisions in contracts. When they are fair and reasonable attempts to fix just compensation for anticipated loss caused by breach of contract, they are enforced * * * They serve a particularly useful function when damages are uncertain in nature or amount or are unmeasurable, as is the case in many government contracts." Priebe & Sons v. United States, 332 U.S. 407, 68 S.Ct. 123, 92 L.Ed. 32. See also Williston on Contracts, Vol. 5, 3rd Ed., § 788, page 760. In 43 Am.Jur., Public Works and Contracts, § 78, page 822 it is pointed out that "In many instances the governing law requires contracts for public work to contain stipulations for liquidated damages for delay, and in the absence of statute it is customary in many jurisdictions to insert such stipulations. Such a provision requiring liquidated damages for delay is not against public policy and is an appropriate means of inducing due performance, or of giving compensation, in case of failure to perform; the courts give effect to a stipulation of this kind in accordance with its terms."

Judged in this light and by the standards established in Anderson v. Cactus Heights Country Club, 80 S.D. 417, 125 N.W.2d 491, the provision in question must be considered to be one for liquidated damages rather than a penalty for the following reasons: I. Damages for delay in constructing a new highway are impossible of measurement. II. The amount stated in the contract as liquidated damages indicates an endeavor to fix fair compensation for the loss, inconvenience, added costs, and deprivation of use caused by delay. Daily damage is graduated according to total amount of work to be performed. It may be assumed that a large project involves more loss than a small one and each day of delay adds to the loss, inconvenience, cost and deprivation of use. As stated in Vol. 5, Williston on

Contracts, 3rd Ed., § 785, page 733 "It is commonly provided in building and construction contracts that there shall be deducted from the contractor's compensation a fixed sum for each day's delay in performing the contract beyond the day fixed therein. Such damages are obviously graded according to the extent of the breach, increasing proportionately with each day's delay. Moreover, each day's delay, while unquestionably injurious, is injurious frequently in ways that are difficult to estimate. Accordingly, unless the sum fixed in the contract is very unreasonable the provision is treated as one for liquidated damages." [Citations omitted] For the same reasons we must conclude the amount stipulated in the contract bears a reasonable relation to probable damages and is not, as a matter of law, disproportionate to any and all damage reasonably to be anticipated from the unexcused delay in performance.

Affirmed.

Questions

1. How does the court define a provision for liquidated damages in a contract?

2. According to the court, under what circumstances will a provision for liquidated damages be upheld?

3. What factors did the court consider in determining that the provision in this case is for liquidated damages rather than a penalty?

4. Why does the court consider damages for delay in constructing a new highway to be impossible to measure?

5. How does the court assess the reasonableness of the amount stipulated as liquidated damages in the contract?

Takeaways – Dave Gustafson v. State

A liquidated damages clause must be a reasonable estimate at the time of contracting of the likely damages from the breach, and the need for estimation at that time must be shown by reference to the likely difficulty of measuring the actual damages from a breach of contract or if the estimate greatly exceeds a reasonable upper estimate of what the damages are likely to be, it is a penalty.

As of what point in time is the reasonableness of a liquidated damages clause determined? Older cases say at the time the contract was executed. The modern trend is towards assessing the reasonableness either at the time of contract formation or at the time of the breach. The UCC and the Restatement Second take the view that reasonableness should be tested "in light of the anticipated or actual loss." (See Rest.2d § 356(1) UCC 2-718(1). Under the Code it is enough if the provision is reasonable with respect to either (1) the harm the parties anticipate will result from the breach at the time of contracting or (2) the actual damages suffered at the time of the breach.

Cellphone Termination Fee Cases
California Court of Appeal, 2011
193 Cal. App. 4th 298; 122 Cal. Rptr. 3d 726

BRUINIERS, J. These consolidated appeals are from a judgment after trial in a consumer class action against wireless telephone carrier Sprint Spectrum, L.P. (Sprint), challenging its policy of charging early termination fees (ETF's) to customers terminating service prior to expiration of defined contract periods. The trial court found the ETF's to be unlawful penalties under Civil Code section 1671, subdivision (d), enjoined enforcement, and granted restitution/damages to the plaintiff class in the amount of ETF's collected by Sprint during the class period, $73,775,975. . . .

Sprint is a national cellular service carrier, providing cellular telephone service in California. In 2003, lawsuits were filed in Alameda County and in Orange County against Sprint and other cellular service providers alleging that the ETF's violated California consumer protection laws and constituted unauthorized penalties under [Civil Code] section 1671. . . .

Testimony concerning Sprint's initial decision to adopt a $150 ETF was presented by Plaintiffs through the video deposition of Bruce Pryor, Sprint's vice-president of consumer marketing. In 1999, Sprint began to study the concept of term contracts with ETF's as a means to reduce its "churn" rates, and tested use of ETF's in selected markets. Sprint reported monthly wireless churn rates in 1998 of 3.3 percent, and in 1999 of 3.4 percent. Sprint adopted term contracts incorporating the $150 ETF nationwide in May 2000. Sprint reduced its churn rate to 2.8 percent in 2000. . . .

The trial court found that an ETF operated primarily as a liquidated damage clause. Because Sprint failed to prove that, in adopting ETF's, it made any effort "to determine what losses it would sustain from breach by the early termination of its contracts" or "to estimate a fair average compensation for such losses," it failed to satisfy the reasonable endeavor test and the ETF's were consequently unlawful penalties under section 1671, subdivision (d).

A provision in a consumer contract "liquidating damages for the breach of the contract is void except that the parties to such a contract may agree therein upon an amount which shall be presumed to be the amount of damage sustained by a breach thereof, when, from the nature of the case, it would be impracticable or extremely difficult to fix the actual damage." (§ 1671, subd. (d); see *id.*, subd. (c)(1).) Because liquidated damage clauses in consumer contracts are presumed void, the burden is on the proponent of the clause to rebut that presumption. (*Garrett v. Coast & Southern Fed. Sav. & Loan Assn.* (1973) 9 Cal.3d 731, 738 [108 Cal. Rptr. 845, 511 P.2d 1197] (*Garrett*).)

Decisions interpreting this statute have created a two-part test for determining whether a liquidated damages provision is valid: (1) fixing the amount of actual damages must be impracticable or extremely difficult, and (2) the amount selected must represent a reasonable endeavor to estimate fair compensation for the loss sustained. (*Utility Consumers' Action Network, Inc. v. AT&T Broadband of Southern Cal., Inc.* (2006) 135 Cal.App.4th 1023, 1029 [37 Cal. Rptr. 3d 827] (*Utility Consumers*).) "Absent *either* of these elements, a liquidated damages provision is void ... ." (*Hitz, supra*, 38 Cal.App.4th at p. 288, italics added.) A liquidated damages provision need not, however, be expressly negotiated by both parties to a form contract in order to be valid. (*Utility Consumers*, at p. 1035.)

Impracticability may be established by showing "that the measure of actual damages would be a comparatively small amount and that it would be economically impracticable in each instance of a default to require a [seller] to prove to the satisfaction of the [consumer] the actual damages by accounting procedures." (*Garrett, supra*, 9 Cal.3d at p. 742.) The trial court found that, although Sprint could readily calculate its lost monthly revenue per customer in the event of a default, it would have been impracticable to determine Sprint's avoidable costs, and therefore impracticable to determine actual damages at the inception of the contracts. Plaintiffs do not challenge this finding.

"Determining whether a reasonable endeavor was made depends upon both (1) the motivation and purpose in imposing the charges, and (2) their effect." (*Utility Consumers, supra*, 135 Cal.App.4th at p. 1029.) "[T]he focus is not ... on whether liquidated damages are disproportionate to the loss from breach, but on whether they were *intended* to exceed loss substantially—a result of which is to generate a profit." (*Hitz, supra*, 38 Cal.App.4th at p. 289.) A liquidated damages provision that "bears no reasonable relationship to the range of actual damages that the parties could have anticipated would flow from a breach" is an unlawful penalty that compels a forfeiture upon a breach of contract. (*Ridgley v. Topa Thrift & Loan Assn.* (1998) 17 Cal.4th 970, 977 [73 Cal. Rptr. 2d 378, 953 P.2d 484].) Such penalties are " 'ineffective, and the wronged party can collect only the actual damages sustained.' [Citations.]" (*Id.* at p. 977.)

In order to establish the reasonable endeavor required, evidence must exist that the party seeking to impose liquidated damages " 'actually engaged in some form of analysis to determine what losses it would sustain from [a] breach, and that it made a genuine and non-pretextual effort to estimate a fair average compensation for the losses to be sustained.' " (*Hitz, supra*, 38 Cal.App.4th at p. 291.) The trial court made a finding that "when Sprint implemented the ETF in 2000, and increased it in 2005, it made no endeavor—reasonable or otherwise—to determine what losses it would sustain from breach or to estimate a fair average compensation for such losses." Sprint "did no analysis that considered the lost revenue from contracts, the avoidable costs, and Sprint's expected lost profits from contract terminations." The ETF amounts were set not based on the basis of any actual or estimated loss, but "from a competitive standpoint." Sprint's purpose in adopting the ETF was to control churn and was implemented "primarily as a means to prevent customers from leaving." After adoption of ETF's, Sprint succeeded in reducing its churn rate to 2.8 percent in 2000.

As discussed above, the court's findings are supported by substantial evidence. The testimony of Bruce Pryor, Sprint's vice-president of consumer marketing, was that Sprint began to study the concept of term contracts with ETF's in 1999 as a means to reduce its churn rates. The decision to implement ETF's was made by members of Sprint's marketing team. Contemporaneous Sprint internal documents referred to the ETF as a "$150 contract penalty fee," and as a "Penalty or Contract Cancellation Fee." Sprint's post merger $200 ETF was based on Nextel's premerger ETF. The trial court found "no evidence at trial that Nextel did any analysis that considered the lost revenue from contracts, the avoidable costs, or Nextel's expected lost profits from contract terminations."

Sprint counters that "undisputed evidence" at trial showed that the ETF's were not intended to exceed losses, and that Sprint officials were "aware that their ETFs would recover only a fraction of the revenue lost as a result of early terminations." Sprint asserts that any charge that "does not overstate actual damages *cannot* be a penalty." Sprint cites testimony that early terminations occurred on average with 13.25 months left on a contract, depriving Sprint of average revenues of $49.16 per month in monthly recurring charges per customer and that it lost over $650 in revenue for each early termination. Sprint points out that the ETF's do not even cover their costs of adding new customers, which averaged $388 dollars during the class period. It contends that the evidence showed that it "well understood that due to competitive forces, the ETF could not be set anywhere near a level that would compensate it for a customer's breach through early termination."

Sprint's expert calculated that Sprint's actual damages from early terminations by the class members was $987 million. Sprint contends that the ETF's on average *reduced* each class member's net obligation under their contract by more than $450, and that a subscriber with a $150 ETF would have reduced his or her net payments to Sprint by voluntarily paying the ETF with at least four months remaining on the contract, and a subscriber with a $200 ETF could have done the same by voluntarily paying an ETF with at least five months left. As we discuss further *post*, the jury found that Sprint's actual damages from early terminations were exactly equal to the amount of its uncollected ETF's ($225,697,433).

Sprint asserts that the trial court erroneously failed to consider the effect of Sprint's ETF's and in requiring a "formal study of estimated damages" to satisfy the motive-and-purpose prong of the reasonable endeavor test. Sprint argues that because the ETF's were not "intended to exceed loss substantially," they do not and cannot violate the motive-and-purpose aspect of the reasonable endeavor test. (*Hitz, supra,* 38 Cal.App.4th at p. 289.)

We note first that, as to Sprint's motive and purpose, whatever information as to costs and revenues Sprint may have been "aware" of, it cites to no evidence in the trial record that any of this information was part of the calculus in deciding to impose ETF's, or in determining the amount of an ETF. Further, we do not second-guess the trial court's factual determinations as to Sprint's motivation and purpose. (*Hitz, supra,* 38 Cal.App.4th at p. 290.)

While Sprint contends that it satisfied both prongs of the reasonable endeavor test in adopting ETF's, the real focus of its argument is on the *effect* of the ETF's. The thrust of that argument is that so long as the ETF amount is shown in practice to be *less than* Sprint's actual damages, the *effect* is not to generate a profit, whatever Sprint's motive and purpose, and nothing more is required to meet the test. . . .

Here, as the trial court found, the evidence fails to establish any endeavor, reasonable or otherwise, to even approximate Sprint's actual damages flowing from breach of the term contracts by consumers, and instead reflects a marketing decision made with an entirely deterrent purpose and focus. We believe that Plaintiffs are correct that the reasonable endeavor test, to have any meaning, must necessarily focus on those circumstances actually considered in evaluating a liquidated damage provision, not post hoc rationalization. . . .

The judgment of the trial court is affirmed.

Questions

1. What two-part test is used to determine the validity of a liquidated damages provision?

2. According to the court's findings, what factors were lacking in Sprint's adoption of the early termination fees (ETFs)?

3. What is the burden of proof for the proponent of a liquidated damages clause in a consumer contract?

4. How does impracticability of determining actual damages factor into the validity of a liquidated damages provision?

5. What is the focus of the reasonable endeavor test in assessing the validity of a liquidated damages provision?

Takeaways – Cellphone Termination Fee Cases

Damages for breach by either party to a contract may be liquidated in the agreement but only at an amount that is reasonable in the light of the anticipated or actual loss caused by the breach and the difficulties of the proof of loss. (Rest.2d § 356). California Civil Code § 1671 places on the party seeking to invalidate the provision the burden of establishing that the liquidated damages clause was unreasonable under the circumstances existing at the time the contract was made. The statute has an important qualification though. It does not apply to a consumer. (Cal.Civ.Code § 1671(c))

ASSESSMENT QUESTIONS, CHAPTER 7

1. Define specific performance as a remedy for breach of contract. Under what circumstances is specific performance typically available?

2. Discuss the principle of mutuality of remedies and its impact on the availability of specific performance.

3. Can specific performance be granted for personal service contracts? Explain the general approach of courts in granting specific performance in such cases.

4. Explain the concept of monetary damages as a remedy for breach of contract. What are the different types of monetary damages that may be awarded?

5. Explain the difference between "expectation damages" and "reliance damages" as remedies for breach of contract. When are each type of damages typically awarded?

6. Describe the principle of foreseeability in awarding damages for breach of contract. How does it affect the calculation of damages?

7. Explain the concept of mitigation of damages. What is the duty of the non-breaching party to mitigate their losses?

8. What are nominal damages? When are they awarded and what purpose do they serve?

9. Explain the concept of "cover" in relation to the calculation of damages for breach of contract under the UCC?

10. Explain the concept of liquidated damages in contract law. Under what

circumstances can parties include liquidated damages clauses in their contracts?

11. What is the distinction between liquidated damages and penalties? How do courts evaluate the enforceability of liquidated damages clauses?

12. Explain the principle of restitution as a remedy for breach of contract. When is restitution awarded and what does it seek to achieve?

13. Can a party seek both specific performance and monetary damages for the same breach of contract? Explain the legal principles involved.

14. Identify the several limitations on awards of monetary damages.

Chapter 8
PERFORMANCE AND BREACH

Introduction

Let's suppose that the parties have exchanged mutual promises and have created an enforceable bilateral contract. Will each party be bound to perform no matter what? If one or both parties want to reserve the right to withhold their performance if a certain event either occurs or does not occur, can they do so? The answer is yes, provided they make the occurrence or nonoccurence of the event a condition.

Suppose a law student wants to make some extra money by walking her neighbor's dog on a daily basis. She wants to enter into a long-term contract but doesn't want to be obligated to walk the dog on rainy days. How can she fashion an enforceable agreement that will assure she will not be in breach of her promise to walk the dog if it rains on a particular day? She could make a non-rainy day a condition of her duty to perform. If it rains, she is relieved of her duty. Such a contract might read, "law student promises to walk Fido every day provided that it is not raining." If it rains on a particular day, she can skip walking the dog and not be in breach.

Contract obligations may be absolute or conditional. When a party is accused of failing to perform under a contract they may respond that they have not breached the contract because any performance they were to render was conditional, i.e., any duty on their part has not yet arisen because some event has not yet occurred or any obligation they were under has been discharged because some event has occurred. (See Cal.Civ.Code § 1434.)

A contractual obligation is conditional when the rights or duties of any party thereto depend upon the occurrence of an uncertain event. (Cal.Civ.Code § 1434.) Hence, a person who makes an absolute or unconditional promise, supported by a sufficient consideration, is bound to perform when the time for performance arrives. A person who makes a conditional promise, supported by a sufficient consideration, is bound to perform only if the condition precedent occurs or is relieved from the duty to perform if the condition subsequent occurs.

Conditions Precedent, Subsequent and Concurrent

A condition is a fact or an event, the happening or non-happening of which creates or extinguishes a duty on the part of a promisor. (Rest.2d § 224) A condition which creates or triggers a duty is a condition precedent. (Cal.Civ.Code § 1436) A condition which extinguishes a duty is a condition subsequent. (Cal.Civ.Code § 1438) Conditions concurrent are those which are mutually dependent, and are to be performed at the same time. (Cal.Civ.Code § 1437) Conditions can be beyond the control of the parties (as in our dog-walking example above) or they can be within the control of the parties (I'll only buy the house if I'm satisfied with the home inspection report").

Express and Constructive (Implied) Conditions

A condition may be express, implied in fact, or implied in law. (1 Witkin, Summary of Cal.Law (10th ed. 2005) Contracts § 777, 794-808.) An express condition is one explicitly agreed to and placed in the contract by the parties. A constructive condition (sometimes called an implied condition) is a condition that is imposed by law in order to do justice.

Luttinger v. Rosen
Supreme Court of Connecticut, 1972
164 Conn 45, 316 A.2d 757

LOISELLE, J. The plaintiffs contracted to purchase for $85,000 premises in the city of Stamford owned by the defendants and paid a deposit of $8500. The contract was "subject to and conditional upon the buyers obtaining first mortgage financing on said premises from a bank or other lending institution in an amount of $45,000 for a term of not less than twenty (20) years and at an interest rate which does not exceed 8½ per cent per annum." The plaintiffs agreed to use due diligence in attempting to obtain such financing. The parties further agreed that if the plaintiffs were unsuccessful in obtaining financing as provided in the contract, and notified the seller within a specific time, all sums paid on the contract would be refunded and the contract terminated without further obligation of either party.

In applying for a mortgage which would satisfy the contingency clause in the contract, the plaintiffs relied on their attorney who applied at a New Haven lending institution for a $45,000 loan at 8¼ percent per annum interest over a period of twenty-five years. The plaintiffs' attorney knew that this lending institution was the only one which at that time would lend as much as $45,000 on a mortgage for a single-family dwelling. A mortgage commitment was obtained for $45,000 with "interest at the prevailing rate at the time of closing but not less than 8-¾%." Since this commitment failed to meet the contract requirement, timely notice was given to the defendants and demand was made for the return of the down payment. The defendants' counsel thereafter offered to make up the difference between the interest rate offered by the bank and the 8½ percent rate provided in the contract for the entire twenty-five years by a funding arrangement, the exact terms of which were not defined. The plaintiffs did not accept this offer and on the defendants' refusal to return the deposit an action was brought. From a judgment rendered in favor of the plaintiffs the defendants have appealed.

The defendants claim that the plaintiffs did not use due diligence in seeking a mortgage within the terms specified in the contract. The unattacked findings by the court establish that the plaintiffs' attorney was fully informed as to the conditions and terms of mortgages being granted by various banks and lending institutions in and out of the area and that the application was made to the only bank which might satisfy the mortgage conditions of the contingency clause at that time. These findings adequately support the court's conclusion that due diligence was used in seeking mortgage financing in accordance with the contract provisions. Brauer v. Freccia, 159 Conn. 289, 293, 268 A.2d 645. The defendants assert that notwithstanding the plaintiffs' reliance on their counsel's knowledge of lending practices, applications should have been made to other lending institutions. This claim is not well taken. The law does not require the performance of a futile act. Vachon v. Tomascak, 155 Conn. 52, 57, 230 A.2d 5; Tracy v. O'Neill, 103 Conn. 693, 699, 131 A. 417; Janulewycz v. Quagliano, 88 Conn. 60, 64, 89 A. 897.

The remaining assignment of error briefed by the defendants is that the court erred in concluding that the mortgage contingency clause of the contract, a condition precedent, was not met and, therefore, the plaintiffs were entitled to recover their deposit. "A condition precedent is a fact or event which the parties intend must exist or take place before there is a right to performance." Lach v. Cahill, 138 Conn. 418, 421, 85 A.2d 481. If the condition precedent is not fulfilled the contract is not enforceable. Lach v. Cahill, supra; Bialeck v. Hartford, 135 Conn. 551, 556, 66 A.2d 610. In this case the language of the contract is unambiguous and clearly indicates that the parties intended that the purchase of the defendants' premises be conditioned on the obtaining by the plaintiffs of a mortgage as specified in the contract. From the subordinate facts found the court could reasonably conclude that since the plaintiffs were unable to obtain a $45,000 mortgage at no more than 8½ percent per annum interest "from a bank or other lending institution" the condition precedent to performance of the contract was not met and the plaintiffs were entitled to the refund of their deposit. Any additional offer by the defendants to fund the difference in interest payments could be rejected by the plaintiffs. See Lach v. Cahill, supra, 420. There was no error in the court's exclusion of testimony relating to the additional offer since the offer was obviously irrelevant.

There is no error.

Questions

1. What obligation did the Luttinger's want to reserve the right to avoid?

2. What act or event would determine whether or not they could avoid it or would have to follow through by performing?

3. Explain why the court concluded that the plaintiffs were entitled to recover their

deposit based on the language of the contract and the fulfillment of the condition precedent.

4. Why did the court exclude testimony relating to the additional offer made by the defendants to fund the difference in interest payments?

Internatio-Rotterdam, Inc. v. River Brand Rice Mills., Inc.
United States Court of Appeals, Second Circuit, 1958
259 F.2d 137

HINCKS, Circuit Judge. Appeal from the United States District Court, Southern District of New York, Walsh, Judge, upon the dismissal of the complaint after plaintiff's case was in.

The defendant-appellee, a processor of rice, in July 1952 entered into an agreement with the plaintiff-appellant, an exporter, for the sale of 95,600 pockets of rice. The terms of the agreement, evidenced by a purchase memorandum, indicated that the price per pocket was to be "$8.25 F.A.S. Lake Charles and/or Houston, Texas"; that shipment was to be "December, 1952, with two weeks call from buyer"; and that payment was to be by "irrevocable letter of credit to be opened immediately payable against" dock receipts and other specified documents. In the fall, the appellant, which had already committed itself to supplying this rice to a Japanese buyer, was unexpectedly confronted with United States export restrictions upon its December shipments and was attempting to get an export license from the government. December is a peak month in the rice and cotton seasons in Louisiana and Texas, and the appellee became concerned about shipping instructions under the contract, since congested conditions prevailed at both the mills and the docks. The appellee seasonably elected to deliver 50,000 pockets at Lake Charles and on December 10 it received from the appellant instructions for the Lake Charles shipments. Thereupon it promptly began shipments to Lake Charles which continued until December 23, the last car at Lake Charles being unloaded on December 31. December 17 was the last date in December which would allow appellee the two week period provided in the contract for delivery of the rice to the ports and ships designated. Prior thereto, the appellant had been having difficulty obtaining either a ship or a dock in this busy season in Houston. On December 17, the appellee had still received no shipping instructions for the 45,600 pockets destined for Houston. On the morning of the 18th, the appellee rescinded the contract for the Houston shipments, although continuing to make the Lake Charles deliveries. It is clear that one of the reasons for the prompt cancellation of the contract was the rise in market price of rice from $8.25 per pocket, the contract price, to $9.75. The appellant brought this suit for refusal to deliver the Houston quota. . . .

The area of contest is also considerably reduced by the appellant's candid concession that the appellee's duty to ship, by virtue of the two-week notice provision, did not arise until two weeks after complete shipping instructions had been given by the appellant. Thus on brief the appellant says: "[w]e concede (as we have done from the beginning) that on a fair interpretation of the contract appellant had a duty to instruct appellee by December 17, 1952 as to the place to which it desired appellee to ship at both ports, and that, being late with its instructions in this respect, appellant could not have demanded delivery (at either port) until sometime after December 31, 1952." This position was taken, of course, with a view to the contract provision for shipment "December, 1952": a two-week period ending December 31 would begin to run on December 17. But although appellant concedes that the two weeks' notice to which appellee was entitled could not be shortened by the failure to give shipping instructions on or before December 17, it stoutly insists that upon receipt of shipping instructions subsequent to December 17 the appellee thereupon became obligated to deliver within two weeks thereafter. We do not agree.

It is plain that a giving of the notice by the appellant was a condition precedent to the appellee's duty to ship. Corbin on Contracts, Vol. 3, § 640. Id. § 724. Obviously, the appellee could not deliver free alongside ship, as the contract required, until the appellant identified its ship and its location. Jacksboro Stone Co. v. Fairbanks Co., 48 Tex.Civ. App. 639, 107 S.W. 567; Fortson Grocery Co. v. Pritchard Rice Milling Co., Tex. Civ.App., 220 S.W. 1116. Thus the giving of shipping instructions was what Professor Corbin would classify as a "promissory condition": the appellant promised to give the notice and the appellee's duty to ship was conditioned on the receipt of the notice. Op. cit.§ 633, p. 523, § 634, footnote 38. The crucial question is whether that condition was performed. And that depends on whether the appellee's duty of shipment was conditioned on notice on or before December 17, so that the appellee would have two weeks wholly within December within which to perform, or whether, as we understand the appellant to contend, the appellant could perform the condition by giving the notice later in December, in which case the appellee would be under a duty to ship within two weeks thereafter. The answer depends upon the proper interpretation of the contract: if the contract properly interpreted made shipment in December of the essence then the failure to give the notice on or before December 17 was nonperformance by the appellant of a condition upon which the appellee's duty to ship in December depended.

In the setting of this case, we hold that the provision for December delivery went to the essence of the contract. In support of the plainly stated provision of the contract there was evidence that the appellee's mills and the facilities appurtenant thereto were working at full capacity in December when the rice market was at peak activity and that appellee had numerous other contracts in January as well as in December to fill. It is reasonable to infer that in July, when the contract was made, each party wanted the protection of the specified delivery period; the appellee so that it could schedule its production without undue congestion of its storage facilities and the appellant so that it could surely meet commitments which it in turn should make to its customers. There was also evidence that prices on the rice market were fluctuating. In view of this factor it is not reasonable to infer that when the contract was made in July for December delivery, the parties intended that the appellant should have an option exercisable subsequent to December 17 to postpone delivery until January. United Irr. Co. v. Carson Petroleum Co., Tex.Civ.App., 283 S.W. 692; Steiner v. United States, D.C., 36 F.Supp. 496. That in effect would have given the appellant an option to postpone its breach of the contract, if one should then be in prospect, to a time when, so far as could have been foreseen when the contract was made, the price of rice might be falling. A postponement in such circumstances would inure to the disadvantage of the appellee who was given no reciprocal option. Further indication that December delivery was of the essence is found in the letter of credit which was provided for in the contract and established by the appellant. Under this letter, the bank was authorized to pay appellee only for deliveries "during December, 1952." It thus appears that the appellant's interpretation of the contract, under which the appellee would be obligated, upon receipt of shipping instructions subsequent to December 17, to deliver in January, would deprive the appellee of the security for payment of the purchase price for which it had contracted.

Since, as we hold, December delivery was of the essence, notice of shipping instructions on or before December 17 was not merely a "duty" of the appellant as it concedes: it was a condition precedent to the performance which might be required of the appellee. The nonoccurrence of that condition entitled the appellee to rescind or to treat its contractual obligations as discharged. Corbin on Contracts, §§ 640, 724 and 1252; Williston on Sales, §§ 452, 457; Restatement, Contracts, § 262; National Commodity Corp. v. American Fruit Growers, 6 Terry 169, 45 Del. 169, 70 A.2d 28; Alpena Portland Cement Co. v. Backus, 8 Cir., 156 F. 944; Jungmann & Co. v. Atterbury Bros., Inc., 249 N.Y. 119, 163 N.E. 123; Arnolt Corp. v. Stansen Corp., 7 Cir., 189 F.2d 5. On December 18th the appellant unequivocally exercised its right to rescind. Having done so, its obligations as to the Houston deliveries under the contract were at an end. And of course its obligations would not revive thereafter when the appellant finally succeeded in obtaining an export permit, a ship and a dock and then gave shipping instructions; when it expressed willingness to accept deliveries in January; or when it accomplished a "liberalization" of the outstanding letter of credit whereby payments might be made against simple forwarder's receipts instead of dock receipts.

The appellant urges that by reason of substantial part performance on its part prior to December 17th, it may not be held to have been in default for its failure sooner to give shipping instructions. The contention has no basis on the facts. As to the Houston shipments the appellant's activities prior to December 17th were not in performance of its contract: they were merely preparatory to its expectation to perform at a later time. The mere establishment of the letter of credit was not an act of performance: it was merely an arrangement made by the appellant for future performance which as to the Houston deliveries because of appellant's failure to give shipping instructions were never made. From these preparatory activities the appellee had no benefit whatever.

The appellant also maintains that the contract was single and "indivisible" and that consequently appellee's continuing shipments to Lake Charles after December 17 constituted an election to reaffirm its total obligation under the contract. This position also, we hold untenable. Under the contract, the appellee concededly had an option to split the deliveries betwixt Lake Charles and Houston. The price had been fixed on a per pocket basis, and payment, under the letter of credit, was to be made upon the presentation of dock receipts which normally would be issued both at Lake Charles or Houston at different times. The fact that there was a world market for rice and that in December the market price substantially exceeded the contract price suggests that it would be more to the appellant's advantage to obtain the Lake Charles delivery than to obtain no delivery at all. The same considerations suggest that by continuing with the Lake Charles delivery the appellee did not deliberately intend to waive its right to cancel the Houston deliveries. Conclusions to the contrary would be so greatly against self-interest as to be completely unrealistic. The only reasonable inference from the totality of the facts is that the duties of the parties as to the Lake Charles shipment were not at all dependent on the Houston shipments. We conclude their duties as to shipments at each port were paired and reciprocal and that performance by the parties as to Lake Charles did not preclude the appellee's right of cancellation as to Houston. Cf. Corbin on Contracts §§ 688, 695; Simms-Wylie Co. v. City of Ranger, Tex.Civ.App., 224 S.W.2d 265.

Finally, we hold that the appellant's claims of estoppel and waiver have no basis in fact or in law.

Affirmed.

Questions

1. What was the event the nonoccurrence of which entitled the seller to rescind or to treat its contractual obligations as discharged?

2. What was the crucial question regarding the appellee's duty to ship in relation to the receipt of shipping instructions?

3. Why did the court consider December delivery to be of the essence in this case?

4. According to the court's interpretation, what effect did the appellant's failure to give shipping instructions on or before December 17 have on the appellee's duty to ship?

Takeaways – Internatio-Rotterdam, Inc.

Reference is made in the opinion to what Professor Corbin classified as a "promissory condition." Performance that one party promises may also be a condition of the other party's legal duty; so that failure by one party to perform would be a breach of contract by that party and would prevent the other party's failure to pay from being a breach of contract. (Corbin, Contracts (One Vol.Ed. §§ 633 and 634) As an example, a law professor agrees to teach a course at a law school in return for a salary. The professor's promise or duty to teach is a condition of the school's obligation to pay and failure of the professor to teach will be a non-occurrence of a condition precedent excusing the school from its duty to pay.

"Pay If Paid" or "Pay When Paid?" Condition or Promise?

Wm. R. Clarke Corp. v. Safeco Ins. Co.
Supreme Court of California, 1997
15 Cal.4th 882, 64 Cal.Rptr.2d 578; 938 P.2d 372

KENNARD, J. In recent years, general contractors in California have begun to insert "pay if paid" provisions into their agreements with subcontractors. A pay if paid provision makes payment by the owner to the general contractor a condition precedent to the general contractor's obligation to pay the subcontractor for work the subcontractor has performed.

In other jurisdictions, the majority view is that, if reasonably possible, clauses in construction subcontracts stating that the subcontractor will be paid when the general contractor is paid will not be construed as establishing true conditions precedent, but rather as merely fixing the usual time for payment to the subcontractor, with the implied understanding that the subcontractor in any event has an unconditional right to payment within a reasonable time. (See, e.g., Koch v. Construction Technology, Inc. (Tenn. 1996) 924 S.W.2d 68; Power & Pollution Svcs. v. Suburban Piping (1991) 74 Ohio App.3d 89 [598 N.E.2d 69]; OBS Co., Inc. v. Pace Const. Corp. (Fla. 1990) 558 So.2d 404; Southern St. Masonry v. J.A. Jones Const. (La. 1987) 507 So.2d 198; Thos. J. Dyer Co. v. Bishop International Engineering Co. (6th Cir. 1962) 303 F.2d 655.) This approach has been followed in California. (Yamanishi v. Bleily & Collishaw, Inc. (1972) 29 Cal.App.3d 457, 462463 [105 Cal.Rptr. 580]; see also Rubin v. Fuchs (1969) 1 Cal.3d 50, 53 [81 Cal.Rptr. 373, 459 P.2d 925] [stating that "provisions of a contract will not be construed as conditions precedent in the absence of language plainly requiring such construction"].) A contract clause that has been construed in this fashion is sometimes referred to as a "pay when paid" rather than a "pay if paid" provision. (See Kirksey, "Minimum Decencies"-A Proposed Resolution of the "Pay-When-Paid"/"Pay-If-Paid" Dichotomy (Jan. 1992) Construction Law. 1.)

If it is not reasonably possible to construe the contractual provision as other than a condition precedent, then courts must decide whether public policy permits enforcement of a contractual provision that may result in the subcontractor's forfeiting all right to payment for work performed. The high court of New York has concluded that a true pay if paid provision in a subcontract for construction work is void as against public policy. (West-Fair Elec. v. Aetna Cas. & Sur. Co. (1995) 87 N.Y.2d 148, 157 [638 N.Y.S.2d 394, 398, 661 N.E.2d 967, 971].) In Illinois, North Carolina, and Wisconsin, pay if paid provisions have been declared void and unenforceable by statute. (770 Ill. Comp. Stat. Ann. 60/21; N.C. Gen. Stat. § 22C-2 (1991); Wis. Stat. § 779.135.) The validity of a true pay if paid provision presents a question of first impression in this court.

We granted review in this case to determine whether a subcontractor may collect on a general contractor's payment bond for work it has performed under a contract containing a pay if paid provision when the owner has not paid the general contractor. We conclude that pay if paid provisions like the one at issue here are contrary to the public policy of this state and therefore unenforceable because they effect an impermissible indirect waiver or forfeiture of the subcontractors' constitutionally protected mechanic's lien rights in the event of nonpayment by the owner. Because they are unenforceable, pay if paid provisions in construction subcontracts do not insulate either general contractors or their payment bond sureties from their contractual obligations to pay subcontractors for work performed.

In 1990, the owner of a commercial building in Los Angeles entered into a contract with Keller Construction Co., Ltd. (Keller), as general contractor, for rehabilitation work on the building. Keller in turn entered into subcontracts for this project with, among others, Wm. R. Clarke Corporation, Barsotti's, Inc., Garvin Fire Protection Systems, Inc., and Church and Larsen, Inc. (collectively, the subcontractors). Each subcontract contained a pay if paid provision and three of the four subcontracts also included an addendum reiterating the pay if paid limitation yet also purporting to preserve the subcontractors' mechanic's lien rights and to make those rights the subcontractors' "sole remedy" in the event the owner failed to pay Keller.

At the owner's insistence, and pursuant to the terms of the general contract, Keller obtained a labor and material payment bond from defendant Safeco Insurance Company of America (Safeco) to protect the owner from mechanic's lien claims by subcontractors and material suppliers. The bond recited that it was a payment bond as defined in Civil Code section 3096 and that it had been executed to comply with title 15 (Works of Improvement) of the Civil Code. The bond stated that Keller, as principal, and Safeco, as surety, "are held and firmly bound unto any and all persons who perform labor upon or bestow skill or other necessary services on, or furnish materials or lease equipment to be used or consumed in, or furnish appliances, teams, or power contributing to the work described in [the general contract between the owner and Keller], a copy of which contract is or may be attached hereto, and is hereby referred to, in the sum of" $16.5 million. The bond further stated: "Now, Therefore, the Condition of This Obligation Is Such, That if the Principal shall pay, or cause to be paid in full, the claims of all persons performing labor upon or bestowing skill or other necessary services on, or furnishing materials or leasing equipment to be used or consumed in or furnishing appliances, teams or power contributing to such work, then this obligation shall be void; otherwise to remain in full force and effect." In the final provision relevant here, the bond stated: "No suit, action or proceeding may be maintained on this bond unless the person claiming hereunder shall previously have either, recorded a mechanic's lien claim pursuant to Title 15, Works of Improvement, of the Civil Code of the State of California or given notice to the Surety on this bond before the expiration of the time prescribed in said statute for recording a lien." The bond was duly executed by the authorized agents of Keller and Safeco, and it was duly recorded.

After substantial work had been completed on the project, the owner stopped making payments to Keller, apparently as a result of the owner's insolvency. Keller then declined to pay the subcontractors, which recorded mechanic's liens and filed separate actions against Safeco seeking recovery under the payment bond. The actions were deemed related and were assigned to the same judge for all purposes. Three of the actions were resolved by summary judgment, the fourth by trial to the court. In each action, the trial court granted judgment for the subcontractors and against Safeco. Safeco appealed from each judgment. After consolidating the appeals, the Court of Appeal affirmed each judgment against Safeco.

Safeco argues here, as it did in the trial court and in the Court of Appeal, that its obligation under the payment bond never matured because the liability of a surety on a private works payment bond is no greater than that of its principal, and Keller, the principal on the payment bond issued by Safeco, never incurred any obligation to pay the subcontractors for their work because a condition precedent to Keller's contractual obligation to pay the subcontractors-that Keller receive payment from the owner for the subcontractors' work-was never satisfied. Safeco's argument thus assumes the validity of the pay if paid provisions in the subcontracts, under which payment from the owner to Keller was a condition precedent to Keller's obligation to pay the subcontractors. As will appear, we conclude that the assumption is false.

Our state Constitution provides: "Mechanics, persons furnishing materials, artisans, and laborers of every class, shall have a lien upon the property upon which they have bestowed labor or furnished material for the value of such labor done and material furnished; and the Legislature shall provide, by law, for the speedy and efficient enforcement of such liens." (Cal. Const., art. XIV, § 3.) . . .

By law, a subcontractor may not waive its mechanic's lien rights except under certain specified circumstances. [Civil Code section 3262 (a)] . . . .

Safeco argues that a pay if paid provision in a construction subcontract does not violate Civil Code section 3262's anti-waiver provisions because, under Civil Code section 3140 (limiting a subcontractor's recovery on a mechanic's lien claim to "such amount as may be due him according to the terms of his contract"), mechanic's lien remedies are available only to subcontractors whose payment rights have vested under the terms of their contracts. Absent a contractual right to payment, a subcontractor has no mechanic's lien remedy to enforce. In Safeco's view, a mechanic's lien is merely one remedy that is granted to subcontractors to enforce a contractual right to payment. Absent such a contractual right, there can be no remedy. Thus, according to Safeco, the subcontractors have not waived their mechanic's lien remedy. Rather, they never acquired the contractual payment right that is a necessary precondition to the enforcement of any mechanic's lien remedy.

Strictly speaking, Safeco is correct. A pay if paid provision in a construction agreement does not take the form of a waiver of mechanic's lien rights. Yet "[t]he law respects form less than substance" (Civ. Code, § 3528), and a pay if paid provision is in substance a waiver of mechanic's lien rights because it has the same practical effect as an express waiver of those rights.

The New York high court put it this way: "As the owner here has become insolvent, the owner may never make another contract payment to the general contractor. Because the lack of future payments by the owner is virtually certain, [the plaintiff subcontractor's] right to receive payment has been indefinitely postponed, and plaintiff has effectively waived its right to enforce its mechanics' liens. The waiver has occurred by operation of the pay-when-paid provision because mechanics' liens may not be enforced until a debt becomes due and payable." (West-Fair Elec. v. Aetna Cas. & Sur. Co., supra, 87 N.Y.2d at p. 158 [638 N.Y.S.2d at p. 398, 661 N.E.2d at p. 971].)

We may agree with Safeco that a pay if paid provision is not precisely a waiver of mechanic's lien rights and yet conclude that a pay if paid provision is void because it violates the public policy that underlies the anti-waiver provisions of the mechanic's lien laws. The Legislature's carefully articulated anti-waiver scheme would amount to little if parties to construction contracts could circumvent it by means of pay if paid provisions having effects indistinguishable from waivers prohibited under Civil Code section 3262.

Safeco advances several arguments against the conclusion that pay if paid provisions in construction subcontracts are void as against public policy. We consider these arguments in turn.

Safeco argues that it is established law in this state that pay if paid provisions in construction subcontracts are valid and enforceable. The authority Safeco cites for this proposition is Michel & Pfeffer v. Oceanside Properties, Inc. (1976) 61 Cal.App.3d 433 [132 Cal.Rptr. 179], which we find to be distinguishable. There, under a modification of the subcontractor's agreement with the general contractor, the subcontractor agreed to accept as payment for the final 15 percent of the contract price a pro rata interest in funds the general contractor would receive from either a secured promissory note or the proceeds of an intended sale of the project property. The Court of Appeal concluded that under this agreement the subcontractor had no right to the final payment until the general contractor received funds from one of the two designated sources. (Id. at p. 441.) The Court of Appeal further reasoned that because the general contractor had not received funds from either source, the general contractor was not in default on its agreement, and the subcontractor therefore could not yet recover its final payment either by proceeding against the surety on a payment bond or by foreclosing a mechanic's lien on the project property. (Ibid.)

Although the agreement provision at issue in Michel & Pfeffer v. Oceanside Properties, Inc., supra, 61 Cal.App.3d 433, raises some of the same concerns as a pay if paid provision, it was not such a provision. Nothing in the Court of Appeal's opinion suggests that the final payment to the subcontractor could be delayed indefinitely, nor did the Court of Appeal consider whether, if so, the provision there at issue violated the public policy underlying the anti-waiver provisions of Civil Code section 3262. Accordingly, we do not find the Court of Appeal's decision in that case relevant or helpful in deciding the issue presented here, and Safeco's reliance upon it is misplaced.

In defense of pay if paid provisions, Safeco argues strenuously that the public policy against waivers of mechanic's lien rights is not the only public policy at issue, and that this court should consider also the fundamental public policy served by freedom of contract. Safeco argues that pay if paid provisions should be held valid because they permit general contractors and subcontractors to allocate the risk of owner insolvency in a mutually agreeable manner.

Safeco's argument assumes that the sole purpose and effect of a pay if paid provision in a subcontract is to allocate the risk of owner insolvency. But the provisions at issue here were not so limited. As noted above, the pay if paid provision in each subcontract made the owner's payment to Keller a condition precedent of Keller's obligation to pay the subcontractor "regardless of the reason for Owner's nonpayment, whether attributable to the fault of the Owner, Contractor, Subcontractor or due to any other cause."

In any event, we find Safeco's "freedom of contract" argument unpersuasive in this context. By closely and carefully circumscribing subcontractors' freedom to waive mechanic's lien rights, and by forbidding waivers not accompanied by payment, or a promise of payment, the Legislature has already determined that there are policy considerations here that override the value of freedom of contract. We merely recognize and enforce that legislative policy determination. . . .

Safeco argues that it incurred no liability on the bond because a surety's obligation on a payment bond is only to answer for the default of its principal. As Safeco observes, the very definition of a surety is "one who promises to answer for the debt, default, or miscarriage of another, or hypothecates property as security therefor." (Civ. Code, § 2787.) Absent a default by the principal, the surety incurs no liability. In this connection, Safeco relies also on Civil Code section 2809, which states that a surety's obligation "must be neither larger in amount nor in other respects more burdensome than that of the principal." Safeco argues that its obligation under the payment bond is simply to answer for any default by Keller in the performance of its contractual payment obligations to the subcontractors. Because payment by the owner was a condition precedent to Keller's contractual payment obligations to the subcontractors, and because that condition was not met, Keller was not in default of any contractual payment obligation to the subcontractors. Therefore, reasons Safeco, as a surety it incurred no liability on the payment bond.

The fallacy of this reasoning (apart from its erroneous assumption that the pay if paid provisions are valid and enforceable and its reliance on a strained construction of Civil Code section 3140) is that it considers only Keller's contractual liability under the subcontracts, while ignoring Keller's separate and independent liability as principal and co-obligor on the payment bond. Keller's contract with the owner required it to obtain a payment bond, the purpose of which is "to create an additional fund or security for the satisfaction of lien claimants [citations], and also to limit the owner's liability to the contract price [citation] ...." . . .The payment bond at issue here refers to Keller's contract with the owner, but makes no mention of the subcontracts. The operative language of the bond states that "[Keller], as Principal, and [Safeco], as Surety, are held and firmly bound unto any and all persons who perform labor upon ... the work described in" the general contract.

Keller's obligation under the bond is measured by the terms of the bond and the statutes referenced in the bond. (Southern Heaters Corp. v. N. Y. Cas. Co. (1953) 120 Cal.App.2d 377, 379 [260 P.2d 1048].) Under the bond, Keller assumed an obligation to pay the lien claims of any and all persons, including subcontractors, that performed work on the project identified in the general contract. Liability on the bond thus extends not only to those with whom Keller has entered into subcontracts, but to "everyone who has a right to claim a lien" . . .And the liability on the bond to pay mechanic's lien claims fell equally on Keller as principal and Safeco as surety. . . .Thus, the default for which Safeco promised to answer was Keller's default under the bond and not Keller's default under the subcontracts. . . .

Having concluded that a general contractor's liability to a subcontractor for work performed may not be made contingent on the owner's payment to the general contractor, we conclude that Keller was liable to the subcontractors under their subcontracts for the work they performed and that Safeco, as Keller's surety, was likewise liable on the payment bond.

The judgment of the Court of Appeal is affirmed.

Questions

1. What is the majority view in other jurisdictions regarding "pay if paid" provisions in construction subcontracts, and how has this approach been followed in California?

2. When determining the validity of a true "pay if paid" provision, what factors must the courts consider, and what is the question of first impression in this case?

3. How does Safeco argue that a pay if paid provision does not violate Civil Code section 3262's anti-waiver provisions, and what is the court's response to this argument?

4. According to Safeco, why should pay if paid provisions be considered valid based on the public policy of freedom of contract? How does the court counter this argument?

Takeaways – Wm R. Clarke v. Safeco

What is the distinction between "language or promise" and "language of condition?" Indeed if it was the parties' intent (or at least the general contractor's intent) that the pay if paid provision would make payment by the owner to the general contractor a condition precedent to the general contractor's obligation to pay the subcontractor for work, what justifies interpreting the clause in a way to circumvent that intent by construing it as language of promise rather than language of condition?

Consider the possible effect of the following rule: "To the extent that the non-occurrence of a condition would cause disproportionate forfeiture, a court may excuse the non-occurrence of that condition unless its occurrence was a material part of the agreed exchange." (Rest.2d § 229) If that means the court can overlook the non-occurrence or failure of a condition to avoid one party forfeiting or losing their right to receive the other party's performance, was it necessary to decide the validity of "pay if paid" clauses on public policy grounds?

Real Estate Brokers and Conditions

As you probably know, real estate brokers work on commission. The seller of a home typically does not want to be obligated to pay a broker a commission unless the home actually sells. A common type of listing agreement is one wherein the broker agrees to produce a buyer ready, willing and able to purchase the described property on the terms and conditions set forth in the listing and the seller agrees to accept the offer on the terms set forth in the agreement. Under such an agreement, it is well settled the broker's commission is earned upon the production of a ready, willing and able buyer. The broker or agent is ordinarily entitled to the commission when he or she produces a purchaser, ready, able and willing to buy the property for the price and on the terms specified by the principal, regardless of whether a valid contract of sale is entered into by the buyer and seller, or whether the sale is ever consummated. (See, *Seck v. Foulks* (1972,) 25 Cal.App.3d 556, 571-572) Production of a buyer ready, willing and able to purchase on the seller's terms is a condition precedent to the broker's right to a commission.

Conditions of Satisfaction

As pointed out earlier, if a party wants to reserve the right to withhold their performance depending upon whether or not a certain fact or event occurs, they need to make that fact or event a condition of their duty to perform. Suppose the fact or event is their satisfaction with the other party's performance?

Gibson v. Cranage
Supreme Court of Michigan, 1878
39 Mich. 49, 33 Am.Rep. 351

MARSTON, J. Plaintiff in error brought assumpsit to recover the contract price for the making and execution of a portrait of the deceased daughter of defendant. It appeared from the testimony of the plaintiff that he at a certain time called upon the defendant and solicited the privilege of making an enlarged picture of his deceased daughter. He says "I was to make an enlarged picture that he would like, a large one from a small one, and one that he would like and recognize as a good picture of his little girl, and he was to pay me."

The defendant testified that the plaintiff was to take the small photograph and send it away to be finished, "and when returned if it was not perfectly satisfactory to me in every particular, I need not take it or pay for it. I still objected and he urged me to do so. There was no risk about it; if it was not perfectly satisfactory to me I need not take it or pay for it."

There was little if any dispute as to what the agreement was. After the picture was finished it was shown to defendant who was dissatisfied with it and refused to accept it. Plaintiff endeavored to ascertain what the objections were, but says he was unable to ascertain clearly, and he then sent the picture away to the artist to have it changed.

On the next day he received a letter from defendant reciting the original agreement, stating that the picture shown him the previous day was not satisfactory and that he declined to take it or any other similar picture, and countermanded the order. A farther correspondence was had, but it was not very material and did not change the aspect of the case. When the picture was afterwards received by the plaintiff from the artist, he went to see defendant and to have him examine it. This defendant declined to do, or to look at it, and did not until during the trial, when he examined and found the same objections still existing.

We do not consider it necessary to examine the charge in detail, as we are satisfied it was as favorable to plaintiff as the agreement would warrant.

The contract (if it can be considered such) was an express one. The plaintiff agreed that the picture when finished should be satisfactory to the defendant, and his own evidence showed that the contract in this important particular had not been performed. It may be that the picture was an excellent one and that the defendant ought to have been satisfied with it and accepted it, but under the agreement the defendant was the only person who had the right to decide this question. Where parties thus deliberately enter into an agreement which violates no rule of public policy, and which is free from all taint of fraud or mistake, there is no hardship whatever in holding them bound by it.

Artists or third parties might consider a portrait an excellent one, and yet it prove very unsatisfactory to the person who had ordered it and who might be unable to point out with clearness or certainty the defects or objections. And if the person giving the order stipulates that the portrait when finished must be satisfactory to him or else he will not accept or pay for it, and this is agreed to, he may insist upon his right as given him by the contract. *McCarren v. McNulty,* 7 Gray, 141; *Brown v. Foster,* 113 Mass., 136: 18 Amer., 465.

The judgment must be affirmed with costs.

Questions

1. How did the court interpret the agreement between the plaintiff and defendant regarding the portrait?

2. Why did the court emphasize that the defendant had the exclusive right to decide whether the portrait was satisfactory?

Takeaways – Gibson v. Cranage

Is *Gibson* another example of a promissory condition? If so, how does it differ from other promissory conditions? A contract can include language which indicates that one of the parties is to have discretion to interpret and apply the contract. Typically this is done by providing that performance must be to the promisee's "satisfaction." Even so, unless it's a contract involving "matters which are dependent upon the personal feelings, taste or judgment of the" promisee, as in a contract to paint a portrait, the party to be satisfied must base his determination on grounds which are reasonable and just. So-called "satisfaction" provisions in a contract either involve the feelings, artistic taste, or sensibilities of the promiser, (as in *Gibson*) or considerations of operative fitness, mechanical utility, or commercial value. *Schliess v. City of Grand Rapids*, 131 Mich. 52, 90 N.W. 700 (1902). In neither case may the promisor avoid the contract at his "whim." In the former, his decision must be genuine, and in the latter, it must be both genuine and reasonable. *Holton v. Monarch Motor Car Company*, 202 Mich. 271, 168 N.W. 539 (1918); *Morehead Manufacturing Company v. Alaska Refrigerator Company*, 203 Mich. 543, 170 N.W. 19 (1918); *Isbell v. Anderson Carriage Company*, 170 Mich. 304, 136 N.W. 457 (1912). These are jury issues, and his expression of dissatisfaction would not be controlling. The fact that the satisfaction clause pertains to acts by the party to be satisfied and not the other party is immaterial. 3A Corbin, Contracts § 644 (1960 ed.). *American Oil Company v. Carey*, 246 F. Supp. 773 (E.D. Mich. 1965).

Concurrent Conditions

Pittman v. Canham
California Court of Appeal, Second District, 1992
2 Cal.App.4th 556, 3 Cal.Rptr.2d 340

GILBERT, J. When is a contract no longer a contract? When it contains concurrent conditions and neither party tenders timely performance. Unlike love or taxes, concurrent conditions do not last forever.

We hold that where a contract creates concurrent conditions and neither party tenders timely performance, both parties are discharged. We affirm the judgment.

Jeffrey A. Pittman was a licensed real estate broker. In 1987 he contacted Lily V. Canham, then 85 years old, to purchase a parcel of property she owned in San Luis Obispo County. After many telephone calls to Canham between May and November 1987, she agreed to sell a 56-acre parcel to Pittman for $250,000.

Pittman drafted the contract dated November 24, 1987, and deposited $1,000 in escrow. The contract called for a further deposit of $24,000 in cash, with the balance of the purchase price to be paid by a note secured by a deed of trust on the property. Closing of escrow was to be within 30 days. The contract provided that "[t]ime is of the essence. All modification or extensions shall be in writing signed by the parties."

The parties executed escrow instructions that provided: "Time is of the essence of these instructions. If this escrow is not in condition to close by the Time Limit Date of December 24, 1987 and written demand for cancellation is received by you from any principal to this escrow after said date, you shall act in accordance with [other provisions of the instructions]. ... [¶] If no demand for cancellation is made, you will proceed to close this escrow when the principals have complied with the escrow instructions." Paragraph 2 of section 4 of the instructions provided, however, that the instructions were not intended to amend, modify or supersede the contract.

About the second week of December Canham gave a signed copy of the escrow instructions to Pittman for delivery to escrow. With the instructions, Canham included a signed deed to the property. The escrow company pointed out, however, that the deed had not been notarized. When Pittman contacted Canham, she told him she would have it notarized at an escrow company near her home.

The December 24 closing date came and went. Canham had not tendered a notarized deed nor had Pittman tendered $24,000, a promissory note or deed of trust.

By March 1988, Canham had been contacted by another broker who wanted to list the property. On March 21 she told Pittman she wanted $10,000 per acre. Pittman embarked on an effort to find out what a fair price for the property was.

In May 1988, Canham told Pittman that she had entered into a contract with other purchasers to buy the property for $600,000. Pittman wrote a letter demanding that she perform on his contract, but she sold the property to the other buyers.

Pittman sued Canham for breach of contract. At trial he attributed the difference in the $250,000 he offered Canham and the $600,000 sales price six months later to an escalating real estate market.

At the end of Pittman's case, Canham moved for a judgment of nonsuit. (Code Civ. Proc., § 581c.) A ruling on the motion was reserved, however, until all the evidence was presented. After the presentation of the evidence, the court granted the motion on the ground that time was of the essence of the contract and neither party tendered performance. The court also gave a statement of decision in which it found that Pittman and not Canham was responsible for the delay in performance, that Canham had not waived time for performance, and that Pittman defaulted when he failed to tender the purchase money, note and deed of trust by December 24, 1987.

Pittman contends the trial court erred in finding he was in default for failing to tender the purchase money note and deed of trust. He concedes that the result reached by the trial court would be proper if his performance had been a condition precedent, but he points out that here the contract provision requiring Canham to deliver a recordable deed into escrow and the provision requiring him to deposit money, a note and a deed of trust are concurrent conditions. Pittman claims that unlike the failure to perform a condition precedent, the failure of both parties to perform concurrent conditions does not automatically terminate the contract, but that one party must tender performance before the other party is in default. (Citing Chan v. Title Ins. & Trust Co. (1952) 39 Cal.2d 253 [246 P.2d 632]; Rubin v. Fuchs (1969) 1 Cal.3d 50 [81 Cal.Rptr. 373, 459 P.2d 925]; 1 Miller & Starr, Cal. Real Estate (2d ed.

1989) § 1:135, p. 488.)

Concurrent conditions are conditions precedent which are mutually dependent, and the only important difference between a concurrent condition and a condition precedent is that the condition precedent must be performed before another duty arises, whereas a tender of performance is sufficient in the case of a concurrent condition. (1 Witkin, Summary of Cal. Law (9th ed. 1987) Contracts, § 737, pp. 667-668.)

Contrary to Pittman's assertion, the failure of both parties to perform concurrent conditions does not leave the contract open for an indefinite period so that either party can tender performance at his leisure. The failure of both parties to perform concurrent conditions during the time for performance results in a discharge of both parties' duty to perform. Thus, where the parties have made time the essence of the contract, at the expiration of time without tender by either party, both parties are discharged. (3A Corbin on Contracts (1960) § 663, p. 181.) Here, because time was made the essence of the contract, the failure of both parties to tender performance by December 24, 1987, discharged both from performing. Neither party can hold the other in default and no cause of action to enforce the contract arises. (See Pitt v. Mallalieu (1948) 85 Cal.App.2d 77, 81 [192 P.2d 24].)

Pittman relies on the portion of the escrow instructions that states: "Time is of the essence of these instructions. ... If this escrow is not in condition to close by the Time Limit Date of December 24, 1987 and ... [i]f no demand for cancellation is made, you will proceed to close this escrow when the principals have complied with the escrow instructions." He claims this provision shows that time was not truly of the essence in this transaction.

But it is difficult to see how a paragraph that begins with the words "[t]ime is of the essence" could reasonably be construed as meaning time is not truly of the essence. The provision relied on by Pittman merely instructs the escrow holder not to cancel escrow on its own initiative, but to close escrow should the parties voluntarily and notwithstanding discharge mutually decide to perform. As we read the paragraph, it does not purport to give a party the unilateral right to demand performance after the time for performance has passed. Such a construction would render meaningless the parties' agreement that time is of the essence.

We appreciate the reluctance of a buyer to act first by placing money into escrow. But in a contract with concurrent conditions, the buyer and seller cannot keep saying to one another, "No, you first." Ultimately, in such a case, the buyer seeking enforcement comes in second; he loses.

Chan v. Title Ins. & Trust Co., supra, 39 Cal.2d 253, is of no help to Pittman. There, the court found no default because time for performance had been waived. (Id., at p. 256.) Here, the trial court held that there has been no waiver, and there is nothing in the record that requires us to disturb that finding.

Nor is Pittman aided by Rubin v. Fuchs, supra, 1 Cal.3d 50. There, buyer promised to deposit cash and a purchase money deed of trust before the date set for close of escrow. Seller promised to record a tract map prior to that date. Recordation of the tract map would supply the legal description for the deed of trust. Seller, however, did not record the tract map, and buyer could therefore not deposit a deed of trust.

Our Supreme Court held that seller could not rescind for buyer's failure to perform because seller's performance was necessarily precedent to performance by the buyer. (Rubin v. Fuchs, supra, 1 Cal.3d 50, 54.) Here there was no impediment to Pittman's tender of performance. . . .

The judgment is affirmed. Costs are awarded to Canham.

Questions

1. What is the distinction between concurrent conditions and conditions precedent in a contract, and how does it impact the parties' obligations?

2. Explain the court's ruling regarding the effect of the failure to tender timely performance by both parties in a contract with concurrent conditions.

3. How did the court interpret the provision in the escrow instructions regarding the time limit for closing the escrow? What was the significance of this interpretation?

4. Why did the court reject the argument that the buyer's performance was a condition precedent in this case, as opposed to a concurrent condition?

Takeaways - Pittman v. Canham

Usually, if a party's duty to perform is conditional, they are not obligated to perform until the condition precedent has occurred. However, with concurrent conditions, a tender of performance is sufficient to trigger the other party's duty to perform. A tender is an offer of performance. An effective tender has the effect of placing the party to whom the tender is made in default if such person refuses to accept the offer of performance.

Prevention

Parsons v. Bristol Development Co.
Supreme Court of California, 1965
62 Cal.2d 861

TRAYNOR, C. J. In December 1960 defendant Bristol Development Company entered into a written contract with plaintiff engaging him as an architect to design an office building for a lot in Santa Ana and to assist in supervising construction. Plaintiff's services were to be performed in two phases. He completed phase one, drafting preliminary plans and specifications, on January 20, 1961, and Bristol paid him $600.

The dispute concerns Bristol's obligation to pay plaintiff under phase two of the contract. The contract provided that "a condition precedent to any duty or obligation on the part of the Owner [Bristol] to commence, continue or complete Phase 2 or to pay Architect any fee therefor, shall be the obtaining of economically satisfactory financing arrangements which will enable Owner, in its sole judgment, to construct the project at a cost which in the absolute decision of the Owner shall be economically feasible." It further provided that when Bristol notified plaintiff to proceed with phase two it should pay him an estimated 25 per cent of his fee, and that it would be obligated to pay the remaining 75 per cent "only from construction loan funds."

Using plaintiff's preliminary plans and specifications, Bristol obtained from a contractor an estimate of $1,020,850 as the cost of construction, including the architect's fee of 6 per cent. On the basis of this estimate, it received an offer from a savings and loan company for a construction loan upon condition that it show clear title to the Santa Ana lot and execute a first trust deed in favor of the loan company.

Shortly after obtaining this offer from the loan company, Bristol wrote plaintiff on March 14, 1961, to proceed under phase two of the contract. In accordance with the contract, Bristol paid plaintiff $12,000, an estimated 25 per cent of his total fee. Thereafter, plaintiff began to draft final plans and specifications for the building.

Bristol, however, was compelled to abandon the project because it was unable to show clear title to the Santa Ana lot and thus meet the requirements for obtaining a construction loan. Bristol's title became subject to dispute on May 23, 1961, when defendant James Freeman filed an action against Bristol claiming an adverse title. (Freeman had previously conveyed the Santa Ana lot to Bristol on October 1, 1960, with the understanding that Bristol would construct an office building upon the lot and pay Freeman an annuity.) On August 15, 1961, Bristol notified plaintiff to stop work on the project.

Plaintiff brought an action against Bristol and Freeman to recover for services performed under the contract and to foreclose a mechanic's lien on the Santa Ana lot. The trial court, sitting without a jury, found that Bristol's obligation to make further payment under the contract was conditioned upon the existence of construction loan funds. On the ground that this condition to plaintiff's right to further payment was not satisfied, the court entered judgment for defendants. Plaintiff appeals. . . .

Since there is no conflict in the extrinsic evidence in the present case we must make an independent determination of the meaning of the contract. After providing for payment of an estimated 25 per cent of plaintiff's fee upon written notice to proceed with phase two, paragraph 4 of the contract makes the following provisions for payment:

"4. ... "(a) ..."(b) Upon completion of final working plans, specifications and engineering, or authorized commencement of construction, whichever is later, a sum equal to Seventy-Five (75%) Per Cent of the fee for services in Phase 2, less all previous payments made on account of fee; provided, however, that this payment shall be made only from construction loan funds.

"(c) The balance of the fee shall be paid in equal monthly payments commencing with the first day of the month following payments as set forth in Paragraph 4(b); provided, however, that Ten (10%) Per Cent of the fee based upon the reasonable estimated cost of construction shall be withheld until thirty (30) days after the Notice of Completion of the project has been filed.

"(d) If any work designed or specified by the Architect is abandoned of [sic] suspended in whole or in part, the Architect is to be paid forthwith to the extent that his services have been rendered under the preceding terms of this paragraph. Should such abandonment or suspension occur before the Architect has completed any particular phase of the work which entitles him to a partial payment as aforesaid, the Architect's fee shall be prorated based upon the percentage of the work completed under that particular phase and shall be payable forthwith."

Invoking the provision that "payment shall be made only from construction loan funds," Bristol contends that since such funds were not obtained it is obligated to pay plaintiff no more than he has already received under the contract.

Plaintiff, on the other hand, contends that he performed 95 per cent of his work on phase two and is entitled to that portion of his fee under subdivision (d) of paragraph 4 less the previous payment he received. He contends that subdivision (d) is a "savings clause" designed to secure partial payment if, for any reason, including the lack of funds, the project was abandoned or suspended, plaintiff would limit the construction loan condition to subdivision (b), for it provides "that this payment shall be made only from construction loan funds" (emphasis added), whereas the other subdivisions are not expressly so conditioned.

The construction loan condition, however, cannot reasonably be limited to subdivision (b), for subdivisions (c) and (d) both refer to the terms of subdivision (b) and must therefore be interpreted with reference to those terms. Thus, the "balance of the fee" payable "in equal monthly payments" under subdivision (c) necessarily refers to the preceding subdivisions of paragraph 4. In the absence of evidence to the contrary, subdivision (d), upon which plaintiff relies, must likewise be interpreted to incorporate the construction loan condition (Civ. Code, § 1641), for it makes explicit reference to payment under preceding subdivisions by language such as "under the preceding terms" and "partial payment as aforesaid." Subdivision (d) merely provides for accelerated payment upon the happening of a contingency. It contemplates, however, that construction shall have begun, for it provides for prorated payment upon the abandonment or suspension in whole or in part of "any work designed or specified by the Architect." Implicit in the scheme is the purpose to provide, after initial payments, for a series of payments from construction loan funds, with accelerated payment from such funds in the event that construction was abandoned or suspended. Although plaintiff was guaranteed an estimated 25 per cent of his fee if the project was frustrated before construction, further payment was contemplated only upon the commencement of construction. This interpretation is supported by evidence that plaintiff knew that Bristol's ability to undertake construction turned upon the availability of loan funds. Accordingly, the trial court properly determined that payments beyond an estimated 25 per cent of plaintiff's fee for phase two were to be made only from construction loan funds.

When "payment of money is to be made from a specific fund, and not otherwise, the failure of such fund will defeat the right of recovery." (Rains v. Arnett, 189 Cal.App.2d 337, 347 [11 Cal.Rptr. 299].) Although there are exceptions to this rule, plaintiff has neither alleged nor proved facts that entitle him to recover on the ground of any exception.

Each party to a contract has a duty to do what the contract presupposes he will do to accomplish its purpose. (Bewick v. Mecham, 26 Cal.2d 92, 99 [156 P.2d 757, 157 A.L.R. 1277].) Thus, "A party who prevents fulfillment of a condition of his own obligation ... cannot rely on such condition to defeat his liability." (Bewick v. Mecham, supra, 26 Cal.2d at p. 99; Pacific Venture Corp. v. Huey, 15 Cal.2d 711, 717 [104 P.2d 641].)plaintiff, however, has not shown that Bristol failed to make the proper and reasonable efforts that were contemplated to secure the loan from which he was to be paid. (Cf. Rosenheim v. Howze, 179 Cal. 309 [176 P. 456].) The risk that a loan might not be obtained even though Bristol acted properly and in good faith was a risk clearly anticipated even though the reason the loan failed may not have been foreseen.

Nor has plaintiff established grounds for applying the doctrine of equitable estoppel to deny Bristol the right to invoke the construction loan condition. (See Code Civ. Proc., § 1962, subd. 3.) If, by its letter of March 14, asking plaintiff to proceed with his work under phase two of the contract, Bristol had induced plaintiff to believe that funds had been obtained, and if plaintiff had reasonably relied upon such representation, Bristol could not invoke the condition to defeat its contractual liability. Reasonable reliance resulting in a foreseeable prejudicial change in position is the essence of equitable estoppel, and therefore a compelling basis for preventing a party from invoking a condition that he represented as being satisfied. (See Crestline Mobile Homes Mfg. Co. v. Pacific Finance Corp., 54 Cal.2d 773, 778-781 [8 Cal.Rptr. 448, 356 P.2d 192]; cf. Drennan v. Star Paving Co., 51 Cal.2d 409, 414-415 [333 P.2d 757].) Bristol, however, did not represent that funds had been obtained, and plaintiff did not reasonably rely upon the existence of construction loan funds when he undertook work under phase two of the contract. A representative of Bristol told plaintiff before he began phase two of his work that although Bristol would be able to pay plaintiff $12,000, an estimated 25 per cent of his fee, "they would not be able to proceed unless actual construction funds were obtained." Plaintiff, knowing that funds had not been obtained, nevertheless chose to proceed with his work on the project.

Finally, plaintiff has not shown that Bristol breached the duty to give him notice when it became clear that construction funds could not be obtained. Without such funds the purpose of the contract would have been frustrated and plaintiff could not have been paid the balance of his fee. Plaintiff therefore would have been excused from performing so long as there was a reasonable doubt as to his compensation. Whether or not such funds were obtained was a matter peculiarly within Bristol's knowledge. Accordingly, Bristol had a duty to notify plaintiff that the project was imperiled when Freeman filed his action against Bristol on May 23, for Bristol then knew or should have known that it would be unable to obtain a loan. Plaintiff, however, has not shown that he failed to receive such notice, and even if it is assumed that he had no notice, he did not prove the extent to which he suffered damages by continuing to work after he should have received notice.

The judgment is affirmed.

Questions

1. What was the condition precedent for Bristol's obligation to pay the architect under phase two of the contract?

2. How did the court interpret subdivision (d) of paragraph 4 in relation to the construction loan condition?

3. What is the general rule regarding payment from a specific fund when it comes to contract obligations?

4. What grounds did the plaintiff fail to establish in order to apply the doctrine of equitable estoppel against Bristol?

Takeaways – Parsons v. Bristol Development

Even though the condition precedent to the owner's obligation to pay the plaintiff never occurred, why did the plaintiff think he was nevertheless entitled to be paid? A party who prevents fulfillment of a condition of his own obligation cannot rely on such condition to defeat his liability. If a party prevents or makes impossible the performance or happening of a condition precedent, the condition is excused.

Waiver and Estoppel

McKenna v. Vernon
Supreme Court of Pennsylvania, 1917
258 Pa. 18, 101 A. 919

[P]laintiff undertook the erection and completion of a moving picture theater in the city of Philadelphia, agreeably to certain plans and specifications which accompanied and were made part of the agreement, he to receive therefor, in full compensation, the sum of $8,750, to be paid by the owner to the contractor wholly upon certificates of the architect as follows: Eighty per cent. of the work set in place as the work proceeds, the first payment within 30 days after the completion of the work; all payments to be due when certificates of the same shall have been issued by the architect; . . . From time to time, as the work progressed, the owner made several payments on account, amounting in all to $6,000. Suit was brought, August 28, 1914, to recover the balance of $2,750. . . . [D]efendant claimed that the building was not completed within the time allowed by the contract, and demanded as a set-off a penalty of $283.35. The trial resulted in a verdict for the plaintiff for $2,500. At the conclusion of the evidence, the defendant asked for a compulsory nonsuit, which was refused.

The several assignments of error, in one form and another, relate directly or indirectly to this one feature of the case, and are all based on the theory that, in the absence of a certificate from the architect of the final completion of the building in accordance with plans and specifications, no right of action existed. Not only is there no express provision to this effect in the contract, but the contract itself shows that no distinction is there made between final payment and the payments on account of the 80 per cent. of work in place.

All payments were to be made only on certificate of the architect, and yet with a single exception each of the seven payments made as the work progressed was made without a certificate being asked for. With such constant and repeated disregard on the part of the owner to exact compliance with this provision in the contract, it is too late now for him to insist that failure on the part of the plaintiff to secure such certificate before suit defeats his right of action. Furthermore, on the trial, the architect, called as a witness, testified that the plaintiff had performed substantial compliance with all the requirements of the contract, that he had not given the certificate to this effect only because it had not been asked for, and that whatever variations there were from the specifications were authorized and directed by him. The provision in the contract for written certificates from the architect is for the benefit and protection of the owner. If he waived it repeatedly, as he did here, during the progress of the work, he cannot complain if he be held to have waived it when he seeks to defend against a final payment for work shown to have been honestly and substantially performed, especially when almost daily he has had the work under his own observation, without remonstrance or complaint at any time with respect to either the work done or materials employed. This being the situation, the court was entirely right in refusing the nonsuit. . . .

The judgment is affirmed.

Questions

1. What was the contractual requirement for payment in the construction agreement?

2. How did the owner's actions during the construction project impact the requirement for a certificate from the architect?

Takeaways – McKenna v. Vernon

Even though the contract provided "all payments to be due when certificates of the same shall have been issued by the architect" why was the owner required to make the final payment without having first received an architect's certificate? Do you think it has anything to do with the fact that he made seven payments without insisting on a certificate? A waiver is a voluntary relinquishment of a known right. If the owner had the right to insist upon an architect's certificate did he relinquish that right when he made payments without requiring the certificate?

When a party has by their words or conduct caused another party to change their position in detrimental reliance on those words or conduct they may be precluded or "estopped" from taking advantage of the other party's change in position. A waiver can be retracted if there has been no change of position in reliance on it, but reliance may change this by turning the waiver into a binding estoppel. Did the plaintiff in *McKenna* rely on the waiver by changing its position?

Drafting Tip – Avoiding Waivers of Breach

If a party desires to avoid the consequences of an implied waiver, he or she may wish to insert the following language into the written agreement:

> *"The failure by one party to require performance of any provision shall not affect that party's right to require performance at any time thereafter, nor shall a waiver of any breach or default of this Contract constitute a waiver of any subsequent breach or default or a waiver of the provision itself."*

Beverly Way Associates v. Barham
California Court of Appeal Second District, 1990
226 Cal.App.3d 49, 276 Cal.Rptr. 240

EPSTEIN, J. This case presents a single principal issue for resolution. It is whether, in a contract for the sale of real estate, the buyer's communicated rejection of a "satisfaction" condition precedent to its obligation to purchase terminates the contract so that the buyer cannot later waive the condition and enforce the agreement. We conclude that it does. We therefore affirm the decision of the trial court, which reached the same conclusion in its order sustaining a demurrer to the buyer's suit to enforce the contract.

This case reaches us on the basis of a successful assertion of a general demurrer without leave to amend. "In assessing the sufficiency of a complaint against a general demurrer, we must treat the demurrer as admitting all material facts properly pleaded." (Glaire v. LaLanne-Paris Health Spa, Inc. (1974) 12 Cal.3d 915, 918 [117 Cal.Rptr. 541, 528 P.2d 357].) Since the demurrer was sustained without leave to amend, we are also mindful of the policy that "the allegations of the complaint must be liberally construed with a view to obtaining substantial justice among the parties." (Youngman v. Nevada Irrigation Dist. (1969) 70 Cal.2d 240, 244-245 [74 Cal.Rptr. 398, 449 P.2d 462].)

The verified complaint in this case incorporates a series of documents by reference that thoroughly chronicle the agreement of the parties. The following summary is based on that pleading, including its incorporated annexes.

In July 1988, the defendant Phyllis Barham (seller) owned a residential building in Long Beach. On July 7, 1988, she executed a contract to sell the building to plaintiff, Beverly Way Associates, a California general partnership (buyer). The purchase price was $3.9 million. The contract provided for the opening of escrow and for a closing within 60 days thereafter. There was no "time is of the essence" provision.

Paragraph 5 of the agreement (contingencies) provided that the "Buyer's obligations to purchase the Property shall be conditioned upon" approval by the buyer of a number of specified inspections and documents, and delivery of clear title and conveyance documents at the close of escrow. The most important provision in the agreement, for purposes of our review, is paragraph 5(a) (Approval by Buyer of Inspection and Documents). The initial portion of that provision states:

"Buyer (and Buyer's consultants) shall have twenty-eight (28) business days after receipt of each of the following items in which to inspect and approve (and Seller shall immediately upon acceptance of this offer deliver to Buyer true copies of the following documents and access to Property to inspect) and it shall be a condition to Buyer's obligation to close escrow that Buyer shall have approved ...." There follows a listing of seven categories of matters to be approved. The fourth of these includes a certified ALTA survey of the property showing all improvements thereon and the location of all exceptions to the title referred to in the preliminary title report.

Although the 60-day provision in the contract would have had escrow close by mid-September, the parties continued to take actions called for under the agreement for a considerable time thereafter. The seller furnished the material required in paragraph 5 on November 15, 1988. On December 2, 1988, a date well within the 28-day period for buyer approval, the buyer wrote the seller rejecting the land survey.

The buyer's letter recites that it had received the survey delivered by the seller, and advised that, "We reluctantly disapprove of the matters disclosed on the Survey and relating to the Property." The following six paragraphs describe the reasons for the rejection in detail. The principal concern appeared to be that a concrete electrical room was constructed on one of the garage parking spaces, and that this reduced the parking spaces to a number below the amount shown on the tract map. According to the buyer's letter, "This fact and its implications represent a serious matter affecting the lawful use, value, title, utility, financeability and marketability of the Property."

The letter continued with an expression of hope that the problems just recited could be surmounted with "some effort, additional time and expense." Rather than cancel, the buyer proposed "some alternatives to keep the deal alive."

Two alternatives were put forward. The first proposed that the seller give the buyer an option until July 1, 1989, to purchase the property for the original price. In return, the seller would have the right to recover $50,000 of the $75,000 deposited in escrow in the event that the buyer should fail to exercise the option.

The second alternative would have reconstructed the agreement into a lease-purchase arrangement, under which the buyer would take possession of the property and pay rent to the seller, and would have an option to purchase "before a certain specified date."

The letter closed with a request to the seller to "advise as to how you wish to proceed with this transaction."

According to the complaint, there was no further communication between the parties until February 2, 1989. On that date, the buyer sent the second letter pertinent to the case. In this correspondence, it advised that, "We are prepared to waive our objections to such items and to proceed to close escrow within 45 days of Ms. Barham's confirmation to us and to escrow that this will be satisfactory to Ms. Barham." The reference to "such items" was to the problems discussed in the December 2, 1988, letter.

The seller then instructed escrow to immediately prepare cancellation instructions and to transmit them to the parties for their inspection. The buyer demanded that seller go forward with the original sale transaction. The seller refused, and the buyer sued for specific performance. (May 19, 1989.) It also filed a lis pendens. The seller demurred and moved to expunge the lis pendens. The demurrer and motion were heard together on July 21, 1989. The demurrer was sustained. The trial court concluded that, "By disapproving the survey on December 12, 1988, plaintiff buyer terminated the contract and cannot sue on same. The court is satisfied that, if plaintiff were granted leave to amend, it would not plead around exhibit D." (The Dec. 2, 1988, letter.) The court therefore declined to grant leave to amend. It also expunged the lis pendens. This appeal followed.

Both sides to this appeal treat the buyer's right of approval under paragraph 5 of the contract as a condition precedent in favor of the buyer. They are quite correct in that characterization.

Section 1436 of the Civil Code (a part of the original 1872 codification) defines a condition precedent as one "which is to be performed before some right dependent thereon accrues, or some act dependent thereon is performed." Although the Restatement avoids the terms "condition precedent" and "condition subsequent," preferring the word "condition" alone to define the former concept (see Rest.2d Contracts, § 224, com. e), the definition it provides is essentially the same for purposes of the issue in this case: "A condition is an event, not certain to occur, which must occur, unless its non-occurrence is excused, before performance under a contract becomes due." (Rest.2d, Contracts, § 224.) This is consistent with the view of the text writers (see 5 Williston, Contracts (3d ed. 1961) §§ 666A, 675A, pp. 141, 189; 3A Corbin, Contracts (1960) § 647, p. 102; 1 Witkin, Summary of Cal. Law (9th ed. 1987) Contracts, § 729, p. 659) and with the national majority view (see Annot., Sale of Realty-Conditions-Financing (1962) 81 A.L.R.2d 1338). It also is consistent with the California authorities. (See Mattei v. Hopper (1958) 51 Cal.2d 119, 122 [330 P.2d 625]; Kadner v. Shields (1971) 20 Cal.App.3d 251, 257 [97 Cal.Rptr. 742].) Finally, we find it significant that the contract language tracks the California statutory definition of a condition precedent as well as the Restatement definition. Paragraph 5(a) specifically provides that "it shall be a condition to Buyer's obligation to close escrow that Buyer shall have approved" of the items specified in the further provisions of the subparagraph, including the property survey.

We turn to an examination of the nature of the buyer's power to approve the condition precedent and to the effect of its disapproval.

Most of the textual and case material on "satisfaction" conditions precedent turns on whether an objective or subjective standard is to be used in reviewing the reasonableness of its exercise, whether good faith is required, and whether such clauses render agreements that include them unenforceable. (See Rest. 2d, Contracts, § 228 (objective standard preferred); 5 Williston, supra, 675A (honest judgment required; contracts generally upheld); Mattei v. Hopper, supra, 51 Cal.2d 119 (contracts not illusory).) We put these issues to one side, since neither party questions the reasonableness, under any standard, of the buyer's exercise of its approval authority in the December 2, 1988, letter, let alone its good faith in doing so.

The effect of a buyer's power to approve documentation required in a contract for the purchase of real estate "is to give the buyer an option not to consummate the purchase if it fails to meet the condition," at least so long as the buyer acts reasonably and in the exercise of good faith. (Crescenta Valley Moose Lodge v. Bunt (1970) 8 Cal.App.3d 682, 687 [87 Cal.Rptr. 428].) Stated another way, the contract gives the buyer the "power and privilege" of termination in the event that it reasonably concludes that the condition has not been fulfilled. (See Mattei v. Hopper, supra, 51 Cal.2d at p. 122 ["satisfactory" lease]; see also Fowler v. Ross (1983) 142 Cal.App.3d 472, 478 [191 Cal.Rptr. 183] [effect of failure of condition that buyer obtain financing was termination of contract, even though contract did not include language that specifically so provided].)

Under the California rule, the holder of a formal option loses the right to exercise it once it has communicated a formal rejection, and this is so even though the purported exercise occurs within the time specified in the option agreement. (Landberg v. Landberg (1972) 24 Cal.App.3d 742, 757 [101 Cal.Rptr. 335].) If anything, the situation of a party who has a power to approve or disapprove a condition precedent and also exercises it by disapproval, presents an a fortiori case.

Except for the judicial gloss that the power of rejection must be exercised reasonably, the party having the power to approve or reject is in the same position as a contract offeree. It is hornbook law that an unequivocal rejection by an offeree, communicated to the offeror, terminates the offer; even if the offeror does no further act, the offeree cannot later purport to accept the offer and thereby create enforceable contractual rights against the offeror. (See Rest.2d, Contracts, § 38, illus. 1, and authority cited in Reporter's Note; 1 Witkin, Summary of Cal. Law, supra, § 172.)

There can be no question but that the buyer exercised its power of disapproval in this case. The December 2, 1988, letter said so expressly ("[w]e reluctantly disapprove the matter disclosed on the Survey and relating to the Property"). This rejection, communicated to the seller, terminated the contract. It left the buyer with no power to create obligations against the seller by a late "waiver" of its objections and acceptance of the proffered documentation.

The fact that the buyer considered the existing contract to be at an end is reflected not only in the unequivocal language of its disapproval, which we have quoted, but also by its effort to keep the "deal alive" by proposing two entirely new formulations that were novel to the agreement of the parties: an option to purchase, and a lease-purchase arrangement. It may be inferred that the buyer was hoping to find a way to acquire the property, but it cannot be doubted that it was unwilling to do so on the basis of what had been presented by the seller.

The buyer presents several arguments in aid of its position that its February 2, 1989, "waiver" and acceptance letter bound the seller to go through with the deal. None of them has merit.

The buyer points out that the contract did not contain a "time is of the essence" clause. From that it argues that it could exercise its power to approve or waive the paragraph 5 documentation within a "reasonable" time, and that whether its doing so two and one-half months after the documents were furnished (instead of within twenty-eight days, as the contract provided) was reasonable is a question of fact. Given the procedural posture of the case, this may be allowed. But it is irrelevant because the buyer exercised its power by rejecting the documentation. The case is entirely different from a simple failure to accept or reject for a period beyond a time specified in the agreement.

For the same reason, we cannot credit the buyer's purported waiver of the objections it had raised in the December 2, 1988, letter. That letter did more than express a concern about the land survey; it disapproved the survey. Approval of the survey was an express condition precedent to the buyer's obligation to perform. The February 2, 1989, letter is consistent with this result. It did not unequivocally do anything. Instead, it stated that the buyer was "prepared" to waive its objection to the survey, and to proceed to close escrow within 45 days of the seller's confirmation that this would be satisfactory to her, and it asked whether it was satisfactory to her. This language reads far more like a renewed offer for a contract than an assertion that the parties have an agreement to which the seller is still bound.

The buyer also argues that since the contract does not specify the effect a failure to approve the documentation, it cannot be concluded that the effect was to terminate the agreement, and that parol evidence should be admitted on that issue. This argument suffers from the same infirmity as buyer's other contentions. The buyer did not just fail to approve the documentation; it disapproved it. Absent a contrary agreement, the legal effect of that act was to terminate the contract. The verified pleading contains no suggestion of a contrary agreement, and none is presented to us in the arguments of the parties. Given that, we see no basis for parol evidence.

As we have seen, the trial court sustained the demurrer without leave to amend because it did not believe that the buyer could plead around the December 2, 1988, rejection letter. Nor do we, and nothing to the contrary has been suggested in the briefs. We conclude that the trial court correctly resolved the issues before it.

The order of dismissal is affirmed.

Questions

1. How did the buyer exercise its power to approve or disapprove a condition precedent in this case?

2. According to the court's reasoning, what is the effect of the buyer's communicated rejection of the condition precedent on the contract?

3. How did the buyer attempt to keep the "deal alive" after rejecting the condition precedent?

4. What arguments did the buyer present to support its position that the seller was bound to go through with the deal? How did the court respond to these arguments?

Avoidance of Forfeiture as a Basis for Excusing a Condition

"To the extent that the non-occurrence of a condition would cause disproportionate forfeiture, a court may excuse the non-occurrence of that condition unless its occurrence was a material part of the agreed exchange." (Rest.2d § 229)

Hicks v. Bush
New York Court of Appeals, 1962
10 N.Y.2d 488, 180 N.E.2d 425

FULD, J. In this action for specific performance of a written agreement, we granted the plaintiff leave to appeal to consider whether the parol evidence rule was violated by the receipt of testimony tending to establish that the parties had orally agreed that the legal effectiveness of the written agreement should be subject to a stated condition precedent.

On July 10, 1956, the plaintiff Frederick Hicks, together with defendant Michael Congero and one Jack McGee, executed a written agreement with the individual defendants, members of defendant Clinton G. Bush Company, whereby the parties were to merge their various corporate interests into a single "holding" company in order to achieve more efficient operation and greater financial strength. The document recited, among other things, that the plaintiff would subscribe for some 425,000 shares of stock in the new holding corporation, known as Bush-Hicks Enterprises, Inc., and that the defendants comprising the Bush Company would subscribe for more than a million shares. The other parties to the agreement were to subscribe for a total of less than 50,000 shares. The principal consideration for the subscription was the transfer to the holding company of stock in the operating corporations which the several parties owned.

The written agreement provided expressly that the subscriptions for the stock in Bush-Hicks Enterprises were to be made "within five days after the date of this Agreement" and that, "If within twenty-five days after the date hereof Bush-Hicks shall have failed to accept any of said subscriptions delivered to it * * * then and in any such event the obligations of all of the parties hereto shall be terminated and cancelled." The subscriptions were promptly made and accepted and, although the plaintiff turned over the stock of his corporations, the defendants did not transfer the stock of their companies to Bush-Hicks Enterprises. In consequence, the plaintiff never received the Bush-Hicks stock as provided in the agreement and the merger never eventuated.

Alleging a breach of contract, the plaintiff brought this suit for specific performance and for an accounting. In their answer, the defendants urged, as an affirmative defense, that the written agreement was executed "upon a parol condition" that it "was not to operate" as a contract and that the contemplated merger was not "to become effective" until so-called "equity expansion funds", amounting to $672,500, were first procured. And, to support that allegation, the defendants upon the trial offered evidence of such an oral understanding. The court admitted the evidence, over the plaintiff's objection that it varied and contradicted the terms of the writing, and, finding that the oral condition asserted had actually been agreed on by the parties, rendered judgment in favor of the defendants.

A reading of the record unquestionably supports the decision of the courts below that the parties, having concluded that $672,500 was essential to successful operation of the proposed merger, agreed that the entire merger deal was to be subject to the condition precedent that that sum be raised. Thus, one witness, the president of the defendant Bush Company, declared that everyone "understood" that the writing was not to become operative as a binding contract until the specified equity expansion funds were obtained. . . . . There is only one understanding, verbal understanding that we have had. That speaks of `Get the money or no deal.'"

The expansion capital of $672,500, which the parties hoped would be procured by December 31, 1956, was never raised.

The applicable law is clear, the relevant principles settled. Parol testimony is admissible to prove a condition precedent to the legal effectiveness of a written agreement (see Saltzman v. Barson, 239 N.Y. 332, 337; Grannis v. Stevens, 216 N.Y. 583, 587; Reynolds v. Robinson, 110 N.Y. 654; see, also, 4 Williston, Contracts [3d ed., 1961], §634, p. 1021; 3 Corbin, Contracts [1960 ed.], § 589, p. 530 et seq.), if the condition does not contradict the express terms of such written agreement. (See Fadex Foreign Trading Corp. v. Crown Steel Corp., 297 N.Y. 903, affg. 272 App. Div. 273, 274-276; see, also, Restatement, Contracts, § 241.) A certain disparity is inevitable, of course, whenever a written promise is, by oral agreement of the parties, made conditional upon an event not expressed in the writing. Quite obviously, though, the parol evidence rule does not bar proof of every orally established condition precedent, but only of those which in a real sense contradict the terms of the written agreement. (See, e.g., Illustration to Restatement, Contracts, § 241.) Upon the present appeal, our problem is to determine whether there is such a contradiction. . . .

There is here no direct or explicit contradiction between the oral condition and the writing; in fact, the parol agreement deals with a matter on which the written agreement, as in some of the cases cited, is silent. The plaintiff, however, contends that, since the written agreement provides in terms that the obligations of the parties were to be terminated if the merged corporation failed to accept any of their stock subscriptions within 25 days, the additional oral condition" that the writing "was [not] to become operative" and that the merger was "not to become effective" until the expansion funds had been raised is irreconcilable with the written agreement.

As already indicated, and analysis confirms it, the two conditions may stand side by side. The oral requirement that the writing was not to take effect as a contract until the equity expansion funds were obtained is simply a further condition a condition added to that requiring the acceptance of stock subscriptions within 25 days and not one which is contradictory. If both provisions had been contained in the written agreement, it is clear that the defendants would not have been under immediate legal duty to transfer the stock in their companies to Bush-Hicks Enterprises until both conditions had been fulfilled and satisfied. And it is equally clear that evidence of an oral condition is not to be excluded as contradictory or "inconsistent" merely because the written agreement contains other conditions precedent. (See, e.g., Hartford Fire Ins. Co. v. Wilson, 187 U. S. 467, 474; Ware v. Allen, 128 U. S. 590, 595-596; Liebling v. Florida Realty Inv. Corp., 24 F.2d 688, 689; Golden v. Meier, 129 Wis. 14, 18; see, also, 3 Corbin, Contracts [1960 ed.], pp. 541-542.) As the Supreme Court wrote in the Hartford Fire Ins. Co. case (187 U. S. 467, 474, supra), "If an instrument containing an absolute promise to pay may be conditionally delivered, it is difficult to perceive any good reason why an instrument containing a promise to pay upon a contingency may not likewise be conditionally delivered."

In short, the parties in the case before us intended that their respective rights and duties with respect to the contemplated transfers of stock in the operating companies to the holding company be subject to two conditions, each independent of the other the acceptance of the stock subscription within a specified period and the procuring of expansion funds of $672,500. As the courts below found, the parties did not contemplate performance of the written agreement until such funds were first received. In other words, it was their desire and understanding that the merger was to be one of proposal only and that, even though the formal preliminary steps were to be taken, the writing was not to become operative as a contract or the merger effective until $672,500 was raised. It is certainly not improbable that parties contracting in these circumstances would make the asserted oral agreement; the condition precedent at hand is the sort of condition which parties would not be inclined to incorporate into a written agreement intended for public consumption. The challenged evidence was, therefore, admissible and, since there was ample proof attesting to the making of the oral agreement, the trial court was fully warranted in holding that no operative or binding contract ever came into existence.

Judgment affirmed.

Questions

1. What was the plaintiff's argument regarding the alleged contradiction between the oral condition and the written agreement in the case?

2. According to the court's reasoning, why did the parol evidence rule not bar the admission of evidence regarding the oral condition?

3. How did the court reconcile the oral condition and the written agreement in relation to the parties' rights and duties?

4. Why did the court find the oral agreement to be admissible and in line with the parties' intentions?

5. How did the court determine that no operative or binding contract existed based on the evidence presented?

Takeaways – Hicks v. Bush

Can the effectiveness of a contract in its entirety be subject to the occurrence of a condition precedent? It the answer is, "yes' might there have been a better way for the parties to this agreement to have handled this situation that might have kept them out of court?

Constructive Conditions of Exchange

Dependent and Independent Promises

Unless the parties clearly express a contrary intent, the law presumes that mutual promises in a contract are dependent. In other words, the law constructs or implies a *condition* that performance by one party is a condition precedent to the duty of the other party to perform. The parties can avoid this presumption by expressly agreeing that each party's duty to perform is independent of the other party's duty to perform.

Kingston v. Preston
Court of King's Bench, 1773
Lofft 194, 2 Doug. 689, 99 Eng. Rep. 437

It was an action of debt, for non-performance of covenants contained in certain articles of agreement between the plaintiff and the defendant. The declaration stated;—That, by articles made the 24th of March, 1770, the plaintiff, for the considerations therein-after mentioned, covenanted, with the defendant, to serve him for one year and a quarter next ensuing, as a covenant-servant, in his trade of a silk-mercer, at £200 a year, and in consideration of the premises, the defendant covenanted, that at the end of the year and a quarter, he would give up his business of a mercer to the plaintiff, and a nephew of the defendant, . . . the defendant would permit the said young traders to carry on the said business in the defendant's house.—Then the declaration stated a covenant by the plaintiff, that he would accept the business and stock in trade, at a fair valuation, with the defendant's nephew. . .and execute such deeds of partnership, and, further, that the plaintiff should, and would, at, and before, the sealing and delivery of the deeds, cause and procure good and sufficient security to be given to the defendant. . . Then the plaintiff averred, that he had performed, and been ready to perform, his covenants, and assigned for breach on the part of the defendant, that he had refused to surrender and give up his business, at the end of the said year and a quarter. The defendant pleaded, 1. That the plaintiff did not offer sufficient security; and, 2. That he did not give sufficient security for the payment of the £250. And the plaintiff demurred generally to both pleas.—

On the part of the plaintiff, the case was argued by Mr. Buller, who contended, that the covenants were mutual and independent, and, therefore, a plea of the breach of one of the covenants to be performed by the plaintiff was no bar to an action for a breach by the defendant of one of which he had bound himself to perform, but that the defendant might have his remedy for the breach by the plaintiff, in a separate action. On the other side, Mr. Grose insisted, that the covenants were dependent in their nature, and, therefore, performance must be alleged: the security to be given for the money, was manifestly the chief object of the transaction, and it would be highly unreasonable to construe the agreement, so as to oblige the defendant to give up a beneficial business, and valuable stock in trade, and trust to the plaintiff's personal security, (who might, and, indeed, was admitted to be worth nothing,) for the performance of his part.

In delivering the judgment of the Court, Lord Mansfield expressed himself to the following effect: There are three kinds of covenants: 1. Such as are called mutual and independent, where either party may recover damages from the other, for the injury he may have received by a breach of the covenants in his favour, and where it is no excuse for the defendant, to allege a breach of the covenants on the part of the plaintiff. 2. There are covenants which are conditions and dependent, in which the [2 Douglas 691] performance of one depends on the prior performance of another, and, therefore, till this prior condition is performed, the other party is not liable to an action on his covenant. 3. There is also [99 Eng. Rep. 438] a third sort of covenants, which are mutual conditions to be performed at the same time; and, in these, if one party was ready, and offered, to perform his part, and the other neglected, or refused, to perform his, he who was ready, and offered, has fulfilled his engagement, and may maintain an action for the default of the other; though it is not certain that either is obliged to do the first act.—His Lordship then proceeded to say, that the dependence, or independence, of covenants, was to be collected from the evident sense and meaning of the parties, and, that, however transposed they might be in the deed, their precedency must depend on the order of time in which the intent of the transaction requires their performance. That, in the case before the Court, it would be the greatest injustice if the plaintiff should prevail: the essence of the agreement was, that the defendant should not trust to the personal security of the plaintiff, but, before he delivered up his stock and business, should have good security for the payment of the money. The giving such security, therefore, must necessarily be a condition precedent.—Judgment was accordingly given for the defendant, because the part to be performed by the plaintiff was clearly a condition precedent.

Questions

1. What were the arguments presented by the plaintiff's counsel regarding the nature of the covenants in the case?

2. How did the defendant's counsel interpret the agreement and justify the defendant's refusal to perform his part?

3. According to Lord Mansfield's judgment, what are the three types of covenants?

4. How did Lord Mansfield determine the dependence or independence of the covenants in this case?

5. Why did Lord Mansfield rule in favor of the defendant and consider the giving of security as a condition precedent in the agreement?

Takeaways – Kingston v. Preston

Did the contract expressly say that the giving of security was a condition precedent to hand over the business? If not, why did the court conclude that the owner was not obligated to hand over the keys to the business until he received security from the purchaser. Would you say the owner's promise to hand over the keys was a "conditional promise?"

Promises are dependent where each promise is conditional on the other side performing their part of the bargain. Although neither party expressly conditions her promise on performance by the other, the law constructs or implies a condition that performance or tender of performance, by one party is a condition precedent to the liability of the other party.

Promises are independent where each promise is absolute, (i.e., must be performed) regardless of the other side performing their part of the bargain. To get around the presumption that mutual promises are dependent, the parties must expressly state that mutual promises in a contract are independent. Why would the parties to a bilateral contract ever want to make their promises anything other than dependent? Consider this example: the typical fire insurance policy is subject to at least two conditions; that there be a loss by fire and that the insurance premiums be paid up. A lender who holds a mortgage on the structure might find itself without security for its loan if the insurance company could site the owner/mortgagor's failure to timely make premium payments as a failure of condition when a claim is made against the policy. To afford even greater protection to the secured creditor, it became customary to modify the loss payable clause to provide that the lender's coverage could not be forfeited by the act or default of any other person. This modified provision came to be known as a standard mortgagee clause. Insurance companies have used standard mortgagee clauses in real estate fire insurance policies since at least 1878. (See, e.g., *Witherow v. United American Ins. Co.* (1929) 101 Cal.App. 334.) In effect it means that the duty to pay the mortgagee in the event of a loss is independent of the duty of the mortgagor to pay premiums.

Time for Performance

Stewart v. Newbury
Court of Appeals of New York, 1917
220 N.Y. 379, 115 N.E. 984

CRANE, J. [Stewart offered to do the excavation work for Newbury's foundry building. Newbury replied, "Confirming the telephone conversation of this morning we accept your bid of July the 18th to do [220 N.Y. 382]the concrete work on our new building. We trust that you will be able to get at this the early part of next week."]

Nothing was said in writing about the time or manner of payment. The plaintiff, however, claims that after sending his letter, and before receiving that of the defendant, he had a telephone communication with Mr. Newbury and said: 'I will expect my payments in the usual manner,' and Newbury said, 'All right, we have got the money to pay for the building.' This conversation over the telephone was denied by the defendants. The custom, the plaintiff testified, was to pay 85 per cent. every 30 days or at the end of each month, 15 per cent. being retained till the work was completed.

In July the plaintiff commenced work and continued until September 29th, at which time he had progressed with the construction as far as the first floor. He then sent a bill for the work done up to that date for $896.35. The defendants refused to pay the bill and work was discontinued. The plaintiff claims that the defendants refused to permit him to perform the rest of his contract, they insisting that the work already done was not in accordance with the specifications. The defendants claimed upon the trial that the plaintiff voluntarily abandoned the work after their refusal to pay his bill.

On October 5, 1911, the defendants wrote the plaintiff a letter containing the following: 'Notwithstanding you promised to let us know on Monday whether you would complete the job or throw up the contract, you have not up to this time advised us of your intention. * * * Under the circumstances, we are compelled to accept your action as being an abandonment of your contract and of every effort upon your part to complete your work on our building. As you know, the bill which you sent us and which we declined to pay is not correct, either in items or amount, nor is there anything due you under our contract as we understand it until you have completed your work on our building.'

To this letter the plaintiff replied the following day. In it he makes no reference to the telephone communication agreeing, as he testified, to make 'the usual payments,' but does say this: 'There is nothing in our agreement which says that I shall wait until the job is completed before any payment is due, nor can this be reasonably implied. * * * As to having given you positive date as to when I should let you know what I proposed doing, I did not do so; on the contrary, I told you that I would not tell you positively what I would do until I had visited the job, and I promised that I would do this at my earliest convenience and up to the present time I have been unable to get up there.'

The defendant Herbert Newbury testified that the plaintiff 'ran away and left the whole thing.' And the defendant F. A. Newbury testified that he was told by Mr. Stewart's man that Stewart was going to abandon the job; that he thereupon telephoned Mr. Stewart, who replied that he would let him know about it the next day, but did not.

In this action, which is brought to recover the amount of the bill presented, as the agreed price and $95.68 damages for breach of contract, the plaintiff had a verdict for the amount stated in the bill, but not for the other damages claimed, and the judgment entered thereon has been affirmed by the Appellate Division.

The appeal to us is upon exceptions to the judge's charge. The court charged the jury as follows:

'Plaintiff says that he was excused from completely performing the contract by the defendants' unreasonable failure to pay him for the work he had done during the months of August and September. * * * Was it understood that the payments were to be made monthly? If it was not so understood, the defendants only obligation was to make payments at reasonable periods, in view of the character of the work, the amount of work being done, and the value of it. In other words, if there was no agreement between the parties respecting the payments, the defendants' obligation was to make payments at reasonable times. * * * But whether there was such an agreement or not, you may consider whether it was reasonable or unreasonable for him to exact a payment at that time and in that amount.'

The court further said, in reply to a request to charge:

'I will say in that connection, if there was no agreement respecting the time of payment, and if there was no custom that was understood by both parties, and with respect to which they made the contract, then the plaintiff was entitled to payments at reasonable times.'

The defendants' counsel thereupon made the following request, which was refused:' I ask your honor to instruct the jury that, if the circumstances existed as your honor stated in your last instruction, then the plaintiff was not entitled to any payment until the contract was completed.'

The jury was plainly told that if there were no agreement as to payments, yet the plaintiff would be entitled to part payment at reasonable times as the work progressed, and if such payments were refused he could abandon the work and recover the amount due for the work performed.

This is not the law. Counsel for the plaintiff omits to call our attention to any authority sustaining such a proposition and our search reveals none. In fact, the law is very well settled to the contrary. This was an entire contract. Ming v. Corbin, 142 N. Y. 334, 340, 341,37 N. E. 105. Where a contract is made to perform work and no agreement is made as to payment, the work must be substantially performed before payment can be demanded.

This case was also submitted to the jury upon the ground that there may have been a breach of contract by the defendants in their refusal to permit the plaintiff to continue with his work, claiming that he had departed from the specifications, and there was some evidence justifying this view of the case; but it is impossible to say upon which of these two theories the jury arrived at its conclusion. The above errors, therefore, cannot be considered as harmless and immaterial. Stokes v. Barber Asphalt Paving Co., 207 N. Y. 252, 257,100 N. E. 597; Condran v. Park & Tilford, 213 N. Y. 341, 107 N. E. 565;Clarke v. Schmidt, 210 N. Y. 211, 215,104 N. E. 613. As the verdict was for the amount of the bill presented and did not include the damages for a breach of contract, which would be the loss of profits, it may well be presumed that the jury adopted the first ground of recovery charged by the court as above quoted and decided that the plaintiff was justified in abandoning work for nonpayment of the installment. The judgment should be reversed . . .

Questions

1. What was the plaintiff's claim regarding the defendants' failure to pay for the work?

2. According to the court's charge, what was the defendants' obligation regarding the timing of payments?

3. Did the court find that there was an agreement or custom regarding the time of payment?

4. What did the court state about the plaintiff's entitlement to payment before completion of the contract?

Takeaways – Stewart v. Newbury

Rest.2d § 234(1) requires simultaneous performance whenever feasible, in the absence of language or circumstances indicating a contrary intention. Rest.2d § 234(2) states that where the performance of one party requires a period of time and the performance of the other party does not, the performance of the party requiring a period of time is due before the performance of the other party. This is why it is sometimes said, "The doing must take place before the giving." Performance of the work is a constructive condition precedent to the duty to pay. If you've ever wondered why you don't get paid until the end of the pay period, i.e., after you've done the work, this is why.

Substantial Performance

A promisor who has rendered a "substantial (albeit incomplete) performance" can get judgment for the contract price, with a deduction for minor defects and nonperformance. I.e., the party who has substantially performed is limited to the contract price less the cost of completing the contract or correcting defects.

"Substantial performance" is defined as whether the performance meets the essential purpose of the contract. Was the performance in Jacob & Youngs v. Kent (which we examined earlier in this book.) where the contractor installed the wrong brand of pipe, resulting in no effect on the overall value of the house, a "substantial performance?"

Express conditions (those that are placed into the contract by the parties) must be completely performed and are not subject to the doctrine of substantial performance. Constructive (implied) conditions may be satisfied by substantial performance.

If one party materially fails to perform his or her promise, or materially delays performance, the other party's duty is discharged. However, a slight or partial delay or failure to perform does not discharge or end the other party's duty to perform.

In determining whether a failure to perform is material, the following circumstances are significant:

(1) The extent to which the injured party will be deprived of the benefit which he or she reasonably expected;

(2) the extent to which the injured party can be adequately compensated for the part of that benefit of which he or she will be deprived.

(3) the extent to which the party failing to perform or to offer to perform will suffer forfeiture;

(4) the likelihood that the party failing to perform or to offer to perform will cure his or her failure, taking account of all the circumstances including reasonable

assurances;

(5) the extent to which the behavior of the party failing to perform or to offer to perform comports with standards of good faith and fair dealing. (See, Rest.2d § 241)

A duty to perform is discharged or ended by a material failure of consideration even though the party owing the duty is unaware of the failure or has breached his or her own promise. (See, 1 Witkin, Summary of Cal.Law (10th ed. 2005) Contracts § 813-815.)

Time Is of the Essence

Delay in performance is a material breach only if time of performance is of the essence, that is, if prompt performance is, by the express language of the contract or by its very nature, a vital matter. A late or delayed performance does not ordinarily give rise to a material breach. If the parties intend that a prompt performance is necessary or that failure to perform in a timely manner shall constitute a material breach they should insert the following language into their agreement:

"Time is of the essence for the completion of the work described in this contract. It is anticipated by the parties that all work described herein will be completed within 30 days of the date of execution, and that any delay in the completion of the work described herein shall constitute a material breach of this contract."

The Perfect Tender Rule

Under UCC § 2-601 a purchaser of goods possesses a legal right to insist upon a "perfect tender" by the seller. If the goods fail to conform exactly to the description in the contract (whether as to quality, quantity or manner of delivery) the buyer may reject the goods and rescind the contract. In reading the next two cases consider whether or not there is any leeway in applying the perfect tender rule.

D.P. Technology Corp. v. Sherwood Tool, Inc.
United States District Court, District of Connecticut, 1990
751 F. Supp. 1038

[The plaintiff seller, D.P. Technology ("DPT"), a California corporation, sues the defendant buyer, Sherwood Tool, Inc. ("Sherwood") a Connecticut corporation, alleging a breach of contract for the purchase and sale of a computer system.]

NEVAS, District Judge. The facts of this case can be easily summarized. On January 24, 1989, the defendant entered into a written contract to purchase a computer system, including hardware, software, installation and training, from the plaintiff. The complaint alleges that the computer system was "specifically" designed for the defendant and is not readily marketable. The contract, executed on January 24, 1989, incorporates the delivery term set forth in the seller's Amended Letter of January 17, 1989 stating that the computer system would be delivered within ten to twelve weeks. The delivery period specified in the contract ended on April 18, 1989. The software was delivered on April 12, 1989 and the hardware was delivered on May 4, 1989. On May 9, 1989, the defendant returned the merchandise to the plaintiff, and has since refused payment for both the software and the hardware. Thus, the plaintiff alleges that the defendant breached the contract by refusing to accept delivery of the goods covered by the contract while the defendant argues that it was rather the plaintiff who breached the contract by failing to make a timely delivery. . . .

Because the contract between the parties was a contract for the sale of goods, the law governing this transaction is to be found in Article 2 of the Uniform Commercial Code ("UCC"); Conn.Gen.Stat. §§ 42a-2-101 *et seq.* In its motion to dismiss, the defendant argues that the plaintiff fails to state a claim upon which relief can be granted because the plaintiff breached the contract which provided for a delivery period of ten to twelve weeks from the date of the order, January 24, 1989. Since the delivery period ended on April 18, 1989, the May 4 hardware delivery was 16 days late. The defendant contends that because the plaintiff delivered the hardware after the contractual deadline, the late delivery entitled the defendant to reject delivery, since a seller is required to tender goods in conformance with the terms set forth in a contract. U.C.C. § 2-301; Conn.Gen.Stat. § 42a-2-301.

In its memorandum in opposition, the plaintiff contends that the defendant waived the original delivery schedule. The plaintiff points to its allegation in the complaint that it designed and developed the computer system pursuant to the contract, Complaint ¶ 3-6. and argues that, in designing and developing a "specifically designed" computer system, consultations with the defendant took place which resulted in adjustment of the delivery schedule, and that the defendant waived the 10-12 week delivery requirement. In *Bradford Novelty Co. v. Technomatic,* 142 Conn. 166, 170, 112 A.2d 214, 216 (1955) (pre-Code), where the buyer acquiesced to a delay in delivery, the court found that the buyer "by its conduct, waived its right to strict compliance with the provisions of the contract as to time of performance." In the instant case, however, the plaintiff failed to allege its waiver claim in the complaint. Consequently, the defendant's motion to dismiss cannot be denied on a claim of waiver.

The plaintiff also states that even if the computers were delivered late, the buyer could not reject the goods pursuant to Conn.Gen.Stat. § 42a-2-602 because the parties had an installment contract. The plaintiff contends that the contract was an installment one, which authorizes the delivery of goods in separate lots to be separately accepted, as illustrated by the separate deliveries of software and hardware. A buyer may reject an installment only if the non-conformity substantially impairs the value of the goods. Conn.Gen.Stat. § 42a-2-612(2)-(3). The defendant has not asserted that the late delivery substantially reduced the computer system's value. Since the allegations in the complaint must be construed in favor of the nonmoving party in a motion to dismiss, if an installment contract was alleged, then UCC Section 2-601 would be superseded by UCC Section 2-612. However, the complaint lacks any reference to an installment contract. Therefore, the defendant's motion to dismiss cannot be denied on the grounds that there was an installment contract.

In addition, the plaintiff argues that the defendant relies on the perfect tender rule, allowing buyers to reject for any non-conformity with the contract. Plaintiff points out that the defendant has not cited one case in which a buyer rejected goods solely because of a late delivery, and that the doctrine of "perfect tender" has been roundly criticized. While it is true that the perfect tender rule has been criticized by scholars principally because it allowed a dishonest buyer to avoid an unfavorable contract on the basis of an insubstantial defect in the seller's tender, *Ramirez v. Autosport,* 88 N.J. 277, 283-85, 440 A.2d 1345, 1348-49 (1982); . . .E. Peters, *Commercial Transactions* 33-37 (1971) (even before enactment of the UCC, the perfect tender rule was in decline), the basic tender provision of the Uniform Commercial Code continued the perfect tender policy developed by the common law and embodied in the Uniform Sales Act. Section 2-601 states that with certain exceptions, the buyer has the right to reject "if the goods or the tender of delivery fail *in any respect* to conform to the contract." (emphasis supplied). Conn.Gen.Stat. § 42a-2-601. The courts that have considered the issue have agreed that the perfect tender rule has survived the enactment of the Code. *See, e.g., Intermeat, Inc. v. American Poultry, Inc.,* 575 F.2d 1017, 1024 (2d Cir. 1978) ("There is no doubt that the perfect tender rule applies to measure the buyer's right of initial rejection of goods under UCC section 2-601."); *Capitol Dodge Sales, Inc. v. Northern Concrete Pipe, Inc.,* 131 Mich.App. 149, 158, 346 N.W.2d 535, 539 (1983) (adoption of 2-601 creates a perfect tender rule replacing pre-Code cases defining performance of a sales contract in terms of substantial compliance); *Texas Imports v. Allday,* 649 S.W.2d 730, 737 (Tex.App.1983) (doctrine of substantial performance is not applicable under 2-601); *Ramirez,* 440 A.2d at 1349 (before acceptance, the buyer may reject goods for any nonconformity); *Sudol v. Rudy Papa Motors,* 175 N.J.Super. 238, 240-241, 417 A.2d 1133, 1134 (1980) (section 2-601 contains perfect tender rule); . . . Similarly, courts interpreting 2-601 have strictly interpreted it to mean any nonconformity, thus excluding the doctrine of substantial performance.[6]*Printing Center of Texas, Inc. v. Supermind Pub. Co. Inc.,* 669 S.W.2d 779, 783 (Tex.App.1984) (the term conform within 2-601 authorizing the buyer to reject the whole if the goods or tender of delivery fail in any respect to conform to the contract does not mean substantial performance but complete performance); . . . Connecticut, however, appears in this regard to be the exception. Indeed, in the one Connecticut case interpreting 2-601, *Franklin Quilting Co., Inc. v. Orfaly,* 1 Conn.App. 249, 251, 470 A.2d 1228, 1229 (1984), in a footnote, the Appellate Court stated that "the `perfect tender rule' requires a *substantial nonconformity* to the contract before a buyer may rightfully reject the goods." *Id.* at 1229 n. 3, citing White & Summers,

Uniform Commercial Code (2d Ed.), section 8-3 (emphasis supplied). Thus, the Connecticut Appellate Court has adopted "the White and Summers construction of 2-601 as in substance a rule that does not allow rejection for insubstantial breach such as a short delay causing no damage." *Id.* (3rd Ed.) section 8-3. *See also National Fleet Supply, Inc. v. Fairchild,* 450 N.E.2d 1015, 1019 n. 4 (Ind.App.1983) (despite UCC's apparent insistence on perfect tender, it is generally understood that rejection is not available in circumstances where the goods or delivery fail in some small respect to conform to the terms of the sales contract (citing White and Summers)); *McKenzie v. Alla-Ohio Coals, Inc.,* 29 U.C.C.Rep.Serv. (Callaghan) 852, 856-57 (D.D.C.1979) (there is substantial authority that where a buyer has suffered no damage, he should not be allowed to reject goods because of an insubstantial nonconformity).

As noted above, a federal court sitting in diversity must apply the law of the highest court of the state whose law applies. Since this court has determined that Connecticut law governs, the next task is to estimate whether the Connecticut Supreme Court would affirm the doctrine of substantial nonconformity, as stated in *Orfaly,* an opinion of the Connecticut Appellate Court. When the highest state court has not spoken on an issue, the federal court must look to the inferior courts of the state and to decisions of sister courts as well as federal courts. As noted, the weight of authority is that the doctrine of substantial performance does not apply to the sale of goods. However, as noted by White and Summers, in none of the cases approving of perfect rather than substantial tender was the nonconformity insubstantial, such as a short delay of time where no damage is caused to the buyer. White and Summers, *Uniform Commercial Code* (3rd Ed.), section 8-3 n. 8. In the instant case, there is no claim that the goods failed to conform to the contract. Nor is there a claim that the buyer was injured by the 16-day delay. There is, however, a claim that the goods were specially made, which might affect the buyer's ability to resell. Thus Connecticut's interpretation of 2-601 so as to mitigate the harshness of the perfect tender rule reflects the consensus of scholars that the rule is harsh and needs to be mitigated. Indeed, Summers and White state that the rule has been so "eroded" by the exceptions in the Code that "relatively little is left of it; the law would be little changed if 2-601 gave the right to reject only upon `substantial' non-conformity," especially since the Code requires a buyer or seller to act in good faith. R. Summers and J. White, *Uniform Commercial Code* (3rd Ed. 1988), 8-3, at 357. *See also Alden Press Inc. v. Block & Co., Inc.,* 123 Ill.Dec. 26, 30, 173 Ill.App.3d 251, 527 N.E.2d 489, 493 (1988) (notwithstanding the perfect tender rule, the reasonableness of buyer's rejection of goods and whether such rejection of goods is in good faith are ultimately matters for the trier of fact); *Printing Center of Texas v. Supermind Pub. Co., Inc.,* 669 S.W.2d 779, 784 (Tex.App.1984) (if the evidence establishes any nonconformity, the buyer is entitled to reject the goods as long as it is in good faith); *Neumiller Farms, Inc. v. Cornett,* 368 So.2d 272, 275 (Ala.1979) (claim of dissatisfaction with delivery of goods so as to warrant their rejection must be made in good faith, rather than in an effort to escape a bad bargain). A rejection of goods that have been specially manufactured for an insubstantial delay where no damage is caused is arguably not in good faith.

Although the Connecticut Supreme Court has not yet addressed the issue of substantial nonconformity, it has stated, in a precode case, *Bradford Novelty Co. v. Technomatic,* 142 Conn. 166, 170, 112 A.2d 214, 216 (1955), that although "[t]he time fixed by the parties for performance is, at law, deemed of the essence of the contract," where, as here, goods have been specially manufactured, "the time specified for delivery is less likely to be considered of the essence ... [since] in such a situation there is a probability of delay, and the loss to the manufacturer is likely to be great if the buyer refuses to accept and pay because of noncompliance with strict performance." *Id.* But see *Marlowe v. Argentine Naval Com'n,* 808 F.2d 120, 124 (D.C.Cir.1986) (buyer within its rights to cancel a contract for 6-day delay in delivery since "time is of the essence in contracts for the sale of goods") (citing *Norrington v. Wright,* 115 U.S. 188, 203, 6 S.Ct. 12, 14, 29 L.Ed. 366 (1885) ("In the contracts of merchants, time is of the essence.")

After reviewing the case law in Connecticut, this court finds that in cases where the nonconformity involves a delay in the delivery of specially manufactured goods, the law in Connecticut requires substantial nonconformity for a buyer's rejection under 2-601, and precludes a dismissal for failure to state a claim on the grounds that the perfect tender rule, codified at 2-601, demands complete performance. Rather, Connecticut law requires a determination at trial as to whether a 16-day delay under these facts constituted a substantial nonconformity.

For the foregoing reasons, the defendant's rule 12(b) (6) motion to dismiss this one count complaint is denied.

Questions

1. What is the "perfect tender rule" mentioned in the case, and how did the plaintiff criticize it?

2. According to the court, what is the requirement for a buyer's rejection under UCC Section 2-601 in cases involving a delay in the delivery of specially manufactured goods in Connecticut?

Takeaways – DP Technologies

Judge Learned Hand stated in *Mitsubishi Goshi Kaisha v. J. Aron & Co., Inc.,* 16 F.2d 185, 186 (2d Cir.1926), that "[t]here is no room in commercial contracts for the doctrine of substantial performance." While Judge Hand wrote in a pre-UCC context, modern courts have reiterated the view that perfect tender does not require substantial performance but complete performance.

Although many jurisdictions hold that the perfect tender rule gives the buyer the right to reject if the goods fail in any respect fail to conform to the contract, the law in some jurisdictions is that in cases where the nonconformity involves a delay in the delivery of specially manufactured goods, substantial nonconformity is required. Note that section 2-601 is only applicable to "one-shot" contracts. It does not apply to installment contracts.

Bartus v. Riccardi
City Court of Utica, 1967
284 N.Y.S. 2d, 222, 55 Misc.2d 3

HAROLD H. HYMES, J. The plaintiff is a franchised representative of Acousticon, a manufacturer of hearing aids. On January 15, 1966, the defendant signed a contract to purchase a Model A-660 Acousticon hearing aid from the plaintiff. The defendant specified Model A-660 because he had been tested at a hearing aid clinic and had been informed that the best hearing aid for his condition was this Acousticon model. An ear mold was fitted to the defendant and the plaintiff ordered Model A-660 from Acousticon.

On February 2, 1966, in response to a call from the plaintiff the defendant went to the plaintiff's office for his hearing aid. At that time he was informed that Model A-660 had been modified and improved, and that it was now called Model A-665. This newer model had been delivered by Acousticon for the defendant's use. The defendant denies that he understood this was a different model number. The hearing aid was fitted to the defendant. The defendant complained about the noise, but was assured by the plaintiff that he would get used to it.

The defendant tried out the new hearing aid for the next few days for a total use of 15 hours. He went back to the hearing clinic, where he was informed that the hearing aid was not the model that he had been advised to buy. On February 8, 1966, he returned to the plaintiff's office complaining that the hearing aid gave him a headache, and that it was not the model he had ordered. He returned the hearing aid to the plaintiff, for which he received a receipt. At that time the plaintiff offered to get Model A-660 for the defendant. The defendant neither consented to nor refused the offer. No mention was made by either party about canceling the contract, and the receipt given by the plaintiff contained no notation or indication that the plaintiff considered the contract canceled or rescinded.

The plaintiff immediately informed Acousticon of the defendant's complaint. By letter dated February 14, 1966, Acousticon, writing directly to the defendant, informed him that Model A-665 was an improved version of Model A-660, and that they would either replace the model that had been delivered to him or would obtain Model A-660 for him. He was asked to advise the plaintiff immediately of his decision so that they could effect a prompt exchange. After receiving this letter the defendant decided that he did not want any hearing aid from the plaintiff, and he refused to accept the tender of a replacement, whether it be Model A-665 or A-660.

The plaintiff is suing for the balance due on the contract. . . . The question before the court is whether or not the plaintiff, having delivered a model which admittedly is not in exact conformity with the contract, can nevertheless recover in view of his subsequent tender of the model that did meet the terms of the contract.

The defendant contends that since there was an improper delivery of goods, the buyer has the right to reject the same under sections 2-601 and 2-602 (subd. [2], par. [c]) of the Uniform Commercial Code. He further contends that, even if the defendant had accepted delivery, he may, under section 2-608 (subd. [1], par. [b]) of the Uniform Commercial Code, revoke his acceptance of the goods because "his acceptance was reasonably induced * * * by the seller's assurances." He also relies on section 2-711, claiming that he may recover not only the down payment but also consequential damages.

The defendant, however, has neglected to take into account section 2-508 of the Uniform Commercial Code which has added a new dimension to the concept of strict performance. This section permits a seller to cure a nonconforming delivery under certain circumstances. Subdivision (1) of this section enacts into statutory law what had been New York case law. This permits a seller to cure a nonconforming delivery *before the expiration of the contract time* by notifying the buyer of his intention to so cure and by making a delivery within the contract period. . . .

However, subdivision (2) of section 2-508 of the Uniform Commercial Code goes further and extends *beyond the contract time* the right of the seller to cure a defective performance. Under this provision, even where the contract period has expired and the buyer has rejected a nonconforming tender or has revoked an acceptance, the seller may "substitute a conforming tender" if he had "reasonable grounds to believe" that the nonconforming tender would be accepted and "if he seasonably notifies the buyer" of his intention "to substitute a conforming tender." (51 N. Y. Jur., Sales, p. 41.)

This in effect extends the contract period beyond the date set forth in the contract itself unless the buyer requires strict performance by including such a clause in the contract.

"The section [§ 2-508, subd. (2)] rejects the time-honored, and perhaps time-worn notion, that the proper way to assure effective results in commercial transactions is to require strict performance. Under the Code a buyer who insists upon such strict performance must rely on a special term in his agreement or the fact that the seller knows as a commercial matter that strict performance is required." (48 Cornell L. Q. 13; 29 Albany L. Rev. 260.)

This section seeks to avoid injustice to the seller by reason of a surprise rejection by the buyer. (Official Comment, McKinney's Cons. Laws of N. Y., Book

62½, Uniform Commercial Code, § 2-508.)

An additional burden, therefore, is placed upon the buyer by this section. "As a result a buyer may learn that even though he rejected or revoked his acceptance within the terms of Sections 2-601 and 2-711, he still may have to allow the seller additional time to meet the terms of the contract by substituting delivery of conforming goods." (3 Bender's Uniform Commercial Code Serv., Sales and Bulk Transfers, § 14-02 [1] [a] [ii].)

Has the plaintiff in this case complied with the conditions of section 2-508?

The model delivered to the defendant was a newer and improved version of the model that was actually ordered. Of course, the defendant is entitled to receive the model that he ordered even though it may be an older type. But, under the circumstances, the plaintiff had reasonable grounds to believe that the newer model would be accepted by the defendant.

The plaintiff acted within a reasonable time to notify the defendant of his tender of a conforming model. (Uniform Commercial Code, § 1-204.) The defendant had not purchased another hearing aid elsewhere. His position had not been altered by reason of the original nonconforming tender.

The plaintiff made a proper subsequent conforming tender pursuant to subdivision (2) of section 2-508 of the Uniform Commercial Code.

Judgment is granted to plaintiff.

Questions

1. What sections of the Uniform Commercial Code (UCC) does the defendant rely on to support his argument? Explain how each section is relevant to the case.

2. What does section 2-508 of the UCC allow the seller to do in terms of curing nonconforming deliveries?

3. According to the court's ruling, did the plaintiff comply with the conditions of section 2-508?

4. What additional burden does section 2-508 place on the buyer? Why is this provision included in the UCC?

Takeaways – Bartus v. Riccardi

The drafters of the UCC carved out exceptions to the perfect tender rule. *See, e.g., Leitchfield Dev't Corp. v. Clark,* 757 S.W.2d 207 (Ky.App. 1988) (perfect tender rule of UCC is modified and limited by UCC § 2-508 that seller has reasonable opportunity to cure improper tender); *T.W. Oil, Inc. v. Consolidated Edison Co. of New York, Inc.,* 457 N.Y.S.2d 458, 463, 57 N.Y.2d 574, 443 N.E.2d 932, 937 (1982) (seller's right to cure defective tender, Section 2-508, was intended to act as a meaningful limitation on the absolutism of the perfect tender rule under which no leeway was allowed for any imperfections.)

The original purpose of the perfect tender rule was to prevent unscrupulous sellers from forcing non-conforming goods upon the buyer. However, section 2-508 of the Uniform Commercial Code which permits a seller to cure a nonconforming delivery under certain circumstances appears to solve the problem. Only sellers who are unable to timely cure will be forced to take the goods back.

Waiver of Breach

Instead of treating a breach as a termination of the contract, the injured party may waive the breach by electing to treat the contract as still alive and remaining ready and able to perform on his or her own part, thereby limiting the claim to damages caused by the breach. A waiver may be express or implied. It is implied when the injured party continues to perform with knowledge of the other's breach and accepts further performance from the breaching party following the breach. (See, 1 Witkin, Summary of Cal. Law (10th ed. 2005) Contracts, § § 856-857.)

Divisible Contracts

Gill v. Johnstown Lumber Co.
Supreme Court of Pennsylvania, 1892
151 Pa. 534, 25 Atl. 120

Action by John L. Gill against the Johnstown Lumber Company for services for driving logs. Verdict was directed for defendant, and plaintiff appeals. Reversed.

Heydrick, J. The single question in this cause is whether the contract upon which the plaintiff sued is entire or severable. If it is entire, it is conceded that the learned court below properly directed a verdict for the defendant; if severable, it is not denied that the cause ought to have been submitted to the jury. The criterion by which it is to be determined to which class any particular contract shall be assigned is thus stated in Parsons on Contracts, 29-31: "If the part to be performed by one party consists of several and distinct items, and the price to be paid by the other is apportioned to each item to be performed, or is left to be implied by law, such a contract will generally be held to be severable. * * * But if the consideration to be paid is single and entire, the contract must be held to be entire, although the "subject of the contract may consist of several distinct and wholly independent items." The rule thus laid down was quoted with approval and applied in Oil Co. v. Brewer, 66

Pa. 351, and followed in Rugg v. Moore, 110 Pa. 236, 1 Atl. 320. It was also applied in Ritchie v. Atkinson, 10 East, 295, a case not unlike the present. There the master and freighter of a vessel of 400 tons mutually agreed that the ship should proved to St. Petersburg, and there load from the freighter's factors a complete cargo of hemp and iron, and deliver the same to the freighter at London on being paid freight, for hemp £5 per ton, for iron 5s. per ton, and certain other charges, one half to be paid on delivery and the other at three months. The vessel proceeded to St. Petersburg, and when about half loaded was compelled by the imminence of a Russian embargo upon British vessels to leave, and returning to London delivered to the freighter so much of the stipulated cargo as had been taken on board. The freighter, conceiving that the contract was entire, and the delivery of a complete cargo a condition precedent to a recovery of any compensation, refused to pay at the stipulated rate for so much as was delivered. Lord Ellenborough said: "The delivery of the cargo is in its nature divisible, and therefore I think it is not a condition precedent; but the plaintiff" is entitled to recover freight in proportion to the extent of such delivery; leaving the defendant to his remedy in damages for the short delivery."

Applying the test of an apportionable or apportioned consideration to the contract in question, it will be seen at once that it is severable. The work undertaken to be done by the plaintiff consisted of several items, viz., driving logs, first, of oak, and, second, of various other kinds of timber, from points upon Stony creek and its tributaries above Johnstown to the defendant's boom at Johnstown, and also driving crossties from some undesignated point or points, presumably under- stood by the parties, to Bethel, in Somerset county, and to some other point or points below Bethel. For this work the consideration to be paid was not an entire sum, but was apportioned among the several items at the rate of $1 per 1,000 feet for the oak logs; 75 cents per 1,000 feet for all other logs ; 3 cents each for cross-ties driven to Bethel ; and 5 cents each for cross-ties driven to points below Bethel. But while the contract is severable, and the plaintiff entitled to compensation at the stipulated rate for all logs and ties delivered at the specified points, there is neither reason nor authority for 'the claim for compensation in respect to logs that were swept by the flood to and through the defendant's boom, whether they had been driven part of the way by plaintiff, or remained untouched by him at the coming of the flood. In respect to each particular log the contract in this case is like a contract of common carriage, which is dependent upon the delivery of the goods at the designated place, and, if by *casus* the delivery is prevented, the carrier cannot recover pro tanto for freight for part of the route over which the goods were taken. Whart. Cont. § 714. Indeed, this is but an application of the rule already stated. The consideration to be paid for driving each log is an entire sum per 1,000 feet for the whole distance, and is not apportioned to parts of the drive.

The judgment is reversed, and a venire facias de novo is awarded.

Questions

1. What is the single question at issue in this case, and why is it significant in determining the outcome?

2. How can a contract be classified as either entire or severable?

3. Why is the claim for compensation in respect to the logs swept by the flood not justified?

Takeaways – Gill v. Johnstown Lumber Co.

A divisible contract, as opposed to an entire contract, is one in which performance can be divided into two or more parts and performance of each part forms a part of an equivalent exchange with the opposing party. For example, a contract to be employed for one year could be divided into 12, 24, 26 or 52 parts, depending on whether the employee was paid once a month, twice a month, bi-weekly or every week. If the contract is divisible, a party that has partially performed is entitled to be paid for the divisible portion of the work that he or she has done. In other, words, partial performance of a divisible contract is not grounds for refusing to pay a portion of the compensation due. Why was the contract in *Gill v. Johnstown Lumber* held to be entire or not divisible?

Restitution for a Party in Default

Britton v. Turner
Supreme Court of Judicature of New Hampshire, 1834
6 N.H. 481

Assumpsit for work and labour, performed by the plaintiff, in the service of the defendant, from March 9th, 1831, to December 27, 1831.

The declaration contained the common counts, and among them a count in *quantum meruit*, for the labor, averring it to be worth one hundred dollars.

At the trial in the C. C. Pleas, the plaintiff proved the performance of the labor as set forth in the declaration.

The defense was that it was performed under a special contract—that the plaintiff agreed to work one year, from some time in March, 1831, to March 1832, and that the defendant was to pay him for said year's labor the sum of one hundred and twenty dollars; and the defendant offered evidence tending to show that such was the contract under which the work was done. Evidence was also offered to show that the plaintiff left the defendant's service without his consent, and it was contended by the defendant that the plaintiff had no good cause for not continuing in his employment. There was no evidence offered of any damage arising from the plaintiffs departure, farther than was to be inferred from his non fulfillment of the entire contract.

The court instructed the jury, that if they were satisfied from the evidence that the labor was performed, under a contract to labor a year, for the sum of one hundred and twenty dollars, and if they were satisfied that the plaintiff labored only the time specified in the declaration, and then left the defendant's service, against his consent, and without any good cause, yet the plaintiff was entitled to recover, under his *quantum meruit* count, as much as the labor he performed was reasonably worth, and under this direction the jury gave a verdict for the plaintiff for the sum of $95.

The defendant excepted to the instructions thus given to the jury.

PARKER, J. delivered the opinion of the court. It may be assumed, that the labor performed by the plaintiff, and for which he seeks to recover a compensation in this action, was commenced under a special contract to labor for the defendant the term of one year, for the sum of one hundred and twenty dollars, and that the [486] plaintiff has labored but a portion of that time, and has voluntarily failed to complete the entire contract.

It is clear, then, that he is not entitled to recover upon the contract itself, because the service, which was to entitle him to the sum agreed upon, has never been performed.

But the question arises, can the plaintiff, under these circumstances, recover a reasonable sum for the service he has actually performed, under the count in *quantum meruit*. Upon this, and questions of a similar nature, the decisions to be found in the books are not easily reconciled.

It has been held, upon contracts of this kind for labor to be performed at a specified price, that the party who voluntarily fails to fulfill the contract by performing the whole labor contracted for, is not entitled to recover any thing for the labor actually performed, however much he may have done towards the performance, and this has been considered the settled rule of law upon this subject. [Citations omitted]

That such rule in its operation may be very unequal, not to say unjust, is apparent. A party who contracts to perform certain specified labor, and who breaks his contract in the first instance, without any attempt to perform it, can only be made liable to pay the damages which the other party has sustained by reason of such non performance, which in many instances may be trifling—whereas a party who in good faith has entered upon the performance of his contract, and nearly completed it, and then abandoned the further performance—although the other party has had the full benefit of all that has been done, and has perhaps sustained no actual damage—is in fact subjected to [487] a loss of all which has been performed, in the nature of damages for the non fulfillment of the remainder, upon the technical rule, that the contract must be fully performed in order to a recovery of any part of the compensation.

By the operation of this rule, then, the party who attempts performance may be placed in a much worse situation than he who wholly disregards his contract, and the other party may receive much more, by the breach of the contract, than the injury which he has sustained by such breach, and more than he could be entitled to were he seeking to recover damages by an action.

The case before us presents an illustration. Had the plaintiff in this case never entered upon the performance of his contract, the damage could not probably have been greater than some small expense and trouble incurred in procuring another to do the labor which he had contracted to perform. But having entered upon the performance, and labored nine and a half months, the value of which labor to the defendant as found by the jury is $95, if the defendant can succeed in this defence, he in fact receives nearly five sixths of the value of a whole year's labor, by reason of the breach of contract by the plaintiff a sum not only utterly disproportionate to any probable, not to say possible damage which could have resulted from the neglect of the plaintiff to continue the remaining two and an half months, but altogether beyond any damage which could have been recovered by the defendant, had the plaintiff done nothing towards the fulfillment of his contract.

Another illustration is furnished in *Lantry* v. *Parks,* 8 Cowen, 83. There the defendant hired the plaintiff for a year, at ten dollars per month. The plaintiff worked ten and an half months, and then left saying he would work no more for him. This was on Saturday—on Monday the plaintiff returned, and offered to resume his work, but the defendant said he would employ him no longer. The court held that the refusal of the defendant on Saturday was a violation of his contract, and that he could recover nothing for the labor performed.

There are other cases, however, in which principles have been adopted leading to a different result.

It is said, that where a party contracts to perform certain work, and to furnish materials, as, for instance, to build a house, and the work is done, but with some variations from the mode prescribed by the contract, yet if the other party has the benefit of the labor and materials he should be bound to pay so much as they are reasonably worth. [Citations Omitted]

A different doctrine seems to have been holden in *Ellis* v. *Hamlen,* 3 Taunt. 52, and it is apparent, in such cases, that if the house has not been built in the manner specified in the contract, the work has not been done. The party has no more performed what he contracted to perform, than he who has contracted to labor for a certain period, and failed to complete the time.

It is in truth virtually conceded in such cases that the work has not been clone, for if it had been, the party performing it would be entitled to recover upon the contract itself, which it is held he cannot do.

Those cases arc not to be distinguished, in principle, from the present, unless it be in the circumstance, that where the party has contracted to furnish materials, and do certain labor, as to build a house in a specified manner, if it is not done according to the contract, the party for whom it is built may refuse to receive it—elect to take no benefit from what has been performed—and therefore if he does receive, he shall be bound to pay the value—whereas in a contract for labor, merely, from day to day, the party is continually receiving the benefit of the con [489] tract under an expectation that it will be fulfilled, and cannot, upon the breach of it, have an election to refuse to receive what has been done, and thus discharge himself from payment.

But we think this difference in the nature of the contracts does not justify the application of a different rule in relation to them. The party who contracts for labor merely, for a certain period, does so with full knowledge that he must, from the nature of the case, be accepting part performance from day to day, if the other party commences the performance, and with knowledge also that the other may eventually fail of completing the entire term If under such circumstances he actually receives a benefit from the labor performed, over and above the damage occasioned by the failure to complete, there is as much reason why lie should pay the reasonable worth of what has thus been done for his benefit, as there is when he enters and occupies the house which has been built for him, but not according to the stipulations of the contract, and which he perhaps enters, not because he is satisfied with what has been done, but because circumstances compel him to accept it such as it is, that he should pay for the value of the house.

Where goods are sold upon a special contract as to their nature, quality, and price, and have been used before their inferiority has been discovered, or other circumstances have occurred which have rendered it impracticable or inconvenient for the vendee to rescind the contract *in toto,* it seems to have been the practice formerly to allow the vendor to recover the stipulated price, and the vendee recovered by a cross action damages for the breach of the contract. "But according to the later and more convenient practice, the vendee in such case is allowed, in an action for the price, to give evidence of the inferiority of the goods in reduction of damages, and the plaintiff who has broken his contract is not entitled to recover more than the value of the benefits which the Turner, defendant has actually derived from the goods; and where the latter has derived no benefit, the plaintiff cannot recover at all." 2 Stark. Ev. 640, 642; 1 Starkie's Rep. 107. . . .

There is a close analogy between all these classes of cases, in which such diverse decisions have been made.

If the party who has contracted to receive merchandise, takes a part and uses it, in expectation that the whole will be delivered, which is never done, there seems to be no greater reason that he should pay for what he has received, than there is that the party who has received labor in part, under similar circumstances, should pay the value of what has been done for his benefit.

It is said, that in those cases where the plaintiff has been permitted to recover there was an acceptance of what had been done. The answer is, that where the contract is to labor from day to day, for a certain period, the party for whom the labor is done in truth stipulates to receive it from day to day, as it is performed, and although the other may not eventually do all he has contracted to do, there has been, necessarily, an acceptance of what has been done in pursuance of the contract, and the party must have understood when he made the contract that there was to be such acceptance.

If then the party stipulates in the outset to receive part performance from time to time, with a knowledge that the whole may not be completed, we see no reason why he should not equally be holden to pay for the amount of value received, as where he afterwards takes the benefit of what has been done, with a knowledge that the whole which was contracted for has not been performed. In neither case has the contract been performed. In neither can an action be sustained on the original contract. In both the party has assented to receive what is done. The only difference is, that in the one case the assent is prior, with a knowledge that all may not be performed, in the other it is subsequent, with a knowledge that the whole has not been accomplished.

We have no hesitation in holding that the same rule should be applied to both classes of cases, especially, as the operation of the rule will be to make the party who has failed to fulfill his contract, liable to such amount of damages as the other party has sustained, instead of subjecting him to an entire loss for a partial failure, and thus making the amount received in many cases wholly disproportionate to the injury. 1 Saund. 320, c; 2 Stark. Evid. 643. It is as "hard upon the plaintiff to preclude him from recovering at all, because he has failed as to part of his entire undertaking," where his contract is to labor for a certain period, as it can be in any other description of contract, provided the defendant has received a benefit and value from the labor actually performed.

We, hold then, that where a party undertakes to pay upon a special contract for the performance of labor, or the furnishing of materials, he is not to be charged upon, such special agreement until the money is earned according to the terms of it, and where the parties have made an express contract the law will not imply and raise a contract different from that which the parties have entered into, except upon some farther transaction between the parties.

In case of a failure to perform such special contract, by the default of the party contracting to do the service, if the money is not due by the terms of the special agreement he is not entitled to recover for his labor, or for the materials furnished, unless the other party receives what has been done, or furnished, and upon the whole case derives a benefit from it. 14 Mass. 282, *Taft* v. *Montague;* 2 Stark. Ev. 644.

But if, where a contract is made of such a character, a party actually receives labor, or materials, and thereby derives a benefit and advantage, over and above the damage which has resulted from the breach of the contract by the other party, the labor actually done, and the value received, furnish a new consideration, and the law thereupon raises a promise to pay to the extent of the reasonable worth of such excess. This may be considered as making a new case, one not within the original agreement, and the party is entitled to "recover on his new case, for the work done, not as agreed, but yet accepted by the defendant." 1 Dane's Abr. 224.

If on such failure to perform the whole, the nature of the contract be such that the employer can reject what has been done, and refuse to receive any benefit from the part performance, he is entitled so to do, and in such case is not liable to be charged, unless he has before assented to and accepted of what has been done, however much the other party may have done towards the performance, lie has in such case received nothing, and having contracted to receive nothing but the entire matter contracted for, he is not bound to pay, because his express promise was only to pay on receiving the whole, and having actually received nothing the law cannot and plight not to raise an implied promise to pay. But where the party receives value—takes and uses the materials, or has advantage from the labor, he is liable to pay the reasonable worth of what he has received. 1 Camp. 38, *Farnsworth* v. *Garrard.* And the rule is the same whether it was received and accepted by the assent of the party prior to the breach, under a contract by which, from its nature, he was to receive labor, from time to time until the completion of the whole contract; or whether it was received and accepted by an assent subsequent to the performance of all which was in fact done. If he received it under such circumstances as precluded him from rejecting it afterwards, that does not alter the case—it has still been received by his assent.

In fact we think the technical reasoning, that the performance of the whole labor is a condition precedent, and the right to recover any thing dependent upon it—that the contract being entire there can be no apportionment—and that there being an express contract no other can be implied, even upon the subsequent performance of service—is not properly applicable to this species of contract, where a beneficial service has been actually performed; for we have abundant reason to believe, that the general understanding of the community is, that the hired laborer shall be entitled to compensation for the service actually performed, though he do not continue the entire term contracted for, and such contracts must be presumed to be made with reference to that understanding, unless an express stipulation shows the contrary. . . .

It is easy, if parties so choose, to provide by an express agreement that nothing shall be earned, if the laborer leaves his employer without having performed the whole service contemplated, and then there can be no pretense for a recovery if he voluntarily deserts the service before the expiration of the time.

The amount, however, for which the employer ought to be charged, where the laborer abandons his contract, is only the reasonable worth, or the amount of advantage lie receives upon the whole transaction, *(ante* 15, *Wadleigh* v. *Sutton,)* and, in estimating the value of the labor, the contract price for the service cannot be exceeded. 7 Green. 78; 4 Wendell, 285, *Dubois* v. *Delaware & Hudson Canal Company;* 7 Wend. 121, *Koon* v. *Greenman.*

If a person makes a contract fairly he is entitled to have it fully performed, and if this is not done he is entitled to damages. He may maintain a suit to recover the amount of damage sustained by the non performance. The benefit and advantage which the party takes by the labor, therefore, is the amount of value which he receives, if any, after deducting the amount of damage; and if he elects to put this in defence he is entitled so to do, and the implied promise which (he law will raise, in such case, is to pay such amount of the stipulated price for the whole labor, as remains after deducting what it would cost to procure a completion of the residue of the service, and also any damage which has been sustained by reason of the non fulfillment of the contract. If in such case it be found that the damages are equal to, or greater than the amount of the labor performed so that the employer, having a right to the full performance of the contract, has not upon the whole case received a beneficial service, the plaintiff cannot recover. . . .

Applying the principles thus laid down, to this case, the plaintiff is entitled to judgment on the verdict. The defendant sets up a mere breach of the contract in defense of the action, but this cannot avail him. He does not appear to have offered evidence to show that he was damnified by such breach, or to have asked that a deduction should be made upon that account. The direction to the jury was therefore correct, that the plaintiff was entitled to recover as much as the labor performed was reasonably worth, and the jury appear to have allowed a *pro rata* compensation, for the time which the plaintiff labored in the defendant's service.

As the defendant has not claimed or had any adjustment of damages, for the breach of the contract, in this action, if he has actually sustained damage he is still entitled to a suit to recover the amount. . . .

Judgment on the verdict.

Questions

1. What was the defense's argument regarding the plaintiff's departure from the defendant's service?

2. What was the court's instruction to the jury regarding the plaintiff's entitlement to recover under the quantum meruit count?

3. According to the court, what is the settled rule of law regarding contracts for labor where the party fails to fulfill the entire contract?

Takeaways – Britton v. Turner

Even breaching parties can furnish value and confer benefits. Is the breaching party that conferred a benefit entitled to be reimbursed for it? Both the UCC and the Restatement say yes. UCC 2-718(2) gives a defaulting buyer a right to restitution. Rest.2d §374 says the party in breach is entitled to restitution for any benefit that he has conferred by way of part performance or reliance in excess of any loss caused by the breach.

Kirkland v. Archbold
Court of Appeals of Ohio, 1953
113 N.E.2d 496

This appeal comes to this court on questions of law from a judgment for the plaintiff in the sum of $200 entered by the court without the intervention of a jury. The action is founded on a written contract dated August 2, 1949, whereby the plaintiff agreed to construct certain alterations and to do certain repairs to a dwelling house located at 2321 East 88th St., in the City of Cleveland for the sum of $6,000.

The plaintiff claims to have started the work called for by said contract about August 5, 1949 and to have continued therewith until November 5, 1949, when he was forcibly and wrongfully ejected from the premises by the defendant's agent. It is plaintiff's claim that at the time he was wrongfully prevented from proceeding further with the work, the reasonable value of the work and materials expended by him and his sub-contractors, in repairing the building at 2331 East 88 Street, was $2,985; that only $800 had been paid thereon, leaving a balance due of $2,185, which he claims as the amount of his damages.

The court committed error prejudicial to the rights of plaintiff in holding that the provisions of the contract were severable. The plaintiff agreed to make certain repairs and improvements on the defendant's property for which he was to be paid $6,000. The total consideration was to be paid for the total work specified in the contract. The fact that a schedule of payments was set up based on the progress of the work does not change the character of the agreement. . . . .

The court found that the plaintiff and not the defendant breached the agreement, leaving the job without just cause, when the work agreed upon was for from completed. In fact, the plaintiff by his pleadings and evidence does not attempt to claim substantial performance on his part. The question is, therefore, clearly presented on the facts as the court found them to be, as to whether or not the plaintiff being found in default can maintain a cause of action for only part performance of his contract.

The earlier case law of Ohio has refused to permit a plaintiff to found an action on the provisions of a contract where he himself is in default. The only exception to the rule recognized is where the plaintiff has substantially performed his part of the agreement. . . . .

The result of decisions which deny a defaulting contractor all right of recovery even though his work has enriched the estate of the other party to the contract is to penalize the defaulting contractor to the extent of the value of all benefit conferred by his work and materials upon the property of the other party. This result comes from unduly emphasizing the technical unity and entirety of contracts. Some decisions permit such result only when the defaulting contractor's conduct was wilful or malicious.

An ever-increasing number of decisions of courts of last resort now modify the severity of this rule and permit defaulting contractors, where their work has contributed substantial value to the other contracting party's property, to recover the value of the work and materials expended on a quantum meruit basis, the recovery being diminished, however, to the extent of such damage as the contractor's breach causes the other party. These decisions are based on the theory of unjust enrichment. The action is not founded on the broken contract but on a quasi-contract to pay for the benefits received, which cannot be returned, diminished by the damages sustained because of the contractor's breach of his contract.

The leading case supporting this theory of the law is Britton v. Turner . . . .Williston on Contracts, Vol. 5, p. 4123, par. 1475, says: "The element of forfeiture in wholly denying recovery to a plaintiff who is materially in default is most strikingly exemplified in building contracts. It has already been seen how, under the name of substantial performance, many courts have gone beyond the usual principles governing contracts in allowing relief in an action on the contract. But many cases of hardship cannot be brought within the doctrine of substantial performance, even if it is liberally interpreted; and the weight of authority strongly supports the statement that a builder, whose breach of contract is merely negligent, can recover the value of his work less the damages caused by his default; but that one who has willfully abandoned or broken his contract cannot recover. The classical English doctrine, it is true, has denied recovery altogether where there has been a material breach even though it was due to negligence rather than willfulness; and a few decisions in the United States follow this rule, where the builder has not substantially performed. But the English court has itself abandoned it and now holds that where a builder has supplied work and labor for the erection or repair of a house under a lump sum contract, but has departed from the terms of the contract, he is entitled to recover for his services and materials, unless (1) the work that he has done has been of no benefit to the owner; (2) the work he has done is entirely different from the work which he has contracted to do; or (3) he has abandoned the work and left it unfinished. The courts often do not discuss the question whether one who has intentionally abandoned the contract did so merely to get out of a bad bargain or whether he acted in a mistaken belief that a just cause existed for the abandonment. Where the latter situation exists, however, it would seem that the defaulter might properly be given recovery for his part performance. It seems probable that the tendency of decisions will favor a builder who has not been guilty of conscious moral fault in abandoning the contract or in its performance.'

The drastic rule of forfeiture against a defaulting contractor who has by his labor and materials materially enriched the estate of the other party, should, in natural justice, be afforded relief to the reasonable value of the work done, less whatever damage the other party has suffered. . . .

We conclude, therefore, that the judgment is contrary to law as to the method by which the right to judgment was determined. . . .

For the foregoing reasons the judgment is reversed and the cause is remanded for further proceedings.

Questions

1. Based on the court's reasoning, what is the basis for the doctrine allowing a defaulting contractor to recover the value of their work and materials, less damages caused by their breach of contract?

2. Citing the court's reasoning, what exceptions to the severe rule of forfeiture are recognized when a defaulting contractor seeks recovery for their work?

3. According to the court's reasoning, what is the appropriate relief to be granted to a defaulting contractor who has materially enriched the other party's estate through their labor and materials?

Takeaways – Britton v. Turner and Kirkland v. Archbold

A defaulting party who has not substantially performed may nevertheless be entitled to restitution as a means of avoiding unjust enrichment. The plaintiff who has defaulted, although unable to recover on the contract, may recover under a theory of quasi contract for the reasonable value of her services less any damages suffered by the defendant. (Rest.2d § 374(1).) The presumption is that payment should be made for any services that were actually rendered and for any benefit that was conferred. A party in default is not treated as an outlaw and they are not deprived of all relief.

Suspending Performance and Terminating the Contract

Walker & Co. v. Harrison
Supreme Court of Michigan, 1957
347 Mich. 630, 81 N.W.2d 352

SMITH, Justice. This is a suit on a written contract. The defendants are in the dry-cleaning business. Walker & Company, plaintiff, sells, rents, and services advertising signs and billboards. These parties entered into an agreement pertaining to a sign. The agreement is in writing and is termed a 'rental agreement.' It specifies in part that:

'The lessor agrees to construct and install, at its own cost, one 18'9" high x 8'8" wide pylon type d.f. neon sign with electric clock and flashing lamps * * *. The lessor agrees to and does hereby lease or rent unto the said lessee the said SIGN for the term, use and rental and under the conditions, hereinafter set out, and the lessee agrees to pay said rental * * *.

'(a) The term of this lease shall be 36 months . . .

'(b) The rental to be paid by lessee shall be $148.50 per month for each and every calendar month during the term of this lease; . . .

'(d) Maintenance. Lessor at its expense agrees to maintain and service the sign together with such equipment as supplied and installed by the lessor to operate in conjunction with said sign under the terms of this lease; this service is to include cleaning and repainting of sign in original color scheme as often as deemed necessary by lessor to keep sign in first class advertising condition and make all necessary repairs to sign and equipment installed by lessor. . . .'

At the 'expiration of this agreement,' it was also provided, 'title to this sign reverts to lessee.' This clause is in addition to the printed form of agreement and was apparently added as a result of defendants' concern over title, they having expressed a desire 'to buy for cash' and the salesman, at one time, having 'quoted a cash price.'

The sign was completed and installed in the latter part of July, 1953. The first billing of the monthly payment of $148.50 was made August 1, 1953, with payment thereof by defendants on September 3, 1953. This first payment was also the last. Shortly after the sign was installed, someone hit it with a tomato. Rust, also, was visible on the chrome, complained defendants, and in its corners were 'little spider cobwebs.' In addition, there were 'some children's sayings written down in here.' Defendant Herbert Harrison called Walker for the maintenance he believed himself entitled to under subparagraph (d) above. It was not forthcoming. He called again and again. 'I was getting, you might say, sorer and sorer. * * * Occasionally, when I started calling up, I would walk around where the tomato was and get mad again. Then I would call up on the phone again.' Finally, on October 8, 1953, plaintiff not having responded to his repeated calls, he telegraphed Walker that:

'You Have Continually Voided Our Rental Contract By Not Maintaining Signs As Agreed As We No Longer Have A Contract With You Do Not Expect Any Further Remuneration.'

Walker's reply was in the form of a letter. After first pointing out that 'your telegram does not make any specific allegations as to what the failure of maintenance comprises,' and stating that 'We certainly would appreciate your furnishing us with such information,' the letter makes reference to a prior collateral controversy between the parties, 'wondering if this refusal on our part prompted your attempt to void our rental contract,' and concludes as follows:

'We would like to call your attention to paragraph G in our rental contract, which covers procedures in the event of a Breach of Agreement. In the event that you carry out your threat to make no future monthly payments in accordance with the agreement, it is our intention to enforce the conditions outlined under paragraph G through the proper legal channels. We call to your attention that your monthly rental payments are due in advance at our office not later than the 10th day of each current month. You are now approximately 30 days in arrears on your September payment. Unless we receive both the September and October payments by October 25th, this entire matter will be placed in the hands of our attorney for collection in accordance with paragraph G which stipulates that the entire amount is forthwith due and payable.'

No additional payments were made and Walker sued in assumpsit for the entire balance due under the contract, $5,197.50, invoking paragraph (g) of the agreement. Defendants filed answer and claim of recoupment, asserting that plaintiff's failure to perform certain maintenance services constituted a prior material breach of the agreement, thus justifying their repudiation of the contract and grounding their claim for damages. The case was tried to the court without a jury and resulted in a judgment for the plaintiff. The case is before us on a general appeal.

Defendants urge upon us again and again, in various forms, the proposition that Walker's failure to service the sign, in response to repeated requests, constituted a material breach of the contract and justified repudiation by them. Their legal proposition is undoubtedly correct. Repudiation is one of the weapons available to an injured party in event the other contractor has committed a material breach. But the injured party's determination that there has been a material breach, justifying his own repudiation, is fraught with peril, for should such determination, as viewed by a later court in the calm of its contemplation, be unwarranted, the repudiator himself will have been guilty of material breach and himself have become the aggressor, not an innocent victim.

What is our criterion for determining whether or not a breach of contract is so fatal to the undertaking of the parties that it is to be classed as 'material'? There is no single touchstone. Many factors are involved. They are well stated in section 275 of Restatement of the Law of Contracts in the following terms:

'In determining the materiality of a failure fully to perform a promise the following circumstances are influential:

'(a) The extent to which the injured party will obtain the substantial benefit which he could have reasonably anticipated;

'(b) The extent to which the injured party may be adequately compensated in damages for lack of complete performance;

'(c) The extent to which the party failing to perform has already partly performed or made preparations for performance;

'(d) The greater or less hardship on the party failing to perform in terminating the contract;

'(e) The willful, negligent or innocent behavior of the party failing to perform;

'(f) The greater or less uncertainty that the party failing to perform will perform the remainder of the contract.'

We will not set forth in detail the testimony offered concerning the need for servicing. Granting that Walker's delay (about a week after defendant Herbert Harrison sent his telegram of repudiation Walker sent out a crew and took care of things) in rendering the service requested was irritating, we are constrained to agree with the trial court that it was not of such materiality as to justify repudiation of the contract, and we are particularly mindful of the lack of preponderant evidence contrary to his determination. The trial court, on this phase of the case, held as follows:

'Now Mr. Harrison phoned in, so he testified, a number of times. He isn't sure of the dates but he sets the first call at about the 7th of August and he complained then of the tomato and of some rust and some cobwebs. The tomato, according to the testimony, was up on the clock; that would be outside of his reach, without a stepladder or something. The cobwebs are within easy reach of Mr. Harrison and so would the rust be. I think that Mr. Bueche's argument that these were not materially a breach would clearly be true as to the cobwebs and I really can't believe in the face of all the testimony that there was a great deal of rust seven days after the installation of this sign. And that really brings it down to the tomato. And, of course, when a tomato has been splashed all over your clock, you don't like it. But he says he kept calling their attention to it, although the rain probably washed some of the tomato off. But the stain remained, and they didn't come. I really can't find that that was such a material breach of the contract as to justify rescission. I really don't think so.'

Nor, we conclude, do we. There was no valid ground for defendants' repudiation and their failure thereafter to comply with the terms of the contract was itself a material breach, entitling Walker, upon this record, to judgment.

The question of damages remains. The parties, particularly appellants, have discussed at some length whether this contract is one of sale or of lease. Through much of its content it appears merely to be an ordinary lease, but when we come to its end we find that title, without more, is to pass to the 'lessee' at the expiration of the agreement. Is the so-called rent merely the payment of a sale price in installments? We need not, in the light of the terms of the particular contract, and upon the record, vex this question, despite illustrious aid offered us by 2 Williston on Sales, § 336, .. .and the comprehensive analysis of Dalzell in 1 Oregon Law Review 9, 'Lease-Contracts as a Means of Conveying Title to Chattels.' For the parties before us have agreed, with particularity, as to remedies in event of breach, the remedy here sought, as provided, being acceleration of 'rentals' due. The trial court cut down such sum by the amount that service would have cost Walker during the unexpired portion of the agreement . . . and as to such diminution Walker does not complain or cross-appeal. Judgment was, therefore, rendered for the cash price of the sign, for such services and maintenance as were extended and accepted, and interest upon the amount in default. There was no error.

Affirmed. Costs to appellee.

Questions

1. According to the court's reasoning, what is the significance of determining whether a breach of contract is "material"?

2. What factors does the court consider in determining the materiality of a failure to fully perform a promise, according to the Restatement of the Law of Contracts?

3. Why did the court conclude that the delay in servicing the sign requested by the defendants was not a material breach of the contract?

4. What did the court determine about the defendants' repudiation of the contract and their failure to comply with its terms?

5. In terms of damages, what remedy did the plaintiff seek and what was the court's decision regarding the calculation of damages in this case?

Takeaways – Walker & Co. v. Harrison

Material failure of consideration discharges the other party's duty. This is what is called a material breach. Slight or partial failure of consideration may not have this effect. This is oftentimes called a "minor breach."

A breach of contract may be total or partial. If the breach is total, the injured party has the right to terminate the contract. If the breach is partial, there is no such right. A total breach occurs if the breach is material. Materiality depends upon the importance or seriousness of the breach and the probability of the injured party obtaining substantial performance. A slight breach at the outset of performance justifies termination and constitutes a total breach. After substantial commencement of performance, a slight breach which does not materially impact upon the contract, does not justify termination, and does not constitute a total breach. Any breach of contract, whether total or partial, causing measurable injury, gives rise to a cause of action for damages. (See, 1 Witkin, Summary of Cal.Law (10th ed. 2005) Contracts § 813-815.)

K & G Construction Co. v. Harris
Court of Appeals of Maryland, 1960
223 Md. 305, 164 A.2d 451

PRESCOTT, Judge. Feeling aggrieved by the action of the trial judge of the Circuit Court for Prince George's County, sitting without a jury, in finding a judgment against it in favor of a subcontractor, the appellant, the general contractor on a construction project, appealed.

The principal question presented is: Does a contractor, damaged by a subcontractor's failure to perform a portion of his work in a workmanlike manner, have a right, under the circumstances of this case, to withhold, in partial satisfaction of said damages, an installment payment, which, under the terms of the contract, was due the subcontractor, unless the negligent performance of his work excused its payment?

[The pertinent provisions of the parties written agreement are as follows:]

"Section 4. (b) Progress payments will be made each month during the performance of the work. Subcontractor will submit to Contractor, by the 25th of each month, a requisition for work performed during the preceding month. Contractor will pay these requisitions, less a retainer equal to ten per cent (10%), by the 10th of the months in which such requisitions are received.

"(c) No payments will be made under this contract until the insurance requirements of Sec. 9 hereof have been complied with.

"Section 8. * * * All work shall be performed in a workmanlike manner, and in accordance with the best practices.

"Section 9. Subcontractor agrees to carry, during the progress of the work, * * * liability insurance against * * * property damage, in such amounts and with such companies as may be satisfactory to Contractor and shall provide Contractor with certificates showing the same to be in force.'

'While in the course of his employment by the Subcontractor on the Project, a bulldozer operator drove his machine too close to Contractor's house while grading the yard, causing the immediate collapse of a wall and other damage to the house. The resulting damage to contractor's house was $3,400.00. Subcontractor had complied with the insurance provision (Sec. 9) of the aforesaid contract. Subcontractor reported said damages to their liability insurance carrier. The Subcontractor and its insurance carrier refused to repair damage or compensate Contractor for damage to the house, claiming that there was no liability on the part of the Subcontractor.

Contractor was generally satisfied with Subcontractor's work and progress as required under Sections 3 and 8 of the contract until September 12, 1958, with the exception of the bulldozer accident of August 9, 1958.

'Subcontractor performed work under the contract during July, 1958, for which it submitted a requisition by the 25th of July, as required by the contract, for work done prior to the 25th of July, payable under the terms of the contract by Contractor on or before August 10, 1958. Contractor was current as to payments due under all preceding monthly requisitions from Subcontractor. The aforesaid bulldozer accident damaging Contractor's house occurred on August 9, 1958. Contractor refused to pay Subcontractor's requisition due on August 10, 1958, because the bulldozer damage to Contractor's house had not been repaired or paid for. Subcontractor continued to work on the project until the 12th of September, 1958, at which time they discontinued working on the project because of Contractor's refusal to pay the said work requisition and notified Contractor by registered letters of their position and willingness to return to the job, but only upon payment. At that time,

September 12, 1958, the value of the work completed by Subcontractor on the project for which they had not been paid was $1,484.50.

'Contractor later requested Subcontractor to return and complete work on the Project which Subcontractor refused to do because of nonpayment of work requisitions of July 25 and thereafter. Contractor's house was not repaired by Subcontractor nor compensation paid for the damage.

Contractor filed suit against the Subcontractor . . . for the $450.00 costs above the contract price in having another excavating subcontractor complete the uncompleted work in the contract. Subcontractor filed a counter-claim for recovery of work of the value of $1,484.50 for which they had not received payment and for loss of anticipated profits on uncompleted portion of work in the amount of $1,340.00. . . . [T]he Contractor's claim and the counter-claims of the Subcontractor, by agreement of the parties, were submitted to the Court for determination, without jury. . . . Circuit Court Judge Fletcher found for counter-plaintiff Subcontractor in the amount of $2,824.50 from which Contractor has entered this appeal. . . .

The vital question, more tersely stated, remains: Did the contractor have a right, under the circumstances, to refuse to make the progress payment due on August 10, 1958?

The answer involves interesting and important principles of contract law. Promises and counter-promises made by the respective parties to a contract have certain relations to one another, which determine many of the rights and liabilities of the parties. Broadly speaking, they are (1) independent of each other, or (2) mutually dependent, one upon the other. They are independent of each other if the parties intend that *performance* by each of them is in no way conditioned upon *performance* by the other. 5 Page, The Law of Contracts, ¶ 2971. In other words, the parties exchange promises for promises, not the *performance* of promises for the *performance* of promises. 3 Williston, Contracts (Rev. Ed.), ¶813, n. 6. A failure to perform an independent promise does not excuse non-performance on the part of the adversary party, but each is required to perform his promise, and, if one does not perform, he is liable to the adversary party for such non-performance. (Of course, if litigation ensues questions of set-off or recoupment frequently arise.) Promises are mutually dependent if the parties intend *performance* by one to be conditioned upon *performance* by the other, and, if they be mutually dependent, they may be (a) precedent, i. e., a promise that is to be performed before a corresponding promise on the part of the adversary party is to be performed, (b) subsequent, i. e., a corresponding promise that is not to be performed until the other party to the contract has performed a precedent covenant, or (c) concurrent, i. e., promises that are to be performed at the same time by each of the parties, who are respectively bound to perform each. Page, op. Cit., ¶¶ 2941, 2951, 2961. . . .

In the early days, it was settled law that covenants and mutual promises in a contract were *prima facie* independent, and that they were to be so construed in the absence of language in the contract clearly showing that they were intended to be dependent. Williston, op. cit., ¶816; Page, op. cit., ¶¶2944, 2945. In the case of Kingston v. Preston, 2 Doug. 689, decided in 1774, Lord Mansfield, contrary to three centuries of opposing precedents, changed the rule, and decided that performance of one covenant might be dependent on prior performance of another, although the contract contained no express condition to that effect. Page, op. cit., ¶2946; Williston, op. cit., ¶817. The modern rule, which seems to be of almost universal application, is that there is a presumption that mutual promises in a contract are dependent and are to be so regarded, whenever possible. Page, op. cit., ¶2946; Restatement, Contracts, ¶ 266. Cf. Williston, op. cit., ¶812. . . .

We hold that when the subcontractor's employee negligently damaged the contractor's wall, this constituted a breach of the subcontractor's promise to perform his work in a 'workmanlike manner, and in accordance with the best practices.' . . . And there can be little doubt that the breach was material: the damage to the wall amounted to more than double the payment due on August 10. . . . 3A Corbin, Contracts, § 708, says: 'The failure of a contractor's [in our case, the subcontractor's] performance to constitute 'substantial' performance may justify the owner [in our case, the contractor] in refusing to make a progress payment * * *. * * * If the refusal to pay an installment is justified on the owner's [contractor's] part, the contractor [subcontractor] is not justified in abandoning work by reason of that refusal. His abandonment of the work will itself be a wrongful repudiation that goes to the essence, even if the defects in performance did not.' See also Restatement, Contracts, § 274; . . . and compare Williston, op. cit., §§ 805, 841 and 842. Professor Corbin, in § 954, states further: 'The unexcused failure of a contractor to render a promised performance when it is due is always a breach of contract * * *. Such failure may be of such great importance as to constitute what has been called herein a 'total' breach. * * *. For a failure of performance constituting such a 'total' breach, an action for remedies that are appropriate thereto is at once maintainable. Yet the injured party is not required to bring such action. He has the option of treating the non-performance as a 'partial' breach only * * *.' In permitting the subcontractor to proceed with work on the project after August 9, the contractor, obviously, treated the breach by the subcontractor as a partial one. As the promises were mutually dependent and the subcontractor had made a material breach in his performance, this justified the contractor in refusing to make the August 10 payment; hence, as the contractor was not in default, the subcontractor again breached the contract when he, on September 12, discontinued work on the project, which rendered him liable (by the express terms of the contract) to the contractor for his increased cost in having the excavating done-a stipulated amount of $450. Cf. Keystone Engineering Corp. v. Sutter, 196 Md. 620, 628, 78 A.2d 191.

The appellees . . . also contend that the contractor had no right to refuse the August 10 payment, because the subcontractor had furnished the insurance against property damage, as called for in the contract. There is little, or no, merit in this suggestion. The subcontractor and his insurance company denied liability. The furnishing of the insurance by him did not constitute a license to perform his work in a careless, negligence, or unworkmanlike manner; and its acceptance by the contractor did not preclude his assertion of a claim for unworkmanlike performance directly against the subcontractor.

Judgment against the appellant reversed; and judgment entered in favor of the appellant against the appellees for $450, the appellees to pay the costs.

Questions

1. According to the court's reasoning, what determines whether promises in a contract are independent or mutually dependent?

2. Why did the court find that the subcontractor's breach of performing the work in a workmanlike manner was material?

3. Was the promise to make progress payments absolute or conditional? If it was conditional, what was it conditioned upon?

Prevention and Cooperation

United States v. Peck
United States. Supreme Court, 1880
102 U.S. 64, 12 Otto 64, 1880 , 26 L.Ed. 46

[Peck, the claimant, entered into a contract with the proper military officer to furnish and deliver a certain quantity of wood and hay to the military station at Tongue River, in the Yellowstone region, on or before a specified day. He furnished the wood, but failed to furnish the hay, which was furnished by other parties at an increased expense. The accounting officers of the government claimed the right to deduct from the claimant's wood account the increased cost of the hay. Whether this could lawfully be done was the principal question in the cause.]

Mr. JUSTICE BRADLEY, after stating the case, delivered the opinion of the court. We think that the facts of the case clearly bring it within the rules allowing the introduction of parol evidence: . . . secondly, for the purpose of showing the conduct of the agents of the defendants by which the claimant was encouraged and led on to rely on a particular means of fulfilling his contract until it was too late to perform it in any other way; and then was prevented by these agents themselves from employing those means. The supply of hay which he depended on, and which under the circumstances he had a right to depend on, was taken away by the defendants themselves. In other words, the defendants prevented and hindered the claimant from performing his part of the contract.... And that the conduct of one party to a contract which prevents the other from performing his part is an excuse for non-performance, see Addison, Contracts, sect. 326; *Fleming* v. *Gilbert*, 3 Johns. (N. Y.) 527. In the case last cited, the defendant was sued on a bond obliging him by a certain time to procure and cancel a mortgage of the plaintiff and deliver the same to him. The defendant was allowed to prove by parol that he procured the mortgage, and, having inquired of the plaintiff what he should do with it, was directed to place it in the hands of a third person. This was held to be an excuse for not having fully performed the condition. Judge Thompson said: 'It is a sound principle that he who prevents a thing being done shall not avail himself of the non-performance he has occasioned. Had not the plaintiff dispensed with a further compliance with the condition of the bond, it is probable that the defendant would have taken measures to ascertain what steps were requisite to get the mortgage discharged of record, and would have literally complied with the condition of the bond.' So when A. gave to B. a bond to convey certain premises, but they subsequently agreed by parol to rescind the contract, and A. thereupon sold the premises to a third person, it was held that though the bond was not cancelled or given up, nor any of the papers changed, yet by the parol agreement and the acts of the parties under it the bond was discharged. *Dearborn* v. *Cross*, 7 Cow. (N. Y.) 48; and see 2 Cowen & Hill's Notes to Phillips on Evid., 605. The principle involved in these cases is applicable to the present. Judgment affirmed.

Questions

1. How did the conduct of the defendants' agents affect the claimant's ability to fulfill the contract?

2. According to the court's opinion, what happens when one party to a contract prevents the other party from performing their obligations?

Takeaways – United States v. Peck

If a party prevents the other party from completing performance then the duty of performance will be excused. What was the duty that Peck had under the contract that was excused?

New England Structures, Inc. v. Loranger
Supreme Judicial Court of Massachusetts, 1968
354 Mass. 62, 234 N.E.2d 888

CUTTER, J. In one case the plaintiffs, doing business as Theodore Loranger & Sons (Loranger), the general contractor on a school project, seek to recover from New England Structures, Inc., a subcontractor (New England), damages caused by an alleged breach of the subcontract. Loranger avers that the breach made it necessary for Loranger at greater expense to engage another subcontractor to complete work on a roof deck. In a cross action, New England seeks to recover for breach of the subcontract by Loranger alleged to have taken place when Loranger terminated New England's right to proceed. The actions were consolidated for trial. A jury returned a verdict for New England in the action brought by Loranger, and a verdict for New England in the sum of $16,860.25 in the action brought by New England against Loranger. The cases are before us on Loranger's exceptions to the judge's charge.

Loranger, under date of July 11, 1961, entered into a subcontract with New England by which New England undertook to install a gypsum roof deck in a school, then being built by Loranger. New England began work on November 24, 1961. On December 18, 1961, New England received a telegram from Loranger which read, "Because of your ... repeated refusal ... or inability to provide enough properly skilled workmen to maintain satisfactory progress, we ... terminate your right to proceed with work at the ... school as of December 26, 1961, in accordance with Article ... 5 of our contract. We intend to complete the work ... with other forces and charge its costs and any additional damages resulting from your repeated delays to your account." New England replied, "Failure on your [Loranger's] part to provide ... approved drawings is the cause of the delay." The telegram also referred to various allegedly inappropriate changes in instructions. . . .

There was conflicting evidence concerning (a) how New England had done certain work; (b) whether certain metal cross pieces (called bulb tees) had been properly "staggered" and whether joints had been welded on both sides by certified welders, as called for by the specifications; (c) whether New England had supplied an adequate number of certified welders on certain days; (d) whether and to what extent Loranger had waived certain specifications; and (e) whether New England had complied with good trade practices. The architect testified that on December 14, 1961, he had made certain complaints to New England's president. The work was completed by another company at a cost in excess of New England's bid. There was also testimony (1) that Loranger's job foreman told one of New England's welders "to do no work at the job site during the five day period following the date of Loranger's termination telegram," and (2) that, "if New England had been permitted to continue its work, it could have completed the entire subcontract ... within five days following the date of the termination telegram."

The trial judge ruled, as matter of law, that Loranger, by its termination telegram, confined the justification for its notice of termination to New England's "repeated refusal ... or inability to provide enough properly skilled workmen to maintain satisfactory progress." He then gave the following instructions: "If you should find that New England ... did not furnish a sufficient number of men to perform the required work under the contract within a reasonable time ... then you would be warranted in finding that Loranger was justified in terminating its contract; and it may recover in its suit against New England.... [T]he termination ... cannot, as ... matter of law, be justified for any ... reason not stated in the telegram of December 18 ... including failure to stagger the joints of the bulb tees or failure to weld properly ... or any other reason, unless you find that inherent in the reasons stated in the telegram, namely, failure to provide enough skilled workmen to maintain satisfactory progress, are these aspects. Nevertheless, these allegations by Loranger of deficiency of work on the part of New England Structures may be considered by you, if you find that Loranger was justified in terminating the contract for the reason enumerated in the telegram. You may consider it or them as an element of damages sustained by Loranger...." Counsel for Loranger claimed exceptions to the portion of the judge's charge quoted above in the body of this opinion.

1. Some authority supports the judge's ruling, in effect, that Loranger, having specified in its telegram one ground for termination of the subcontract, cannot rely in litigation upon other grounds, except to the extent that the other grounds may directly affect the first ground asserted. See Railway Co. v. McCarthy, 96 U.S. 258, 267-268 ("Where a party gives a reason for his conduct and decision touching ... a controversy, he cannot, after litigation has begun, change his ground, and put his conduct upon ... a different consideration. He is not permitted thus to mend his hold. He is estopped from doing it by a settled principle of law" [emphasis supplied]); Luckenbach S.S. Co. Inc. v. W.R. Grace & Co. Inc. 267 Fed. 676, 679 (4th Cir.); Chevrolet Motor Co. v. Gladding, 42 F.2d 440 (4th Cir.), cert. den. 282 U.S. 872. See also Rode & Brand v. Kamm Games, 181 F.2d 584, 587 (2d Cir.); Cummings v. Connecticut Gen. Life Ins. Co. 102 Vt. 351, 359-362. In each of these cases, there is reference to estoppel or "waiver" as the legal ground behind the principle.

Our cases somewhat more definitely require reliance or change of position based upon the assertion of the particular reason or defence before treating a person, giving one reason for his action, as estopped later to give a different reason. See Bates v. Cashman, 230 Mass. 167, 168-169. There it was said, "The defendant is not prevented from setting up this defense. Although he wrote respecting other reasons for declining to perform the contract, he expressly reserved different grounds for his refusal.[4] While of course one cannot fail in good faith in presenting his reasons as to his conduct touching a controversy, he is not prevented from relying upon one good defence among others urged simply because he has not always put it forward, when it does not appear that he has acted dishonestly or that the other party has been misled to his harm, or that he is estopped on any other ground." See Brown v. Henry, 172 Mass. 559, 567; St. John Bros. Co. v. Falkson, 237 Mass. 399, 402-403; Moss v. Old Colony Trust Co. 246 Mass. 139, 150; Sheehan v. Commercial Travelers Mut. Acc. Assn. of America, 283 Mass. 543, 551-553; Restatement: Contracts, § 304; Williston, Contracts (3d ed.) § 742 (and also §§ 678, 679, 691; Corbin, Contracts, §§ 762, 1218, 1266 (and also §§ 265, 721, 727, 744, 756). See also Randall v. Peerless Motor Car Co. 212 Mass. 352, 376.

We think Loranger is not barred from asserting grounds not mentioned in its telegram unless New England establishes that, in some manner, it relied to its detriment upon the circumstance that only one ground was so asserted. Even if some evidence tended to show such reliance, the jury did not have to believe this evidence. They should have received instructions that they might consider grounds for termination of the subcontract and defenses to New England's claim (that Loranger by the telegram had committed a breach of the subcontract), other than the ground raised in the telegram, unless they found as a fact that New England had relied to its detriment upon the fact that only one particular ground for termination was mentioned in the telegram.

2. As there must be a new trial, we consider whether art. 5 of the subcontract (fn. 1) afforded New England any right during the five-day notice period to attempt to cure its default, and, in doing so, to rely on the particular ground stated in the telegram . . . . [W]e interpret it as giving New England no period in which to cure continuing defaults, but merely as directing that New England be told when it must quit the premises and as giving it an opportunity to take steps during the five-day period to protect itself from injury. Nothing in art. 5 suggests that a termination pursuant to its provisions was not to be effective in any event at the conclusion of the five-day period, even if New England should change its conduct.

If Loranger in fact was not justified by New England's conduct in giving the termination notice, it may have subjected itself to liability for breach of the subcontract. The reason stated in the notice, however, for giving the notice cannot be advanced as the basis of any reliance by New England in action taken by it to cure defaults. After the receipt of the notice, as we interpret art. 5, New England had no further opportunity to cure defaults.

Exceptions sustained.

Questions

1. According to the judge's ruling, can Loranger rely on grounds not mentioned in its termination telegram?

2. Can New England rely on the reason stated in the termination notice as a basis for its reliance in taking action to cure defaults?

Takeaways – New England Structures v. Loranger

Failure to specify or particularize reasons for rejecting the other party's performance may result in a waiver of unstated reasons. See Rest.2d §248 and UCC § 2-605(1). "Just as the injured party is not, as a general rule, precluded from relying on a reason for rejection because he stated no reasons, he is not precluded by the mere fact that he stated an insufficient reason, even though he knew or had reason to know of a sufficient one. The giving of an insufficient reason may, however, so mislead the other party as to induce his failure to cure the defective performance or offer of performance within the time allowed by the agreement. If it does so, the non-occurrence of the condition is excused. The giving of an insufficient reason must contribute materially to the failure to cure." (Comment a to Rest.2d §248)

Repudiation and Anticipatory Breach

An unjustified or unexcused failure to perform a contractual duty at the time performance is due is an actual breach. A repudiation (which is a positive, unequivocal statement of an intention not to perform [Rest.2d § 250]) that occurs before the time when performance is due gives rise to an anticipatory breach. When an anticipatory breach occurs, the injured party may either sue immediately, or wait until the time for performance and then exercise his or her rights for actual breach of contract. Where one of the parties repudiates the contract and absolutely refuses to perform the duties and obligations required of him or her, the other party need not go through the useless act of tendering or offering their own performance. (*Laredo Hides Co., Inc. v. H & H Meat Products Co., Inc.* 513 S.W.2d 210 (1974))

An anticipatory repudiation or breach may be express or implied. A person who expressly repudiates the contract by an unequivocal refusal to perform commits an express anticipatory breach or repudiation. [Rest.2d § 250(a)] A person, who puts it out of his or her power to perform the promise commits an implied anticipatory breach or repudiation [Rest.2d § 250(b)]. (See, 1 Witkin, Summary of Cal.Law (10th ed. 2005) Contracts § 861-864.)

Although an anticipatory breach or repudiation of a contract by one party permits the other party to sue for damages without performing or offering to perform its own obligations, this does not mean damages can be recovered without evidence that, but for the defendant's breach, the plaintiff would have had the ability to perform. (*Dickey v. Kuhn* (1930) 106 Cal.App. 300, 303-304 [289 P. 242]) In other words, plaintiff must be able to prove that he was ready, willing and able to perform in order to recover damages.

Hochster v. De La Tour
Queen's Bench, 1853
2. E & B 678, 118 Eng.Rep. 922

Declaration: "for that, heretofore, to wit on 12th April 1852, in consideration that plaintiff, at the request of defendant, would agree with the defendant to enter into the service and employ of the defendant in the capacity of a courier, on a certain day-then to come, to wit the 1st day of June 1852, and to serve the defendant in that capacity, and travel with him on the continent of Europe as a courier for three months certain from the day and year last aforesaid, and to be ready to start with the defendant on such travels on the day and year last aforesaid, at and for certain wages or salary, to wit " 10l. per month of such service, "the defendant then agreed with the plaintiff, and then promised him, that he, the defendant, would engage and employ the plaintiff in the capacity of a courier on and from the said 1st day of June 1852 for three months " on these terms; "and to start on such travels with the plaintiff on the day and year last aforesaid, and to pay the plaintiff" on these terms: averment that plaintiff, confiding in the said agreement and promise of the defendant-, "agreed with the defendant" to fulfill these terms on his part, "and to be ready to start with the defendant on such travels on the day and year last aforesaid, at and for the wages and salary aforesaid." That, "from the time of the making of said agreement of the said promise of the defendant until the time when the defendant wrongfully refused to perform and broke his said promise, and absolved, exonerated and discharged the plaintiff from the performance of his agreement as hereinafter mentioned, he the plaintiff was always ready and willing to enter into the service and employ of the defendant, in the capacity aforesaid, on the said 1st June 1852, and to serve the defendant in that capacity, and to travel with him on the continent of Europe as a courier for three months certain from the day and year last aforesaid, and to start with the defendant on such travels on the day and year last aforesaid, at and for the wages and salary aforesaid; and the plaintiff, but for the breach by the defendant of his said promise as hereinafter mentioned, would, on the said 1st June 1852, have entered into the said service and employ of the defendant in the capacity, and upon the terms and for the time aforesaid: of all which several premises the defendant always had notice and knowledge: yet the defendant, not regarding the said agreement, nor his said promise, afterwards and before the said 1st June 1852, wrongfully wholly refused and declined to engage or employ the defendant in the capacity and for the purpose aforesaid, on or from the said 1st June 1852 for three months, or on, from or for, any other time, or to start on 'such travels with the plaintiff on the day and year last aforesaid, or in any manner whatsoever to perform or fulfill his said promise, and then wrongfully wholly absolved, exonerated and discharged the plaintiff from his said agreement, and from the performance of the same agreement on his the plaintiff's part, and from being ready and willing to perform the same on the plaintiff's part; and the defendant then wrongfully wholly broke, put an end to and determined his said promise and engagement:" to the damage of the plaintiff. The writ was dated on the 22d of May 1852.

Pleas: 1. That defendant did not agree or promise in manner and form etc.: conclusion to the country. Issue thereon.

2. That plaintiff did not agree with defendant in manner and form etc.: conclusion to the country. Issue thereon.

3. That plaintiff was not ready and willing, nor did defendant absolve, exonerate or discharge plaintiff from being ready and willing, in manner and form etc.: conclusion to the country. Issue thereon.

4. That defendant did not refuse or decline, nor wrongfully absolve, exonerate or discharge, nor wrongfully break, put an end to or determine, in manner and form &c.: conclusion to the country. Issue thereon.

On the trial, before Erle J., at the London sittings in last Easter Term, it appeared that plaintiff was a courier, who, in April, 1852, was engaged by defendant to accompany him on a tour, to commence on 1st June 1852, on the terms mentioned in the declaration. On the 11th May 1852, defendant wrote to plaintiff that he had changed his mind, and declined his services. He refused to make him any compensation. The action was commenced on 22d May. The plaintiff, between the commencement of the action and the 1st June, obtained an engagement with Lord Ashburton, on equally good terms, but not commencing till 4th July. The defendant's counsel objected that there could be no breach of the contract before the 1st of June. The learned Judge was of a contrary opinion, but reserved leave to enter a nonsuit on this objection. The other questions were left to the jury, who found for plaintiff.

Lord Campbell C.J. now delivered the judgment of the Court. On this motion in arrest of judgment, the question arises, whether, if there be an agreement between A. and B., whereby B. engages to employ A. on and from a future day for a given period of time, to travel with him into a foreign country as a courier, and to start with him in that capacity on that day, A. being to receive a monthly salary during the continuance of such service, B. may, before the day, refuse to perform the agreement and break and renounce it, so as to entitle A. before the day to commence an action against B. to recover damages for breach of the agreement; A. having been ready and willing to perform it, till it was broken and renounced by B. The defendant's counsel very powerfully contended that, if the plaintiff was not contented to dissolve the contract, and to abandon all remedy upon it, he was bound to remain ready and willing to perform it till the day when the actual employment as courier in the service of the defendant was to begin; and that there could be no breach of the agreement, before that day, to give a right of action. But it cannot be laid down as a universal rule that, where by agreement an act is to be done on a future day, no action can be brought for a breach of the agreement till the day for doing the act has arrived. If a man promises to marry a woman on a future day, and before that day marries another woman, he is instantly liable to an action for breach of promise of marriage; *Short v. Stone* (8 Q. B. 358). If a man contracts to execute a lease on and from a future day for a certain term, and, before that day, executes a lease to another for the same term, he may be immediately sued for breaking the contract; *Ford v. Tiley* (6 B. & C. 325). So, if a man contracts to sell and deliver specific goods on a future day, and before the day he sells and delivers them to another, he is immediately liable to an action at the suit of the person with whom he first contracted to sell and deliver them; *Bowdell v. Parsons* (10 East, 359).

One reason alleged in support of such an action is, that the defendant has, before the day, rendered it impossible for him to perform the contract at the day: but this does not necessarily follow; for, prior to the day fixed for doing the act, the first wife may have died, a surrender of the lease executed might be obtained, and the defendant might have repurchased the goods so as to be in a situation to sell and deliver them to the plaintiff. Another reason may be, that, where there is a contract to do an act on a future day, there is a relation constituted between the parties in the meantime by the contract, and that they impliedly promise that in the meantime neither will do any thing to the prejudice of the other inconsistent with that relation. As an example, a man and woman engaged to marry are affianced to one another during the period between the time of the engagement and the celebration of the marriage. In this very case, of traveler and courier, from the day of the hiring till the day when the employment was to begin, they were engaged to each other; and it seems to be a breach of an implied contract if either of them renounces the engagement. This reasoning seems in accordance with the unanimous decision of the Exchequer Chamber in *Elderton v. Emmens*, which we have followed in subsequent cases in this Court.

The declaration in the present case, in alleging a breach, states a great deal more than a passing intention on the part of the defendant which he may repent of, and could only be proved by evidence that he had utterly renounced the contract, or done some act which rendered it impossible for him to perform it. If the plaintiff has no remedy for breach of the contract unless he treats the contract as in force, and acts upon it down to the 1st June 1852, it follows that, till then, he must enter into no employment which will interfere with his promise "to start with the defendant on such travels on the day and year," and that he must then be properly equipped in all respects as a courier for a three months' tour on the continent of Europe. But it is surely much more rational, and more for the benefit of both parties, that, after the renunciation of the agreement by the defendant, the plaintiff should be at liberty to consider himself absolved from any future performance of it, retaining his right to sue for any damage he has suffered from the breach of it. Thus, instead of remaining idle and laying out money in preparations which must be useless, he is at liberty to seek service under another employer, which would go in mitigation. of the damages to which he would otherwise be entitled for a breach of the contract.

It seems strange that the defendant, after renouncing the contract, and absolutely declaring that he will never act under it, should be permitted to object that faith is given to his assertion, and that an opportunity is not left to him of changing his mind. If the plaintiff is barred of any remedy by entering into an engagement inconsistent with starting as a courier with the defendant on the 1st June, he is prejudiced by putting faith in the defendant's assertion: and it would be more consonant with principle, if the defendant were precluded from saying that he had not broken the contract when he declared that he entirely renounced it. Suppose that the defendant, at the time of his renunciation, had embarked on a voyage for Australia, so as to render it physically impossible for him to employ the plaintiff as a courier on the continent of Europe in the months of June, July and August 1852: according to decided cases, the action might have been brought before the 1st June; but the renunciation may have been founded on other facts, to be given in evidence, which would equally have rendered the defendant's performance of the contract impossible. The man who wrongfully renounces a contract into which he has deliberately entered cannot justly complain if he is immediately sued for a compensation in damages by the man whom he has injured: and it seems reasonable to allow an option to the injured party, either to sue immediately, or to wait till the time when the act was to be done, still holding it as prospectively binding for the exercise of this option, which may be advantageous to the innocent party, and cannot be prejudicial to the wrongdoer.

An argument against the action before the 1st of June is urged from the difficulty of calculating the damages: but this argument is equally strong against an action before the 1st of September, when the three months would expire. In either case, the jury in assessing the damages would be justified in looking to all that had happened, or was likely to happen, to increase or mitigate the loss of the plaintiff down to the day of trial. We do not find any decision contrary to the view we are taking of this case. *Leigh v. Patterson* (8 Taunt. 540) only shews that, upon a sale of goods to be delivered at a certain time, if the vendor before the time gives information to the vendee that he cannot deliver them, having sold them, the vendee may calculate the damages according to the state of the market when they ought to have been delivered. . . . .

If it should be held that, upon a contract to do an act on a future day, a renunciation of the contract by one party dispenses with a condition to be performed in the meantime by the other, there seems no reason for requiring that other to wait till the day arrives before seeking his remedy by action: and the only ground on which the condition can be dispensed with seems to be, that the renunciation may be treated as a breach of the contract.

Upon the whole, we think that the declaration in this case is sufficient. It gives us great satisfaction to reflect that, the question being on the record, our opinion may be reviewed in a Court of Error. In the meantime we must give judgment for the plaintiff.

Judgment for plaintiff.

Questions

1. How does the court's ruling in this case affect the rights and options of the injured party when the other party renounces a contract before the performance date?

2. What are some reasons that allow for an action to be brought for breach of a contract before the date for performance is due?

Takeaways – Hochster v. De La Tour

So what constitutes a *repudiation*? "In order to constitute a repudiation, a party's language must be sufficiently positive to be reasonably interpreted to mean that the party will not or cannot perform. Mere expression of doubt as to his willingness or ability to perform is not enough to constitute a repudiation." (Comment b to Rest.2d § 250)

A repudiation by the obligor generally gives rise to a claim for damages for total breach even though it is not accompanied or preceded by a breach by nonperformance. (Rest.2d §253(1).) Repudiation gives rise to an *anticipatory breach* because it occurs before there is any breach by non-performance. If a party to an obligation gives notice to another, before the latter is in default, that he or she will not perform their obligation, and does not retract such notice before the time at which performance upon his part is due, such other party is entitled to enforce the obligation without previously performing or offering to perform any conditions upon his part in favor of the former party. (Cal.Civ.Code § 1440)

Minor v. Minor
California Court of Appeal, First District 1960
184 Cal.App.2d 118

TOBRINER, J. Appellant wife must fail in her chief contention here that because of the alleged repudiation of respondent husband she is entitled to the total sum due on a property settlement agreement which provides only for monthly installment payments. Since the wife had fully performed her part of the agreement, and since the doctrine of anticipatory breach does not apply to a unilateral contract, the trial court correctly denied the wife's claim for the sum total due on the contract.

On September 25, 1957, appellant and respondent signed the contract upon which this action rests. This contract provides that, in consideration of appellant's waiver of any future claim to alimony, respondent will pay her $1,000 within 15 days, and a balance of $9,000 in monthly installments of $175 for a total of $10,000. The contract contains no acceleration clause to the effect that in the event of a default in payment the whole amount should become due. On the day of execution of the agreement appellant obtained an uncontested divorce from respondent; the trial court specifically found, however, that the contract "was not merged in the Decree of Divorce."

Appellant's complaint sets up a first cause of action upon the ground that the agreement provided for payment of the total sum in installments; that respondent refused to pay the first installment and paid only after a threatened levy of execution upon his place of business; that appellant obtained the December, 1957, payment by means of execution, and the January payment because of threatened contempt proceedings; that respondent repudiated the contract and refused to pay the installments due. The second cause of action, incorporating these allegations of the first, and further alleging that respondent threatened to dispose of his property and leave the state, sought injunctive relief against such disposition. The complaint did not request judgment for two installments delinquent at the time of filing suit.

At the trial appellant testified that immediately after she obtained the divorce, respondent renounced his obligation under this contract; appellant's brother corroborated this repudiation. Appellant also testified that respondent failed to make the initial $1,000 payment and the first installment of $175 within the agreed time; that, upon her questioning him on a number of occasions about these defaults, respondent replied that he was not going to pay her. And, indeed, respondent had made no payments after the commencement of this action (April 16, 1958) to the time of the trial (April 1, 1959), a period of approximately one year. Respondent did, however, on May 21, 1958, following the filing of the action, remit a check to appellant's lawyer, payable to her, covering the payments due in February and March, 1958. Appellant's counsel deposited this check in his account, purportedly in trust for appellant. According to appellant's testimony respondent had at no time paid her voluntarily but only under the compulsion of legal process. Appellant contends that respondent committed an anticipatory breach of the contract resulting in his liability for the total amount of $10,000 provided in it, because he allegedly stated he would not honor the contract and subsequently dishonored it.

Denying his wife's allegations that he intended to dishonor the contract, to dispose of his property or to leave the state, respondent admitted he had failed to make several payments under the agreement, contending that the failures were due to his "dire financial straits." In holding appellant "take nothing by reason of her complaint" the trial court found "that the doctrine of anticipatory breach does not apply to the contract in question before the Court," and neither rendered findings on issues which it considered immaterial in view of its ruling on anticipatory breach nor accepted appellant's proposed findings upon such breach. The court likewise refused the requested relief as to appellant's claim to payments due at the time of trial and as to an injunction.

We consider, first, the issue as to the findings and the alleged anticipatory breach; second, the failure to give relief as to amounts allegedly due and unpaid at the time of trial.

The issue as to the findings is inseparable from that of the anticipatory breach. While appellant contends the court both failed to find upon issues raised by the pleadings and refused to adopt proposed findings, the court was neither compelled to make findings upon immaterial issues nor to adopt appellant's proposed findings on such issues. (Robb v. Cardoza (1932), 127 Cal.App. 588 [16 P.2d 325]; Gornstein v. Priver (1923), 64 Cal.App. 249, 255 [221 P. 396]; Imperial Water Co. No. 1 v. Imperial Irrigation Dist. (1923), 62 Cal.App. 286, 290 [217 P. 88].) Findings on the allegations of appellant's first cause of action relating to respondent's alleged failure to pay two installments, his alleged repudiation, and his threats of refusal to pay, etc. (Paragraphs IV, V, VI, VII, IX and X), as well as findings as to these paragraphs incorporated by reference in the second count, become immaterial in the face of the court's finding that the doctrine of anticipatory breach does not apply to the contract. Appellant's reliance upon Del Ruth v. Del Ruth (1946), 75 Cal.App.2d 638, 644 [171 P.2d 34], does not affect the point, since, there, the only question related to the ineffectiveness of a waiver of specific findings in a divorce action when such findings were required in the absence of such waiver. Thus the court's failure in the instant case to find on the above-mentioned pleadings or to adopt appellant's proposed findings should be upheld if the court correctly resolved the basic issue of the anticipatory breach.

The question, here, pertains to the breach of a unilateral contract. Since the bilateral contract had been fully performed by the wife, it congealed, so far as the husband was concerned, into a unilateral contract. That the wife had completed her performance becomes manifest from the fact that she had no more to do; she renounced her rights to alimony, present and future, and at the time of the signature of the agreement, the renunciation was final. As appellant herself states, "the right to alimony once waived cannot be regained." (Fox v. Fox (1954), 42 Cal.2d 49 [265 P.2d 881]; Lane v. Lane (1953), 117 Cal.App.2d 247 [255 P.2d 110]; Carson v. Carson (1960), 179 Cal.App.2d 665 [4 Cal.Rptr. 38].)

Despite appellant's cases and authorities, the trial court's ruling that the doctrine of anticipatory breach does not apply to a contract which has become unilateral because of the opposite party's full performance, finds uncontradicted support in California law. The leading California case, Cobb v. Pacific Mutual Life Ins. Co. (1935), 4 Cal.2d 565 [51 P.2d 84], holding that upon repudiation of a health and disability insurance policy the company does not become liable for the whole amount of future installments not yet due, states: "There can be no anticipatory breach of a unilateral contract. ... It is also the law that a bilateral contract becomes unilateral when the promisee has fully performed. In the case at bar the promisee had fully performed." (P. 573.) "He was therefore within the exception stated in the rule which holds that no repudiation can amount to an anticipatory breach of the rest of the installments not yet due." (P. 573.) Likewise, in a comparable action for installments due in the amount of $600 upon a contract for rendition of services for $1,000 payable in monthly installments, the court in Farmer v. Mountain Lake Club (1928), 94 Cal.App. 663 [271 P. 780], said: "While the contract recited a total consideration of $1,000, it was payable in weekly installments, and contained no provision that the whole amount should become due and payable upon a failure to pay any one installment." (P. 664.) The court held "... as each installment fell due it created a cause of action, and a suit therefor would not be premature." (P. 664.)

The decision of the Court of Appeals, for the Ninth Circuit, in John Hancock Mutual Life Insurance Co. v. Cohen (1958), 254 F.2d 417, summarizes the California cases: "... we find no indication in the law of ... California of an intent to depart from the majority view that unconditional unilateral contracts for the payment of money in installments are not the proper subjects for the doctrine of anticipatory breach." (P. 427.) [Citations omitted]

Appellant cites cases which do not involve the exact situation of anticipatory breach of a unilateral contract, and she relies upon authorities which question the theory above stated. We shall consider both points; we turn first to the cases.

In Guitron v. Rodriguez (1930), 105 Cal.App. 513 [288 P. 134], cited by appellant, defendant entered into an oral contract for the purchase of a grocery store, promising to pay $3,700: $1,000 down and the balance in installments of $150 per month. Having made the initial payment, defendant took possession, then repudiated the contract, and refused to make any further payments. The District Court of Appeal held that plaintiffs could recover damages based on future as well as presently due payments since "... the repudiation of an executory contract [emphasis added] results in a violation of the contract 'in omnibus.' " Ibid., page 514. The court neither discussed the fact that the contract, having been fully performed on one side, became unilateral, nor the effect of such performance on the applicability of the doctrine of anticipatory breach; instead, it assumed the contract to be bilateral.

Pollack v. Pollack (Tex. Com. App., 1931), 39 S.W.2d 853, appellant's next cited case, characterized by Williston as "extreme" (5 Williston on Contracts, 1330B, p. 3743) applies to the instant situation only by way of dicta, and the dicta, indeed, is not persuasive. In overruling a second motion for rehearing (Pollack v. Pollack (1932), 46 S.W.2d 292, 293), the court construes the contract as executory on both sides rather than as performed. The court further declares that, even assuming plaintiff's full performance, the doctrine of anticipatory breach still governs, explaining that the English authorities, who originated the doctrine, apply it only to contracts not yet performed. The court recognizes that the "great weight of authority in America adheres to the English rule" (p. 293) but proceeds to state that, "Notwithstanding all this, we are constrained to hold that, since to except contracts performed on one side from the rule violates every reason that can be given for its existence in the first instance, and since this court has never committed itself to the exception, it should not now do so."

In support of Pollack v. Pollack (1931), supra, appellant cites Pierce v. Tennessee C. I. & R. Co. (1898), 173 U.S. 1 [19 S.Ct. 335, 43 L.Ed. 591]; Roehm v. Horst (1899), 178 U.S. 1 [20 S.Ct. 780, 44 L.Ed. 953], and Parker v. Russell (1882), 133 Mass. 74. In Pierce the contract in issue was executory on both sides. Such was also the situation in Roehm, although there several executory contracts, rather than one agreement, were in issue. Indeed, Chief Justice Fuller states, "In the case of an ordinary money contract, such as a promissory note, or a bond, the consideration has passed; there are no mutual obligations; and cases of that sort do not fall within the reason of the rule [of anticipatory breach]." (P. 17.) Assuming that the early Parker case expresses the Massachusetts rule, it is no more applicable in California than the previously discussed Pierce and Roehm cases.

Appellant's citation of comment (a), section 316, volume 1, Restatement of Contracts, succumbs to the section to which it is appended. The section states that "Where a unilateral contract, or a bilateral contract that has been wholly performed on one side, is for the payment of money in installments or for the performance of other acts, not connected with one another by a condition having reference to more than one of them or otherwise, a breach as to any number less than the whole of such installments or acts is partial." The comment elaborates upon the exception as to either installments or acts which are not connected by a condition relating to the remaining acts or installments; indeed it points out that the "... acts in such a series are more likely to be connected with one another than installments of money." (Emphasis added.) Appellant cannot rely upon the Restatement as authority for the proposition that an anticipatory breach of contract is total in the instant case, in which "acts" are not involved but only "installments," which are themselves not interrelated.

The cases cited by appellant in connection with the comment, Coughlin v. Blair (1953), 41 Cal.2d 587 [262 P.2d 305] and Gold Min. & Water Co. v. Swinerton (1943), 23 Cal.2d 19 [142 P.2d 22], entailed the repudiation of obligations calling for the performance of acts rather than the payment of money in installments. In Coughlin the acts composed the rendition of certain improvements to real estate; in Gold Min. & Water Co., the involved lease provided for the maintenance, improvement and working of the leased mine, as well as for the payment of royalties; indeed, the court stated, "It is not like the case of money payable in fixed installments." (P. 30.) In both cases, therefore, the comment applied "because of the comparative importance of having all the acts performed in order to achieve the object of the contract." (Comment (a), § 316, vol. 1, Rest., Contracts.) (Emphasis added.)

In the instant case we have a converse situation. The main objective of the contract is not frustrated by the repudiation; the payment of the amount due upon the fixed dates fulfills its underlying purpose. The payments are separable and divisible. The default in one, even though concomitant with a renunciation of the whole contract, does not preclude performance of the remainder. The series of acts are not so connected that the omission of one affects the totality; the purpose of the covenant may be achieved even though a single payment may fail.

Professor Corbin has severely criticized the nonapplicability of the anticipatory breach doctrine to a contract which the complaining party has fully performed (4 Corbin on Contracts, § 962 ff, p. 864 ff). The rationale for the orthodox position resides in the fact that the party who has fully performed need only await counter-performance; he is entitled to no more than such performance upon the future dates to which he has agreed. On the other hand, the party who has not yet performed must be ready to, or actually, undertake, further performance. To call upon him to do so in the face of a repudiation of the other contracting party may cause him unmerited hardship. Hence his claim for immediate total performance is greater than that of his dormant counterpart who has fully performed. But the dissenting critics point out that to gain a rather tenuous "logical consistency," we incongruously award judgment for future installments to the party who has not yet performed, and deny such judgment to the party who has fully performed.

In an age in which the installment contracts have had a wide and varied application, and a large proportion of the population has become obligated upon them, we cannot facilely change the accepted rules. "Since the World War ending in 1918, there has been a tremendous expansion in the volume of consumption goods bought on the installment plan. This has now become the customary and accepted method of buying homes, automobiles, electric refrigerators, air conditioning and heating plants and other types of expensive household furnishings and equipment." ("Installment Selling,") 12 Encyclopedia Britannica (1954), page 425. A ruling that the whole amount becomes due upon an installment contract, when executed by one party and repudiated by the other, could work social consequences which we are neither prepared to evaluate nor to engender.

Whatever the theoretical considerations may be, the courts, as we have shown supra, have not applied the doctrine of anticipatory breach, which is itself a judicial innovation in the preexisting rules of the common law, to the breach of unilateral contracts or agreements fully performed by the complaining party. (1 Witkin, Summary of California Law, § 302; 5 Williston on Contracts, § 1328.) That the judicial journey of improvisation should not have stopped at the point of the bilateral agreement, but should have proceeded to the unilateral agreement and to the bilateral contract fully performed on one side, may be argued persuasively; California law, however, has marked the stopping place, and we accept it. . . .

In conclusion upon the main issue, we hold that the total recovery sought here is foreclosed by the embedded rule that the doctrine of anticipatory breach does not apply to an installment contract which has been fully performed by the adverse party.

We affirm the judgment in all respects except as to installments due and unpaid at the date of trial; with respect to such installments, we reverse the judgment and direct the trial court to determine the amount of installments due and unpaid, at the date of trial and to render judgment to appellant for such amount. Appellant shall recover costs on appeal.

Questions

1. Why did the trial court deny the wife's claim for the total sum due on the property settlement agreement?

2. What is the effect of the wife's full performance on the contract in question?

3. According to California law, is the doctrine of anticipatory breach applicable to unilateral contracts?

Takeaways – Minor v. Minor

As noted in the opinion, Professor Corbin is critical of the distinction between unilateral and bilateral contracts as a basis for not applying the doctrine of anticipatory breach to the former category. He has pointed out the logical inconsistency in permitting one who has not performed to sue, while denying the same right to a party who has fully performed. (4 Corbin on Contracts, § 962 et seq.)

So how can a creditor avoid the exception to the rule of anticipatory breach and protect herself? The answer would be to make sure to include an acceleration clause in the installment contract that provides if any payment is made late, the outstanding balance shall become immediately due and payable.

Responding to a Repudiation

Must the recipient of a repudiation always treat it as final and sue immediately? Can the recipient of a repudiation ignore the repudiation and await performance? Is it safe for the recipient of the repudiation to sit and do nothing?

Cosden Oil & Chemical Co. v. Karl O. Helm Aktiengesellschaft
United States Court of Appeals for the Fifth Circuit, 1984
736 F.2d 1064

REAVLEY, Circuit Judge: We must address one of the most difficult interpretive problems of the Uniform Commercial Code--the appropriate time to measure buyer's damages where the seller anticipatorily repudiates a contract and the buyer does not cover. The district court applied the Texas version of Article 2 and measured buyer's damages at a commercially reasonable time after seller's repudiation. We affirm, but remand for modification of damages on another point.

This contractual dispute arose out of events and transactions occurring in the first three months of 1979, when the market in polystyrene, a petroleum derivative used to make molded products, was steadily rising. During this time Iran, a major petroleum producer, was undergoing political turmoil. Karl O. Helm Aktiengesellschaft (Helm or Helm Hamburg), an international trading company based in Hamburg, West Germany, anticipated a tightening in the world petrochemical supply and decided to purchase a large amount of polystyrene. Acting on orders from Helm Hamburg, Helm Houston, a wholly-owned subsidiary, initiated negotiations with Cosden Oil & Chemical Company (Cosden), a Texas-based producer of chemical products, including polystyrene. . .

Negotiating over the telephone and by telex, the parties agreed to the purchase and sale of 1250 metric tons of high impact polystyrene at $.2825 per pound and 250 metric tons of general purpose polystyrene at $.265 per pound. The parties also discussed options on each polystyrene type. . . .

Cosden shipped 90,000 pounds of high impact polystyrene to Helm on or about January 26. Cosden then sent an invoice for that quantity to Helm Houston on or about January 31. The front of the invoice stated, "This order is subject to the terms and conditions shown on the reverse hereof." Among the "Conditions of Sale" listed on the back of the invoice was a force majeure provision. Helm paid for the first shipment in accordance with the agreement.

As Helm had expected, polystyrene prices began to rise in late January, and continued upward during February and March. Cosden also experienced problems at two of its plants in late January. . . .Late in January Cosden notified Helm that it was experiencing problems at its production facilities and that the delivery under 04 might be delayed. On February 6, Smith telephoned Scholtyssek and informed him that Cosden was canceling orders 05, 06, and 07 because two plants were "down" and it did not have sufficient product to fill the orders.. . . .

Cosden sued Helm, seeking damages for Helm's failure to pay for delivered polystyrene. Helm counterclaimed for Cosden's failure to deliver polystyrene as agreed. The jury found on special verdict that Cosden had agreed to sell polystyrene to Helm under all four orders. The jury also found that Cosden anticipatorily repudiated orders 05, 06, and 07 and that Cosden cancelled order 04 before Helm's failure to pay for the second 04 delivery constituted a repudiation. The jury fixed the per pound market prices for polystyrene under each of the four orders at three different times: when Helm learned of the cancellation, at a commercially reasonable time thereafter, and at the time for delivery.

The district court, .. determined that Helm was entitled to recover $628,676 in damages representing the difference between the contract price and the market price at a commercially reasonable time after Cosden repudiated its polystyrene delivery obligations and that Cosden was entitled to an offset of $355,950 against those damages for polystyrene delivered, but not paid for, under order 04.

Both parties find fault with the time at which the district court measured Helm's damages for Cosden's anticipatory repudiation of orders 05, 06, and 07. Cosden argues that damages should be measured when Helm learned of the repudiation. Helm contends that market price as of the last day for delivery--or the time of performance--should be used to compute its damages under the contract-market differential. We reject both views, and hold that the district court correctly measured damages at a commercially reasonable point after Cosden informed Helm that it was canceling the three orders.

Article 2 of the Code has generally been hailed as a success for its comprehensiveness, its deference to mercantile reality, and its clarity. Nevertheless, certain aspects of the Code's overall scheme have proved troublesome in application. The interplay among sections 2.610, 2.711, 2.712, 2.713, and 2.723, Tex.Bus. & Com.Code Ann. (Vernon 1968), represents one of those areas, and has been described as "an impossible legal thicket." J. White & R. Summers, Uniform Commercial Code Sec. 6-7 at 242 (2d ed. 1980). The aggrieved buyer seeking damages for seller's anticipatory repudiation presents the most difficult interpretive problem. Section 2.713 describes the buyer's damages remedy:

Buyer's Damages for Non-Delivery or Repudiation

(a) Subject to the provisions of this chapter with respect to proof of market price (Section 2.723), the measure of damages for non-delivery or repudiation by the seller is the difference between the market price at the time when the buyer learned of the breach and the contract price together with any incidental and consequential damages provided in this chapter (Section 2.715), but less expenses saved in consequence of the seller's breach.

Courts and commentators have identified three possible interpretations of the phrase "learned of the breach." If seller anticipatorily repudiates, buyer learns of the breach:

(1) When he learns of the repudiation;

(2) When he learns of the repudiation plus a commercially reasonable time; or

(3) When performance is due under the contract. . . .

We do not doubt, and Texas law is clear, that market price at the time buyer learns of the breach is the appropriate measure of section 2.713 damages in cases where buyer learns of the breach at or after the time for performance. This will be the common case, for which section 2.713 was designed. See Peters, Remedies for Breach of Contracts Relating to the Sale of Goods Under the Uniform Commercial Code: A Roadmap for Article Two, 73 Yale L.J. 199, 264 (1963). In the relatively rare case where seller anticipatorily repudiates and buyer does not cover, see Anderson, supra, at 318, the specific provision for anticipatory repudiation cases, section 2.610, authorizes the aggrieved party to await performance for a commercially reasonable time before resorting to his remedies of cover or damages.

In the anticipatory repudiation context, the buyer's specific right to wait for a commercially reasonable time before choosing his remedy must be read together with the general damages provision of section 2.713 to extend the time for measurement beyond when buyer learns of the breach. Comment 1 to section 2.610 states that if an aggrieved party "awaits performance beyond a commercially reasonable time he cannot recover resulting damages which he should have avoided." This suggests that an aggrieved buyer can recover damages where the market rises during the commercially reasonable time he awaits performance. To interpret 2.713's "learned of the breach" language to mean the time at which seller first communicates his anticipatory repudiation would undercut the time that 2.610 gives the aggrieved buyer to await performance.

The buyer's option to wait a commercially reasonable time also interacts with section 2.611, which allows the seller an opportunity to retract his repudiation. Thus, an aggrieved buyer "learns of the breach" a commercially reasonable time after he learns of the seller's anticipatory repudiation. The weight of scholarly commentary supports this interpretation. See J. Calamari & J. Perillo, Contracts Sec. 14-20 (2d ed. 1977); Sebert, Remedies Under Article Two of the Uniform Commercial Code: An Agenda for Review, 130 U. Pa. L. Rev. 360, 372-80 (1981); Wallach, Anticipatory Repudiation and the UCC, 13 U.C.C.L.J. 48 (1980); Peters, supra, at 263-68.

Typically, our question will arise where parties to an executory contract are in the midst of a rising market. To the extent that market decisions are influenced by a damages rule, measuring market price at the time of seller's repudiation gives seller the ability to fix buyer's damages and may induce seller to repudiate, rather than abide by the contract. By contrast, measuring buyer's damages at the time of performance will tend to dissuade the buyer from covering, in hopes that market price will continue upward until performance time.

Allowing the aggrieved buyer a commercially reasonable time, however, provides him with an opportunity to investigate his cover possibilities in a rising market without fear that, if he is unsuccessful in obtaining cover, he will be relegated to a market-contract damage remedy measured at the time of repudiation. The Code supports this view. While cover is the preferred remedy, the Code clearly provides the option to seek damages. See Sec. 2.712(c) & comment 3. If " [t]he buyer is always free to choose between cover and damages for non-delivery," and if 2.712 "is not intended to limit the time necessary for [buyer] to look around and decide as to how he may best effect cover," it would be anomalous, if the buyer chooses to seek damages, to fix his damages at a time before he investigated cover possibilities and before he elected his remedy. See id. comment 2 & 3; Dura-Wood Treating Co. v. Century Forest Industries, Inc., 675 F.2d 745, 754 (5th Cir.), cert. denied, 459 U.S. 865, 103 S. Ct. 144, 74 L. Ed. 2d 122 (1982) ("buyer has some time in which to evaluate the situation"). Moreover, comment 1 to section 2.713 states, "The general baseline adopted in this section uses as a yardstick the market in which the buyer would have obtained cover had he sought that relief." See Sec. 2.610 comment 1. When a buyer chooses not to cover, but to seek damages, the market is measured at the time he could have covered--a reasonable time after repudiation. See Secs. 2.711 & 2.713.

Persuasive arguments exist for interpreting "learned of the breach" to mean "time of performance," consistent with the pre-Code rule. See J. White & R. Summers, supra, Sec. 6-7; Anderson, supra. If this was the intention of the Code's drafters, however, phrases in section 2.610 and 2.712 lose their meaning. If buyer is entitled to market-contract damages measured at the time of performance, it is difficult to explain why the anticipatory repudiation section limits him to a commercially reasonable time to await performance. See Sec. 2.610 comment 1. Similarly, in a rising market, no reason would exist for requiring the buyer to act "without unreasonable delay" when he seeks to cover following an anticipatory repudiation. See Sec. 2.712(a).

The interplay among the relevant Code sections does not permit, in this context, an interpretation that harmonizes all and leaves no loose ends. We therefore acknowledge that our interpretation fails to explain the language of section 2.723(a) insofar as it relates to aggrieved buyers. We note, however, that the section has limited applicability--cases that come to trial before the time of performance will be rare. Moreover, the comment to section 2.723 states that the "section is not intended to exclude the use of any other reasonable method of determining market price or of measuring damages...." In light of the Code's persistent theme of commercial reasonableness, the prominence of cover as a remedy, and the time given an aggrieved buyer to await performance and to investigate cover before selecting his remedy, we agree with the district court that "learned of the breach" incorporates section 2.610's commercially reasonable time....

At trial Cosden argued that Helm's purchases of polystyrene from other sources in early February constituted cover. Helm argued that those purchases were not intended to substitute for polystyrene sales cancelled by Cosden. Helm, however, contended that it did cover by purchasing large amounts of high impact polystyrene from other sources late in February and around the first of March. Cosden claimed that these purchases were not made reasonably and that they should not qualify as cover. The jury found that none of Helm's purchases of polystyrene from other sources were cover purchases.

Now Cosden argues that the prices of polystyrene for the purchases that Helm claimed were cover should act as a ceiling for fixing market price under section 2.713. We refuse to accept this novel argument. Although a buyer who has truly covered may not be allowed to seek higher damages under section 2.713 than he is granted by section 2.712, see Sec. 2.713 comment 5; J. White & R. Summers, supra, Sec. 6-4 at 233-34, in this case the jury found that Helm did not cover. We cannot isolate a reason to explain the jury's finding: it might have concluded that Helm would have made the purchases regardless of Cosden's nonperformance or that the transactions did not qualify as cover for other reasons. Because of the jury's finding, we cannot use those other transactions to determine Helm's damages....

The cause is remanded to the district court to modify Helm's damages under orders 05 and 07.

Questions

1. How did the district court measure the buyer's damages for the seller's anticipatory repudiation in this case?

2. According to the court, when does the buyer "learn of the breach" in the context of anticipatory repudiation?

3. Why did the court reject the arguments to measure damages at the time when the buyer learned of the repudiation or at the time of performance?

4. How does the buyer's option to wait a commercially reasonable time before choosing a remedy interact with the seller's opportunity to retract the repudiation?

Takeaways – Cosden v. Karl O. Helm

According to the *Cosden* court a buyer "learns of the breach" a commercially reasonable time after he learns of the seller's anticipatory repudiation. What is the rational behind that?

Permitting a buyer to wait a commercially reasonable time affords time to assess the seriousness of the seller's repudiation and legitimate business needs of the aggrieved party. Once that time has expired, the buyer's losses should be measured at the time when it should have covered on the open market. (31 Stan.L.Rev. 69)

Retracting a Repudiation

Can a party that has repudiated, withdraw their repudiation? (See Rest.2d § 256, UCC § 2-611)

United States v. Seacoast Gas Co.
United States Court of Appeals, Fifth Circuit, 1953
204 F. 2d 709

Suit against gas company and its surety on gas company's performance bond, for damages alleged to have resulted from an anticipatory breach of contract in nature of notice of intent to cancel contract as of November 15, 1947. The United States District Court for the Southern District of Georgia entered judgment in favor of gas company and surety, and plaintiff appealed. . . .

HUTCHESON, Chief Judge. Brought against Seacoast Gas Company and the surety on it performance bond, the suit was for damages alleged to have resulted from the anticipatory breach by the Gas Company of its contract with plaintiff to supply gas to a federal housing project during the period from April 15, 1947, to June 15, 1948. The claim was: that on October 7, 1947, while performance of the contract was in progress, Seacoast anticipatorily breached the contract by writing plaintiff unequivocally that, because of plaintiff's breach of the contract, Seacoast intended to cancel same as of November 15, 1947; that the plaintiff immediately notified Seacoast that it did not recognize any right in it to cease performance and that it proposed to advertise for bids to insure a continued supply of gas if Seacoast's breach persisted; that, thereafter, having advertised for bids and on November 6th, having received the low bid from Trion Company, it on that date notified Seacoast by letter that unless it retracted its repudiation of the contract within three days from the letter date, Trion's bid would be accepted and Seacoast and its surety would be held liable for breach of contract; and that thereafter Seacoast not having retracted within the time fixed, plaintiff on November 10, accepted Trion's bid and, pursuant thereto, began its preparations to execute with Trion a contract for a price in excess of that provided in the Seacoast contract, and Seacoast is liable to plaintiff for this excess.

Defendant Seacoast, admitting in its pleading and its testimony that the facts were substantially as claimed by plaintiff, defended on the ground: that it had retracted its notice of repudiation and given assurance of its intention to continue to perform before the plaintiff had actually signed the new contract; and that, since, as it claimed, plaintiff had not then substantially changed its position or suffered any damages as a result of Seacoast's notice to terminate the contract and cease performance under it, the retraction was timely and healed the breach.

Upon the issue thus joined, the cause was tried to the court without a jury, and the court stating the question for decision thus, "The question in this case is as to whether Seacoast Gas Company, Inc. withdrew its notice of cancellation of its contract prior to the rendering of the contract to the Trion Gas Company, found that it had done so. On the basis of this finding and a further finding that on November 13, two days before the termination date which Seacoast had fixed in its notice, Zell, who was president both of Seacoast and of Trion Company, to whom the new contract was awarded, notified the regional counsel for the Public Housing Authority that Seacoast admitted it had no right to cancel the contract and was rescinding its notice, the court held that the anticipatory breach had been healed and plaintiff could not recover.

Appealing from this judgment, plaintiff is here insisting that under the settled law governing anticipatory breaches not only as it is laid down in Georgia but generally, Seacoast's retraction came too late to heal the breach, and the judgment must be reversed.

Appellees, on their part, insist that the judgment appealed from was soundly based in law and in fact and must be affirmed.

We do not think so. The undisputed facts establish: that Zell, president of both companies, was present at the opening of the new bids on November 6, 1947, and upon being asked to withdraw Seacoast's notice that it would cease performing the contract, refused to do so; that on that date the Public Housing Administration regional counsel wrote Seacoast by registered mail, addressed "Attention Zell", advising of the steps the government had taken and stating that unless Seacoast retracted its repudiation within three days from the date of the letter, Trion's bid would be accepted and Seacoast and its sureties would be held liable for breach of contract; and that having received no response from Seacoast within the three days specified, and Zell again asked on November 10th, to retract the notice of repudiation having refused to do so, the government accepted Trion's bid and proceeded with the execution of the contract. The record standing thus, under settled law not only of Georgia but generally elsewhere, the breach was not healed, the judgment was wrong, and it must be reversed.

A comparison of the briefs and arguments of appellant and appellees will show that the case is in quite small compass. Both agree that Seacoast's letter of October 24th operated as an anticipatory breach and that unless effectively withdrawn during the *locus poenitentiae* it operated to put Seacoast in default and to render it liable for the loss to the government of the difference in price between the old and the new contract.

Appellees, after quoting from Anson on Contracts, 6th Ed. Sec. 385, p. 444:

"The repudiator has the power of retraction prior to any change of position by the other party, but not afterwards."

go on to say:

"So we see that the authorities seem to be unanimous that a person who gives notice of his intention not to perform a contract may withdraw such notice and offer to perform prior to the time the other party acted or relied thereon."

Based upon these premises, they insist that "the undisputed evidence is that appellant did not `accept the bid of Trion Gas' until November 17th, which was after the notice of cancellation had been withdrawn in writing."

We think: that this statement is erroneous; that it represents the crucial difference between the parties; and that the error of the statement lies in the fact that it confuses the acceptance of the bid with the signing of the contract.

It is true that the contract was not signed until the 17th, after Seacoast had retracted its notice and if appellees were correct in its position that the date of the signing of the new contract was determinative of this case, they would be correct in their conclusion that the judgment should be affirmed.

But that position is not correct. In fact and in law, when the government took bids and notified Seacoast that unless it retracted within three days it would proceed to accept the Trion bid and award the contract to it, the *locus poenitentiae* ended with these three days. The fact that Seacoast claims that it did not receive the notice is completely immaterial both because it was not necessary for the government to give any notice or fix any time and because Zell, on November 10th, repeated to the Regional Counsel his refusal to retract.

All that is required to close the door to repentance is definite action indicating that the anticipatory breach has been accepted as final, and this requisite can be supplied either by the filing of a suit or a firm declaration, as here, that unless within a fixed time the breach is repudiated, it will be accepted.

Here, in addition to this firm declaration, the record shows the taking of bids and the awarding of the contract to the lowest bidder. The error of the district judge lies, we think, in holding that the *locus poenitentiae* was extended until the 17th, when the contract was signed, and that Seacoast having repented before the signing of the contract, had healed the breach and restored the contract to its original vitality.

Whatever of doubt there may be, and we have none with respect to this view, as a matter of strict law, there can be none with respect to the justice or equity of this determination when it is considered; that Zell, the president and practically sole owner of Seacoast, was the organizer, the president and practically sole owner of Trion; that he organized Trion for the sole purpose of the bidding; and that on the date the bids were opened and later on the date the contract was awarded, he, though requested to do so, refused to withdraw Seacoast's repudiation and continued in that refusal until a day or two before the contract was signed.

The evidence showing, as it does, without contradiction, that the signing of the contract was not delayed because of a purpose on the part of the government to extend the time for Seacoast's repentance, but because until that date Trion had not furnished his bond, we think it clear that, in entering judgment for the defendants, the court erred. The judgment is, therefore, reversed and the cause is remanded with directions to enter judgment for plaintiff for the loss Seacoast's breach of contract has caused it.

Question

What actions taken by the plaintiff and the government indicated the acceptance of the anticipatory breach as final?

Takeaways – Seacoast Gas

A repudiation may be retracted before a change of position in reliance thereon. (Rest.2d § 256) It is too late to retract a repudiation after the injured party changes position. see also UCC § 2-611)

"One who has committed an anticipatory breach by a manifestation of intention not to perform his contract has power to nullify its effect as a breach by notifying the promisee that he has changed his wrongful intention and will perform the contract. This power of retraction will cease to exist as soon as the promisee has materially changed his position in reliance on the repudiation." (Corbin, Contracts (One Vol.Ed.) § 980)

McCloskey & Co. v. Minweld Steel Co.
United States Court of Appeals, Third Circuit, 1955
220 F. 2d 101

McLAUGHLIN, Circuit Judge. Plaintiff-appellant, a general contractor, sued on three contracts alleging an anticipatory breach as to each. At the close of the plaintiff's case the district judge granted the defense motions for judgment on the ground that plaintiff had not made out a cause of action.

By the contracts involved the principal defendant, a fabricator and erector of steel, agreed to furnish and erect all of the structural steel required on two buildings to be built on the grounds of the Hollidaysburg State Hospital, Hollidaysburg, Pa. and to furnish all of the long span steel joists required in the construction of one of the two buildings. Two of the contracts were dated May 1, 1950 and the third May 26, 1950. By Article V of each of the contracts "Should the Sub-Contractor [the defendant herein] * * * at any time refuse or neglect to supply a sufficiency * * * of materials of the proper quality, * * * in and about the performance of the work required to be done pursuant to the provisions of this agreement * * *, or fail, in the performance of any of the agreements herein contained, the Contractor shall be at liberty, without prejudice to any other right or remedy, on two days' written notice to the Sub-Contractor, either to provide any such * * * materials and to deduct the cost thereof from any payments then or thereafter due the Sub-Contractor, or to terminate the employment of the Sub-Contractor for the said work and to enter upon the premises . . . ."

There was no stated date in the contracts for performance by the defendant subcontractor. Article VI provided for completion by the subcontractor of its contract work "by and at the time or times hereafter stated to-wit:

"Samples, Shop Drawings and Schedules are to be submitted in the quantities and manner required by the Specifications, for the approval of the Architects, immediately upon receipt by the Sub-Contractor of the contract drawings, or as may be directed by the Contractor. All expense involved in the submission and approval of these Samples, Shop Drawings and Schedules shall be borne by the Sub-Contractor.

"All labor, materials and equipment required under this contract are to be furnished at such times as may be directed by the Contractor, and in such a manner so as to at no time delay the final completion of the building.

"It being mutually understood and agreed that prompt delivery and installation of all materials required to be furnished under this contract is to be the essence of this Agreement."

Appellee Minweld Steel Co., Inc., the subcontractor, received contract drawings and specifications for both buildings in May, 1950. On June 8, 1950, plaintiff McCloskey & Co. wrote appellee asking when it might "expect delivery of the structural steel" for the buildings and "also the time estimated to complete erection." Minweld replied on June 13, 1950, submitting a schedule estimate of expecting to begin delivery of the steel by September 1, and to complete erection approximately November 15. On July 20, 1950 plaintiff wrote Minweld threatening to terminate the contracts unless the latter gave unqualified assurances that it had effected definite arrangements for the procurement, fabrication and delivery within thirty days of the required materials. On July 24, 1950 Minweld wrote McCloskey & Co. explaining its difficulty in obtaining the necessary steel. It asked McCloskey's assistance in procuring it and stated that "We are as anxious as you are that there be no delay in the final completion of the buildings or in the performance of our contract, ..."

Plaintiff-appellant claims that by this last letter, read against the relevant facts, defendant gave notice of its positive intention not to perform its contracts and thereby violated same. Some reference has already been made to the background of the July 24th letter. It concerned Minweld's trouble in securing the steel essential for performance of its contract. Minweld had tried unsuccessfully to purchase this from Bethlehem Steel, U. S. Steel and Carnegie-Illinois. It is true as appellant urges that Minweld knew and was concerned about the tightening up of the steel market. And as is evident from the letter it, being a fabricator and not a producer, realized that without the help of the general contractor on this hospital project particularly by it enlisting the assistance of the General State Authority, Minweld was in a bad way for the needed steel. However, the letter conveys no idea of contract repudiation by Minweld. That company admittedly was in a desperate situation. Perhaps if it had moved earlier to seek the steel its effort might have been successful. But that is mere speculation for there is no showing that the mentioned producers had they been solicited sooner would have been willing to provide the material.

Minweld from its written statement did, we think, realistically face the problem confronting it. As a result it asked its general contractor for the aid which the latter, by the nature of the construction, should have been willing to give. Despite the circumstances there is no indication in the letter that Minweld had definitely abandoned all hope of otherwise receiving the steel and so finishing its undertaking. One of the mentioned producers might have relented. Some other supplier might have turned up. It was McCloskey & Co. who eliminated whatever chance there was. That concern instead of aiding Minweld by urging its plea for the hospital construction materials to the State Authority which represented the Commonwealth of Pennsylvania took the position that the subcontractor had repudiated its agreement and then moved quickly to have the work completed. Shortly thereafter, and without the slightest trouble as far as appears, McCloskey & Co. procured the steel from Bethlehem and brought in new subcontractors to do the work contemplated by the agreement with Minweld.

Under the applicable law Minweld's letter was not a breach of the agreement. . . . . "In order to give rise to a renunciation amounting to a breach of contract, there must be an absolute and unequivocal refusal to perform or a distinct and positive statement of an inability to do so." Minweld's conduct is plainly not that of a contract breaker under that test. [Citation omitted] Restatement of Contracts, Comment (i) to Sec. 318 (1932) speaks clearly on the point saying:

"Though where affirmative action is promised mere failure to act, at the time when action has been promised, is a breach, failure to take preparatory action before the time when any performance is promised is not an anticipatory breach, even though such failure makes it impossible that performance shall take place, and though the promisor at the time of the failure intends not to perform his promise." See Williston on Contracts, Vol. 5, Sec. 1324 (1937), Corbin on Contracts, Vol. 4, Sec. 973 (1951).

Appellant contends that its letter of July 20, requiring assurances of arrangements which would enable appellee to complete delivery in thirty days, constituted a fixing of a date under Article VI of the contracts. The short answer to this is that the thirty day date, if fixed, was never repudiated. Appellee merely stated that it was unable to give assurances as to the preparatory arrangements. There is nothing in the contracts which authorized appellant to demand or receive such assurances.

The district court acted properly in dismissing the actions as a matter of law on the ground that plaintiff had not made out a prima facie case.

The order of the district court of July 14, 1954 denying the plaintiff's motions for findings of facts, to vacate the judgments and for new trials will be affirmed.

Questions

1. How did the court interpret the letter from the subcontractor, Minweld, in relation to the anticipatory breach claim?

2. According to the court's reasoning, what is required for a renunciation to amount to a breach of contract?

3. What legal test did the court apply to determine whether Minweld's conduct constituted a breach of the agreement?

Takeaways – McCloskey & Co. v. Minweld Steel Co.

An express repudiation must be clear, positive and unequivocal in order to give rise to an anticipatory breach. (1 Witkin, Summary of Cal.Law (10th ed. 2005) Contracts § 863.)

Adequate Assurance of Due Performance

When a party to a contract has reasonable grounds for being uncertain or insecure about the other party's ability to perform, the concerned party may make a demand for "adequate assurances of due performance. UCC § 2-609 provides: 1) the aggrieved party is permitted to suspend his performance; 2) he is given the right to require adequate assurance; 3) failure to supply adequate assurances may create an anticipatory breach and thus give rise to all of the remedies available for such a repudiation. Some jurisdictions have extended the doctrine to contracts of all types, not just those for the sale of "goods." (See, *Norcon Power Partners v. Niagara Mohawk Power Corp.* 92 N.Y.2d 458, 705 N.E.2d 656 (1998))

Pittsburgh-Des Moines Steel v. Brookhaven Manor Water Co.
United States Court of Appeals, Seventh Circuit, 1976
532 F. 2d 572

[At the request of the Water Company (Brookhaven), Pittsburgh-Des Moines Steel Company (PDM) submitted a revised proposal to build an elevated tank for $175,000. The original proposal called for progress Payments to PDM; the revised offer called for no payment until the tank had been built and tested. After Brookhaven's acceptance, PDM heard something about a loan that Brookhaven was negotiating for. The credit manager for PDM wrote the prospective lender (copy to Brookha-ven) asking for a notice that $175,000 had been put in escrow for the job, and adding: "As a matter of good business we are holding this matter in abeyance until receipt of such notification." The loan did not go through. Then the credit manager wrote the president of Brookhaven asking for his personal guarantee of payment, "to protect us between now and the time your loan is completed." The letter mentioned the escrow again, this time as a requirement. The president sent a state mont of his personal worth. PM stopped fabricating parts, and the tank was never built. PDM sued Brookhaven, charging repudiation of the contract, and Brookhaven entered a counterclaim. A jury returned a verdict for PDM bro the trial court entered a judgment notwithstanding the verdict, in Brookhaven's favor. PDM appealed.]

PELL, Circuit Judge. . . . PDM argues that its position was in accordance with Section 2-609 of the Uniform Commercial Code (UCC) enacted into law in Illinois as Ill.Rev.Stat. ch. 26, sec. 2-609. That section which "creates a new contract enforcement procedure for the situation where one party feels insecure as to the other's performance" reads in pertinent portion as follows:

"Right to Adequate Assurance of Performance. (1) A contract for sale imposes an obligation on each party that the other's expectation of receiving due performance will not be impaired. When reasonable grounds for insecurity arise with respect to the performance of either party the other may in writing demand adequate assurance of due performance and until he receives such assurance may if commercially reasonable suspend any performance for which he has not already received the agreed return.

"(2) Between merchants the reasonableness of grounds for insecurity and the adequacy of any assurance offered shall be determined according to commercial standards. . . .

"(4) After receipt of a justified demand failure to provide within a reasonable time not exceeding 30 days such assurance of due performance as is adequate under the circumstances of the particular case is a repudiation of the contract."

There appears to be considerable doubt that a seller was entitled to this protection prior to the adoption of the UCC; . . .

The question remaining is whether PDM's actions subsequent to the execution of the contract were within the protection provided by § 2-609. We hold that they were not.

The performance to which PDM was entitled was the full payment of the purchase price within a specified time after the completion of the tank. While we have a substantial question as to whether PDM made a written demand as required by the statute, in keeping with our concept that the UCC should be liberally construed, we do not desire to rest our decision on a formalistic approach. Letters were written which conveyed what PDM wanted done before they would pursue their obligations under the contract. The fundamental problem is that these letters, if they be deemed to be in the nature of a demand, demanded more than that to which PDM was entitled and the demand was not founded upon what in our opinion was an actuating basis for the statute's applicability.

We do not construe § 2-609 as being a vehicle without more for an implied term being inserted in a contract when a substantially equivalent term was expressly waived in the contract. The something more to trigger applicability of the statute is that the expectation of due performance on the part of the other party entertained at contracting time no longer exists because of "reasonable grounds for insecurity" arising. We find that PDM's actions in demanding either the escrowing of the purchase price or a personal guarantee lacked the necessary predicate of reasonable grounds for insecurity having arisen. The contract negates the existence of any basis for insecurity at the time of the contract when PDM was willing to wait 30 days beyond completion for payment. The fact that Brookhaven had not completed its loan negotiations does not constitute reasonable grounds for insecurity when the money in question was not to be needed for some months. Reasonable business men prefer in the absence of some compulsive reason not to commence paying interest on borrowed money until the time for the use for that money is at hand. The credit manager's January letter that the order was being held in abeyance until receipt of notification of escrowing was based upon a "matter of good business," but not upon any change of condition bearing upon Brookhaven's ability to discharge its payment obligation under the contract. With regard to the later request for a personal guarantee, it is not uncommon for an individual to decline assuming obligations of a corporation in which he is a shareholder. Indeed, the use of the corporate device frequently has as a principal purpose the limitation on individual exposure to liability. If an unfavorable risk in dealing with a corporation exists at contracting time, good business judgment may well indicate that an assurance be secured before contracting that there will be individual shareholder backup. None of this occurred and the record is silent as to any reasonable grounds for insecurity arising thereafter.

It is true that one officer of PDM testified that the company did not send a crew because we questioned whether we might be paid for the project "at that time." Some more objective factual basis than a subjective questioning, in our opinion, is needed to demonstrate reasonable grounds for insecurity. Likewise, another PDM officer testified that it was the company's normal and regular procedure not to erect a structure "until we have reason to believe that the funds to pay for the structure *are* available." The time of which he was speaking was a time at which there was no contractual requirement that the funds be available. The funds were only required to be available after completion of installation. He testified further that the normal procedure was not to erect until satisfactory arrangements were made. None of this subjectively normal procedure was imposed as a provision in the contract which in view of the withdrawn provision for progress payments showed reasonably to Brookhaven that not only payment, but arrangements for payment, would not be necessary until after completion.

We, of course, would not deprive PDM of resort to § 2-609 if there had been a demonstration that reasonable grounds for insecurity had arisen. The proof in that respect was lacking. The comptroller and supervisor of PDM's credit department testified that he had access to all of the credit information that the company had regarding Brookhaven, that he had reviewed that information, and that he was unaware of any change in the financial condition of Brookhaven between November of 1968 and the end of 1969. Finally, we note that despite the professed subjective questioning in April as to whether PDM might be paid, the credit manager as early as January had said that the job would be held in abeyance until arrangements had been made for escrowing and a month after the questioning, the questioning officer had offered to proceed with construction in exchange for an interest in Brookhaven, an unlikely course if Brookhaven were financially in a questionable condition. There was also testimony with the same inference that PDM was not fearful of Brookhaven's financial stability or ability to pay in connection with PDM lending to Brookhaven the amount involved at an interest rate of 9½% which rate was then unacceptable to Brookhaven. If the buyer was unable to pay for the performance of the contract, it is difficult to see that it was better able to pay a promissory note. We do not fault Brookhaven for its rejection of various proposals advanced by PDM each of which amounted to a rewriting of the contract in the absence of a proper § 2-609 basis. The fact, if it were a fact, that Brookhaven may not have had a large amount of cash lying in the bank in a checking account, not an unusual situation for a real estate developer, does not support the belief that it, as a company with substantial assets, would fail to meet its obligations as they fell due. Section 2-609 is a protective device when reasonable grounds for insecurity arise; it is not a pen for rewriting a contract in the absence of those reasonable grounds having arisen, particularly when the proposed rewriting involves the very factors which had been waived by the one now attempting to wield the pen. The situation is made no more persuasive for PDM when it is recalled that that company was the original scrivener.

Brookhaven's request to put off the contract for a year clearly came after PDM's repudiation of the contract and was indicative of nothing more than that Brookhaven was willing to undertake a new arrangement with PDM a year hence. Pursuant to § 2-610 of the UCC, Brookhaven was entitled to suspend its own performance by virtue of the anticipatory repudiation by PDM and to resort to available remedies, including damages pursuant to § 2-711 of the Code.

Affirmed

CUMMINGS, CIRCUIT JUDGE (concurring). Although I agree with the result reached in the majority opinion, I differ with the reasoning. Reasonable men could certainly conclude that PDM had legitimate grounds to question Brookhaven's ability to pay for the water tank. When the contract was signed, the parties understood that Brookhaven would obtain a loan to help pay for the project. When the loan failed to materialize, a prudent businessman would have "reasonable grounds for insecurity." I disagree that there must be a fundamental change in the financial position of the buyer before the seller can invoke the protection of UCC § 2-609. Rather, I believe that the Section was designed to cover instances where an underlying condition of the contract, even if not expressly incorporated into the written document, fails to occur. See Comment 3 to UCC § 2-609. Whether, in a specific case, the breach of the condition gives a party "reasonable grounds for insecurity" is a question of fact for the jury.

UCC § 2-609, however, does not give the alarmed party a right to redraft the contract. The district court could properly conclude as a matter of law that these requests by PDM demanded more than a commercially "adequate assurance of due performance."

Questions

1. According to the court's reasoning, what is the purpose of Section 2-609 of the Uniform Commercial Code?

2. Why did the court determine that PDM's actions did not fall within the protection provided by Section 2-609?

3. What specific requirement did PDM demand from Brookhaven in their letters, and why did the court find this demand to be unreasonable?

Takeaways – Pittsburgh-Des Moines Steel Co. v. Brookhaven Manor Water Co.

As the dissenting justice in this case pointed out, UCC § 2-609, does not give the alarmed party a right to redraft the contract. There is a distinction between a party invoking that provision and merely requesting an assurance that performance will be forthcoming a party that attempts to alter the contract.

Insolvent Buyers

An exception to the rule that insecurity only gives rise to a right to demand adequate assurance and nothing more exists when the contract is for the sale of goods and the seller discovers that a buyer is insolvent. UCC § 2-702 provides that upon discovery that the buyer is insolvent, the seller may refuse delivery, stop delivery or condition delivery upon payment in cash. Short of insolvency, 2-609 would not give the insecure seller the right to demand payment at an earlier time or on different terms than were originally provided for in the contract.

ASSESSMENT QUESTIONS, CHAPTER 8

1. Discuss the distinction between conditions precedent and conditions subsequent in contract law. Provide examples for each.

2. What is a concurrent condition?

3. Explain the difference between a dependent promise and an independent promise in contract law. How does the distinction affect the parties' obligations?

4. Describe the doctrine of substantial performance and its impact on the discharge of a contract. Under what circumstances can a party claim substantial performance?

5. What is the effect of a material breach of contract on the non-breaching party's obligations? How does it impact the breaching party's right to payment?

6. Discuss the concept of anticipatory breach in contract law. What happens when one party anticipatorily breaches the contract?

7. Explain the options available to the non-breaching party when faced with an anticipatory breach. What options do they have?

8. Describe the doctrine of election of remedies in relation to breach of contract. How does it apply when a party faces a breach?

9. What is the doctrine of waiver in contract law? How does it affect the non-breaching party's rights and obligations?

Chapter 9
MISTAKE, IMPRACTICABILITY AND FRUSTRATION OF PURPOSE

Introduction

In this chapter we consider several doctrines by which the parties may avoid their contractual obligations. Suppose their basic assumptions at the time they enter into the contract prove to be wrong? Suppose some unexpected event occurs and the non-occurrence of that unexpected event was a basic assumption upon which they agreed? Suppose some unexpected event occurs that, although it doesn't make performance impossible or impractical, means that suddenly one party will not be getting anything in return for their money.

Mistake

Consent to a bargain is not real or free when obtained through mistake. (Cal.Civ.Code § 1567) A mistake is a belief that is not in accord with the facts. (Rest.2d § 151) Mistake may be either of fact or of law. (Cal.Civ.Code § 1576)

Mistake of fact is a mistake not caused by the neglect of a legal duty on the part of the person making the mistake, and consisting of:

(1) An unconscious ignorance or forgetfulness of a fact past or present, material to the contract; or,

(2) Belief in the present existence of a thing material to the contract, which does not exist, or in the past existence of such a thing, which has not existed. (Cal.Civ.Code § 1577)

Mistake of law constitutes a mistake only when it arises from:

(1) A misapprehension of the law by all parties, all supposing that they knew and understood it, and all making substantially the same mistake as to the law; or,

(2) A misapprehension of the law by one party, of which the others are aware at the time of contracting, but which they do not rectify. (Cal.Civ.Code § 1578)

The law divides mistake into two categories, mutual mistake and unilateral mistake.

Mutual Mistake

A mistake of fact, shared by both parties, which goes to the basis of the bargain, entitles either party to rescind the contract. (Rest.2d Contracts § 152)

Sherwood v. Walker
Supreme Court of Michigan, 1887
66 Mich. 568, 33 N.W. 919

MORSE, Justice. Replevin for a cow. Suit commenced in justice's court; judgment for plaintiff; appealed to circuit court of Wayne county, and verdict and judgment for plaintiff in that court. The defendants bring error, and set out 25 assignments of the same.

The defendants reside at Detroit, but are in business at Walkerville, Ontario, and have a farm at Greenfield, in Wayne county, upon which were some blooded cattle supposed to be barren as breeders. The Walkers are importers and breeders of polled Angus cattle. The plaintiff is a banker living at Plymouth, in Wayne county. He called upon the defendants at Walkerville for the purchase of some of their stock, but found none there that suited him. Meeting one of the defendants afterwards, he was informed that they had a few head upon their Greenfield farm. He was asked to go out and look at them, with the statement at the time that they were probably barren, and would not breed. May 5, 1886, plaintiff went out to Greenfield, and saw the cattle. A few days thereafter, he called upon one of the defendants with the view of purchasing a cow, known as "Rose 2d of Aberlone." After considerable talk, it was agreed that defendants would telephone Sherwood at his home in Plymouth in reference to the price. The second morning after this talk he was called up by telephone, and the terms of the sale were finally agreed upon. He was to pay five and one-half cents per pound, live weight, fifty pounds shrinkage. He was asked how he intended to take the cow home, and replied that he might ship her from King's cattle-yard. He requested defendants to confirm the sale in writing, which they did by sending him the following letter:

"WALKERVILLE, May 15, 1886.

"T.C. Sherwood, President, etc.--DEAR SIR: We confirm sale to you of the cow Rose 2d of Aberlone, lot 56 of our catalogue, at five and half cents per pound, less fifty pounds shrink. We inclose herewith order on Mr. Graham for the cow. You might leave check with him, or mail to us here, as you prefer.

"Yours, truly
HIRAM WALKER & SONS."

The order upon Graham inclosed in the letter read as follows:

"WALKERVILLE, May 15, 1886." George Graham: You will please deliver at King's cattle-yard to Mr. T.C. Sherwood, Plymouth, the cow Rose 2d of Aberlone, lot 56 of our catalogue. Send halter with the cow, and have her weighed.

"Yours truly,
HIRAM WALKER & SONS."

On the twenty-first of the same month the plaintiff went to defendants' farm at Greenfield, and presented the order and letter to Graham, who informed him that the defendants had instructed him not to deliver the cow. Soon after, the plaintiff tendered to Hiram Walker, one of the defendants, $80, and demanded the cow. Walker refused to take the money or deliver the cow. The plaintiff then instituted this suit. After he had secured possession of the cow under the writ of replevin, the plaintiff caused her to be weighed by the constable who served the writ, at a place other than King's cattle-yard. She weighed 1,420 pounds. . . .

The defendants then introduced evidence tending to show that at the time of the alleged sale it was believed by both the plaintiff and themselves that the cow was barren and would not breed; that she cost $850, and if not barren would be worth from $750 to $1,000; that after the date of the letter, and the order to Graham, the defendants were informed by said Graham that in his judgment the cow was with calf, and therefore they instructed him not to deliver her to plaintiff, and on the twentieth of May, 1886, telegraphed plaintiff what Graham thought about the cow being with calf, and that consequently they could not sell her. The cow had a calf in the month of October following. On the nineteenth of May, the plaintiff wrote Graham as follows:

"Mr. George Graham, Greenfield--DEAR SIR: I have bought Rose or Lucy from Mr. Walker, and will be there for her Friday morning, nine or ten o'clock. Do not water her in the morning.

"Yours, etc.,
T.C. SHERWOOD."

Plaintiff explained the mention of the two cows in this letter by testifying that, when he wrote this letter, the order and letter of defendants was at his home, and, writing in a hurry, and being uncertain as to the name of the cow, and not wishing his cow watered, he thought it would do no harm to name them both, as his bill of sale would show which one he had purchased. Plaintiff also testified that he asked defendants to give him a price on the balance of their herd at Greenfield, as a friend thought of buying some, and received a letter dated May 17, 1886, in which they named the price of five cattle, including Lucy, at $90, and Rose 2d at $80. When he received the letter he called defendants up by telephone, and asked them why they put Rose 2d in the list, as he had already purchased her. They replied that they knew he had, but thought it would make no difference if plaintiff and his friend concluded to take the whole herd.

The foregoing is the substance of all the testimony in the case.

The circuit judge instructed the jury that if they believed the defendants, when they sent the order and letter to plaintiff, meant to pass the title to the cow, and that the cow was intended to be delivered to plaintiff, it did not matter whether the cow was weighed at any particular place, or by any particular person; and if the cow was weighed afterwards, as Sherwood testified, such weighing would be a sufficient compliance with the order. If they believed that defendants intended to pass the title by writing, it did not matter whether the cow was weighed before or after suit brought, and the plaintiff would be entitled to recover. . . . The court also charged the jury that it was immaterial whether the cow was with calf or not. . . .

It appears from the record that both parties supposed this cow was barren and would not breed, and she was sold by the pound for an insignificant sum as compared with her real value if a breeder. She was evidently sold and purchased on the relation of her value for beef, unless the plaintiff had learned of her true condition, and concealed such knowledge from the defendants. Before the plaintiff secured the possession of the animal, the defendants learned that she was with calf, and therefore of great value, and undertook to rescind the sale by refusing to deliver her. The question arises whether they had a right to do so. The circuit judge ruled that this fact did not avoid the sale and it made no difference whether she was barren or not. I am of the opinion that the court erred in this holding. I know that this is a close question, and the dividing line between the adjudicated cases is not easily discerned. But it must be considered as well settled that a party who has given an apparent consent to a contract of sale may refuse to execute it, or he may avoid it after it has been completed, if the assent was founded, or the contract made, upon the mistake of a material fact,--such as the subject- matter of the sale, the price, or some collateral fact materially inducing the agreement; and this can be done when the mistake is mutual. . . .

If there is a difference or misapprehension as to the substance of the thing bargained for; if the thing actually delivered or received is different in substance from the thing bargained for, and intended to be sold,--then there is no contract; but if it be only a difference in some quality or accident, even though the mistake may have been the actuating motive to the purchaser or seller, or both of them, yet the contract remains binding. . . .

It seems to me, however, in the case made by this record, that the mistake or misapprehension of the parties went to the whole substance of the agreement. If the cow was a breeder, she was worth at least $750; if barren, she was worth not over $80. The parties would not have made the contract of sale except upon the understanding and belief that she was incapable of breeding, and of no use as a cow. It is true she is now the identical animal that they thought her to be when the contract was made; there is no mistake as to the identity of the creature. Yet the mistake was not of the mere quality of the animal, but went to the very nature of the thing. A barren cow is substantially a different creature than a breeding one. There is as much difference between them for all purposes of use as there is between an ox and a cow that is capable of breeding and giving milk. If the mutual mistake had simply related to the fact whether she was with calf or not for one season, then it might have been a good sale, but the mistake affected the character of the animal for all time, and for its present and ultimate use. She was not in fact the animal, or the kind of animal, the defendants intended to sell or the plaintiff to buy. She was not a barren cow, and, if this fact had been known, there would have been no contract. The mistake affected the substance of the whole consideration, and it must be considered that there was no contract to sell or sale of the cow as she actually was. The thing sold and bought had in fact no existence. She was sold as a beef creature would be sold; she is in fact a breeding cow, and a valuable one. The court should have instructed the jury that if they found that the cow was sold, or contracted to be sold, upon the understanding of both parties that she was barren, and useless for the purpose of breeding, and that in fact she was not barren, but capable of breeding, then the defendants had a right to rescind, and to refuse to deliver, and the verdict should be in their favor.

The judgment of the court below must be reversed, and a new trial granted, with costs of this court to defendants.

SHERWOOD, Justice (dissenting). I do not concur in the opinion given by my brethren in this case. I think the judgments before the justice and at the circuit were right. . . .

I entirely agree with my brethren that the right to rescind occurs whenever "the thing actually delivered or received is different in substance from the thing bargained for, and intended to be sold; but if it be only a difference in some quality or accident, even though the misapprehension may have been the actuating motive" of the parties in making the contract, yet it will remain binding. In this case the cow sold was the one delivered. What might or might not happen to her after the sale formed no element in the contract. . . .

Questions

1. What was the basis of the defendants' argument for rescinding the sale of the cow?

2. According to the court, under what circumstances can a party refuse to execute or avoid a completed contract of sale?

3. What was the main contention of the defendants regarding the mistake in the sale?

4. Why did the court consider the mistake in this case to be a material fact that could lead to the rescission of the sale?

5. How did the court differentiate between a mistake that affects the substance of the agreement and a mistake that relates to a mere quality or accident of the item being sold?

Takeaways – Sherwood v. Walker

What was the basic assumption of the parties in *Sherwood v. Walker*? On the purported sale of personal property the parties to the proposed contract are not bound where it appears that each of them is honestly mistaken or in error with reference to the identity of the subject-matter of the contract. In other words, in such circumstances, no enforceable sale has taken place. (*Smith v. Zimbalist* (1934) 2 Cal.App.2d 324) In what respect were the parties in *Sherwood* mistaken with reference to the identity of the subject matter of their contract.

Wood v. Boynton
Supreme Court of Wisconsin, 1885
25 N.W. 42

Taylor, J. This action was brought in the circuit court for Milwaukee county to recover the possession of an uncut diamond of the alleged value of $1,000. The case was tried in the circuit court and, after hearing all the evidence in the case, the learned circuit judge directed the jury to find a verdict for the defendants. The plaintiff excepted to such instruction, and, after a verdict was rendered for the defendants, moved for a new trial upon the minutes of the judge. The motion was denied, and the plaintiff duly excepted, and, after judgment was entered in favor of the defendants, appealed to this court.

The defendants are partners in the jewelry business. On the trial it appeared that on and before the 28th of December, 1883, the plaintiff was the owner of and in the possession of a small stone of the nature and value of which she was ignorant; that on that day she sold it to one of the defendants for the sum of one dollar. Afterwards it was ascertained that the stone was a rough diamond, and of the value of about $700. After learning this fact the plaintiff tendered the defendants the one dollar, and ten cents as interest, and demanded a return of the stone to her. The defendants refused to deliver it, and therefore she commenced this action.

The plaintiff testified to the circumstances attending the sale of the stone to Mr. Samuel B. Boynton, as follows: "The first time Boynton saw that stone he was talking about buying the topaz, or whatever it is, in September or October. I went into his store to get a little pin mended, and I had it in a small box, --the pin, -- a small earring; . . . this stone, and a broken sleeve-button were in the box. Mr. Boynton turned to give me a check for my pin. I thought I would ask him what the stone was, and I took it out of the box and asked him to please tell me what that was. He took it in his hand and spent some time looking at it. I told him I had been told it was a topaz, and he said it might be. He says, 'I would buy this; would you sell it?'" I told him I did not know but what I would. What would it be worth? And he said he did not know; he would give me a dollar and keep it as a specimen, and I told him I would not sell it; and it was certainly pretty to look at. He asked me where I found it, and I told him in Eagle. He asked about how far out, and I said right in the village, and I went out. Afterwards, and about the 28th of December, I needed money pretty badly, and thought every dollar would help, and I took it back to Mr. Boynton and told him I had brought back the topaz and he says "Well, yes; what did I offer you for it?," and I says, "One dollar"; and he stepped to the change drawer and gave me the dollar, and I went out.

In another part of her testimony she says: "Before I sold the stone I had no knowledge whatever that it was a diamond. I told him that I had been advised that it was probably a topaz, and he said probably it was. The stone was about the size of a canary bird's egg, nearly the shape of an egg, -- worn pointed at one end; it was nearly straw color, -- a little darker." She also testified that before this action was commenced she tendered the defendants $1.10, and demanded the return of the stone, which they refused. This is substantially all the evidence of what took place at and before the sale to the defendants, as testified to by the plaintiff herself. She produced no other witness on that point.

The evidence on the part of the defendant is not very different from the version given by the plaintiff, and certainly is not more favorable to the plaintiff. Mr. Samuel B. Boynton, the defendant to whom the stone was sold, testified that at the time he bought this stone, he had never seen an uncut diamond; had seen cut diamonds, but they are quite different from the uncut ones; "he had no ideas this was a diamond, and it never entered his brain at the time." Considerable evidence was given as to what took place after the sale and purchase, but that evidence has very little if any bearing upon the main point in the case.

This evidence clearly shows that the plaintiff sold the stone in question to the defendants, and delivered it to them in December, 1883, for a consideration of one dollar. . . .

The only question in the case is whether there was anything in the sale which entitled the vendor (the appellant) to rescind the sale and so revest the title in her. The only reasons we know of for rescinding a sale and revesting the title in the vendor so that he may maintain an action at law for the recovery of the possession against his vendee are (1) that the vendee was guilty of some fraud in procuring a sale to be made to him; (2) that there was a mistake made by the vendor in delivering an article which was not the article sold, -- a mistake in fact as to the identify of the thing sold with the thing delivered upon the sale. This last is not in reality a rescission of the sale made, as the thing delivered was not the thing sold, and no title ever passed to the vendee by such delivery.

In this case, upon the plaintiff's own evidence, there can be no just ground for alleging that she was induced to make the sale she did by any fraud or unfair dealings on the part of Mr. Boynton. Both were entirely ignorant at the time of the character of the stone and of its intrinsic value. Mr. Boynton was not an expert in uncut diamonds, and had made no examination of the stone, except to take it in his hand and look at it before he made the offer of one dollar, which was refused at the time, and afterwards accepted without any comment or further examination made by Mr. Boynton. The appellant had the stone in her possession for a long time, and it appears from her own statement that she had made some inquiry as to its nature and qualities. If she chose to sell it without further investigation as to its intrinsic value to a person who was guilty of no fraud or unfairness which induced her to sell it for a small sum, she cannot repudiate the sale because it is afterwards ascertained that she made a bad bargain.

The argument would appear to be that Wood chose to sell the stone based on her limited knowledge of its nature, and hence that she assumed the risk that the stone would turn out to be more valuable than she thought.

There is no pretense of any mistake as to the identity of the thing sold. It was produced by the plaintiff and exhibited to the vendee before the sale was made, and the thing sold was delivered to the vendee when the purchase price was paid. . . . Suppose the appellant had produced the stone, and said she had been told that it was a diamond, and she believed it was, but had no knowledge herself as to its character or value, and Mr. Boynton had given her $500 for it, could he have rescinded the sale on the ground of mistake? Clearly not, nor could he rescind it on the ground that there had been a breach of warranty, because there was no warranty, nor could he rescind it on the ground of fraud, unless he could show that she falsely declared that she had been told it was a diamond, or, if she had been so told, still she knew it was not a diamond. . . .

When this sale was made the value of the thing sold was open to the investigation of both parties, neither knew its intrinsic value, and, so far as the evidence in this case shows, both supposed that the price paid was adequate. How can fraud be predicated upon such a sale, even though after investigation showed that the intrinsic value of the thing sold was hundreds of times greater than the price paid? It certainly shows no such fraud as would authorize the vendor to rescind the contract and bring an action at law to recover the possession of the thing sold . . . .

We can find nothing in the evidence from which it could be justly inferred that Mr. Boynton, at the time he offered the plaintiff one dollar for the stone, had any knowledge of the real value of the stone, or that he entertained even a belief that the stone was a diamond. It cannot, therefore, be said that there was a suppression of knowledge on the part of the defendant as to the value of the stone which a court of equity might seize upon to avoid the sale. . . .

However unfortunate the plaintiff may have been in selling this valuable stone for a mere nominal sum, she has failed entirely to make out a case either of fraud or mistake in the sale such as will entitle her to a rescission of such sale so as to recover the property sold in an action at law.

By the Court -- The judgment of the circuit court is affirmed.

Questions

1. What are the two main reasons that may entitle a vendor to rescind a sale and recover the property?

2. Why does the court take the position that there was no mistake as to the identity of the thing sold?

3. Could the plaintiff have rescinded the sale if she had sold the stone for a higher price based on her belief that it was a diamond?

4. What reasons does the court provide for rejecting the plaintiff's claim for rescission and recovery of the stone?

Takeaways – Wood v. Boynton

Can the facts of this case be distinguished from *Sherwood v. Walker*? Would you say in this case that the seller of the stone assumed the risk that she didn't know the true nature of what she was selling?

Renner v. Kehl
Supreme Court of Arizona, 1986
150 Ariz. 94, 722 P.2d 262

GORDON, Vice Chief Justice. This Petition for Review was granted in order to determine the measure of damages available to the plaintiff upon rescission of a land contract. . . .

In 1981 the petitioners, defendants below, acquired from the State of Arizona agricultural development leases covering 2,262 acres of unimproved desert land near Yuma. The petitioners made no attempt to develop the property themselves, but instead decided to sell their interest in the land. The respondents, plaintiffs below, were residents of the state of Washington interested in the large scale commercial cultivation of jojoba. The respondents and their agent, who was familiar with commercial jojoba development, were shown the petitioners' property and became interested in purchasing it. The property appeared to be ideal for the respondents' purposes; the soil and climate were good and both parties were of the opinion that sufficient water was available beneath the land to sustain jojoba production. The respondents made it clear that they were interested in the property only for jojoba production and required adequate water supplies.

The respondents decided to buy the leases and on June 5, 1981, executed a Real Estate Purchase Contract to that effect. Respondents agreed to pay $222,200 for the leases, and paid petitioners $80,200 as a down payment, the remainder to be paid in annual installments. In November of 1981 respondents began development of the property for jojoba production. As part of the development process the respondents had five test wells drilled, none of which produced water of sufficient quantity or quality for commercial jojoba cultivation. After spending approximately $229,000 developing the land respondents determined that the aquifer underlying the property was inadequate for commercial development of jojoba. At this point the project was abandoned and the respondents sued to rescind the purchase contract. The petitioners counterclaimed for the balance of payments due under the contract.. . .

The [trial] court found that the respondents were entitled to rescission based on mutual mistake of fact and failure of consideration, and ordered the respondents to reassign the lease to the petitioners. The petitioners were ordered to pay the respondents $309,849.84 ($80,200 representing the down payment and $229,649.48 representing the cost of developing the property) together with costs and attorney's fees.

The petitioners appealed to the court of appeals, which affirmed the trial court. . . . The petitioners raise the same arguments before this Court, viz., that rescission was not justified, or if rescission was appropriate petitioners are not liable for consequential damages.

Mutual mistake of fact is an accepted basis for rescission. Amos Flight Operations, Inc. v. Thunderbird Bank, 112 Ariz. 263, 540 P.2d 1244 (1975); Mortensen v. Berzell Investment Company, 102 Ariz. 348, 429 P.2d 945 (1967). See Restatement (Second) of Contracts § 152. In Arizona a contract may be rescinded when there is a mutual mistake of material fact which constitutes "an essential part and condition of the contract." Mortensen v. Berzell Investment Company, 102 Ariz. at 350, 429 P.2d at 947. The trial court found that the sole purpose of the contract was to enable respondents to grow jojoba, which depends upon an adequate water supply. The trial court specifically found that "There would have been no sale if both sellers and buyers had not believed it was possible to grow jojoba commercially on the leased acres ...." and that "[b]ased upon the factual data available, all parties were of the opinion that there would be sufficient good quality water for commercial jojoba production, and that it would be close enough to the surface that it would be economically feasible to pump it for irrigation of large acreages." Consequently, the trial court concluded that "[p]laintiffs are entitled to rescind the purchase agreement because of the mutual mistake of fact and because there was a total failure of consideration."

The belief of the parties that adequate water supplies existed beneath the property was "a basic assumption on which both parties made the contract," Restatement (Second) of Contracts § 152 comment b, and their mutual mistake "ha[d] such a material effect on the agreed exchange of performances as to upset the very bases of the contract." Id. comment a. The contract was therefore voidable and the respondents were entitled to rescission.

The trial court also ordered that petitioners pay the respondents $309,849.84 together with costs and attorney's fees. Of the $309,849.84 awarded to the respondents, $229,649.84 represents reimbursement of the costs borne by the respondents in developing the property for jojoba production. The petitioners challenge the $229,649.84 awarded as an improper grant of "consequential damages".

The court of appeals upheld the full award "[b]ecause the plaintiffs have not received a double recovery in the award of rescission and consequential damages...." Slip op. at 4. The appeals court relied upon Fousel v. Ted Walker Mobile Homes, Inc., 124 Ariz. 126, 602 P.2d 507 (App. 1979), for the proposition that rescission can support an award of consequential damages.

In Fousel the plaintiffs purchased a mobile home from the defendants, who engaged in a series of misrepresentations which cost the plaintiffs considerable inconvenience and expense. The plaintiffs prevailed upon their claim for fraud and breach of contract and were awarded $2,705.26 in consequential damages and $10,000 in punitive damages. The sole issue on appeal was whether any damages could be awarded where the plaintiffs elected to sue for rescission. The court of appeals held that the doctrine of election of remedies does not necessarily bar an award of consequential or punitive damages, only "benefit of the bargain" damages. 124 Ariz. at 129, 602 P.2d

We are dealing with a rescission based upon mutual mistake, which implies freedom from fault on the part of both parties. See Restatement (Second) of Contracts § 152. There was no determination that fraud or misrepresentation occurred; indeed, the trial court concluded that "[t]here was no fraud or misrepresentation on the part of the defendants or their agents...." The reliance of the court of appeals upon Fousel was misplaced; we hold that absent proof of breach for fraud or misrepresentation a party who rescinds a contract may not recover consequential damages. Accordingly, we reverse that portion of the trial court's order awarding consequential damages and vacate that portion of the court of appeals' decision which affirms the award of consequential damages.

This does not mean, however, that the respondents are entitled only to recover their down payment. When a party rescinds a contract on the ground of mutual mistake he is entitled to restitution for any benefit that he has conferred on the other party by way of part performance or reliance. Restatement (Second) of Contracts § 376. Restitutionary recoveries are not designed to be compensatory; their justification lies in the avoidance of unjust enrichment on the part of the defendant. D. Dobbs, Remedies § 4.1 p. 224 (1973). Thus the defendant is generally liable for restitution of a benefit that would be unjust for him to keep, even though he gained it honestly. Id; Restatement (Second) of Contracts § 376 comment a. The issue we must now address is the proper measure of the restitutionary interest.

The first step determining the proper measure of restitution requires that the rescinding party return or offer to return, conditional on restitution, any interest in property that he has received in the bargain. Restatement (Second) of Contracts § 384(1)(a). In Arizona this includes reimbursement for the fair market value of the use of the property. With respect to land contracts we have noted that "[i]t is of course essential to justify the rescinding of a contract that the rescinding party offer to place the other in status quo, and this includes the offer to credit the vendors with a reasonable rental value for the time during which the land was occupied." Mortensen v. Berzell Investment Company, 102 Ariz. at 351, 429 P.2d at 948. Earlier we stated that "[t]he offer to surrender possession of property received under the contract need not be unqualified, but may be made conditional upon the vendor's restitution of amounts paid on the contract, less proper allowances in respect of vendee's use of the premises." Mahurin v. Schmeck, 95 Ariz. 333, 341, 390 P.2d 576, 581 (1964). Thus the respondents were obliged to return the land to the petitioners in exchange for their down payment, and in addition to pay the petitioners the fair rental value of the land for the duration of their occupancy.

However, to avoid unjust enrichment the petitioners must pay the respondents a sum equal to the amount by which their property has been enhanced in value by the respondents' efforts. The Restatement (Second) of Contracts § 376 provides that "[i]f [a party] has received and must return land ... he may have made improvements on the land in reliance on the contract and he is entitled to recover the reasonable value of those improvements.... The rule stated in this section applies to avoidance on any ground, including ... mistake...." comment a. The reasonable value of any improvements is measured by "the extent to which the other party's property has been increased in value or his other interests advanced." Restatement (Second) of Contracts § 371(b). Thus the petitioners must pay to the respondents that amount of money which represents the enhanced value of the land due to the respondents' development efforts. In short, the respondents are entitled to their down payment, plus the amount by which their efforts increased the value of the petitioners' property, minus an amount which represents the fair rental value of the land during their occupancy. They are not entitled to the $229,649.84 expended upon development, because that would shift the entire risk of mistake onto the petitioners, which is incompatible with equitable rescission.

The respondents were entitled to rescind the contract, but may not recover the costs of developing the land in the form of consequential damages. The respondents are entitled to restitution of their down payment and any amount by which the value of the land was enhanced, but in turn the respondents must pay petitioners the fair rental value of the tenancy. Accordingly, the trial court is affirmed in part and reversed in part and the court of appeals' decision is approved in part and vacated in part. The case is remanded to the trial court for further proceedings not inconsistent with this opinion.

Questions

1. What is the basis for the trial court's decision to grant rescission in this case?

2. According to the court, under what circumstances can a party who rescinds a contract recover consequential damages?

3. What is the rationale behind the court's decision to award restitutionary interest in this case?

4. What is the measure of restitutionary interest as determined by the court?

5. How does the court address the issue of unjust enrichment in this case?

Takeaways – Renner v. Kehl

What was the basic assumption of the parties in *Renner v. Kehl*?

Should there have been relief for mistake where the purchasers failed to investigate the sufficiency of the water supply? The failure to make a thorough investigation of the facts prior to signing the contract does not preclude rescission where the risk of mistake was not allocated among the parties and the mistake is material and relates to a basic assumption on which the contract was made.(Rest.2d § 152 comment a, illustration 1.)

Unilateral Mistake

Donovan v. RRL Corp.
Supreme Court of California, 2001
26 Cal.4th 261, 109 Cal.Rptr.2d 807; 27 P.3d 702

[Facts were previously set forth at p. 63.]

Having concluded that defendant's advertisement for the sale of the Jaguar automobile constituted an offer that was accepted by plaintiff's tender of the advertised price, and that the resulting contract satisfied the statute of frauds, we next consider whether defendant can avoid enforcement of the contract on the ground of mistake.

A party may rescind a contract if his or her consent was given by mistake. (Civ. Code, § 1689, subd. (b)(1).) A factual mistake by one party to a contract, or unilateral mistake, affords a ground for rescission in some circumstances. Civil Code section 1577 states in relevant part: "Mistake of fact is a mistake, not caused by the neglect of a legal duty on the part of the person making the mistake, and consisting in: [¶] 1. An unconscious ignorance or forgetfulness of a fact past or present, material to the contract . . . ."

The Court of Appeal determined that defendant's error did not constitute a mistake of fact within the meaning of Civil Code section 1577. In support of this determination, the court relied upon the following principle: "[A] unilateral misinterpretation of contractual terms, without knowledge by the other party at the time of contract, does not constitute a mistake under either Civil Code section 1577 [mistake of fact] or 1578 [mistake of law]." (*Hedging Concepts, Inc. v. First Alliance Mortgage Co.* (1996) 41 Cal.App.4th 1410, 1422 (*Hedging Concepts*).)

The foregoing principle has no application to the present case. In *Hedging Concepts*, the plaintiff believed that he would fulfill his contractual obligations by introducing potential business prospects to the defendant. The contract, however, required the plaintiff to procure a completed business arrangement. The Court of Appeal held that the plaintiff's subjective misinterpretation of the terms of the contract constituted, at most, a mistake of law. Because the defendant was unaware of the plaintiff's misunderstanding at the time of the contract, the court held that rescission was not a proper remedy. (*Hedging Concepts, supra*, 41 Cal.App.4th at pp. 1418-1422; citing 1 Witkin, *supra*, Contracts, § 379, pp. 345-346 [relief for unilateral mistake of law is authorized only where one party knows of, does not correct, and takes advantage or enjoys the benefit of another party's mistake].) Defendant's mistake in the present case, in contrast, did not consist of a subjective misinterpretation of a contract term, but rather resulted from an unconscious ignorance that the Daily Pilot advertisement set forth an incorrect price for the automobile. Defendant's lack of knowledge regarding the typographical error in the advertised price of the vehicle cannot be considered a mistake of law. Defendant's error constituted a mistake of fact, and the Court of Appeal erred in concluding otherwise. As we shall explain, the Court of Appeal also erred to the extent it suggested that a unilateral mistake of fact affords a ground for rescission only where the other party is aware of the mistake.

Under the first Restatement of Contracts, unilateral mistake did not render a contract voidable unless the other party knew of or caused the mistake. (1 Witkin, *supra*, Contracts, § 370, p. 337; see Rest., Contracts, § 503.) In *Germain etc. Co. v. Western Union etc. Co.* (1902) 137 Cal. 598, 602, this court endorsed a rule similar to that of the first Restatement. Our opinion indicated that a seller's price quotation erroneously transcribed and delivered by a telegraph company contractually could bind the seller to the incorrect price, unless the buyer knew or had reason to suspect that a mistake had been made. Some decisions of the Court of Appeal have adhered to the approach of the original Restatement. (See, e.g., *Conservatorship of O'Connor* (1996) 48 Cal.App.4th 1076, 1097-1098, and cases cited therein.) Plaintiff also advocates this approach and contends that rescission is unavailable to defendant, because plaintiff was unaware of the mistaken price in defendant's advertisement when he accepted the offer.

The Court of Appeal decisions reciting the traditional rule do not recognize that in *M. F. Kemper Const. Co. v. City of L. A.* (1951) 37 Cal.2d 696, 701 (*Kemper*), we acknowledged but rejected a strict application of the foregoing Restatement rule regarding unilateral mistake of fact. The plaintiff in *Kemper* inadvertently omitted a $301,769 item from its bid for the defendant city's public works project-- approximately one-third of the total contract price. After discovering the mistake several hours later, the plaintiff immediately notified the city and subsequently withdrew its bid. Nevertheless, the city accepted the erroneous bid, contending that rescission of the offer was unavailable for the plaintiff's unilateral mistake.

Our decision in *Kemper* recognized that the bid, when opened and announced, resulted in an irrevocable option contract conferring upon the city a right to accept the bid, and that the plaintiff could not withdraw its bid unless the requirements for rescission of this option contract were satisfied. (*Kemper, supra,* "37 Cal.2d at pp. 700, 704.) We stated: "Rescission may be had for mistake of fact if the mistake is material to the contract and was not the result of neglect of a legal duty, if enforcement of the contract as made would be unconscionable, and if the other party can be placed in statu quo. [Citations.]" (*Id.* at p. 701.) Although the city knew of the plaintiff's mistake before it accepted the bid, and this circumstance was relevant to our determination that requiring the plaintiff to perform at the mistaken bid price would be unconscionable (*id.* at pp. 702-703), we authorized rescission of the city's option contract even though the city had not known of or contributed to the mistake before it opened the bid.

The decisions . . .establish that California law does not adhere to the original Restatement's requirements for rescission based upon unilateral mistake of fact--i.e., only in circumstances where the other party knew of the mistake or caused the mistake. [T]he Restatement Second of Contracts authorizes rescission for a unilateral mistake of fact where "the effect of the mistake is such that enforcement of the contract would be unconscionable." (Rest.2d Contracts, § 153, subd. (a).) fn. 6 The comment following this section recognizes "a growing willingness to allow avoidance where the consequences of the mistake are so grave that enforcement of the contract would be unconscionable." (*Id.*, com. a, p. 394.) Indeed, two of the illustrations recognizing this additional ground for rescission in the Restatement Second of Contracts are based in part upon this court's decisions in *Kemper* and *Elsinore*. (Rest.2d Contracts, § 153, com. c, illus. 1, 3, pp. 395, 396, and Reporter's Note, pp. 400-401; see also *Schultz v. County of Contra Costa* (1984) 157 Cal.App.3d 242, 249-250 [applying section 153, subdivision (a), of the Restatement Second of Contracts], disagreed with on another ground in *Van Petten v. County of San Diego* (1995) 38 Cal.App.4th 43, 50-51; 1 Witkin, *supra*, Contracts, § 370, p. 337 [reciting the rule of the same Restatement provision].) Although the most common types of mistakes falling within this category occur in bids on construction contracts, section 153 of the Restatement Second of Contracts is not limited to such cases. (Rest.2d Contracts, § 153, com. b, p. 395.)

Because the rule in section 153, subdivision (a), of the Restatement Second of Contracts, authorizing rescission for unilateral mistake of fact where enforcement would be unconscionable, is consistent with our previous decisions, we adopt the rule as California law. As the author of one treatise recognized more than 40 years ago, the decisions that are inconsistent with the traditional rule "are too numerous and too appealing to the sense of justice to be disregarded." (3 Corbin, Contracts (1960) § 608, p. 675, fn. omitted.) We reject plaintiff's contention and the Court of Appeal's conclusion that, because plaintiff was unaware of defendant's unilateral mistake, the mistake does not provide a ground to avoid enforcement of the contract.

Having concluded that a contract properly may be rescinded on the ground of unilateral mistake of fact as set forth in section 153, subdivision (a), of the Restatement Second of Contracts, we next consider whether the requirements of that provision, construed in light of our previous decisions, are satisfied in the present case. Where the plaintiff has no reason to know of and does not cause the defendant's unilateral mistake of fact, the defendant must establish the following facts to obtain rescission of the contract: (1) the defendant made a mistake regarding a basic assumption upon which the defendant made the contract; (2) the mistake has a material effect upon the agreed exchange of performances that is adverse to the defendant; (3) the defendant does not bear the risk of the mistake; and (4) the effect of the mistake is such that enforcement of the contract would be unconscionable. We shall consider each of these requirements below.

A significant error in the price term of a contract constitutes a mistake regarding a basic assumption upon which the contract is made, and such a mistake ordinarily has a material effect adverse to the mistaken party. (See, e.g., *Elsinore, supra*, 54 Cal.2d at p. 389 [7 percent error in contract price]; *Lemoge Electric v. County of San Mateo* (1956) 46 Cal.2d 659, 661-662 [6 percent error]; *Kemper, supra*, 37 Cal.2d at p. 702 [28 percent error]; *Brunzell Const. Co. v. G. J. Weisbrod, Inc.* (1955) 134 Cal.App.2d 278, 286 [20 percent error]; Rest.2d Contracts, § 152, com. b, illus. 3, p. 387 [27 percent error].) In establishing a material mistake regarding a basic assumption of the contract, the defendant must show that the resulting imbalance in the agreed exchange is so severe that it would be unfair to require the defendant to perform. (Rest.2d Contracts, § 152, com. c, p. 388.) Ordinarily, a defendant can satisfy this requirement by showing that the exchange not only is less desirable for the defendant, but also is more advantageous to the other party. (*Ibid.*)

Measured against this standard, defendant's mistake in the contract for the sale of the Jaguar automobile constitutes a material mistake regarding a basic assumption upon which it made the contract. Enforcing the contract with the mistaken price of $25,995 would require defendant to sell the vehicle to plaintiff for $12,000 less than the intended advertised price of $37,995--an error amounting to 32 percent of the price defendant intended. The exchange of performances would be substantially less desirable for defendant and more desirable for plaintiff. Plaintiff implicitly concedes that defendant's mistake was material.

The parties and amici curiae vigorously dispute, however, whether defendant should bear the risk of its mistake. Section 154 of the Restatement Second of Contracts states: "A party bears the risk of a mistake when [¶] (a) the risk is allocated to him by agreement of the parties, or [¶] (b) he is aware, at the time the contract is made, that he has only limited knowledge with respect to the facts to which the mistake relates but treats his limited knowledge as sufficient, or [¶] (c) the risk is allocated to him by the court on the ground that it is reasonable in the circumstances to do so." Neither of the first two factors applies here. Thus, we must determine whether it is reasonable under the circumstances to allocate to defendant the risk of the mistake in the advertisement.

Civil Code section 1577, as well as our prior decisions, instructs that the risk of a mistake must be allocated to a party where the mistake results from that party's neglect of a legal duty. (*Kemper, supra,* "37 Cal.2d at p. 701.) It is well established, however, that ordinary negligence does not constitute neglect of a legal duty within the meaning of Civil Code section 1577. (*Kemper, supra,* "37 Cal.2d at p. 702.) For example, we have described a careless but significant mistake in the computation of the contract price as the type of error that sometimes will occur in the conduct of reasonable and cautious businesspersons, and such an error does not necessarily amount to neglect of legal duty that would bar equitable relief. (*Ibid.*; see also *Sun 'n Sand, Inc. v. United California Bank* (1978) 21 Cal.3d 671, 700-701 (plur. opn. of Mosk, J.); *Elsinore, supra,* "54 Cal.2d at pp. 388-389.)

A concept similar to neglect of a legal duty is described in section 157 of the Restatement Second of Contracts, which addresses situations in which a party's fault precludes relief for mistake. Only where the mistake results from "a failure to act in good faith and in accordance with reasonable standards of fair dealing" is rescission unavailable. (Rest.2d Contracts, § 157.) This section, consistent with the California decisions cited in the preceding paragraph, provides that a mistaken party's failure to exercise due care does not necessarily bar rescission under the rule set forth in section 153.

"The mere fact that a mistaken party could have avoided the mistake by the exercise of reasonable care does not preclude . . . avoidance . . . [on the ground of mistake]. Indeed, since a party can often avoid a mistake by the exercise of such care, the availability of relief would be severely circumscribed if he were to be barred by his negligence. Nevertheless, in *extreme cases* the mistaken party's fault is a proper ground for denying him relief for a mistake that he otherwise could have avoided. . . . [T]he rule is stated in terms of good faith and fair dealing. . . . [A] failure to act in good faith and in accordance with reasonable standards of fair dealing during pre-contractual negotiations does not amount to a breach. Nevertheless, under the rule stated in this Section, the failure bars a mistaken party from relief based on a mistake that otherwise would not have been made. During the negotiation stage each party is held to a degree of responsibility appropriate to the justifiable expectations of the other. The terms 'good faith' and 'fair dealing' are used, in this context, in much the same sense as in . . . Uniform Commercial Code § 1-203." (Rest.2d Contracts, § 157, com. a, pp. 416-417, Section 1201, subdivision (19), of the California Uniform Commercial Code defines "good faith," as used in section 1203 of that code, as "honesty in fact in the conduct or transaction concerned."

Because of its erroneous conclusion that defendant's error was not a mistake of fact, the Court of Appeal did not reach the question whether the mistake resulted from defendant's neglect of a legal duty. The Court of Appeal did make an independent finding of fact on appeal that, in light of the statutory duties imposed upon automobile dealers, defendant's failure to review the proof sheet for the advertisement constituted *negligence.* This finding, however, was relevant only to the Court of Appeal's determination that defendant's concurrent negligence rendered it unnecessary for the court to consider the application of *Germain etc. Co. v. Western Union etc. Co., supra,* 137 Cal. 598, to the present case, because *Germain* involved a mistaken offer resulting solely from the negligence of an intermediary. In any event, as established above, ordinary negligence does not constitute the neglect of a legal duty within the meaning of Civil Code section 1577 and the governing decisions. (See also 3 Corbin, Contracts, *supra,* § 606, pp. 649-656 [negligence is no bar to relief from unilateral mistake if other party can be placed in statu quo].) Accordingly, we shall consider in the first instance whether defendant's mistake resulted from its neglect of a legal duty, barring the remedy of rescission. . . .

In *Sun 'n Sand, Inc. v. United California Bank, supra,* 21 Cal.3d 671, for example, a bank contended that a customer's violation of its statutory duty to examine bank statements and returned checks for alterations or forgeries (Cal. U. Com. Code, § 4406) constituted the neglect of a legal duty within the meaning of Civil Code section 1577, thus barring relief for the customer's mistake of fact. We rejected the bank's defense: "It does not follow . . . that breach of this duty by failure to exercise reasonable care in discharging it constitutes the 'neglect of a legal duty' such that a cause of action for mistake of fact must be barred. . . . We have . . . recognized on a number of occasions that 'ordinary negligence does not constitute the neglect of a legal duty as that term is used in section 1577 of the Civil Code.' [Citations.] The rule developed in these cases reflects a determination that the 'neglect of a legal duty' qualification derives content from equitable considerations and principles, and that it would be inequitable to bar relief for mistake because of the breach of a duty of care when the [other] party . . . suffers no loss. That [the plaintiff] may have failed to exercise care in examining its bank statements is thus not a sufficient basis for denying it equitable relief for mistake." (*Sun 'n Sand, Inc. v. United California Bank, supra*, 21 Cal.3d at pp. 700-701 (plur. opn. of Mosk, J.); see *id.* at p. 709 (conc. & dis. opn. of Sullivan, J.) [agreeing with conclusion of plur. opn. on this claim].)

Plaintiff also seeks to preclude relief for defendant's mistake on the ground that defendant's alleged violation of Vehicle Code section 11713.1(e) constitutes negligence per se pursuant to Evidence Code section 669, which provides that an individual's violation of a statute can lead to a presumption that he or she failed to exercise due care. As we have seen, however, a failure to exercise due care, by itself, does not constitute the neglect of a legal duty. Without evidence of bad faith on the part of defendant, its alleged violation of any duty of care arising from section 11713.1(e) constitutes, at most, ordinary negligence. Accordingly, a negligent violation of any duty imposed by section 11713.1(e) does not constitute the neglect of a legal duty or a sufficient basis for denying defendant equitable relief for its good faith mistake. . . .

The municipal court made an express finding of fact that "the mistake on the part of [defendant] was made in good faith[;] it was an honest mistake, not intended to deceive the public . . . ." The Court of Appeal correctly recognized that "[w]e must, of course, accept the trial court's finding that there was a 'good faith' mistake that caused the error in the advertisement." The evidence presented at trial compellingly supports this finding.

Defendant regularly advertises in five local newspapers. Defendant's advertising manager, Crystal Wadsworth, testified that ordinarily she meets with Kristen Berman, a representative of the Daily Pilot, on Tuesdays, Wednesdays, and Thursdays to review proof sheets of the advertisement that will appear in the newspaper the following weekend. When Wadsworth met with Berman on Wednesday, April 23, 1997, defendant's proposed advertisement listed a 1995 Jaguar XJ6 Vanden Plas without specifying a price, as it had the preceding week. On Thursday, April 24, a sales manager instructed Wadsworth to substitute a 1994 Jaguar XJ6 with a price of $25,995. The same day, Wadsworth met with Berman and conveyed to her this new information. Wadsworth did not expect to see another proof sheet reflecting this change, however, because she does not work on Friday, and the Daily Pilot goes to press on Friday and the edition in question came out on Saturday, April 26.

Berman testified that the revised advertisement was prepared by the composing department of the Daily Pilot. Berman proofread the advertisement, as she does all advertisements for which she is responsible, but Berman did not notice that it listed the 1995 Jaguar XJ6 Vanden Plas for sale at $25,995, instead of listing the 1994 Jaguar at that price. Both Berman and Wadsworth first learned of the mistake on Monday, April 28, 1997. Defendant's sales manager first became aware of the mistake after plaintiff attempted to purchase the automobile on Sunday, April 27.

Berman confirmed in a letter of retraction that Berman's proofreading error had led to the mistake in the advertisement.

Defendant's erroneous advertisement in the Daily Pilot listed 16 used automobiles for sale. Each of the advertisements prepared for several newspapers in late April 1997, except for the one in the Daily Pilot, correctly identified the 1994 Jaguar XJ6 for sale at a price of $25,995. In May 1997, defendant's advertisements in several newspapers listed the 1995 Jaguar XJ6] Vanden Plas for sale at $37,995, and defendant subsequently sold the automobile for $38,399. Defendant had paid $35,000 for the vehicle.

Evidence at trial established that defendant adheres to the following procedures when an incorrect advertisement is discovered. Defendant immediately contacts the newspaper and requests a letter of retraction. Copies of any erroneous advertisements are provided to the sales staff, the error is explained to them, and the mistake is circled in red and posted on a bulletin board at the dealership. The sales staff informs customers of any advertising errors of which they are aware.

No evidence presented at trial suggested that defendant knew of the mistake before plaintiff attempted to purchase the automobile, that defendant intended to mislead customers, or that it had adopted a practice of deliberate indifference regarding errors in advertisements. Wadsworth regularly reviews proof sheets for the numerous advertisements placed by defendant, and representatives of the newspapers, including the Daily Pilot, also proofread defendant's advertisements to ensure they are accurate. Defendant follows procedures for notifying its sales staff and customers of errors of which it becomes aware. The uncontradicted evidence established that the Daily Pilot made the proofreading error resulting in defendant's mistake.

Defendant's fault consisted of failing to review a proof sheet reflecting the change made on Thursday, April 24, 1997, and/or the actual advertisement appearing in the April 26 edition of the Daily Pilot--choosing instead to rely upon the Daily Pilot's advertising staff to proofread the revised version. Although, as the Court of Appeal found, such an omission might constitute negligence, it does not involve a breach of defendant's duty of good faith and fair dealing that should preclude equitable relief for mistake. In these circumstances, it would not be reasonable for this court to allocate the risk of the mistake to defendant.

As indicated above, the Restatement Second of Contracts provides that during the negotiation stage of a contract "each party is held to a degree of responsibility appropriate to the justifiable expectations of the other." (Rest.2d Contracts, § 157, com. a, p. 417.) No consumer reasonably can expect 100 percent accuracy in each and every price appearing in countless automobile advertisements listing numerous vehicles for sale. The degree of responsibility plaintiff asks this court to impose upon automobile dealers would amount to strict contract liability for any typographical error in the price of an advertised automobile, no matter how serious the error or how blameless the dealer. We are unaware of any other situation in which an individual or business is held to such a standard under the law of contracts. Defendant's good faith, isolated mistake does not constitute the type of extreme case in which its fault constitutes the neglect of a legal duty that bars equitable relief. Therefore, whether or not defendant's failure to sell the automobile to plaintiff could amount to a violation of section 11713.1(e)--an issue that is not before us--defendant's conduct in the present case does not preclude rescission. . . .

Having determined that defendant satisfied the requirements for rescission of the contract on the ground of unilateral mistake of fact, we conclude that the municipal court correctly entered judgment in defendant's favor.

The judgment of the Court of Appeal is reversed.

Questions

1. What rule did the Court of Appeal decisions recite regarding rescission based on unilateral mistake of fact, and why did the court reject this rule?

2. According to the court's decision, what are the requirements for obtaining rescission of a contract based on unilateral mistake of fact?

3. How did the court determine that the defendant's mistake in the price term of the contract constituted a material mistake regarding a basic assumption of the contract?

Impracticability/Impossibility of Performance

Life is full of surprises. Suppose a law student decides to rent out her home for the month of July while she is away in Europe. Then suppose that, without fault of the law student owner, the night before the one-month rental is to begin the home is unexpectedly destroyed by a fire. Is the owner excused from her duty to provide a home which can be occupied by the renter? The rule is when a party's performance is made impracticable without their fault by the occurrence of an event the non-occurrence of which was a basic assumption on which the contract was made, his duty to render the performance is discharged. (Rest.2d § 261)

In contracts in which performance depends on the continued existence of a given person or thing, an implied condition is that the perishing of the person or thing shall excuse performance. A thing is impossible in legal contemplation when it is not practicable; and a thing is impracticable when it can only be done at an excessive and unreasonable cost. (*City of Vernon v. City of Los Angeles* (1955) 45 Cal.2d 710, 720.) In other words, "impossibility" is defined as not only strict impossibility but as impracticability because of extreme and unreasonable difficulty, expense, injury, or loss involved. "Impossibility" is the traditional term used in such a situation however, both the Restatement Second and the Uniform Commercial Code now use the term "impracticability." (See, Rest.2d Contracts, § 261; UCC § 2-615) Temporary impossibility of the character which, if it should become permanent, would discharge a promisor's entire contractual duty, operates as a permanent discharge if performance after the impossibility ceases would impose a substantially greater burden upon the promisor; otherwise, the duty is suspended while the impossibility exists. (*Autry v. Republic Productions, Inc.* (1947) 30 Cal.2d 144)

Taylor v. Caldwell
Queen's Bench, 1863
13 Best & S. 826, 122 Eng. Rep. 310

BLACKBURN, J. In this case the plaintiffs and defendants had, on the 27th May, 1861, entered into a contract by which the defendants agreed to let the plaintiffs have the use of The Surrey Gardens and Music Hall on four days then to come, viz., the 17th June, 15th July, 5th August and 19th August, for the purpose of giving a series of four grand concerts, and day and night fetes at the Gardens and Hall on those days respectively; and the plaintiffs agreed to take the Gardens and Hall on those days, and pay £100 for each day.

The parties inaccurately call this a "letting," and the money to be paid a "rent;" . . . Nothing however, in our opinion, depends on this. . . . The effect of the whole is to shew that the existence of the Music Hall in the Surrey Gardens in a state fit for a concert was essential for the fulfilment of the contract,—such entertainments as the parties contemplated in their agreement could not be given without it.

After the making of the agreement, and before the first day on which a concert was to be given, the Hall was destroyed by fire. This destruction, we must take it on the evidence, was without the fault of either party, and was so complete that in consequence the concerts could not be given as intended. And the question we have to decide is whether, under these circumstances, the loss which the plaintiffs have sustained is to fall upon the defendants. The parties when framing their agreement evidently had not present to their minds the possibility of such a disaster, and have made no express stipulation with reference to it, so that the answer to the question must depend upon the general rules of law applicable to such a contract.

There seems no doubt that where there is a positive contract to do a thing, not in itself unlawful, the contractor must perform it or pay damages for not doing it, although in consequence of unforeseen accidents, the performance of his contract has become unexpectedly burthensome or even impossible. The law is so laid down in 1 Roll. Abr. 450, Condition (G), and in the note (2) to Walton v. Waterhouse (2 Wms. Saund. 421 a. 6th ed.), and is recognised as the general rule by all the Judges in the much discussed case of Hall v. Wright (E. B. & E. 746). But this rule is only applicable when the contract is positive and absolute, and not subject to any condition either express or implied: and there are authorities which, as we think, establish the principle that where, from the nature of the contract, it appears that the parties must from the beginning have known that it could not be fulfilled unless when the time for the fulfilment of the contract arrived some particular specified thing continued to exist, so that, when entering into the contract, they must have contemplated such continuing existence as the foundation of what was to be done; there, in the absence of any express or implied warranty that the thing shall exist, the contract is not to be construed as a positive contract, but as subject to an implied condition that the parties shall be excused in case, before breach, performance becomes impossible from the perishing of the thing without default of the contractor.

There seems little doubt that this implication tends to further the great object of making the legal construction such as to fulfill the intention of those who entered into the contract. For in the course of affairs men in making such contracts in general would, if it were brought to their minds, say that there should be such a condition.

Accordingly, in the Civil law, such an exception is implied in every obligation of the class which they call obligatio de certo corpore. . . . The examples are of contracts respecting a slave, which was the common illustration of a certain subject used by the Roman lawyers, just as we are apt to take a horse; and no doubt the propriety, one might almost say necessity, of the implied condition is more obvious when the contract relates to a living animal, whether man or brute, than when it relates to some inanimate thing (such as in the present case a theatre) the existence of which is not so obviously precarious as that of the live animal, but the principle is adopted in the Civil law as applicable to every obligation of which the subject is a certain thing. The general subject is treated of by Pothier, who in his Traite des Obligations, partie 3, chap. 6, art. 3, § 668 states the result to be that the debtor corporis certi is freed from his obligation when the thing has perished, neither by his act, nor his neglect, and before he is in default, unless by some stipulation he has taken on himself the risk of the particular misfortune which has occurred.

Although the Civil law is not of itself authority in an English Court, it affords great assistance in investigating the principles on which the law is grounded. And it seems to us that the common law authorities establish that in such a contract the same condition of the continued existence of the thing is implied by English law. . . .

These are instances where the implied condition is of the life of a human being, but there are others in which the same implication is made as to the continued existence of a thing. For example, where a contract of sale is made amounting to a bargain and sale, transferring presently the property in specific chattels, which are to be delivered by the vendor at a future day; there, if the chattels, without the fault of the vendor, perish in the interval, the purchaser must pay the price and the vendor is excused from performing his contract to deliver, which has thus become impossible.

... [T]he case of Williams v. Lloyd W. Jones, 179), above cited, shews that the same law had been already adopted by the English law as early as The Book of Assizes. The principle seems to us to be that, in contracts in which the performance depends on the continued existence of a given person or thing, a condition is implied that the impossibility of performance arising from the perishing of the person or thing shall excuse the performance.

In none of these cases is the promise in words other than positive, nor is there any express stipulation that the destruction of the person or thing shall excuse the performance; but that excuse is by law implied, because from the nature of the contract it is apparent that the parties contracted on the basis of the continued existence of the particular person or chattel. In the present case, looking at the whole contract, we find that the parties contracted on the basis of the continued existence of the Music Hall at the time when the concerts were to be given; that being essential to their performance.

We think, therefore, that the Music Hall having ceased to exist, without fault of either party, both parties are excused, the plaintiffs from taking the gardens and paying the money, the defendants from performing their promise to give the use of the Hall and Gardens and other things. Consequently the rule must be absolute to enter the verdict for the defendants.

Questions

1. What principle of law applies when a contract becomes impossible to fulfill due to the destruction of a specific thing necessary for its performance?

2. According to the court's reasoning, what conditions must be met for an implied condition of continued existence to be applied to a contract?

Takeaways – Taylor v. Caldwell

The three categories of cases where the general rule stated in *Taylor v. Caldwell* has been applied are: (1) supervening death or incapacity of a person necessary for performance, (2) supervening destruction of a specific thing necessary for performance, (3) supervening prohibition or prevention by law. (Rest.2d § 261 comment a.) In order for a supervening event to discharge a duty, the non-occurrence of that event must have been "a basic assumption" on which both parties made the contract.

Cazares v. Saenz
Court of Appeals of California, Fourth Appellate District
208 Cal.App.3d 279, 256 Cal.Rptr. 209 (1989)

WIENER, Acting P. J. On one level, the issue in this case is simply one of attorney's fees. Are plaintiffs Roy Cazares and Thomas Tosdal, former partners in the law firm of Cazares & Tosdal, entitled to one-half of a contingent fee promised them by defendant Phil Saenz when he associated the firm on a particular personal injury case, notwithstanding that Cazares became a municipal court judge before the case was settled? More fundamentally, however, the issue before us requires that we review not only the nature of contingent attorney fee arrangements but also basic contract law regarding frustration of purpose, incapacitation of parties to a contract, and the proper measure of quantum meruit recovery in such circumstances. We decide that where one member of a two-person law firm becomes incapable of performing on a contract of association with another lawyer, the obligations of the parties to the contract are discharged if it was contemplated that the incapacitated attorney would perform substantial services under the agreement. We therefore hold that Cazares and Tosdal are not entitled to 50 percent of the contingent fee as provided in the association agreement. They may, however, recover the reasonable value of the legal services rendered before Cazares's incapacitation, prorated on the basis of the original contract price.

Defendant Phil Saenz was an attorney of limited experience in November 1978 when he was contacted by the Mexican consulate in San Diego regarding a serious accident involving a Mexican national, Raul Gutierrez. Gutierrez had been burned after touching a power line owned by San Diego Gas & Electric Company (SDG&E). He retained Saenz to represent him in a lawsuit against SDG&E and other defendants. The written retainer agreement authorized Saenz to "retain co-counsel if he deems it necessary" and provided that "[a]ttorney fees shall be 33 $^1/_3$% of the net recovery; i.e., after all costs and medical expenses."

Saenz shared office space with the law firm of Cazares & Tosdal, which was composed of partners Roy Cazares and Thomas Tosdal, the plaintiffs in this action. In September 1979, Saenz agreed with Cazares to associate Cazares & Tosdal on the Gutierrez case. According to Saenz, he wanted to work with Cazares because Cazares spoke Spanish and could communicate directly with Gutierrez and because he (Saenz) respected Cazares's work in the Mexican-American community. In contrast, Saenz did not feel comfortable with Tosdal: "Basically, he was an Anglo, a surfer. In my opinion, he was just too liberal for me ...." Saenz testified he had no reason to doubt Tosdal's competence as a lawyer. In fact, Saenz did not object to Tosdal's working on the case as long as he (Saenz) had nothing to do with him.

Cazares, on behalf of his firm, and Saenz agreed Saenz would continue to maintain client contact with Gutierrez and would handle a pending immigration matter to prevent Gutierrez from being deported. Saenz also wanted to actively assist in the preparation and trial of the case as a learning experience. Cazares & Tosdal was to handle most of the legal work on the case. Saenz and Cazares orally agreed they would evenly divide the contingent fee on the Gutierrez case. Both Cazares and Saenz testified they expected and assumed Cazares would prosecute the case to its conclusion.

Gutierrez's complaint filed in November 1979 listed both Saenz and Cazares & Tosdal as counsel of record. During the next two and one-half years, Cazares performed most of the legal work in the case. Saenz maintained client contact, performed miscellaneous tasks and attended depositions including some defense depositions which Cazares did not attend. For all intents and purposes Tosdal performed no work on the case. Neither Cazares nor Saenz kept time records.

In June 1981, the Cazares & Tosdal partnership dissolved. The two partners decided to retain some cases, including the Gutierrez matter, as partnership assets. No formal substitution of counsel was filed in the case. Cazares and Saenz moved to a new office and continued to work on the case together for the next year.

In May 1982 Cazares was appointed a municipal court judge. Cazares urged Saenz to seek Tosdal's help in prosecuting the Gutierrez case. Saenz refused. In January 1983 Tosdal wrote Saenz stating that he remained "ready, willing and available to assist you in any aspect of the preparation of the case in which you may desire my aid."

Saenz never responded to Tosdal's offer. . . .

In April 1983, Saenz settled the Gutierrez case for $1.1 million, entitling him to a fee slightly in excess of $366,000. . . . About two weeks later, Saenz visited Cazares and offered to pay him $40,000 for his work on the case. Cazares declined, claiming Saenz owed the now defunct Cazares & Tosdal partnership more than $183,000. This litigation ensued.

The case was tried to a referee by stipulation. . . .The referee concluded in pertinent part as follows: "The partnership of Tosdal and Cazares entered into an agreement with Saenz, which was in effect a joint venture agreement. The partnership performed fully up until the time Cazares took the bench. At that time, Saenz rejected any help from the remaining partner, therefore preventing the performance by the partnership in further prosecution of the case. The case of Jewel v. Boxer, 156 Cal.App.3d 171 would appear to govern. The joint venture entered into by [the] partnership [with] Saenz entitled the partnership to receive 50% of the fees received by Defendant Saenz." The referee went on to conclude that Saenz was entitled to deduct the $47,000 paid to Khoury and Mazella before calculating the 50 percent due Cazares and Tosdal. Accordingly, judgment was entered in favor of Cazares and Tosdal in the amount of $159,833.00 plus interest.

The initial question is whether Saenz breached the association agreement with Cazares & Tosdal when, after Cazares's appointment to the municipal court, he refused to work with Tosdal on the Gutierrez case. Here, the referee in effect held that Saenz was obligated to accept Tosdal as a substitute for Cazares even though the record firmly establishes both parties to the association agreement contemplated that most if not all of the work on the Gutierrez case would be performed by Cazares. We conclude that Saenz acted within his rights in refusing to work with Tosdal after Cazares became a judge.

Where a contract contemplates the personal services of a party, performance is excused when that party dies or becomes otherwise incapable of performing. (Rest.2d Contracts, §§ 261, 262; 1 Witkin, Summary of Cal. Law (9th ed. 1987) Contracts, § 782, p. 705.) Here, the parties contemplated Cazares would personally perform the firm's obligations under the contract with Saenz, which he in fact did for two and one-half years after the execution of the contract. Cazares became legally incapable of performing the contract after his appointment to the bench. (See State Bar of California v. Superior Court (1929) 207 Cal. 323, 337 [278 P. 432].) Of course, the contract was not between Saenz and Cazares but between Saenz and the firm of Cazares & Tosdal; thus, performance by the firm was not technically impossible. Nonetheless, the Restatement Second of Contracts, section 262 addresses this issue because its language is not limited to the death or incapacity of a party to the contract: "If the existence of a particular person is necessary for the performance of a duty, his death or such incapacity as makes performance impracticable is an event the non-occurrence of which was a basic assumption on which the contract was made." (Italics added.) Here, both Saenz and Cazares testified that Cazares's prosecution of the case to completion was a "basic assumption on which the contract was made."

We have been unable to locate any cases -- California or otherwise -- addressing this issue in the context of an association agreement between lawyers. A similar situation occurs, however, whenever a client hires a firm of lawyers with the expectation of obtaining the services of a particular attorney. Of course under California law, a client may discharge an attorney at any time for any reason; there is no requirement that the discharge be for "cause." The client's only obligation is to compensate the discharged attorney in quantum meruit for the reasonable value of any services rendered. (Fracasse v. Brent (1972) 6 Cal.3d 784, 790-791 [100 Cal.Rptr. 385, 494 P.2d 9].) Thus, if the relationship with Cazares & Tosdal had been terminated by Gutierrez rather than Saenz, there would be no question that the termination was proper.

It is unnecessary in this case for us to decide whether the rights of an attorney acting on behalf of the client in associating other counsel mirror the client's broad rights under Fracasse. Even before Fracasse, when good cause was required to discharge an attorney (see Zurich G. A. & L. Ins. Co., Ltd. v. Kinsler (1938) 12 Cal.2d 98, 100-101 [81 P.2d 913]; Baldwin v. Bennett (1854) 4 Cal. 392, 393), the rule was that where a client contracts with a law firm to obtain the services of a particular attorney and that attorney dies or becomes incapacitated, the client at his option may discharge the firm subject only to the obligation to compensate the firm for the reasonable value of services rendered before the discharge. [Citations omitted] We see no reason why a similar rule should not apply when an attorney on behalf of a client enters into an association agreement with another firm of lawyers. A lawyer who associates a firm on a specific case in order to obtain the services of a particular professional colleague is certainly no less likely than the client to be relying on that colleague's unique legal talents. Here, in fact, Gutierrez specifically delegated to Saenz the discretion to associate co-counsel "if he deem[ed] it necessary." (Ante, p. 282.)

It may be helpful to consider a hypothetical situation in which the roles here were reversed, i.e., if Saenz sought to compel Tosdal to perform after Cazares was appointed to the bench. One of the illustrations to Restatement Second of Contracts, section 262 addresses this precise situation, stating the rule that the death or incapacity of one partner discharges the firm's obligations under the contract. At least where the contract contemplates the unique personal services of a firm member, the rationale of the illustration necessarily leads to the conclusion that the obligations of the party retaining the firm are also discharged in such a situation.

The judgment is reversed. The case is remanded to the superior court for further proceedings consistent with this opinion.

Questions

1. According to the court's decision, under what circumstances can the obligations of parties to a contract be discharged?

2. Why did the court conclude that the obligations of the parties to the contract were discharged?

3. What was the underlying assumption of this contract and what was the unexpected contingency that occurred?

Impracticability Under the UCC

Under UCC 2-615, three conditions must be satisfied before performance is excused: (1) a contingency has occurred; (2) the contingency has made performance impracticable; and (3) the non-occurrence of that contingency was a basic assumption upon which the contract was made.

Transatlantic Financing Corporation v. United States
U.S. Court of Appeals for the District of Columbia Circuit, 1966
363 F.2d 312

J. SKELLY WRIGHT, Circuit Judge: This appeal involves a voyage charter between Transatlantic Financing Corporation, operator of the SS CHRISTOS, and the United States covering carriage of a full cargo of wheat from a United States Gulf port to a safe port in Iran. The District Court dismissed a libel filed by Transatlantic against the United States for costs attributable to the ship's diversion from the normal sea route caused by the closing of the Suez Canal. We affirm.

On July 26, 1956, the Government of Egypt nationalized the Suez Canal Company and took over operation of the Canal. On October 2, 1956, during the international crisis which resulted from the seizure, the voyage charter in suit was executed between representatives of Transatlantic and the United States. The charter indicated the termini of the voyage but not the route. On October 27, 1956, the SS CHRISTOS sailed from Galveston for Bandar Shapur, Iran, on a course which would have taken her through Gibraltar and the Suez Canal. On October 29, 1956, Israel invaded Egypt. On October 31, 1956, Great Britain and France invaded the Suez Canal Zone. On November 2, 1956, the Egyptian Government obstructed the Suez Canal with sunken vessels and closed it to traffic.

On or about November 7, 1956, Beckmann, representing Transatlantic, contacted Potosky, an employee of the United States Department of Agriculture, who appellant concedes was unauthorized to bind the Government, requesting instructions concerning disposition of the cargo and seeking an agreement for payment of additional compensation for a voyage around the Cape of Good Hope. Potosky advised Beckmann that Transatlantic was expected to perform the charter according to its terms, that he did not believe Transatlantic was entitled to additional compensation for a voyage around the Cape, but that Transatlantic was free to file such a claim. Following this discussion, the CHRISTOS changed course for the Cape of Good Hope and eventually arrived in Bandar Shapur on December 30, 1956.

Transatlantic's claim is based on the following train of argument. The charter was a contract for a voyage from a Gulf port to Iran. Admiralty principles and practices, especially stemming from the doctrine of deviation, require us to imply into the contract the term that the voyage was to be performed by the "usual and customary" route. The usual and customary route from Texas to Iran was, at the time of contract, via Suez, so the contract was for a voyage from Texas to Iran via Suez. When Suez was closed this contract became impossible to perform. Consequently, appellant's argument continues, when Transatlantic delivered the cargo by going around the Cape of Good Hope, in compliance with the Government's demand under claim of right, it conferred a benefit upon the United States for which it should be paid in *quantum meruit*.

The doctrine of impossibility of performance has gradually been freed from the earlier fictional and unrealistic strictures of such tests as the "implied term" and the parties' "contemplation." Page, *The Development of the Doctrine of Impossibility of Performance*, 18 Mich. L. Rev. 589, 596 (1920). See generally 6 CORBIN, CONTRACTS §§ 1320-1372 (rev.ed. 1962); 6 WILLISTON, CONTRACTS §§ 1931-1979 (rev. ed. 1938). It is now recognized that "`A thing is impossible in legal contemplation when it is not practicable; and a thing is impracticable when it can only be done at an excessive and unreasonable cost.'" Mineral Park Land Co. v. Howard, 172 Cal. 289, 293, 156 P. 458, 460, L.R.A. 1916F, 1 (1916). *Accord*, Whelan v. Griffith

Consumers Company, D.C.Mun.App., 170 A.2d 229 (1961); RESTATEMENT, CONTRACTS § 454 (1932); UNIFORM COMMERCIAL CODE (U. L.A.) § 2-615, comment 3. The doctrine ultimately represents the ever-shifting line, drawn by courts hopefully responsive to commercial practices and mores, at which the community's interest in having contracts enforced according to their terms is outweighed by the commercial senselessness of requiring performance. When the issue is raised, the court is asked to construct a condition of performance based on the changed circumstances, a process which involves at least three reasonably definable steps. First, a contingency — something unexpected — must have occurred. Second, the risk of the unexpected occurrence must not have been allocated either by agreement or by custom. Finally, occurrence of the contingency must have rendered performance commercially impracticable. Unless the court finds these three requirements satisfied, the plea of impossibility must fail.

The first requirement was met here. It seems reasonable, where no route is mentioned in a contract, to assume the parties expected performance by the usual and customary route at the time of contract. Since the usual and customary route from Texas to Iran at the time of contract was through Suez, closure of the Canal made impossible the expected method of performance. But this unexpected development raises rather than resolves the impossibility issue, which turns additionally on whether the risk of the contingency's occurrence had been allocated and, if not, whether performance by alternative routes was rendered impracticable.

Proof that the risk of a contingency's occurrence has been allocated may be expressed in or implied from the agreement. Such proof may also be found in the surrounding circumstances, including custom and usages of the trade. See 6 CORBIN, *supra*, § 1339, at 394-397; 6 WILLISTON, *supra*, § 1948, at 5457-5458. The contract in this case does not expressly condition performance upon availability of the Suez route. Nor does it specify "via Suez" or, on the other hand, "via Suez or Cape of Good Hope." Nor are there provisions in the contract from which we may properly imply that the continued availability of Suez was a condition of performance. Nor is there anything in custom or trade usage, or in the surrounding circumstances generally, which would support our constructing a condition of performance. The numerous cases requiring performance around the Cape when Suez was closed, see *e. g.*, Ocean Tramp Tankers Corp. v. V/O Sovfracht (The Eugenia), [1964] 2 Q.B. 226, and cases cited therein, indicate that the Cape route is generally regarded as an alternative means of performance. So the implied expectation that the route would be via Suez is hardly adequate proof of an allocation to the promisee of the risk of closure. In some cases, even an express expectation may not amount to a condition of performance. The doctrine of deviation supports our assumption that parties normally expect performance by the usual and customary route, but it adds nothing beyond this that is probative of an allocation of the risk.

If anything, the circumstances surrounding this contract indicate that the risk of the Canal's closure may be deemed to have been allocated to Transatlantic. We know or may safely assume that the parties were aware, as were most commercial men with interests affected by the Suez situation, see The Eugenia, *supra*, that the Canal might become a dangerous area. No doubt the tension affected freight rates, and it is arguable that the risk of closure became part of the dickered terms. UNIFORM COMMERCIAL CODE § 2-615, comment 8. We do not deem the risk of closure so allocated, however. Foreseeability or even recognition of a risk does not necessarily prove its allocation. Compare UNIFORM COMMERCIAL CODE § 2-615, Comment 1; RESTATEMENT, CONTRACTS § 457 (1932). Parties to a contract are not always able to provide for all the possibilities of which they are aware, sometimes because they cannot agree, often simply because they are too busy. Moreover, that some abnormal risk was contemplated is probative but does not necessarily establish an allocation of the risk of the contingency which actually occurs. In this case, for example, nationalization by Egypt of the Canal Corporation and formation of the Suez Users Group did not necessarily indicate that the Canal would be blocked even if a confrontation resulted. The surrounding circumstances do indicate, however, a willingness by Transatlantic to assume abnormal risks, and this fact should legitimately cause us to judge the impracticability of performance by an alternative route in stricter terms than we would were the contingency unforeseen.

We turn then to the question whether occurrence of the contingency rendered performance commercially impracticable under the circumstances of this case. The goods shipped were not subject to harm from the longer, less temperate Southern route. The vessel and crew were fit to proceed around the Cape. Transatlantic was no less able than the United States to purchase insurance to cover the contingency's occurrence. If anything, it is more reasonable to expect owner-operators of vessels to insure against the hazards of war. They are in the best position to calculate the cost of performance by alternative routes (and therefore to estimate the amount of insurance required), and are undoubtedly sensitive to international troubles which uniquely affect the demand for and cost of their services. The only factor operating here in appellant's favor is the added expense, allegedly $43,972.00 above and beyond the contract price of $305,842.92, of extending a 10,000 mile voyage by approximately 3,000 miles. While it may be an overstatement to say that increased cost and difficulty of performance never constitute impracticability, to justify relief there must be more of a variation between expected cost and the cost of performing by an available alternative than is present in this case, where the promisor can legitimately be presumed to have accepted some degree of abnormal risk, and where impracticability is urged on the basis of added expense alone.

We conclude, therefore, as have most other courts considering related issues arising out of the Suez closure that performance of this contract was not rendered legally impossible. Even if we agreed with appellant, its theory of relief seems untenable. When performance of a contract is deemed impossible it is a nullity. In the case of a charter party involving carriage of goods, the carrier may return to an appropriate port and unload its cargo, The Malcolm Baxter, Jr., 277 U.S. 323, 48 S.

Ct. 516, 72 L. Ed. 901 (1928), subject of course to required steps to minimize damages. If the performance rendered has value, recovery in *quantum meruit* for the entire performance is proper. But here Transatlantic has collected its contract price, and now seeks *quantum meruit* relief for the additional expense of the trip around the Cape. If the contract is a nullity, Transatlantic's theory of relief should have been *quantum meruit* for the entire trip, rather than only for the extra expense. Transatlantic attempts to take its profit on the contract, and then force the Government to absorb the cost of the additional voyage. When impracticability without fault occurs, the law seeks an equitable solution, see 6 CORBIN, *supra*, § 1321, and *quantum meruit* is one of its potent devices to achieve this end. There is no interest in casting the entire burden of commercial disaster on one party in order to preserve the other's profit. Apparently the contract price in this case was advantageous enough to deter appellant from taking a stance on damages consistent with its theory of liability. In any event, there is no basis for relief. Affirmed.

Questions

1. According to the court's reasoning, what are the three requirements that must be satisfied for the plea of impossibility to be successful?

2. How did the court determine whether the risk of the contingency (closure of the Suez Canal) had been allocated between the parties?

3. What factors did the court consider when assessing whether performance by an alternative route was commercially impracticable?

4. Why did the court reject Transatlantic's claim for quantum meruit relief for the additional expense of the trip around the Cape of Good Hope?

5. What is the court's stance on allocating the burden of commercial disaster between the parties involved in a contract when impracticability without fault occurs?

Takeaways – Transatlantic Financing

The plaintiff in *Transatlantic* actually succeeded in making the voyage to its destination so plaintiff certainly couldn't claim that performance was "impossible." Why did plaintiff think it had a chance to prevail on an impracticability theory? The modern trend is to allow the defense of impossibility when performance is impracticable because of excessive and unreasonable difficulty or expense. However, where one agrees to do, for a fixed sum, a thing possible to be performed, he will not be excused or become entitled to additional compensation, because unforeseen difficulties are encountered. (*Day v. U.S.*, 245 U.S. 159 (1917).)

Canadian Industrial Alcohol Co. v. Dunbar Molasses Co.
New York Court of Appeals, 1932
258 N.Y. 194, 179 N.E. 383

CARDOZO, Ch. J. A buyer sues a seller for breach of an executory contract of purchase and sale.

The subject-matter of the contract was "approximately 1,500,000 wine gallons Refined Blackstrap [molasses] of the usual run from the National Sugar Refinery, Yonkers, N.Y., to test around 60% sugars."

The order was given and accepted December 27, 1927, but shipments of the molasses were to begin after April 1, 1928, and were to be spread out during the warm weather.

After April 1, 1928 the defendant made delivery from time to time of 344,083 gallons. Upon its failure to deliver more, the plaintiff brought this action for the recovery of damages. The defendant takes the ground that, by an implied term of the contract, the duty to deliver was conditioned upon the production by the National Sugar Refinery at Yonkers of molasses sufficient in quantity to fill the plaintiff's order. The fact is that the output of the refinery, while the contract was in force, was 485,848 gallons, much less than its capacity, of which amount 344,083 gallons were allotted to the defendant and shipped to the defendant's customer. The argument for the defendant is that its own duty to deliver was proportionate to the refinery's willingness to supply, and that the duty was discharged when the output was reduced.

The contract, read in the light of the circumstances existing at its making, or more accurately in the light of any such circumstances apparent from this record, does not keep the defendant's duty within boundaries so narrow. We may assume, in the defendant's favor that there would have been a discharge of its duty to deliver if the refinery had been destroyed *(Stewart v. Stone,* 127 N.Y. 500; *Dexter v. Norton,* 47 N.Y. 62; *Nitro Powder Co. v. Agency of C. C. & F. Co.,* 233 N.Y. 294, 297), or if the output had been curtailed by the failure of the sugar crop *(Pearson v. McKinney,* 160 Cal. 649; *Howell v. Coupland,* 1 Q.B.D. 258; 3 Williston on Contracts, § 1949) or by the ravages of war *(Matter of Badische Co.,* [1921] 2 Ch. 331; *Horlock v. Beal,* [1916] 1 A.C. 486) or conceivably in some circumstances by unavoidable strikes *(American Union Line v. Oriental Navigation Corp.,* 239 N.Y. 207, 219; *Normandie Shirt Co. v. Eagle, Inc.,* 238 N.Y. 218, 229; *Delaware, L. & W. Co. v. Bowns,* 58 N.Y. 573; and cf. *Blackstock v. New York & Erie R. R. Co.,* 20 N.Y. 48; also 2 Williston on Contracts, § 1099, pp. 2045, 2046). We may even assume that a like result would have followed if the plaintiff had bargained not merely for a quantity of molasses to be supplied from a particular refinery, but for molasses to be supplied in accordance with 8, particular contract between the defendant and the refiner, and if thereafter such contract had been broken without fault on the defendant's part *(Scialli v. Correale,* 97 N.J.L. 165; cf., however, *Marsh* v. *Johnston,* 125 App. Div. 597; 196 N.Y. 511). The inquiry is merely this, whether the continuance of a special group of circumstances appears from the terms of the contract interpreted in the setting of the occasion, to have been a tacit or implied presupposition in the minds of the [199] contracting parties, conditioning their belief in a continued obligation *(Tamplin S. S. Co.* v. *Anglo-Mexican P. P. Co.,* [1916] 2 A.C. 397, 406, 407; *Blackburn Bobbin Co.* v. *Allen & Sons, Ltd.,* L.R. [1918] 1 K.B. 540; Lorillard v. Clyde, 142 N.Y. 456; 3 Williston on Contracts, § 1952).

Accepting that test, we ask ourselves the question what special group of circumstances does the defendant lay before us as one of the presuppositions immanent in its bargain with the plaintiff? The defendant asks us to assume that a manufacturer, having made a contract with a middleman for a stock of molasses to be procured from a particular refinery would expect the contract to lapse whenever the refiner chose to diminish his production, and this in the face of the middleman's omission to do anything to charge the refiner with a duty to continue. Business could not be transacted with security or smoothness if a presumption so unreasonable were at the root of its engagements. There is nothing to show that the defendant would have been unable by a timely contract with the refinery to have assured itself of a supply sufficient for its needs. There is nothing to show that the plaintiff in giving the order for the molasses, was informed by the defendant that such a contract had not been made, or that performance would be contingent upon obtaining one thereafter. If the plaintiff had been so informed, it would very likely have preferred to deal with the refinery directly, instead of dealing with a middleman. The defendant does not even show that it tried to get a contract from the refinery during the months that intervened between the acceptance of the plaintiff's order and the time when shipments were begun. It has wholly failed to relieve itself of the imputation of contributory fault (3 Williston on Contracts, § 1959). So far as the record shows, it put its faith in the mere chance that the output of the refinery would be the same from year to year, and finding its faith vain, it tells us that its customer must have expected to take a chance as great. We see no reason for importing into the bargain this aleatory element. The defendant is in no better position than a factor who undertakes in his own name to sell for future delivery a special grade of merchandise to be manufactured by a special mill. The duty will be discharged if the mill is destroyed before delivery is due. The duty will subsist if the output is reduced because times turn out to be hard and labor charges high. . . .

The judgment should be affirmed with costs.

Questions

1. What was the defendant's argument regarding the implied terms of the contract and the duty to deliver?

2. How did the court interpret the defendant's duty to deliver in light of the circumstances surrounding the contract?

3. What factors did the court consider in determining whether the defendant's duty to deliver was discharged?

4. According to the court, what would have been necessary for the defendant to relieve itself of contributory fault in the performance of the contract?

5. How did the court compare the defendant's position to that of a factor selling merchandise manufactured by a special mill for future delivery?

Selland Pontiac-GMC, Inc. v. King
Court of Appeals of Minnesota, 1986
384 N.W.2d 490

RANDALL, Judge. Buyer, Selland Pontiac-GMC, Inc., sued seller, George King, for breach of contract. After a one-day bench trial the court granted judgment for King. The trial court denied Selland's motion for a new trial and/or amended findings of fact and conclusions of law and entered judgment. Selland appeals. We affirm.

Selland contracted with King (doing business as King's Superior Bus Sales) to buy four school bus bodies. The oral agreement made in April, 1983, was reduced to a writing dated May 12, 1983. King was to supply the bodies, which would be built on top of chassis provided by Selland. The written agreement indicates that the bodies would be manufactured by Superior Manufacturing, which was located in Morris, Manitoba. The written agreement contains no completion date. King was aware that Selland's customer needed the buses by late August for the start of the school year. The contract price was $47,660. The writing contained no escape clause excusing King's performance should his source of supply fail.

In reliance on the contract, Selland ordered four bus chassis from General Motors. They arrived at Superior's entry point in Pembina, North Dakota, in June and early July, 1983.

Superior went into receivership on July 7, 1983, and King learned of this on July 8. King informed Selland of the receivership on August 12. The parties do not agree on what happened afterwards. Selland claims that King assured Selland that the buses would be completed on time. King claims that Selland, fully advised of Superior's status, decided to wait and see if Superior would come out of receivership able to supply and install the bus bodies. The trial court found that "[a]fter receiving notice of the receivership, Selland acquiesced to the delay in production."

The bodies were never manufactured. The Superior plant was operated by a new company from approximately late July to September or October. For some time after that, different individuals expressed interest in buying and operating the plant. Finally it was purchased, moved to Oklahoma, and it began production in 1985. Superior went out of business. In December, 1983, Selland's customer (Chief Auto Sales) cancelled their order. Selland sold the chassis at a loss. . . .

. . . Selland questions the trial court's finding that the contract identified Superior as King's supplier, and that the contract contemplated that the bodies would be manufactured by Superior. This finding is supported by the contract which states that Superior bus bodies were being sold.

Selland also questions the trial court's finding that it acquiesced in the delay when it became apparent that the buses would not be completed near the beginning of the school year. King's testimony indicates that from August 12, 1983, he notified Selland of all information relevant to Superior's production schedule and business status as it became known to him. The receiver continually negotiated with another company which operated the Superior plant for a short period. Selland did not cancel its order until December, 1983, and was in contact with both its customer and King throughout August and September. These facts indicate that reasons existed for Selland to wait and see whether the bodies would be produced. The trial court did not err in finding that Selland acquiesced to the delay.

II. Application of § 336.2-615 Except so far as a seller may have assumed a greater obligation and subject to the preceding section on substituted performance: (a) Delay in delivery or nondelivery in whole or part by a seller who complied with paragraphs (b) and (c) is not a breach of his duty under a contract for sale if performance as agreed has been made impracticable by the occurrence of a contingency the non-occurrence of which was a basic assumption on which the contract was made or by compliance in good faith with any applicable foreign or domestic governmental regulation or order whether or not it later proves to be invalid. * * * (c) The seller must notify the buyer seasonably that there will be delay or nondelivery * * *.

Minn. Stat. § 336.2-615 (1984). Supply of Superior bus bodies was a basic assumption on which the contract was made. These became impracticable to supply when Superior ceased manufacturing.

Appellant argues that the trial court improperly applied § 336.2-615. In Barbarossa & Sons v. Iten Chevrolet, Inc., 265 N.W.2d 655 (Minn.1978) the supreme court applied § 336.2-615 and affirmed judgment for the buyer where the manufacturer's supply of seller's order was not a basic assumption of the contract and the contract contained no escape clause. The manufacturer, General Motors, was not mentioned in the contract as the source of supply. General Motors had cancelled several orders at this time due to a shortage. The court stated:

A partial failure of a seller's source of supply generally has been treated as a foreseeable contingency, the risk of which is allocated to the seller absent a specific provision to the contrary in the contract. Id. at 659-60 (citations omitted).

The trial court's finding of no breach of contract here is consistent with Barbarossa's holding that the contract was breached under § 336.2-615. Here the seller's supplier was specified in the contract. Superior was also specified in King's price quotation to Selland. In Barbarossa the supplier did not cease to manufacture, but simply cancelled the orders of some of its dealers. Here both parties testified that they had no knowledge of Superior's questionable financial circumstances when they contracted and King did not expressly assume the risk of Superior's ceasing production.

Appellant claims that the trial court erred in concluding that King gave seasonable notice of nondelivery. The trial court found that King's August 12 notification of the receivership and King's passing on all information as he received it constituted seasonable notice of delay and nondelivery. Whether or not there was seasonable notice of nondelivery is an issue of fact, and we will not disturb the trial court's assessment of the credibility of conflicting testimony. . . . Although King did not ultimately advise Selland of nondelivery, this was not necessary under the facts of this case where Selland canceled the contract before such notice could be given.

The trial court did not clearly err in finding that the contract contemplated that the bus bodies would be manufactured by Superior and that Selland acquiesced to the delay in delivery. The trial court did not err in its application of Minn. Stat. § 336.2615.

Affirmed.

Questions

1. What argument did the appellant make regarding the trial court's application of UCC 2-615? How did the court address this argument?

2. What was the significance of specifying Superior as the supplier in the contract?

Takeaways – Canadian Industrial Alcohol and Selland Pontiac

So, in *Selland*, the source of supply stops cranking out bus bodies and King gets excused. In *Canadian Industrial* the refinery curtails its output but Dunbar isn't excused. Can you explain the differing outcomes? Case law has told us that a partial failure of the seller's source of supply generally has been treated as a foreseeable contingency, and therefore not an excuse under the doctrine of impracticability. (See, *Barbarossa & Sons v. Iten Chevrolet, Inc.,* 265 N.W.2d 655 (Minn.1978)) Why did the court excuse performance in *Selland*? Was it because it was a total failure of the seller's source of supply? Was it because Superior was specifically mentioned in the contract?

Drafting Tip – Force Majeure Clauses

Perhaps some of the defendants in the preceding cases, could have avoided being sued by including a *force* majeure clause into their contract. A *force majeure* clause is an exculpatory clause inserted into a contract that excuses performance upon the occurrence of an event beyond a party's control. A typical such clause might read:

"The Company shall not be liable for any failure in the performance of its obligations under this agreement which may result from strikes or acts of labor unions, fires, floods, earthquakes, or acts of God, war or other contingencies beyond its control."

Crop Failures

Squillante v. California Lands, Inc.
California Court of Appeal, Fourth Appellate District, 1935
5 Cal.App.2d 89, 42 P.2d 81

Allyn, J., pro tem. Plaintiff brought suit for damages for breach of contract to buy ten carloads of Zinfandel grapes "of good quality and color and of good sugar content" from the defendant. The agreement was made through an exchange of telegrams after the plaintiff had inspected defendant's vineyards and arranged that the grapes be packed by a certain packer and under defendant's brand. Five cars were delivered and then, due to heat damage, defendant was unable to harvest or ship any further grapes of the quality agreed upon. Plaintiff was so notified and in due course this action was brought and judgment given for the defendant. The defendant was a grower and not a dealer in grapes except in so far as was necessary to dispose of its own products.

Upon this appeal plaintiff submits that defendant was not relieved from its obligation to deliver the grapes by the crop losses caused by adverse weather conditions and hence that it was error to admit evidence on this issue. It is argued that the contract was a general undertaking to sell grapes of a given quality which the seller was to have ready at all events when delivery was due. This might well be true if the defendant were in the general business of packing and selling grapes (Eskew v. California Fruit Exchange, 203 Cal. 257 [263 P. 804]), but it is apparent here that the parties intended the sale and purchase of ten cars of grapes of a particular quality to be grown and produced in the vineyards of the defendant, to be packed by a named packer under the defendant's established brand which was used by it in marketing its own products. The sale being of a designated quality of a specific variety of grapes growing or to be grown in specific vineyards, and these vineyards being so far affected by extraordinary heat conditions that they did not produce sufficient grapes of the variety and quality named to comply with the contract, the defendant could be compelled to perform the contract only so far as it was possible for it so to do. It could not be compelled to perform impossibilities nor was it liable in damages for a failure to comply with its contract resulting from vis major not attributable to any fault on its part (Ontario Deciduous Fruit Growers Assn. v. Cutting Fruit Packing Co., 134 Cal. 21 [66 P. 28, 86 Am.St.Rep. 231, 53 L.R.A. 681]; Operators' Oil Co. v. Barbre, 65 Fed.2d 857, 861).

The finding of the trial court on this issue is conclusive and is sufficient to sustain the judgment for the defendant. . . .

The judgment is therefore affirmed.

Questions

1. What was the plaintiff's claim in the case?

2. What was the defendant's argument?

3. What was the basis for the court's decision?

4. What legal principles did the court rely on to support its conclusion that the defendant was not liable for a failure to comply with the contract due to extraordinary heat conditions?

Takeaways – Squillante v. California Lands Inc.

"One who contracts to sell and deliver a crop of fruit, vegetables, grain or hay then growing on a specific tract of land, or to be grown on such a tract within a specified growing season is discharged from duty by the destruction of that crop without fault. [However, there is] no discharge if they are not required to be the product of a particular tract of land during a particular season." (Corbin,, Contracts (One Vol. Ed.) §1339)

Frustration of Purpose

Where a party's principal purpose is frustrated by the occurrence of an event, the non-occurrence of which was a basic assumption on which the contract was made, the duty of performance is discharged. (Rest.2d § 265.) The doctrine of frustration addresses situations where, because of the occurrence of an unforeseen supervening event, one party's performance becomes virtually worthless to the other.

Krell v. Henry
Court of Appeal, 1903
L.R. 2 K.B. 740

[By a contract in writing of June 20, 1902, the defendant agreed to hire from the plaintiff a flat in Pall Mall for June 26 and 27, on which days it had been announced that the coronation processions would take place and pass along Pall Mall. The contract contained no express reference to the coronation processions, or to any other purpose for which the flat was taken. A deposit was paid when the contract was entered into, As the processions did not take place on the days originally fixed, the defendant declined to pay the balance of the agreed rent.]

VAUGHAN WILLIAMS L.J. read the following written judgment:—The real question in this case is the extent of the application in English law of the principle of the Roman law which has been adopted and acted on in many English decisions, and notably in the case of Taylor v. Caldwell. That case at least makes it clear that "where, from the nature of the contract, it appears that the parties must from the beginning have known that it could not be fulfilled unless, when the time for the fulfilment of the contract arrived, some particular specified thing continued to exist, so that when entering into the contract they must have contemplated such continued existence as the foundation of what was to be done; there, in the absence of any express or implied warranty that the thing shall exist, the contract is not to be considered a positive contract, but as subject to an implied condition that the parties shall be excused in case, before breach, performance becomes impossible from the perishing of the thing without default of the contractor."

Thus far it is clear that the principle of the Roman law has been introduced into the English law. The doubt in the present case arises as to how far this principle extends. The Roman law dealt with obligationes de certo corpore. Whatever may have been the limits of the Roman law, the case of Nickoll v. Ashton makes it plain that the English law applies the principle not only to cases where the performance of the contract becomes impossible by the cessation of existence of the thing which is the subject-matter of the contract, but also to cases where the event which renders the contract incapable of performance is the cessation or non-existence of an express condition or state of things, going to the root of the contract, and essential to its performance. It is said, on the one side, that the specified thing, state of things, or condition the continued existence of which is necessary for the fulfilment of the contract, so that the parties entering into the contract must have contemplated the continued existence of that thing, condition, or state of things as the foundation of what was to be done under the contract, is limited to things which are either the subject-matter of the contract or a condition or state of things, present or anticipated, which is expressly mentioned in the contract. But, on the other side, it is said that the condition or state of things need not be expressly specified, but that it is sufficient if that condition or state of things clearly appears by extrinsic evidence to have been assumed by the parties to be the foundation or basis of the contract, and the event which causes the impossibility is of such a character that it cannot reasonably be supposed to have been in the contemplation of the contracting parties when the contract was made. In such a case the contracting parties will not be held bound by the general words which, though large enough to include, were not used with reference to a possibility of a particular event rendering performance of the contract impossible. I do not think that the principle of the civil law as introduced into the English law is limited to cases in which the event causing the impossibility of performance is the destruction or non-existence of some thing which is the subject-matter of the contract or of some condition or state of things expressly specified as a condition of it. I think that you first have to ascertain, not necessarily from the terms of the contract, but, if required, from necessary inferences, drawn from surrounding circumstances recognised by both contracting parties, what is the substance of the contract, and then to ask the question whether that substantial contract needs for its foundation the assumption of the existence of a particular state of things. If it does, this will limit the operation of the general words, and in such case, if the contract becomes impossible of performance by reason of the non-existence of the state of things assumed by both contracting parties as the foundation of the contract, there will be no breach of the contract thus limited. Now what are the facts of the present case? The contract is contained in two letters of June 20 which passed between the defendant and the plaintiff's agent, Mr. Cecil Bisgood. These letters do not mention the coronation, but speak merely of the taking of Mr. Krell's chambers, or, rather, of the use of them, in the daytime of June 26 and 27, for the sum of £75, £25. then paid, balance £50 to be paid on the 24th. But the affidavits, which by agreement between the parties are to be taken as stating the facts of the case, shew that the plaintiff exhibited on his [750] premises, third floor, 56A, Pall Mall, an announcement to the effect that windows to view the Royal coronation procession were to be let, and that the defendant was induced by that announcement to apply to the housekeeper on the premises, who said that the owner was willing to let the suite of rooms for the purpose of seeing the Royal procession for both days, but not nights, of June 26 and 27.

In my judgment the use of the rooms was let and taken for the purpose of seeing the Royal procession. It was not a demise of the rooms, or even an agreement to let and take the rooms. It is a licence to use rooms for a particular purpose and none other. And in my judgment the taking place of those processions on the days proclaimed along the proclaimed route, which passed 56A, Pall Mall, was regarded by both contracting parties as the foundation of the contract; and I think that it cannot reasonably be supposed to have been in the contemplation of the contracting parties, when the contract was made, that the coronation would not be held on the proclaimed days, or the processions not take place on those days along the proclaimed route; and I think that the words imposing on the defendant the obligation to accept and pay for the use of the rooms for the named days, although general and unconditional, were not used with reference to the possibility of the particular contingency which afterwards occurred. It was suggested in the course of the argument that if the occurrence, on the proclaimed days, of the coronation and the procession in this case were the foundation of the contract, and if the general words are thereby limited or qualified, so that in the event of the non-occurrence of the coronation and procession along the proclaimed route they would discharge both parties from further performance of the contract, it would follow that if a cabman was engaged to take some one to Epsom on Derby Day at a suitable enhanced price for such a journey, say £10, both parties to the contract would be discharged in the contingency of the race at Epsom for some reason becoming impossible; but I do not think this follows, for I do not think that in the cab case the happening of the race would be the foundation of the contract. No doubt the purpose of the engager would be to go to see the Derby, and the price would be proportionately high; but the cab had no special qualifications for the purpose which led to the selection of the cab for this particular occasion. Any other cab would have done as well. Moreover, I think that, under the cab contract, the hirer, even if the race went off, could have said, "Drive me to Epsom; I will pay you the agreed sum; you have nothing to do with the purpose for which I hired the cab," and that if the cabman refused he would have been guilty of a breach of contract, there being nothing to qualify his promise to drive the hirer to Epsom on a particular day. Whereas in the case of the coronation, there is not merely the purpose of the hirer to see the coronation procession, but it is the coronation procession and the relative position of the rooms which is the basis of the contract as much for the lessor as the hirer; and I think that if the King, before the coronation day and after the contract, had died, the hirer could not have insisted on having the rooms on the days named. It could not in the cab case be reasonably said that seeing the Derby race was the foundation of the contract, as it was of the licence in this case. Whereas in the present case, where the rooms were offered and taken, by reason of their peculiar suitability from the position of the rooms for a view of the coronation procession, surely the view of the coronation procession was the foundation of the contract, which is a very different thing from the purpose of the man who engaged the cab—namely, to see the race—being held to be the foundation of the contract. Each case must be judged by its own circumstances. In each case one must ask oneself, first, what, having regard to all the circumstances, was the foundation of the contract? Secondly, was the performance of the contract prevented? Thirdly, was the event which prevented the performance of the contract of such a character that it cannot reasonably be said to have been in the contemplation of the parties at the date of the contract? If all these questions are answered in the affirmative (as I think they should be in this case), I think both parties are discharged from further performance of the contract. I think that the coronation procession was the foundation of this contract, and that the non-happening of it prevented the performance of the contract; and, secondly, I think that the non-happening of the procession, to use the words of Sir James Hannen in Baily v. De Crespigny, was an event "of such a character that it cannot reasonably be supposed to have been in the contemplation of the contracting parties when the contract was made . . . Appeal dismissed

Questions

1. What was the defendant's agreement with the plaintiff?

2. What was the basis for the defendant's refusal to pay the balance of the agreed rent?

3. What is the principle of the Roman law that has been introduced into English law?

4. What was the unexpected event that occurred and how did it destroy or lessen the value of what defendant had contracted to pay for?

Lloyd v. Murphy
Supreme Court of California, 1944
25 Cal.2d 48, 153 P.2d 47

TRAYNOR, J. On August 4, 1941, plaintiff leased to defendant for a five-year term beginning September 15, 1941, certain premises located at the corner of Almont Drive and Wilshire Boulevard in the city of Beverly Hills, Los Angeles County, "for the sole purpose of conducting thereon the business of displaying and selling new automobiles (including the servicing and repairing thereof and of selling the petroleum products of a major oil company) and for no other purpose whatsoever without the written consent of the lessor" except "to make an occasional sale of a used automobile." Defendant agreed not to sublease or assign without plaintiffs' written consent. On January 1, 1942, the federal government ordered that the sale of new automobiles be discontinued. It modified this order on January 8, 1942, to permit sales to those engaged in military activities, and on January 20, 1942, it established a system of priorities restricting sales to persons having preferential ratings of A-1-j or higher. On March 10, 1942, defendant explained the effect of these restrictions on his business to one of the plaintiffs authorized to act for the others, who orally waived the restrictions in the lease as to use and subleasing and offered to reduce the rent if defendant should be unable to operate profitably. Nevertheless defendant vacated the premises on March 15, 1942, giving oral notice of repudiation of the lease to plaintiffs, which was followed by a written notice on March 24, 1942. Plaintiffs affirmed in writing on March 26th their oral waiver and, failing to persuade defendant to perform his obligations, they rented the property to other tenants pursuant to their powers under the lease in order to mitigate damages. On May 11, 1942, plaintiffs brought this action praying for declaratory relief to determine their rights under the lease, and for judgment for unpaid rent. Following a trial on the merits, the court found that the leased premises were located on one of the main traffic arteries of Los Angeles County; that they were equipped with gasoline pumps and in general adapted for the maintenance of an automobile service station; that they contained a one-story storeroom adapted to many commercial purposes; that plaintiffs had waived the restrictions in the lease and granted defendant the right to use the premises for any legitimate purpose and to sublease to any responsible party; that defendant continues to carry on the business of selling and servicing automobiles at two other places. Defendant testified that at one of these locations he sold new automobiles exclusively and when asked if he were aware that many new automobile dealers were continuing in business replied: "Sure. It is just the location that I couldn't make a go, though, of automobiles." Although there was no finding to that effect, defendant estimated in response to inquiry by his counsel, that 90 per cent of his gross volume of business was new car sales and 10 per cent gasoline sales. The trial court held that war conditions had not terminated defendant's obligations under the lease and gave judgment for plaintiffs, declaring the lease as modified by plaintiffs' waiver to be in full force and effect, and ordered defendant to pay the unpaid rent with interest, less amounts received by plaintiffs from re- renting. Defendant brought this appeal, contending that the purpose for which the premises were leased was frustrated by the restrictions placed on the sale of new automobiles by the federal government, thereby terminating his duties under the lease.

Although commercial frustration was first recognized as an excuse for nonperformance of a contractual duty by the courts of England (Krell v. Henry [1903] 2 K.B. 740 [C.A.]; [Citations omitted]) its soundness has been questioned by those courts (see Maritime National Fish, Ltd., v. Ocean Trawlers, Ltd. [1935] A.C. 524, 528-29, 56 L.Q.Rev. 324, arguing that Krell v. Henry, supra, was a misapplication of Taylor v. Caldwell, 3 B.&S 826 [1863], the leading case on impossibility as an excuse for nonperformance), and they have refused to apply the doctrine to leases on the ground that an estate is conveyed to the lessee, which carries with it all risks [Citations omitted] but the modern cases have recognized that the defense may be available in a proper case, even in a lease. As the author declares in 6 Williston, Contracts (rev. ed. 1938), § 1955, pp. 5485-87, "The fact that lease is a conveyance and not simply a continuing contract and the numerous authorities enforcing liability to pay rent in spite of destruction of leased premises, however, have made it difficult to give relief. That the tenant has been relieved, nevertheless, in several cases indicates the gravitation of the law toward a recognition of the principle that fortuitous destruction of the value of performance wholly outside the contemplation of the parties may excuse a promisor even in a lease. ...

"Even more clearly with respect to leases than in regard to ordinary contracts the applicability of the doctrine of frustration depends on the total or nearly total destruction of the purpose for which, in the contemplation of both parties, the transaction was entered into."

The principles of frustration have been repeatedly applied to leases by the courts of this state [Citations omitted] and the question is whether the excuse for nonperformance is applicable under the facts of the present case.

Although the doctrine of frustration is akin to the doctrine of impossibility of performance (see Civ. Code, § 1511; 6 Cal.Jur. 435-450; 4 Cal.Jur. Ten-year Supp.

187-192; Taylor v. Caldwell, supra) since both have developed from the commercial necessity of excusing performance in cases of extreme hardship, frustration is not a form of impossibility even under the modern definition of that term, which includes not only cases of physical impossibility but also cases of extreme impracticability of performance [Citations omitted] Performance remains possible but the expected value of performance to the party seeking to be excused has been destroyed by a fortuitous event, which supervenes to cause an actual but not literal failure of consideration (Krell v. Henry, supra; Blakely v. Muller, supra; Marks Realty Co. v. Hotel Hermitage Co., 170 App.Div. 484 [156 N.Y.S. 179]; 6 Williston, op. Cit. Supra, §§ 1935, 1954, pp. 5477, 5480; Restatement, Contracts, § 288).

The question in cases involving frustration is whether the equities of the case, considered in the light of sound public policy, require placing the risk of a disruption or complete destruction of the contract equilibrium on defendant or plaintiff under the circumstances of a given case [Citations omitted], and the answer depends on whether an unanticipated circumstance, the risk of which should not be fairly thrown on the promisor, has made performance vitally different from what was reasonably to be expected (6 Williston, op.cit. supra, § 1963, p. 5511; Restatement, Contracts, § 454). The purpose of a contract is to place the risks of performance upon the promisor, and the relation of the parties, terms of the contract, and circumstances surrounding its formation must be examined to determine whether it can be fairly inferred that the risk of the event that has supervened to cause the alleged frustration was not reasonably foreseeable. If it was foreseeable there should have been provision for it in the contract, and the absence of such a provision gives rise to the inference that the risk was assumed.

The doctrine of frustration has been limited to cases of extreme hardship so that businessmen, who must make their arrangements in advance, can rely with certainty on their contracts (Anglo-Northern Trading Co. v. Emlyn Jones and Williams, 2 K.B. 78; 137 A.L.R. 1199, 1216-1221). The courts have required a promisor seeking to excuse himself from performance of his obligations to prove that the risk of the frustrating event was not reasonably foreseeable and that the value of counterperformance is totally or nearly totally destroyed, for frustration is no defense if it was foreseeable or controllable by the promisor, or if counterperformance remains valuable. (La Cumbre Golf & Country Club v. Santa Barbara Hotel Co., 205 Cal. 422, 425 [271 P. 476]; [Citations omitted]

Thus laws or other governmental acts that make performance unprofitable or more difficult or expensive do not excuse the duty to perform a contractual obligation [Citations omitted]

At the time the lease in the present case was executed the National Defense Act (Public Act No. 671 of the 76th Congress [54 Stats. 601], § 2A), approved June 28, 1940, authorizing the President to allocate materials and mobilize industry for national defense, had been law for more than a year. The automotive industry was in the process of conversion to supply the needs of our growing mechanized army and to meet lend-lease commitments. Iceland and Greenland had been occupied by the army. Automobile sales were soaring because the public anticipated that production would soon be restricted. These facts were commonly known and it cannot be said that the risk of war and its consequences necessitating restriction of the production and sale of automobiles was so remote a contingency that its risk could not be foreseen by defendant, an experienced automobile dealer. Indeed, the conditions prevailing at the time the lease was executed, and the absence of any provision in the lease contracting against the effect of war, gives rise to the inference that the risk was assumed. Defendant has therefore failed to prove that the possibility of war and its consequences on the production and sale of new automobiles was an unanticipated circumstance wholly outside the contemplation of the parties.

Nor has defendant sustained the burden of proving that the value of the lease has been destroyed. The sale of automobiles was not made impossible or illegal but merely restricted and if governmental regulation does not entirely prohibit the business to be carried on in the leased premises but only limits or restricts it, thereby making it less profitable and more difficult to continue, the lease is not terminated or the lessee excused from further performance [Citations omitted] Defendant may use the premises for the purpose for which they were leased. New automobiles and gasoline continue to be sold. Indeed, defendant testified that he continued to sell new automobiles exclusively at another location in the same county.

Defendant contends that the lease is restrictive and that the government orders therefore destroyed its value and frustrated its purpose. Provisions that prohibit subleasing or other uses than those specified affect the value of a lease and are to be considered in determining whether its purpose has been frustrated or its value destroyed (see Owens, The Effect of the War Upon the Rights and Liabilities of Parties to a Contract, 19 California State Bar Journal 132, 143). It must not be forgotten, however, that "The landlord has not covenanted that the tenant shall have the right to carry on the contemplated business or that the business to which the premises are by their nature or by the terms of the lease restricted shall be profitable enough to enable the tenant to pay the rent but has imposed a condition for his own benefit; and, certainly, unless and until he chooses to take advantage of it, the tenant is not deprived of the use of the premises." (6 Williston, Contracts, op. Cit. Supra, § 1955, p. 5485; see, also, People v. Klopstock, 24 Cal.2d 897, 901 [151 P.2d 641].)

In the present lease plaintiffs reserved the rights that defendant should not use the premises for other purposes than those specified in the lease or sublease without plaintiff's written consent. Far from preventing other uses or subleasing they waived these rights, enabling defendant to use the premises for any legitimate purpose and to sublease them to any responsible tenant. This waiver is significant in view of the location of the premises on a main traffic artery in Los Angeles County and their adaptability for many commercial purposes. The value of these rights is attested by the fact that the premises were rented soon after defendants vacated them. It is therefore clear that the governmental restrictions on the sale of new cars have not destroyed the value of the lease. Furthermore, plaintiffs offered to lower the rent if defendant should be unable to operate profitably, and their conduct was at all times fair and cooperative.

The consequences of applying the doctrine of frustration to a leasehold involving less than a total or nearly total destruction of the value of the leased premises would be undesirable. Confusion would result from different decisions purporting to define "substantial" frustration. Litigation would be encouraged by the repudiation of leases when lessees found their businesses less profitable because of the regulations attendant upon a national emergency. Many leases have been affected in varying degrees by the widespread governmental regulations necessitated by war conditions.

The cases that defendant relies upon are consistent with the conclusion reached herein. In Industrial Development & Land Co. v. Goldschmidt, supra, the lease provided that the premises should not be used other than as a saloon. When national prohibition made the sale of alcoholic beverages illegal, the court excused the tenant from further performance on the theory of illegality or impossibility by a change in domestic law. The doctrine of frustration might have been applied, since the purpose for which the property was leased was totally destroyed and there was nothing to show that the value of the lease was not thereby totally destroyed. In the present case the purpose was not destroyed but only restricted, and plaintiffs proved that the lease was valuable to defendant. In Grace v. Croninger, supra, the lease was for the purpose of conducting a "saloon and cigar store and for no other purpose" with provision for subleasing a portion of the premises for bootblack purposes. The monthly rental was $650. It was clear that prohibition destroyed the main purpose of the lease, but since the premises could be used for bootblack and cigar store purposes, the lessee was not excused from his duty to pay the rent. In the present case new automobiles and gasoline may be sold under the lease as executed and any legitimate business may be conducted or the premises may be subleased under the lease as modified by plaintiff's waiver. Colonial Operating Corp. v. Hannon Sales & Service, Inc., 34 N.Y.S.2d 116, was reversed in 265 App.Div. 411 [39 N.Y.S.2d 217, and Signal Land Corp. v. Loecher, 35 N.Y.S.2d 25; Schantz v. American Auto Supply Co., Inc., 178 Misc. 909 [36 N.Y.S.2d 747]; and Canrock Realty Corp. v. Vim Electric Co., Inc., 37 N.Y.S.2d 139, involved government orders that totally destroyed the possibility of selling the products for which the premises were leased. No case has been cited by defendant or disclosed by research in which an appellate court has excused a lessee from performance of his duty to pay rent when the purpose of the lease has not been totally destroyed or its accomplishment rendered extremely impracticable or where it has been shown that the lease remains valuable to the lessee.

The judgment is affirmed.

Questions

1. What is the court's view on the doctrine of frustration as it applies to leases?

2. How does the court define frustration in relation to impossibility of performance?

3. According to the court, what factors are considered when determining whether the doctrine of frustration applies?

4. Why does the court conclude that the risk of war and its consequences on the production and sale of new automobiles was reasonably foreseeable?

5. How does the court distinguish the present case from cases where the doctrine of frustration was applied to excuse nonperformance of a contractual obligation?

Takeaways – Lloyd v. Murphy

For performance to be excused under the doctrine of frustration, the frustration must be total or substantial. Partial frustration is not enough. Why was the car dealer's hardship not extreme enough to excuse him from the duty to perform?

20th Century Lites, Inc. v. Goodman
California Superior Court, Appellate Department, 1944
64 Cal.App.2d Supp. 938

KINCAID, J. This appeal arises out of an action commenced by plaintiff to recover certain monthly payments claimed due under a written contract whereby plaintiff leased neon sign installations to defendant in consideration of agreed payments to be made by defendant for the contractual period. The defendant, among other defenses, alleges that by reason of the governmental order of August 5, 1942, prohibiting the illumination of all outside neon or lighting equipment between the hours of sunset and sunrise, he has been prevented, without fault on his part, from using such installations during the nighttime, and that such use was the desired object and effect contemplated by the parties at the time of the execution of the contract.

The lease contract of September 3, 1941, is one wherein plaintiff retains the title to the neon signs and tubing which it installed and maintained on the exterior of defendant's "drive-in" restaurant. The court found from the evidence that the parties had each performed all terms and conditions of the contract to August 4, 1942; that on August 5, 1942, the Government of the United States, as an emergency war measure, ordered a cessation of all outside lighting, including neon illuminated signs, at all hours between sunset and sunrise, covering the district in which defendant's place of business is located; that said proclamation of cessation has, during all the time in question, remained in full force and effect, and that, because of this fact, the defendant has been prevented from illuminating such signs during such hours; that subsequent to August 5, 1942, defendant offered to surrender to plaintiff such contract, to terminate same, and to permit plaintiff to remove such signs, but plaintiff refused to accept the offer and thereafter, beginning September 1, 1942, defendant failed to pay the monthly rental payments in the contract set forth.

The trial court properly concluded and found that, by reason of such governmental proclamation, the desired object or effect that the parties to the contract intended to attain at the time it was entered into, was frustrated without the fault of either party on and after August 5, 1942, and that defendant was harmed thereby. It further found that on and after said date both parties to said contract were excused from any further performance of any one of the terms or conditions thereof, and that said contract thereupon terminated.

The legal principles which are here applicable are set forth in the case of Johnson v. Atkins (1942), 53 Cal.App.2d 430, 433 [127 P.2d 1027], wherein the court quotes with approval from Restatement of the Law of Contracts, section 288, as follows: "'Where the assumed possibility of a desired object or effect to be attained by either party to a contract forms the basis on which both parties enter into it, and this object or effect is or surely will be frustrated, a promisor who is without fault in causing the frustration, and who is harmed thereby, is discharged from the duty of performing his promise unless a contrary intention appears.'" To the same general effect such decision further quotes (p. 434), from 13 Corpus Juris 642: "'Where from the nature of the contract it is evident that the parties contracted on the basis of the continued existence of the person or thing, condition or state of things, to which it relates, the subsequent perishing of the person or thing, or cessation of existence of the condition, will excuse the performance, a condition to such effect being implied, in spite of the fact that the promise may have been unqualified.'" These principles are apparently recognized by Civil Code, section 1511, subdivision 1. Among the California cases in support thereof are Johnson v. Atkins (supra); H. Hackfeld & Co. v. Castle (1921), 186 Cal. 53 [198 P. 1041]; and La Cumbre G. & Co. Club v. Santa Barbara Hotel Co. (1928), 205 Cal. 422 [271 P. 476].

Plaintiff contends that the foregoing principles of law, which have been called the doctrine of commercial frustration, are inapplicable under the terms and conditions of the contract made by the parties herein; that the contractual provisions for block lettering of the signs, thus making them visible in the daytime when they are not illuminated, and the availability of the illumination of the sign during daylight as well as dark hours, demonstrate that there has been no destruction of the subject matter of the contract and that the desired object was not completely frustrated. It argues that the enforced termination of illumination of the signs during the night hours caused only a condition rendering the transaction less attractive and less profitable to defendant.

In considering the soundness of plaintiff's position, it is first necessary to examine the contract in order to ascertain the nature of the "desired object or effect to be attained" by the transaction which the agreement represents. The contract describes the thing leased to defendant as an "electrical advertising display." The defendant is required to use it at his place of business and not elsewhere. Ordinarily, words of a contract are to be understood in their ordinary or popular sense. (Civ. Code, § 1644.) Webster's New International Dictionary defines the noun "display" as "An opening or unfolding; exhibition; manifestation. Ostentatious show; exhibition for effect; parade." When qualified by the adjective "electrical" it becomes an electrical exhibition or electrical manifestation. In order to be an electrical display, it must use electricity, in which event it then becomes illuminated and is an "electrical advertising display." Unelectrified, it is merely a display. While illuminated, it would remain as a sign, still it would not be the "electrical advertising display" which the contract called for and which manifestly was the "desired object or effect to be attained."

The contract is silent as to what hours of the day or night the signs were to be illuminated, although it requires the use of the "electrical advertising display" for a period of thirty-six months. The absence from the contract of any provision fixing hours of the day or night during which the sign is to be illuminated does not create an uncertainty. The parol evidence was inadmissible for the purpose of interpreting any such claimed uncertainty, but it was properly admitted to show a state of facts to which the doctrine of commercial frustration was applicable. The cases do not hold that such facts must appear on the face of the contract, and the purpose of proving them is not to vary the terms of the contract itself, but to show that a state of facts has arisen which results in its termination. The evidence is admissible, not for the purpose of inserting in the contract a provision requiring the defendant to use the sign at night or forbidding him to use it at any other time, but only to show that its illumination at night was the desired object to be obtained by the parties, and that the possibility of such illumination formed the basis on which both parties entered into the contract.

The defendant testified that he had never at any time illuminated the signs in the daytime, and that at the time of his negotiations with plaintiff's representative for such signs defendant advised plaintiff that he was interested in a neon sign for nighttime illumination for his place of business, which he needed because he was "blocked off more or less on a side street." Plaintiff's agent then demonstrated a tube which he said was a much larger and brighter neon tube than the ordinary one, and that by installing it in the tower of the building, it would give illumination at night from a great distance and would bring traffic into his place. Such a tube was ultimately installed as a part of the display.

It is apparent, therefore, that the "desired object or effect to be obtained" by defendant in his hiring of the "electrical advertising display" was the dual purpose of illuminating the exterior of his place of business at night, and the advertising thereof by means of the electrically illuminated signs during the nighttime, whereby passing trade would be notified of the presence of his place of business and would be attracted thereto. The merely incidental facts, that it remained physically possible to illuminate the display with electricity in the daytime and the signs were visible even though unlighted during the daylight hours, are of such inconsequential moment as to have no effect on the application of the rule.

When considered with the fact that all of such neon installations were on the exterior of the building, the required termination of the use of electricity in such signs, between the hours of sunset and sunrise, constituted a "cessation of existence of the condition" which was the "desired object or effect" and was the essential, primary and principal basis for which the signs were rented. The court's finding that such were the facts is substantially supported by the evidence.

We cannot agree with plaintiff's contention that the doctrine of commercial frustration may not be applied unless the defendant can show that the legal prohibition of the use to which the electrical equipment may be put was complete and that such use was entirely prevented for any purpose permitted under the contract of letting. The weight of authority in the United States is to the contrary, and is to the effect that such doctrine may be invoked whenever official governmental action prevents the hirer from using the property for the primary and principal purpose for which it was hired. In such event the contract of hiring is terminated even though other incidental uses might remain available for the thing hired.

Such governmental proclamation having, without the fault of either party to the contract, frustrated the "desired object or effect to be obtained," the doctrine of commercial frustration is applied through the means of implying a condition to exist in the contract whereby under such circumstances as are here found, the parties shall be excused from any further performance of its terms. This rule is cited in Johnson v. Atkins (supra, p. 431), wherein an excerpt from the case of Straus v. Kazemekas, 100 Conn. 581 [124 A. 234, 238] is quoted as follows: "'Where from the nature of the contract and the surrounding circumstances the parties from the beginning must have known that it could not be fulfilled unless when the time for fulfillment arrived, some particular thing or condition of things continued to exist so that they must be deemed, when entering into the contract, to have contemplated such continuing existence as the foundation of what was to be done; in the absence of any express or implied warranty that such thing or condition of things shall exist the contract is to be construed as subject to an implied condition that the parties shall be excused in case, before breach, performance becomes impossible or the purpose of the contract frustrated from such thing or condition ceasing to exist without default of either of the parties. 12 A.L.R. 1275.'"

The lease contract herein contains no provisions with regard to the contingencies here considered. The right to illuminate the signs at night being the primary foundation essential to the desirability and usefulness of the contract, the termination of that right under the conditions here found results in a situation wherein the contract must be deemed subject to the implied condition that the parties had in mind, at the inception of the contract, that such primary foundation should be continuing in existence. Such being the case the trial court properly held that from and after August 5, 1942, the contract was terminated and both parties thereto were excused from further performance.

Plaintiff argues that, even conceding the facts above referred to as being true, the doctrine of commercial frustration cannot be invoked in this case, because of the fact that it has been put to an expense in manufacturing and installing the signs; that the termination of the contract on such grounds would violate the principles of equity. It relies strongly on the case of San Joaquin L. & P. Corp. v. Costaloupes (1929), 96 Cal.App. 322 [274 P. 84], in support of this contention. The latter case may be distinguished from the one here under consideration, as the court there held the contract to be one to deliver electrical energy to a certain described piece of land irrespective of its use. Although a fire had destroyed the factory wherein it had been contemplated that the electricity would be used, the court said (p. 327): "All that appears here is that by reason of the premises the defendants could not use any more power or light in these particular buildings, but if at any time they chose to rebuild or make other use or application of the light and power they could have enforced their right of delivery of electrical energy." This is a vastly different situation than is presented by the contract and the facts of our case. Here, the plaintiff agreed to furnish an "electrical advertising display" which contemplated its being continuously operatable by electrified illumination at night. Furthermore, the defendant was not in the position of the user of electricity in the cited case, in that he could not relieve his situation by any voluntary act of his own, such as rebuilding his factory or making other use of the hired product. The facts herein are such as to prohibit the application of this exception to the general rule.

The defendant, by way of petition for rehearing, for the first time advanced the proposition that, because of the governmental order of November 1, 1943, abolishing the dim-out requirements, the effect of such dim-out regulation was to merely suspend, rather than terminate, the contract during the approximately fourteen months' existence of such regulation. Rehearing was granted, and this proposition was argued and considered.

Such is not the rule in cases where the doctrine of commercial frustration applies. On the application of such doctrine, the promisor "is discharged from the duty of performing his promise ..." (Johnson v. Atkins, supra, p. 434.) (Italics added.) On page 433, we find, "... such a frustration brings the contract to an end forthwith, without more and automatically."

This rule has been recognized by the United States Supreme Court in the case of Allanwilde Transport Corp. v. Vacuum Oil Co. (1918), 248 U.S. 377 [39 S.Ct. 147,

63 L.Ed. 312], where it was urged that the government's embargo on ships leaving American ports during a part of World War I, because of the enemy submarine menace, constituted but a temporary impediment, and therefore did not terminate the contract. In holding to the contrary, the court said: "The duration was of indefinite extent. Necessarily, the embargo would be continued as long as the cause of its imposition,-- that is, the submarine menace,--and that, as far as then could be inferred, would be the duration of the war, of which there could be no estimate or reliable speculation. The condition was, therefore, so far permanent as naturally and justifiably to determine business judgment and action depending upon it."

The cases where the doctrine of commercial frustration, with its immediate termination of the obligations of the promisor applies, are to be distinguished from that type of case wherein such doctrine is inapplicable and the governmental embargo or regulation is not a permanent prohibition but is temporary only. The case of United States Trading Corp. v. Newmark G. Co. (1922), 56 Cal.App. 176, 186 [205 P. 29], is of the latter class, and does not conflict with the rule heretofore enunciated.

The judgment is affirmed, respondent to recover his costs of appeal.

Questions

1. Why did the court consider the termination of the right to illuminate the signs at night as a "cessation of existence of the condition?"

2. What is the doctrine of commercial frustration, and how did the court apply it in this case?

3. Can the doctrine of commercial frustration be invoked when official governmental action prevents the hirer from using the property for its primary and principal purpose?

4. Why did the court reject the argument that the doctrine of commercial frustration should not apply because the plaintiff had incurred expenses in manufacturing and installing the signs?

Takeaways - 20th Century Lites

Although the doctrines of frustration and impossibility are akin, frustration is not a form of impracticability of performance. It more properly relates to the consideration for performance. Under it, performance remains possible, but is excused whenever a fortuitous event supervenes to cause a failure of the consideration or a practically total destruction of the expected value of the performance. (*20th Century Lites, Inc. v. Goodman, supra*; Rest,2d § 265)

Swift Canadian Co. v. Banet
United States Court of Appeals, Third Circuit, 1955
224 F.2d 36

GOODRICH, Circuit Judge. This is an action on the part of a seller of goods to recover against the buyer for breach of contract. In the trial court each party, following the filing of a stipulation of facts, moved for summary judgment. The court granted the motion of the defendant. Plaintiff here says that it should have had the summary judgment or, at the worst, that the case should be remanded for trial on the facts.

The one point presented is both interesting and elusive. The seller is a Canadian corporation. It entered into an agreement with defendant buyers who do business as Keystone Wool Pullers in Philadelphia. By this contract Keystone agreed to purchase a quantity of lamb pelts at a stipulated price. Part of the quantity was delivered on board railroad cars at Toronto and shipped to Keystone in Philadelphia. On or about March 12, 1952, Swift advised Keystone of its readiness to deliver the remaining pelts to the buyer on board railroad cars in Toronto for shipment to Philadelphia. The parties have stipulated that on or about that day the government of the United States by its agency, the Bureau of Animal Industry, had issued stricter regulations for the importation of lamb pelts into the United States. The parties have stipulated that "pursuant to these regulations, the importation into the United States of these lamb pelts by Keystone was prevented." They have also stipulated that for the reasons just stated Keystone then and thereafter refused to accept delivery of the pelts and the loading and shipment of the car did not occur.

From an inspection of the contract made between the parties it appears that the seller agreed to sell the pelts:

"all at $3.80 each U. S. Funds F. O. B. Toronto."

Below this an approximate time was stipulated for shipment and then there were shipping directions in the following form:

"Note .... Frankford Via: Buffalo-Penna. R. R. to

~~Broad & Washington Ave~~.

Freight Sta. Penna. R. R. Delivery."

Following this appears the terms and method of payment.

Two additional conditions of sale should be stated. There was a provision that neither party is to be liable for "orders or acts of any government or governmental agency . . ." And there was a provision that "when pelts are sold F.O.B. seller's plant title and risk of loss shall pass to buyer when product is loaded on cars at seller's plant."

The one question in this case is the legal effect of this agreement between the parties. If the seller's obligation was performed when it delivered, or offered to deliver, the pelts to the railroad company in Toronto, we think it is entitled to recovery. If the seller did fulfill its obligation, when it did so deliver, of course it is clear that when it failed to load the pelts because the buyer had signified his refusal to accept them, the seller may assert the same rights as though he had loaded them. A party is not obligated to do the vain thing of performing, assuming that he is ready to perform, when the other party has given notice of refusal to accept performance. 3 Williston on Sales, § 586 (Rev. ed., 1948); Restatement, Contracts, §§ 280, 306; Leonard Seed Co. v. Lustig Burgerhoff Co., 1923, 81 Pa. Super. 499. See also Uniform Commercial Code, § 2-610(c); Pa.Stat.Ann. tit. 12A, § 2-610(c) (1954).

The argument for the buyer must rest on the fact that the shipping directions in the contract showed that what the parties had in mind was such kind of performance by the seller as would start the goods to the buyer in Philadelphia. This, coupled with the stipulation that, in consequence of the stiffening of federal regulations, "the importation into the United States of these lamb pelts by Keystone was prevented," forms the basis for the argument that the carrying out of the agreement was prevented by governmental agency and the buyer is therefore excused.

The validity of this argument depends upon what effect we give to a provision for shipment of the goods to the buyer via Pennsylvania R. R., destination Philadelphia. We do not think that this is any more than a shipping direction which the buyer could have changed to any other destination in the world had it so desired. Suppose the buyer had found that it wanted the goods in New York, could it not have directed such a change in destination without any violation of the contract? Could the seller have insisted that it would ship to Philadelphia and nowhere else? We think that authority in general regards these shipping directions as simply inserted for the convenience of the buyer and subject to change by him. Dwight v. Eckert, 1888, 117 Pa. 490, 12 A. 32; Hocking v. Hamilton, 1893, 158 Pa. 107, 27 A. 836; Richter v. Zoccoli, 1930, 150 A. 1, 8 N.J.Misc. 289; 1 & 2 Williston on Sales, §§ 190, 457 (Rev. ed., 1948). See also Uniform Commercial Code, § 2-319(3); Pa.Stat. Ann. tit. 12A, § 2-319(3) (1954).

If the contract in this case had called for performance "F.O.B. seller's plant" a provision of the contract itself would clearly have indicated when the seller's responsibility was finished and the buyer's had begun. Here the provision in the earlier part of the contract was simply "F.O.B. Toronto" and it was not specifically provided that the sale was delivery at the seller's plant. We think the provision shows what the parties means by "F.O.B." and can see no difference, so far as this expressed meaning goes, between F.O.B. at seller's plant and F.O.B. Toronto.

The general rule on this subject is pretty clear. Williston points out that when goods are delivered "free on board" pursuant to contract the presumption is that the property passes thereupon. Williston on Sales, § 280(b) (Rev. ed., 1948). It is agreed that this is a presumption and that the phrase F.O.B. is not one of iron-clad meaning. Seabrook Farms Co. v. Commodity Credit Corp., 206 F.2d 93 (C.A. 3, 1953). There is nothing in this case, however, to counteract the effect of such a presumption. When the shipper had made his delivery he was to send bill of lading and draft through a Philadelphia bank. His part of the agreement would have been fully performed when the goods were delivered F.O.B. at Toronto. We think both the risk of loss and the possibility of profit if the market advanced, were in the buyer from then on. Even if the goods could not be imported into the United States under the then existing regulations, the rest of the world was free to the buyer, so far as we know, as destination for the shipment. If he did not care to accept them under the circumstances and his expectation of a profitable transaction was disappointed, nevertheless, the seller having performed or being ready, able and willing to perform, was entitled to the value of his bargain. . . .

The judgment of the district court will be reversed with instructions to enter judgment for the plaintiff for the difference between the contract price and the price at which the goods were sold.

Questions

1. Explain the buyer's argument for why the agreement was prevented by a governmental agency and why it should excuse the buyer from performing.

2. How did the court interpret the shipping directions in the contract? Was the buyer obligated to receive the goods only in Philadelphia?

3. What does "F.O.B." mean in the context of this case, and why was it significant in determining the passing of property and risk of loss?

Takeaways – Swift Canadian Co. v. Banet

Make sure you understand why the buyer's obligation to pay for the pelts was not excused by the court. The contract provided that the sale was "F.O.B. Toronto," UCC § 2-319(b) provides when the term is F.O.B. the place of destination, the seller must at their own expense and risk transport the goods to that place and tender delivery of them. In the absence of some contractual restriction, the purchaser may dispose of the goods in any manner after that point. Once the seller delivered the pelts to the F.O.B. Toronto destination, the seller had fulfilled all of its obligations. Once the purchaser took possession of the goods in Toronto the seller did not assume responsibility for the purchaser's ability (or inability) to ship the goods to any particular location beyond that. Even though one particular resale may have been frustrated, the purchaser was free to sell the goods elsewhere.

Chase Precast v. John J. Paonessa Co.
Supreme Judicial Court of Massachusetts, 1991
409 Mass. 371, 566 N.E.2d 603

LYNCH, J. This appeal raises the question whether the doctrine of frustration of purpose may be a defense in a breach of contract action in Massachusetts, and, if so, whether it excuses the defendant John J. Paonessa Company, Inc. (Paonessa), from performance.

The claim of the plaintiff, Chase Precast Corporation (Chase), arises from the cancellation of its contracts with Paonessa to supply median barriers in a highway reconstruction project of the Commonwealth. Chase brought an action to recover its anticipated profit on the amount of median barriers called for by its supply contracts with Paonessa but not produced. Paonessa brought a cross action against the Commonwealth for indemnification in the event it should be held liable to Chase. After a jury-waived trial, a Superior Court judge ruled for Paonessa on the basis of impossibility of performance.[2] Chase and Paonessa cross appealed. The Appeals Court affirmed, noting that the doctrine of frustration of purpose more accurately described the basis of the trial judge's decision than the doctrine of impossibility. Chase Precast Corp. v. John J. Paonessa Co., 28 Mass. App. Ct. 639 (1990). We agree. We allowed Chase's application for further appellate review, and we now affirm.

The pertinent facts are as follows. In 1982, the Commonwealth, through the Department of Public Works (department), entered into two contracts with Paonessa for resurfacing and improvements to two stretches of Route 128. Part of each contract called for replacing a grass median strip between the north and southbound lanes with concrete surfacing and precast concrete median barriers. Paonessa entered into two contracts with Chase under which Chase was to supply, in the aggregate, 25,800 linear feet of concrete median barriers according to the specifications of the department for highway construction. The quantity and type of barriers to be supplied were specified in two purchase orders prepared by Chase.

The highway reconstruction began in the spring of 1983. By late May, the department was receiving protests from angry residents who objected to use of the concrete median barriers and removal of the grass median strip. Paonessa and Chase became aware of the protest around June 1. On June 6, a group of about 100 citizens filed an action in the Superior Court to stop installation of the concrete median barriers and other aspects of the work. On June 7, anticipating modification by the department, Paonessa notified Chase by letter to stop producing concrete barriers for the projects. Chase did so upon receipt of the letter the following day. On June 17, the department and the citizens' group entered into a settlement which provided, in part, that no additional concrete median barriers would be installed. On June 23, the department deleted the permanent concrete median barriers item from its contracts with Paonessa.

Before stopping production on June 8, Chase had produced approximately one-half of the concrete median barriers called for by its contracts with Paonessa, and had delivered most of them to the construction sites. Paonessa paid Chase for all that it had produced, at the contract price. Chase suffered no out-of-pocket expense as a result of cancellation of the remaining portion of barriers.

This court has long recognized and applied the doctrine of impossibility as a defense to an action for breach of contract. See, e.g., Boston Plate & Window Glass Co. v. John Bowen Co., 335 Mass. 697 (1957); Baetjer v. New England Alcohol Co., 319 Mass. 592 (1946); Butterfield v. Byron, 153 Mass. 517 (1891). Under that doctrine, "where from the nature of the contract it appears that the parties must from the beginning have contemplated the continued existence of some particular specified thing as the foundation of what was to be done, then, in the absence of any warranty that the thing shall exist ... the parties shall be excused ... [when] performance becomes impossible from the accidental perishing of the thing without the fault of either party." Boston Plate & Window Glass Co., supra at 700, quoting Hawkes v. Kehoe, 193 Mass. 419, 423 (1907).

On the other hand, although we have referred to the doctrine of frustration of purpose in a few decisions, we have never clearly defined it. See Mishara Constr. Co. v. Transit-Mixed Concrete Corp., 365 Mass. 122, 128-129 (1974); Essex-Lincoln Garage, Inc. v. Boston, 342 Mass. 719, 721-722 (1961); Baetjer v. New England Alcohol Co., supra at 602. Other jurisdictions have explained the doctrine as follows: when an event neither anticipated nor caused by either party, the risk of which was not allocated by the contract, destroys the object or purpose of the contract, thus destroying the value of performance, the parties are excused from further performance. See Howard v. Nicholson, 556 S.W.2d 477, 482 (Mo. Ct. App. 1977); Perry v. Champlain Oil Co., 101 N.H. 97 (1957); Lloyd v. Murphy, 25 Cal.2d 48 (1944).

In Mishara Constr. Co., supra at 129, we called frustration of purpose a "companion rule" to the doctrine of impossibility. Both doctrines concern the effect of supervening circumstances upon the rights and duties of the parties. The difference lies in the effect of the supervening event. Under frustration, "[p]erformance remains possible but the expected value of performance to the party seeking to be excused has been destroyed by [the] fortuitous event.... Lloyd v. Murphy, supra at 53. The principal question in both kinds of cases remains "whether an unanticipated circumstance, the risk of which should not fairly be thrown on the promisor, has made performance vitally different from what was reasonably to be expected." See Lloyd, supra at 54 (frustration); Mishara Constr. Co., supra at 129 (impossibility).

Since the two doctrines differ only in the effect of the fortuitous supervening event, it is appropriate to look to our cases dealing with impossibility for guidance in treating the issues that are the same in a frustration of purpose case. The trial judge's findings with regard to those issues are no less pertinent to application of the frustration defense because they were considered relevant to the defense of impossibility.

Another definition of frustration of purpose is found in the Restatement (Second) of Contracts § 265 (1981):

"Where, after a contract is made, a party's principal purpose is substantially frustrated without his fault by the occurrence of an event the non-occurrence of which was a basic assumption on which the contract was made, his remaining duties to render performance are discharged, unless the language or the circumstances indicate the contrary.

This definition is nearly identical to the defense of "commercial impracticability," found in the Uniform Commercial Code, G.L.c. 106, § 2-615 (1988 ed.), which this court, in Mishara Constr. Co., supra at 127-128, held to be consistent with the common law of contracts regarding impossibility of performance. It follows, therefore, that the Restatement's formulation of the doctrine is consistent with this court's previous treatment of impossibility of performance and frustration of purpose.

Paonessa bore no responsibility for the department's elimination of the median barriers from the projects. Therefore, whether it can rely on the defense of frustration turns on whether elimination of the barriers was a risk allocated by the contracts to Paonessa. Mishara Constr. Co., supra at 129, articulates the relevant test:

"The question is, given the commercial circumstances in which the parties dealt: Was the contingency which developed one which the parties could reasonably be thought to have foreseen as a real possibility which could affect performance? Was it one of that variety of risks which the parties were tacitly assigning to the promisor by their failure to provide for it explicitly? If it was, performance will be required. If it could not be so considered, performance is excused."

This is a question for the trier of fact. Id. At 127, 130.

Paonessa's contracts with the department contained a standard provision allowing the department to eliminate items or portions of work found unnecessary. The purchase order agreements between Chase and Paonessa do not contain a similar provision. This difference in the contracts does not mandate the conclusion that Paonessa assumed the risk of reduction in the quantity of the barriers. It is implicit in the judge's findings that Chase knew the barriers were for department projects. The record supports the conclusion that Chase was aware of the department's power to decrease quantities of contract items. The judge found that Chase had been a supplier of median barriers to the department in the past. The provision giving the department the power to eliminate items or portions thereof was standard in its contracts. See Standard Specifications for Highways and Bridges, Commonwealth of Massachusetts Department of Public Works § 4.06 (1973). The judge found that Chase had furnished materials under and was familiar with the so-called "Unit Price Philosophy" in the construction industry, whereby contract items are paid for at the contract unit price for the quantity of work actually accepted. Finally, the judge's finding that "[a]ll parties were well aware that lost profits were not an element of damage in either of the public works projects in issue" further supports the conclusion that Chase was aware of the department's power to decrease quantities, since the term prohibiting claims for anticipated profit is part of the same sentence in the standard provision as that allowing the engineer to eliminate items or portions of work.

In Mishara Constr. Co., supra at 130, we held that, although labor disputes in general cannot be considered extraordinary, whether the parties in a particular case intended performance to be carried out, even in the face of a labor difficulty, depends on the facts known to the parties at the time of contracting with respect to the history of and prospects for labor difficulties. In this case, even if the parties were aware generally of the department's power to eliminate contract items, the judge could reasonably have concluded that they did not contemplate the cancellation for a major portion of the project of such a widely used item as concrete median barriers, and did not allocate the risk of such cancellation.

Our opinion in Chicopee Concrete Serv., Inc. v. Hart Eng'g Co., 398 Mass. 476 (1986), does not lead to a different conclusion. Although we held there that a provision of a prime contract requiring city approval of subcontractors was not incorporated by reference into the subcontract, id. at 478, we nevertheless stated that, if the record had supported the conclusion that the subcontractor knew, or at least had notice of, the approval clause, the result might have been different. Id. At 478-479. . . .

Judgment affirmed.

Questions

1. How does the court differentiate between the doctrines of impossibility and frustration of purpose?

2. According to the court's decision, under what circumstances can the defense of frustration of purpose be invoked?

3. What factors did the court consider in determining whether Paonessa assumed the risk of reduction in the quantity of the barriers?

Takeaways – Chase Precast v. John J. Paonessa, Co.

Clearly frustration of purpose is a more accurate label for the defense argued in this case than impossibility of performance, since, as the lower court in this case pointed out, "[p]erformance was not literally impossible. Nothing prevented Paonessa from honoring its contract to purchase the remaining sections of median barrier, whether or not the [department] would approve their use in the road construction." 28 Mass. App. Ct. 639, 644 n. 5 (1990).

Northern Indiana Public Service Co. v. Carbon County Coal
United States Court of Appeals, Seventh Circuit, 1986
799 F.2d 265

POSNER, Circuit Judge. These appeals bring before us various facets of a dispute between Northern Indiana Public Service Company (NIPSCO), an electric utility in Indiana, and Carbon County Coal Company, a partnership that until recently owned and operated a coal mine in Wyoming. In 1978 NIPSCO and Carbon County signed a contract whereby Carbon County agreed to sell and NIPSCO to buy approximately 1.5 million tons of coal every year for 20 years, at a price of $24 a ton subject to various provisions for escalation which by 1985 had driven the price up to $44 a ton.

NIPSCO's rates are regulated by the Indiana Public Service Commission. In 1983 NIPSCO requested permission to raise its rates to reflect increased fuel charges. Some customers of NIPSCO opposed the increase on the ground that NIPSCO could reduce its overall costs by buying more electrical power from neighboring utilities for resale to its customers and producing less of its own power. Although the Commission granted the requested increase, it directed NIPSCO, in orders issued in December 1983 and February 1984 (the "economy purchase orders"), to make a good faith effort to find, and wherever possible buy from, utilities that would sell electricity to it at prices lower than its costs of internal generation. The Commission added ominously that "the adverse effects of entering into long-term coal supply contracts which do not allow for renegotiation and are not requirement contracts, is a burden which must rest squarely on the shoulders of NIPSCO management." Actually the contract with Carbon County did provide for renegotiation of the contract price--but one-way renegotiation in favor of Carbon County; the price fixed in the contract (as adjusted from time to time in accordance with the escalator provisions) was a floor. And the contract was indeed not a requirements contract: it specified the exact amount of coal that NIPSCO must take over the 20 years during which the contract was to remain in effect. NIPSCO was eager to have an assured supply of low-sulphur coal and was therefore willing to guarantee both price and quantity.

Unfortunately for NIPSCO, as things turned out it was indeed able to buy electricity at prices below the costs of generating electricity from coal bought under the contract with Carbon County; and because of the "economy purchase orders," of which it had not sought judicial review, NIPSCO could not expect to be allowed by the Public Service Commission to recover in its electrical rates the costs of buying coal from Carbon County. NIPSCO therefore decided to stop accepting coal deliveries from Carbon County, at least for the time being; and on April 24, 1985, it brought this diversity suit against Carbon County in a federal district court in Indiana, seeking a declaration that it was excused from its obligations under the contract either permanently or at least until the economy purchase orders ceased preventing it from passing on the costs of the contract to its ratepayers. In support of this position it argued that the contract violated section 2(c) of the Mineral Lands Leasing Act of 1920, 30 U.S.C. § 202, because of Carbon County's affiliation with a railroad (Union Pacific), and that in any event NIPSCO's performance was excused or suspended--either under the contract's force majeure clause or under the doctrines of frustration or impossibility--by reason of the economy purchase orders.

On May 17, 1985, Carbon County counterclaimed for breach of contract and moved for a preliminary injunction requiring NIPSCO to continue taking delivery under the contract. On June 19, 1985, the district judge granted the preliminary injunction, from which NIPSCO has appealed. Also on June 19, rejecting NIPSCO's argument that it needed more time for pretrial discovery and other trial preparations, the judge scheduled the trial to begin on August 26, 1985. Trial did begin then, lasted for six weeks, and resulted in a jury verdict for Carbon County of $181 million. The judge entered judgment in accordance with the verdict, rejecting Carbon County's argument that in lieu of damages it should get an order of specific performance requiring NIPSCO to comply with the contract. Upon entering the final judgment the district judge dissolved the preliminary injunction, and shortly afterward the mine--whose only customer was NIPSCO--shut down. NIPSCO has appealed from the damage judgment, and Carbon County from the denial of specific performance.

All that those orders [the forece majeure clause] do is tell NIPSCO it will not be allowed to pass on fuel costs to its ratepayers in the form of higher rates if it can buy electricity cheaper than it can generate electricity internally using Carbon County's coal. Such an order does not "prevent," whether wholly or in part, NIPSCO from using the coal; it just prevents NIPSCO from shifting the burden of its improvidence or bad luck in having incorrectly forecasted its fuel needs to the backs of the hapless ratepayers. The purpose of public utility regulation is to provide a substitute for competition in markets (such as the market for electricity) that are naturally monopolistic. Suppose the market for electricity were fully competitive, and unregulated. Then if NIPSCO signed a long-term fixed-price fixed-quantity contract to buy coal, and during the life of the contract competing electrical companies were able to produce and sell electricity at prices below the cost to NIPSCO of producing electricity from that coal, NIPSCO would have to swallow the excess cost of the coal. It could not raise its electricity prices in order to pass on the excess cost to its consumers, because if it did they would buy electricity at lower prices from NIPSCO's competitors. By signing the kind of contract it did, NIPSCO gambled that fuel costs would rise rather than fall over the life of the contract; for if they rose, the contract price would give it an advantage over its (hypothetical) competitors who would have to buy fuel at the current market price. If such a gamble fails, the result is not force majeure.

This is all the clearer when we consider that the contract price was actually fixed just on the downside; it put a floor under the price NIPSCO had to pay, but the escalator provisions allowed the actual contract prices to rise above the floor, and they did. This underscores the gamble NIPSCO took in signing the contract. It committed itself to paying a price at or above a fixed minimum and to taking a fixed quantity at that price. It was willing to make this commitment to secure an assured supply of low sulphur coal, but the risk it took was that the market price of coal or substitute fuels would fall. A force majeure clause is not intended to buffer a party against the normal risks of a contract. The normal risk of a fixed-price contract is that the market price will change. If it rises, the buyer gains at the expense of the seller (except insofar as escalator provisions give the seller some protection); if it falls, as here, the seller gains at the expense of the buyer. The whole purpose of a fixed-price contract is to allocate risk in this way. A force majeure clause interpreted to excuse the buyer from the consequences of the risk he expressly assumed would nullify a central term of the contract. . . .

The Indiana Public Service Commission is a surrogate for the forces of competition, and the economy fuel orders are a device for simulating the effects in a competitive market of a drop in input prices. The orders say to NIPSCO, in effect: "With fuel costs dropping, and thus reducing the costs of electricity to utilities not burdened by long-term fixed-price contracts, you had better substitute those utilities' electricity for your own when their prices are lower than your cost of internal generation. In a freely competitive market consumers would make that substitution; if you do not do so, don't expect to be allowed to pass on your inflated fuel costs to those consumers." Admittedly the comparison between competition and regulation is not exact. In an unregulated market, if fuel costs skyrocketed NIPSCO would have a capital gain from its contract (assuming the escalator provisions did not operate to raise the contract price by the full amount of the increase in fuel costs, a matter that would depend on the cause of the increase). This is because its competitors, facing higher fuel costs, would try to raise their prices for electricity, thus enabling NIPSCO to raise its price, or expand its output, or both, and thereby increase its profits. The chance of this "windfall" gain offsets, on an ex ante (before the fact) basis, the chance of a windfall loss if fuel costs drop, though NIPSCO it appears was seeking a secure source of low-sulphur coal rather than a chance for windfall gains. If as is likely the Public Service Commission would require NIPSCO to pass on any capital gain from an advantageous contract to the ratepayers (which is another reason for thinking NIPSCO wasn't after windfall gains--it would not, in all likelihood, have been allowed to keep them), then it ought to allow NIPSCO to pass on to them some of the capital loss from a disadvantageous contract--provided that the contract, when made, was prudent. Maybe it was not; maybe the risk that NIPSCO took was excessive. But all this was a matter between NIPSCO and the Public Service Commission, and NIPSCO did not seek judicial review of the economy purchase orders.

If the Commission had ordered NIPSCO to close a plant because of a safety or pollution hazard, we would have a true case of force majeure. As a regulated firm NIPSCO is subject to more extensive controls than unregulated firms and it therefore wanted and got a broadly worded force majeure clause that would protect it fully (hence the reference to partial effects) against government actions that impeded its using the coal. But as the only thing the Commission did was prevent NIPSCO from using its monopoly position to make consumers bear the risk that NIPSCO assumed when it signed a long-term fixed-price fuel contract, NIPSCO cannot complain of force majeure; the risk that has come to pass was one that NIPSCO voluntarily assumed when it signed the contract.

The district judge refused to submit NIPSCO's defenses of impracticability and frustration to the jury, ruling that Indiana law does not allow a buyer to claim impracticability and does not recognize the defense of frustration. . . .

Section 2-615 of the Uniform Commercial Code takes this approach. It provides that "delay in delivery ... by a seller ... is not a breach of his duty under a contract for sale if performance as agreed has been made impracticable by the occurrence of a contingency the non-occurrence of which was a basic assumption on which the contract was made...." Performance on schedule need not be impossible, only infeasible--provided that the event which made it infeasible was not a risk that the promisor had assumed. Notice, however, that the only type of promisor referred to is a seller; there is no suggestion that a buyer's performance might be excused by reason of impracticability. The reason is largely semantic. Ordinarily all the buyer has to do in order to perform his side of the bargain is pay, and while one can think of all sorts of reasons why, when the time came to pay, the buyer might not have the money, rarely would the seller have intended to assume the risk that the buyer might, whether through improvidence or bad luck, be unable to pay for the seller's goods or services. To deal with the rare case where the buyer or (more broadly) the paying party might have a good excuse based on some unforeseen change in circumstances, a new rubric was thought necessary, different from "impossibility" (the common law term) or "impracticability" (the Code term, picked up in Restatement (Second) of Contracts Sec. 261 (1979)), and it received the name "frustration." Rarely is it impracticable or impossible for the payor to pay; but if something has happened to make the performance for which he would be paying worthless to him, an excuse for not paying, analogous to impracticability or impossibility, may be proper. See Restatement, supra, Sec. 265, comment a.

The leading case on frustration remains Krell v. Henry, [1903] 2 K.B. 740 (C.A.). Krell rented Henry a suite of rooms for watching the coronation of Edward VII, but Edward came down with appendicitis and the coronation had to be postponed. Henry refused to pay the balance of the rent and the court held that he was excused from doing so because his purpose in renting had been frustrated by the postponement, a contingency outside the knowledge, or power to influence, of either party. The question was, to which party did the contract (implicitly) allocate the risk? Surely Henry had not intended to insure Krell against the possibility of the coronation's being postponed, since Krell could always relet the room, at the premium rental, for the coronation's new date. So Henry was excused.

NIPSCO is the buyer in the present case, and its defense is more properly frustration than impracticability; but the judge held that frustration is not a contract defense under the law of Indiana. He relied on an Indiana Appellate Court decision which indeed so states, Ross Clinic, Inc. v. Tabion, 419 N.E.2d 219, 223 (Ind.App.1981), but solely on the basis of an old decision of the Indiana Supreme Court, Krause v. Board of Trustees, 162 Ind. 278, 283-84, 70 N.E. 264, 265 (1904), that doesn't even discuss the defense of frustration and anyway precedes by years the recognition of the defense by American courts. At all events, the facts of the present case do not bring it within the scope of the frustration doctrine, so we need not decide whether the Indiana Supreme Court would embrace the doctrine in a suitable case.

For the same reason we need not decide whether a force majeure clause should be deemed a relinquishment of a party's right to argue impracticability or frustration, on the theory that such a clause represents the integrated expression of the parties' desires with respect to excuses based on supervening events; or whether such a clause either in general or as specifically worded in this case covers any different ground from these defenses; or whether a buyer can urge impracticability under section 2-615 of the Uniform Commercial Code, which applies to this suit. . . .

Whether or not Indiana recognizes the doctrine of frustration, and whether or not a buyer can ever assert the defense of impracticability under section 2-615 of the Uniform Commercial Code, these doctrines, so closely related to each other and to force majeure as well, see International Minerals & Chemical Corp. v. Llano, Inc., 770 F.2d 879, 885-87 (10th Cir. 1985), cannot help NIPSCO. All are doctrines for shifting risk to the party better able to bear it, either because he is in a better position to prevent the risk from materializing or because he can better reduce the disutility of the risk (as by insuring) if the risk does occur. . . .

Since impossibility and related doctrines are devices for shifting risk in accordance with the parties' presumed intentions, which are to minimize the costs of contract performance, one of which is the disutility created by risk, they have no place when the contract explicitly assigns a particular risk to one party or the other. As we have already noted, a fixed-price contract is an explicit assignment of the risk of market price increases to the seller and the risk of market price decreases to the buyer, and the assignment of the latter risk to the buyer is even clearer where, as in this case, the contract places a floor under price but allows for escalation. If, as is also the case here, the buyer forecasts the market incorrectly and therefore finds himself locked into a disadvantageous contract, he has only himself to blame and so cannot shift the risk back to the seller by invoking impossibility or related doctrines. See Farnsworth, supra, at 680 and n. 18; White & Summers, Handbook of the Law Under the Uniform Commercial Code 133 (2d ed. 1980). It does not matter that it is an act of government that may have made the contract less advantageous to one party. See, e.g., Connick v. Teachers Ins. & Annuity Ass'n, 784 F.2d 1018, 1022 (9th Cir. 1986); Waegemann v. Montgomery Ward & Co., 713 F.2d 452, 454 (9th Cir. 1983). Government these days is a pervasive factor in the economy and among the risks that a fixed-price contract allocates between the parties is that of a price change induced by one of government's manifold interventions in the economy. Since "the very purpose of a fixed price agreement is to place the risk of increased costs on the promisor (and the risk of decreased costs on the promisee)," the fact that costs decrease steeply (which is in effect what happened here--the cost of generating electricity turned out to be lower than NIPSCO thought when it signed the fixed-price contract with Carbon County) cannot allow the buyer to walk away from the contract. . . .[Affirmed]

Questions

1. According to the court's reasoning, why was the force majeure clause in the contract not applicable in this case?

2. Why did the court reject NIPSCO's defense of impracticability and frustration?

3. What was the rationale behind the court's explanation of the purpose of public utility regulation?

4. Why did the court conclude that the risk NIPSCO took when signing the contract was not a force majeure event?

Takeaways – Northern Indiana Public Service Corp.

Does UCC § 2-615 apply to both buyers and sellers?

As the court noted, NIPSCO's defense is more properly frustration than impracticability. Why is that so? (Compare Rest.2d § 261 with § 265.)

Remedies in the Event of Discharge

The general rule is that when a contract is discharged by impracticability or frustration of purpose, the parties must return any benefits that were conferred upon them. (Rest.2d § 377)

Young v. City of Chicopee
Supreme Judicial Court of Massachusetts, 1904
186 Mass. 518, 72 N.E. 63

This is an action to recover for work and materials furnished under a written contract, providing for the repair of a wooden bridge forming a part of the highway across the Connecticut River. While the work was in progress the [Mass. Page 519] bridge was totally destroyed by fire without the fault of either party, so that the contract could not be performed.

The specifications required that the timber and other woodwork of the carriage way, wherever decayed, should be replaced by sound material securely fastened, so that the way should be in a "complete and substantial condition." As full compensation both for work and materials the plaintiff was to receive a certain sum per thousand feet for the lumber used "on measurements made after laying and certified by both engineers," or, in other words, the amount of the plaintiff's compensation was measured by the number of feet of new material wrought into the bridge. That the public travel might not be interfered with more than was reasonably necessary, the contract provided that no work should be begun until material for at least one half of the repairs contemplated should be "upon the job." With this condition the plaintiff complied, the lumber, which at the time of the fire had not been used, being distributed "all along the bridge" and upon the river banks. Some of this lumber was destroyed by the fire.

At the trial the defendant did not dispute its liability to pay for the work done upon and materials wrought into the structure at the time of the fire; (Angus v. Scully,176 Mass. 357, and cases there cited;) and the only question before us is whether it was liable for the damage to the lumber which was distributed as above stated and had not been used.

It is to be noted that there had been no delivery of this lumber to the defendant. It was brought "upon the job" and kept there as the lumber of the plaintiff. The title to it was in him and not in the defendant. Nor did the defendant have any care or control over it. No part of it belonged to the defendant until wrought into the bridge. The plaintiff could have exchanged it for other lumber. If at any time during the progress of the work before the fire the plaintiff had refused to proceed, the defendant against his consent could not lawfully have used it. Indeed had it not been destroyed it would have remained the property of the plaintiff after the fire. Nor is the situation changed, so far as respects the question before us, by the fact that the lumber was brought there in compliance with the condition relating to the commencement of the work. This condition manifestly was inserted [Mass. Page 520] to insure the rapid progress of the work, and it has no material bearing upon the rights of the parties in relation to the lumber. It is also to be borne in mind in this connection that the compensation for the whole job was to be determined by the amount of lumber wrought into the bridge.

The contract was entire. By the destruction of the bridge each party was excused from further performance and the plaintiff could recover for partial performance. The principle upon which the plaintiff can do this is sometimes said to rest upon the doctrine that there is an implied contract upon the owner of the structure upon which the work is to be done that it shall continue to exist, and therefore, if it is destroyed, even without his fault, still he must be regarded as in default and so liable to pay for what has been done. [Citations omitted] In Butterfield v. Byron,153 Mass. 517, 523, it was said by Knowlton, J. that there was "an implied assumpsit for what has properly been done by either [of the parties], the law dealing with it as done at the request of the other, and creating a liability to pay for it its [N.E. Page 64] value." In whatever way the principle may be stated, it would seem that the liability of the owner in a case like this should be measured by the amount of the contract work done which, at the time of the destruction of the structure, had become so far identified with it as that but for the destruction it would have enured to him as contemplated by the contract.

In the present case the defendant, in accordance with this doctrine, should be held liable for the labor and materials actually wrought into the bridge. To that extent it insured the plaintiff. But it did not insure the plaintiff against the loss of lumber owned by him at the time of the fire, which had not then come into such relations with the bridge as, but for the fire, to enure to the benefit of the defendant as contemplated by the contract. The cases of Haynes v. Second Baptist Church, 88 Mo. 285, and Rawson v. Clark,70 Ill. 656, cited by the plaintiff, seem to us to be distinguishable from this case.

The exceptions therefore must be sustained and the verdict set aside. In accordance with the terms of the statement contained in the bill of exceptions, judgment should be entered for the plaintiff in the sum of $584 damages, and it is so ordered.

Questions

1. Explain the court's interpretation of the principle underlying the plaintiff's right to recover for partial performance despite the destruction of the bridge.

2. What condition in the contract did the plaintiff comply with to ensure the progress of the work? How did the court view this condition in relation to the rights of the

parties regarding the lumber?

3. In the court's view, what was the extent of the defendant's liability for the labor and materials in the bridge? How did this differ from the plaintiff's claim for the loss of lumber?

Takeaways – Young v. City of Chicopee

California Civil Code section 1514 provides that if performance is prevented by any cause excusing performance, other than the act of the creditor, the debtor is entitled to a ratable proportion of the consideration to which he or she would have been entitled upon full performance, according to the benefit which the creditor receives from the actual performance.

ASSESSMENT QUESTIONS, CHAPTER 9

1. Define the concept of impracticability of performance and discuss the requirements for establishing impracticability. Under what circumstances can a party claim impracticability as a defense?

2. Describe the impact of unforeseen events or supervening circumstances on the defense of impracticability of performance.

3. Discuss the concept of frustration of purpose and explain the requirements for establishing frustration. When can a party claim frustration of purpose as a defense?

4. Describe the difference between frustration of purpose and impracticability of performance as defenses in contract law. How do these defenses differ in their application?

5. Discuss the doctrine of foreseeability and its relevance to the defenses of impracticability and frustration. How does foreseeability impact the availability of this defense?

6. Explain the effect of a force majeure clause in a contract on the defense of impracticability or frustration of purpose. How does such a clause impact the parties' rights and obligations?

7. Describe the options available to a party who successfully invokes the defense of either impracticability or frustration of purpose. What remedies can they seek?

8. Discuss the principle of risk allocation in relation to impracticability of performance and frustration of purpose. How does risk allocation impact the availability of these defenses?

9. Describe the impact of temporary impossibility or temporary frustration on the parties' obligations. Can a contract be temporarily suspended or discharged due to these factors?

10. Discuss the effect of economic hardship or financial difficulty on the defense of impracticability of performance. Can a party be excused from performing under a contract if it becomes more difficult or expensive than anticipated?

Chapter 10
THIRD PARTY RIGHTS

Introduction

Parties to a contract are said to be in privity of contract. Can parties who are not in privity of contract ever have the right to enforce contractual promises made by the parties who are in privity? Can a party in privity transfer their right to receive the other party's performance to a non-party? Can a party who is in privity appoint a non-party to perform their contractual duties and obligations? These concepts will be examined in this chapter.

Third Party Beneficiary Contracts

A contract, made expressly for the benefit of a third person, may be enforced by him at any time before the parties thereto rescind it. (Cal.Civ. Code, § 1559)

Lawrence v. Fox
Court of Appeals of New York, 1859
20 N.Y. 268

[The transaction which gave rise to this case took place in the City of Buffalo on Canal Street which was: ". . . more than a street. It was the name of a district, a small and sinful neighborhood . . . . As late as the 1800's, there were 93 saloons there, among which were sprinkled 15 other dives known as concert halls plus sundry establishments designed to separate the sucker from his money as swiftly as possible, painlessly by preference, but painfully if necessary. . . . . It must have been an eternal mystery to the clergy and the good people of the town why the Lord never wiped out this 19th century example of Sodom and Gomorrah with a storm or a great wave from Lake Erie." (93 Harv. L.R. 1109, 1126) A gentleman by the name of Holly, owed $300 to Lawrence. Holly loaned $300 to Fox in exchange for Fox's promise to pay $300 to Lawrence. When Fox failed to pay, Lawrence sued to enforce Fox's promise to Holly. Lawrence won in the trial court and got a verdict for $344.66 which was the amount of the loan plus interest. Defendant appealed.]

H. GRAY, J. The first objection raised on the trial amounts to this: That the evidence of the person present, who heard the declarations of Holly giving directions as to the payment of the money he was then advancing to the defendant, was mere hearsay and therefore not competent. Had the plaintiff sued Holly for this sum of money no objection to the competency of this evidence would have been thought of; and if the defendant had performed his promise by paying the sum loaned to him to the plaintiff, and Holly had afterwards sued him for its recovery, and this evidence had been offered by the defendant, it would doubtless have been received without an objection from any source. All the defendant had the right to demand in this case was evidence which, as between Holly and the plaintiff, was competent to establish the relation between them of debtor and creditor. For that purpose the evidence was clearly competent; it covered the whole ground and warranted the verdict of the jury.

But it is claimed that notwithstanding this promise was established by competent evidence, it was void for the want of consideration. It is now more than a quarter of a century since it was settled by the Supreme Court of this State—in an able and pains-taking opinion by the late Chief Justice SAVAGE, in which the authorities were fully examined and carefully analysed—that a promise in all material respects like the one under consideration was valid; and the judgment of that court was unanimously affirmed by the Court for the Correction of Errors. *(Farley v. Cleaveland,* 4 Cow., 432; same case in error, 9 id., 639.) In that case one Moon owed Farley and sold to Cleaveland a quantity of hay, in consideration of which Cleaveland promised to pay Moon's debt to Farley; and the decision in favor of Farley's right to recover was placed upon the ground that the hay received by Cleaveland from Moon was a valid consideration for Cleaveland's promise to pay Farley, and that the subsisting liability of Moon to pay Farley was no objection to the recovery. The fact that the money advanced by Holly to the defendant was a loan to him for a day, and that it thereby became the property of the defendant, seemed to impress the defendant's counsel with the idea that because the defendant's promise was not a trust fund placed by the plaintiff in the defendant's hands, out of which he was to realize money as from the sale of a chattel or the collection of a debt, the promise although made for the benefit of the plaintiff could not enure to his benefit. The hay which Cleveland delivered to Moon was not to be paid to Farley, but the debt incurred by Cleveland for the purchase of the hay, like the debt incurred by the defendant for money borrowed, was what was to be paid.

That case has been often referred to by the courts of this State, and has never been doubted as sound authority for the principle upheld by it. *(Barker v. Buklin,* 2 Denio, 45; Hudson Canal *Company v. The Westchester Bank,* 4 id., 97.) It puts to rest the objection that the defendant's promise was void for want of consideration. The report of that case shows that the promise was not only made to Moon but to the plaintiff Farley. In this case the promise was made to Holly and not expressly to the plaintiff; and this difference between the two cases presents the question, raised by the defendant's objection, as to the want of privity between the plaintiff and defendant. . . .

But it is urged that because the defendant was not in any sense a trustee of the property of Holly for the benefit of the plaintiff, the law will not imply a promise. I agree that many of the cases where a promise was implied were cases of trusts, created for the benefit of the promiser. The case *of Felton v. Dickinson* (10 Mass., 189, 190), and others that might be cited, are of that class; but concede them all to have been cases of trusts, and it proves nothing against the application of the rule to this case. The duty of the trustee to pay the cestuis que trust, according to the terms of the trust, implies his promise to the latter to do so. In this case the defendant, upon ample consideration received from Holly, promised Holly to pay his debt to the plaintiff; the consideration received and the promise to Holly made it as plainly his duty to pay the plaintiff as if the money had been remitted to him for that purpose, and as well implied a promise to do so as if he had been made a trustee of property to be converted into cash with which to pay. The fact that a breach of the duty imposed in the one case may be visited, and justly, with more serious consequences than in the other, by no means disproves the payment to be a duty in both. The principle illustrated by the example so frequently quoted (which concisely states the case in hand) "that a promise made to one for the benefit of another, he for whose benefit it is made may bring an action for its breach," has been applied to trust cases, not because it was exclusively applicable to those cases, but because it was a principle of law, and as such applicable to those cases.

It was also insisted that Holly could have discharged the defendant from his promise, though it was intended by both parties for the benefit of the plaintiff, and therefore the plaintiff was not entitled to maintain this suit for the recovery of a demand over which he had no control. It is enough that the plaintiff did not release the defendant from his promise, and whether he could or not is a question not now necessarily involved . . . .

The cases cited, and especially that of *Farley v. Cleveland,* establish the validity of a parol promise; it stands then upon the footing of a written one. Suppose the defendant had given his note in which, for value received of Holly, he had promised to pay the plaintiff and the plaintiff had accepted the promise, retaining Holly's liability. Very clearly Holly could not have discharged that promise, be the right to release the defendant as it may. No one can doubt that he owes the sum of money demanded of him, or that in accordance with his promise it was his duty to have paid it to the plaintiff; nor can it be doubted that whatever may be the diversity of opinion elsewhere, the adjudications in this State, from a very early period, approved by experience, have established the defendant's liability; if, therefore, it could be shown that a more strict and technically accurate application of the rules applied, would lead to a different result (which I by no means concede), the effort should not be made in the face of manifest justice. . . .

The judgment should be affirmed.

COMSTOCK, J. (Dissenting.) The plaintiff had nothing to do with the promise on which he brought this action. It was not made to him, nor did the consideration proceed from him. If he can maintain the suit, it is because an anomaly has found its way into the law on this subject. In general, there must be privity of contract. The party who sues upon a promise must be the promi*see,* or he must have some legal interest in the undertaking. In this case, it is plain that Holly, who loaned the money to the defendant, and to whom the promise in question was made, could at any time have claimed that it should be performed to himself personally. He had lent the money to the defendant, and at the same time directed the latter to pay the sum to the plaintiff. This direction he could countermand, and if he had done so, manifestly the defendant's promise to pay according to the direction would have ceased to exist. The plaintiff would receive a benefit by a complete execution of the arrangement, but the arrangement itself was between other parties, and was under their exclusive control. If the defendant had paid the money to Holly, his debt would have been discharged thereby. So Holly might have released the demand or assigned it to another person, or the parties might have annulled the promise now in question, and designated some other creditor of Holly as the party to whom the money should be paid. It has never been claimed, that in a case thus situated, the right of a third person to sue upon the promise rested on any sound principle of law. We are to inquire whether the rule has been so established by positive authority. . . .

If A delivers money or property to B, which the latter accepts upon a trust for the benefit of C, the latter can enforce the trust by an appropriate action for that purpose. *(Berly v. Taylor,* 5 Hill, 577.) If the trust be of money, I think the beneficiary may assent to it and bring the action for money had and received to his use. If it be of something else than money, the trustee must account for it according to the terms of the trust, and upon principles of equity. There is some authority even for saying that an express promise founded on the possession of a trust fund may be enforced by an action at law in the name of the beneficiary, although it was made to the creator of the trust. Thus, in Comyn's Digest (Action on the case upon Assumpsit, B. 15), it is laid down that if a man promise a pig of lead to A, and his executor give lead to make a pig to B, who assumes to deliver it to A, an assumpsit lies by A against him. The case of The Delaware and *Hudson Canal Company v. The Westchester County Bank* (4 Denio, 97), involved a trust because the defendants had received from a third party a bill of exchange under an agreement that they would endeavor to collect it, and would pay over the proceeds when collected to the plaintiffs. A fund received under such an agreement does not belong to the person who receives it. He must account for it specifically; and perhaps there is no gross violation of principle in permitting the equitable owner of it to sue upon an express promise to pay it over. Having a specific interest in the thing, the undertaking to account for it may be regarded as in some sense made with him through the author of the trust. But further than this we cannot go without violating plain rules of law. In the case before us there was nothing in the nature of a trust or agency. The defendant borrowed the money of Holly and received it as his own. The plaintiff had no right in the fund, legal or equitable. The promise to repay the money created an obligation in favor of the lender to whom it was made and not in favor of any one else.

Question

What is the significance of the court's reference to the concept of privity between the plaintiff and defendant in this case? How does the court respond to the objection raised regarding the lack of privity?

Takeaways – Lawrence v. Fox

The usual presumption of the law is that parties contract for their own benefit and not for the benefit of third parties who are not in privity of contract. However, a third party who is not a promisee and who gave no consideration has an enforceable right by reason of a contract made by two others (1) if he is a creditor of the promisee or some other person and the contract calls for a performance by the promisor in satisfaction of the obligation; or (2) if the promised performance will be of pecuniary benefit to him and the contract is so expressed as to give the promisor reason to know that such benefit is contemplated by the promisee as one of the motivating causes of his making the contract. (Corbin, Contracts (One Volume Ed.) § 776) These two categories were recognized in the First Restatement as "creditor" and "donee" beneficiaries respectively. A third party who fails to qualify as either a creditor or a donee beneficiary is an incidental beneficiary who has no right to enforce the contract.

The three classes of beneficiaries [donee, creditor, and incidental] were abandoned (although not entirely) in favor of the Second Restatement's two divisions [intended and incidental] which permitted review of intent without further distinction. (See, Rest.2d § 302)

Intended Beneficiaries

Seaver v. Ransom
Court of Appeals of New York, 1918
224 N.Y. 223

POUND, J. Judge Beman and his wife were advanced in years. Mrs. Beman was about to die. She had a small estate consisting of a house and lot in Malone and little else. Judge Beman drew his wife's will according to her instructions. It gave $1,000 to plaintiff, $500 to one sister, plaintiff's mother, and $100 each to another sister and her son, the use of the house to her husband for life, remainder to the American Society for the Prevention of Cruelty to Animals. She named her husband as residuary legatee and executor. Plaintiff was her niece, thirty-four years old, in ill health, sometimes a member of the Beman household. When the will was read to Mrs. Beman she said that it was not as she wanted it; she wanted to leave the house to plaintiff. She had no other objection to the will, but her strength was waning and although the judge offered to write another will for her, she said she was afraid she would not hold out long enough to enable her to sign it. So the judge said if she would sign the will he would leave plaintiff enough in his will to make up the difference. He avouched the promise by his uplifted hand with all solemnity and his wife then executed the will. When he came to die it was found that his will made no provision for the plaintiff.

This action was brought and plaintiff recovered judgment in the trial court on the theory that Beman had obtained property from his wife and induced her to execute the will in the form prepared by him by his promise to give plaintiff $6,000, the value of the house, and that thereby equity impressed his property with a trust in favor of plaintiff. Where a legatee promises the testator that he will use property given him by the will for a particular purpose, a trust arises. (O'Hara v. Dudley, 95 N. Y. 403; Trustees of Amherst College v. Bitch, 151 N. Y. 282; Ahrens v. Jones, 169 N. Y. 555.) Beman received nothing under his wife's will but the use of the house in Malone for life. Equity compels the application of property thus obtained to the purpose of the testator, but equity cannot so impress a trust except on property obtained by the promise. Beman was bound by his promise, but no property was bound by it; no trust in plaintiff's favor can be spelled out.

An action on the contract for damages or to make the executors trustees for performance stands on different ground. (Farmers Loan & Trust Co. v. Mortimer, 219 N. Y. 290, 294, 295.) The Appellate Division properly passed to the consideration of the question whether the judgment could stand upon the promise made to the wife, upon a valid consideration, for the sole benefit of plaintiff. The judgment of the trial court was affirmed by a return to the general doctrine laid down in the great case of Lawrence v. Fox (20 N. Y. 268) which has since been limited as herein indicated.

Contracts for the benefit of third persons have been the prolific source of judicial and academic discussion. (Williston, Contracts for the Benefit of a Third Person, 15 Harvard Law Review, 767; Corbin, Contracts for the Benefit of Third Persons, 27 Yale Law Review, 1008.) The general rule, both in law and equity (Phalen v. U. S. Trust Co., 186 N. Y. 178, 186), was that privity between a plaintiff and a defendant is necessary to the maintenance of an action on the contract. The consideration must be furnished by the party to whom the promise was made. The contract cannot be enforced against the third party and, therefore, it cannot be enforced by him. On the other hand, the right of the beneficiary to sue on a contract made expressly for his benefit has been fully recognized in many American jurisdictions, either by judicial decision or by legislation, and is said to be "the prevailing rule in this country." (Hendrick v. Lindsay, 93 U. S. 143; Lehow v. Simonton, 3 Col. 346.) It has been said that "the establishment of this doctrine has been gradual, and is a victory of practical utility over theory, of equity over technical subtlety." (Brantly on Contracts [2d ed.], p. 253.) The reasons for this view are that it is just and practical to permit the person for whose benefit the contract is made to enforce it against one whose duty it is to pay. Other jurisdictions still adhere to the present English rule (7 Halsbury's Laws of England, 342, 343; Jenks' Digest of English Civil Law, § 229) that a contract cannot be enforced by or against a person who is not a party. (Exchange Bank v. Rice, 107 Mass. 37; but see, also, Forbes v. Thorpe, 209 Mass. 570; Gardner v. Denison, 217 Mass. 492.)

In New York the right of the beneficiary to sue on contracts made for his benefit is not clearly or simply defined. It is at present confined, first, to cases where there is a pecuniary obligation running from the promisee to the beneficiary; "a legal right founded upon some obligation of the promisee in the third party to adopt and claim the promise as made for his benefit." (Farley v. Cleveland, 4 Cow. 432; Lawrence v. Fox, supra; [238] Garnsey v. Rogers, 47 N. Y. 233; Vrooman v. Turner, 69 N. Y. 280; Lorillardv. Clyde, 122 N. Y. 498; Durnherr v. Rau, 135 N. Y. 219; Townsend v. Rackham, 143 N. Y. 516; Sullivan v. Sullivan, 161 N. Y. 554.) Secondly, to cases where the contract is made for the benefit of the wife (Buchanan v. Tilden, 158 N. Y. 109; Bouton v. Welch, 170 N. Y. 554), affianced wife (De Cicco v. Schweizer, 221 N. Y. 431), or child (Todd v. Weber, 95 N. Y. 181, 193; Matter of Kidd, 188 N. Y. 274) of a party to the contract. The close relationship cases go back to the early King's Bench case (1677), long since repudiated in England, of Button v. Poole (2 Lev. 210; s. c, 1 Ventris, 318, 332). (Schemerhorn v. Vanderheyden, 1 Johns. 139.) The natural and moral duty of the husband or parent to provide for the future of wife or child sustains the action on the contract made for their benefit. "This is the farthest the cases in this state have gone," says CULLEN, J., in the marriage settlement case of Borland v. Welch (162 N. Y. 104, 110).

The right of the third party is also upheld in, thirdly, the public contract cases (Little v. Banks, 85 N. Y. 258; Pond v. New Rochelle Water Co., 183 N. Y. 330; Smyth v. City of New York, 203 N. Y. 106; Farnsworth v. Boro Oil & Gas Co., 216 N. Y. 40, 48; Rigney v. N. Y. C. & H. R. R. R. Co., 217 N. Y. 31; Matter of International Ry. Co. v. Rann, 224 N. Y. 83; cf. German Alliance Ins. Co. v. Home Water Supply Co., 226 U. S. 220) where the municipality seeks to protect its inhabitants by covenants for their benefit and, fourthly, the cases where, at the request of a party to the contract, the promise runs directly to the beneficiary although he does not furnish the consideration. (Rector, etc., v. Teed, 120 N. Y. 583; F. N. Bank of Sing Sing v. Chalmers, 144 N. Y. 432, 439; Hamilton v. Hamilton, 127 App. Div. 871, 875.) It may be safely said that a general rule sustaining recovery at the suit of the third party would include but few classes of cases not included in these groups, either categorically or in principle.

The desire of the childless aunt to make provision for a beloved and favorite niece differs imperceptibly in law or in equity from the moral duty of the parent to make testamentary provision for a child. The contract was made for the plaintiff's benefit. She alone is substantially damaged by its breach. The representatives of the wife's estate have no interest in enforcing it specifically. It is said in Buchanan v. Tilden that the common law imposes moral and legal obligations upon the husband and the parent not measured by the necessaries of life. It was, however, the love and affection or the moral sense of the husband and the parent that imposed such obligations in the cases cited rather than any common-law duty of husband and parent to wife and child. If plaintiff had been a child of Mrs. Beman, legal obligation would have required no testamentary provision for her, yet the child could have enforced a covenant in her favor identical with the covenant of Judge Beman in this case. (De Cicco v. Schweizer, supra.) The constraining power of conscience is not regulated by the degree of relationship alone. The dependent or faithful niece may have a stronger claim than the affluent or unworthy son. No sensible theory of moral obligation denies arbitrarily to the former what would be conceded to the latter. We might consistently either refuse or allow the claim of both, but I cannot reconcile a decision in favor of the wife in Buchanan v. Tilden based on the moral obligations arising out of near relationship with a decision against the niece here on the ground that the relationship is too remote for equity's ken. No controlling authority depends upon so absolute a rule. In Sullivan v. Sullivan (supra) the grandniece lost in a litigation with the aunt's estate founded on a certificate of deposit payable to the aunt "or in case of her death to her niece," but what was said in that case of the relations of plaintiff's intestate and defendant does not control here, any more than what was said in Durnherr v. Rau (supra) on the relation of husband and wife, and the inadequacy of mere moral duty, as distinguished from legal or equitable obligation, controlled the decision in Buchanan v. Tilden. Borland v. Welch (supra) deals only with the rights of volunteers under a marriage settlement not made for the benefit of collaterals. KELLOGG, P. J., writing for the court below well said:

> "The doctrine of Lawrence v. Fox is progressive, not retrograde. The course of the late decisions is to enlarge, not to limit the effect of that case."

The court in that leading case attempted to adopt the general doctrine that any third person, for whose direct benefit a contract was intended, could sue on it. . . .

But, on principle, a sound conclusion may be reached. If Mrs. Beman had left her husband the house on condition that he pay the plaintiff $6,000 and he had accepted the devise, he would have become personally liable to pay the legacy and plaintiff could have recovered in an action at law against him, whatever the value of the house. (Gridley v. Gridley, 24 N. Y. 130; Brown v. Knapp, 79 N. Y. 136, 143; Dinan v. Coneys, 143 N. Y. 544, 547; Blackmore v. White, [1899] 1 Q. B. 293, 304.) That would be because the testatrix had in substance bequeathed the promise to plaintiff and not because close relationship or moral obligation sustained the contract. The distinction between an implied promise to a testator for the benefit of a third party to pay a legacy and an unqualified promise on a valuable consideration to make provision for the third party by will is discernible but not obvious. The tendency of American authority is to sustain the gift in all such cases and to permit the donee-beneficiary to recover on the contract. (Matter of Edmundson's Estate, [1918, Pa.] 103 Atl. Rep. 277.) The equities are with the plaintiff and they may be enforced in this action, whether it be regarded as an [242] action for damages or an action for specific performance to convert the defendants into trustees for plaintiff's benefit under the agreement.

The judgment should be affirmed, with costs.

Questions

1. According to the court's analysis, what are the requirements for a beneficiary to sue on a contract made for their benefit?

2. The court refers to the prevailing rule in the United States regarding contracts made for the benefit of third persons. How does the court describe the development of this doctrine and its application in different jurisdictions?

Takeaways – Seaver v. Ransom

Only third parties who are "intended beneficiaries" have enforceable contract rights. In order to qualify as an intended beneficiary the third party must meet two requirements;

(1) the third party must show that recognition of a right to performance in the beneficiary is appropriate to effectuate the intention of the parties

and

(2) the performance of the promise will satisfy an obligation of the promisee to pay money to the beneficiary or the circumstances indicate that the promisee intends to give the beneficiary the benefit of the promised performance in the form of a gift. (Rest.2d § 302) This is known as the "intent to benefit" test.

Johnson v. Holmes Tuttle Lincoln-Mercury

California Court of Appeal, Second District, 1958
160 Cal.App.2d 290, 325 P.2d 193

VALLEE, J. Appeal from a judgment for plaintiffs as third party beneficiaries of an oral agreement to procure public liability and property damage insurance.

The agreement is alleged to have been entered into between Holmes Tuttle Lincoln-Mercury, Inc., called defendant, and Phillip R. Caldera and his wife, Ruth, in connection with the purchase by the Calderas of a new Mercury automobile from defendant on November 23, 1953.

On December 11, 1953, about three weeks after the Calderas purchased the car, Phillip Caldera was involved in an accident with the Mercury. Plaintiffs, Willie Mae Johnson and Fletcher Jones, a passenger, were injured and Johnson's car was damaged.

Separate actions were filed by plaintiffs against Phillip Caldera. Judgments were entered May 23, 1955, in favor of plaintiff Johnson for $4,413.89, and in favor of plaintiff Jones for $2,070. These judgments remain unsatisfied.

Plaintiffs allege defendant, by its salesman Harry Rozany, had agreed with Caldera at the time the Mercury was purchased to procure "full coverage" insurance for Caldera, including public liability and property damage, for the operation of the Mercury; both Caldera and defendant understood the insurance was to be obtained for the usual term and for no less than the minimum legal limits; defendant failed to obtain the public liability and property damage insurance after Caldera had performed all of the terms of the agreement on his part. The prayer is for the amounts of the judgments obtained against Caldera with interest. In a jury trial the verdict was for plaintiffs as prayed. Defendant appeals from the judgment which followed.

On November 23, 1953, Caldera appeared with his wife, Ruth, at the showroom of defendant for the purpose of purchasing a new Mercury. One of defendant's salesmen, Harry Rozany, approached the Calderas and discussed with them the prospective purchase of a new Mercury like the one then in the showroom. After about five minutes Rozany took them to a "closing room" where terms were discussed for about an hour and the purchase consummated. The Calderas told Rozany they had a 1948 Chevrolet as a trade-in and $900 cash as a down payment. They indicated they could not afford to make payments of over $80 a month on the balance. During the discussion Caldera told Rozany he wanted "full coverage insurance," and Rozany replied, "Oh, yes, you are getting it." Rozany made out the papers and sold them "another insurance," a policy by which the insurer engaged to pay the balance of the purchase price of the car in the event of the death or disability of Caldera. The premium of $2.50 to $3.00 a month was to be included in the installment payments. Rozany computed the figures in the transaction on "scratch paper." He had Caldera sign the car order and the conditional sale contract in blank. Rozany took the papers "upstairs," saying he was going to complete filling them out.

About December 2, 1953, Mrs. Caldera received by mail a copy of the conditional sale contract dated December 1, 1953, which showed fire, theft, comprehensive, and $50 deductible collision insurance thereon, but which made no reference to public liability and property damage insurance. Mrs. Caldera read only the figures. She called defendant to talk to Rozany but as he was not there she did not talk to him or to anyone. Caldera did not see this copy of the conditional sale contract received by Mrs. Caldera. Neither of the Calderas saw the original sales order until after the first of the year when Caldera went to put in the new certificate of registration and discovered the folded document with the stamped notation "No liability insurance sold on this car," which had been placed in the registration holster and fastened on the wheel by Rozany shortly after he had returned to the closing room with the approved order at the time of the purchase. Caldera first learned he had no public liability and property damage insurance after his wife went to the office of Olympic Insurance Company "to find out about the insurance." That company had issued the collision policy dated December 15, 1953, which the Calderas received December 17, 1953, four days after the accident.

To Caldera, who was 36 years old, employed as a mechanic, and who had been through the ninth grade in school, "full coverage insurance" meant everything that is supposed to be in insurance, including public liability and property damage. The public liability and property damage insurance on the 1948 Chevrolet automobile used as a trade-in had expired in August of 1953, and Caldera testified that since it was an old car and they intended trading it in on a new one any day he thought there was no use in renewing it.

Defendant had a licensed insurance department. Its salesman, Rozany, had been a new car salesman there about three years, during which time he had sold about 300 cars, and on at least one occasion the sale involved the purchase of public liability and property damage insurance. Rozany's experience as a new car salesman was continuous from 1937.

Plaintiffs' expert witness, James P. Bennett, an experienced insurance salesman, testified over objection of defendant that the term "full coverage" when used by a layman meant in the automobile insurance business insurance against damage to his car and against damage caused by his car; it would include a term of one year, basic limits of $5,000 for injuries to one person, $10,000 for injuries to all persons in one accident, and $5,000 for property damage, as well as $500 medical payments. The premium for such insurance by one using his car to travel to and from work in the particular territory in which Caldera drove would be $63. He also testified there was sufficient information on the purchaser's statement which was signed by Caldera to order the coverage, so long as he had the sales order to identify the car.

Defendant first asserts the evidence does not support the implied finding of the jury that there was a contract to procure public liability and property damage insurance between Caldera and defendant; nor does the evidence support the implied finding that plaintiffs were third party beneficiaries of a contract between Caldera and defendant. It is argued there was no consideration paid by Caldera for defendant's agreement to procure full coverage insurance, including public liability and property damage. The agreement alleged and proved was that in consideration of Caldera's purchasing the Mercury defendant would procure full coverage insurance, including public liability and property damage. Mutual promises constitute consideration. (Civ. Code, § 1605; [Citations omitted]) A single consideration may support several counterpromises. (H. S. Crocker Co., Inc. v. McFaddin, 148 Cal.App.2d 639, 645 [307 P.2d 429].)

It is interesting to note that the conditional sale contract which Caldera signed in blank recites a total contract balance due of $2,505.73. The policy received by Caldera shows the amount of the contract as $2,598.73, a difference of $93. The insurer must have obtained the contract figure from defendant. The uncontradicted evidence shows that the cost of public liability and property damage in basic limits plus $500 medical payments coverage was $63. Figuring the transaction with one year's premiums in advance as Rozany did with the other coverages, the total charges equal the $93 difference.

The evidence recited, contrary to defendant's claim, shows there was a meeting of minds. It is argued that because Rozany testified he did not know what the term "full coverage" meant there could be no meeting of minds. The jury was not compelled to believe Rozany. He was thoroughly impeached. The jury may have inferred his knowledge from his experience. He had been a new car salesman since 1937, three years with defendant, and had sold around 300 cars "or better." Defendant was a licensed insurance broker with an insurance department operated in connection with its auto sales business. Rozany told Mrs. Caldera full coverage "includes everything."

Referring to the testimony of the witness Bennett, which was admitted over its objection, defendant argues it was erroneously admitted in that it was proof of custom and usage for the purpose of creating a contract, which may not be done. Custom and usage was not relied on to create a contract. It was admitted for the purpose of explaining and interpreting the phrase, "full coverage," and for that purpose it was admissible. (Code Civ. Proc., § 1870, subd. 12.) Furthermore, the testimony was in effect merely a statement of the law which every person is presumed to know and of which the court could take judicial notice. (Veh. Code, § 415.)

Defendant contends plaintiffs were not third party beneficiaries. "A contract, made expressly for the benefit of a third person, may be enforced by him at any time before the parties thereto rescind it." (Civ. Code, § 1559.) Where one person for a valuable consideration engages with another to do some act for the benefit of a third person, and the agreement thus made has not been rescinded, the party for whose benefit the contract or promise was made, or who would enjoy the benefit of the act, may maintain an action against the promisor for the breach of his engagement. While the contract remains unrescinded, the relations of the parties are the same as though the promise had been made directly to the third party. Although the party for whose benefit the promise was made was not cognizant of it when made, it is, if adopted by him, deemed to have been made to him. He may sue on the promise. Where a promise is made to benefit a third party on the happening of a certain contingency, the third party may enforce the contract on the occurrence of that contingency. (12 Cal.Jur.2d 493, § 261.) The action by a third party beneficiary for the breach of the promisor's engagement does not rest on the ground of any actual or supposed relationship between the parties but on the broad and more satisfactory basis that the law, operating on the acts of the parties, creates the duty, establishes a privity, and implies the promise and obligation on which the action is founded. (Washer v. Independent Min. & Dev. Co., 142 Cal. 702, 708-9 [76 P. 654].)

It is not necessary that the beneficiary be named and identified as an individual; a third party may enforce a contract if he can show he is a member of a class for whose benefit it was made. [Citations omitted] It is no objection to the maintenance of an action by a third party that a suit might be brought also against the one to whom the promise was made. [Citations omitted]

The test for determining whether a contract was made for the benefit of a third person is whether an intent to benefit a third person appears from the terms of the contract. (Le Ballister v. Redwood Theatres, Inc., 1 Cal.App.2d 447, 449 [36 P.2d 827].) If the terms of the contract necessarily require the promisor to confer a benefit on a third person, then the contract, and hence the parties thereto, contemplate a benefit to the third person. The parties are presumed to intend the consequences of a performance of the contract. It is held that a person injured may sue on a contract for the benefit of all members of the public who are so injured since the happening of the injury sufficiently determines his identity and right of action. (Levy v. Daniels' U-Drive Auto Renting Co., 108 Conn. 333 [143 A. 163, 165, 61 A.L.R. 846].)

Section 11580 of the Insurance Code reads:

"A policy insuring against losses set forth in subdivision (a) shall not be issued or delivered to any person in this State unless it contains the provisions set forth in subdivision (b). Such policy, whether or not actually containing such provisions, shall be construed as if such provisions were embodied therein.

"(a) Unless it contains such provisions, the following policies of insurance shall not be thus issued or delivered:

"(1) Against loss or damage resulting from liability for injury suffered by another person other than a policy of workmen's compensation insurance.

"(2) Against loss of or damage to property caused by draught animals or any vehicle, and for which the insured is liable.

"(b) Such policy shall not be thus issued or delivered to any person in this State unless it contains all the following provisions:

"(1) A provision that the insolvency or bankruptcy of the insured will not release the insurer from the payment of damages for injury sustained or loss occasioned during the life of such policy.

"(2) A provision that whenever judgment is secured against the insured or the executor or administrator of a deceased insured in an action based upon bodily injury, death, or property damage, then an action may be brought against the insurer on the policy and subject to its terms and limitations, by such judgment creditor to recover on the judgment."

The statute is a part of every policy and creates a contractual relation which inures to the benefit of any and every person who might be negligently injured by the insured as completely as if such injured person had been specifically named in the policy. [Citations omitted] The primary purpose of the statute is to protect an injured person when the insured is bankrupt or insolvent. [Citations omitted] The complaint here alleges Caldera is insolvent and there was evidence to that effect. The statute in effect makes the tortfeasee a creditor beneficiary. It makes the benefit of the policy available to the creditor beneficiary tortfeasee. (See 27 Cal.L.Rev. 497, 529.)

In James Stewart & Co. v. Law, 149 Tex. 392 [233 S.W.2d 558, 22 A.L.R.2d 639], a corporation--the owner--entered into a contract with a contractor for the erection of certain buildings. The contract expressly obligated the contractor to maintain certain insurance, and also provided that in case any part of the contract was sublet by the contractor the latter should require of its subcontractor the maintenance of automobile liability insurance. The contractor sublet part of the work to a subcontractor who in turn contracted with a truck owner for the hauling of gravel in connection with the performance of his subcontract. Neither the contractor nor the subcontractor required his respective subcontractor to carry automobile insurance and none was carried by the truck owner. While hauling gravel, the latter injured an employee of the owner, and the employee brought suit against the contractor to recover damages on the theory that the contractor had breached its contract with the owner by failing to see that all subcontractors carried automobile liability insurance, and that he, the employee, was a third party beneficiary of such contract. The court held the injured employee was a third party beneficiary under the contract and as such entitled to maintain suit against the contractor. . . .

There is no escape from the conclusion that the agreement between defendant and Caldera was not for the sole benefit of the latter but that it was intended to inure to the benefit of third persons who might be protected by a full coverage policy. [Citations omitted] The intent to confer a benefit on anyone to whom Caldera might become liable as a result of a hazard incident to ownership and operation of the Mercury is obvious. This is precisely what Caldera wanted as a means of obtaining a benefit to himself. It must have been in the contemplation of the parties when Rozany agreed to procure public liability and property damage insurance that injury to third persons might result from ownership and operation of the Mercury. It was reasonable for the jury to infer that Caldera, in making the agreement with defendant, desired and intended that such persons be protected in the event of an accident with the Mercury. The jury's finding that there was a third party beneficiary contract breached by defendant to plaintiffs' damage is amply supported by the record.

The action is for breach of an oral contract to procure insurance; it is not based on fraud, as defendant asserts. Proof of fraud was merely incidental to proof of the contract. Defendant filed a general and special demurrer to the complaint which was overruled. Error is asserted. It is said there is no "allegation that the alleged agreement was for the express benefit of plaintiffs." Sufficient facts are alleged to show that it was for plaintiffs' benefit. While there are some uncertainties in the complaint, no prejudice is shown. Depositions were taken before trial, the cause was fully and fairly tried, defendant does not claim surprise, and the error, if any, in overruling the special demurrer did not affect defendant's substantial rights in any way.

Other points made do not require discussion.

Affirmed.

Questions

1. What legal principles apply to determine whether plaintiffs qualify as third-party beneficiaries in this case?

2. Explain the requirements for a third party to enforce a contract made for their benefit.

3. Can the action by plaintiffs be maintained if the contract between Caldera and defendant was rescinded? What would be the effect of rescission on the rights of a third-party beneficiary and the ability to sue for breach of contract?

Takeaways – Johnson v. Holmes-Tuttle

Insurance contracts are classic examples of third-party beneficiary contracts. Who is the promisor? Who is the promisee? Who is the third-party beneficiary? Note, that it is not necessary that the contract identify the third party by name as long as the third party can show that he or she is one of a class of persons for whose benefit it was made. (*Watson v. Aced* (1957) 156 Cal.App.2d 87, 91-92)

Lucas v. Hamm
Supreme Court of California, 1961
56 Cal.2d 583, 364 P.2d 685, 15 Cal.Rptr. 821

GIBSON, C. J. Plaintiffs, who are some of the beneficiaries under the will of Eugene H. Emmick, deceased, brought this action for damages against defendant L. S. Hamm, an attorney at law who had been engaged by the testator to prepare the will. They have appealed from a judgment of dismissal entered after an order sustaining a general demurrer to the second amended complaint without leave to amend. . . .

Defendant agreed with the testator, for a consideration, to prepare a will and codicils thereto for him by which plaintiffs were to be designated as beneficiaries of a trust provided for by paragraph Eighth of the will and were to receive 15 per cent of the residue as specified in that paragraph. Defendant, in violation of instructions and in breach of his contract, negligently prepared testamentary instruments containing phraseology that was invalid by virtue of section 715.2 and former sections 715.1 and 716 of the Civil Code relating to restraints on alienation and the rule against perpetuities.... After the death of the testator the instruments were admitted to probate. Subsequently defendant, as draftsman of the instruments and as counsel of record for the executors, advised plaintiffs in writing that the residual trust provision was invalid and that plaintiffs would be deprived of the entire amount to which they would have been entitled if the provision had been valid unless they made a settlement with the blood relatives of the testator.... As the direct and proximate result of the negligence of defendant and his breach of contract in preparing the testamentary instruments and the written advice referred to above, plaintiffs were compelled to enter into a settlement under which they received a share of the estate amounting to $75,000 less than the sum which they would have received pursuant to testamentary instruments drafted in accordance with the directions of the testator....

It was held in Buckley v. Gray, 110 Cal. 339 [42 P. 900, 52 Am.St.Rep. 88, 31 L.R.A. 862], that an attorney who made a mistake in drafting a will was not liable for negligence or breach of contract to a person named in the will who was deprived of benefits as a result of the error.... For the reasons hereinafter stated the case is overruled.... [Discussion of the claim that sounded in tort is omitted.]

Neither do we agree with the holding in Buckley that beneficiaries damaged by an error in the drafting of a will cannot recover from the draftsman on the theory that they are third-party beneficiaries of the contract between him and the testator. Obviously the main purpose of a contract for the drafting of a will is to accomplish the future transfer of the estate of the testator to the beneficiaries named in the will, and therefore it seems improper to hold, as was done in Buckley, that the testator intended only "remotely" to benefit those persons. It is true that under a contract for the benefit of a third person performance is usually to be rendered directly to the beneficiary, but this is not necessarily the case. (See Rest., Contracts, § 133, comment d; 2 Williston on Contracts (3d ed. 1959) 829.) For example, where a life insurance policy lapsed because a bank failed to perform its agreement to pay the premiums out of the insured's bank account, it was held that after the insured's death the beneficiaries could recover against the bank as third-party beneficiaries. (Walker Bank & Trust Co. v. First Security Corp., 9 Utah 2d 215 [341 P.2d 944, 945 et seq.].)persons who had agreed to procure liability insurance for the protection of the promisees but did not do so were also held liable to injured persons who would have been covered by the insurance, the courts stating that all persons who might be injured were third-party beneficiaries of the contracts to procure insurance. (Johnson v. Holmes Tuttle Lincoln-Merc., 160 Cal.App.2d 290, 296 et seq. [325 P.2d 193]; James Stewart & Co. v. Law, 149 Tex. 392 [233 S.W.2d 558, 561-562, 22 A.L.R.2d 639].) Since, in a situation like those presented here and in the Buckley case, the main purpose of the testator in making his agreement with the attorney is to benefit the persons named in his will and this intent can be effectuated, in the event of a breach by the attorney, only by giving the beneficiaries a right of action, we should recognize, as a matter of policy, that they are entitled to recover as third-party beneficiaries. (See 2 Williston on Contracts (3d ed. 1959) pp. 843-844; 4 Corbin on Contracts (1951) pp. 8, 20.)

Section 1559 of the Civil Code, which provides for enforcement by a third person of a contract made "expressly" for his benefit, does not preclude this result. The effect of the section is to exclude enforcement by persons who are only incidentally or remotely benefited. (See Hartman Ranch Co. v. Associated Oil Co., 10 Cal.2d 232, 244 [73 P.2d 1163]; cf. 4 Corbin on Contracts (1951) pp. 23-24.) As we have seen, a contract for the drafting of a will unmistakably shows the intent of the testator to benefit the persons to be named in the will, and the attorney must necessarily understand this.

Defendant relies on language in Smith v. Anglo- California Trust Co., 205 Cal. 496, 502 [271 P. 898], and Fruitvale Canning Co. v. Cotton, 115 Cal.App.2d 622, 625 [252 P.2d 953], that to permit a third person to bring an action on a contract there must be "an intent clearly manifested by the promisor" to secure some benefit to the third person. This language, which was not necessary to the decision in either of the cases, is unfortunate. Insofar as intent to benefit a third person is important in determining his right to bring an action under a contract, it is sufficient that the promisor must have understood that the promisee had such intent. (Cf. Rest., Contracts, § 133, subds. 1(a) and 1(b); 4 Corbin on Contracts (1951) pp. 16-18; 2 Williston on Contracts (3d ed. 1959) pp. 836-839.) No specific manifestation by the promisor of an intent to benefit the third person is required. The language relied on by defendant is disapproved to the extent that it is inconsistent with these views.

We conclude that intended beneficiaries of a will who lose their testamentary rights because of failure of the attorney who drew the will to properly fulfill his obligations under his contract with the testator may recover as third-party beneficiaries. . . .

Questions

1. According to the court's opinion, can beneficiaries of a will be considered third-party beneficiaries of the contract between the testator and the attorney who drafted the will?

2. How does the court address the argument raised by the defendant regarding Section 1559 of the Civil Code?

3. What is the court's response to the defendant's reliance on the language in Smith v. Anglo-California Trust Co. and Fruitvale Canning Co. regarding the intent of the promisor to benefit the third person?

Takeaways – Lucas v. Hamm

Were the beneficiaries in this case creditor beneficiaries or donee beneficiaries? As this case demonstrates, is not necessary that the intent to benefit the third party be manifested by the promisor (the attorney in this particular case); it is sufficient that the promisor understand that the promisee has such intent.

Schauer v. Mandarin Gems of Cal.
California Court of Appeal, Fourth District, 2005
125 Cal.App.4th 949

IKOLA, J. Sarah Jane Schauer (plaintiff) appeals from a judgment of dismissal in favor of Mandarin Gems of California, Inc., dba Black, Starr & Frost (defendant) after the court sustained defendant's demurrer to plaintiff's second amended complaint without leave to amend. Plaintiff sought to recover on various theories based on her discovery that a diamond ring given to her as an engagement gift prior to her marriage to her now former husband, Darin Erstad, allegedly was not worth the $43,000 he paid defendant for it in 1999. Erstad is not a party to this action.

We reverse the judgment and remand. We conclude plaintiff has standing as a third party beneficiary of the sales contract between Erstad and defendant, and she has adequately pleaded a contract cause of action based on allegations of defendant's breach of express warranty. Defendant must answer to that claim.. . . .

Plaintiff and Erstad went shopping for an engagement ring on August 15, 1999. After looking at diamonds in premier jewelry establishments such as Tiffany and Company and Cartier, they went to defendant's store, where they found a ring that salesperson Joy said featured a 3.01 carat diamond with a clarity grading of "'SI1.'" Erstad bought the ring the same day for $43,121.55. The following month, for insurance purposes, defendant provided Erstad a written appraisal verifying the ring had certain characteristics, including an SI1 clarity rating and an average replacement value of $45,500. Paul Lam, a graduate gemologist with the European Gemological Laboratory (EGL), signed the appraisal.

The couple's subsequent short term marriage was dissolved in a North Dakota judgment awarding each party, "except as otherwise set forth in this Agreement," "the exclusive right, title and possession of all personal property . . . which such party now owns, possesses, holds or hereafter acquires." Plaintiff's personal property included the engagement ring given to her by Erstad.

On June 3, 2002, after the divorce, plaintiff had the ring evaluated by the "'Gem Trade Laboratory,'" which gave the diamond a rating of "'SI2' quality," an appraisal with which "multiple other [unidentified] jewelers, including one at [defendant's store]" agreed. That was how plaintiff discovered defendant's alleged misrepresentation, concealment, and breach of express warranty regarding the true clarity of the diamond and its actual worth, which is -- on plaintiff's information and belief -- some $23,000 less than what Erstad paid for it.

Plaintiff sued defendant on several theories. . . . In its general demurrer to the second amended complaint and each cause of action, defendant asserted plaintiff had no viable claim under any theory because: (1) plaintiff was neither the purchaser of the ring nor a third party beneficiary of the contract between defendant and Erstad, who was not alleged to have assigned his rights to plaintiff [.] . . .

The trial court . . . sustained the demurrer . . . without further leave to amend. The judgment of dismissal followed, and plaintiff appeals. As we will explain, the court erred. Although the complaint is fatally defective in some respects, plaintiff is entitled as a matter of law to pursue her contract claim as a third party beneficiary. . . .

[A]lthough plaintiff does not have Erstad's rights by virtue of the divorce judgment, she nonetheless has standing in her own right to sue for breach of contract as a third party beneficiary under the allegation, inter alia, that "[d]efendant entered into a written contract with Plaintiff's fiancée [*sic*] to purchase the subject engagement ring for the sole and stated purpose of giving it [to] Plaintiff."

Civil Code section 1559 provides: "A contract, made expressly for the benefit of a third person, may be enforced by him [or her] at any time before the parties thereto rescind it." Because third party beneficiary status is a matter of contract interpretation, a person seeking to enforce a contract as a third party beneficiary "'must plead a contract which was made expressly for his [or her] benefit and one in which it clearly appears that he [or she] was a beneficiary.'" (*California Emergency Physicians Medical Group v. PacifiCare of California* (2003) 111 Cal.App.4th 1127, 1138.)

"Expressly," [as used in the statute and case law,] means "in an express manner; in direct or unmistakable terms; explicitly; definitely; directly.'" [Citations.] '[A]n intent to make the obligation inure to the benefit of the third party must have been clearly manifested by the contracting parties.'" (*Sofias v. Bank of America* (1985) 172 Cal.App.3d 583, 587.) Although this means persons only incidentally or remotely benefited by the contract are not entitled to enforce it, it does not mean both of the contracting parties must intend to benefit the third party: Rather, it means the promisor -- in this case, defendant jeweler -- "must have understood that the promisee [Erstad] had such intent. [Citations.] No specific manifestation by the promisor of an intent to benefit the third person is required." (*Lucas v. Hamm* (1961) 56 Cal.2d 583, 591; see also, *Johnson v. Superior Court* (2000 80 Cal.App.4th 1050, 1064-1065; *Don Rose Oil Co., Inc. v. Lindsley* (1984) 160 Cal.App.3d 752, 757, and *Zigas v. Superior Court* (1981) 120 Cal.App.3d 827, 837.)

We conclude the pleading here meets the test of demonstrating plaintiff's standing as a third party beneficiary to enforce the contract between Erstad and defendant. The couple went shopping for an engagement ring. They were together when plaintiff chose the ring she wanted or, as alleged in the complaint, she "caused [the ring] to be purchased for her." Erstad allegedly bought the ring "for the sole and *stated* purpose of giving [the ring]" to plaintiff. (Italics added.) Under the alleged facts, the jeweler *must* have understood Erstad's intent to enter the sales contract for plaintiff's benefit. Thus, plaintiff has adequately pleaded her status as a third party beneficiary, and she is entitled to proceed with her contract claim against defendant to the extent it is not time-barred. . . .

Plaintiff has attempted to plead a separate cause of action for rescission. She is not entitled to that remedy. Civil Code section 1559 provides, "A contract, made expressly for the benefit of a third person, may be *enforced* by him [or her] at any time before *the parties thereto rescind it.*" (Italics added.) But only the parties to the contract may rescind it. Civil Code section 1689 provides, in pertinent part, "(a) A contract may be rescinded if all the *parties* thereto consent. [¶] (b) A *party to a contract* may rescind the contract in the following cases: [¶] (1) If the consent of the *party* rescinding, or of any party *jointly contracting* with him [or her], was given by mistake, or obtained through duress, menace, fraud, or undue influence, exercised by or with the connivance of the *party* as to whom he [or she] rescinds, or of any other *party to the contract jointly interested with such party*. [¶] (2) If the consideration for the obligation of the rescinding *party* fails, in whole or in part, through the fault of the *party* as to whom he [or she] rescinds." (Italics added.)

We have found no cases specifically holding the rescission remedy unavailable to a third party beneficiary, but the proposition is self-evident to a degree that might well explain the absence of precedent. Civil Code section 1559 grants a third party beneficiary the right to *enforce* the contract, not rescind it, and Civil Code section 1689 limits its grant of rescission rights to the contracting parties. Not only do the relevant statutes demand making rescission unavailable to a third party beneficiary, but common sense compels the conclusion. The interest of the third party beneficiary is as the intended recipient of the *benefits* of the contract, and a direct right to those benefits, i.e., specific performance, or damages in lieu thereof, will protect the beneficiary's interests. Rescission, on the other hand, extinguishes a contract between the parties. (Civ. Code, § 1688.) Plaintiff, not having participated in the agreement, not having undertaken any duty or given any consideration, is a stranger to the agreement, with no legitimate interest in voiding it. As a matter of law, without an assignment of Erstad's contract rights, plaintiff cannot rescind the sales contract to which she was not a party. . . .

The judgment is reversed. The case is remanded with directions to the trial court to overrule defendant's demurrer to plaintiff's cause of action for breach of contract and order defendant to answer. . . .

Questions

1. According to the court's decision, under what circumstances can a third party beneficiary enforce a contract?

2. Explain the court's interpretation of "expressly" and the promisor's understanding of the promisee's intent.

3. Can a third party beneficiary seek rescission of a contract?

Incidental Beneficiaries

If a contract is not made expressly for the benefit of a particular third person, such person cannot enforce the contract even though he or she would receive some benefit from the performance of the contract. In other words, anyone who fails to meet the "intent to benefit" test is an incidental beneficiary and incidental beneficiaries do not have enforceable rights.

Jones v. Aetna Casualty & Surety Co.
California Court of Appeal, First District, 1994
26 Cal.App.4th 1717, 33 Cal.Rptr.2d 291

MERRILL, J. Frank N. Jones, Donna M. Jones and Snowcreek, Inc. (Jones), appeal from the judgment entered in favor of respondent Aetna Casualty and Surety Company (Aetna), following the order sustaining the demurrer without leave to amend to Jones's first amended complaint for tortious breach of insurance contract. . . .

Jones had leased commercial property in Danville from Danville L&M Limited (lessor) for the operation of their restaurant. Pursuant to the lease agreement, lessor was obligated to maintain rental income insurance providing coverage for damage or destruction from fire or other perils. The lease stated this coverage would be at Jones's expense and the policy would provide that the loss would be payable to lessor. The lease also stated that during any repairs to the premises after damage or destruction from a peril, Jones's rent would be equitably reduced to the extent lessor received proceeds from the rental income insurance. The insurance policy lessor obtained, through Aetna, included a "rental value endorsement" which stated Aetna would be liable for the "Actual Loss Sustained by the insured resulting directly from necessary untenantability, caused by damage to or destruction of the building(s) or structure(s) as furnished and equipped by the insured, by a peril not excluded in this policy...."

In 1989 and 1990, the restaurant premises suffered damage from the intrusion of water from a variety of sources. Patronage was reduced to the extent that Jones was unable to meet its rent obligations. On August 10, 1990, Jones vacated the premises.

Aetna was notified of the loss by Jones in 1989. It failed to provide coverage benefits on the claim for loss of rental income or damage to the structure. Jones alleged that Aetna's actions constituted a breach of the covenant of good faith and fair dealing and that such breach caused lessor to sue Jones for nonpayment of rent and for structural damage to the premises. In the first cause of action, Jones claimed Aetna breached its "obligations to the plaintiffs as implied-in-law co-insureds under the policy of insurance." In the second cause of action, Jones charged Aetna breached its obligations to Jones as third party beneficiaries under the insurance policy. A third cause of action stated that Aetna's actions were intentional and entitled Jones to punitive damages.

Aetna's general demurrer to the original complaint was sustained with leave to amend. Its general demurrer to the amended complaint was sustained without leave to amend. Aetna maintained Jones had no standing to sue as an implied-in-law coinsured under the contract of insurance or as a third party beneficiary. . . .

While an action for breach of the covenant of good faith and fair dealing sounds in tort, the duty of good faith and fair dealing arises from and exists solely because of the contractual relationship between the parties. (Gruenberg v. Aetna Ins. Co. (1973) 9 Cal.3d 566, 577-578 [108 Cal.Rptr. 480, 510 P.2d 1032].) Thus, someone who is not a party to the contract has no standing to enforce it or to recover extracontractual damages for the wrongful withholding of benefits to the contracting party. (Hatchwell v. Blue Shield of California (1988) 198 Cal.App.3d 1027, 1034 [244 Cal.Rptr. 249].) However, in the context of insurance policies, "[a] nonparty who is nevertheless entitled to policy benefits, such as an 'insured' person under the terms of the policy or an express beneficiary, has standing only if [he or] she is the claimant whose benefits are wrongfully withheld." (Ibid.)

Jones does not allege he was a contracting party for the insurance policy. Neither does he allege that he was a claimant. Instead, he submits that the facts as pled demonstrate standing as an implied-in-law coinsured under the terms of the policy. Jones states that as the lease agreement required lessor to purchase rental income insurance at Jones's expense, that insurance is deemed to mutually benefit both parties and as such he is a coinsured under the policy with standing to sue. However, the authority he cites for this proposition is unpersuasive.

[The court rejected Jones' argument that principles set forth in subrogation cases are applicable to the instant case or that he pled sufficient facts to establish standing under the implied-in-law coinsured theory.] . . .

Neither are we persuaded by Jones's alternative argument that he has standing to prosecute the action as a third party beneficiary of the insurance policy. Civil Code section 1559 provides: "A contract, made expressly for the benefit of a third person, may be enforced by him at any time before the parties thereto rescind it." A third party may qualify as a beneficiary under a contract where the contracting parties must have intended to benefit that third party and such intent appears on the terms of the contract. (Ascherman v. General Reinsurance Corp. (1986) 183 Cal.App.3d 307, 311 [228 Cal.Rptr. 1].) However, it is well settled that Civil Code section 1559 excludes enforcement of a contract by persons who are only incidentally or remotely benefited by it. (Lucas v. Hamm (1961) 56 Cal.2d 583, 590 [15 Cal.Rptr. 821, 364 P.2d 685], cert. den. (1962) 368 U.S. 987 [7 L.Ed.2d 525, 82 S.Ct. 603]; Walters v. Marler (1978) 83 Cal.App.3d 1, 31 [147 Cal.Rptr. 655].) [7a] " 'A third party should not be permitted to enforce covenants made not for his benefit, but rather for others. He is not a contracting party; his right to performance is predicated on the contracting parties' intent to benefit him....' " (Cancino v. Farmers Ins. Group (1978) 80 Cal.App.3d 335, 344 [145 Cal.Rptr. 503], quoting Lucas v. Hamm, supra, 56 Cal.2d at pp. 590-591; see also Murphy v. Allstate Ins. Co. (1976) 17 Cal.3d 937, 944 [132 Cal.Rptr. 424, 553 P.2d 584].) [8] An insurer's duty of good faith and fair dealing is owed solely to its insured and, perhaps, any express beneficiary of the insurance policy. Incidental or remote beneficiaries of the policy cannot state a cause of action against the insurer for a breach of the duty. (Cancino v. Farmers Ins. Group, supra, 80 Cal.App.3d at p. 342, citing Austero v. National Cas. Co., supra, 62 Cal.App.3d at pp. 516-517.)

The fact that the third party is only incidentally named in the contract or that the contract, if carried out to its terms, would inure to the third party's benefit is insufficient to entitle him or her to demand enforcement. (Walters v. Marler, supra, 83 Cal.App.3d at p. 33.) Whether a third party is an intended beneficiary or merely an incidental beneficiary to the contract involves construction of the parties' intent, gleaned from reading the contract as a whole in light of the circumstances under which it was entered. (Ibid.)

It is apparent from the terms of the insurance policy in the instant case that Jones was not an intended beneficiary. The fact that, by virtue of the lease provision for rent abatement, Jones would have received some benefit in the event Aetna indemnified the lessor for loss of rental income only makes him an incidental beneficiary under the policy. The policy itself and surrounding circumstances do not demonstrate that Aetna and lessor intended Jones to benefit from their agreement.

The implied covenant of good faith and fair dealing in the insurance policy at issue was intended to benefit the insured lessor. Jones has no standing as a third party beneficiary to enforce the covenant made for the benefit of the lessor.

We conclude the trial court properly determined the facts as pleaded did not state a cause of action. There is no reasonable possibility that the lack of standing can be cured by amendment.

The judgment is affirmed.

Questions

1. How does the court distinguish between an intended beneficiary and an incidental beneficiary?

2. Explain why the court concluded that the plaintiff did not have standing to sue as a third party beneficiary in this case.

3. What factors did the court consider in determining that the plaintiff was an incidental beneficiary rather than an intended beneficiary?

Takeaways – Jones v. Aetna Casualty

In deciding whether the third party is an intended beneficiary with enforceable rights or an incidental beneficiary with no right to enforce the contract, what is the most critical factor?

Municipal Contracts and Third Parties

Luis v. Orcutt Town Water Co.
California Court of Appeal, Second District, 1962
204 Cal.App.2d 433

BALTHIS, J. This action was brought to recover damages resulting from a fire which destroyed the mercantile store of plaintiff Luis in the Town of Orcutt. The second amended complaint (hereinafter referred to as the "complaint") contains six causes of action; three for plaintiff Luis and three for plaintiff Great American Insurance Company (New York); the term "plaintiff" as used in the singular hereafter refers to plaintiff Luis. The claims of the insurance company are derivative from plaintiff Luis and are based upon subrogation by reason of the company's having paid a portion of the loss. The liability of defendants is alleged to be both contractual and tortious.

A demurrer to plaintiffs' complaint was sustained without leave to amend and, after judgment was entered for defendants, plaintiffs appeal. The question presented by the appeal is whether the complaint states facts sufficient to constitute a cause of action against defendants; defendant Union Oil Company of California is referred to herein as "Union" and defendant Orcutt Town Water Company is referred to as "Water Company."

The allegations of the first cause of action of the complaint may be summarized as follows:

Prior to 1940 Union owned and operated a private water system in the Town of Orcutt which also supplied water to third persons for domestic and commercial purposes. The portion of the water system supplying water to third persons in the Town of Orcutt was acquired in 1940 by Water Company with permission of the Public Utilities Commission.

The complaint refers to two contracts between Union and Water Company. The principal agreement provides that Union will supply Water Company with such quantities of water from Union's wells located at Union's property adjoining the Town of Orcutt as Water Company may require for distribution to domestic and commercial consumers within the Town of Orcutt; that said water is to be delivered to Water Company's facilities at Union's Orcutt pump station and that Water Company will maintain and operate the pumps and lines for receiving and transporting the water to its own storage facilities.

Paragraph 2 of the principal agreement provides in part as follows: "Union further agrees to furnish water to Water Company's Orcutt town storage tank from Union's separate high pressure line in case of emergency when Water Company is prevented from or is unable to take water at its connection at Union's Orcutt property." . . .

The complaint also states that a fire department is maintained in the Town of Orcutt as a volunteer fire department requiring regular annual taxes to be collected by the county. Plaintiff Luis is a resident and taxpayer of Orcutt and was and is a customer of Water Company.

It is further alleged that as a matter of practice and conduct on the part of defendants, the word "emergency" contained in the principal agreement above mentioned was recognized and acknowledged to include emergency by fire and it was further "recognized and acknowledged that the practical method of supplying additional water in the case of emergency by fire would be to open a high pressure valve which existed in the vicinity of a fire hydrant maintained for fire purposes in the vicinity of the Orcutt pump station and which would provide an increase in water from a two inch to a six inch water flow under pressure when said valve was opened." (Complaint, par. VIII.) Defendants advised the local fire officials that in the event water was needed to combat a fire, defendants would open said high-pressure valve at once, but that defendants did not advise the local fire authorities as to the location of said valve. Defendants communicated the various facts to other interested persons including plaintiff.

The complaint then states that plaintiff owned and operated a store building and mercantile business in the Town of Orcutt; that on November 10, 1951, the building and its contents were destroyed by fire; that at the time of fire urgent demand was made upon defendants to supply water to combat the fire but defendants "failed to promptly and immediately operate the valve and delayed in doing so for a highly unreasonable length of time exceeding one hour," and that as a result "plaintiff's building and contents were totally destroyed" (complaint, par. X); that defendants breached the contract and plaintiff has suffered damages in the sum of $140,000. . . .

In the third cause of action it is alleged that defendants voluntarily assumed an obligation "that in the event of emergency by fire a high pressure valve which existed in the vicinity of a fire hydrant maintained for fire purposes in the vicinity of the Orcutt pump station, and which would provide an increase in water from a two inch to a six inch water flow under pressure when said valve was opened, would be opened immediately upon the occurrence of any such emergency by fire." . . . The complaint states that this assumption of obligation by defendants was made known by means of communications to the local officials of the fire district and to other interested persons including plaintiff. One of the individuals responsible for turning on the valve was an employee of Union; the other individual was responsible to both defendants and was unavailable at the time of fire because he was on vacation; no other provision for emergency by fire was made by either defendant or the local fire authorities or by plaintiff; by reason of the failure to provide water for such emergency by fire and because of such negligence plaintiff suffered the property losses mentioned. . . .

The rule is well established in California that a water company is not liable to one of its consumers for failure to furnish water (or at sufficient pressure) for fire protection unless an express contract for that purpose has been made. Liability for loss resulting from fire is not an incident of the ordinary relation of water distributor and consumer; it can only be created by an express private contract whereby the water company agreed to furnish water as a protection against fire. It is only where the contract calls for water service for the purposes of extinguishing fires that loss of the premises by fire may be compensated in damages as having been reasonably supposed to have been within the contemplation of the parties.

The reasons for the above rule are stated in one of the leading cases (Niehaus Bros. Co. v. Contra Costa etc. Water Co. (1911) 159 Cal. 305, 318-319 [113 P. 375, 36 L.R.A. N.S. 1045], as follows:

"Applying the reasoning of these authorities to the relation between the company and the consumer here ... no obligation to furnish water for fire protection is implied, nor can it be said to exist in the absence of an express contract. Keeping in mind ... that the primary business of a water company is to furnish water as a commodity, and not to extinguish fires, and further recognizing that under the law of this state the defendant is a quasi public corporation engaged in the exercise of a public use and discharging a public duty which would otherwise devolve upon the municipality itself and furnishing water at rates fixed exclusively by the municipality, it would appear plain that it was never contemplated that from the simple relation of distributor and consumer the former undertook to assume liability for failure to furnish water to extinguish fires. In the nature of things the compensation fixed by the municipality has no relation to the assumption of any such liability; that compensation is based on the expense of furnishing water simply as a commodity; liability for destruction of premises to which the company may be required to supply water was not taken into consideration in fixing the rate, nor, we apprehend, was it even thought that any such liability could be imposed by the ordinance, or was to be assumed by the company in doing so."

The court further points out that if a water company were to be held liable for damages resulting from a failure on the part of the water company to supply sufficient water at sufficient pressure to extinguish a fire, it would place upon the water company a staggering insurance burden not covered by the rates charged. The court said at page 321:

"It is common knowledge that, notably in large manufacturing centers within municipalities, hydrants are installed on the premises and connected with a public water company's system as a precautionary measure in case of fire. This is particularly true when the enterprise in which the owners are engaged is more readily exposed to danger from fire, either from the inflammable material which is being used in the factories, or on account of the proximity of others which are of that character. The various factories or mills in which hydrants are placed and connections with the public water system made may represent property worth millions of dollars which is subject to danger of destruction by fire and where the water to be used should fire arise is not furnished under any express contract between the parties but is being supplied simply under the ordinance rates as to water and hydrant charges established by law. Of course, if the position of the respondent is correct, then in all these instances a public water company is assuming liability practically as an insurer of millions of dollars worth of property upon which, either from the nature of the business conducted on the premises or the locality in which the property is situated, an insurance company itself would not think of assuming the risk." ...

A municipality may not recover damages against a water company for failure to furnish water under sufficient pressure for fire protection (City of Ukiah v. Ukiah Water & Imp. Co. (1904) 142 Cal. 173 [75 P. 773, 100 Am.St.Rep. 107, 64 L.R.A. 231]).

It is helpful to examine the pertinent provisions of the principal contract and to analyze the relationships involved in the instant case.

First to be considered is the fact that there is no contract involved here to which plaintiff Luis is a party. The two agreements referred to in the complaint are between Union and Water Company; the contracts are essentially between the water producer and the water distributor and have nothing to do with the consumer. They refer to the supply and sale of water for "domestic and commercial purposes," not for fire purposes. The contracts are not the type or classification referred to in the exception to the general rule, that is, an express private contract by a consumer with a water company to obtain water service for a particular purpose, fire protection (Niehaus Bros. Co. v. Contra Costa etc. Co., supra, 159 Cal. 305, 312-313).

Further, plaintiff is not an express beneficiary under the principal contract which as pointed out above, is between water supplier and water distributor.

Section 1559, Civil Code, reads: "A contract, made expressly for the benefit of a third person, may be enforced by him at any time before the parties thereto rescind it." This code section has been explained and interpreted by a large number of cases but the most concise statement of the law is found in the Restatement of Contracts, section 133, where third-party beneficiaries are classified as follows:

A person is a donee beneficiary:

"(a) ... if it appears from the terms of the promise in view of the accompanying circumstances that the purpose of the promisee in obtaining the promise of all or part of the performance thereof is to make a gift to the beneficiary or to confer upon him a right against the promisor to some performance neither due nor supposed or asserted to be due from the promisee to the beneficiary." A person is a creditor beneficiary:

"(b) ... if no purpose to make a gift appears from the terms of the promise in view of the accompanying circumstances and performance of the promise will satisfy an actual or supposed or asserted duty of the promisee to the beneficiary, or a right of the beneficiary against the promisee which has been barred by the Statute of Limitations or by a discharge in bankruptcy, or which is unenforceable because of the Statute of Frauds."

A person is an incidental beneficiary:

"(c) ... if neither the facts stated in Clause (a) nor those stated in Clause (b) exist."

Although Civil Code section 1559 makes no reference to the different types of beneficiaries, the California cases generally rely on these Restatement classifications (Hartman Ranch Co. v. Associated Oil Co. (1937) 10 Cal.2d 232, 244 [73 P.2d 1163]).

Under the foregoing rules a plaintiff must plead a contract which was made expressly for his benefit and one in which it clearly appears that he was a beneficiary, e.g., Steinberg v. Buchman (1946) 73 Cal.App.2d 605, 609 [167 P.2d 207]. The fortuitous fact that he may have suffered detriment by reason of the nonperformance of the contract does not give him a cause of action. (Shutes v. Cheney (1954) 123 Cal.App.2d 256, 262 [266 P.2d 902].) The test in deciding whether a contract inures to the benefit of a third person is whether an intent to so benefit the third person appears from the terms of the agreement (Le Ballister v. Redwood Theatres, Inc. (1934) 1 Cal.App.2d 447, 448-449 [36 P.2d 827]). Where a claim is made that the parties to an agreement intended to benefit a third party, but no attempt is made to reform the contract nor has any mistake or fraud been alleged, the courts must be guided by the terms of the written instrument (Shutes v. Cheney, supra, 123 Cal.App.2d 256, 261).

We hold that the principal contract involved here, and relied upon by plaintiff for his first and second causes of action, was not made expressly for the benefit of plaintiff; the terms of such agreement do not indicate that the parties to it contemplated or intended expressly to benefit plaintiff Luis, or to protect him against fire losses, or to entitle him to sue upon such agreement. Plaintiff could only be considered a most remote and incidental beneficiary in a relationship not recognized by the law. . . .

The judgment appealed from is affirmed.

Questions

1. Why was the plaintiff in this case not able to recover damages from the water company for the loss resulting from the fire?

2. Discuss the court's analysis of the relationships between the parties involved in the case.

3. Based on the court's reasoning, what would be the implications if a water company were held liable for damages resulting from a failure to supply sufficient water for fire protection? How would it affect the water company and the rates charged for water services?

Takeaways – Luis v. Orcutt Town Water Co.

Subject to certain exceptions, a promisor who contracts with a government or governmental agency to do an act or render a service to the public is not subject to contractual liability to a member of the public for consequential damages resulting from performance or failure to perform. (Rest.2d § 313(2).) In other words, individual members of the public are treated as incidental beneficiaries unless a different intention is manifested . I.e.,. (Comment a to Rest.2d § 313)

Vesting of Third Party's Rights

Once the original parties have entered into an enforceable contract may they change or modify it without the consent of the third party beneficiary?

Karo v. San Diego Symphony Orchestra Ass'n.
U.S. Court of Appeals, Ninth Circuit (Cal.), 1985
762 F.2d 819

BOOCHEVER, Circuit Judge: Karo appeals from a district court order dismissing his hybrid suit for breach of a collective bargaining agreement and breach of the duty of fair representation on the ground that he lacked standing. Although Karo is a union member, he is not an employee within the collective bargaining unit. We affirm the dismissal.

Karo is a percussionist and a member of the Musicians Association of San Diego Local 325, American Federation of Musicians (Local 325). In 1969 he was employed by the San Diego Symphony Orchestra Association (Symphony) as substitute percussionist for one concert, but has not been employed by the Symphony since that time.

On May 4, 1983, Karo filed a complaint against Local 325 and the Symphony (defendants) pursuant to section 301 of the Labor Management Relations Act of 1947 (LMRA), 29 U.S.C. § 185 (1982). The complaint was triggered by Karo's desire to obtain a contract chair in the percussion section of the Symphony. Karo alleged that Local 325 had breached its duty of fair representation by agreeing to a contract modification which bypassed the audition procedures and by failing to act on his grievance concerning the matter; that the Symphony breached the collective bargaining agreement by failing to hold auditions for the percussion chair; and that the Symphony and Local 325 conspired to modify the agreement in order to eliminate auditions so that another musician could be hired for the percussion chair without having to audition.

In 1980 Karo learned that the Symphony had an opening for a percussionist, and that auditions were to be scheduled during the Symphony's 1981-1982 season. At that time the relationship between the Symphony and Local 325 was governed by a collective bargaining agreement entered into on September 1, 1979, which specified the terms and conditions of employment for Local 325 members with the Symphony. Local 325 was recognized as the exclusive representative of Symphony musicians for the purpose of collective bargaining. It is undisputed that although Karo was a union member, he was never a member of the bargaining unit. The agreement, which was to terminate on August 31, 1982, was modified and extended for one year in February 1982.

The audition procedures in the original agreement provided that when a vacancy occurred the Symphony would give fifteen days written notice to the union.

The Symphony was required to conduct blind auditions with the players performing behind a screen, and to follow elaborate procedures for impartially selecting the best applicant.

The 1982 modification permitted the Symphony to offer contracts without auditions to noncontract musicians with six years of service within ten years preceding April 10, 1982. Mr. Plank, a noncontract percussionist with the required years of service, was awarded a seat without an audition under this provision. . . .

[E]ven if Karo could be considered a third party beneficiary of the 1979 agreement he still cannot prevail. The agreement was amended to provide specifically for filling positions without auditions when noncontract musicians had prior service for specified periods. Under the modified agreement Karo had no right to audition for the seat.

The Restatement (Second) of Contracts provides that in the absence of terms in a third party beneficiary contract prohibiting change or modification of a duty to an intended beneficiary, the promisor and promisee retain power to discharge or modify the duty by subsequent agreement. Restatement (Second) of Contracts § 311(1), (2) (1981). The power to modify terminates when the beneficiary materially changes position in justifiable reliance on the promise before receiving notification of the modification. Id. § 311(3). Karo does not allege any such change of position. Thus, assuming that Karo could be regarded as a third party beneficiary under the 1979 contract, no rights he might have acquired thereunder had vested when the contract was modified in 1982. Accordingly the union and Symphony had the power to modify the agreement eliminating the open audition provisions when non-contract musicians had requisite experience for filling the position. . . .

Karo . . . . does not have standing to sue as a third party beneficiary because he had no vested rights at the time that the agreement was amended. . . .

The judgment of dismissal is AFFIRMED.

Questions

1. According to the Restatement Second of Contracts, when can a duty owed to an intended beneficiary in a third party beneficiary contract be modified by the promisor and promisee?

2. Why did the court conclude that Karo did not have standing to sue as a third party beneficiary?

Takeaways – Karo v. San Diego Symphony

The right of the original parties to rescind or modify a third party beneficiary contract, without the assent of the beneficiary, ceases once the beneficiary learns of the contract and assents to it or materially changes his position in justifiable reliance on it or brings suit on it. (Rest.2d § 311(3).) Did Karo, come close to doing any of those things so that his rights would have vested?

Detroit Bank & Trust v. Chicago Flame Hardening
United States District Court, N. D. Indiana, 1982
541 F. Supp. 1278

LEE, District Judge. . . . *Findings of Fact* . . . 4. On July 29, 1964, Marvin R. Scott, Gainor D. Scott and John R. Keeler, the owners of the entire issue of Chicago Flame's capital stock, unanimously agreed by corporate resolution that upon the death of these specifically named shareholders (M. R. Scott, G. D. Scott and J. D. Keeler), the corporation would pay to his wife, if then living, commencing with the date of her husband's death, a graduated monthly stipend over a fifteen (15) year period totaling $150,300 to terminate in the event of her death if prior to the expiration of the payment period.

5. The signatories to this 1964 resolution did not expressly reserve the right to alter and/or amend.

6. Despite the fact that the potential beneficiaries of this resolution lacked experience or independent expertise in the flame hardening industry, they were, as recipient widows under the terms of the resolution, to make themselves available for consulting work and to agree not to compete with Chicago Flame for the duration of their receipt of benefits as consideration for the same under this corporate agreement.

7. This 1965 resolution further provided that the capital shares of the then deceased original shareholder be retained in a voting trust with the surviving original shareholders acting as trustees until the death of the last surviving original shareholder.

8. Within a reasonable time following the adoption of this resolution Marvin R. Scott's wife, Roxanne, became aware that this document's beneficial terms were potentially available to her in the future. She then "forgot the whole thing." (Transcript of testimony, December 22, 1980, pp. 19-20).

9. The provisions of the 1964 widow's resolution were initially implemented on July 12, 1967 when Marjorie Scott Keeler signed the requisite statement agreeing to abide by the resolution's consideration requirements, following the July 8, 1967 death of her husband, John R. Keeler.

10. Marjorie Scott Keeler thereinafter continually received a monthly stipend pursuant to the express terms of this agreement, except for an eighteen (18) month period during 1971 and 1972 when she voluntarily consented to a postponement in recognition of Chicago Flame's deteriorating financial posture.

11. Marvin R. Scott's wife, Roxanne, was fully and continuously aware that Marjorie Scott Keeler (her sister-in-law) was receiving the benefits provided by the 1964 resolution for surviving spouses of the original signatories.

12. On February 15, 1971 Marvin R. Scott participated in and approved the adoption of a second corporate resolution along with the other owners of the entire issue of Chicago Flame's capital stock, Gainor D. Scott and Marjorie Scott Keeler. This subsequent agreement was executed to rescind the right of Marvin R. Scott's surviving spouse to receive graduated monthly payments as formerly provided in the 1964 resolution.

13. Marvin R. Scott's motivation for entering into this second resolution was to sustain the future financial integrity of Chicago Flame.

14. Following a lengthy period of convalescence, Marvin R. Scott died on October 31, 1971 leaving plaintiff's current ward, Roxanne Scott, as his surviving spouse.

15. Although there remains conflicting testimony, it is the determination of the Court that, while Mrs. Roxanne Scott may not have actually seen the February 15, 1971 rescission document prior to the instigation of this suit, she became aware of her husband's relinquishment of the widow's benefits during the interim following his death and the filing of this suit.

16. Following the death of her husband, Roxanne Scott moved to Florida. Due to a continuing emotional illness, she was adjudicated incompetent by a Florida court and a guardianship was established in March of 1972 which was maintained for approximately two years.

17. Roxanne Scott returned to Michigan in 1975 where she suffered a recurrence of the same mental illness in August of 1975. She remained hospitalized in various facilities until her release in December of 1975. A guardianship was established solely over her estate in November, 1975. This same guardianship remains in force. Although mentally competent today, Mrs. Scott continues to be under a physician's care.

18. Mrs. Roxanne Scott did not request the monthly stipend available to surviving spouses through the 1964 resolution prior to the initiation of this litigation on September 19, 1977; nor was she approached in that regard by Chicago Flame.

19. Mrs. Roxanne Scott made no expenditure, nor did she change position or perform any act in reliance on the 1964 widow's resolution prior to the commencement of this litigation.

20. Following the January, 1977 death of Gainor Scott, Chicago Flame executed the same "consideration" agreement with his widow, Cecelia Scott, as they had previously done with Marjorie Scott Keeler. Thereinafter, Chicago Flame continued to provide benefits to these two fully vested surviving spouses as mandated by the operative terms of the 1964 widow's resolution.

21. On June 16, 1977 Mr. Thomas Farnsworth purchased a majority of Chicago Flame's capital shares from Marjorie Scott Keeler Lanning (since remarried) and Cecelia Scott. At the time of the purchase, Mr. Farnsworth fully perceived the continuing obligation imposed pursuant to the still effective terms of the 1964 resolution and the relief believed provided by Marvin R. Scott's prior rescission of these same benefits.

Plaintiff initiated this litigation on September 19, 1977 by way of a complaint which seeks to enforce the terms of the 1964 widow's resolution for the benefit of its ward, Mrs. Roxanne Scott. Plaintiff asserts its contentions on the basis of (1) the failure to expressly reserve the right to rescind, (2) a presumption of acceptance for a donee beneficiary, (3) Roxanne Scott's medical condition precluding the earlier assertion of her rights as a means of acceptance, and (4) that this agreement vested a right in its ward which could not be denied by the 1971 rescission. Given the fact that this disputed resolution was executed in Indiana by a domestic corporation of that state, Indiana law clearly controls and will dictate the determination of this matter. *Royal v. Keny Co.,* 528 F.2d 184 (7th Cir. 1975).

The old Restatement rule provided that the promisor and promisee could make no change in the promise made to a donee beneficiary unless such a power is reserved. Restatement of Contracts § 142 at 168 (1932). Nor could a change be made by the promisor and promisee in their promise to a creditor beneficiary if he has changed his position in reliance on that promise. *Id.; see* Page, *The Power of Contracting Parties to Alter a Contract for Rendering Performance to a Third Person,* 12 Wis.L.Rev. 141, 149-50 (1937). Evolutionary changes in the law, however, have transformed the aforementioned position of the original Restatement. The Second Restatement of Contracts as adopted and promulgated, eliminates this distinction between a donee and creditor beneficiary and recognizes that modification on the part of the promisor and promisee is ineffective only if the agreement so provides, unless the third party beneficiary has changed his position in reliance on the promise or has accepted, adopted or acted upon it. Restatement (Second) of Contracts § 142 (1979). *See also* Note, *Gratuitous Promise,* 6 Val.L.Rev. 353 (1972); 17 Am.Jur.2d Contracts § 317 (1979); 97 A.L.R.2d 1262 (1964).

Indiana specifically reaffirmed its adoption of this majority view as later expressed in the Second Restatement. In the case of *In Re Estate of Fanning,* 263 Ind. 414, 333 N.E.2d 80 (1975), the Indiana Supreme Court examined the posture of a third party beneficiary and determined that the right to rescind or modify a third party beneficiary contract, without the assent of the beneficiary, ceases once the contract is accepted, adopted or acted upon by the third party.

The plaintiff, on behalf of its ward, asserts that the 1971 rescission was invalid for the parties failed to expressly reserve the right to rescind the 1964 widow's resolution. Indiana has long recognized that even a party without right may rescind a contract if the other party fails to object to it and permits the rescission to occur; such a rescission would be by mutual consent. *Ralya v. Atkins,* 157 Ind. 331, 61 N.E. 726 (1901); *see generally* Corbin on Contracts §§ 772-776 (1951 ed. & Supp. 1980); 3 Williston, *Contracts* § 1826 (3d ed. 1959). In the case of contracts entered into for the benefit of a third party, Indiana follows the rule found in most jurisdictions. That is, the parties to a third party beneficiary contract may rescind, vary or abrogate the contract as they see fit, without the approval of the third party, at any time before the contract is accepted, adopted or acted upon by a third party beneficiary. *Fanning,* 333 N.E.2d at 84; *accord Jackman Cigar Co. v. Berger,* 114 Ind.App. 437, 52 N.E.2d 363 (1944). A rescission prior to the required change in position by a third party deprives that third party of any rights under or because of the contract. *Id.; see* 17 Am.Jur.2d Contracts § 317 (1979).

In this case the 1964 agreement was adopted as a corporate resolution by Chicago Flame Hardening, Inc. All of the officers and shareholders of the corporation approving the initial agreement. On February 15, 1971 the officers and shareholders mutually agreed to rescind the July 29, 1964 resolution. Recognizing the majority view followed by Indiana, the rescission of the prior agreement is valid without a specific reservation of the power to rescind so long as the third-party beneficiary, Mrs. Roxanne Scott, had not accepted, adopted or acted upon the original widow's resolution. Therefore, an express reservation of the right to rescind is not required to abrogate the third party beneficiary agreement.

Plaintiff next contends that since Mrs. Roxanne Scott had knowledge of the original 1964 resolution, her acceptance of this beneficial agreement must be presumed. In support of this position plaintiff offers three vintage cases which recognize a presumption of acceptance.

These cases are clearly distinguishable from the present cause. The primary and controlling distinction is that while acceptance was presumed in cases cited by plaintiff, the intended beneficiaries were infants at the time of the transaction. A presumption is necessary in such instances to protect the interests of minor beneficiaries. Mrs. Scott, however, was an adult at the time of the 1964 widow's resolution, completely able to assert her own rights, and as such is not afforded the same protection. Moreover, the same authority submitted by plaintiff in support of a presumption of acceptance provides *a fortiori* a strong argument for the opposite proposition a lack of such protection for a competent adult through negative implication.

Plaintiff's cases and contention here are effectively nothing more than a camouflaged application of gift theory which recognizes that once a gift is consummated, it remains irrevocable except by consent of the donee. Although the contract theory applicable to this cause has been extended in some instances as an equitable means of avoiding the delivery requirement necessitated by the gift theory, it would be an oversimplification to also attempt to inject into this same contract theory a substitute for acceptance. The determinative legal theory in this matter is therefore a stricter contract theory which does not provide the presumption of acceptance claimed by plaintiff for its beneficiary ward donee. *Fanning*, 333 N.E.2d at 85.

Plaintiff's next focus theorizes that "but for" Roxanne Scott's declining health, she would have instituted this litigation at an earlier date. Plaintiff attempts thereby to utilize its ward's acknowledged mental and physical difficulties as a vehicle to excuse not only the failure to sue before rescission, but also to demonstrate why prompt commencement of this action to preserve her benefits was prevented. The net effect of this proposition is to attempt to transform this 1977 litigation into a belated substitute for acceptance prior to rescission.

Although the Court recognizes that the filing of a suit by a third party beneficiary may be considered as acceptance by that individual, *Zimmerman v. Zehender*, 164 Ind. 466, 73 N.E. 920 (1905); *Blackard v. Monarch*, 131 Ind.App. 514, 169 N.E.2d 735 (1960), the Court may not consider Mrs. Scott's health as dispositive of the issue before it. Perhaps equity might demand some presumption of acceptance had Mrs. Scott been totally incapacitated prior to rescission;[19] however, plaintiff's own evidence makes it clear that the February 15, 1971 rescission took place before Mrs. Scott's inhibiting physical and mental decline occurred and the appointment of guardians to represent her interests.

As early as 1903, the Indiana Supreme Court stated that "[A] contract for the benefit of a competent third person may become available to that person, provided that it is not rescinded by the parties thereto before such third person gives notice that he accepts it." *Johnson v. Central Co.*, 159 Ind. 605, 65 N.E. 1028 (1903). Therefore, this Court cannot accept plaintiff's novel preclusion argument. Mrs. Scott was a "competent" adult third party beneficiary at the time of this rescission. Consequently, this Court may not fictionalize the initiation of this suit as an act of acceptance prior to the 1971 rescission. *See Zimmerman, supra*, 73 N.E. at 922.

The attenuated circumstance surrounding this litigation resulted in the submission of numerous briefs by opposing counsel. Three cases which appear to be somewhat significant to this cause have emerged. However, different interpretations of each have been offered. To resolve this conflict, the Court believes a review of the cases must be provided.

First, the case of *In Re Estate of Fanning,* 263 Ind. 414, 333 N.E.2d 80 (1975) (previously cited), dealt with the ownership of certificates of deposit. Wildus Fanning purchased certificates of deposit which, upon their face, were payable to "Wildus Fanning or Marcella Seavey either of them with the right of survivorship and not as tenants in common." Since the certificates were discovered in Fanning's safety deposit box after her death and since no signature card or deposit agreement had been executed, her daughter (Seavey) could not claim the certificates under a gift theory as there was no actual or constructive delivery. The Indiana Supreme Court held that where a certificate of deposit creates a joint account with rights of survivorship in clear and unequivocal language, donative intent of the donor is presumptively established. The thrust of the holding was that principles of contract law, rather than that of gifts, should be the governing substantive law due to the inherent contractual nature of certificates. The daughter who was unaware of the existence of the certificates until after the death of her mother, was found to be a third party beneficial owner. Therefore, the essence of *Fanning* is that as a third party contract, the donor could rescind during her lifetime; otherwise, the presumptive donative intent could be refuted only by parol evidence of fraud, duress, undue influence or mistake. *See Moore v. Bowyer,* Ind.App., 388 N.E.2d 611, 612 (1976).

The Court's reading of *Fanning* does not support plaintiff's contention that knowledge on the part of the donee beneficiary constitutes acceptance. In fact, *Fanning* provides authority for this Court's position concerning rescission by citing with approval 17 Am.Jur.2d Contracts § 314 (1964), which states in part, "[t]he parties to a contract entered into for the benefit of a third person may rescind, vary, or abrogate the contract as they see fit, without the assent of the third person, at any time before the contract is accepted, adopted, or acted upon by him ..." Although *Fanning* acknowledges the right of rescission in third party beneficiary contracts, it is distinguishable from this instant case for rescission was never attempted by the decedent certificate purchase.

The next case for consideration is *Matter of Estate of Bannon,* 171 Ind.App. 610, 358 N.E.2d 215 (1976), which addressed the inheritance tax aspects of an annuity. The decedent accepted employment for a fixed term with a specific salary. The agreement provided that if he died before expiration of the term survived by his wife then the corporation was to pay her $5,000 per year for the balance of the original term. That court in applying an ownership tax theory determined that the decedent did not have an interest in the property which passed to his wife after his death. Again, there was no attempt by the decedent to rescind the annuity agreement. The *Bannon* court questioned whether the widow was a third party beneficiary to the annuity agreement whose rights were vested. Moreover, in a footnote on this point *Fanning* is cited in recognition of the right to modify a third party beneficiary contract. *Bannon, supra,* at 218 n. 7.

The final case for review is *Salesky v. Hat Corporation of America*, 20 A.D. 114, 244 N.Y.S.2d 965 (1963). In *Salesky*, a majority of the shareholders approved a corporate resolution which provided $10,000 for six years to the wife of their president upon his death. The interested wife voted with the majority in adopting the resolution. The contracting parties to this agreement also expressly reserved the right to terminate the agreement upon proper notice. Later, this resolution was amended without shareholder approval by substituting the president's sister as the intended beneficiary. Upon the president's death both his wife and sister claimed to be the equitable beneficiary. The court found for the sister.

This case is also distinguishable for Mr. M. R. Scott and Chicago Flame did not expressly reserve the right to terminate its 1964 resolution and Mrs. Roxanne Scott did not vote to approve the same. Therefore, the language in *Salesky* concerning vested rights and retention of control is not dispositive in this cause.

The Court's review of these cases fails to resolve the decisive question remaining before the Court. Neither plaintiff's assertions concerning acceptance, nor defendant's position on rescission are directly supported by the cases presented. The Court must therefore return to the issue of whether Roxanne Scott accepted, adopted or acted upon the 1964 resolution prior to the 1971 rescission.

The analysis above establishes that acceptance may not be presumed by this Court and that this contract for the benefit of a third party is enforceable only if the third party beneficiary has accepted, adopted or acted upon it prior to rescission. Because prior decisions fail to provide an adequate definition, the Court must examine the somewhat nebulous term "acceptance" in an effort to identify if some form of assent took place on the part of Mrs. Roxanne Scott if it is to conclude that the 1971 rescission was ineffective and that her derivative rights were preserved. *See e.g., United States v. Winnicki*, 151 F.2d 56, 57 (7th Cir. 1945) (words "receive" and "accept" are legal equivalents).

Acceptance may be an overt act, or the adoption of a benefit which is a question of intent and thereby also a factual determination. *See* Corbin, *supra*, §§ 782-793; Jones, *Legal Protection of Third Party Beneficiaries: On Opening Courthouse Doors*, 46 Cinn.L.Rev. 313 (1977). Nevertheless, even in instances such as this where plaintiff has provided no specific evidence of an overt act or of a change in position, it must still be remembered that "the power of promisor and promisee to vary the promisor's duty to an intended beneficiary is terminated when the beneficiary manifests assent to the promise in a manner invited by the promisor or promisee." Restatement (Second) on Contracts, *supra*, § 311 at comment (h). This rule utilizes an analogy to the law of offer and acceptance by recognizing that a third party beneficiary may well rely in ways difficult or impossible to prove. *Id.*

Fortunately for this Court, the narrow question currently before it does not present this circumstance characterized by an impossibility of proof. The converse is true as the Court's determination of the factual question regarding Roxanne Scott's intent to accept the benefits afforded by the 1964 resolution was answered in the negative by her own sworn testimony. While facing cross-examination, Mrs. Scott was specifically asked whether she made any long range plans or depended upon the 1964 widow's resolution. Her answer was, "No, I forgot the whole thing." (Transcript of testimony, December 22, 1980, pp. 19-20). In addition to this testimonial controversion, the Court also failed to discern any other corroborative evidence which might sustain plaintiff's claim of acceptance or change in position in reliance on that resolution. *See generally* Note, *The Requirements of Promissory Estoppel as Applied to Third Party Beneficiaries,* 30 U.Pitt.L.Rev. 174 (1968). Furthermore, the Court's position regarding the failure to establish adoptive intent is not gleaned from this single negatory response, but is supported by a detailed review of the entire record. It is therefore the conclusion of the Court that Roxanne Scott failed to accept, adopt or act upon the 1964 resolution prior to the 1971 rescission. Consequently, the Court must hold that Mrs. Scott's failure to act or rely upon the original agreement extinguished any benefits which might have accrued to her from the 1964 agreement.

It is the final determination of the Court that Mrs. Roxanne Scott failed to accept, adopt or act upon the 1964 resolution prior to the contracting parties' valid rescission on February 15, 1971.

Questions

1. Did the signatories to the 1964 resolution reserve the right to alter or amend it?

2. Under what circumstances can a party rescind or modify a third party beneficiary contract in Indiana?

3. According to Indiana law, when does the right to rescind or modify a third party beneficiary contract cease?

4. What is the difference between the "old" Restatement rule and the current Restatement rule on vesting?

Takeaways – Detroit Bank

The original parties to the contract can expressly agree to reserve the right to modify or terminate the rights of the third-party and such an agreement will trump any vesting rights.

Vesting only becomes an issue if the promisor and promisee purport to vary or discharge the rights of the beneficiary by a subsequent agreement. If there is no purported modification or discharge, there is no necessity to consider whether the beneficiary's rights have vested.

Assignment

A right arising out of a contract may be transferred by the holder of the right to another person. (Rest.2d § 317, Cal.Civ.Code § 1458) Such a transfer is called an *assignment*. The person making the transfer is the *assignor*. The person receiving the transfer is the *assignee*. If an assignment is effectively made, the assignor retains no further interest or claim in the right that has been assigned.

The general rule is that contract rights are freely assignable unless the assignment would materially change the duty of the obligor, materially increase the burden or risk imposed upon the obligor by his contract, impair the obligor's chance of obtaining return performance, or materially reduce the value of the return performance to the obligor. (See Rest.2d § 317) Unless it falls into one of the above exceptions, the assignment of a right cannot be objected to by the obligor.

Herzog v. Irace
Supreme Judicial Court of Maine, 1991
594 A.2d 1106

BRODY, Justice. Anthony Irace and Donald Lowry appeal from an order entered by the Superior Court affirming a District Court judgment in favor of Dr. John P. Herzog in an action for breach of an assignment to Dr. Herzog of personal injury settlement proceeds collected by Irace and Lowry, both attorneys, on behalf of their client, Gary G. Jones. On appeal, Irace and Lowry contend that the District Court erred in finding that the assignment was valid and enforceable against them. They also argue that enforcement of the assignment interferes with their ethical obligations toward their client. Finding no error, we affirm.

The facts of this case are not disputed. Gary Jones was injured in a motorcycle accident and retained Irace and Lowry to represent him in a personal injury action. Soon thereafter, Jones dislocated his shoulder, twice, in incidents unrelated to the motorcycle accident. Dr. Herzog examined Jones's shoulder and concluded that he needed surgery. At the time, however, Jones was unable to pay for the surgery and in consideration for the performance of the surgery by the doctor, he signed a letter dated June 14, 1988, written on Dr. Herzog's letterhead stating:

I, Gary Jones, request that payment be made directly from settlement of a claim currently pending for an unrelated incident, to John Herzog, D.O., for treatment of a shoulder injury which occurred at a different time.

Dr. Herzog notified Irace and Lowry that Jones had signed an "assignment of benefits" from the motorcycle personal injury action to cover the cost of surgery on his shoulder and was informed by an employee of Irace and Lowry that the assignment was sufficient to allow the firm to pay Dr. Herzog's bills at the conclusion of the case. Dr. Herzog performed the surgery and continued to treat Jones for approximately one year.

In May, 1989, Jones received a $20,000 settlement in the motorcycle personal injury action. He instructed Irace and Lowry not to disburse any funds to Dr. Herzog indicating that he would make the payments himself. Irace and Lowry informed Dr. Herzog that Jones had revoked his permission to have the bill paid by them directly and indicated that they would follow Jones's directions. Irace and Lowry issued a check to Jones for $10,027 and disbursed the remaining funds to Jones's other creditors. Jones did send a check to Dr. Herzog but the check was returned by the bank for insufficient funds and Dr. Herzog was never paid.

Dr. Herzog filed a complaint in District Court against Irace and Lowry seeking to enforce the June 14, 1988 "assignment of benefits." The matter was tried before the court on the basis of a joint stipulation of facts. The court entered a judgment in favor of Dr. Herzog finding that the June 14, 1988 letter constituted a valid assignment of the settlement proceeds enforceable against Irace and Lowry. Following an unsuccessful appeal to the Superior Court, Irace and Lowry appealed to this court. Because the Superior Court acted as an intermediate appellate court, we review the District Court's decision directly. See Brown v. Corriveau, 576 A.2d 200, 201 (Me.1990). . . .

Validity of Assignment

An assignment is an act or manifestation by the owner of a right (the assignor) indicating his intent to transfer that right to another person (the assignee). See Shiro v. Drew, 174 F.Supp. 495, 497 (D.Me.1959). For an assignment to be valid and enforceable against the assignor's creditor (the obligor), the assignor must make clear his intent to relinquish the right to the assignee and must not retain any control over the right assigned or any power of revocation. Id. The assignment takes effect through the actions of the assignor and assignee and the obligor need not accept the assignment to render it valid. Palmer v. Palmer, 112 Me. 149, 153, 91 A. 281, 282 (1914). Once the obligor has notice of the assignment, the fund is "from that time forward impressed with a trust; it is ... impounded in the [obligor's] hands, and must be held by him not for the original creditor, the assignor, but for the substituted creditor, the assignee." Id. at 152, 91 A. 281. After receiving notice of the assignment, the obligor cannot lawfully pay the amount assigned either to the assignor or to his other creditors and if the obligor does make such a payment, he does so at his peril because the assignee may enforce his rights against the obligor directly. Id. at 153, 91 A. 281.

Ordinary rights, including future rights, are freely assignable unless the assignment would materially change the duty of the obligor, materially increase the burden or risk imposed upon the obligor by his contract, impair the obligor's chance of obtaining return performance, or materially reduce the value of the return performance to the obligor, and unless the law restricts the assignability of the specific right involved. See Restatement (Second) Contracts § 317(2)(a) (1982). In Maine, the transfer of a future right to proceeds from pending litigation has been recognized as a valid and enforceable equitable assignment. McLellan v. Walker, 26 Me. 114, 117-18 (1896). An equitable assignment need not transfer the entire future right but rather may be a partial assignment of that right. Palmer, 112 Me. at 152, 91 A. 281. We reaffirm these well established principles.

Relying primarily upon the Federal District Court's decision in Shiro, 174 F.Supp. 495, a bankruptcy case involving the trustee's power to avoid a preferential transfer by assignment, Irace and Lowry contend that Jones's June 14, 1988 letter is invalid and unenforceable as an assignment because it fails to manifest Jones's intent to permanently relinquish all control over the assigned funds and does nothing more than request payment from a specific fund. We disagree. The June 14, 1988 letter gives no indication that Jones attempted to retain any control over the funds he assigned to Dr. Herzog. Taken in context, the use of the word "request" did not give the court reason to question Jones's intent to complete the assignment and, although no specific amount was stated, the parties do not dispute that the services provided by Dr. Herzog and the amounts that he charged for those services were reasonable and necessary to the treatment of the shoulder injury referred to in the June 14 letter. Irace and Lowry had adequate funds to satisfy all of Jones's creditors, including Dr. Herzog, with funds left over for disbursement to Jones himself. Thus, this case simply does not present a situation analogous to Shiro because Dr. Herzog was given preference over Jones's other creditors by operation of the assignment. Given that Irace and Lowry do not dispute that they had ample notice of the assignment, the court's finding on the validity of the assignment is fully supported by the evidence and will not be disturbed on appeal.

Ethical Obligations

Next, Irace and Lowry contend that the assignment, if enforceable against them, would interfere with their ethical obligation to honor their client's instruction in disbursing funds. Again, we disagree.

Under the Maine Bar Rules, an attorney generally may not place a lien on a client's file for a third party. M.Bar R. 3.7(c). The Bar Rules further require that an attorney "promptly pay or deliver to the client, as requested by the client, the funds, securities, or other properties in the possession of the lawyer which the client is entitled to receive." M.Bar R. 3.6(f)(2)(iv). The rules say nothing, however, about a client's power to assign his right to proceeds from a pending lawsuit to third parties.

Because the client has the power to assign his right to funds held by his attorney, McLellan v. Walker, 26 Me. at 117-18, it follows that a valid assignment must be honored by the attorney in disbursing the funds on the client's behalf. The assignment does not create a conflict under Rule 3.6(f)(2)(iv) because the client is not entitled to receive funds once he has assigned them to a third party. Nor does the assignment violate Rule 3.7(c), because the client, not the attorney, is responsible for placing the incumbrance upon the funds. Irace and Lowry were under no ethical obligation, and the record gives no indication that they were under a contractual obligation, to honor their client's instruction to disregard a valid assignment. The District Court correctly concluded that the assignment is valid and enforceable against Irace and Lowry.

The entry is: Judgment affirmed.

Questions

1. What is the definition of an assignment?

2. What is the legal requirement for an assignment to be valid and enforceable against the assignor's creditor?

3. What happens to the funds once the obligor receives notice of the assignment?

4. Under what circumstances are ordinary rights freely assignable?

Takeaways – Herzog v. Irace

This case involves the assignment of proceeds from a personal injury action, not an assignment of the cause of action itself. If the assignor had assigned his right to sue the person who injured him that would be an assignment of the cause of action. And yes, a cause of action can be assigned. In other wordss, a cause of action for damages is itself personal property. (See Civ.Code, § 953 ["A thing in action is a right to recover money or other personal property by a judicial proceeding"]; *Parker v. Walker* (1992) 5 Cal.App.4th 1173, 1182-1183, 6 Cal.Rptr.2d 908 ["A cause of action to recover money in damages ... is a chose in action and therefore a form of personal property"]; see also *Iszler v. Jorda* (N.D.1957) 80 N.W.2d 665, 668-669 [a chose in action is property].) *Hamer v. Sidway* in Chapter 1, is an example of an assignment of a cause of action.

Assignment Need Not Be in Any Particular Form

There are no magic words that are necessary to create an assignment. To be valid an assignment only has to manifest a present transfer and relinquishment of control of an existing right. (Rest.2d § 324) A notification which does not reasonably identify the rights assigned is ineffective. Unless some law provides otherwise, an assignment may be oral, written, or partly oral and partly written.

The Importance of Notice of Assignment

As noted in *Herzog*, after receiving notice of the assignment, the obligor must deal with the assignee and should no longer deal with the assignor. If the obligor makes payment to the assignor, he subjects himself to double liability because the assignee may enforce his rights against the obligor directly and getting the money wrongfully paid to the assignor back, will be the problem of the obligor.

Assignment of Future Rights

Rights expected to arise out of a contract not yet in existence (future rights) are generally not assignable. (Rest.2d §321(2)) I.e., you cannot presently assign what you don't yet have. However, the assignment of a conditional or unmatured right must be distinguished from the transfer of a right that has not yet been created, but is expected to arise in the future. The former can be validly assigned while the latter cannot. A promise to assign an existing right in the future does not constitute a valid assignment.

Gratuitous Gift Assignments vs. Assignments for Value

An assignment need not be supported by consideration in order to be valid. That may come as surprise in light of all you have learned up to now, but the reason for this rule comes from the law of personal property. A gift is complete upon delivery. Once the gift has been delivered the donor has no legal right to get it back. So, if a valid assignment requires the present transfer of an existing right with the assignor retaining no claim or interest in the thing that has been assigned, an effective assignment has been made. A gratuitous assignment is just as final and complete as an assignment made for value. This impeccable logic breaks down a little though upon examining Restatement Second section 332(2). That section provides that a gratuitous assignment (as opposed to an assignment for value) is terminable by the death of the assignor, by a subsequent assignment of the same right or by notice of termination communicated to the assignee. Each of the foregoing examples assumes that the assignee has not taken possession of the thing that has been assigned. If the assignee has taken possession, the assignment is irrevocable. Assignments for value (i.e., those supported by consideration) are irrevocable. The delivery of a signed writing expressing an intent to assign makes a gratuitous assignment irrevocable. (*Berl v. Rosenberg* (1959) 169 Cal.App.2d 125, 336 P2d 975)

A verbal gift is not valid, unless the means of obtaining possession and control of the thing are given, nor if it is capable of delivery, unless there is an actual or symbolical delivery of the thing to the donee. (Cal.Civ.Code § 1147)

Anti-Assignment Clauses

Can the right to make an assignment be prohibited?

Bel-Ray Company, Inc. v. Chemrite (Pty) Ltd.
United States Court of Appeals, Third Circuit, 1999
181 F.3d 435

[The Bel-Ray Company, a New Jersey corporation, makes specialty lubricants, using formulas and technology that it maintains in the highest con-fidentiality. Over a period of years, Bel-Ray entered into a series of agree. ments-the Trade Agreements, or "Agreements" with a South African corporation, Chemrite Ltd., for the blending and distribution of Bel-Ray products in South Africa. In 1996, a newly formed firm named Lubritene Ltd. acquired Chemrite's lubricant business, including rights under the Agreements. Bel-Ray was informed of the transfer. Business went on as before, under the Agreements. Four persons who had been shareholders and officeholders in Chemrite took similar positions in Lubritene.

Bel-Ray brought an action in New Jersey against Lubritene, charging it with fraud and other torts, and with violations of the Agreements. In the trial court, Bel-Ray got an order compelling Lubritene to arbitrate the Bel-Ray claims. The basis for this order was a provision in the most recent Agreement requiring arbitration, in New Jersey, of "any and all disputes relating to the agreement or its breach."

Appealing, Lubritene relied on provisions in the Chemrite/Bel-Ray Agreements that required Bel-Ray's written consent to any assignment of Chemrite's interests under the Agreements.]

Stapleton, Circuit Judge . . .Under the Federal Arbitration Act ("FAA"), a court may only compel a party to arbitrate where that party has entered into a written agreement to arbitrate that covers the dispute. See 9 U.S.C.§§ 2 & 206. The arbitration clauses in the Trade Agreements are the only written agreements to arbitrate offered in this case. It is undisputed that these agreements were entered into by Chemrite and Bel-Ray, and that Chemrite subsequently assigned the agreements to Lubritene. If these assignments are effective, then the District Court's order should be affirmed. Lubritene, however, contends that the assignments are ineffective because Bel-Ray did not consent to the assignments in writing as the Trade Agreements require. They therefore argue that there is no written agreement to arbitrate and we must reverse the District Court's order.

Thus, according to Lubritene, this case turns on the effect to be given to the Trade Agreements' requirement that Bel-Ray consent in writing to any assignment of Chemrite's interest. . . .

. . . . The New Jersey Supreme Court has not yet addressed the effect of contractual provisions limiting or prohibiting assignments. Nevertheless, we are not without guidance because the Superior Court's Appellate Division recently addressed this issue in Garden State Buildings L.P. v. First Fidelity Bank, N.A., 702 A.2d 1315 (N.J. Super. Ct. App. Div. 1997). There, a partnership had entered a loan agreement with Midatlantic Bank for the construction of a new hotel. The parties subsequently entered into a modification agreement to extend the loan's maturity date, which provided that: "No party hereto shall assign this Letter Agreement (or assign any right or delegate any obligation contained herein) without the prior written consent of the other party hereto and any such assignment shall be void." Id. at 1318. Midatlantic subsequently assigned the loan to Starwood without obtaining the partnership's prior written consent. The partnership acknowledged Starwood's rights under the loan agreement by making payments to, and eventually entering a settlement agreement with, Starwood. Nonetheless, the partnership filed suit against Midatlantic for damages arising from its breach of the modification agreement's assignment clause. It argued that it was not required to void the assignment, but could recognize its validity while still preserving its right to sue Midatlantic for breach of its covenant not to assign without the partnership's written consent.

To resolve this claim the Appellate Division looked to § 322 of the Restatement (Second) of Contracts, which provides in relevant part: "

(2) A contract term prohibiting assignment of rights under the contract, unless a different intention is manifested . . . . "(b) gives the obligor a right to damages for breach of the terms forbidding assignment *but does not render the assignment ineffective* . . .

"Restatement (Second) of Contracts § 322 (1981) (emphasis added). The Court, distinguished between an assignment provision's effect upon a party's "power" to assign, as opposed to its "right" to assign. A party's "power" to assign is only limited where the parties clearly manifest a different intention. According to the Court:

> "` [t]o reveal the intent necessary to preclude the power to assign, or cause an assignment violative of contractual provisions to be wholly void, such clause must contain express provisions that any assignment shall be void or invalid if not made in a certain specified way.' Otherwise, the assignment is effective, and the obligor has the right to damages."
>
> Garden State, 702 A.2d at 1321 (quoting University Mews Assoc's v. Jeanmarie, 471 N.Y.S.2d 457, 461 (N.Y. Sup. Ct. 1984)). The Court concluded that the parties had sufficiently manifested their intent to limit Midatlantic's power to assign the loan because the anti-assignment clause clearly provided that assignments without the other party's written consent "shall be void." Id. At 1322.

In adopting § 322, New Jersey joins numerous other jurisdictions that follow the general rule that contractual provisions limiting or prohibiting assignments operate only to limit a parties' right to assign the contract, but not their power to do so, unless the parties' manifest an intent to the contrary with specificity. [Citations omitted] To meet this standard the assignment provision must generally state that non-conforming assignments (i) shall be "void" or "invalid," or (ii) that the assignee shall acquire no rights or the non-assigning party shall not recognize any such assignment. See Garden State, 702 A.2d at 1321 ("clause must contain express provisions that any assignment shall be void or invalid if not made in a certain specified way"); [Citations omitted] In the absence of such language, the provision limiting or prohibiting assignments will be interpreted merely as a covenant not to assign, or to follow specific procedures--typically obtaining the non-assigning party's prior written consent--before assigning. Breach of such a covenant may render the assigning party liable in damages to the non-assigning party. The assignment, however, remains valid and enforceable against both the assignor and the assignee. [Citations omitted]

The Trade Agreements in this case contain the following assignment provisions: (i) the Distributor Sales Agreement § 7.06 provides that the "Agreement and the obligations and rights under this Agreement will not be assignable by [Chemrite] without express prior written consent of Bel-Ray, which may be withheld at the sole discretion of Bel-Ray"; (ii) the Blending and Manufacturing License Agreement § 7.05 provides that the "Agreement and the obligations and rights hereunder will not be assignable by [Chemrite] without the express prior written consent of BEL-RAY"; and (iii) the License Agreement to Trade Name § 6.06 provides that the "Agreement, and the obligations and rights under this agreement will not be assignable without the express written consent of all Parties to this Agreement." (A39, A61, A83). None contain terms specifically stating that an assignment without Bel-Ray's written consent would be void or invalid. Several courts have considered virtually identical clauses and concluded that they did not contain the necessary express language to limit the assigning party's power to assign. See Lomas, 812 F. Supp. at 844; Macklowe, 566 N.Y.S.2d at 606-07; Sullivan, 465 N.Y.S.2d at 236-38.

The Trade Agreements' assignment clauses do not contain the requisite clear language to limit Chemrite's "power" to assign the Trade Agreements. Chemrite's assignment to Lubritene is therefore enforceable, and Lubritene is bound to arbitrate claims "relating to" the Trade Agreements pursuant to their arbitration clauses. We therefore agree with the District Court that Bel-Ray was entitled to an order compelling Lubritene to arbitrate. . . .

Questions

1. What was the basis for Lubritene's argument that the assignments were ineffective?

2. How did the court interpret the effect of contractual provisions limiting or prohibiting assignments?

3. Did the assignment clauses in the Trade Agreements contain the necessary language to limit Chemrite's power to assign?

Takeaways – Bel Ray v. Chemrite

As a general rule, there are no restrictions on the right to assign nor can the obligor's consent to an assignment be required. (UCC § 9–406(d)) The UCC overrides anti-assignment clauses in most contracts. UCC § 9–406(d) provides that a term in an agreement between an account debtor and an assignor . . . is ineffective to the extent that it: (1) prohibits, restricts, or requires the consent of the account debtor . . . to the assignment or transfer of . . . the account. . .

An assignment in violation of a covenant or promise not to assign is not void or ineffective and the only remedy for violation of the promise not to assign is an action for breach. (*Randal v. Tatum* (1893) 98 Cal. 390)

Where a commercial lease provides for assignment only with the prior consent of the lessor, such consent may be withheld only where the lessor has a commercially reasonable objection to the assignee or the proposed use. (*Kendall v. Ernest Pestana, Inc.* (1985) 40 Cal.3d 488, 220 Cal.Rptr. 818; 709 P.2d 837)

Assignee Stands In Shoes of Assignor

The assignee takes the assignment subject to all of the claims and defenses that could have been asserted against the assignor. (Rest.2d § 336, UCC § 9-404) The general rule in sales transactions that the assignee takes his assignment subject to the purchaser's defenses, set-offs and counterclaims against the seller. 39 FLR 3d 518. A written contract for the payment of money or personal property may be transferred. Such a transfer conveys all of the rights of the assignor to the assignee, subject to all equities and defenses existing in favor of the maker or obligor at the time of the assignment. (Cal.Civ.Code § 1459)

Delacy Investments, Inc. v. Thurman & Re/Max Real Estate
Minnesota Court of Appeals, 2005
693 N.W.2d 479

HALBROOKS, Judge. . . . Appellant Delacy Investments, Inc., d/b/a Commission Express (CE), is in the business of factoring receivables from real-estate agents. In this business, a real-estate agent can assign or sell his future receivable or commission to CE in exchange for immediate funds. Respondent Re/Max Real Estate Guide, Inc. (Re/Max) is a real-estate brokerage company.

On November 11, 2001, defendant Steven Thurman, a licensed real-estate agent, entered into a master repurchase and security agreement (MRSA) with CE. The substance of the MRSA "grant[ed] to CE a security interest under the [UCC] in all of [Thurman's] right, title and interest in and to [Thurman's] current and future accounts receivable . . . ." CE perfected its security interest by filing a UCC financing statement with the Minnesota Secretary of State.

On February 25, 2003, Thurman entered into a standard independent-contractor agreement with Re/Max. The agreement details the employment relationship between the two, whereby Thurman agreed to pay Re/Max certain overhead expenses. The agreement explains how Thurman will receive his "commission" from Re/Max and certain "nonpayment remedies." In pertinent part, the agreement states:

[Thurman] shall be deemed entitled only to 100 percent of the amount by which commissions generated by [Thurman's] efforts exceed past-due financial obligations imposed by the terms of Paragraphs 4 and 5 of the Agreement. That portion of commissions which does not exceed past-due financial obligations shall be deemed to belong to RE/MAX and shall be used by RE/MAX first to offset arrearages owed by [Thurman].

(Emphasis added.) Thus, in terms of the legal relationships that exist here, CE is an "assignee," having accepted Thurman's assignment of his commission by the MRSA. Thurman, in turn, is an "assignor," having assigned his right of commission to CE. Re/Max is an "account debtor" by virtue of its independent-contractor agreement with Thurman, whereby Re/Max possesses the potential right to receipt of that which Thurman assigned to CE.

In April 2003, Re/Max executed an acknowledgement of CE's security interest in Thurman's account receivable from the sale of a home on Javelin Avenue and directed that Thurman's commission from that sale be paid directly to CE.[1] On April 22, 2003, CE and Thurman entered into an Account Receivable Sale and Assignment Agreement (assignment agreement), whereby CE agreed to purchase a $10,000 receivable related to Thurman's sale of a property on Keller Lake Drive in Burnsville (Keller Lake property).

On June 7, Re/Max terminated Thurman as a real-estate agent for poor performance, failure to deposit earnest-money payments in a timely manner, and customer complaints. Re/Max asserts that at the time of his termination, Thurman had accumulated $11,126.38 in overhead debts owed to Re/Max. As a result, Re/Max refused to pay the assigned receivable and "applied the commission to Thurman's balance in accordance with [the independent-contractor agreement]," claiming a right of setoff based on the overhead expenses that Thurman owed. In Re/Max's words, "because the commissions earned by Re/Max as a result of Thurman's services did not exceed his past-due financial obligation to Re/Max, Thurman was entitled to no compensation at the Keller Lake closing, and so nothing was paid to CE pursuant to the assignment."

In June 2003, CE sent Re/Max a demand for immediate payment of the Keller Lake account receivable and sent a notice of default to Thurman. Re/Max did not pay. CE then filed a complaint in district court. Re/Max answered and counterclaimed against Thurman. Both parties moved for summary judgment. The district court denied CE's motion and granted Re/Max's, finding that "[CE's] ability to receive a commission from Re/Max is based upon Thurman's assignment of a contractual right to receive a commission from Re/Max." Therefore, the district court determined that "Thurman was not entitled to a commission at the time of the Keller Lake [p]roperty closing." As a result, it was "impossible for [CE] to obtain a greater right in the commission than Thurman had in the commission." This appeal follows.

Did the district court err by granting summary judgment to respondent based on its interpretation of article 9 of the Uniform Commercial Code as to assignment of an account receivable? . . .

In granting Re/Max's motion for summary judgment, the district court determined that Thurman was not entitled to a commission at the time of the Keller Lake property closing. The court stated:

. . . Under Minn. Stat. § 336.9-404, an assignee's rights are subject to "(1) all terms of the agreement between the account debtor and the assignor . . . [.]" Minn. Stat. § 336.9-404 (2002). "A valid assignment generally operates to vest in the assignee the same right, title, or interest that the assignor had in the thing assigned. Ill. Farmers Ins. Co. v. Glass Service Co. [], 669 N.W.2d 420, 424 (Minn. [] App. 2003) (citation omitted), [rev'd on other grounds, 683 N.W.2d 792 (Minn. 2004)].

In the present action, Thurman was not entitled to collect a commission while his fees were in arrears. There is no question that at the time of the closing on the Keller Lake [p]roperty, Thurman was in arrears in his fees to Re/Max in the amount of approximately $11,126.38. The [c]ourt, therefore, finds that Thurman was not entitled to a commission at the time of the Keller Lake [p]roperty closing and that it is impossible for [CE] to obtain a greater right in the commission than Thurman had in the commission. . . .

[T]he U.C.C. provision governing assignment in account receivables, which states:

(a) Assignee's rights subject to terms, claims, and defenses; exceptions. Unless an account debtor has made an enforceable agreement not to assert defenses or claims, and subject to subsections (b) through (e), the rights of an assignee are subject to:

(1) all terms of the agreement between the account debtor and assignor and any defense or claim in recoupment arising from the transaction that gave rise to the contract; and

(2) any other defense or claim of the account debtor against the assignor which accrues before the account debtor receives a notification of the assignment authenticated by the assignor or assignee.

Id. (emphasis added). The official comment to the provision further explains its meaning:

Subsection (a) . . . provides that an assignee generally takes an assignment subject to defenses and claims of an account debtor. Under subsection (a)(1), if the account debtor's defenses on an assigned claim arise from the transaction that gave rise to the contract with the assignor, it makes no difference whether the defense or claim accrues before or after the account debtor is notified of the assignment.

Minn. Stat. § 336.9-404 cmt. 2 (emphasis added); see also Restatement (Second) of Contracts § 336, cmt. b (1981) (explaining that an assignor can assign "only what he has" and "is subject to limitations imposed by the terms of that contract [creating the right] and to defenses which would have been available against the [account debtor] had there been no assignment"). The particular issue presented here is one of first impression in Minnesota.

Under Minn. Stat. § 336.9-404(a)(1) (2004), because the rights of CE are subject to all terms of the agreement between Re/Max and Thurman namely, the independent-contractor agreement giving CE a right to all of Thurman's commissions which exceed past-due financial obligations to Re/Max we conclude that CE cannot collect from Re/Max because the commissions earned by Re/Max as a result of Thurman's sales do not exceed his past-due financial obligations to Re/Max. As we recently explained, "[i]t is black-letter law that an assignee of a claim take no other or greater rights than the original assignor and cannot be in a better position than the assignor." Ill. Farmers Ins. Co., 669 N.W.2d at 424. This most basic principle of commercial law is reflected in the Latin phrase nemo dat qui non habetor, "no one may transfer more than he owns." Commerce Bank, N.A. v. Chrysler Realty Corp., 244 F.3d 777, 780 (10th Cir. 2001).

Our decision is further supported by a number of courts across the country interpreting former § 9-318(1) and revised § 9-404 of the UCC. See Minn. Stat. § 645.22 (2004) ("Laws uniform with those of other states shall be interpreted and construed to effect their general purpose to make uniform the laws of those states which enact them."). As the Texas Court of Appeals has explained, "when [an] assignee brings suit against the [account-debtor] . . . to enforce rights conferred by the contract, the courts will almost universally agree that the [account-debtor] may assert any defense that might have been asserted against the assignor, being one of the original contract parties." Irrigation Assoc. v. First Nat'l Bank of Frisco, 773 S.W.2d 346, 348 (Tex. App. 1989) (emphasis added). The Sixth Circuit has more recently interpreted the same UCC provision to "clearly limit[] the rights of . . . the assignee, to those of the assignor . . . and make its right to accounts receivable subject to the provisions of [the account debtor's] contract with [the assignor]." Nat'l. City Bank, Northwest v. Columbian Mut. Life Ins. Co., 282 F.3d 407, 410 (6th Cir. 2002) (emphasis added). In that case, the court concluded that "[t]here is no authority for the proposition that a perfected assignment to a third person takes precedence over a right of recoupment created between the original contracting parties in their contract." *Id.*

"[I]f [the assignee] did not want to arbitrate disputes over collections from account debtors, it could have contracted with [the assignor] to prevent it from entering into any agreement that contained arbitration clauses. Because it did not do so, it is bound by the arbitration clause." 252 F. Supp. 2d at 506.

Similarly, here, if CE did not want to be bound by the independent-contractor agreement between Re/Max and Thurman, it could have contracted otherwise. But it did not, and CE is thereby bound by the independent-contractor agreement between Re/Max and Thurman. As the assignee, CE cannot assume greater rights than Thurman, the assignor.

But CE also argues that Minn. Stat. § 336.9-404(a)(2) (2004) does not permit an account debtor to contract away the rights of an assignee after having received notice of a previously-executed assignment. According to CE, subsection (a)(2) limits which setoffs an account debtor may assert against a payment to an assignee after notice of the assignment. CE contends that Re/Max had notice of the assignment on three separate occasions: (1) statutory notice by CE's filing of the financing statement with the Secretary of State on November 14, 2001, after Thurman's execution of the MRSA; (2) actual notice that CE was entitled to all of the Thurman receivables when a notice of default regarding the Javelin Avenue property was delivered by certified mail on March 12, 2003; and (3) actual notice from the assignment of the Keller Lake receivable on April 22, 2003. CE argues that Thurman signed the MRSA with CE, giving CE a right to his commission, before Thurman signed the independent-contractor agreement with Re/Max.

The UCC defines "notice" as:

(d) A person "notifies" or "gives" a notice or notification to another person by taking such steps as may be reasonably required to inform the other person in ordinary course, whether or not the other person actually comes to know of it.

(e). . . [A] person "receives" a notice or notification when:

(1) it comes to that person's attention; or

(2) it is duly delivered in a form reasonable under the circumstances at the place of business through which the contract was made or at another location held out by that person as the place for receipt of such communications. Minn. Stat. § 336.1-202(d)-(e) (2004).

It therefore appears that Re/Max had notice of the assignment between Thurman and CE before its independent-contractor agreement with Thurman.

A perfected security interest is generally effective against creditors "[e]xcept as otherwise provided in the Uniform Commercial Code." Minn. Stat. § 336.9-201(a) (2004) (emphasis added). Minn. Stat. § 336.9-404(a)(1) provides otherwise. See Nat'l. City Bank, Northwest, 282 F.3d at 409-10 (explaining that the subsection clearly limits the rights of the assignee to those of the assignor). As one commentator explains, "[i]t makes no difference whether the defense or claim accrues before or after the account debtor is notified of the assignment if the account debtor's defenses on an assigned claim arise from the transaction that gave rise to the contract with the assignor." 20 Brent A. Olson, Minnesota Practice § 10.7.04 (2004). Minn. Stat. § 336.9-404(a)(2) does not govern the dispute here.

The plain language of Minn. Stat. § 336.9-404(a)(1) makes clear that the rights of CE (as an assignee) "are subject to . . . all terms of the agreement between the account debtor and assignor." Id. Here, the independent-contractor agreement between Re/Max and Thurman limited payment to Thurman to those commissions that exceeded his past-due financial obligations to Re/Max. Because CE can take no greater rights nor be in a better position than Thurman by recovering a commission when Thurman, himself, was not entitled to the commission, the district court did not err by granting summary judgment to Re/Max.

[W]e affirm the district court's grant of summary judgment in favor of respondent.

Questions

1. According to the UCC provision, what are the rights of an assignee subject to?

2. According to the district court's interpretation, what rights does an assignee have under the UCC?

Takeaways – Delacy Investments, Inc.

UCC § 9-404(a)(1) makes it clear that the rights of an assignee are subject to all of the terms of the agreement between the obligor and the assignor. Where the right being assigned is an obligation to pay money, any defense that the obligor could have asserted against the assignor, can be asserted against the assignee. The assignee's rights can never be greater than his or her assignor and the assignee never acquires greater rights by virtue of the assignment.

Avoiding The Rule The Assignee Stands in the Shoes of the Assignor

A number of rules and principles have developed that allow the assignee to get around the rule that normally the assignment of a right is subject to all of the claims and defenses that could be asserted against it. Among them are waiver of defense clauses and the holder in due course rule.

Waiver of Defense Clauses

Chemical Bank v. Rinden Professional Association
Supreme Court of New Hampshire. 1985
126 N.H. 688, 498 A.2d 706

DOUGLAS, J. This case presents the issue whether the defendant, Rinden Professional Association (Rinden), validly waived its defenses against the plaintiff-assignee, Chemical Bank, upon the assignment of its lease-purchase agreement. We hold that the waiver was valid and affirm the judgment in favor of plaintiff.

On April 25, 1974, Rinden, a law firm in Concord, entered into a lease-purchase agreement with Intertel Communications Corporation (Intertel) for an office phone system for the defendant's place of business. Under the contract, Rinden was to pay Intertel $158.00 per month for 96 months. At the end of this period, Rinden had the option to purchase the equipment for $1.00.

Shortly thereafter, Rinden received a document executed by Intertel, which gave notice of an assignment to Chemical Bank of the right to receive payments from Rinden as provided for in the lease-purchase agreement. Also contained in the notice was a so-called "hell or high water" clause, the purpose of which was to waive as to the assignee any defenses Rinden might have against Intertel. The clause specifically stated that such defenses could still be raised against the assignor, Intertel. The waiver of defenses clause was required by Chemical Bank as a precondition of its purchase from Intertel of Rinden's contract. After reading it, John Satterfield, office manager of Rinden, signed the document on June 11, 1974.

After receiving the document signed by Satterfield on behalf of Rinden, Chemical Bank paid Intertel the sum of $8,804.39 and received from Intertel an assignment of the right to payment under the lease. Contractual duties, such as maintenance of the phone system, were not delegated, but remained with Intertel. Around June 18, 1974, Rinden received a letter from Chemical Bank informing it that the assignment had been completed and that Rinden was now obliged to make its payments to Chemical Bank.

Rinden made payments to Chemical Bank for nearly three years, until the phone system began to malfunction seriously in 1977. It notified Intertel of the problems and ceased payments. Rinden eventually replaced the phone system with that of another company.

Rinden refused to pay Chemical Bank, and litigation ensued. . . . The Master . . . found that the June 11, 1974, document from Intertel to Rinden contained a valid notice of assignment and waiver of defenses and that Chemical Bank is a holder in due course entitled to collect the balance of its payments from Rinden. This report was approved by the Superior Court (*Cann,* J.) on January 30, 1984. . . .The defendant appeals the decision, claiming error in the finding that the waiver of defenses clause is enforceable . . .

Under Mass. Gen. Laws Ann. ch. 106, § 9-206(1), warranties contained in a commercial sales contract may be modified so that a buyer agrees not to assert defenses against an assignee of the contract. *Credit Alliance Corp. v. David O. Crump Sand and Fill,* 470 F.Supp. 489, 491 (S.D.N.Y. 1979). The requirements of a valid waiver are that there was an agreement by a buyer, who is not a consumer, to waive defenses against an assignee and that the assignment was made for value, in good faith, and without notice of a claim or defense. Additionally, under the terms of the contract in issue here, modification of it could only be by a "like signed agreement." We find that these requirements were met so that the defendant validly waived his defenses against Chemical Bank.

The master found that Rinden agreed to the waiver of defenses clause, and the evidence supports this view. . . .

The defendant does not claim that it is a consumer so as to make Mass. Gen. Laws Ann. ch. 106, § 9-206(1) inapplicable on that account. The defendant is a professional association, a law firm, not in need of special protections often provided for unwary consumers. . . .

Next we must determine whether there is sufficient evidence to support the master's findings that Chemical Bank took the assignment for value, in good faith, and without notice of a claim or defense. As to the first issue, Chemical Bank paid Intertel over $8,800 for the assignment of Intertel's rights in the defendant's contract.

As to the next requirement, the defendant asserts that Chemical Bank is not a good faith purchaser, mainly because the plaintiff and Intertel were too closely connected. Nothing in the record indicates, however, that the relationship between Intertel and Chemical Bank was anything other than an arms-length commercial relationship.

William Tupka, the Chemical Bank employee in charge of the Intertel account, testified that Chemical Bank's course of dealing in purchasing the rights to the Rinden contract from Intertel was typical of its transactions with hundreds of other clients with which it had entered into similar agreements. Chemical Bank and Intertel were not related corporations, having common directors or owning shares of stock in each other. Nor was Chemical Bank the only bank to lend to Intertel.

Finally, the facts that Chemical Bank checked Rinden's credit rating and insisted upon an insertion of a waiver of defenses clause, before it would purchase the assignment, certainly do not prove lack of good faith as Rinden claims. Both Mr. Tupka and Kenneth Barron, former president of Intertel, testified that these actions were standard procedure for a bank extending credit. Moreover, even if there was any evidence of interrelatedness, Massachusetts law appears to look with disfavor on the admission of past dealings between parties to show bad faith, absent some other indications of bad faith by the holder. *See Bowling Green, Inc. v. State Street Bank and Trust Co.,* 425 F.2d 81, 85 (1st Cir. 1970) (citing *Universal C.I.T. Credit Corp. v. Ingel,* 347 Mass. 119, 125, 196 N.E.2d 847, 852 (1964)).

There is also no basis to conclude that the master erred in finding that Chemical Bank took the assignment without notice of a claim or defense. Mr. Tupka testified that he came across nothing in his investigation of the Intertel account which would indicate that Rinden might have some kind of claim or defense relating to the lease agreement between it and Intertel. No evidence was introduced to contradict this testimony

Having found the requirements of Mass. Gen. Laws Ann. ch. 106, § 9-206(1) met, the master also found that the June 11 document was a "like, signed agreement" as required for modification under the lease-purchase contract. This finding is supported by the fact that they were both written documents, signed by the same parties, dealing with terms of payment for the same equipment. Also, as discussed above, the language of the second document was that of a contract. . . .

We note that our decision today is in accord with the policy of the UCC in general, and of § 9-206(1) in particular, "to encourage the supplying of credit for the buying of goods by insulating the [institutional] lender from lawsuits over the quality of the goods." *Massey-Ferguson Credit Corp. v. Brown,* 169 Mont. 396, 402, 547 P.2d 846, 850 (1976) (quoting *Massey-Ferguson, Inc. v. Utley,* 439 S.W.2d 57, 60 (Ky. 1969)). "A contrary holding would not only have a chilling effect on loans made by financial institutions but would mean that the law allows the plain meaning of covenants to be declared nugatory whenever a bad bargain results." *B.V.D. Co. v. Marine Midland Bank-New York,* 46 A.D.2d 51, 53, 360 N.Y.S.2d 901, 904 (1974). . . .

Affirmed.

Questions

1. What is the purpose of the "hell or high water" clause in the assignment document signed by Rinden?

2. What are the requirements for a valid waiver of defenses against an assignee under Massachusetts law?

Takeaways – Chemical Bank v. Rinden Professional

As you have seen, a valid waiver of defense clause can be a powerful device to avoid the general rule that an obligor can assert against the assignee any defense he/she could have asserted against the assignor. However, a number of states deprive waiver-of-defense clauses and holder-in-due-course status of their effectiveness in ordinary consumer transactions. Hence, for the most part, a waiver of defense clause will only be effective in commercial business-to-business transactions.

Holder in Due Course

Another way an assignee can take an assignment free of defenses is to be a "holder in due course." (UCC § 3-302) To qualify as a holder in due course the right being assigned has to be in the form of a negotiable instrument (defined at UCC § 3-104). One who (1) possesses (i.e,. holds) (2) a negotiable instrument (3) for value (i.e., they didn't find it or steal it) (4) in good faith and (5) without any notice that it is overdue or has been dishonored or of any claims or defenses against it, takes the assignment of it free of any claims or defenses.

Notice of Assignment Cuts Off Right to Assert Certain Defenses

Earlier in this chapter, reference was made to the consequences of notice of assignment. Notice of assignment has another important effect. It cuts off the right to set-off defenses that are unrelated to the right that has been assigned. Defenses that are related to the right that has been assigned can be recouped regardless of when they accrued. (Rest.2d § 336(2)) So what is a "recoupment" and what is a "set-off?" The *Delacy case* distinguishes between a right of "recoupment" and "setoff." A right of ?recoupment arises from the same transaction or contract that gave rise to the assignment whereas setoff is a broader term referring to any claim or demand that the obligor has against the assignor even though it is unrelated to the right that has been assigned. (*Nat'l. City Bank, Northwest v. Columbian Mutual Life Ins., Co.* 282 F.3d 407, 409 (2002) (citing Black's Law Dictionary 1439-40 (4th ed. 1968)).

In order to cut off potential set-off defenses the assignee should notify the assignor immediately of an assignment. By doing so the assignee can accept the assignment with assurance that, after his or her notification to the obligor, he or she is protected from any new defenses that may accrue to the obligor independent of the contract right that has been assigned.

Example: Moe hires Curly to paint his house for $1,000. In a separate transaction Moe sells his car to Curly on credit for $500. Moe intends to collect what he is owed for the car by setting off the price of the car against the money he owes Curly for painting the house. Curly then assigns his right to receive the $1,000 to Larry. Moe fails to pay and Larry sues Moe for the $1,000. How much does Moe owe Larry? I.e., can he deduct the $500 he has coming to him for the car from the $1,000 debt that was assigned to Larry? Since this claim did not arise out of the house painting contract it can be set-off only if it accrued (i.e. came into existence) *before* notification of the assignment. If Larry gave Moe notice of the assignment before the car was sold then the full $1000 is owed. If notice of assignment was not given until after the car had been sold, Moe can set-off against Larry the $500 price of the car. Note that if the defense was related to the house painting contract (e.g. Curly failed to complete the job or did a shoddy job) the obligor could recoup the amount owed (that is, assert it as a defense against the assignee) regardless of whether it accrued before or after notice of assignment was given.

Implied Warranty of Assignment

The house painting example given above raises another issue. What if Curly made the assignment of the $1,000 claim to Larry without disclosing the fact that it was subject to being set off by the $500 claim for the debt over the car? Larry thinks he is being assigned a right worth $1,000 where in fact, the right is only worth $500. If Larry paid value for the assignment, he might be really upset. The answer would be that in this situation Curly has violated the implied warranty of assignment. Every assignment carries with it an implied promise that the assignor will not do anything to defeat or impair the value of the assignment and knows of no fact which would do so. (Rest.2d § 333)

Priority of Assignees of the Same Right

Suppose an assignor assigns the same right to two different assignees. Which of the assignees has the superior claim to the right that has been assigned? If it is a gratuitous assignment, the answer is easy. A gratuitous assignment is revoked by a subsequent assignment of the same right. (Rest.2d § 332(2)) If it is an assignment for value, there are two different views on this. Restatement 2d § 342 says that the right of an assignee is superior to that of a subsequent assignee of the same right. This is the "first in time" rule.

The California rule is different. As between bona fide assignees of the same right for value, the assignee first giving written notice thereof to the obligor has priority among multiple assignees. (Cal.Civ.Code § 955.1(b)) In other words, the first to give notice of assignment will be the holder of the assigned right.

Delegation

A delegation is an appointment of another person or entity to perform one's duties. (Rest.2d § 318; UCC § 2-210) In a delegation the person making the appointment remains liable in the event of a breach by the delegate.

Assignment and Delegation Contrasted

An assignment is a transfer of rights. A delegation is an appointment of another to perform one's duties. Rights are assigned. Duties are delegated. In an assignment, the assignor has no further claim or interest in the right being assigned. In a delegation, the original obligor is still liable and may be sued in the event of the delegate's total failure to perform or a partial or defective performance. In other words, you can delegate your duties but you can't escape them. In order for the original obligor to escape their duties and avoid liability when they wish to appoint someone else to discharge their duties they must enter into a novation.

Non-Delegable Duties

As a general rule, a party may discharge its contractual obligations through a delegate. The only exception is, if "the other party has a substantial interest in having the original promisor perform or control the acts required by the contract." (See, UCC § 2-210)

The classic example of a non-delegable duty is the so-called "personal service contract," a contract entered into on the basis of the "character, reputation, taste, skill, or discretion of the party that is to render [performance]." 3 E. Allan Farnsworth, Farnsworth on Contracts Sec. 11.10, at 129 (1990). Suppose a concert promoter contracted with Luciano Pavarotti to sing in its opera hall, Pavarotti could not delegate his duty to perform to pop-star Michael Jackson. On the other hand, the payment of rent pursuant to a lease is hardly the type of performance that depends upon the identity of the party that is to perform, i.e., the lessee. (See, *Metropolitan Airports Comm'n. v. Northwest Airlines, Inc.*, 6 F3d 492 (7th Circuit, 1993).)

Taylor v. Palmer
Supreme Court of California, 1866
31 Cal. 240

[Smith & Co. entered into a contract with the City and County of San Francisco to do some grading work on some streets to prepare them to be paved. They then got the plaintiff to do the work and the City and County refused to pay.]

SANDERSON, J. The contract in suit was made by the Superintendent with Smith & Co., who assigned to the plaintiff, by whom the work was performed, and it is next claimed that the contract belongs to that class which the party who is to perform the stipulated work is not permitted to assign by reason of the trust and confidence reposed in his skill and ability by the other contracting party. . . .

[I]t is clear to us that this contract does not belong to the class suggested. There is nothing in the statute or the contract or the nature of the work suggestive of such a theory. On the contrary, the public generally are invited to bid for and take these contracts regardless of professions, trades or occupations. Aside from the discretion vested in the Board of Supervisors to reject all bids when they deem it for the public good, or the bid of any party who may have proved delinquent or unfaithful in any previous contract with the city, there is no restriction upon the capacity of the contractor. He is not expected nor required to perform the work in person. Were it so, street improvements in San Francisco would make slow progress. Whether he knows anything about road making, or can tell the difference between a mud turnpike and a Nicholson pavement, or whether a sewer should be constructed in the shape of a longitudinal section of an egg shell, or which end of the section should be uppermost, is of no consequence, for the contract is not awarded to him because of his supposed knowledge or skill, but because his bid is the lowest and his bond for the performance of the work in a workmanlike manner and according to the specifications is good. All painters do not paint portraits like Sir Joshua Reynolds, nor landscapes like Claude Lorraine, nor do all writers write dramas like Shakespeare or fiction like Dickens. Rare genius and extraordinary skill are not transferable, and contracts for their employment are therefore personal, and cannot be assigned. But rare genius and extraordinary skill are not indispensable to the workmanlike digging down of a sand hill or the filling up of a depression to a given level, or the construction of brick sewers with manholes and covers, and contracts for such work are not personal, and may be assigned.

Questions

1. According to the court, why does this contract not fall into the category of contracts that are not permitted to be delegated?

2. What factors determine the capacity of the contractor to perform the work under the contract?

3. How does the court differentiate between contracts requiring rare genius or extraordinary skill and contracts involving general workmanship?

Takeaways – Taylor v. Palmer

Taylor v. Palmer is an old case. Although the court uses the term, "assignment" don't they really mean "delegation?" You will recall that an assignment is a transfer of rights. A delegation is an appointment of another to perform one's duties. Enlightenment may exist in UCC § 2-210 (5) which provides: "An assignment of 'the contract' or of 'all my rights under the contract' or an assignment in similar general terms is an assignment of rights and unless the language or the circumstances, . . . indicate the contrary, it is also a delegation of performance of the duties of the assignor." (See also, Rest.2d §328)

Sally Beauty Company, Inc. v. Nexxus Products Company, Inc.
United States Court of Appeals, Seventh Circuit, 1986
801 F.2d 1001

CUDAHY, Circuit Judge. Nexxus Products Company ("Nexxus") entered into a contract with Best Barber & Beauty Supply Company, Inc. ("Best"), under which Best would be the exclusive distributor of Nexxus hair care products to barbers and hair stylists throughout most of Texas. When Best was acquired by and merged into Sally Beauty Company, Inc. ("Sally Beauty"), Nexxus cancelled the agreement. Sally Beauty is a wholly-owned subsidiary of Alberto-Culver Company ("Alberto-Culver"), a major manufacturer of hair care products and a competitor of Nexxus'. Sally Beauty claims that Nexxus breached the contract by canceling; Nexxus asserts by way of defense that the contract was not assignable or, in the alternative, not assignable to Sally Beauty. The district court granted Nexxus' motion for summary judgment, ruling that the contract was one for personal services and therefore not assignable. We affirm on a different theory--that this contract could not be assigned to the wholly-owned subsidiary of a direct competitor under section 2-210 of the Uniform Commercial Code. . . . [Nexxus had written to Sally Beauty:]

... [W]e have great reservations about allowing our NEXXUS Products to be distributed by a company which is, in essence, a direct competitor. We appreciate your argument of autonomy for your business, but the fact remains that you are totally owned by Alberto-Culver.

Since we see no way of justifying this conflict, we cannot allow our products to be distributed by Sally Beauty Company.

In August 1983 Sally Beauty commenced this action by filing a complaint in the Northern District of Illinois, claiming that Nexxus had violated the federal antitrust laws and breached the distribution agreement. In August 1984 Nexxus filed a counterclaim alleging violations of the Lanham Act, the Racketeer Influenced and Corrupt Organizations Act ("RICO") and the unfair competition laws of North Carolina, Tennessee and unidentified "other states." On October 22, 1984 Sally Beauty filed a motion to dismiss the counterclaims arising under RICO and "other states' law." Nexxus filed a motion for summary judgment on the breach of contract claim the next day.

The district court ruled on these motions in a Memorandum Opinion and Order dated January 31, 1985. It granted Sally's motion to dismiss the two counterclaims and also granted Nexxus' motion for summary judgment. In May 1985 it dismissed the remaining claims and counterclaims (pursuant to stipulation by the parties) and directed the entry of an appealable final judgment on the breach of contract claim.

Sally Beauty's breach of contract claim alleges that by acquiring Best, Sally Beauty succeeded to all of Best's rights and obligations under the distribution agreement. It further alleges that Nexxus breached the agreement by failing to give Sally Beauty 120 days notice prior to terminating the agreement and by terminating it on other than an anniversary date of its formation. Complaint, Count III, Appellant's Appendix at 54-55. Nexxus, in its motion for summary judgment, argued that the distribution agreement it entered into with Best was a contract for personal services, based upon a relationship of personal trust and confidence between Reichek and the Redding family. As such, the contract could not be assigned to Sally without Nexxus' consent.

In opposing this motion Sally Beauty argued that the contract was freely assignable because (1) it was between two corporations, not two individuals and (2) the character of the performance would not be altered by the substitution of Sally Beauty for Best. . . .

In ruling on this motion, the district court framed the issue before it as "whether the contract at issue here between Best and Nexxus was of a personal nature such that it was not assignable without Nexxus' consent." It ruled:

[I]n this case the circumstances surrounding the contract's formation support the conclusion that the agreement was not simply an ordinary commercial contract but was one which was based upon a relationship of personal trust and confidence between the parties. Specifically, Stephen Redding, Nexxus's vice-president, traveled to Texas and met with Best's president personally for several days before making the decision to award the Texas distributorship to Best. Best itself had been in the hair care business for 40 years and its president Mark Reichek had extensive experience in the industry. It is reasonable to conclude that Stephen Redding and Nexxus would want its distributor to be experienced and knowledgeable in the hair care field and that the selection of Best was based upon personal factors such as these....

.Sally Beauty contends that the distribution agreement is freely assignable because it is governed by the provisions of the Uniform Commercial Code (the "UCC" or the "Code"), as adopted in Texas.....Texas applies the "dominant factor" test to determine whether the UCC applies to a given contract or transaction: was the essence of or dominant factor in the formation of the contract the provision of goods or services?.... We are confident that a Texas court would find the sales aspect of this contract dominant and apply the majority rule that such a distributorship is a contract for "goods" under the UCC....

We are concerned here with the delegation of Best's duty of performance under the distribution agreement, as Nexxus terminated the agreement because it did not wish to accept Sally Beauty's substituted performance....

In the exclusive distribution agreement before us, Nexxus had contracted for Best's "best efforts" in promoting the sale of Nexxus products in Texas. UCC Sec. 2-306(2) .... It was this contractual undertaking which Nexxus refused to see performed by Sally.

[We] hold that Sally Beauty's position as a wholly-owned subsidiary of Alberto-Culver is sufficient to bar the delegation of Best's duties under the agreement.

We do not believe that our holding will work the mischief with our national economy that the appellants predict. We hold merely that the duty of performance under an exclusive distributorship may not be delegated to a competitor in the market place--or the wholly-owned subsidiary of a competitor--without the obligee's consent. We believe that such a rule is consonant with the policies behind section 2-210, which is concerned with preserving the bargain the obligee has struck. Nexxus should not be required to accept the "best efforts" of Sally Beauty when those efforts are subject to the control of Alberto-Culver. It is entirely reasonable that Nexxus should conclude that this performance would be a different thing than what it had bargained for. At oral argument, Sally Beauty argued that the case should go to trial to allow it to demonstrate that it could and would perform the contract as impartially as Best. It stressed that Sally Beauty is a "multi-line" distributor, which means that it distributes many brands and is not just a conduit for Alberto-Culver products. But we do not think that this creates a material question of fact in this case. When performance of personal services is delegated, the trier merely determines that it is a personal services contract. If so, the duty is per se nondelegable. There is no inquiry into whether the delegate is as skilled or worthy of trust and confidence as the original obligor: the delegate was not bargained for and the obligee need not consent to the substitution. And so here: it is undisputed that Sally Beauty is wholly owned by Alberto-Culver, which means that Sally Beauty's "impartial" sales policy is at least acquiesced in by Alberto-Culver--but could change whenever Alberto-Culver's needs changed. Sally Beauty may be totally sincere in its belief that it can operate "impartially" as a distributor, but who can guarantee the outcome when there is a clear choice between the demands of the parent-manufacturer, Alberto-Culver, and the competing needs of Nexxus? The risk of an unfavorable outcome is not one which the law can force Nexxus to take. Nexxus has a substantial interest in not seeing this contract performed by Sally Beauty, which is sufficient to bar the delegation under section 2-210, Tex. Bus. Com. Code Ann. Sec. 2-210 (Vernon 1968). Because Nexxus should not be forced to accept performance of the distributorship agreement by Sally, we hold that the contract was not assignable without Nexxus' consent.

The judgment of the district court is AFFIRMED.

Questions

1. According to the court, what factors determine whether a contract is of a personal nature and not assignable?

2. How does the court interpret the provisions of the Uniform Commercial Code (UCC) in relation to the contract in question?

3. What is the significance of Sally Beauty being a wholly-owned subsidiary of a competitor in determining the assignability of the contract?

4. Why does the court conclude that the contract was not assignable without Nexxus' consent?

5. So what was the "substantial interest" Nexxus had in seeing the original promisor perform?

Novation

A novation involves one of the original parties substituting out of a contract, and a new party substituting into the contract in place of and in stead of the original party and all three parties agreeing to the arrangement. A successful novation involves one of the original parties and the newly substituted-in party now being in privity of contract.

ASSESSMENT QUESTIONS, CHAPTER 10

1. Define the concept of a third party beneficiary in contract law. How does a third party beneficiary acquire rights under a contract?

2. Discuss the difference between an intended third party beneficiary and an incidental third party beneficiary.

3. Explain the doctrine of vesting in relation to third party beneficiary rights. When do the rights of a third party beneficiary vest?

4. Can a third party beneficiary enforce a contract directly against the promisor?

5. Describe the concept of assignment in contract law. What rights can be assigned, and what rights cannot be assigned?

6. Explain the difference between an assignment and a delegation in contract law. When does a delegation of duties occur?

7. Discuss the requirements for a valid assignment of rights. What elements must be present for a valid assignment to take place?

8. Can contractual rights be assigned without the consent of the obligor? Explain the general rule and any exceptions.

9. Explain the concept of a novation. How does a novation differ from a mere assignment or delegation?

10. Describe the impact of an anti-assignment clause in a contract. Under what circumstances can a contractual right still be assigned despite such a clause?

11. Discuss the liability of an assignor or delegator after the assignment or delegation takes place. What responsibilities do they still retain?

12. Explain the concept of an obligor's defenses against an assignee. What defenses can the obligor raise against the assignee's enforcement of the assigned right?

13. Describe the impact of a delegation of duties on the delegating party's liability. Can the delegating party still be held responsible for the performance of the delegated duty?

14. Explain the concept of an incidental beneficiary in relation to third party rights. Can an incidental beneficiary enforce a contract?

INDEX

A

Acceptance, 79

Acceptance Varying Offer, 128

accord and satisfaction, 263

Accord and Satisfaction, 263

Assurance of Due Performance, 647

adhesion contract, 145

Advertisements as Offers, 60

Anti-Assignment, 767

Anticipatory Breach, 624

assignee, 762

Assignment of Future Rights, 766

assignment of rights, 768, 783, 787

Assignments for Value, 766

assignor, 762

B

Bargained for Exchange, 22

bilateral contract, 42, 60, 79, 90, 91

blue pencil rule, 307, 309

C

Capacity to Contract, 243

Certainty Damage Limitation, 526

chose in action, 765

commercial paper, 17

Concealment, 270

Concealment / Non-Disclosure, 270

Concurrent Conditions, 565

Condition Subsequent, 549

Conditions, 549

Conditions Precedent, 549

CONSIDERATION, 8

constructive condition, 550

Conditions of Exchange, 584

contract defined, 1

Counter Offer, 128

Course of Dealing, 390

Course of Performance, 396

creditor beneficiary, 750

Crop Failures, 690

D

Damage Limitations, 540

Definiteness, 162

Delegation, 781

Dependent Promises, 584

Detriment, 8

Disclaiming Implied Warranties, 425

Divisible Contracts, 599

donee beneficiary, 750

Duress, 252

duty to mitigate, 499

E

email signatures, 214

Emotional Distress, 517

Equitable estoppel, 40

equitable remedy, 450

estoppel in pais, 40, 41

Excuse of Condition, 580

executory contract, 262

expectation interest, 473

Express Conditions, 550, 590

express contracts, 48

Express Warranties, 429

extrinsic evidence, 348

F

Filling Gaps, 416

force majeure clause, 690, 714, 715

Foreseeability of Damages, 505

Forfeiture, 580

789

four corners rule, 371
fraud exception parol evidence, 370
Frustration of Purpose, 691

G

gambling, 291
General Damages, 508
General Rules Interpretation, 384
Good Faith, 441
Gratuitous Gift Assignments, 766

H

hell or high water clause, 776, 779
Holder in Due Course, 779

I

illegal contracts, 286
Illusory Promise, 17
implied condition, 550
Implied In Fact Contracts, 1
Implied Terms, 416
Implied Terms UCC Contracts, 416
Implied Warranty Assignment, 780
Implied Warranty of Fitness, 421
Implied Warranty Merchantability, 416
Impossibility, 673
Impracticability, 673
in pari delicto, 290
Incidental Beneficiaries, 743
Incomplete Construction, 491
Independent Promises, 584
Injunctions, 466
Insolvent Buyers, 651
integration clause, 358
Intended Beneficiaries, 727
Interpretation, 348

L

Leading Object Rule Exception, 188

legal remedy, 450
Liability for Non-Disclosure, 270
Licensing Laws, 300
Limitations On Damages, 497
Liquidated Damages, 540
lost volume seller, 489

M

Mailbox Rule, 113
Merchant's Firm Offer, 156
Merger Clauses, 355
Minors, 243
Mirror Image Rule, 128, 133, 134
Misrepresentation, 270
Mistake, 270
Mistaken Offers, 69
modification, 21
Municipal Contracts/3rd Parties, 746
Mutual Assent, 51
mutual mistake, 72, 260, 360, 361

N

negotiable instrument, 779
No Oral Modification Clauses, 371
Non-Competition Clauses, 300
Non-Delegable Duties, 781
Non-Disclosure, 270
Non Objecting Merchant Rule, 230
Notice of Assignment, 766
notification of acceptance, 73, 82, 99, 132
Novation, 786

O

Offer, 51
Omitted Terms, 416
Option Contracts, 153
oral contract, 176, 222, 224, 225, 231, 2
Overreaching, 252

P

parol evidence rule, 348, 349, 351, 352,
Parol Evidence Rule, 348
Party to be Charged, 177
Past Consideration, 28
Perfect Tender Rule, 591
Performance and Breach, 549
Personal Service Contracts, 466
Persons of Unsound Mind, 243
plain meaning rule, 371
Pre-Existing Duty Rule, 252, 259, 263
Precontractual Liability, 166
Prenuptial Agreements, 310
Pressure in Bargaining, 252
Prevention, 569
price quotation, 60, 76, 110, 194, 666
Priority of Assignees 781
procedural unconscionability, 333, 334,
promissory estoppel, 34, 37, 41, 42, 43
Punitive Damages, 514

Q

Quasi Contracts, 43

R

Real Estate Brokers and Conditions, 562
reliance interest, 473
Remedies, 450
repudiation, 191, 241, 482, 484, 486, 498
Rescission, 469
restitution, 473
Restitution for a Party in Default, 601
Restraints on Trade, 300
retraction, 644
Revocation of Offers, 117
ribbon matching rule, 136
rule of reasonableness, 306
Rules of Contract Interpretation, 384

S

Satisfying, 198
severable contracts, 600
Shipment of Goods as Acceptance, 108
Signature Requirement, 212
Silence as acceptance, 112
Special Damages, 508
Specific Performance, 450
Statute of Frauds, 176
Substantial Performance, 590
Substantive unconscionability, 333, 334,
Suretyship Clause, 185
Suspending Performance, 611

T

Take It or Leave It Contracts, 341
tende rdefined, 568
Termination Power of Acceptance, 116
Implied Warranty of Merchantability, 416
Third Party Beneficiary, 723
Third Party Rights, 723
Time for Performance, 587
Time Is of the Essence, 591

U

Unconscionability, 326
Unconscionable Contracts, 286
Undue Influence, 252, 264
Unilateral Mistake, 665
Unjust Enrichment, 43
Usage of Trade, 390

V

Vesting of Third Party's Rights, 752
void contract, 250
voidable contract, 243

W

Waiver and Estoppel, 573

Waiver of Breach, 599

Writing Requirement, 198